Renault Mégane
Owners Workshop Manual

M R Storey

Models covered

(5955 - 320)

Renault Mégane Hatchback, Sport Tourer (Estate) & Coupe
Petrol: 1.6 litre (1598cc)
Diesel: 1.5 litre (1461cc)

Does NOT cover 1.2, 1.4 or 2.0 litre petrol engined models, 1.6, 1.9 or 2.0 litre diesel engined models, Renaultsport versions or features specific to Coupe Cabriolet

ABCDE
FGHIJ
KLMNO
PQR

A book in the **Haynes Owners Workshop Manual Series**

ISBN **978 0 85733 955 3**

British Library Cataloguing in Publication Data
A catalogue record for this book is available from the British Library.

Printed in India

Haynes Group Limited
Sparkford, Yeovil, Somerset BA22 7JJ, England

Haynes North America, Inc
2801 Townsgate Road, Suite 340 Thousand Oaks, CA 91361

Disclaimer

There are risks associated with automotive repairs. The ability to make repairs depends on the individual's skill, experience and proper tools. Individuals should act with due care and acknowledge and assume the risk of performing automotive repairs.

The purpose of this manual is to provide comprehensive, useful and accessible automotive repair information, to help you get the best value from your vehicle. However, this manual is not a substitute for a professional certified technician or mechanic.

This repair manual is produced by a third party and is not associated with an individual vehicle manufacturer. If there is any doubt or discrepancy between this manual and the owner's manual or the factory service manual, please refer to the factory service manual or seek assistance from a professional certified technician or mechanic.

Even though we have prepared this manual with extreme care and every attempt is made to ensure that the information in this manual is correct, neither the publisher nor the author can accept responsibility for loss, damage or injury caused by any errors in, or omissions from, the information given.

Contents

LIVING WITH YOUR RENAULT MÉGANE

Introduction Page **0•4**

Safety first! Page **0•5**

Roadside repairs

If your car won't start Page **0•6**

Jump starting Page **0•7**

Wheel changing Page **0•8**

Identifying leaks Page **0•9**

Towing Page **0•9**

Weekly checks

Introduction Page **0•10**

Underbonnet check points Page **0•10**

Engine oil level Page **0•11**

Coolant level Page **0•11**

Brake and clutch fluid level Page **0•12**

Screen washer fluid level Page **0•12**

Tyre condition and pressure Page **0•13**

Wiper blades Page **0•14**

Battery Page **0•14**

Electrical systems Page **0•15**

Lubricants and fluids Page **0•16**

Tyre pressures Page **0•16**

MAINTENANCE

Routine maintenance and servicing

Renault Mégane petrol models Page **1A•1**

- Servicing specifications Page **1A•2**
- Maintenance schedule Page **1A•3**
- Maintenance procedures Page **1A•5**

Renault Mégane diesel models Page **1B•1**

- Servicing specifications Page **1B•2**
- Maintenance schedule Page **1B•3**
- Maintenance procedures Page **1B•6**

Contents

REPAIRS AND OVERHAUL

Engine and associated systems

Petrol engine in-car repair procedures Page **2A•1**
Diesel engine in-car repair procedures Page **2B•1**
Engine removal and overhaul procedures Page **2C•1**
Cooling, heating and air conditioning systems Page **3•1**
Petrol engine fuel & exhaust systems Page **4A•1**
Diesel engine fuel & exhaust systems Page **4B•1**
Emission control systems Page **4C•1**
Starting and charging systems Page **5A•1**
Ignition system – petrol engines Page **5B•1**
Pre/post-heating system – diesel engines Page **5C•1**

Transmission

Clutch Page **6•1**
Manual transmission Page **7•1**
Driveshafts Page **8•1**

Brakes and suspension

Braking system Page **9•1**
Suspension and steering Page **10•1**

Body equipment

Bodywork and fittings Page **11•1**
Body electrical system Page **12•1**

Wiring diagrams Page **12•21**

REFERENCE

Dimensions and weights Page **REF•1**
Fuel economy Page **REF•2**
Conversion factors Page **REF•6**
Buying spare parts Page **REF•7**
Jacking and vehicle support Page **REF•7**
General repair procedures Page **REF•8**
Vehicle identification Page **REF•9**
Tools and working facilities Page **REF•10**
MOT test checks Page **REF•12**
Fault finding Page **REF•16**
Glossary of technical terms Page **REF•23**

Index Page **REF•27**

The third generation Renault Mégane was introduced into the UK in November 2008, replacing the previous Mégane range. The third version of the Mégane has a more conventional design than previous versions. Gone is the angular shape and controversial rear end of the previous version, to be replaced by a more rounded, conservative design.

The engine range is essentially carried over from the previous Mégane, but all units feature upgrades to boost engine power, while reducing fuel consumption and emissions. In the new Mégane, the petrol engine covered by this manual is a 16-valve double overhead camshaft design, with variable valve timing (VVT). The diesel engine is the well proven direct-injection common-rail 1.5 litre unit, first seen in the Clio.

In common with the rest of the modern Renault range, the new Mégane offers class-leading levels of passenger safety, scoring a full five stars in the Euro NCAP safety tests. To an impact-absorbing bodyshell and highly-rigid cabin are added adaptive front airbags, side and curtain airbags, side impact bars, and seat belt tensioners with load limiters. In addition, some models feature 'anti-submarining' airbags in the front seats, to prevent occupants sliding under the seat belt in a heavy impact. With all-wheel disc brakes, ABS, EBD and Brake Assist on every model, it's clear that Renault have made a big commitment to active as well as passive safety with the new car.

The Mégane range comprises a 5-door Hatchback model, a 5 door estate model (called the 'Sport Tourer' by Renault) and a 3 door Coupe model. A Cabriolet model is available but is not covered by this manual.

All models have front-wheel-drive, with a choice of five or six speed manual transmissions. The front suspension is of conventional MacPherson strut type, incorporating lower arms, and an anti-roll bar; at the rear, a semi-independent beam axle is combined with compact underfloor springs and inclined shock absorbers to maximise the load area.

The car has a high equipment level, even at the lower end of the model range. Besides the valuable safety equipment already mentioned, all feature variable electric power steering, trip computer, engine immobiliser, rear seat headrests, radio/CD, remote central locking, electric front windows and air conditioning. Satellite navigation, climate control and electric door mirrors are among the equipment fitted higher up the range.

Your Renault Mégane manual

The aim of this manual is to help you get the best value from your car. It can do so in several ways. It can help you decide what work must be done (even should you choose to get it done by a garage). It will also provide information on routine maintenance and servicing, and give a logical course of action and diagnosis when random faults occur. However, it is hoped that you will use the manual by tackling the work yourself. On simpler jobs it may even be quicker than booking the car into a garage and going there twice, to leave and collect it. Perhaps most important, a lot of money can be saved by avoiding the costs a garage must charge to cover its labour and overheads.

The manual has drawings and descriptions to show the function of the various components so that their layout can be understood. Tasks are described and photographed in a clear step-by-step sequence.

References to the 'left' and 'right' of the car are in the sense of a person in the driver's seat, facing forwards.

Acknowledgements

Thanks are due to Draper tools Limited, who provided some of the workshop tools, and to all those people at Sparkford who helped in the production of this manual.

We take great pride in the accuracy of information given in this manual, but car manufacturers make alterations and design changes during the production run of a particular car of which they do not inform us. No liability can be accepted by the authors or publishers for loss, damage or injury caused by any errors in, or omissions from, the information given.

Working on your car can be dangerous. This page shows just some of the potential risks and hazards, with the aim of creating a safety-conscious attitude.

General hazards

Scalding

• Don't remove the radiator or expansion tank cap while the engine is hot.

• Engine oil, transmission fluid or power steering fluid may also be dangerously hot if the engine has recently been running.

Burning

• Beware of burns from the exhaust system and from any part of the engine. Brake discs and drums can also be extremely hot immediately after use.

Crushing

• When working under or near a raised vehicle, always supplement the jack with axle stands, or use drive-on ramps. ***Never venture under a car which is only supported by a jack.***

• Take care if loosening or tightening high-torque nuts when the vehicle is on stands. Initial loosening and final tightening should be done with the wheels on the ground.

Fire

• Fuel is highly flammable; fuel vapour is explosive.

• Don't let fuel spill onto a hot engine.

• Do not smoke or allow naked lights (including pilot lights) anywhere near a vehicle being worked on. Also beware of creating sparks (electrically or by use of tools).

• Fuel vapour is heavier than air, so don't work on the fuel system with the vehicle over an inspection pit.

• Another cause of fire is an electrical overload or short-circuit. Take care when repairing or modifying the vehicle wiring.

• Keep a fire extinguisher handy, of a type suitable for use on fuel and electrical fires.

Electric shock

• Ignition HT and Xenon headlight voltages can be dangerous, especially to people with heart problems or a pacemaker. Don't work on or near these systems with the engine running or the ignition switched on.

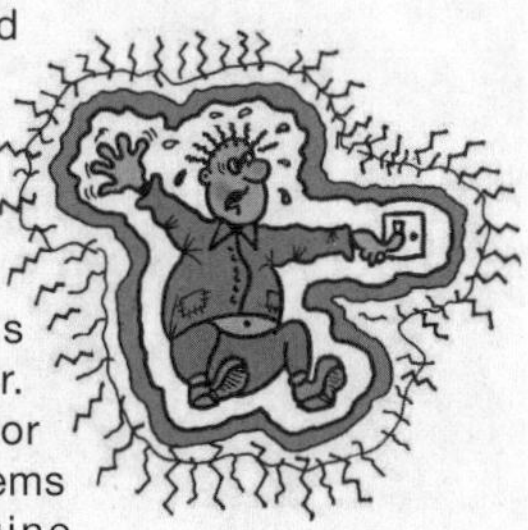

• Mains voltage is also dangerous. Make sure that any mains-operated equipment is correctly earthed. Mains power points should be protected by a residual current device (RCD) circuit breaker.

Fume or gas intoxication

• Exhaust fumes are poisonous; they can contain carbon monoxide, which is rapidly fatal if inhaled. Never run the engine in a confined space such as a garage with the doors shut.

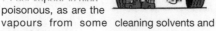

• Fuel vapour is also poisonous, as are the vapours from some cleaning solvents and paint thinners.

Poisonous or irritant substances

• Avoid skin contact with battery acid and with any fuel, fluid or lubricant, especially antifreeze, brake hydraulic fluid and Diesel fuel. Don't syphon them by mouth. If such a substance is swallowed or gets into the eyes, seek medical advice.

• Prolonged contact with used engine oil can cause skin cancer. Wear gloves or use a barrier cream if necessary. Change out of oil-soaked clothes and do not keep oily rags in your pocket.

• Air conditioning refrigerant forms a poisonous gas if exposed to a naked flame (including a cigarette). It can also cause skin burns on contact.

Asbestos

• Asbestos dust can cause cancer if inhaled or swallowed. Asbestos may be found in gaskets and in brake and clutch linings. When dealing with such components it is safest to assume that they contain asbestos.

Special hazards

Hydrofluoric acid

• This extremely corrosive acid is formed when certain types of synthetic rubber, found in some O-rings, oil seals, fuel hoses etc, are exposed to temperatures above 4000C. The rubber changes into a charred or sticky substance containing the acid. *Once formed, the acid remains dangerous for years. If it gets onto the skin, it may be necessary to amputate the limb concerned*.

• When dealing with a vehicle which has suffered a fire, or with components salvaged from such a vehicle, wear protective gloves and discard them after use.

The battery

• Batteries contain sulphuric acid, which attacks clothing, eyes and skin. Take care when topping-up or carrying the battery.

• The hydrogen gas given off by the battery is highly explosive. Never cause a spark or allow a naked light nearby. Be careful when connecting and disconnecting battery chargers or jump leads.

Air bags

• Air bags can cause injury if they go off accidentally. Take care when removing the steering wheel and trim panels. Special storage instructions may apply.

Diesel injection equipment

• Diesel injection pumps supply fuel at very high pressure. Take care when working on the fuel injectors and fuel pipes.

Warning: Never expose the hands, face or any other part of the body to injector spray; the fuel can penetrate the skin with potentially fatal results.

Remember...

DO

• Do use eye protection when using power tools, and when working under the vehicle.

• Do wear gloves or use barrier cream to protect your hands when necessary.

• Do get someone to check periodically that all is well when working alone on the vehicle.

• Do keep loose clothing and long hair well out of the way of moving mechanical parts.

• Do remove rings, wristwatch etc, before working on the vehicle – especially the electrical system.

• Do ensure that any lifting or jacking equipment has a safe working load rating adequate for the job.

DON'T

• Don't attempt to lift a heavy component which may be beyond your capability – get assistance.

• Don't rush to finish a job, or take unverified short cuts.

• Don't use ill-fitting tools which may slip and cause injury.

• Don't leave tools or parts lying around where someone can trip over them. Mop up oil and fuel spills at once.

• Don't allow children or pets to play in or near a vehicle being worked on.

The following pages are intended to help in dealing with common roadside emergencies and breakdowns. You will find more detailed fault finding information at the back of the manual, and repair information in the main chapters.

If your car won't start and the starter motor doesn't turn

- ☐ Open the bonnet and make sure that the battery terminals are clean and tight.
- ☐ Switch on the headlights and try to start the engine. If the headlights go very dim when you're trying to start, the battery is probably flat. Get out of trouble by jump starting (see next page) using another car.

If your car won't start even though the starter motor turns as normal

- ☐ Is there fuel in the tank?
- ☐ Has the engine immobiliser been deactivated? This should happen automatically, or when the keycard is inserted into the facia slot. However, if a faulty card causes the card reader slot to flash rapidly, consult a Renault dealer for advice.
- ☐ On manual transmission models, if the car is in gear, the clutch must be depressed; otherwise, the footbrake must be applied.
- ☐ If it's a model with automatic transmission, the footbrake must be applied, and the selector must be in N or P.
- ☐ Is there moisture on electrical components under the bonnet? With the ignition off, wipe off any obvious dampness with a dry cloth. Spray a water-repellent aerosol product (WD-40 or equivalent) on ignition and fuel system electrical connectors like those shown in the photos. Pay special attention to the ignition coil wiring connectors.

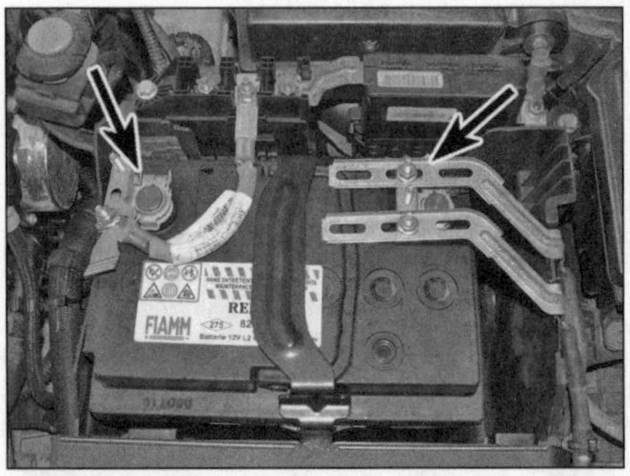

A Remove the battery cover and check the condition and security of the battery connections.

B With the ignition off, check that the wiring connectors are securely connected to the four ignition coils (petrol models).

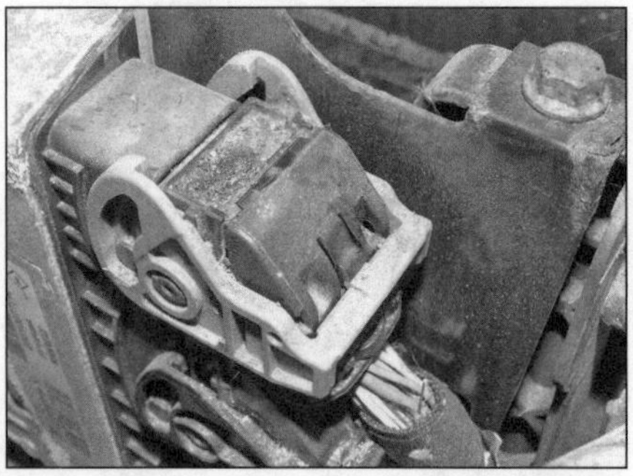

C Lift off the cover and check the security of the engine management ECU connectors and any other accessible electrical connectors.

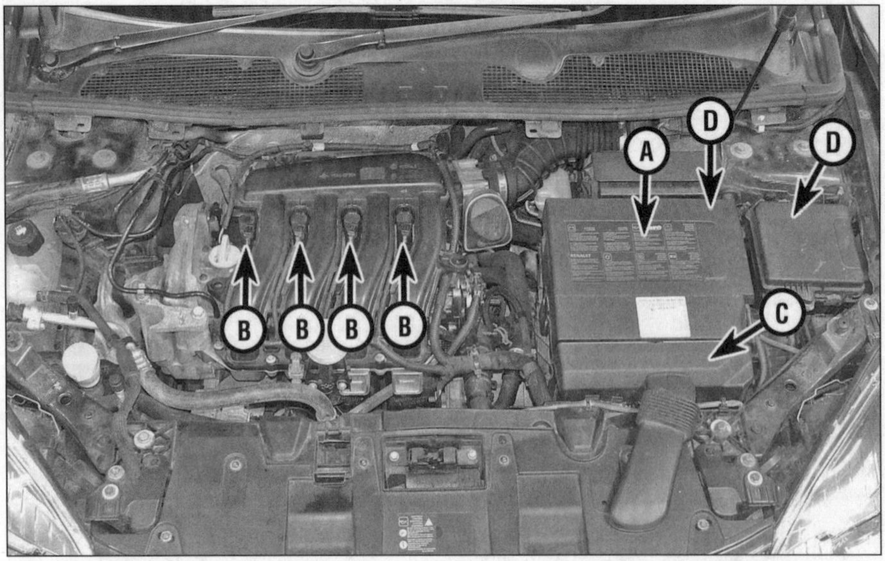

Check that electrical connections are secure (with the ignition switched off) and spray them with a water-dispersant spray like WD-40 if you suspect a problem due to damp.

D With the ignition off, check the fuses.

Jump starting

HAYNES HiNT *Jump starting will get you out of trouble, but you must correct whatever made the battery go flat in the first place. There are three possibilities:*

***1** The battery has been drained by repeated attempts to start, or by leaving the lights on.*

***2** The charging system is not working properly (alternator drivebelt slack or broken, alternator wiring fault or alternator itself faulty).*

***3** The battery itself is at fault (electrolyte low, or battery worn out).*

When jump-starting a car, observe the following precautions:

- ✓ Before connecting the booster battery, remove the key card from the facia slot.
- ✓ Ensure that all electrical equipment (lights, heater, wipers, etc) is switched off.
- ✓ Take note of any special precautions printed on the battery case.
- ✓ Make sure that the booster battery is the same voltage as the discharged one in the vehicle.
- ✓ If the battery is being jump-started from the battery in another vehicle, the two vehicles MUST NOT TOUCH each other.
- ✓ Make sure that the transmission is in neutral (or PARK, in the case of automatic transmission).
- ✓ Once the booster battery has been connected, insert the key card into the facia slot

HAYNES HiNT ***Budget jump leads can be a false economy, as they often do not pass enough current to start large capacity or diesel engines. They can also get hot.***

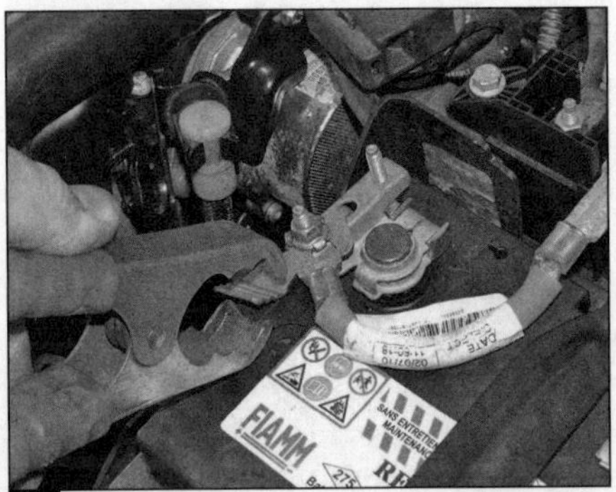

1 Connect one end of the red jump lead to the positive (+) terminal of the flat battery

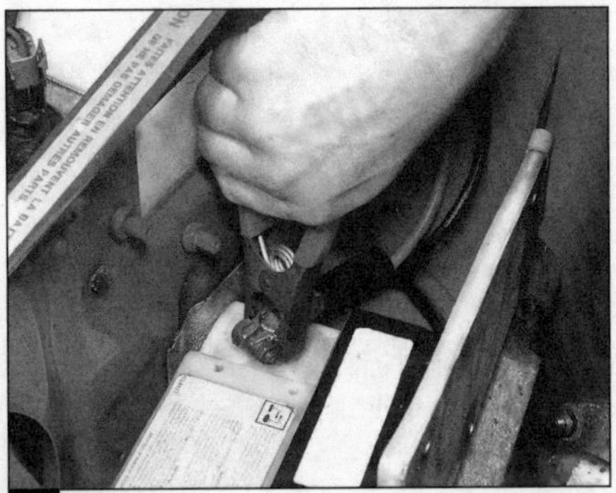

2 Connect the other end of the red lead to the positive (+) terminal of the booster battery.

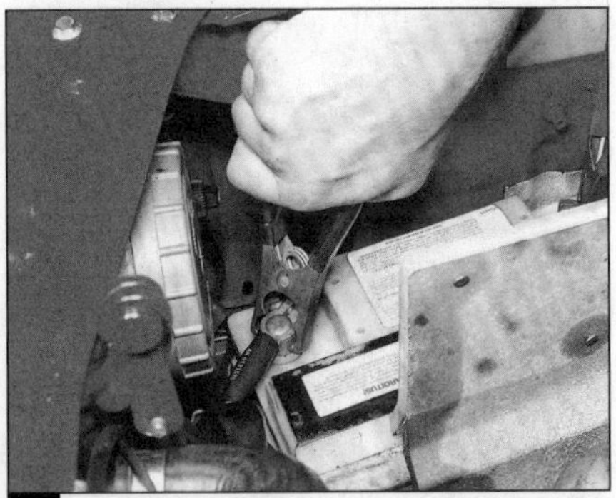

3 Connect one end of the black jump lead to the negative (-) terminal of the booster battery

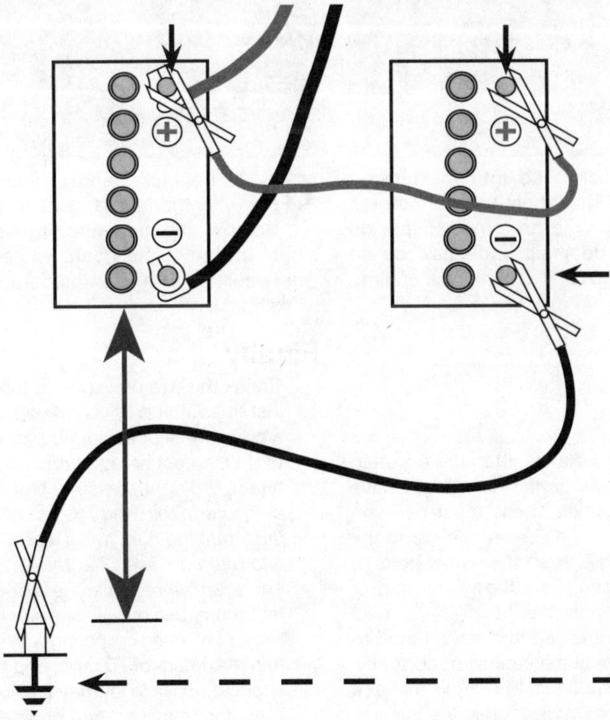

4 Connect the other end of the black jump lead to a bolt or bracket on the engine block, well away from the battery, on the vehicle to be started.

5 Make sure that the jump leads will not come into contact with the fan, drive-belts or other moving parts of the engine.

6 Start the engine using the booster battery and run it at idle speed. Switch on the lights, rear window demister and heater blower motor, then disconnect the jump leads in the reverse order of connection. Turn off the lights etc.

Wheel changing

Warning: ***Do not change a wheel in a situation where you risk being hit by other traffic. On busy roads, try to stop in a lay-by or a gateway. Be wary of passing traffic while changing the wheel – it is easy to become distracted by the job in hand.***

Preparation

- ☐ When a puncture occurs, stop as soon as it is safe to do so.
- ☐ Park on firm level ground, if possible, and well out of the way of other traffic.
- ☐ Use hazard warning lights if necessary.
- ☐ If you have one, use a warning triangle to alert other drivers of your presence.
- ☐ Apply the handbrake and engage first or reverse gear (or P on models with automatic transmission).
- ☐ Chock the wheel diagonally opposite the one being removed – a couple of large stones will do for this.
- ☐ If the ground is soft, use a flat piece of wood to spread the load under the jack.

Changing the wheel

1 The emergency spare wheel and tools are located in the luggage compartment, under the boot carpet. Release the turn buckles and lift up the carpet. Unscrew the spare wheel retainer anti-clockwise, and lift out the spare wheel. Place the spare wheel under the vehicle close to the jacking point.

2 The vehicle jack is stored in the tool tray at the side of the spare wheel. Lift out the tool tray, which also contains the wheelbrace, towing eye, and hub cap removal tool. Where alloy wheels are fitted there should also be a set of wheel bolts.

3 Remove the wheel trim or centre cap from the punctured wheel, using the tool provided. Use the wheelbrace to loosen each wheel bolt by half a turn.

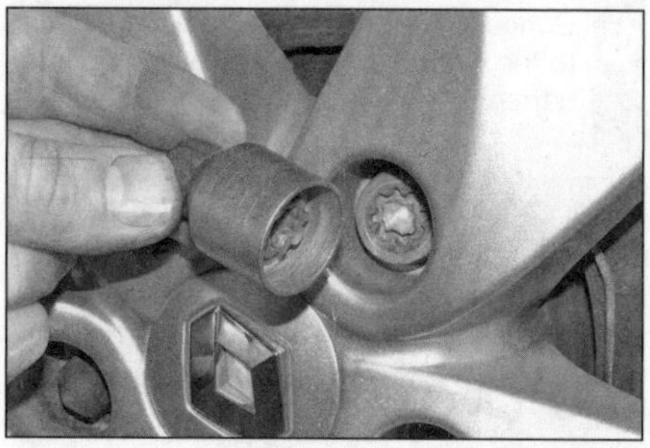

4 Models with alloy wheels may have a special locking wheel bolt fitted.

5 Locate the jack head into the jacking point nearest the wheel to be changed. The jacking points are small 'cups' on the base of the door sill, indicated by an arrowhead marking. Only use the jack on firm, level ground.

6 Turn the jack handle clockwise until the wheel is raised clear of the ground. Remove the bolts and lift the punctured wheel clear. Fit the spare wheel. Refit the wheel bolts, and tighten moderately with the wheelbrace.

7 Where alloy wheels are fitted there should be a set of spare bolts that do not have a separate washer. These must be used on the steel spare wheel. Lower the car to the ground, then finally tighten the wheel bolts in a diagonal sequence. Refit the wheel trim or centre cap, where possible. Ideally, the wheel bolts should be slackened and retightened to the specified torque at the earliest opportunity. Remove the wheel chocks and stow the jack and tools in the correct location in the car.

Finally . . .

- ☐ Check the tyre pressure on the wheel just fitted. If it is low, or if you don't have a pressure gauge with you, drive slowly to the nearest garage and inflate the tyre to the right pressure. **Note:** *The tyre pressure monitoring system will register a fault until the punctured wheel is repaired and refitted – see Chapter 10.*
- ☐ The spare wheel on some models is for temporary use only. Drive with extra care, especially when cornering – limit yourself to a maximum of 70 mph, and to the shortest possible journeys, while it is fitted.
- ☐ Have the damaged tyre or wheel repaired as soon as possible.

Identifying leaks

Puddles on the garage floor or drive, or obvious wetness under the bonnet or underneath the car, suggest a leak that needs investigating. It can sometimes be difficult to decide where the leak is coming from, especially if an engine undershield is fitted. Leaking oil or fluid can also be blown rearwards by the passage of air under the car, giving a false impression of where the problem lies.

Warning: Most automotive oils and fluids are poisonous. Wash them off skin, and change out of contaminated clothing, without delay.

HAYNES HiNT ***The smell of a fluid leaking from the car may provide a clue to what's leaking. Some fluids are distinctively coloured. It may help to remove the engine undershield, clean the car carefully and to park it over some clean paper overnight as an aid to locating the source of the leak. Remember that some leaks may only occur while the engine is running.***

Sump oil

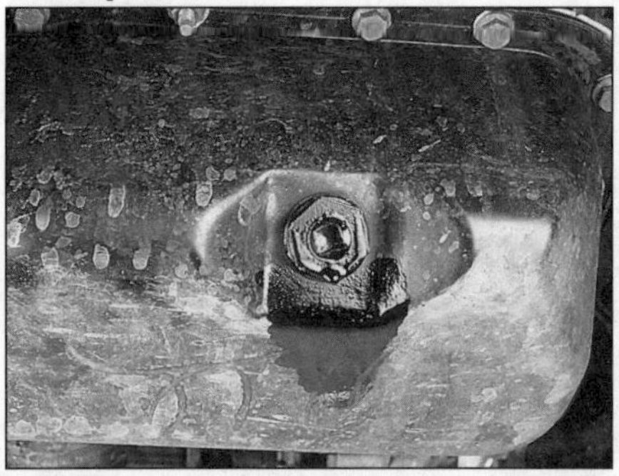

Engine oil may leak from the drain plug...

Oil from filter

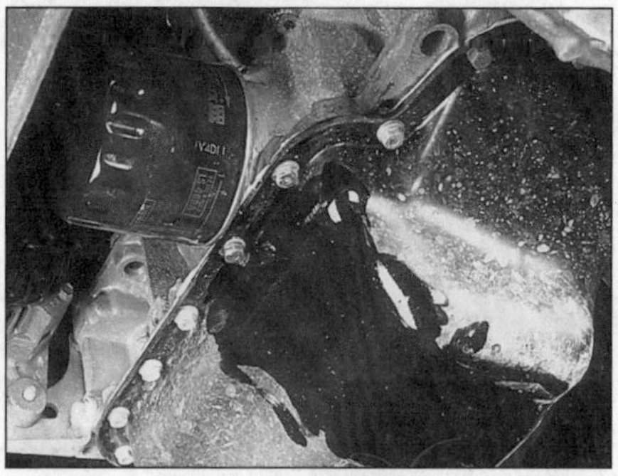

...or from the base of the oil filter.

Gearbox oil

Gearbox oil can leak from the seals at the inboard ends of the driveshafts.

Antifreeze

Leaking antifreeze often leaves a crystalline deposit like this.

Brake fluid

A leak occurring at a wheel is almost certainly brake fluid.

Power steering fluid

Power steering fluid may leak from the pipe connectors on the steering rack.

Towing

When all else fails, you may find yourself having to get a tow home – or of course you may be helping somebody else. Long-distance recovery should only be done by a garage or breakdown service. For shorter distances, DIY towing using another car is easy enough, but observe the following points:

☐ A towing eye is located with the jack in the luggage compartment (see *Wheel changing*). To fit the towing eye, prise out the cover on the side of the bumper, and remove it. Screw the towing eye in as far as it will go. Tighten the towing eye with the wheelbrace.

☐ Insert the keycard into its slot and press the starter button (to turn on the ignition) when the vehicle is being towed, so that the steering lock is released, and that the direction indicator and brake lights will work. A vehicle with a flat battery can not be towed as the steering lock will not release. Charge or replace the battery before towing.

☐ Use a proper tow-rope – they are not expensive. The vehicle being towed must display an ON TOW sign in its rear window.

☐ Always turn the ignition key to the 'on' position when the vehicle is being towed, so that the steering lock is released, and the direction indicator and brake lights work.

☐ Before being towed, release the handbrake and select neutral on the transmission. On models with automatic transmission, the car **must** be towed with its front wheels raised clear of the ground, or transmission damage may occur. Otherwise, the safe towing speed is no more than 12 mph, for no further than 18 miles.

☐ Note that greater-than-usual pedal pressure will be required to operate the brakes, since the vacuum servo unit is only operational with the engine running.

☐ The driver of the car being towed must keep the tow-rope taut at all times to avoid snatching.

☐ Make sure that both drivers know the route before setting off.

☐ Only drive at moderate speeds and keep the distance towed to a minimum. Drive smoothly and allow plenty of time for slowing down at junctions.

Introduction

There are some very simple checks which need only take a few minutes to carry out, but which could save you a lot of inconvenience and expense.

These checks require no great skill or special tools, and the small amount of time they take to perform could prove to be very well spent, for example:

☐ Keeping an eye on tyre condition and pressures, will not only help to stop them wearing out prematurely, but could also save your life.

☐ Many breakdowns are caused by electrical problems. Battery-related faults are particularly common, and a quick check on a regular basis will often prevent the majority of these.

☐ If your car develops a brake fluid leak, the first time you might know about it is when your brakes don't work properly. Checking the level regularly will give advance warning of this kind of problem.

☐ If the oil or coolant levels run low, the cost of repairing any engine damage will be far greater than fixing the leak, for example.

Underbonnet check points

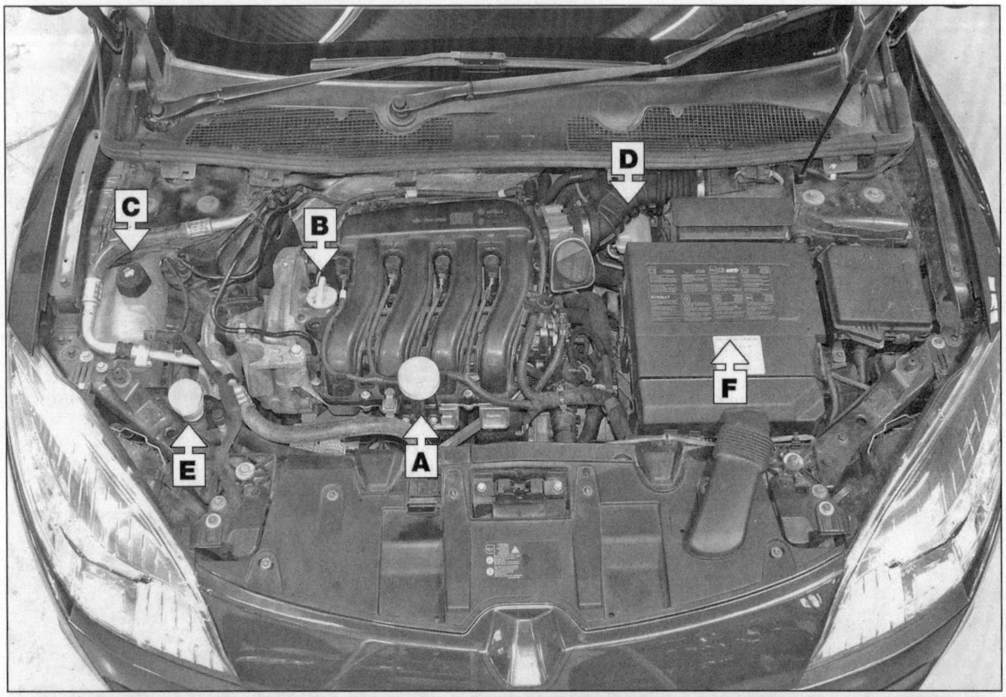

◀ Petrol engine

A *Engine oil level dipstick*
B *Engine oil filler cap*
C *Coolant reservoir (expansion) tank*
D *Brake and clutch fluid reservoir*
E *Washer fluid reservoir*
F *Battery (under cover)*

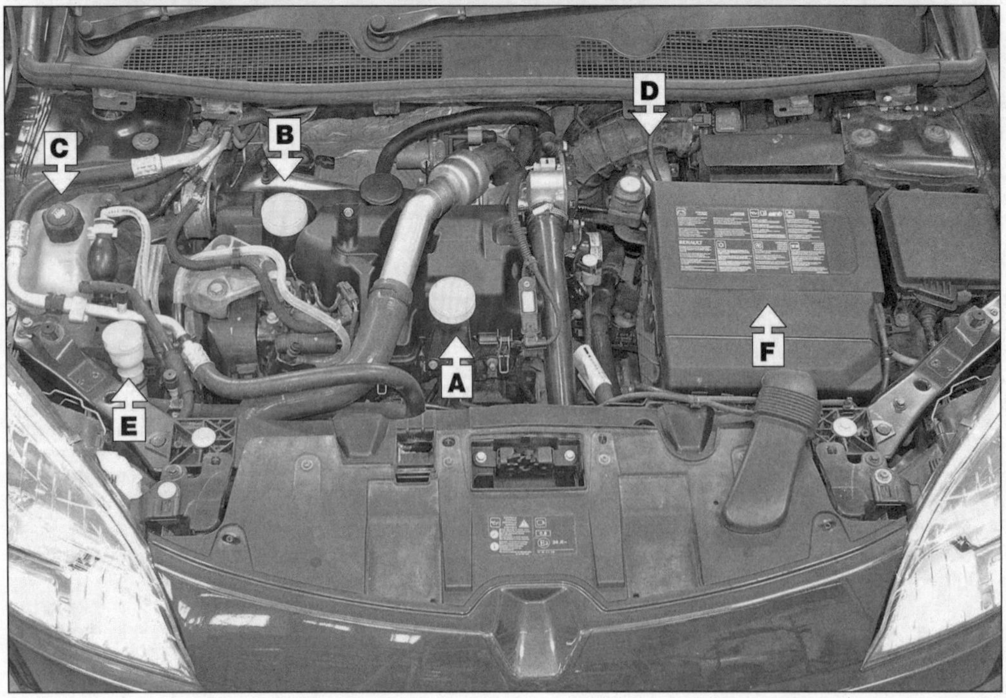

◀ Diesel engine

A *Engine oil level dipstick*
B *Engine oil filler cap*
C *Coolant reservoir (expansion) tank*
D *Brake and clutch fluid reservoir*
E *Washer fluid reservoir*
F *Battery (under cover)*

Engine oil level

Before you start

✔ Make sure that the car is on level ground.

✔ Check the oil level before the car is driven, or at least 5 minutes after the engine has been switched off.

> HAYNES HiNT
> ***If the oil is checked immediately after driving the vehicle, some of the oil will remain in the upper engine components, resulting in an inaccurate reading on the dipstick.***

The correct oil

Modern engines place great demands on their oil. It is very important that the correct oil for your car is used (see *Lubricants and fluids*).

Car care

- If you have to add oil frequently, you should check whether you have any oil leaks. Place some clean paper under the car overnight, and check for stains in the morning. If there are no leaks, then the engine may be burning oil.
- Always maintain the level between the upper and lower dipstick marks. If the level is too low, severe engine damage may occur. Oil seal failure may result if the engine is overfilled by adding too much oil.

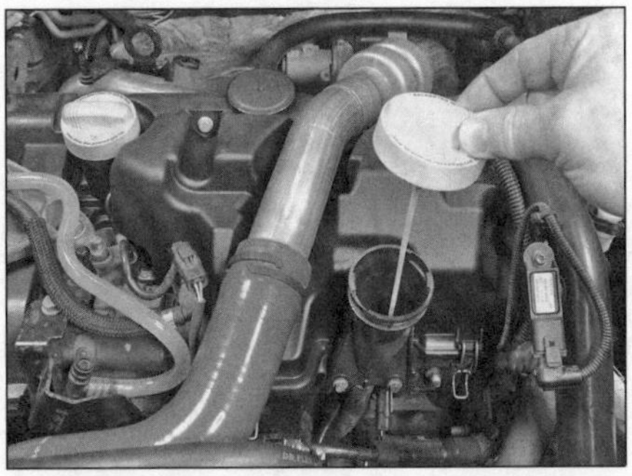

1 Pull out the dipstick. The dipstick is located at the front of the engine on all engines. Unscrew and remove the dipstick.

2 Using a clean rag or paper towel, wipe all the oil from the dipstick. Insert the clean dipstick into the tube (or screw the oil filler cap fully on) as far as it will go, then withdraw/unscrew it again.

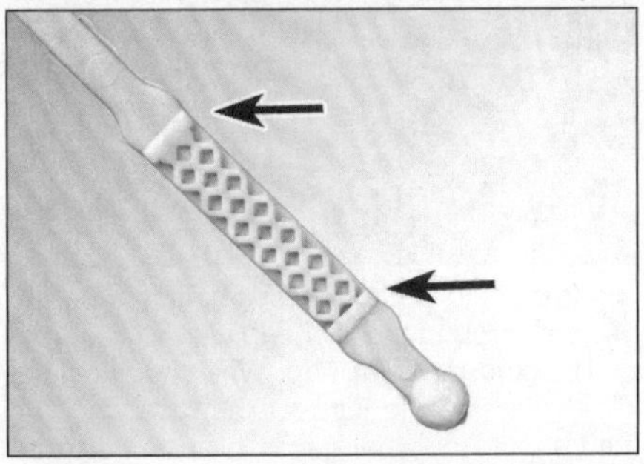

3 Note the oil level on the end of the dipstick, which should be within the 'hatched' area, between the upper and lower marks. Approximately 1.5 to 2.0 litres of oil will raise the level from the lower to the upper mark.

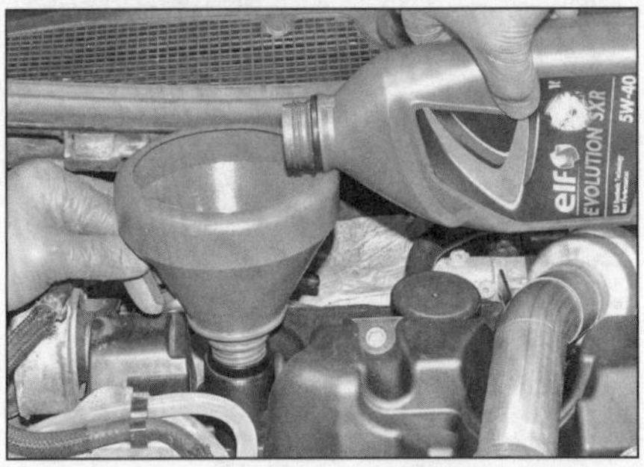

4 Oil is added through the filler cap. Unscrew the filler cap, then top-up the level. A funnel may help to reduce spillage. Add the oil slowly, checking the level on the dipstick often. Don't overfill.

Coolant level

> ***Warning: Do not attempt to remove the expansion tank pressure cap when the engine is hot, as there is a very great risk of scalding. Do not leave open containers of coolant about, as it is poisonous.***

Car care

- With a sealed-type cooling system, adding coolant should not be necessary on a regular basis. If frequent topping-up is required, it is likely there is a leak. Check the radiator, all hoses and joint faces for signs of staining or wetness, and rectify as necessary.
- It is important that antifreeze is used in the cooling system all year round, not just during the winter months. Don't top up with water alone, as the antifreeze will become diluted.

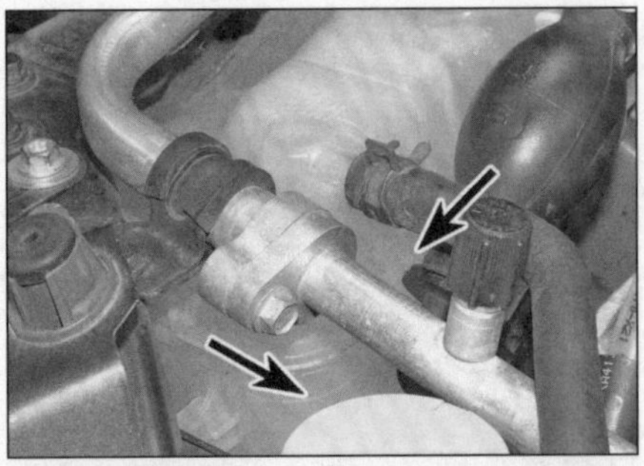

1 The coolant level varies with the temperature of the engine. The expansion tank has MAX and MIN level markings (visible from the right-hand side of the engine compartment). When cold, the level should be between the two marks. When the engine is hot, the level may rise slightly above the MAX mark.

2 If topping-up is necessary, wait until the engine is cold, then remove the cap on the expansion tank.

3 Add a mixture of water (ideally distilled water) and antifreeze to the expansion tank, until the coolant is up to the MAX mark. Use antifreeze of the same type as that which is already in the system. Refit the cap securely.

Brake and clutch* fluid level

**The brake fluid reservoir also supplies fluid to the clutch master cylinder.*

Warning: Brake fluid can harm your eyes and damage painted surfaces, so use extreme caution when handling and pouring it. Do not use fluid that has been standing open for some time, as it absorbs moisture from the air, which can cause a dangerous loss of braking effectiveness.

Safety first!

- If the reservoir requires repeated topping-up this is an indication of a fluid leak somewhere in the system, which should be investigated immediately.
- The fluid level in the reservoir will drop slightly as the brake pads wear down, but the fluid level must never be allowed to drop below the MIN mark.
- If a leak is suspected, the car should not be driven until the braking system has been checked. Never take any risks where brakes are concerned.

1 The MAX and MIN marks are indicated on the side of the reservoir, which is located at the back of the engine compartment, on the transmission side. The fluid level must be kept between these two marks.

2 If topping-up is necessary, first wipe the area around the filler cap with a clean rag, then unscrew the cap. When adding fluid, it's a good idea to inspect the reservoir. The fluid should be changed if it appears to be dark, or if dirt is visible.

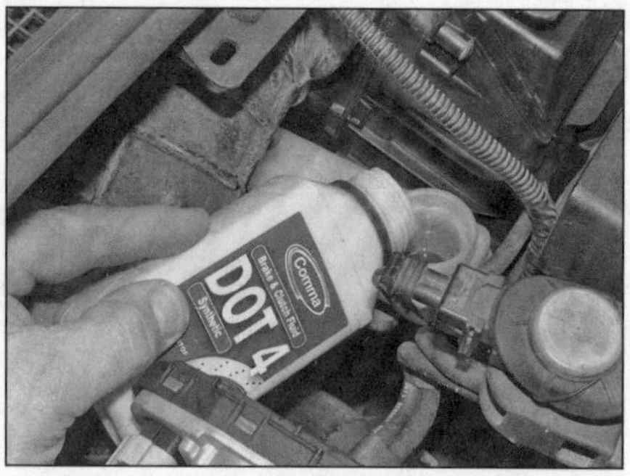

3 Carefully add fluid, avoiding spilling it on surrounding paintwork. Use only the specified hydraulic fluid; mixing different types of fluid can cause damage to the system and/or a loss of braking effectiveness. After filling to the correct level, refit the cap securely. Wipe off any spilt fluid.

Screen washer fluid level

- Screenwash additives not only keep the windscreen clean during bad weather, they also prevent the washer system freezing in cold weather – which is when you are likely to need it most. Don't top-up using plain water, as the screenwash will become diluted, and will freeze in cold weather.

Warning: On no account use engine coolant antifreeze in the screen washer system – this may damage the paintwork.

1 The windscreen/tailgate washer fluid reservoir filler neck is located at the front of the engine compartment, behind the right-hand headlight. Lift up the cap.

2 When topping-up the reservoir, a screenwash additive should be added in the quantities recommended on the bottle. The bottle can safely be filled until the level is visible inside.

Tyre condition and pressure

It is very important that tyres are in good condition, and at the correct pressure - having a tyre failure at any speed is highly dangerous.

Tyre wear is influenced by driving style - harsh braking and acceleration, or fast cornering, will all produce more rapid tyre wear. As a general rule, the front tyres wear out faster than the rears. Interchanging the tyres from front to rear ("rotating" the tyres) may result in more even wear. However, if this is completely effective, you may have the expense of replacing all four tyres at once!

Remove any nails or stones embedded in the tread before they penetrate the tyre to cause deflation. If removal of a nail does reveal that the tyre has been punctured, refit the nail so that its point of penetration is marked. Then immediately change the wheel, and have the tyre repaired by a tyre dealer.

Regularly check the tyres for damage in the form of cuts or bulges, especially in the sidewalls. Periodically remove the wheels, and clean any dirt or mud from the inside and outside surfaces. Examine the wheel rims for signs of rusting, corrosion or other damage. Light alloy wheels are easily damaged by "kerbing" whilst parking; steel wheels may also become dented or buckled. A new wheel is very often the only way to overcome severe damage.

New tyres should be balanced when they are fitted, but it may become necessary to re-balance them as they wear, or if the balance weights fitted to the wheel rim should fall off. Unbalanced tyres will wear more quickly, as will the steering and suspension components. Wheel imbalance is normally signified by vibration, particularly at a certain speed (typically around 50 mph). If this vibration is felt only through the steering, then it is likely that just the front wheels need balancing. If, however, the vibration is felt through the whole car, the rear wheels could be out of balance. Wheel balancing should be carried out by a tyre dealer or garage.

1 ***Tread Depth - visual check***
The original tyres have tread wear safety bands (B), which will appear when the tread depth reaches approximately 1.6 mm. The band positions are indicated by a triangular mark on the tyre sidewall (A).

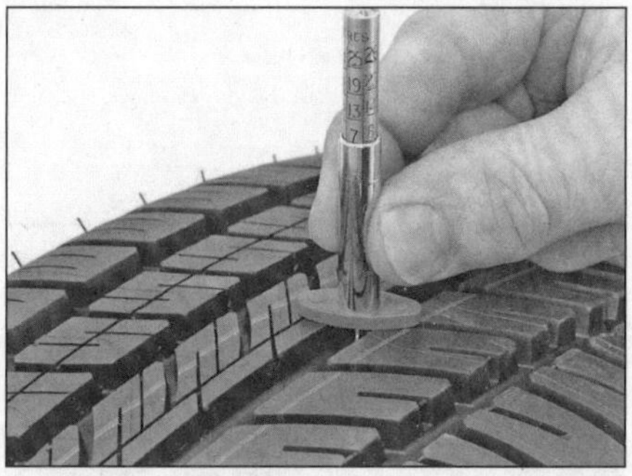

2 ***Tread Depth - manual check***
Alternatively, tread wear can be monitored with a simple, inexpensive device known as a tread depth indicator gauge.

3 ***Tyre Pressure Check***
Check the tyre pressures regularly with the tyres cold. Do not adjust the tyre pressures immediately after the vehicle has been used, or an inaccurate setting will result.

Tyre tread wear patterns

Shoulder Wear

Underinflation (wear on both sides)
Under-inflation will cause overheating of the tyre, because the tyre will flex too much, and the tread will not sit correctly on the road surface. This will cause a loss of grip and excessive wear, not to mention the danger of sudden tyre failure due to heat build-up.
Check and adjust pressures
Incorrect wheel camber (wear on one side)
Repair or renew suspension parts
Hard cornering
Reduce speed!

Centre Wear

Overinflation
Over-inflation will cause rapid wear of the centre part of the tyre tread, coupled with reduced grip, harsher ride, and the danger of shock damage occurring in the tyre casing.
Check and adjust pressures

If you sometimes have to inflate your car's tyres to the higher pressures specified for maximum load or sustained high speed, don't forget to reduce the pressures to normal afterwards.

Uneven Wear

Front tyres may wear unevenly as a result of wheel misalignment. Most tyre dealers and garages can check and adjust the wheel alignment (or "tracking") for a modest charge.
Incorrect camber or castor
Repair or renew suspension parts
Malfunctioning suspension
Repair or renew suspension parts
Unbalanced wheel
Balance tyres
Incorrect toe setting
Adjust front wheel alignment
Note: *The feathered edge of the tread which typifies toe wear is best checked by feel.*

Wiper blades

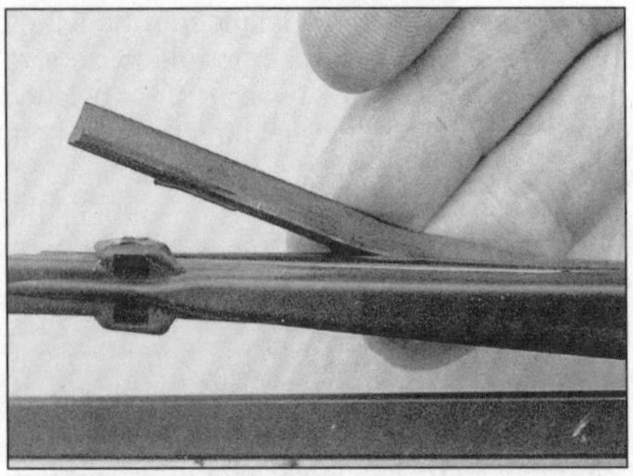

1 Check the condition of the wiper blades; if they are cracked or show any signs of deterioration, or if the glass swept area is smeared, renew them. For maximum clarity of vision, wiper blades should be renewed annually, as a matter of course.

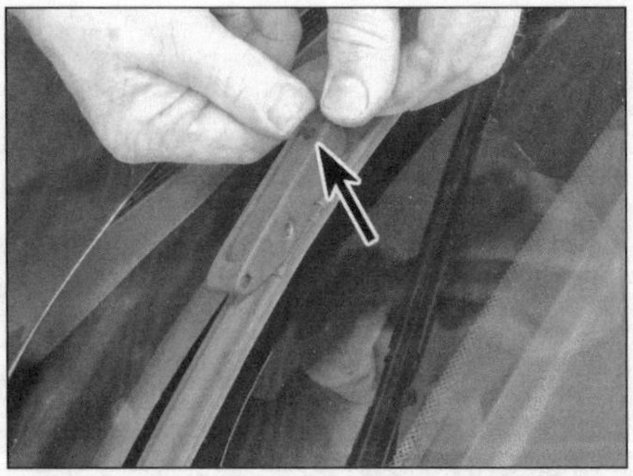

2 To remove a windscreen wiper blade, depress the clip (arrowed) rotate the blade slightly and slide it off the arm.

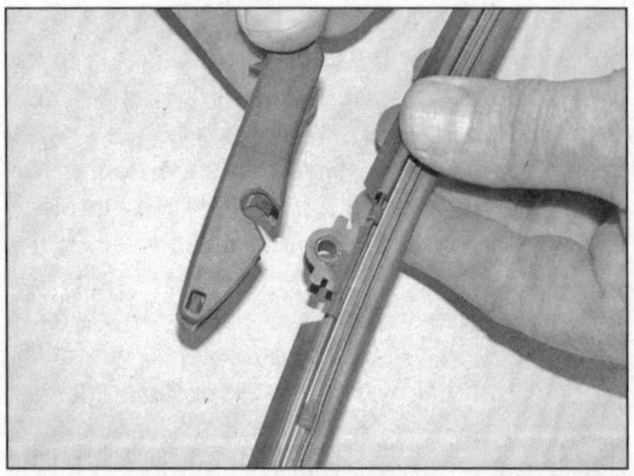

3 Don't forget to check the tailgate wiper blade as well, which unclips directly from the arm.

Battery

Caution: Before carrying out any work on the vehicle battery, read the precautions given in 'Safety first!' at the start of this manual.

✔ Make sure that the battery tray is in good condition, and that the clamp is tight. Corrosion on the tray, retaining clamp and the battery itself can be removed with a solution of water and baking soda. Thoroughly rinse all cleaned areas with water. Any metal parts damaged by corrosion should be covered with a zinc-based primer, then painted.

✔ Periodically (approximately every three months), check the charge condition of the battery, as described in Chapter 5A.

✔ If the battery is flat, and you need to jump start your vehicle, see *Roadside repairs*.

HAYNES HiNT ***Battery corrosion can be kept to a minimum by applying a layer of petroleum jelly to the clamps and terminals after they are reconnected.***

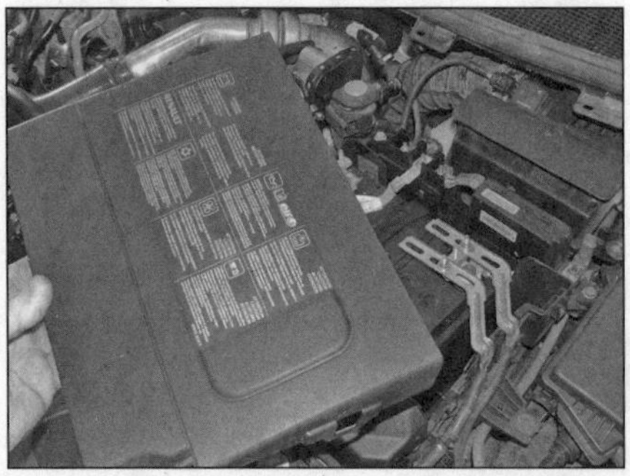

1 The battery is located at the front of the engine compartment, behind the left-hand headlight. To access the battery unclip the cover. The exterior of the battery should be inspected periodically for damage such as a cracked case or cover.

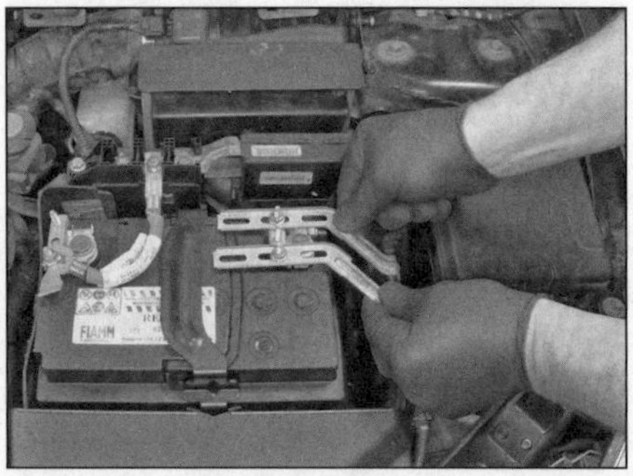

2 Check the tightness of the battery cable clamps to ensure good electrical connections. You should not be able to move them. Also check each cable for cracks and frayed conductors.

3 If corrosion (white, fluffy deposits) is evident, remove the cables from the battery terminals, clean them with a small wire brush, then refit them. Automotive stores sell a tool for cleaning the battery post . . .

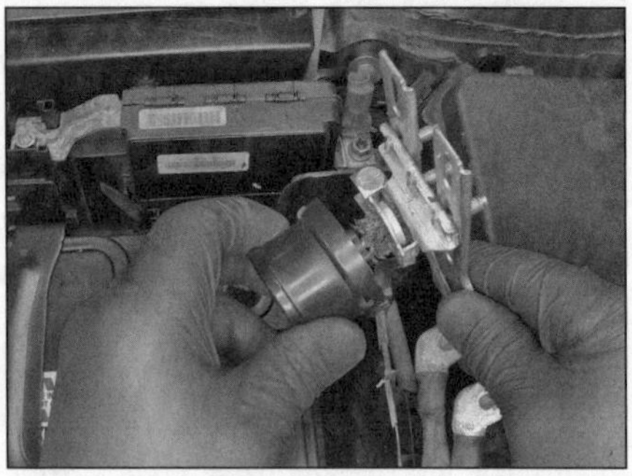

4 . . . as well as the battery cable clamps.

Electrical systems

✔ Check all external lights and the horn. Refer to Chapter 12 Section 2 for details if any of the circuits are found to be inoperative.

✔ Visually check all accessible wiring connectors, harnesses and retaining clips for security, and for signs of chafing or damage.

HAYNES HiNT ***If you need to check your brake lights and indicators unaided, back up to a wall or garage door and operate the lights. The reflected light should show if they are working properly.***

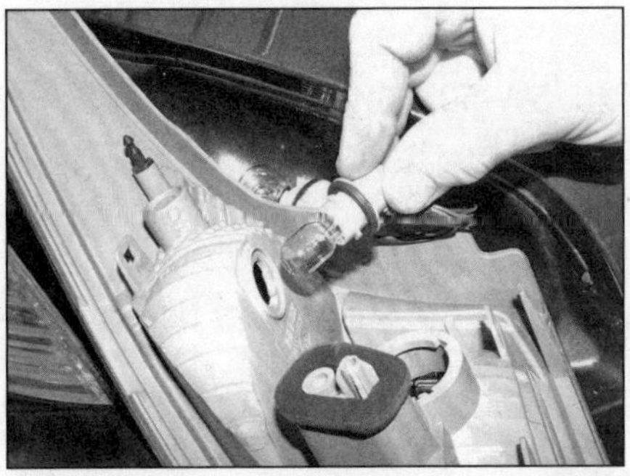

1 If a single indicator light, brake light or headlight has failed, it is likely that a bulb has blown and will need to be renewed. Refer to Chapter 12 for details. If both brake lights have failed, it is possible that the brake light switch operated by the brake pedal has failed. Refer to Chapter 9 for details.

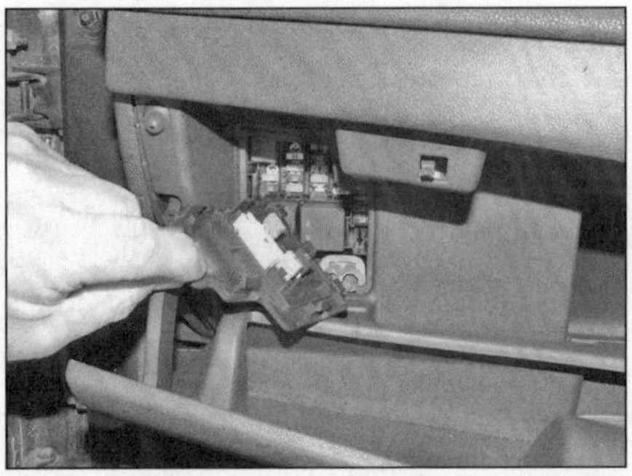

2 If more than one indicator light or headlight has failed, it is likely that either a fuse has blown, or that there is a fault in the circuit (see Chapter 12). The main fuses are mounted behind a panel inside the glovebox. Open the glovebox and release the fuse panel at the top.

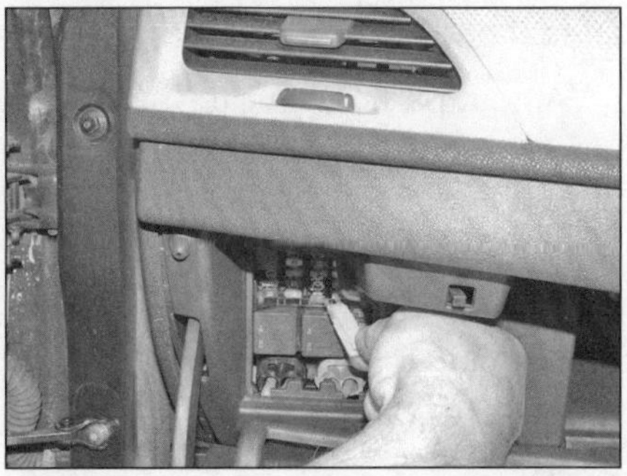

3 To renew a blown fuse, remove it using the plastic tweezer tool provided (where applicable). Fit a new fuse of the same rating, available from car accessory shops. It is important that you find the reason that the fuse blew (see *Electrical fault finding* in Chapter 12).

Lubricants and fluids

Petrol engine	Engine oil, SAE 10W-30, 10W-40 or 10W-50, to specification ACEA A3, A5, B4 or B5
Diesel engine:	
Without particulate filter	Engine oil, SAE 5W-40, 5W-50, 10W-40 or 10W-50, specification ACEA A3 or B4
With particulate filter	Engine oil, SAE 5W-30 or 5W-40 to specification ACEA C3
Cooling system	Ethylene glycol-based antifreeze suitable for use in mixed-metal engines – Glacéol RX type D
Manual transmission	TransElf TRJ 75W-80
Brake and clutch systems	Hydraulic fluid to DOT 4

Tyre pressures

Note: *Pressures given here are a guide only, and apply to original-equipment tyres – the recommended pressures may vary if any other make or type of tyre is fitted. Renault suggest different pressures depending on use, rather than based on load. Check with the car handbook for latest recommendations, and for usage other than that quoted below.*

Urban use	**Front**	**Rear**
195/65 R15 91H tyres	2.3 bar (33 psi)	2.0 bar (29 psi)
195/65 R15 91T tyres	2.3 bar (33 psi)	2.0 bar (29 psi)
205/55 R16 91H tyres	2.3 bar (33 psi)	2.0 bar (29 psi)
Motorway use		
195/65 R15 91H tyres	2.4 bar (35 psi)	2.2 bar (32 psi)
195/65 R15 91T tyres	2.4 bar (35 psi)	2.2 bar (32 psi)
205/55 R16 91H tyres	2.4 bar (35 psi)	2.2 bar (32 psi)
Emergency spare tyre		
All usage, front or rear	2.3 bar (33 psi)	

Chapter 1 Part A:
Routine maintenance and servicing – petrol models

Contents

	Section number
Air conditioning system check	20
Air filter element renewal	17
Auxiliary drivebelt check	7
Auxiliary drivebelt renewal	23
Bodywork and underbody condition check	13
Brake fluid renewal	21
Braking system check	5
Clutch check	6
Coolant renewal	22
Driveshaft gaiter check	12
Electrical systems check	9
Engine oil and filter renewal	3
Exhaust system check	10
Front wheel alignment check	19
Hose and fluid leak check	14
Introduction	1
Manual transmission oil level check	18
Pollen filter renewal	4
Regular maintenance	2
Road test	15
Seat belt check	8
Spark plug renewal	16
Suspension and steering check	11
Timing belt renewal	24

Degrees of difficulty

Easy, suitable for novice with little experience	**Fairly easy,** suitable for beginner with some experience	**Fairly difficult,** suitable for competent DIY mechanic	**Difficult,** suitable for experienced DIY mechanic	**Very difficult,** suitable for expert DIY or professional

Lubricants and fluids

Refer to *Weekly checks* on page 0•16

Capacities

Engine oil (including oil filter)	5.0 litres
Cooling system	5.3 litres
Manual transmission:	
JR5 (5 speed)	2.4 litres
TL4 (6 speed)	2.0 litres
Fuel tank	60 litres approximately (13 gallons)

Cooling system

Antifreeze mixture:	**Antifreeze**
Protection to –23°C	35%
Protection to –40°C	50%

Fuel system

System pressure	3.5 bar
Specified idle speed (non-adjustable)	700 ± 40 rpm
Idle mixture CO content (non-adjustable)	0.5% max (0.3% max at 2000 rpm)

Ignition system

Firing order	1-3-4-2
Location of No 1 cylinder	Flywheel end
Ignition timing	Controlled by ECU – see Chapter 5B
Spark plug gap	0.95 ± 0.05 mm

Brakes

Brake pad friction material minimum thickness	1.5 mm

Torque wrench settings

	Nm	lbf ft
Auxiliary drive belt tensioner*	40	30
Ignition coil bolts	14	10
Clutch pedal nuts	21	15
Roadwheel bolts	110	81
Spark plugs	25	18
Sump plug	20	15
Transmission drain plug	24	18

** A new bolt must be used*

The maintenance intervals in this manual are provided with the assumption that you, not the dealer, will be carrying out the work. These are the minimum maintenance intervals recommended by us for cars driven daily. If you wish to keep your car in peak condition at all times, you may wish to perform some of these procedures more often. We encourage frequent maintenance, because it enhances the efficiency, performance and resale value of your car.

If the car is driven in dusty areas, used to tow a trailer, or driven frequently at slow speeds (idling in traffic) or on short journeys, more frequent maintenance intervals are recommended.

Every 250 miles (400 km) or weekly

☐ Refer to *Weekly checks*

Every 9000 miles (15 000 km)

☐ Renew the engine oil and filter (Section 3)

Note: *Frequent oil and filter changes are good for the engine. We recommend changing the oil at the mileage specified here, or at least once a year.*

Note: *All petrol models featured in this manual are fitted with an 'oil control system' (OCS). The system monitors the style and type of driving and calculates the need for an oil change based on these parameters. For example a vehicle used primarily for urban driving will require more frequent oil changes than a vehicle that Is used for long distance motorway driving. When an oil change is due the instrument panel will display 'service or oil change Interval'.*

Every 18 000 miles (30 000 km) or 2 years, whichever comes first

In addition to all the items listed previously, carry out the following:

☐ Renew the pollen filter (Section 4)
☐ Check the braking system (Section 5)
☐ Check the operation of the clutch (Section 6)
☐ Check the condition of the auxiliary drivebelt (Section 7)
☐ Check the condition of the seat belts (Section 8)
☐ Check the operation of all electrical systems (Section 9)
☐ Check the condition of the exhaust system and mountings (Section 10)
☐ Check the suspension and steering components (Section 11)
☐ Check the condition of the driveshaft gaiters (Section 12)
☐ Check the bodywork and underbody for damage and corrosion (Section 13)
☐ Check all underbonnet components and hoses for fluid leaks (Section 14)
☐ Carry out a road test (Section 15)

Every 36 000 miles (60 000 km) or 4 years, whichever comes first

In addition to all the items listed previously, carry out the following:

☐ Renew the spark plugs (Section 16)
☐ Renew the air filter element (Section 17)
☐ Check the manual transmission oil level (Section 18)
☐ Check the front wheel alignment (Section 19)
☐ Check the operation of the air conditioning system (Section 20)
☐ Renew the brake fluid (Section 21)
☐ Renew the coolant (Section 22)

Every 72 000 miles (120 000 km) or 6 years, whichever comes first

☐ Renew the auxiliary drive belt (Section 23)*
☐ Renew the timing belt (Section 24)*

*** Note:** *Although the normal interval for timing belt and auxiliary drive belt renewal is 72 000 miles (120 000 km), it is strongly recommended that the interval is reduced to 36 000 miles (60 000 km) or 4 years on cars which are subjected to intensive use, ie, mainly short journeys or a lot of stop-start driving. The actual belt renewal interval is therefore very much up to the individual owner, but bear in mind that severe engine damage may result if the belt breaks.*

 Component location – petrol models

Underbonnet view

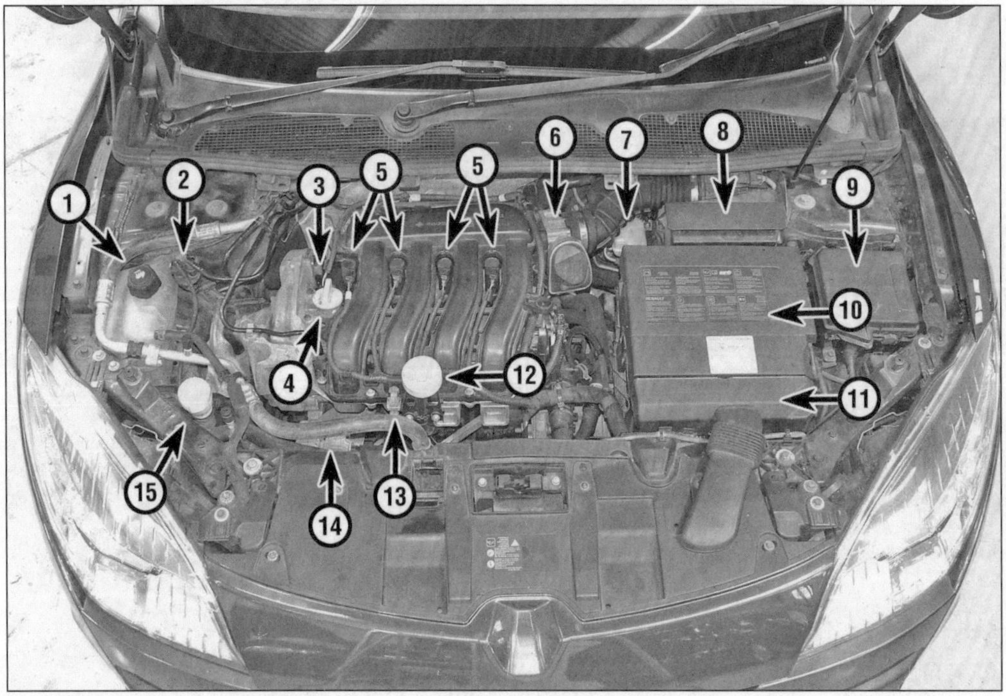

1 Coolant expansion tank
2 Canister purge valve
3 VVT solenoid valve
4 Engine oil filler cap
5 Ignition coils
6 Throttle body
7 Brake/clutch fluid reservoir
8 Air filter housing
9 Engine compartment fusebox
10 Battery (under cover)
11 Engine management ECU (under cover)
12 Engine oil dipstick
13 Inlet air temperature sensor
14 Alternator
15 Fuel supply hose

Front underbody view

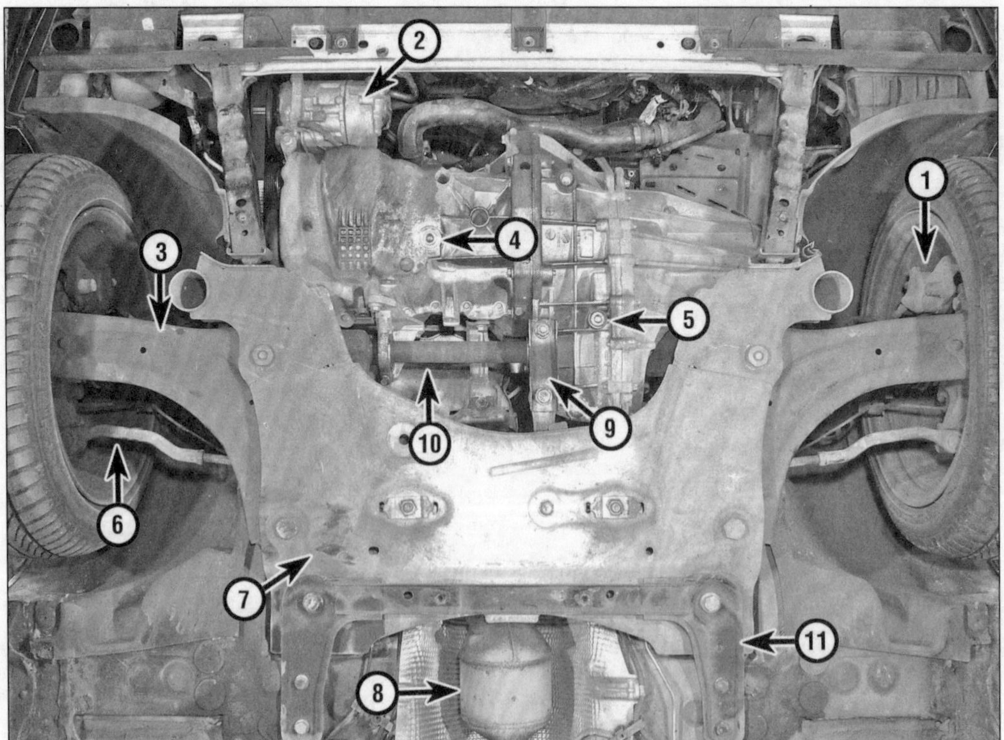

1 Front brake caliper
2 Air conditioning compressor
3 Front suspension lower arm
4 Engine oil drain plug
5 Transmission oil drain plug
6 Track rod
7 Subframe
8 Catalytic converter
9 Engine rear mounting link
10 Right-hand driveshaft
11 Rear crossmember

Rear underbody view

1 *Exhaust rear silencer*
2 *Spare wheel well*
3 *Rear shock absorber*
4 *Rear axle*
5 *Rear brake pipes/hoses*
6 *Exhaust mounting*
7 *Heat shield*
8 *Fuel tank*
9 *Charcoal canister*

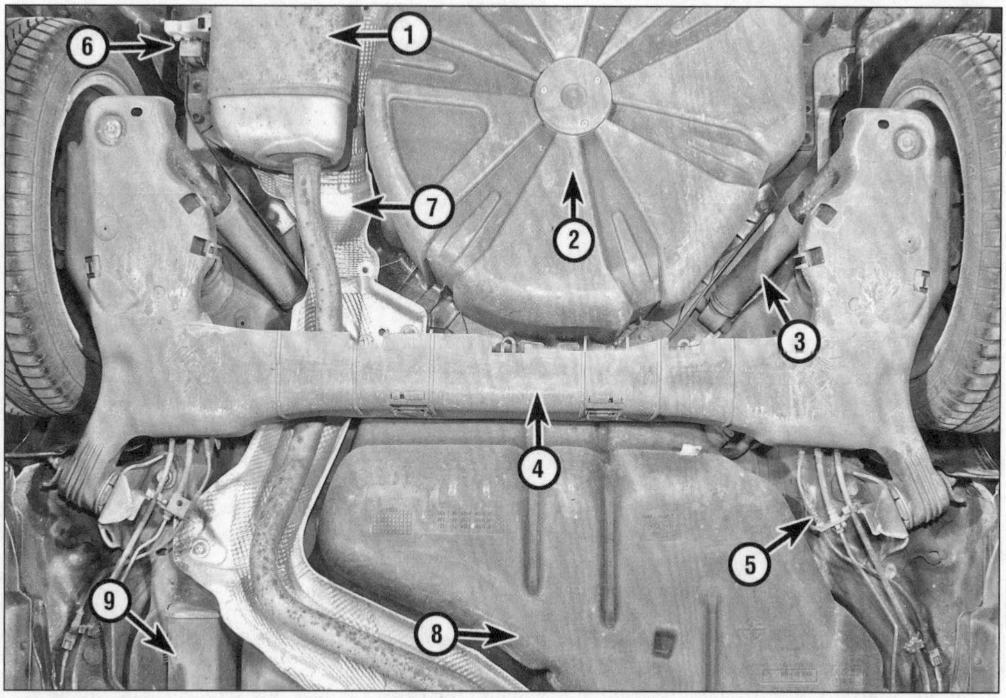

Maintenance procedures

1 Introduction

This Chapter is designed to help the home mechanic maintain his/her car for safety, economy, long life and peak performance.

The Chapter contains a master maintenance schedule, followed by Sections dealing specifically with each task in the schedule. Visual checks, adjustments, component renewal and other helpful items are included. Refer to the accompanying illustrations of the engine compartment and the underside of the car for the locations of the various components.

Servicing your car in accordance with the mileage/time maintenance schedule and the following Sections will provide a planned maintenance programme, which should result in a long and reliable service life. This is a comprehensive plan, so maintaining some items but not others at the specified service intervals will not produce the same results.

As you service your car, you will discover that many of the procedures can – and should – be grouped together, because of the particular procedure being performed, or because of the proximity of two otherwise-unrelated components to one another. For example, if the car is raised for any reason, the exhaust can be inspected at the same time as the suspension and steering components.

The first step in this maintenance programme is to prepare yourself before the actual work begins. Read through all the Sections relevant to the work to be carried out, then make a list and gather all the parts and tools required. If a problem is encountered, seek advice from a parts specialist, or a dealer service department.

Resetting the service light

To reset the service warning light on the instrument panel, switch on the ignition, then scroll through the trip computer's displayed options until the 'oil change interval' is displayed. Now press and hold the button for 10 seconds. The value will flash 4 times and then the new interval will be displayed. When the new value flashes 4 times release the button.

Special precautions for vehicles fitted with Stop/Start technology

Some models feature Stop/Start technology, where under normal operating conditions the engine will automatically stop (and restart) to reduce fuel consumption and the production of greenhouse gases. Precautions must be taken to ensure that the vehicle will not restart whilst service and maintenance operations are taking place. This can be achieved by pressing the Stop/Start switch on the dashboard (the dashboard will display 'Stop and Start deactivated') opening the bonnet, or by leaving the drivers door open. However the safest way to ensure the system will not restart is to disconnect the battery *-see Disconnecting the battery in Chapter 5A.*

2 Regular maintenance

If, from the time the car is new, the routine maintenance schedule is followed closely, and frequent checks are made of fluid levels and high-wear items, as suggested throughout this manual, the engine will be kept in relatively good running condition, and the need for additional work will be minimised.

It is possible that there will be times when the engine is running poorly due to the lack of regular maintenance. This is even more likely if a used car, which has not received regular and frequent maintenance checks, is purchased. In such cases, additional work may need to be carried out, outside of the regular maintenance intervals.

If engine wear is suspected, a compression test (refer to Chapter 2A) will provide valuable information regarding the overall performance of the main internal components. Such a test can be used as a basis to decide on the extent of the work to be carried out. If, for example, a compression test indicates serious internal engine wear, conventional maintenance as described in this Chapter will not greatly improve the performance of the engine, and may prove a waste of time and money, unless extensive overhaul work is carried out first.

The following series of operations are those most often required to improve the performance of a generally poor-running engine:

Primary operations

a) Clean, inspect and test the battery (refer to 'Weekly checks').
b) Check all the engine-related fluids (refer to 'Weekly checks').
c) Check the condition of the auxiliary drivebelt(s) (Section 7).
d) Check the condition of all hoses, and check for fluid leaks (Section 14).
e) Renew the spark plugs (Section 16).
f) Check the condition of the air filter, and renew if necessary (Section 17).

If the above operations do not prove fully effective, carry out the following secondary operations:

Secondary operations

All items listed under *Primary operations*, plus the following:

a) Check the charging system (Chapter 5A).
b) Check the ignition system (Chapter 5B).
c) Check the fuel system (refer to Chapter 4A).

Every 9000 miles (15 000 km)

3 Engine oil and filter renewal

1 Frequent oil and filter changes are the most important preventative maintenance procedures which can be undertaken by the home mechanic. As engine oil ages, it becomes diluted and contaminated, which leads to premature engine wear.

2 Before starting this procedure, gather together all the necessary tools and materials. Also make sure that you have plenty of clean rags and newspapers handy, to mop-up any spills. Ideally, the engine oil should be warm, as it will drain more easily, and more built-up sludge will be removed with it.

3 Take care not to touch the exhaust or any other hot parts of the engine when working under the car. To avoid any possibility of scalding, and to protect yourself from possible skin irritants and other harmful contaminants in used engine oils, it is advisable to wear gloves when carrying out this work.

4 Firmly apply the handbrake, then jack up the front of the car and support it on axle stands (see *Jacking and vehicle support*).

5 Remove the fasteners and lower out the engine undertray. Remove the oil filler cap, then position a container beneath the sump. Clean the drain plug and the area around it, then slacken it half a turn – all models have a drain plug which requires an 8 mm square key to remove it **(see illustrations)**.

6 Allow some time for the old oil to drain, noting that it may be necessary to reposition the container as the oil flow slows to a trickle.

7 After all the oil has drained, wipe off the drain plug with a clean rag and fit a new sealing washer **(see illustration)**. Clean the area around the drain plug opening, then refit and tighten the plug securely.

8 Move the container into position under the oil filter, which is located horizontally on the front face of the engine **(see illustration)**. Access is not easy, but it is possible without removing any body or engine components.

9 Using an oil filter removal tool where possible, slacken the filter initially. Loosely wrap some rags around the oil filter, then unscrew it and immediately position it with its open end uppermost to prevent further spillage of oil. Remove the oil filter from the engine compartment, and empty the oil into the container.

10 Use a clean rag to remove all oil, dirt and sludge from the filter sealing area on the engine. Check the old filter to make sure that the rubber sealing ring hasn't stuck to the engine. If it has, carefully remove it.

11 Apply a light coating of clean oil to the sealing ring on the new filter **(see illustration)**, then screw it into position on the engine. Tighten the filter firmly by hand only – do not use any tools. Wipe clean the exterior of the oil filter.

12 Remove the old oil and all tools from under the car, refit the undertray where necessary, and lower the car to the ground.

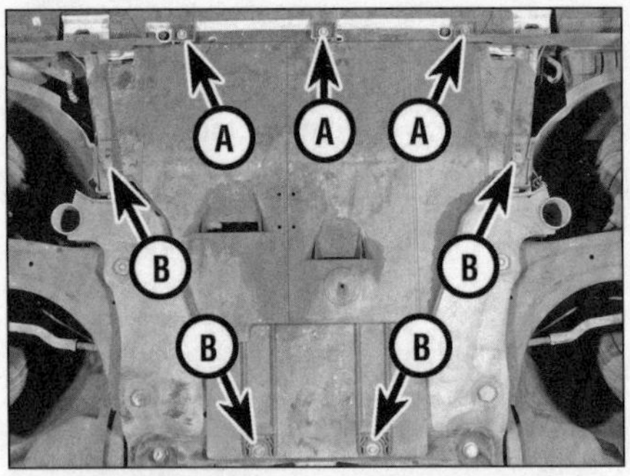

3.5a Slacken the front bolts (A) and remove the rear bolts (B)

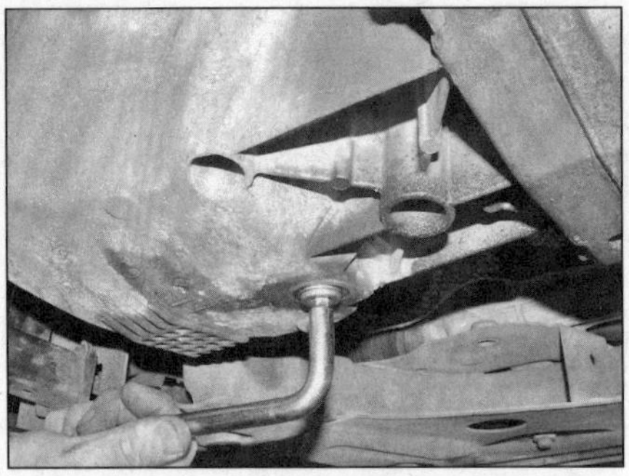
3.5b The engine oil drain plug is removed using a square-section key

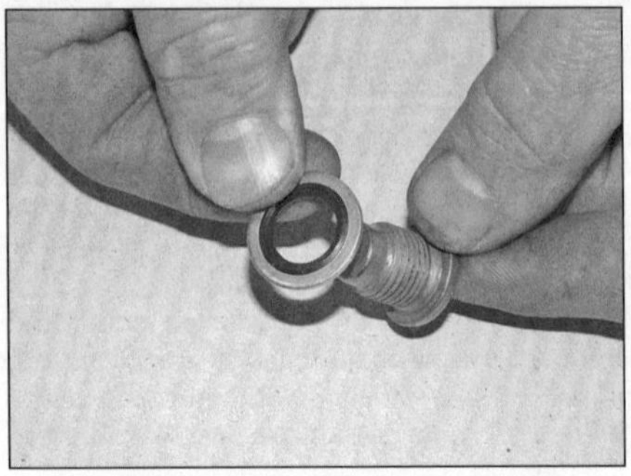
3.7 Fit a new seal to the drain plug

3.8 Oil filter location (arrowed) on the front of the engine

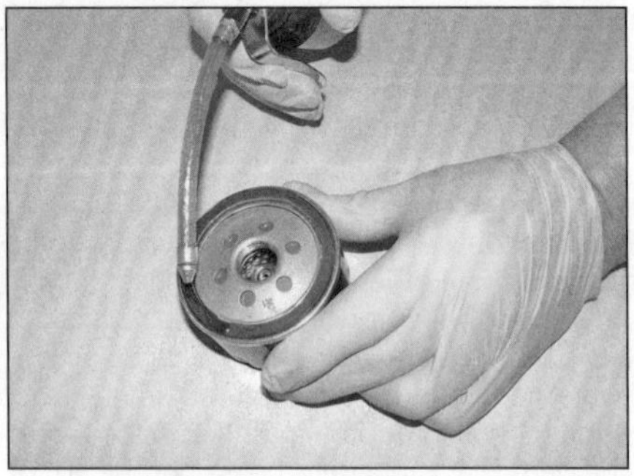
3.11 Lubricate the seal on the new oil filter

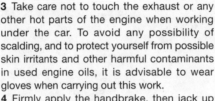

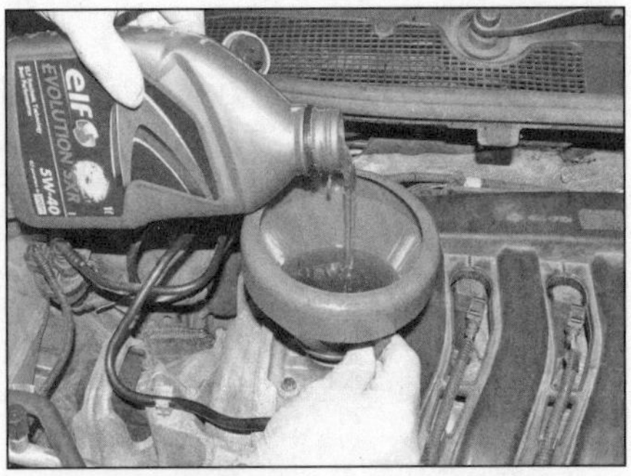

3.13a Slowly fill the engine with correct amount of oil...

3.13b ...checking that the oil is up to the maximum mark on the dipstick

3.13c ...and then refit the oil filler cap

13 Fill the engine with the specified quantity and grade of oil, as described in *Weekly checks*. Pour the oil in slowly, in small amounts, waiting each time for the oil to drain into the sump. When the oil level is up to the maximum mark on the dipstick, refit and tighten the oil filler cap **(see illustrations)**.

14 Start the engine and run it for a few minutes, checking that there are no leaks around the oil filter seal and the sump drain plug. Note that when the engine is first started, there will be a delay of a few seconds before the oil pressure warning light goes out while the new filter fills with oil. Do not race the engine while the warning light is on.

15 Switch off the engine and wait a few minutes for the oil to settle in the sump once more. With the new oil circulated and the filter now completely full, recheck the level on the dipstick and add more oil if necessary.

16 Dispose of the used engine oil safely with reference to *General repair procedures* in the Reference section of this manual.

Every 18 000 miles (30 000 km) or 2 years

4 Pollen filter renewal

1 Remove the side panel from the centre console on the drivers side and then remove the lower fascia panel **(see illustration)** on the same side (as described in Chapter 11).

2 Remove the air distribution duct and then carefully release the clutch hydraulic fluid pipes from the retaining clips on the pedal box.

3 Release the wiring loom and then unbolt the clutch pedal mounting bolts. There is no need to disconnect the wiring plug.

4 Carefully rotate and lower the pedal into the foot well **(see illustration)**.

5 Unclip the wiring loom from the side of the air distribution housing.

6 On some models the filter cover is held in place by screws, on other models it is a simple clip fit. Remove the screws or unclip the cover as appropriate **(see illustrations)**.

7 Pull the filter from the housing. The filter will have to be deformed to clear the steering column and pedal assembly **(see illustration)**.

4.1 Remove the lower panel

4.4 Rotate and lower the clutch pedal assembly

4.6a Where fitted remove the screws (arrowed)...

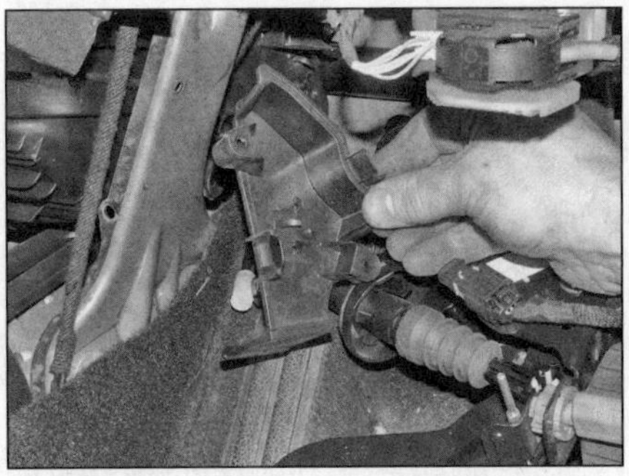

4.6b ...and remove the filter cover

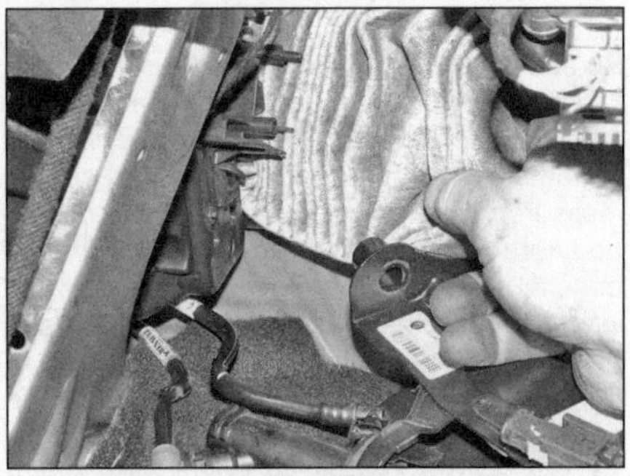

4.7 Manoeuvre the pollen filter out from the housing

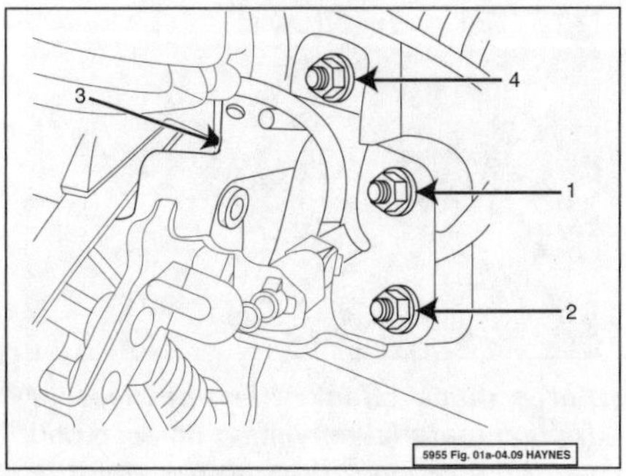

4.9 Tighten the clutch pedal bolts in the order shown

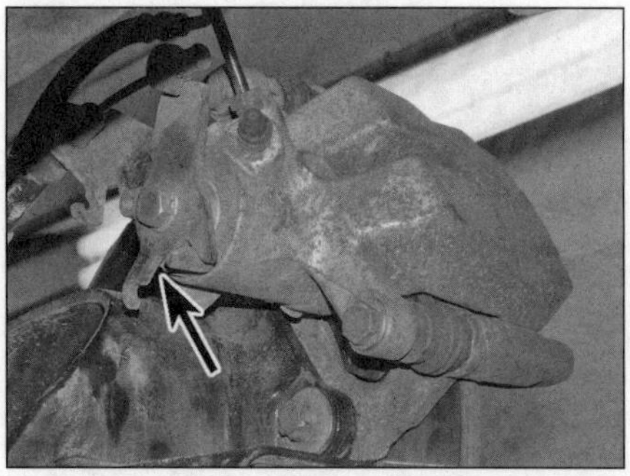

5.5 With the handbrake on, there should be a gap between the caliper lever and its stop

5.8a Prise free the rear storage compartment of the centre console to access the handbrake adjustment

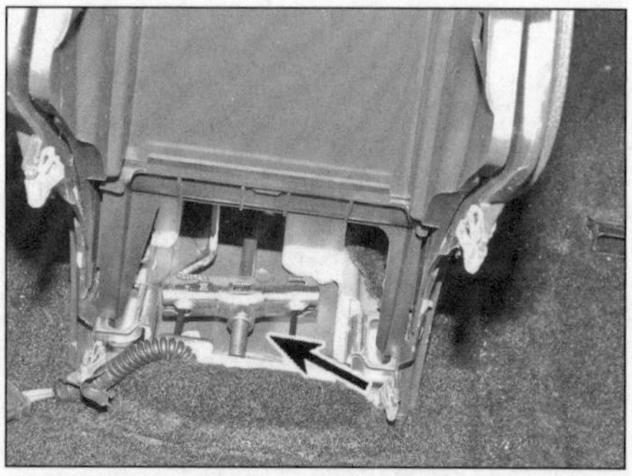

5.8b If necessary, use the nut (arrowed) to adjust the handbrake

Note the direction of the airflow arrows on the filter - they should point into the cabin.

8 Inspect the housing for any debris and vacuum it out if necessary.

9 Refitting is a reversal of removal. Remember to tighten the pedal assembly nuts to the correct torque **(see illustration)**.

5 Braking system check

Handbrake check and adjustment

Note: *Models fitted with an automatic (motorised) handbrake do not require adjustment or checking as part of a routine service.*

1 The handbrake should be capable of holding the parked car stationary, even on steep slopes, when applied with moderate force. The mechanism should be firm and positive in feel, with no trace of stiffness or sponginess from the cables, and should release immediately the handbrake lever is released. If the mechanism is faulty in any of these respects, it must be checked immediately as follows.

2 Handbrake adjustment is made inside the car, after removing the rear section of the centre console (as described in Chapter 11).

3 Jack up the rear of the car and support it on axle stands (see *Jacking and vehicle support*).

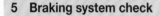

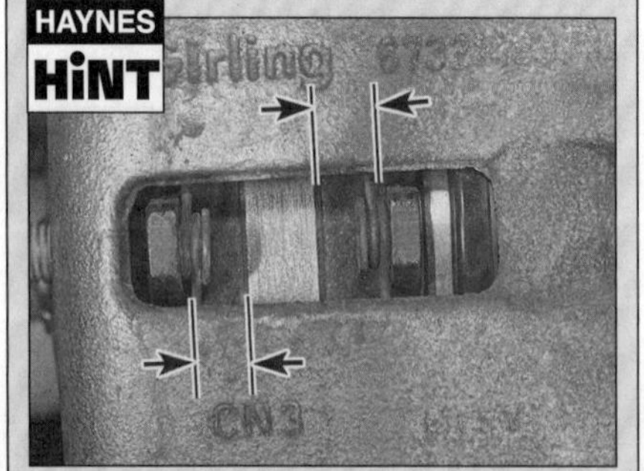

For a quick check, the thickness of friction material remaining on each pad can be measured through the aperture on the caliper body.

4 Operate the handbrake several times, and leave it applied as normal.

5 Check that the handbrake operating lever on each rear caliper is sitting off its stop by approximately 1 mm **(see illustration)**. If not, further adjustment may be required, or the cable on the side affected may have seized.

6 Check that the handbrake cables slide freely by pulling on their front ends, and check that the operating levers on the rear brake calipers move smoothly.

7 If the cables have stretched over time, the cables may need to be adjusted beyond the nominal setting. Bear in mind that the adjuster nut has a plastic insert, which loses its effectiveness over time – if the adjustment is being lost regularly, a new nut should be fitted.

8 Move both of the caliper operating levers as far rearwards as possible, then tighten the adjuster nut inside the car until all free play is removed from both cables. With the aid of an assistant, adjust the nut so that the operating lever on each rear brake caliper starts to move as the handbrake lever is moved between the first and second notch (click) of its ratchet mechanism **(see illustrations)**.

9 After adjustment, release the handbrake fully, and check that the wheels are free to turn.

10 On completion, lower the car to the ground.

Brake pad and disc check

11 Firmly apply the handbrake, then jack up the front or rear of the car and support it securely on axle stands (see *Jacking and vehicle support*). Remove the roadwheels. Remember, the car has disc brakes all round, so all four calipers should be checked.

12 For a quick check, the thickness of friction material remaining on each brake pad can be measured through the aperture in the caliper body **(see Haynes Hint)**. If any pad's friction material is worn to the specified thickness or less, all four pads must be renewed as a set. Pad wear warning contacts may be fitted to the inboard pads, but this should not be used as an excuse for omitting a visual check.

13 For a comprehensive check, the brake pads should be removed and cleaned. This will allow the operation of the caliper to be checked, and the brake disc itself to be fully examined for condition on both sides. Refer to Chapter 9 for further information.

6 Clutch check

Check that the clutch pedal moves smoothly and easily through its full travel, and that the clutch itself functions correctly, with no trace of slip or drag. If the clutch action is less than precise, this may indicate the need for bleeding the system – it could also indicate the presence of a fluid leak (see Chapter 6).

7 Auxiliary drivebelt check

1 The auxiliary drivebelt is located at the right-hand side of the engine, providing drive for the alternator and the air conditioning compressor.

2 The drivebelt features an automatic tensioner.

3 Due to their function and material makeup, drivebelts are prone to failure after a period of time, and should therefore be inspected regularly.

4 Loosen the right-hand front wheel bolts, then jack up the front of the car, and support it on axle stands (see *Jacking and vehicle support*). Remove the wheel.

5 Remove the screws and clips securing the front section of the wheel arch liner, and remove it.

6 With the engine stopped, inspect the full length of the drivebelt for cracks and separation of the belt plies. Small cracks in the belt ribs are no cause for concern, unless they are deep into the belt itself. Also check for fraying, and glazing which gives the belt a shiny appearance **(see illustration)**.

7 Turn the engine (using a spanner or socket on the crankshaft pulley bolt) so that the belt can be inspected thoroughly. Twist the belt between the pulleys so that both sides can be viewed. Check the pulleys for nicks, cracks, distortion and corrosion.

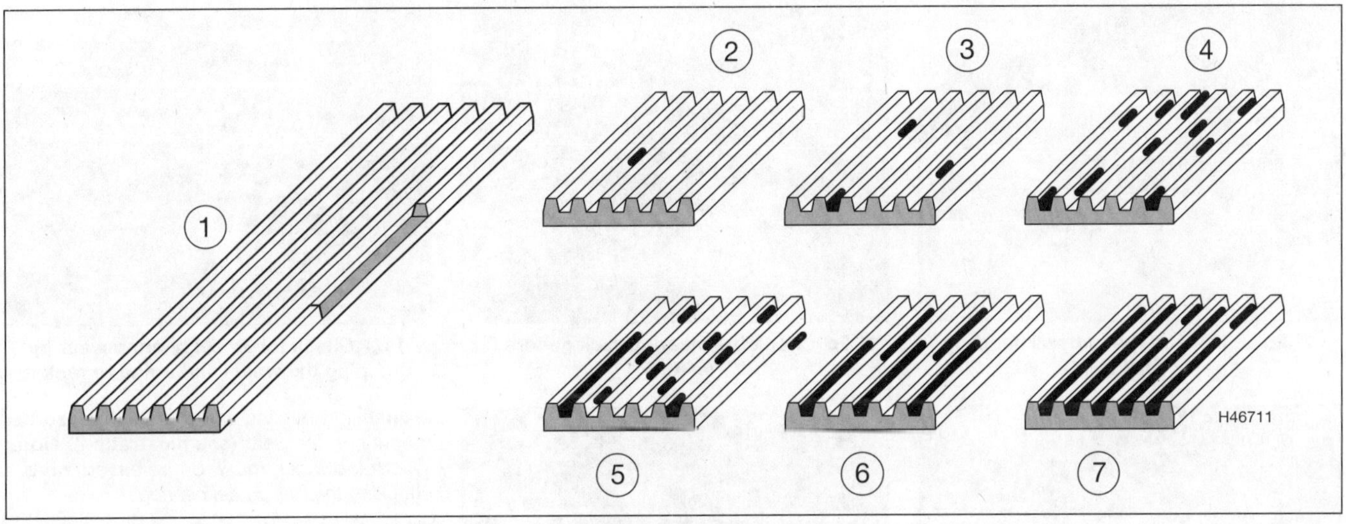

7.6 Check for drivebelt wear

1 If sections are missing renew the belt
2 Small deposits in the grooves are not a concern
3 Small scattered deposits are not a concern
4 Deposits up to half of the rib height: renew the belt if noisy
5 Deposits up to half the rib height: renew the belt if noisy
6 Heavy deposits: renew the belt
7 Heavy deposits: renew the belt

8 If the belt is satisfactory, refit the components removed to access it, then refit the wheel and lower the car to the ground. Tighten the wheel bolts to the specified torque.

8 Seat belt check

1 Carefully examine the seat belt webbing for cuts, or any signs of serious fraying or deterioration. If the belt is of the retractable type, pull the belt all the way out of the inertia reel, and examine the full extent of the webbing.
2 Fasten and unfasten the belt, ensuring that the locking mechanism holds securely, and releases properly when intended. If the belt is of the retractable type, check also that the retracting mechanism operates correctly when the belt is released.
3 Check the security of all seat belt mountings and attachments which are accessible without removing any trim or other components.

9 Electrical systems check

1 Check the operation of all electrical equipment, ie, lights, direction indicators, horn, etc. Refer to the appropriate Sections of Chapter 12 for details if any of the circuits are found to be inoperative.
2 Note that stop-light switch adjustment is described in Chapter 9.
3 Visually check all accessible wiring connectors, harnesses and retaining clips for security, and for signs of chafing or damage. Rectify any faults found.

10 Exhaust system check

1 With the engine cold (at least an hour after the car has been driven), check the complete exhaust system from the engine to the end of the tailpipe. Ideally, the inspection should be carried out with the car on a hoist to permit unrestricted access, but if a hoist is not available, raise and support the car safely on axle stands (see *Jacking and vehicle support*).
2 Check the exhaust pipes and connections for evidence of leaks, severe corrosion and damage. Make sure that all brackets and mountings are in good condition and tight. Leakage at any of the joints or in other parts of the system will usually show up as a black sooty stain in the vicinity of the leak.
3 Rattles and other noises can often be traced to the exhaust system, especially the brackets and mountings. Try to move the pipes and silencers. If the components can come into contact with the body or suspension parts, secure the system with new mountings or if possible, separate the joints and twist the pipes as necessary to provide additional clearance.
4 Run the engine at idling speed. Have an assistant place a cloth or rag over the rear end of the exhaust pipe, and listen for any escape of exhaust gases that would indicate a leak.
5 On completion, lower the car to the ground.

11 Suspension and steering check

Front suspension and steering

1 Raise the front of the car, and securely support it on axle stands (see *Jacking and vehicle support*).
2 Visually inspect the balljoint dust covers and the steering rack-and-pinion gaiters for splits, chafing or deterioration **(see illustrations)**. Any wear of these components will cause loss of lubricant, together with dirt and water entry, resulting in rapid deterioration of the balljoints or steering gear.
3 Grasp the roadwheel at the 12 o'clock and 6 o'clock positions, and try to rock it **(see illustration)**. Very slight free play may be felt, but if the movement is appreciable, further investigation is necessary to determine the source. Continue rocking the wheel while an assistant depresses the footbrake. If the

11.2a Check the balljoint rubber gaiters on the track rod ends . . .

11.2b . . . and on the anti-roll bar drop links

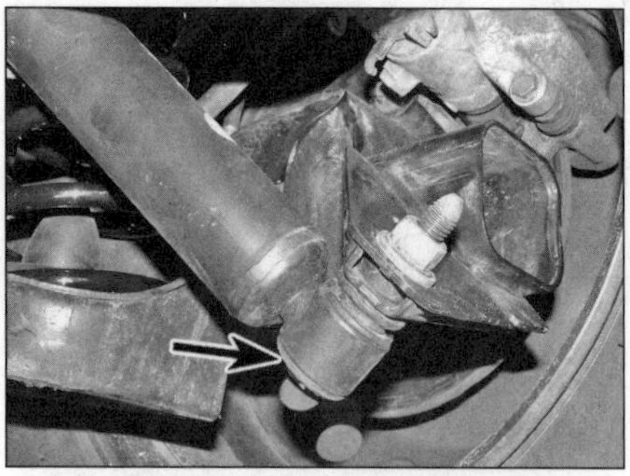

11.8 Check the rear shock absorber for fluid leaks and mounting damage

movement is now eliminated or significantly reduced, it is likely that the hub bearings are at fault. If the free play is still evident with the footbrake depressed, then there is wear in the suspension joints or mountings.

4 Now grasp the wheel at the 9 o'clock and 3 o'clock positions, and try to rock it as before. Any movement felt now may again be caused by wear in the hub bearings or the steering track rod balljoints. If the outer balljoint is worn, the visual movement will be obvious. If the inner joint is suspect, it can be felt by placing a hand over the rack-and-pinion rubber gaiter and gripping the track rod. If the wheel is now rocked, movement will be felt at the inner joint if wear has taken place.

5 Using a large screwdriver or flat bar, check for wear in the suspension mounting bushes by levering between the relevant suspension component and its attachment point. Some movement is to be expected, as the mountings

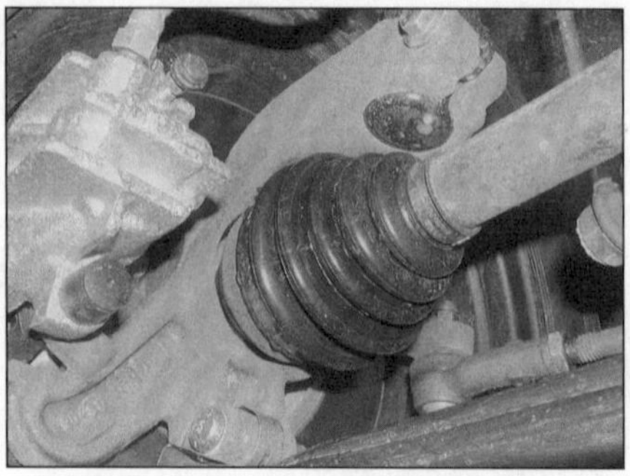

12.1a Check the outer CV joint gaiters for splits or signs of perishing

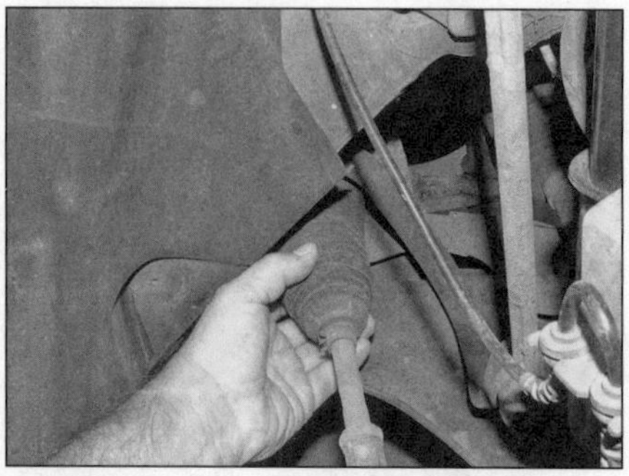

11.2c Check the steering rack gaiters for splitting

11.9 Check around the front strut piston rod gaiter for fluid leaks

are made of rubber, but excessive wear should be obvious. Also check the condition of any visible rubber bushes, looking for splits, cracks or contamination of the rubber.

6 With the car standing on its wheels, have an assistant turn the steering wheel back-and-forth, about an eighth of a turn each way. There should be very little, if any, lost movement between the steering wheel and roadwheels. If this is not the case, closely observe the joints and mountings previously described. In addition, check the steering column universal joints for wear, and also check the rack-and-pinion steering gear itself.

Rear suspension

7 Chock the front wheels, then jack up the rear of the car and support securely on axle stands (see *Jacking and vehicle support*).

8 Working as described previously for the front suspension, check the rear hub bearings, the

12.1b Similarly check the inner CV joint gaiters

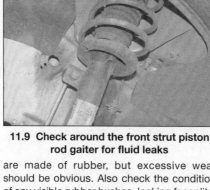

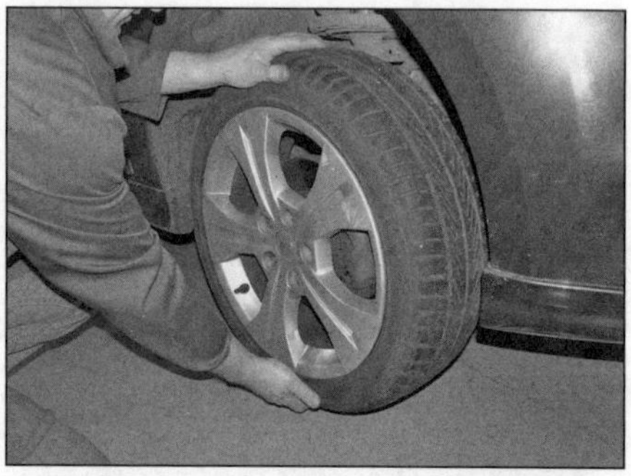

11.3 Check for wheel bearing wear by grasping the wheel and trying to rock it

suspension bushes and the shock absorber mountings for wear **(see illustration). Note:** *The handbrake must be released before checking the rear wheel bearings.*

Shock absorber check

9 Check for any signs of fluid leakage around the shock absorber body, or from the rubber gaiter around the piston rod **(see illustration)**. Should any fluid be noticed, the shock absorber is defective internally, and should be renewed. **Note:** *Shock absorbers should always be renewed in pairs on the same axle.*

10 The efficiency of the shock absorber may be checked by bouncing the car at each corner. Generally speaking, the body will return to its normal position and stop after being depressed. If it rises and returns on a rebound, the shock absorber is probably suspect.

Roadwheel bolt check

11 Remove the wheel trims or wheel centre caps, as applicable, then slacken the roadwheel bolts slightly.

12 Tighten the bolts to the specified torque, using a torque wrench.

12 Driveshaft gaiter check

1 With the car raised and securely supported on stands, turn the steering onto full lock, then slowly rotate the roadwheel. Inspect the condition of the outer constant velocity (CV) joint rubber gaiters while squeezing the gaiters to open out the folds. Check for signs of cracking, splits or deterioration of the rubber which may allow the grease to escape and lead to water and grit entry into the joint. Also check the security and condition of the retaining clips. Repeat these checks on the inner CV joints **(see illustrations)**. If any damage or deterioration is found, the gaiters should be renewed as described in Chapter 8.

2 At the same time, check the general condition of the CV joints themselves by first holding the driveshaft and attempting to rotate the wheel. Repeat this check by holding the inner joint and attempting

to rotate the driveshaft. Any appreciable movement indicates wear in the joints, wear in the driveshaft splines, or a loose driveshaft retaining nut.

13 Bodywork and underbody condition check

1 Once the car has been washed and all tar spots and other surface blemishes have been cleaned off, carefully check all paintwork, looking closely for chips or scratches. Pay particular attention to vulnerable areas such as the front panels (bonnet and bumper), and around the wheel arches. Any damage to the paintwork must be rectified as soon as possible to comply with the terms of the manufacturer's anti-corrosion warranties; check with a Renault dealer for details.

2 If a chip or light scratch is found which is recent and still free from rust, it can be touched-up using the appropriate touch-up stick which can be obtained from Renault dealers. Any more serious damage, or rusted stone chips, can be repaired as described in Chapter 11, but if damage or corrosion is so severe that a panel must be renewed, seek professional advice as soon as possible.

3 Always check that the door and ventilation opening drain holes and pipes are completely clear, so that water can drain out.

4 The wax-based underbody protective coating should be inspected annually, preferably just prior to Winter, when the underbody should be washed down as thoroughly as possible without disturbing the protective coating (see Chapter 11, Section 2, regarding the use of steam cleaners). Any damage to the coating should be repaired using a wax-based sealer. If any of the body panels are disturbed for repair or renewal, do not forget to replace the coating and to inject wax into door panels, sills and box sections, to maintain the level of protection provided by the manufacturer.

14 Hose and fluid leak check

1 Visually inspect the engine joint faces, gaskets and seals for any signs of water or oil leaks. Pay particular attention to the areas around the top of the engine, cylinder head, oil filter and sump joint faces **(see illustration)**. Bear in mind that, over a period of time, some very slight seepage from these areas is to be expected – what you are really looking for is any indication of a serious leak. Should a leak be found, renew the offending gasket or oil seal by referring to the appropriate Chapters in this manual.

2 Also check the security and condition of all the engine-related pipes and hoses, and all hydraulic and braking system pipes and hoses

14.1 Check along the sump joint for signs of oil leaks

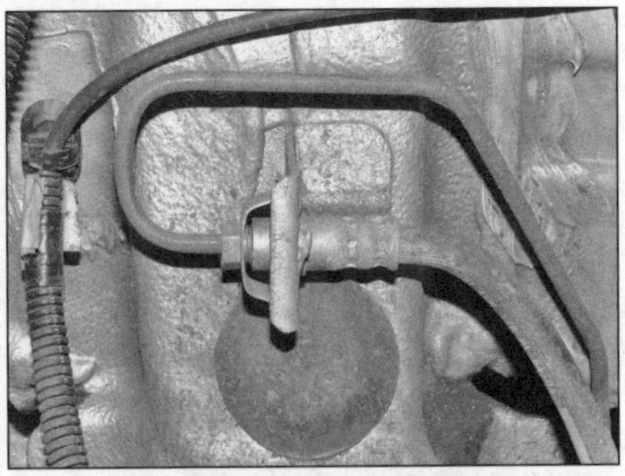

14.2 Check the brake pipes very carefully, especially at joints

14.3a Check the large-diameter radiator hoses for signs of damage

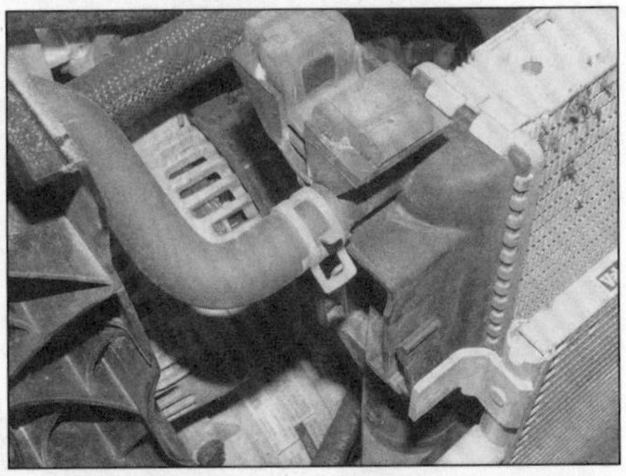

14.3b Spring-type hose clips can pinch and puncture hoses

(see illustration). Ensure that all cable-ties or securing clips are in place, and in good condition. Clips which are broken or missing can lead to chafing of the hoses, pipes or wiring, which could cause more serious problems in the future.

3 Carefully check the radiator hoses and heater hoses along their entire length. Renew any hose which is cracked, swollen or deteriorated. Cracks will show up better if the hose is squeezed. Pay close attention to the hose clips that secure the hoses to the cooling system components. Hose clips can pinch and puncture hoses, resulting in cooling system leaks. If the crimped-type hose clips are used, it may be a good idea to use Jubilee clips **(see illustrations)**.

4 Inspect all the cooling system components

HAYNES HiNT

A leak in the cooling system will usually show up as white- or rust-coloured deposits on the area surrounding the joint.

(hoses, joint faces, etc) for leaks **(see Haynes Hint)**. Where any problems are found on system components, renew the component or gasket with reference to Chapter 3.

5 With the car raised, inspect the fuel tank and filler neck for punctures, cracks and other damage. The connection between the filler neck and tank is especially critical **(see illustration)**. Sometimes a rubber filler neck or connecting hose will leak due to loose retaining clamps or deteriorated rubber.

6 Carefully check all rubber hoses and metal fuel lines leading away from the fuel tank. Check for loose connections, deteriorated hoses, crimped lines, and other damage. Pay particular attention to the vent pipes and hoses, which often loop up around the filler neck and can become blocked or crimped. Follow the lines to the front of the car, carefully inspecting them all the way. Renew damaged sections as necessary. Similarly, whilst the car

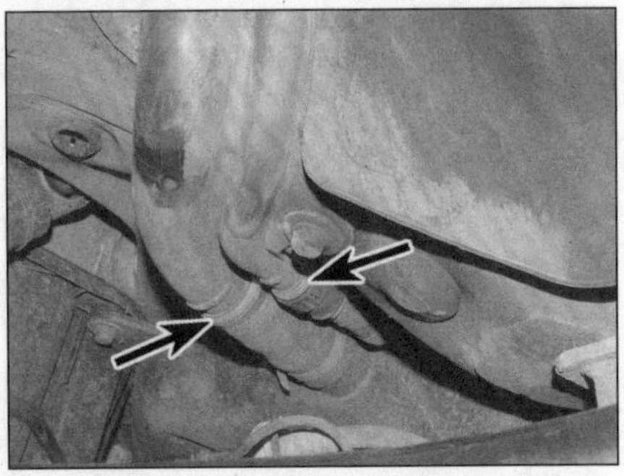

14.5 Check the fuel tank filler neck hoses for signs of leakage

is raised, take the opportunity to inspect all underbody brake fluid pipes and hoses.

7 From within the engine compartment, check the security of all fuel, vacuum and brake hose attachments and pipe unions, and inspect all hoses for kinks, chafing and deterioration.

15 Road test

Instruments and electrical equipment

1 Check the operation of all instruments and electrical equipment.

2 Make sure that all instruments read correctly, and switch on all electrical equipment in turn, to check that it functions properly.

Steering and suspension

3 Check for any abnormalities in the steering, suspension, handling or road 'feel'.

4 Drive the car, and check that there are no unusual vibrations or noises.

5 Check that the steering feels positive, with no excessive 'sloppiness', or roughness, and check for any suspension noises when cornering and driving over bumps.

Drivetrain

6 Check the performance of the engine, clutch, transmission and driveshafts.

7 Listen for any unusual noises from the engine, clutch and transmission.

8 Make sure that the engine runs smoothly when idling, and that there is no hesitation when accelerating.

9 Check that, where applicable, the clutch action is smooth and progressive, that the drive is taken up smoothly, and that the pedal travel is not excessive. Also listen for any noises when the clutch pedal is depressed.

10 Check that all gears can be engaged smoothly without noise, and that the gear lever action is smooth and not abnormally vague or 'notchy'.

11 Listen for a metallic clicking sound from the front of the car, as the car is driven slowly in a circle with the steering on full-lock. Carry out this check in both directions. If a clicking noise is heard, this indicates wear in a driveshaft joint (see Chapter 8).

Braking system

12 Make sure that the car does not pull to one side when braking, and that the wheels do not lock when braking hard.

13 Check that there is no vibration through the steering when braking.

14 Check that the handbrake operates correctly, without excessive movement of the lever, and that it holds the car stationary on a slope.

15 Test the operation of the brake servo unit as follows. Depress the footbrake four or five times to exhaust the vacuum, then start the engine. As the engine starts, there should be a noticeable 'give' in the brake pedal as vacuum builds-up. Allow the engine to run for at least two minutes, and then switch it off. If the brake pedal is now depressed again, it should be possible to detect a hiss from the servo as the pedal is depressed. After about four or five applications, no further hissing should be heard, and the pedal should feel considerably harder.

Every 36 000 miles (60 000 km) or 4 years

16 Spark plug renewal

Warning: High voltages are produced by the electronic ignition system. Extreme care must be taken when working on the system with the ignition switched on. Persons with surgically-implanted cardiac pacemaker devices should keep well clear of the ignition circuits, components and test equipment.

16.3 Disconnect the coil electrical connectors

16.4 Remove the ignition coils

16.6a Unscrew the plugs using a long extension bar...

16.6b ...and a suitable deep socket

1 The correct functioning of the spark plugs is vital for the correct running and efficiency of the engine. It is essential that the plugs fitted are appropriate for the engine, the type being specified at the start of this Chapter. If the correct type of plug is used and the engine is in good condition, the spark plugs should not need attention between scheduled servicing intervals. Spark plug cleaning is rarely necessary, and should not be attempted. If there is any doubt as to the condition of the spark plugs they should be replaced.

2 To remove the plugs, first open the bonnet and (where fitted) unclip the engine upper cover.

3 Release the wiring loom and disconnect the wiring pugs from each ignition coil **(see illustration)**.

4 Remove the ignition coil retaining bolts and work the coils free from the spark plugs **(see illustration)**. Keep the coils in the correct order.

5 It is advisable to remove any dirt from the spark plug recesses using a clean brush, a vacuum cleaner or compressed air before removing the plugs, to prevent the dirt dropping into the cylinders. However, since the plugs are deeply recessed in the engine, this may be difficult.

6 Unscrew the plugs using a spark plug spanner, box spanner or a deep socket and extension bar **(see illustrations)**. Keep the socket in alignment with the spark plug, otherwise if it is forcibly moved to either side, the ceramic top of the spark plug may be broken off. As each plug is removed, examine it as follows:

7 Examination of the spark plugs will give a good indication of the condition of the engine. If the insulator nose of the spark plug is clean and white, with no deposits, this is indicative

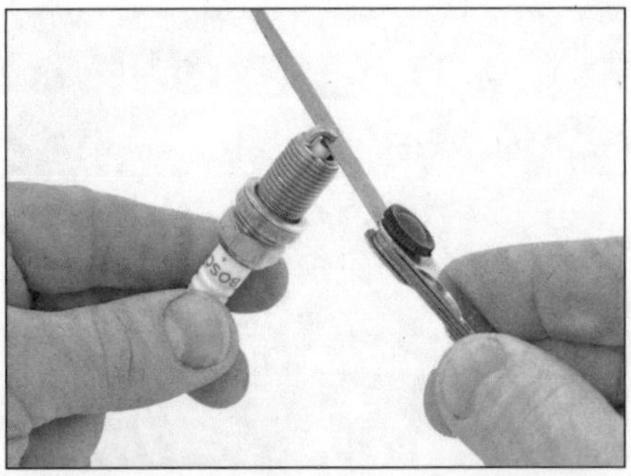

16.12 Measuring the spark plug gap with a feeler blade

of a weak mixture or too hot a plug (a hot plug transfers heat away from the electrode slowly, a cold plug transfers heat away quickly).

8 If the tip and insulator nose are covered with hard black-looking deposits, then this is indicative that the mixture is too rich. Should the plug be black and oily, then it is likely that the engine is fairly worn, as well as the mixture being too rich.

9 If the insulator nose is covered with light tan to greyish-brown deposits, then the mixture is correct and it is likely that the engine is in good condition.

10 If the spark plug has not completed its service interval, it may be refitted, however, check that the condition of the plug and the gap is correct before refitting. If, due to engine condition, the spark plug is not serviceable, it should be renewed.

11 The spark plug gap is of considerable importance as, if it is too large or too small, the size of the spark and its efficiency will be seriously impaired. For best results, the spark plug gap should be checked against the Specifications at the start of this Chapter.

12 Measure the gap with a feeler blade **(see illustration)**. If the gap is outside the specifications it should be renewed. Whilst it is possible to adjust the gap with the correct tools this practise is not recommended.

13 Special spark plug electrode gap measuring (and adjusting tools) are available from most motor accessory shops.

14 Before fitting the spark plugs, check that the threaded connector sleeves are tight, and that the plug exterior surfaces and threads are

HAYNES HiNT

It's often difficult to insert spark plugs into their holes without cross-threading them. To avoid this possibility, fit a short length of rubber or plastic hose over the end of the spark plug. The flexible hose acts as a universal joint, to help align the plug with the plug hole. Should the plug begin to cross thread, the hose will slip on the spark plug, preventing thread damage to the aluminium cylinder head.

clean. Apply a little anti-seize compound to the threads.

15 Insert each spark plug into the cylinder head and screw them in by hand, taking extra care to enter the plug threads correctly **(see Haynes Hint)**.

16 Tighten the plugs to the specified torque **(see illustration)** using the spark plug socket and a torque wrench.

17 Before refitting the coils over the new plugs, Renault recommend that the rubber boots are first lightly lubricated inside, using Fluostar 2L silicon free grease (part number 82 00 168 855).

18 Refit the ignition HT coils with reference to Chapter 5B, then refit the engine cover to complete.

17 Air filter element renewal

Removal

1 The air filter is located behind the battery.

2 Unscrew and remove the two filter housing

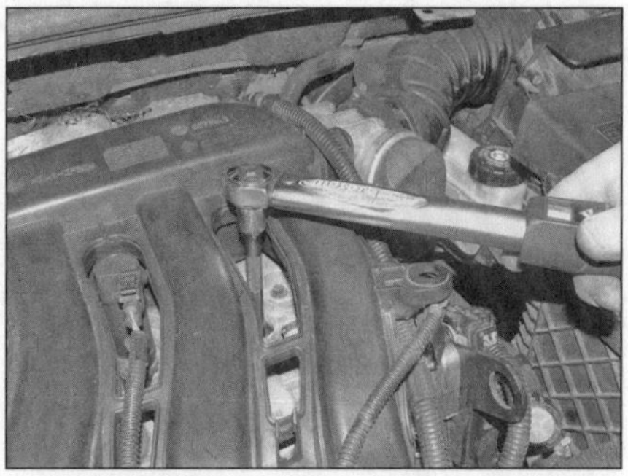

16.16 Tighten the plug to the specified torque

mounting screws – access is limited and may require the use of a stubby or cranked screwdriver **(see illustration)**.

3 Slide the filter housing out upwards to remove it **(see illustration)**.

4 Withdraw the filter element from the housing **(see illustration)**.

Refitting

5 Clean the inside of the air cleaner body and housing/cover, being careful not to get dirt into the inlet duct.

6 Fit the new element using a reversal of the removal procedure.

18 Manual transmission oil level check

1 Either position the car over an inspection pit, or jack up the front and rear of the car and support it on axle stands (see *Jacking and vehicle support*). The car must be level for the check to be accurate.

2 Remove the engine undertray

3 Locate the plastic filler/level plug, and clean the area around it before removal. The plug is located close to the left-hand driveshaft on the six speed transmission and on the front-facing side of the transmission on five speed models **(see illustrations)**.

4 Unscrew and remove the plug – this could be very tight **(see illustration)**. Check the condition of the filler plug seal, and obtain a new one if necessary.

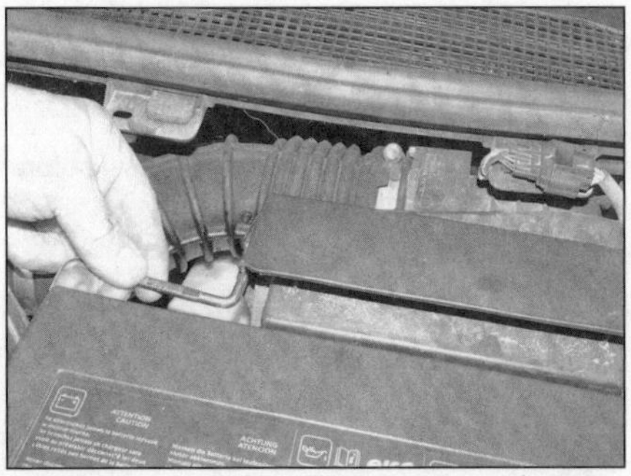

17.2 Use a cranked screwdriver to release the screws

17.3 Remove the cover complete with the air filter

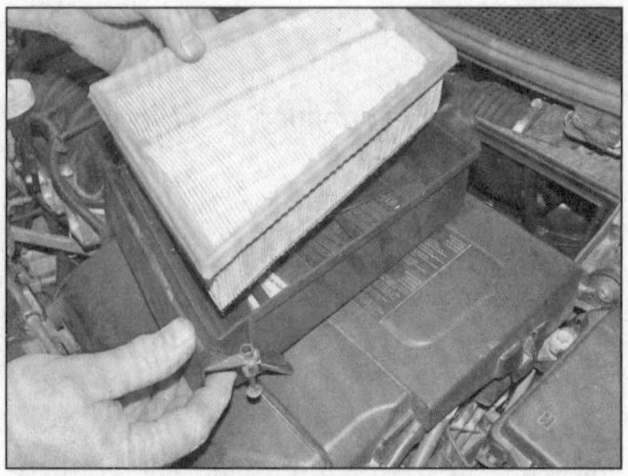

17.4 Remove the air filter from the housing

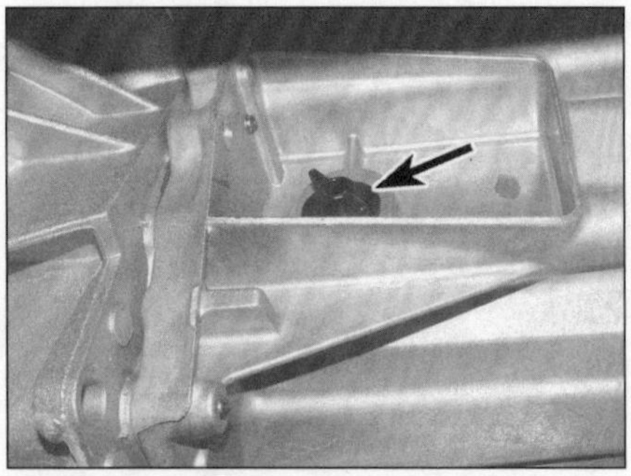

18.3a The transmission filler/level plug is on the front (5-speed)...

18.3b ...or on the side (6-speed)

18.4 Unscrew the filler/level plug

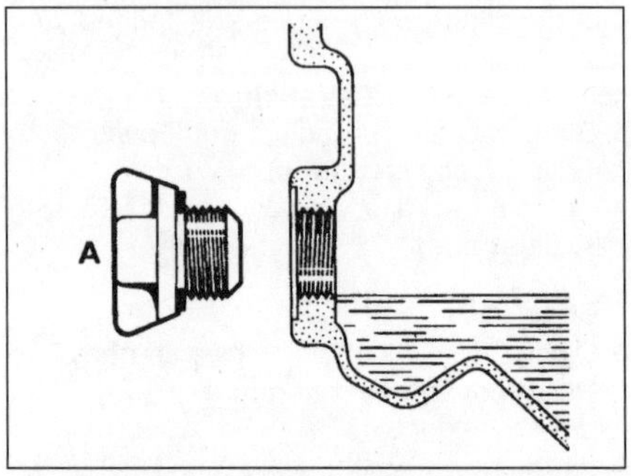

18.5 Manual transmission level/filler plug (A) – correct level shown

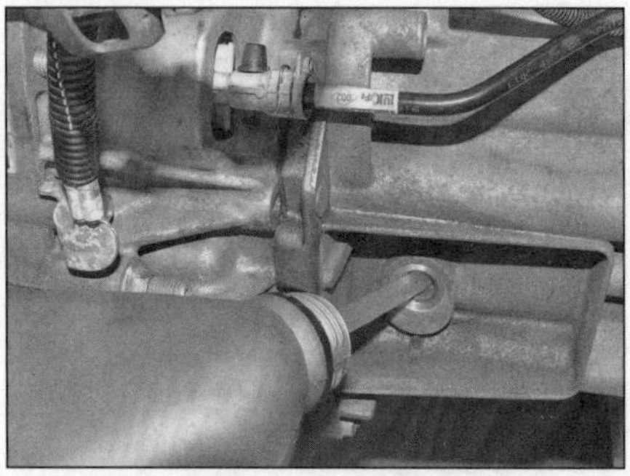

18.6a Topping-up the oil level through the filler hole (5 speed transmission)...

18.6b ... and on the 6 speed transmission

5 The oil level should be up to the lower edge of the filler/level plug aperture **(see illustration)**.

6 If necessary, top-up using the specified type of lubricant until the transmission oil level is correct. Fill the transmission until oil starts to flow out, and allow excess oil to drain out. Access to the filler plug on the six speed transmission is limited **(see illustrations)**.

7 Once the transmission oil level is correct, refit the filler/level plug and tighten it securely – by hand only.

8 Refit the engine undertray cover and then lower the car to the ground. Note that frequent need for topping-up indicates a leak, possibly through an oil seal. The cause should be investigated and rectified.

19 Front wheel alignment check

Refer to the information given in Chapter 10.

20 Air conditioning system check

The air conditioning system should be checked by a Renault dealer or suitably equipped garage using dedicated test equipment.

21 Brake fluid renewal

Warning: Brake hydraulic fluid can harm your eyes and damage painted surfaces, so use extreme caution when handling and pouring it. Do not use fluid that has been standing open for some time, as it absorbs moisture from the air. Excess moisture can cause a dangerous loss of braking effectiveness.

1 The procedure is similar to that for the bleeding of the hydraulic system as described in Chapter 9, except that the brake fluid reservoir should be emptied by syphoning, using a clean poultry baster or similar before starting, and allowance should be made for the old fluid to be expelled when bleeding a section of the circuit.

2 Working as described in Chapter 9, open the first bleed screw in the sequence, and pump the brake pedal gently until nearly all the old fluid has been emptied from the master cylinder reservoir **(see illustration)**. Top-up to the MAX level with new fluid, and continue pumping until only the new fluid remains in the reservoir, and new fluid can be seen emerging from the bleed screw. Tighten the screw, and top the reservoir level up to the MAX level line.

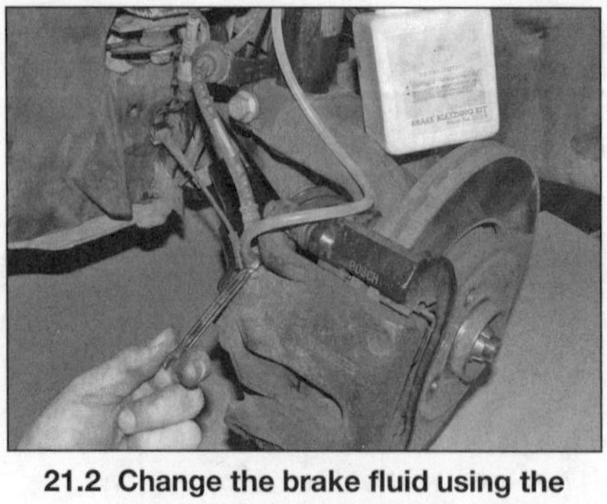

21.2 Change the brake fluid using the same method as for brake bleeding

HAYNES HiNT ***Old hydraulic fluid is invariably much darker in colour than the new, making it easy to distinguish the two.***

3 Work through all the remaining bleed screws in the sequence until new fluid can be seen at all of them. Be careful to keep the master cylinder reservoir topped-up to above the MIN level at all times, or air may enter the system and greatly increase the length of the task.

4 When the operation is complete, check that all bleed screws are securely tightened, and that their dust caps are refitted. Wash off all traces of spilt fluid, and recheck the master cylinder reservoir fluid level.

5 Check the operation of the brakes before taking the car on the road.

22 Coolant renewal

Warning: Wait until the engine is cold before starting this procedure. Do not allow antifreeze

22.5 The coolant drain tap (arrowed)

22.6a Open the bleed screw on the thermostat housing (arrowed)...

22.6b ...and on the heater hose (arrowed) next to the bulkhead

to come in contact with your skin, or with the car's painted surfaces. Rinse off spills immediately with plenty of water. Never leave antifreeze lying around in an open container, or in a puddle in the driveway or on the garage floor. Children and pets are attracted by its sweet smell, but antifreeze can be fatal if ingested.

Cooling system draining

1 With the engine completely cold, remove the expansion tank filler cap. Turn the cap anti-clockwise, wait until any pressure remaining in the system is released, then unscrew it and lift it off.

2 Jack up and support the front of the vehicle(see *Jacking and vehicle support* in the reference section).

3 Remove both front road wheels and then (with reference to Chapter 11) remove the front sections of both wing liners and then remove the front bumper.

4 Remove the engine undertray and then position a container beneath the radiator drain tap.

5 Open the drain tap and allow the coolant to drain into the container **(see illustration)**.

6 To assist draining, open the cooling system bleed screws on the thermostat housing, and on the heater hose **(see illustrations)**.

7 If draining of the coolant is only required to remove the waterpump, thermostat or heater matrix then the system can be drained by removal of one of the main coolant hoses. This avoid the need to remove the front bumper cover

8 If compressed air is available, Renault suggest inserting an air line into the expansion tank to drive out as much water as possible.

9 Flush the system if necessary as described in the following paragraphs and then close the drain tap. Refill the system as described later in this Section. Refit the bumper, wing liners and road wheels. Lowe the vehicle to the ground

Cooling system flushing

10 If coolant renewal has been neglected, or if the antifreeze mixture has become diluted, then in time, the cooling system may gradually lose efficiency, as the coolant passages become restricted due to rust, scale deposits, and other sediment. The cooling system efficiency can be restored by flushing the system clean.

11 The simplest method for flushing the system is to drain the system and then refill the system with clean water. When the system is full drain the system a second time. Check the condition of the water drained – if it is clean, flushing is complete; if not, repeat the process.

Radiator flushing

12 Disconnect the top and bottom hoses and any other relevant hoses from the radiator, with reference to Chapter 3.

13 Insert a garden hose into the radiator top inlet. Direct a flow of clean water through the radiator, and continue flushing until clean water emerges from the radiator bottom outlet.

14 If after a reasonable period, the water still does not run clear, the radiator can be flushed with a good proprietary cleaning agent. It is important that the manufacturer's instructions are followed carefully. If the contamination is particularly bad, insert the hose in the radiator bottom outlet, and reverse-flush the radiator.

Engine flushing

15 To flush the engine, remove the thermostat as described in Chapter 3, and disconnect the bottom hose.

16 Insert a garden hose into the thermostat housing and direct a clean flow of water through the engine. Continue flushing until clean water emerges from the radiator bottom hose.

17 On completion, refit the thermostat and reconnect the bottom hose. Where applicable, refit the engine undertray.

Antifreeze mixture

18 The antifreeze should always be renewed at the specified intervals. This is necessary not only to maintain the antifreeze properties, but also to prevent corrosion which would otherwise occur as the corrosion inhibitors become progressively less effective.

19 Always use an ethylene-glycol based antifreeze which is suitable for use in mixed-metal cooling systems. The quantity of antifreeze and levels of protection are given in the Specifications.

20 Before adding antifreeze, the cooling system should be completely drained, preferably flushed, and all hoses checked for condition and security.

21 After filling with antifreeze, a label should be attached to the expansion tank, stating the type and concentration of antifreeze used, and the date installed. Any subsequent topping-up should be made with the same type and concentration of antifreeze.

22 Do not use engine antifreeze in the windscreen/tailgate washer system, as it will cause damage to the vehicle's paintwork. A screenwash additive should be added to the washer system in the quantities stated on the bottle.

Cooling system filling

23 Before attempting to fill the cooling system, make sure that all hoses and clips are in good condition, and that the clips are tight. Note that an antifreeze mixture must be used all year round, to prevent corrosion of the engine components.

24 Remove the expansion tank filler cap **(see illustration)**.

25 If not already done, open the cooling system bleed screws.

26 Slowly fill the system until the coolant level reaches the MAX mark on the expansion tank. Close the bleed screws in turn when coolant free from air bubbles emerges from each one.

27 Start the engine, and run it at a fast idle speed (approximately 2000 rpm). As soon as the engine is running, top-up the level in the expansion tank if necessary, then refit and tighten the expansion tank filler cap – the cap should not normally be removed when the engine is running, nor when the system is hot.

22.24 Remove the coolant expansion tank filler cap

28 Allow the engine to run at 2000 rpm until the cooling fan has cut in and out three times.

29 Stop the engine and allow the engine to cool for at least an hour, and preferably, overnight.

30 Recheck the coolant level with reference to *Weekly checks*. Top-up the level if necessary and refit the expansion tank filler cap.

Airlocks

31 If, after draining and refilling the system, symptoms of overheating are found which did not occur previously, then the fault is almost certainly due to trapped air at some point in the system, causing an airlock and restricting the flow of coolant; usually, the air is trapped because the system was refilled too quickly.

32 If an airlock is suspected, first try gently squeezing all visible coolant hoses. A coolant hose which is full of air feels quite different to one full of coolant when squeezed. After refilling the system, most airlocks will clear once the system has cooled, and been topped-up.

33 While the engine is running at operating temperature, switch on the heater and heater fan, and check for heat output. Provided there is sufficient coolant in the system, any lack of heat output could be due to an airlock in the system.

34 Airlocks can have more serious effects than simply reducing heater output – a severe airlock could reduce coolant flow around the engine. Check that the radiator top hose is hot when the engine is at operating temperature – a top hose which stays cold could be the result of an airlock (or a non-opening thermostat).

35 If the problem persists, stop the engine and allow it to cool down **completely**, before unscrewing the radiator and expansion tank caps, or loosening the hose clips and squeezing the hoses to bleed out the trapped air. In the worst case, the system will have to be at least partially drained (this time, the coolant can be saved for re-use) and flushed to clear the problem.

Every 72 000 miles (120 000 km) or 6 years

23 Auxiliary belt renewal

1 Jack up and support the front of the vehicle (see *Jacking and vehicle support* in the reference section).

2 Remove the right-hand road wheel and the front section of the wing liner as described in Chapter 11.

3 Access can be improved by supporting the right-hand end of the engine on a suitable jack and then removing the right-hand engine mounting as described in Chapter 2A.

4 Using a 16 mm spanner turn the tensioner pulley clockwise to release the tension on the belt. Some versions of the tensioner have a slot provided to lock the tensioner in position by inserting a 6mm hex key into the slot. On other versions the tensioner must held in the slack position with the spanner.

5 Noting its routing, remove the drivebelt from the pulleys **(see illustration)**.

6 Renault recommend that both the tensioner and the belt are replaced once removed.

7 Unbolt and remove the tensioner pulley. With the belt and pulley removed, check and clean if necessary the grooves in the crankshaft pulley.

8 Fit the new tensioner **(see illustration)** and tighten the new retaining bolt to the specified torque.

9 Fit the belt loosely around the AC compressor, the alternator and the tensioner pulleys, making sure that it is correctly located in the grooves.

10 Rotate the new tensioner to the slack position and slip the belt over the crankshaft pulley. Ensure the belt is correctly position in the pulley grooves and then slowly allow the belt to be tensioned.

11 Turn the engine through a few complete revolutions, using a spanner or socket on the crankshaft pulley bolt. Check that the belt is running properly on its pulleys, and that the tensioner is working correctly (check that the belt is taut, midway along its bottom run).

12 On completion, refit the components removed to access the belt, then refit the wheel and lower the car to the ground. Tighten the wheel bolts to the specified torque.

24 Timing belt renewal

Refer to Chapter 2A.

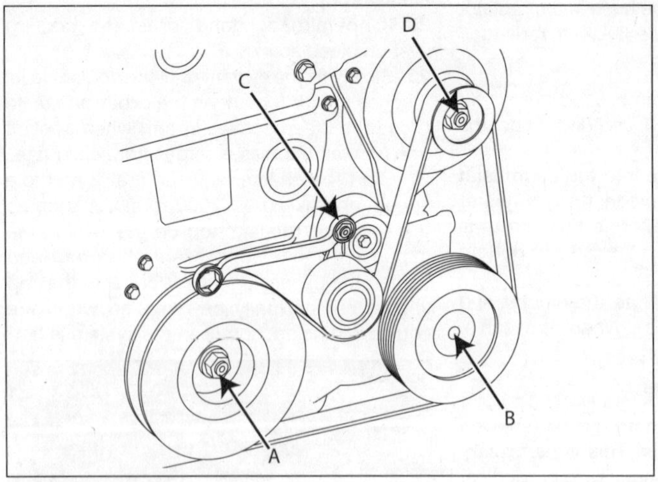

23.5 The belt routing

A Crankshaft pulley
B AC compressor
C Automatic tensioner
D Alternator

23.8 Fit a new automatic belt tensioner

Chapter 1 Part B:
Routine maintenance and servicing – diesel models

Contents

	Section number
Air conditioning system check	22
Air filter element renewal	17
Auxiliary drivebelt check	7
Auxiliary drivebelt renewal	19
Bodywork and underbody condition check	14
Brake fluid renewal	24
Braking system check	5
Clutch check	6
Coolant renewal	25
Driveshaft gaiter check	13
Electrical systems check	10
Engine oil and filter renewal	3
Exhaust system check	11
Front wheel alignment check	21
Fuel filter renewal	18
Fuel filter water draining	8
Hose and fluid leak check	15
Introduction	1
Manual transmission oil level check	20
Pollen filter renewal	4
Regular maintenance	2
Road test	16
Seat belt check	9
Suspension and steering check	12
Timing belt renewal	23

Degrees of difficulty

Easy, suitable for novice with little experience	**Fairly easy,** suitable for beginner with some experience	**Fairly difficult,** suitable for competent DIY mechanic	**Difficult,** suitable for experienced DIY mechanic	**Very difficult,** suitable for expert DIY or professional

Lubricants and fluids

Refer to *Weekly checks* on page 0•16

Capacities

Engine oil (including oil filter)

All engines	4.5 litres
Difference between MAX and MIN dipstick marks	1.5 to 2.0 litres
Cooling system	
All engines	6.5 litres
Manual transmission	
JR5 (5 speed)	2.4 litres
TL4 (6 speed)	2.0 litres
Fuel tank	60 litres approximately (13 gallons)

Cooling system

Antifreeze mixture:	**Antifreeze**
Protection to –23°C	35%
Protection to –40°C	50%

Fuel system

Specified idle speed (non-adjustable):	800± 50 rpm

Brakes

Brake pad friction material minimum thickness	1.5 mm

Torque wrench settings

	Nm	lbf ft
Auxiliary belt tensioner bolt*	40	30
Clutch pedal nuts	21	15
Roadwheel bolts	110	81
Sump plug	20	15
Transmission drain plug	24	18

** A new bolt must be used*

The maintenance intervals in this manual are provided with the assumption that you, not the dealer, will be carrying out the work. These are the minimum maintenance intervals recommended by us for vehicles driven daily. If you wish to keep your vehicle in peak condition at all times, you may wish to perform some of these procedures more often. We encourage frequent maintenance, because it enhances the efficiency, performance and resale value of your vehicle.

If the vehicle is driven in dusty areas, used to tow a trailer, or driven frequently at slow speeds (idling in traffic) or on short journeys, more frequent maintenance intervals are recommended.

When the vehicle is new, it should be serviced by a factory-authorised dealer service department, in order to preserve the factory warranty.

Every 250 miles (400 km) or weekly

- ☐ Refer to *Weekly checks*

Every 9000 miles (15 000 km)

- ☐ Renew the engine oil and filter (Section 3)

Note: *Frequent oil and filter changes are good for the engine. We recommend changing the oil at the mileage specified here, or at least once a year.*

Note: *All diesel models featured in this manual are fitted with an 'oil control system' (OCS). The system monitors the style and type of driving and calculates the need for an oil change based on these parameters. For example a vehicle used primarily for urban driving will require more frequent oil changes than a vehicle that Is used for long distance motorway driving. When an oil change is due the instrument panel will display 'service or oil change Interval'.*

Every 18 000 miles (30 000 km) or 2 years, whichever comes first

In addition to all the items listed previously, carry out the following:

- ☐ Renew the pollen filter (Section 4)
- ☐ Check the braking system (Section 5)
- ☐ Check the operation of the clutch (Section 6)
- ☐ Check the condition of the auxiliary drivebelt (Section 7)
- ☐ Drain any water from the fuel filter (Section 8)
- ☐ Check the condition of the seat belts (Section 9)
- ☐ Check the operation of all electrical systems (Section 10)
- ☐ Check the condition of the exhaust system and mountings (Section 11)
- ☐ Check the suspension and steering components (Section 12)
- ☐ Check the condition of the driveshaft gaiters (Section 13)
- ☐ Check the bodywork and underbody for damage and corrosion (Section 14)
- ☐ Check all underbonnet components and hoses for fluid leaks (Section 15)
- ☐ Carry out a road test (Section 16)

Every 36 000 miles (60 000 km) or 4 years, whichever comes first

In addition to all the items listed previously, carry out the following:

- ☐ Renew the air filter element (Section 17)
- ☐ Renew the fuel filter element (Section 18)
- ☐ Renew the auxiliary drivebelt (Section 19)
- ☐ Check the manual transmission oil level (Section 20)
- ☐ Check the front wheel alignment (Section 21)
- ☐ Check the operation of the air conditioning system (Section 22)
- ☐ Renew the brake fluid (Section 23)
- ☐ Renew the coolant (Section 24)

Every 96 000 miles (154 000 Km) or 6 years, whichever comes first

- ☐ Renew the timing belt (Section 25)*

* **Note:** *This is the standard interval, but on vehicles which are subjected to intensive use, ie, mainly short journeys or a lot of stop-start driving, we would recommend that this interval is reduce to 60,000 miles or 4 years. The actual belt renewal interval is therefore very much up to the individual owner, but bear in mind that severe engine damage may result if the belt breaks.*

Underbonnet view

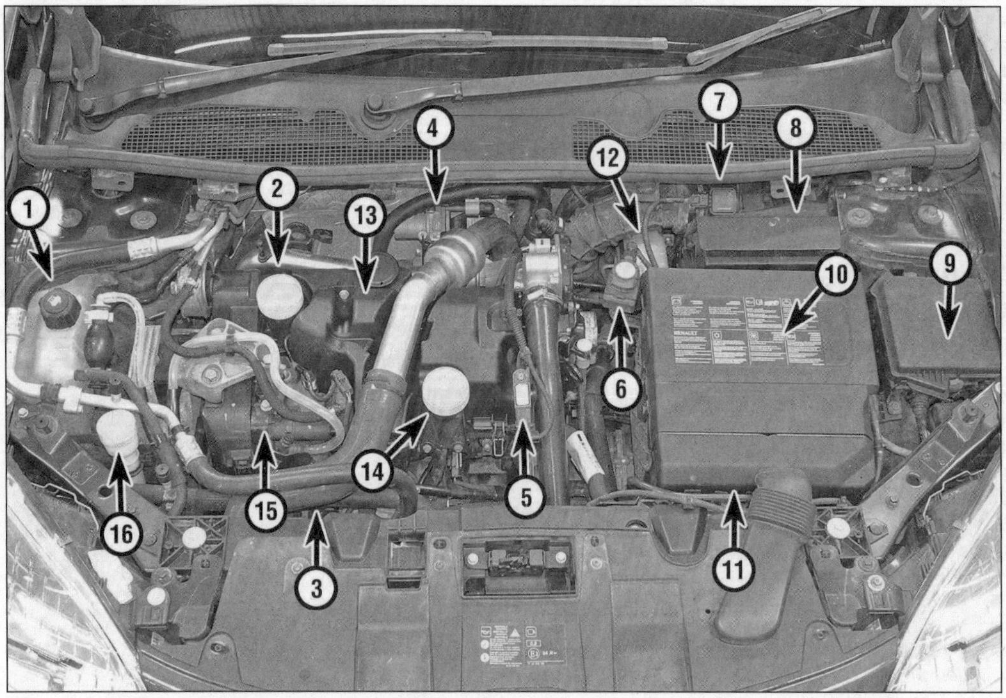

1 *Coolant expansion tank*
2 *Engine oil filler cap*
3 *Intercooler air duct*
4 *EGR housing*
5 *Turbo pressure sensor*
6 *Boost pressure solenoid*
7 *Airflow meter*
8 *Air cleaner housing*
9 *Engine compartment fusebox*
10 *Battery (under cover)*
11 *Engine management ECU (under cover)*
12 *Brake/clutch fluid reservoir*
13 *Injectors (under cover)*
14 *Engine oil dipstick*
15 *Injection pump*
16 *Washer fluid reservoir*

Front underbody view

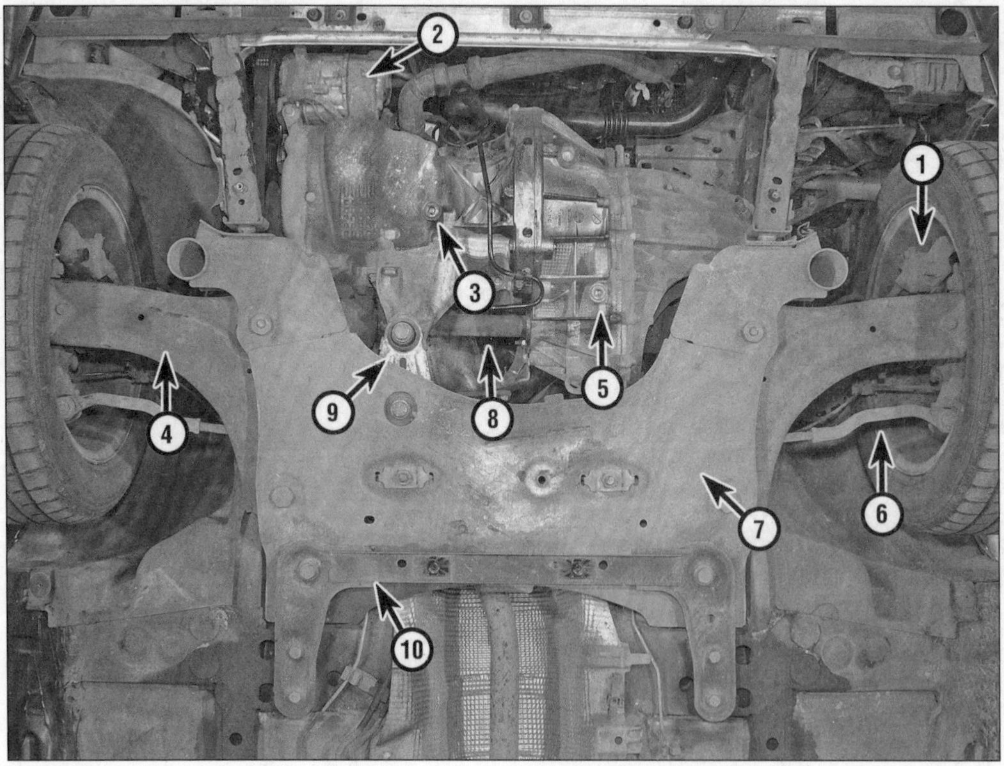

1 *Front brake caliper*
2 *Air conditioning compressor*
3 *Engine oil drain plug*
4 *Front suspension lower arm*
5 *Transmission oil drain plug*
6 *Track rod*
7 *Subframe*
8 *Right-hand driveshaft*
9 *Engine rear mounting link*
10 *Subframe rear crossmember*

Rear underbody view

1 *Exhaust rear silencer*
2 *Spare wheel well*
3 *Rear shock absorber*
4 *Handbrake cables*
5 *Rear axle*
6 *Fuel tank*
7 *Heat shield*

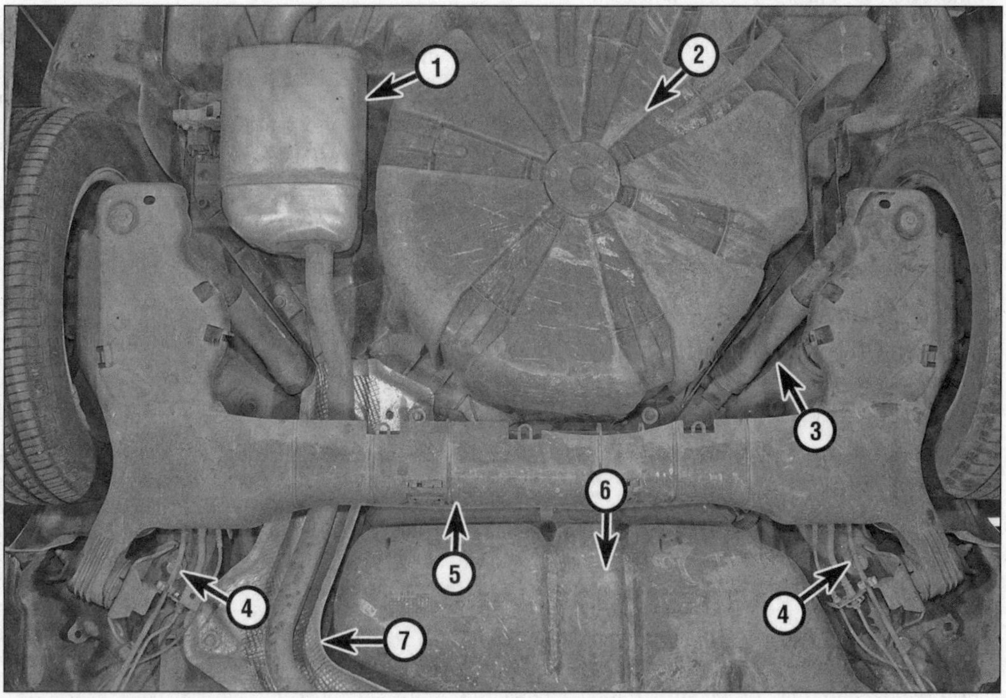

Maintenance procedures

1 Introduction

This Chapter is designed to help the home mechanic maintain his/her vehicle for safety, economy, long life and peak performance.

The Chapter contains a master maintenance schedule, followed by Sections dealing specifically with each task in the schedule. Visual checks, adjustments, component renewal and other helpful items are included. Refer to the accompanying illustrations of the engine compartment and the underside of the vehicle for the locations of the various components.

Servicing your vehicle in accordance with the mileage/time maintenance schedule and the following Sections will provide a planned maintenance programme, which should result in a long and reliable service life. This is a comprehensive plan, so maintaining some items but not others at the specified service intervals will not produce the same results.

As you service your vehicle, you will discover that many of the procedures can – and should – be grouped together, because of the particular procedure being performed, or because of the proximity of two otherwise-unrelated components to one another. For example, if the vehicle is raised for any reason, the exhaust can be inspected at the same time as the suspension and steering components.

The first step in this maintenance programme is to prepare yourself before the actual work begins. Read through all the Sections relevant to the work to be carried out, then make a list and gather all the parts and tools required. If a problem is encountered, seek advice from a parts specialist, or a dealer service department.

Resetting the service light

To reset the service warning light on the instrument panel, switch on the ignition, then scroll through the trip computer's displayed options until the 'oil change interval' is displayed. Now press and hold the button for 10 seconds. The value will flash 4 times and then the new interval will be displayed. When the new value flashes 4 times release the button.

Special precautions for vehicles fitted with Stop/Start technology

Some models feature Stop/Start technology, where under normal operating conditions the engine will automatically stop (and restart) to reduce fuel consumption and the production of greenhouse gases. Precautions must be taken to ensure that the vehicle will not restart whilst service and maintenance operations are taking place. This can be achieved by pressing the Stop/Start switch on the dashboard (the dashboard will display 'Stop and Start deactivated') opening the bonnet, or by leaving the drivers door open. However the safest way to ensure the system will not restart is to disconnect the battery *-see Disconnecting the battery in Chapter 5A.*

2 Regular maintenance

If, from the time the vehicle is new, the routine maintenance schedule is followed closely, and frequent checks are made of fluid levels and high-wear items, as suggested throughout this manual, the engine will be kept in relatively good running condition, and the need for additional work will be minimised.

It is possible that there will be times when the engine is running poorly due to the lack of regular maintenance. This is even more likely if a used vehicle, which has not received regular and frequent maintenance checks, is purchased. In such cases, additional work may need to be carried out, outside of the regular maintenance intervals.

If engine wear is suspected, a compression test (refer to Chapter 2B or 2C) will provide valuable information regarding the overall performance of the main internal components. Such a test can be used as a basis to decide on the extent of the work to be carried out. If, for example, a compression test indicates serious internal engine wear, conventional maintenance as described in this Chapter will not greatly improve the performance of the engine, and may prove a waste of time and money, unless extensive overhaul work is carried out first.

The following series of operations are those most often required to improve the performance of a generally poor-running engine:

Primary operations

a) Clean, inspect and test the battery (refer to 'Weekly checks').
b) Check all the engine-related fluids (refer to 'Weekly checks').
c) Check the condition of the auxiliary drivebelt (Section 7).
d) Check the condition of all hoses, and check for fluid leaks (Section 15).
e) Check the condition of the air filter, and renew if necessary (Section 17).
f) Check the fuel filter, and renew if necessary (Section 18).

If the above operations do not prove fully effective, carry out the following secondary operations:

Secondary operations

All items listed under *Primary operations*, plus the following:

a) Check the charging system (refer to Chapter 5A).
b) Check the preheating system (refer to Chapter 5C).
c) Check the fuel system (refer to Chapter 4B).

Every 9000 miles (15 000 km)

3 Engine oil and filter renewal

1 Frequent oil and filter changes are the most important preventative maintenance procedures which can be undertaken by the DIY owner. As engine oil ages, it becomes diluted and contaminated, which leads to premature engine wear.

2 Before starting this procedure, gather together all the necessary tools and materials. Also make sure that you have plenty of clean rags and newspapers handy, to mop-up any spills. Ideally, the engine oil should be warm, as it will drain more easily, and more built-up sludge will be removed with it.

3 Take care not to touch the exhaust or any other hot parts of the engine when working under the car. To avoid any possibility of scalding, and to protect yourself from possible skin irritants and other harmful contaminants in used engine oils, it is advisable to wear gloves when carrying out this work.

4 Firmly apply the handbrake, then jack up the front of the car and support it on axle stands (see *Jacking and vehicle support*).

5 Remove the fasteners and lower out the engine undertray. Remove the oil filler cap, then position a container beneath the sump. Clean the drain plug and the area around it, then slacken it half a turn – all models have a drain plug which requires an 8 mm square key to remove it **(see illustrations)**.

6 Allow some time for the old oil to drain, noting that it may be necessary to reposition the container as the oil flow slows to a trickle.

7 After all the oil has drained, wipe off the drain plug with a clean rag and fit a new sealing washer **(see illustration)**. Some models have a copper washer, others have bonded washer (often called a 'Dowty seal'). Clean the area around the drain plug opening, then refit and tighten the plug securely.

8 Move the container into position under the oil filter, which is located horizontally on the front face of the engine **(see illustration)**. Access is not easy, but it is possible without removing any body or engine components.

9 Using an oil filter removal tool where possible, slacken the filter initially. Loosely wrap some rags around the oil filter, then unscrew it and immediately position it with its open end uppermost to prevent further spillage of oil. Remove the oil filter from the engine compartment, and empty the oil into the container.

10 Use a clean rag to remove all oil, dirt and sludge from the filter sealing area on the engine. Check the old filter to make sure that the rubber sealing ring hasn't stuck to the engine. If it has, carefully remove it.

11 Apply a light coating of clean oil to the sealing ring on the new filter, then screw it into position on the engine **(see illustration)**. Tighten the filter firmly by hand only – do not use any tools. Wipe clean the exterior of the oil filter.

12 Remove the old oil and all tools from under

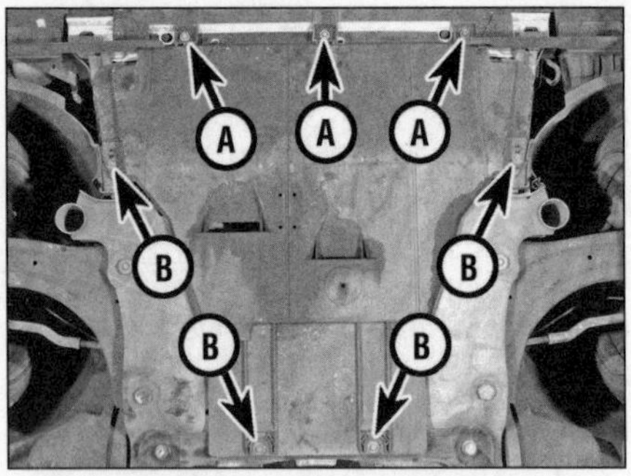

3.5a Slacken the front bolts (A) and remove the rear bolts (B)

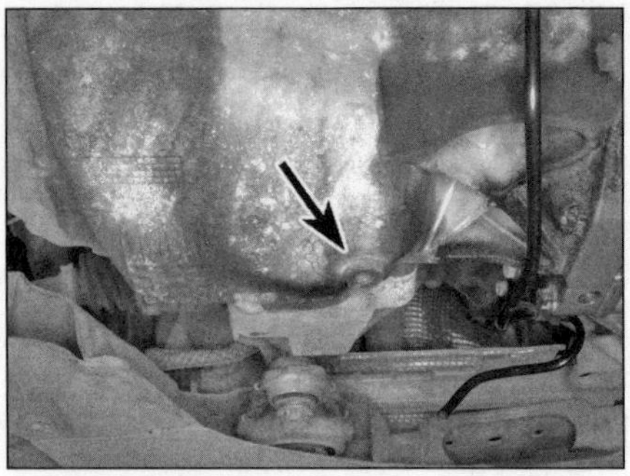
3.5b Engine oil drain plug (arrowed)

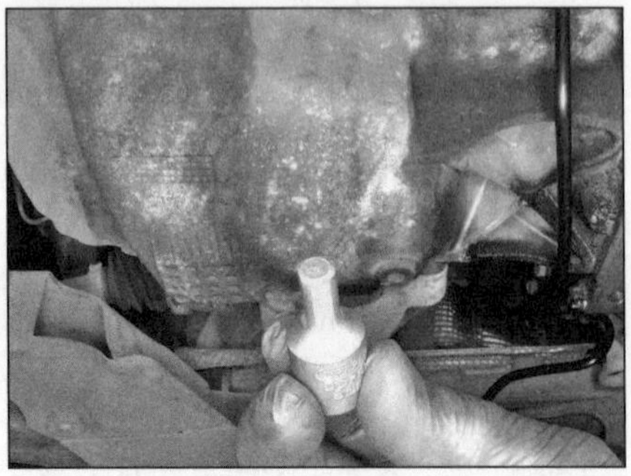
3.5c The correct sump plug drain key will be required

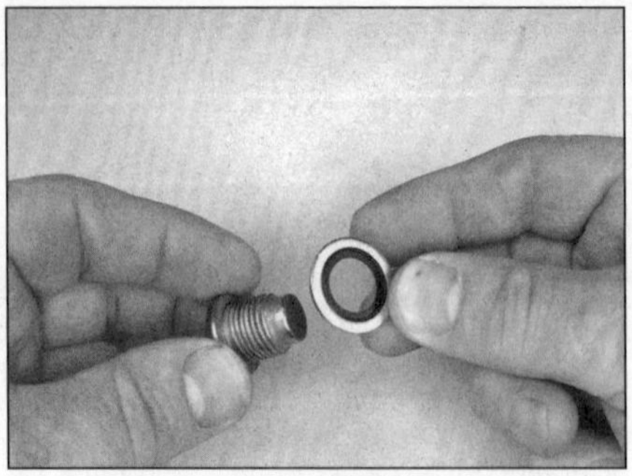
3.7 Fit a new sealing washer

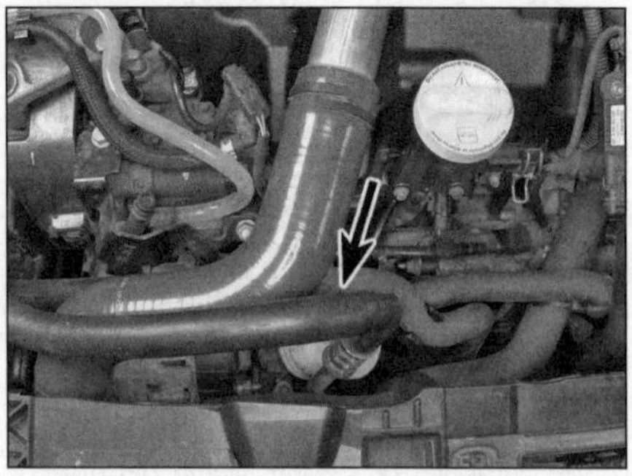
3.8 The oil filter (arrowed)

3.11 Oil the new filter sealing ring before fitting

3.13 Slowly fill the engine with oil

3.15 Once the engine has been run, check the oil level and add more if required

the car, refit the undertray where necessary, and lower the car to the ground.

13 Fill the engine with the specified quantity and grade of oil, as described in *Weekly checks*. Pour the oil in slowly, in small amounts, waiting each time for the oil to drain into the sump **(see illustration)**. When the oil level is up to the maximum mark on the dipstick, refit and tighten the oil filler cap.

14 Start the engine and run it for a few minutes, checking that there are no leaks around the oil filter seal and the sump drain plug. Note that when the engine is first started, there will be a delay of a few seconds before the oil pressure warning light goes out while the new filter fills with oil. Do not race the engine while the warning light is on.

15 Switch off the engine and wait a few minutes for the oil to settle in the sump once more. With the new oil circulated and the filter now completely full, recheck the level on the dipstick and add more oil if necessary **(see illustration)**.

16 Dispose of the used engine oil safely with reference to *General repair procedures* in the Reference section of this manual.

Every 18 000 miles (30 000 km) or 2 years

4 Pollen filter renewal

1 Remove the side panel from the centre console on the drivers side and then remove the lower fascia panel **(see illustration)** on the same side (as described in Chapter 11).

2 Remove the air distribution duct and then carefully release the clutch hydraulic fluid pipes from the retaining clips on the pedal box.

3 Release the wiring loom and then unbolt the clutch pedal mounting bolts. There is no need to disconnect the wiring plug.

4 Carefully rotate and lower the pedal into the foot well **(see illustration)**.

5 Unclip the wiring loom from the side of the air distribution housing.

6 On some models the filter cover is held in place by screws, on other models it is a simple clip fit. Remove the screws or unclip the cover as appropriate **(see illustrations)**.

7 Pull the filter from the housing. The filter will have to be deformed to clear the steering column and pedal assembly **(see illustration)**. Note the direction of the airflow arrows on the filter - they should point into the cabin.

8 Inspect the housing for any debris and vacuum it out if necessary.

4.1 Remove the lower panel

4.4 Rotate and lower the clutch pedal assembly

4.6a Where fitted remove the screws (arrowed)...

4.6b ...and remove the filter cover

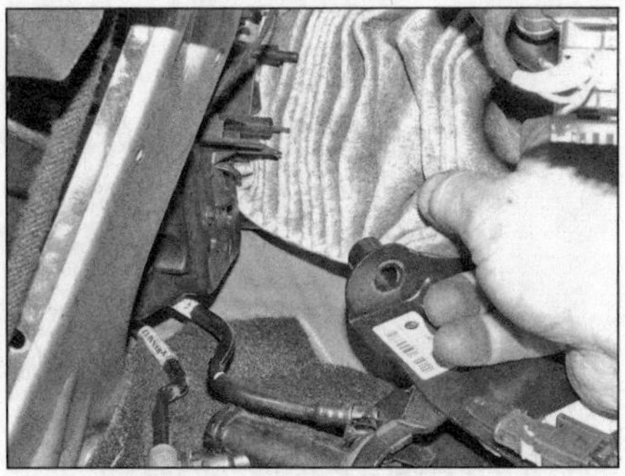

4.7 Manoeuvre the pollen filter out from the housing

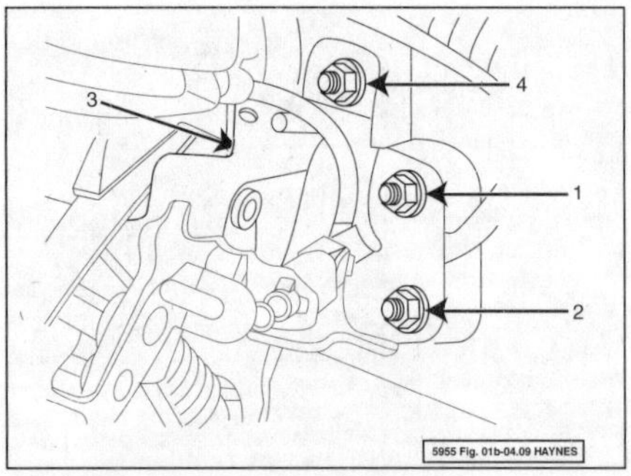

4.9 Tighten the clutch pedal bolts in the order shown

9 Refitting is a reversal of removal. Remember to tighten the pedal assembly nuts to the correct torque **(see illustration)**.

5 Braking system check

Handbrake check and adjustment

1 The handbrake should be capable of holding the parked car stationary, even on steep slopes, when applied with moderate force. The mechanism should be firm and positive in feel, with no trace of stiffness or sponginess from the cables, and should release immediately the handbrake lever is released. If the mechanism is faulty in any of these respects, it must be checked immediately as follows.

2 Handbrake adjustment is made inside the car, after removing the centre console as described in Chapter 11.

3 Jack up the rear of the car and support it on axle stands (see *Jacking and vehicle support*).

4 Operate the handbrake several times, and leave it applied as normal.

5 Check that the handbrake operating lever on each rear caliper is sitting off its stop by approximately 1 mm **(see illustration)**. If not, further adjustment may be required, or the cable on the side affected may have seized.

6 Check that the handbrake cables slide freely by pulling on their front ends, and check that the operating levers on the rear brake calipers move smoothly.

7 If the cables have stretched over time, the cables may need to be adjusted beyond the nominal setting. Bear in mind that the adjuster nut has a plastic insert, which loses its effectiveness over time – if the adjustment is being lost regularly, a new nut should be fitted.

8 Move both of the caliper operating levers as far rearwards as possible, then tighten the adjuster nut inside the car until all free play is removed from both cables. With the aid of an assistant, adjust the nut so that the operating lever on each rear brake caliper starts to move as the handbrake lever is moved between the first and second notch (click) of its ratchet mechanism **(see illustration)**.

9 After adjustment, release the handbrake fully, and check that the wheels are free to turn.

10 On completion, lower the car to the ground.

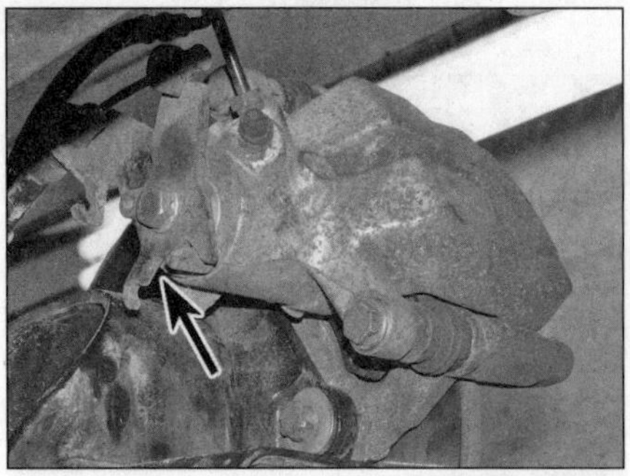

5.5 With the handbrake on, there should be a gap between the caliper lever and its stop

5.8a Prise free the rear storage compartment of the centre console to access the handbrake adjustment

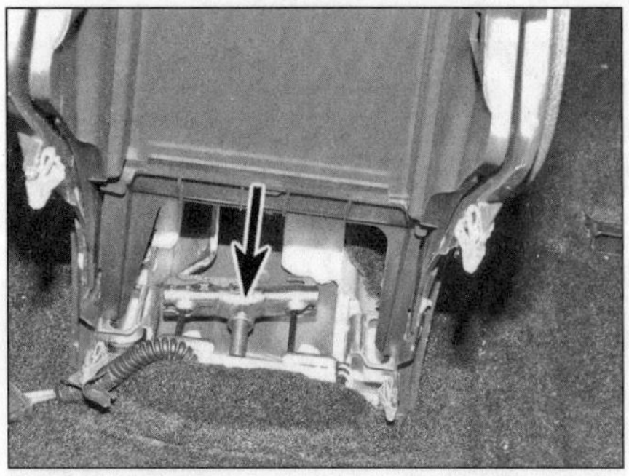

5.8b If necessary, use the nut (arrowed) to adjust the handbrake

HAYNES HiNT

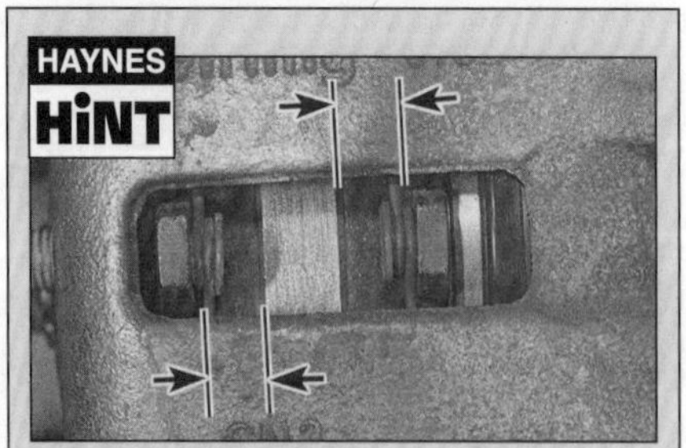

For a quick check, the thickness of friction material remaining on each pad can be measured through the aperture on the caliper body.

Brake pad and disc check

11 Firmly apply the handbrake, then jack up the front or rear of the car and support it securely on axle stands (see *Jacking and vehicle support*). Remove the roadwheels. Remember, the car has disc brakes all round, so all four calipers should be checked.

12 For a quick check, the thickness of friction material remaining on each brake pad can be measured through the aperture in the caliper body **(see Haynes Hint)**. If any pad's friction material is worn to the specified thickness or less, all four pads must be renewed as a set. Pad wear warning contacts may be fitted to the inboard pads, but this should not be used as an excuse for omitting a visual check.

13 For a comprehensive check, the brake pads should be removed and cleaned. This will allow the operation of the caliper to be checked, and the brake disc itself to be fully examined for condition on both sides. Refer to Chapter 9 for further information.

6 Clutch check

Check that the clutch pedal moves smoothly and easily through its full travel, and that the clutch itself functions correctly, with no trace of slip or drag. If the clutch action is less than precise, this may indicate the need for bleeding the system – it could also indicate the presence of a fluid leak (see Chapter 6).

7 Auxiliary drivebelt check

1 The auxiliary drivebelt is located at the right-hand side of the engine, providing drive for the alternator and the air conditioning compressor.

2 The drivebelt features an automatic tensioner.

3 Due to their function and material makeup, drivebelts are prone to failure after a period of time, and should therefore be inspected regularly.

4 Loosen the right-hand front wheel bolts, then jack up the front of the car, and support it on axle stands (see *Jacking and vehicle support*). Remove the wheel.

5 Remove the screws and clips securing the front section of the wheel arch liner, and remove it.

6 With the engine stopped, inspect the full length of the drivebelt for cracks and separation of the belt plies. Small cracks in the belt ribs are no cause for concern, unless they are deep into the belt itself. Also check

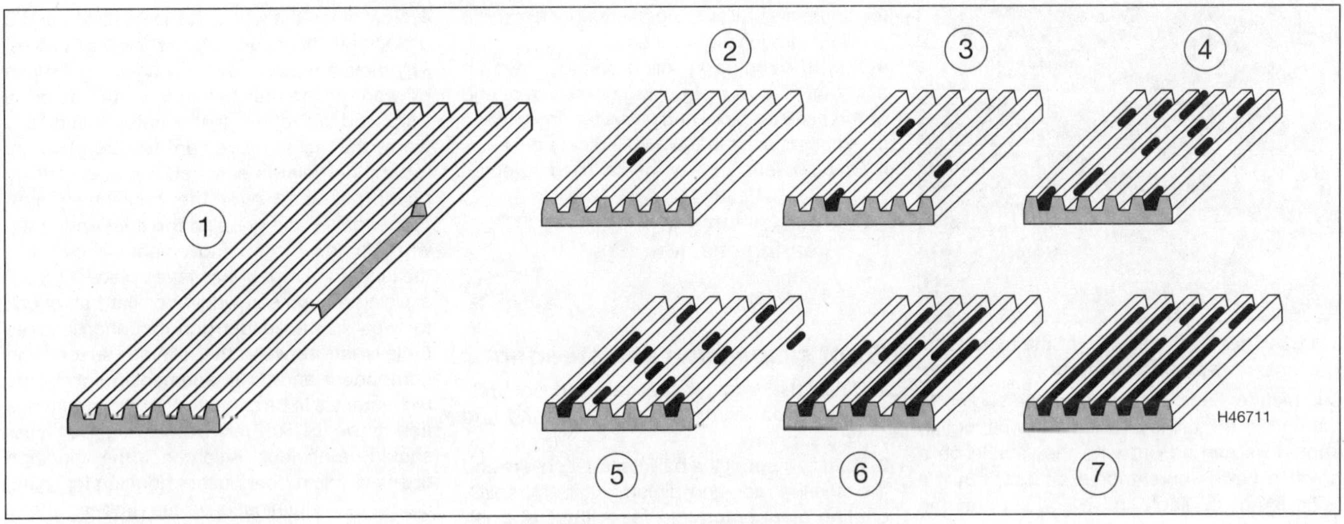

7.6 Check for drivebelt wear

1 If sections are missing renew the belt
2 Small deposits in the grooves are not a concern
3 Small scattered deposits are not a concern
4 Deposits up to half of the rib height: renew the belt if noisy
5 Deposits up to half the rib height: renew the belt if noisy
6 Heavy deposits: renew the belt
7 Heavy deposits: renew the belt

for fraying, and glazing which gives the belt a shiny appearance **(see illustration)**.

7 Turn the engine (using a spanner or socket on the crankshaft pulley bolt) so that the belt can be inspected thoroughly. Twist the belt between the pulleys so that both sides can be viewed. Check the pulleys for nicks, cracks, distortion and corrosion.

8 If the belt is satisfactory, refit the components removed to access it, then refit the wheel and lower the car to the ground. Tighten the wheel bolts to the specified torque.

8 Fuel filter water draining

Note: *It is advisable to wear gloves when carrying out this procedure.*

1 The fuel filter is located under the right-hand wheel arch – remove the front section of the wheel arch liner as described in Chapter 11.

2 Some models have a water sensor fitted to the base, other models have a simple drain tap.

3 Place a suitable container beneath the drain tap.

4 Open the drain tap, and allow fuel and water to drain until water-free fuel emerges **(see illustrations)**. Typically, only a very small amount should have to be drained – if a large amount of fuel is drained, the engine may have to be cranked for a long time before the engine will start. Close the drain tap securely.

5 On models fitted with a sensor, disconnect the wiring plug and hold a suitable container beneath the filter.

6 Slacken the sensor and let the water and fuel mix drain into the container. Tighten the sensor and reconnect the wiring pug.

7 Dispose of the drained fuel safely.

8 Start the engine. If difficulty is experienced, bleed the fuel system (Chapter 4B).

9 Seat belt check

1 Carefully examine the seat belt webbing for cuts, or any signs of serious fraying or deterioration. If the belt is of the retractable type, pull the belt all the way out of the inertia reel, and examine the full extent of the webbing.

2 Fasten and unfasten the belt, ensuring that the locking mechanism holds securely, and releases properly when intended. If the belt is of the retractable type, check also that the retracting mechanism operates correctly when the belt is released.

3 Check the security of all seat belt mountings and attachments which are accessible without removing any trim or other components.

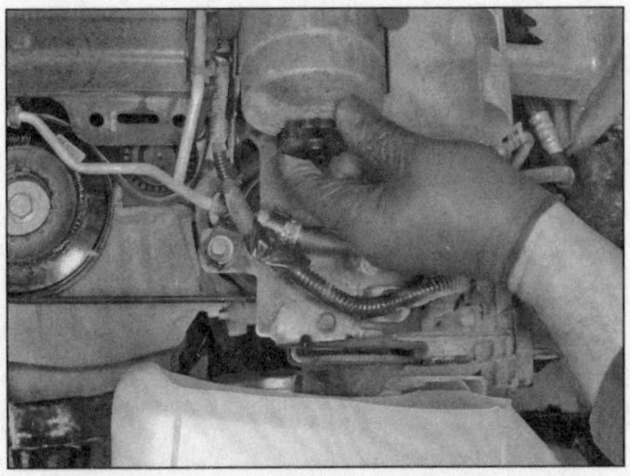

8.4a Open the drain tap...

10 Electrical systems check

1 Check the operation of all electrical equipment, ie, lights, direction indicators, horn, etc. Refer to the appropriate Sections of Chapter 12 for details if any of the circuits are found to be inoperative.

2 Note that stop-light switch adjustment is described in Chapter 9.

3 Visually check all accessible wiring connectors, harnesses and retaining clips for security, and for signs of chafing or damage. Rectify any faults found.

11 Exhaust system check

1 With the engine cold (at least an hour after the vehicle has been driven), check the

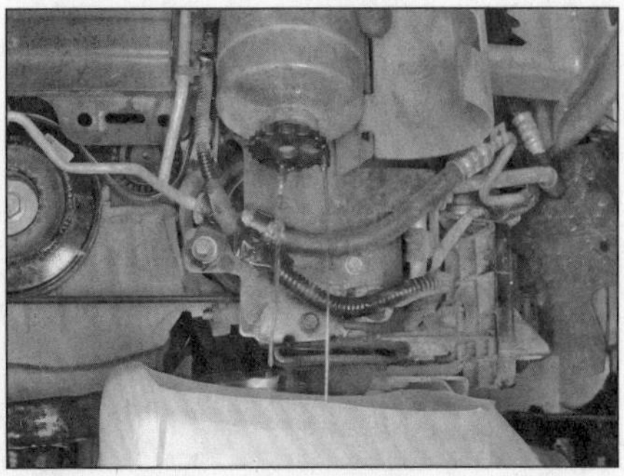

8.4b ...and drain of the fuel/water

11.3 Check the security of the exhaust pipes and joints

complete exhaust system from the engine to the end of the tailpipe. Ideally, the inspection should be carried out with the vehicle on a hoist to permit unrestricted access, but if a hoist is not available, raise and support the vehicle safely on axle stands (see *Jacking and vehicle support*).

2 Check the exhaust pipes and connections for evidence of leaks, severe corrosion and damage. Make sure that all brackets and mountings are in good condition and tight. Leakage at any of the joints or in other parts of the system will usually show up as a black sooty stain in the vicinity of the leak.

3 Rattles and other noises can often be traced to the exhaust system, especially the brackets and mountings **(see illustration)**. Try to move the pipes and silencers. If the components can come into contact with the body or suspension parts, secure the system with new mountings or if possible, separate the joints and twist the pipes as necessary to provide additional clearance.

4 Run the engine at idling speed. Have an assistant place a cloth or rag over the rear end of the exhaust pipe, and listen for any escape of exhaust gases that would indicate a leak.

5 On completion, lower the car to the ground.

12 Suspension and steering check

Front suspension and steering

1 Raise the front of the car, and securely support it on axle stands (see *Jacking and vehicle support*).

2 Visually inspect the balljoint dust covers and the steering rack-and-pinion gaiters for splits, chafing or deterioration **(see illustrations)**. Any wear of these components will cause loss of lubricant, together with dirt and water entry, resulting in rapid deterioration of the balljoints or steering gear.

3 Grasp the roadwheel at the 12 o'clock and 6 o'clock positions, and try to rock it **(see illustration)**. Very slight free play may be felt, but if the movement is appreciable, further investigation is necessary to determine the source. Continue rocking the wheel while an assistant depresses the footbrake. If the movement is now eliminated or significantly reduced, it is likely that the hub bearings are at fault. If the free play is still evident with the footbrake depressed, then there is wear in the suspension joints or mountings.

12.2a Check the balljoint rubber gaiters on the track rod ends...

12.2b ...and on the anti-roll bar drop links

4 Now grasp the wheel at the 9 o'clock and 3 o'clock positions, and try to rock it as before. Any movement felt now may again be caused by wear in the hub bearings or the steering track rod balljoints. If the outer balljoint is worn, the visual movement will be obvious. If the inner joint is suspect, it can be felt by placing a hand over the rack-and-pinion rubber gaiter and gripping the track rod. If the wheel is now rocked, movement will be felt at the inner joint if wear has taken place.

5 Using a large screwdriver or flat bar, check for wear in the suspension mounting bushes by levering between the relevant suspension component and its attachment point. Some movement is to be expected, as the mountings are made of rubber, but excessive wear should be obvious. Also check the condition of any visible rubber bushes, looking for splits, cracks or contamination of the rubber.

6 With the car standing on its wheels, have an assistant turn the steering wheel back-and-forth, about an eighth of a turn each way. There should be very little, if any, lost movement between the steering wheel and roadwheels. If this is not the case, closely observe the joints and mountings previously described. In addition, check the steering column universal joints for wear, and also check the rack-and-pinion steering gear itself.

Rear suspension

7 Chock the front wheels, then jack up the rear of the car and support securely on axle stands (see *Jacking and vehicle support*).

8 Working as described previously for the front suspension, check the rear hub bearings, the suspension bushes and the shock absorber mountings for wear **(see illustration). Note:** *The handbrake must be released before checking the rear wheel bearings.*

Shock absorber check

9 Check for any signs of fluid leakage around the shock absorber body, or from the rubber gaiter around the piston rod **(see illustration)**. Should any fluid be noticed, the shock absorber is defective internally, and should be renewed. **Note:** *Shock absorbers should always be renewed in pairs on the same axle.*

10 The efficiency of the shock absorber may be checked by bouncing the car at each

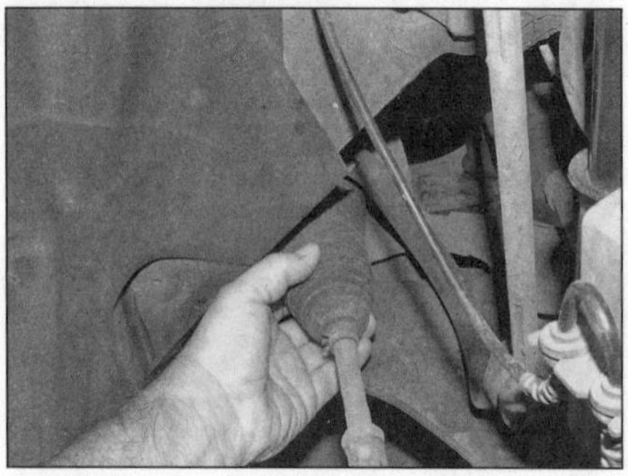

12.2c Check the steering rack gaiters for splitting

12.3 Check for wheel bearing wear by grasping the wheel and trying to rock it

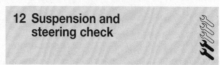

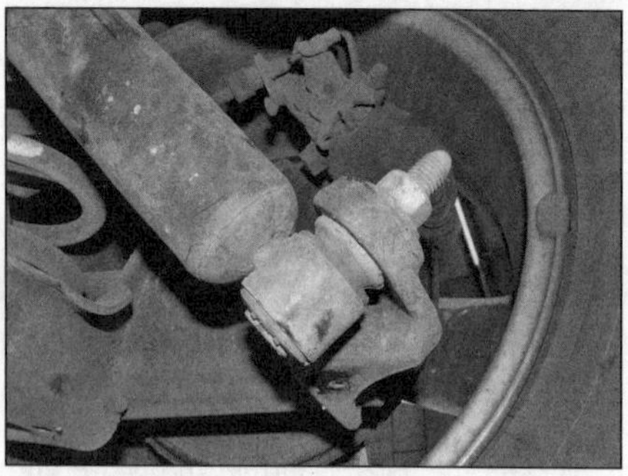

12.8 Check the rear shock absorber for fluid leaks and mounting damage

corner. Generally speaking, the body will return to its normal position and stop after being depressed. If it rises and returns on a rebound, the shock absorber is probably suspect.

Roadwheel bolt check

11 Remove the wheel trims or wheel centre caps, as applicable, then slacken the roadwheel bolts slightly.

12 Tighten the bolts to the specified torque, using a torque wrench.

13 Driveshaft gaiter check

1 With the car raised and securely supported on stands, turn the steering onto full lock, then slowly rotate the roadwheel. Inspect the condition of the outer constant velocity (CV) joint rubber gaiters while squeezing the gaiters to open out the folds. Check for signs of cracking, splits or deterioration of the rubber which may allow the grease to escape and lead to water and grit entry into the joint. Also check the security and condition of the retaining clips. Repeat these checks on the inner CV joints **(see illustration)**. If any damage or deterioration is found, the gaiters should be renewed as described in Chapter 8.

2 At the same time, check the general condition of the CV joints themselves by first holding the driveshaft and attempting to rotate the wheel. Repeat this check by holding the inner joint and attempting to rotate the driveshaft. Any appreciable movement indicates wear in the joints, wear in the driveshaft splines, or a loose driveshaft retaining nut.

14 Bodywork and underbody condition check

1 Once the car has been washed and all tar spots and other surface blemishes have been cleaned off, carefully check all paintwork, looking closely for chips or scratches. Pay particular attention to vulnerable areas such as the front panels (bonnet and spoiler), and around the wheel arches. Any damage to the paintwork must be rectified as soon as possible to comply with the terms of the manufacturer's anti-corrosion warranties; check with a Renault dealer for details.

2 If a chip or light scratch is found which is recent and still free from rust, it can be touched-up using the appropriate touch-up stick which can be obtained from Renault dealers. Any more serious damage, or rusted stone chips, can be repaired as described in Chapter 11, but if damage or corrosion is so severe that a panel must be renewed, seek professional advice as soon as possible.

3 Always check that the door and ventilation opening drain holes and pipes are completely clear, so that water can drain out.

12.9 Check around the front strut piston rod gaiter for fluid leaks

13.1 Check the CV joint gaiters for splits or signs of perishing

15.1 Check along the sump joint for signs of oil leaks

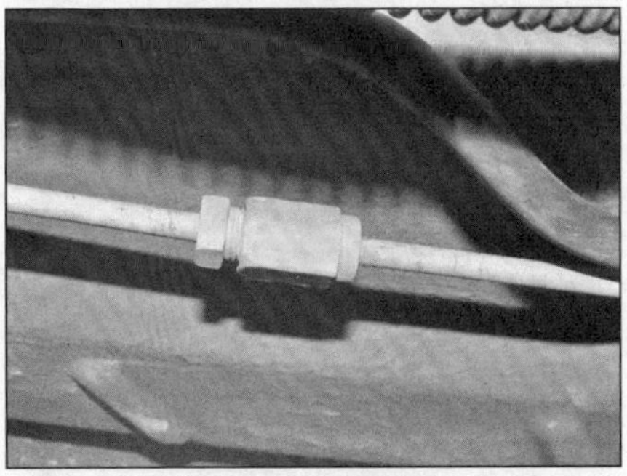

15.2 Check the brake pipes very carefully, especially at joints

4 The wax-based underbody protective coating should be inspected annually, preferably just prior to Winter, when the underbody should be washed down as thoroughly as possible without disturbing the protective coating (see Chapter 11, Section 2, regarding the use of steam cleaners). Any damage to the coating should be repaired using a suitable wax-based sealer. If any of the body panels are disturbed for repair or renewal, do not forget to replace the coating and to inject wax into door panels, sills and box sections, to maintain the level of protection provided by the manufacturer.

15 Hose and fluid leak check

1 Visually inspect the engine joint faces, gaskets and seals for any signs of water or oil leaks. Pay particular attention to the areas around the top of the engine, cylinder head, oil filter and sump joint faces **(see illustration)**. Bear in mind that, over a period of time, some very slight seepage from these areas is to be expected – what you are really looking for is any indication of a serious leak. Should a leak be found, renew the offending gasket or oil seal by referring to the appropriate Chapters in this manual.

2 Also check the security and condition of all the engine-related pipes and hoses, and all hydraulic and braking system pipes and hoses **(see illustration)**. Ensure that all cable-ties or securing clips are in place, and in good condition. Clips which are broken or missing can lead to chafing of the hoses, pipes or wiring, which could cause more serious problems in the future.

3 Carefully check the radiator hoses and heater hoses along their entire length. Renew any hose which is cracked, swollen or deteriorated. Cracks will show up better if the hose is squeezed. Pay close attention to the hose clips that secure the hoses to the cooling system components. Hose clips can pinch and puncture hoses, resulting in cooling system leaks. If the crimped-type hose clips are used, it may be a good idea to use Jubilee clips.

4 Inspect all the cooling system components (hoses, joint faces, etc) for leaks **(see Haynes Hint)**. Where any problems are found on system components, renew the component or gasket with reference to Chapter 3.

HAYNES HiNT

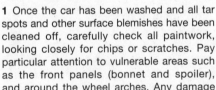

A leak in the cooling system will usually show up as white- or rust-coloured deposits on the area surrounding the joint.

5 With the car raised, inspect the fuel tank and filler neck for punctures, cracks and other damage. The connection between the filler neck and tank is especially critical. Sometimes a rubber filler neck or connecting hose will leak due to loose retaining clamps or deteriorated rubber.

6 Carefully check all rubber hoses and metal fuel lines leading away from the fuel tank. Check for loose connections, deteriorated hoses, crimped lines, and other damage. Pay particular attention to the vent pipes and hoses, which often loop up around the filler neck and can become blocked or crimped. Follow the lines to the front of the car, carefully inspecting them all the way. Renew damaged sections as necessary. Similarly, whilst the car is raised, take the opportunity to inspect all underbody brake fluid pipes and hoses.

7 From within the engine compartment, check the security of all fuel, vacuum and brake hose attachments and pipe unions, and inspect all hoses for kinks, chafing and deterioration.

8 Where applicable, check the condition of the automatic transmission fluid cooler pipes and hoses.

16 Road test

Instruments and electrical equipment

1 Check the operation of all instruments and electrical equipment.

2 Make sure that all instruments read correctly, and switch on all electrical equipment in turn, to check that it functions properly.

Steering and suspension

3 Check for any abnormalities in the steering, suspension, handling or road 'feel'.

4 Drive the car, and check that there are no unusual vibrations or noises.

5 Check that the steering feels positive, with no excessive 'sloppiness', or roughness, and check for any suspension noises when cornering and driving over bumps.

Drivetrain

6 Check the performance of the engine, clutch, transmission and driveshafts.

7 Listen for any unusual noises from the engine, clutch and transmission.

8 Make sure that the engine runs smoothly when idling, and that there is no hesitation when accelerating.

9 Check that, where applicable, the clutch action is smooth and progressive, that the drive is taken up smoothly, and that the pedal travel is not excessive. Also listen for any noises when the clutch pedal is depressed.

10 Check that all gears can be engaged smoothly without noise, and that the gear lever action is smooth and not abnormally vague or 'notchy'.

11 Listen for a metallic clicking sound from the front of the car, as the car is driven slowly in a circle with the steering on full-lock. Carry out this check in both directions. If a clicking noise is heard, this indicates wear in a driveshaft joint (see Chapter 8).

Braking system

12 Make sure that the car does not pull to one side when braking, and that the wheels do not lock when braking hard.

13 Check that there is no vibration through the steering when braking.

14 Check that the handbrake operates correctly, without excessive movement of the lever, and that it holds the car stationary on a slope.

15 Test the operation of the brake servo unit as follows. Depress the footbrake four or five times to exhaust the vacuum, then start the engine. As the engine starts, there should be a noticeable 'give' in the brake pedal as vacuum builds-up. Allow the engine to run for at least two minutes, and then switch it off. If the brake pedal is now depressed again, it should be possible to detect a hiss from the servo as the pedal is depressed. After about four or five applications, no further hissing should be heard, and the pedal should feel considerably harder.

Every 36 000 miles (60 000 km) or 4 years

17 Air filter element renewal

Removal

1 The air filter is located behind the battery.

2 Access can be improved by removing the battery cover. Unclip the cover **(see illustration)**.

3 Unscrew and remove the two filter housing mounting screws – access to the one nearest the engine is hampered by the engine ECU, and may require the use of a stubby or cranked screwdriver.

4 Slide the filter housing out upwards to remove it **(see illustration)**.

5 Withdraw the filter element from the housing

Refitting

6 Clean the inside of the air cleaner body and housing/cover, being careful not to get dirt into the inlet duct. Use a vacuum cleaner if necessary.

7 Fit the new element using a reversal of the removal procedure.

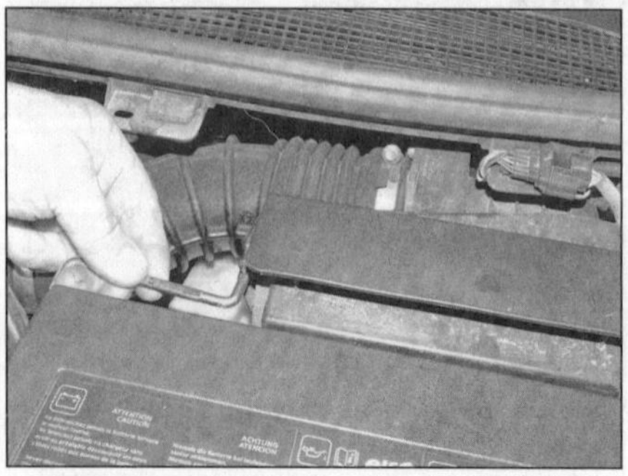

17.2 Remove the battery cover

17.4 Slide the filter housing upwards to remove

18 Fuel filter renewal

Note: *It is advisable to wear gloves when carrying out this procedure.*

1 The fuel filter is located behind the right-hand headlight, and is accessed through the wheel arch. Access can be improved by removing the right-hand headlight as described in Chapter 12.

2 Loosen the right-hand front wheel bolts, then jack up the front of the car, and support it on axle stands (see *Jacking and vehicle support*). Remove the wheel.

3 Remove the front section of the wheel arch liner as described in Chapter 11.

4 Position a suitable container beneath the filter

5 Disconnect the wiring plug from the filter heater **(see illustration)**.

6 Remove the mounting nut from the filter

18.5 Disconnect the wiring plug

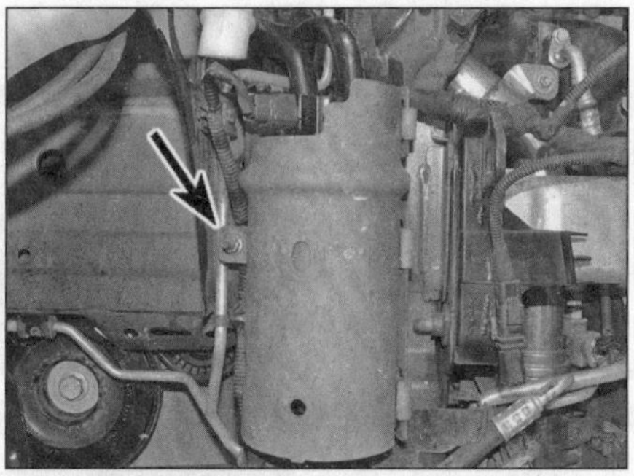

18.6a Remove the nut (arrowed)...

18.6b ...and open the protective cover

crash protection cage **(see illustrations)** and then either lower the lower the filter assembly to access the fuel lines or release them from above after removing the headlight.

7 Squeeze the quick-release fittings and disconnect the two fuel pipes, noting their fitted positions – anticipate some loss of fuel as this is done **(see illustration)**. Remove the filter unit completely.

8 Unless a new filter is being fitted immediately, cap or plug the open fuel pipe connections, to prevent the entry of dirt into the system.

9 New filters are supplied with a comprehensive set of O-rings **(see illustration)**.

10 Over a suitable container, remove the drain plug and heater element **(see illustration)**.

11 Replace the O-ring seals **(see illustration)**. Wear gloves and lubricate the seals with clean diesel before fitting. Refit the drain plug and heating element.

> **HAYNES HiNT** ***When fitting a new filter (where possible) fill it with clean fuel before fitting. This will greatly reduce the length time for priming and bleeding the system on completion.***

18.7 Depress the locking ring (arrowed) and remove the fuel pipes

12 Fit the new filter back into position under the wheel arch, making sure the fuel pipes and wiring plugs are reconnected correctly and securely.

13 On completion, refit the components removed to access the filter, then refit the wheel and lower the car to the ground. Tighten the wheel bolts to the specified torque.

14 Squeeze the hand-priming pump a few times to prime the system, then start the engine as normal. If the engine is reluctant to start, refer to Chapter 4B for more information on priming and bleeding the fuel system.

15 With the engine running, check for any sign of fuel leakage under the wheel arch.

16 Dispose of the old filter responsibly.

18.9 The new filter should be supplied with new seals

19 Auxiliary drivebelt renewal

Note: *If the belt is removed, the belt, tensioner and tensioner bolt must be replaced.*

Removal and refitting

1 Jack up and support the front of the vehicle (see *Jacking and vehicle support* in the reference section).

2 Remove the right-hand road wheel and the front section of the wing liner as described in Chapter 11.

18.10 Remove the heater element

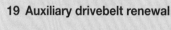

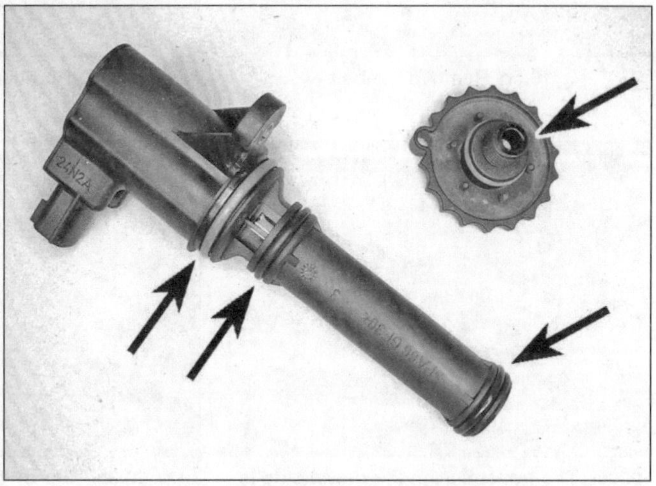

18.11 Replace the seals (arrowed)

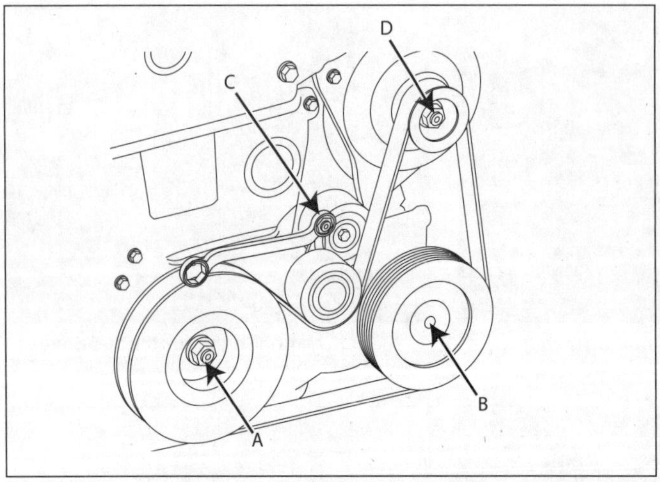

19.5a Note the belt routing

A Crankshaft pulley
B AC compressor
C Automatic tensioner
D Alternator

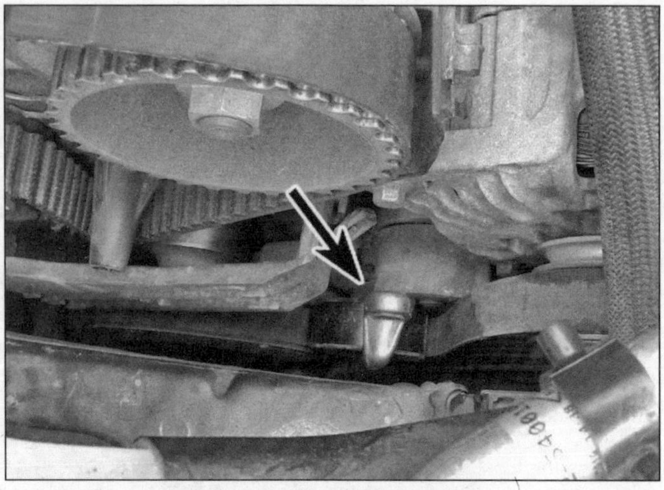

19.5b The tensioner (arrowed)

3 Remove the engine undershield and then to further improve access unclip the fuel lines from the top of the engine mounting.

4 Using a 16 mm spanner turn the tensioner pulley clockwise to release the tension on the belt.

5 Noting its routing remove the drivebelt from the pulleys **(see illustrations)**. This is best accomplished with an assistant holding the spanner whilst the belt is remove from below.

6 Renault recommend that the tensioner, tensioner bolt and the belt are replaced once removed.

7 Unbolt and remove the tensioner pulley **(see illustration)**. With the belt and pulley removed, check and clean if necessary the grooves in the crankshaft pulley.

8 Fit the new tensioner and tighten the new retaining bolt to the specified torque.

9 Turn the tensioner clockwise and then fit the belt loosely around the main pulleys, making sure that it is correctly located in the grooves.

10 Slowly release the tensioner and allow the belt to be tensioned.

11 Turn the engine through a few complete revolutions, using a spanner or socket on the crankshaft pulley bolt. Check that the belt is running properly on its pulleys, and that the tensioner is working correctly (check that the belt is taut, midway along its bottom run).

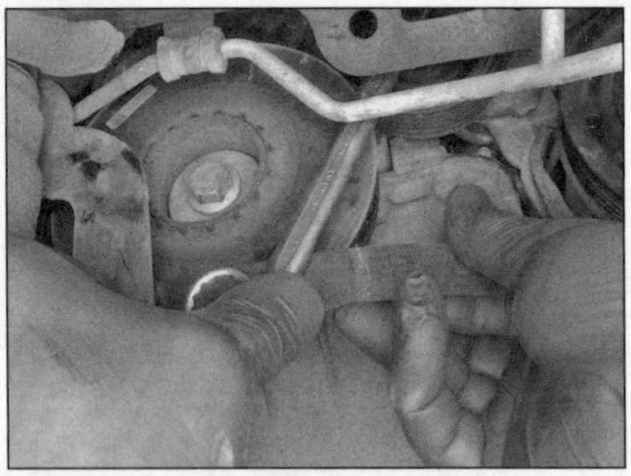

19.5c Remove the belt

19.7 Remove the tensioner

12 On completion, refit the components removed to access the belt, then refit the wheel and lower the car to the ground. Tighten the wheel bolts to the specified torque.

20 Manual transmission oil level check

1 Either position the car over an inspection pit, or jack up the front and rear of the car and support it on axle stands (see *Jacking and vehicle support*). The car must be level for the check to be accurate.

2 Remove the engine undertray

3 Locate the plastic filler/level plug, and clean the area around it before removal. The plug is located close to the left-hand driveshaft on the six speed transmission and on the front-facing side of the transmission on five speed models **(see illustrations)**.

4 Unscrew and remove the plug – this could be very tight **(see illustration)**. Check the condition of the filler plug seal, and obtain a new one if necessary.

5 The oil level should be up to the lower

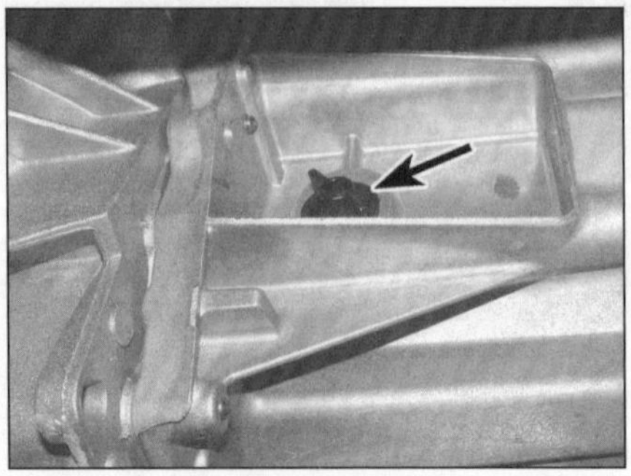

20.3a The transmission filler/level plug is on the front (5-speed)...

20.3b ...or on the side (6-speed)

20.4 Unscrew the filler/level plug

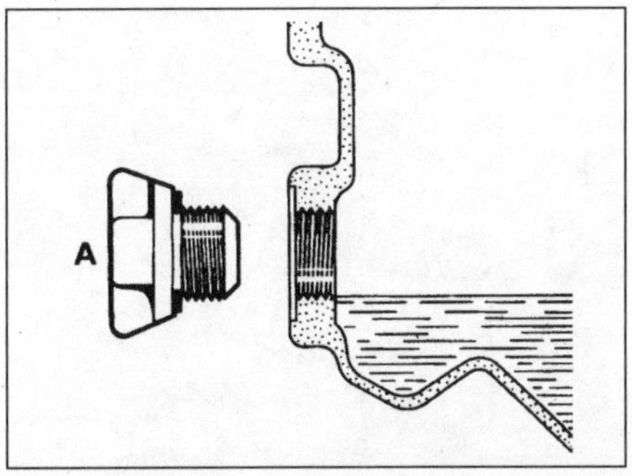

20.5 Manual transmission level/filler plug (A) – correct level shown

edge of the filler/level plug aperture **(see illustration)**.

6 If necessary, top-up using the specified type of lubricant until the transmission oil level is correct. Fill the transmission until oil starts to flow out, and allow excess oil to drain out. Access to the filler plug on the six speed transmission is limited **(see illustration)**. We used a large syringe and a length of tubing.

7 Once the transmission oil level is correct, refit the filler/level plug and tighten it securely – by hand only.

8 Refit the engine undertray cover and then lower the car to the ground. Note that frequent need for topping-up indicates a leak, possibly through an oil seal. The cause should be investigated and rectified.

21 Front wheel alignment check

Refer to the information given in Chapter 10.

22 Air conditioning system check

The air conditioning system must be checked by a Renault dealer or a suitably equipped garage using dedicated test equipment.

23 Brake fluid renewal

Warning: Brake hydraulic fluid can harm your eyes and damage painted surfaces, so use extreme caution when handling and pouring it. Do not use fluid that has been standing open for some time, as it absorbs moisture from the air. Excess moisture can cause a dangerous loss of braking effectiveness.

20.6a Topping-up the oil level through the filler hole (5 speed transmission)...

1 The procedure is similar to that for the bleeding of the hydraulic system as described in Chapter 9, except that the brake fluid reservoir should be emptied by syphoning, using a clean poultry baster or similar before starting, and allowance should be made for the old fluid to be expelled when bleeding a section of the circuit.

2 Working as described in Chapter 9, open the first bleed screw in the sequence, and pump the brake pedal gently until nearly all the old fluid has been emptied from the master cylinder reservoir **(see illustration)**. Top-up to the MAX level with new fluid, and continue pumping until only the new fluid remains in the reservoir, and new fluid can be seen emerging from the bleed screw. Tighten the screw, and top the reservoir level up to the MAX level line.

Old hydraulic fluid is invariably much darker in colour than the new, making it easy to distinguish the two.

3 Work through all the remaining bleed screws in the sequence until new fluid can be seen at all of them. Be careful to keep the master cylinder reservoir topped-up to above the MIN level at all times, or air may enter the system and greatly increase the length of the task.

4 When the operation is complete, check that all bleed screws are securely tightened, and that their dust caps are refitted. Wash off all traces of spilt fluid, and recheck the master cylinder reservoir fluid level.

5 Check the operation of the brakes before taking the car on the road.

23.2 Change the brake fluid using the same method as for brake bleeding

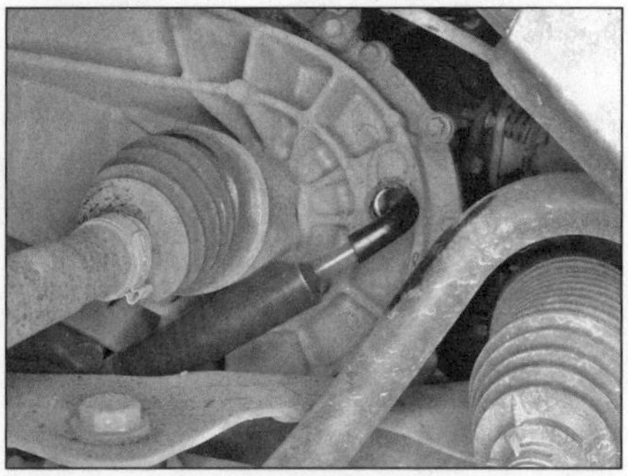

20.6b ... and on the 6 speed transmission

24 Coolant renewal

Warning: Wait until the engine is cold before starting this procedure. Do not allow antifreeze to come in contact with your skin, or with the painted surfaces of the vehicle. Rinse off spills immediately with plenty of water. Never leave antifreeze lying around in an open container, or in a puddle in the driveway or on the garage floor. Children and pets are attracted by its sweet smell, but antifreeze can be fatal if ingested.

Cooling system draining

1 With the engine completely cold, remove the expansion tank filler cap. Turn the cap anti-clockwise, wait until any pressure remaining in the system is released, then unscrew it and lift it off.

2 Jack up and support the front of the vehicle(see *Jacking and vehicle support* in the reference section).

3 Remove both front road wheels and then (with reference to Chapter 11) remove the front sections of both wing liners and then remove the front bumper.

4 Remove the engine undertray and then position a container beneath the radiator drain tap.

5 Open the drain tap and allow the coolant to drain into the container **(see illustration)**.

6 To assist draining, open the cooling system

24.5 The coolant drain tap (arrowed)

24.6a Open the bleed screw on the thermostat housing (arrowed)...

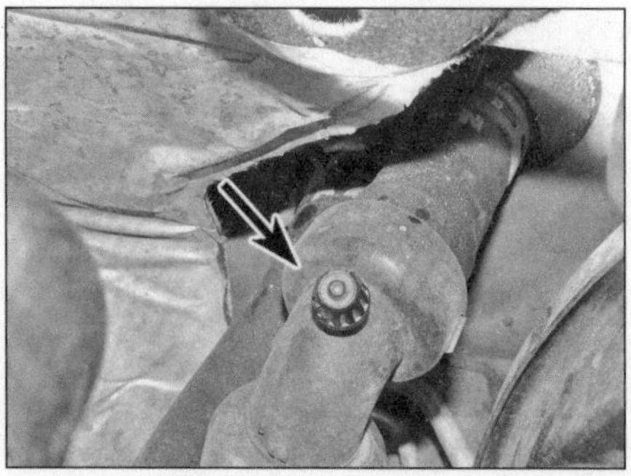

24.6b ...and on the heater hose (arrowed) next to the bulkhead

24.7a Remove the spring clip (arrowed) from the hose...

bleed screws on the thermostat housing, and on the heater hose **(see illustrations)**.

7 If draining of the coolant is only required to remove the waterpump, thermostat or heater matrix then the system can be drained by removal of the one of the main coolant hoses **(see illustrations)**. This avoid the need to remove the front bumper cover

8 If compressed air is available, Renault suggest inserting an air line into the expansion tank to drive out as much water as possible.

9 Flush the system if necessary as described in the following paragraphs and then close the drain tap. Refill the system as described later in this Section. Refit the bumper, wing liners and road wheels. Lowe the vehicle to the ground

Cooling system flushing

10 If coolant renewal has been neglected, or if the antifreeze mixture has become diluted, then in time, the cooling system may gradually lose efficiency, as the coolant passages become restricted due to rust, scale deposits, and other sediment. The cooling system efficiency can be restored by flushing the system clean.

11 The simplest method for flushing the system is to drain the system and then refill the system with clean water. When the system is full drain the system a second time. Check the condition of the water drained – if it is clean, flushing is complete; if not, repeat the process.

Radiator flushing

12 Disconnect the top and bottom hoses and any other relevant hoses from the radiator, with reference to Chapter 3.

13 Insert a garden hose into the radiator top inlet. Direct a flow of clean water through the radiator, and continue flushing until clean water emerges from the radiator bottom outlet.

14 If after a reasonable period, the water still does not run clear, the radiator can be flushed with a good proprietary cleaning agent. It is important that the manufacturer's instructions are followed carefully. If the contamination is particularly bad, insert the hose in the radiator bottom outlet, and reverse-flush the radiator.

Engine flushing

15 To flush the engine, remove the thermostat as described in Chapter 3, and disconnect the bottom hose.

16 Insert a garden hose into the thermostat housing and direct a clean flow of water through the engine. Continue flushing until clean water emerges from the radiator bottom hose.

17 On completion, refit the thermostat and reconnect the bottom hose. Where applicable, refit the engine undertray.

Antifreeze mixture

18 The antifreeze should always be renewed at the specified intervals. This is necessary not only to maintain the antifreeze properties, but also to prevent corrosion which would otherwise occur as the corrosion inhibitors become progressively less effective.

19 Always use an ethylene-glycol based antifreeze which is suitable for use in mixed-metal cooling systems. The quantity of antifreeze and levels of protection are given in the Specifications.

20 Before adding antifreeze, the cooling system should be completely drained, preferably flushed, and all hoses checked for condition and security.

21 After filling with antifreeze, a label should be attached to the expansion tank, stating the type and concentration of antifreeze used, and the date installed. Any subsequent topping-up should be made with the same type and concentration of antifreeze.

22 Do not use engine antifreeze in the windscreen/tailgate washer system, as it will cause damage to the vehicle's paintwork. A screenwash additive should be added to the washer system in the quantities stated on the bottle.

Cooling system filling

23 Before attempting to fill the cooling system, make sure that all hoses and clips are in good condition, and that the clips are tight. Note that an antifreeze mixture must be used all year round, to prevent corrosion of the engine components.

24 Remove the expansion tank filler cap **(see illustration)**.

25 If not already done, open the cooling system bleed screws.

26 Slowly fill the system until the coolant level reaches the MAX mark on the expansion tank. Close the bleed screws in turn when coolant free from air bubbles emerges from each one.

27 Start the engine, and run it at a fast idle speed (approximately 2000 rpm). As soon as

24.7b ...with a suitable tool

24.7c Release the hose and catch the coolant in a suitable container

24.24 Remove the coolant expansion tank filler cap

the engine is running, top-up the level in the expansion tank if necessary, then refit and tighten the expansion tank filler cap – the cap should not normally be removed when the engine is running, nor when the system is hot.

28 Allow the engine to run at 2000 rpm until the cooling fan has cut in and out three times.

29 Stop the engine and allow the engine to cool for at least an hour, and preferably, overnight.

30 Recheck the coolant level with reference to *Weekly checks*. Top-up the level if necessary and refit the expansion tank filler cap.

Airlocks

31 If, after draining and refilling the system, symptoms of overheating are found which did not occur previously, then the fault is almost certainly due to trapped air at some point in the system, causing an airlock and restricting the flow of coolant; usually, the air is trapped because the system was refilled too quickly.

32 If an airlock is suspected, first try gently squeezing all visible coolant hoses. A coolant hose which is full of air feels quite different to one full of coolant when squeezed. After refilling the system, most airlocks will clear once the system has cooled, and been topped-up.

33 While the engine is running at operating temperature, switch on the heater and heater fan, and check for heat output. Provided there is sufficient coolant in the system, any lack of heat output could be due to an airlock in the system.

34 Airlocks can have more serious effects than simply reducing heater output – a severe airlock could reduce coolant flow around the engine. Check that the radiator top hose is hot when the engine is at operating temperature – a top hose which stays cold could be the result of an airlock (or a non-opening thermostat).

35 If the problem persists, stop the engine and allow it to cool down **completely**, before unscrewing the radiator and expansion tank caps, or loosening the hose clips and squeezing the hoses to bleed out the trapped air. In the worst case, the system will have to be at least partially drained (this time, the coolant can be saved for re-use) and flushed to clear the problem.

Every 96 000 miles (154 000 km) or 6 years

25 Timing belt renewal

Refer to Chapter 2B.

Notes

Chapter 2 Part A:
Petrol engine in-car repair procedures

Contents

	Section number
Camshaft oil seal – renewal	6
Camshafts – removal, inspection and refitting	7
Compression test – description and interpretation	2
Crankshaft oil seals – renewal	11
Cylinder head – dismantling and overhaul See Chapter 2C	
Cylinder head – removal, inspection and refitting	8
Engine oil and filter renewal	See Chapter 1A
Engine oil level check	See *Weekly checks*
Engine/transmission mountings – inspection and renewal	12
Flywheel – removal, inspection and refitting	13
General information	1
Oil pump and sprockets – removal, inspection and refitting	10
Sump – removal and refitting	9
Timing belt – removal, inspection and refitting	4
Timing belt sprockets and tensioner – removal, inspection and refitting	5
Top Dead Centre (TDC) for No 1 piston – locating	3

Degrees of difficulty

Easy, suitable for novice with little experience	**Fairly easy,** suitable for beginner with some experience	**Fairly difficult,** suitable for competent DIY mechanic	**Difficult,** suitable for experienced DIY mechanic	**Very difficult,** suitable for expert DIY or professional

Specifications

General

Type	Four-cylinder, in-line, double overhead camshaft (DOHC) with VVT (Variable Valve Timing)
Designation:	K4M
Bore	79.5 mm
Stroke	80.5 mm
Capacity	1598 cc
Firing order	1-3-4-2 (No 1 cylinder at flywheel end)
Direction of crankshaft rotation	Clockwise viewed from pulley end
Compression ratio	10 : 1

Camshaft

Endfloat	0.04 to 0.08 mm
Camshaft bearing journal diameters:	
No 1 to No 5 bearings	24.979 to 25.000 mm
No 6 bearing	27.979 to 28.000 mm

Cylinder head

Maximum distortion	0.05 mm

Lubrication system

System pressure:		
At idle	0.5 bar	
At 3000 rpm	3.1 bar	
Oil pump clearances:	**Minimum**	**Maximum**
Gear to body	0.110 mm	0.249 mm
Gear endfloat	0.020 mm	0.086 mm

Torque wrench settings	Nm	lbf ft
Alternator support bracket bolt	25	18
Camshaft phase-shifter cover	15	11
Camshaft phase-shifter sprocket bolt*	100	74
Camshaft sprocket (exhaust)*:		
Stage 1	30	22
Stage 2	Angle-tighten a further 84°	
Connecting rod cap nuts (oiled):*		
Stage 1	20	15
Stage 2	Angle-tighten a further 110° ± 6°	
Connecting rod cap bolts (oiled):*		
Stage 1	20	15
Stage 2	Angle-tighten a further 45° ± 6°	
Crankshaft pulley bolt*:		
Stage 1	40	30
Stage 2	Angle-tighten a further 145° ± 15°	
Cylinder head bolts*:		
Stage 1	20	15
Stage 2	Angle-tighten a further 240° ± 6°	
Driveshaft bearing support bracket (to block and sump)	44	32
Driveshaft bearing support bracket (clamp bolt)	21	16
Engine/transmission mountings:		
Right-hand mounting to engine/body	62	46
Left-hand mounting to transmission/body	62	46
Rear mounting	105	77
Flywheel bolts*:		
Stage 1	25	18
Stage 2	Angle-tighten a further 50° ± 6°	
Front suspension strut-to-swivel hub bolts	See Chapter 10	
Main bearing cap:		
Stage 1	25	18
Stage 2	Angle-tighten a further 47° ± 5°	
Oil level sensor	28	20
Oil pump bolts	25	18
Oil separator to cylinder head upper section	15	11
Roadwheel bolts	110	81
Strengthening bracket/flywheel cover:		
On engine	50	37
On transmission	25	18
Sump	14	10
Sump to gearbox bellhousing:	44	32
Timing belt idler pulley*	50	37
Timing belt tensioner pulley*:		
Pretighten	7	5
Final	27	20
Timing cover:		
Upper cover (nuts and bolts)	46	34
Lower cover	12	9
Throttle valve bolts	10	7
Valve cover bolts:		
Bolts, 1 to 17, 20,21 and 22	12	9
Bolts 23, 18, 19 and 24	14	10

** Use new nuts/bolts when refitting*

1 General information

How to use this Chapter

This Part of Chapter 2 is devoted to in-car repair procedures for the petrol engine. Similar information covering the diesel engine can be found in Part B. All procedures concerning engine removal and refitting, and engine block/cylinder head overhaul can be found in Part C of this Chapter.

Refer to *Vehicle identification numbers* in the Reference Section at the end of this manual for details of engine code locations.

Most of the operations included in this Part are based on the assumption that the engine is still installed in the car. Therefore, if this information is being used during a complete engine overhaul, with the engine already removed, many of the steps included here will not apply.

Engine description

The engine is of four cylinder, in-line, overhead camshaft type, mounted transversely in the front of the car. Double overhead camshafts are fitted.

The overhead camshafts are each mounted in the cylinder head by six plain bearings with matching caps, and are driven by the crankshaft by a toothed rubber timing belt, which also drives the water pump. The inlet camshaft sprocket incorporates a phase-shifter which provides variable valve timing by advancing the inlet valve timing during certain operating conditions. The phase-shifter is activated by the engine management ECU via an electrically-controlled solenoid valve located on the top, right-hand side of the cylinder head. The camshafts operate the valves by hydraulic tappets and roller cam followers located below the camshafts in the cylinder head.

The cylinder block is of cast iron. The engine has conventional dry liners bored directly into the cylinder block. The crankshaft is supported within the cylinder block on five shell-type main bearings. Thrustwashers are fitted at the upper centre main bearing to control crankshaft endfloat.

The connecting rods are attached to the crankshaft by horizontally-split shell type big-end bearings and to the pistons by gudgeon pins which are an interference fit in the connecting rods. The aluminium alloy pistons are fitted with three piston rings, comprising two compression rings and a scraper-type oil control ring.

A fully-enclosed crankcase ventilation system is employed; crankcase fumes are drawn from an oil separator on the cylinder head, and passed via a hose to the inlet manifold.

Lubrication is by pressure feed from a gear-type oil pump, which is chain-driven direct from the crankshaft.

Operations with engine in place

The following operations can be carried out without having to remove the engine from the car:

a) Removal and refitting of the cylinder head.
b) Removal and refitting of the timing belt and sprockets.
c) Renewal of the camshaft oil seal.
d) Removal and refitting of the camshaft.
e) Removal and refitting of the pressed steel sump.
*f) Removal and refitting of the connecting rods and pistons.**
g) Removal and refitting of the oil pump.
h) Renewal of the crankshaft timing belt end oil seal.
i) Renewal of the engine mountings.

* **Note:** *Although the operation marked with an asterisk can be carried out with the engine in the car after removal of the sump, it is better for the engine to be removed, in the interests of cleanliness and improved access. For this reason, these procedures are described in Part C of this Chapter.*

2 Compression test – description and interpretation

Note: *A compression gauge will be required for this test.*

1 A compression check will tell you what mechanical condition the top end (pistons, rings, valves, head gasket) of the engine is in. Specifically, it can tell you if the compression is down due to leakage caused by worn piston rings, defective valves and seats or a blown head gasket. **Note:** *The battery must be fully-charged, for this check.*

2 Begin by cleaning the area around the spark plugs before you remove them (compressed air should be used, if available, otherwise a small brush or even a bicycle tyre pump will work). The idea is to prevent dirt from getting into the cylinders as the compression check is being done.

3 Remove all the spark plugs from the engine (see Chapter 1A).

4 Disable the engine management system by removing the engine protection fuse from the engine compartment fusebox.

5 Fit the compression gauge into the No 1 spark plug hole – the type of tester which screws into the plug thread is to be preferred.

6 Have an assistant hold the accelerator pedal fully depressed, while at the same time cranking the engine over several times on the starter motor. Observe the compression gauge – the compression should build-up quickly in a healthy engine. Low compression on the first stroke, followed by gradually increasing pressure on successive strokes, indicates worn piston rings. A low compression reading on the first stroke, which does not build-up during successive strokes, indicates leaking valves or a blown head gasket (a cracked head could also be the cause). Deposits on the undersides of the valve heads can also cause low compression. Record the highest gauge reading obtained, then repeat the procedure for the remaining cylinders.

7 Add some engine oil (about three squirts from a plunger-type oil can) to each cylinder, through the spark plug hole and repeat the test.

8 If the compression increases after the oil is added, the piston rings are worn. If the compression does not increase significantly, the leakage is occurring at the valves or head gasket. Leakage past the valves may be caused by burned valve seats and/or faces, or warped, cracked or bent valves.

9 If two adjacent cylinders have equally low compression, there is a strong possibility that the head gasket between them is blown. The appearance of coolant in the combustion chambers or the crankcase would verify this condition.

10 Actual compression pressures for the engines covered by this manual are not specified by the manufacturer. However, bearing in mind the information given in the preceding paragraphs, the results obtained should give a good indication of engine condition and what course of action, if any, to take.

3 Top Dead Centre (TDC) for No 1 piston – locating

Note: *A TDC pin from a Renault dealer (Mot. 1489) or automotive tool shop is required for this operation. This pin Is normally included in an engine timing tool kit, such as AST tools AST4964* ***(see illustration)*** *or Draper 32812*

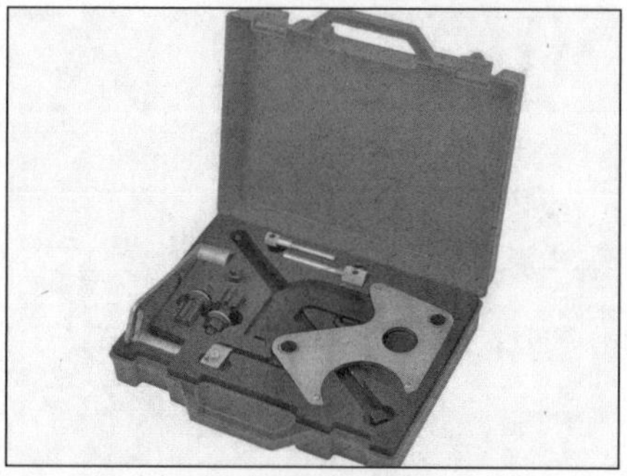

3.0 A suitable set of timing tools will be required

1 Top Dead Centre (TDC) is the highest point in the cylinder that each piston reaches as the crankshaft turns. Each piston reaches TDC at the end of the compression stroke and again at the end of the exhaust stroke; however, for the purpose of timing the engine, TDC refers to the position of No 1 piston at the end of its compression stroke. No 1 piston is at the **flywheel** end of the engine.

2 Apply the handbrake, then jack up the front right-hand side of the car and support it on axle stands. Remove the right-hand roadwheel.

3 Remove the front section of the wing liner from within the right-hand wheel arch to give access to the crankshaft pulley bolt.

4 Remove the spark plugs as described in Chapter 1A, so that the engine can be turned over easily.

5 The engine must now be turned in order to check for pressure in No 1 cylinder as the piston rises on the compression stroke. As the spark plug holes are deeply recessed, it is not possible to place a finger over them, however, the inverted handle of a screwdriver may be used instead, or alternatively simply listen for air being forced out of the No 1 spark plug hole. Turn the engine in a clockwise direction, using a socket or spanner on the crankshaft pulley bolt, until air is forced from No 1 cylinder; this indicates that No 1 piston is rising on its compression stroke.

6 Unscrew the hose clips and remove the air filter housing to throttle body hose **(see illustration)**.

7 Disconnect the wiring plug from the throttle body and then unbolt the throttle body. As

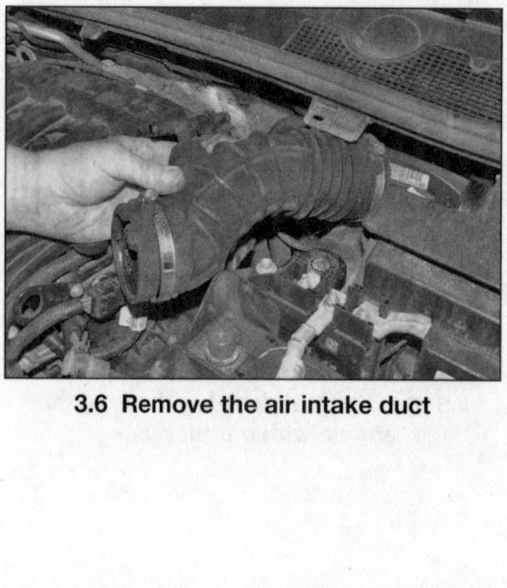

3.6 Remove the air intake duct

3.7 Disconnect the vapour hose

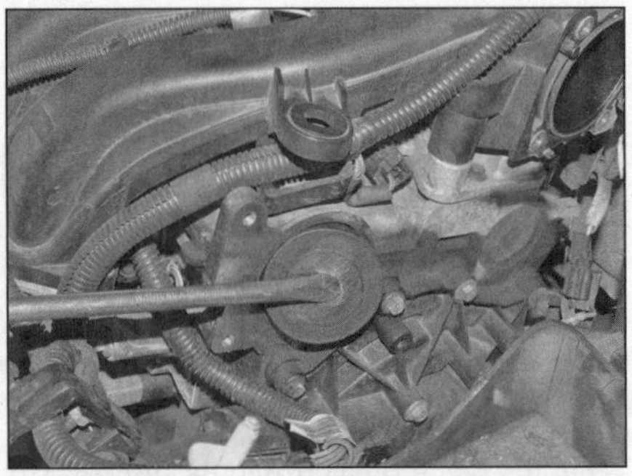

3.8 Using a screwdriver, prise the camshaft sealing plugs from the left-hand end of the cylinder head

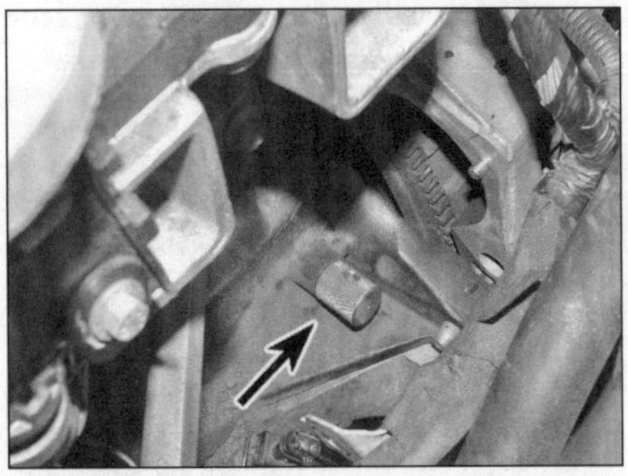

3.9 Fit the timing pin (arrowed) into the cylinder block – shown with the starter motor removed

3.10 The special Renault tool used to lock the camshafts in the TDC position

the throttle body is removed disconnect the vapour house from the body **(see illustration)**. Unclip the wiring loom at the inlet camshaft and then unbolt the engine lifting eye.

8 Using a screwdriver, pierce the centres of the two plastic plugs at the left-hand end of the cylinder head, and pull out the plugs **(see illustration)**. With No 1 piston approaching TDC, the grooves in the ends of the camshafts should be positioned approximately at 30° angle from the horizontal, with the offset below the centreline.

9 Unscrew the TDC plug from the left-hand front of the cylinder block, then fully screw in the TDC pin **(see illustration)**. Access to the plug can be greatly improved by removing the starter motor, as described in Chapter 5A.

10 Carefully turn the crankshaft clockwise until the crankshaft web is in contact with the TDC pin. At this point, the No 1 piston is at TDC on its compression stroke, and the grooves in the ends of the camshafts will now be positioned horizontally. Insert the special tool and lock the camshafts in the TDC position **(see illustration)**. A similar tool may be fabricated from metal plate if necessary.

11 Note that on some models the crankshaft sprocket is not keyed to the crankshaft, therefore if the crankshaft pulley/sprocket is removed it is important to have an accurate method of determining the TDC position of No 1 piston.

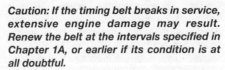

4.8 Support the right-hand end of the engine with a trolley jack

4 Timing belt – removal, inspection and refitting

Caution: If the timing belt breaks in service, extensive engine damage may result. Renew the belt at the intervals specified in Chapter 1A, or earlier if its condition is at all doubtful.

Note: *A set of timing tools will be required. These are available from Renault (Mot. 1489, Mot 1750 Mot 1496, Mot 1488 and Mot 1490-01). Alternatively after market specialists tool suppliers list these tools. For example the correct tools are listed by AST tools as AST4964* ***(see illustration 3.0)*** *and by Draper tools (32812).*

Note: *Renault state that the timing belt must be renewed whenever it is removed, and also that the tensioner and idler pulley must be renewed whenever the timing belt is renewed.*

Removal

1 Where fitted remove the engine cover and then disconnect the battery negative lead (see Disconnecting the battery in Chapter 5A).

2 Apply the handbrake, then jack up the front of the vehicle and support on axle stands (*see Jacking and vehicle support*). Remove the right-hand roadwheel.

3 Remove the engine compartment undertray and then remove the front section of the right-hand wheel arch liner, after pulling out the plastic retainers and removing the screws.

4 Remove the air filter inlet duct and then remove the throttle body **(see illustrations 3.6 and 3.7)** as described in Chapter 4A. Disconnect the vapour (EVAP) hose from the throttle body as it is removed. Access can be further improved by removing the battery.

5 Remove the wiring loom from the right-hand end of the engine by disconnecting it from the inlet manifold and unbolting the engine lifting eye at the right-hand front of the cylinder head.

6 Where fitted, unclip the fuel line from the lower timing cover. On other models the fuel line runs over the right-hand engine mounting. On these models disconnect (and immediately seal both the line and the stub on the fuel rail.

7 Working from below unbolt the lower rear engine to subframe tie bar.

8 Carefully, position a trolley jack and a large block of wood under the sump to support the right-hand side of the engine. Raise the jack to just take the weight of the engine **(see illustration)**.

9 Remove the right-hand upper engine mounting from the engine and body with reference to Section 12.

10 Remove the auxiliary drivebelt as described in Chapter 1A and then set the engine at TDC for No 1 piston as described in Section 3. Remove the TDC locating pin.

11 The crankshaft pulley must now be removed. To do this the engine must be locked. On engines with the suffix 858 and 866 remove the crankshaft position sensor and lock the flywheel with an 8mm hex key or socket extension. Note that this method effectively uses the crankshaft sensor pick up point on the flywheel to lock the engine. If this is damaged the engine will not start. On all other engines remove the blanking plug from the bell housing and jam a screwdriver into the flywheel ring gear to lock the engine.

12 Having said that, the best method of locking the flywheel is to remove the starter motor (as described in Chapter 5A) and use a screwdriver or pry bar jammed into the ring gear (or one of the slots in the flywheel) to lock the engine **(see illustration)**. This has the advantage that with the starter motor removed the TDC locating pin can easily be fitted and removed.

13 With an assistant locking the engine with

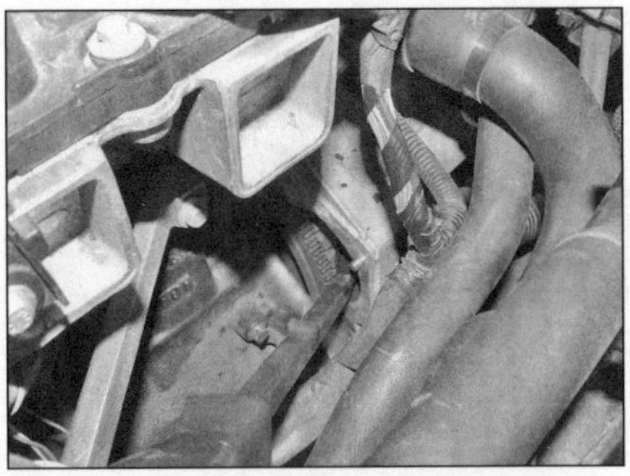

4.12 Lock the engine with a suitable pry bar

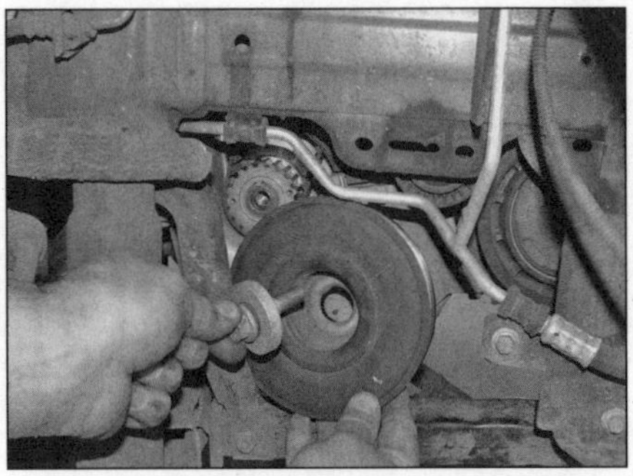

4.13 Remove the bolt and the crankshaft pulley

one of the methods suggested, remove the crankshaft pulley bolt. Discard the bolt – a new one must be used **(see illustration)**.

14 Using a screwdriver, pierce the centres of the two plastic plugs at the left-hand end of the camshafts, and pull the plugs from the cylinder head **(see illustration 3.8)**. With No 1 piston approaching TDC, the grooves in the ends of the camshafts should be as shown **(see illustration)**.

15 Refit the TDC pin. If the crankshaft has remained stationary whilst the crankshaft pulley was removed the engine should be still at TDC on the compression stroke. If the crankshaft has moved, reposition the crankshaft at TDC as described in Section 3

16 With the engine set at TDC insert the special tool (Renault Mot 1496 or equivalent) into the slots in the ends of the camshafts. Alternatively a length of metal bar may be fabricated **(see illustration 3.10** and **Tool Tip 1** to replicate the special tool**)**.

17 Unbolt the upper and lower timing belt covers **(see illustrations)**.

18 Make suitable alignment marks between the camshaft sprockets and the cylinder head cover. Loosen the timing belt tensioner, then turn the tensioner hub anti-clockwise to release the tension. Tighten the tensioner.

19 Unbolt and remove the idler pulley **(see illustration)**. Discard the pulley – a new one must be fitted.

20 Release the belt from the camshaft sprockets, water pump pulley, crankshaft sprocket and tensioner pulley. Remove the belt from the engine **(see illustration)**.

21 Unbolt and remove the tensioner pulley **(see illustration)**. Discard the pulley – a new one must be fitted.

22 Renault tool Mot 1490-01 or alternative must now be fitted to the camshaft sprockets

TOOL TiP

Tool Tip 1 To make a camshaft holding tool, obtain a length of steel strip and cut it to length so that it will fit across the rear of the cylinder head. Obtain a second length of steel strip of suitable thickness to fit snugly in the slots in the camshafts. Cut the second strip into two lengths and drill accordingly so that they can be bolted to the first strip in the correct position to engage with the camshaft slots. Secure a suitably drilled small piece of steel angle to the first strip so that the tool can be bolted to the threaded hole in the cylinder head upper section.

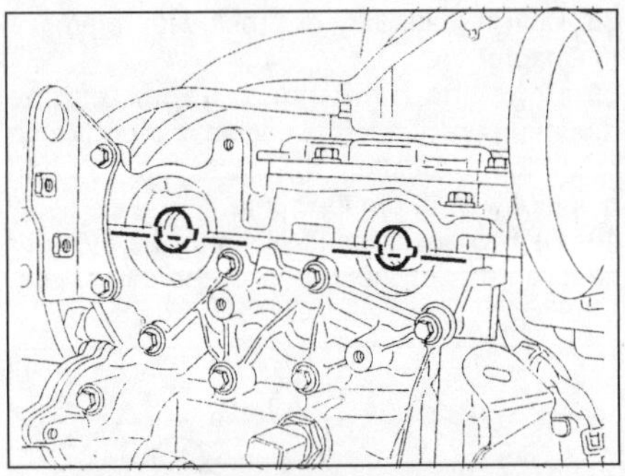

4.14 With the crankshaft at TDC the grooves in the end of the camshafts will be positioned horizontally

4.17a Removing the upper timing cover...

4.17b ...and the lower timing cover

4.19 Remove the idler pulley

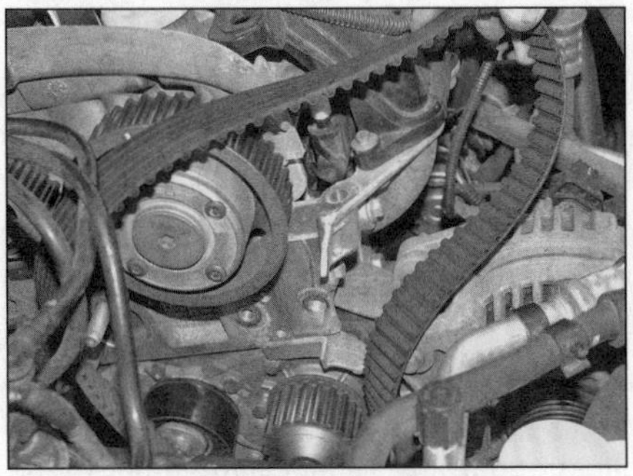

4.20 Remove the belt

4.21 Remove the tensioner pulley

4.22a Use the correct tool or...

4.22b ...alternatively use a sprocket holding tool for the exhaust camshaft sprocket ...

4.22c ...and a strap wrench for the inlet camshaft VVT sprocket

TOOL TiP

Tool Tip 2 To make a camshaft sprocket holding tool, obtain two lengths of steel strip 6 mm thick by 30 mm wide or similar, one 600 mm long, the other 200 mm long (all dimensions approximate). Bolt the two strips together to form a forked end, leaving the bolt slack so that the shorter strip can pivot freely. At the end of each 'prong' of the fork, drill a suitable hole and fit a nut and bolt to engage with the holes in the sprocket.

(see illustrations and **Tool Tip 2)**. On the inlet sprocket, remove the blanking plug and then remove the sprockets from the camshafts.

23 Clean the sprockets and wipe them dry. Also clean the cylinder head and block behind the timing belt running area.

Inspection

24 Examine the timing belt carefully for any signs of cracking, fraying or general wear, particularly at the roots of the teeth.

4.29 Note the index mark (arrowed) on the exhaust camshaft sprocket

25 The belt **must** be renewed if it has been removed.

26 Where a free running crankshaft sprocket is fitted, thoroughly clean the nose of the crankshaft and the bore of the crankshaft sprocket. Also clean the contact surfaces of the camshaft sprockets and the accessory drivebelt pulley. This is necessary to prevent the possibility of the sprockets slipping in use.

27 Check the waterpump while the belt is removed. There should be no signs of coolant leaking and the pump should turn freely. Serous consideration should be given to replacing the waterpump whilst the belt is removed. It is not uncommon for a previously sound waterpump to start to leak after the timing belt has been replaced due to the change in belt tension.

Refitting

28 Fit the new tensioner as described in Section 5.Check that the lug on the rear of the tensioner is correctly located in the groove. Note that if the belt is being replaced at the specified interval, it is strongly recommended that the waterpump is also replaced, as described in Chapter 3.

29 Using new bolts and ensuring that the VVT (variable valve timing) inlet sprocket is in the locked position (see Section 5) refit the sprockets. They should be free to rotate. The exhaust sprocket should have the Renault logo at the 12 o'clock position. The VVT sprocket should have the index mark in the 12 o'clock position **(see illustration)**. Check that the camshafts and No 1 piston are still at TDC. Fit the timing belt on the crankshaft sprocket, then locate it around the water pump, over the camshafts and around the tensioner.

30 Fit the idler pulley and tighten the bolt to the specified torque. The belt must be taut between the camshaft sprockets.

31 Refit the special tool and tighten the new camshaft sprocket bolts to the specified torque. The sprockets must not move and the belt must be taut between the sprockets.

32 Using a 6.0 mm Allen key, turn the index pointer until it is opposite the shallow notch at the front of the fixed notched plate **(see illustration)**, then pretighten the nut to the specified torque. Check that the camshafts and crankshaft are still at TDC.

33 Refit the lower timing belt cover and then remove the small access panel.

34 Lock the crankshaft in position and refit the crankshaft pulley. Tighten the new bolt to the specified torque.

35 Remove the locking tools from the camshafts and the TDC pin from the cylinder block. Turn the crankshaft clockwise two complete turns. Refit the TDC and camshaft timing tools and then recheck the tensioner index setting. If necessary, loosen the nut and use the Allen key to reposition the index pointer in line with the shallow notch. Finally, fully-tighten the tensioner to the specified torque.

36 Refit the access door and then the upper timing belt cover. Tighten the bolts securely.

37 Refit the TDC plug to the cylinder block and tighten securely. Where removed, refit the starter motor.

38 Refit the auxiliary drivebelt with reference to Chapter 1A.

39 Refit the right-hand upper engine mounting bracket to the engine and body with reference to Section 12. Lower the jack and block of wood from the sump.

40 Fit two new plastic plugs in the cylinder head on the left-hand end of the camshafts.

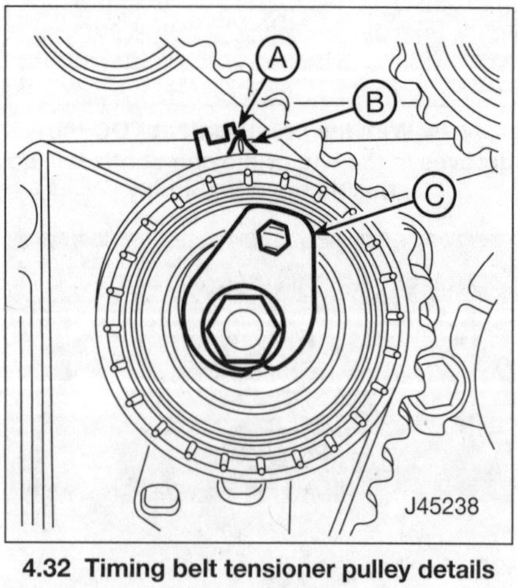

4.32 Timing belt tensioner pulley details

A Shallow notch
B Adjustable index
C Eccentric adjustment

Renault technicians use special tools to drive the plugs into position, although suitable sockets or blocks of wood may be used instead **(see illustration)**.

41 Refit the throttle body and air intake pipe, not forgetting the evaporative emissions pipe at the rear of the throttle body.

42 Clip the fuel pipes to the lower timing cover or reconnect the fuel line at the top of the engine mounting.

43 Refit the engine lifting eye and tighten the bolts. Where unclipped, reconnect the wiring loom.

44 Refit the right-hand wheel arch liners, and engine compartment undertray, then refit the roadwheel and lower the vehicle to the ground.

45 Reconnect the battery negative lead.

5 Timing belt sprockets and tensioner – removal, inspection and refitting

Caution: The timing belt sprockets are not keyed to the camshafts, neither is the crankshaft sprocket keyed to the crankshaft. Before starting work, make sure that you have the necessary tooling to accurately set the camshafts and crankshaft to TDC.

Removal

1 Remove the timing belt as described in Section 4.

2 Slide the crankshaft sprocket from the nose of the crankshaft, noting which way round it is fitted.

3 On the inlet camshaft sprocket remove the blanking plug to access the sprocket retaining bolt. Mark the position of both camshaft sprockets in relation to the cylinder head **(see illustration 4.29)**.

4 Use a suitable tool to hold each camshaft sprocket stationary while the fasteners are loosened, then unscrew and remove the fasteners and withdraw the sprockets from the camshafts.

5 To remove the tensioner, unscrew the centre fastener and withdraw the unit from the stud on the water pump. Note the groove in the water pump cover for the tensioner lug.

6 To remove the idler, unscrew the centre bolt and withdraw it from the cylinder head.

Inspection

7 Inspect the teeth of the sprockets for signs of nicks and damage.

8 Spin the tensioner pulley by hand and check it for any roughness or tightness. Do not attempt to clean it with solvent, as this may enter the bearing. If wear is evident, renew the tensioner. **Note:** *Renault state that the tensioner and idler pulley must be renewed whenever the timing belt is renewed.*

Refitting

9 Locate the idler on the cylinder head, then insert the bolt and tighten to the specified torque.

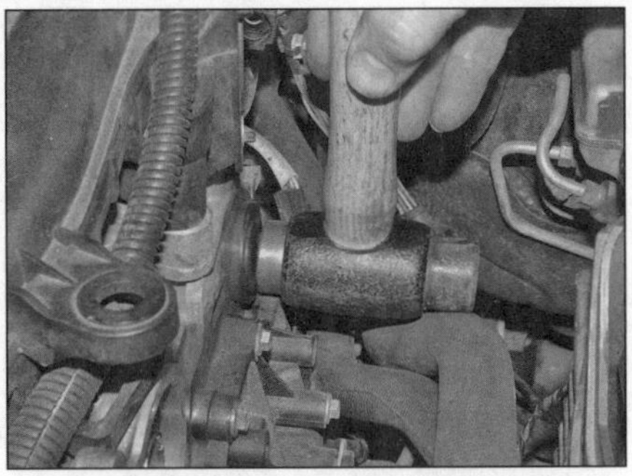

4.40 Fitting new plastic plugs to the cylinder head using a large socket or gently tap them in place with a hammer. Ensure they fit flush with the cylinder head

10 Locate the tensioner on the stud on the water pump cover, making sure that the lug engages the groove. Fit the fastener loosely at this stage.

11 Set the engine at TDC for No 1 piston as described in Section 3. Slip the crankshaft sprocket off the end of the crankshaft and check that the keyway in the crankshaft is uppermost. Note that on all engines there is a keyway in both the crankshaft and crankshaft sprocket, but there may not necessarily be a Woodruff key fitted.

12 Using a suitable solvent, thoroughly clean the end of the crankshaft, crankshaft sprocket bore, and the crankshaft and sprocket mating faces. Similarly clean the camshaft ends, camshaft sprocket bores and mating faces. It is essential that all traces of oil and grease are removed from these areas to allow the sprockets to be securely clamped when the pulley and retaining bolt/nuts are refitted. If the sprockets slip in service, serious engine damage will result.

13 Check that the camshafts are still correctly positioned with their slots parallel to the join between the upper and lower cylinder head sections, and the offsets below the centreline. If necessary, temporarily refit the old camshaft sprocket fastener and turn the camshafts slightly using a spanner to correctly align the slots.

14 The camshafts must now be retained in this position either by using Renault special tool Mot. 1496, or by fabricating a home made alternative **(see Tool Tip 1)**. Engage the Renault special tool or the home-made alternative with the slots in the camshafts and secure the tool to the cylinder head using a suitable bolt. With the crankshaft against the TDC pin and the camshafts secured with the holding tool, refit the crankshaft sprocket to the end of the crankshaft.

15 Before fitting the inlet camshaft sprocket check that it is in the locked position – there should be no movement between the hub and the sprocket. If the sprocket can move in relation to the hub, fit the sprocket in a vice equipped with suitable soft jaws. Fit a nut and bolt through the hub and rotate the hub to lock it to the sprocket. If the hub and sprocket will not lock together the assembly must be replaced.

16 Locate the camshaft sprockets on the camshafts so that the Renault logo is in the 12 o'clock position on the exhaust camshaft and the index mark is at the 12 o'clock position on the inlet camshaft. Fit the special tool (Mot 1490 or equivalent) and tighten the new bolts to the specified torque. Refit the blanking plug to the inlet camshaft sprocket.

17 Slide the crankshaft sprocket onto the nose of the crankshaft, making sure it is the correct way round.

18 Locate the new timing belt over the crankshaft and camshaft sprockets, and around the tensioner pulley, making sure that the sprocket marks remain vertical.

19 Refit the crankshaft pulley and fit a new bolt. Tighten the new bolt to the specified torque.

20 Tension the new timing belt as described in Section 4.

21 Refit the remaining components in reverse order of removal.

6 Camshaft oil seal – renewal

Note: *Replacement oil seals are supplied with a protective sleeve. Do not touch or lubricate either the seal or the camshaft.*

1 Remove the camshaft sprocket as described in Section 5.

2 Note the fitted depth of the old oil seal. Using a small screwdriver, prise out the oil seal from the cylinder head taking care not to damage the sealing surface on the camshaft. Alternatively, the oil seal can be removed by drilling two small holes diagonally opposite each other and inserting self tapping screws in them. A pair of grips can then be used to pull out the oil seals, by pulling on each side in turn.

3 Inspect the seal rubbing surface on the camshaft. If it is grooved or rough in the area where the old seal was fitted, the new seal should be fitted slightly less deeply, so that it rubs on an unworn part of the surface.

4 Renault technicians use a special tool (Mot. 1632) to fit the oil seal. The tool consists of a threaded rod, metal tube and nut, and a machined shoulder to locate the protector/guide on **(see illustrations)**. The rod is screwed into the end of the camshaft, and the protector/guide located on the shoulder. The metal tube is then fitted against the oil seal and the nut tightened to press the seal into the cylinder head/bearing cap. If the Renault tool cannot be obtained, a similar tool can be made out of a threaded rod, metal tube, washer and nut.

5 Wipe clean the oil seal seating, and then slide the seal with the protective sleeve onto the camshaft. Press the oil seal squarely into position and recover the protective sleeve.

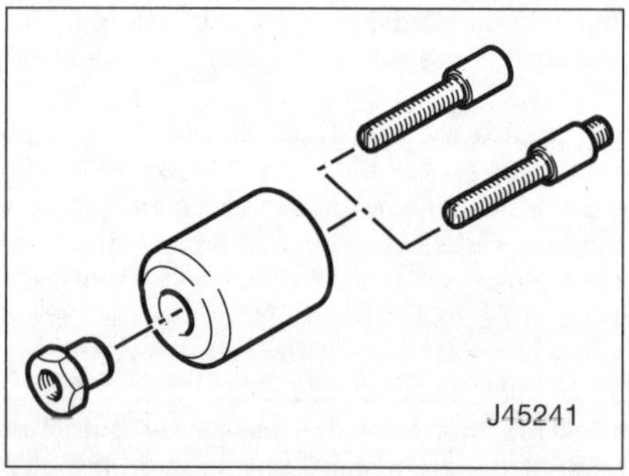

6.4a Renault tool for fitting the camshaft oil seal

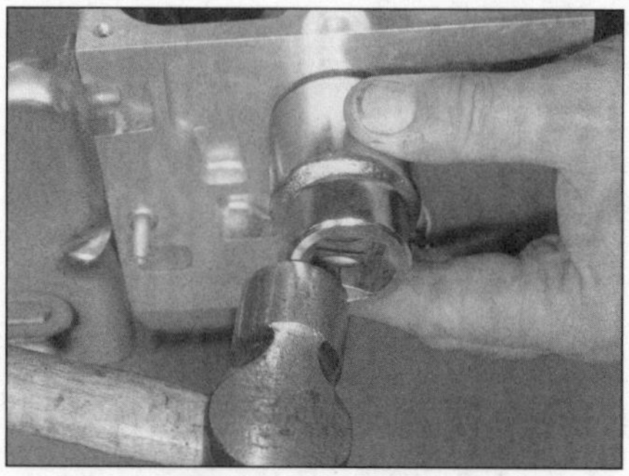

6.4b Alternatively drive the seal into position using a suitable socket

Note that the Renault tool is designed to locate the seal at the original depth, however, if the camshaft sealing surface is excessively worn, position it less deeply so that it locates on the unworn surface.

6 After fitting the oil seal, remove the protector/guide and tool.

7 Wipe away any excess oil, then refit the camshaft sprocket as described in Section 5.

7 Camshafts – removal, inspection and refitting

Removal

1 Disconnect the battery negative lead and position it away from the terminal. Cover the exposed terminal with a suitable insulator.

2 Remove the timing belt as described in Section 4.

3 Remove the camshaft sprockets as described in Section 5.

4 Remove the air inlet duct and throttle body as described in Chapter 4A.

5 Disconnect the fuel supply hose from the fuel rail with reference to Chapter 4A.

6 Disconnect the brake vacuum pipe from the inlet manifold.

7 Disconnect the wiring plugs from the ignition coils and move the loom to one side.

8 Unbolt and remove the upper section of the inlet manifold.

9 Remove the injector gallery protector, then disconnect the wiring plugs from the injectors. Disconnect the wiring plugs from the camshaft sensor and the VVT control solenoid. Release the loom and position it to one side.

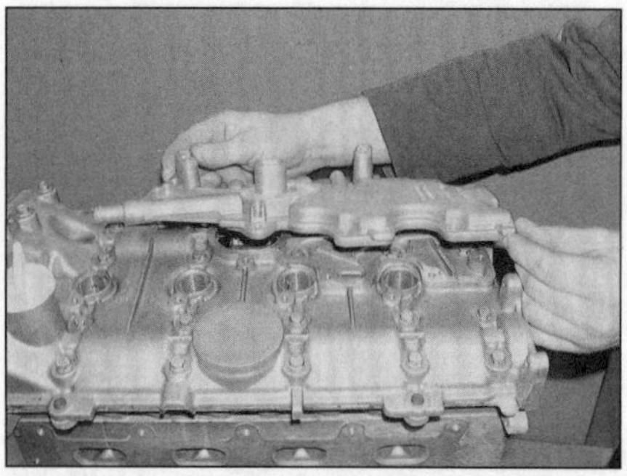

7.11 Undo the eight bolts and remove the oil separator housing

7.12 Removing the valve cover/bearing cap from the cylinder head

7.14 Lift out the cam followers and place them in a marked box or containers

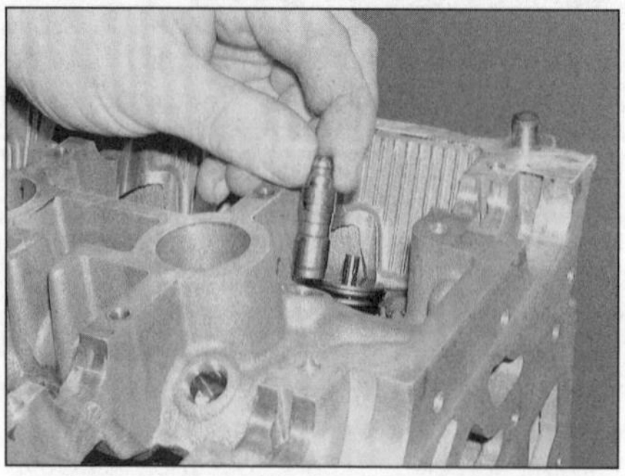

7.15 Lift out the tappets and place them upright in a marked box or containers filled with oil

10 Remove the ignition coils as described in Chapter 5B and then remove the camshaft sensor and VVT control solenoid.

11 Unbolt and remove the oil separator unit **(see illustration)**

12 Progressively unscrew the valve cover/bearing cap retaining bolts, then release the cover by using a copper mallet to tap the lugs at each rear corner and using a screwdriver to lever up the lugs on the front of the cover. Once the cover is free, lift it squarely from the cylinder head **(see illustration)**. The camshafts will rise up slightly under the pressure of the valve springs – be careful they don't tilt and jam. Remove the cover/bearing cap.

13 Identify each camshaft for location and TDC position, then carefully lift them from the cylinder head. The inlet camshaft should have the marking AM on it and the exhaust should have the marking EM. If these are not visible, identify the camshafts with dabs of paint. Remove the oil seals from the camshafts, noting their fitted positions.

14 Obtain a box with 16 compartments and mark the valve positions clearly on it. Remove each hydraulic cam follower and place it in its compartment for safe-keeping **(see illustration)**.

15 Obtain a metal box with 16 compartments identified with the valve positions, and fill it with fresh engine oil. Remove the hydraulic tappets from the cylinder head and place them in their correct compartments, making sure that they are completely immersed in the oil **(see illustration)**.

Inspection

16 Inspect the cam lobes and the camshaft bearing journals for scoring or other visible evidence of wear.

17 If the camshafts appear satisfactory, measure the bearing journal diameters and compare the figures obtained with those given in the Specifications. If the diameters are not as specified, consult a Renault dealer or engine overhaul specialist. Wear of the camshaft bearings will almost certainly be accompanied by similar wear of the bearings in the cylinder head, which will entail renewal of the cylinder head upper and lower sections, together with the camshafts.

18 Inspect the cam followers and hydraulic tappets for scuffing, cracking or other damage and renew any components as necessary. Also check the condition of the tappet bores in the cylinder head. As with the camshafts, any wear in this area will necessitate cylinder head renewal.

Refitting

19 Clean the sealant from the mating surfaces of the valve cover/bearing cap and cylinder head.

20 To prevent any possibility of the valves contacting the pistons when the camshafts are refitted, remove the TDC pin or dowel rod used to lock the crankshaft, and turn the crankshaft clockwise a quarter turn.

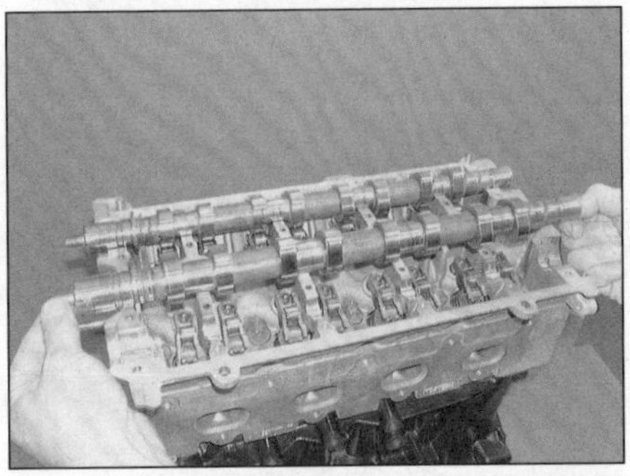

7.25a Refit the camshafts in the cylinder head

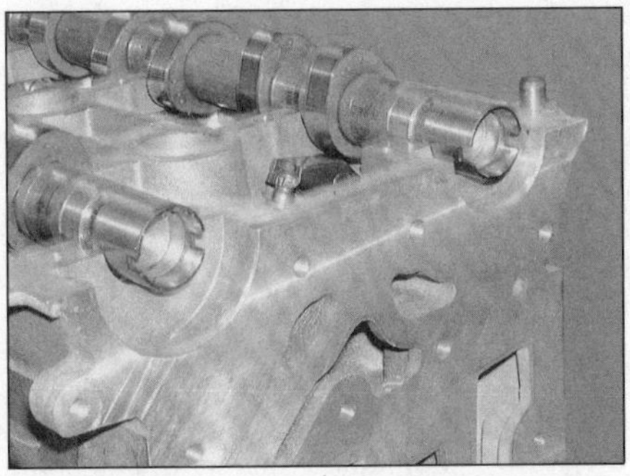

7.25b Position the camshafts in their TDC position so that the grooves are horizontal and the offset is below the centreline

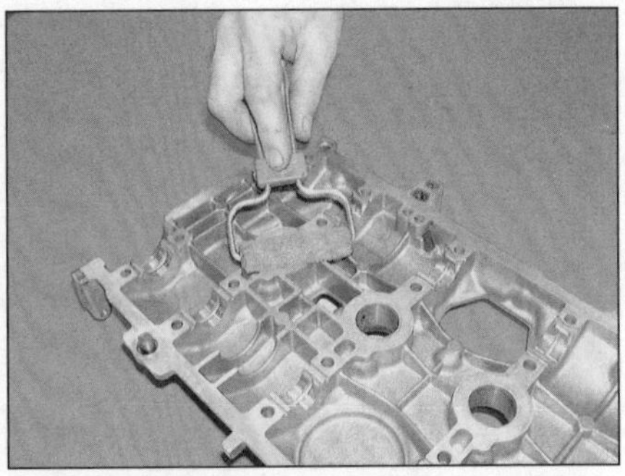

7.26 Apply an even coating of Loctite 518 gasket solution to the mating face of the valve cover/bearing cap

21 Lubricate the tappet bores in the cylinder head with clean engine oil.

22 If the hydraulic tappets have not been kept immersed in oil, the oil will drain from them and they will need to be reprimed before refitting. To check whether they require repriming, depress the top of the tappet with a thumb – if the piston goes down, the tappet requires repriming. Renault recommend that the tappets are immersed in diesel fuel and operated until they are primed.

23 Remove the hydraulic tappets from their compartments and insert them in their correct positions in the head.

24 One at a time, remove the cam followers from their compartments and locate them on the hydraulic tappets and valve stems.

25 Lubricate the bearings and journals of the inlet and exhaust camshafts with fresh engine oil, then carefully locate them on the cylinder head in their correct positions and at TDC as previously-noted. The grooves at the left-hand end of the camshafts must be horizontal **(see illustrations)**.

26 Check that the valve cover/bearing cap mating surfaces are clean and dry, then apply Loctite 518 (or a suitable alternative) to the cover surface using a roller **(see illustration)**. Make several applications until the colour is **reddish.**

27 Locate the valve cover/bearing cap on the cylinder head, insert the bolts, and progressively tighten them to the specified torque in the sequence and stages given in the Specifications **(see illustration)**. Make sure that the camshafts are located correctly on the cam followers and in the cover.

28 Check that the oil separator mating surfaces are clean and dry, then apply Loctite 518 (or a suitable alternative) to the separator surface using a roller **(see illustration)**. Make several applications until the colour is **reddish.**

29 Locate the oil separator on the valve cover, insert the bolts, and tighten them to the specified torque in sequence **(see illustration)**.

30 Refit the ignition coils with reference to Chapter 5B and then refit the camshaft sensor and the VVT control solenoid.

31 Reconnect the wiring to the fuel injectors.

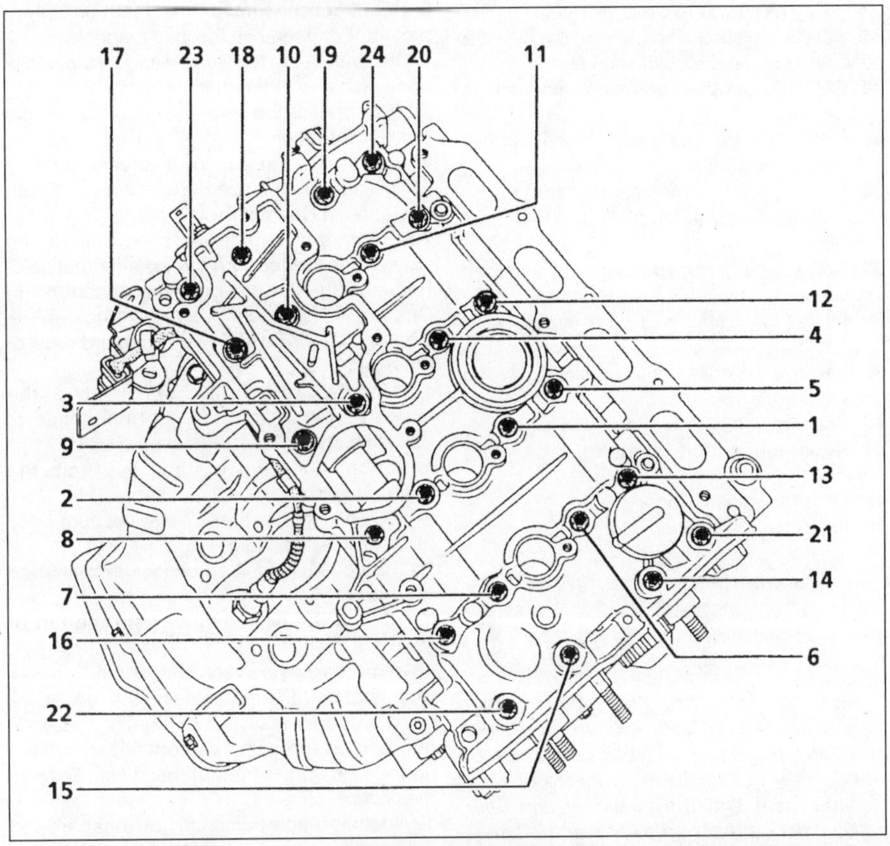

7.27 Valve cover/bearing cap retaining bolt identification (see Specifications for tightening sequence)

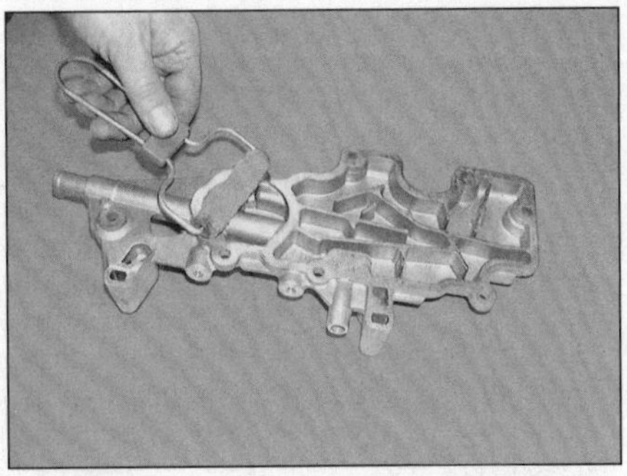

7.28 Apply an even coating of Loctite 518 gasket solution to the mating face of the oil separator housing

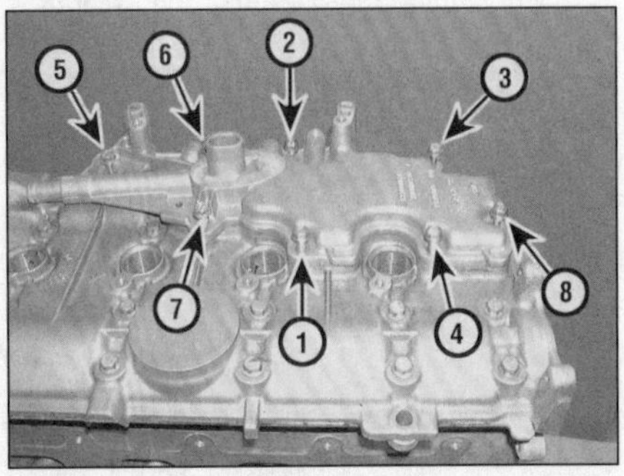

7.29 Oil separator housing retaining bolt tightening sequence

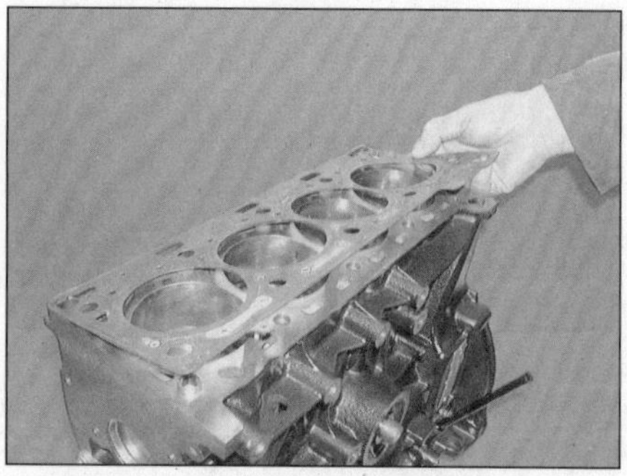

8.34 Locate a new cylinder head gasket on the cylinder block . . .

32 Refit the inlet manifold together with new seals with reference to Chapter 4A.
33 Refit the engine lifting eye to the cylinder head and tighten the bolts securely.
34 Refit the throttle body with reference to Chapter 4A.
35 Reconnect the brake servo vacuum hose to the inlet manifold.
36 Reconnect the fuel supply and return hoses to each end of the fuel rail, and tighten the clips.
37 Refit the camshaft sprockets as described in Section 5.
38 Fit a new timing belt with reference to Section 4 of this Chapter.
39 Remove the trolley jack and block of wood from under the sump.
40 Reconnect the battery negative lead.
41 Refill the engine with fresh oil, with reference to Chapter 1A.
42 Refit the engine undertray and lower the vehicle to the ground.

8 Cylinder head – removal, inspection and refitting

Note: *In addition to any other parts required, have a new timing belt, cylinder head and cylinder head cover gaskets, and a set of new cylinder head bolts ready for reassembly. Renault state that the tensioner and idler pulley must be renewed whenever the timing belt is renewed.*
1 Disconnect the battery negative lead (refer to *Disconnecting the battery* in the Reference

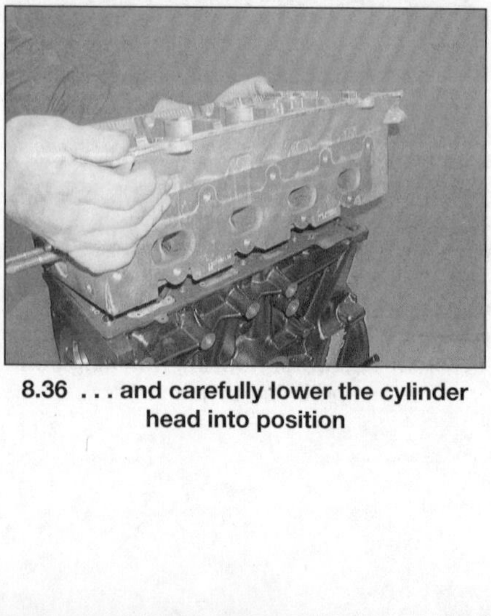

8.36 . . . and carefully lower the cylinder head into position

Section).
2 Pull up and remove the engine cover.
3 Jack up and support the front of the vehicle (see *Jacking and vehicle support* in the reference section).
4 Remove the engine undertray, then drain the cooling system with reference to Chapter 1A.
5 Carefully, position a trolley jack and a large block of wood under the sump to support the engine. Raise the jack to just take the weight of the engine.
6 Remove the timing belt and camshaft sprockets with reference to Sections 4 and 5 of this Chapter.
7 Unplug the wiring from the throttle body.
8 Unbolt and remove the injector gallery protector and remove the inlet manifold.
9 Disconnect the fuel supply and return hoses from each end of the fuel rail.
10 Disconnect the engine wiring loom at the front of the engine, and also disconnect the wiring from the ignition coil and fuel injectors.
11 Unbolt and remove the inlet manifold with reference to Chapter 4A.
12 Refer to Chapter 4A and remove the catalytic converter from the exhaust manifold. Remove the throttle body as described in Chapter 4A. Disconnect the wiring for the oxygen sensor on the rear left-hand side of the engine.
13 Unscrew the bolts and remove the support bracket from the right-hand side of the exhaust manifold.
14 Unbolt the engine lifting eye from the cylinder head.
15 Disconnect the brake servo vacuum hose from the inlet manifold.
16 Remove the ignition coils with reference to Chapter 5B.
17 Unbolt the oil separator from the top of the valve cover.
18 Progressively unscrew the valve cover retaining bolts, then release the cover by using a copper mallet to tap the lugs at each rear corner and using a screwdriver to lever up the lugs on the front of the cover. Remove the cover.
19 Identify each camshaft for location and TDC position, then carefully lift them from the cylinder head. The inlet camshaft should have the marking AM on it and the exhaust should have the marking EM. If these are not visible, identify the camshafts with dabs of paint.
20 Obtain a box with 16 compartments and mark the valve positions clearly on it. Remove each cam follower and place it in its compartment for safe-keeping.
21 Obtain a metal box with 16 compartments identified with the valve positions, and fill it with fresh engine oil. Carefully remove the hydraulic tappets from the cylinder head and place them in their correct compartments, making sure that they are completely immersed in the oil.
22 Disconnect the wiring from the temperature sensor on the thermostat housing at the left-hand end of the cylinder head.
23 Release the clips and disconnect the radiator top hose, heater hoses and expansion tank hose from the thermostat housing.
24 Unbolt the wiring loom support bracket from the left-hand end of the cylinder head.
25 Remove the spark plugs as described in Chapter 1A.
26 Progressively unscrew and remove the cylinder head bolts in the **reverse** order to that shown in **illustration 8.38**.
27 Lift the cylinder head from the block. Recover the gasket.

Inspection

28 The mating faces of the cylinder head and block must be perfectly clean before refitting the head. Use a scraper to remove all traces of gasket and carbon and also clean the tops of the pistons. Take particular care with the aluminium cylinder head, as the soft metal is easily damaged. Also, make sure that debris is not allowed to enter the oil and water channels – this is particularly important for the oil circuit, as carbon could block the oil supply to the camshaft and cam followers or crankshaft bearings. Using adhesive tape and paper, seal the water, oil and bolt holes in the cylinder block. Clean the piston crowns in the same way.
29 Check the block and head for nicks, deep scratches and other damage. If slight, they may be removed carefully with a file. It may be possible to repair more serious damage by machining, but this is a specialist job.
30 If warpage of the cylinder head is suspected, use a straight edge to check it for distortion, as this can be associated with the head gasket blowing. No regrinding of the cylinder head is allowed. Refer to Part C of this Chapter for further information.
31 Clean out all the bolt holes in the block using a pipe cleaner, or a rag and screwdriver. Make sure that all oil is removed, otherwise there is a possibility of the block being cracked by hydraulic pressure when the bolts are tightened.
32 Examine the bolt threads and the threads in the cylinder block for damage. If necessary, use the correct size tap to chase out the threads in the block. Renew the bolts.

Refitting

33 It is recommended that No 1 piston is positioned halfway up its cylinder before refitting the cylinder head as a safeguard against the valves touching the tops of the pistons. Turn the crankshaft clockwise until No 1 piston rises to the mid-cylinder position.
34 Position a new gasket on the block making sure it is the correct way up **(see illustration)**.
35 If the lower inlet manifold was removed, it can be refitted at this stage, with reference to Chapter 4A, making sure that the timing end is flush with the end of the cylinder head before tightening the bolts.
36 Carefully lower the cylinder head onto the block making sure that the gasket is not displaced **(see illustration)**.

37 Locate the new bolts in position. **Note:** *New bolts must be used. **Do not** lubricate their threads.*
38 Tighten the cylinder head bolts to the specified torques in sequence and in the stages given in the Specifications **(see illustrations)**. The first stage compresses the gasket and the second stage is the main tightening procedure. When angle-tightening the bolts, put paint marks on the bolt heads and cylinder head as a guide for the correct angle, or obtain a special angle-tightening tool. Note that, provided the bolts are tightened exactly as specified, there will be no need to retighten them once the engine has been started and run after reassembly.
39 Refit the spark plugs with reference to Chapter 1A.
40 Refit the engine lifting eye to the left-hand end of the cylinder head.
41 Refit the wiring loom support bracket to the cylinder head and tighten the bolts.
42 Reconnect the radiator top hose, heater hoses and expansion tank to the thermostat housing and tighten the clips.
43 Reconnect the wiring to the temperature sensor on the thermostat housing.
44 If the hydraulic tappets have not been kept immersed in oil, the oil will drain from them and they will need to be reprimed before refitting. To check whether they require repriming, depress the top of the tappet with a thumb – if the piston goes down, the tappet requires repriming. Renault recommend that the tappets are immersed in diesel fuel and operated until they are primed.
45 Remove the hydraulic tappets from their compartments and insert them in their correct positions in the head.
46 One at a time, remove the cam followers from their compartments and locate them on the hydraulic tappets and valve stems.
47 Lubricate the bearings and journals of the inlet and exhaust camshafts with fresh engine oil, then carefully locate them on the cylinder head in their correct positions and at TDC as previously-noted. The grooves at the left-hand end of the camshafts must be horizontal.
48 Turn the crankshaft clockwise to position No 1 piston at TDC. Refer to Section 3 if necessary.
49 Check that the valve cover/bearing cap mating surfaces are clean and dry, then apply Loctite 518 (or a suitable alternative) to the cover surface using a roller. Make several applications until the colour is **reddish.**
50 Locate the valve cover on the cylinder head, insert the bolts, and tighten them to the specified torque in the sequence and stages given in the Specifications **(see illustration 7.31)**.
51 Check that the oil separator mating surfaces are clean and dry, then apply Loctite 518 (or a suitable alternative) to the separator surface using a roller. Make several applications until the colour is reddish.
52 Locate the oil separator on the valve cover, insert the bolts, and tighten them to the specified torque in sequence **(see illustration 7.29)**.
53 Refit the ignition coils with reference to Chapter 5B.
54 Refit the engine lifting eye to the cylinder head and tighten the bolts securely.
55 Refit the support bracket to the right-hand side of the exhaust manifold, and tighten the bolts securely.
56 Reconnect the wiring to the oxygen sensor on the rear left-hand side of the engine.
57 Refit the throttle body with reference to Chapter 4A.
58 Refit the catalytic converter to the exhaust manifold with reference to Chapter 4A.
59 Refit the inlet manifold together with new seals with reference to Chapter 4A.
60 Reconnect the brake servo vacuum hose to the inlet manifold.
61 Reconnect the wiring to the ignition coil and fuel injectors, and attach the wiring loom to the front of the engine.
62 Reconnect the fuel supply and return hoses to each end of the fuel rail, and tighten the clips.
63 Refit the injector gallery protector.
64 Refit the timing belt and camshaft sprockets with reference to Sections 4 and 5 of this Chapter.
65 Remove the trolley jack and block of wood from under the sump.
66 Refit the bonnet with reference to Chapter 11.
67 Reconnect the battery negative lead.
68 Refill the engine with fresh oil, with reference to Chapter 1A.
69 Refill and bleed the cooling system with reference to Chapter 1A.
70 Refit the engine undertray and lower the vehicle to the ground.

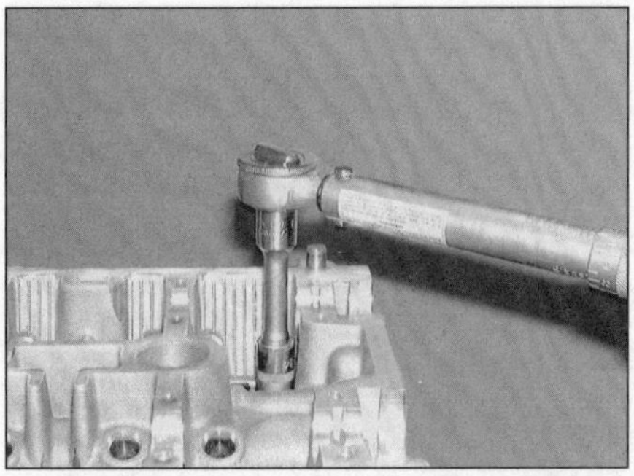

8.38a Tighten the cylinder head retaining bolts to the Stage 1 torque setting using a torque wrench

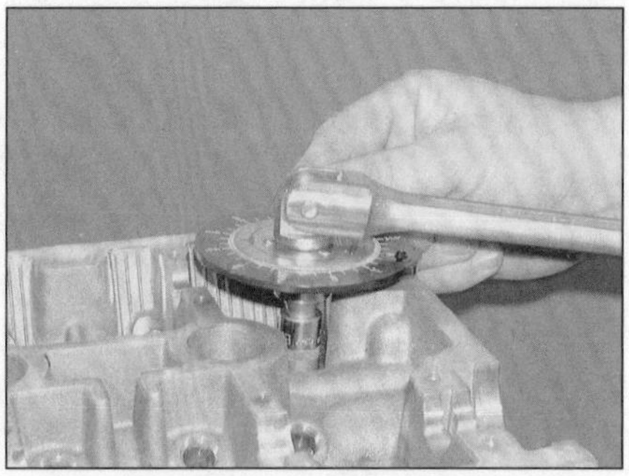

8.38b Using an angle tightening gauge to tighten the cylinder head retaining bolts through the Stage 2 angle

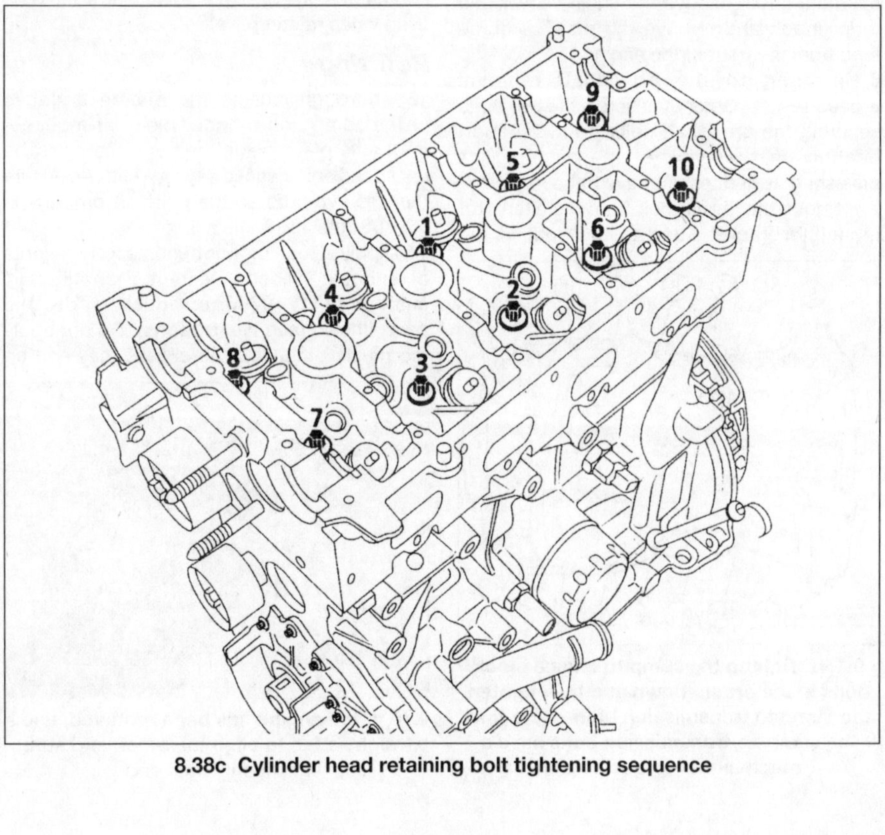

8.38c Cylinder head retaining bolt tightening sequence

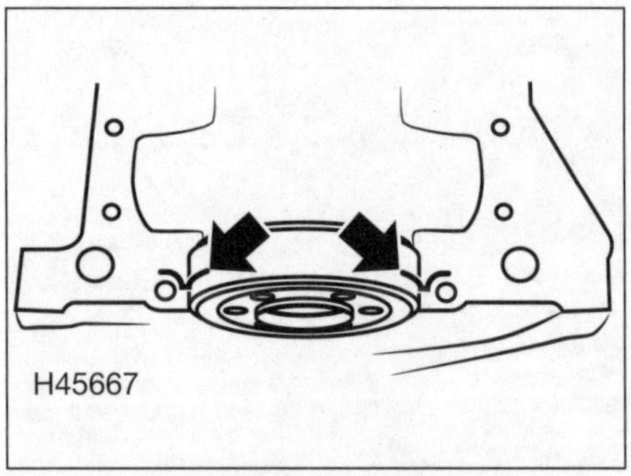

9.14a Apply two 5mm beads to the area shown (flywheel end)

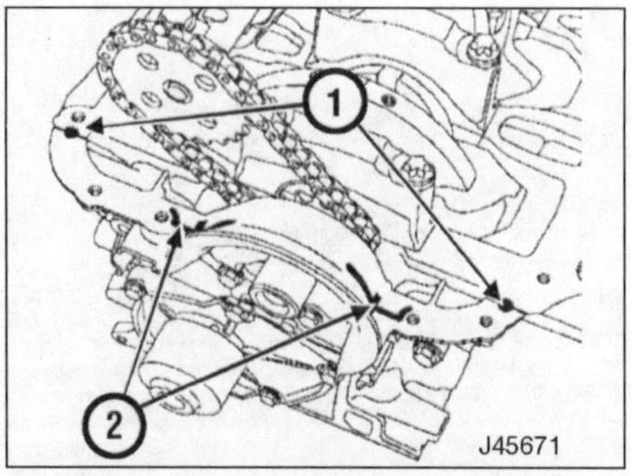

9.14b Apply a 7 mm diameter spot of sealant at (1) and a 5 mm bead at (2) – timing end

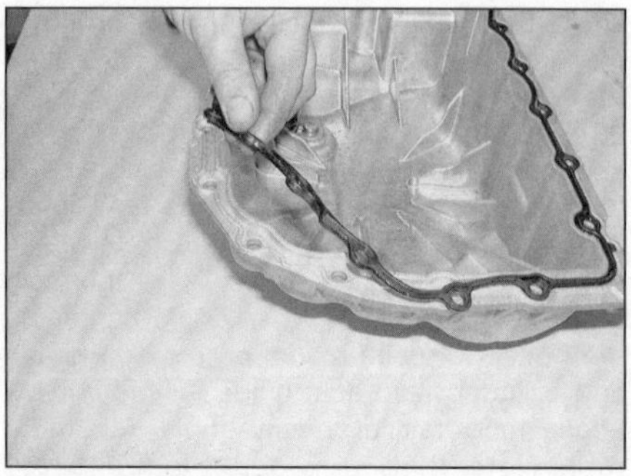

9.15a Locate a new gasket on the sump

9 Sump – removal and refitting

Removal

1 Disconnect the battery negative lead (refer to *Disconnecting the battery* in the Reference Section).

2 Jack up the front of the car and support on axle stands. Remove the engine compartment undertray.

3 Drain the engine oil referring to Chapter 1A, then refit and tighten the drain plug. Though not essential, it makes sense to fit a new oil filter on completion, before the sump is refilled with fresh oil.

4 Remove both front roadwheels, then remove both wheel arch liners (see Chapter 11).

5 Where fitted, remove the engine cover and then unbolt and remove the dipstick guide tube from the front of the engine.

6 Referring to the driveshaft removal procedure in Chapter 8, unscrew the two bolts securing the driveshaft collar to the support bearing on the back of the engine. The driveshaft itself does not have to be removed.

7 Remove the lowest bolt from the alternator mounting bracket fitted to the front of the engine. The bracket itself does not have to be removed, but the lowest bolt is screwed into the sump.

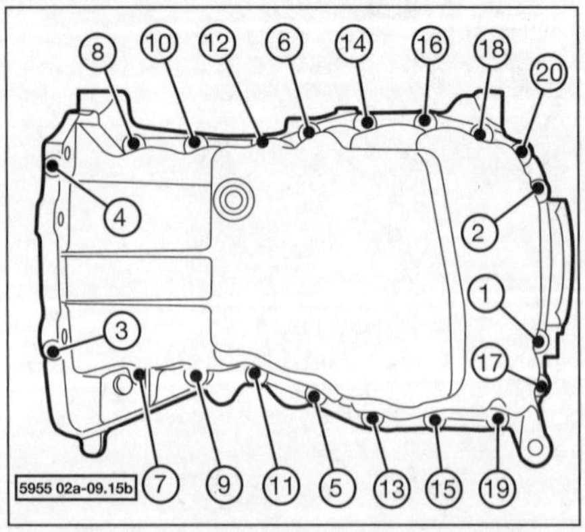

9.15b Tighten the sump to engine block bolts in the order shown and then tighten the sump to transmission bolts. Note that the sump-to-transmission bolts have a much higher torque setting

8 Unbolt and remove the engine steady bar at the rear of the engine – this will allow the engine to move slightly on its remaining right and left-hand mountings, but providing they are not disturbed, this is not dangerous.

9 Disconnect the wiring plug from the oil level sensor.

10 Remove the 4 bolts securing the sump to the transmission bell housing.

11 Loosen and remove the nineteen bolts used to secure the sump. In addition to the bolts, the sump is secured by several spots of sealant – tap the sump with a hide or plastic mallet to break the seal, or prise it very carefully, so as not to damage the sealing surfaces.

12 Lower the sump out from under the car, and recover the gasket – a new one should be used when refitting.

Refitting

13 Thoroughly clean the mating surfaces of the sump and cylinder block. If required, the baffle plate inside the sump can also be unclipped and cleaned – when refitting, ensure that the five tabs on the plate sit properly in the cut-outs inside the sump.

14 Apply a total of four beads and two spots of suitable silicone sealant (Renault part number 7711219706, or equivalent) to the areas shown **(see illustrations)**. Do not apply too much, otherwise the excess may end up inside the sump, where it could get sucked into the engine.

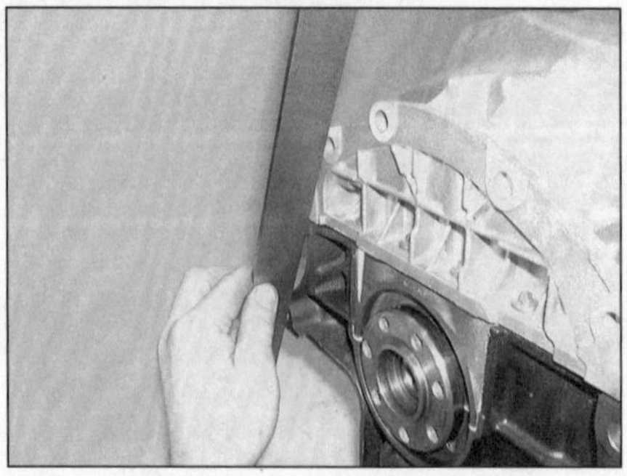

9.16 If the engine has been removed, use a straight-edge to align the block and sump at the flywheel end

15 Locate the new gasket in position on the sump, and lift the sump into position on the cylinder block. Insert the bolts and tighten them progressively in order to the specified torque **(see illustrations)**.

16 If the engine is removed from the car, use a straight-edge to maintain the alignment between the left-hand end of the sump and cylinder block **(see illustration)**.

17 Further refitting is a reversal of removal, noting the following points:

a) Tighten all nuts/bolts to the specified torque.

b) Refer to Chapter 8 when refitting the right-hand driveshaft collar to the support bearing.

c) Allow sufficient time for the sealant used to cure, then fill the engine with fresh oil (see Chapter 1A). On completion, start the engine, and check for signs of leakage.

10 Oil pump and sprockets – removal, inspection and refitting

Removal

1 To remove the oil pump alone, first remove the sump as described in Section 9.

2 Unscrew the oil pump mounting bolts and the additional bolt(s) securing the anti-emulsion/baffle plate to the crankcase **(see illustration)**.

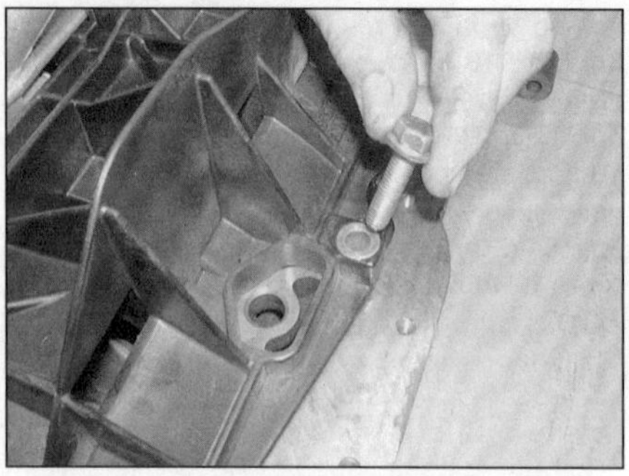

10.2 Unscrew the anti-emulsion plate retaining bolt(s)

10.3a Remove the anti-emulsion plate...

10.3b ...then tilt the pump to disengage its sprocket from the drive chain

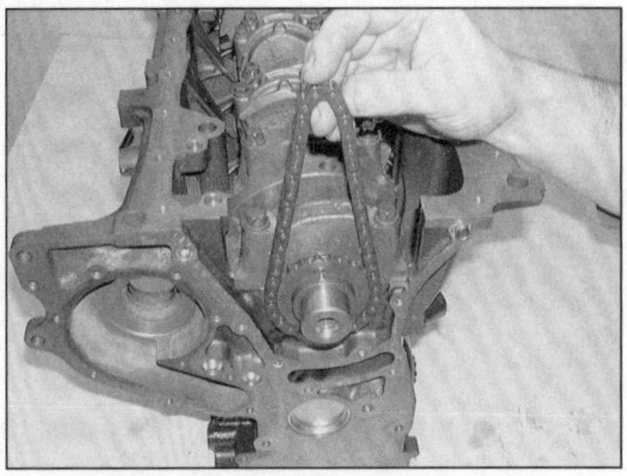

10.6 Slide the drive sprocket together with the chain from the crankshaft

10.7a Extract the oil pressure relief valve retaining clip...

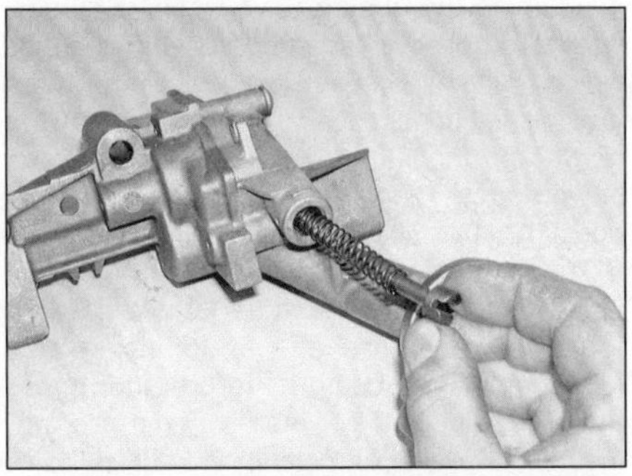

10.7b ...remove the oil pressure relief valve spring retainer and spring...

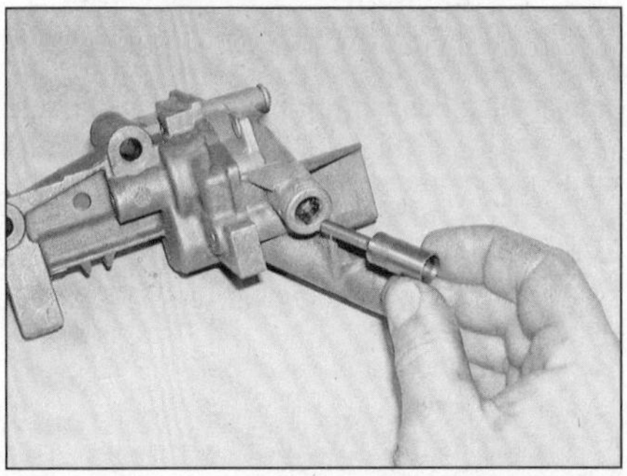

10.7c ...followed by the plunger

3 Withdraw the oil pump slightly and remove the anti-emulsion plate. Tilt the pump to disengage its sprocket from the drive chain and lift away the pump **(see illustrations)**. If the locating dowels are displaced, refit them in their locations.

4 To remove the pump complete with its drive chain and sprockets, first remove the sump as described in Section 9, then remove the crankshaft timing belt end oil seal housing as described in Section 11.

5 Remove the oil pump as described in paragraphs 1 and 2 above.

6 Slide the drive sprocket together with the chain from the crankshaft **(see illustration)**. Note that the drive sprocket is not keyed to the crankshaft, but relies on the pulley bolt being tightened correctly to clamp the sprocket.

Inspection

7 Extract the retaining clip, and remove the oil pressure relief valve spring retainer, spring and plunger **(see illustrations)**.

8 Unscrew the retaining bolts, and lift off the pump cover **(see illustration)**.

9 Carefully examine the gears, pump body and relief valve plunger for any signs of scoring or wear. Renew the pump complete if excessive wear is evident.

10 If the components appear serviceable, measure the clearance between the pump body and the gears using feeler blades. Also measure the gear endfloat, and check the flatness of the end cover **(see illustrations)**. If the clearances exceed the specified tolerances, the pump must be renewed.

11 If the pump is satisfactory, reassemble the components in the reverse order of removal. Fill the pump with oil, then refit the cover and tighten the bolts securely **(see illustration)**.

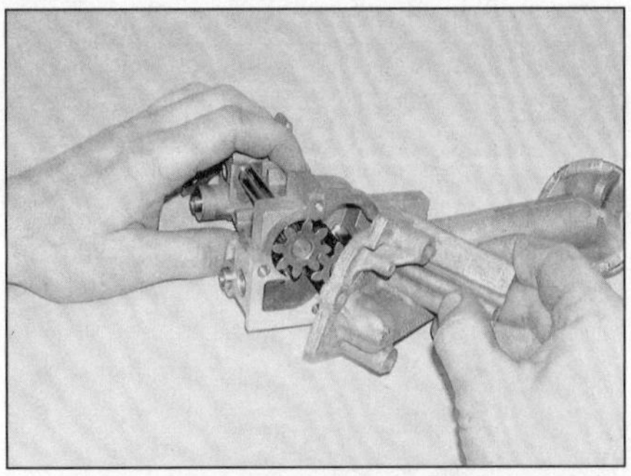

10.8 Unscrew the retaining bolts, and lift off the oil pump cover

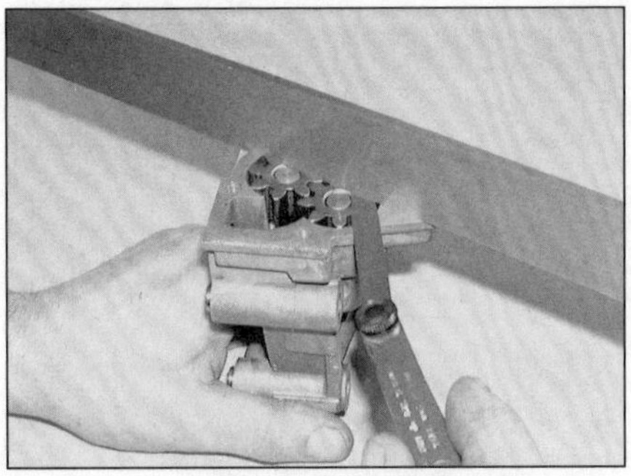

10.10b ...and measure the gear endfloat

Refitting

12 Wipe clean the oil pump and cylinder block mating surfaces.

13 Locate the drive sprocket onto the end of

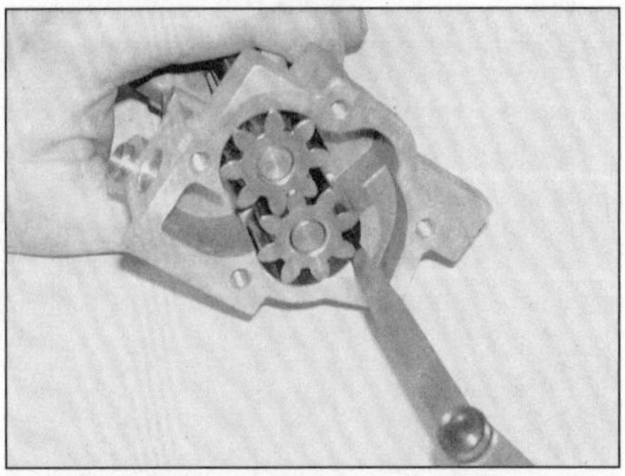

10.10a Using feeler blades, measure the clearance between the pump body and the gears...

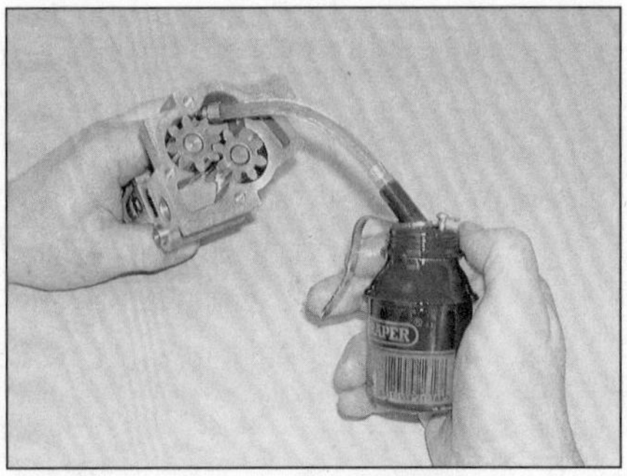

10.11 Fill the pump with oil, then refit the cover

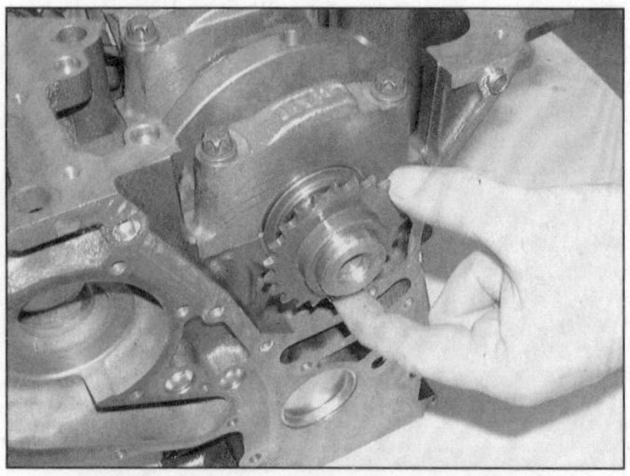

10.13 Ensure that the oil pump drive sprocket is fitted with the projecting boss facing away from the crankshaft

the crankshaft, ensuring that it is fitted with the projecting boss facing away from the crankshaft **(see illustration)**. Engage the pump with the dowels, fit the two retaining bolts and tighten them to the specified torque.

14 Refit the anti-emulsion plate and secure with the retaining bolt(s).

15 Refit the oil seal housing as described in Section 11.

16 Refit the sump as described in Section 9.

11 Crankshaft oil seals – renewal

Timing belt end oil seal

1 Remove the timing belt and the crankshaft sprocket with reference to Sections 4 and 5. Where fitted remove the woodruff key. An alternative, though longer, method is to remove the sump and oil seal housing, and fit the new oil seal on the bench.

2 Note the fitted position of the old seal, then prise it out of the oil seal housing using a screwdriver or suitable hooked instrument. An alternative method of removing the oil seal is to drill carefully two small holes opposite each other in the oil seal and insert self-tapping screws, then pull on the screws with grips. Take care not to damage the surface of the spacer or the seal housing.

3 With the oil seal removed, where applicable slide the spacer from the crankshaft, noting which way round it is fitted.

4 Examine the spacer for excessive oil seal wear and polish off any burrs or raised edges which may have caused the seal to fail in the first place. If necessary, the spacer can be refitted so that the new oil seal contacts an unworn area. Clean the oil seal seating in the housing with a suitable solvent.

5 The new seal must be installed dry. Do not lubricate it or the crankshaft. Locate the new seal over the crankshaft with its closed side facing outwards. Using hand pressure, press the oil seal squarely into the housing a little way, then use a socket or metal tube to drive the oil seal to the previously-noted position – take great care not to damage the seal lips during fitting **(see illustration)**. Do not drive it in too far or it will have to be removed and possibly renewed.

6 Slide the spacer onto the crankshaft and carefully press it into the oil seal, while twisting it to prevent damage.

7 Wipe away any excess oil, then refit the crankshaft sprocket and fit the new timing belt with reference to Sections 5 and 4.

11.5 Using a socket to drive the new crankshaft oil seal into the housing

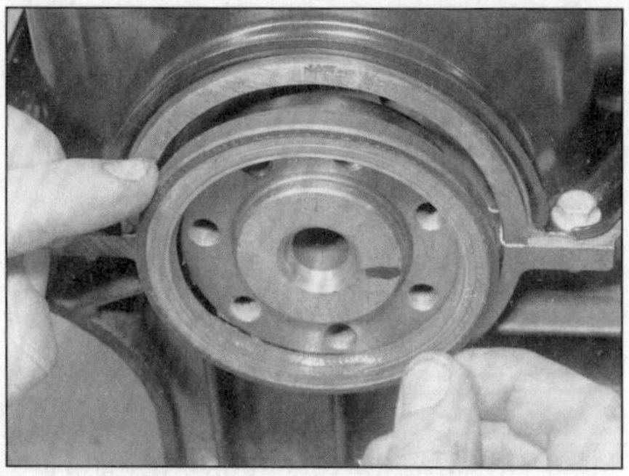

11.11 Fitting a new crankshaft flywheel end oil seal

Flywheel/driveplate end oil seal

8 Renewal of the crankshaft left-hand oil seal requires the transmission to be removed as described in Chapter 7. The clutch (see Chapter 6) and the flywheel (see Section 13 of this Chapter) must also be removed.

9 Prise out the old oil seal using a small screwdriver, taking care not to damage the surface on the crankshaft. Alternatively, the oil seal can be removed by drilling two small holes diagonally opposite each other and inserting self tapping screws in them. A pair of grips can then be used to pull out the oil seal, by pulling on each side in turn.

10 Inspect the seal rubbing surface on the crankshaft. If it is grooved or rough in the area where the old seal was fitted, the new seal should be fitted slightly less deeply, so that it rubs on an unworn part of the surface.

11 Wipe clean the oil seal seating. To ensure a perfect seal the crankshaft and housing must be clean and dry. Locate the seal over the crankshaft with its closed side facing outwards **(see illustration)**. Make sure that the oil seal lip is not damaged as it is located on the crankshaft.

12 Using a metal tube, drive the oil seal squarely into the bore until flush. A block of wood cut to pass over the end of the crankshaft may be used instead.

13 Refit the flywheel with reference to Section 13. Refit the clutch as described in Chapter 6 and then refit the transmission to the engine as described in the relevant Chapter of this Manual.

12 Engine/transmission mountings – inspection and renewal

Inspection

1 Apply the handbrake, then jack up the front of the car and support it on axle stands (see *Jacking and vehicle support*). Remove the engine compartment undertray.

2 Visually inspect the rubber pads on the two front and one rear engine/transmission mountings for signs of cracking and deterioration. Careful use of a lever will help to determine the condition of the rubber pads. If there is excessive movement in the mounting, or if the rubber has deteriorated, the mounting should be renewed.

3 Lower the vehicle to the ground.

Renewal

Right-hand front mounting

4 If not already done so jack up the front of the vehicle and support it on axle stands (see *Jacking and vehicle support* in the reference section). Remove the engine undertray.

5 Support the right-hand end of the engine with a jack and block of wood beneath the sump **(see illustration)**.

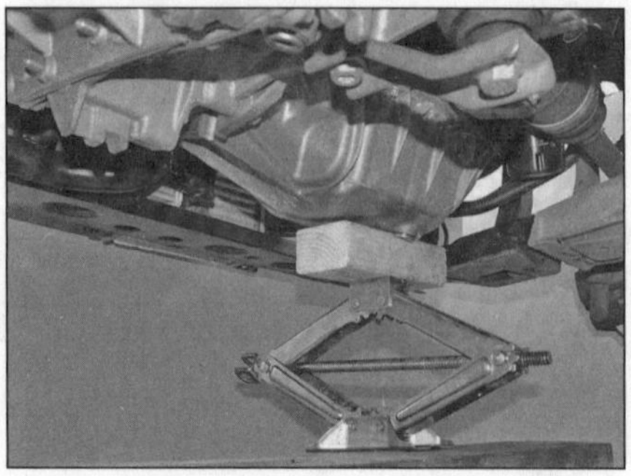

12.5 Support the engine with a suitable jack

12.6 Disconnect the fuel line

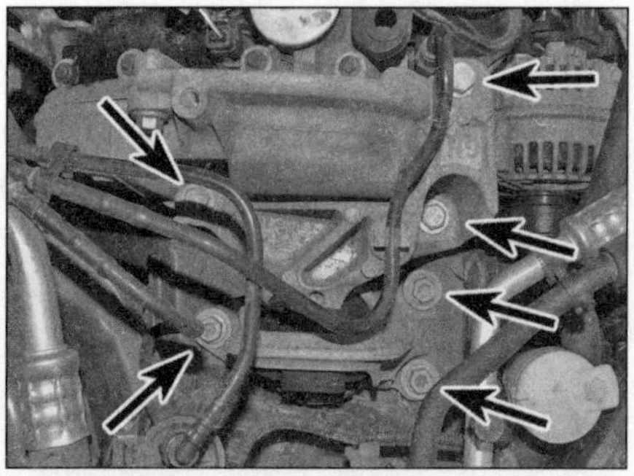

12.8a Remove the bolts (arrowed) and then...

12.8b ...remove the mounting

12.13 Remove the centre bolt (arrowed)

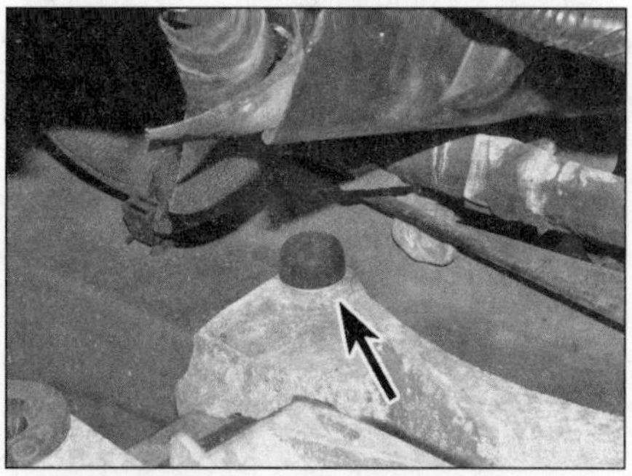

12.14a Remove the loom protector (arrowed) from the rear mounting...

12.14b ...and then unbolt and remove the mounting

12.15 Unclip the clutch pipe, unbolt and remove the mounting from the transmission

6 Disconnect the fuel line from the fuel rail and seal the pipe **(see illustration)**. Unclip the fuel lines from the mounting and inner wing.

7 Mark the relationship between the upper and lower sections of the engine mounting.

8 Unbolt the mounting from the engine and inner wing panel and remove it **(see illustrations)**.

9 Fit the new mounting using a reversal of the removal procedure, but tighten the nuts/bolts to the specified torque wrench settings.

Left-hand mounting

10 Remove the battery and battery box as described in Chapter 5A.

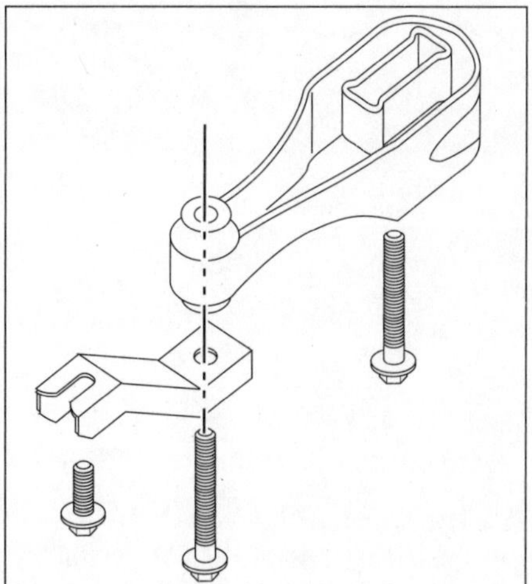

12.21 The rear engine mounting

11 With the front of the car supported on axle stands, remove the left-hand roadwheel.

12 Using a jack and block of wood, support the weight of the transmission/engine.

13 Unscrew the centre bolt (or nut on some models) securing the lower mounting to the upper/body bracket **(see illustration)** then slightly lower the transmission/engine. If necessary, release the stud from the upper bracket using a soft-faced mallet.

14 Unscrew the bolts from the chassis leg and remove the upper bracket from the body **(see illustrations)**.

15 Unscrew the bolts and remove the lower mounting/bracket from the transmission **(see illustration)**.

16 Locate the new mounting/bracket on the transmission, insert the bolts and tighten to the specified torque.

17 Refit the upper bracket to the body, insert the bolts and tighten to the specified torque.

12.22 Remove the bracket bolts (arrowed)

18 Raise the transmission/engine making sure that the mounting stud enters the upper bracket correctly. Refit the centre nut and tighten to the specified torque. Remove the hoist or trolley jack.

19 Refit the battery with reference to Chapter 5A.

20 Refit the roadwheel and lower the car to the ground.

Rear mounting

21 Apply the handbrake, then jack up the front of the vehicle and support it on axle stands (see *Jacking and vehicle support*). Note the rear mounting does not support the weight of the engine **(see illustration)**.

22 Unbolt the bracket from the transmission **(see illustration)**.

23 Unbolt the mounting from the subframe **(see illustration)** and remove it from the vehicle.

24 Fit the new mounting using a reversal of the removal procedure, but tighten the nuts/bolts to the specified torque setting.

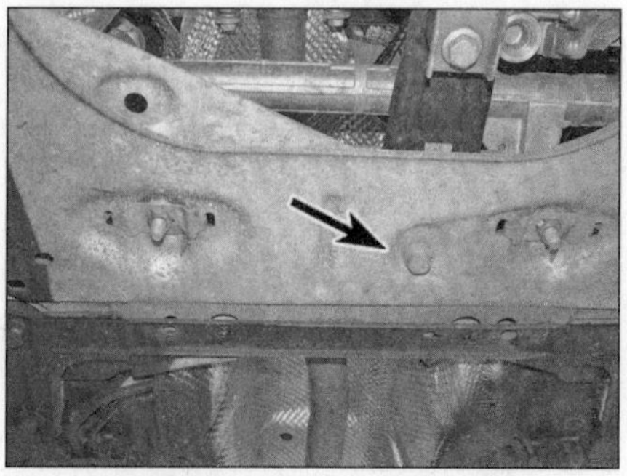

12.23 Remove the bolt from the rear subframe and then remove the mounting

13 Flywheel – removal, inspection and refitting

Note: *Removal of the flywheel requires the transmission to be removed as described in Chapter 7.*

Removal

1 Remove the manual gearbox as described in Chapter 7.

2 Remove the clutch as described in Chapter 6.

3 Mark the flywheel in relation to the crankshaft to aid refitting. Note that the flywheel can only be refitted in one position, as the bolts are unequally spaced.

4 The flywheel must now be held stationary while the bolts are loosened. To do this, locate a long bolt in one of the transmission to engine mounting bolt holes, and either insert a wide-bladed screwdriver in the starter ring gear, or use a piece of bent metal bar engaged with the ring gear.

5 Unscrew the mounting bolts, and withdraw the flywheel – take care as it is heavy.

Inspection

6 Examine the flywheel for wear or chipping of the ring gear teeth. If the ring gear is worn or damaged, it may be possible to renew it separately. Note however that Renault do not supply the ring gear as a separate part, it is only available with the flywheel.

7 Check the flywheel carefully for signs of distortion, and for hairline cracks around the bolt holes, or radiating outwards from the centre. If damage of this sort is found, it must be renewed.

8 Examine the flywheel for scoring of the clutch face. If the clutch face is scored, the flywheel may be machined until flat, but renewal is preferable.

Refitting

9 Clean the flywheel and crankshaft mating surfaces, then locate the flywheel on the crankshaft, making sure that any previously made marks are aligned.

10 Fit the new bolts and tighten them in a diagonal sequence to the specified torque wrench setting.

11 Refit the clutch (Chapter 6) and the manual gearbox as described in Chapter 7.

Chapter 2 Part B:
Diesel engine in-car repair procedures

Contents

Section	Section number
Camshaft and tappets – removal, inspection and refitting	9
Camshaft oil seals – renewal	8
Compression and leakdown tests – description and interpretation	2
Crankshaft oil seals – renewal	13
Cylinder head – dismantling and overhaul	See Chapter 2C
Cylinder head – removal, inspection and refitting	10
Engine assembly/valve timing holes – general information and usage	3
Engine mountings – renewal	15
Engine oil and filter renewal	See Chapter 1B
Engine oil level check	See *Weekly checks*
Flywheel – removal, inspection and refitting	14
General information	1
Oil pressure switch – removal and refitting	16
Oil pump and sprockets – removal, inspection and refitting	12
Sump – removal and refitting	11
Timing belt – removal, inspection and refitting	6
Timing belt sprockets, idler pulley and tensioner – removal and refitting	7
Valve clearances – checking and adjustment	5
Valve cover – removal and refitting	4

Degrees of difficulty

Easy, suitable for novice with little experience	**Fairly easy,** suitable for beginner with some experience	**Fairly difficult,** suitable for competent DIY mechanic	**Difficult,** suitable for experienced DIY mechanic	**Very difficult,** suitable for expert DIY or professional

Specifications

General

Type	Four cylinder, in-line, single overhead camshaft
Designation	K9K-834, K9K-836 and K9K-837
Capacity	1461 cc
Bore	76.0 mm
Stroke	80.5 mm
Firing order	1-3-4-2 (No 1 cylinder at flywheel end)
Direction of crankshaft rotation	Clockwise viewed from timing belt end
Maximum distortion of cylinder head	0.05 mm

Compression pressures

Engine warm – approximately 80°C:	
Minimum pressure	18 bars
Maximum difference between cylinders	4 bars

Camshaft

Drive	Toothed belt
Number of bearings	6
Camshaft endfloat	0.08 to 0.178 mm

Valve clearances (cold)

Inlet	0.125 - 0.25 mm
Exhaust	0.325 - 0.45 mm

Lubrication system

System pressure (at 80°C):	
At idle	0.8 bar minimum
At 4000 rpm	3.4 bars minimum
Maximum	5.2 bars
Oil pump type	Gear-type, chain-driven off the crankshaft right-hand end

Torque wrench settings

	Nm	lbf ft
Alternator	25	18
Big-end bearing caps:*		
Stage 1	25	18
Stage 2	Angle-tighten a further 110° ± 6°	
Brake vacuum pump	25	18
Camshaft bearing caps	10	7
Camshaft adjustable bolts	14	10
Camshaft hub:*		
Stage 1	30	22
Stage 2	Angle-tighten a further 86° ± 6°	
Clutch pressure plate:		
M6 bolts	14	10
M7	20	15
Crankshaft end plate	10	7
Crankshaft main bearing caps:		
Stage 1	25	18
Stage 2	Angle-tighten a further 47°± 6°	
Crankshaft pulley bolt:*		
Stage 1	120	88
Stage 2	Angle-tighten a further 95° ± 15°	
Cylinder block TDC blanking plug	25	18
Cylinder head bolts:*		
Stage 1	20	15
Stage 2	25	18
Stage 2	Angle-tighten a further 270° ± 10°	
Cylinder head coolant outlet	10	7
Driveshaft support bracket	44	33
Engine right-hand cover	10	7
Engine/transmission mountings:		
Right-hand mounting to engine/body	62	46
Right-hand upper tie bar to the engine	115	85
Right-hand upper tie bar to the body	105	77
Left-hand mounting to transmission	62	46
Left-hand mounting to body	62	46
Left-hand mounting central nut/bolt	62	46
Rear mounting link to subframe	105	77
Rear mounting link to transmission	105	77
Exhaust gas recirculation valve	21	15
Exhaust manifold	26	19
Flywheel*		
Stage 1	20	15
Stage 2	Angle-tighten a further 36° ± 6°	
Glow plugs	15	11
High-pressure fuel pump	23	17
High-pressure fuel pump sprocket	70	52
High-pressure pipe	28	21
High-pressure rail	21	15
Injector flanges	27	20
Knock sensor	20	15
Multifunction support bracket lower bolt	25	18
Oil filter support	28	21
Oil level sensor	25	18
Oil pressure sensor	35	26
Oil pump	25	18
Roadwheel bolts	110	81
Sump to block bolts	14	10
Sump to transmission bolts	44	33
Timing belt tensioner	27	20
Turbocharger oil delivery pipe (on cylinder head)	25	18
Turbocharger oil delivery (banjo bolt)	14	10
Turbocharger oil return pipe	12	9
Turbocharger to exhaust manifold	26	19
Valve cover	11	8
Water pump	10	7
Water pump inlet pipe	25	18

* **Note:** *Use new bolts.*

1 General information

How to use this Chapter

1 This Part of Chapter 2 is devoted to in-car repair procedures for the diesel engine. Similar information covering the petrol engine can be found in Part A. All procedures concerning engine removal and refitting, and engine block/cylinder head overhaul can be found in Part C of this Chapter.

2 Refer to *Vehicle identification numbers* in the Reference Section at the end of this manual for details of engine code locations.

3 Most of the operations included in this Part are based on the assumption that the engine is still installed in the car. Therefore, if this information is being used during a complete engine overhaul, with the engine already removed, many of the steps included here will not apply.

Engine description

4 The engine is of four cylinder, in-line, single overhead camshaft type, mounted transversely at the front of the vehicle.

5 The cylinder block is of cast iron with conventional dry liners bored directly into the cylinder block. The crankshaft is supported in five shell-type main bearings. Thrustwashers are fitted to No 3 main bearing to control crankshaft endfloat.

6 The connecting rods are attached to the crankshaft by 'cracked' horizontally split shell-type big-end bearings and to the pistons by gudgeon pins. The gudgeon pins are fully-floating and are retained by circlips. The aluminium alloy pistons are fitted with three piston rings, comprising two compression rings and a scraper-type oil control ring.

7 The single overhead camshaft is mounted directly in the cylinder head, and is driven by the crankshaft via a toothed timing belt.

8 The camshaft operates the valves via inverted bucket type tappets, which operate in bores machined directly in the cylinder head. The valve clearances are adjusted by changing the tappet buckets which are available in 25 different thicknesses. The inlet and exhaust valves are mounted vertically in the cylinder head and are each closed by a single valve spring.

9 The high-pressure fuel injection pump is driven by the timing belt and is described in further detail in Chapter 4B.

10 A semi-closed crankcase ventilation system is employed, and crankcase fumes are drawn from the cylinder block and passed via a hose to the inlet tract (see Chapter 4C for further details).

11 Engine lubrication is by pressure feed from a gear type oil pump located beneath the crankshaft. Engine oil is fed through an externally-mounted oil filter to the main oil gallery feeding the crankshaft, auxiliary shaft (where fitted) and camshaft. Oil spray jets are fitted to the cylinder block to supply oil to the underside of the pistons. An oil cooler is mounted between the oil filter and the cylinder block.

Operations with engine in place

12 The following operations can be carried out without having to remove the engine from the vehicle:

a) Removal and refitting of the cylinder head.
b) Removal and refitting of the timing belt and sprockets.
c) Renewal of the camshaft oil seals.
d) Removal and refitting of the camshaft.
e) Removal and refitting of the sump.
*f) Removal and refitting of the connecting rods and pistons.**
g) Removal and refitting of the oil pump.
h) Renewal of the crankshaft oil seals.
i) Renewal of the engine mountings.
j) Removal and refitting of the flywheel.

** Although the operation marked with an asterisk can be carried out with the engine in the car after removal of the sump, it is better for the engine to be removed in the interests of cleanliness and improved access. For this reason, the procedure is described in Chapter 2C.*

2 Compression and leakdown tests – description and interpretation

Compression test

Note: *A compression tester specifically designed for diesel engines must be used for this test.*

1 When engine performance is down, or if misfiring occurs which cannot be attributed to a fault in the fuel system, a compression test can provide diagnostic clues as to the engine's condition. If the test is performed regularly it can give warning of trouble before any other symptoms become apparent.

2 A compression tester is connected to an adaptor which screws into the glow plug hole. It is unlikely to be worthwhile buying such a tester for occasional use, but it may be possible to borrow or hire one – if not, have the test performed by a garage.

3 Unless specific instructions to the contrary are supplied with the tester, observe the following points:

a) The battery must be in a good state of charge, the air filter must be clean and the engine should be at normal operating temperature.
b) All the glow plugs must be removed before starting the test and the wiring disconnected from the injectors.

4 There is no need to hold the accelerator pedal down during the test.

5 The actual compression pressures measured are not so important as the balance between cylinders. Values are given in the Specifications.

6 The cause of poor compression is less easy to establish on a diesel engine than on a petrol one. The effect of introducing oil into the cylinders ('wet' testing) is not conclusive, because there is a risk that the oil will sit in the swirl chamber or in the recess on the piston crown instead of passing to the rings. However, the following can be used as a rough guide to diagnosis.

7 All cylinders should produce very similar pressures; any difference greater than that specified indicates the existence of a fault. Note that the compression should build-up quickly in a healthy engine; low compression on the first stroke, followed by gradually increasing pressure on successive strokes, indicates worn piston rings. A low compression reading on the first stroke, which does not build-up during successive strokes, indicates leaking valves or a blown head gasket (a cracked head could also be the cause).

8 A low reading from two adjacent cylinders is almost certainly due to the head gasket having blown between them.

Leakdown test

9 A leakdown test measures the rate at which compressed air fed into the cylinder is lost. It is an alternative to a compression test and in many ways it is better, since the escaping air provides easy identification of where pressure loss is occurring (piston rings, valves or head gasket).

10 The equipment needed for leakdown testing is unlikely to be available to the home mechanic. If poor compression is suspected, have the test performed by a suitably-equipped garage.

3 Engine assembly/valve timing holes – general information and usage

Caution: Do not attempt to rotate the engine whilst the crankshaft and camshaft timing pins are in position. If the engine is to be left in this state for a long period of time, it is a good idea to place suitable warning notices inside the vehicle, and in the engine compartment. This will reduce the possibility of the engine being accidentally cranked on the starter motor, which would cause considerable damage.

Note: *Special timing tools are required for this work. These are available from Renault or specialist tool suppliers, such as AST tools or Draper tools.*

1 Top Dead Centre (TDC) is the highest point in the cylinder that each piston reaches as the crankshaft turns. Each piston reaches TDC at the end of the compression stroke and again at the end of the exhaust stroke; however, for the purpose of timing the engine, TDC refers to the position of No 1 piston at the end of its compression stroke. No 1 piston is at the **flywheel** end of the engine.

3.8a Remove the upper timing belt cover

3.8b With the cover removed, note how the retaining clips fit together...

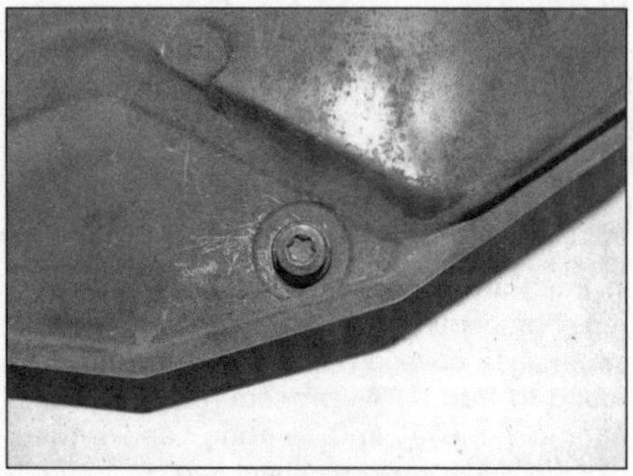

3.8c ...and the position of the plastic screw

2 When No 1 piston is at TDC, the timing hole in the camshaft sprocket will be aligned with the hole in the cylinder head so that the timing pin can be inserted. Additionally, if the crankshaft timing pin is fully screwed into the cylinder block, it will just contact the timing flat on the crankshaft web.

3 Setting the TDC timing is necessary to ensure that the valve timing is maintained during operations that require removal and refitting of the timing belt. Note that the engine does not have a conventional diesel injection pump, however it is still necessary to align a mark on the pump sprocket the pump body. The mark should be one tooth to the right of vertical.

4 To set the engine at TDC, the right-hand engine mounting support and cover must be removed for access to the camshaft sprocket as described in Section 15 of this Chapter. First jack up the front of the car and support on axle stands (see *Jacking and vehicle support* in the reference section)..

5 Remove the engine undertray and then remove the rear lower engine mounting. The engine will still be supported by the left and right-hand upper mountings. Remove the front right wheel and then remove the front section of the wheel arch liner.

6 To improve access further remove the windscreen wipers and both the upper and lower windscreen cowl panels as described in Chapter 11. Whilst not essential this will allow the engine to be moved forward slightly (on a suitable jack) as well as up and down.

7 Remove the auxiliary drivebelt with reference to Chapter 1B.

8 Support the right-hand end of the engine with a jack and block of wood beneath the sump. Unbolt the right-hand engine mounting from the engine and body (as described in Section 15 of this Chapter) and unclip the upper timing cover. Note that on some models the upper cover may be in one, or two pieces. Where it is a single item release the lower clips and remove the plastic retaining screw **(see illustrations)**. Access to the screw is limited, but it can if necessary be prized out from the expansion plug – a replacement will be require for refitting. Note that considerable dexterity will be required to remove the upper cover.

3.11 Remove the support bracket

3.12 Remove the blanking plug (arrowed)

3.15 Fitting the crankshaft TDC pin

3.16 Fit the camshaft timing pin

9 Where the upper cover is in two sections, unclip and remove the upper and then remove the plastic retaining screw. Unclip and remove the lower section of the upper cover.

10 Remove the lower timing cover by releasing the clips. It will be necessary to slightly raise and lower the engine to facilitate removal of the timing cover.

11 With the covers removed, unbolt and remove the engine mounting support bracket **(see illustration)**.

12 Unscrew and remove the plug from the TDC hole on the left-hand front of the cylinder block. This is directly below the starter motor **(see illustration)**. If you are just checking the timing leave the starter motor in position, however if you are accessing the TDC timing hole for timing belt replacement, consider removing the starter motor (as described in Chapter 5A) as this gives easy access to the TDC timing hole, as well as making locking the crankshaft (for the removal of the crankshaft pulley) considerably easier.

13 The crankshaft must now be turned using a spanner on the crankshaft pulley bolt.

14 Turn the crankshaft clockwise until the timing hole in the camshaft sprocket is approaching the hole in the cylinder head – the hole will be in the eight o'clock position. The mark on the high pressure fuel pump should be in the ten o'clock position. If the pump timing mark is not in the correct position, rotate the crankshaft as required to obtain the correct position.

15 Insert and tighten the special TDC pin into the cylinder block timing hole **(see illustration)**.

16 Slowly turn the crankshaft clockwise until its web contacts the timing pin. Now insert the remaining timing pin through the hole in the camshaft sprocket and into the cylinder head **(see illustration)**. The engine is now positioned with No 1 piston at TDC on its compression stroke.

17 Check that the mark on the high-pressure injection pump sprocket is one tooth to the right of vertical **(see illustration)**. If the timing belt is to be replaced at this point mark the position of the fuel pump sprocket in relation the pump mounting.

18 On completion, remove the timing pins and refit all removed components.

3.17 The mark on the high-pressure pump sprocket (arrowed) must be one tooth to the right of vertical

4 Valve cover – removal and refitting

Removal

1 Jack up and support the front of the vehicle - (see *Jacking and vehicle support* in the reference section). Remove both front road wheels.

2 Remove the front section of the wheel arch liners and then remove engine undershield.

3 Open the bonnet, disconnect the battery and where fitted remove the engine cover. Whilst not strictly necessary access can be improved if the upper and lower sections of the windscreen cowl panels are removed

4 Support the right-hand end of the engine using a trolley jack with a block of wood on the jack head to spread the load on the engine sump.

5 Raise the engine slightly and remove the right-hand engine mount (see Section 15). With the mount removed, unclip and remove the upper section of the timing belt cover as described in Section 3.

6 Remove the turbocharger outlet pipe by rotating and releasing the clip at the turbocharger and the inter cooler. Remove the bolt and remove the pipe **(see illustrations)**.

7 Remove the air inlet pipe and disconnect the wiring plugs from the valve and camshaft position sensor. Unbolt and then remove the damper valve assembly **(see illustrations)**.

8 Release the wiring loom from the cover and then unclip and unbolt the soundproofing from the valve cover **(see illustrations)**.

4.6a Release the clip (arrowed)

4.6b Remove the bolt...

4.6c ...and remove the outlet hose

4.7a Remove the inlet hose

4.7b Disconnect the wiring plugs from the valve and the camshaft position sensor

4.7c Remove the valve

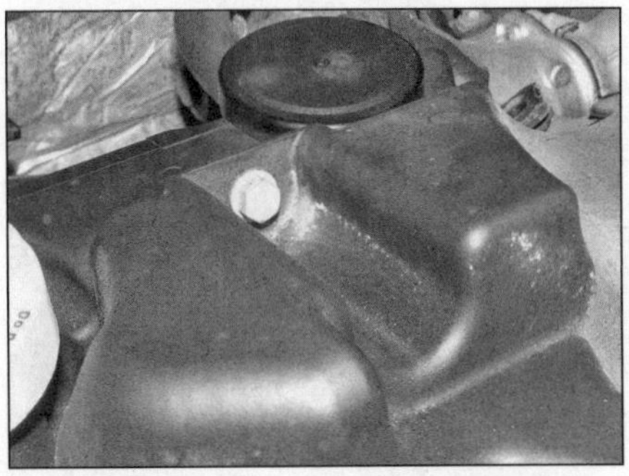

4.8a Remove the bolts (one shown)...

4.8b ...release the clips...

4.8c ...and remove the cover

4.9a Remove the breather pipe

4.9c Disconnect the wiring plugs from the fuel injectors

9 Disconnect the wiring plugs from the injectors and remove the breather hose **(see illustrations)**.

10 Remove the bleed pipe from the injectors and then (where the pipe runs along the back of the cover) remove the fuel return pipe. Note that Renault recommend that this pipe is replaced if removed.

11 Remove the vacuum hose and then disconnect the wiring plug from the exhaust gas temperature sensor. Unclip the wiring loom for the sensor and move it to one side.

12 At the left-hand end of the cylinder head, remove the engine lifting eye and bracket. To avoid damaging the sensor, unbolt and

4.9b Remove the support bracket

4.12 Remove the camshaft position sensor

remove the camshaft position sensor **(see illustration)**.

13 Slacken and then remove the valve cover bolts. Remove the cover and recover the gasket.

Refitting

14 Refitting is a reversal of removal, but bear in mind the following:

a) Clean the mounting surfaces

b) Apply a 2 mm wide and 10 mm long bead of sealant at the points shown **(see illustration)**

c) Tighten the bolts in the order shown to the correct torque **(see illustration)**

d) Fit new seals to the injectors and fit new high pressure supply pipes

e) Fit a new gasket to the turbo outlet pipe

f) Refit the remainder of the components in reverse order.

5 Valve clearances – checking and adjustment

Note: *This operation is not part of the maintenance schedule. It should be undertaken if noise from the valve gear becomes evident, or if loss of performance gives cause to suspect that the clearances may be incorrect. Adjustment involves removing the camshaft and changing the tappet buckets which are available in 25 different thicknesses.*

Checking

1 Remove the valve cover as described in Section 4 of this Chapter.

2 During the following procedure, the crankshaft must be turned using a spanner on the crankshaft pulley bolt. Improved access to the pulley bolt can be obtained by jacking up the front right-hand corner of the vehicle and removing the roadwheel and the lower wheel arch cover (secured by plastic clips).

3 If desired, to enable the crankshaft to be turned more easily, remove the glow plugs (Chapter 5C).

4 Draw the valve positions on a piece of paper, numbering them 1 to 8 from the flywheel end of the engine. Identify them as inlet or exhaust (ie, 1E, 2I, 3E, 4I, 5E, 6I, 7E, 8I).

5 Turn the crankshaft until the valves of No 1 cylinder (flywheel end) are 'rocking'. The exhaust valve will be closing and the inlet valve will be opening. The piston of No 4 cylinder will be at the top of its compression stroke, with both valves fully closed. The clearances for both valves of No 4 cylinder may be checked at the same time.

6 Insert a feeler blade of the correct thickness

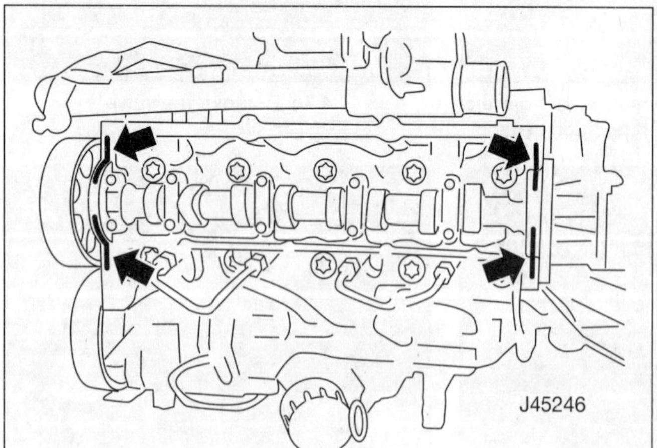

4.14a Apply 1.0 mm wide and 10mm long beads of sealant to the camshaft end bearing caps

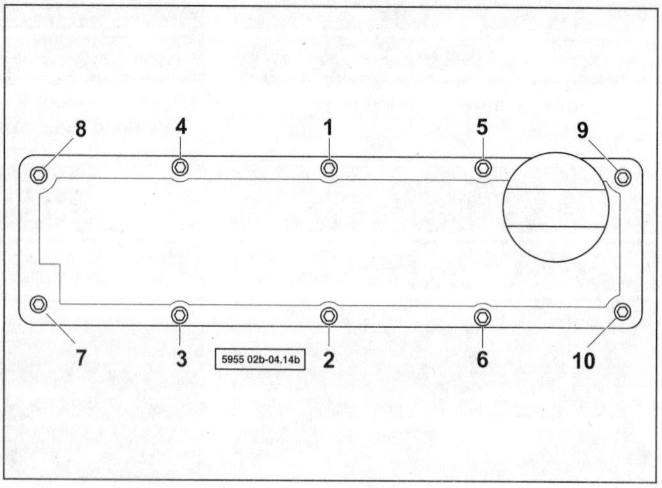

4.14b Tighten the valve cover bolts in the order shown

5.6 Using a feeler blade to check the valve clearances

(see Specifications) between the cam lobe and the top of the tappet bucket, and check that it is a firm sliding fit **(see illustration)**. If it is not, use the feeler blades to ascertain the exact clearance, and record this for use when calculating the thickness of the new tappet bucket required. Note that the inlet and exhaust valve clearances are different (see Specifications).

7 With No 4 cylinder valve clearances checked, turn the engine through half a turn so that No 3 valves are 'rocking', then check the valve clearances of No 2 cylinder in the same way. Similarly check the remaining valve clearances in the sequence shown **(see illustration)**.

Adjustment

Note: *A micrometer or dial gauge and probe will be required for this operation.*

8 Where a valve clearance differs from the specified value, the tappet bucket for that valve must be changed with a thinner or thicker one accordingly. On new tappets, the thickness is stamped on the bottom face of the tappet, however, the original tappets do have any thickness stamped on them. It is therefore prudent to use a micrometer or dial gauge to measure the true thickness of any tappet removed, as it may have been reduced by wear **(see illustration)**.

9 To access the tappet buckets, first remove the camshaft as described in Section 9. Remove and refit each bucket separately, to avoid confusion **(see illustration)**.

10 The size of tappet required is calculated as follows. If the measured clearance is less than specified, subtract the measured clearance from the specified clearance, and deduct the result from the thickness of the existing tappet. For example:

Sample calculation – clearance too small

Clearance measured (A) = 0.15 mm
Desired clearance (B) = 0.20 mm
Difference (B – A) = 0.05 mm
Tappet bucket thickness fitted = 3.70 mm
Tappet bucket thickness required = 3.70 – 0.05 = 3.65 mm

11 If the measured clearance is greater than specified, subtract the specified clearance from the measured clearance, and add the result to the thickness of the existing tappet. For example:

Sample calculation – clearance too big
Clearance measured (A) = 0.50 mm
Desired clearance (B) = 0.40 mm
Difference (A – B) = 0.10 mm
Tappet bucket thickness fitted = 3.45 mm
Tappet bucket thickness required = 3.45 + 0.10 = 3.55 mm

12 Working on each separately, lift out the bucket to be renewed, then oil the new one and carefully locate it in the cylinder head **(see illustration)**

13 Refit the camshaft with reference to Section 9.

14 Where removed, refit the glow plugs (Chapter 5C).

15 Remove the spanner from the crankshaft pulley bolt.

16 Wipe clean the contact surfaces on the valve cover and cylinder head, then apply four beads of sealant, 2.0 mm wide, to the camshaft end bearing caps (Nos 1 and 6) **(see illustration 4.14a)**.

17 Refit the valve cover and tighten the bolts to the specified torque in the order given **(see illustration 4.14b)**.

18 Refit the remaining components in reverse order to removal.

6 Timing belt – removal, inspection and refitting

Caution: If the timing belt breaks in service, extensive engine damage will result. Renew the belt at the intervals specified in Chapter 1B, or earlier if its condition is at all doubtful.

Note: *The belt and tensioner must be replaced if removed.*

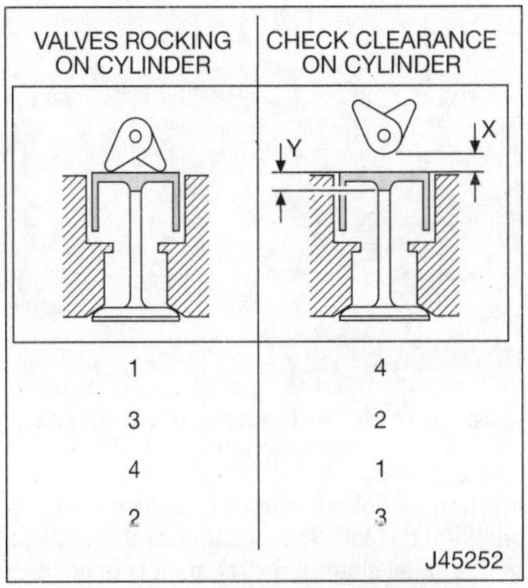

5.7 Valve clearance measurement
X Clearance *Y Tappet thickness*

Removal

1 Disconnect the battery negative lead (refer to *Disconnecting the battery* in Reference). To improve access remove the upper and lower windscreen cowl panels (as described in Chapter 11).

2 Jack up the front of the car and support on axle stands (see *Jacking and vehicle support* in the reference section). Remove the front right wheel, engine/radiator undertray and wheel arch liner. Where fitted remove the engine cover.

3 Remove the auxiliary drivebelt with reference to Chapter 1B, then unbolt and remove the drivebelt tensioner.

4 The crankshaft pulley must now be removed. There is a small gap beneath the starter motor into which a screwdriver or similar tool can be jammed into the starter ring gear teeth. Note however that access to both the ring gear and the TDC timing plug (below the starter motor) is considerably easier if the starter motor is removed first.

5 Using a long knuckle bar and socket remove the crankshaft pulley bolt. With

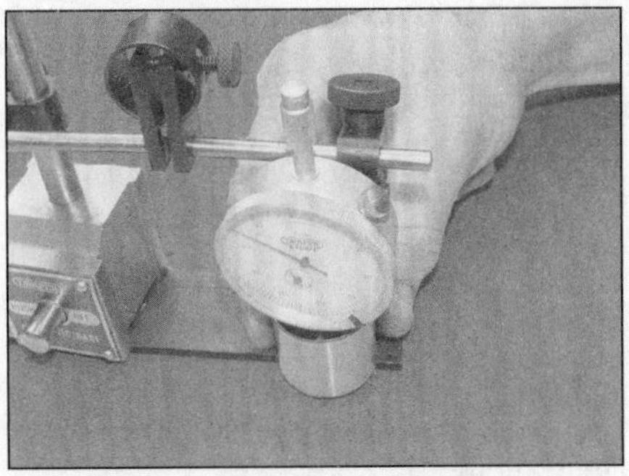

5.8 Using a dial gauge to measure the thickness of the removed tappet

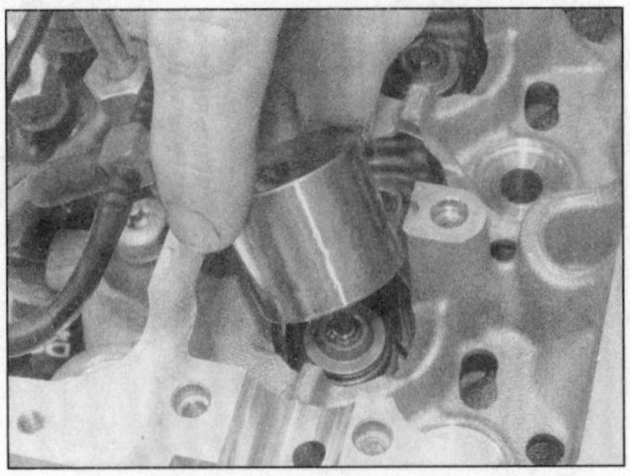

5.9 Removing a tappet bucket

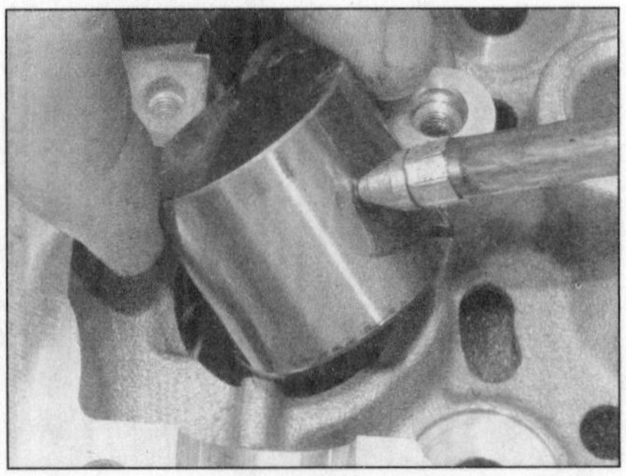

5.12 Lubricate the tappet bucket before refitting it

6.5a Unscrew and remove the crankshaft pulley bolt...

6.5b ...and remove the pulley

6.5c Refit the bolt and mark the position of the keyway

the bolt removed, ease the pulley from the crankshaft. Mark the position of the keyway on the crankshaft sprocket, as it is difficult to see once the bolt is refitted **(see illustrations)**. Refit the bolt with a suitable spacer.

6 Remove the rear lower engine mounting. The engine will still be supported by the left and right-hand upper mountings. Support the right-hand end of the engine with a jack. Place a block of wood on the head of the jack to spread the load on the sump.

7 Unbolt the right-hand engine mounting from the engine and body, then release and unclip the timing belt covers as described in Section 3 of this Chapter.

8 Unbolt and remove the engine mounting support bracket **(see illustration)**.

9 Unscrew and remove the blanking plug from the TDC hole on the left-hand front of the cylinder block **(see illustration 3.12)**.

6.8 Remove the support bracket

6.16a Loosen the tensioner locknut (arrowed)...

10 The crankshaft must now be turned to the TDC position using a spanner on the crankshaft pulley bolt.

11 Turn the crankshaft clockwise until the timing hole in the camshaft sprocket is approaching the hole in the cylinder head. The hole will be approaching the nine o'clock position.

12 Insert and tighten the special TDC pin into the cylinder block timing hole **(see illustration 3.15)**.

13 Slowly turn the crankshaft clockwise until its web contacts the timing pin. Now insert the timing pin (or a suitable bolt) through the hole in the camshaft sprocket and into the cylinder head **(see illustration 3.16)**. The engine is now positioned with No 1 piston at TDC on its compression stroke.

14 Check that the mark on the high-pressure injection pump sprocket is one tooth to the right of vertical. It may be necessary to rotate the crankshaft again to align the mark on the pump sprocket **(see illustration)**.

6.14 Check that the position of the pump is correct. Note the alignment mark (arrowed) on the belt

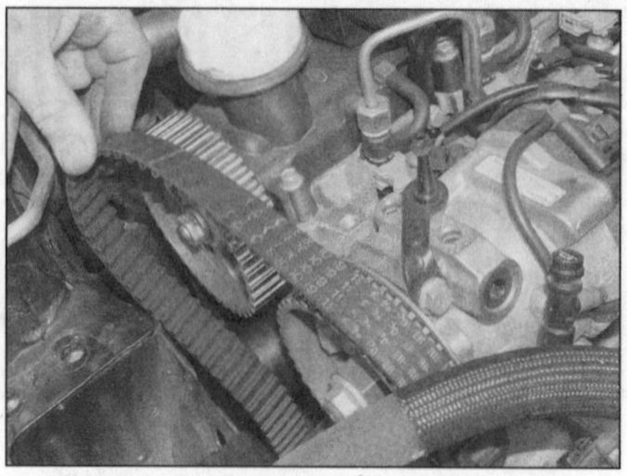

6.16b ...then release the timing belt

15 Check that the keyway on the crankshaft pulley is in the 12 O'clock position. For reference mark the position of all the sprockets in relation to the engine before removing the timing belt.

16 Loosen the tensioner bolt, then turn the tensioner clockwise to release the tension. If necessary, use a 6.0 mm Allen key in the eccentric hub plate to move the tensioner. Lock the tensioner in the relaxed position and remove the belt **(see illustrations)**.

17 Do not turn the camshaft or the crankshaft whilst the timing belt is removed, as there is a risk of piston-to-valve contact. If it is necessary to turn the camshaft for any reason, before doing so, turn the crankshaft anti-clockwise (viewed from the timing belt end of the engine) by a quarter turn to position all four pistons half-way down their bores. Leave the TDC pin tightened into the cylinder block.

18 Unbolt and remove the timing belt tensioner. Discard the tensioner – a new one must be fitted.

19 Clean the sprockets, water pump pulley and tensioner and wipe them dry, although do not apply excessive amounts of solvent to the water pump and tensioner pulleys otherwise the bearing lubricant may be contaminated. Also clean the rear timing belt cover, and the cylinder head and block.

Inspection

20 The belt and tensioner must be replaced once removed, however an examination of the old belt may indicate other problems, such as worn or misaligned sprockets. Vehicles with build codes BZOB, KZOB and DZOB must have the high pressure pump adjusted (as described in Chapter 4B). If the pump has been adjusted there should be a blue sticker (with an 'X' marked on it) fixed to the suspension tower. However this may have been removed, so it will always be worth checking and adjusting the pump alignment if the old timing belt shows any damage to the edge of the belt **(see illustration)**.

21 Check the waterpump for play and any signs of a coolant leak. Consider replacing the waterpump regardless of its condition as it is not uncommon for a waterpump to leak after timing belt replacement due to the change in loading on the waterpump bearing.

22 Thoroughly clean the nose of the crankshaft and the bore of the crankshaft sprocket, and also the contact surfaces of the sprocket and pulley.

Refitting

23 Check that the crankshaft, camshaft and high-pressure fuel injection pump sprockets are still positioned at TDC, and that the groove in the crankshaft nose is pointing upwards. If the pistons have been positioned half-way down their bores, turn the crankshaft clockwise until the web contacts the TDC tool.

24 Fit the new tensioner and check that the tensioner peg is correctly located in the groove in the cylinder head.

25 Slacken the 2 upper bolts on the camshaft sprocket and remove the lower bolt **(see illustration)**. The sprocket should be free to rotate on the hub.

26 Align the timing marks on the belt with those on the camshaft and fuel injection pump sprockets **(see illustration)**, ensuring that the running direction arrows on the belt are pointing clockwise (viewed from the timing belt end of the engine). Note that the belt should be marked with lines across its width to act as timing marks. Fit the timing belt over the crankshaft sprocket first, followed by the water pump pulley, fuel injection pump sprocket, camshaft sprocket, and tensioner. There should be19 belt grooves between the timing marks on the camshaft and injection pump sprockets. And 51 belt grooves between the mark on the high pressure pump and the crankshaft sprocket – at the six o'clock position.

27 With the timing marks still aligned, use the 6.0 mm Allen key to pretension the belt by turning the tensioner anti-clockwise until the index pointer is positioned below the timing window **(see illustrations)**. Hold the tensioner stationary and tighten the locknut to the specified torque. This torque is critical, since if the nut were to come loose, considerable engine damage would result.

28 Refit the missing bolt from the camshaft sprocket and tighten all 3 bolts. Note that the bolts should not be tight against the adjustable slots in the sprocket.

29 Refit the crankshaft pulley, then insert the old bolt. After tightening the bolt, remove the timing pins from the cylinder block and camshaft sprocket.

30 Turn the crankshaft two complete turns in the normal direction of rotation, but just before the camshaft sprockets are aligned, refit and tighten the crankshaft timing pin. Slowly turn the crankshaft clockwise until its web is contacting the timing pin. Insert the timing pin through the hole in the camshaft sprocket and into the cylinder head. Slacken the 3 bolts in the camshaft sprocket.

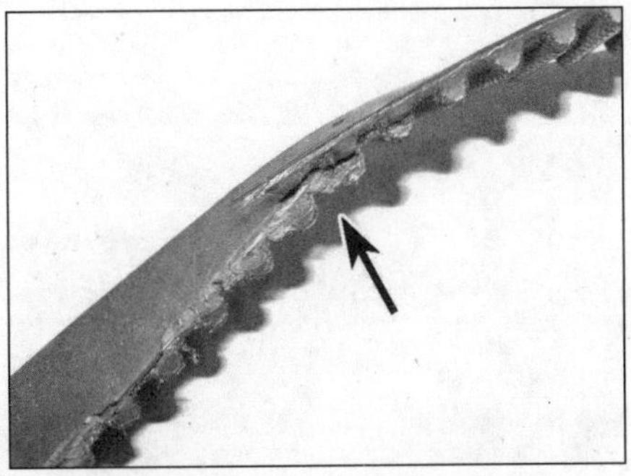

6.20 This belt is clearly damaged. Identify the cause before replacing the belt

6.25 Slacken the upper bolts (arrowed) and remove the lower

6.26 Align the timing marks on the belt with those on the camshaft and fuel injection pump sprockets

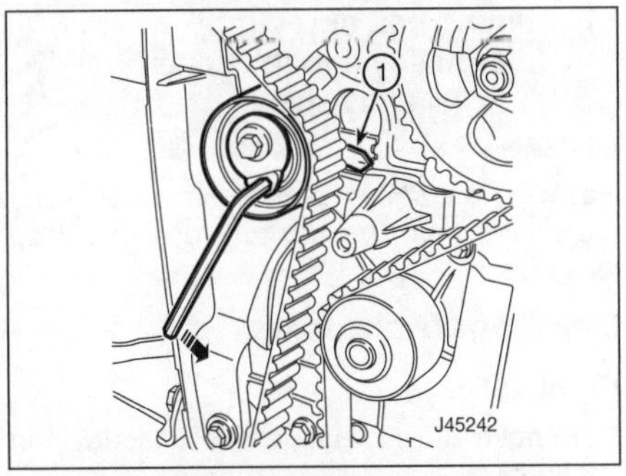

6.27a Pretension the timing belt by positioning the tensioner pointer (1) as shown

31 Hold the tensioner with the Allen key, then loosen the locknut a maximum of one turn, and turn the tensioner clockwise until the index pointer is positioned in the middle of the timing window **(see illustration)**. Tighten the locknut to the specified torque and then tighten the camshaft sprocket bolts to the specified torque.

32 Remove the TDC timing pin and the camshaft sprocket timing pin. Rotate the engine two complete revolutions and refit the timing pins. Check that the pointer on the tensioner is at the mid point on the index marks. Repeat the tensioning procedure if this is incorrect.

33 Remove the camshaft timing pin and then remove the old crankshaft pulley bolt. Fit a new bolt and tighten it to the specified torque.

34 Remove the TDC timing pin from the engine block. Apply sealant to the threads, then refit the blanking plug to the cylinder block and tighten it to the specified torque.

35 Refit the engine mounting support bracket and tighten the bolts to the specified torque.

36 Refit the timing covers, using a new plastic screw if required.

37 Refit the right-hand engine mounting to the engine and body and tighten the bolts to the specified torque.

38 Fit a new auxiliary drivebelt and tensioner with reference to Chapter 1B.

39 Refit the engine undertray and wheel arch liner.

40 Refit the front right wheel and lower the car to the ground. Tighten the wheel bolts to the specified torque.

41 Refit the windscreen cowl panels.

42 Reconnect the battery negative lead (refer to *Disconnecting the battery* in the Chapter 5A).

6.27b Pretensioning the timing belt

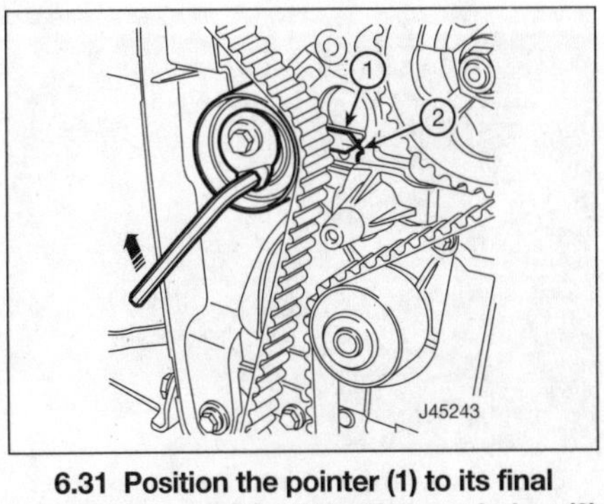

6.31 Position the pointer (1) to its final setting in the middle of the timing window (2)

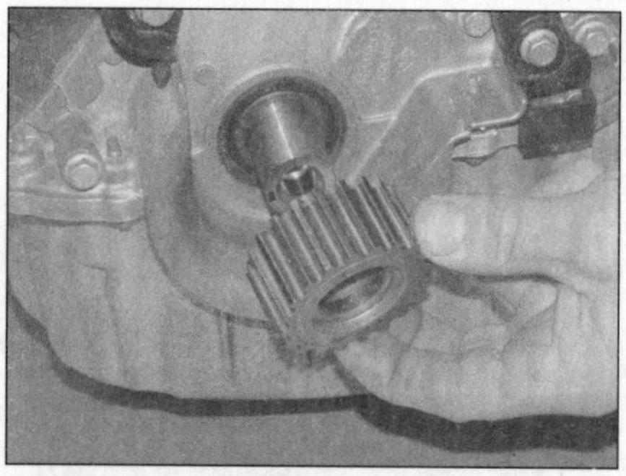

7.2 Removing the crankshaft sprocket

7.10 Angle-tightening the camshaft sprocket retaining bolt

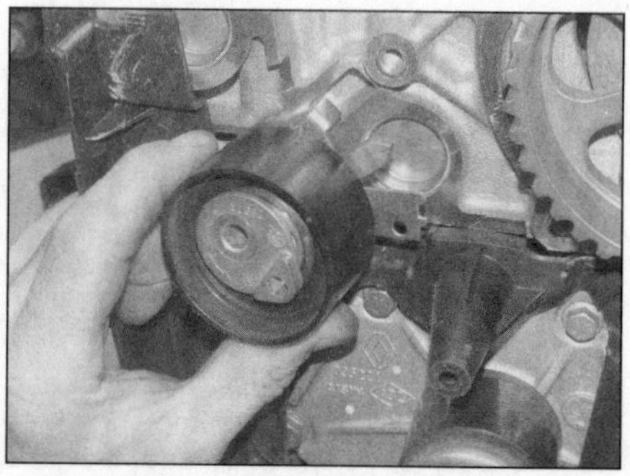

7.13 Removing the timing belt tensioner

7 Timing belt sprockets, idler pulley and tensioner – removal and refitting

Note: *If the timing belt is removed, both the timing belt and the tensioner must be replaced.*

Crankshaft sprocket

Removal

1 Remove the timing belt as described in Section 6.

2 Slide the sprocket from the crankshaft, noting which way around it is fitted **(see illustration)**.

Refitting

3 Thoroughly clean the nose of the crankshaft and the bore of the crankshaft sprocket, and also the contact surfaces of the sprocket and pulley. This is necessary to prevent the possibility of the sprocket slipping in use.

4 Slide the sprocket onto the crankshaft the correct way around.

5 Refit the timing belt as described in Section 6.

Camshaft sprocket

Removal

6 Remove the timing belt as described in Section 6.

7 Hold the sprocket stationary using a suitable gear holding tool. Alternatively, an old timing belt can be wrapped around the sprocket and held firmly with a pair of grips. Unscrew and remove the central securing nut.

8 Release the sprocket from the camshaft, noting the integral spline on the sprocket and the corresponding cut-out in the end of the camshaft.

9 If the stud in the end of the camshaft comes loose it must be replaced.

Refitting

10 Refit the camshaft sprocket, making sure that the integral spline locates in the camshaft cut-out. Insert the bolt and tighten it to the specified torque and angle, holding the sprocket stationary as during removal **(see illustration)**.

11 Refit and tension the timing belt as described in Section 6.

Tensioner

Removal

12 Remove the timing belt as described in Section 6.

13 Unscrew the securing bolt, then withdraw the tensioner assembly from the engine **(see illustration)**.

Refitting

14 Refitting is a reversal of removal. Refit and tension the timing belt as described in Section 6.

High-pressure pump sprocket

Note: *A suitable puller will be required for this operation.*

Removal

15 Remove the timing belt and then remove the high pressure pump as described in Chapter 4B.

16 Clamp the pump firmly in a vice and then using a 32mm spanner to lock the pump, remove the sprocket retaining bolt.

17 Use a puller to release the sprocket from the taper on the pump shaft. Recover the Woodruff key from the groove in the pump shaft.

Refitting

18 Refitting is a reversal of removal, bearing in mind the following points.

a) *Ensure that the Woodruff key is correctly engaged with the pump shaft and sprocket.*
b) *Tighten the sprocket securing nut to the specified torque.*
c) *Refit and tension the timing belt as described in Section 6.*

8 Camshaft oil seals – renewal

Timing belt end oil seal

1 Remove the camshaft sprocket as described in Section 7.

2 Note the fitted depth of the old oil seal. Using a small screwdriver, prise out the oil seal from the cylinder head taking care not to damage the sealing surface on the camshaft. Alternatively, the oil seal can be removed by drilling two small holes diagonally opposite each other and inserting self tapping screws in them. A pair of grips can then be used to pull out the oil seals, by pulling on each side in turn.

3 Inspect the seal rubbing surface on the camshaft. If it is grooved or rough in the area where the old seal was fitted, the new seal should be fitted slightly less deeply, so that it rubs on an unworn part of the surface.

4 Renault technicians use a tool (Mot. 1632) to fit the oil seal. The tool consists of a threaded rod, metal tube and nut, and a machined shoulder to locate the protector/guide on. The rod is screwed into the end of the camshaft, and the protector/guide located on the shoulder. The metal tube is then fitted against the oil seal and the nut tightened to press the seal into the cylinder head/bearing cap **(see illustrations)**. If the Renault tool cannot be

8.4a Screw the rod into the end of the camshaft...

8.4b ...locate the new oil seal and protector onto the camshaft...

8.4c ...then tighten the tool to press the seal into position

obtained, a similar tool can be made out of a threaded rod, metal tube, washer and nut.

5 Wipe clean the oil seal seating and the camshaft nose with a suitable solvent. **Do not** apply any lubricate to the housing, or the camshaft then press the oil seal squarely into position. Note that the Renault tool is designed to locate the seal at the original depth, however, if the camshaft sealing surface is excessively worn, position it less deeply so that it locates on the unworn surface.

6 After fitting the oil seal, remove the protector/guide and tool.

Flywheel end sealing

7 No oil seal is fitted to the flywheel end of the camshaft. The sealing is provided by a gasket between the cylinder head and the vacuum pump housing, and on certain models by an O-ring fitted between the vacuum pump and the housing. The gasket and the O-ring, where applicable, can be renewed after unbolting the vacuum pump from the cylinder head (see Chapter 9).

9 Camshaft and tappets – removal, inspection and refitting

Note: *A new camshaft oil seal will be required, and suitable sealant will be required for the camshaft bearing caps and valve cover.*

Removal

1 Removal of the camshaft will normally only be required for access to the tappet buckets (eg, for valve clearance adjustment) or during cylinder head overhaul. For cylinder head overhaul, remove the head as described in Section 10.

2 Remove the camshaft sprocket as described in Section 7.

3 Remove the valve cover as described in Section 4.

4 Remove the brake vacuum pump with reference to Chapter 9. Note the position of the offset drive inside the pump which engages the slot in the end of the camshaft **(see illustrations)**.

5 Using a dial gauge, measure the camshaft endfloat, and compare with the value given in the Specifications. This will give an indication of the amount of wear present on the thrust surfaces.

6 If the original camshaft is to be refitted, it is advisable to measure the valve clearances at this stage as described in Section 5, so that any different thickness tappets required can be obtained before the camshaft is refitted.

7 Check the camshaft bearing caps for identification marks, and if none are present, make identifying marks so that they can be refitted in their original positions and the same way round. Number the caps from the flywheel end of the engine **(see illustration)**.

8 Progressively slacken the bearing cap bolts until the valve spring pressure is relieved. Remove the bolts and the bearing caps themselves.

9 Lift out the camshaft together with the oil seal **(see illustration)**.

10 Remove the tappets, keeping each identified for position **(see illustration)**. Place them in a compartmented box, or on a sheet of card marked into eight sections, so that they may be refitted to their original locations. If any of the valve clearances measured in paragraph 9 is incorrect, use a micrometer to measure the thickness of the old tappet from its upper surface to the inner surface which contacts the valve stem. Refer to Section 5 and obtain new tappets of the correct thickness.

Inspection

11 Examine the camshaft bearing surfaces and cam lobes for wear ridges, pitting or scoring. Renew the camshaft if evident.

12 Renew the oil seal at the end of the camshaft as a matter of course. Lubricate the lips of the new seal before fitting, and store the camshaft so that its weight is not resting on the seal. Alternatively, the seal may be fitted after refitting the camshaft.

13 Examine the camshaft bearing surfaces in the cylinder head and bearing caps. Deep scoring or other damage means that the cylinder head must be renewed.

14 Inspect the tappet buckets for scoring, pitting and wear ridges. Renew as necessary.

Refitting

15 Oil the tappets (inside and out) and fit them to the bores from which they were removed; where applicable, fit the new tappets to their correct bores.

16 Oil the camshaft bearings. Place the camshaft without the oil seal onto the cylinder head.

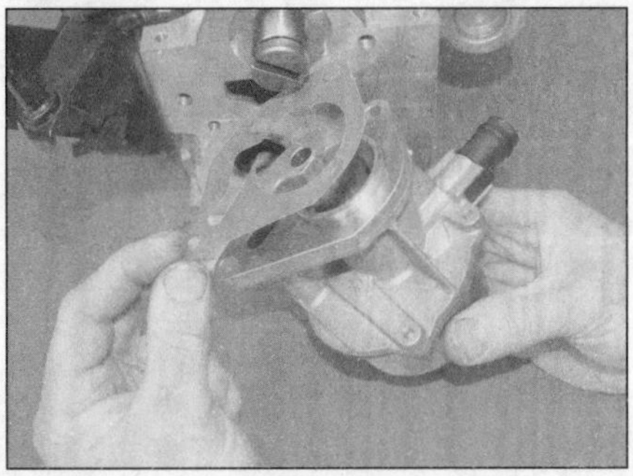

9.4a Removing the brake vacuum pump and gasket

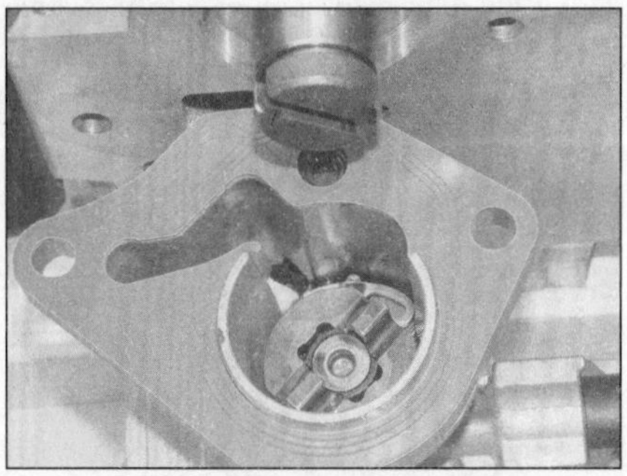

9.4b Offset drive in the pump which engages the slot in the end of the camshaft

9.7 The camshaft bearing caps are numbered from the flywheel end of the engine

9.9 Removing the camshaft from the cylinder head

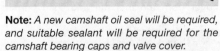

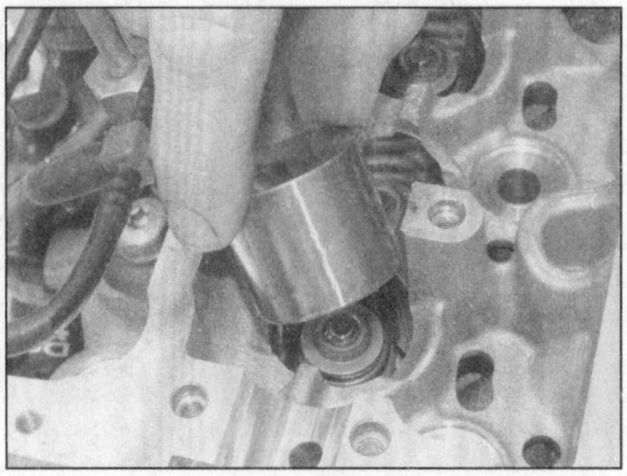

9.10 Removing the tappets

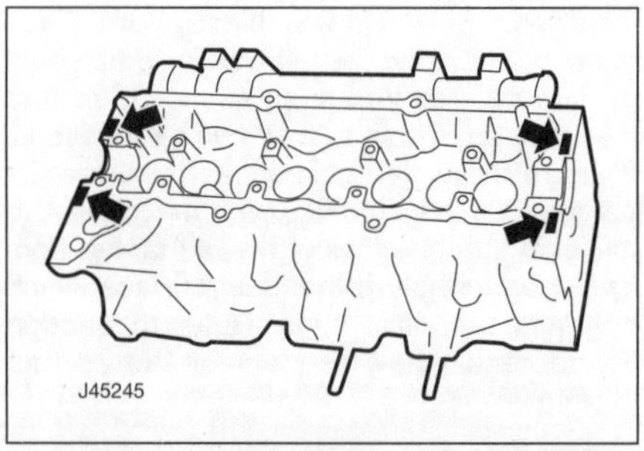

9.17a Apply 7.0 mm wide beads of sealant to the camshaft end bearing cap-to-cylinder head contact areas as shown

9.17b Apply the beads of sealant...

9.18a ...then refit the camshaft bearing caps

17 Wipe clean the upper sealing edge of the cylinder head, then apply four beads of sealant, 7.0 mm wide, to the camshaft end bearing cap (Nos 1 and 6) contact areas as shown **(see illustrations).**

18 Refit the camshaft bearing caps to their original locations, then insert the bearing cap bolts and progressively tighten them to the specified torque **(see illustration).**

19 If a new camshaft has been fitted, measure the endfloat using a dial gauge, and check that it is within the specified limits.

20 Fit the new oil seal with reference to Section 8.

21 Refit the brake vacuum pump with reference to Chapter 9.

22 Wipe clean the contact surfaces on the valve cover and cylinder head and then refit the valve cover as described in Section 4.

23 Fit a new timing belt as described in Section 6.

24 Fit the remaining components in reverse order to removal.

10 Cylinder head – removal, inspection and refitting

Note: *A new cylinder head gasket must be fitted and all cylinder head bolts must be renewed. Sealant for the valve cover will also be required.*

Note: *The cylinder head can be removed complete with the turbocharger, high pressure pump, fuel rail and injectors if necessary. This is a cost effective method if only the cylinder head gasket requires removal. An assistant will be require If this method Is adopted as the cylinder head Is a heavy Item. If the cylinder head requires machining for example it will be simpler to remove as many components as possible with the cylinder head in situ.*

Removal

1 Before starting work, allow the engine to cool for as long as possible, to ensure the fuel pressure in the high-pressure lines, and the fuel temperature, are at a minimum (refer to Chapter 4B).

2 Disconnect the battery negative lead (see *Disconnecting the battery* as described in Chapter 5A).

3 Jack up and support the front of the vehicle (see *jacking and vehicle support* in the reference section).

4 Remove the engine undertray and then drain the cooling system with reference to Chapter 1B.

5 With reference to Chapters 11 and 12 remove the wiper arms and the windscreen cowl panel.

6 Remove the catalytic convertor and (where fitted) the particulate filter at the manifold **(see illustration)** as described in Chapter 4A. Note, however, that the converter cannot be completely removed from the engine compartment, as the right-hand driveshaft is still in position; place or tie it to one side.

7 Unscrew the union nuts and remove the turbocharger oil return pipe from the cylinder block and turbocharger. To remove the turbocharger, unbolt the two support struts.

8 Unbolt and remove the rear engine mount – see Section 15.

9 Support the right-hand end of the sump on a suitable jack. Protect the sump by spreading the load with a suitable block of wood.

10 Remove the right-hand engine mount, the timing belt (Section 6) and, if necessary, the camshaft sprocket (Section 7).

11 Remove the inter cooler inlet and outlet pipes and then disconnect the oil breather pipes from the engine and air filter housing **(see illustration).**

12 Unclip and unbolt the sound proofing cover from the fuel rail and then unbolt

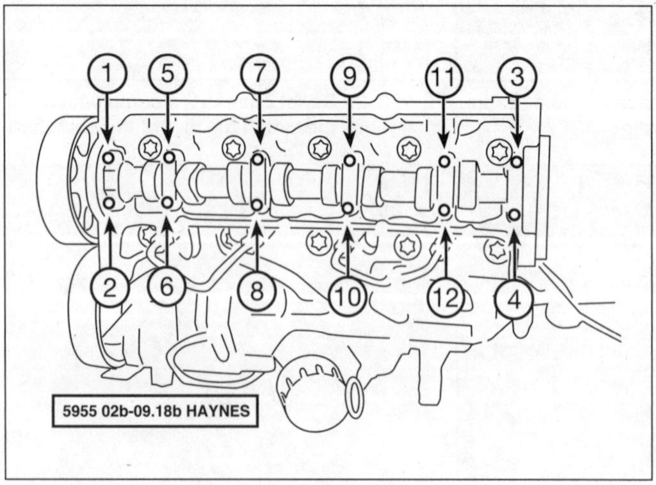

9.18b Tighten the bearing caps in the order shown

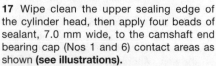

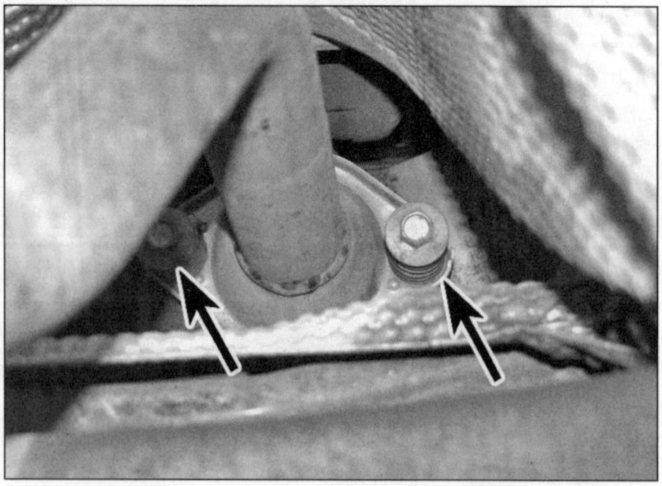

10.6 Disconnect the exhaust at the flexible mounting (arrowed)

10.11 Disconnect the breather pipe (arrowed)

10.13 Disconnect the wiring from the coolant temperature sensor

10.14 Disconnect the fuel pressure regulator wiring plug (arrowed)

and remove the pump high pressure pump protective cover - as described in Section 3.

13 Disconnect the wiring from the following sensors:

a) Air intake temperature (before turbocharger).
b) Air intake temperature (after turbocharger).
c) Air pressure (after turbocharger).
d) EGR valve control.
e) Air filter.
*f) Coolant temperature sensor **(see illustration).***
g) Camshaft position sensor

14 At the rear of the high-pressure injection pump, disconnect the wiring from the fuel temperature sensor and the fuel pressure regulator **(see illustration)**.

15 Disconnect the wiring from the four fuel injectors and glow plugs. If necessary, remove the glow plugs from the cylinder head.

16 Before removing the injectors, consider that Renault stipulate the high-pressure fuel lines must be renewed after removing them. If the removal of the cylinder head is just to renew the gasket, leave the injectors in position together with the fuel lines and high-pressure pump. If the cylinder head is to be stripped completely remove the fuel lines, fuel rail and fuel injectors as described in Chapter 4B.

17 Refer to Chapter 4B and observe the precautions necessary when disconnecting the high-pressure fuel injection pipes. In particular, all disconnected pipes and components in the following paragraphs must be plugged to prevent entry of dust and dirt into the fuel system, and all removed high-pressure pipes must be renewed after removal.

18 Loosen the union nuts and disconnect the four high-pressure pipes between the fuel rail and injectors **(see illustration)**.

19 Loosen the union nut and disconnect the fuel supply pipe from the fuel rail.

20 Disconnect the wiring from the fuel pressure sensor on the fuel rail **(see illustration)**.

21 Release the clip securing the fuel return pipe and wiring, and release the wiring from the lifting eye.

22 Remove the hoses and coolant temperature sensor from the left-hand end of the cylinder head **(see illustration)**.

23 Unbolt and remove the timing belt tensioner from the cylinder head **(see illustration)**.

24 Remove the upper bolt from the alternator, slacken the lower bolt and move the alternator away from the cylinder head

25 Unbolt and remove the inner timing cover from the cylinder block and head **(see illustration)**.

26 Remove the air filter hoses and then remove the air filter housing.

27 Release the injector fuel return pipes from the clips on the valve cover.

28 Unscrew the bolts and remove the valve cover from the top of the cylinder head.

29 Disconnect the quick-release vacuum pipe from the brake vacuum pump on the left-hand end of the cylinder head **(see illustration)**.

30 Unbolt the engine oil level dipstick tube from the cylinder head and remove it from the sump **(see illustration)**.

31 The cylinder head assembly complete with high-pressure pump and ancillaries is

10.18 Removing the high-pressure pipes

10.20 Disconnect the wiring plug (arrowed) from the fuel pressure sensor

10.22 Remove the coolant hoses (arrowed) from the thermostat housing

10.23 Removing the timing belt tensioner

10.25 Remove the inner timing cover

10.29 Disconnect the quick-release vacuum pipe from the brake vacuum pump

10.30 Unbolt and remove the engine oil level dipstick tube

10.33 Remove the cylinder head bolts

very heavy. If they are to be left attached, it is advisable to use a hoist and suitable lifting tackle connected to the lifting eyes to lift the cylinder head. Alternatively, before loosening the cylinder head bolts, remove the turbocharger, manifolds, and high-pressure pump from the cylinder head with reference to the relevant Sections of Chapter 4B.

32 Before removing the cylinder head, turn the crankshaft anti-clockwise (viewed from the timing belt end of the engine) by a quarter turn to position all four pistons half-way down their bores. The TDC pin can remain in the cylinder block if necessary, however, remember that it is in position and do not turn the crankshaft further anti-clockwise.

33 Progressively slacken the cylinder head bolts in the **reverse** sequence to that shown **(see illustration 10.43).** With all the bolts loose, remove them **(see illustration)**.

34 Lift the cylinder head upwards off the cylinder block. If it is stuck, tap it with a hammer and block of wood to release it. **Do not** try to turn the cylinder head (it is located by two dowels), nor attempt to prise it free using a screwdriver inserted between the block and head faces.

35 If necessary, remove the camshaft and tappets (Section 8).

Inspection

36 The mating faces of the cylinder head and block must be perfectly clean before refitting the head. Use a scraper to remove all traces of gasket and carbon, and also clean the tops of the pistons. Take particular care with the aluminium cylinder head, as the soft metal is damaged easily. Also, make sure that debris is not allowed to enter the oil and water channels – this is particularly important for the oil circuit, as carbon could block the oil supply to the camshaft or crankshaft bearings. Using adhesive tape and paper, seal the water, oil and bolt holes in the cylinder block. Clean the piston crowns in the same way.

37 Check the block and head for nicks, deep scratches and other damage. If slight, they may be removed carefully with a file. Machining of the cylinder head or cylinder block is not recommended by the manufacturers.

38 If warpage of the cylinder head is suspected, use a straight-edge to check it for distortion. Refer to Chapter 2C if necessary; if the warpage is more than the maximum, the cylinder head must be renewed, as regrinding is not allowed.

39 Clean out the cylinder head bolt holes in the block using a pipe cleaner, or a rag and screwdriver. Make sure that all oil is removed, otherwise there is a possibility of the block being cracked by hydraulic pressure when the bolts are tightened. Examine the bolt threads in the cylinder block for damage, and if necessary, use the correct size tap to chase out the threads. The cylinder head bolts must be renewed each time they are removed, and must not be oiled before being fitted.

Refitting

40 Where removed, refit the tappets, camshaft and camshaft sprocket with reference to Section 9 and 7. Turn the camshaft so that the sprocket is at its TDC position.

41 Ensure that the cylinder head locating dowels are fitted to the cylinder block, then fit the new gasket the right way round on the cylinder block **(see illustration)**.

42 Carefully lower the cylinder head onto the dowels and gasket, then insert the new bolts and hand-tighten. **Do not** oil the threads or heads of the new bolts.

43 Tighten the bolts in sequence, and in the stages given in the Specifications **(see illustration)**.

44 Turn the crankshaft clockwise by a quarter turn until the internal web contacts the TDC timing pin.

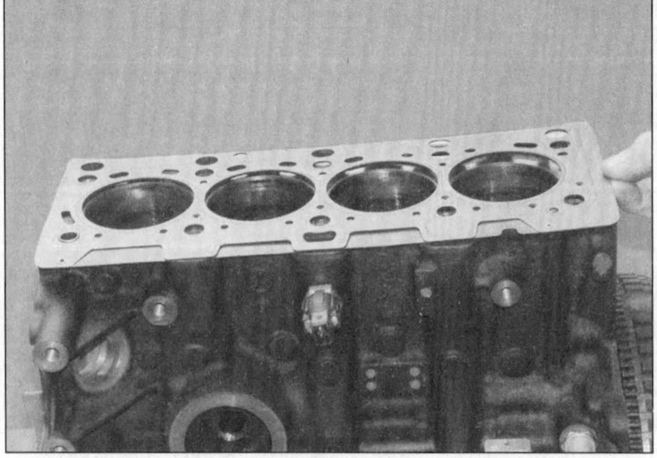

10.41 Locate the new gasket on the cylinder block

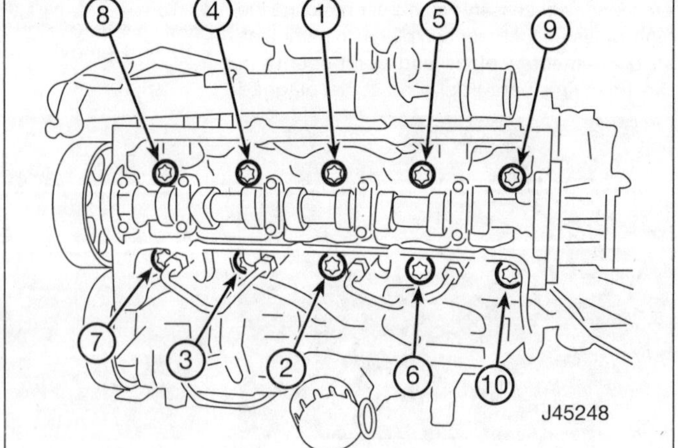

10.43 Cylinder head bolt tightening sequence

45 Refit the turbocharger, manifolds and injection pump to the cylinder head with reference to the relevant Sections of Chapter 4B.
46 Refit the air filter support bracket and tighten securely.
47 Reconnect the vacuum pipe to the brake vacuum pump.
48 Reconnect the wiring to the fuel pressure sensor on the fuel rail.
49 Reconnect the fuel supply pipe to the fuel rail and tighten the union nut.
50 Refit the four fuel injectors as described in Chapter 4B.
51 Refit the four high-pressure pipes to the fuel rail and injectors and tighten the union nuts to the specified torque.
52 Wipe clean the contact surfaces on the valve cover and cylinder head, then apply four beads of sealant, 2.0 mm wide, to the camshaft end bearing caps (Nos 1 and 6) and refit the cover with reference to Section 3. Secure the fuel return pipes in the clips on the valve cover and reconnect the crankcase ventilation hose.
53 Refit the air filter assembly and tighten the mounting bolt, then reconnect the air hose.
54 Refit the inner timing cover and tighten the mounting bolts.
55 Refit the auxiliary drivebelt tensioner and tighten the mounting bolt.
56 Locate the timing belt tensioner roller on the cylinder head and hand-tighten the securing nut at this stage.
57 Refit the turbocharger oil return pipe and tighten the union nuts.
58 Refit the turbocharger and reconnect the exhaust downpipe and catalytic converter with reference to Chapter 4B.
59 Refit the coolant temperature sensor and coolant hoses.
60 Secure the fuel return pipe and wiring with the clip.
61 Reconnect the wiring to the fuel temperature sensor and low-pressure flow adjuster on the rear of the high-pressure injection pump.
62 Reconnect the wiring to the air intake temperature sensors, air pressure sensor, EGR valve and air filter.
63 Refit the timing belt as described in Section 6.

11.08 Remove the oil level sensor

64 Reconnect the battery negative lead (refer to *Disconnecting the battery* in Chapter 5A).
65 Prime and bleed the fuel system as described in Chapter 4B.
66 Refill and bleed the cooling system as described in Chapter 1B.
67 Start the engine and run it up to temperature, checking constantly for fuel, oil and coolant leaks.

11 Sump – removal and refitting

Removal

1 Disconnect the battery negative lead (refer to *Disconnecting the battery* in Chapter 5A).
2 Jack up the front of the vehicle and support on axle stands (see *Jacking and vehicle support* in the reference section). Remove the engine undertray and both front wheels.
3 Drain the engine oil referring to Chapter 1B, then refit and tighten the drain plug using a new washer.
4 Remove the bolts from the driveshaft intermediate bearing housing – there is no need to remove the driveshaft.
5 Unbolt and remove the rear engine mounting/tie bar.
6 Remove the lower bolt from the alternator/AC compressor mounting bracket.
7 Remove the drain hose (from the injector rail) from the transmission and the sump.

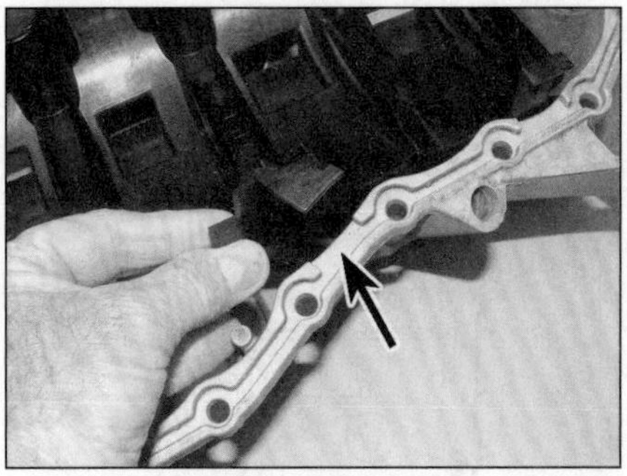

11.12 Make sure the tabs are located in the cut-outs when refitting the baffle plate

8 Disconnect the wiring plug from the oil level sensor and then remove the sensor **(see illustration)**.
9 Remove the 4 sump to transmission bolts and then remove the sump to block bolts.
10 If the sump can not be fully removed at this point (it will be fouling the oil pick up strainer) then (working through the gap between the sump and the block) slacken the oil pump mounting bolts sufficiently so that the sump can pass over the strainer.
11 Remove the sump and recover the gasket.

Refitting

12 Thoroughly clean the mating surfaces of the sump and cylinder block. Where removed, refit the baffle plate making sure that the tabs are correctly located in the cut-outs near the sump joint face **(see illustration)**.
13 Apply 2 drops 5 mm in diameter of Rhodorseal 5661 (or similar) sealant to the two points where the engine right-hand cover meets the cylinder block. Apply 12 mm long and 5 mm diameter beads of sealant to the angled areas on the right-hand cover and oil seal housing. Fit a new gasket on the sump. The gasket must be located over the baffle plate tabs **(see illustrations)**.
14 Partially fit the sump. If the oil pump mounting bolts were slackened then tighten them to the specified torque. Fit the sump and tighten the sump to transmission bolts

11.13a Apply sealant where the right-hand cover meets the cylinder block...

11.13b ...then locate a new gasket on the sump...

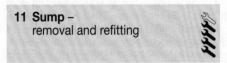

11.13c ...before refitting the sump

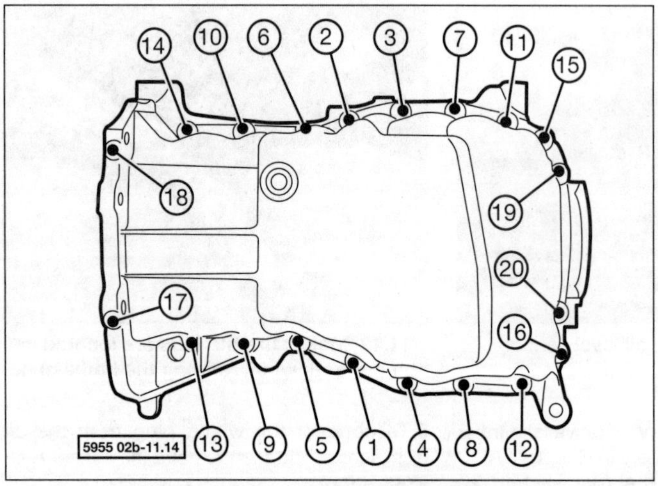

11.14 Sump bolt tightening sequence

12.3 Fitting a new oil seal to the right-hand cover

followed by the sump to block bolts. Tighten the bolts to the specified torque in the sequence shown **(see illustration)**.

15 Refit the remainder of the components in reverse order to removal.

16 Refill the engine with oil and then disconnect the crankshaft sensor to stop the engine from starting. Crank the engine over on the starter motor for several seconds until the engine oil warning light extinguishes. Refit the crankshaft sensor, sart the engine and check for oil leaks.

12 Oil pump and sprockets – removal, inspection and refitting

Removal

1 Remove the sump as described in Section 11.

2 Unscrew the two mounting bolts and withdraw the oil pump, tilting it to disengage its sprocket from the drive chain. If the two locating dowels are displaced, refit them in their locations.

3 To remove the drive chain, first remove the crankshaft sprocket as described in Section 7, then unbolt the engine right-hand cover from the cylinder block. Prise out the oil seal with a screwdriver, and discard it as a new one must be fitted on reassembly. If necessary, the new oil seal may be fitted with the right-hand cover on the bench **(see illustration)**.

4 Slide the oil pump drive sprocket and drive chain from the nose of the crankshaft **(see illustrations)**. Note that the drive sprocket is not keyed to the crankshaft, but relies on the pulley bolt being tightened correctly to clamp the sprocket. It is most important that the pulley bolt is correctly tightened otherwise there is the possibility of the oil pump not functioning properly.

5 Unhook the drive chain from the drive sprocket.

Inspection

6 Unscrew the retaining bolts and lift the pump cover over the driveshaft. Withdraw the idler gear and the drivegear/shaft. Mark the gears before removal, so that they can be refitted in their original position.

7 Extract the retaining clip and remove the oil pressure relief valve spring retainer, spring, spring seat and plunger.

8 Clean the components and carefully examine the gears, pump body and relief valve plunger for any signs of scoring or wear. Renew the complete pump assembly if excessive wear is evident (no spare parts are available).

9 If the components appear serviceable, measure the clearance between the pump body and the gears using feeler gauges. Also measure the gear endfloat and check the flatness of the end cover. If the clearances exceed the specified tolerances, the pump must be renewed. There should be no discernible wear or distortion of the cover.

10 If the pump is satisfactory, reassemble the components in the reverse order of removal. Fill the pump with oil, then refit the cover and tighten the bolts securely.

Refitting

11 Wipe clean the oil pump and cylinder block mating surfaces and check that the two locating dowels are fitted in the cylinder block.

12 Engage the drive chain with the drive sprocket, then slide the sprocket onto the nose of the crankshaft.

13 Fit a new gasket to the right-hand cover. Refit the engine right-hand cover, insert the bolts and tighten them to the specified torque. If a new oil seal has already been fitted, wrap tape around the nose of the crankshaft to protect the oil seal, and remove it on completion **(see illustrations)**.

14 Fit a new gasket to the closure plate and tighten the bolts to the specified torque.

15 Tilt the oil pump and engage the sprocket

12.4a Oil pump and mounting bolts

12.4b Removing the oil pump and drive chain

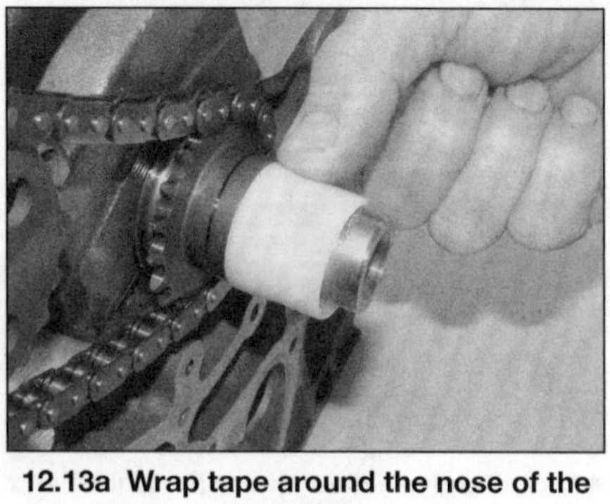

12.13a Wrap tape around the nose of the crankshaft...

with the drive chain, then position it on the dowels and insert the two mounting bolts. Tighten the bolts to the specified torque.
16 Refit the sump with reference to Section 11.

13 Crankshaft oil seals – renewal

Timing end cover oil seal

Note: *The new oil seal is extremely fragile and must only be handled by the protector.* ***Do not*** *touch the surface of the oil seal.*
1 Remove the crankshaft sprocket, as described in Section 7.
2 Note the fitted position of the old seal, then prise it out of the right-hand cover/housing using a screwdriver or suitable hooked instrument, taking care not to damage the surface of the crankshaft. Alternatively, the oil seal can be removed by drilling two small holes diagonally opposite each other and inserting self tapping screws in them. A pair of grips can then be used to pull out the oil seal, by pulling on each side in turn.
3 Inspect the seal rubbing surface on the crankshaft. If it is grooved or rough in the area where the old seal was fitted, the new seal should be fitted slightly less deeply, so that it rubs on an unworn part of the crankshaft surface.
4 Renault technicians use a tool (Mot. 1586) to fit the oil seal. The tool consists of a threaded rod, metal tube and nut, and a machined shoulder to locate the protector/guide on. The rod is screwed into the end of the crankshaft, and the protector/guide located on the shoulder. The metal tube is then fitted against the oil seal and the nut tightened to press the seal into the right-hand cover. If the Renault tool cannot be obtained, a similar tool can be made out of a threaded rod, metal tube, washer and nut.
5 Using a suitable solvent clean the oil seal housing and the crankshaft nose. Do not apply any lubricant – the seal is designed to be fitted dry. Press the oil seal squarely into position. Note that the Renault tool is designed to locate the seal at the original depth, however, if the crankshaft sealing surface is excessively worn, position it less deeply so that it locates on the unworn surface.
6 After fitting the oil seal, remove the protector/guide and tool.
7 Refit the crankshaft sprocket as described in Section 7.

Flywheel end oil seal

8 Remove the transmission as described in Chapter 7.
9 Remove the clutch assembly as described in Chapter 6.
10 Remove the flywheel as described in Section 14.
11 Renew the oil seal as described in paragraphs 2 to 6 inclusive **(see illustration)**.

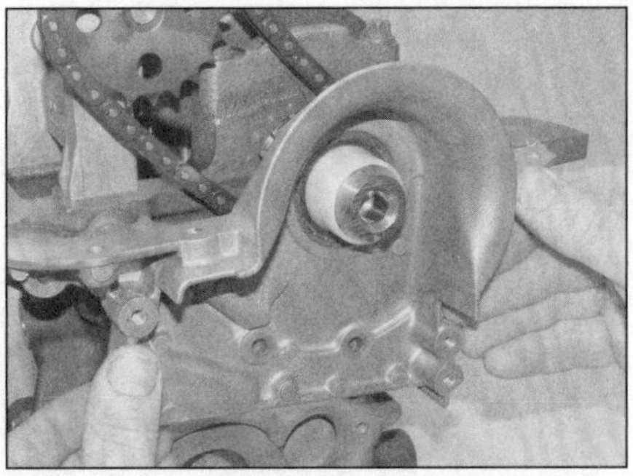

12.13b ...and fit the right-hand cover

12 Refit the flywheel with reference to Section 14 and then refit (or replace) the clutch assembly. Refit the transmission.

14 Flywheel – removal, inspection and refitting

Note: *New flywheel bolts must be used on refitting.*

Removal

1 Remove the transmission as described in Chapter 7.
2 Remove the clutch as described in Chapter 6.
3 The flywheel must now be held stationary while the securing bolts are loosened. To do this, locate a long bolt in one of the engine-to-gearbox mounting bolt holes and insert a wide-bladed screwdriver or length of bent metal bar in the starter ring gear or use a suitable locking tool **(see illustration)**.
4 Unscrew the securing bolts and withdraw the flywheel from the crankshaft. Note that the flywheel bolt holes are offset so that the flywheel can only be fitted in one position. Discard the old bolts as new ones must be used on refitting.

Inspection

5 Examine the flywheel for scoring of the clutch face and for wear or chipping of the ring gear teeth. If the clutch face is scored, the flywheel may be machined until flat, but renewal is preferable.

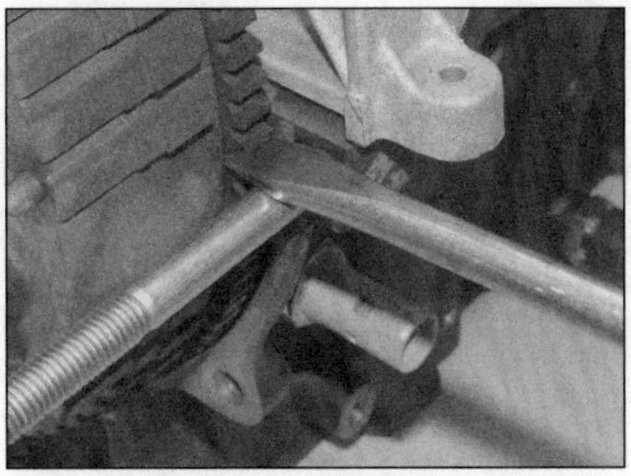

14.3 Hold the flywheel stationary using a screwdriver in the starter ring gear

13.11 Fitting a new oil seal to the flywheel end of the crankshaft

6 If the ring gear teeth are worn or damaged, the flywheel must be renewed.

Refitting

7 Clean the flywheel and crankshaft faces.
8 Locate the flywheel on the crankshaft and insert the new bolts. Tighten the new bolts in a diagonal sequence to the specified torque. Hold the flywheel stationary as during removal **(see illustration). Do not** oil the new bolt threads as they are supplied with locking compound.
9 Refit (or replace) the clutch as described in Chapter 6.
10 Refit the manual transmission with reference to Chapter 7.

15 Engine mountings – renewal

Inspection

1 Apply the handbrake, then jack up the front of the car and support it on axle stands (see *Jacking and vehicle support*). Where fitted, remove the engine compartment undertray.
2 Visually inspect the rubber pads on the right and left-hand engine mountings and the rear torque link, for signs of cracking and deterioration. Careful use of a lever will help to determine the condition of the rubber pads. Check that all the mounting bolts are securely tightened; use a torque wrench to check if possible. If there is excessive movement, or if the rubber has deteriorated, the mounting should be renewed.

14.8 Fit new flywheel bolts

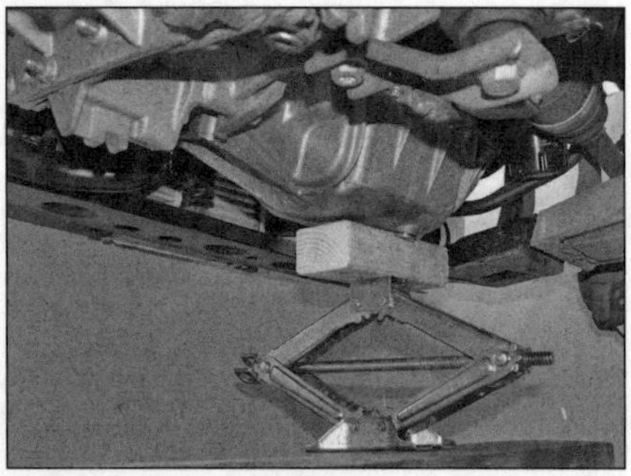

15.5 Support the engine with a suitable jack

15.7a Remove the bolts (arrowed)...

15.7b ...and remove the tie bar

Renewal

Right-hand mounting

3 Jack up and support the front of the vehicle (see *Jacking and vehicle support* in the reference section).

4 Remove then engine undertray and then in order to allow the engine to be moved easily remove the rear mounting (torque link) as described below.

5 Using a jack and a suitable block of wood to spread the load under the sump **(see illustration)** *raise the right-hand end of the engine slightly.*

6 Unclip or disconnect the fuel lines from the inner wing. Immediately seal the openings.

7 Models fitted with K9K-836 and 837 engines have an additional tie bar fitted to the upper mounting. Where fitted unbolt and remove the tie bar **(see illustrations)**.

8 Mark the position of the mounting on the inner wing.

9 Unscrew the bolts and remove the mounting from the engine and the body **(see illustration)**.

10 Locate the new mounting/bracket on the body, insert the bolts and tighten to the specified torque.

11 Lower the engine making sure that the bracket locates on the body mounting correctly. Remove the trolley jack.

Left-hand mounting

12 Remove the battery and battery box as described in Chapter 5A.

13 With the front of the car supported on axle stands, remove the left-hand roadwheel.

14 Using a jack and block of wood, support the weight of the transmission/engine.

15 Unscrew the centre bolt (or nut on some models) securing the lower mounting to the upper/body bracket **(see illustration)** then slightly lower the transmission/engine. If necessary, release the stud from the upper bracket using a soft-faced mallet.

16 Unscrew the bolts from the chassis leg and remove the upper bracket from the body **(see illustrations)**.

17 Unscrew the bolts and remove the lower mounting/bracket from the transmission **(see illustration)**.

18 Locate the new mounting/bracket on the transmission, insert the bolts and tighten to the specified torque.

19 Refit the upper bracket to the body, insert the bolts and tighten to the specified torque.

20 Raise the transmission/engine making sure that the mounting stud enters the upper bracket correctly. Refit the centre nut and tighten to the specified torque. Remove the hoist or trolley jack.

21 Refit the battery with reference to Chapter 5A.

22 Refit the roadwheel and lower the car to the ground.

Rear torque link

23 With the car supported on axle stands, unscrew the bolts securing the rear link to the subframe **(see illustration)**.

24 Unbolt the tie bar from the engine/transmission. Note some models have an additional small bracket fitted – where fitted remove the bracket. Withdraw the link from under the car **(see illustration)**.

15.9 Remove the mounting

15.15 Remove the centre bolt (arrowed)

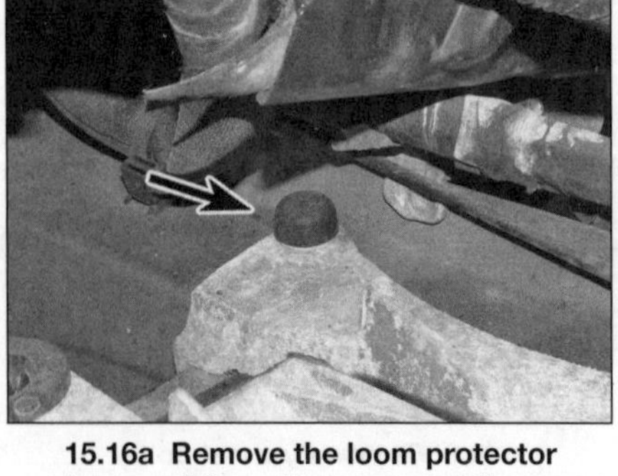

15.16a Remove the loom protector (arrowed) from the rear mounting...

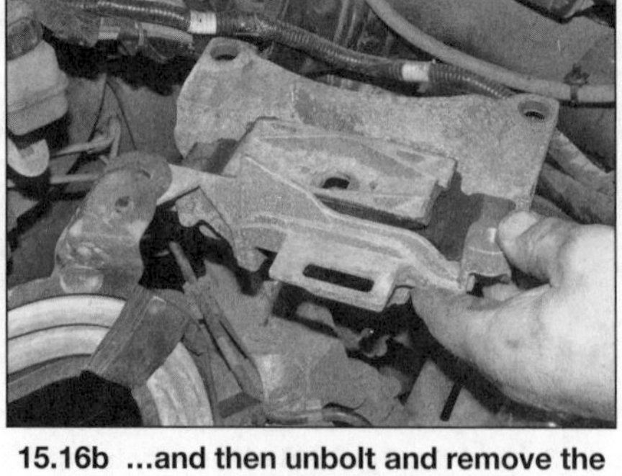

15.16b ...and then unbolt and remove the mounting

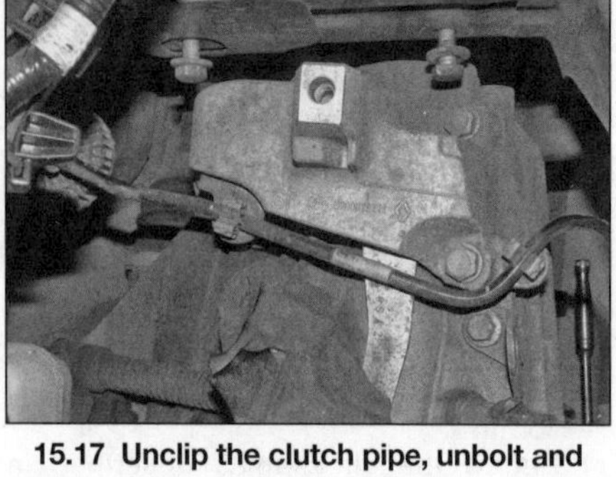

15.17 Unclip the clutch pipe, unbolt and remove the mounting from the transmission

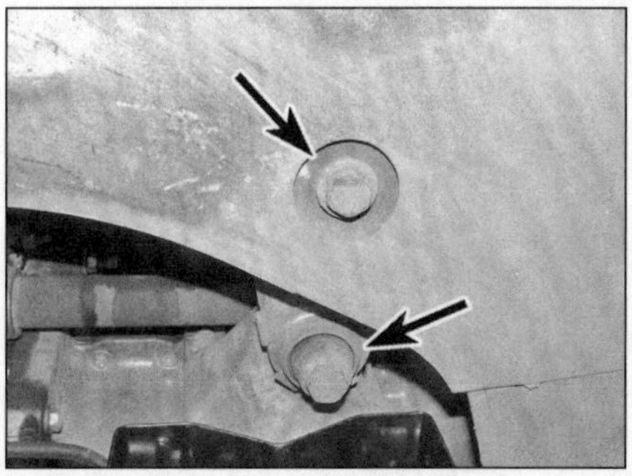

15.23 The rear torque link mounting bolts (arrowed)

15.24 Removing the engine rear torque link

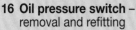

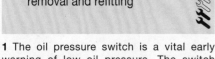

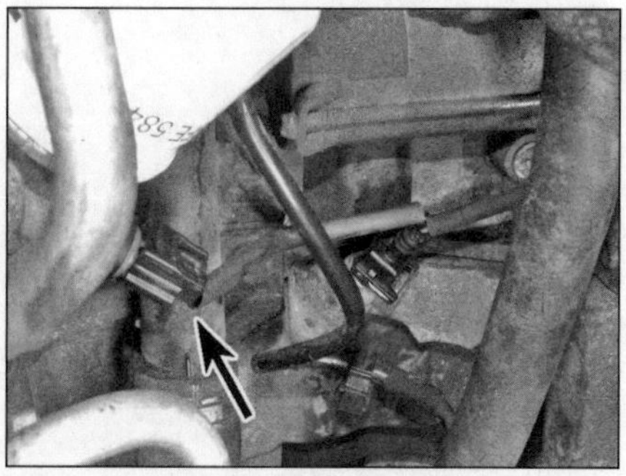

16.6 Disconnect the wiring plug from the oil pressure warning switch

25 Refitting is a reversal of the removal procedure, but before fully tightening the bolts attempt to rock the engine/transmission assembly in order to settle the mountings. Tighten the mounting bolts to the specified torque.

16 Oil pressure switch – removal and refitting

1 The oil pressure switch is a vital early warning of low oil pressure. The switch operates the oil warning light on the instrument panel – the light should come on with the ignition, and go out almost immediately when the engine starts.

2 If the light does not come on, there could be a fault on the instrument panel, the switch wiring, or the switch itself. If the light does not go out, low oil level, worn oil pump (or sump pick-up blocked), blocked oil filter, or worn main bearings could be to blame – or again, the switch may be faulty.

3 If the light comes on while driving, the best advice is to turn the engine off immediately, and not to drive the car until the problem has been investigated – ignoring the light could mean expensive engine damage.

Removal

4 The oil pressure switch is located on the front face of the engine, next to the oil filter.

5 Jack up the front of the car, and support it on axle stands (see *Jacking and vehicle support*) – to improve access, remove the oil filter, referring to Chapter 1B if necessary.

6 Disconnect the wiring plug from the switch **(see illustration)**.

7 Unscrew the switch from the block, and remove it together with its sealing washer. There should only be a very slight loss of oil when this is done.

Inspection

8 Examine the switch for signs of cracking or splits. If the top part of the switch is loose, this is an early indication of impending failure.

9 Check that the wiring terminals at the switch are not loose, then trace the wire from the switch connector until it enters the main loom – any wiring defects will give rise to apparent oil pressure problems.

Refitting

10 Refitting is the reverse of the removal procedure, noting the following points:

a) *Clean the switch threads before fitting. Tighten the switch securely.*
b) *Reconnect the switch connector, making sure it clicks home properly. Ensure that the wiring is routed away from any hot or moving parts.*
c) *Lower the car to the ground, then check the engine oil level and top-up if necessary (see 'Weekly checks').*
d) *Check for signs of oil leaks once the engine has been restarted and warmed-up to normal operating temperature.*

Chapter 2 Part C:
Engine removal and overhaul procedures

Contents

	Section number
Crankshaft – inspection	14
Crankshaft – refitting	17
Crankshaft – removal	11
Cylinder block/crankcase – cleaning and inspection	12
Cylinder head – dismantling	7
Cylinder head – reassembly	9
Cylinder head and valves – cleaning and inspection	8
Engine – initial start-up after overhaul	19
Engine (diesel models) – removal and refitting	5
Engine (petrol models) – removal and refitting	4
Engine overhaul – dismantling sequence	6
Engine overhaul – general information	2
Engine overhaul – reassembly sequence	16
Engine removal – methods and precautions	3
General information	1
Main and big-end bearings – inspection	15
Piston/connecting rod assemblies – inspection	13
Piston/connecting rod assemblies – refitting	18
Piston/connecting rod assemblies – removal	10

Degrees of difficulty

Easy, suitable for novice with little experience	**Fairly easy,** suitable for beginner with some experience	**Fairly difficult,** suitable for competent DIY mechanic	**Difficult,** suitable for experienced DIY mechanic	**Very difficult,** suitable for expert DIY or professional

Specifications

General

Engine codes:	
1.6 litre DOHC petrol engine	K4M
1.5 litre SOHC diesel engine	K9K

Valves

Valve spring free length:	
K4M engine	51.83 mm
K9K engine	43.31 mm

Cylinder head

Height:	
K4M engine	137.0 mm
K9K engine	127.0 mm
Maximum acceptable gasket face distortion	0.05mm
Refinishing limit	No refinishing permitted
Valve protrusion/depth in relation to head surface	0.00 ± 0.07 mm

Cylinder block

Bore diameter:	
K4M engines:	
Class A	79.500 to 79.510mm
Class B	79.510 to 79.520 mm
Class C	79.520 to 79.530 mm
K9K engine - nominal	76.000 mm

Pistons and piston rings

Piston diameter:	
K4M engine (measured 42.0 mm from crown):	
Class A	79.475 ± 0.005mm
Class B	79.485 ± 0.005 mm
Class C	79.495 ± 0.005 mm
K9K engine (measured 56.0 mm from crown)	75.94 ± 0.007 mm
Piston ring end gaps (installed):	
K4M engine:	
Top compression	0.15 to 0.35 mm
Second compression	0.40 to 0.60 mm
Oil control (2 rails and expander)	0.20 to 0.90 mm
K9K engine:	
Top compression	0.2 to 0.35 mm
Second compression	0.7 to 0.9 mm
Oil control (2 rails and expander)	0.25 to 0.5 mm
Ring gap spacing (all engines)	120°
Piston protrusion (K9K engine)	0.192 ± 0.093 mm

Crankshaft

Main bearing journal diameter:	
K4M and K9K engines:	
Standard	47.990 to 47.997 mm
1st undersize	47.997 to 48.003 mm
2nd undersize	48.003 to 48.010 mm
Crankpin (big-end) journal diameter:	
K4M and K9K engines:	
Standard	43.97 ± 0.01 mm
Crankshaft endfloat:	
K4M and K9K engines:	
New	0.045 to 0.252 mm
Maximum	0.852 mm

Torque wrench settings

Refer to Parts A and B of this Chapter.

1 General information

How to use this Chapter

This Part of Chapter 2 is devoted to engine/transmission removal and refitting, to those repair procedures requiring the removal of the engine/transmission from the car, and to the overhaul of engine components. It includes only the Specifications relevant to those procedures. Refer to Parts A or B for additional Specifications, and for all torque wrench settings.

General information

The information ranges from advice concerning preparation for an overhaul and the purchase of new parts, to detailed step-by-step procedures covering removal and installation of internal engine components and the inspection of parts.

The following Sections have been written based on the assumption that the engine has been removed from the car. For information concerning in-car engine repair, as well as removal and installation of the external components necessary for the overhaul, see Parts A or B this Chapter.

When overhauling the engine, it is essential to establish first exactly what replacement parts are available. At the time of writing, very few under- or oversized components are available for engine reconditioning (the exception being for the diesel engine). In many cases, it would appear that the easiest and most economically-sensible course of action is to replace a worn or damaged engine with an exchange unit.

2 Engine overhaul – general information

It is not always easy to determine when, or if, an engine should be completely overhauled, as a number of factors must be considered.

High mileage is not necessarily an indication that an overhaul is needed, while low mileage does not preclude the need for an overhaul. Frequency of servicing is probably the most important consideration. An engine which has had regular and frequent oil and filter changes, as well as other required maintenance, will most likely give many thousands of miles of reliable service. Conversely, a neglected engine may require an overhaul very early in its life.

Excessive oil consumption is an indication that piston rings, valve stem oil seals and/or valves and valve guides are in need of attention. Make sure that oil leaks are not responsible before deciding that the rings and/or guides are bad. Perform a cylinder compression check to determine the extent of the work required.

Check the oil pressure with a gauge fitted in place of the oil pressure warning light switch, and compare it with the value given in the Specifications. If it is extremely low, the main and big-end bearings and/or the oil pump are probably worn out.

Loss of power, rough running, knocking or metallic engine noises, excessive valve gear noise and high fuel consumption may also point to the need for an overhaul, especially if they are all present at the same time. If a complete tune-up does not remedy the situation, major mechanical work is the only solution.

An engine overhaul involves restoring all internal parts to the specification of a new engine. **Note:** *Always check first what parts are available before planning any overhaul operation – refer to Section 1. Manufacturer main dealers, or a good engine reconditioning specialist/automotive parts supplier, may be able to suggest alternatives which will enable you to overcome the lack of parts.*

During an overhaul, it is usual to renew the piston rings, and to rebore and/or hone the cylinder bores; where the rebore is done by an automotive machine shop, new oversize pistons and rings will also be installed – all these operations, of course, assume the availability of suitable parts. The main and big-end bearings are generally renewed and, if necessary, the crankshaft may be reground to restore the journals.

Generally, the valves are serviced as well during an overhaul, since they're usually in less-than-perfect condition at this point. While the engine is being overhauled, other components, such as the starter and alternator, can be renewed as well, or rebuilt, if the necessary parts can be found. The end result should be an as-new engine that will give many trouble-free miles.

Critical cooling system components such as the hoses, drivebelt, thermostat and coolant pump MUST be renewed when an engine is overhauled. The radiator should be checked carefully, to ensure that it isn't clogged or leaking (see Chapter 3). Also, as a general rule, the oil pump should be renewed when an engine is rebuilt.

Before beginning the engine overhaul, read through the entire procedure to familiarise yourself with the scope and requirements of the job. Overhauling an engine isn't difficult, but it is time-consuming. Plan on the car being off the road for a minimum of two weeks, especially if parts must be taken to an automotive machine shop for repair or reconditioning. Check on availability of parts, and make sure that any necessary special tools and equipment are obtained in advance.

Most work can be done with typical hand tools, although a number of precision measuring tools are required for inspecting parts to determine if they must be renewed. Often, an automotive machine shop will handle the inspection of parts, and will offer advice concerning reconditioning and renewal.

Always wait until the engine has been completely dismantled, and all components, especially the cylinder block/crankcase, have been inspected, before deciding what service and repair operations must be performed by an automotive machine shop. Since the block's condition will be the major factor to consider when determining whether to overhaul the original engine or buy a rebuilt one, never purchase parts or have machine work done on other components until the cylinder block/crankcase has been thoroughly inspected.

As a general rule, time is the primary cost of an overhaul, so it doesn't pay to install worn or sub-standard parts.

As a final note, to ensure maximum life and minimum trouble from a rebuilt engine, everything must be assembled with care, in a spotlessly-clean environment.

3 Engine removal – methods and precautions

If you have decided that an engine must be removed for overhaul or major repair work, several preliminary steps should be taken.

Locating a suitable place to work is extremely important. Adequate work space, with storage space for the car, will be needed. If a garage is not available, at the very least a flat, level, clean work surface is required.

Cleaning the engine compartment and engine before beginning the removal procedure will help keep tools clean and organised.

The engine can be removed complete with the transmission by unbolting the front-end components (bumper, radiator, etc) and lifting it out forwards. An engine hoist will be necessary; make sure the equipment is rated in excess of the combined weight of the engine and transmission. Safety is of primary importance, considering the potential hazards involved in removing the engine/transmission from the car.

If this is the first time you have removed an engine, a helper should ideally be available. Advice and aid from someone more experienced would also be useful. There are many instances when one person cannot simultaneously perform all of the operations required when removing the engine/ transmission from the car.

Plan the operation ahead of time. Arrange for, or obtain, all of the tools and equipment you'll need prior to beginning the job. Some of the equipment necessary to perform engine/ transmission removal and installation safely and with relative ease, and which may have to be hired or borrowed, includes (in addition to the engine hoist) a heavy-duty trolley jack, a strong pair of axle stands, some wooden blocks, and an engine dolly (a low, wheeled platform capable of taking the weight of the engine/transmission, so that it can be moved easily when on the ground). A complete set of spanners and sockets (as described in the Reference section of this manual) will obviously be needed, together with plenty of rags and cleaning solvent for mopping-up spilled oil, coolant and fuel. If the hoist is to be hired, make sure that you arrange for it in advance, and perform all of the operations possible without it beforehand. This will save you money and time.

Plan for the car to be out of use for quite a while. A machine shop will be required to perform some of the work which the home mechanic can't accomplish without special equipment. These establishments often have a busy schedule, so it would be a good idea to consult them before removing the engine, to accurately estimate the amount of time required to rebuild or repair components that may need work.

Always be extremely careful when removing and installing the engine/transmission. Serious injury can result from careless actions. By planning ahead and taking your time, the job (although a major task) can be accomplished successfully.

4.1 Unbolt and disconnect the distribution panel

4 Engine (petrol models) – removal and refitting

Note: *Read through the entire Section, as well as reading the advice in the preceding Section, before beginning this procedure. In this procedure, the engine and transmission are removed as a unit and lifted out of the engine bay. If preferred, the transmission can be removed from the engine first (as described in Chapter 7) – this leaves the engine free to be lifted out on its own.*

Note: *If the services of a mobile air conditioning specialist are not available have the AC system drained by a suitably equipped garage before starting work.*

Removal

1 Remove the battery and battery tray as described in Chapter 5A. Disconnect the wiring plugs from the distribution panel at the rear of the battery tray **(see illustration)**.

2 Though not essential, access to the engine will be improved (particularly for attaching the engine hoist) by removing the bonnet as described in Chapter 11.

3 Jack up the front of the car, and support it on axle stands (see *Jacking and vehicle support*).

4 Remove the engine undertray, then drain the cooling system with reference to Chapter 1A. If the engine is to be dismantled, drain the engine oil also.

5 As part of the removal procedure, the driveshafts must be disconnected from the transmission, which will result in significant loss of oil/fluid. To avoid this drain the transmission first, as described in Chapter 7 **(see illustration)**.

6 On all models the refrigerant circuit should be evacuated by a garage equipped with suitable AC recovery equipment. Mobile specialists also provide this service.

7 Remove both front roadwheels, then remove both wheel arch liners (see Chapter 11).

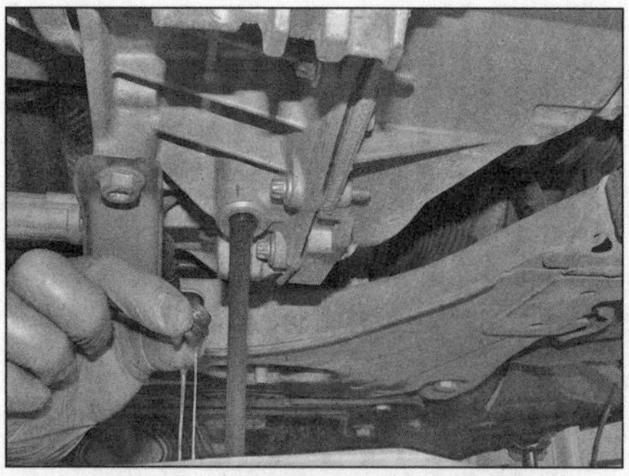
4.5 Drain the transmission fluid

4.8 Remove the bolts (arrowed)

4.9a Remove the air deflector

4.9b Remove the front bumper reinforcement

4.13 Preparing to remove the complete front panel

4.17 Disconnect the fuel supply pipe from the fuel rail

8 Remove the front bumper cover as described in Chapter 11. Remove the headlight support panels **(see illustration)**.

9 Unclip and remove the air deflectors from the radiator and then remove the bumper reinforcement panel **(see illustrations)**.

10 If working alone, disconnect the refrigerant lines from the condenser and then disconnect the coolant hoses from the radiator.

11 Unclip and then remove the condenser (as described in Chapter 3). Seal the refrigerant pipe and the condenser openings immediately.

12 Remove the radiator as described in Chapter 3.

13 Release the wiring loom from the cooling fan and from the top of the front panel. Disconnect the bonnet release cable and then unbolt the complete front panel assembly. If an assistant is available it is possible to remove the front panel with the radiator and condenser installed **(see illustration)**.

14 With the front panel removed access to many of the components is considerably simpler.

15 Remove the air cleaner (and if not already done, the engine ECU) as described in Chapter 4A.

16 Unbolt the fusebox and switching unit from the left-hand inner wing and then disconnect the wiring plugs from both units.

17 Disconnect the fuel supply pipe from the fuel rail, and cap both open connections, to prevent fuel loss and dirt entry **(see illustration)**.

18 Disconnect the brake servo vacuum hose from the inlet manifold and the vapour hose from the throttle body.

19 Disconnect the coolant hoses from the thermostat housing, the front of the engine and the bulkhead.

20 Disconnect the compressor wiring plug and then release the loom. Remove the refrigerant pipes from the compressor. Remove them completely or secure them to one side. Seal the openings in the compressor and the refrigerant pipes.

21 With reference to Chapter 7, disconnect the gearchange control cables from the transmission.

22 Disconnect the clutch hydraulic pipe at the transmission **(see illustrations)** referring to Chapter 6 if necessary. Plug the pipes to reduce fluid loss, and to prevent dirt entry.

23 Unbolt and remove the earth connections from the transmission.

24 Remove the driveshafts as described in Chapter 8.

25 Trace the wiring from the exhaust oxygen sensors to their connector plugs, and disconnect them.

26 Disconnect the exhaust downpipe from the manifold as described in Chapter 4A. Detach the front mountings and lower the exhaust.

27 Unbolt and remove the engine rear

4.22a Disconnect the clutch fluid pipe by removing the clip (arrowed)...

4.22b ...and disconnect the reversing light switch

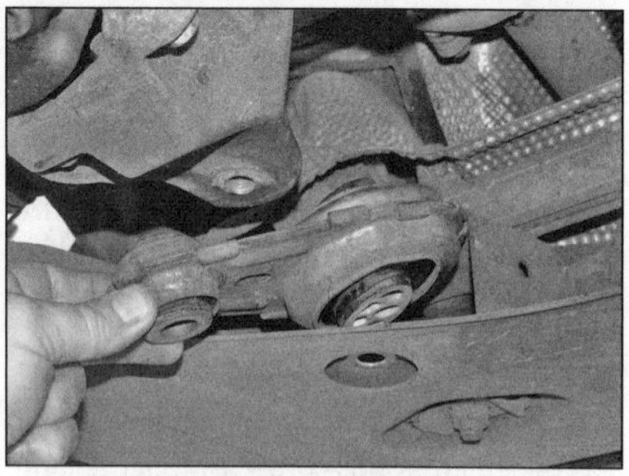
4.27 Remove the rear engine mount/ steady bar

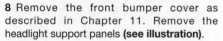

mounting as described in Chapter 2A **(see illustration)**.

28 Make a final check round the engine and transmission, to make sure nothing (apart from the left- and right-hand mountings) remains attached or in the way which will prevent it from being lifted out.

29 Securely attach the engine/transmission unit to a suitable engine crane or hoist, and raise it so that the weight is just taken off the two remaining engine mountings. It is helpful at this stage to have an assistant available, either to work the crane or to guide the engine out.

30 Referring to Chapter 2A, unbolt the left and right-hand mountings from the body.

31 With the help of an assistant, lift the engine, and guide it out through the front of the car. When clear of the car, lower it to the ground. Be prepared to steady the engine when it touches down, to stop it toppling over.

Separation

32 To separate the transmission from the engine, first remove the starter motor with reference to Chapter 5A.

33 Progressively unscrew and remove the transmission-to-engine bolts, noting where each one goes, and the location of any brackets attached, for guidance when refitting.

34 With the help of an assistant, withdraw the transmission directly from the engine, making sure that its weight is not allowed to bear on the clutch friction disc. Note that there are two locating dowels used.

Refitting

35 Refitting is a reversal of removal, noting the following additional points:

a) *Make sure that all mating faces are clean, and use new gaskets where necessary.*

b) *Tighten all nuts and bolts to the specified torque setting, where given.*

c) *If the transmission was removed, refit it to the engine.*

d) *Delay fully tightening the engine left- and right-hand mountings until the engine has settled into place.*

e) *Fit new circlips to the grooves in the inner end of each driveshaft CV joint, and ensure that they fully engage as they are fitted into the transmission.*

f) *Check and if necessary adjust the transmission cables as described in Chapter 7.*

g) *Refill or top-up the transmission oil with reference to Chapter 1A.*

h) *Top-up and bleed the clutch hydraulic system as described in Chapter 6.*

i) *Refill the cooling system as described in Chapter 1A.*

j) *Fit new seals to all the air conditioning. Lubricate the seals with compressor oil. If the system has been left open to atmosphere for any length of time the receiver/drier should be replaced. On completion, have the system recharged by a specialist or a Renault dealer.*

5 Engine (diesel models) – removal and refitting

Note: *Read through the entire Section, as well as reading the advice in the preceding Section, before beginning this procedure. In this procedure, the engine and transmission are removed as a unit and lifted out of the engine bay. If preferred, the transmission can be removed from the engine first (as described in Chapter 7) – this leaves the engine free to be lifted out on its own.*

Note: *If the services of a mobile air conditioning specialist are not available have the AC system drained by a suitably equipped garage before starting work.*

Removal

1 Remove the battery and battery tray as described in Chapter 5A.

2 Though not essential, access to the engine will be improved (particularly for attaching the engine hoist) by removing the bonnet as described in Chapter 11.

3 Jack up the front of the car, and support it on axle stands (see *Jacking and vehicle support*).

4 Remove the engine undertray, then drain the cooling system with reference to Chapter 1B. If the engine is to be dismantled, drain the engine oil also.

5 As part of the removal procedure, the driveshafts must be disconnected from the transmission, which will result in significant loss of oil/fluid. To avoid this, drain the transmission first, as described in Chapter 7.

6 The refrigerant circuit should be evacuated by a garage equipped with suitable AC recovery equipment. Mobile specialists also provide this service.

7 Remove both front roadwheels, then remove both wheel arch liners (see Chapter 11).

8 Remove the front bumper cover as described in Chapter 11. Remove the headlight support panels **(see illustration 4.8)**.

9 Unclip and remove the air deflectors from the radiator and then remove the bumper reinforcement panel **(see illustrations 4.9a and 4.9b)**.

10 If working alone, disconnect the refrigerant lines from the condenser and then disconnect the coolant hoses from the radiator.

11 Unclip and then remove the condenser (as described in Chapter 3). Seal the refrigerant pipe and the condenser openings immediately.

12 Remove the intercooler (as described in Chapter 4B) and then remove the radiator as described in Chapter 3.

13 Release the wiring loom from the cooling fan and from the top of the front panel. Disconnect the bonnet release cable and then unbolt the complete front panel assembly. If an assistant is available it is possible to remove the front panel with the radiator, intercooler and condenser installed.

5.18 Disconnect the vacuum hoses

14 With the front panel removed access to many of the components is considerably simpler.

15 Remove the air cleaner (and if not already done, the engine ECU) as described in Chapter 4A.

16 Unbolt the fusebox and switching unit from the left-hand inner wing and then disconnect the wiring plugs from both units.

17 Disconnect the fuel supply pipe from the fuel pump and cap both open connections, to prevent fuel loss and dirt entry.

18 Disconnect the brake servo vacuum hose from the vacuum pump **(see illustration)** and then disconnect the air inlet duct from the turbocharger – seal the opening in the turbocharger with a suitable rag.

19 Disconnect the coolant hoses from the thermostat housing, the front of the engine and the bulkhead.

20 Disconnect the compressor wiring plug and then release the loom. Remove the refrigerant pipes from the compressor. Remove them completely or secure them to one side. Seal the openings in the compressor and the refrigerant pipes.

21 With reference to Chapter 7, disconnect the gearchange control cables from the transmission.

22 Disconnect the clutch hydraulic pipe at the transmission **(see illustrations 4.22a and 4.22b)** referring to Chapter 6 if necessary. Plug the pipes to reduce fluid loss, and to prevent dirt entry.

23 Disconnect the wiring plug from the glow plug controller and then unbolt and remove the earth connections from the transmission.

24 Remove the driveshafts as described in Chapter 8.

25 Disconnect the wiring plug from the diesel fuel heater **(see illustration)** and then unclip and remove the wiring loom

26 Disconnect the exhaust downpipe from the manifold as described in Chapter 4A. Detach the front mountings and lower the exhaust.

27 Unbolt and remove the engine rear mounting as described in Chapter 2A **(see illustration 4.27)**.

28 Make a final check round the engine and transmission, to make sure nothing (apart from the left- and right-hand mountings) remains attached or in the way which will prevent it from being lifted out.

5.25 Disconnect the wiring plug

5.30 Removing the upper engine mount/ steady bar

29 Securely attach the engine/transmission unit to a suitable engine crane or hoist, and raise it so that the weight is just taken off the two remaining engine mountings. It is helpful at this stage to have an assistant available, either to work the crane or to guide the engine out.

30 Referring to Chapter 2A, unbolt the left and right-hand mountings from the body **(see illustration)**.

31 With the help of an assistant, lift the engine, and guide it out through the front of the car. When clear of the car, lower it to the ground. Be prepared to steady the engine when it touches down, to stop it toppling over.

Separation

32 To separate the transmission from the engine, first remove the starter motor with reference to Chapter 5A.

33 Progressively unscrew and remove the transmission-to-engine bolts, noting where each one goes, and the location of any brackets attached, for guidance when refitting.

34 With the help of an assistant, withdraw the transmission directly from the engine, making sure that its weight is not allowed to bear on the clutch friction disc. Note that there are two locating dowels used.

Refitting

35 Refitting is a reversal of removal, noting the following additional points:

a) *Make sure that all mating faces are clean, and use new gaskets where necessary.*
b) *Tighten all nuts and bolts to the specified torque setting, where given.*
c) *If the transmission was removed, refit it to the engine.*
d) *Delay fully tightening the engine left- and right-hand mountings until the engine has settled into place.*
e) *Fit new circlips to the grooves in the inner end of each driveshaft CV joint, and ensure that they fully engage as they are fitted into the transmission.*
f) *Check and if necessary adjust the transmission cables as described in Chapter 7.*
g) *Refill or top-up the transmission oil with reference to Chapter 1A.*
h) *Top-up and bleed the clutch hydraulic system as described in Chapter 6.*
i) *Refill the cooling system as described in Chapter 1A.*
j) *Fit new seals to all the air conditioning. Lubricate the seals with compressor oil. If the system has been left open to atmosphere for any length of time the receiver/drier should be replaced. On completion, have the system recharged by a specialist or a Renault dealer.*

6 Engine overhaul – dismantling sequence

1 It is much easier to dismantle and work on the engine if it is mounted on a portable engine stand. These stands can often be hired from a tool hire shop. Before the engine is mounted on a stand, the flywheel should be removed (Part A or B of this Chapter) so that the stand bolts can be tightened into the end of the cylinder block/crankcase.

2 If a stand is not available, it is possible to dismantle the engine with it mounted on blocks, on a sturdy workbench or on the floor. Be extra careful not to tip or drop the engine when working without a stand.

3 If you are going to obtain a reconditioned engine, all external components must be removed first, to be transferred to the new engine (just as they will if you are doing a complete engine overhaul yourself). **Note:** *When removing the external components from the engine, pay close attention to details that may be helpful or important during refitting. Note the fitted position of gaskets, seals, spacers, pins, washers, bolts and other small items. These external components include the following* ***(see illustrations):***

a) *Alternator, air conditioning compressor and mounting bracket (Chapter 5A).*
b) *Coolant hoses.*
c) *Spark plugs or glow plugs (Chapter 1A or 5B).*
d) *Fuel system components (Chapter 4A or 4B).*
e) *Brake vacuum pump – diesel models (Chapter 9).*
f) *Thermostat and housing (Chapter 3).*
g) *Dipstick and tube, where applicable.*
h) *All electrical switches and sensors, and the related wiring harness.*
i) *Intake and exhaust manifolds (Chapter 4A or 4B).*

6.3a Remove the alternator and compressor mounting bracket

6.3b Pull the pipe from the coolant pump inlet

6.3c Remove the thermostat housing

6.3d Unbolt the oil cooler cover...

6.3e ...disconnect the hoses...

6.3f ...unscrew the special bolt...

6.3g ...and remove the oil cooler

j) Oil filter (Chapter 1A or 1B) and oil cooler, where applicable.
k) Engine/transmission mounting brackets (Chapter 2A or 2B).
l) Flywheel (Chapter 2A or 2B).

4 If you are obtaining a 'short' engine (which consists of the engine cylinder block/crankcase, crankshaft, pistons and connecting rods all assembled), then the cylinder head, sump, oil pump and timing belt will have to be removed also.

5 If you are planning a complete overhaul, the engine can be dismantled and the internal components removed in the following order:

a) Alternator and mounting bracket (Chapter 5A).
b) Intake and exhaust manifolds (Chapter 4A or 4B).
c) Timing belt and pulleys (Chapter 2A or 2B).
d) Water pump (Chapter 3).
e) Cylinder head (Chapter 2A or 2B).
f) Flywheel (Chapter 2A or 2B).
g) Sump (Chapter 2A or 2B).
h) Oil pump (Chapter 2A or 2B).
i) Piston/connecting rod assemblies (Section 10).
j) Crankshaft (Section 11).

6 Before beginning the dismantling and overhaul procedures, make sure that you have all of the correct tools necessary. Refer to the Reference section at the end of this manual for further information.

7 Cylinder head – dismantling

Note: *New and reconditioned cylinder heads are available from the manufacturers and from engine overhaul specialists. Due to the fact that some specialist tools are required for the dismantling and inspection procedures, and new components may not be readily available (refer to Section 1), it may be more practical and economical for the home mechanic to purchase a reconditioned head rather than to dismantle, inspect and recondition the original head.*

1 Referring to Chapter 2A or 2B remove the camshaft(s), tappets, followers and shims, as applicable.

2 On diesel engines, remove the brake vacuum pump (see Chapter 9), thermostat housing, the fuel injectors, injection pump (if removed with the cylinder head) and glow plugs (Chapter 4B or 5C).

3 Remove the inlet and exhaust manifolds, the engine lifting eyes and top cover mountings, and the coolant outlet elbow.

4 Using a valve spring compressor, compress each valve spring in turn until the split collets can be removed. Release the compressor and lift off the cap and spring. If, when the valve spring compressor is screwed down, the valve spring cap refuses to free and expose the split collets, gently tap the top of the tool, directly over the cap, with a light hammer. This will free the cap **(see illustrations)**.

5 Remove the valves from the combustion chambers. It is essential that the valves and associated components are kept in their correct order, unless they are so badly worn that they are to be renewed. If they are going to be kept and used again, place them in labelled polythene bags, or in a compartmented box **(see illustrations)**.

6 On all petrol engines, the valve stem seals

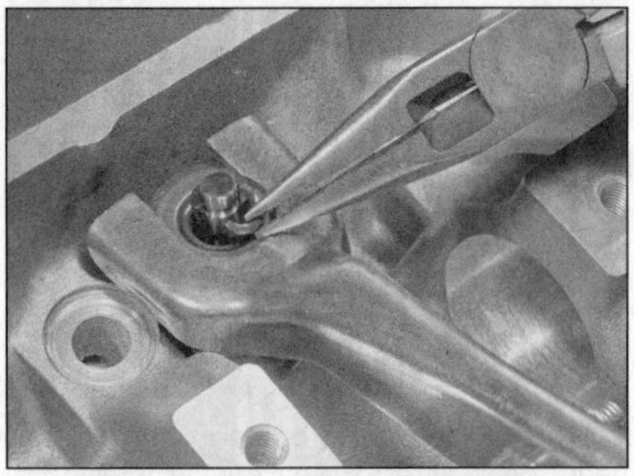

7.4a Remove the split collets...

7.4b ...then lift off the cap...

7.4c ...and valve spring

7.4d ...followed by the spring seat

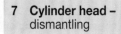

7.5a Withdrawing a valve from the combustion chamber

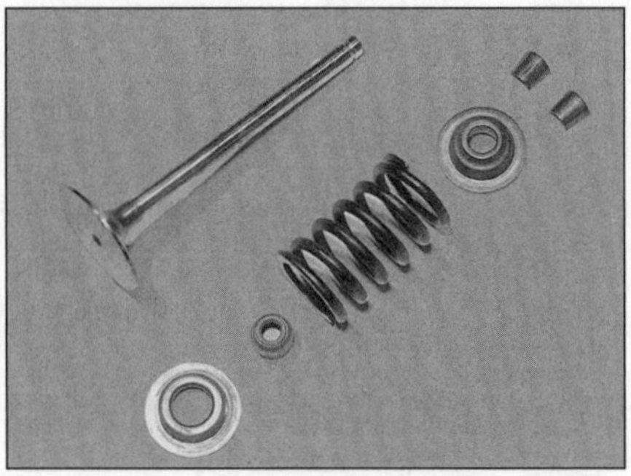

7.5b Valve components

7.5c Store the valve components in a labelled polythene bag

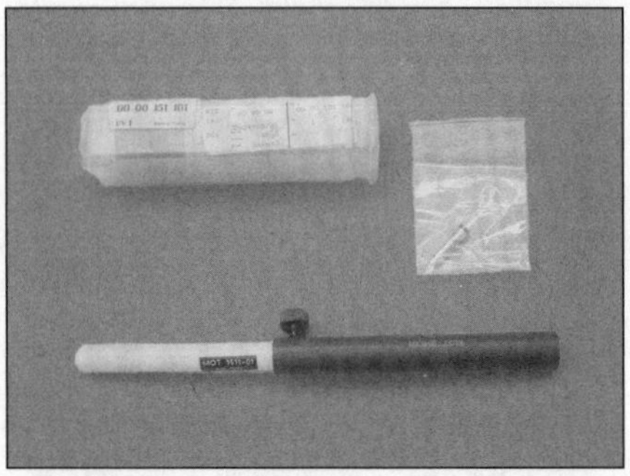

7.7a Renault tool for measuring the fitted height of the old valve stem oil seals

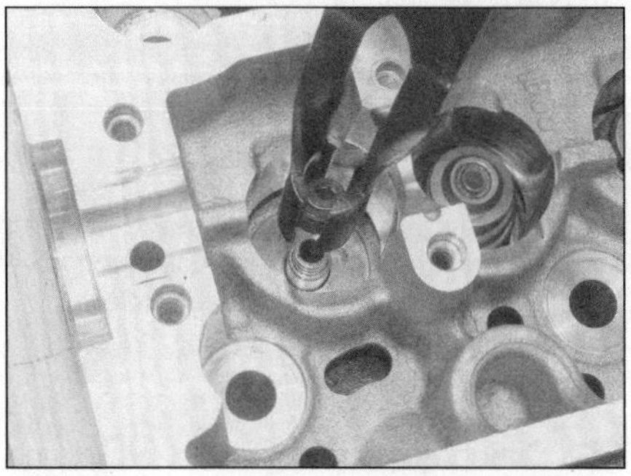

7.7b Removing the oil seal from the top of the valve guide

are integral with the valve spring lower seats, and may be difficult to remove.

7 On the K9K diesel engine, before removing the valve stem oil seals, measure their fitted height above the cylinder head and record it. Renault technicians use a special tool which is adjusted according to the fitted height of the old seals; the tool is then used to tap the new seals to an identical height. Use a pair of pliers to pull the oil seals from the valve guides **(see illustrations)**.

8 Cylinder head and valves – cleaning and inspection

1 Thorough cleaning of the cylinder head and valve components, followed by a detailed inspection, will enable you to decide how much valve service work must be carried out during the engine overhaul. **Note:** *If the engine has been severely overheated, and/or if the head gasket had failed, it is best to assume that the cylinder head is warped, and to check carefully for signs of this.*

Cleaning

2 Scrape away all traces of old gasket material and sealing compound from the cylinder head. Take care not to damage the cylinder head surfaces.

3 Scrape away the carbon from the combustion chambers and ports, then wash the cylinder head thoroughly with paraffin or a suitable solvent.

4 Scrape off any heavy carbon deposits that may have formed on the valves, then use a power-operated wire brush to remove deposits from the valve heads and stems.

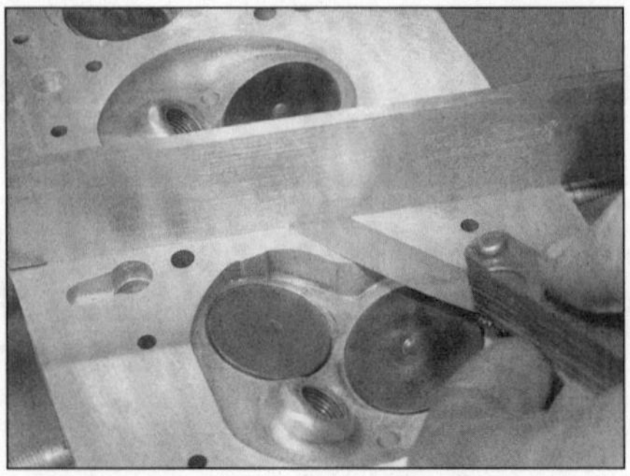

8.6 Checking the cylinder head surface for distortion with feeler blades

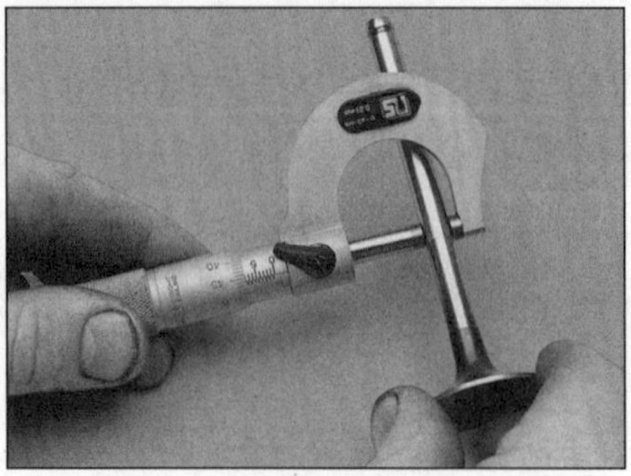

8.13 Measuring a valve stem using a micrometer

Inspection and renovation

Note: *Be sure to perform all the following inspection procedures before concluding that the services of a machine shop or engine overhaul specialist are required. Make a list of all items that require attention.*

Cylinder head

5 Inspect the head very carefully for cracks, evidence of coolant leakage and other damage. If cracks are found, consult an automotive engineering specialist or manufacturer dealership, before purchasing a new head.

6 If warpage of the cylinder head gasket surface is suspected, use a straight-edge to check it for distortion **(see illustration)**. If feeler blades are used, the degree of distortion can be assessed more accurately, and compared with the value specified. Check for distortion along the length and across the width of the head, and along both diagonals. If the head is warped, it may be possible to have it machined flat ('skimmed') at an engineering works – check with an engine specialist.

7 Examine the valve seats in each of the combustion chambers. If they are severely pitted, cracked or burned, then they will need to be renewed or recut by an engine overhaul specialist. If they are only slightly pitted, this can be removed by grinding-in the valve heads and seats with fine valve-grinding compound, as described below. Note that on diesel engines the valve seats can only be recut to a limited depth, to avoid decreasing the compression ratio. Using a dial test indicator, check that valve depth below the cylinder head gasket surface is within the limits given in the Specifications.

8 If the valve guides are worn, indicated by a side-to-side motion of the valve, new guides must be fitted.

9 The renewal of valve guides is best carried out by an engine overhaul specialist, since if it is not done skilfully, there is a risk of damaging the cylinder head.

10 If the valve seats are to be recut, consult an automotive engineering specialist or manufacturer dealership.

11 Check the tappet bores in the cylinder head for wear. If excessive wear is evident, the cylinder head must be renewed.

Valves

12 Examine the head of each valve for pitting, burning, cracks and general wear, and check the valve stem for scoring and wear ridges. Rotate the valve, and check for any obvious indication that it is bent. Look for pits and excessive wear on the tip of each valve stem. Renew any valve that shows any such signs of wear or damage.

13 If the valve appears satisfactory at this stage, measure the valve stem diameter at several points, using a micrometer **(see illustration)**. Any significant difference in the readings obtained indicates wear of the valve stem. Should any of these conditions be apparent, the valve(s) must be renewed.

14 If the valves are in satisfactory condition, they should be ground (lapped) into their respective seats, to ensure a smooth gas-tight seal. If the seat is only lightly pitted, or if it has been recut, fine grinding compound only should be used to produce the required finish. Coarse valve-grinding compound should not be used unless a seat is badly burned or deeply pitted; if this is the case, the cylinder head and valves should be inspected by an expert, to decide whether seat recutting, or even the renewal of the valve or seat insert, is required.

15 Valve grinding is carried out as follows. Place the cylinder head upside-down on a bench, with a block of wood at each end to give clearance for the valve stems.

16 Smear a trace of valve-grinding compound on the seat face, and press a suction grinding tool onto the valve head. With a semi-rotary action, grind the valve head to its seat, lifting the valve occasionally to redistribute the grinding compound **(see illustration)**. A light spring placed under the valve head will greatly ease this operation. If coarse grinding compound is being used, work only until a dull, matt even surface is produced on both the valve seat and the valve, then wipe off the used compound, and repeat the process with fine compound.

17 When a smooth unbroken ring of light grey matt finish is produced on both the valve and seat, the grinding operation is complete. Do not grind in the valves any further than absolutely necessary, or the seat will be prematurely sunk into the cylinder head.

18 When all the valves have been ground-in, carefully wash off all traces of grinding compound, using paraffin or a suitable solvent, before reassembly of the cylinder head.

Valve components

19 Examine the valve springs for signs of damage and discoloration and also measure their free length using vernier calipers or a steel rule **(see illustration)** or by comparing the existing spring with a new component.

20 Stand each spring on a flat surface and check it for squareness. If any of the springs are damaged, distorted or have lost their tension, obtain a complete new set of springs.

Valve stem oil seals

21 The valve stem oil seals should be renewed as a matter of course.

8.16 Grinding a valve to its seat – lift the valve to redistribute the paste

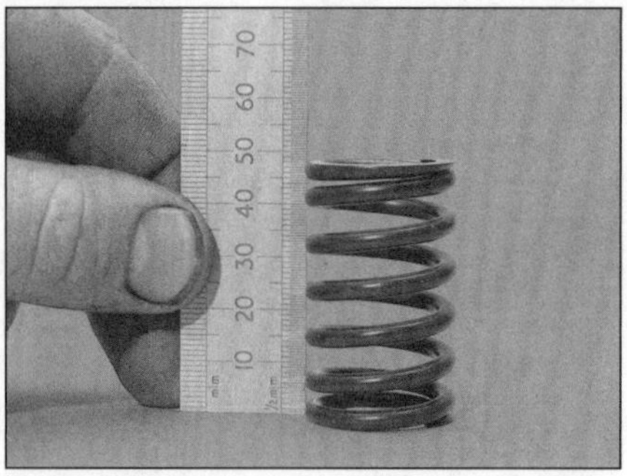

8.19 Checking a valve spring free length

9 Cylinder head – reassembly

1 Regardless of whether or not the head was sent away for repair work, make sure that it is clean before beginning reassembly. Be sure to remove any metal particles and abrasive grit that may still be present from operations such as valve grinding or head resurfacing. Use compressed air, if available, to blow out all the oil holes and passages.

2 Lubricate the valve stems, then insert the valves into their original locations. If new valves are being fitted, insert them into the locations to which they have been ground **(see illustration)**.

3 On petrol engines, ease the valve stem oil seals/seats over the valve stems, then press them onto the valve guides, using a large socket on the seat area. On the K9K diesel engine, press the new valve stem oil seals onto the guides to their previously-noted position, using the special guide to locate the seals over the valve stems **(see illustrations)**. **Do not** lubricate the oil seals before fitting them. Remove the guide after fitting the seal.

4 Working on each valve separately, locate the spring and cap over the valve stem. On the K9K diesel engine, the springs are tapered and the smaller-diameter taper must be positioned at the top.

5 Compress the valve spring and locate the split collets in the recess in the valve stem. Release the compressor, then repeat the procedure on the remaining valves. Use a little grease to hold the collets in place **(see illustration)**.

6 With all the valves installed, place the cylinder head on the bench supported by blocks of wood and, using a hammer and

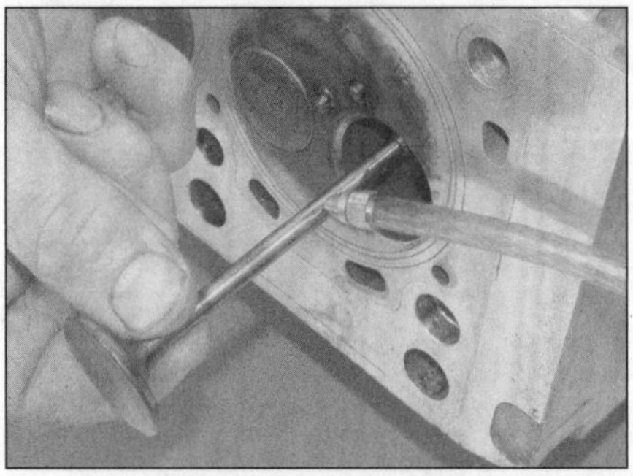

9.2 Lubricate the valve stems before inserting the valves

9.3a Fit the special guide onto the valve stem...

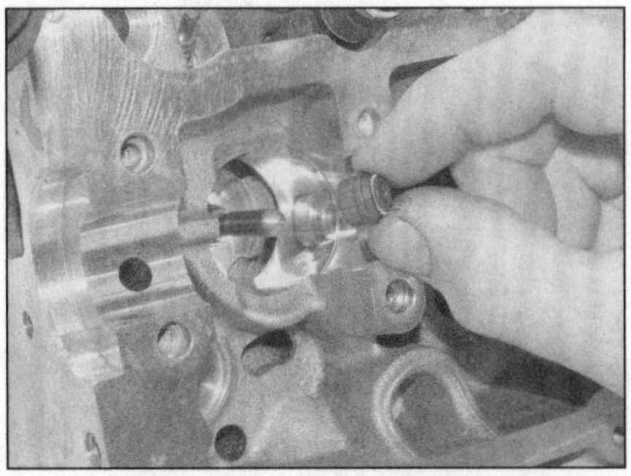

9.3b ...then fit the oil seal...

9.3c ...and press it on to its previously-noted position on the guide

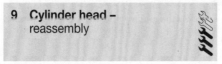

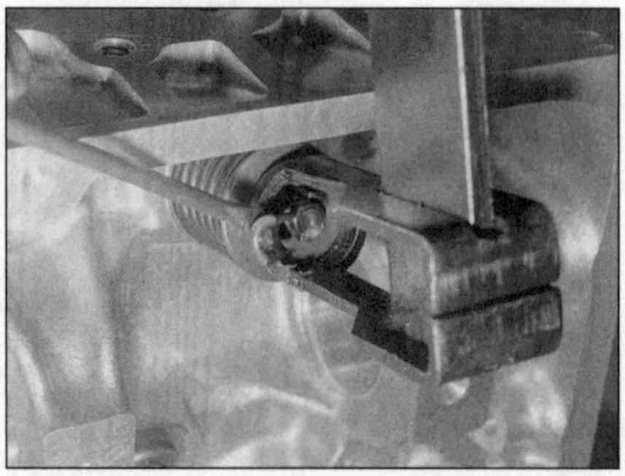

9.5 Use a little grease to hold the collets in place

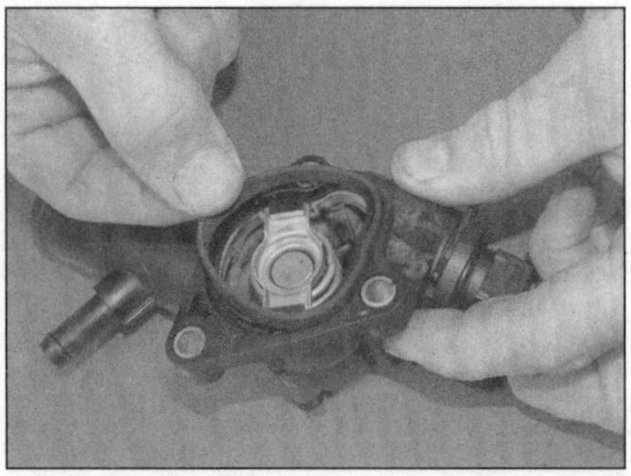

9.8 Locating a new seal on the thermostat housing (diesel engine)

interposed block of wood, tap the end of each valve stem to settle the components.

7 Refit as necessary the manifolds, lifting eyes and coolant outlet elbow.

8 On diesel engines, refit the brake vacuum pump (see Chapter 9), thermostat housing with a new seal **(see illustration)**, the fuel injectors, injection pump and glow plugs (Chapter 4B or 5C).

9 Referring to Chapter 2A or 2B, refit the tappets, followers and shims, and camshaft(s), as applicable.

10 Piston/connecting rod assemblies – removal

Note: *Although this task is theoretically possible with the engine in the car, in practice, owners are advised to remove the engine first. The following paragraphs assume the engine is removed from the car.*

1 With the cylinder head, sump and oil pump removed (see Chapter 2A or 2B), proceed as follows.

2 Rotate the crankshaft so that No 1 big-end cap (nearest the flywheel position) is at the lowest point of its travel. If the big-end cap and rod are not already numbered, mark them with a centre-punch **(see illustration)**. Mark both cap and rod to identify the cylinder they operate in.

3 Unscrew the big-end bearing cap nuts (petrol engine) or bolts (diesel engine). Withdraw the cap, complete with shell bearing, from the connecting rod **(see illustration)**.

4 If only the bearing shells are being attended to, push the connecting rod up and off the crankpin and remove the upper bearing shell **(see illustration)**. Keep the bearing shells and cap together in their correct sequence if they are to be refitted.

5 Each piston has an arrow stamped on its crown, pointing towards the flywheel end of the engine.

6 Push the connecting rod up and remove the piston and rod from the top of the bore. Note that if there is a pronounced wear ridge at the top of the bore, there is a risk of damaging the piston rings as they foul the ridge. However, it is reasonable to assume that a rebore and new pistons will be required in any case if the ridge is so pronounced.

7 Repeat the procedure for the remaining piston/connecting rod assemblies. Ensure that the caps and rods are marked before removal, as described previously, and keep all components in order.

8 On diesel engines only, the gudgeon pins are a floating fit in the pistons, and can be removed after releasing the circlips. On petrol engines, do not attempt to separate the pistons from the connecting rods; have an engine overhaul specialist carry out the work.

11 Crankshaft – removal

1 Remove the timing belt, crankshaft sprocket, oil pump (and drive sprocket), and flywheel with reference to Chapters 2A or 2B.

2 The pistons/connecting rods must be free of the crankshaft journals, as described later in this Section, however it is not essential to remove them completely from the cylinder block.

3 Before the crankshaft is removed, check the endfloat using a dial gauge in contact with the end of the crankshaft **(see illustration)**. Push the crankshaft fully one way and then zero the gauge. Push the crankshaft fully the other way and check the endfloat. The result can be compared with the specified amount and will give an indication as to whether new thrustwashers are required.

4 If a dial gauge is not available, feeler gauges can be used. First push the crankshaft fully towards the flywheel end of the engine, then slip the feeler gauge between the web of No 2 (or No 1) crankpin and the thrustwasher.

5 Identification numbers should already be cast onto the base of each main bearing cap, together with arrows pointing towards the flywheel end of the engine. If not, number them 1 to 5 from the flywheel end of the engine using a centre-punch, as was done for the connecting rods and caps **(see illustration)**. Also mark the crankcase, so that the caps will be refitted the correct way round.

6 Unscrew the main bearing cap retaining bolts and withdraw the caps, complete with bearing shells **(see illustration)**. Tap the caps with a wooden or copper mallet if they are stuck. Note that No 1 main bearing cap is sealed to the sides of the cylinder block with a semi-permanent silicone-based sealant.

10.2 Big-end caps marked with a centre-punch

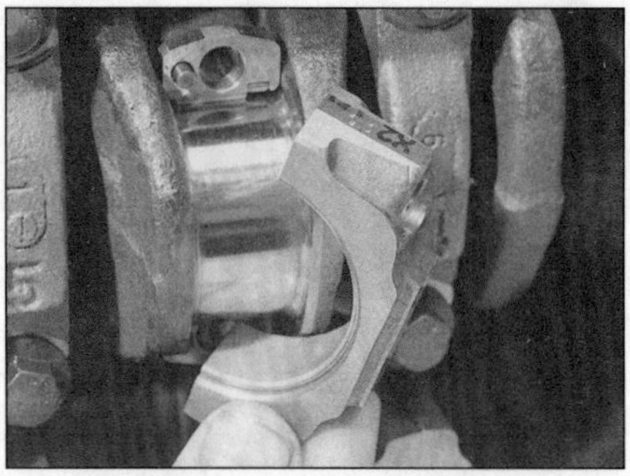

10.3 Removing a big-end bearing cap

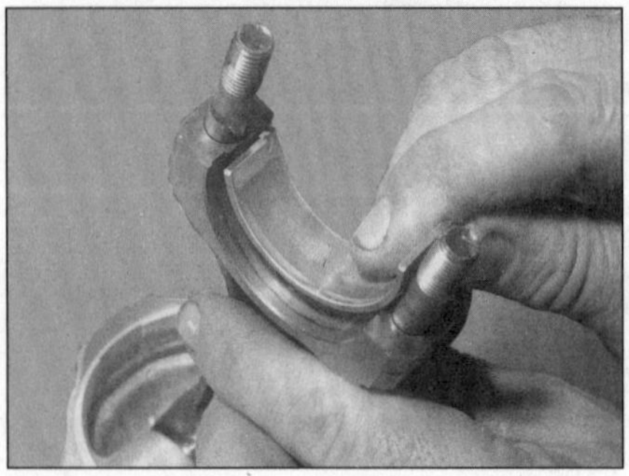

10.4 Removing a big-end bearing upper shell

11.3 Checking the crankshaft endfloat with a dial gauge

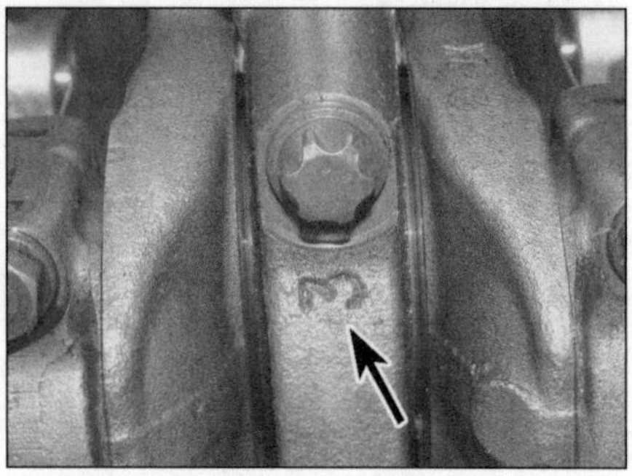

11.5 The main bearing caps are numbered for position

11.6 Removing a main bearing cap bolt

11.7 Lifting the crankshaft from the crankcase

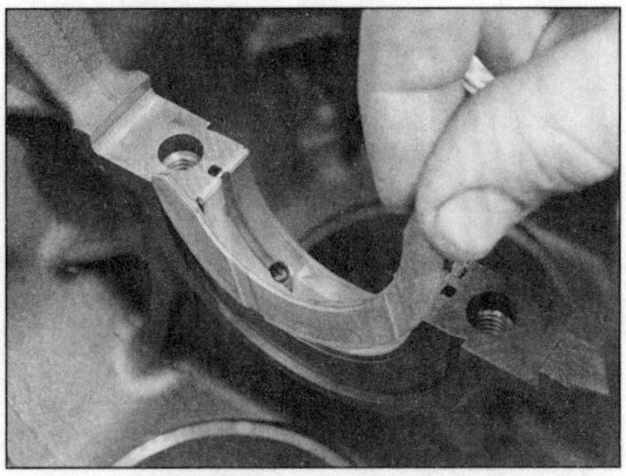

11.8 Removing the crankshaft thrustwashers (diesel engine)

As there is very little clearance between the crankshaft and cylinder block in this area in which to tap or prise the cap free, it may be necessary to use Renault special tool Mot. 1423 for removal or alternatively, use a home-made alternative.

7 Carefully lift the crankshaft from the crankcase **(see illustration)**.

8 Remove the thrustwashers, then remove the bearing shell upper halves from the crankcase **(see illustration)**. Place each shell with its respective bearing cap, noting that the grooved shells are fitted on the crankcase and the plain shells in the caps.

12 Cylinder block/crankcase – cleaning and inspection

Cleaning

1 For complete cleaning, remove all external components and brackets, and all electrical switches/sensors. The piston-cooling oil jets are pressed into the cylinder block, and must be drilled in order to fit a removal tool; this work is best left to a specialist. If necessary, the core plugs can be removed. Drill a small hole in them, then insert a self-tapping screw and pull out the plugs using a pair of grips or a slide-hammer.

2 Scrape all traces of gasket or sealant from the cylinder block, taking care not to damage the head and sump mating faces.

3 If the block is extremely dirty, it should be steam-cleaned.

4 After the block has been steam-cleaned, clean all oil holes and oil galleries one more time. Flush all internal passages with warm water until the water runs clear, dry the block thoroughly and wipe all machined surfaces with a light rust-preventative oil. If you have access to compressed air, use it to speed up the drying process and to blow out all the oil holes and galleries.

5 If the block is not very dirty, you can do an adequate cleaning job with hot soapy water and a stiff brush. Take plenty of time and do a thorough job. Regardless of the cleaning method used, be sure to clean all oil holes and galleries very thoroughly, dry the block completely and coat all machined surfaces with light oil.

6 The threaded holes in the block must be clean to ensure accurate torque wrench readings during reassembly. Run the proper-size tap into each of the holes to remove rust, corrosion, thread sealant or sludge and to restore damaged threads. If possible, use compressed air to clear the holes of debris produced by this operation. Now is a good time to clean the threads on the head bolts and the main bearing cap bolts as well.

7 Refit the main bearing caps and tighten the bolts finger-tight.

8 After coating the mating surfaces of the new core plugs with suitable sealant, refit them in the cylinder block. Make sure that they are driven in straight and seated properly, or leakage could result. Special tools are available for this purpose, but a large socket, with an outside diameter that will just slip into the core plug, will work just as well.

9 If the engine is not going to be reassembled right away, cover it with a large plastic bag to keep it clean and prevent it rusting.

Inspection

10 Visually check the castings for cracks and corrosion. Look for stripped threads in the threaded holes. If there has been any history of internal coolant leakage, it may be worthwhile having an engine overhaul specialist check the cylinder block/crankcase for cracks with special equipment. If defects are found, have them repaired, if possible, or renew the assembly.

11 Check each cylinder bore for scuffing and scoring.

12 If in any doubt as the condition of the cylinder block, have the block/bores inspected and measured by an engine reconditioning specialist. They will be able to advise on whether the block is serviceable, whether a rebore is necessary, and supply the appropriate replacement pistons and rings.

13 If the bores are in fairly good condition and not excessively worn, then it may only be necessary to renew the piston rings.

14 If this is the case, the bores should be honed, to allow the new rings to bed-in correctly and provide the best possible seal. Consult an engine reconditioning specialist

15 The cylinder block/crankcase should now be completely clean and dry, with all components checked for wear or damage, and repaired or overhauled as necessary. Refit as many ancillary components as possible, for safe-keeping. If reassembly is not to start immediately, cover the block with a large plastic bag to keep it clean, and protect the machined surfaces as described above to prevent rusting.

13 Piston/connecting rod assemblies – inspection

1 Before the inspection process can begin, the piston/connecting rod assemblies must be cleaned and the original piston rings removed from the pistons.

2 Carefully expand the old rings over the top of the pistons. The use of two or three old feeler blades will be helpful in preventing the rings dropping into empty grooves **(see illustration)**. Note that the oil control ring is in two sections.

3 Scrape away all traces of carbon from the top of the piston. A wire brush or a piece of fine emery cloth can be used once the majority of the deposits have been scraped away.

4 Remove the carbon from the ring grooves using a special groove-cleaning tool. If a tool is not available, use an old ring. Break the ring in half to do this. Be very careful to remove only the carbon deposits; do not remove any metal, or scratch the sides of the ring grooves. Protect your fingers – piston rings are sharp.

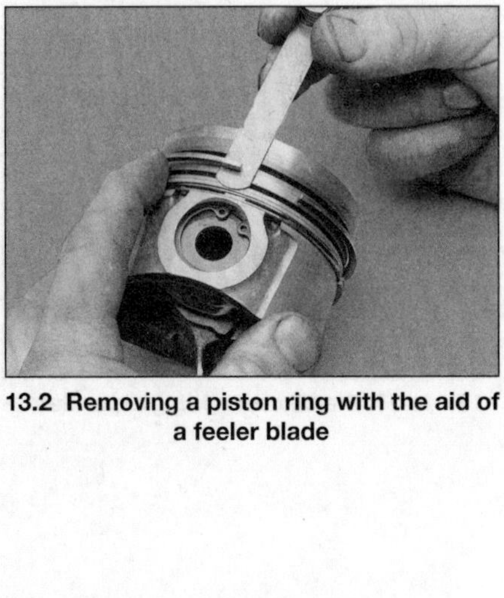

13.2 Removing a piston ring with the aid of a feeler blade

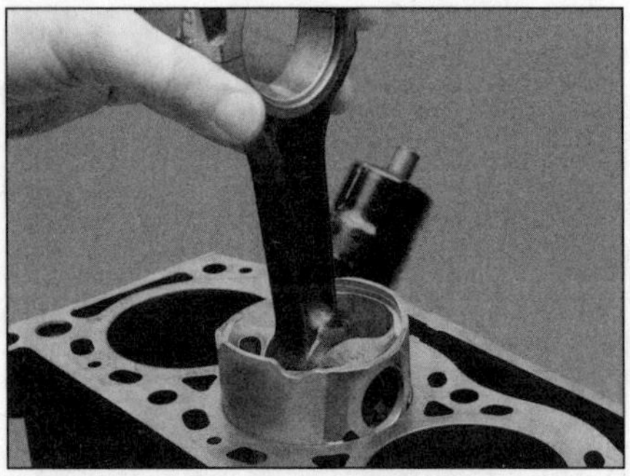

13.12a Use the piston to push the rings into the cylinder bores...

13.12b ...then measure the ring end gaps

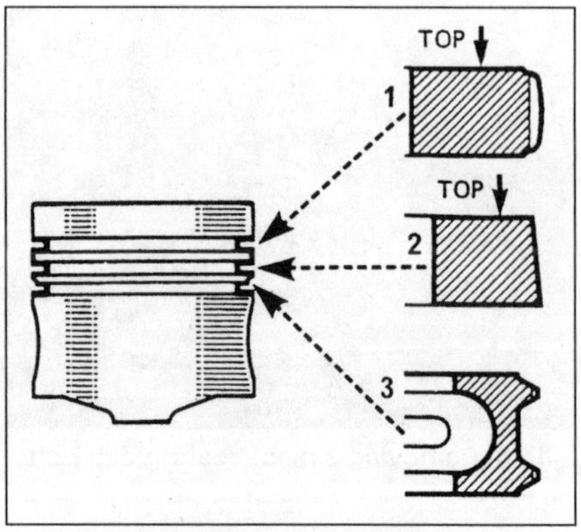

13.13 Piston ring profiles

1 Top compression ring
2 Lower compression ring
3 Oil control ring
Position the TOP markings as shown

5 Once the deposits have been removed, clean the piston/connecting rod assembly with paraffin or a suitable solvent and dry thoroughly. Make sure the oil return holes in the ring grooves are clear.

6 If the pistons and cylinder bores are not damaged or worn excessively and if the cylinder block does not need to be rebored, the original pistons can be re-used. Normal piston wear appears as even vertical wear on the piston thrust surfaces and slight looseness of the top ring in its groove. New piston rings should always be used when the engine is reassembled.

7 Carefully inspect each piston for cracks around the skirt, at the gudgeon pin bosses and at the piston ring lands (between the piston ring grooves).

8 Look for scoring and scuffing on the sides of the skirt, holes in the piston crown and burned areas at the edge of the crown. If the skirt is scored or scuffed, the engine may have been suffering from overheating and/or abnormal combustion, which caused excessively-high operating temperatures. The cooling and lubricating systems should be checked thoroughly.

9 Scorch marks on the sides of the pistons show that blow-by has occurred and the rings are not sealing correctly. A hole in the piston crown is an indication that abnormal combustion (pre-ignition, knocking or detonation) has been occurring. If any of the above problems exist, the causes must be corrected, or the damage will occur again.

10 Corrosion of the piston, in the form of small pits, indicates that coolant is leaking into the combustion chamber and/or the crankcase. Again, the cause must be corrected, or the problem may persist in the rebuilt engine.

11 Check the fit of the gudgeon pin by twisting the piston and connecting rod in opposite directions. Any noticeable play indicates excessive wear, which must be corrected. The piston/connecting rod assemblies should be taken to a dealer or engine reconditioning specialist to have the pistons, gudgeon pins and rods checked, and new components fitted as required.

12 Before refitting the rings to the pistons, check their end gaps by inserting each of them in their cylinder bores. Use the piston to make sure that they are square **(see illustrations)**. Renault rings are supplied pre-gapped; no attempt should be made to adjust the gaps by filing.

13 Refit the piston rings as follows. Where the original rings are being refitted, use the marks or notes made on removal, to ensure that each ring is refitted to its original groove and the same way up. New rings generally have their top surfaces identified by markings (often an indication of size, such as STD, or the word TOP) – the rings must be fitted with such markings uppermost **(see illustration). Note:** *Always follow the instructions printed on the ring package or box.*

14 The oil control ring (lowest one on the piston) is usually installed first, and is composed of three separate elements. Slip the spacer/expander into the groove. Next, install the lower side rail. Place one end of the side rail into the groove between the spacer/expander and the ring land, hold it firmly in place, and slide a finger around the piston while pushing the rail into the groove. Next, install the upper side rail in the same manner **(see illustrations)**. After the three oil ring components have been installed, check that both the upper and lower side rails can be turned smoothly in the ring groove.

15 The second compression (middle) ring is installed next, followed by the top compression ring – ensure their marks are uppermost. Do not expand either ring any more than necessary to slide it over the top of the piston.

16 With all the rings in position, space the ring gaps (including the elements of the oil control ring) uniformly around the piston at 120° intervals **(see illustration)**. Repeat the procedure for the remaining pistons and rings.

13.14a Fit the oil control ring expander...

13.14b ...followed by the ring

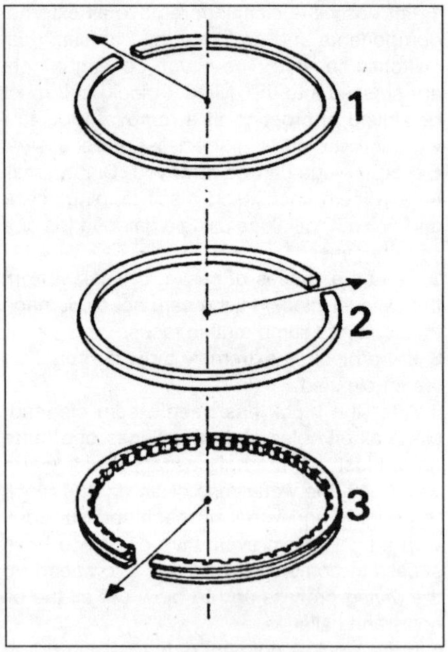

13.16 Position the piston ring end gaps 120° apart

1 Top compression ring
2 Lower compression ring
3 Oil control ring

14 Crankshaft - inspection

1 Clean the crankshaft and dry it with compressed air if available. Be sure to clean the oil holes with a pipe cleaner or similar probe.

Warning: Wear eye protection when using compressed air.

2 Check the main and big-end bearing journals for uneven wear, scoring, pitting and cracking.

3 If the crankshaft has been reground, check for burrs around the crankshaft oil holes (the holes are usually chamfered, so burrs should not be a problem unless regrinding has been carried out carelessly). Remove any burrs with a fine file or scraper and thoroughly clean the oil holes as described previously.

4 Using a micrometer, measure the diameter of the main bearing and connecting rod journals and compare the results with the Specifications at the beginning of this Chapter **(see illustration)**. If in any doubt, take the crankshaft to an engine reconditioning specialist and have it measured.

5 By measuring the diameter at a number of points around each journal's circumference, you will be able to determine whether or not the journal is out-of-round. Take the measurement at each end of the journal, near the webs, to determine if the journal is tapered.

6 If the crankshaft journals are damaged, tapered, out-of-round, or worn beyond the limits specified in this Chapter, the crankshaft must be taken to an engine overhaul specialist, who will regrind it, and who can supply the necessary undersize bearing shells, where available. **Note:** *Renault state that regrinding the crankshaft on the K9K diesel engine is not allowed.*

7 Check the oil seal journals at each end of the crankshaft for wear and damage. If either seal has worn an excessive groove in its journal, consult an engine overhaul specialist, who will be able to advise whether a repair is possible, or whether a new crankshaft is necessary.

15 Main and big-end bearings - inspection

1 Even though the main and big-end bearing shells should be renewed during the engine overhaul (where possible), the old shells should be retained for close examination, as they may reveal valuable information about the condition of the engine.

2 Bearing failure occurs because of lack of lubrication, the presence of dirt or other foreign particles, overloading the engine, and corrosion **(see illustration)**. Regardless of the cause of bearing failure, it must be corrected before the engine is reassembled, to prevent it from happening again.

3 When examining the bearing shells, remove them from the cylinder block/ crankcase and main bearing caps and from the connecting rods and the big-end bearing caps, then lay them out on a clean surface in the same general position as their location in the engine. This will enable you to match any bearing problems with the corresponding crankshaft journal. Do not touch any shell's bearing surface with your fingers while checking it, or the delicate surface may be scratched.

4 Dirt or other foreign matter gets into the engine in a variety of ways. It may be left in the engine during assembly, or it may pass through filters or the crankcase ventilation system. It may get into the oil, and from there into the bearings. Metal chips from machining operations and normal engine wear are often present. Abrasives are sometimes left in engine components after reconditioning, especially when parts are not thoroughly cleaned using the proper cleaning methods. Whatever the source, these foreign objects often end up embedded in the soft bearing material, and are easily recognised. Large particles will not embed in the material, and will score or gouge the shell and journal. The best prevention for this cause of bearing failure is to clean all parts thoroughly, and to keep everything spotlessly-clean during engine assembly. Frequent and regular engine oil and filter changes are also recommended.

5 Lack of lubrication (or lubrication breakdown) has a number of inter-related causes. Excessive heat (which thins the oil), overloading (which squeezes the oil from the bearing face) and oil leakage (from excessive bearing clearances, worn oil pump or high engine speeds) all contribute to lubrication breakdown. Blocked oil passages, which usually are the result of misaligned oil holes in a bearing shell, will also starve a bearing of oil, and destroy it. When lack of lubrication is the cause of bearing failure, the bearing material is wiped or extruded from the shell's steel backing. Temperatures may increase to the point where the steel backing turns blue from overheating.

6 Driving habits can have a definite effect on bearing life. Full-throttle, low-speed operation (labouring the engine) puts very high loads on bearings, which tends to squeeze out the oil film. These loads cause the shells to flex, which produces fine cracks in the bearing face (fatigue failure). Eventually, the bearing material will loosen in pieces, and tear away from the steel backing. Short-distance driving leads to corrosion of bearings, because insufficient engine heat is produced to drive off condensed water and corrosive gases. These products collect in the engine oil, forming acid and sludge. As the oil is carried to the engine bearings, the acid attacks and corrodes the bearing material.

14.4 Measuring a main bearing journal diameter using a micrometer

7 Incorrect shell refitting during engine assembly will lead to bearing failure as well. Tight-fitting shells leave insufficient bearing running clearance, and will result in oil starvation. Dirt or foreign particles trapped behind a bearing shell result in high spots on the bearing, which lead to failure. Do not touch any shell's bearing surface with your fingers during reassembly; there is a risk of scratching the delicate surface, or of depositing particles of dirt on it.

16 Engine overhaul - reassembly sequence

1 Before starting, ensure all new parts have been obtained and all necessary tools are available. Read through the entire procedure to familiarise yourself with the work involved and to ensure all items necessary for engine reassembly are at hand.

2 In addition to all normal tools and materials, obtain any necessary sealant and thread-locking fluid.

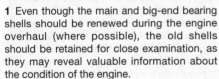

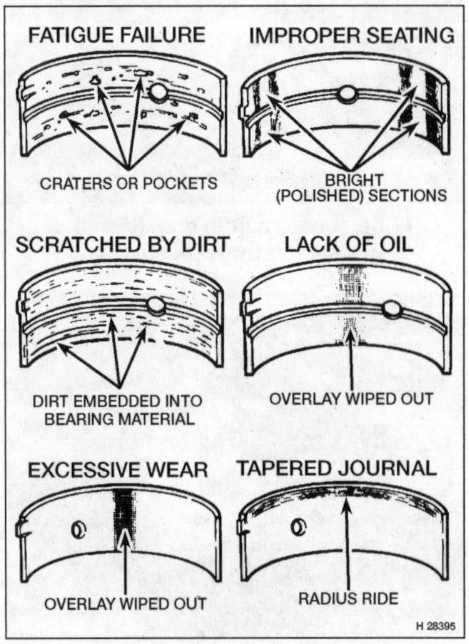

15.2 Typical bearing shell failures

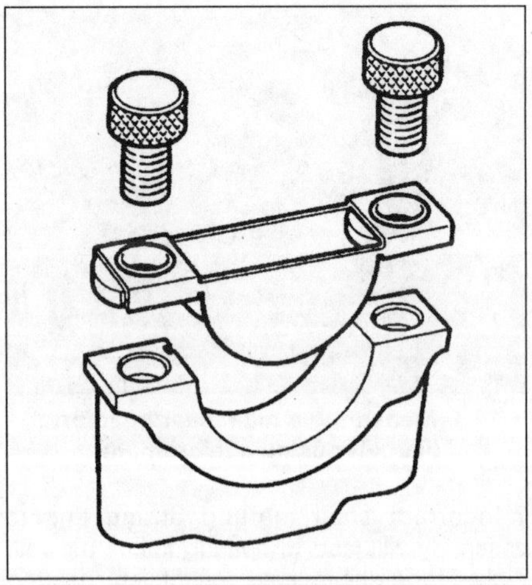

17.5a Tool for fitting main bearing shells (petrol engines)

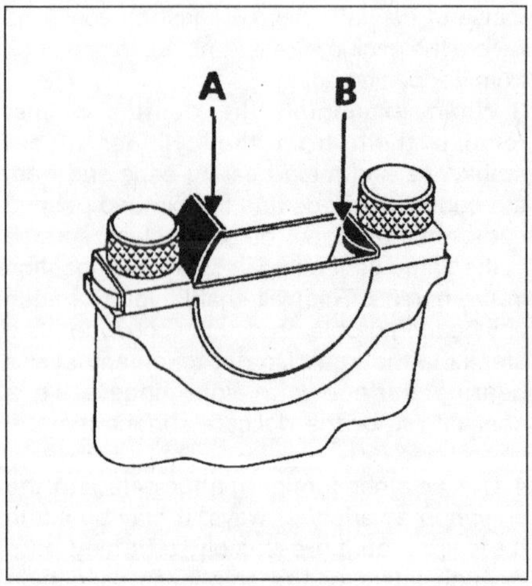

17.5b Press the bearing shell at (A) until it contacts (B)

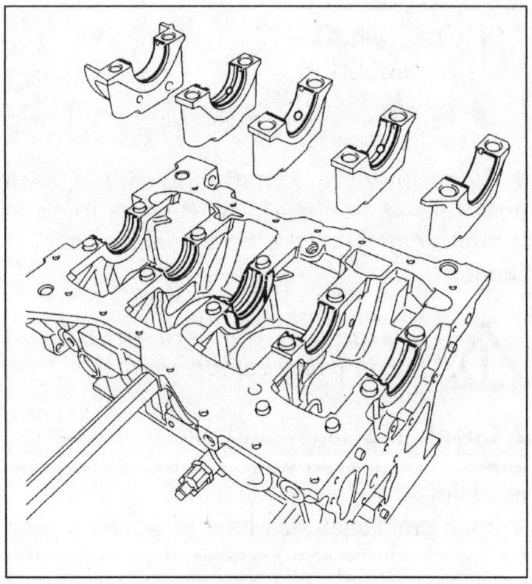

17.5c Bearing shell positions (petrol engines)

3 To save time and avoid problems, assembly can be carried out in the following order:
a) Crankshaft.
b) Pistons/connecting rod assemblies.
c) Oil pump.
d) Sump.
e) Flywheel.
f) Cylinder head.
g) Timing belt and sprockets.
h) Engine external components.

4 At this stage, all engine components should be absolutely clean and dry, with all faults repaired. All components should be neatly arranged on a completely clean work surface or in individual containers.

17 Crankshaft – refitting

1 Crankshaft refitting is the first major step in engine reassembly. It is assumed at this point that the cylinder block/crankcase and crankshaft have been cleaned, inspected and repaired or reconditioned as necessary. Position the engine upside-down.

2 If temporarily refitted, remove the main bearing cap bolts, and lift out the caps. Lay the caps out in the proper order, to ensure correct installation.

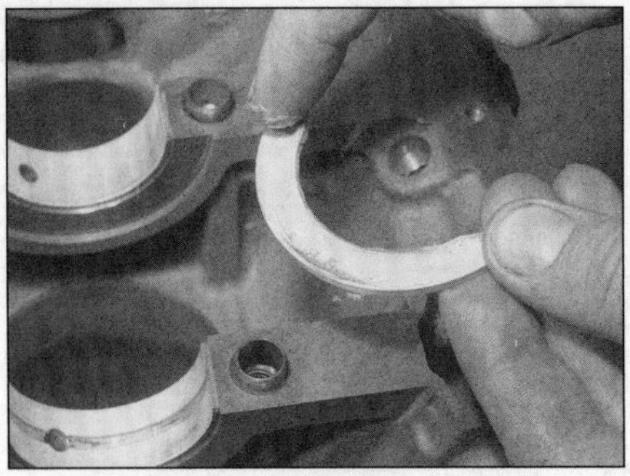

17.6a Smear a little grease on the crankshaft thrustwashers...

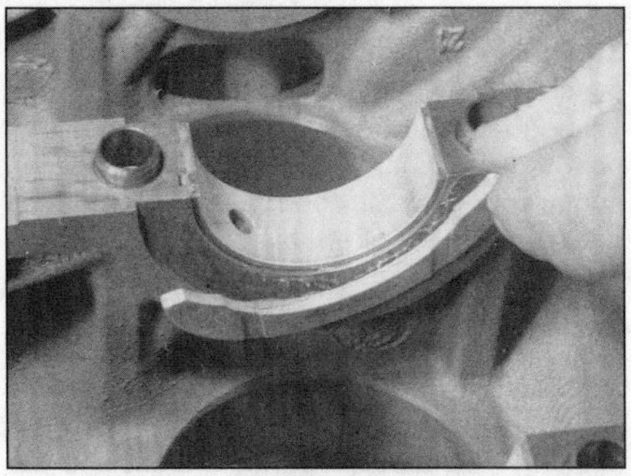

17.6b ...and stick them to the centre main bearing

17.7 Lubricate the main bearing shells before fitting the crankshaft

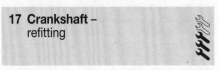

17.9 Lay the crankshaft in position in the crankcase

3 If they are still in place, remove the old bearing shells from the block and the main bearing caps. Wipe the bearing recesses with a clean, lint-free cloth. They must be kept spotlessly clean.

4 Clean the backs of the new main bearing shells. Fit the shells with an oil groove in each main bearing location in the block. Note that on petrol engines, the shells with the oil grooves are fitted to the cylinder block and to main bearing caps 2 and 4. The shells without oil grooves are fitted to main bearing caps 1, 3 and 5.

5 Make sure the tag where fitted on each bearing shell fits into the notch in the block or cap/lower crankcase. On engines where tags are not incorporated in the shells, it is recommended that the Renault tool Mot. 1493 or 1493-01 is obtained, though if care is taken the shells can be lined up accurately enough without it **(see illustrations)**. Note that the oil holes in the block must line up with the oil holes in the bearing shell.

6 Using a little grease, stick the thrustwashers to each side of the centre main bearing upper location (petrol engines) or to each side of No 2 (1.9 litre) or No 3 (1.5 litre) main bearing upper location (diesel engines); ensure that the oilway grooves on each thrustwasher face outwards (away from the cylinder block) **(see illustrations)**.

7 Clean the bearing surfaces of the shells in the block, then apply a thin, uniform layer of clean molybdenum disulphide-based grease, engine assembly lubricant, or clean engine oil to each surface **(see illustration)**. Coat the thrustwasher surfaces as well.

8 Lubricate the crankshaft oil seal journals with molybdenum disulphide-based grease, engine assembly lubricant, or clean engine oil.

9 Make sure the crankshaft journals are clean, then lay the crankshaft back in place in the block **(see illustration)**.

10 Ensure that the cap locating dowels are in position and fit main bearing caps 2 to 5 to

17.10 Fitting No 5 main bearing cap (petrol engine)

17.12a Tighten the main bearing cap bolts to the specified torque...

17.12b ...and angle

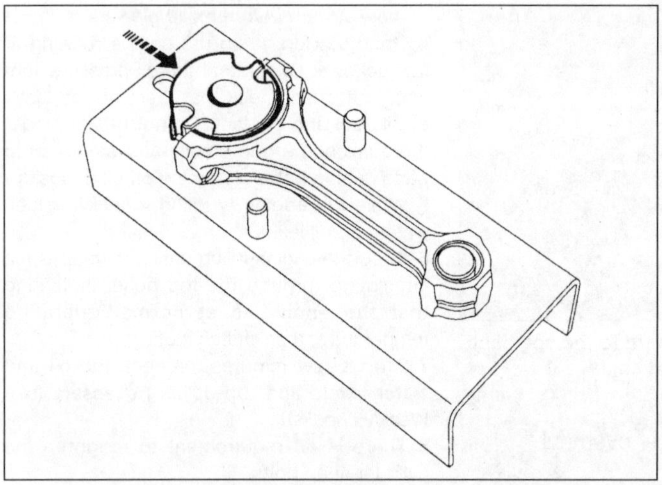

18.2 Using tool Mot. 1492 to fit the big-end shells

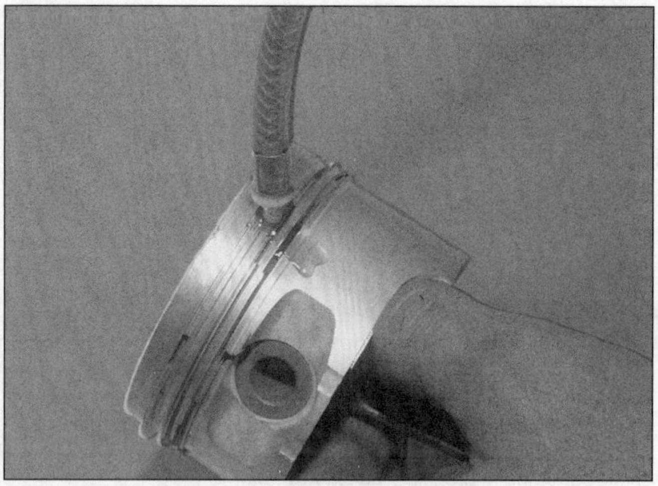

18.3a Lubricating the piston rings...

their correct locations and the correct way round **(see illustration)**.

11 Apply a thin coating of Rhodorseal 5661 sealant (available from Renault dealers) to the mating surface of No 1 main bearing cap, taking great care not to block the oil return grooves, then fit the cap.

12 Insert the new main bearing cap bolts and tighten them to the specified Stage 1 torque setting using a torque wrench. Once all the bolts have been tightened to their Stage 1 setting, angle-tighten the bolts through the specified Stage 2 angle, using a socket and extension bar. It is recommended that an angle-measuring gauge is used during this stage of the tightening, to ensure accuracy **(see illustrations)**.

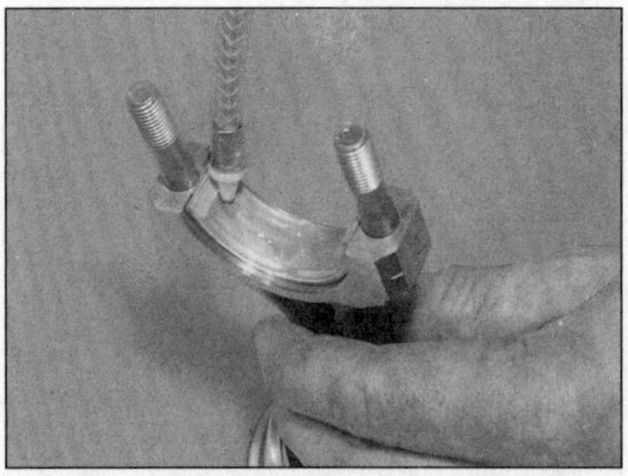

18.3b ...and big-end bearing shell in the connecting rod

13 Check that the crankshaft is free to turn without stiffness or tight spots.

14 Check the crankshaft endfloat with reference to Section 11.

15 Lubricate the oil seal location, the crankshaft, and a new oil seal. Fit the seal, lips inwards, and use a piece of tube (or the old seal, inverted) to tap it into place until flush.

16 Continue with the engine reassembly procedures as described in the relevant Sections of this Chapter and Chapter 2A or 2B.

18 Piston/connecting rod assemblies – refitting

1 Clean the backs of the big-end bearing shells and the recesses in the connecting rods and big-end caps. If new shells are being fitted, ensure that all traces of the protective grease are cleaned off using paraffin. Wipe the shells and connecting rods dry with a lint-free cloth.

2 Press the big-end bearing shells into the connecting rods and caps in their correct positions. Note that locating tags are not incorporated in the shells and, to ensure correct fitting, it is recommended that the Renault tool Mot. 1492 is obtained **(see illustration)**. However, if care is taken and the shells are accurately fitted, the tool is not necessary.

3 Lubricate No 1 piston and piston rings and check that the ring gaps are still spaced at 120° intervals to each other. Also, lubricate the big-end bearing shell in the connecting rod **(see illustrations)**.

4 Fit a ring compressor to No 1 piston, then insert the piston and connecting rod into No 1 cylinder. The V arrow must point to the flywheel end of the engine. With No 1 crankpin at its lowest point, drive the piston carefully into the cylinder with the wooden handle of a hammer, at the same time guiding the connecting rod onto the crankpin **(see illustration)**.

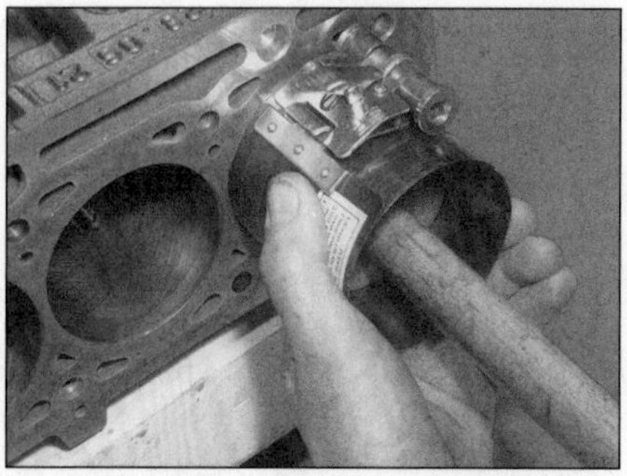

18.4 Using the wooden handle of a hammer to drive the piston into the bore

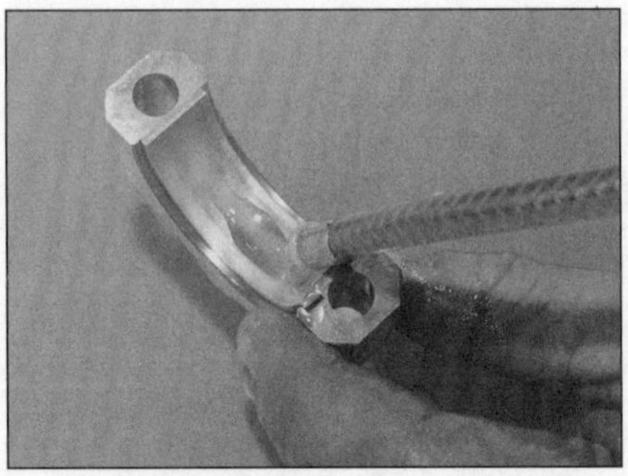

18.5a Lubricate the big-end cap bearing shell...

18.5b ...then refit the cap...

18.5c ...screw on the nuts...

18.5d ...and tighten them to the specified torque and angle

5 Liberally lubricate the crankpin journal and big-end cap bearing shells, then refit the correct cap and insert the nuts/bolts. Tighten them to the specified torque and angle **(see illustrations)**. Turn the crankshaft to make sure that it is free before moving on to the next assembly.

6 Repeat the above procedures on the remaining piston/connecting rod assemblies.

7 On completion, refit the oil pump, sump and cylinder head as described in Chapter 2A or 2B.

19 Engine – initial start-up after overhaul

1 With the engine refitted in the car, double-check the engine oil and coolant levels. Make a final check that everything has been reconnected, and that there are no tools or rags left in the engine compartment.

2 On petrol models, carry out the following:

a) Remove the ignition HT coil assemblies as described in Chapter 5B and the spark plugs as described in Chapter 1A.

b) Crank the engine on the starter motor until the oil pressure light goes out.

c) Refit the spark plugs and HT coil assemblies.

d) Start the engine, noting that this may take a little longer than usual while the fuel system is primed.

3 On diesel models, carry out the following:

a) Prime the fuel system as described in Chapter 4B.

b) Start the engine as normal. Additional cranking may be necessary to bleed the fuel system before the engine starts.

4 Once started, keep the engine running at fast tickover. Check that the oil pressure light goes out, then check that there are no leaks of oil, fuel and coolant. Do not be alarmed if there are some odd smells and smoke from parts getting hot and burning off oil deposits.

5 While the engine is idling, check for fuel, water and oil leaks.

6 Keep the engine idling until hot water is felt circulating through the top hose, indicating that the engine is at normal operating temperature, then switch it off.

7 After a few minutes, recheck the oil and water levels and top-up as necessary (see *Weekly checks*).

8 There is no requirement to retighten the cylinder head bolts.

9 If new pistons, rings or crankshaft bearings have been fitted, the engine must be run-in for the first 500 miles (800 km). Do not operate the engine at full-throttle, nor allow it to labour in any gear during this period. It is recommended that the oil and filter be changed at the end of this period.

Chapter 3
Cooling, heating and air conditioning systems

Contents

	Section number
Air conditioning system – checking and maintenance	13
Air conditioning system – component removal and refitting	14
Air conditioning system – general information and precautions	12
Antifreeze mixture	See Chapter 1A or 1B
Coolant draining	See Chapter 1A or 1B
Coolant filling	See Chapter 1A or 1B
Coolant level check	See *Weekly checks*
Coolant temperature sensor – testing, removal and refitting	8
Cooling system hoses – renewal	2
Expansion bottle – removal, inspection and refitting	4
General cooling system checks	See Chapter 1A or 1B
General information	1
Heater/ventilation system components – removal and refitting	11
Heating system – general information and checks	10
Radiator – removal, inspection, cleaning and refitting	3
Radiator cooling fan – removal and refitting	6
Radiator cooling fan switch – general information	7
System flushing	See Chapter 1A or 1B
Thermostat – removal and refitting	5
Water pump – removal and refitting	9

Degrees of difficulty

Easy, suitable for novice with little experience	**Fairly easy,** suitable for beginner with some experience	**Fairly difficult,** suitable for competent DIY mechanic	**Difficult,** suitable for experienced DIY mechanic	**Very difficult,** suitable for expert DIY or professional

Specifications

General

Cooling system type	Pressurised sealed system, with timing belt-driven water pump, front-mounted radiator and electric cooling fan
Cooling system pressure	1.4 bar
Air conditioning oil type:	
Original oil	ND-OIL 8
Replacement type	SP10
Air conditioning refrigerant type	R134a
Air conditioning refrigerant quantity	480g ± 35g
Air conditioning oil quantities:	
Split pipe or rapid leak	Quantity recovered + 100 ml
Replacement pipe	Quantity recovered + 10 ml
Condenser replacement	Quantity recovered + 30 ml
Evaporator replacement	Quantity recovered + 30 ml
Receiver/Drier replacement	Quantity recovered + 15 ml

Thermostat

Starts to open:	
K4M (petrol)	89°C
K9K (diesel)	83°C
Fully open:	
K4M (petrol)	99°C
K9K (diesel)	95°C

Coolant temperature sensor

Resistance:	
At 25°C	2252 ± 112 ohms
At 80°C	280 ± 8 ohms

Torque wrench settings	Nm	lbf ft
Air conditioning compressor mounting bolts	25	18
Air conditioning condenser unions	10	7
Alternator bolts	25	18
Crossmember support panel bolts	21	15
Water pump bolts*:		
Petrol engines:		
Bolt 1	27	20
Bolts 2-8	10	7
Diesel engine	10	7
Thermostat housing		
Petrol engines:		
Stage 1	4	3
Stage 2	12	9
Diesel engines	12	9

** With thread-locking fluid applied – see text*

1 General information

The cooling system is of the pressurised type. The main components are a timing belt-driven pump, an aluminium cross-flow radiator, an expansion bottle, an electric cooling fan, a thermostat, and the associated hoses. Diesel models also feature a coolant-fed oil cooler, mounted at the base of the oil filter

The system functions as follows. When the engine is cold, coolant is pumped around the cylinder block and head passages. After cooling the cylinder bores, combustion surfaces and valve seats, the coolant passes through the heater and inlet manifold, and is returned to the water pump.

When the coolant reaches a predetermined temperature, the thermostat opens, and the hot coolant passes through the top hose to the radiator. As the coolant circulates through the radiator, it is cooled by the inrush of air when the car is in motion. The airflow is supplemented by the action of the electric cooling fan when necessary. Upon reaching the bottom of the radiator, the coolant returns to the pump via the radiator bottom hose, and the cycle is repeated.

As the coolant warms up, it expands; the increased volume is accommodated in an expansion bottle. The bottle is 'hot', which means the coolant circulates through the bottle all the time the engine is running.

The electric cooling fan is mounted behind the radiator and is controlled by the engine ECU, see Section 7 for details.

For details of the air conditioning system refer to Section 14.

Precautions

Warning: Do not attempt to remove the expansion bottle filler cap, or to disturb any part of the cooling system, while the engine is hot, as there is a high risk of scalding. If the expansion bottle filler cap must be removed before the engine and radiator have fully cooled (even though this is not recommended), the pressure in the cooling system must first be relieved. Cover the cap with a thick layer of cloth to avoid scalding, and slowly unscrew the filler cap until a hissing sound is heard. When the hissing has stopped, indicating that the pressure has reduced, slowly unscrew the filler cap until it can be removed; if more hissing sounds are heard, wait until they have stopped before unscrewing the cap completely. At all times, keep well away from the filler cap opening, and protect your hands.

Warning: Do not allow antifreeze to come into contact with your skin, or with the painted surfaces of the car. Rinse off spills immediately, with plenty of water. Never leave antifreeze lying around in an open container, or in a puddle in the driveway or on the garage floor. Children and pets are attracted by its sweet smell, but antifreeze can be fatal if ingested.

Warning: If the engine is hot, the electric cooling fan may start rotating even if the engine is not running. Be careful to keep your hands, hair, and any loose clothing well clear when working in the engine compartment.

Warning: Refer to Section 14 for precautions to be observed when working on models equipped with air conditioning.

2 Cooling system hoses – renewal

Note: *Refer to the warnings given in Section 1 of this Chapter before proceeding. Hoses should only be disconnected once the engine has cooled sufficiently to avoid scalding.*

1 The number, routing and pattern of hoses will vary according to model, but the same basic procedure applies. Before commencing work, make sure that the new hoses are to hand, along with new hose clips if needed. It is good practice to renew the hose clips at the same time as the hoses.

2 Drain the cooling system, as described in Chapter 1A or 1B, saving the coolant if it is fit for re-use. Squirt a little penetrating oil onto the hose clips if they are rusty.

3 Release the hose clips from the hose concerned. Almost all the standard clips fitted at the factory are the spring type, released by squeezing the tangs together with pliers, at the same time working the clip away from the hose stub **(see illustrations)**. These clips can be awkward to use, can pinch old hoses, and may become less effective with age, so may have been updated with Jubilee clips (released by turning the screw).

4 Unclip any wires, cables or other hoses which may be attached to the hose being removed. Make notes for reference when reassembling if necessary.

5 Note that the coolant unions are fragile (most are made of plastic); do not use

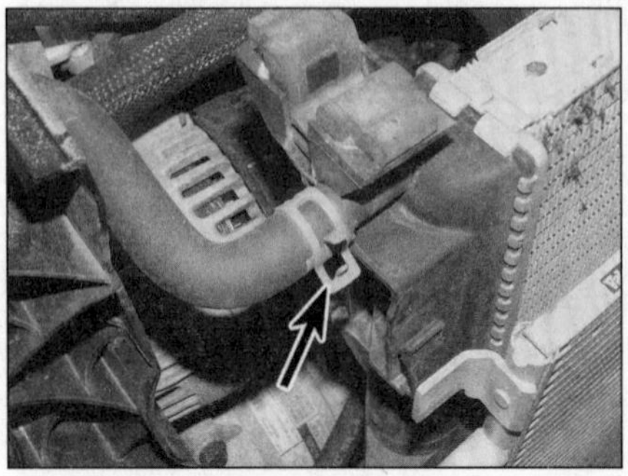

2.3a Most of the coolant hose clips are of the spring type...

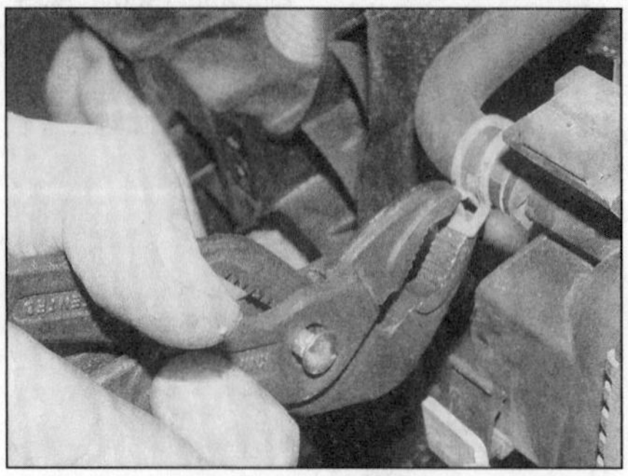

2.3b ...released by squeezing the tangs together with pliers

2.3c ...or by using a special cable operated release tool

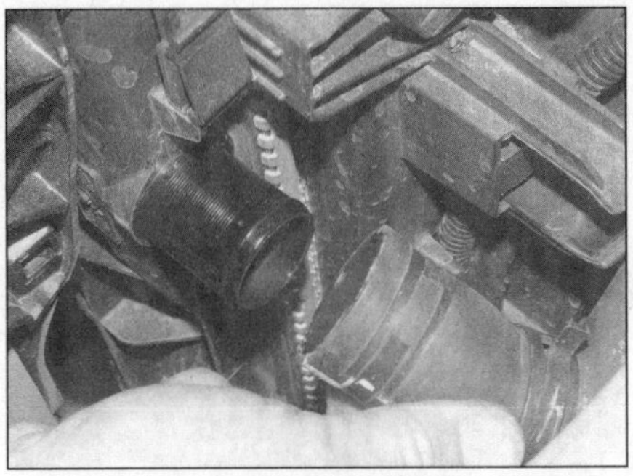

2.5a Note that the radiator hose fittings are made of plastic

2.5b A blunt pick tool can be used to free off the hose

excessive force when attempting to remove the hoses. If a hose proves to be difficult to remove, try to release it by rotating the hose ends before attempting to free it – if this fails, try gently prising up the end of the hose with a small screwdriver or hook type tool to 'break' the seal **(see illustrations)**.

6 Before fitting the new hose, smear the stubs with washing-up liquid or a suitable rubber lubricant to aid fitting. **Do not** use oil or grease, which may attack the rubber.

7 Fit the hose clips over the ends of the hose, then fit the hose over its stubs. Work the hose into position. When satisfied, locate and tighten the hose clips.

8 Refill the cooling system as described in Chapter 1A or 1B. Run the engine, and check that there are no leaks.

9 Recheck the tightness of the hose clips on any new hoses after a few hundred miles.

3 Radiator – removal, inspection, cleaning and refitting

Note: *If the radiator is to be removed for a period of more than 48 hours, precautions must be taken against internal corrosion. Either rinse the radiator with clean water and dry it thoroughly by blowing air through it, or fill it with coolant and plug the hose stubs.*

Removal

1 Jack up the front of the car, and support it on axle stands (see *Jacking and vehicle support*).

2 Remove both front wheels and then remove both the front sections of both front wing liners.

3 Remove the engine undertray and then remove the front bumper cover as described in Chapter 11.

4 Where fitted, remove the engine cover and then drain the radiator – see Chapter 1A or 1B.

5 With reference to Chapter 12 remove both front headlights.

6 Unclip the air deflector from the top and side of the radiator **(see illustration)**.

7 On diesel models remove the intercooler as described in Chapter 4B.

8 Disconnect the horn wiring plug, unbolt and then remove the horns from the front cross member **(see illustration)**.

9 Release the retaining clips and separate the AC condenser form the radiator **(see illustrations)**. Secure the radiator to the front crossmember with suitable straps or plastic ties. If necessary protect the condenser with card whilst the radiator is removed.

3.6a Unclip the ends...

3.6b ...and then remove the upper section of the air deflector...

3.6c ...followed by the side sections

3.8 Remove the horns

3.9a Open the clip (arrowed)...

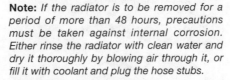

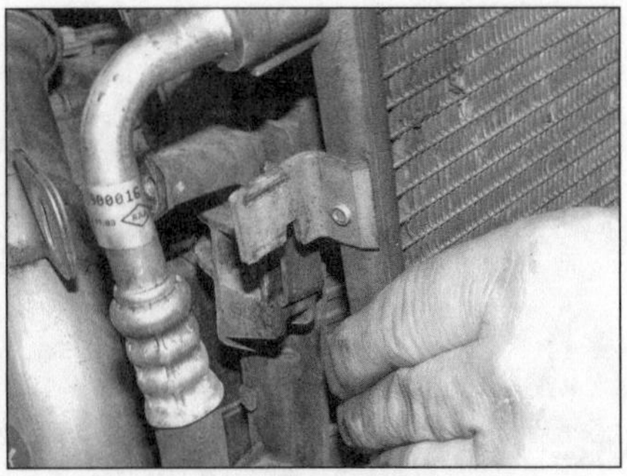

3.9b ...and release the condenser

3.10a Remove the left-hand coolant hose...

3.10b ...the right-hand hose...

3.10c ...and the vent hose

3.11a Remove the bolts...

3.11b ...and recover the brackets

3.11c Lift the radiator up and out from the front panel

10 Disconnect the radiator hoses. **(see illustrations)**.

11 At each side remove the mounting brackets. Lift the radiator out, taking care not to damage the fins in the process, and remove it from the car **(see illustrations)**.

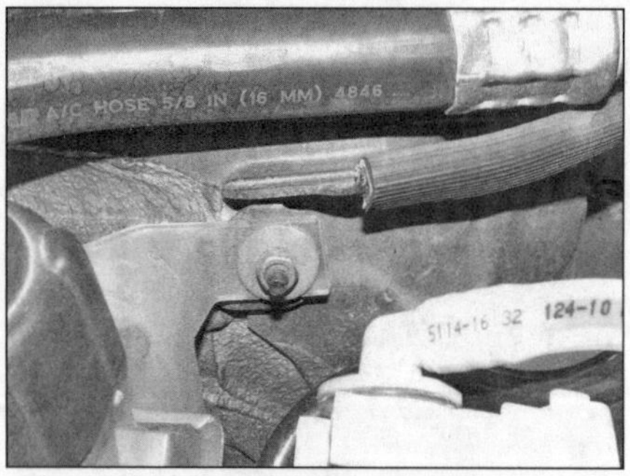
4.3 Remove the mounting bolt

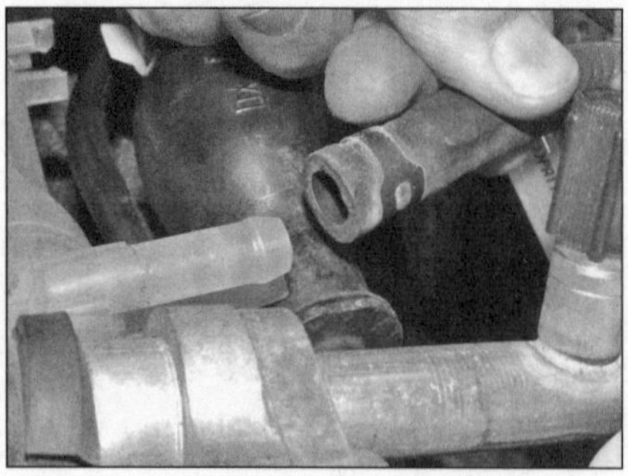
4.5a Remove the vent (de-gas) hose...

Inspection and cleaning

12 If the radiator has been removed due to suspected blockage, reverse-flush it as described in Chapter 1A or 1B. Clean dirt and debris from the radiator fins, using an airline (in which case, wear eye protection) or a soft brush. Be careful, as the fins are sharp, and easily damaged.

13 If necessary, a radiator specialist can perform a 'flow test' on the radiator, to establish whether an internal blockage exists.

14 A leaking radiator should be replaced. In some case a specialist may be able to repair it, but it is usually more cost effective to replace it. Do not attempt to weld or solder a leaking radiator, as damage to the plastic components may result.

15 Inspect the condition of the mounting rubbers, and renew them if necessary.

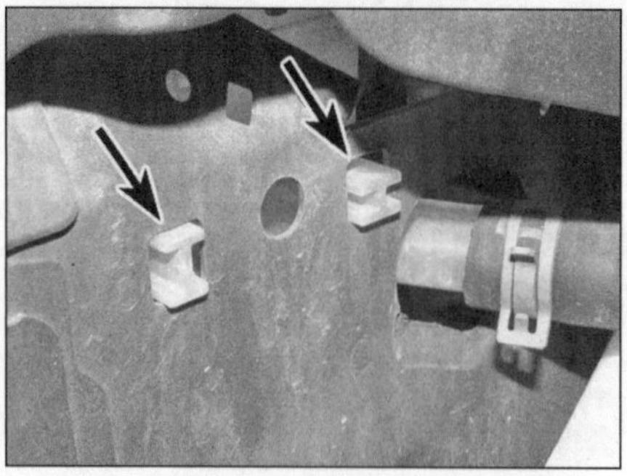
4.5b ...and the main hose. Note the expansion bottle locating pegs (arrowed)

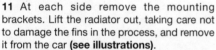

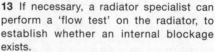

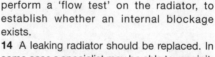

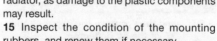

Refitting

16 Refitting is a reversal of removal, bearing in mind the following points:

a) Take care not to damage the radiator fins (nor the condenser, where applicable) during refitting.
b) On diesel models, refit the intercooler as described in Chapter 4B.
c) Refit the front bumper with reference to Chapter 11.
d) On completion, refill the cooling system as described in Chapter 1A or 1B.

4 Expansion bottle – removal, inspection and refitting

Removal

1 With the engine cold, drain some coolant from the system (see Chapter 1A or 1B) until the expansion bottle is empty.

2 On diesel models unclip the hand priming pump.

3 Undo the retaining nut at the bulkhead which secures the expansion bottle **(see illustration)**.

4 Where fitted, unclip the wiring loom form the expansion bottle.

5 Disconnect the coolant hoses from the bottle. The lower hose can be accessed by either removing the left-hand headlight, or by rotating the bottle to expose the hose **(see illustrations)**.

6 Hold the air conditioning pipework and (where applicable the) diesel fuel priming hose

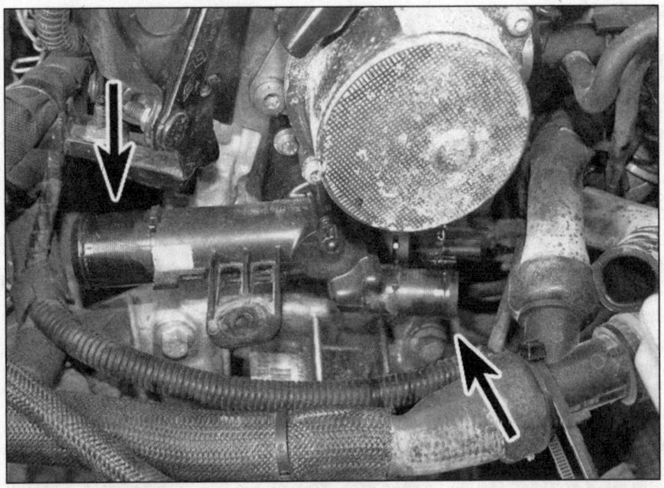

5.16 Remove the coolant hoses (arrowed). Diesel model shown

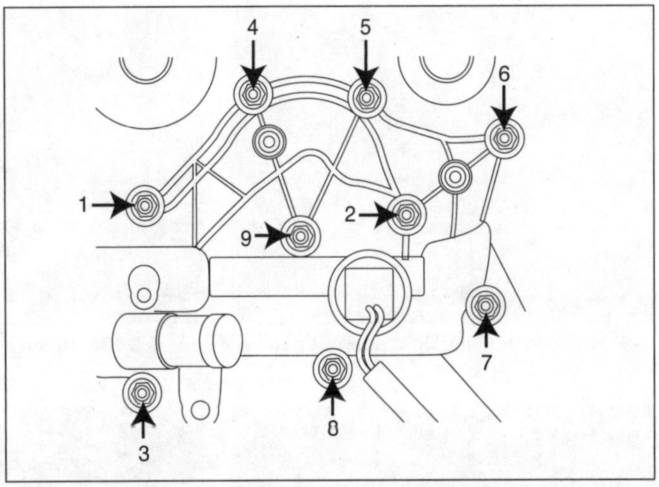

5.19 Tighten the bolts in the order shown

aside, and manoeuvre the bottle out from its location.

Inspection

7 Clean the bottle and inspect it for cracks and other damage. Renew it if necessary. Also inspect the cap; if there is evidence that coolant has been vented through the cap, renew it.

Refitting

8 Refitting is a reversal of removal, but remember to refill and bleed the cooling system as described in Chapter 1A or 1B.

5 Thermostat – removal and refitting

Note: *Renault only supply the thermostat complete with the housing. Aftermarket suppliers may supply the thermostat as a separate part.*

1 As the thermostat ages, it will become slower to react to changes in water temperature ('lazy'). Ultimately, the unit may stick in the open or closed position, and this causes problems. A thermostat which is stuck open will result in a very slow warm-up; a thermostat which is stuck shut will lead to rapid overheating.

2 Before assuming the thermostat is to blame for a cooling system problem, check the coolant level. If the system is draining due to a leak, or has not been properly filled, there may be an airlock in the system (refer to the coolant renewal procedure in Chapter 1A or 1B).

3 If the engine seems to be taking a long time to warm up (based on heater output), the thermostat could be stuck open. Don't necessarily believe the temperature gauge reading – some gauges never seem to register very high in normal driving.

4 A lengthy warm-up period might suggest that the thermostat is missing – it may have been removed or inadvertently omitted by a previous owner or mechanic. Don't drive the car without a thermostat – the engine management system's ECU will then stay in warm-up mode for longer than necessary, causing emissions and fuel economy to suffer.

5 If the engine runs hot, use your hand to check the temperature of the radiator top hose. If the hose isn't hot, but the engine clearly is, the thermostat is probably stuck closed, preventing the coolant inside the engine from escaping to the radiator – renew the thermostat. Again, this problem may also be due to an airlock (refer to the coolant renewal procedure in Chapter 1A or 1B).

6 If the radiator top hose is hot, it means that the coolant is flowing (at least as far as the radiator) and the thermostat is open. Consult the *Fault diagnosis* section at the end of this manual to assist in tracing possible cooling system faults, but a lack of heater output would now definitely suggest an airlock or a blockage.

7 To gain a rough idea of whether the thermostat is working properly when the engine is warming up, without dismantling the system, proceed as follows.

8 With the engine completely cold, start the engine and let it idle, while checking the temperature of the radiator top hose. Periodically check the temperature indicated on the coolant temperature gauge – if overheating is indicated, switch the engine off immediately.

9 The top hose should feel cold for some time as the engine warms up, and should then get warm quite quickly as the thermostat opens.

10 The above is not a precise or definitive test of thermostat operation, but if the system does not perform as described, remove and test the thermostat as described below.

11 The thermostat is located in the cylinder head outlet elbow housing on the left-hand side of the engine.

Removal

12 Partially drain the cooling system, as described in Chapter 1A or 1B, so that the coolant level is below the thermostat location.

13 Where fitted, unclip the engine cover, and remove it.

14 To improve access remove the air inlet hoses as necessary, referring to Chapter 4A or 4B.

15 Though not essential, access to the thermostat housing will be improved by removing the battery as described in Chapter 5A.

16 Disconnect the hoses from the thermostat housing, noting their locations **(see illustration)**.

17 Disconnect the wiring plug from the coolant temperature sensor.

18 Unbolt the housing and remove it, recovering the sealing ring/gasket. If the thermostat can be renewed separately, it should lift out of the housing – note how it is fitted (any vent hole should be at the top).

Refitting

19 Refitting is a reversal of removal, bearing in mind the following points:

a) Fit a new sealing ring or gasket.
b) Transfer the coolant temperature sensor to the new housing. Renew the seal on the sensor.
c) On petrol models tighten the bolts in the order shown ***(see illustration).***
d) On completion, refill the cooling system as described in Chapter 1A or 1B.

6 Radiator cooling fan – removal and refitting

Removal

1 Jack up and support the front of the vehicle (see *jacking and vehicle* support in the reference section).

2 Disconnect the battery negative lead - see *Disconnecting the battery in Chapter 5A*.

3 Unbolt and then remove the engine under shield.

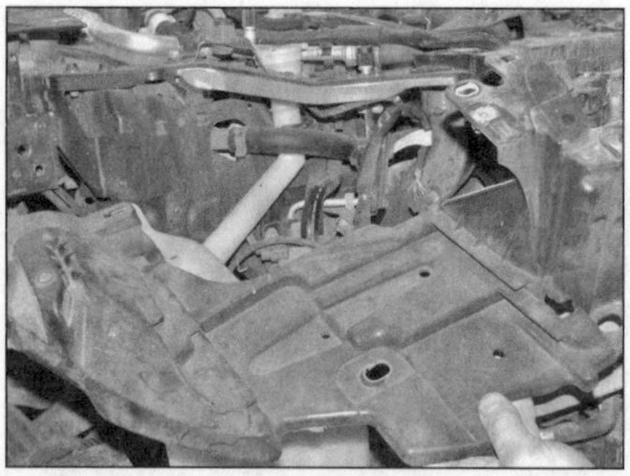

6.9 Remove the headlight support panels

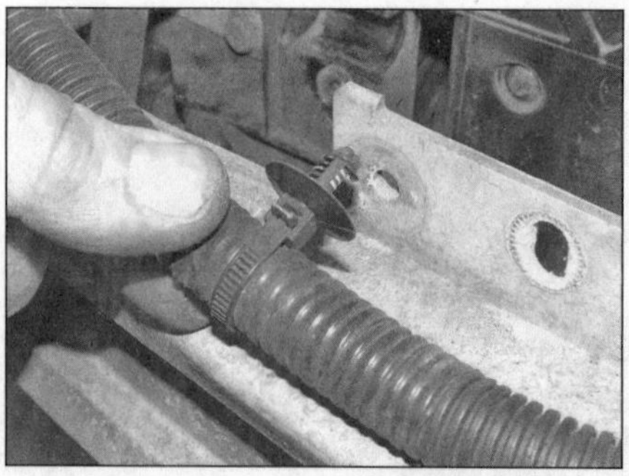

6.13a Release the wiring loom

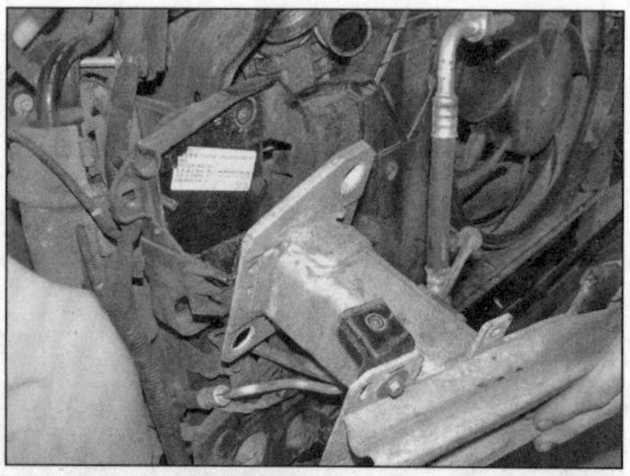

6.13b Unbolt and then remove the bumper reinforcement

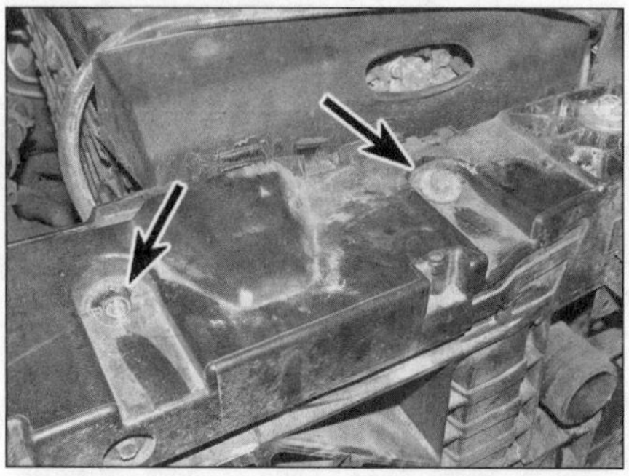

6.15 Remove the bolts (arrowed)

6.16a Slacken the lower bolts...

6.16b ...and remove the upper ones

Petrol models

4 At the top of the fan housing unclip the coolant pipe.

5 Disconnect the wiring plugs from fan and the fan speed controller. Release the loom from the fan shroud and move the loom and wiring plugs to the side.

6.17 Prise out the plastic clips

6 Remove the retaining bolts and carefully lower the fan assembly from vehicle.

Diesel models

7 Remove the front bumper as described in Chapter 11.

8 Release the inlet and outlet pipes from the intercooler - as described in Chapter 4B (there is no need to remove the intercooler).

9 Remove both front headlights as described in Chapter 12 and then remove both headlight support panels **(see illustration)**.

10 Disconnect the wiring plug from the horns and then remove the horns.

11 Unclip and then remove the air deflector panels from in front of the radiator.

12 Unbolt the bonnet release lock. Release the cable form the top of the bonnet slam panel and move it to one side.

13 Unclip the wiring loom and then unbolt and remove the bumper reinforcement panel **(see illustrations)**.

14 Partially drain the coolant and then disconnect the small vent hose on the right-hand side of the radiator.

15 Remove the bolts on the left-hand end of the front panel and release the wiring loom from the rear of the panel **(see illustration)**.

16 Remove the front panel upper mounting bolts and then slacken off (but do not remove) the lower mounting bolts **(see illustrations)**.

17 Prise out the plastic clips from the top of the front panel **(see illustration)**.

18 It should now be possible to tip the complete panel (with the radiator and AC condenser still attached) forward to access the cooling fan. As the panel is tipped, check that the coolant and AC hoses are not unduly strained.

19 Disconnect the wiring pugs from the fan and the fan speed controller **(see illustration)**.

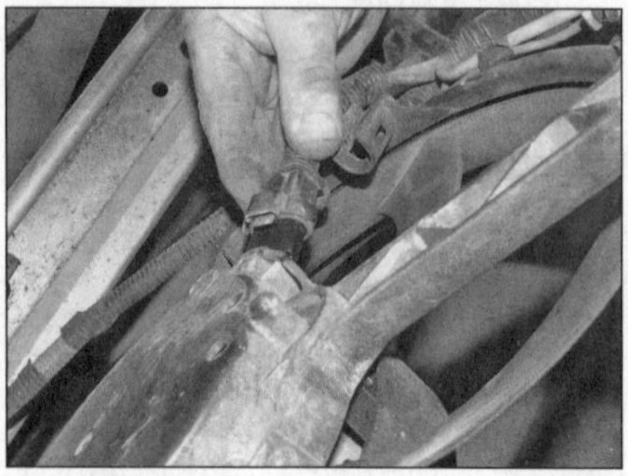

6.19a Disconnect the wiring plug from the fan motor...

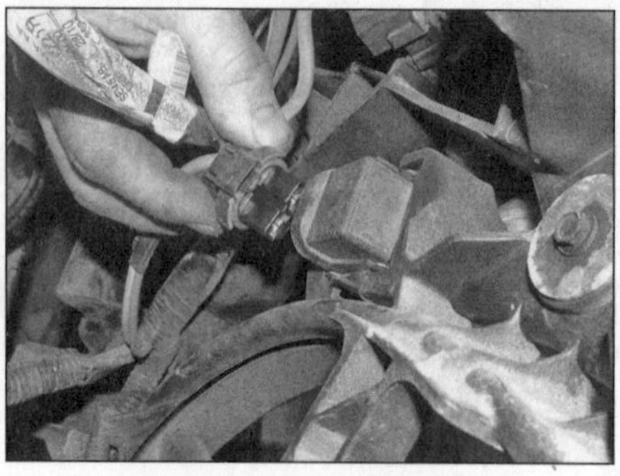

6.19b ...the controller...

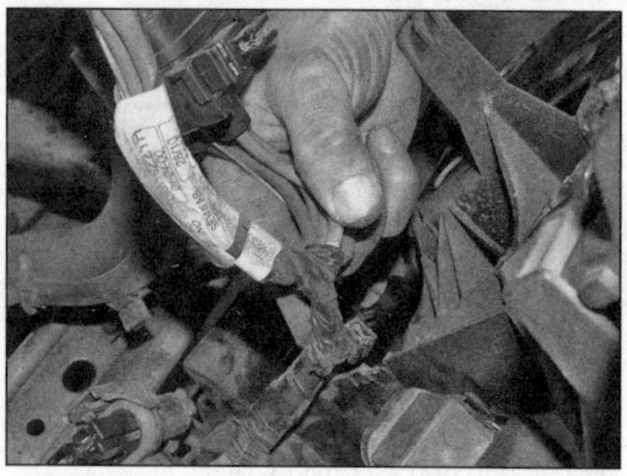

6.19c ...and then unclip the relay

Unclip the relay – there is no need to disconnect the wiring plug.

20 Remove the fan mounting bolts and manoeuvre the fan upwards from the engine bay.

Refitting

21 Refit by reversing the removal operations. On diesel models refill the radiator and fit a new seal to the intercooler pipe.

7 Radiator cooling fan switch – general information

The operation of the radiator fan is controlled by the main engine control ECU and the UCH (Unite Centrale Habitacle) control unit – located beneath the glovebox. The fan has a slow and high speed setting, controlled when the air conditioning is switched on or when the engine coolant temperature reaches predefined temperatures. A faulty or non operational cooling fan will lead to the engine over heating, especially at warm ambient temperatures and in slow or stationary traffic. The fan operates at the following engine temperatures:

a) Slow speed – if the coolant temperature is greater than 99°C, the fan will operate at its slow speed. When the coolant temperature is lower than 96°C, the fan stops operating.

b) High speed – if the coolant temperature is greater than 102°C, the fan will operate at its high speed. When the coolant temperature is lower than 99°C, the fan stops operating.

c) The coolant temperature warning light will illuminate if the temperature is greater than 114°C. When the coolant temperature drops below111°C, the light will go out.

Note: *If there is a fault on the slow-speed circuit, the fan will run at the high-speed setting.*

8 Coolant temperature sensor – testing, removal and refitting

1 The temperature sensor is located in the thermostat housing at the left-hand of the cylinder head.

Testing

2 The temperature sensor contains a thermistor – an electronic component whose electrical resistance decreases as its temperature rises. When the coolant is cold, the sender resistance is high, current flow through the gauge is reduced, and the gauge points towards the cold end of the scale. As the coolant temperature rises and the sender resistance falls, current flow increases, and the gauge needle moves towards the upper end of the scale. If the sender is faulty, it must be renewed.

3 If the gauge develops a fault, first check the other sensor and warning lights on the instrument panel. If one or more the warning lights or gauges are faulty the problem is unlikely to be confined to the coolant temperature sensor. In this case a full diagnostic check will be required at either a Renault dealer (who will have access to the factory approved diagnostic tool) or at a suitably equipped independent garage.

4 If the gauge remains at the 'cold' end of the scale when the engine is hot, remove the sender (as described below) and check the resistance of the sensor **(see illustration)**. Check the resistance at room temperature first and then suspend the sensor in a pan of water and raise the temperature, checking that the resistance changes as the temperature rises. A sensor who's resistance changes with the rise in temperature is likely to be good. If there is any doubt, replace the sensor – they are not expensive.

5 If the gauge needle remains at the 'hot' end of the scale when the engine is cold, disconnect the sender wire. If the needle then returns to the 'cold' end of the scale when the ignition is switched on, the sender unit is proved faulty, and should be renewed. If the needle still does not move, check the remainder of the circuit as described previously.

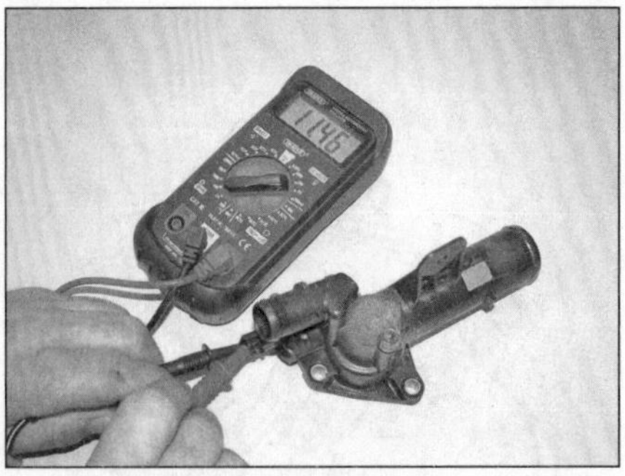

8.4 Checking the sensor resistance with the thermostat housing removed

Removal and refitting

6 Drain the cooling system as described in Chapter 1A or 1B. Alternatively, remove the expansion bottle cap to depressurise the system, and have the new temperature sensor or a suitable bung to hand.

7 Disconnect the multi-plug, then either release the securing clip and withdraw the temperature sensor from the coolant housing, or unscrew it **(see illustrations)**.

8 Refit the temperature sensor into the coolant housing using a reversal of the removal procedure. Make sure it is either securely held by the clip, or screwed in tightly enough to prevent leaks.

9 Top-up or refill the cooling system, with reference to *Weekly checks,* Chapter 1A or 1B.

8.7a Temperature sensor location (arrowed) – diesel models

8.7b Disconnect the wiring plug...

8.7c ...then pull out the securing clip and withdraw the sensor

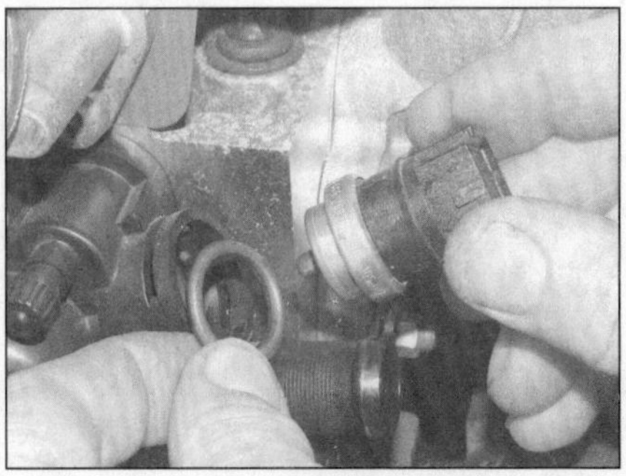

8.8d Recover the sensor sealing ring

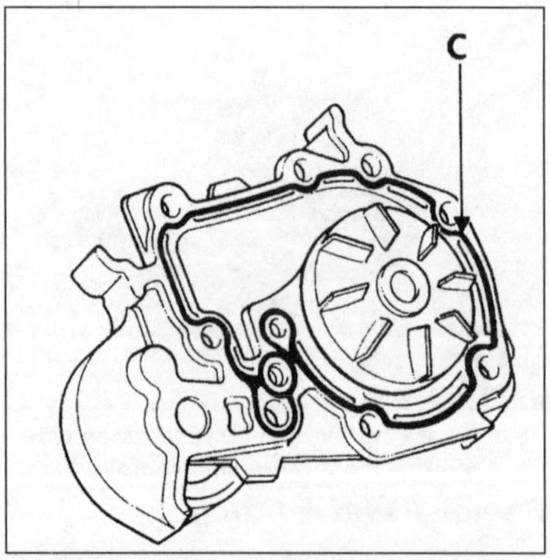

9.8 Apply a bead of sealant (C) to the coolant mating surface – petrol engines

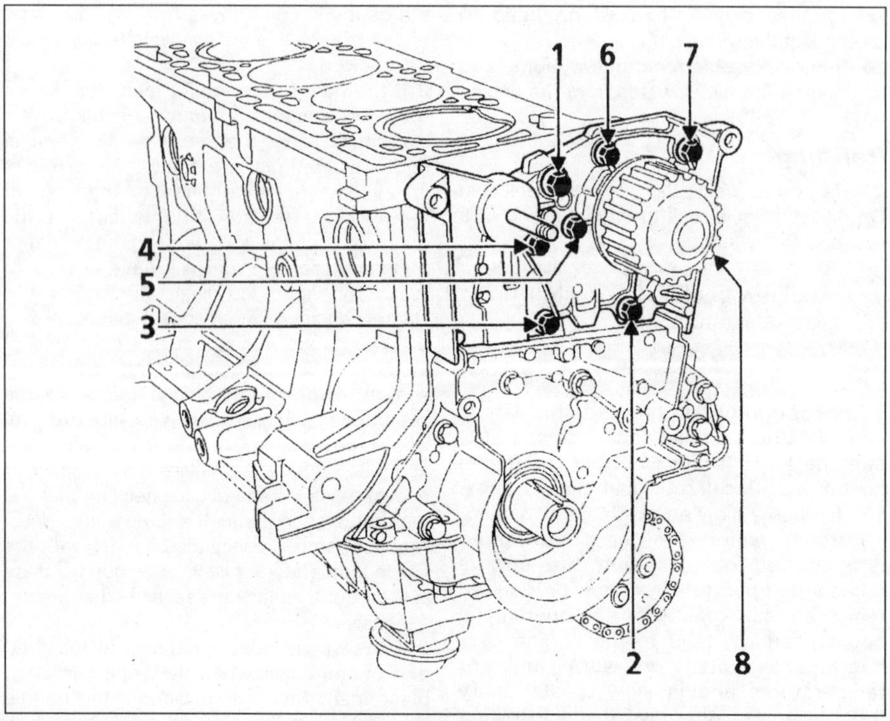

9.10 Coolant pump retaining bolt tightening sequence – petrol engines. Note the different torque figure specified for bolt number 1

9 Water pump – removal and refitting

1 If the water pump is leaking, or is noisy in operation, it must be renewed. If in doubt as to whether a pump is leaking, examine the weep hole at the base of the pump – if water staining (typically white) can be seen around this hole, a new pump is needed. Note that a pump in this condition may only leak when the engine is running.

2 The water pump is driven by the engine's timing belt, which has to be removed when renewing the pump. In light of this, if a new timing belt is being fitted after a high mileage, for peace of mind, some owners will also fit a new pump.

Petrol engine

Note: *A tube of Loctite 518 (or equivalent) sealant will be required on refitting.*

Removal

3 Drain the cooling system as described in Chapter 1A.

4 Remove the timing belt as described in Chapter 2A.

5 Slacken and remove the eight coolant pump retaining bolts, noting the locations of the different-size bolts.

6 Withdraw the pump from the block, tapping it with a soft-faced mallet if it is stuck.

Refitting

7 Commence refitting by thoroughly cleaning the mating surfaces of the pump and cylinder block, ensuring that all traces of sealant are removed.

8 Apply a 0.6 to 1.0mm wide band of Loctite 518 (or equivalent) sealant to the pump mating face **(see illustration).**

9 Locate the pump in position. Apply a little thread-locking fluid to water pump bolts 1 and 4 in the tightening sequence, and refit them to their correct locations.

10 Working in sequence **(see illustration)**, tighten all the bolts (1 to 8) to the specified torque setting and then tighten bolt number 1 to the specified torque.

11 Refit the timing belt as described in Chapter 2A. Note that Renault insist the timing belt (and tensioner) must be replaced if removed.

12 On completion, refill the cooling system as described in Chapter 1A.

Diesel engine

Removal

13 Drain the cooling system as described in Chapter 1B.

14 Remove the timing belt as described in Chapter 2B.

15 Unbolt the auxiliary drivebelt tensioner and remove it.

16 Disconnect the alternator wiring, then remove the alternator upper mounting bolt. Loosen the lower mounting bolt, and pivot the alternator outwards.

17 Undo the retaining bolts and remove the timing belt backplate from the cylinder block **(see illustration).**

18 Unscrew the five retaining bolts, then manoeuvre the water pump out of position **(see illustration).** The original factory fitted gasket is part of the crankshaft end cover gasket. To remove the gasket fold it over and then cut through the gasket. Recover the pump gasket and discard it; a new one must be used on refitting.

Refitting

19 Ensure that pump and cylinder block/ housing mating faces are clean and dry, and that the locating dowels are correctly positioned.

20 Offer up the new gasket (dry) and fit the pump assembly **(see illustration).**

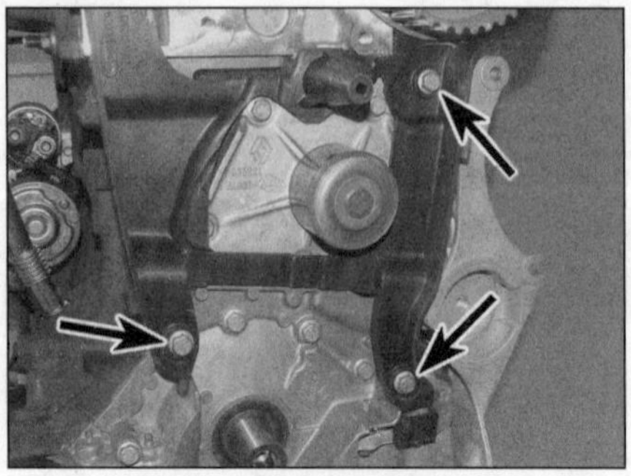

9.17 Unscrew the timing belt backplate securing bolts (arrowed)

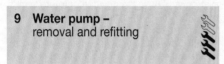

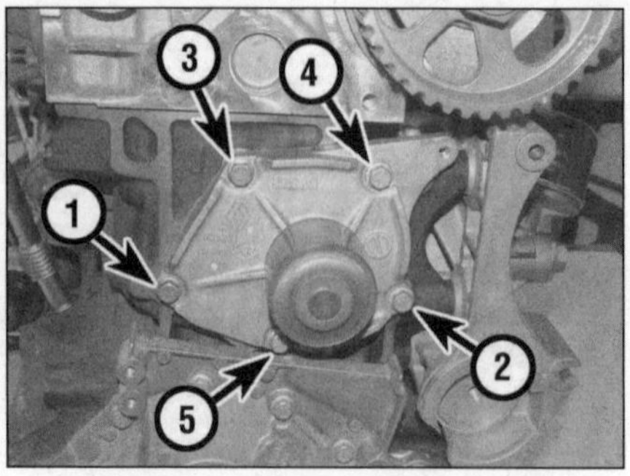

9.18 Undo the pump retaining bolts (arrowed)

21 Apply a little thread-locking fluid to the pump retaining bolts, then refit and tighten them to their specified torque in the order show **(see illustration 9.18)**.

22 Refit the timing belt backplate cover to the cylinder block, and securely tighten the retaining bolts.

23 Refit the timing belt as described in Chapter 2B –a new belt and tensioner must be fitted.

24 On completion, refill the cooling system as described in Chapter 1B.

10 Heating system – general information and checks

General information

1 The heater and fresh air ventilation unit works on the principle of mixing hot and cold air in the proportions selected by means of the central outer (temperature) control knob. Coolant flows through the heater radiator all the time that the engine is running, regardless of the temperature selected.

2 Air distribution is selected by the right-hand control knob on models fitted with manual AC. On models with fully automatic Climate Control (CC) distribution is controlled by the upper right-hand switch. Additional control is possible by opening, closing or redirecting individual vents in the facia panel.

3 An air recirculation control (the left-hand switch on manual AC models and the lower left, but one switch on models with CC) enables the outside air supply to be closed off, while the air inside the car is recirculated. This can be useful to prevent unpleasant odours entering from outside the car – for instance, when driving in heavy traffic – but should only be used briefly, as the recirculated air inside the car will soon become stale and may cause light misting.

4 A four-speed blower fan is controlled by the central inner knob on models with manual AC or by the left-hand upper and lower switches on models with CC.

5 Temperature is controlled by the left-hand switch on manual AC models and by the left and right outer switches on models fitted with CC.

Checks

6 Periodically check that all the controls operate as intended. Problems related to the temperature and air distribution controls may be due to cables being broken or disconnected (see Section 11).

7 If the blower does not operate at all, check the fuse and the blower multi-plug before condemning the motor. If one or two speeds do not work, the fault is almost certainly in the heater blower resistor (see Section 11).

8 Check the condition and security of the coolant hoses which feed the heater radiator. The radiator-to-hose joints are at the bulkhead under the bonnet. If water leaks inside the car seem to be coming from the heater, establish whether the leak is of coolant (indicating a leaking heater radiator) or of rainwater (indicating a defective scuttle seal). Cooling system antifreeze has a distinctive sweet smell.

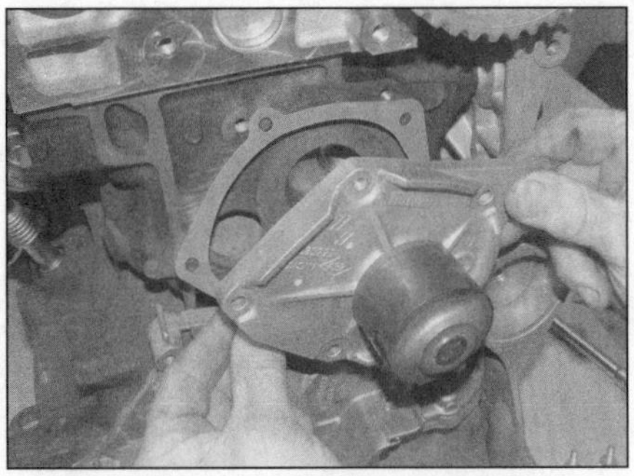

9.20 Fitting a new gasket to the water pump

11 Heater/ventilation system components – removal and refitting

Note: *Access to many of the heating and ventilation system component parts is extremely limited. The only components that are relatively simple to remove are the heater matrix, auxiliary heater and the control panel. All the remaining components require considerable time (and dexterity) to remove. If you are replacing a component that is difficult to access – the heater blower motor would be a good example – then consideration should be given to replacing other components with a high failure rate such as the blower motor control whilst they are easily accessible.*

Heater control panel

Removal

1 Disconnect the battery negative lead, and move the lead away from the battery (see *Disconnecting the battery).*

2 Prise off the outer surround panel. Disconnect the wiring plugs as the panel is removed **(see illustrations)**.

3 Whilst not strictly necessary, remove the audio unit as described in Chapter 12. Removing the audio unit allows the control panel to be fully rotated to access the control cables (manual AC models only) without fear of damaging the audio unit front panel.

4 Remove the panel mounting screws **(see illustration)** and then depress the locking pins to release the panel from the facia

5 Carefully rotate the panel to access the control cables – manual AC models only. Note the position of the cables and then disconnect the left-hand (air mixture cable) followed by the right-hand cable (air distribution). Access is difficult and some dexterity will be required **(see illustrations)**.

6 Disconnect the wiring plug(s) from the back of the panel **(see illustration)**.

Refitting

7 Refitting is a reversal of removal. Ensure that the control cables are correctly and

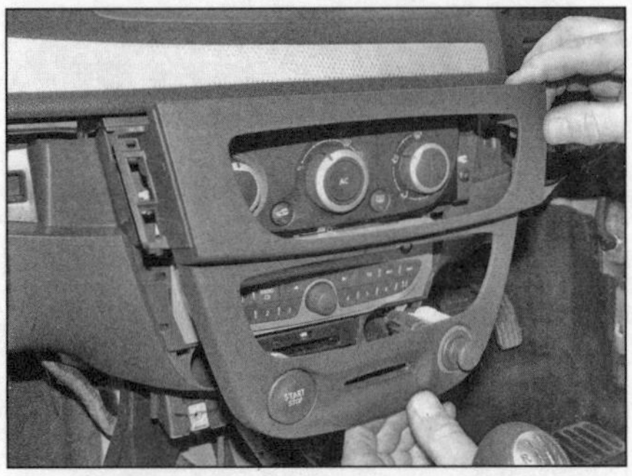

11.2a Remove the outer panel ...

11.2b ...disconnecting the wiring plugs as the panel is removed

11.4 Remove the mounting screws (arrowed)

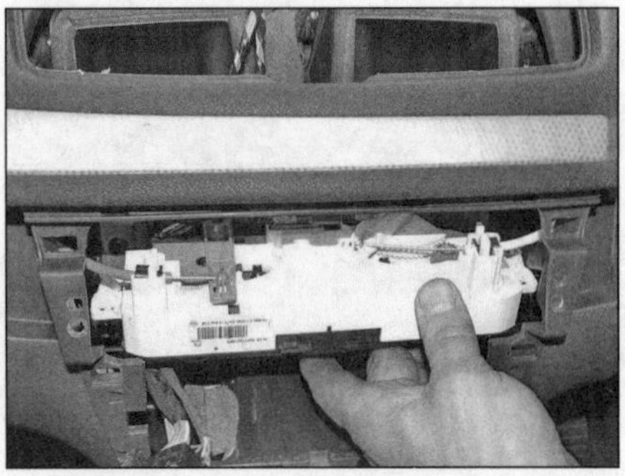

11.5a Rotate the panel and...

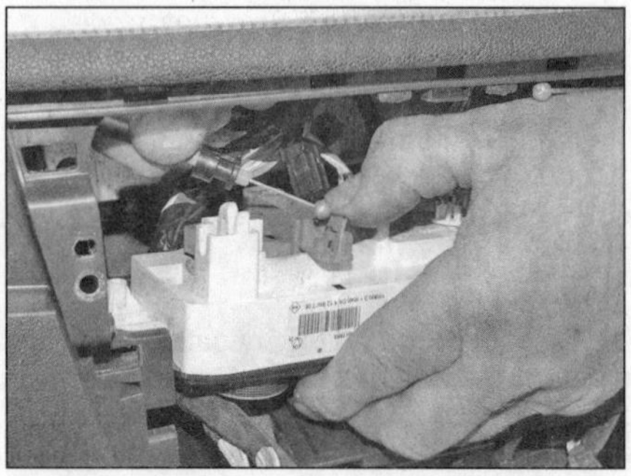

11.5b ...disconnect the left-hand cable...

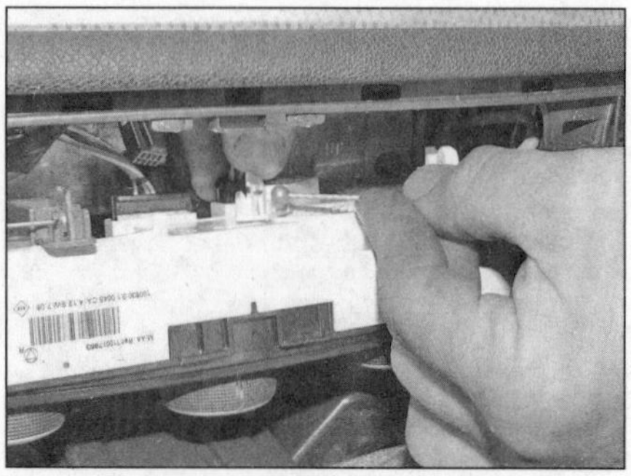

11.5c ...followed by the right-hand cable

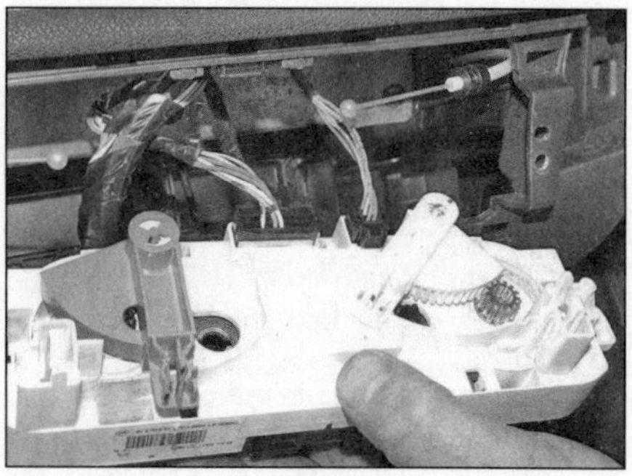

11.6 Disconnect the wiring plugs

securely refitted – the cables do not require adjustment.

Air distribution cable

Removal

8 Start by removing the heater control panel as described previously in this Section, and disconnect the cable from the back of the panel. If just the cable is to be removed, the panel need not be removed completely, though removing it does improve working room.

9 Remove the lower facia panels from the right-hand side as described in Chapter 11.

10 Partially remove the carpet in the right-hand side footwell, so that the metal facia crossmember support panel can be removed. Remove the bolts and remove the crossmember support.

11 Note the routing of the cable and then disconnect it from the control arm **(see illustration)**.

11.11 The location of the distribution air cable (arrowed). Shown with the facia removed for clarity

Refitting

12 Refitting is a reversal of removal.

Air mixture cable

13 Remove the glovebox as described in Chapter 11.

14 Remove the control panel and cable as described above.

15 Remove the retaining clip and then remove the air distribution duct from above the left-hand side.

16 Note the routing of the cable and then unclip it from the control arm. Remove the cable

Refitting

17 Refitting is a reversal of removal.

Recirculation cable

Removal

18 Remove the complete facia as described in Chapter 11.

11.20a Release the cable at the left-hand end and...

19 The cable is located on top of the heater distribution unit.

20 Unclip the cable at the left-hand end and then at the right-hand end **(see illustrations)**.

Refitting

21 Refitting is a reversal of removal.

Blower motor

Removal

22 Disconnect the battery negative lead, and move the lead away from the battery (see *Disconnecting the battery*).

23 Renault suggest it is possible to remove the motor after the steering column has been removed. We found this to be impossible, so had to remove the complete heater/air distribution assembly from the vehicle, as described below.

24 Before the heater assembly can be accessed the facia panel and the main crossmember must be removed as described in Chapter 11.

25 With the heater assembly removed (or at least pulled away from the bulkhead) access to the blower motor is relatively simple.

26 Disconnect the air recirculation control cable and then unplug the wiring connector from the cable control motor. Note the routing of the wiring loom and move it to one side **(see illustration)**.

27 Remove the fixing screws and then remove the air recirculation duct **(see illustrations)**.

28 With difficulty release the wiring plug from the blower motor.

29 A special tool (Ms1909) is available to release the motor from the housing. This is

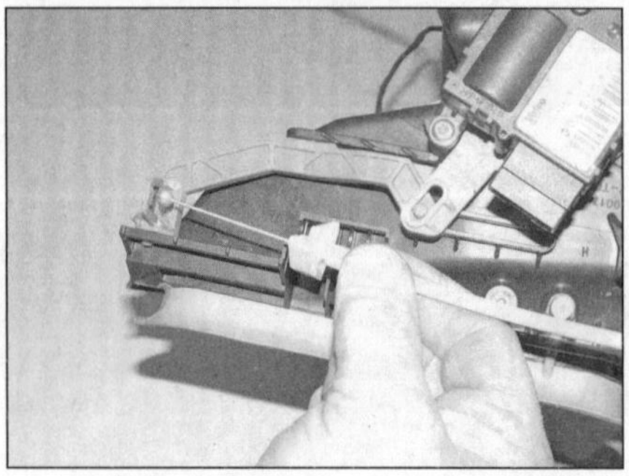

11.20b ...then the right-hand end

11.26 Release the loom and then disconnect the wiring plug

11.27a Remove the screws and...

11.27b ..and release the housing

11.30a A screwdriver can be used to release the blower motor

11.30b Remove the blower motor

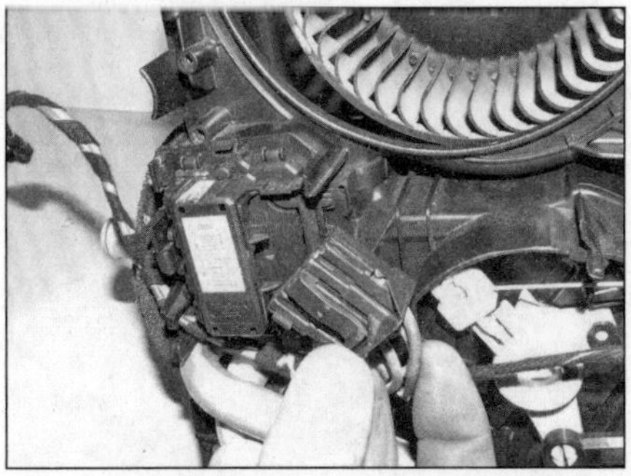

11.36 Disconnect the wiring plug

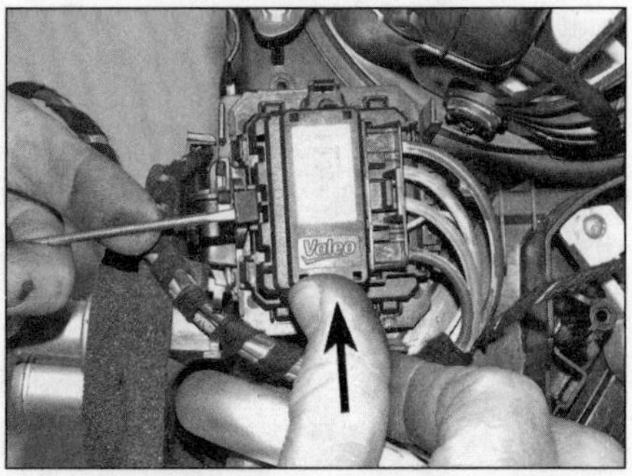

11.37a Release the assembly by pushing in the direction shown

11.37b Withdraw the resistor pack

a three legged tool that passes through the holes in the fan and engages in the main motor body. Rotating the tool turns the complete fan assembly inside the housing allowing it to be removed. Where the tool is not available a pair of screwdrivers can be used to release the blower motor assembly.

30 Lift the locking catch and using either the special tool or a pair of screwdrivers rotate the motor assembly anti-clockwise and pull it forward out of the housing **(see illustrations)**.

Refitting

31 Refitting is a reversal of removal. Ensure the locking catch engages correctly.

Blower motor resistor

Removal

32 Disconnect the battery negative lead, and move the lead away from the battery (see *Disconnecting the battery*).

33 Remove the glovebox as described in Chapter 11.

34 Unclip and remove the air distribution duct.

35 The resistor pack is located high up on the left-hand side of the heater/air distribution assembly. Access is extremely limited.

36 Working blind, depress the locking tab and disconnect the wiring plug **(see illustration)**. Note that all the illustrations show removal of the resister pack with the air distribution housing removed from the vehicle for clarity.

37 The resistor is a sliding fit in the housing. Release the locking tab (at the rear) and then push up the resistor pack to release it **(see illustration)**. Note that this is an extremely difficult operation, requiring considerable patience and dexterity.

Refitting

38 Refit by reversing the removal operations.

Heater blower motor switch

Removal

39 Remove the heater control panel as described previously in this Section.

40 The switch is part of the panel, and cannot be renewed separately.

Refitting

41 Refitting is a reversal of removal.

Heater matrix

Removal

42 Disconnect the battery negative lead, and move the lead away from the battery (see *Disconnecting the battery*).

11.47a Remove the retaining clips (arrowed)

43 Working in the engine compartment, trace the two heater hoses to the bulkhead connections, which must be disconnected – do not confuse these coolant hoses with the rigid refrigerant pipes which should not be disturbed. The cooling system does not necessarily have to be drained for this operation – either clamp the hoses beforehand, or turn their hose ends upwards afterwards to minimise coolant loss.

44 Remove the glovebox as described in Chapter 11.

45 Remove the side extension panel from the centre console and then unclip and remove the air distribution duct.

46 Place a waterproof sheet inside the car, below the heater matrix, to protect it from coolant spillage. Have ready a shallow container to catch the coolant which will be lost when the heater pipes are disconnected (this applies even if the cooling system was drained, as coolant will remain in the matrix).

47 Slide off the horseshoe clips from the matrix pipes and then (anticipating some coolant spillage) gently work the pipes free from the matrix **(see illustrations)**.

48 Move the pipes to the side and then remove the matrix retaining screws. Remove the cover and then pull the matrix from the housing **(see illustrations)**.

Refitting

49 Refitting is a reversal of removal, noting the following points:

a) Fit new sealing rings to the matrix pipes.

b) On completion, fill and bleed the cooling system as described in Chapter 1A or 1B.

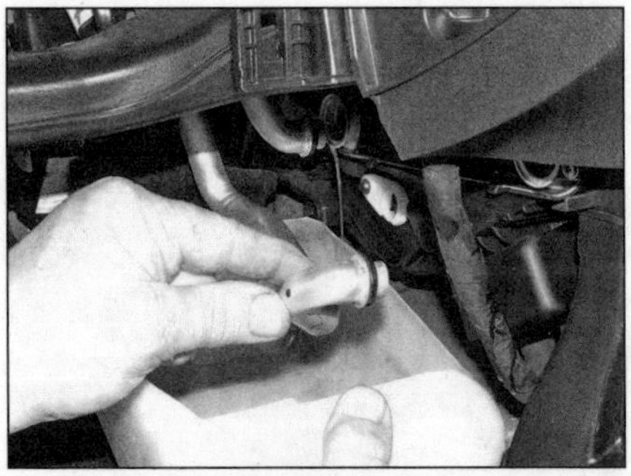

11.47b Release the pipes and catch any escaping coolant

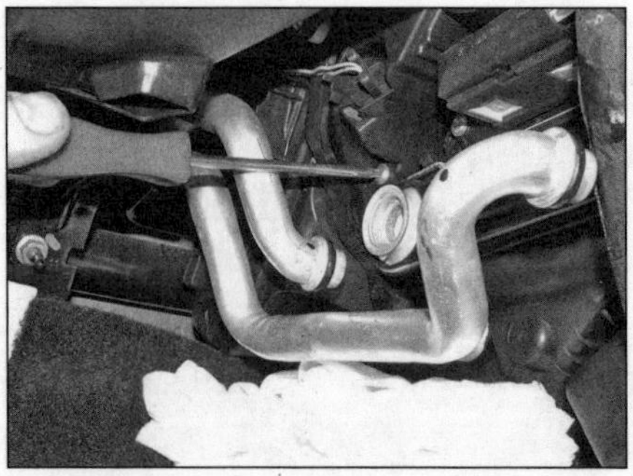

11.48a Remove the screws and...

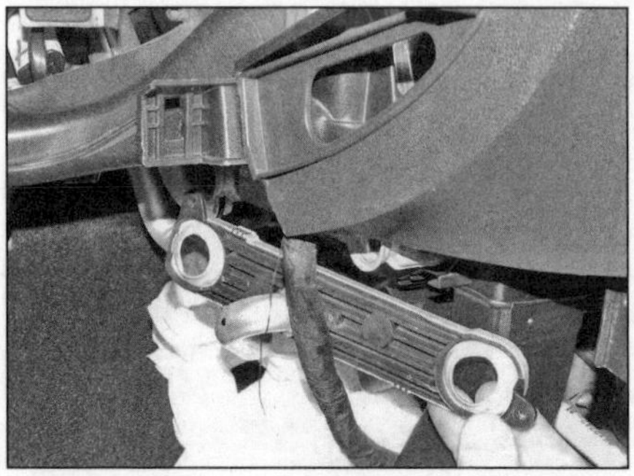

11.48b ...pull off the cover

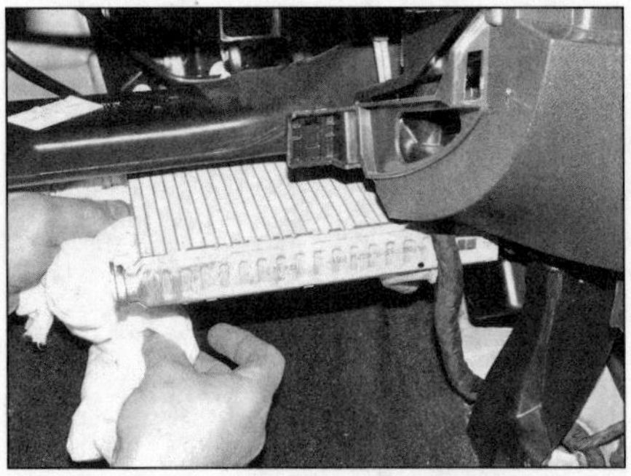

11.48c Withdraw the matrix

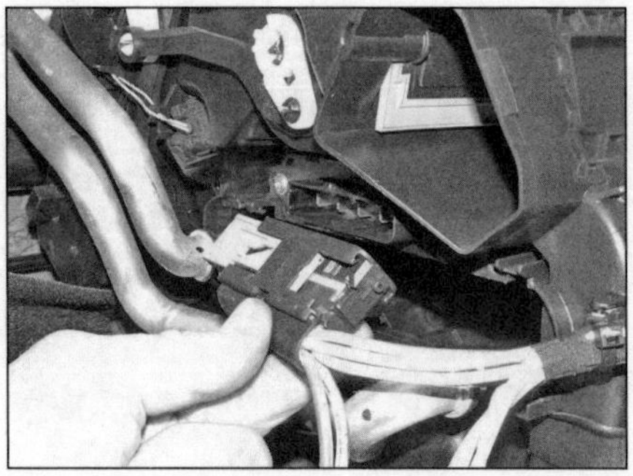

11.55 Release the wiring plug

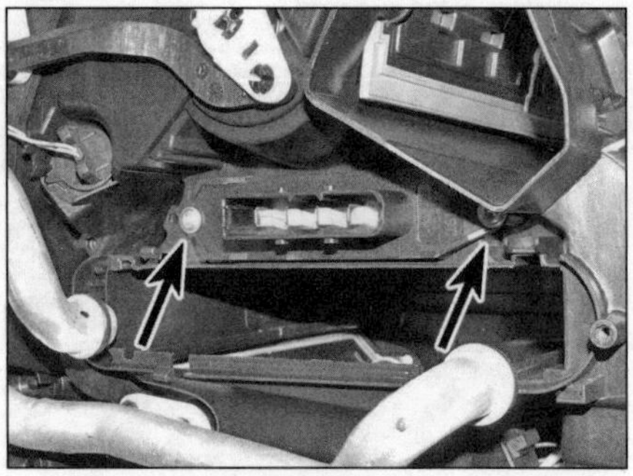

11.56 Remove the screws (arrowed)

Auxiliary heater

Removal

50 Fitted to some models is an electric heater element. This is fitted to the base of the main heater assembly. It provides 'instant' heat from cold when required, and will also be employed to supplement the heat from the main heater matrix as necessary, to maintain the selected cabin temperature.

51 The auxiliary heater is located just above the heater matrix.

52 Disconnect the battery negative lead, and move the lead away from the battery (see *Disconnecting the battery*).

53 Remove the glovebox as described in Chapter 11.

54 Remove the side extension panel from the centre console and then unclip and remove the air distribution duct.

55 Slide the wiring plug locking catch upwards to release it, and pull off the plug **(see illustration)**.

56 Remove the two screws from the heater end plate **(see illustration)**.

57 Withdraw the heater unit by sliding it sideways into the footwell **(see illustration)**.

58 If required the heater control relays can also be removed. These are located below the heater matrix. Unclip the box, disconnect the wiring plug and remove the control unit **(see illustration)**.

Refitting

59 Refitting is a reversal of removal.

Heater assembly/Air distribution housing

Warning: The air conditioning system must be discharged before starting this procedure. Discharging the air conditioning system must be carried out by a suitably equipped specialist, or a Renault dealer. It is a criminal offence to knowingly discharge refrigerant into the atmosphere.

Removal

60 Have the air conditioning system professionally discharged.

61 With reference to Chapter 11 remove the upper and lower windscreen cowl panels.

62 Working in the engine compartment, trace the two heater hoses to the bulkhead connections. Disconnect the hoses. The cooling system does not necessarily have to be drained for this operation – either clamp the hoses beforehand, or turn their hose ends upwards afterwards to minimise coolant loss.

63 Remove the bolts and disconnect the refrigerant pipes. **Do not** disturb the refrigerant pipes unless the system has been discharged first. Immediately seal the refrigerant pipes with suitable plugs.

64 Remove the facia panel and the complete crossmember as described in Chapter 11.

65 Place a waterproof sheet inside the car, below the heater matrix, to protect it from coolant spillage. Have ready a shallow container to catch the coolant which will be lost when the heater pipes are disconnected (this applies even if the cooling system was drained, as coolant will remain in the matrix).

66 Slide off the horseshoe clips from the matrix pipes and then (anticipating some coolant spillage) gently work the pipes free from the matrix.

67 Move the rigid pipes forwards to clear the matrix, and remove them.

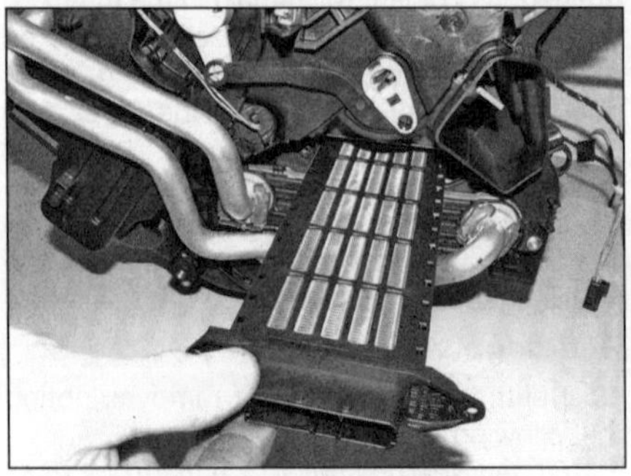

11.57 Remove the heater

11.58 Remove the relay/control unit

68 If not already done so, disconnect the wiring plugs from the housing.

69 With the aid of an assistant lift the assembly upwards, disconnect the evaporator drain hose and remove the assembly from the vehicle.

Refitting

70 Refitting is a reversal of removal, noting the following points:

a) *Fit new seals to the heater matrix pipes.*

b) *On completion, fill and bleed the cooling system as described in Chapter 1A or 1B.*

c) *Fit new O-ring seals to the refrigerant pipes. Have the system recharged and checked by an air conditioning specialist or a Renault dealer.*

Centre vent panel

Removal

71 Taking great care not to mark the finish, prise up the vent panel **(see illustration)**.

72 Disconnect the wiring plugs on the underside of the facia vent panel. Remove the panel from the facia.

Refitting

73 Refitting is a reversal of removal.

Facia end vents

Removal

74 On the right-hand side remove the facia end panel and then taking care not to mark the surface of the facia, prise and push out (from the rear) the vent.

75 Withdraw the vent from its location, and remove it.

76 On the left hand side carefully remove the cosmetic trim panel that extends along the top of the glovebox. This panel is extremely fragile and care must be taken removing it **(see illustration)**. Note that after the glovebox has been removed it is possible to partially release some of the clips from the rear.

77 With the trim panel removed, prise out the vent.

Refitting

78 Refitting is a reversal of removal.

12 Air conditioning system – general information and precautions

General information

An Air Conditioning (AC) system is fitted to all models. It enables the temperature of incoming air to be lowered; it also dehumidifies the air, which makes for rapid demisting and increased comfort. Two types of air conditioning are fitted – manual and automatic (climate control).

The cooling side of the system works in the same way as a domestic refrigerator. Refrigerant gas is drawn into a belt-driven compressor, and passes into a condenser in front of the radiator, where it loses heat and becomes liquid. The liquid passes through an expansion valve to an evaporator, where it changes from liquid under high pressure to gas under low pressure. This change is accompanied by a drop in temperature, which cools the evaporator. The refrigerant returns to the compressor and the cycle begins again.

Air blown through the evaporator passes to the air distribution unit, where it is mixed with hot air blown through the heater matrix, to achieve the desired temperature in the passenger compartment.

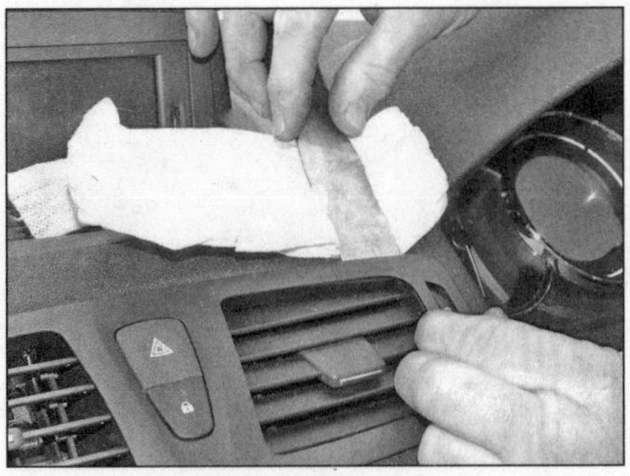

11.71 Protect the facia whilst releasing the vent

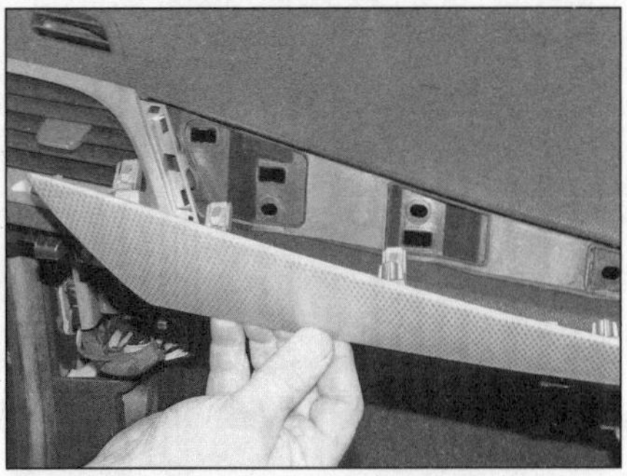

11.76 Prise out the trim panel

Precautions

Warning: The refrigerant is potentially dangerous, and should only be handled by qualified persons. If it is splashed onto the skin, it can cause frostbite. It is not itself poisonous, but in the presence of a naked flame (including a cigarette) it forms a poisonous gas.

Uncontrolled discharging of the refrigerant is dangerous, and damaging to the environment. It is a criminal offence to knowingly discharge refrigerant into the atmosphere. Before beginning any work on the AC system it must be professionally discharged. This service is provide by an increasing number of garages or by your Renault dealer. If the vehicle is not roadworthy many air conditioning specialist offer a mobile service.

As soon as any part of the AC system is opened to the atmosphere (after discharging the system) all parts of the system should be sealed immediately with suitable sealing plugs.

13 Air conditioning system – checking and maintenance

Routine maintenance is limited to checking the tension and condition of the compressor (auxiliary) drivebelt, as described in Chapter 1A or 1B.

Periodic recharging of the system will be required, since there is inevitably a slow loss of refrigerant. It is suggested that the system be inspected by a specialist every other year, or at once if a loss of performance is noticed.

14 Air conditioning system – component removal and refitting

Warning: The air conditioning system must be discharged before starting this procedure. Discharging the air conditioning system must be carried out by a suitably equipped specialist, or a Renault dealer. It is a criminal offence to knowingly discharge refrigerant into the atmosphere.

Compressor drivebelt

1 Refer to the auxiliary drivebelt procedures in Chapter 1A or 1B.

Compressor

Removal

2 Before starting work have the AC system discharged by a suitably equipped garage or Renault dealer.

3 Jack up and support the front of the vehicle (see *Jacking and vehicle support* in the reference section). Remove the front right-hand road wheel.

4 Disconnect the battery negative terminal (see *Disconnecting the battery*).

5 Remove both front headlights (as described in Chapter 12) and then remove the support panel from beneath the headlights.

6 Remove the front section of the right-hand wing liner and then (with reference to Chapter 11) remove the front bumper cover.

7 With the bumper cover removed, disconnect the wiring plug from the horns and the remove the bumper reinforcement.

8 Unbolt the bonnet lock from the slam panel and move it to one side.

9 At the right-hand end of the slam panel remove the bolts and release the wiring loom.

10 Slacken off the front panel lower mounting bolts and then remove the upper bolts and plastic retaining clips.

11 Tilt the panel forwards and (on diesel models) remove the outlet pipe from the intercooler.

12 Remove the auxiliary drivebelt with reference to Chapter 1A or 1B.

13 Disconnect the refrigerant pipes from the compressor. Seal the pipe ends and the

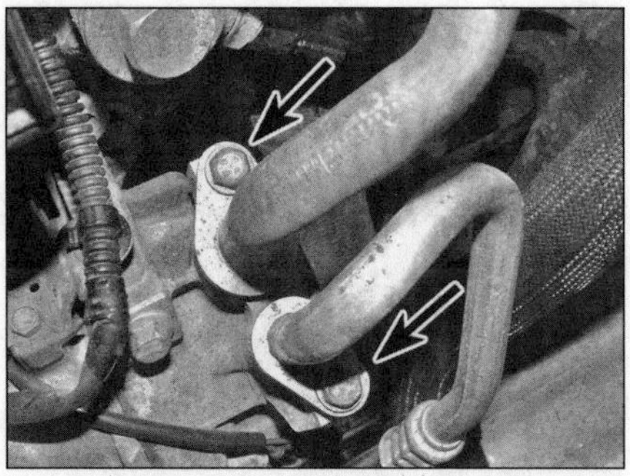

14.13 Remove the bolts (arrowed) and release the refrigerant pipes

14.14 Disconnect the wiring plug (arrowed)

14.15 Remove the bolts (arrowed)

compressor openings with suitable sealing plugs immediately **(see illustration).**

14 Disconnect the wiring plug from the top of the compressor **(see illustration).**

15 Remove the bolts and then remove the compressor **(see illustration).**

Refitting

16 Refitting is a reversal of removal, noting the following points:

a) Clean the refrigerant pipes, fit new O-ring seals and lubricate the seal with compressor oil before refitting the refrigerant pipes.

b) Fit an new auxiliary drivebelt.

c) Have the system recharged and checked by an air conditioning specialist or a Renault dealer.

Condenser

Removal

17 Before starting work have the AC system discharged by a suitably equipped garage or Renault dealer.

18 To access the condenser, first remove the front bumper as described in Chapter 11.

19 Remove the right-hand headlight as described in Chapter 12.

20 Unclip and remove the air deflector top and both sides.

21 Disconnect the wiring plug from the pressure sensor.

22 Unbolt and remove the refrigerant pipes **(see illustrations).** Seal the pipe ends and the condenser openings with suitable sealing plugs immediately.

23 Release the retaining clips and then pull up the condenser to remove it **(see illustration 3.9).**

Refitting

24 Refitting is a reversal of removal, noting the following points:

a) Clean the refrigerant pipes, fit new O-ring seals and lubricate the seals with compressor oil before refitting the refrigerant pipes.

b) Have the system recharged and checked by an air conditioning specialist or a Renault dealer.

Receiver/drier (Dehydrator)

Removal

25 The receiver drier is designed to absorb any moisture in the refrigerant circuit. It should be replaced on any AC system that has been open to the atmosphere fro an extended period.

26 Before starting work have the AC system discharged by a suitably equipped garage or Renault dealer.

27 To access the drier first remove the front bumper as described in Chapter 11 and then remove the condenser as described in paragraphs 17 to 23 of this Section.

28 With the condenser on the bench fit an M5 bolt into the end cap of the drier.

29 Using circlip pliers remove the circlip and then using pliers on the M5 bolt pull out the drier. It may be necessary to use locking pliers and a hammer to gently tap the pliers upwards to release the receiver drier. Remove the drier and dispose of it. A new one must be fitted.

Refitting

30 Refitting is a reversal of removal, noting the following points:

a) Fit new O-ring seals and lubricate the seals with compressor oil before fitting the new drier.

b) Have the system recharged and checked by an air conditioning specialist or a Renault dealer.

Pressure sensor

Note: *The pressure sensor is located beside the condenser on the right-hand side. Where a label is fitted next to the AC charging port the system must be drained before the sensor can be removed. On all other models a Schrader valve is fitted below the sensor. On these models the sensor can be removed and replaced without draining the AC system. If there is any doubt as to which type of sensor is fitted the AC system must be drained first.*

Removal

31 Remove the front bumper for access to the sensor, as described in Chapter 11.

32 Remove the central air deflector and the right-hand side deflector.

33 Disconnect the wiring connector from the sensor **(see illustration).**

34 Observing the precautions outlined above, slacken and remove the pressure sensor from the high-pressure pipe.

Refitting

35 Refitting is a reversal of removal. Check the condition of the sensor seal, and fit a new one if necessary.

14.22a Remove the upper...

14.22b ...and lower refrigerant pipes

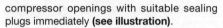

14.33 Disconnect the wiring plug

Evaporator

Removal

Note: *Whilst not a difficult task, it is complex and time consuming. An evaporator will normally only require replacement if it is leaking. Have an AC specialist, or Renault dealer confirm that the evaporator is faulty before starting work.*

36 Before starting work have the AC system discharged by a suitably equipped garage or Renault dealer.

37 Disconnect the battery negative terminal (see *Disconnecting the battery*).

38 Remove the complete facia and crossmember as described in Chapter 11.

39 At the bulkhead, disconnect the refrigerant and coolant pipes.

40 Check that all the wiring plugs have been disconnected and then lift up the complete air distribution housing. Disconnect the evaporator drain pipe and then lift the assembly from the vehicle.

41 Start the disassembly of the air distribution housing by removing the pollen filter, the wiring plug from the blower motor, the motor cover **(see illustration)** and then the blower motor.

42 Remove the foam insulation and then remove the cover plate from the heater matrix pipes **(see illustration)**. Remove the heater matrix as described Section 11 of this Chapter.

43 Where fitted remove the auxiliary heater – see Section 11 of this Chapter for details.

44 Note the position of the air distribution flaps and then partially release them.

45 Separate the two main sections of the main housing, remove the foam insulation and then slide out the small panel that covers the refrigerant pipes **(see illustrations)**.

46 Remove the evaporator from the housing **(see illustration)**.

Refitting

47 Refitting is a reversal of removal, but if the evaporator is to be replaced, remove the expansion valve and transfer it to the new evaporator. Before refitting to the vehicle check the operation of all control cables and flaps.

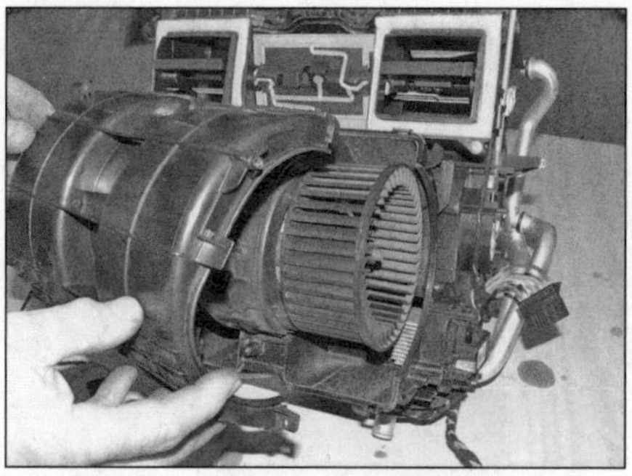

14.41 Remove the motor cover

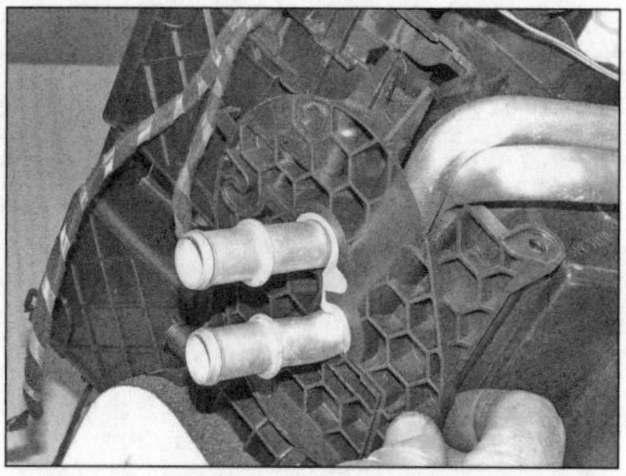

14.42 Remove the cover

Expansion valve

Removal

48 Before starting work have the AC system discharged by a suitably equipped garage or Renault dealer.

49 Remove both wiper arms and then remove the upper and lower windscreen cowl panels as described in Chapter 11.

50 Partially remove the sound proofing panel from the bulk head.

51 Unbolt the refrigerant pipes from the expansion valve **(see illustration)**.

52 Carefully move the refrigerant pipes to the side and then remove the bolt securing the valve to the evaporator. Withdraw the expansion valve from the bulkhead.

Refitting

53 Refitting is a reversal of removal, but fit new seals to the expansion valve. Lubricate the seals with compressor oil and then have the system leak tested and refilled with refrigerant. Entrust this work to a suitably equipped garage or your Renault dealer.

Heating/ventilation control motors

Note: *On models with automatic air conditioning (climate control), electric motors are used instead of cables. Control cables are still used on models with manual air conditioning.*

Recirculation motor

54 Remove the complete facia as described in Chapter 11.

55 Disconnect the control cable.

56 Remove the two mounting screws and the disconnect the wiring plug **(see illustration)**.

57 Refitting is a reversal of removal.

Air mixing motors

58 Mixture motors are located at the left

14.45a Separate the main sections of the housing...

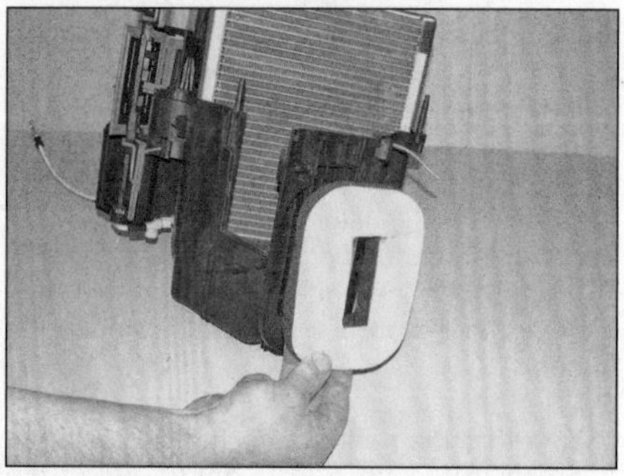

14.45b ...remove the foam insulation...

14.45c ...and then slide out the pipe cover

14.46 Remove the evaporator

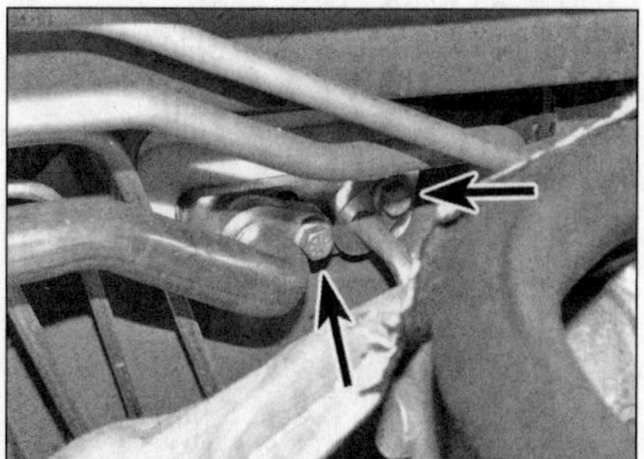

14.51 Remove the bolts (arrowed)

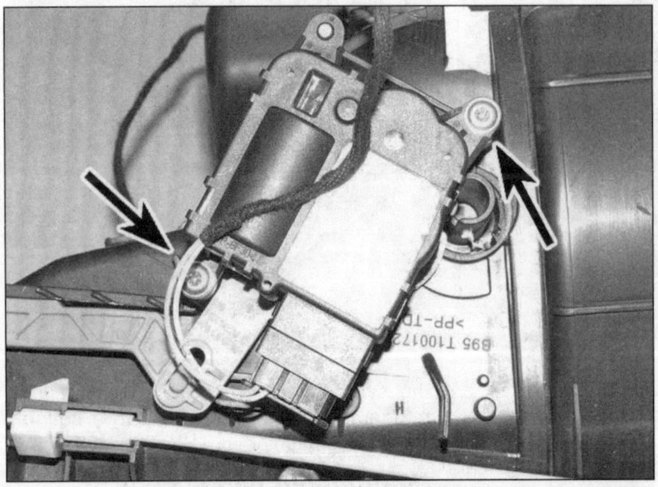

14.56 Remove the mounting screws

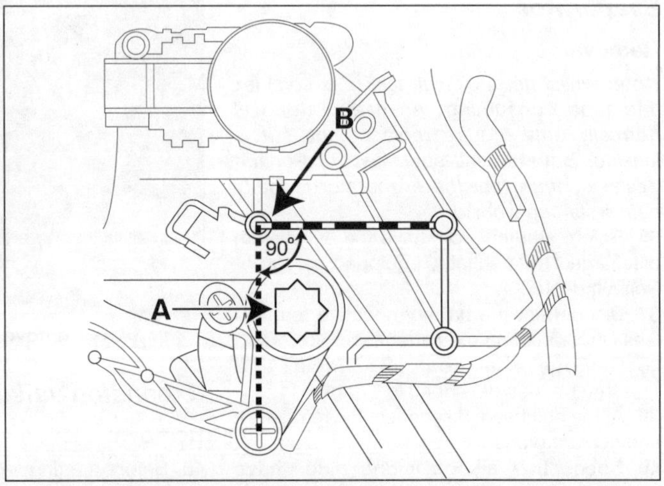

14.61 The flat section of the control flap (A), must be at 90 degrees to the horizontal

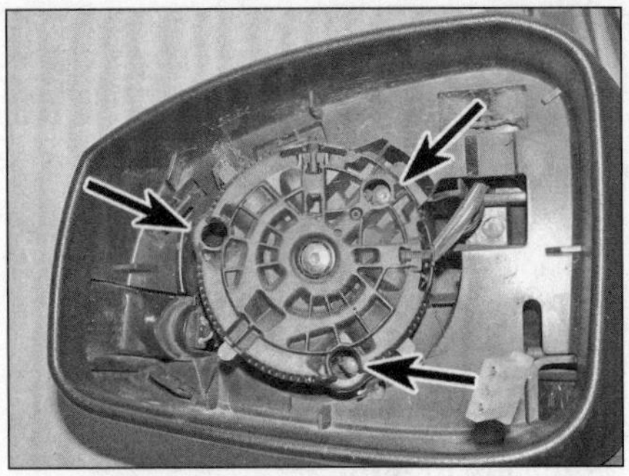

14.72 Remove the motor mounting screws (arrowed)

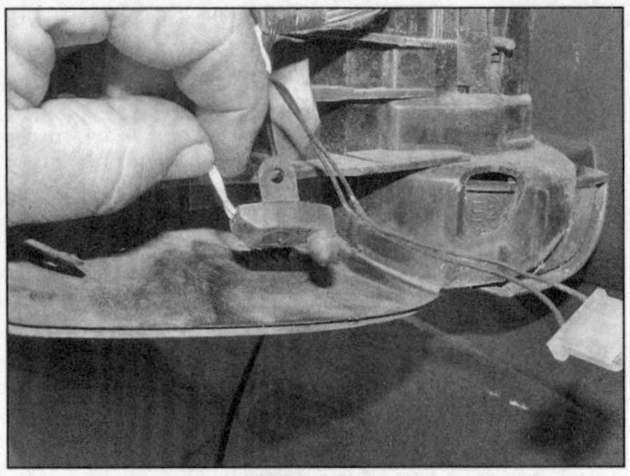

14.73 Remove the sensor

and right-hand sides of the air distribution housing.

59 The right-hand motor can be accessed by following the procedure outlined in Chapter 1A or 1B for pollen filter removal, but do not remove the pollen filter.

60 With the clutch pedal assembly moved to the side, disconnect the wiring plug and then remove the motor fixing screws. Remove the motor.

61 Refitting is a reversal of removal, but ensure that the control flap flat side is at 90 degrees to the horizontal before fitting the motor **(see illustration)**. Adjust the position of the flap manually if necessary.

62 The left-hand motor can be accessed after the glovebox and front side section of the centre console have been removed - as described in Chapter 11.

63 Disconnect the wiring plug, remove the mounting screws and then remove the motor.

64 Refitting is a reversal of removal, but ensure that the control flap flat side is at 90 degrees to the horizontal before fitting the motor **(see illustration 11.61)**. Adjust the position of the flap manually if necessary.

Air distribution motor

65 The motor is located on the right-hand side of the air distribution housing. The motor can be accessed by following the procedure outlined in Chapter 1A or 1B for pollen filter removal, but do not remove the pollen filter. The distribution motor is the upper motor.

66 Disconnect the wiring plug, remove the mounting screws and then remove the motor.

67 Refitting is a reversal of removal, but ensure that the control flap flat side is at 90 degrees to the horizontal before fitting the motor **(see illustration 11.61)**. Adjust the position of the flap manually if necessary.

Cabin temperature sensor

68 The sensor is located in the rear view mirror.

69 Unclip the lower trim piece, disconnect the wiring plug and remove the sensor complete with the trim panel.

70 Refitting is a reversal of removal.

Exterior temperature sensor

71 The exterior temperature sensor is located in the left-hand exterior mirror.

72 Remove the mirror glass, the motor **(see illustration)** and the mirror front shell as described in Chapter 11.

73 Unclip the sensor from its mounting on the mirror body **(see illustration)**.

74 No wiring plug is provided, so the two sensor wires have to be cut to remove the sensor. When doing this, leave as much wire as possible on the car, to make fitting the new sensor easier.

75 Refitting is a reversal of removal. Solder the new sensor wires to the old ones, observing the wire colour-coding, and insulate the two joints with tape or heat-shrink tubing.

Chapter 4 Part A:
Petrol engine fuel and exhaust systems

Contents

	Section number
Accelerator pedal – removal and refitting	3
Air cleaner assembly and inlet ducts – removal and refitting	2
Air filter element renewal	See Chapter 1A
Exhaust emission check	See Chapter 1A
Exhaust system – general information, removal and refitting	15
Exhaust system check	See Chapter 1A
Fuel gauge sender unit and pressure regulator – testing, removal and refitting	9
Fuel injection system – depressurisation	6
Fuel injection system – testing and adjustment	12
Fuel injection systems – general information	5
Fuel pipes and fittings - general information and disconnection	7
Fuel pump – removal and refitting	8
Fuel tank – removal and refitting	10
General information and precautions	1
Hose and leak check	See Chapter 1A
Manifolds – removal and refitting	14
Multipoint injection system components – removal and refitting	13
Throttle body/housing – removal and refitting	11
Unleaded petrol – general information and usage	4

Degrees of difficulty

Easy, suitable for novice with little experience	**Fairly easy,** suitable for beginner with some experience	**Fairly difficult,** suitable for competent DIY mechanic	**Difficult,** suitable for experienced DIY mechanic	**Very difficult,** suitable for expert DIY or professional

Specifications

System type

All models	Valeo V40 multipoint injection

Recommended fuel

Minimum octane rating	95 or 98 RON unleaded (if unavailable, 91 RON may be used). Leaded fuel or LRP must **not** be used

Fuel system data

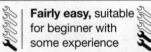

Fuel pressure regulator control pressure	3.5 ± 0.06 bars
Fuel pump flow output	
Minimum	80 litres/hour
Maximum	120 litres/hour
Air temperature sensor resistance:	
At 0°C	5290 to 6490 ohms
At 20°C	2400 to 2600 ohms
At 40°C	1070 to 1270 ohms
Coolant temperature sensor resistance:	
At 20°C	3060 to 4045 ohms
At 40°C	1315 to 1600 ohms
At 80°C	300 to 370 ohms
At 90°C	210 to 270 ohms
Injector resistance	14.5 ± 1.5 ohms at 20°C
TDC sensor resistance	200 to 270 ohms
Fuel tank level sender unit resistance at height of float pin (approx):	
At 164 mm	3.5 ± 3.5 ohms
At 143 mm	61 ± 7 ohms
At 110 mm	110 ± 10 ohms
At 81 mm	190 ± 16 ohms
At 52 mm	280 ± 20 ohms
At 47 mm	310 ± 10 ohms
Specified idle speed (non-adjustable):	660-740 rpm
Idle mixture CO content (non-adjustable)	
At idle	0.5% maximum
At fast idle	0.3% maximum (2500-2800 rpm)

Torque wrench settings	Nm	lbf ft
Crankshaft position sensor	8	6
Exhaust manifold:		
Nuts	26	19
Heat shield	10	7
Support bracket	44	32
Fuel rail	10	7
Fuel tank	21	15
Inlet manifold:		
Bolts 1-5	9	6
Bolts 6-8	12	9
Knock sensor	20	15
Oxygen sensor	44	32
Throttle body	10	7

1 General information and precautions

The fuel system consists of a fuel tank which is mounted under the rear of the vehicle with an electric fuel pump immersed in it, and a fuel feed line leading to the fuel rail on the engine. A further line from the fuel tank leads to the charcoal canister. In comparison to the fuel system on earlier models, there is no return line to the fuel tank. This is commonly referred to as a 'returnless system' **(see illustration).** The fuel pump supplies fuel to the fuel rail, which acts as a reservoir for the four fuel injectors which inject fuel into the inlet tracts. The fuel pressure regulator is located in the base of the fuel pump and not in the fuel rail as on earlier models. The Electronic Control Unit (ECU) is located on the left-hand side of the engine compartment, and the system includes various sensors, electrical components and related wiring.

Refer to Section 5 for further information on the operation of each fuel injection system, and to Section 15 for information on the exhaust system.

Warning: Many of the procedures in this Chapter require the removal of fuel lines and connections, which may result in some fuel spillage. Before carrying out any operation on the fuel system, refer to the precautions given in 'Safety first!' at the beginning of this manual, and follow them implicitly. Petrol is a highly dangerous and volatile liquid, and the precautions necessary when handling it cannot be overstressed

Note: *Residual pressure will remain in the fuel lines long after the vehicle was last used. When disconnecting any fuel line, first depressurise the fuel system as described in Section 6.*

2 Air cleaner assembly and inlet ducts – removal and refitting

Removal

1 Disconnect and remove the battery. Remove the battery tray as described in Chapter 5A.

2 Loosen the hose clip from the outlet pipe and pull it free **(see illustration).**

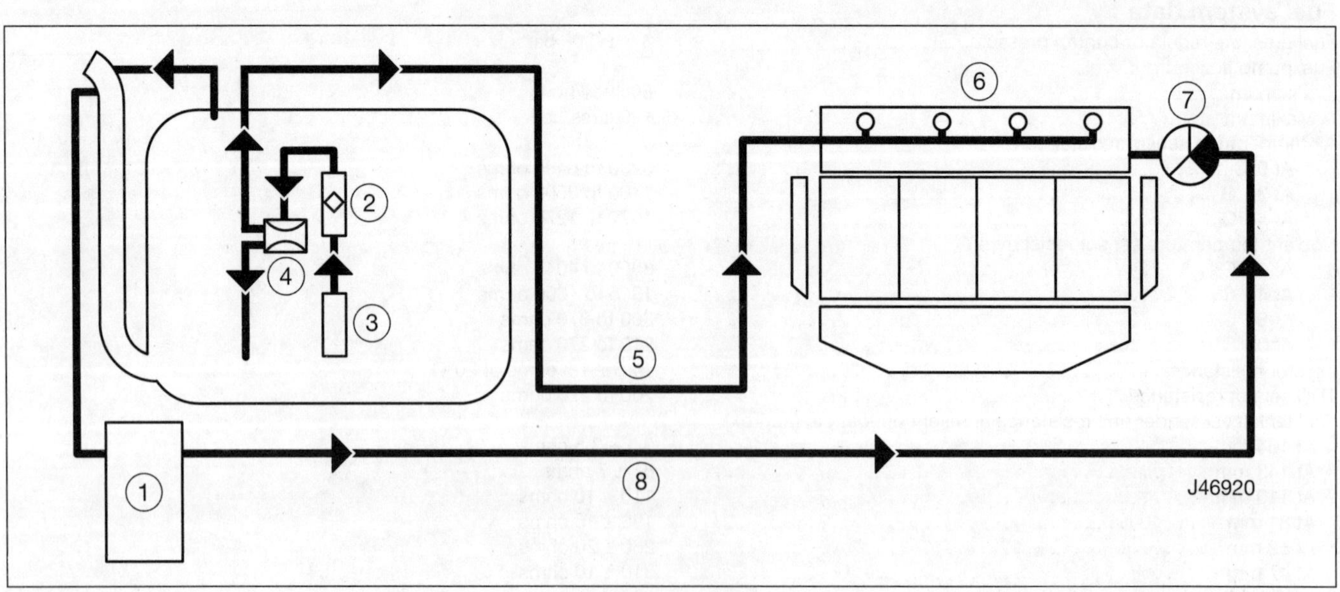

1.1 The fuel circuit

1 *Fuel vapour canister*
2 *Filter*
3 *Fuel pump*
4 *Pressure regulator*
5 *Supply pipe*
6 *Fuel rail*
7 *Vapour control solenoid*
8 *Vapour line*

2.2 Loosen the hose clip and pull the outlet pipe free from the air cleaner housing

2.3 Remove the bolt

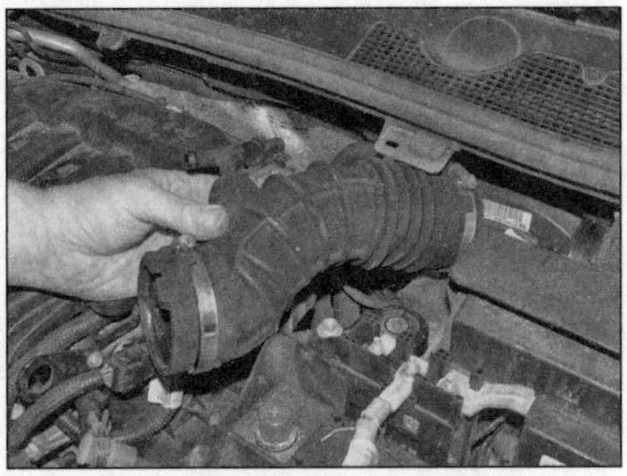

2.4 Remove the outlet duct

3 Remove the single bolt and then pull the housing free **(see illustration)** unclipping it from the inlet pipe on the inner wing as it is removed.
4 If required the duct between the air filter and the throttle body can be removed after slackening the house clip on the throttle body **(see illustration)**.
5 To fully remove the air cleaner inlet duct, jack up and support the front of the vehicle (see *Jacking and vehicle support* in the reference section) and then remove the front bumper cover as described in Chapter 11. Remove the front section of the left-hand wing liner and then prise the inlet pipe free.

Refitting

6 Refitting is a reversal of removal.

3 Accelerator pedal – removal and refitting

Removal

1 Remove the lower trim panel from under the steering column as described in Chapter 11.
2 Disconnect the wiring plug from the accelerator pedal.
3 Remove the bolts securing the accelerator pedal in position **(see illustration)**.
4 Unhook and then withdraw the accelerator pedal.
5 Examine the pedal and pivot for signs of wear and renew as necessary.

Refitting

6 Refitting is a reversal of removal.

4 Unleaded petrol – general information and usage

All petrol models are designed to run on fuel with an octane rating of 95 or 98 RON, however, if unavailable, 91 octane fuel may be used. All models have a catalytic converter, and so must be run on unleaded fuel only. Under no circumstances should leaded fuel or LRP be used, as this will damage the converter.

5 Fuel injection systems – general information

1 All models equipped with a sequential multipoint fuel injection/ignition system.
2 The system is of closed-loop type incorporating two oxygen (lambda) sensors, one located upstream and the other downstream of the catalytic converter. The downstream oxygen sensor monitors the catalytic convertor efficiency. An evaporative emission control system is fitted.
3 The multipoint injection system uses one injector and one ignition coil for each cylinder, and the injectors are operated individually and sequentially at the beginning of the inlet stroke. The electronic control unit (ECU) is able to determine which cylinder is on its inlet stroke without the use of a camshaft position sensor, however if the unit is renewed, the car must be taken for a road test lasting at least 25 minutes to enable the ECU to reprogramme itself.
4 The system incorporates a closed-loop catalytic converter and an evaporative emission control system. The fuel injection side of the system operates as follows (refer to Chapter 5B for information on the ignition system):
5 The fuel pump is immersed in the fuel tank, and pumps fuel from the fuel tank to the fuel rail on the engine. Fuel supply pressure is controlled by a pressure regulator in the fuel pump. The regulator operates by allowing excess fuel to return to the tank. There are four injectors (one per cylinder) located in the inlet manifold downstream of the throttle valve. All the injectors are fed from the fuel rail.

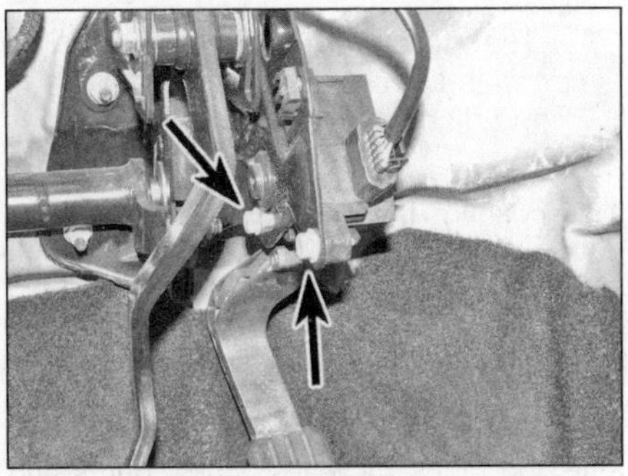

3.3 The accelerator retaining nuts (arrowed)

6 All models are 'fly by wire' There is no throttle cable. The throttle valve is motorised and has an integral potentiometer; the accelerator pedal also incorporates a potentiometer.
7 The electrical control system consists of the ECU, along with the following sensors:

a) Throttle potentiometer – informs the ECU of the throttle position, and the rate of throttle opening or closing.
b) Coolant temperature sensor – informs the ECU of engine temperature.
c) Inlet air temperature sensor – informs the ECU of the temperature of the air passing through the throttle body.
d) Oxygen (lambda) sensors – informs the ECU of the oxygen content of the exhaust gases and the efficiency of the catalytic converter (explained in greater detail in Part C of this Chapter).
e) Idle speed regulation stepper motor (where fitted) – controls the idle speed.
f) Crankshaft speed/position (TDC) sensor – informs the ECU of engine speed and crankshaft position.
g) Knock sensor – informs the ECU when pre-ignition ('pinking') is occurring (explained in greater detail in Part B of Chapter 5).
h) Manifold absolute pressure (MAP) sensor – informs the ECU of the engine load by monitoring the pressure in the inlet manifold.
i) Fuel vapour recirculation valve – operates the fuel evaporative control system (explained in greater detail in Part C of this Chapter).
j) Vehicle speed sensor – informs the ECU of the vehicle speed.
k) Brake pedal switch – reduces the fuelling under braking.

8 All the above information is analysed by the ECU and, based on this, the ECU determines the appropriate ignition and fuelling requirements for the engine. The ECU controls the fuel injector by varying its pulse width – the length of time the injector is held open – to provide a richer or weaker mixture, as appropriate. The mixture is constantly

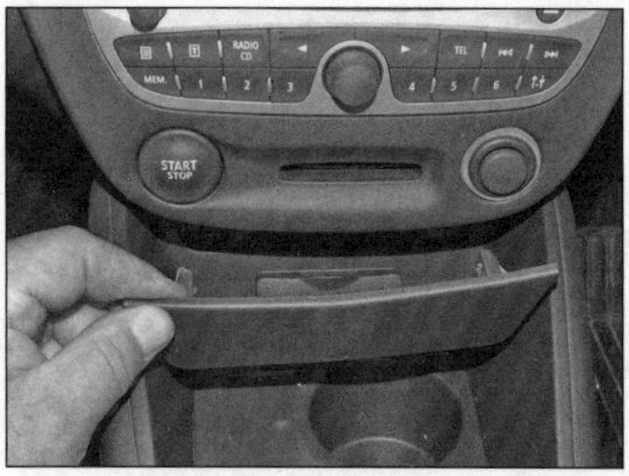

5.12a Remove the cover to access the diagnostic socket

varied by the ECU, to provide the best setting for cranking, starting (with either a hot or cold engine), warm-up, idle, cruising and acceleration.

9 The ECU also has full control over the engine idle speed, via a stepper motor which is fitted to the throttle body. The motor pushrod rests against a cam on the throttle spindle. When the throttle is closed (accelerator pedal released), the ECU uses the motor to vary the opening of the throttle valve and so control the idle speed.

10 The ECU also controls the exhaust and evaporative emission control systems, which are described in detail in Part C of this Chapter.

11 If there is an abnormality in any of the readings obtained from either the coolant temperature sensor, the inlet air temperature sensor or the oxygen sensor, the ECU enters its back-up mode. In this event, the ECU ignores the abnormal sensor signal, and assumes a pre-programmed value which will allow the engine to continue running (albeit at reduced efficiency). If the ECU enters this back-up mode (also referred to as 'limp mode') the warning light on the instrument panel will come on, and the relevant fault code will be stored in the ECU memory.

12 If the warning light comes on, the vehicle should be taken to a Renault dealer or suitably equipped garage at the earliest opportunity. A complete test of the engine management system can then be carried out, using a special electronic diagnostic test unit, which is plugged into the system's diagnostic connector **(see illustrations)**.

5.12b A suitable code reader can be plugged into the connector

6 Fuel injection system – depressurisation

Warning: Refer to the warning note in Section 1 before proceeding. The following procedure will merely relieve the pressure in the fuel system – remember that fuel will still be present in the system components, and take precautions accordingly before disconnecting any of them.

Note: *The fuel system referred to in this Section includes the tank mounted fuel pump, the fuel injectors, the pressure regulator, the fuel rail and the metal pipes and flexible hoses of the fuel lines between these components. All these contain fuel which will be under pressure while the engine is running, and/or while the ignition is switched on. The pressure will remain for some time after the ignition has been switched off, and it must be relieved when any of these components are disturbed for servicing work.*

Method 1

1 Disconnect the battery negative lead (refer to *Disconnecting the battery* in Chapter 5A).

2 Place a suitable container beneath the connection or union to be disconnected, and have a large rag ready to soak up any escaping fuel not being caught by the container.

3 Slowly loosen the connection or union nut to avoid a sudden release of pressure, and position the rag around the connection, to catch any fuel spray which may be expelled. Once the pressure is released, disconnect the fuel line. Plug the pipe ends, to minimise fuel loss and prevent the entry of dirt into the fuel system.

Method 2

4 Lift up the rear seat, remove the cover and disconnect the fuel pump wiring plug (see Section 8 of this Chapter).

5 Start the engine and allow it to idle until it stops due to lack of fuel. Operate the starter motor a couple more times, to ensure that all fuel pressure has been relieved.

6 Switch off the ignition and refit the fuel wiring connector.

7 Fuel pipes and fittings - general information and disconnection

1 Disconnect the cable from the negative battery terminal (see Chapter 5A Section 4) before proceeding.

2 The fuel supply pipe connects the fuel pump in the fuel tank to the fuel rail on the engine.

3 Whenever you're working under the vehicle, be sure to inspect all fuel and evaporative emission pipes for leaks, kinks, dents and other damage. Always replace a damaged fuel pipe immediately.

4 If you find signs of dirt in the pipes during disassembly, disconnect all pipes and blow them out with compressed air. Inspect the fuel strainer on the fuel pump pick-up unit for damage and deterioration.

Steel tubing

5 It is critical that the fuel pipes be replaced with pipes of equivalent type and specification.

6 Some steel fuel pipes have threaded fittings. When loosening these fittings, hold the stationary fitting with a spanner while turning the union nut.

Plastic tubing

Warning: When removing or installing plastic fuel tubing, be careful not to bend or twist it too much, which can damage it. Also, plastic fuel tubing is NOT heat resistant, so keep it away from excessive heat.

7 When replacing fuel system plastic tubing, use only original equipment replacement plastic tubing.

Flexible hoses

8 When replacing fuel system flexible hoses, use original equipment replacements, or hose to the same specification.

9 Don't route fuel hoses (or metal pipes) within 100 mm of the exhaust system or within 280 mm of the catalytic converter. Make sure that no rubber hoses are installed directly against the vehicle, particularly in places where there is any vibration. If allowed to touch some vibrating part of the vehicle, a hose can easily become chafed and it might start leaking. A good rule of thumb is to maintain a minimum of 8.0 mm clearance around a hose (or metal pipe) to prevent contact with the vehicle underbody.

8 Fuel pump – removal and refitting

Warning: Refer to the warning note in Section 1 before proceeding.

Removal

1 Disconnect the battery negative lead (refer to *Disconnecting the battery* as described in Chapter 5A).

2 Remove the rear seat, or rear seat cushion as described in Chapter 11, for access to the fuel pump cover.

3 Remove the screws, remove the protective metal cover and then prise out the plastic cover **(see illustrations)**.

4 Disconnect the wiring connector from the fuel pump, and tape the connector to the vehicle body, to prevent it disappearing behind the tank **(see illustration)**.

5 Anticipating some fuel spillage, disconnect the fuel lines. Immediately seal the fuel lines and tank openings **(see illustration)**.

6 Noting the alignment arrows on the pump

8.3a Remove the metal plate...

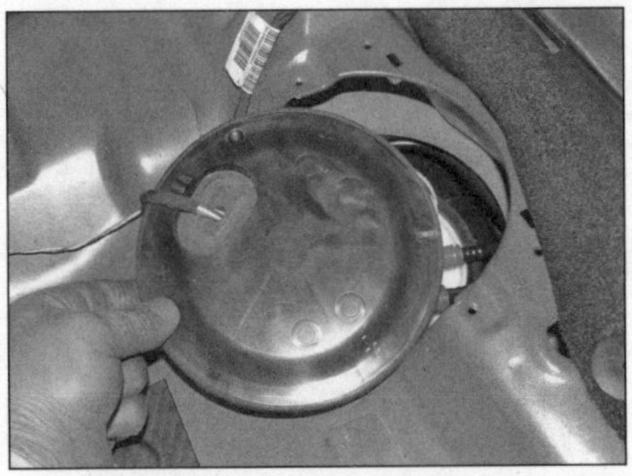

8.3b ...and then the plastic cover

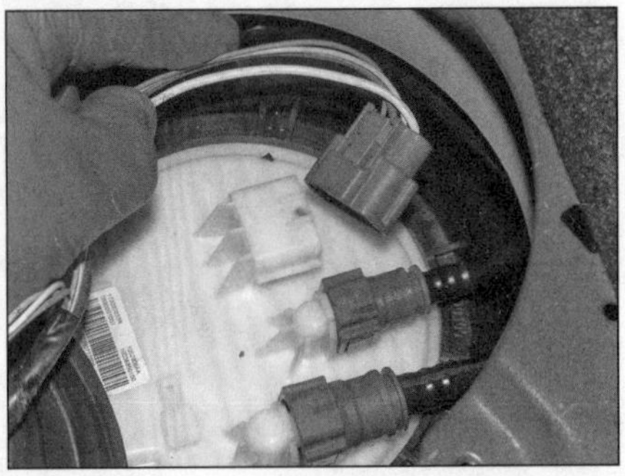

8.4 Disconnect the wiring plug

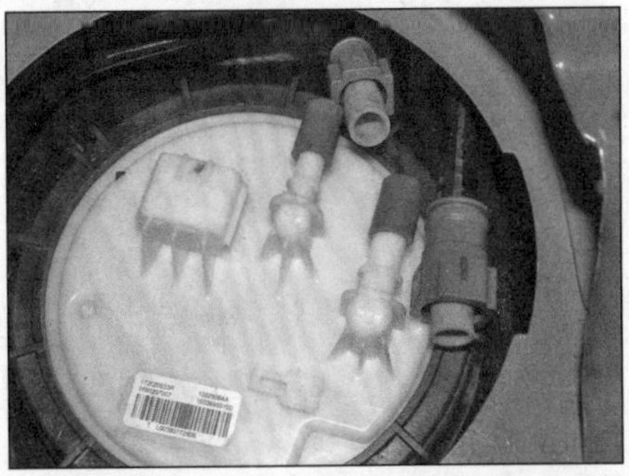

8.5 Disconnect the fuel lines

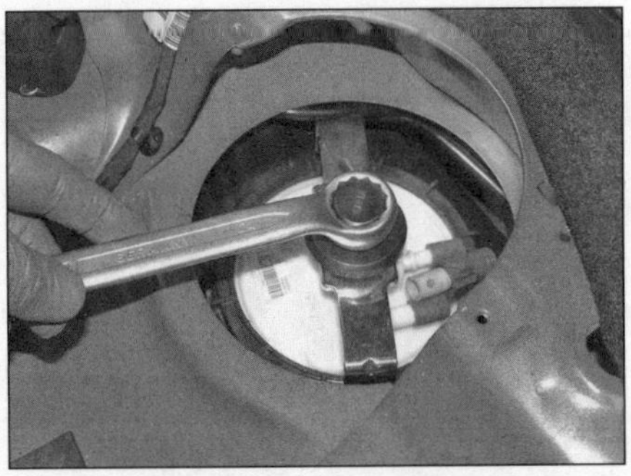

8.6a Use the correct tool...

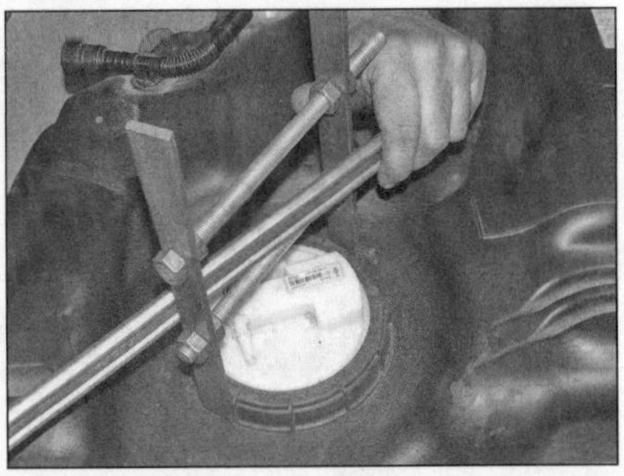

8.6b ...or fabricate one

cover, locking ring and fuel tank, unscrew the locking ring and remove it from the tank. This can be accomplished by using either the correct tool or by fabricating a suitable tool out of metal bar and two bolts **(see illustrations)**.

7 Carefully lift the fuel pump assembly out of the fuel tank, taking great care not to damage the fuel level gauge sender arm, or to spill fuel in the interior of the vehicle. Remove the rubber sealing ring and dispose of it – a new one must be fitted. If the pump is to remain out of the fuel tank for several hours, the locking ring should be refitted temporarily to prevent any possibility of the opening or the threads on the fuel tank from distorting. Renault recommend that the locking ring is always replaced whenever it is removed.

8 Note that the fuel pump/fuel gauge sender unit is only available as a complete assembly – no components are available separately.

Refitting

9 Ensure that the fuel pump pick-up filter is clean and free of debris. Fit the new sealing ring to the top of the fuel tank.

10 Carefully manoeuvre the pump assembly into the fuel tank. There is a lug on the pump and a recess in the tank that must be aligned.

11 Press down on the pump assembly and fit the new locking ring. Securely tighten the locking ring until the arrow on the ring aligns with the mark on the tank **(see illustration)**.

12 Reconnect the fuel line to the top of the fuel pump.

13 Reconnect the wiring connector.

14 Reconnect the battery and start the engine. Check the fuel pump and hose(s) for signs of leakage.

15 Refit the plastic access cover and metal plate. Replace the rear seat cushion.

9 Fuel gauge sender unit and pressure regulator – testing, removal and refitting

Testing

1 The fuel gauge sender unit is supplied as part of the fuel pump assembly, however it is possible to test its operation and remove it.

2 To test the sender unit, first remove the pump as described in Section 8.

3 Disconnect the wiring plug from the cover and connect an ohmmeter to the two terminals **(see illustration)**.

4 With the pump assembly upright on the bench, measure the resistance of the sender unit at the different heights given in the Specifications **(see illustration)**. The

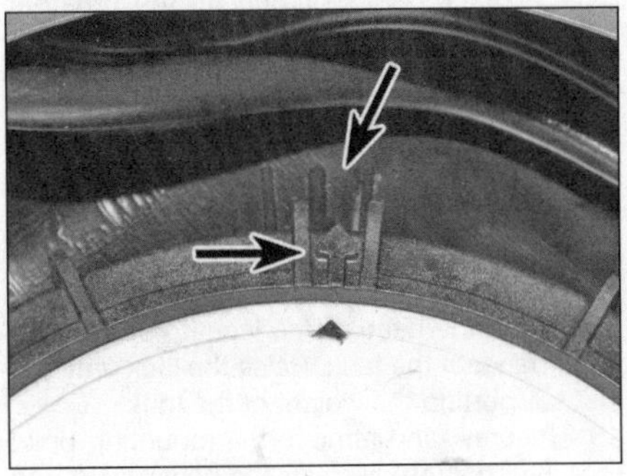

8.11 Align the arrows

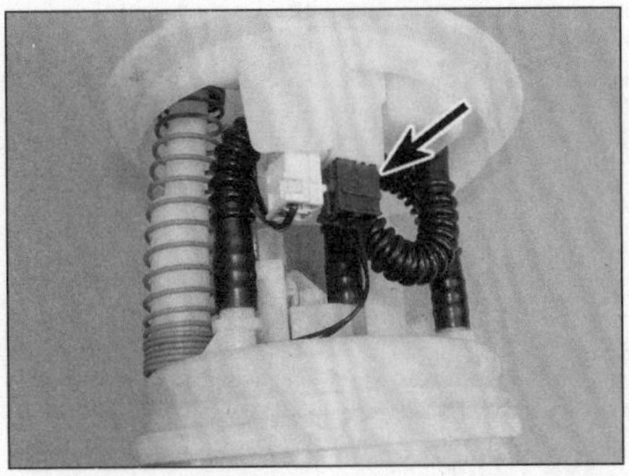

9.3 Disconnect the wiring from the cover

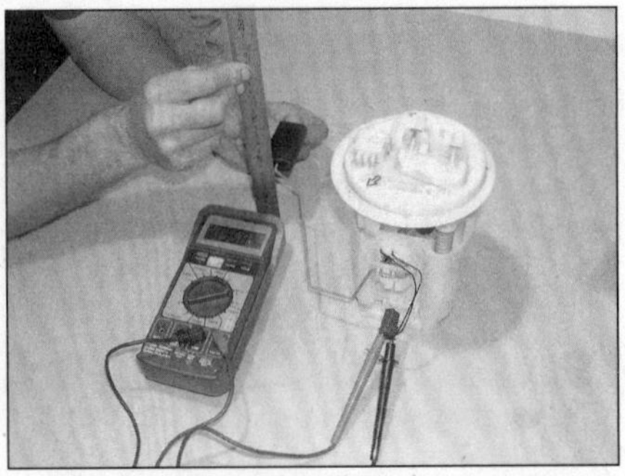

9.4 Testing the sender unit with an ohmmeter

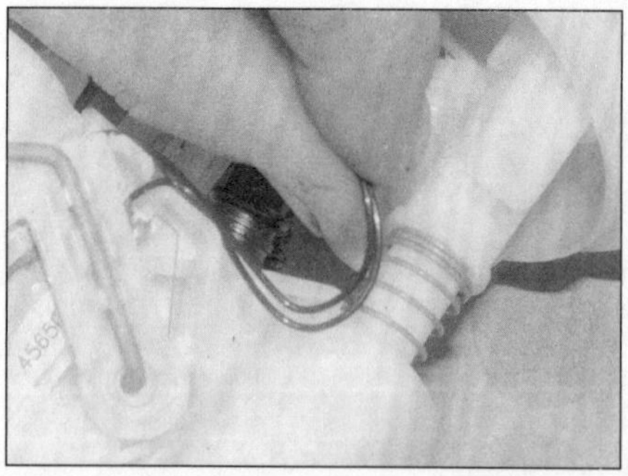

9.5a Remove the wiring from the clips...

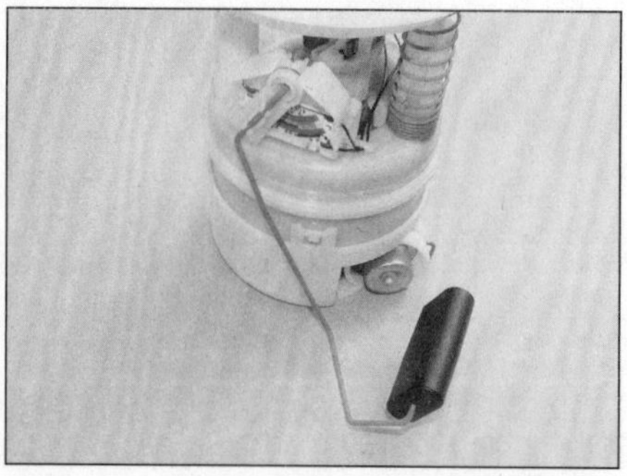

9.5b ...then unclip the unit from the main body

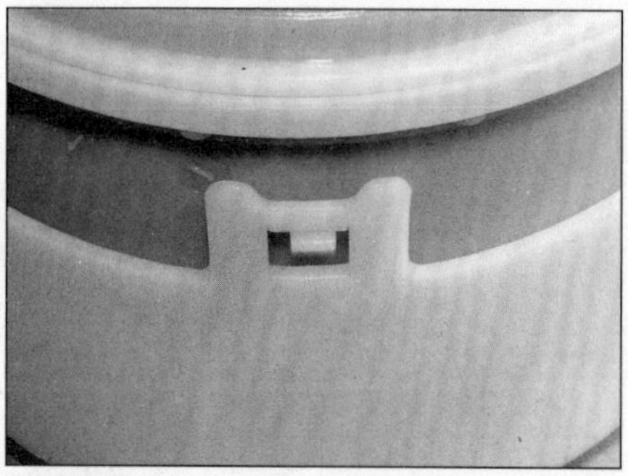

9.6a Release the clips and remove the base cover...

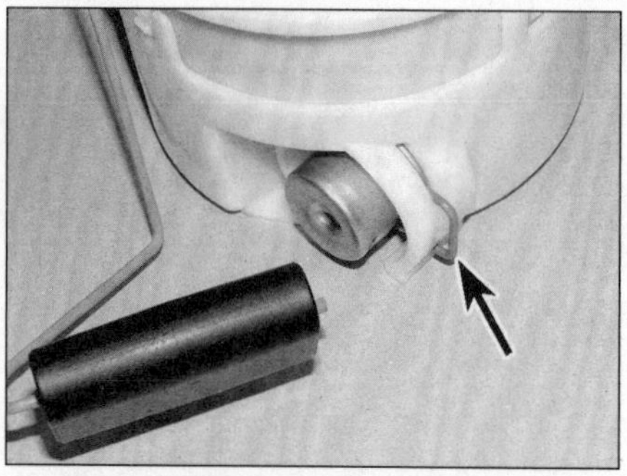

9.6b ...then pull out the spring clip to remove the pressure regulator

resistances are approximate but it should be clear if the sender unit is not operating correctly.

Removal

5 To remove the sender unit, first release the wiring from the clips, then unclip the unit from the main body **(see illustrations)**.

6 To remove the fuel pressure regulator, unclip the base cover, then pull out the retaining spring clip and remove the regulator **(see illustrations)**.

7 Use a screwdriver to prise off the gauze filter, then clean any sediment from the filter and cover.

Refitting

8 Refitting is a reversal of removal, but test the unit before refitting the pump assembly to the tank.

10 Fuel tank – removal and refitting

Warning: Refer to the warning note in Section 1 before proceeding

Removal

1 Before removing the fuel tank, all fuel must be drained from it. Since a drain plug is not provided, it is preferable to carry out the removal operation when the tank is nearly empty.

2 Remove the rear seat, or rear seat cushion (Chapter 11), for access to the fuel pump cover.

3 Remove the metal cover and then prise out the plastic cover.

4 Disconnect the battery negative lead (refer to *Disconnecting the battery* in Chapter 5A).

5 Disconnect the wiring connector from the fuel gauge sender.

6 Chock the front wheels, then jack up the rear of the vehicle and support on axle stands (see *Jacking and vehicle support*).

7 Lower the exhaust system from its mountings **(see illustration)** and let it rest on the rear axle. There is no need to remove it from the vehicle, however if the system has been previously replaced it will be easier to split the exhaust at the clamps and remove it.

8 Partially remove the heat shield from above the exhaust **(see illustration)**. Note that the fuel tank and heat shield share a common mounting at the rear.

9 Remove the hose clips from the fuel filler and breather pipes. Note that some models have a quick release fitting on the breather pipe **(see illustration)**. Dispose of the clips – new ones must be used.

10 Work around the tank and release the rigid brake liens from the clips on the fuel tank **(see illustration)**.

11 Unclip the fuel lines from the tank and move them to one side.

12 Place a trolley jack with of piece wood placed on the head of the jack (to spread the load) beneath the tank. Raise the jack until it is just supporting the weight of the tank.

13 Unscrew and remove the mounting bolts **(see illustration)** recover the heat shield and then slowly lower the fuel tank out of position,

10.7 Remove the exhaust hangers by unbolting them

10.8 The heat shield is held in place by several screw clips, best removed with a pair of sliding joint (waterpump) pliers

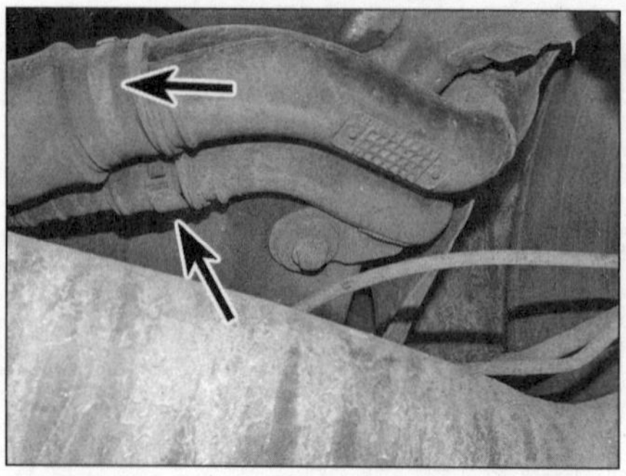

10.9 Remove the hose clips (arrowed)

10.10 Unclip the brake lines

disconnecting any other relevant pipes as they become accessible.

14 Separate the filler neck from the fuel tank as it is lowered.

15 With the help of an assistant remove the tank from underneath the vehicle, working it around the exhaust as necessary.

16 If the tank is contaminated with sediment or water, remove the fuel sender unit (Section 9), and swill the tank out with clean fuel. The tank is injection moulded from a synthetic material – if seriously damaged, it should be renewed. However, in certain cases, it may be possible to have small leaks or minor damage repaired. Seek the advice of a specialist before attempting to repair the fuel tank.

Refitting

17 Refitting is the reverse of the removal procedure, noting the following points:

- a) *When lifting the tank back into position, take care to ensure that the hoses are not trapped between the tank and vehicle body.*
- b) *Ensure that all pipes and hoses are correctly routed. Make sure the sealing rings are in position in the quick-release fittings prior to fitting and make sure they are securely clipped in position.*
- c) *Renault recommend the replacement of the filler and breather pipe hose clips.*
- c) *On completion, refill the tank with a small amount of fuel, and check for signs of leakage prior to taking the vehicle out on the road.*

11 Throttle body/housing – removal and refitting

Warning: Refer to the warning note in Section 1 before proceeding

Note: *It is not possible to repair the throttle body/housing – if faulty it must be renewed as a complete assembly.*

Removal

1 Disconnect the battery negative lead (see *Disconnecting the battery* as described in Chapter 5A).

2 Loosen the hose clips and remove the inlet hose from the throttle body **(see illustration)**.

3 Unplug the electrical connector **(see illustration)**.

4 Remove the mounting bolts **(see illustration)**.

5 Withdraw the throttle body and recover the gasket **(see illustration)**.

Refitting

6 Refitting is a reversal of removal, but a new gasket should be fitted. After reconnecting the battery, turn the ignition on and wait for a minimum of 30 seconds. During this time, the ECU will adapt the throttle minimum and maximum operating range. Note that the idle

10.13 Remove the tank mounting bolts

speed may be initially unstable, until the ECU adapts the throttle body fully to the engine. This will be completed over several varying drive cycles.

12 Fuel injection system – testing and adjustment

Testing

1 If a fault appears in the fuel injection system, first ensure that all the system wiring connectors are securely connected and free of corrosion. Ensure that the fault is not due to poor maintenance; ie, check that the air cleaner filter element is clean, the spark plugs are in good condition and correctly gapped, the cylinder compression pressures are correct, the ignition timing is correct, and that the engine breather hoses are clear and undamaged, referring to the relevant part of Chapters 1, 2 and 5 for further information.

2 If these checks fail to reveal the cause of the problem, the vehicle should be taken to a Renault dealer or suitably-equipped garage for testing. A diagnostic connector (located beneath the ashtray on the centre console) is incorporated in the engine management circuit, into which a special electronic diagnostic tester can be plugged **(see illustration 5.12b)**. The tester will help locate the fault quickly and simply, alleviating the need to test all the system components individually, which is a time-consuming operation that carries a risk of damaging the ECU. The Renault Clip diagnostic tester is specific for Renault dealerships Several aftermarket tools are also available, but none have the depth of coverage of the official factory tool. The diagnostic tool can display fault codes and live data from many components. In the hands of a skilled technician, faults can be quickly traced and rectified. However, it must be remembered that the diagnostic tool is only the first stage in the repair process. The fault must be confirmed by individual testing of the component identified.

3 If the 'electronic incident' warning light illuminates on the instrument panel whilst driving, or remains illuminated longer than 3 seconds after switching on the ignition, then the ECU has detected a fault within the system. The warning light is more commonly known as a MIL (malfunction indicator lamp). If the vehicle has no driving faults, then it is worth completing a few drive cycles to see

11.2 Remove the inlet hose from the throttle body

11.3 Remove the wiring plug

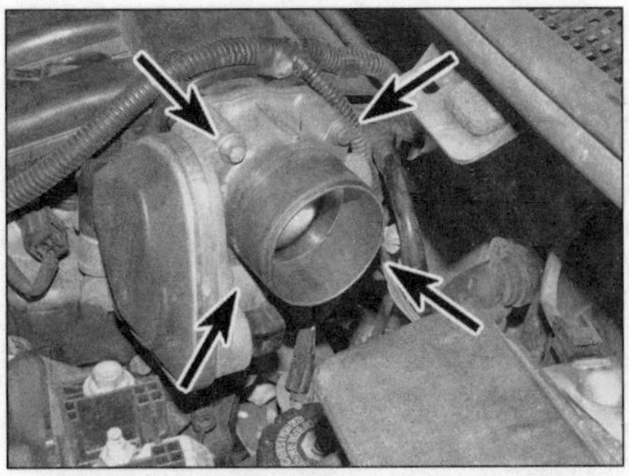

11.4 Remove the throttle body mounting bolts (arrowed – two bolts hidden)

11.5 Disconnect the vapour hose as the throttle body is removed

if the lamp has been falsely triggered by a software glitch (or intermittent fault) before having a diagnostic check carried out.

4 Basic fault code readers are now available at a reasonable cost. These testers will only display the mandatory EOBD (European On Board Diagnostic) emissions related fault codes. Most of these simple code readers will not display manufacturer specific fault codes. Some individual components may be tested for resistance after removal using the information given in the Specifications, however other items (such as the idle speed stepper motor) cannot be checked and are not adjustable.

Adjustment

5 Experienced home mechanics with a considerable amount of skill and equipment (including a tachometer and an accurately calibrated exhaust gas analyser) may be able to check the exhaust CO level and the idle speed. However, if these are found to be in need of adjustment, the car *must* be taken to a suitably-equipped garage for further testing. Neither the mixture adjustment (exhaust gas CO level) nor the idle speed are adjustable, and should either be incorrect, a fault must be present in the fuel injection system.

13 Multipoint injection system components – removal and refitting

Warning: Refer to the warning note in Section 1 before proceeding

Fuel rail and injectors

Note: *If a faulty injector is suspected, before condemning the injector, it is worth trying the effect of one of the proprietary injector cleaning treatments.*

Removal

1 Depressurise the fuel system as described in Section 6, then disconnect the battery negative lead.

2 Remove the inlet manifold as described in Section 14.

3 Disconnect the wiring plugs from the injectors and then (anticipating some fuel spillage) disconnect the fuel supply.

4 Unscrew the two bolts and gently free the fuel rail from the inlet manifold. The use of a lubricant may help free the injectors from the cylinder head **(see illustration)**.

5 There may be fuel still in the rail, so be prepared to mop it up and then plug the end of the fuel rail.

6 To remove the fuel injectors from the fuel rail, release the spring clips from the fuel rail and pull the injectors free. Keep the injectors in the correct order **(see illustrations)**.

7 With the injectors in the right order on the bench, check the resistance of each injector (see the Specifications at the beginning of this Chapter). They should all show a similar resistance, but any major variation will require further investigation. If any of the injectors are suspect they can be tested and ultrasonically cleaned by a garage with the correct specialist equipment.

Refitting

8 Refitting is a reversal of removal, but renew the O-rings at the top and bottom of each injector **(see illustration).** Ensure that the fuel rail is securely reconnected (the spring clip should click securely into position).

9 Refit the fuel rail assembly to the cylinder head, making sure the sealing rings remain correctly positioned, and tighten the retaining bolts to the specified torque. Refit the inlet manifold.

10 On completion start the engine and check for fuel leaks.

Inlet air temperature sensor

Removal

11 The sensor is fitted to the front of the inlet manifold, next to the oil dipstick tube. Unplug and remove the sensor **(see illustrations)**.

12 The air temperature sensor is easily checked with a meter. Its resistance will vary according to the air temperature. Check the resistance and compare it with the specification given at the beginning of this Chapter. Check that the resistance changes with a change in temperature. Placing it in a refrigerator for 20 minutes is a good method of checking that the resistance changes with the air temperature.

Refitting

13 Refitting is a reversal of removal, but check the condition of the seal.

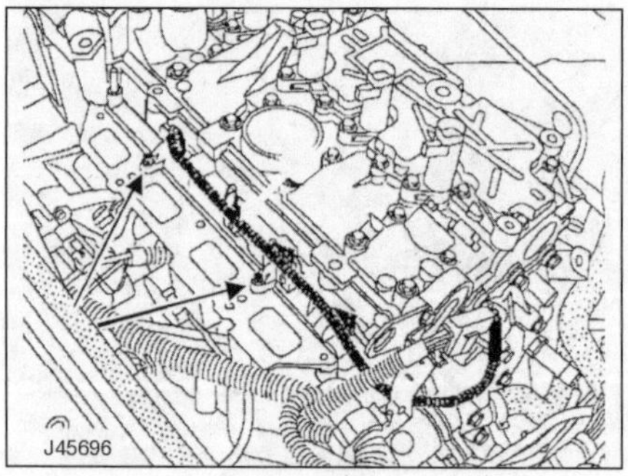

13.4 Remove the fuel rail complete with the injectors

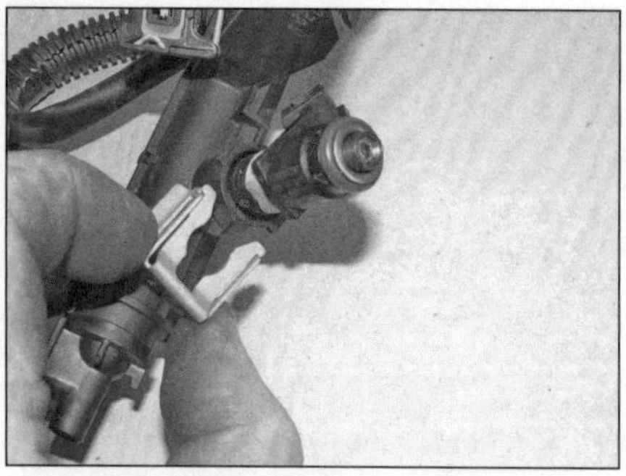

13.6a Remove the spring clip...

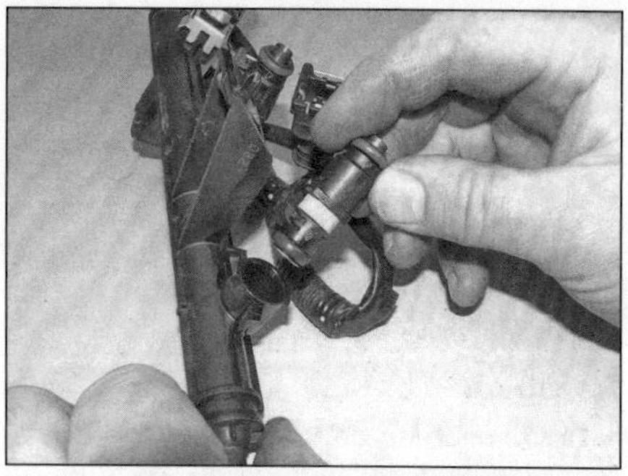

13.6b ...and then the injector

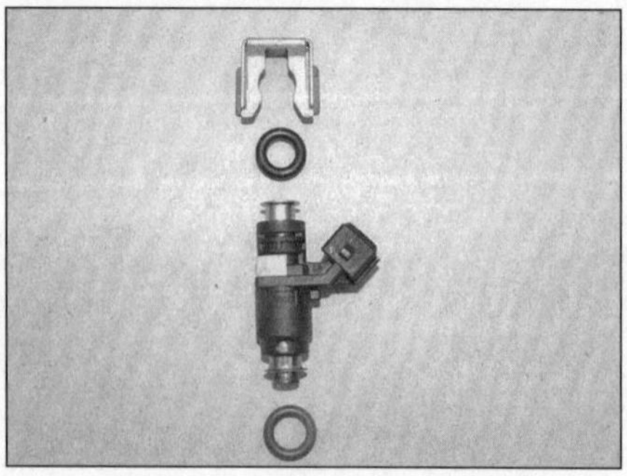

13.8 The injector components. Note that the lower seal is coloured green

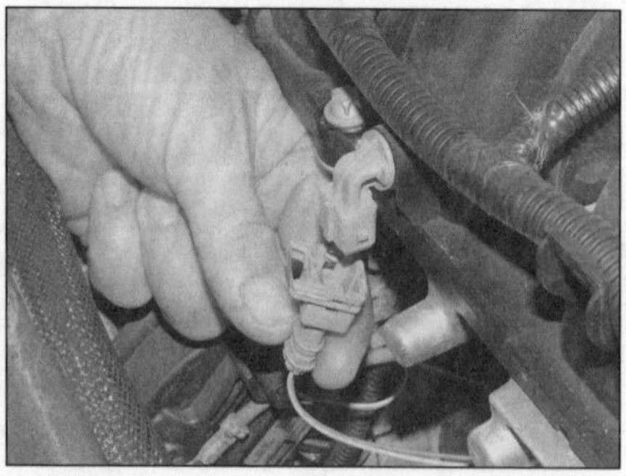

13.11a Disconnect the wiring plug...

13.11b ...then twist and remove the air temperature sensor

Coolant temperature sensor

14 The sensor is located on the thermostat housing or at the left-hand end of the cylinder head above the gearbox bellhousing **(see illustrations)**. Refer to Chapter 3 for removal and refitting details.

Knock sensor

15 The knock sensor is located on the front of the cylinder block.
16 Refer to Chapter 5B for the removal and refitting procedures.

Manifold absolute pressure sensor

Removal

17 The manifold absolute sensor is mounted at the rear of the inlet manifold.
18 Disconnect the wiring plug, unscrew the mounting nuts and remove the sensor **(see illustration)**.

Refitting

19 Refitting is a reversal of removal.

Fuel system and fuel pump relays

20 The system does not have separate relays. All switching functions are controlled by the switching and control unit, located on the front left-hand side of the engine bay – next to the battery.

Crankshaft position sensor

Removal

21 Jack up and support the front of the vehicle (see *jacking and vehicle support* in the reference section).
22 Remove the engine undershield.
23 Unclip the wiring plug from the sensor.
24 Unscrew the retaining bolt and remove the sensor.

Refitting

25 Refitting is a reversal of removal.

Electronic control unit (ECU)

Note: *The ECU is electronically-coded to match the engine immobiliser and certain other engine components. If the ECU is being removed in order to fit a new unit, it is highly recommended that the work be carried out by a Renault dealer.*

13.14 The coolant temperature sensor

Removal

26 The ECU is located in the left-hand side of the engine compartment in front of the battery.
27 First disconnect the battery negative lead (refer to *Disconnecting the battery* in Chapter 5A).
28 Remove the battery cover as described in Chapter 5A.
29 Unclip and remove the cooling inlet duct and the ECU cover **(see illustration)**.
30 Remove the mounting bolts and withdraw the control unit **(see illustration)**.
31 Unlock and remove the three electrical connectors from the ECU **(see illustration)**. Access can be improved if the left-hand headlight is removed as described in Chapter 12.

Refitting

32 Refitting is a reverse of the removal procedure ensuring that the wiring is securely reconnected. After the battery is reconnected the ECU must be adapted to the vehicle. To do this:

a) *Turn on the ignition and wait for a minimum of 30 seconds. The throttle body will operate and adapt the maximum and minimum position of the throttle plate.*
b) *Allow the vehicle to idle until the normal operating temperature is reached.*
c) *Drive the vehicle in third gear with an engine speed of between 3000 to 5000rpm. Decelerate, without braking for at least 5 seconds.*
d) *Drive the vehicle in third gear with an engine speed of between 2000 to 4000 rpm and decelerate without braking for at least 5 seconds*

13.18 Disconnect the wiring plug from the MAP sensor

Note: *The ECU will continue to adapt to the engine for several drive cycles. During this time the idle speed and acceleration may be compromised.*

14 Manifolds – removal and refitting

Inlet manifold

1 Disconnect the battery negative (earth) lead and position it away from the terminal.
2 Remove the throttle body inlet pipe.
3 Disconnect the wiring from the throttle valve, absolute pressure sensor, ignition coils and air temperature sensor.
4 Unclip the wiring and move it to one side.
5 Unscrew and remove the throttle body mounting bolts and position the throttle body to one side.
6 Unbolt and remove the ignition coils.
7 At the rear of the cylinder head disconnect the breather pipe and the servo vacuum pipe.
8 Disconnect the vent pipe from the vapour canister and then unclip the oxygen sensor wiring loom.
9 Disconnect the wiring plug from the camshaft control solenoid.
10 Progressively unscrew and remove the bolts in the reverse order to that shown **(see illustration 14.12)**.
11 Withdraw the inlet manifold and recover the gasket.

13.29 Remove the cover

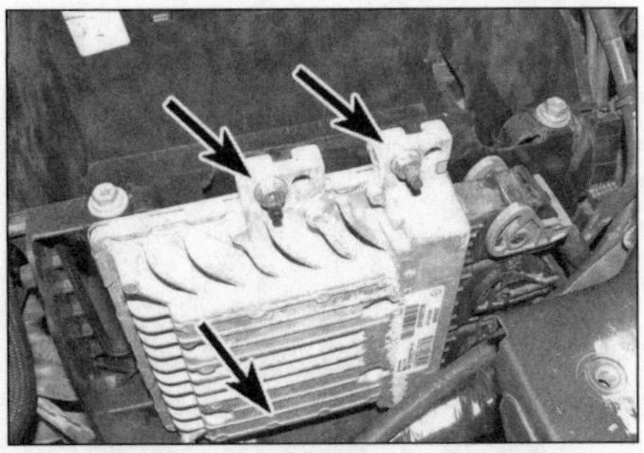

13.30 Remove the mounting bolts (arrowed). One bolt hidden and shown with the front panel removed for clarity

13.31 Disconnect the wiring plugs

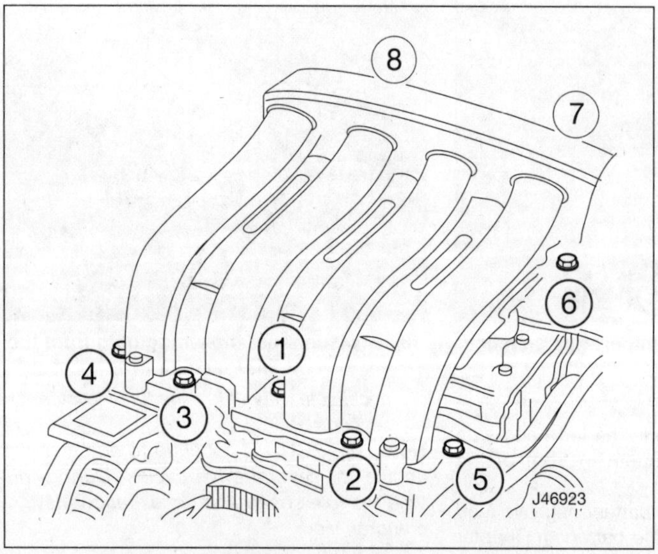

14.12 Tighten the bolts in the order shown

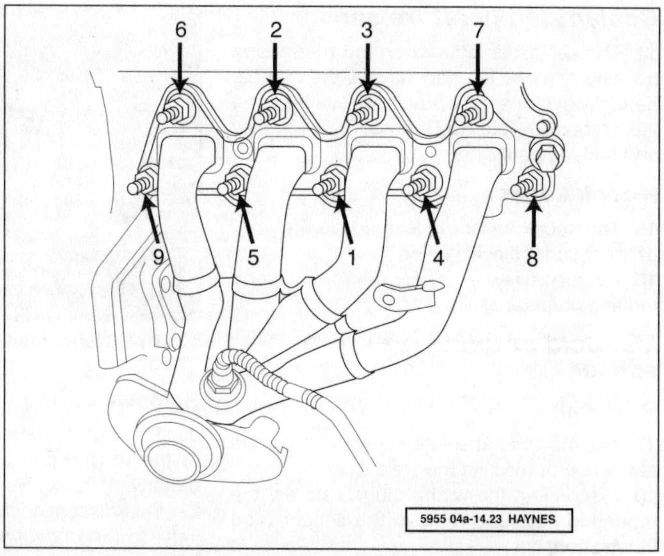

14.23 Tighten the bolts in the order shown

12 Refitting is a reversal of removal but use a new gasket and tighten the mounting bolts to the specified torque **(see illustration)**.

Exhaust manifold

13 Disconnect the battery negative (earth) lead and position it away from the terminal.
14 Remove the air cleaner assembly as described in Section 2.
15 With reference to Chapter 11 remove both sections of the windscreen cowl.
16 Remove the inlet manifold as described in this section.
17 Apply the handbrake, then jack up the front of the vehicle and support it on axle stands (see *Jacking and vehicle support)*. Remove the engine undertray.
18 Disconnect the exhaust front downpipe from the exhaust manifold with reference to Section 14.
19 Remove the oxygen sensor as described in Chapter 4C. Alternatively, leave the sensor in position and remove it from the manifold on the bench.
20 Remove the manifold support bracket and then unclip the coolant pipes from the bracket. Remove the bracket.
21 Unbolt and remove the manifold heat shield.
22 Unbolt the exhaust manifold (in the reverse order to that shown in **illustration 14.23**) and remove it from the vehicle. With the manifold on the bench remove the lower heat shield (if required).
23 Refitting is a reversal of removal but use a new gasket and tighten the mounting nuts, in the correct order to the specified torque **(see illustration)**. Ensure that the cylinder head and manifold mating surfaces are clean.

15 Exhaust system – general information, removal and refitting

General information

1 On new vehicles the exhaust system consists of a single section including the catalytic convertor **(see illustration)**.
2 Each section however can be renewed

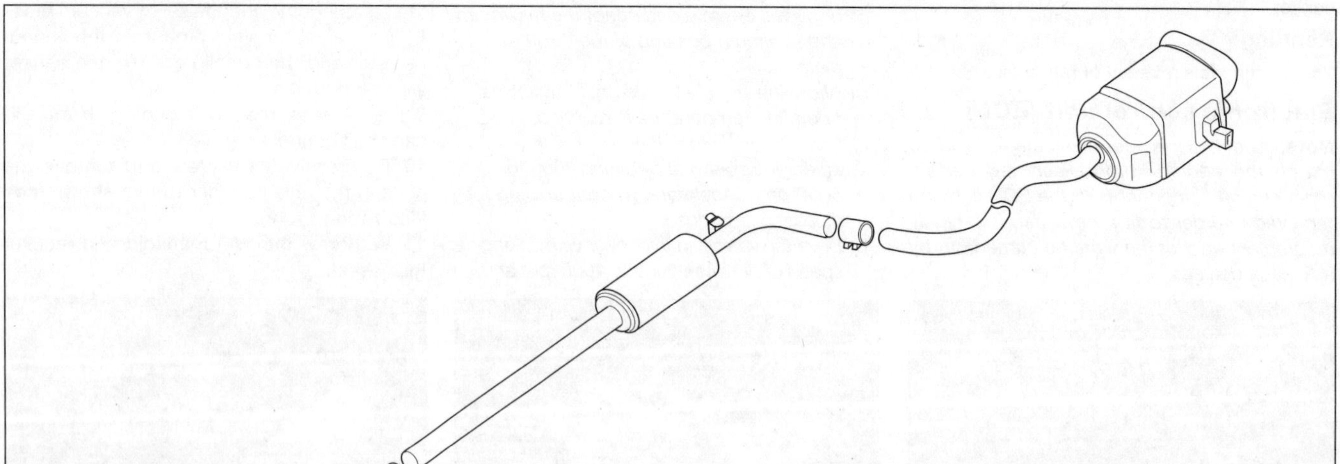

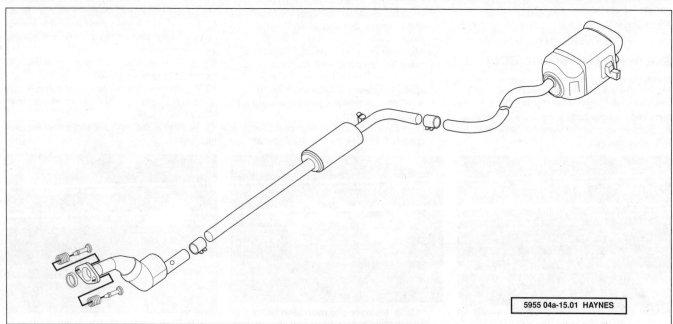

15.1 Replacement exhausts are supplied as individual sections

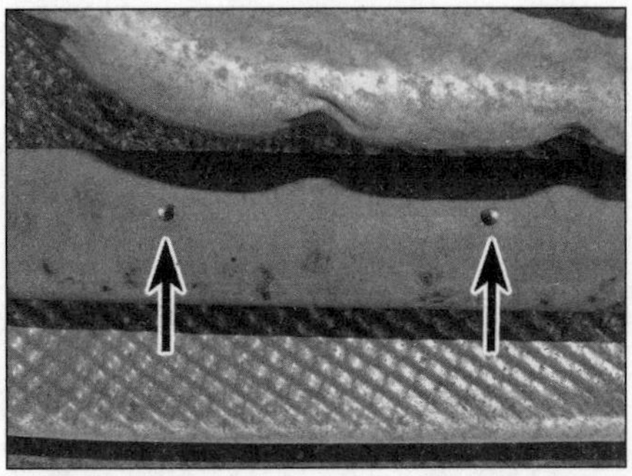

15.2a Locate the cutting points (arrowed)

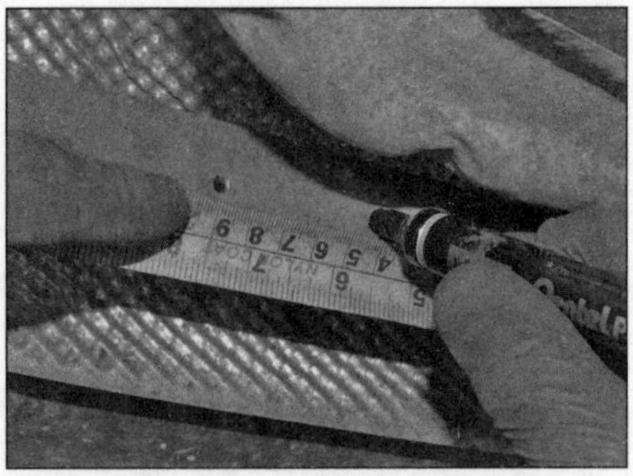

15.2b Locate the centre point and mark it for cutting

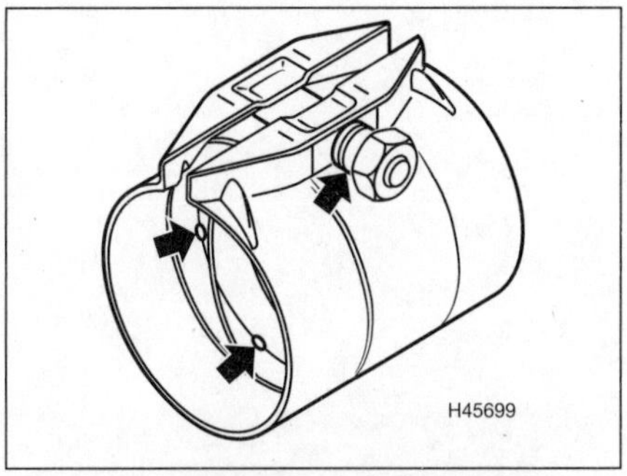

15.2c The special pipe clamp. Insert the exhaust pipe to the inner marks

separately. Renault have provided cutting points on the factory system to enable this. A special clamp is also available to join the old section to the new. **(see illustrations)**.

3 A flexible section (or joint) is incorporated into the exhaust or catalytic converter front section and the system is supported throughout on rubber mountings.

Removal

4 To remove a part of the system, first jack up the front or rear of the car, and support it on axle stands (see *Jacking and vehicle support*). Alternatively, position the car over an inspection pit, or on car ramps. Remove the engine compartment undertray.

Catalytic converter

5 Trace the wiring back from the oxygen sensors and disconnect it at the wiring connectors. Free the wiring from any relevant retaining clips so the sensors are free to be removed with the front pipe.

6 If the original system is still in place, locate the cutting point and saw through the pipe with a hacksaw **(see illustration 15.2a)**. If the system has been renewed previously, unscrew and remove the clamp and disconnect the catalytic converter from the rear section.

7 Unscrew and remove the bolts securing the catalytic convertor to the exhaust manifold. Recover the springs and gasket **(see illustration)**. Withdraw the pipe from under the vehicle.

Intermediate pipe and resonator

8 If the original rear section is fitted, it must be cut , first from the catalytic convertor and then from the rear silencer. Locate the cutting areas. The cutting points are marked with two circular punch marks on the side of the pipe. The punch marks are 80 mm apart and the exhaust section should be cut at the mid-point between the two punch marks.

9 Make the two cuts and unbolt the exhaust mounting **(see illustration)** and remove the intermediate pipe from the vehicle.

15.7 Recover the sealing ring

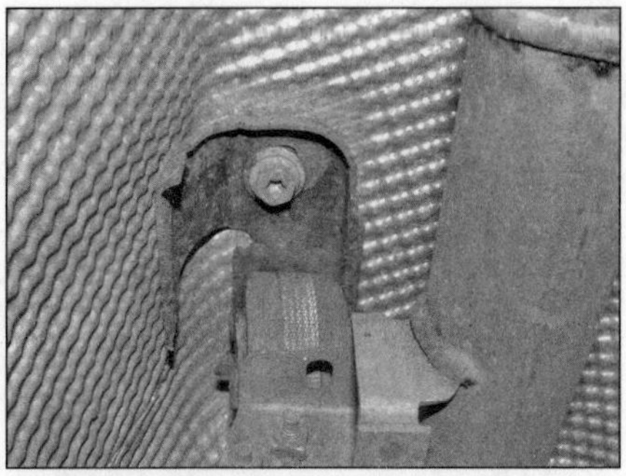

15.9 Unbolt the exhaust mounting

10 If the rear section gas previously been replaced, unscrew the bolt and slide the clamp sleeve on to the rear section then release the rubber mountings and withdraw the intermediate section from under the vehicle.

Rear tailpipe and silencer

11 If the original rear section is fitted locate the cutting point and the rear section from the intermediate section.

12 If the rear section is in two halves, unscrew the bolt and slide the clamp sleeve on to the intermediate section then release the rubber mountings and withdraw the tailpipe and silencer from under the vehicle.

Heat shields

13 The heat shields are secured to the underbody by various nuts and bolts. Each shield can be removed separately but note that they overlap, making it necessary to loosen another section first. If a shield is being removed to gain access to a component located behind it, it may prove sufficient in some cases to remove the retaining nuts and/or bolts, and simply lower the shield, without disturbing the exhaust system. Otherwise remove the exhaust section as described earlier.

Refitting

14 Each section is refitted by reversing the removal sequence, noting the following points:

a) *Ensure that all traces of corrosion have been removed from the joints.*
b) *Inspect the rubber mountings for signs of damage or deterioration, and renew as necessary.*
c) *When reconnecting the intermediate pipe to the tailpipe, apply a smear of exhaust system jointing paste (Renault recommend the use of Sodicam) to the sleeve inner surface, to ensure a gas-tight seal. Make sure both inner ends of the cut pipe are positioned squarely against the stop of the clamp sleeve. Position the sleeve bolt vertically on the left-hand side of the pipe and securely tighten the nut until it is heard to click; the clamp bolt has a groove in it to ensure that the nut is correctly tightened (equivalent to a tightening torque of approximately 25 Nm/18 lbf ft).*
d) *Prior to tightening the exhaust system fasteners, ensure that all rubber mountings are correctly located, and that there is adequate clearance between the exhaust system and vehicle underbody.*
e) *Fit a new gasket to the catalytic converter before fitting it to the exhaust manifold.*

Chapter 4 Part B:
Diesel engine fuel and exhaust systems

Contents

	Section number
Accelerator pedal – removal and refitting	8
Air cleaner assembly – removal and refitting	2
Air filter renewal	See Chapter 1B
Engine management ECU – removal and refitting	9
Exhaust system – general information and component renewal	17
Exhaust system check	See Chapter 1B
Fuel filter renewal	See Chapter 1B
Fuel gauge sender unit – removal, testing and refitting	3
Fuel injectors – testing, removal and refitting	11
Fuel pipes and fittings - general information and disconnection	6
Fuel system – priming and bleeding	5
Fuel tank – removal and refitting	4
General information	1
High-pressure pump – removal and refitting	10
Idle speed – general	7
Injector rail (common rail) – removal and refitting	12
Intercooler – removal and refitting	16
Manifolds – removal and refitting	13
Turbocharger – description	14
Turbocharger – removal and refitting	15

Degrees of difficulty

Easy, suitable for novice with little experience	**Fairly easy,** suitable for beginner with some experience	**Fairly difficult,** suitable for competent DIY mechanic	**Difficult,** suitable for experienced DIY mechanic	**Very difficult,** suitable for expert DIY or professional

Specifications

General

Type	Siemens/Continental
System type	Rear-mounted fuel tank, high-pressure pump with common-rail, direct injection
Firing order	1-3-4-2 (number 1 at flywheel end)
Idle speed	800 ± 50 rpm
Maximum no-load speed	4500 ± 150 rpm
Maximum under-load speed	5000 ± 150 rpm

High-pressure pump

Type	Bosch
Direction of rotation	Clockwise viewed from sprocket end

Injectors

Type	Siemans/Continental solenoid injector
Maximum pressure	1400 bars

Turbocharger

Type	Garrett
Boost pressure	1300 ± 2 mbars

Fuel tank

Fuel tank level sender unit resistance at height of float pin (approx):

At 164 mm	3.5 ± 3.5 ohms
At 143 mm	61 ± 7 ohms
At 110 mm	110 ± 10 ohms
At 81 mm	190 ± 16 ohms
At 52 mm	280 ± 20 ohms
At 47 mm	310 ± 10 ohms

Torque wrench settings

	Nm	lbf ft
Catalytic converter:		
Rear mounting	21	15
To side mounting strut	25	18
To turbocharger	26	19
Strut to engine	44	32
EGR solenoid valve	10	7
EGR valve heat shield	12	9
Engine lifting eye	21	15
Exhaust manifold	26	19
Exhaust pipe clamp	21	15
Fuel injectors to cylinder head	27	20
Fuel tank	21	15
High-pressure fuel rail	21	15
High-pressure pipe union nuts	28	21
High-pressure pump	23	17
High-pressure pump sprocket nut	70	52
Particulate filter temperature sensor	44	32
Particulate filter pressure sensor pipe	21	15
Turbocharger oil supply pipe:		
On cylinder head	35	26
On turbocharger	14	10
Turbocharger oil return pipe	12	9
Turbocharger to exhaust manifold	28	21
Turbocharger outlet elbow	28	21

1 General information

1 The fuel system consists of a rear-mounted fuel tank, a fuel filter with integral water separator, a high-pressure pump with common rail injection system, electronic injectors and associated components.

2 The main components of the system are as follows:

a) Priming bulb on the low-pressure circuit.
b) Fuel filter.
c) High-pressure pump incorporating a low-pressure transfer pump.
d) Flow actuator attached to the pump.
e) Injector rail.
f) Pressure sensor located on the injector rail.
g) Four electronic solenoid injectors.
h) Fuel temperature sensor.
i) Coolant temperature sensor.
j) Upstream air temperature sensor.
k) Downstream air temperature sensor.
l) Cylinder reference sensor.
m) Engine speed sensor.
n) Turbocharging pressure sensor.
o) Accelerometer.
p) EGR solenoid valve.
q) Accelerator pedal potentiometer.
r) Atmospheric pressure sensor.
s) ECU.

TOOL TIP

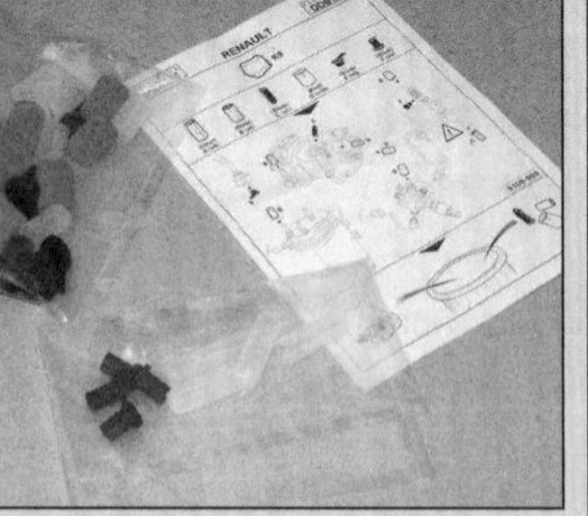

The fuel system is very sensitive to contamination; even a small amount could be sufficient to cause extensive damage to fuel system components such as the high-pressure pump and electronic injectors. It is highly recommended that a set of fuel line plugs is obtained from a Renault dealership.

3 The common rail injection system operates as follows. Fuel is drawn from the fuel tank to the high-pressure pump by a low-pressure transfer pump integrated in the high-pressure pump. Before reaching the high-pressure pump, the fuel passes through a fuel filter, where foreign matter and water are removed. As the fuel passes through the filter, it is heated by an electric heater. On reaching the high-pressure pump, the fuel is pressurised to a maximum of 1400 bars according to demand, and accumulates in the injection common rail. The pressure is accurately maintained in the fuel rail by a flow actuator located on the rear of the pump, the actuator being controlled by the engine management ECU. This arrangement keeps heat generation to a minimum, and improves engine output. The rail pressure is also maintained by the injectors themselves; short electrical pulses which are not long enough to open the injector allow fuel into the return (leak-off) circuit, and also the normal pulses which open the injectors cause a reduction in pressure. The ECU determines the exact timing and duration of the injection period according to engine operating conditions.

4 The four fuel injectors inject a homogeneous spray of fuel into the combustion chambers located in the cylinder head. The injectors operate sequentially according to the firing order of the cylinders, and each injector needle is lubricated by fuel, which accumulates in the spring chamber. Each injector has its own unique flow characteristics which are used by the system ECU to calculate the exact quantity of fuel to inject.

5 Provided that the specified maintenance is carried out, the fuel injection equipment will give long and trouble-free service. The main potential cause of damage to the high-pressure pump and injectors is dirt or water in the fuel **(see Tool tip)**.

6 Servicing of the high-pressure pump, injectors, and electronic equipment and sensors is very limited for the home mechanic, and any dismantling or adjustment other than that described in this Chapter must be entrusted to a Renault dealer or a diesel fuel injection specialist.

7 If a fault appears in the injection system, first ensure that all the system wiring connectors are securely connected and free of corrosion. Should the fault persist, the vehicle should be taken to a Renault dealer or suitably equipped garage who can test the system on a diagnostic tester. The tester will locate the fault quickly and simply, alleviating the need to test all the system components individually, which is a time-consuming operation that carries a risk of damaging the ECU. It is advisable to have any faulty components renewed by the dealer as in many instances the tester is required to reprogramme the ECU in the event of component or sensor renewal.

Warning: It is necessary to take certain precautions when working on the fuel system components, particularly the fuel injectors and high-pressure pump. Before carrying

out any operations on the fuel system, refer to the precautions given in 'Safety first!' at the beginning of this manual, and to any additional warning notes at the start of the relevant Sections. Allow the engine to cool for 5 to 10 minutes to ensure the fuel pressure and temperature are at a minimum.

2 Air cleaner assembly – removal and refitting

Removal

1 Where fitted, remove the engine top cover.
2 Disconnect the battery (see *Disconnecting the battery* in Chapter 5A).
3 Remove the battery and battery tray as described in Chapter 5A.
4 Disconnect the wiring plug from the air flow sensor **(see illustration)** and (where fitted) unclip the electrical connector from the bulkhead.
5 Loosen the hose clip and remove the outlet pipe from the air filter housing **(see illustration)**.
6 Remove the mounting bolt from the housing **(see illustration)** and if necessary the inlet duct.
7 Pull the air filter housing up, separate it from the inlet duct and remove it **(see illustration)**.

Refitting

8 Refitting is a reversal of removal.

2.4 Disconnect the air flow sensor wiring plug

2.5 Release the outlet duct

2.6 Remove the mounting bolt

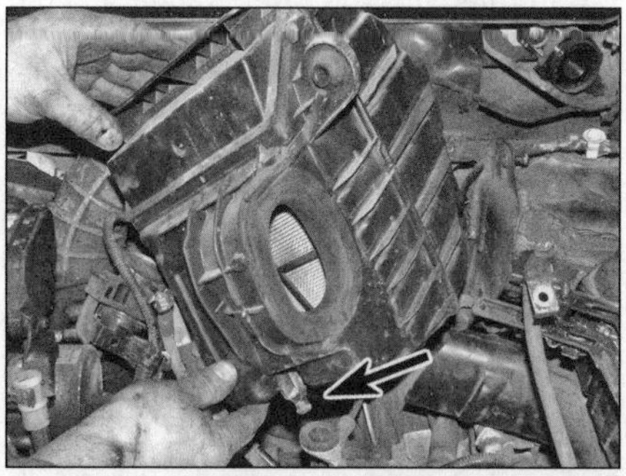

2.7 Remove the air filter housing. Note the locating peg (arrowed)

3 Fuel gauge sender unit – removal, testing and refitting

Warning: Refer to the warning note in Section 1 before proceeding.

Removal

1 Disconnect the battery negative lead (refer to *Disconnecting the battery* as described in Chapter 5A).
2 Remove the rear seat, or rear seat cushion as described in Chapter 11, for access to the fuel pump cover.
3 Remove the screws, remove the protective metal cover and then prise out the plastic cover **(see illustrations)**.
4 Disconnect the wiring connector from the fuel gauge sender, and tape the connector to the vehicle body, to prevent it disappearing behind the tank **(see illustration)**.
5 Anticipating some fuel spillage, disconnect the fuel lines **(see illustration)**.
6 Noting the alignment arrows on the gauge sender cover, locking ring and fuel tank, unscrew the locking ring and remove it from the tank. This can be accomplished by using either the correct tool or by fabricating a suitable tool out of metal bar and two bolts **(see illustrations)**.

3.3a Remove the metal plate...

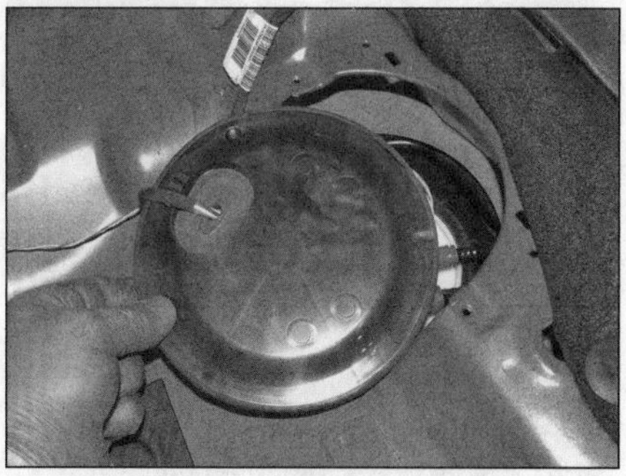

3.3b ...and then the plastic cover

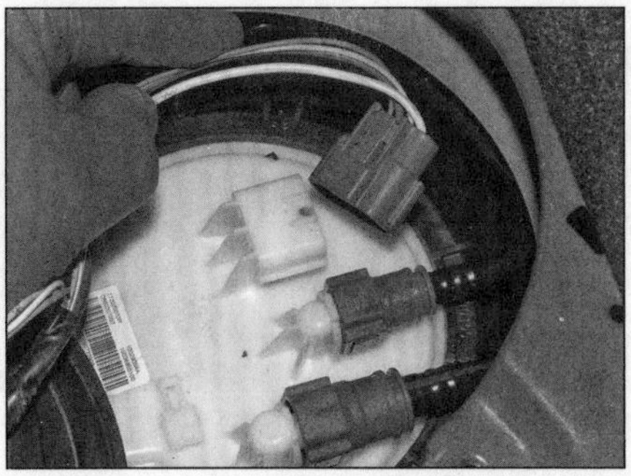

3.4 Disconnect the wiring plug

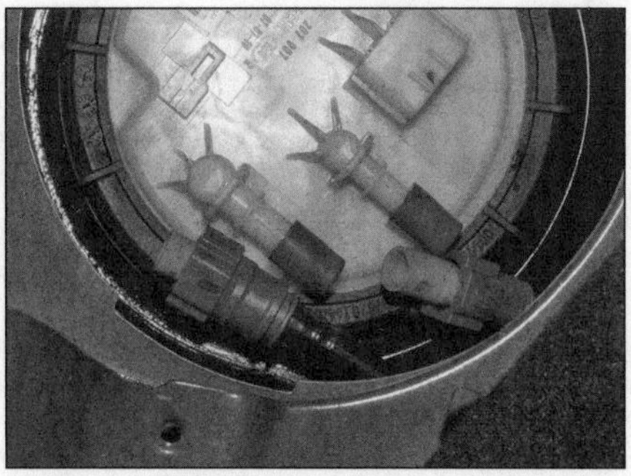

3.5 Disconnect and immediately seal the fuel lines

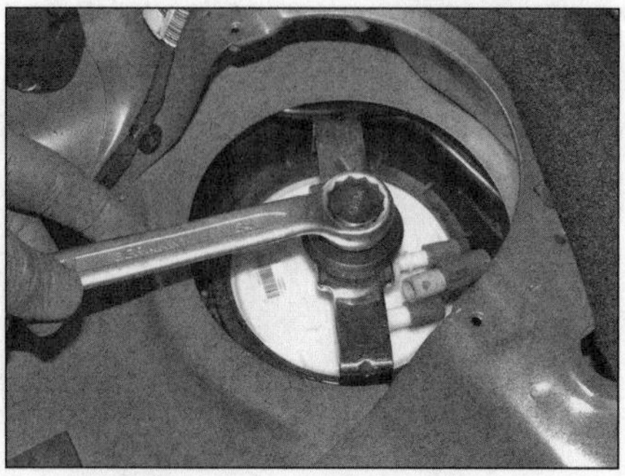

3.6a Use the correct tool...

3.6b ...or fabricate one

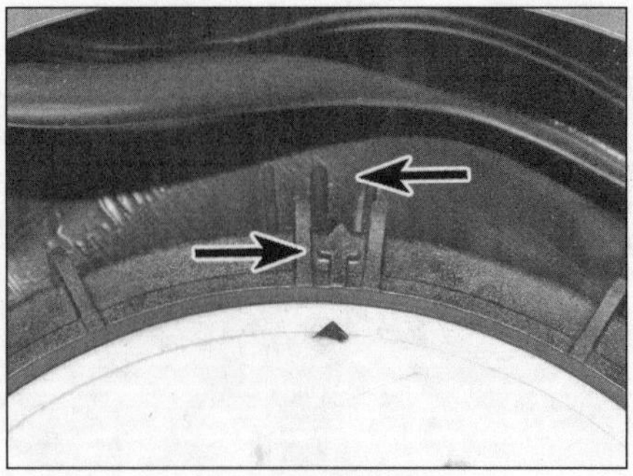

3.11 Align the arrows

7 Carefully lift the fuel gauge sender assembly out of the fuel tank, taking great care not to damage the fuel gauge sender arm, or to spill fuel in the interior of the vehicle. Remove the rubber sealing ring and dispose of it – a new one must be fitted. If the sender is to remain out of the fuel tank for several hours, the locking ring should be refitted temporarily to prevent any possibility of the opening, or the threads on the fuel tank from distorting. Renault recommend that the locking ring is always replaced whenever it is removed.

8 Note that the fuel gauge sender unit is only available as a complete assembly – no components are available separately.

Refitting

9 Ensure that the fuel pick-up filter is clean and free of debris. Fit the new sealing ring to the top of the fuel tank.

10 Carefully manoeuvre the sender assembly into the fuel tank. There is a lug on the sender and a recess in the tank that must be aligned.

11 Press down on the assembly and fit the new locking ring. Securely tighten the locking ring until the arrow on the ring aligns with the mark on the tank **(see illustration)**.

12 Reconnect the fuel line to the top of the fuel pump.

13 Reconnect the wiring connector.

14 Reconnect the battery and start the engine. Check the sender and hoses for signs of leakage.

15 Refit the plastic access cover and metal plate. Replace the rear seat cushion.

4 Fuel tank – removal and refitting

Warning: Refer to the warning note in Section 1 before proceeding.

Removal

1 Before removing the fuel tank, all fuel must be drained from it. Since a drain plug is not provided, it is preferable to carry out the removal operation when the tank is nearly empty.

2 Remove the rear seat, or rear seat cushion (Chapter 11), for access to the fuel pump cover.

3 Remove the metal cover and then prise out the plastic cover.

4 Disconnect the battery negative lead (refer to *Disconnecting the battery* in Chapter 5A).

5 Disconnect the wiring connector from the fuel gauge sender.

6 Chock the front wheels, then jack up the rear of the vehicle and support on axle stands (see *Jacking and vehicle support*).

7 Lower the exhaust system from its mountings **(see illustration)** and let it rest on the rear axle. There is no need to remove it from the vehicle, however if the system has been previously replaced it will be easier to split the exhaust at the clamps and remove it.

8 Partially remove the heat shield from above the exhaust **(see illustration)**. Note that the fuel tank and heat shield share a common mounting at the rear.

9 Remove the hose clips from the fuel filler and breather pipes. Note that some models have a quick release fitting on the breather pipe **(see illustration)**. Dispose of the clips – new ones must be used.

10 Work around the tank and release the rigid brake lines from the clips on the fuel tank **(see illustration)**.

11 Unclip the fuel lines from the tank and move them to one side.

12 Place a trolley jack with of piece wood placed on the head of the jack (to spread the load) beneath the tank. Raise the jack until it is just supporting the weight of the tank.

13 Unscrew and remove the mounting bolts **(see illustration)** recover the heat shield and

4.7 Remove the exhaust hangers by unbolting them

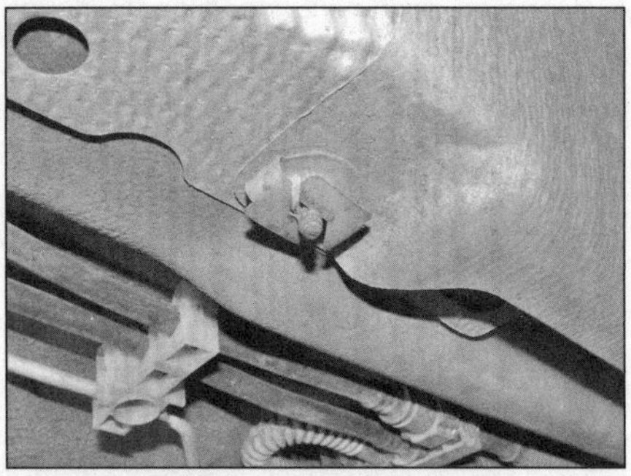

4.8 The heat shield is held in place by several screw clips, best removed with a pair of sliding joint (waterpump) pliers

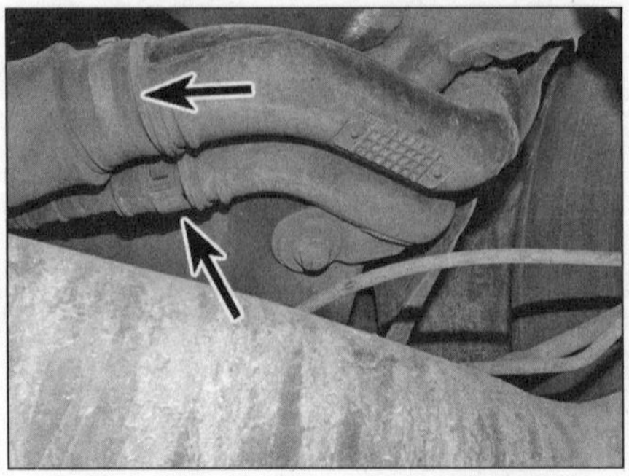

4.9 Remove the hose clips (arrowed)

4.10 Unclip the brake lines

4.13 Remove the tank mounting bolts

then slowly lower the fuel tank out of position, disconnecting any other relevant pipes as they become accessible.

14 Separate the filler neck from the fuel tank as it is lowered.

15 With the help of an assistant remove the tank from underneath the vehicle, working it around the exhaust as necessary.

16 If the tank is contaminated with sediment or water, remove the fuel sender unit (Section 3), and swill the tank out with clean fuel. The tank is injection moulded from a synthetic material – if seriously damaged, it should be renewed. However, in certain cases, it may be possible to have small leaks or minor damage repaired. Seek the advice of a specialist before attempting to repair the fuel tank.

Refitting

17 Refitting is the reverse of the removal procedure, noting the following points:

a) When lifting the tank back into position, take care to ensure that the hoses are not trapped between the tank and vehicle body.

b) Ensure that all pipes and hoses are correctly routed. Make sure the sealing rings are in position in the quick-release fittings prior to fitting and make sure they are securely clipped in position.

c) Renault recommend the replacement of the filler and breather pipe hose clips.

c) On completion, refill the tank with a small amount of fuel, and check for signs of leakage prior to taking the vehicle out on the road.

5 Fuel system – priming and bleeding

Warning: Refer to the precautions in Section 1 before proceeding. Do not attempt to bleed the system by loosening any of the unions on the high-pressure circuit.

Note: *Priming of the fuel system after filter renewal will be improved if the filter is filled with clean diesel fuel before securing it to the filter head. To avoid spillages of fuel, keep the filter upright during refitting.*

1 After disconnecting part of the fuel supply system or running out of fuel, it is necessary to prime the system low-pressure circuit before restarting the engine.

2 All models are fitted with a hand operated priming bulb located next to the coolant expansion tank **(see illustration)**.

3 Squeeze the priming bulb several times to purge the low-pressure circuit of air.

4 Attempt to start the engine normally, however, do not operate the starter motor for more than 5 seconds. If necessary squeeze the priming bulb several more times. Operate the starter motor in 4 to 5 second bursts followed by pauses of 8 to 10 seconds. As soon as the engine starts, let it run at fast idle speed until a regular idle speed is reached.

5.2 The fuel priming bulb

5 Now low pressure fuel lines are supplied with a bleed valve in the open position. The system can be bleed through these valves, however once closed **(see illustration)** they are not designed to be opened again (although it may be possible).

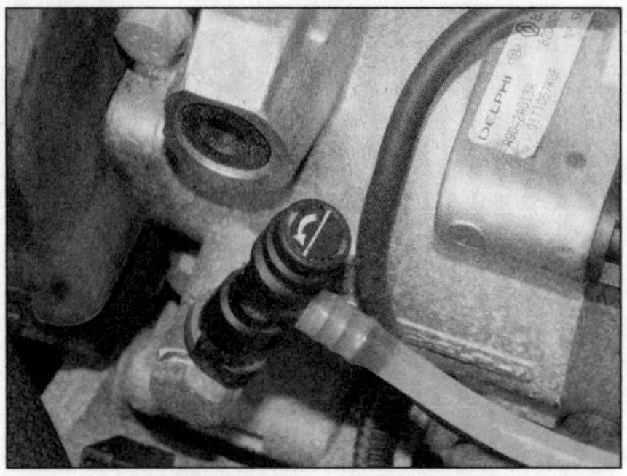

5.5 The bleed valve is not designed to be opened, once closed

6 Fuel pipes and fittings – general information and disconnection

1 Disconnect the cable from the negative battery terminal (see Chapter 5A Section 4) before proceeding.

2 The fuel supply pipe connects the fuel pump in the fuel tank to the fuel filter on the engine.

3 Whenever you're working under the vehicle, be sure to inspect all fuel and evaporative emission pipes for leaks, kinks, dents and other damage. Always replace a damaged fuel pipe immediately.

4 If you find signs of dirt in the pipes during disassembly, disconnect all pipes and blow them out with compressed air. Inspect the fuel strainer on the fuel pump pick-up unit for damage and deterioration.

Steel tubing

5 It is critical that the fuel pipes be replaced with pipes of equivalent type and specification.

6 Some steel fuel pipes have threaded fittings. When loosening these fittings, hold the stationary fitting with a spanner while turning the union nut.

Plastic tubing

Warning: When removing or installing plastic fuel tubing, be careful not to bend or twist it too much, which can damage it. Also, plastic fuel tubing is NOT heat resistant, so keep it away from excessive heat.

7 When replacing fuel system plastic tubing, use only original equipment replacement plastic tubing.

Flexible hoses

8 When replacing fuel system flexible hoses, use original equipment replacements, or hose to the same specification.

9 Don't route fuel hoses (or metal pipes) within 100 mm of the exhaust system or within 280 mm of the catalytic converter. Make sure that no rubber hoses are installed directly against the vehicle, particularly in places where there is any vibration. If allowed to touch some vibrating part of the vehicle, a hose can easily become chafed and it might start leaking. A good rule of thumb is to maintain a minimum of 8.0 mm clearance around a hose (or metal pipe) to prevent contact with the vehicle underbody.

7 Idle speed – general

1 The engine management ECU uses the following inputs to calculate the recommended idle speed according to the varying load on the engine by peripheral electrical or mechanical components.

a) Engine coolant temperature.

b) Battery voltage.

c) The gear selected.

d) Electrical consumers (heater fan, climate control system, lighting, etc).

2 At normal engine temperature with no electrical consumers switched on and neutral selected, the engine idle speed will be 850 rpm.

3 If the accelerator pedal potentiometer internal tracks are faulty, the ECU will override the idle speed to 1100 rpm, and the injection warning light will be illuminated on the instrument panel. If there is no output from the potentiometer, the idle speed will be 1300 rpm. In each case, if the brake pedal is depressed, the idle speed will revert to its normal level.

4 If there is an injector fault, the idle speed will be set to 1300 rpm and the warning light will be illuminated.

5 With Neutral, 1st or 2nd gear selected, the idle speed will be 850 rpm at an ambient temperature of more than 20°C; below this temperature the idle speed will increase accordingly. In 3rd, 4th or 5th gear, the idle speed will be 900 rpm.

6 Should the idle speed be incorrect, the car should be taken to a Renault dealer or suitably equipped garage who will have the necessary diagnostic equipment to pin-point the faulty component responsible.

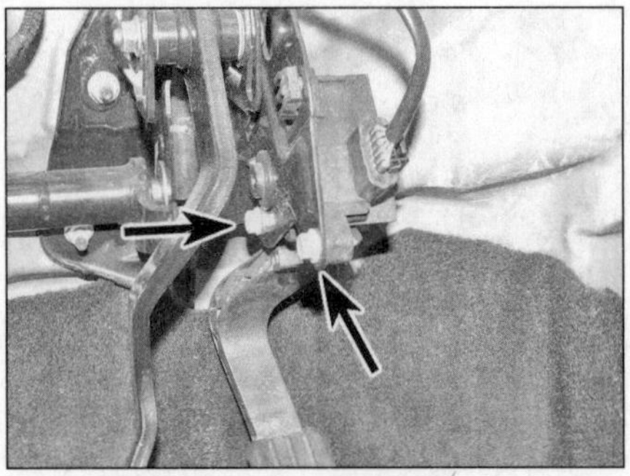

8.3 The accelerator retaining nuts (arrowed)

9.4 Remove the cover

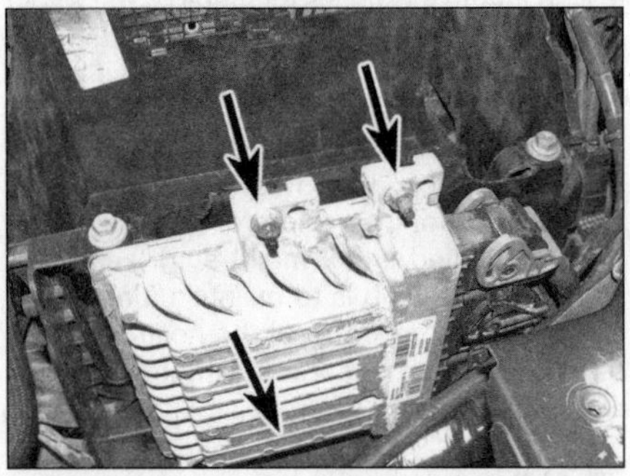

9.5 Remove the mounting bolts (arrowed). One bolt hidden and shown with the front panel removed for clarity

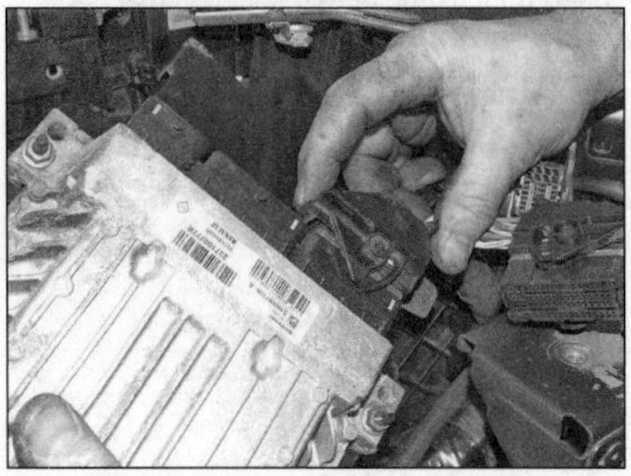

9.6 Disconnect the wiring plugs

8 Accelerator pedal – removal and refitting

Removal

1 Remove the lower trim panel from under the steering column as described in Chapter 11.

2 Disconnect the wiring plug from the accelerator pedal.

3 Remove the bolts securing the accelerator pedal in position **(see illustration)**.

4 Unhook and then withdraw the accelerator pedal.

5 Examine the pedal and pivot for signs of wear and renew as necessary.

Refitting

6 Refitting is a reversal of removal.

9 Engine management ECU – removal and refitting

Note: *The ECU is electronically-coded to match the engine immobiliser and certain other engine components. If the ECU is being removed in order to fit a new unit, it is highly recommended that the work be carried out by a Renault dealer or suitably equipped garage.*

Removal

1 The ECU is located in the left-hand side of the engine compartment in front of the battery.

2 First disconnect the battery negative lead (refer to *Disconnecting the battery* in Chapter 5A).

3 Remove the battery cover as described in Chapter 5A.

4 Unclip and remove the cooling inlet duct and the ECU cover **(see illustration)**.

5 Remove the mounting bolts and withdraw the control unit **(see illustration)**.

6 Unlock and remove the three electrical connectors from the ECU **(see illustration)**. Access can be improved if the left-hand headlight is removed as described in Chapter 12.

Refitting

7 Refitting is a reverse of the removal procedure ensuring that the wiring is securely reconnected. After the battery is reconnected it may take several drive cycles for the ECU to adapt itself to the vehicle. During the period the idle speed, economy and drivability may be compromised.

10 High-pressure pump – removal and refitting

Warning: Refer to the warning note in Section 1 before proceeding.

Caution: Before starting work, allow the engine to cool for 5 to 10 minutes, to ensure the fuel pressure and temperature are at a minimum.

Note: *Cleanliness is of critical importance when working on the fuel system of any modern diesel engine. The smallest speck of grit or dirt can cause extensive damage to the pump and injectors. Always clean thoroughly the pump and injector unions before dismantling. Immediately plug and seal all pipes and components. Components that are removed from the engine should immediately be placed in clean plastic bags.*

Note: *Renault do not supply individual pump parts. If the pump is faulty it must be replaced. This will normally be on an exchange basis.*

Removal

1 Disconnect the battery negative lead (refer to *Disconnecting the battery* in Chapter 5A).

2 Where fitted, remove the engine cover and then the turbocharger outlet pipe from the top of the engine **(see illustrations)**.

3 Jack up the right-hand front of the car and support on axle stands (see *Jacking and vehicle support* in the reference section).

10.2a Remove the bolt

10.2b At the intercooler end, lever the spring clip (arrowed) free

10.2c Release the spring clip at the turbocharger end and pull out the pipe

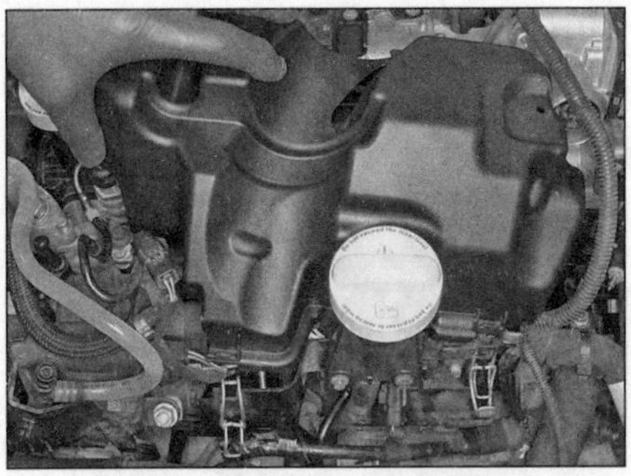
10.9 Remove the cover

10.10a Disconnect the wiring plug

10.10b Remove the main bolts (arrowed)...

10.10c ...and the single bolt (arrowed) beneath the pump

10.10d Remove the cover

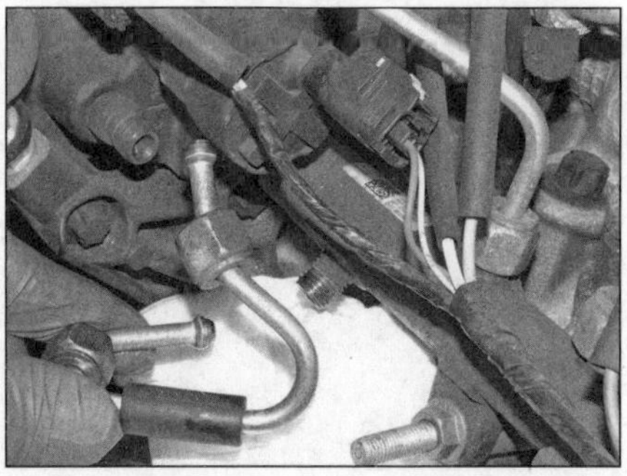
10.11 Remove the high pressure pipe

4 Remove the front right wheel, engine undertray and the front section of the wheel arch liner.

5 Remove the front bumper cover as described in Chapter 11 and then remove the auxiliary drivebelt with reference to Chapter 1B.

6 Support the right-hand end of the engine with a support bar across the engine compartment, with a hoist, or alternatively with a jack and block of wood beneath the sump.

7 Remove the rear engine steady bar and then unbolt the right-hand engine mounting.

8 Remove the timing belt covers and then remove the timing belt as described in Chapter 2B.

9 Unbolt and then unclip the sound proofing/ protective cover from the top of the engine **(see illustration).**

10 Remove the dipstick tube bolts. Move the dipstick aside or remove it completely. Release the wiring loom and then unbolt and remove the fuel rail cover **(see illustrations)**.

11 Place a clean rag over the alternator and then remove the fuel pipes from the pump. Remove the high-pressure outlet pipe **(see illustration)**. Seal the pump and pipes immediately. Do not allow fuel to contaminate the alternator.

12 Unclip and remove the support bracket from the top of the pump and then disconnect the electrical connectors from the pump.

13 Loosen the alternator lower bolt and remove the top bolt. Tip the alternator away from the engine.

14 Unbolt and remove the pump **(see illustration)**. Place the pump in a vice and remove the sprocket retaining nut. Use a strap wrench and a ring spanner to do this. A puller will then be required to remove the sprocket from the pump.

Refitting

Note: *The high-pressure pipe between the pump and the common rail must be replaced.*

15 Refitting is a reversal of removal, but take care not to place the new high-pressure pipe under any stress. If fitting a new pump, it is highly recommended that the pump is primed with diesel on the bench before fitting.

16 If when removing the timing belt damage was evident **(see illustration)** and the vehicle build code is BZOB, KZOB or DZOB, then the pump must be rotated fully anti-clockwise before fully tightening the pump mounting bolts.

17 New high-pressure pipes are supplied with a lubricant for the threads on the pipe. If no lubricant is supplied the pipes are self-lubricating and lubricant should not be applied.

18 Tighten all nuts and bolts to the specified torque and angle as applicable. When tightening the pipe union nuts onto the injectors, counter-hold the injectors with a further spanner. Prime and bleed the fuel system as described in Section 5.

19 Fit a new timing belt and refit the remaining components in reverse order to removal.

11 Fuel injectors – testing, removal and refitting

Warning: Exercise extreme caution when working on the high-pressure fuel system. Do

10.14 Remove the pump mounting bolts (arrowed)

10.16 Typical belt damage, caused by an incorrectly aligned fuel pump

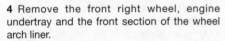

11.4 Release the spring clip (arrowed) and remove the pipe from the turbocharger

11.5a Disconnect the wiring plug

11.5b Remove the hose from the control valve

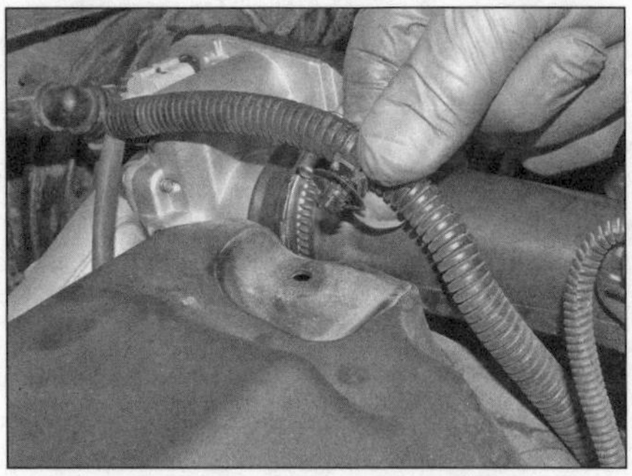
11.5c Release the wiring loom

11.6 Remove the protective cover

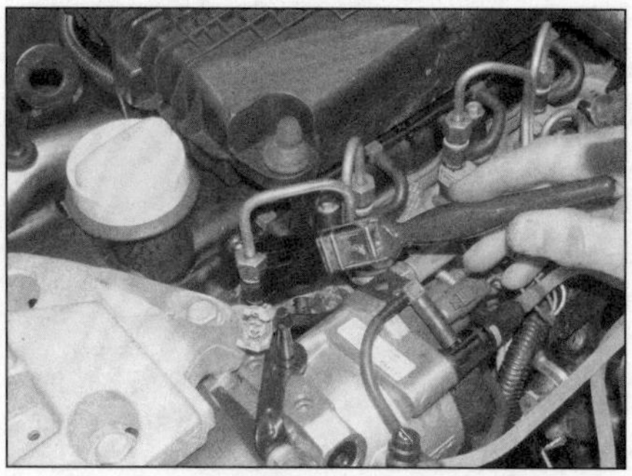
11.7 Thoroughly clean around the injectors and high pressure pipes

not attempt to test the fuel injectors or disconnect the high-pressure lines with the engine running. Never expose the hands or any part of the body to injector spray, as the high working pressure can cause the fuel to penetrate the skin, with possibly fatal results. You are strongly advised to have any work which involves testing the injectors under pressure carried out by a dealer or fuel injection specialist. Refer to the precautions given in Section 1 of this Chapter before proceeding. After switching off the engine, allow the engine to cool for 5 to 10 minutes to allow the fuel pressure to drop before disconnecting any of the high-pressure fuel pipes.

Note: *Each new injector is supplied with a unique 16-digit code which specifies its flow characteristics. This code must be programmed into the engine management ECU with a special diagnostic tool, therefore this work should be entrusted to a Renault dealer or suitably equipped garage.*

Testing

1 It is not possible to test the fuel injectors without specialist equipment, therefore, if they are thought to be faulty, consult a Renault dealer or diesel specialist.

Removal

Note: *Take care not to allow dirt into the injectors or fuel pipes during this procedure; clean around the area before commencing work. Note that all high-pressure pipes removed must be renewed as a matter of course. The injector flame shield washers must also be renewed.*

2 Disconnect the battery negative lead (refer to *Disconnecting the battery* in Chapter 5A).

3 Where fitted, remove the engine top cover.

4 Unbolt and remove the turbocharger to intercooler pipe from the top of the engine **(see illustration)**.

5 At the left-hand end of the engine, disconnect the wiring plug from the boost pressure sensor. Release the hose clip from the intercooler pipe and move it to the side. Release the wiring loom from the boost pressure sensor and the damper valve at the end of the cylinder head **(see illustrations)**.

6 Unclip and unbolt the protective cover/ sound proofing from the fuel rail and injectors **(see illustration)**.

7 Thoroughly clean the area around the injectors, fuel rail and high pressure fuel lines **(see illustration)**.

8 Disconnect the wiring plugs from the fuel injectors **(see illustration)**.

9 Disconnect the fuel leak-off pipes from the injectors. Tape over or plug all fuel apertures to prevent entry of dust and dirt **(see illustrations)**.

11.8 Disconnecting the fuel injector wiring

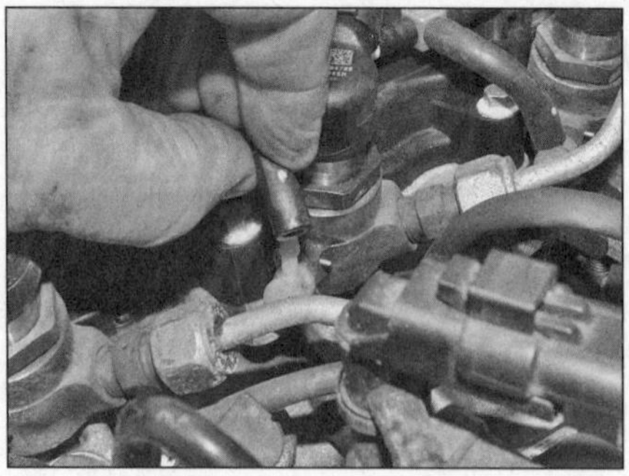
11.9a Fuel leak-off pipes on the injectors

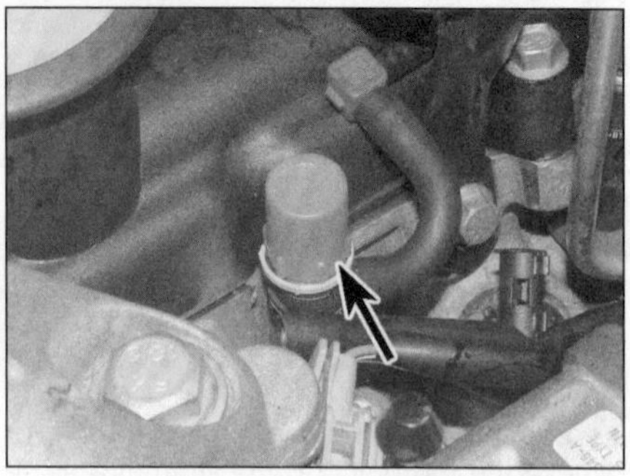
11.9b Fit protective caps to prevent entry of dust

11.10a Unscrew the high pressure pipe union nuts...

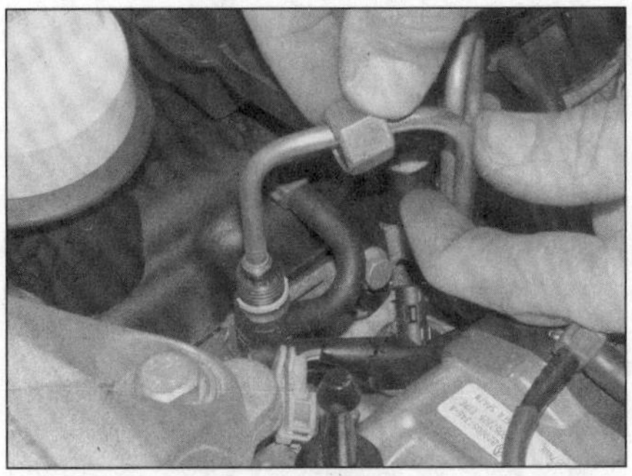
11.10b ...and move them away before releasing the pipe

11.11a Unscrew the securing bolt...

11.11b ...remove the clamp plate...

11.11c ...and then remove the injector from the cylinder head

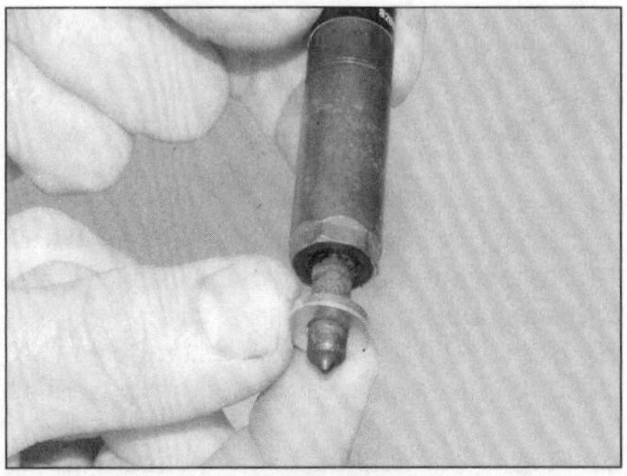
11.11d Recover the flame shield washer

10 While holding the injector central unions with one spanner, unscrew the high-pressure pipe union nuts with a further spanner. Take care not to damage the leak-off stubs on the injectors, and wrap them in cloth rag before loosening them. Similarly, unscrew the union nuts from the fuel rail, then remove the pipes. Move the nuts and olives along the pipes when releasing the pipes from the rail and injectors **(see illustrations)**.

11 Using a Torx key (or socket) unscrew the bolt securing each injector clamp plate to the cylinder head. Lift off the clamp plates and remove the injectors then recover the flame shield washers between the injectors and the cylinder head. Take care not to drop the injectors or allow the needles at their tips to become damaged. The injectors are precision-made to fine limits and must not be handled roughly. In particular, do not mount them in a bench vice. It is recommended that the injectors are stored vertically at all times **(see illustrations)**.

12 If the injectors are stuck in the cylinder head several tools are available to aid their removal **(see illustration)**. In extreme cases a special hydraulic puller maybe required to remove the injectors. A well equipped garage or a diesel specialist will have access to this equipment.

Refitting

13 Clean the cylinder head, taking care to prevent foreign matter entering the fuel apertures. The injectors can be cleaned with a lint-free cloth soaked in brake cleaning fluid or fresh diesel. **Do not** clean them with a wire brush or emery cloth.

14 Carefully inspect the injector housings in the cylinder head. It is not uncommon for a build up of carbon to contaminate the seat of the housing. Specialist seat cutting tools are available to remove any contamination and to clean the seat in the bore **(see illustration)**.

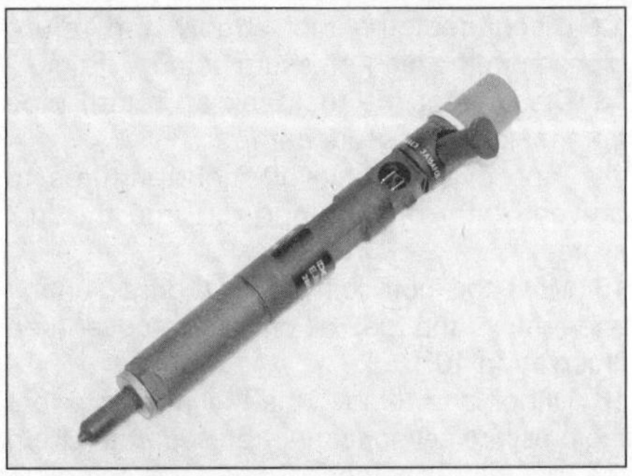
11.11e Fuel injector removed from the cylinder head

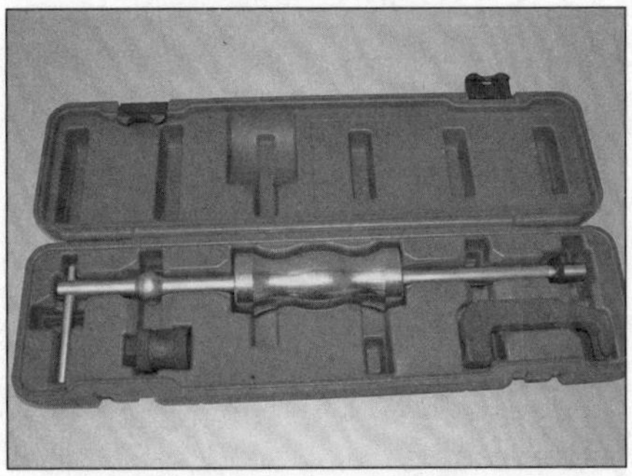
11.12 Slide hammer and adaptor kit for injector removal

15 Fit new sealing shims between the injectors and the cylinder head. Insert the injectors then fit the clamp plates. Tighten the clamp plate bolts to the specified torque.

16 Refit the leak-off pipes, then fit the new high-pressure fuel pipes. Before fitting the

11.11f A suitable storage rack can be easily fabricated

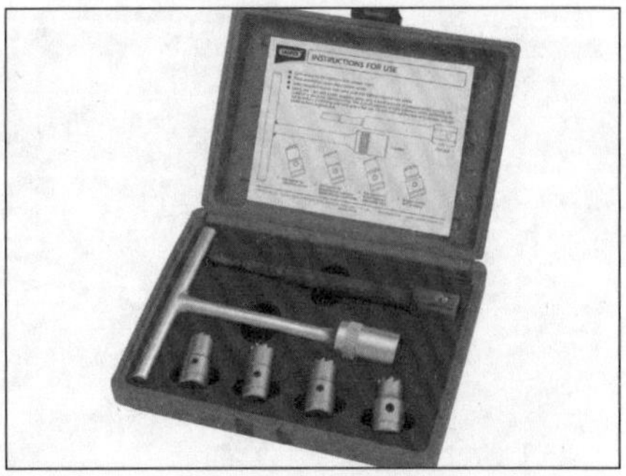
11.14 Injector seat cutting tool kit

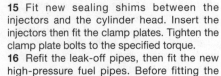

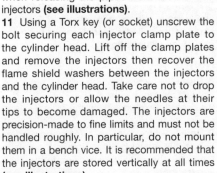

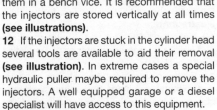

12.10 Remove the bolts (arrowed) from the dipstick guide tube

new pipes, lubricate the threads of the union nuts with oil from the sachet provided, and finger-tighten the nuts before tightening them to the specified torque.

17 Reconnect the fuel injector wiring.

18 Temporarily refit the intercooler pipes and the boost pressure sensor.

19 Reconnect the battery negative lead (refer to *Disconnecting the battery*).

20 Start the engine. If difficulty is experienced, bleed the fuel system as described in Section 5.

21 Run the engine up to temperature whilst watching for any fuel leaks from the injectors, high pressure pipes and the fuel return (bleed off) pipes. If no leaks are present stop the engine, remove the intercooler pipes and boost pressure sensor wiring. Refit the protective cover/sound proofing to the injectors and fuel rail. Refit the remainder of the components in reverse order to removal.

12 Injector rail (common rail) – removal and refitting

Warning: Refer to the warning note in Section 1 before proceeding. After switching off the engine, allow several minutes for the fuel pressure so subside before disconnecting any of the high-pressure fuel pipes.

Note: *Take care not to allow dirt into the fuel pipes during this procedure; clean around the area before commencing work. Note that all high-pressure pipes removed must be renewed as a matter of course.*

Removal

1 Disconnect the battery negative lead (refer to *Disconnecting the battery* in Chapter 5A).

2 Where fitted remove the engine top cover.

3 Unbolt and remove the turbocharger to intercooler pipe from the top of the engine **(see illustration 11.4)**.

4 At the left-hand end of the engine, disconnect the wiring plug from the boost pressure sensor. Release the hose clip from the intercooler pipe and move it to the side. Release wiring loom from the boost pressure sensor and the damper valve at the end of the cylinder head **(see illustrations 11.5a, 11.5b and 11.5c)**.

5 Unclip and unbolt the protective cover/ sound proofing from the fuel rail and injectors **(see illustration 11.6)**.

6 Thoroughly clean the area around the injectors, fuel rail and high pressure fuel lines **(see illustration 11.7)**.

7 Disconnect the wiring plugs from the fuel injectors

8 Unbolt and remove the high pressure pipes from between the fuel rail and the injectors.

9 Disconnect the wiring plugs from the glow plugs and then unclip the coolant hose from above the alternator.

10 Remove the dipstick and then unbolt the dipstick guide tube **(see illustration)**. Move the guide tube to the side – there is no need to remove it completely.

11 Disconnect the wiring plugs from the high pressure pump and the fuel rail.

12 Disconnect the fuel supply and return pipes from the high-pressure pump.

13 Disconnect the fuel leak-off return pipe from the high-pressure pump.

14 Tape over or plug all fuel apertures to prevent entry of dust and dirt into the fuel system.

15 Move the loom to the side and then unbolt and remove the fuel rail protective cover **(see illustration 10.10d)**.

16 Unbolt and remove the fuel rail. Note that the pressure sensor cannot be separated from the fuel rail; if the sensor fails, the complete rail must be renewed.

Refitting

17 Refitting is a reversal of removal, but take care not to place the new high-pressure pipe under any stress. Before fitting the new pipe, lubricate the threads of the union nuts with oil from the sachet provided, and finger-tighten the nuts before tightening them to the specified torque. When tightening the pipe union nuts onto the injectors, counter-hold the injectors with a further spanner.

13 Manifolds – removal and refitting

Removal

1 The inlet manifold is incorporated into the cylinder head and therefore cannot be removed separately. To remove the exhaust manifold, first apply the handbrake, then jack up the front of the vehicle and support it on axle stands (*see Jacking and vehicle support*).

2 Disconnect the exhaust downpipe from the exhaust manifold and support it to one side with reference to Section 17.

3 Remove the turbocharger as described in Section 14. If the reason for removing the manifold is simply to renew the gasket, the turbocharger can remain attached to the manifold.

4 Loosen the two clamps, then remove the EGR metal tube between the inlet and exhaust manifolds. Renault recommend that the metal tube and clamps are renewed as a matter of course.

5 Unscrew the mounting bolts and remove the EGR unit from the inlet manifold.

6 Progressively unscrew the mounting nuts and remove the exhaust manifold from the studs on the cylinder head. Recover the metal gasket **(see illustrations)**.

Refitting

7 Clean the surfaces of the cylinder head and exhaust manifold.

8 Locate a new gasket on the cylinder head studs.

9 Refit the exhaust manifold and finger-tighten the retaining nuts. Tighten the nuts in the order shown to the specified torque **(see illustration)**.

10 Refit the EGR unit to the inlet manifold and tighten the mounting nuts to the specified torque.

11 Fit the new metal tube between the inlet and exhaust manifolds and secure with new clamps. Renault technicians use a special tool to tighten the clamps, however, it should be possible to tighten them using pliers and a screwdriver if care is taken.

12 Refit the turbocharger with reference to Section 14.

13 Refit the exhaust downpipe to the manifold with reference to Section 17.

14 Lower the vehicle to the ground.

13.6a Removing the exhaust manifold together with the turbocharger

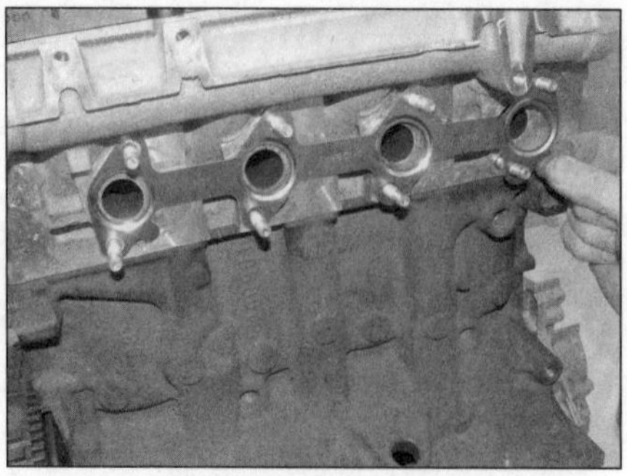

13.6b Removing the exhaust manifold gasket

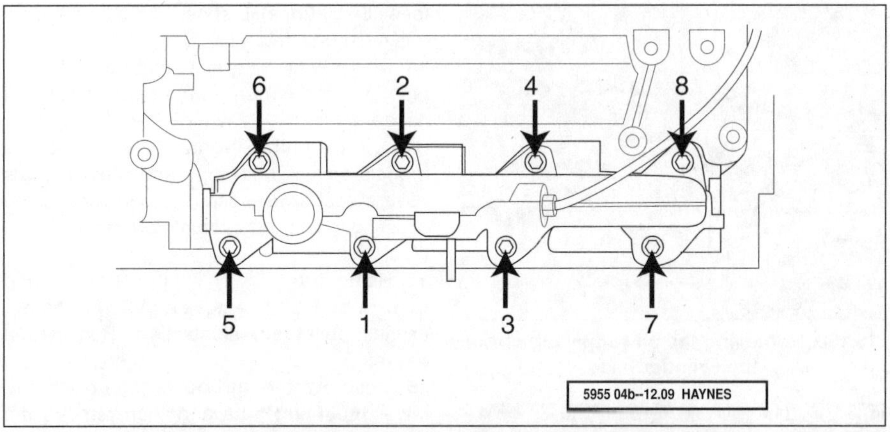

13.9 Tighten the nuts in the order shown

14 Turbocharger – description

1 A turbocharger increases engine efficiency by raising the pressure in the inlet manifold above atmospheric pressure **(see illustration)**. Instead of the air simply being sucked into the cylinders, it is forced in. Additional fuel is supplied in proportion to the increased air intake.

2 Energy for the operation of the turbocharger comes from the exhaust gas. The gas flows through a specially-shaped housing (the turbine housing) and in so doing, spins the turbine wheel. The turbine wheel is attached to a shaft, at the end of which is another vaned wheel known as the compressor wheel. The compressor wheel spins in its own housing and compresses the inducted air on the way to the inlet manifold.

3 Between the turbocharger and the inlet manifold the compressed air passes through an intercooler. This is an air-to-air heat exchanger, mounted behind the front bumper, next to the air conditioning condenser and the coolant radiator. The purpose of the intercooler is to remove some of the heat gained in being compressed from the inducted air. Because cooler air is denser, removal of this heat further increases engine efficiency.

4 Boost pressure (the pressure in the inlet manifold) is limited by a wastegate, which diverts the exhaust gas away from the turbine wheel in response to a pressure-sensitive actuator. Turbocharging boost pressure is controlled by a pressure sensor located on the intercooler outlet pipe **(see illustration)**.

5 The turbo shaft is pressure-lubricated by an oil feed pipe from the main oil gallery. The shaft 'floats' on a cushion of oil. A drain pipe returns the oil to the sump.

Precautions

- The turbocharger operates at extremely high speeds and temperatures. Certain precautions must be observed to avoid premature failure of the turbo or injury to the operator.
- Do not race the engine immediately after start-up, especially if it is cold. Give the oil a few seconds to circulate.
- Always allow the engine to return to idle speed before switching it off – do not blip the throttle and switch off, as this will leave the turbo spinning without lubrication.
- Allow the engine to idle for several minutes before switching off after a high speed run.
- Observe the recommended intervals for oil and filter changing, and use a reputable oil of the specified quality. Neglect of oil changing, or use of inferior oil, can cause carbon formation on the turbo shaft and subsequent failure.

Warning: Do not operate the turbo with any parts exposed. Foreign objects falling onto the rotating vanes could cause excessive damage and (if ejected) personal injury.

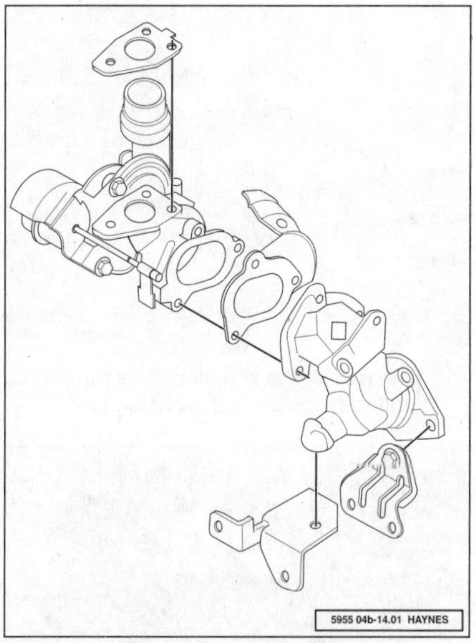

14.1 The turbocharger

15 Turbocharger – removal and refitting

Note: *New oil supply pipe O-rings and copper washers must be used on refitting.*

Removal

1

2 Disconnect the battery negative lead (refer to *Disconnecting the battery* in Chapter 5A).

3 Where fitted, remove the engine top cover, then remove the air cleaner unit (as described in Section 2).

4 Remove the battery and battery tray as described in Chapter 5A.

5 Remove the upper and lower windscreen cowl panels as described in Chapter 11.

6 Remove the turbocharger inlet and outlet pipes from the top of the engine.

7 Disconnect the wiring plug and then unbolt and remove the damper (anti-shudder) valve **(see illustrations)**.

8 Release the clamps and remove the EGR rigid pipe and then (with reference to Chapter 4C) remove the EGR valve assembly.

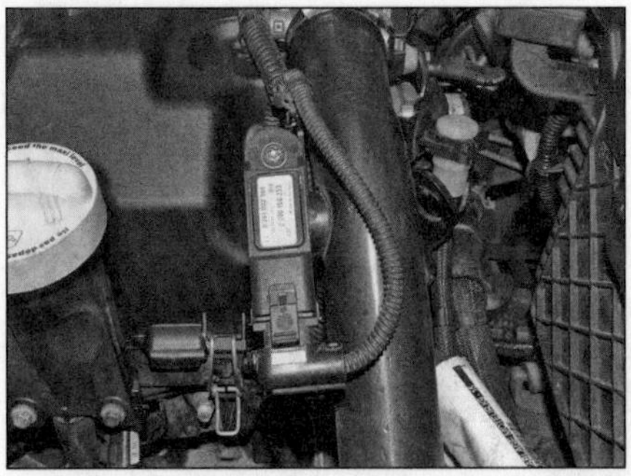

14.4 Turbocharger boost pressure sensor

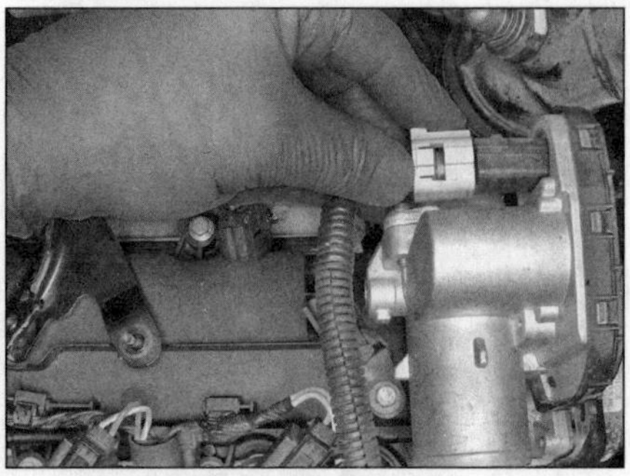

15.7a Disconnect the wiring plug

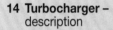

15.7b Remove the valve

15.13a Removing the oil supply pipe and sealing rings from the turbocharger

15.13b Removing the oil supply pipe from the cylinder head

15.14a Oil return pipe flange bolts on the bottom of the turbocharger

15.14b Removing the oil return pipe

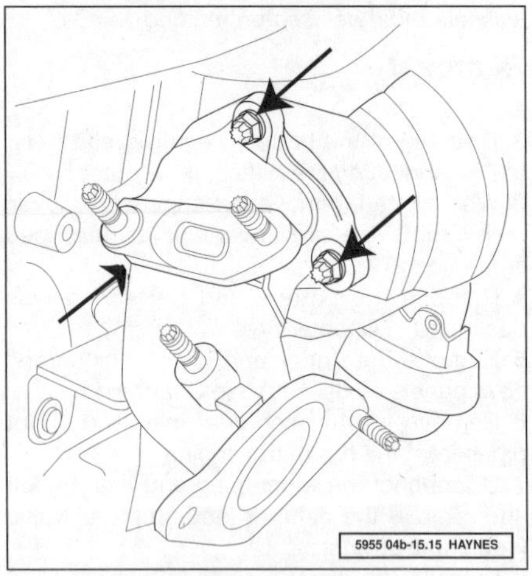

15.15 Remove the nuts (arrowed)

9 Apply the handbrake, then jack up the front of the vehicle, and support securely on axle stands (see *Jacking and vehicle support*).

10 Remove the engine undershield and then remove the right-hand front roadwheel.

11 Remove the vacuum hose from the wastegate control.

12 Working form below disconnect the particulate filter (later models) or catalytic convertor from the turbocharger. Some models fitted with a particulate filter may also have a low pressure fuel injector and a cooler fitted. Where fitted disconnect the wiring plug. Disconnect the fuel line (seal the line immediately) and then remover the cooler/heat sink.

13 Unscrew the union and disconnect the oil supply pipe from the turbocharger, collect the sealing rings, then unscrew the union nut and disconnect the pipe from the cylinder head **(see illustrations)**. Dispose of the pipe – anew one must be fitted.

14 Unscrew the bolts and detach the oil return pipe from the bottom of the turbocharger – if necessary, remove the pipe from the cylinder block **(see illustrations)**. Note that some models have a rigid pipe and other models have a section of hose (secured with spring clips) connecting the drain pipe to the engine block.

15 Remove the lower support bracket and then unbolt and remove the turbocharger exhaust outlet **(see illustration)**. Recover the gasket.

16 Unscrew the turbocharger upper and lower mounting nuts and then remove the turbocharger together with the oil return pipe from the exhaust manifold. With the assembly on the bench, remove the oil return pipe. Do not attempt to separate the inlet and exhaust sections of the turbocharger.

Refitting

17 Refitting is a reversal of removal, but renew any damaged hose clamps and use new turbocharger-to-exhaust manifold nuts which should be tightened to the specified torque. Fit new a oil supply pipe, O-rings and copper seals to the pipe and tightening the union nuts to the specified torque. Fit a new gasket to the top of the oil return pipe, and new O-ring seals to the grooves in the bottom of the pipe **(see illustrations)**. On completion, the following procedure must be observed before starting the engine in order to establish initial oil pressure in the turbocharger.

a) Disconnect the wiring from the fuel injectors.

b) Crank the engine on the starter motor until the instrument panel oil pressure warning light goes out (this may take several seconds).

c) Reconnect the wiring to the injectors, then start the engine using the normal procedure.

d) Run the engine at idle speed, and check the turbocharger oil unions for leakage.

e) After the engine has been run, check the engine oil level, and top-up if necessary.

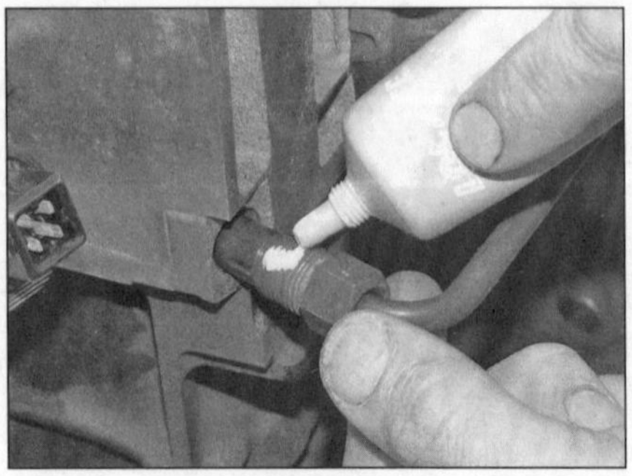

15.17a Applying sealant to the threads of the oil supply pipe union

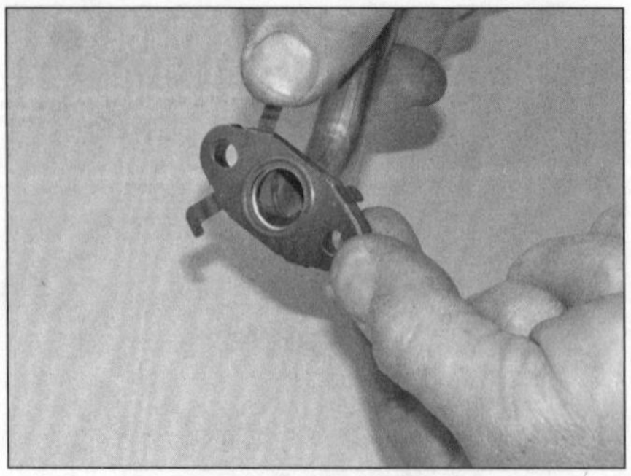

15.17b Fitting a new gasket to the top of the oil return pipe...

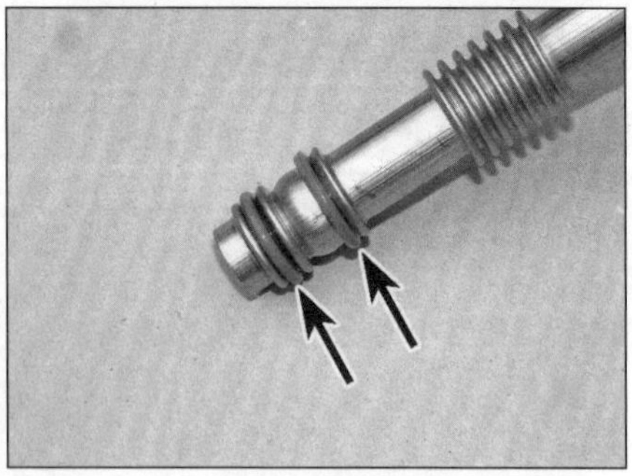

15.17c ...and fit new O-ring seals to the grooves in the bottom of the pipe

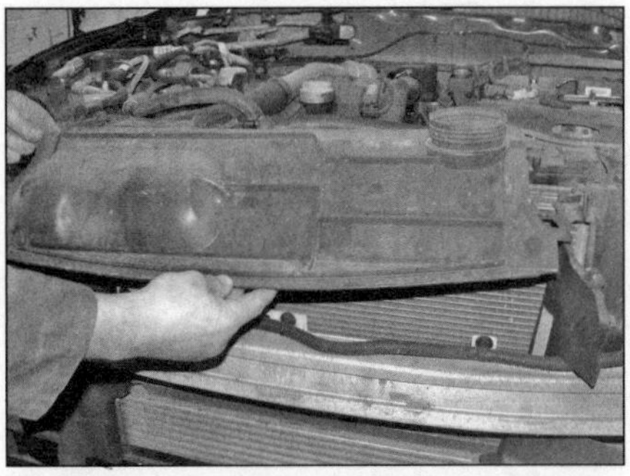
16.3 Removing the central air deflector

16.4 Remove both headlight support panels

16.5a Remove the upper (arrowed)...

16.5b ...and the lower spring retaining clips and...

16.5c ...then remove the mounting bolt

16.6 Release the locking clip (arrowed)

16 Intercooler – removal and refitting

Removal

1 The intercooler is located below the air conditioning condenser and in front of the radiator.

2 Remove the front bumper as described in Chapter 11.

3 Remove the centre and side air deflector panels **(see illustration)**.

4 Remove both headlight support panels **(see illustration)**.

5 Loosen the clips and disconnect the air inlet and outlet ducts from the intercooler **(see illustrations)**. Remove the ducts from both sides.

6 Depress the locking clip **(see illustration)** slide the intercooler to the right and remove it.

Refitting

7 Refitting is a reversal of removal, but tighten all nuts and bolts to the specified torque where given.

17 Exhaust system – general information and component renewal

General information

1 On new vehicles the exhaust system consists of a single section that includes the catalytic convertor. Later models have a particulate filter and catalytic convertor integrated into a single unit. The complete assembly is attached to the turbocharger with a flexible mounting.

2 The intermediate pipe and tailpipe may be renewed separately by cutting the intermediate pipe with a hacksaw. The system is suspended throughout its entire length by rubber mountings.

Removal

3 To remove a part of the system, first jack up the front or rear of the car, and support it on axle stands (see *Jacking and vehicle support*). Alternatively, position the car over an inspection pit, or on car ramps. Remove the engine compartment undershield.

Catalytic converter/particulate filter

4 Chock the rear wheels and firmly apply the handbrake, then jack up the front of the vehicle and support it on axle stands (see *Jacking and vehicle support*).

5 On models fitted with a particulate filter, unscrew and remove the temperature sensor from the filter.

6 On models fitted with a particulate filter, unscrew and remove the pressure sensor and then remove the support bracket.

7 If the original system is still in place, locate the cutting point and saw through the pipe with a hacksaw **(see illustration)**. If the

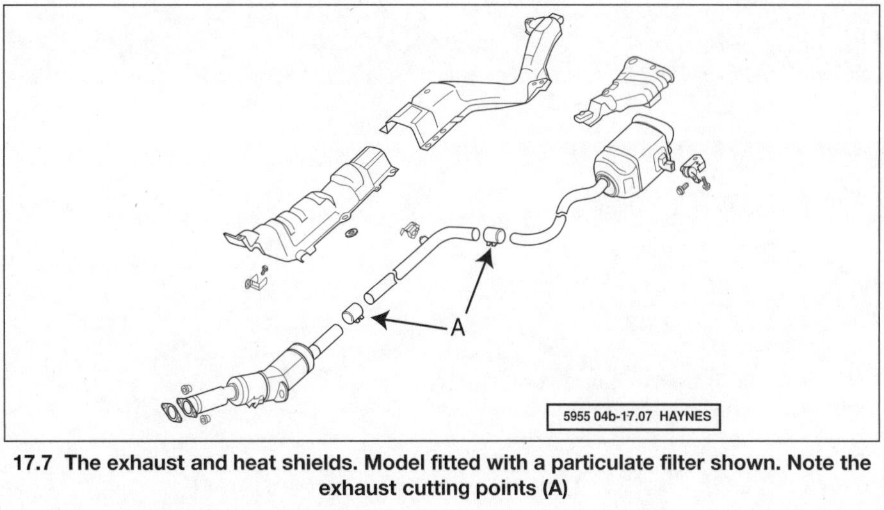

17.7 The exhaust and heat shields. Model fitted with a particulate filter shown. Note the exhaust cutting points (A)

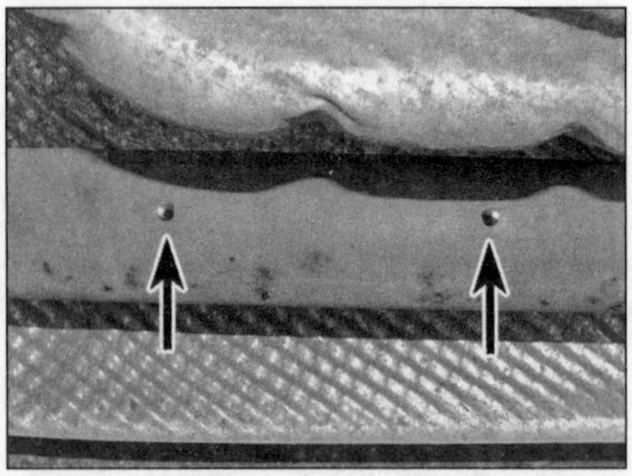

17.13a Locate the marks (arrowed)...

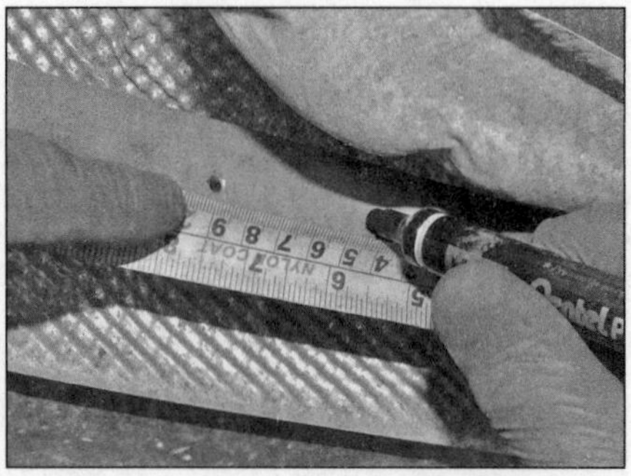

17.13b ...and then mark the centre

system has been renewed previously, unscrew and remove the clamp and disconnect the catalytic converter from the rear section.

8 Unbolt the filter from the turbocharger. Recover the gasket and dispose of it – a new one must be used.

9 Remove the bolts from the support bracket and then with the aid of an assistant remove the filter from beneath the vehicle

Intermediate pipe

10 If the original exhaust and particulate filter is fitted, it must be cut at the particulate filter/catalytic convertor and just in front of the rear suspension using either a hacksaw or pipe cutter. The cutting points are marked with two circular punch marks on the side of the pipe. The punch marks are 90 mm apart and the exhaust section should be cut at the mid-point between the two punch marks. **Note:** *Ensure that the exhaust pipe is cut squarely, or else it will be difficult to obtain a gas-tight seal when the exhaust is refitted.*

11 With the intermediate pipe cut, withdraw the intermediate exhaust section from under the vehicle.

12 If the intermediate section has been replaced before unscrew the bolts and slide the clamp sleeves up (or down) the pipe. Release the rubber mountings and withdraw the intermediate section from under the vehicle.

Rear tailpipe and silencer

13 If the original rear section is fitted cut the pipe between the marks **(see illustrations)** and then unhook (or unbolt) the exhaust hanger.

14 If the rear section is in two halves, unscrew the bolt and slide the clamp sleeve on to the intermediate section then release the rubber mountings and withdraw the tailpipe and silencer from under the vehicle.

Heat shield(s)

15 The heat shields are secured to the underbody by various nuts and bolts. Each shield can be removed separately but note that they overlap making it necessary to loosen another section first. If a shield is being removed to gain access to a component located behind it, it may prove sufficient in some cases to remove the retaining nuts and/or bolts and simply lower the shield without disturbing the exhaust system. Otherwise remove the exhaust section as described earlier.

Refitting

16 Each section is refitted by reversing the removal sequence, noting the following points:

a) Ensure that all traces of corrosion have been removed from the joints.

b) Inspect the rubber mountings for signs of damage or deterioration, and renew as necessary.

c) When reconnecting the intermediate pipe to the tailpipe, apply a smear of exhaust system jointing paste (Renault recommend the use of Sodicam) to the sleeve inner surface, to ensure a gas-tight seal. Make sure both inner ends of the cut pipe are positioned squarely against the stop of the clamp sleeve. Position the sleeve bolt vertically on the left-hand side of the pipe and securely tighten the nut until it is heard to click; the clamp bolt has a groove in it to ensure that the nut is correctly tightened (equivalent to a tightening torque of approximately 25 Nm/18 lbf ft).

d) Prior to tightening the exhaust system fasteners, ensure that all rubber mountings are correctly located, and that there is adequate clearance between the exhaust system and vehicle underbody.

e) Fit a new gasket to the particulate filter before fitting it to the turbocharger.

Chapter 4 Part C:
Emission control systems

Contents

	Section number
Catalytic converter and particulate filter – general information and precautions	4
Diesel engine emissions control systems – testing and component renewal	3
General information and precautions	1
Petrol engine emissions control systems – testing and component renewal	2

Degrees of difficulty

Easy, suitable for novice with little experience	**Fairly easy,** suitable for beginner with some experience	**Fairly difficult,** suitable for competent DIY mechanic	**Difficult,** suitable for experienced DIY mechanic	**Very difficult,** suitable for expert DIY or professional

Specifications

Torque wrench setting	**Nm**	**lbf ft**
Oxygen (lambda) sensor	44	32

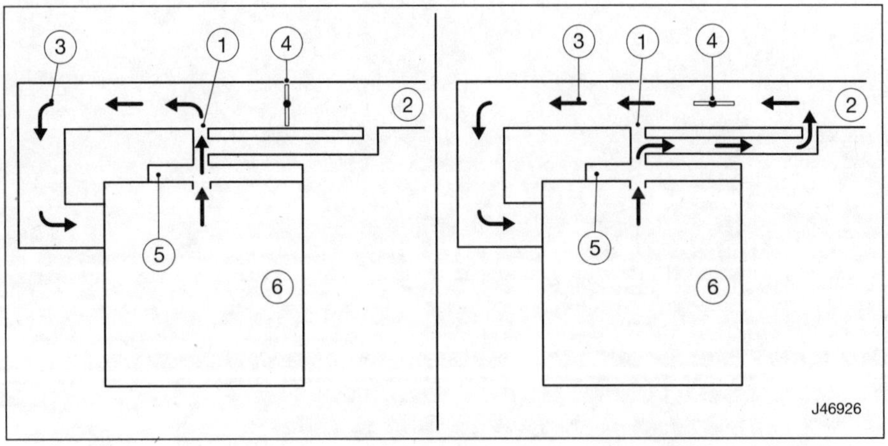

1.4 Crankcase emission control system – petrol engine

1 Calibrated choke
2 Air inlet
3 Inlet manifold
4 Throttle plate
5 Vapour recovery plate
6 Engine

1 General information and precautions

Petrol models

1 All petrol engines are designed to use unleaded petrol and also have various other features built into the fuel system to help minimise harmful emissions.

2 All models are equipped with a crankcase emissions control system, a catalytic converter and an evaporative emissions control system.

3 The emissions control systems function as follows.

Crankcase emissions control

4 To reduce the emission of unburned hydrocarbons from the crankcase into the atmosphere, the engine is sealed and the blow-by gases and oil vapour are drawn from inside the crankcase into the inlet manifold or throttle body to be burned by the engine during normal combustion **(see illustration)**.

5 Under all conditions the gases are forced out of the crankcase by the (relatively) higher crankcase pressure.

6 The crankcase ventilation hoses and restrictors should be periodically cleaned to ensure correct operation of the system.

Exhaust emissions control

7 To minimise the amount of pollutants which escape into the atmosphere, all models are fitted with a catalytic converter in the exhaust system. The system is of the closed loop type, in which an oxygen (lambda) sensor in the exhaust system provides the fuel injection/ ignition system ECU with constant feedback, enabling the ECU to adjust the mixture to provide the best possible conditions for the converter to operate. To comply with legislation all petrol vehicles also have an oxygen sensor fitted after the catalytic converter. This sensor monitors the efficiency of the converter.

8 The oxygen sensor has a heating element built-in that is controlled by the ECU through the sensor relay to bring the sensor's tip to an efficient operating temperature quickly. The sensor's tip is sensitive to oxygen and sends the ECU a varying voltage depending on the amount of oxygen in the exhaust gases; if the inlet air/fuel mixture is too rich, the exhaust gases are low in oxygen so the sensor sends a low voltage signal, the voltage rising as the mixture weakens and the amount of oxygen rises in the exhaust gases. Peak conversion efficiency of all major pollutants occurs if the inlet air/fuel mixture is maintained at the chemically correct ratio for the complete combustion of petrol of 14.7 parts (by weight) of air to 1 part of fuel (the 'stoichiometric' ratio). The sensor output voltage alters in a large step at this point, the ECU using the signal change as a reference point and correcting the inlet air/fuel mixture accordingly by altering the fuel injector pulse width.

Evaporative emissions control

9 To minimise the escape into the atmosphere of unburned hydrocarbons, an evaporative emissions control system is also fitted to all models **(see illustration)**. The fuel tank filler cap is sealed and a charcoal canister is fitted. The canister collects the petrol vapours generated in the tank when the car is parked and stores them until they can be cleared from the canister (under the control of the fuel injection/ignition system ECU) via the purge valve into the inlet manifold to be burned by the engine during normal combustion.

10 To ensure that the engine runs correctly when it is cold and/or idling and to protect the catalytic converter from the effects of an over-rich mixture, the purge control valve is not opened by the ECU until the engine has warmed-up, and the engine is under load; the valve solenoid is then modulated on and off to allow the stored vapour to pass into the inlet manifold.

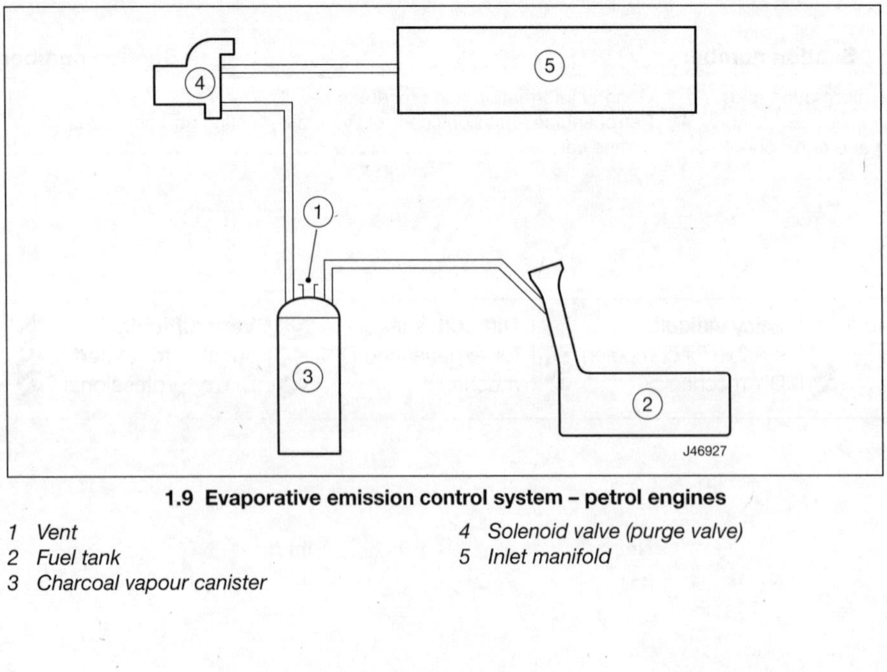

1.9 Evaporative emission control system – petrol engines

1 Vent
2 Fuel tank
3 Charcoal vapour canister
4 Solenoid valve (purge valve)
5 Inlet manifold

Diesel models

11 All diesel engine models are designed to meet strict emission requirements and are also equipped with a crankcase emissions control system. In addition to this, all models are fitted with an unregulated catalytic converter to reduce harmful exhaust emissions. Later models also have a particulate filter fitted. To further reduce emissions, an exhaust gas recirculation (EGR) system is also fitted.

12 The emissions control systems function as follows.

Crankcase emissions control

13 To reduce the emission of unburned hydrocarbons from the crankcase into the atmosphere, the engine is sealed and the blow-by gases and oil vapour are drawn from inside the crankcase, through the cylinder head cover, then through a pressure sensitive recirculation valve into the turbocharger. From the turbocharger, the gases enter the inlet

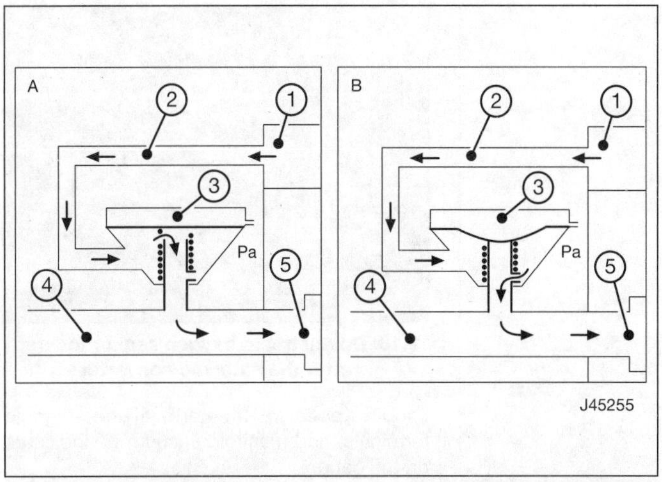

1.13 Crankcase emissions control system – diesel engine

A Low load conditions
B Medium to high load conditions
Pa Atmospheric pressure
1 Cylinder head cover
2 Oil vapour rebreathing hose
3 Pressure-sensitive recirculation valve
4 Air inlet duct
5 Turbocharger

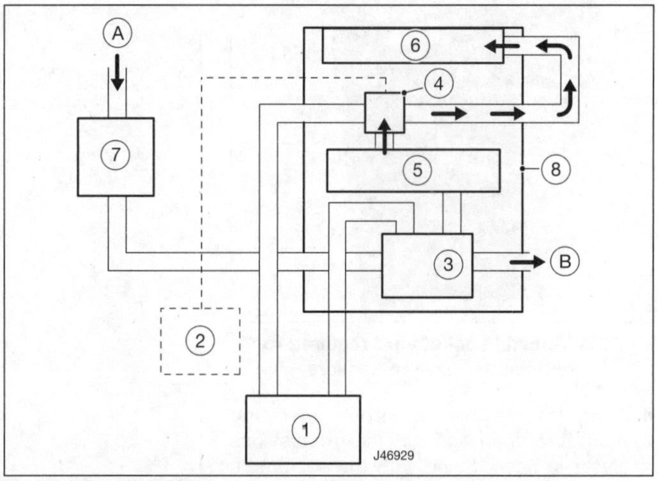

1.18 Exhaust gas recirculation system – diesel engine

A Air inlet
B Outlet to exhaust system
1 Intercooler
2 Engine management ECU
3 Turbocharger
4 Water-cooled EGR unit with solenoid valve
5 Exhaust manifold
6 Plenum
7 Air filter
8 Engine

manifold to be burned by the engine during normal combustion **(see illustration)**.

14 There are no restrictors in the system hoses, since the minimal depression in the inlet manifold remains constant during all engine operating conditions.

Exhaust emissions control – catalytic converter

15 To minimise the amount of pollutants which escape into the atmosphere, an unregulated catalytic converter is fitted in the exhaust system. The catalytic converter consists of a canister containing a fine mesh impregnated with a catalyst material, over which the exhaust gases pass. The catalyst speeds up the oxidation of harmful carbon monoxide, unburnt hydrocarbons and soot, effectively reducing the quantity of harmful products reaching the atmosphere. The catalytic converter operates remotely in the exhaust system, and there is no oxygen sensor as fitted to the petrol engines.

Exhaust emissions control – particulate filter

16 Many of the diesel vehicles covered by this manual have a diesel particulate filter fitted as well as a catalytic converter. The catalytic converter is combined with the particulate filter into a single unit. A major by product of combustion in diesel engines is the production of soot – effectively small particle of carbon, that are a recognised health hazard. The particulate filter traps these particles. Like all filters it will become saturated over time, however unlike an air or oil filter routine replacement is not a simple or low cost exercise. To this end particulate filters are regenerated by effectively burning off, of the accumulated soot in the filter.

17 Regeneration is triggered by the feedback from a filter mounted pressure sensor. A combination of post top dead centre fuel injection, glow plug activation and the secondary injection of fuel (via a manifold mounted injector) regenerates the filter by burning off the accumulated soot. Regeneration only takes place with the engine at normal operating temperatures and above road speeds of 12 mph. For this reason diesel vehicles that are only used for short distance stop/start urban driving should be driven for a longer distance at a constant speed occasionally. Renault do not make any recommendations as to how often this should take place, but we would recommend (in line with other manufacturers) that the vehicle is driven at a constant speed for a minimum of twenty minutes every 1,000 miles. For example, a twenty minute journey on a dual carriage way or motorway at 60 mph would be ideal.

Exhaust gas recirculation system

18 The system is designed to recirculate small quantities of exhaust gas into the inlet tract, and therefore into the combustion process **(see illustration)**, reducing the level of oxides of nitrogen present in the final exhaust gas which is released into the atmosphere. The system is controlled by the engine management ECU which uses several sensors to determine when to switch the system on and off. The system is switched on if:

a) The air temperature is greater than 15°C and the coolant temperature is greater than 70°C.
b) The air temperature is greater than 50°C and the coolant temperature is greater than 40°C.
c) The engine speed is between 850 and 1000 rpm.
d) The injected diesel fuel flow is between 2.0 and 5.0 mg/stroke.
e) The atmospheric pressure is between 980 and 1000 mbars.

The system is switched off if the battery voltage is less than 9 volts, if the engine speed is less than 500 rpm, the mapping (engine speed/load) exceeds a given threshold, or the air conditioning compressor is activated.

19 The volume of exhaust gas recirculated is controlled by an electrically-operated exhaust gas recirculation (EGR) valve on the exhaust manifold, activated by the engine management ECU.

2 Petrol engine emissions control systems – testing and component renewal

Crankcase emissions control

Testing

1 There is no specific test procedure for the crankcase emissions control system. If problems are suspected, check that the hoses are clean internally, and that the restrictors are not blocked or missing.

Component renewal

2 This is self-evident. Mark the various hoses before disconnecting them if there is any possibility of confusion on reassembly.

Exhaust emissions control

Testing

3 An exhaust gas analyser (CO meter) will be needed. The ignition system must be in good condition, the air cleaner element must be clean, and the engine must be in good mechanical condition.

2.9a Special sockets are required to remove the oxygen sensors

4 Bring the engine to normal operating temperature, then connect the exhaust gas analyser in accordance with the equipment maker's instructions.

5 Run the engine at 2500 rpm for about 30 seconds, then allow it to idle and check the CO level (Chapter 4A Specifications). If the CO level is within the specified limits, the system is operating correctly.

6 If the CO level is higher than specified, then the next step (or where available the first step) will be to connect a suitable code reader to the vehicle. Cost effective code readers are now widely available to the home mechanic, but most of them will only display the mandatory EOBD (European On Board Diagnostic) fault codes. As these mandatory codes are restricted to emission related faults they are ideal for checking emissions related fault codes.

7 Renew the oxygen sensor if it is proved faulty.

Oxygen sensors renewal

8 To remove the upstream sensor on all engines, trace the wiring from the sensor located on the exhaust manifold to the connector and disconnect it.

9 Unscrew the sensor from the manifold using a special deep socket **(see illustrations)**.

10 To remove the downstream sensor raise the front of the vehicle and support it on axle stands (see *Jacking and vehicle support*). Remove the engine compartment

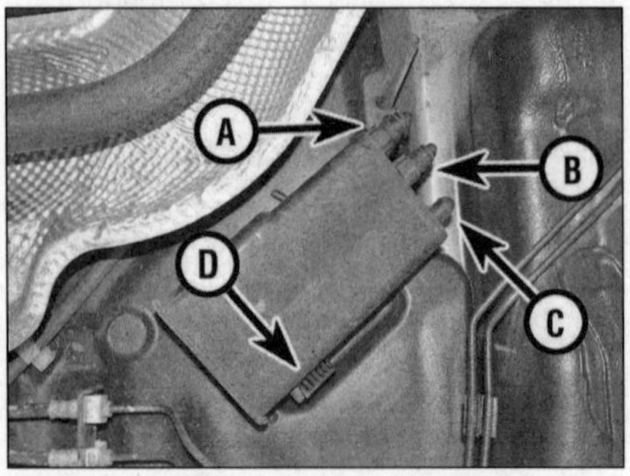

2.27 Connections to the top of the fuel evaporative charcoal canister

A To engine
B From fuel tank
C Canister breather
D Release clip

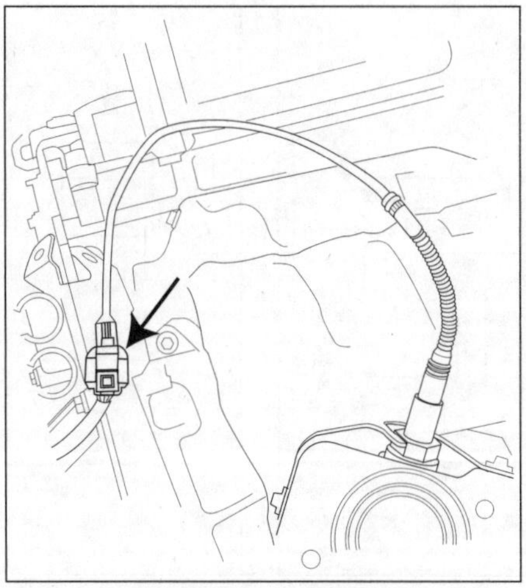

2.9b The upstream oxygen sensor

undertray and then disconnect the sensor wiring. Unscrew the sensor from the exhaust downpipe and remove it **(see illustration)**.

11 Clean the threads of the sensor (if it is to be refitted) and the threads in the exhaust pipe or manifold (as applicable).

12 Note that if the sensor wires are broken, the sensor must be renewed. No attempt should be made to repair them.

13 Apply high temperature anti-seize compound to the sensor threads. Screw the sensor in by hand, then tighten it to the specified torque.

14 Reconnect the sensor wiring, and where applicable refit the undertray and lower the vehicle to the ground.

Catalytic converter – renewal

15 The catalytic converter is renewed as part of the exhaust system. Refer to Part A of this Chapter.

Evaporative emissions control

Testing

16 The operating principle of the system is that the solenoid valve is open only when the engine is warm with the throttle at least at the part throttle position.

17 Bring the engine to normal operating temperature, then switch it off. Connect a vacuum gauge (range 0 to 1000 mbars) into the hose between the canister and the solenoid valve. Connect a voltmeter to the solenoid valve terminals.

18 Start the engine and allow it to idle. There should be no vacuum shown on the gauge, and no voltage present at the solenoid.

19 If manifold vacuum is indicated although no voltage is present, the solenoid valve may be stuck open. Temporarily disconnect the hoses from the solenoid valve and blow through the outlets to dislodge any particles of carbon.

20 If voltage is present at idle, there is a fault in the wiring or the computer.

21 Depress the accelerator slightly. Voltage

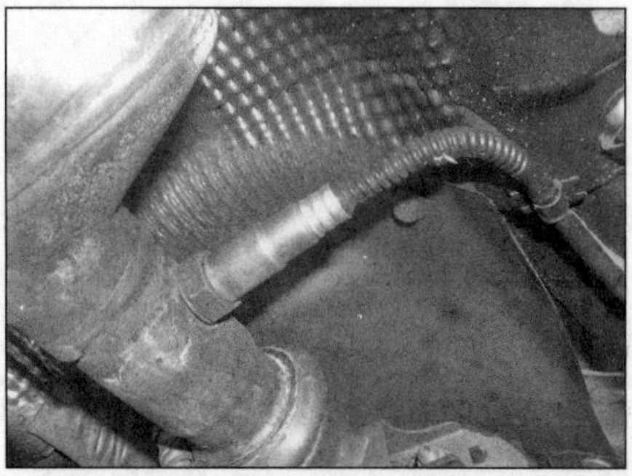

2.10 Downstream oxygen sensor located after the catalytic converter

should appear momentarily at the solenoid terminals, and manifold vacuum be indicated on the gauge.

22 If vacuum is not indicated even though voltage is present, either there is a leak in the hoses, or the valve is not opening.

23 If no voltage appears, there is a fault in the wiring or the computer.

Charcoal canister renewal

24 Apply the handbrake, then jack up the rear of the vehicle and support it on axle stands (see *Jacking and vehicle support*).

25 Disconnect the battery negative lead (refer to *Disconnecting the battery* in Chapter 5A).

26 The canister is located at the rear of the vehicle close to the rear axle.

27 Note the location of the hoses, then disconnect the vapour inlet hose leading from the fuel tank, and the hose leading to the inlet manifold. Prise free the release clip and withdraw the canister from the vehicle **(see illustration)**.

28 Dispose of the old canister safely, bearing in mind that it may contain liquid fuel and/or fuel vapour.

29 Fit the new canister using a reversal of the removal procedure. Make sure that the hoses are connected correctly.

Solenoid valve

30 The solenoid valve is located on the right-hand strut tower **(see illustration)**.

31 Disconnect the wiring plug and the vacuum hoses from the valve, noting the fitted locations of the hoses.

32 Unbolt, or unclip the valve.

2.30 The control valve for the evaporative emissions circuit

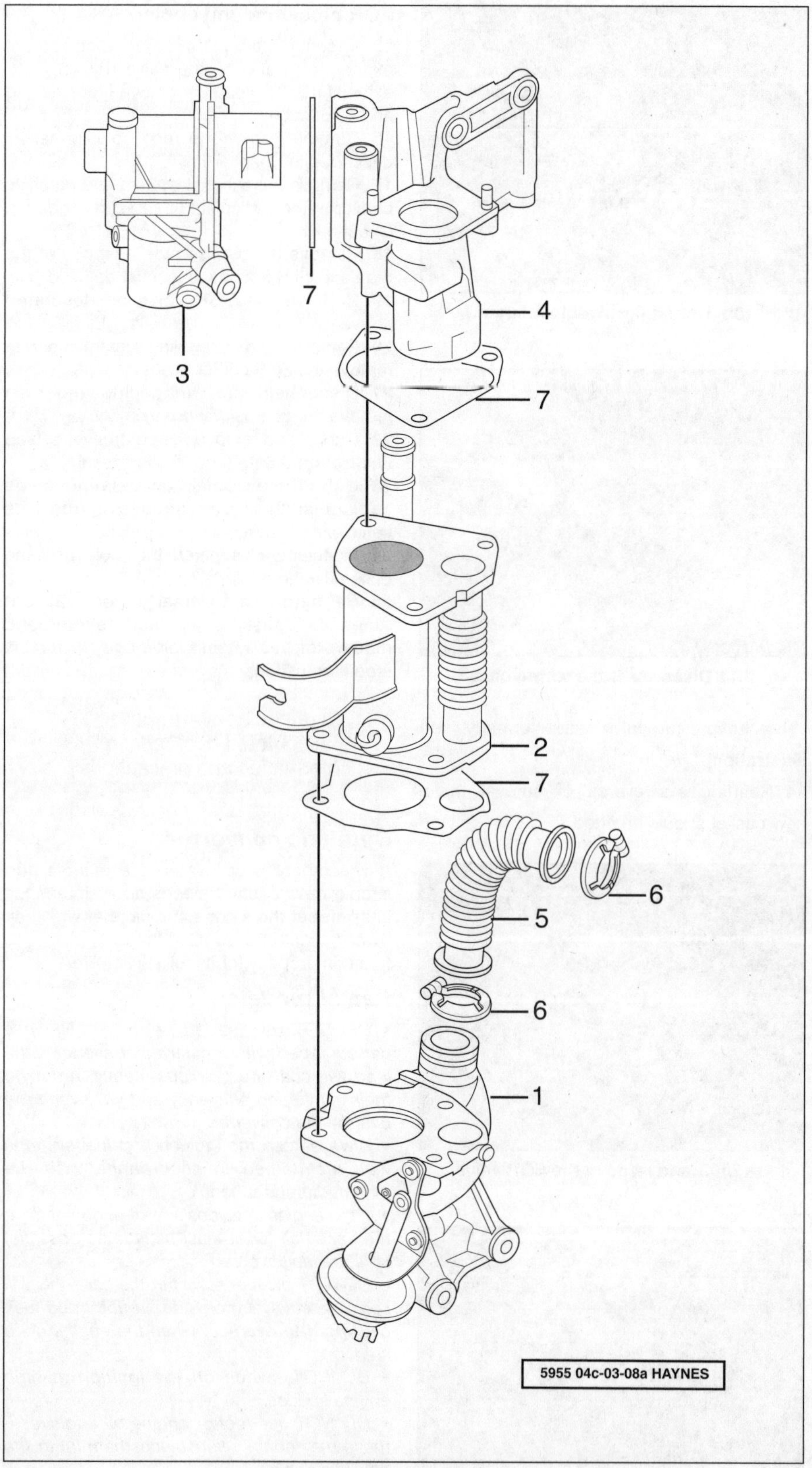

3.8a Typical EGR components

1 *By pass valve*
2 *Heat exchanger*
3 *Control valve*
4 *Control valve housing*
5 *By pass hose*
6 *Hose clip*
7 *Gasket*

3 Diesel engine emissions control systems – testing and component renewal

Crankcase emissions control

Testing

1 If the system is thought to be faulty, first check that the hoses are unobstructed.

2 Periodically inspect the system components for security and damage, and renew them as necessary.

Component renewal

3 This is self-evident. Mark the various hoses before disconnecting them if there is any possibility of confusion on reassembly.

Exhaust emissions control

Testing

4 The system can only be tested accurately using a suitable exhaust gas analyser (suitable for use with diesel engines).

Catalytic converter renewal

5 The catalytic converter is renewed as part of the exhaust system. Refer to Part B of this Chapter.

Particulate filter renewal

6 The particulate filter is renewed as part of the exhaust system. Refer to Part B of this Chapter.

Exhaust gas recirculation

Testing

7 Testing of the EGR system is best left to a Renault dealer who will have the dedicated equipment necessary to carry out the test.

EGR valve unit

8 The EGR valve is mounted on the inlet manifold at the rear of the cylinder head **(see illustrations)**. Several variants are fitted, depending on the year of production. All are similar.

9 Disconnect the battery negative lead (refer to *Disconnecting the battery* in Chapter 5A).

10 Where fitted remove the engine top cover and then remove the intercooler pipes **(see illustrations)**.

3.8b EGR solenoid valve

3.10a Release the spring clip (arrowed)

3.10b Unbolt (arrowed) and then...

3.10c ...unclip and remove the pipe

3.11 Disconnect the wiring plug

11 Disconnect the wiring from the EGR solenoid valve **(see illustration)**.
12 Unbolt and remove the EGR valve **(see illustrations)**. Recover the gasket.
13 Thoroughly clean and inspect the EGR valve. Ensure the valve seats correctly **(see illustration)**.
14 Refitting is a reversal of removal, but a new gasket should be fitted.

3.12a Unbolt...

3.12b ...and remove the EGR valve

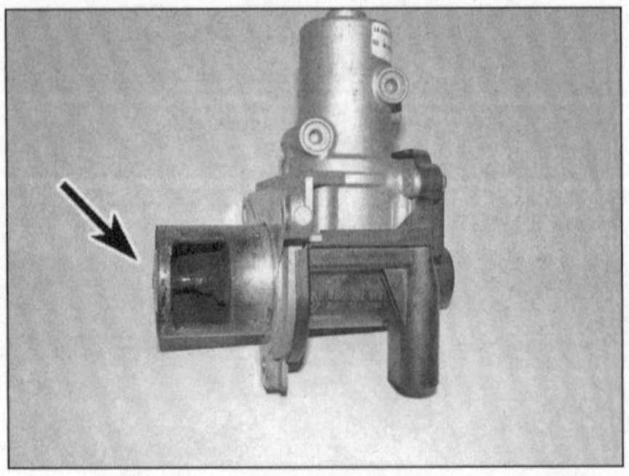
3.13 Clean and inspect the valve seat (arrowed)

3.25 Use pincers to tighten the clamp

EGR pipework and cooler

15 If required, the pipework and cooler (heat exchanger) between the valve housing and exhaust manifold can be removed for cleaning and inspection.
16 Remove the windscreen cowl panel as described in Chapter 11.
17 Remove the exhaust system and catalytic converter (or particulate filter) as described in Chapter 4B.
18 Remove the bypass pipe. Dispose of the pipe and clips – a new one must be used.
19 Remove the EGR valve as described above.
20 Partially drain the cooling system and then remove the EGR cooler hoses
21 Disconnect the wiring plug and then remove the damper valve assembly.
22 Unbolt and remove the control valve **(see illustration 3.8a)**. Recover the gasket.
23 Unbolt the cooler, anticipating some coolant spillage and remove it from the vehicle.
24 On the bench separate the cooler from the EGR valve housing.
25 Refitting is a reversal of removal, but renew tall gaskets. Renault recommend renewal of the by pass pipe and hose clips **(see illustration)**.

4 Catalytic converter and particulate filter - general information and precautions

Catalytic converter

The catalytic converter is a reliable and simple device which needs no maintenance in itself, but there are some facts of which an owner should be aware if the converter is to function properly for its full service life.

Petrol models

- *DO NOT use leaded petrol or LRP in a car equipped with a catalytic converter – the lead will coat the precious metals, reducing their converting efficiency and will eventually destroy the converter.*
- *Always keep the ignition and fuel systems well maintained in accordance with the manufacturer's schedule.*
- *If the engine develops a misfire, do not drive the car at all (or at least as little as possible) until the fault is cured.*
- *DO NOT push or tow start the car – this will soak the catalytic converter in unburned fuel, causing it to overheat when the engine does start.*
- *DO NOT switch off the ignition at high engine speeds.*
- *DO NOT use fuel or engine oil additives – these may contain substances harmful to the catalytic converter.*
- *DO NOT continue to use the car if the engine burns oil to the extent of leaving a visible trail of blue smoke.*
- *Remember that the catalytic converter*

operates at very high temperatures. DO NOT park the car on dry undergrowth, over long grass or piles of dead leaves after a long run.

- *Remember that the catalytic converter is FRAGILE – do not strike it with tools during servicing work or drop it.*
- *In some cases a sulphurous smell (like that of rotten eggs) may be noticed from the exhaust. This is common to many catalytic converter equipped cars and once the car has covered a few thousand miles the problem should disappear.*
- *The catalytic converter, used on a well maintained and well driven car, should last for between 50 000 and 100 000 miles – if the converter is no longer effective it must be renewed.*

Diesel models

- *DO NOT use fuel or engine oil additives – these may contain substances harmful to the catalytic converter.*
- *DO NOT continue to use the car if the engine burns oil to the extent of leaving a visible trail of blue smoke.*
- *Remember that the catalytic converter operates at very high temperatures. DO NOT park the car on dry undergrowth, over long grass or piles of dead leaves after a long run.*
- *Remember that the catalytic converter is FRAGILE – do not strike it with tools during servicing work or drop it.*

Particulate filter

- Regeneration of the filter only takes place above 12 mph once the engine is fully warmed up.
- There may be a slight drop in performance whilst regeneration is taking place.
- If the vehicle is used mostly in stop/start traffic, it may never get up to operating temperature. Always use the vehicle for an extended high speed run every 1000 miles or so.
- All models fitted with a Diesel Particulate Filter (DPF) have an oil quality monitoring system fitted. Regeneration tends to dilute the engine oil as fuel is injected post compression. If the oil qulity warning appears, check the oil level and change the oil at the earliest opportunity.
- Do not use 'home brew' diesel oils – they will rapidly block the filter.

Notes

Chapter 5 Part A:
Starting and charging systems

Contents

	Section number
Alternator – removal and refitting	7
Alternator – testing	6
Auxiliary drivebelt checking and renewal	See Chapter 1A or 1B
Battery – disconnecting, removal and refitting	4
Battery – testing and charging	3
Battery check	See *Weekly checks*
Charging system – testing	5
Electrical fault finding – general information	2
Electrical system check	See Chapter 1A or 1B
General information, precautions and battery disconnection	1
Starter motor – removal and refitting	9
Starting system – testing	8

Degrees of difficulty

Easy, suitable for novice with little experience	**Fairly easy,** suitable for beginner with some experience	**Fairly difficult,** suitable for competent DIY mechanic	**Difficult,** suitable for experienced DIY mechanic	**Very difficult,** suitable for expert DIY or professional

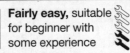

Specifications

Battery

Type	Lead-acid, 'maintenance-free'
Charge condition:	
Poor	11.5 volts
Normal	12.0 volts
Good	12.5 volts

Alternator

Type	Valeo or Bosch
Output:	
Petrol engines	120 amp
Diesel engines	150 amps
Regulated voltage	13.5 to 14.8 volts

Starter motor

Type	Bosch, Valeo or Mitsubishi

Torque wrench settings

	Nm	lbf ft
Alternator mounting bolts	25	18
Alternator support strut	25	18
Starter motor mounting bolts	44	32

1 General information, precautions and battery disconnection

General information

The engine electrical system consists mainly of the charging and starting systems. Because of their engine-related functions, these components are covered separately from the body electrical devices such as the lights, instruments, etc (which are covered in Chapter 12). On petrol engine models, refer to Part B for information on the ignition system, and on diesel models, refer to Part C for information on the preheating system.

The electrical system is of the 12 volt negative-earth type.

The original-equipment battery is of the 'maintenance-free' (sealed for life) type, and is charged by the alternator, which is belt-driven from the crankshaft pulley.

The starter motor is of the pre-engaged type, incorporating an integral solenoid. On starting, the solenoid moves the drive pinion into engagement with the flywheel ring gear before the starter motor is energised. Once the engine has started, a one-way clutch prevents the motor armature being driven by the engine until the pinion disengages from the flywheel.

Precautions

- It is necessary to take extra care when working on the electrical system to avoid damage to semi-conductor devices (diodes and transistors), and to avoid the risk of personal injury. In addition to the precautions given in *Safety first!* at the beginning of this manual, observe the following when working on the system:
- *Always remove rings, watches, etc, before working on the electrical system.* Even with the battery disconnected, capacitive discharge could occur if a component's live terminal is earthed through a metal object. This could cause a shock or nasty burn.
- *Do not reverse the battery connections.* Components such as the alternator, electronic control units, or any other components having semi-conductor circuitry could be irreparably damaged.
- If the engine is being started using jump leads and a slave battery, connect the batteries *positive-to-positive* and *negative-to-negative* (see *Jump starting*). This also applies when connecting a battery charger.
- Never disconnect the battery terminals, the alternator, any electrical wiring or any test instruments when the engine is running.
- Do not allow the engine to turn the alternator when the alternator is not connected.
- Never 'test' for alternator output by 'flashing' the output lead to earth.
- Never use an ohmmeter of the type incorporating a hand-cranked generator for circuit or continuity testing.
- Always ensure that the battery negative lead is disconnected when working on the electrical system.
- Before using electric-arc welding equipment on the car, disconnect the battery, alternator and components such as the fuel injection/ignition electronic control unit to protect them from the risk of damage.

2 Electrical fault finding – general information

Refer to Chapter 12.

3 Battery – testing and charging

Testing

Low-maintenance battery

1 If the car covers a small annual mileage, it is worthwhile checking the specific gravity of the electrolyte every three months to determine the state of charge of the battery. Use a hydrometer to make the check and compare the results with the following table. Note that the specific gravity readings assume an electrolyte temperature of 15°C (60°F); for every 10°C (18°F) below 15°C (60°F) subtract 0.007. For every 10°C (18°F) above 15°C (60°F) add 0.007.

	Ambient temperature Above 25°C	Below 25°C
Fully-charged	*1.210 to 1.230*	*1.270 to 1.290*
70% charged	*1.170 to 1.190*	*1.230 to 1.250*
Discharged	*1.050 to 1.070*	*1.110 to 1.130*

2 If the battery condition is suspect, first check the specific gravity of electrolyte in each cell. A variation of 0.040 or more between any cells indicates loss of electrolyte or deterioration of the internal plates.

3 If the specific gravity variation is 0.040 or more, the battery should be renewed. If the cell variation is satisfactory but the battery is discharged, it should be charged as described later in this Section.

Maintenance-free battery

4 In cases where a 'sealed for life' maintenance-free battery is fitted, topping-up and testing of the electrolyte in each cell is not possible. The condition of the battery can therefore only be tested using a battery condition indicator or a voltmeter.

All battery types

5 If testing the battery using a voltmeter, connect the voltmeter across the battery and compare the result with those given in the Specifications under 'charge condition'. The test is only accurate if the battery has not been subjected to any kind of charge for the previous six hours. If this is not the case, switch on the headlights for 30 seconds, then wait four to five minutes before testing the battery after switching off the headlights. All other electrical circuits must be switched off, so check that the doors and tailgate/boot lid are fully shut when making the test.

6 If the voltage reading is less than 12.0 volts, then the battery is discharged.

7 If the battery is to be charged, remove it from the car (Section 4) and charge it as described later in this Section.

Charging

Note: *The following is intended as a guide only. Always refer to the manufacturer's recommendations (often printed on a label attached to the battery), and always disconnect both terminal leads before charging a battery.*

Low-maintenance battery

8 Charge the battery at a rate of 3.5 to 4 amps and continue to charge the battery at this rate until no further rise in specific gravity is noted over a four hour period.

9 Alternatively, a trickle charger charging at the rate of 1.5 amps can safely be used overnight.

10 Specially rapid 'boost' charges which are claimed to restore the power of the battery in 1 to 2 hours are not recommended, as they can cause serious damage to the battery plates through overheating.

11 While charging the battery, note that the temperature of the electrolyte should never exceed 37.8°C (100°F).

Maintenance-free battery

12 This battery type takes considerably longer to fully recharge than the standard type, the time taken being dependent on the extent of discharge, but it can take anything up to three days.

13 A constant voltage type charger is required, to be set, when connected, to 13.9 to 14.9 volts with a charger current below 25 amps. Using this method, the battery should be usable within three hours, giving a voltage reading of 12.5 volts, but this is for a partially-discharged battery and, as mentioned, full charging can take considerably longer.

14 If the battery is to be charged from a fully-discharged state (condition reading less than 12.2 volts), have it recharged by your Renault dealer or local automotive electrician, as the charge rate is higher and constant supervision during charging is necessary.

4 Battery – disconnecting, removal and refitting

Note: *Refer to the precautions given in 'Safety first!' and in Section 1 of this Chapter.*

Disconnection

1 The battery is located at the front left-hand corner of the engine compartment, under a plastic cover. Lower the drivers window and then release the bonnet. Remove the keycard, open the bonnet and then remove the battery cover **(see illustration)**.

4.1 Remove the battery cover

4.2 Note how close the earth connections are to the positive pole (arrowed)

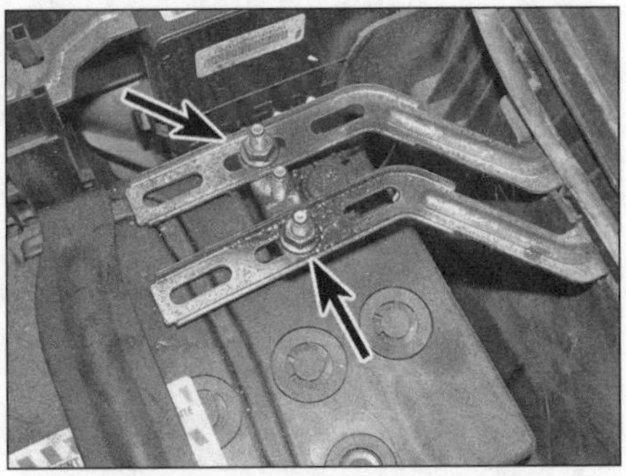

4.3 The battery negative earth cables. Remove both nuts (arrowed)

2 The battery earth (marked negative on the battery) connections are close to exposed battery positive connections **(see illustration)**. Cover the exposed positive connections with a suitable insulation material (a plastic bag is ideal) to avoid any possibility of the spanner shorting on the positive cable.

3 Slacken and then remove the earth (negative) cable connections **(see illustration)**. Place a protective cover over the exposed negative battery terminal and/or place the removed earth connections in a plastic bag. On models fitted with 'Stop and Start' disconnect the battery current monitor wiring plug.

4 Reconnecting is a reversal of disconnecting. Before starting the vehicle, reach in through the open drivers window and turn on the sidelights for a few minutes. This will allow any surface charge on the battery to dissipate. Enter the vehicle and turn the ignition on. Wait a few seconds to allow any ignition controlled components to initialise and stabilise and then start the vehicle. Note that several drive cycles may be required before full engine performance is restored.

Removal

5 Disconnect the battery negative (earth) terminal as described above.

6 Disconnect the battery positive terminal and then unbolt the battery retaining bracket. Remove the bracket **(see illustrations)**.

7 Where applicable, pull out the battery vent pipe from the top of the battery, and move it to one side. Make sure the vent pipe cannot be trapped when the battery is refitted.

8 Lift out the battery, using the handles provided on top where applicable **(see illustration)**. Particularly on diesel models, the battery is heavy.

9 If required, the battery tray can also be removed. Start by removing the ECU cooling duct and the ECU cover **(see illustration)**.

10 At the rear of the battery unclip and unbolt the fusebox and fusible links **(see illustrations)**. On diesel models remove the vacuum solenoid from the rear.

11 At the front unbolt and remove the main engine management ECU and then remove the cooling duct from beneath the front wing **(see illustrations)**.

12 Unclip the wiring loom from the side of the battery compartment and then remove the bolts from the main section of the battery tray. Lift out the tray, disconnecting the drain hose as the tray is removed **(see illustrations)**.

Refitting

13 Refitting is a reversal of removal. Smear petroleum jelly on the battery terminals after

4.6a Remove the positive terminal

4.6b Remove the retaining bracket

4.8 Remove the battery

4.9 Remove the ECU cover

4.10a Unbolt the starter motor supply cable (arrowed)...

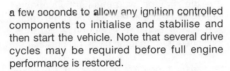

4.10b ...and then unclip the fusebox and terminal rail

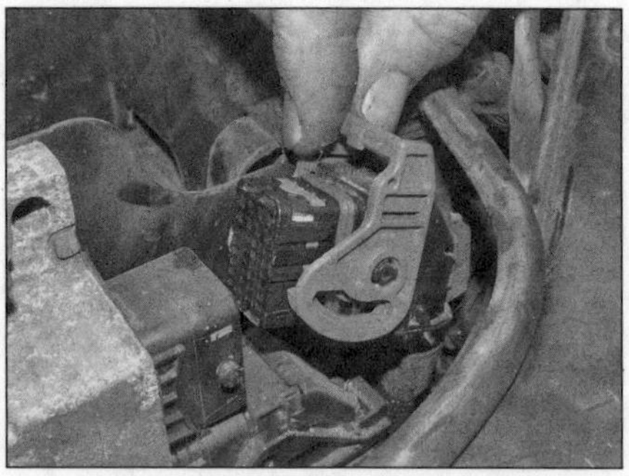

4.11a Disconnect and then unbolt...

4.11b ...and remove the engine ECU

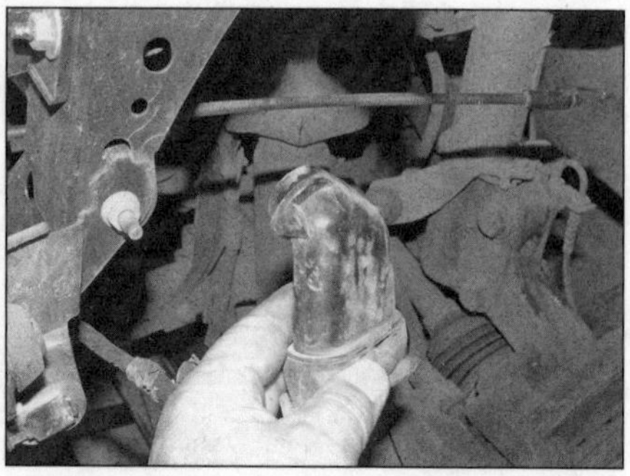

4.11c Remove the ventilation duct

reconnecting the leads, to reduce corrosion. Always reconnect the positive lead first, and the negative lead last. Follow the procedure outlined in paragraph 4 and restart the vehicle.

5 Charging system – testing

Note: *Refer to the warnings given in 'Safety first!' and in Section 1 of this Chapter before starting work.*

1 If the no-charge warning light fails to illuminate when the ignition is switched on, first check the alternator wiring connections for security. A conventional bulb is not fitted to the instrument panel. If the light still fails to illuminate refer the vehicle to a Renault dealer or suitably equipped garage.

2 If the ignition warning light illuminates when the engine is running, stop the engine and check that the drivebelt is correctly tensioned (see Chapter 1A or 1B) and that the alternator connections are secure. If all is so far satisfactory, have the alternator checked by an auto-electrician for testing and repair.

3 If the alternator output is suspect even though the warning light functions correctly, the regulated voltage may be checked as follows.

4 Connect a voltmeter across the battery terminals and start the engine.

5 Increase the engine speed until the voltmeter reading remains steady; the reading should be between 13.2 and 14.8 volts.

6 Switch on as many electrical accessories (eg, the headlights, heated rear window and heater blower) as possible, and check that the alternator maintains the regulated voltage between 13.2 and 14.8 volts.

4.12a Remove the control unit support bolt (arrowed)

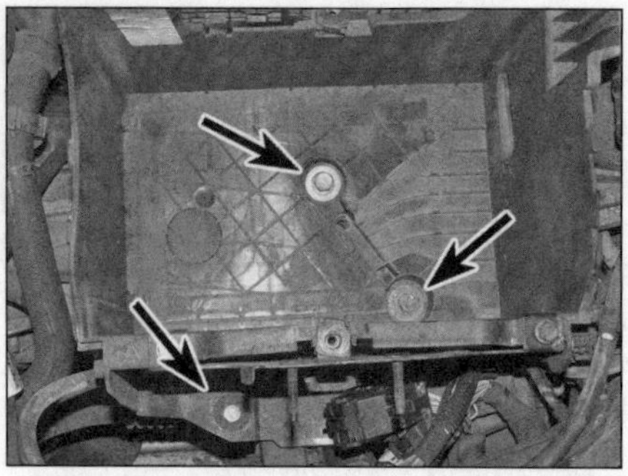

4.12b Remove the battery tray mounting bolts (arrowed)

7 If the regulated voltage is not as stated, the fault may be due to worn brushes, weak brush springs, a faulty voltage regulator, a faulty diode, a severed phase winding, or worn or damaged slip-rings. The alternator should be renewed or taken to an auto-electrician for testing and repair.

6 Alternator – testing

If the alternator is thought to be suspect, it should be removed from the vehicle and taken to an auto-electrician for testing. Most auto-electricians will be able to supply and fit brushes at a reasonable cost. However, check on the cost of repairs before proceeding, as it may prove more economical to obtain a new or exchange alternator.

7 Alternator – removal and refitting

Removal

1 Disconnect the battery negative lead (refer to Section 4 of this Chapter).

2 Jack up and support the front of the vehicle (see *Jacking and vehicle support* in the reference section) and then remove the headlights (as described in Chapter 12) and the front bumper cover as described in Chapter 11.

3 Remove the air deflector sides and centre

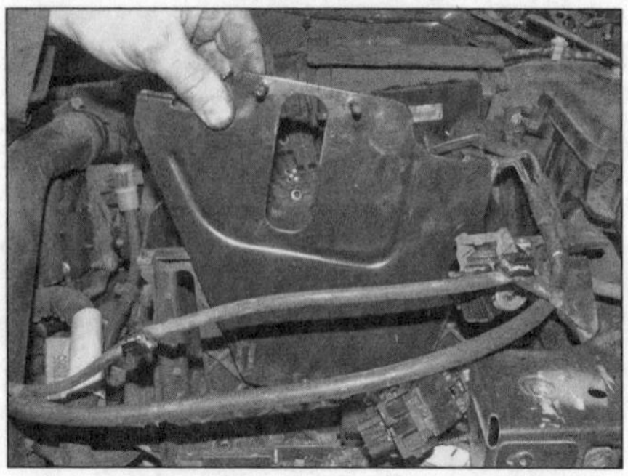

4.12c Note that the ECU support tray can be removed separately if required

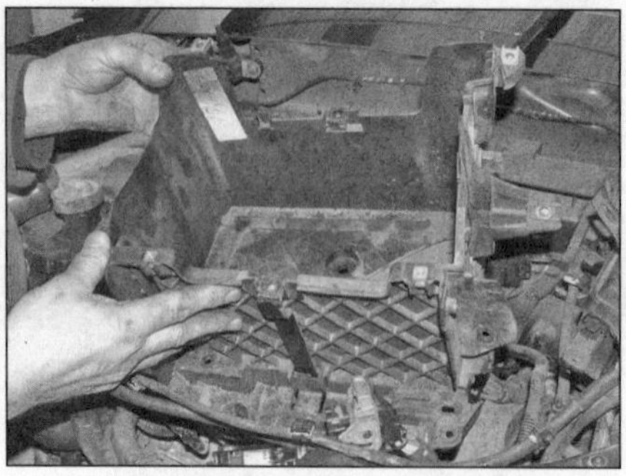

4.12d Remove the tray

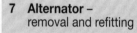

4.12e Disconnect the drain hose

and then remove the bumper reinforcement -as described in Chapter 11.

4 On diesel models remove the pipe from the between the intercooler and turbocharger and then remove the coolant hose from the expansion bottle. Anticipate some loss of coolant as the hose is removed.

5 Unbolt the bonnet lock and then disconnect the bonnet lock cable. Move the cable to the side. On diesel models remove the bolts from the left-hand end of the front panel and then release the wiring loom **(see illustrations)**.

6 Remove the front panel upper mounting bolts and then slacken the panel lower mounting bolts.

7 Remove the plastic clips from the ends of the front panel and ensuring that no hoses or electrical connections are unduly strained pivot the panel away from the engine **(see illustrations)**. Pay particular attention to the AC pipes and hoses as the panel is pivoted . If necessary replace the lower mounting bolts with longer bolts (or threaded bar) and pull the panel away at the bottom as well.

8 Remove the front section of the wing liner and then remove the auxiliary drivebelt as described in Chapter 1A or 1B.

9 On petrol models unbolt and remove the support strut from the rear of the alternator.

10 On diesel models (where fitted) remove the protective shield form the top of the alternator.

11 Disconnect the alternator wiring plug, then (after removing the access cap if necessary) unscrew the nut and remove the main battery supply lead from the terminal **(see illustrations)**.

12 On all petrol models (working under the wheel arch) unbolt and remove the auxiliary drivebelt tensioner pulley – this is necessary to gain access to the alternator lower mounting bolt.

13 Partially remove the alternator upper mounting bolt. Slacken, but do not remove the lower mounting bolt. The mounting is slotted, to allow the partially-withdrawn bolts to pass out forwards with the alternator itself **(see illustrations)**.

14 It is likely that (thanks to the spacers fitted to its mounting lugs) the alternator will prove difficult to remove from its mountings, and may even have to be prised forwards – take care when prising to avoid damaging it or any surrounding components. Remove the alternator from the engine.

Refitting

15 Refitting is a reversal of removal. Refer to the relevant part of Chapter 1A or 1B for details of fitting the auxiliary drivebelt. Note that the alternator mounting holes are fitted with adjustable spacers which are clamped to the mounting bracket when the bolts are tightened. This makes the task of refitting the alternator difficult, and it is suggested that the spacers are tapped out slightly to provide additional clearance.

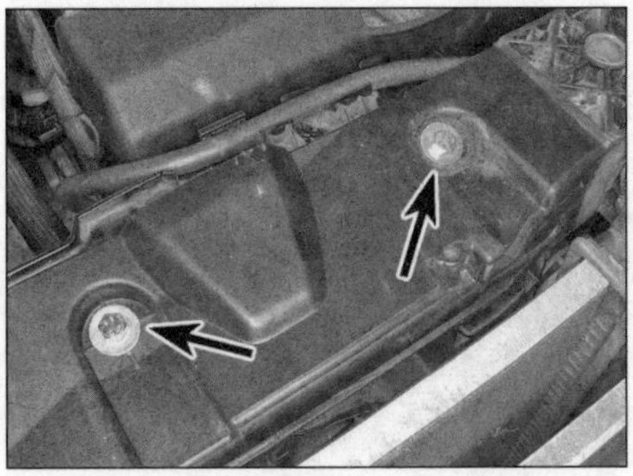

7.5a Remove the bolts (arrowed) and...

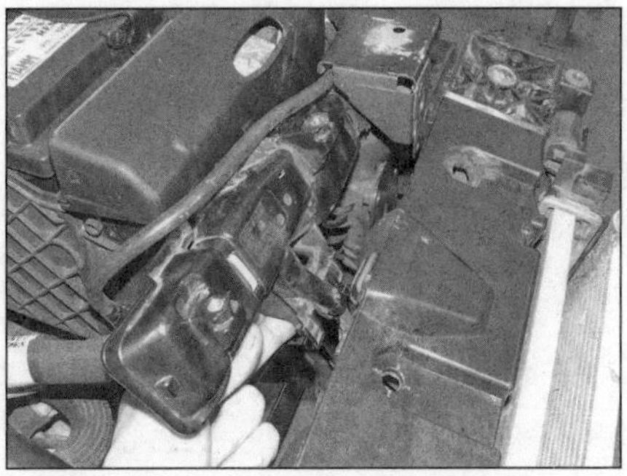

7.5b ...unclip the loom carrier

7.7a Pivot the panel forwards to...

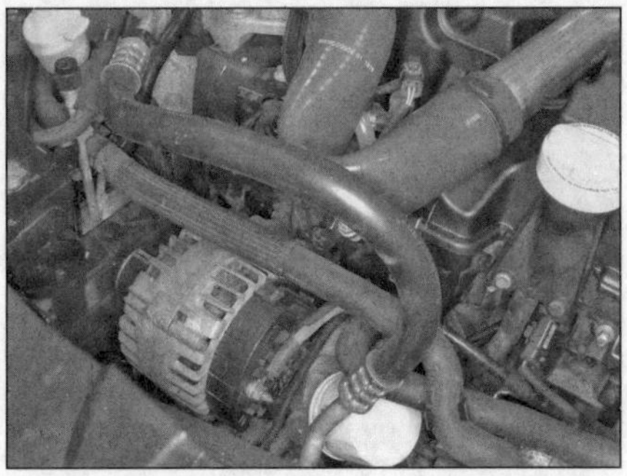

7.7b ...allow access to the alternator

7.11a Release the wiring plug and then...

7.11b ...unbolt the main terminal

7.13a Slacken the upper bolt

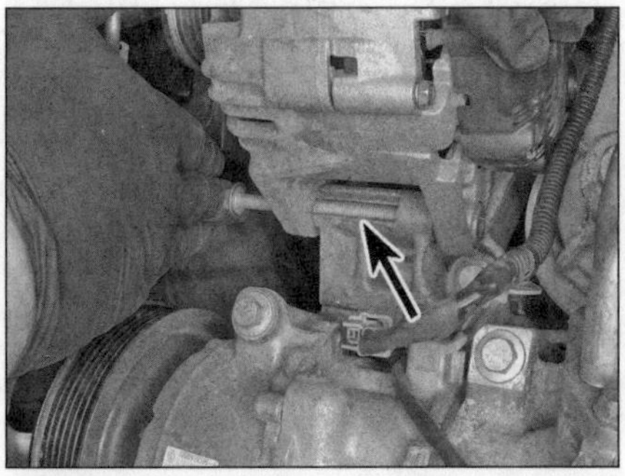

7.13b Note the slotted mounting (arrowed)

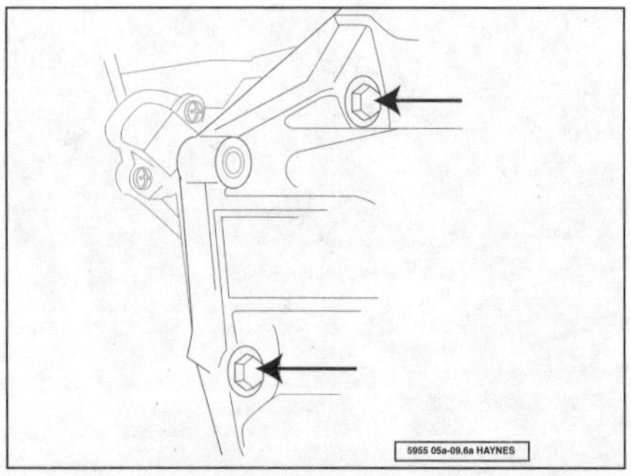
9.6a Starter motor mounting bolts (arrowed) – petrol engines

9.6b Remove the starter motor

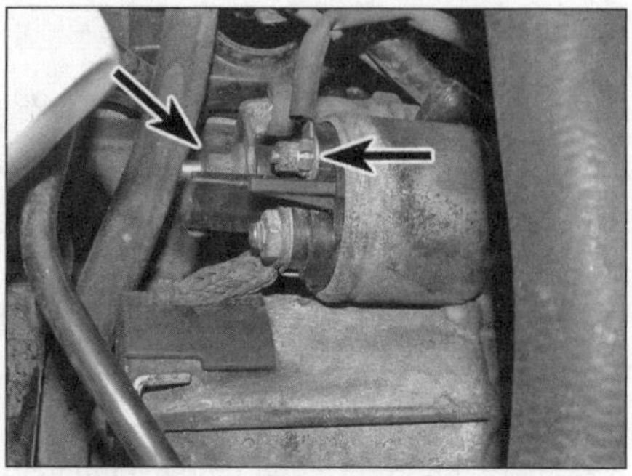
9.10 Remove the cables (arrowed)

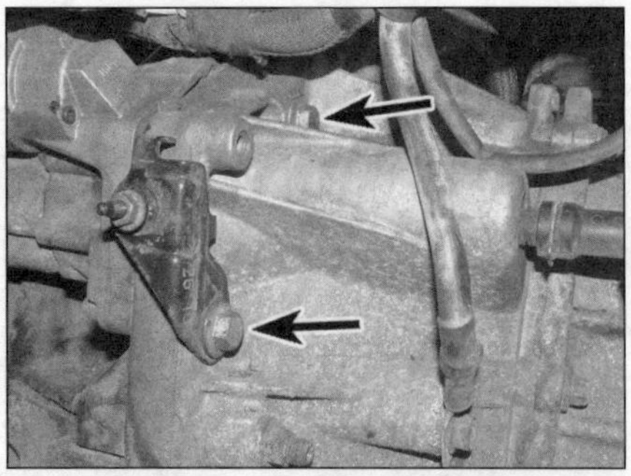
9.11a Remove the mounting bolts (arrowed) and...

9.11b ...then remove the starter motor (diesel engines)

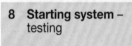

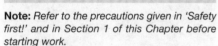

8 Starting system – testing

Note: *Refer to the precautions given in 'Safety first!' and in Section 1 of this Chapter before starting work.*

1 If the starter motor fails, the following may be possible causes:

a) The battery is faulty.
b) The electrical connections between the switch, solenoid, battery and starter motor are somewhere failing to pass the necessary current from the battery through the starter to earth.
c) The solenoid is faulty.
d) The starter motor is mechanically or electrically defective.

2 To check the battery, switch on the headlights. If they dim after a few seconds, this indicates that the battery is discharged – recharge (see Section 3) or renew the battery. If the headlights glow brightly, press the starter button and observe the lights. If they dim, then this indicates that current is reaching the starter motor, therefore the fault must lie in the starter motor. If the lights continue to glow brightly (and no clicking sound can be heard from the starter motor solenoid), this indicates that there is a fault in the circuit or solenoid – see the following paragraphs. If the starter motor turns slowly when operated, but the battery is in good condition, then this indicates that either the starter motor is faulty, or there is considerable resistance somewhere in the circuit.

3 If a fault in the circuit is suspected, disconnect the battery leads (including the earth connection to the body), the starter/ solenoid wiring and the engine/ transmission earth strap. Thoroughly clean the connections, and reconnect the leads and wiring, then use a voltmeter or test light to check that full battery voltage is available at the battery positive lead connection to the solenoid, and that the earth is sound. Smear petroleum jelly around the battery terminals to prevent corrosion – corroded connections are amongst the most frequent causes of electrical system faults.

4 If the battery and all connections are in good condition, check the circuit by disconnecting the wire from the solenoid blade terminal. Connect a voltmeter or test light between the wire end and a good earth (such as the battery negative terminal), and check that the wire is live when the starter button is pressed. If it is, then the circuit is sound – if not the circuit wiring can be checked as described in Chapter 12.

5 The solenoid contacts can be checked by connecting a voltmeter or test light between the battery positive feed connection on the starter side of the solenoid and earth. When the starter button is pressed, there should be a reading or lighted bulb, as applicable. If there is no reading or lighted bulb, the solenoid is faulty and should be renewed.

6 If the circuit and solenoid are proved sound, the fault must lie in the starter motor. In this event, it may be possible to have the starter motor overhauled by a specialist, but check on the cost of spares before proceeding, as it may prove more economical to obtain a new or exchange motor.

9 Starter motor – removal and refitting

1 The starter motor is located at the front of the engine.

2 Jack up and support the front of the vehicle (see *Jacking and vehicle support* in the reference section). Remove the engine undershield.

Removal

3 Disconnect the battery negative lead (refer to *Disconnecting the battery in Section 4 of this Chapter*).

Petrol engines

4 Disconnect the wiring plug from the oil level sensor.

5 Noting their locations, disconnect the wires from the starter motor and solenoid.

6 Unscrew the starter motor mounting bolts and withdraw the starter motor from the transmission **(see illustrations)**. Check that the centring dowel has not fallen out as the motor is removed, and refit it to the transmission face if necessary.

Diesel engines

7 Where fitted, remove the engine top cover.

8 Loosen the clamps and remove the intercooler outlet pipe.

9 Disconnect the wiring plugs from the oil pressure sensor and the oil level sensor.

10 Note the location of the wires on the starter motor and solenoid, then disconnect them **(see illustration)**.

11 Unscrew the mounting bolts and withdraw the starter motor from the transmission **(see illustrations)**. Check that the centring dowel has not fallen out as the motor is removed, and refit it to the transmission face if necessary.

Refitting

12 Refitting is a reversal of removal – position the starter motor on the location dowel as it is offered into place. Finally, tighten the mounting bolts to the specified torque.

Chapter 5 Part B:
Ignition system – petrol engines

Contents

	Section number
General information and precautions	1
Ignition HT coils – removal, testing and refitting	3
Ignition system – testing	2
Ignition timing – checking and adjustment	5
Knock sensor – removal and refitting	4
Spark plug renewal	See Chapter 1A

Degrees of difficulty

Easy, suitable for novice with little experience	**Fairly easy,** suitable for beginner with some experience	**Fairly difficult,** suitable for competent DIY mechanic	**Difficult,** suitable for experienced DIY mechanic	**Very difficult,** suitable for expert DIY or professional

Specifications

General

Ignition system type	Fully-electronic, computer-controlled, with four individual ignition coils, one on each spark plug
Firing order	1-3-4-2
Location of No 1 cylinder	Flywheel end

Ignition timing	Controlled by the ECU

Ignition HT coil resistances

Typical:	
Primary resistance	0.54 ± 0.02 ohms
Secondary resistance	9.0 to 12.5 kohms

Torque wrench settings

	Nm	lbf ft
Alternator support strut	20	15
Ignition coil	15	11
Knock sensor	20	15
Spark plugs	25 to 30	18 to 22

1 General information and precautions

General information

The ignition system is integrated with the fuel injection system to form a combined engine management system under the control of one ECU (see Chapter 4A for further information). All engines are fitted with a distributorless ignition system.

The ignition system uses one coil for each cylinder, with each coil mounted on the relevant spark plug.

The crankshaft speed/position sensor (see Chapter 4A) is used to determine piston position as well as engine speed.

The power module for the ignition is integrated in the engine management ECU. The ECU uses the inputs from the sensors to calculate the required ignition advance setting and coil charging time – an integral amplifier circuit within the ECU switches the ignition coil primary (LT) circuit.

The knock sensor is mounted on the cylinder block to inform the ECU when the engine is 'pinking'. Its sensitivity to a particular frequency of vibration allows it to detect the impulses which are caused by the shock waves set up when the engine starts to 'pink' (pre-ignite). The knock sensor sends an electrical signal to the ECU which retards the ignition advance setting until the 'pinking' ceases – the ignition timing is then gradually returned to the 'normal' setting. This maintains the ignition timing as close to the knock threshold as possible – the most efficient setting for the engine under normal running conditions.

Precautions

The following precautions must be observed, to prevent damage to the ignition system components and to reduce risk of personal injury.

a) Ensure the ignition is switched off before disconnecting any of the ignition wiring.

b) Ensure that the ignition is switched off before connecting or disconnecting any ignition test equipment, such as a timing light.

c) Do not earth the coil primary or secondary circuits.

Warning: Voltages produced by an electronic ignition system are considerably higher than those produced by conventional ignition systems. Extreme care must be taken when working on the system with the ignition switched on. Persons with surgically-implanted cardiac pacemaker devices should keep well clear of the ignition circuits, components and test equipment

2 Ignition system – testing

1 The components of ignition systems are normally very reliable; most faults are far more likely to be due to loose or dirty connections, or to 'tracking' of HT voltage due to dirt, dampness or damaged insulation than to the failure of any of the system's components. Always check all wiring thoroughly before condemning an electrical component and work methodically to eliminate all other possibilities before deciding that a particular component is faulty.

3.2 Disconnect the wiring plug

3.3a Remove the bolt (arrowed) and...

3.3b ...withdraw the pencil coil

2 The old practice of checking for a spark by holding the live end of a spark plug HT lead (or in this case, the individual coils) a short distance away from the engine is not recommended; not only is there a high risk of a powerful electric shock, but the coil or ECU may be damaged. However, if necessary each plug can be checked individually by removing it, then reconnecting the coil and connecting the body of the spark plug to a suitable earthing point on the engine using a battery jumper lead. It is important to make a good earth connection if using this method. Never try to 'diagnose' misfires by pulling off one coil at a time.

Engine will not start

3 If the engine either will not turn over at all, or only turns very slowly, first check the battery and starter motor as described in Chapter 5A.
4 Use an ohmmeter to check the resistances of the coils, and compare with the information given in the Specifications.
5 If these checks fail to reveal the cause of the problem, the vehicle should be taken to a Renault dealer or suitably equipped garage for testing. A diagnostic socket is provided – often referred to as the 'Data Link Connector (or DLC) into which a special electronic diagnostic tester can be plugged. The tester will guide a skilled technician to the source of the problem without the need to test all the components individually. If necessary, the system wiring and wiring connectors can be checked as described in Chapter 12.

Engine misfires

6 An irregular misfire suggests either a loose connection or intermittent fault in the primary circuit, or an HT fault between the coils and spark plugs.
7 With the ignition switched off, check carefully through the system ensuring that all connections are clean and securely fastened.
8 Check that the HT coils and their associated wiring connections are clean and dry.
9 Regular misfiring of one spark plug may be due to a faulty spark plug, faulty injector, a faulty coil or loss of compression in the relevant cylinder. Regular misfiring of cylinders 1 and 4 only, or 2 and 3 only suggests a fault on the relevant coil. Regular misfiring of all the cylinders suggests a fuel supply fault, such as a clogged fuel filter or faulty fuel pump.
10 All the vehicles covered by this manual comply with the European On Board Diagnostic (EOBD) protocols for emissions standards. A miss-fire count is one of the mandatory trouble codes required by legislation.
11 Low cost simple code readers that will give access to the mandatory emissions related fault codes are now available to the home mechanic. They are limited in there scope, as most will only give access to the mandatory codes, with little explanation other than a fault code and a description.

3 Ignition HT coils – removal, testing and refitting

Removal

1 Disconnect the battery negative lead (refer to *Disconnecting the battery* in Reference).
2 The ignition coils are accessible through the holes in the inlet manifold. Where fitted remove the engine top cover, then carefully disconnect the wiring from each coil. Take care not to damage the connectors **(see illustration)**.
3 Unscrew the single mounting bolt and withdraw each coil from its spark plug **(see illustrations)**.
4 Check the condition of the O-rings where the coils enter the valve cover, and if necessary renew them.

Testing

5 Each coil can be tested as described in the previous Section, using an ohmmeter to check for the resistances given in the Specifications.
6 Further testing of the ignition system should be carried out by a Renault dealer or suitably equipped garage using specialised equipment connected to the engine management diagnostic socket.

Refitting

7 Refitting is a reversal of removal, noting the following points:

a) *Before refitting the coils over the plugs, Renault recommend that the rubber boots are first lightly lubricated inside, using fluorine grease (part number 82 00 168 855).*
b) *Tighten the mounting bolts to the specified torque, and ensure that the wiring connectors are correctly and securely refitted.*

4 Knock sensor – removal and refitting

Removal

1 The knock sensor is located on the front, centre of the cylinder block.
2 To remove the sensor unbolt the dipstick guide tube and move it to the side.
3 Unbolt the support strut from the rear of the alternator and the engine block.
4 Disconnect the wiring plug and then unscrew the sensor from the cylinder block.

Refitting

5 Refitting is a reversal of removal. Ensure that the sensor and its seating on the cylinder block or head are completely clean and tighten the sensor to the specified torque wrench setting. It is essential that these measures are scrupulously observed, as if the sensor is not correctly secured to a clean mating surface it may not be able to detect the impulses caused by pre-ignition. If this were to happen, the correction of ignition timing would not take place, with the consequent risk of severe engine damage.

5 Ignition timing – checking and adjustment

The ignition timing is constantly being monitored and adjusted by the engine management ECU, and nominal checking values cannot be given. Therefore, it is not possible for the home mechanic to check the ignition timing. The only way in which the ignition timing can be checked is using special electronic test equipment, connected to the engine management system diagnostic connector (refer to Chapter 4A). No adjustment of the ignition timing is possible. Should the ignition timing be incorrect, then a fault must be present in the engine management system.

Chapter 5 Part C:
Pre/post-heating system – diesel engines

Contents

	Section number		Section number
Coolant temperature sensor – removal, testing, and refitting	4	Pre/post-heating system – description and testing	1
Glow plugs – removal, inspection and refitting	2	Pre/post-heating system control unit – removal and refitting	3

Degrees of difficulty

Easy, suitable for novice with little experience	**Fairly easy,** suitable for beginner with some experience	**Fairly difficult,** suitable for competent DIY mechanic	**Difficult,** suitable for experienced DIY mechanic	**Very difficult,** suitable for expert DIY or professional

Specifications

Glow plugs

Resistance	0.6 ohms

Coolant temperature sensor

Resistance at (all figures are approximate):	
-10° C	12 500 ± 7000 ohms
25° C	2252 ± 112 ohms
50° C	810 ± 40 ohms
80° C	280 ± 8 ohms
110° C	115 ± 3 ohms
120° C	88 ± 2 ohms

Fuel temperature sensor

Resistance at 25°C	2.2 kohms

Torque wrench setting	**Nm**	**lbf ft**
Glow plugs	15	11

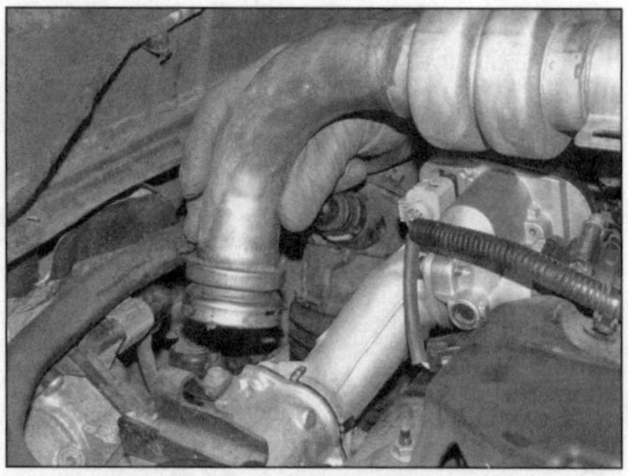
2.2a Remove the intercooler inlet duct

2.2b Release the wiring loom (arrowed)

2.2c Move the outlet pipe to the side

1 Pre/post-heating system – description and testing

Description

1 The preheating/post-heating system consists of glow plugs screwed into the combustion chambers, a control unit mounted next to the battery on the left-hand side of the engine compartment, and a coolant temperature sensor located on the thermostat housing. The control unit is itself activated by the engine management ECU.

2 The glow plugs are supplied with current from the control unit in several phases, namely variable preheating, fixed preheating, starting heating, and variable post-heating.

3 The variable preheating phase occurs when the ignition is switched on, and during this phase the preheating warning light is illuminated on the instrument panel. The period of preheating depends on the temperature of the coolant and battery voltage. The maximum period of 15 seconds occurs if the coolant temperature is low and the battery voltage is less than 9.3 volts. The period varies from 15 seconds to zero seconds according to the temperature of the coolant, and when the temperature reaches 80°C, no preheating occurs. With normal battery voltage the maximum period is 10 seconds.

4 The fixed preheating phase occurs straight after the variable phase finishes, after the warning light has extinguished, and lasts for up to 5 seconds. Normally, the driver will start the engine at some point during this phase.

5 During the period when the starter motor is in operation, the glow plugs are continuously supplied with current.

6 The variable post-heating phase occurs immediately after the engine has been started, and the period of post-heating depends on the temperature of the coolant. The maximum period of variable post-heating is 60 seconds, at which point the system is switched off. Variable post-heating will cease if the coolant temperature exceeds 80°C.

7 On models fitted with a particulate filter the glow plugs maybe initialised to aid regeneration of the particulate filter.

Testing

8 If the system malfunctions, testing is best carried out by a Renault dealer (or suitably-equipped garage) using dedicated test equipment, however, some preliminary checks may be made as follows.

9 Connect a voltmeter or 12 volt test lamp between the glow plug supply cable and earth (engine or vehicle metal). Make sure that the live connection is kept clear of the engine and bodywork. Have an assistant switch on the ignition and check that voltage is applied to the glow plugs. Note the time for which the warning light is lit and the total time for which voltage is applied before the system cuts out, and compare to the times given in the description above.

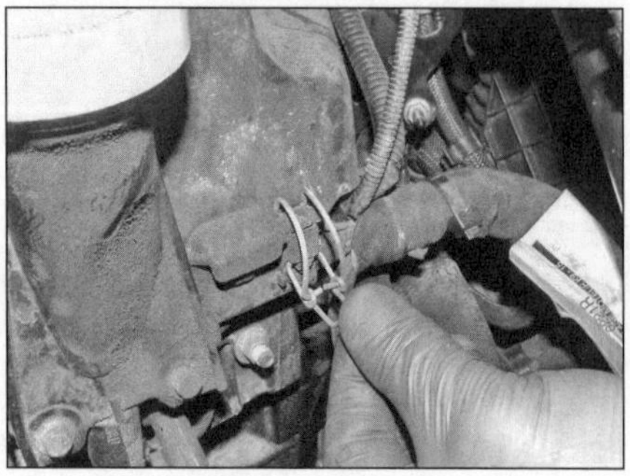
2.3a Unclip and then...

2.3b ...remove the cover

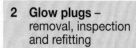

10 If there is no supply at all, the relay, control unit or associated wiring is at fault.

11 To locate a defective glow plug, disconnect the main supply cable and the interconnecting wire from the top of the glow plugs. Using an ohmmeter, check for continuity between each glow plug terminal and earth. The resistance of a glow plug in good condition is very low (less than 1 ohm), so if the test lamp does not light or the continuity tester shows a high resistance, the glow plug is defective.

12 If an ammeter is available, the current draw of each glow plug can be checked. After an initial surge of around 15 to 20 amps, each plug should draw around 10 amps. Any plug which draws much more or less than 10 amps is probably defective.

13 As a final check, the glow plugs can be removed and inspected as described in Section 2.

14 If the pre/post-heating system is faulty, first check the wiring to each individual component. If this does not locate the fault, ideally each component should be substituted with known good units until the fault is located. If this is not possible, take the vehicle to a Renault dealer or diesel specialist who will have the diagnostic equipment necessary to pin point the fault quickly.

2 Glow plugs – removal, inspection and refitting

Caution: If the preheating system has just been energised, or if the engine has been running, the glow plugs may be very hot.

Removal

1 Disconnect the battery negative (earth) lead and position it away from the terminal (refer to *Disconnecting the battery* in Chapter 5A).

2 Remove the intercooler inlet pipe from the top of the engine and then disconnect the wiring plug from the boost pressure sensor. Release the wiring loom from the top of the cover. Slacken the hose clip on the intercooler outlet pipe and move the pipe to the side. **(see illustrations)**.

3 Unbolt an then unclip the protective cover fitted to the pump and injector rail **(see illustrations)**.

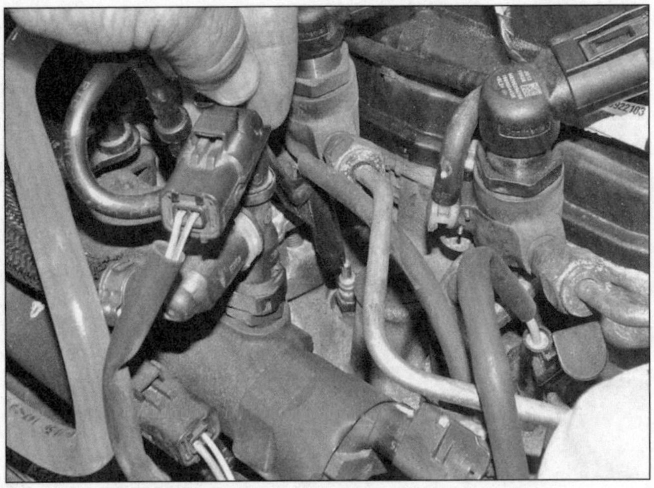

2.4 Disconnecting the wiring from the glow plugs

2.5a Clean the surrounding area...

4 Disconnect the wiring plugs from the glow plugs **(see illustration)**.

5 Clean the surrounding area, then apply penetrating fluid to the base of the glow plug. Allow the fluid to penetrate and then unscrew and remove the glow plugs from the cylinder head **(see illustrations)**. To ensure that the glow plugs do not snap off in the cylinder head, use a torque wrench to initially slacken the plug. Renault recommend a maximum reverse torque of 40 Nm.

6 If the glow plugs are stuck in the cylinder head then if possible, refit the removed components and run the engine up to operating temperature. Remove the glow plugs whilst the engine is still warm. Exercise caution in the vicinity of any engine parts that may still be hot. If the glow plugs still refuse to move then consider soaking them again in penetrating and leaving them to soak over night.

7 If a glow plug breaks during removal, it may be possible to drill out the plug and use a specialist removal tool to extract the remains. However this method does carry the risk of damaging the cylinder head, as well as the possibility of debris entering the combustion chamber. The safest option will always be to remove the cylinder head and have a machine shop remove the glow plugs and repair the glow plug holes as required.

Inspection

8 Inspect the glow plugs for physical damage. Burnt or eroded glow plug tips can be caused by a bad injector spray pattern. Have the injectors checked if this sort of damage is found.

9 If the glow plugs are in good physical condition, check them electrically using a 12 volt test lamp or continuity tester with reference to the previous Section.

10 The glow plugs can be energised by applying 12 volts to them to verify that they heat up evenly and in the required time. Observe the following precautions:

a) Support the glow plug by clamping it carefully in a vice or self-locking pliers. Remember it will become red-hot.

b) Make sure that the power supply or test lead incorporates a fuse or overload trip to protect against damage from a short-circuit.

c) After testing, allow the glow plug to cool for several minutes before attempting to handle it.

11 A glow plug in good condition will start to glow red at the tip after drawing current for 5 seconds or so. Any plug which takes much longer to start glowing, or which starts glowing in the middle instead of at the tip, is defective.

Refitting

12 Refit by reversing the removal operations. Apply a smear of copper based anti-seize compound to the plug threads and tighten the glow plugs to the specified torque **(see illustration)**. Do not overtighten, as this can damage the glow plug element.

3 Pre/post-heating system control unit – removal and refitting

Removal

1 The pre/post-heating control unit is located behind the air filter inlet on the left-hand inner wing **(see illustration)**.

2 Disconnect the battery as described in Chapter 5A.

3 Remove the front bumper cover and the front section of the wing liner as described in Chapter 11.

4 Remove the air filter inlet and then disconnect the wiring plug from the control unit.

5 Unscrew the mounting nuts/bolts and remove the control unit from the mounting bracket.

Refitting

6 Refitting is a reversal of removal.

2.5b ...then unscrew and remove the glow plugs

2.12 Tightening the glow plugs

3.1 The glow plug control unit (arrowed)

4.3a Pull out the retaining clip (housing removed for clarity)...

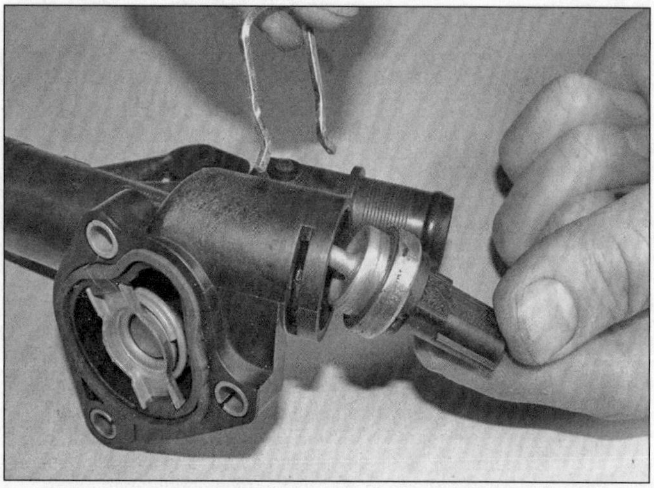

4.3b ...and ease the sensor from the thermostat housing

4 Coolant temperature sensor – removal, testing, and refitting

Note: *Also refer to Chapter 3, Section 8.*

Removal

1 The coolant temperature sensor is located on the thermostat housing on the left-hand end of the cylinder head.

2 Drain the cooling system as described in Chapter 1B. Alternatively, have the new sensor or a suitable bung to hand to quickly plug the hole and prevent liquid from being spilt while the sensor is being removed.

3 Pull out the retaining clip, then ease the sensor from the thermostat housing **(see illustrations)**. If necessary recover the sealing (O-ring) ring from the housing.

Refitting

4 Refitting is the reverse of removal, but fit a new sealing ring.

5 On completion, top-up or refill and bleed the cooling system, as necessary, as described in Chapter 1B.

Chapter 6
Clutch

Contents

	Section number		Section number
Clutch – general check	See Chapter 1A or 1B	Clutch pedal – removal and refitting	6
Clutch assembly – removal, inspection and refitting	8	Clutch pedal switches – removal and refitting	7
Clutch hydraulic hoses – removal and refitting	4	Clutch slave cylinder – removal and refitting	3
Clutch hydraulic system – bleeding	5	General information	1
Clutch master cylinder – removal and refitting	2		

Degrees of difficulty

Easy, suitable for novice with little experience	**Fairly easy,** suitable for beginner with some experience	**Fairly difficult,** suitable for competent DIY mechanic	**Difficult,** suitable for experienced DIY mechanic	**Very difficult,** suitable for expert DIY or professional

Specifications

General

Clutch type	Single dry plate, diaphragm spring, hydraulically-operated release mechanism

Clutch disc

Diameter:	
Petrol engines	215.0 mm
Diesel engines	
5 speed transmission	215.0 mm
6 speed transmission	225.0 mm
Friction material thickness (new)	7.0 mm (approximate)

Torque wrench settings

Torque wrench settings	Nm	lbf ft
Clutch pedal mounting bracket nuts	21	15
Clutch slave cylinder/release bearing	21	15
Clutch slave cylinder flange bolts (5-speed transmission)	9	7
Pressure plate-to-flywheel bolts:	15	11

2.4 Connect a piece of tubing over the bleed nipple

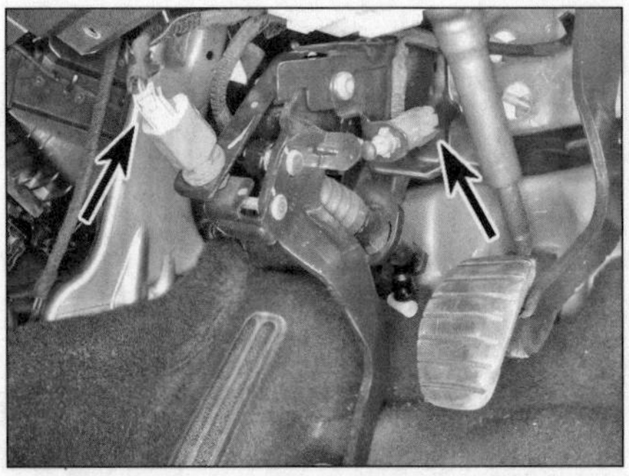

2.6 Disconnect the wiring plugs (arrowed)

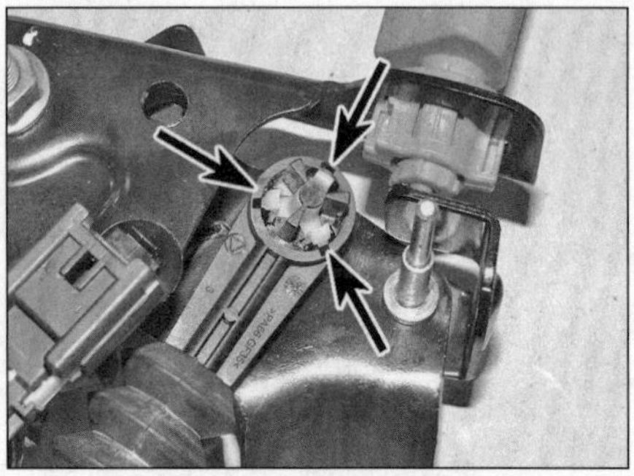

2.9 Depress the clips (arrowed)

1 General information

The clutch consists of a friction disc, a pressure plate assembly, a release bearing and hydraulic slave cylinder; all of these components are contained in the large cast-aluminium alloy bellhousing, sandwiched between the engine and the transmission.

The hydraulic master cylinder is located in the pedal bracket on the bulkhead, and the clutch fluid reservoir is shared with the brake fluid reservoir on the top of the brake master cylinder. Inside the reservoir each circuit has its own compartment, so that in the event of fluid loss in the clutch circuit, the brake circuit remains fully operational.

The clutch disc (friction disc) is fitted between the engine flywheel and the clutch pressure plate, and is allowed to slide on the transmission input shaft splines.

The pressure plate assembly is bolted to the engine flywheel. When the engine is running, drive is transmitted from the crankshaft, via the flywheel, to the friction disc (these components being clamped securely together by the pressure plate assembly) and from the friction disc to the transmission input shaft.

To interrupt the drive, the spring pressure must be relaxed by the hydraulically-operated release mechanism. Depressing the clutch pedal operates the master cylinder which in turn operates the slave cylinder and presses the release bearing against the pressure plate spring fingers. This causes the springs to deform and releases the clamping force on the pressure plate.

2.10 Rotate the master cylinder to remove it from the pedal assembly

When the pedal is released, the diaphragm spring forces the pressure plate into contact with the friction linings on the friction disc. The disc is now firmly sandwiched between the pressure plate and the flywheel, thus transmitting engine power to the transmission.

Wear of the friction material on the friction disc is automatically compensated for by the operation of the hydraulic system. As the friction material on the disc wears, the pressure plate moves towards the flywheel causing the clutch diaphragm spring inner fingers to move outwards. When the clutch pedal is released, excess fluid is expelled through the master cylinder into the fluid reservoir.

Warning: Hydraulic fluid is poisonous; wash off immediately and thoroughly in the case of skin contact, and seek immediate medical advice if any fluid is swallowed or gets into the eyes. Certain types of hydraulic fluid are flammable, and may ignite when allowed into contact with hot components; when servicing any hydraulic system, it is safest to assume that the fluid is flammable, and to take precautions against the risk of fire as though it is petrol that is being handled. Hydraulic fluid is also an effective paint stripper, and will attack plastics; if any is spilt, it should be washed off immediately, using copious quantities of fresh water. Finally, it is hygroscopic (it absorbs moisture from the air) – old fluid may be contaminated and unfit for further use. When topping-up or renewing the fluid, always use the recommended type, and ensure that it comes from a freshly-opened sealed container.

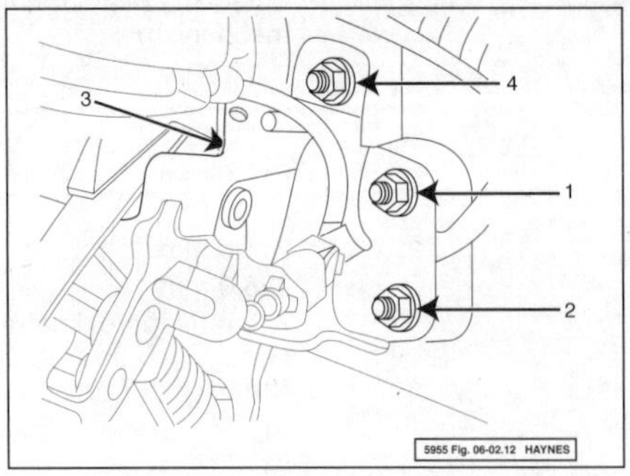

2.12 Tighten the nuts in the order shown

2 Clutch master cylinder – removal and refitting

Note: *Refer to the warning in Section 1 before proceeding.*

Removal

1 Gain access to the clutch bleed nipple by removing the battery and battery tray as described in Chapter 5A.

2 Unscrew the brake fluid reservoir cap.

3 Connect a piece of tubing which is a tight fit over the clutch bleed nipple located on the pipe at the front of the transmission **(see illustration)**. Place the other end of the tube into a container large enough to hold the contents of the brake fluid reservoir.

4 Following the procedure in Section 5 for bleeding the clutch, but pump the clutch pedal until all the fluid is drained from the master cylinder and brake fluid reservoir.

5 Remove the driver's lower facia trim panel as described in Chapter 11, Section 24.

6 Disconnect the wiring plugs from the clutch pedal switches, noting their fitted positions **(see illustration)**.

7 Place some absorbent cloth below the pipe connections on the master cylinder. Remove the clips from the master cylinder unions, and disconnect the pipes. Cap or tape over the open pipe connections, to prevent further loss of fluid.

8 Unscrew the pedal bracket mounting nuts **(see illustration 2.12)** and withdraw the pedal from the bulkhead.

9 With the master cylinder and pedal assembly removed from the vehicle, release the master cylinder balljoint fitting from the pedal by pressing the clips **(see illustration)**.

10 Release the master cylinder from the pedal assembly by turning it a quarter-turn clockwise **(see illustration)**.

11 If the master cylinder is faulty it must be renewed

Refitting

12 Refitting is a reversal of removal, noting the following points:

3.2a Unscrew the two mounting bolts...

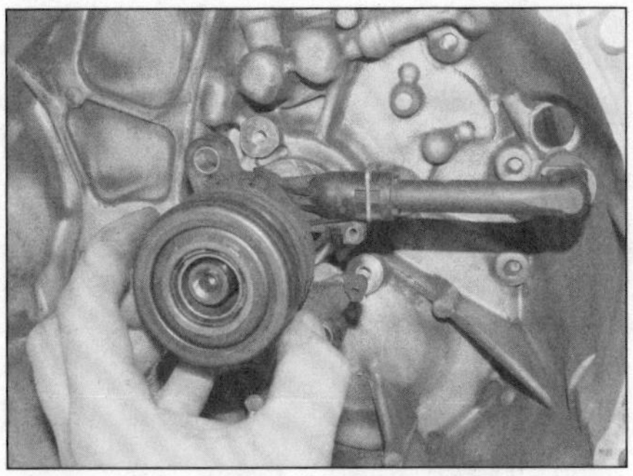

3.2b ...and withdraw the release bearing and slave cylinder

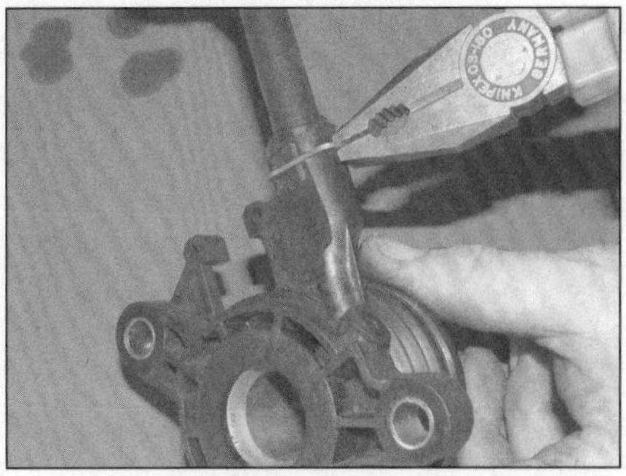

3.3 Pull out the clip to separate the slave cylinder from the supply pipe

a) *Check the condition of the pipe seals, and renew if necessary.*
b) *Ensure that all fluid hose connections are clean, and are securely made.*
c) *Tighten the clutch pedal mounting bracket nuts to the specified torque in the correct order* ***(see illustration).***
d) *Fill and bleed the clutch system on completion, as described in Section 5. Also check the operation of the brakes, and if necessary, bleed the system as described in Chapter 9.*

3 Clutch slave cylinder – removal and refitting

Note: *Refer to the warning in Section 1 before proceeding.*

Note: *All models feature a concentric slave cylinder (CSC) where the slave cylinder and release bearing are combined into a single assembly.*

Removal

1 Remove the transmission as described in Chapter 7.

2 Inside the bellhousing, unscrew and remove the two mounting bolts, then withdraw the slave cylinder and release bearing over the transmission input shaft **(see illustrations)**.

3 Most models have a removable supply pipe. Where fitted pull out the joining clip **(see illustration)**. Note that replacement slave cylinders are normally supplied with this pipe fitted

Refitting

4 Refitting is a reversal of removal, noting the following points:

a) *Always replace the release bearing/slave cylinder.*
b) *Pre-fill the cylinder with clean brake fluid (seal the pipe) before fitting*
c) *Tighten the release bearing mounting bolts to the specified torque.*
d) *Refit the transmission as described in Chapter 7.*
e) *On completion, bleed the clutch as described in Section 5.*

4 Clutch hydraulic hoses – removal and refitting

Note: *Refer to the warning in Section 1 before proceeding.*

Removal

1 Remove the battery and battery tray as described in Chapter 5A.

2 Remove the engine ECU as described in Chapter 4A or 4B, as applicable.

3 Remove the air cleaner and inlet ducts as described in Chapter 4A or 4B, as applicable.

4 Unscrew the brake fluid reservoir cap.

5 Empty the system of fluid as described in Section 2.

6 Prise the slave cylinder pipe clip out carefully (do not try to remove the clip completely), and pull the pipe off **(see illustration)**. Plug or tape over the slave cylinder connection, to prevent further fluid loss.

7 Trace the pipe back to the bulkhead connections, releasing it from the mounting clips **(see illustration)**.

8 A pair of link pipes allow the supply pipe (from the brake fluid reservoir) and the return pipe (to the slave cylinder) to be removed. Place a suitable rag beneath the pipe connections and then prise out the circlips. Remove the supply and return pipes.

9 Remove the driver's lower facia trim panel and the glovebox as described in Chapter 11.

10 Place some absorbent cloth below the pipe connections on the master cylinder. Remove the clips from the master cylinder unions, and disconnect the pipes **(see illustration)**. Access to the pipes is considerably easier if the pedal assembly is first removed from the bulkhead. Cap or tape over the open pipe connections, to prevent further loss of fluid.

11 Place some absorbent cloth below the pipe connections on the bulkhead, at the front of the passenger footwell. Remove the clips from the unions where the pipes pass through the bulkhead, and separate the pipes.

12 Remove the clutch pipes from the rear of the air distribution housing and then remove them from the vehicle.

Refitting

13 Refitting is a reversal of removal, noting the following points:

a) *Fill and bleed the clutch system on completion, as described in Section 5.*
b) *Check the operation of the brakes, and if necessary, bleed the system as described in Chapter 9.*

4.6 Disconnect the fluid supply pipe from the slave cylinder. Partially release the circlip (arrowed)

4.7 Release the pipes from the clips

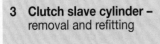

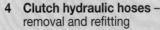

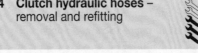

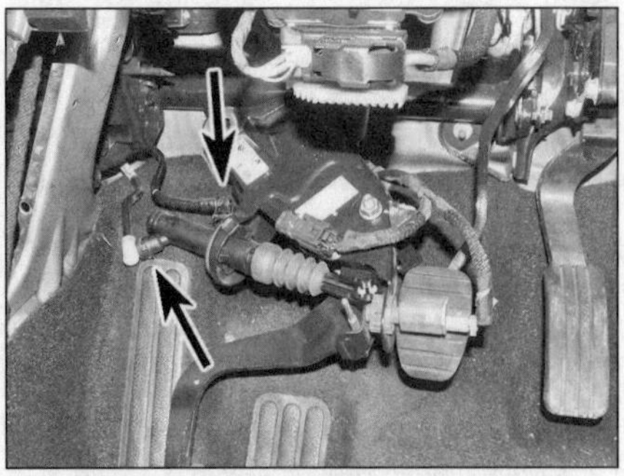

4.10 Master cylinder pipe connections (arrowed)

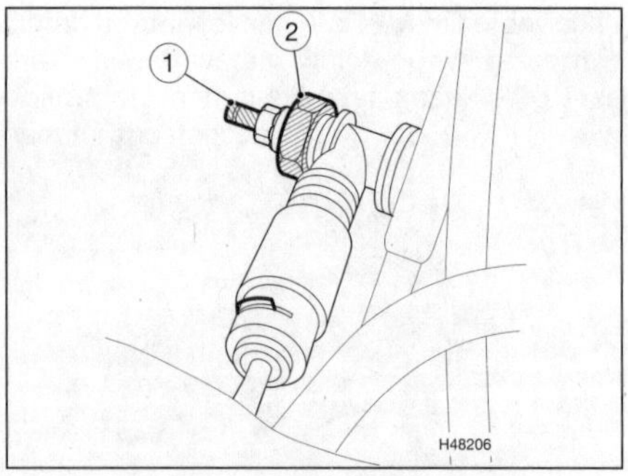

5.5a Conventional bleed screw

1 Bleed screw 2 Plastic union

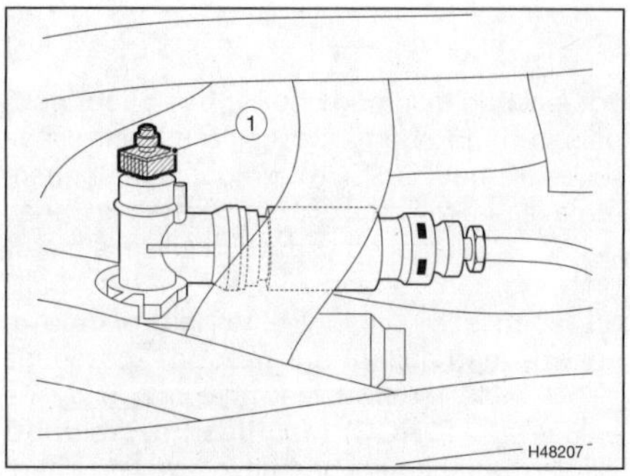

5.5b Half-turn bleed screw

1 Bleed screw

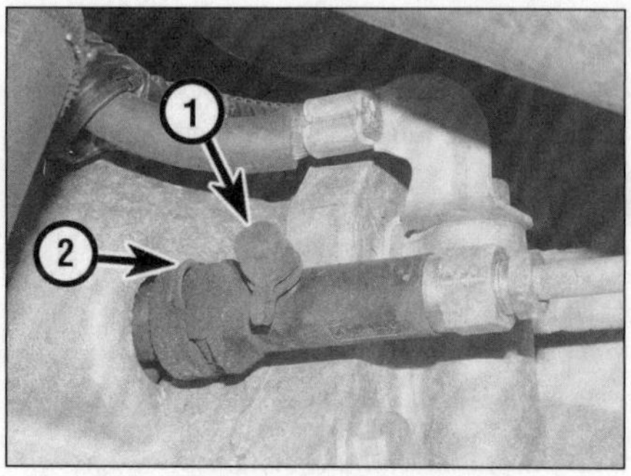

5.5c Press-clip bleed nipple

1 Bleed screw 2 Press-clip

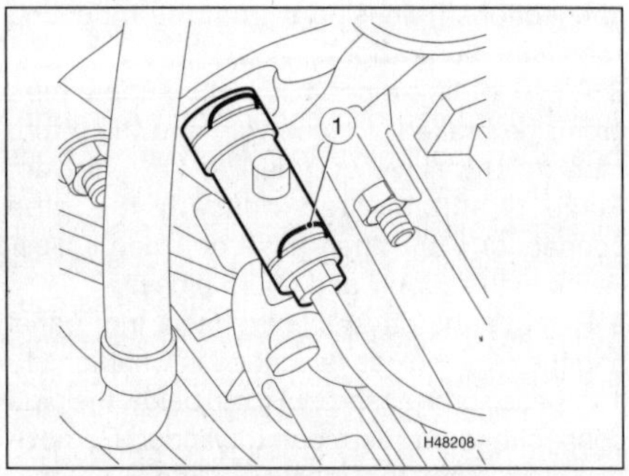

5.5d Pull-clip bleed nipple

1 Pull-clip

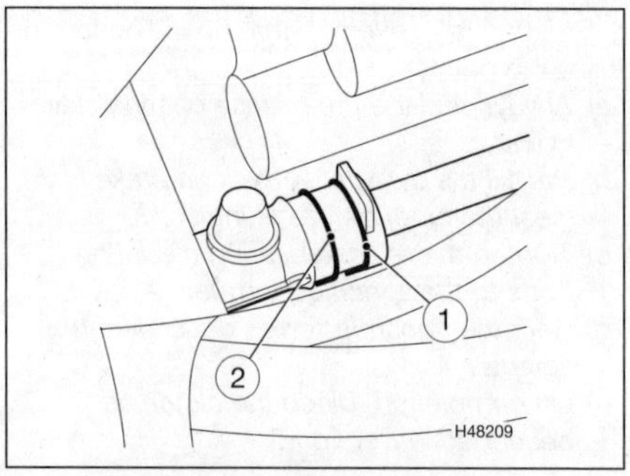

5.5e Double-clip bleed nipple

Lower clip 1 and lift clip 2

5 Clutch hydraulic system – bleeding

Note: *Refer to the warning in Section 1 before proceeding.*

Note: *A large capacity syringe will be needed to bleed the hydraulic system.*

1 The correct operation of any hydraulic system is only possible after removing all air from the components and circuit; this is achieved by bleeding the system.

2 During the bleeding procedure, add only clean, unused hydraulic fluid of the recommended type; never re-use fluid that has already been bled from the system. Ensure that sufficient fluid is available before starting work.

3 If there is any possibility of incorrect fluid being already in the system, the hydraulic circuit must be flushed completely with uncontaminated, correct fluid.

4 If hydraulic fluid has been lost from the system, or air has entered because of a leak, ensure that the fault is cured before continuing further.

5 The bleed screw/nipple is fitted in the slave cylinder hydraulic supply pipe at the front of the transmission bellhousing, however there are several possible types as shown, each one requiring a different release method **(see illustrations)**:

a) Conventional bleed screw in a plastic union – to open, hold the union with one spanner and undo the screw with another.

b) Half-turn bleed screw – to open, undo the screw by hand.

c) Press-clip bleed nipple – to open, press and hold the clip while pulling out the pipe by one notch.

d) Pull-clip bleed nipple – to open, lift and hold the clip while pulling out the pipe by one notch.

e) Double-clip bleed nipple – to open, lower the clip furthest from the bleed nipple and lift the remaining clip, while pulling out the pipe by one notch.

6 Access to the bleed screw/nipple is awkward. Either raise the front of the vehicle and support it on axle stands (see *Jacking and vehicle support*) and then remove the engine undertray for access from under the engine, or carry out the following for access from the top of the engine:

a) Remove the battery, battery tray and ECU as described in Chapter 5A.

c) Remove the air cleaner and inlet ducts as described in Chapter 4A or 4B, as applicable.

7 Unscrew the brake fluid reservoir cap, and top-up (or remove) the fluid level to the MIN mark.

8 Secure the clutch pedal in the upright position with a suitable strap or block of wood.

9 Connect a piece of transparent tube to the bleed screw/nipple. The tube should be long enough so that it is above the height of the brake fluid reservoir. Open the bleed nipple as described above.

10 Fill a large syringe with at least 60 ml of clean brake fluid and connect it to the transparent tube.

11 Keeping the syringe above the height of the brake fluid reservoir, slowly inject the contents of the syringe whilst monitoring the height of the fluid in the brake fluid reservoir. Remove fluid from the reservoir if necessary.

12 Close the bleed nipple and check the operation of the clutch. Repeat the bleeding procedure if necessary.

13 Discard any hydraulic fluid that has been bled from the system as it will not be fit for re-use.

14 If the clutch is not operating correctly after repeated bleeding, the master cylinder or slave cylinder may be faulty. If new parts are fitted, it may be that there is an air-lock in the system; disconnect the hoses from each component in turn to check there is fluid at that point. Place some absorbent cloth below the pipe connections as they are removed, to soak up the fluid that escapes. The system will then need further bleeding. **Note:** *If any fluid is spilt, it should be washed off immediately, using copious quantities of fresh water.*

15 Refit the remaining components in reverse order to removal.

6 Clutch pedal – removal and refitting

The clutch pedal is removed as an assembly with the clutch master cylinder – refer to Section 2. If required, the pedal could be removed after unhooking the return spring, unscrewing the pivot shaft nut, and withdrawing the pivot shaft.

7 Clutch pedal switches – removal and refitting

1 Two or three clutch pedal switches are fitted. The one on top of the pedal bracket signals the start of pedal travel and the lower switch (on the side on some models) signals the end of pedal travel **(see illustration)**. Models fitted with an electric parking brake (EPB) also have a third switch fitted.

2 The signals from the start and end of travel are used by used by the engine ECU to permit smoother gearchanging, and to enable other related control functions, such as idle speed control when the pedal is depressed. The third switch controls the release of the parking brake.

3 The end of pedal travel switch is used by the keyless card system, to signal that the clutch is fully depressed, to allow the engine to be started. The monitoring of the clutch pedal position is also used on vehicles fitted with stop/start technology.

Removal

4 Remove the driver's lower facia trim panel as described in Chapter 11, Section 24.

5 Disconnect the wiring plugs from the relevant switch.

6 Twist the switch through a quarter-turn, and remove it from the pedal mounting bracket.

Refitting

7 Refitting is a reversal of removal, noting the following points:

a) The start of travel switch and lock ring must be replaced once removed.

b) Raise the pedal and check that a gap of 1 to 2.5 mm exists between the bracket and the start of travel switch plunger.

c) Check the extension of the plunger on the end of travel switch – this must be between 28 to 29 mm. Adjust the plunger to this dimension by pushing (or pulling) the plunger ***(see illustration)****. Note that the plunger can only be adjusted a maximum of three times before it must be replaced.*

8 Clutch assembly – removal, inspection and refitting

Warning: Dust created by clutch wear and deposited on the clutch components may contain asbestos, which is a health hazard. DO NOT blow it out with compressed air, or inhale any of it. DO NOT use petrol or petroleum-based solvents to clean off the dust. Brake system cleaner should be used to flush the dust into a suitable receptacle. After the clutch components are wiped clean with rags, dispose of the contaminated rags and cleaner in a sealed, marked container.

Note: *Although some friction materials may no longer contain asbestos, it is safest to assume that they do, and to take precautions accordingly.*

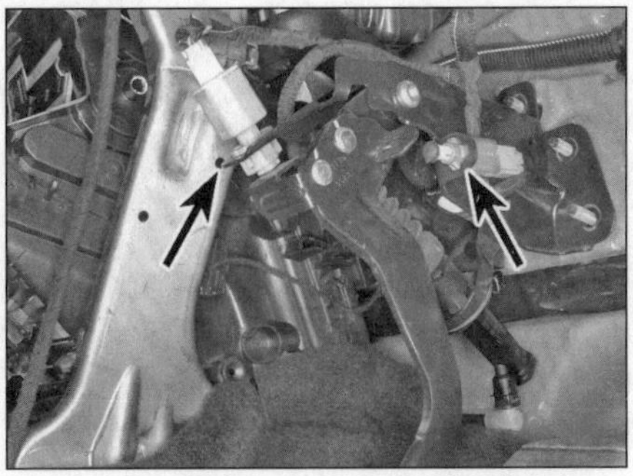

7.1 The clutch pedal travel switches

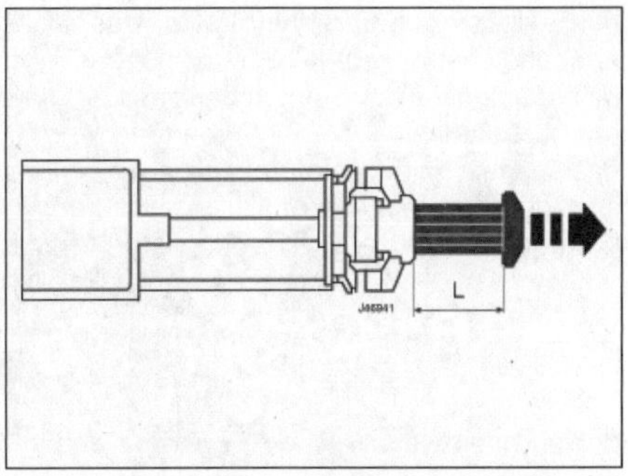

7.7 Adjust the plunger so that the dimension L is 19 to 20mm

Removal

1 Unless the complete engine/transmission has to be removed from the car (see Chapter 2C), the clutch can be reached by removing the transmission as described in Chapter 7 **(see illustration)**.

2 Before disturbing the clutch, use chalk or a marker pen to mark the relationship of the pressure plate assembly to the flywheel **(see illustration)**.

3 Hold the flywheel stationary using a suitable tool engaged with the starter ring gear teeth – a piece of metal can be tightened to one of the bolt holes, or alternatively an assistant can use a wide-bladed screwdriver engaged with the teeth **(see illustration)**.

4 Working in a diagonal sequence, slacken the pressure plate bolts by half a turn at a time, until spring pressure is released and the bolts can be unscrewed by hand. Discard the bolts – new ones should be used when refitting.

5 Prise the pressure plate assembly off its locating dowels, and collect the friction disc, noting which way round the disc is fitted **(see illustrations)**.

Inspection

Note: *Due to the amount of work necessary to remove and refit clutch components, it is usually considered good practice to renew the clutch friction disc, pressure plate assembly and release bearing (slave cylinder) as a matched set, even if only one of these*

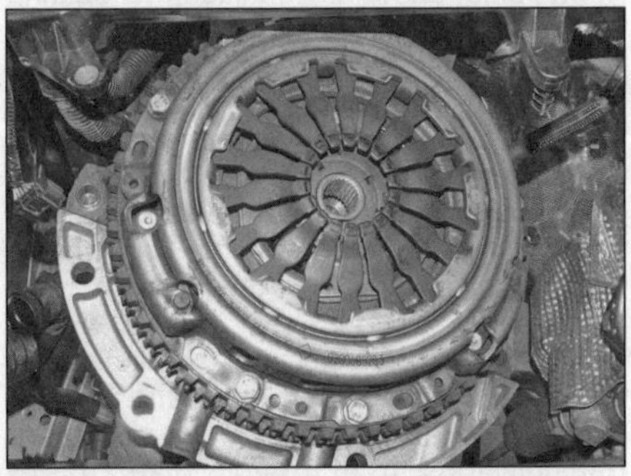

8.1 View of the clutch assembly with the transmission removed

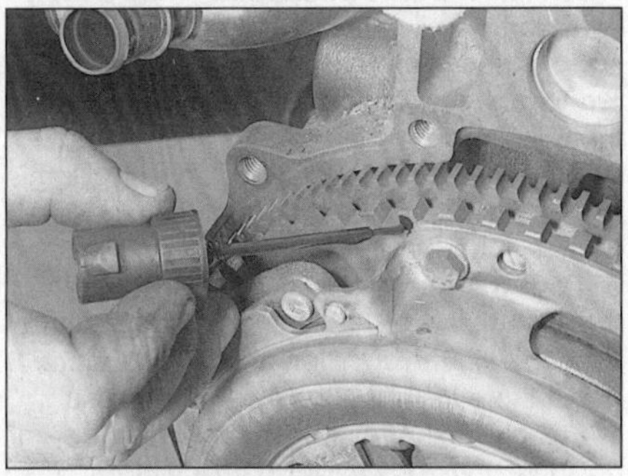

8.2 Mark the relationship of the pressure plate to the flywheel

8.3 Using a screwdriver in the ring gear teeth while unscrewing the clutch cover bolts

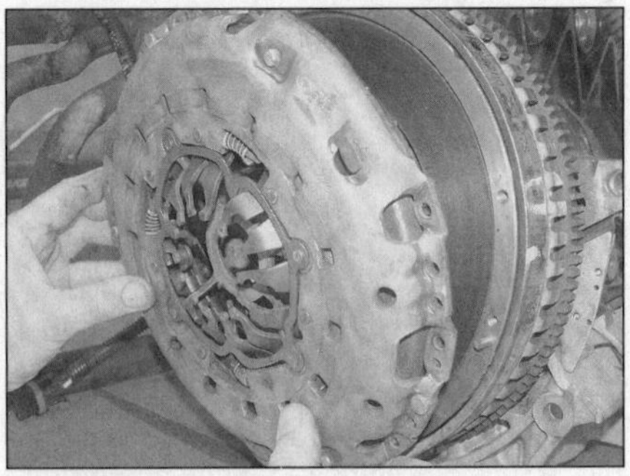

8.5a Withdraw the pressure plate assembly...

8.5b ...and the friction disc, noting which way round it is fitted

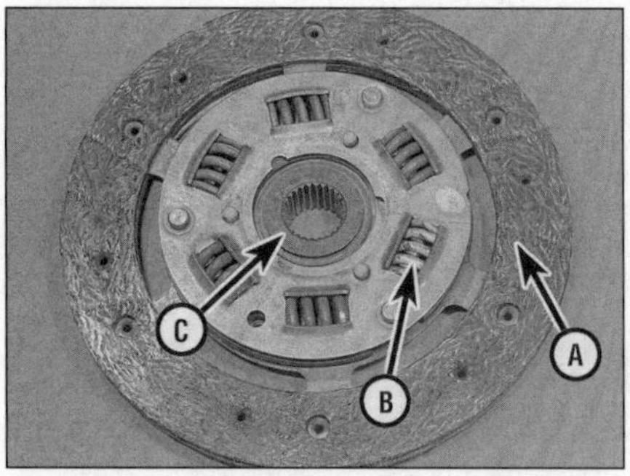

8.7 Inspect the friction disc linings (A), springs (B – where applicable) and splines (C)

8.10 Check the diaphragm spring fingers for wear, especially at the tips

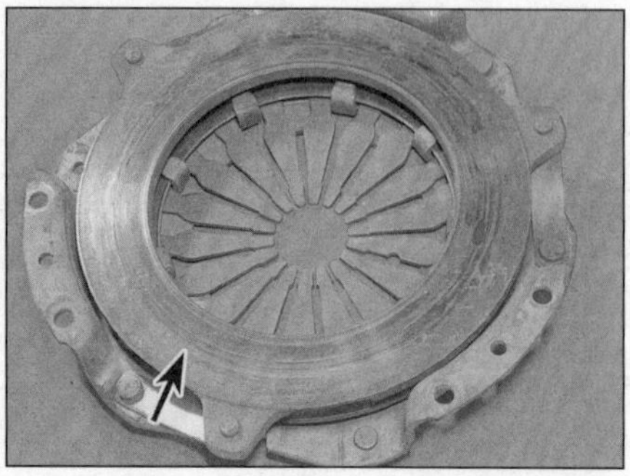
8.11 Check the machined face of the pressure plate

is actually worn enough to require renewal. It is also worth considering the renewal of the clutch components on a preventive basis if the engine and/or transmission have been removed for some other reason.

6 When cleaning clutch components, read first the warning at the beginning of this Section; remove the dust using a clean, dry cloth, and working in a well-ventilated atmosphere.

7 Check the friction disc linings for signs of wear, damage or oil contamination. If the friction material is cracked, burnt, scored or damaged, or if it is contaminated with oil or grease (shown by shiny black patches), the friction disc must be renewed **(see illustration)**. Check the depth of the rivets below the friction material surface. If any are at or near the surface of the friction material, then the friction disc must be renewed.

8 If the friction material is still serviceable, check that the centre boss splines are unworn, that the torsion springs are in good condition and securely fastened and that all the rivets are tight. If any wear or damage is found, the friction disc must be renewed.

9 If the friction material is fouled with oil, this must be due to an oil leak from the crankshaft oil seal, from the sump-to-cylinder block joint, or from the transmission input shaft. Renew the seal or repair the joint, as appropriate, as described in the appropriate part of Chapter 2 or 7, before installing the new friction disc.

10 Check the pressure plate assembly for obvious signs of wear or damage; shake it to check for loose rivets or worn or damaged fulcrum rings, and check that the drive straps securing the pressure plate to the cover do not show signs of overheating (such as a deep yellow or blue discoloration). If the diaphragm spring is worn or damaged, or if its pressure is in any way suspect, the pressure plate assembly should be renewed **(see illustration)**

11 Examine the machined bearing surfaces of the pressure plate and of the flywheel; they should be clean, completely flat, and free from scratches or scoring **(see illustration)**. If either is discoloured from excessive heat, or shows signs of cracks, it should be renewed – although minor damage of this nature can sometimes be polished away using emery paper.

12 Check that the release bearing contact surface rotates smoothly and easily, with no sign of noise or roughness. Also check that the surface itself is smooth and unworn, with no signs of cracks, pitting or scoring. If there is any doubt about its condition, the bearing must be renewed.

Refitting

13 On reassembly, ensure that the disc contact surfaces of the flywheel and pressure plate are completely clean, smooth, and free from oil or grease. Use solvent to remove any protective grease from new components.

14 Fit the friction disc so that its spring hub assembly faces away from the flywheel (5-speed transmissions); on 6-speed transmissions, the friction plate has a protruding small-diameter centre bush which locates into the crankshaft spigot bearing. There may also be a marking showing which way round the plate is to be refitted. Depending on the type of centralising tool being used, the friction disc may be held in position at this stage.

15 Refit the pressure plate assembly, aligning the marks made on dismantling (if the original pressure plate is re-used), and locating the pressure plate on its locating dowels. Fit the pressure plate bolts, but tighten them only finger-tight, so that the friction disc can still be moved.

16 The friction disc must now be centralised, so that when the transmission is refitted, its input shaft will pass through the splines at the centre of the friction disc.

17 Centralisation can be achieved by passing a screwdriver or other long bar through the friction disc and into the hole in the crankshaft; the friction disc can then be moved around until it is centred on the crankshaft hole.

18 Alternatively, a clutch-aligning-tool can be used to eliminate the guesswork; these can be obtained from most accessory shops. The normal type consists of a spigot bar with several different adapters, but a home-made aligning tool can be fabricated from a length of metal rod or wooden dowel which fits closely inside the crankshaft hole, and has insulating tape wound around it to match the diameter of the friction disc splined hole **(see illustration)**.

19 A more recent type of aligning tool works by clamping the friction disc to the pressure plate before locating the two items on the flywheel **(see illustrations)**.

8.18 Using a clutch alignment tool to centralise the friction disc

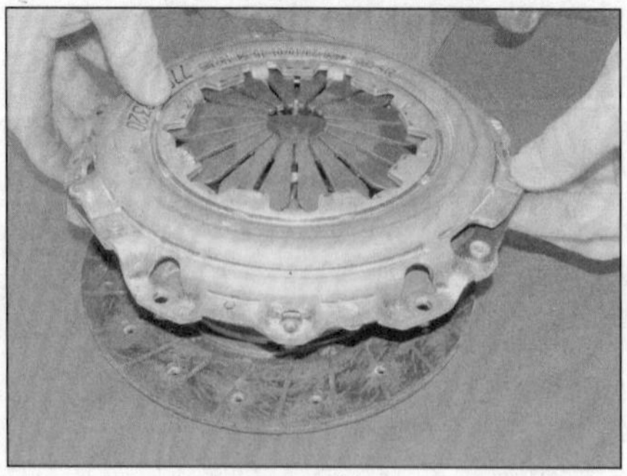
8.19a Centralise the pressure plate on the disc...

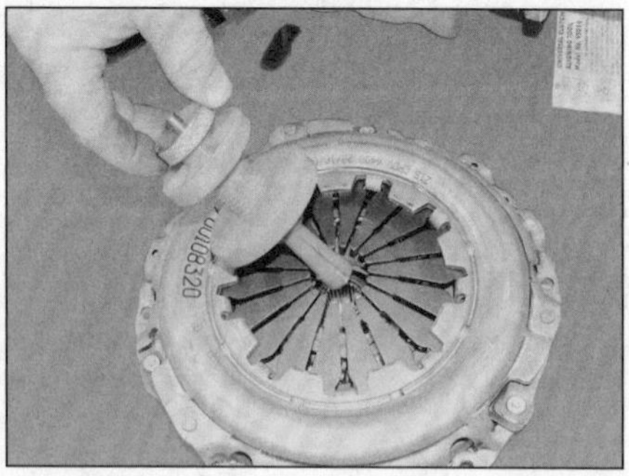
8.19b ...fit the tool and tighten to clamp the disc to the pressure plate...

20 When the friction disc is centralised, tighten the pressure plate bolts evenly and in a diagonal sequence to the specified torque setting **(see illustration)**.

21 Renault recommend not greasing the splines the transmission input shaft, to avoid potential damage to the clutch release bearing.

22 Refit the transmission as described in Chapter 7.

8.19c ...then locate the assembly on the flywheel

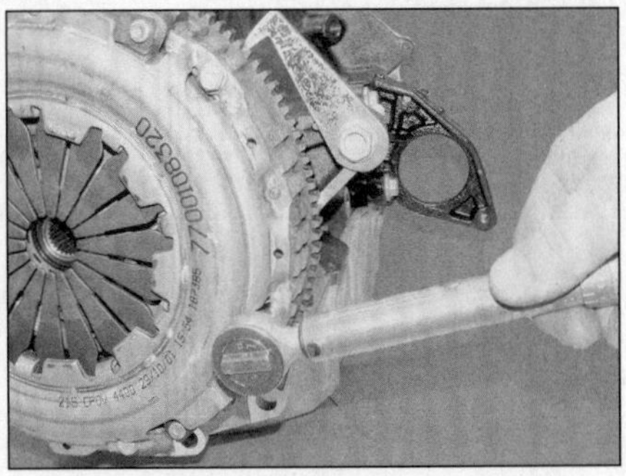

8.20 Hold the flywheel stationary while tightening the clutch cover bolts

Chapter 7
Manual transmission

Contents

	Section number
Gearchange mechanism – adjustment	3
Gearchange mechanism – removal and refitting	4
General information	1
Manual transmission – removal and refitting	7
Manual transmission overhaul – general information	8
Oil seals – renewal	5
Reversing light switch – testing, removal and refitting	6
Transmission oil – draining and refilling	2
Transmission oil level check	See Chapter 1A or 1B

Degrees of difficulty

Easy, suitable for novice with little experience	**Fairly easy,** suitable for beginner with some experience	**Fairly difficult,** suitable for competent DIY mechanic	**Difficult,** suitable for experienced DIY mechanic	**Very difficult,** suitable for expert DIY or professional

Specifications

General

Type	Five or six forward speeds (all synchromesh) and reverse, cable-operated gearchange mechanism. Final drive differential integral with main transmission

Designation

Five speed	JR5
Six speed	TL4

Lubrication

Type	Tranself TRJ 75W80
Capacity:	
JR5 transmission	2.4 litres
TL4 transmission	2.0 litres

Torque wrench settings

Torque wrench settings	Nm	lbf ft
Radiator crossmember:		
Front bolt	180	133
Side support bolts	21	15
Roadwheel bolts	110	81
Reverse light switch	23	17
Starter motor mounting bolts	44	32
Transmission bellhousing to engine	44	32
Transmission mounting:		
Centre nut	62	46
Mounting to transmission bolts	62	46
Mounting to body	62	46
Transmission oil drain plug	24	17

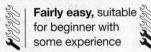

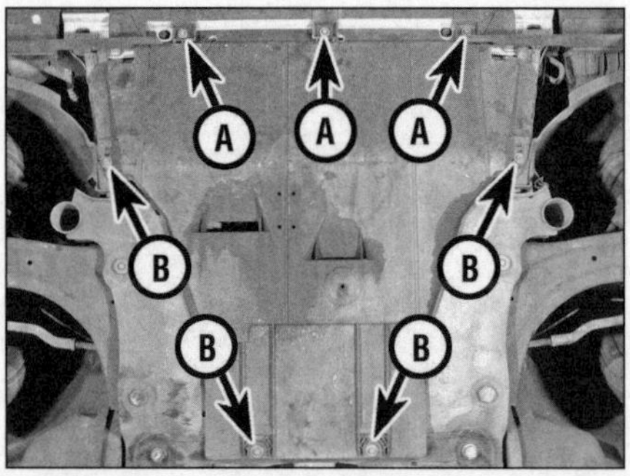

2.2 Slacken the front bolts (A) and remove the rear bolts (B)

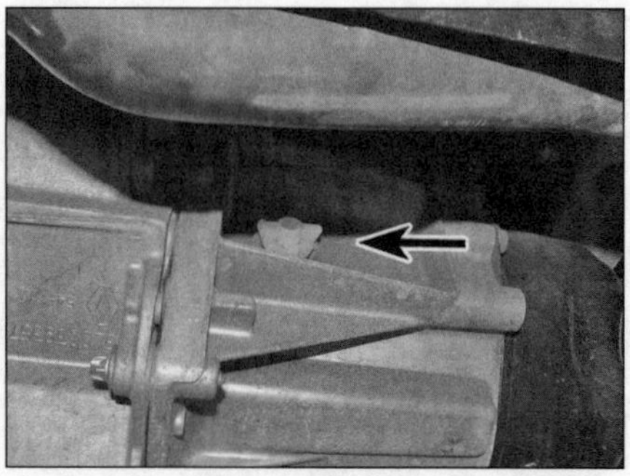
2.3a On 5-speed models, the filler plug is on the front...

2.3b ...while 6-speed models have the plug on the side

1 General information

The transmission is equipped with five or six forward gears, one reverse gear and a final drive differential, incorporated in one casing bolted to the left-hand end of the engine. The transmission type code is stamped into the transmission casing, either on top or on the underside.

Drive is transmitted from the crankshaft via the clutch to the input shaft which rotates in sealed ball-bearings, and has a splined extension to accept the clutch friction disc. From the input shaft, drive is transmitted to the output shaft, which rotates in a roller bearing at its right-hand end, and a sealed ball-bearing at its left-hand end. From the output shaft, drive is transmitted to the differential crown wheel, which rotates with the differential case and planetary gears, thus driving the side gears and driveshafts. The rotation of the planetary gears on their shaft allows the inner roadwheel to rotate at a slower speed than the outer roadwheel when the car is cornering.

The input and output shafts are arranged side-by-side, parallel to the crankshaft and driveshafts, so that their gear pinion teeth are in constant mesh. In the neutral position, the output shaft gear pinions rotate freely, so that drive cannot be transmitted to the crown wheel. Synchromesh is provided on all forward speeds. Gear selection is via a floor-mounted lever and twin cable mechanism.

The transmission selector cable causes the appropriate selector fork to move its respective synchro-sleeve along the shaft, in order to lock the gear pinion to the synchro-hub. Since the synchro-hubs are splined to the output shaft, this locks the pinion to the shaft, so that drive can be transmitted. To ensure that gearchanging can be made quickly and quietly, a synchromesh system is fitted to all forward gears, consisting of baulk rings and spring-loaded fingers, as well as the gear pinions and synchro-hubs. The synchromesh cones are formed on the mating faces of the baulk rings and gear pinions.

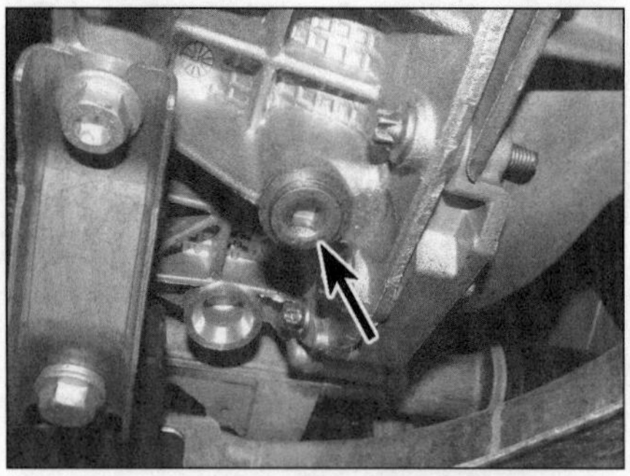
2.3c The 5-speed unit drain plug (arrowed)...

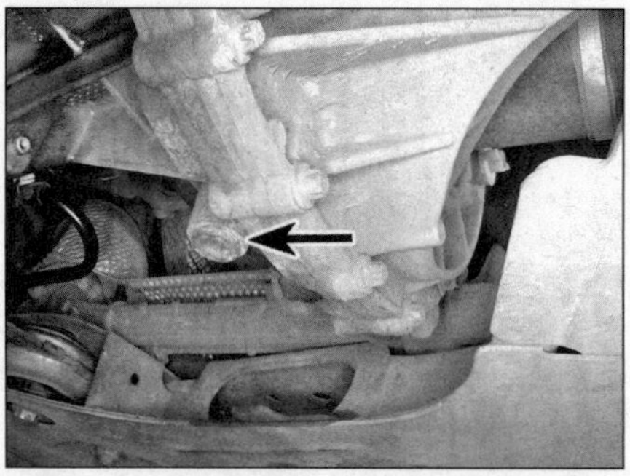
2.3d ...and the 6-speed version (arrowed)

2.4 Unscrew the filler/level plug (6 speed shown)

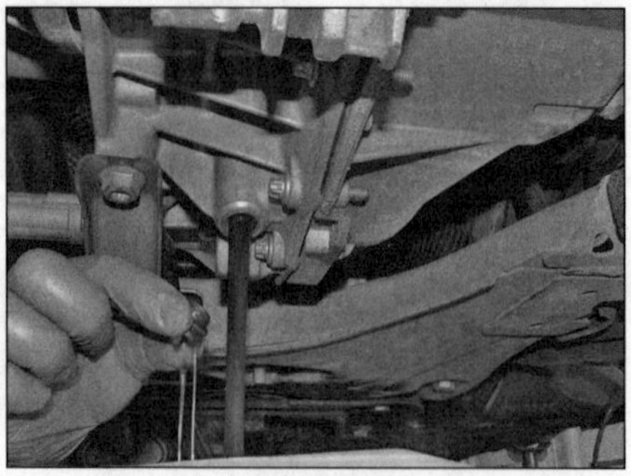
2.5 Unscrew the drain plug, and allow the oil to drain (5 speed shown)

2 Transmission oil – draining and refilling

1 This operation is much quicker and more efficient if the car is first taken on a journey of sufficient length to warm the engine/transmission up to operating temperature.

2 Park the car on level ground, switch off the engine and apply the handbrake firmly. For improved access, jack up the car and support it securely on axle stands (see *Jacking and vehicle support*), or alternatively position the car over an inspection pit or on car ramps. Note that, to ensure accuracy, the car must be level when checking the oil level. Remove the engine compartment undershield **(see illustration)**.

3 Remove all traces of dirt from around the drain and filler/level plugs. On 5-speed transmissions, the filler/level plug is located on the front-facing side of the transmission, while 6-speed units have the plug on the left-hand end face, at the front. The drain plug on 5-speed transmissions is underneath, while the 6-speed transmission drain plug is on the left-hand face, at the rear **(see illustrations)**.

4 Unscrew and remove the filler/level plug – this will probably be very tight **(see illustration)**.

5 Position a suitable container under the transmission, then unscrew the drain plug and allow the oil to drain completely into the container **(see illustration)**. If the oil is hot, take precautions against scalding. Clean both the filler/level and the drain plugs, being especially careful to wipe any metallic particles off the magnetic inserts, where applicable. The sealing washers should be renewed whenever they are disturbed.

6 When the oil has finished draining, clean the drain plug threads and those of the transmission casing. Fit a new seal to the drain plug **(see illustration)**. Fit the drain plug and tighten it to the specified torque.

7 Refilling the transmission is an extremely awkward operation, especially on the 6 speed transmission. Above all, allow plenty of time for the oil level to settle properly before checking it. Note that the car must be level when checking the oil level.

8 Refill the transmission with the exact amount of the specified type of oil The oil should be just below the filler plug hole. Refit the filler/level plug and tighten securely **(see illustration)**.

9 Refit the engine undershield and then lower the car to the ground.

3 Gearchange mechanism – adjustment

Note: *Adjustment is only possible on the 6-speed transmission.*

1 Remove the centre console **(see illustration)** as described in Chapter 11, Section 23.

2 The transmission must be in the neutral position.

3 Release the locking catch on the selector cable by prising it up using a small screwdriver **(see illustration)**.

4 Fabricate a suitable 'spacer' (eg, a thin strip of wood, or similar) 5.0 ± 0.5 mm thick, into the gap between the right-hand side of the lever and the housing **(see illustration)**.

5 Hold the gear lever in the 3rd gear position, tight up against the inserted 'spacer'.

6 Refasten the locking catch on the selector cable by pushing it fully home **(see illustration)**.

7 Check that all gears can be selected satisfactorily, then refit the removed components. Road test the car to confirm the adjustment.

4 Gearchange mechanism – removal and refitting

Gear lever

Removal

1 Ensure that the gear lever is in Neutral.

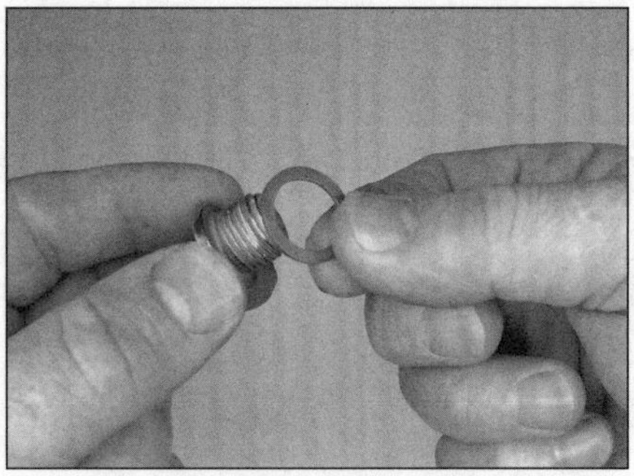

2.6 Fit a new seal

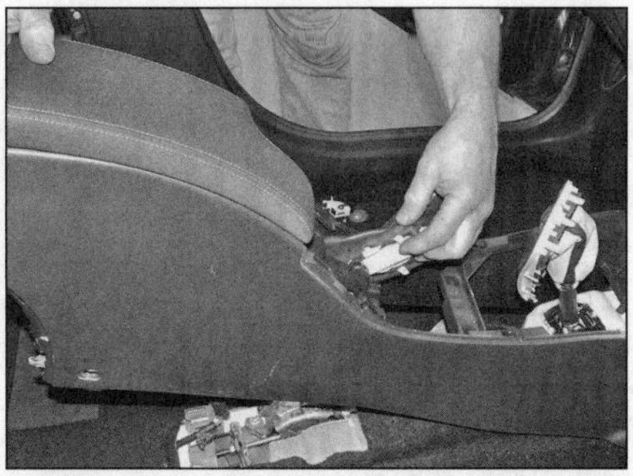

3.1 Remove the centre console

2 Disconnect the battery and then remove the centre console as described in Chapter 11, Section 23. Unclip the wiring loom from the side of the gear lever.

3 At the base of the gear lever, press the locking button and release the lower selector cable. Using an open ended spanner prise off the upper cable.

4 Make a 200 mm cut in the carpet **(see illustration)** at the rear of the gear lever and then move the soundproofing material to the side.

5 Lift of the protective cover from the airbag controller (discard the cover – Renault insist that it must be replaced).

6 Remove the mounting bolts and lift the gear lever assembly from the vehicle.

Refitting

7 Refitting is a reversal of removal, but check and adjust (if necessary) the gear change mechanism as described in Section 3.

2.8 Filling the transmission with oil

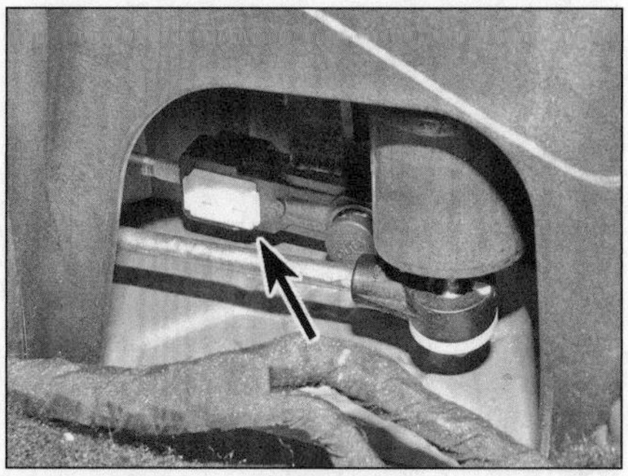

3.3 Prise up the locking catch (arrowed)

Gear selector cables

Removal

8 Remove the battery, battery tray and ECU as described in Chapter 5A.

9 Using an open ended spanner prise the gear change cables from the ball joints on the transmission. Unclip the outer cable stops from the top of the transmission **(see illustration)**.

10 Remove the centre console as described in Chapter 11, Section 23. Unclip the wiring loom from the side of the gear lever.

11 At the base of the gear lever, press the locking button and release the lower selector cable. Using an open ended spanner prise off the upper cable.

12 Remove the outer cable sleeves from the stops at the front of the gear change **(see illustration)**.

13 The cover plate at the front of the transmission tunnel must now be removed.

3.4 Fit a suitable 5mm spacer

3.6 Note how the locking catch engages with the threaded section of the cable (arrowed)

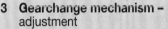

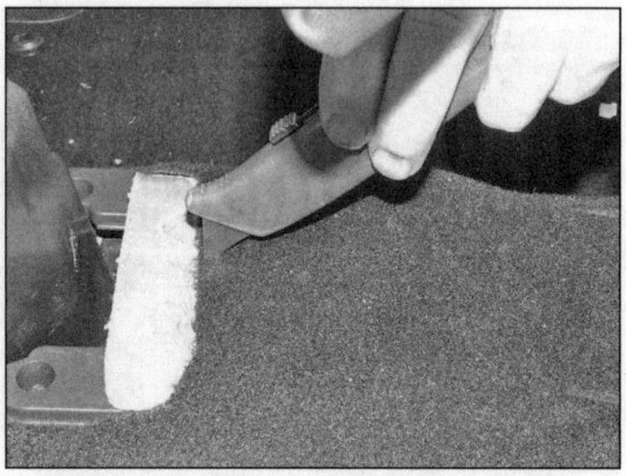

4.4 Make a short cut in the carpet

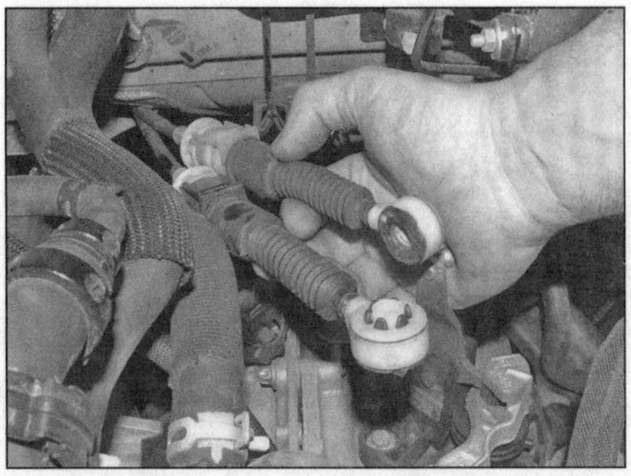

4.9 Remove the cables

4.12 Remove the outer sleeves

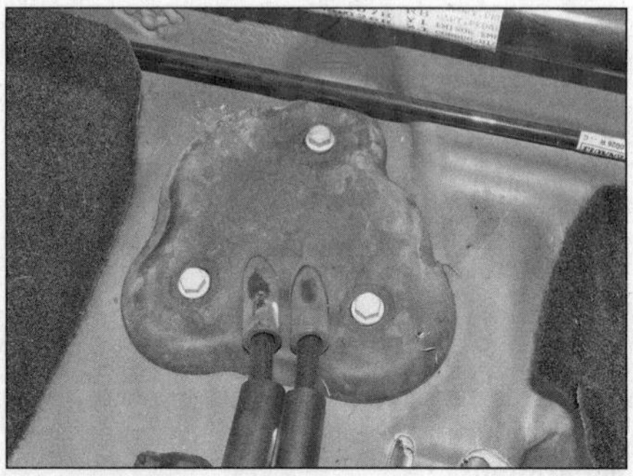

4.13 Remove the cover bolts (shown with heater distribution unit removed)

Access is extremely limited, but can be improved by partial removal of the carpet. Remove the three bolts **(see illustration)**.

14 Jack up and support the front of the vehicle (see *Jacking and vehicle support* in the reference section).

15 Working underneath the vehicle remove the exhaust system as described in Chapter 4A or 4B and then remove the heatshield.

16 With the aid of an assistant remove the cables by withdrawing them Into the engine bay.

Refitting

17 Refitting is a reversal of removal, but check and (if necessary) adjust the gear change mechanism as described in Section 3

5 Oil seals - renewal

Driveshaft seals

1 Apply the handbrake, then jack up the front of the car and support it on axle stands (see *Jacking and vehicle support*). Remove the right-hand wheel.

2 Drain the transmission oil as described in Section 2.

3 Referring to Chapter 8 remove the appropriate driveshaft from the transmission.

4 Wipe clean the old oil seal, and measure its fitted depth below the casing edge. This is necessary to determine the correct fitted position of the new oil seal.

5 Free the old oil seal, either by levering it out **(see illustration)** or using a small drift to tap the outer edge of the seal inwards so that the opposite edge of the seal tilts out of the casing.

6 Wipe clean the oil seal seating in the casing.

7 Lubricate the sealing lip of the new oil seal with clean transmission oil and making sure its sealing lip is facing inwards, carefully slide it into position. Press the seal squarely into the transmission until it is positioned at the same depth as the original was prior to removal. If necessary, the seal can be tapped into position using a piece of metal tube or a socket which bears only on the hard outer edge of the seal **(see illustrations)**.

8 Reconnect the driveshaft to the transmission as described in Chapter 8.

9 Refill the transmission with oil as described in Section 2.

10 Refit the roadwheel and lower the car to the ground. Tighten the wheel bolts to the specified torque.

Input shaft seal

11 It is not possible to renew the input shaft oil seal without first dismantling the transmission. The guide tube assembly is a press-fit in the housing, and is removed inwards. Oil seal renewal should therefore be entrusted to a Renault dealer or transmission overhaul specialist.

6 Reversing light switch - testing, removal and refitting

Testing

1 The reversing light circuit is controlled by a plunger-type switch. On 5-speed units, the switch is screwed into the left-hand side of the transmission casing, next to the driveshaft inner joint, while 6-speed units have the switch on the top of the casing. If a fault develops in the circuit, first ensure that the circuit fuse has not blown.

2 To test the switch, disconnect the wiring connector, and use a multimeter (set to the resistance function) or a battery-and-bulb test circuit to check that there is continuity between the switch terminals only when reverse gear is selected. If this is not the case, and there are no obvious breaks or other damage to the wires, the switch is faulty, and must be renewed.

Removal

5-speed models

3 Firmly apply the handbrake, then jack up the front of the car and support it on axle stands (see *Jacking and vehicle support*). Remove the engine compartment undershield.

4 Disconnect the wiring plug.

5 Have a replacement switch (or suitable sealing plug) to hand and unscrew the switch

5.5 Carefully remove the oil seal

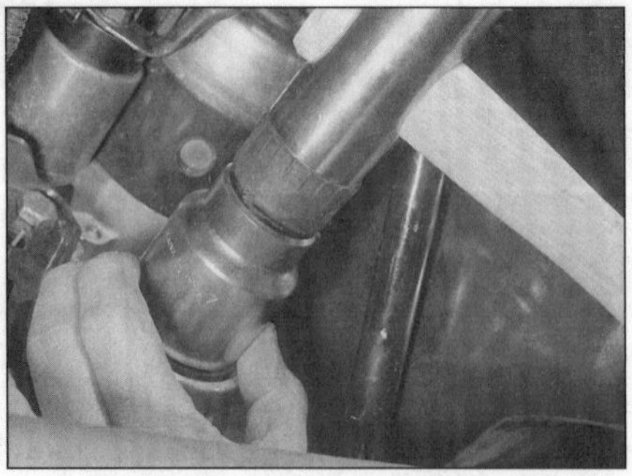

5.7a Tap the new seal into position using a socket or metal tube...

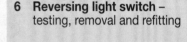

5.7b ...until it is at the required fitted depth

(see illustration). Immediately seal the hole. If this action is performed quickly enough there will be little if any fluid loss. If fluid escapes check the oil level and top up as required - as described in Section 2 of this Chapter.

6-speed models

6 Remove the battery and battery tray as described in Chapter 5A.

7 Disconnect the wiring plug **(see illustration)** and then unscrew the switch from the transmission. Recover the sealing washer.

Refitting

8 Fit a new sealing washer to the switch, then screw it back into the transmission casing and tighten it securely. Reconnect the wiring, and test the operation of the circuit. If any oil was lost when the switch was removed, check the oil level as described in Chapter 1A or 1B.

7 Manual transmission – removal and refitting

Note: *This Section describes the removal of the transmission leaving the engine in position in the car. Alternatively, the engine and transmission can be removed together, as described in Chapter 2C, then separated on the bench.*

Removal

1 Disconnect the battery - see *Disconnecting the battery* in Chapter 5A.

2 Where fitted remove the engine cover and

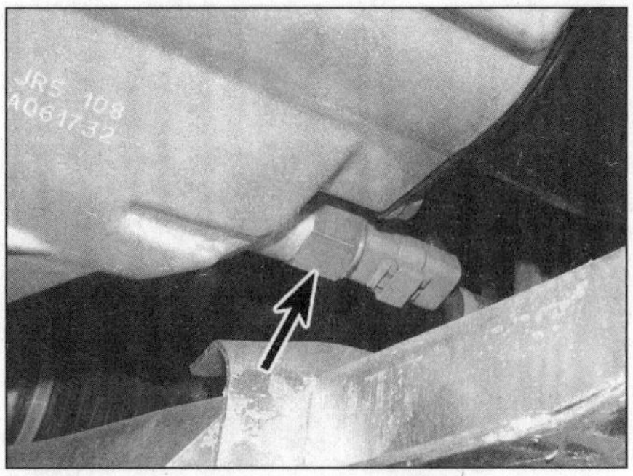

6.5 The reversing light switch on the 5-speed transmission

then remove the battery, ECU and battery tray as described in Chapter 5A **(see illustrations)**. On diesel models move the boost control solenoid to one side.

3 Remove the air inlet duct and air filter housing as described in Chapter 4A or 4B.

4 On diesel models disconnect and remove the inter cooler hoses from the top of the engine.

5 Disconnect the gearchange cables from the top of the transmission, as described in Section 4 and then remove the transmission breather pipe **(see illustration)**.

6 Using the information in Chapter 6, first drain the clutch system via the bleed nipple, then disconnect the hydraulic fluid pipe from the slave cylinder.

7 Alternatively clamp the master cylinder supply hose (with a brake pipe clamp at the supply pipe on the brake master cylinder. Disconnect the clutch hydraulic pipe as

6.7 Disconnecting the wiring plug on 6-speed transmissions

described in Chapter 6 and then seal the end of the pipe.

8 Unbolt the earth cable (s) and release the wiring harness from the top of the transmission. Move the wiring to one side **(see illustration)**.

9 Disconnect the reversing light switch on 6 speed transmissions using the information in Section 6.

10 Apply the handbrake, then jack up the front of the car and support it on axle stands (see *Jacking and vehicle support*). Remove the engine compartment undershield **(see illustration)** and both front roadwheels.

11 Drain the transmission oil as described in Section 2 and on 5 speed transmissions disconnect the reversing light switch.

12 Remove the front bumper cover and the wing liners as described in Chapter 11.

13 Remove the driveshafts as described in Chapter 8.

7.2a Remove the battery and...

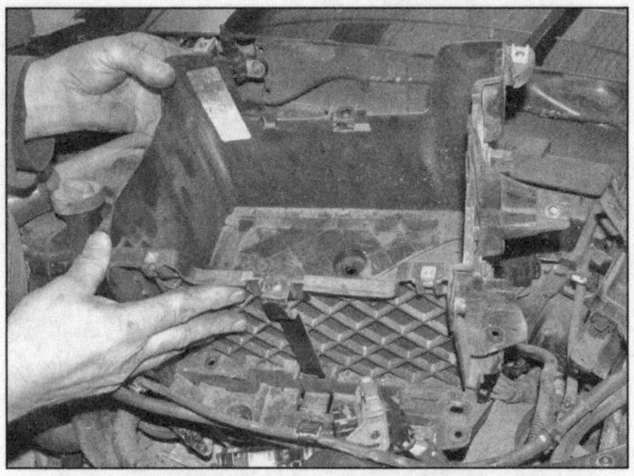

7.2b ...the battery tray

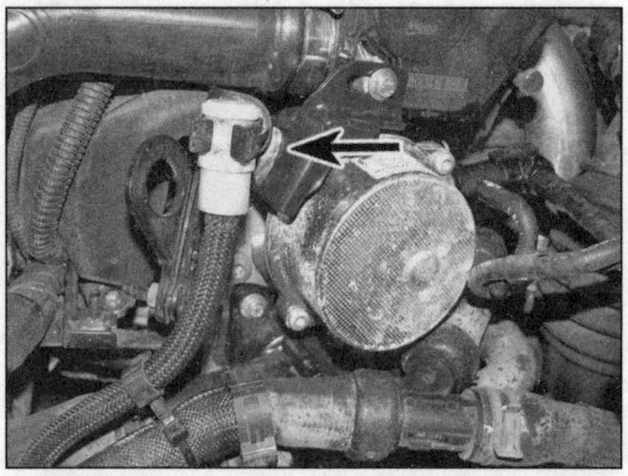

7.5 Unclip and remove the breather hose (arrowed)

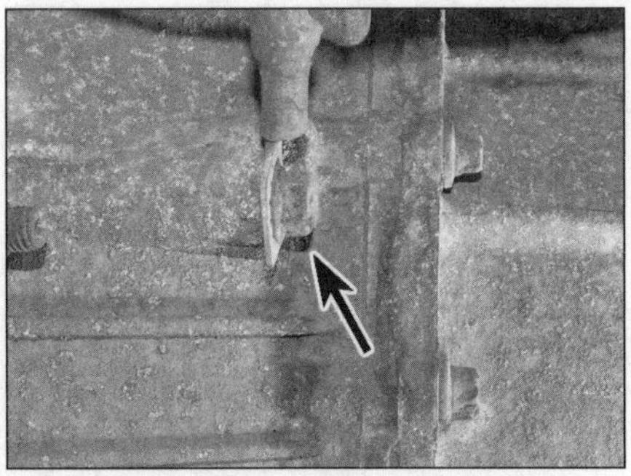

7.8a Remove the earth connection from the transmission (arrowed)

7.8b Remove the wiring loom and secure it to the side

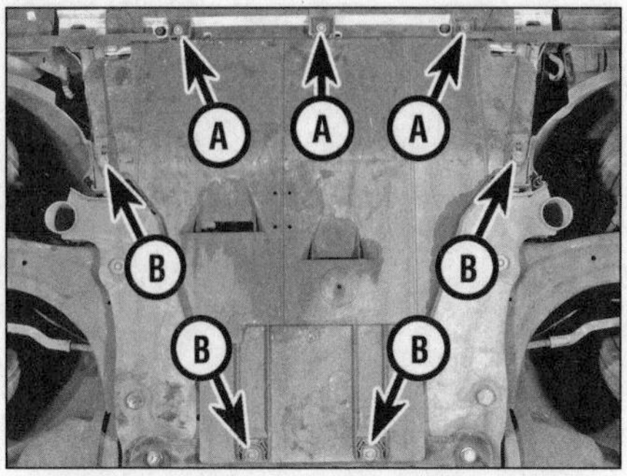

7.10 Slacken the front bolts (A) and remove the rear bolts (B)

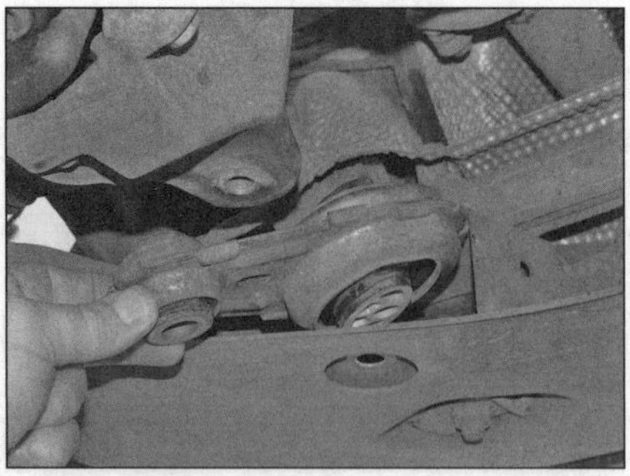

7.14 Remove the rear mounting/steady bar

7.15 Remove the lower bolts (arrowed)

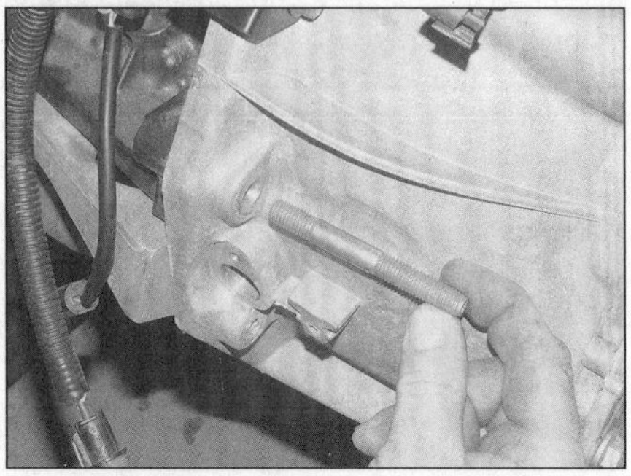

7.19 6-speed models have an engine-to-transmission stud at the front

7.20 With care, the transmission can be supported from below

14 Remove the lower engine support (steady bar) as described in Chapter 2A or 2B and then remove the starter motor as described in Chapter 5A **(see illustration)**.

15 At both sides remove the radiator lower support panel side struts. Unclip the wiring loom and then unbolt and remove the support panel from beneath the radiator. There are two bolts at the front and one below **(see illustration)**.

16 Remove the front suspension subframe as described in Chapter 10.

17 Disconnect the crankshaft speed/position sensor wiring connector as described in Chapter 4A or 4B.

18 Where applicable, release the clip securing the coolant pipes to the front of the transmission, and move the pipes to one side.

19 Loosen the transmission-to-engine nuts, bolts and studs – do not remove all of them at this stage **(see illustration)**.

20 The weight of the transmission must now be supported, as the engine left-hand mounting must be unscrewed and removed. Although this can be accomplished from below, with the aid of an assistant, it is recommended that an engine support bar or engine crane is used, to support the weight from above **(see illustration)**. Note that, especially with the 6-speed unit, it will be necessary to lower the engine/transmission at the transmission end during the removal procedure.

21 With the transmission weight supported, loosen and remove the bolts securing the engine left-hand mounting to the chassis leg and the top of the transmission – access to the rear bolt in particular is not easy. Remove the bracket from the top of the transmission **(see illustration)**.

22 Lower the transmission until the housing is clear of the chassis on the left-hand side.

23 Unscrew and remove the transmission-to-engine nuts, bolts and studs, noting that some of them are used to retain other mounting brackets **(see illustration)**.

24 Withdraw the transmission off the engine, taking care that its weight is not allowed to hang on the input shaft **(see illustration)**. The

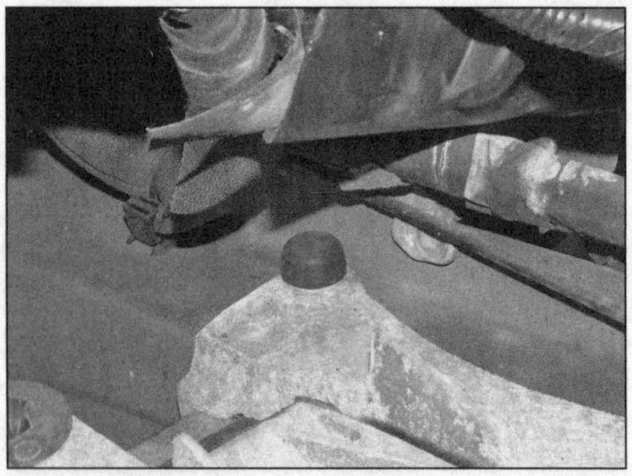

7.21a Remove the protective cap from the rear mounting bolt

7.21b Remove the bolts (arrowed)...

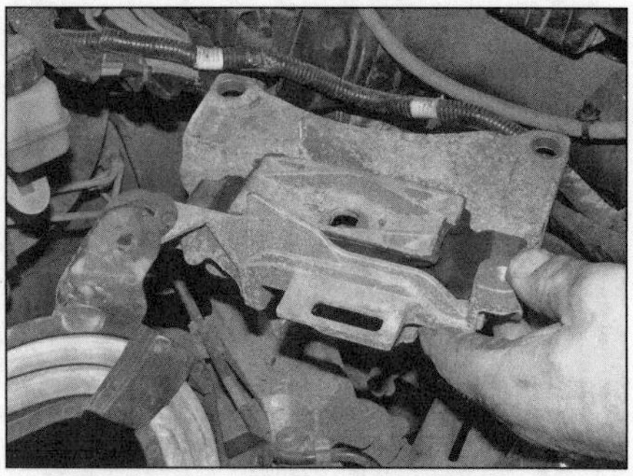

7.21c ...and remove the bracket

7.21d Remove the bracket from the transmission

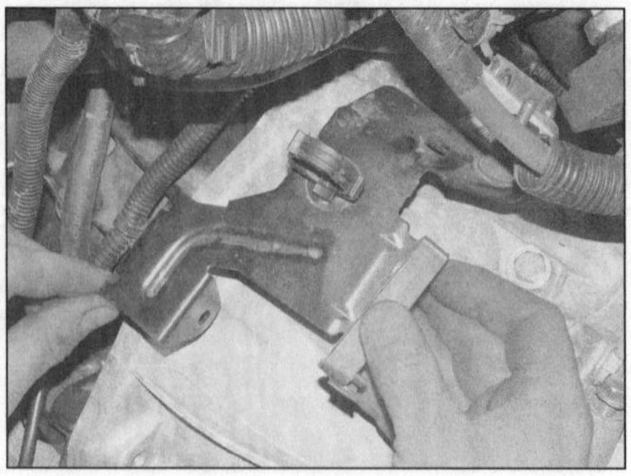

7.23 Note that some of the engine-to-transmission bolts also secure brackets

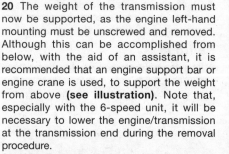

7.24 Withdraw the transmission off the engine

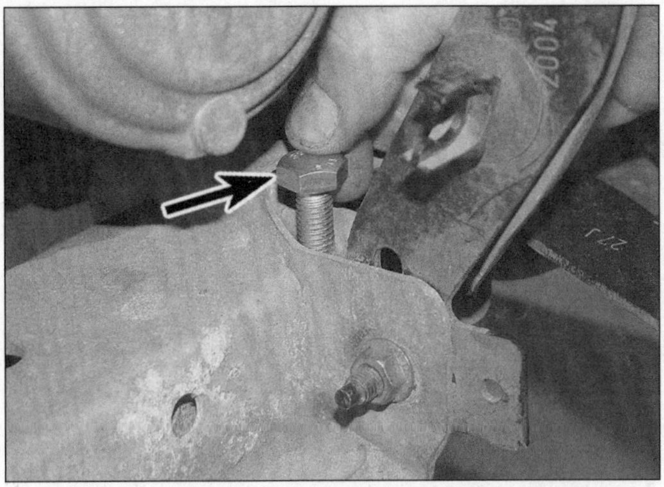

7.25a Insert a suitable 13 mm spacer (such as this M13 bolt)...

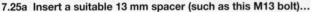

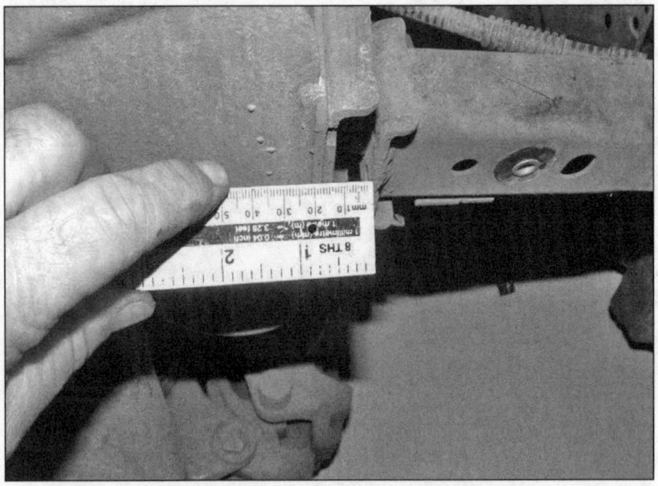

7.25b ...or simply measure the gap to ensure it is correct

6-speed transmission in particular is a heavy unit, and it is recommended that an assistant is on hand to help. Lower the unit to the ground, and remove from under the car.

Refitting

25 Refitting is a reversal of removal, noting the following additional points:

a) Make sure that the location dowels are correctly positioned in the transmission.

b) **Do not** *grease the splines the transmission input shaft. (a special lubricant is supplied with most clutch kits).*

c) When refitting the radiator lower crossmember/support panel, fit the fasteners and side plates loosely, then insert a 13 mm spacer between it and the subframe, at the rear. We used a 13 mm diameter bolt – this should be withdrawn once the nuts have been tightened each side ***(see illustrations)****. The crossmember forms part of the deformable front structure of the car, and the gap left by using the spacer is essential.*

d) Check the transmission oil level with reference to Chapter 1A or 1B.

e) Tighten all nuts and bolts to the specified torque.

f) On 6-speed transmissions, adjust the gearchange mechanism if necessary, as described in Section 3.

8 Manual transmission overhaul – general information

Overhauling a manual transmission is a difficult and involved job for the DIY home mechanic. In addition to dismantling and reassembling many small parts, clearances must be precisely measured and, if necessary, changed by selecting shims and spacers. Transmission internal components are also often difficult to obtain, and in many instances, extremely expensive. Because of this, if the transmission develops a fault or becomes noisy, the best course of action is to have the unit overhauled by a specialist repairer, or to obtain an exchange reconditioned unit.

Nevertheless, it is not impossible for the more experienced mechanic to overhaul a transmission, provided the special tools are available and the job is done in a deliberate step-by-step manner so that nothing is overlooked.

The tools necessary for an overhaul include internal and external circlip pliers, bearing pullers, a slide-hammer, a set of pin punches, a dial test indicator, and possibly a hydraulic press. In addition, a large, sturdy workbench and a vice will be required.

During dismantling of the transmission, make careful notes of how each component is fitted, to make reassembly easier and more accurate.

Before dismantling the transmission, it will help if you have some idea what area is malfunctioning. Certain problems can be closely related to specific areas in the transmission, which can make component examination and renewal easier. Refer to the *Fault finding* Section at the end of this manual for more information.

Chapter 8
Driveshafts

Contents

	Section number
Driveshaft – removal and refitting	2
Driveshaft gaiter and constant velocity (CV) joint check	See Chapter 1A or 1B
Driveshaft overhaul – general information	5
General information	1
Outer constant velocity joint gaiter – renewal	3
Driveshaft inner joint gaiter – renewal	4

Degrees of difficulty

Easy, suitable for novice with little experience	**Fairly easy,** suitable for beginner with some experience	**Fairly difficult,** suitable for competent DIY mechanic	**Difficult,** suitable for experienced DIY mechanic	**Very difficult,** suitable for expert DIY or professional

Specifications

General

Driveshaft type	Solid steel shafts, splined to inner and outer constant velocity joints, vibration damper fitted on some right-hand driveshafts

Torque wrench settings	**Nm**	**lbf ft**
Anti-roll bar link rod nut	44	32
Driveshaft retaining nut*	280	207
Driveshaft support bearing bolts*	21	16
Roadwheel bolts	110	81
Suspension strut to swivel hub bolts	180	133
Track rod end balljoint nut	37	27

** Use new nuts/bolts*

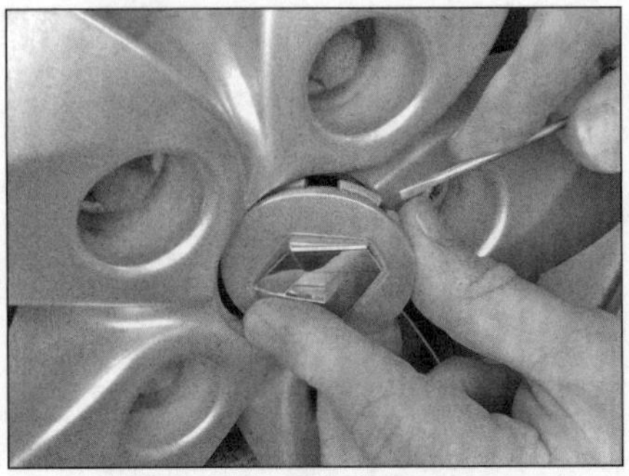

2.2a Remove the centre cap

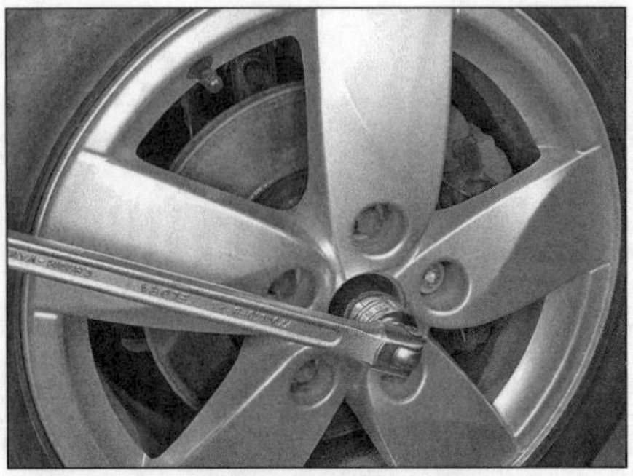

2.2b Slacken the driveshaft nut with the car resting on its wheels

1 General information

Drive is transmitted from the differential to the front wheels by means of two, unequal-length driveshafts.

Each driveshaft is fitted with an inner and outer constant velocity (CV) joint. The inner constant velocity joint is of the spider-and-yoke type and the outer joint is of the ball-and-cage type. Each outer joint is splined to engage with the wheel hub, and is threaded so that it can be fastened to the hub by a large nut. The inner joint is also splined to engage with the differential.

On the right-hand driveshaft, the inner constant velocity (CV) joint is located approximately halfway along the shaft length, and the joint is supported by the rear of the cylinder block via a support bearing and bracket.

2 Driveshaft – removal and refitting

Removal

1 Drain the transmission oil/fluid as described in Chapter 7. Alternatively raise the side of the vehicle you are working on high enough to minimise (or eliminate) the loss of fluid from the transmission.

2 Remove the wheel trim/centre cap (as applicable), then slacken the driveshaft nut with the car resting on its wheels **(see illustrations)**. Also slacken the wheel bolts.

3 Chock the rear wheels of the car, firmly apply the handbrake, then jack up the front of the car and support it on axle stands (see *Jacking and vehicle support*). Remove the appropriate front roadwheel.

TOOL TiP

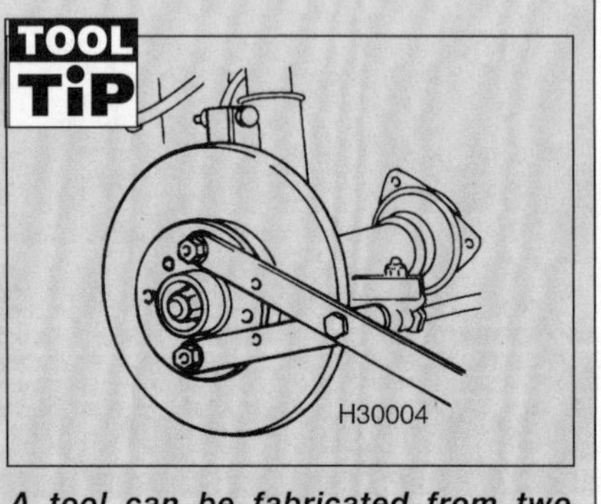

A tool can be fabricated from two lengths of steel strip (one long, one short) and a nut and bolt; the nut and bolt forming the pivot of a forked tool

4 If the driveshaft nut was not slackened with the wheels on the ground (see paragraph 1), refit at least two roadwheel bolts to the front hub, tightening them securely, then have an assistant firmly depress the brake pedal to prevent the front hub from rotating, whilst you slacken and remove the driveshaft retaining nut. Alternatively, a tool can be fabricated from two lengths of steel strip (one long, one short) and a nut and bolt; the nut and bolt forming the pivot of a forked tool **(see Tool Tip)**.

5 Slacken the nut securing the steering gear track rod end balljoint to the swivel hub. Use a torx key to counter hold the ball joint taper. Leave the nut attached by just a few threads. Release the balljoint tapered shank using a universal balljoint separator, then unscrew the nut completely, and separate the joint **(see illustrations)**.

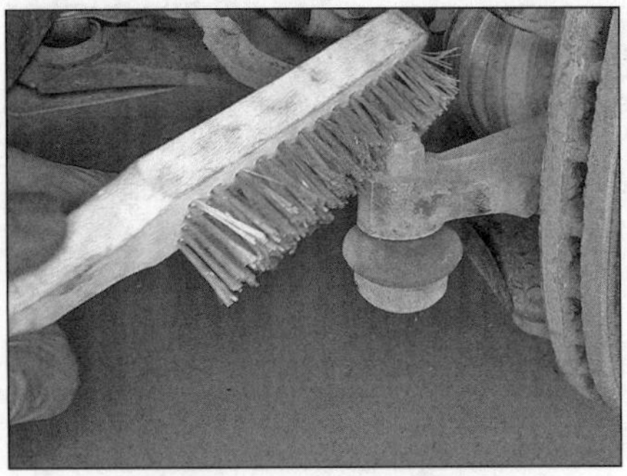

2.5a Clean the exposed threads

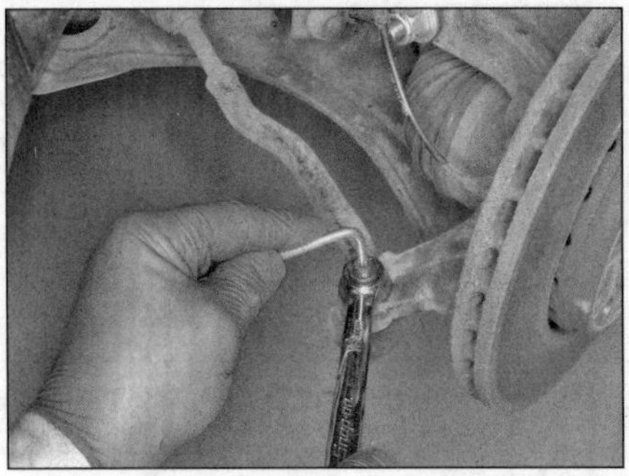

2.5b Loosen the track rod end balljoint nut...

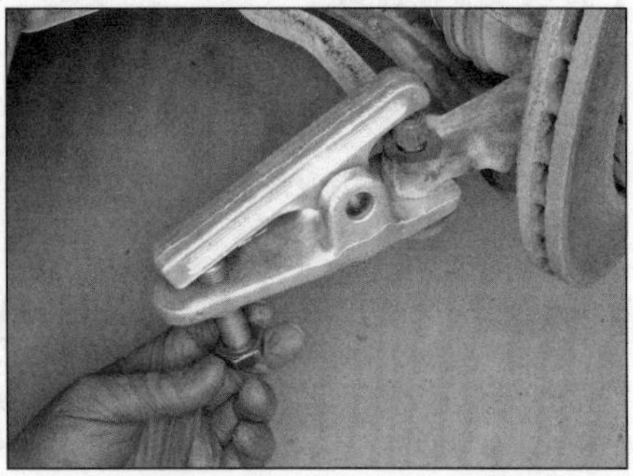

2.5c ...then use a balljoint separator tool...

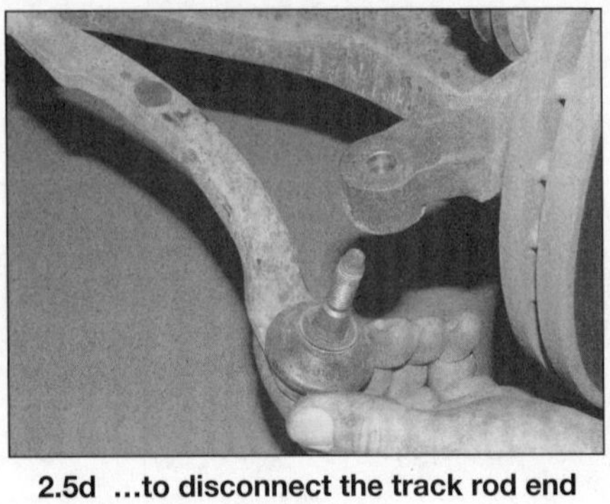

2.5d ...to disconnect the track rod end balljoint

2.6a Unscrew the link rod upper nut, using an Allen key to hold the stud...

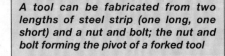

2.6b ...and separate the link rod from the strut bracket

6 Unscrew the upper nut from the anti-roll bar link rod, using a hex key to prevent the stud turning. Pull the link rod away from the strut mounting bracket **(see illustrations)**.

7 Disconnect the ABS wheel sensor wiring connector from the base of the swivel hub. Mark the position of the brake hose on the bracket and then prise it free. Unbolt the bracket and remove it strut/hub **(see illustrations)**.

8 Before removing the strut to swivel hub nut/bolts ensure the driveshaft is free to move in the hub. Apply penetrating fluid and then using a copper headed hammer drive the shaft into the hub **(see illustration)**. Fit the old driveshaft hub nut if there is any change of damaging the threads on the driveshaft.

9 Note the orientation of the bolts and then remove the nuts and bolts from the hub/strut. Lever the swivel hub free from the strut with a suitable lever **(see illustrations)**.

10 The splined end of the driveshaft now has to be fully released from its location in the hub.

11 Pull the disc/hub outwards, and turn it to allow the driveshaft to be withdrawn through the hub. It's helpful to have an assistant on hand here, to pull the hub outwards, while you slide out the driveshaft **(see illustration)**. **Note:** *Once the left-hand driveshaft has been removed from the hub, there is nothing to prevent it dropping out of the transmission – be prepared to catch it.*

12 If working on the right-hand driveshaft, unscrew the bolt securing the driveshaft collar to the support bearing on the back of the engine **(see illustration)**. On some models a single bolt is fitted and the bracket pivots away. Other models have two bolts and a separate bracket. Discard the bolt(s) – new ones must be fitted.

13 Pull the driveshaft out of the transmission, and remove it, ensuring that neither of the CV joints is bent excessively during the procedure. Also take care that the joint gaiters do not suffer unnecessary damage during removal. On the right-hand driveshaft, recover the support bearing collar **(see illustration)**.

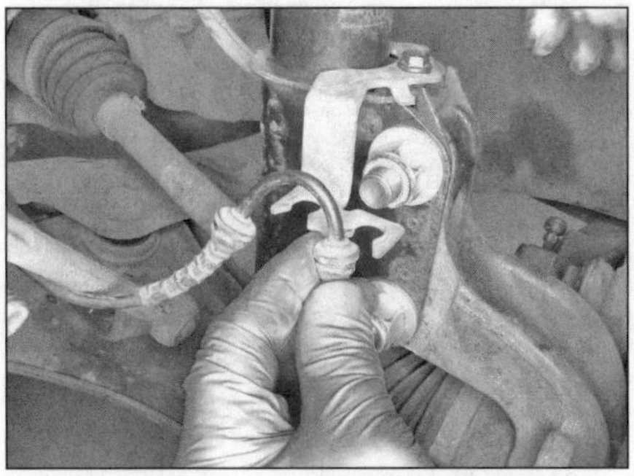

2.7a Prise free the ABS sensor loom...

2.7b ...and the brake flexible hose

2.7c Remove the bracket

2.8 Drive the shaft into the hub

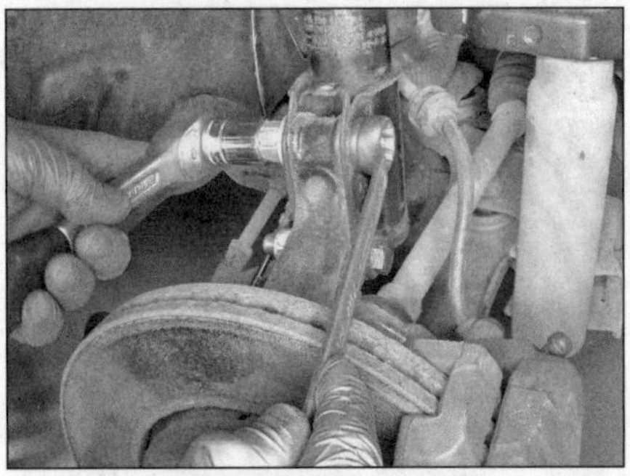

2.9a Remove the nuts...

2.9b ...and drive out the bolts

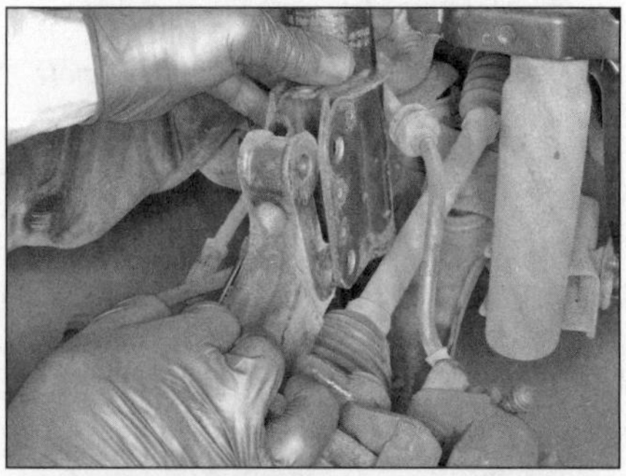

2.9c Release the hub from the strut

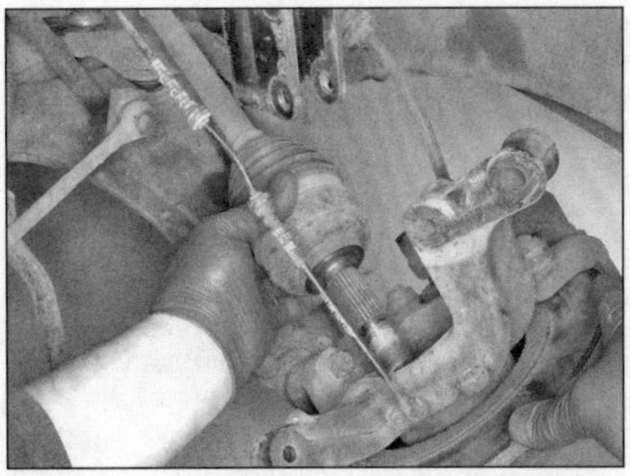

2.11 Pull the disc/hub out, and turn it to remove the driveshaft splined end

2.12 On the right-hand driveshaft, undo the two support plate bolt (arrowed)

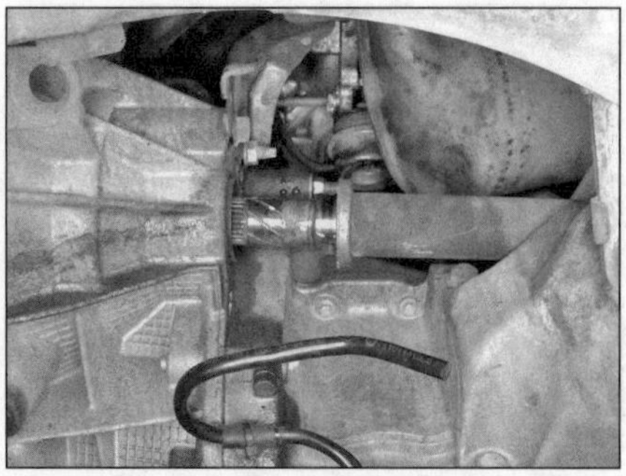

2.13 Removing the right-hand driveshaft

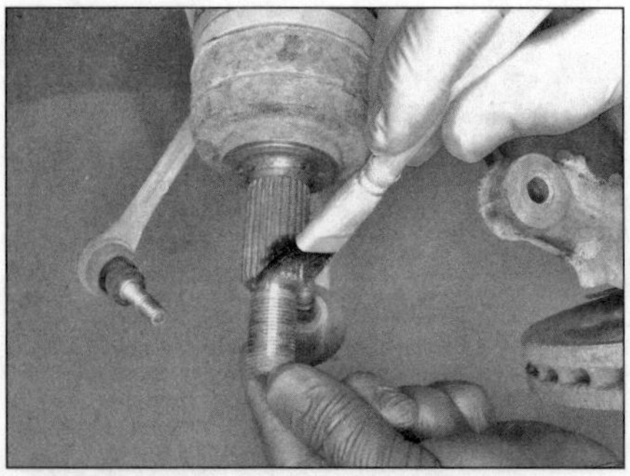

2.14 Apply an anti-seize compound to the driveshaft splines

3.3 Pull back the gaiter

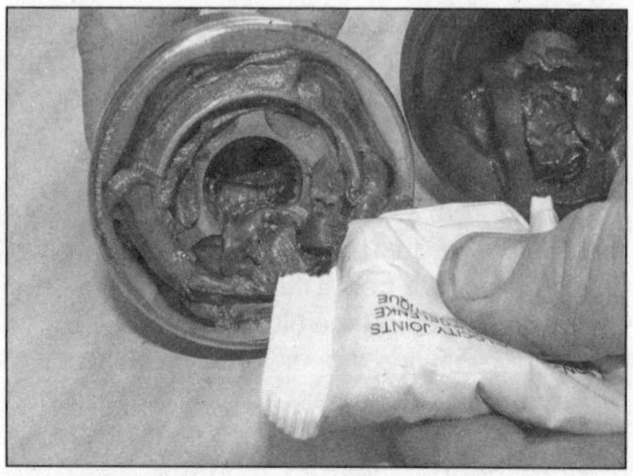

3.5 Fill the joint with fresh grease

3.8a Crimp the large clip in place...

Refitting

14 Refitting is a reversal of removal, noting the following points:

a) Whenever a driveshaft is removed, the driveshaft oil seals in the transmission should be replaced - as described in Chapter 7.

b) Clean and grease the driveshaft support bearing, and apply a little oil to the driveshaft oil seals and splines.

c) Clean the splines on the outer end of the driveshaft and apply a suitable anti-seize compound ***(see illustration)****.*

d) Tighten all nuts and bolts to the specified torque.

e) Once the driveshaft has been re-inserted in the hub, tighten the new driveshaft nut as fully as possible by hand initially – delay tightening to the specified torque until the car is resting back on its wheels.

3.8b ...and the smaller one

3 Outer constant velocity joint gaiter – renewal

Note1: *Check on the availability of a joint repair kit before removal. The type of retaining clip for the gaiter may vary; check the fitment of the clip is correct according to the type supplied with the kit.*

Note 2: *Plastic type gaiter clips are not suitable for thermoplastic gaiters. A metal clip must always be used with these gaiters.*

1 Remove the driveshaft as described in Section 2.

2 If required, mount the driveshaft in a vice.

3 Note the fitted locations of both of the outer joint gaiter retaining clips, then release the clips from the gaiter, and slide the gaiter back along the driveshaft **(see illustration)**.

4 With the shaft secured in a suitable vice strike the inner section of the joint with brass drift or similar. It may take several hard blows to force the joint off the shaft. Recover the circlip from the end of the shaft.

5 Scoop out all of the old grease, and then pack the joint with new grease (see Specifications at the beginning of this Chapter). Take care that the fresh grease does not become contaminated with dirt or grit as it is being applied **(see illustration)**.

6 Fit the inner clip and gaiter to the drive- shaft, and with a soft-faced hammer drive the outer joint over the new circlip and onto the shaft. The small diameter end of the gaiter must be located in the groove on the driveshaft.

7 Ensure that the gaiter is not twisted or distorted, and then insert a small screwdriver under the lip of the gaiter at the housing end to allow any trapped air to escape.

8 Remove the screwdriver, fit the new retaining clips in the previously-noted positions, and tighten them **(see illustrations)**.

4 Driveshaft inner joint gaiter – renewal

1 Remove the driveshaft from the car, as described in Section 2.

2 If required, mount the driveshaft in a vice.

3 Note the fitted location of both of the inner joint gaiter retaining clips, then release the clips from the gaiter, and slide the gaiter back along the driveshaft a little way **(see illustrations)**.

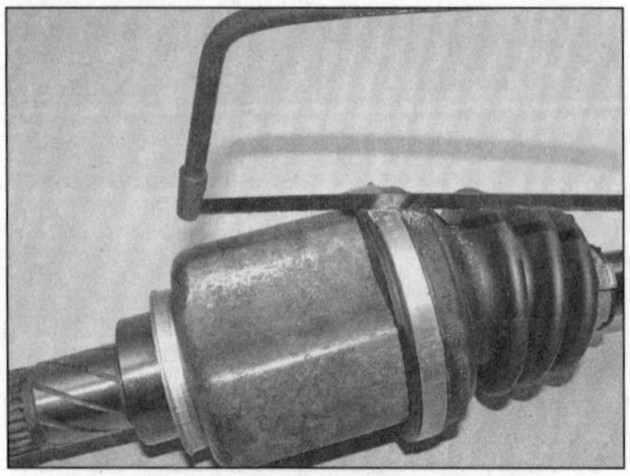

4.3a Cut through the large clip with a hacksaw...

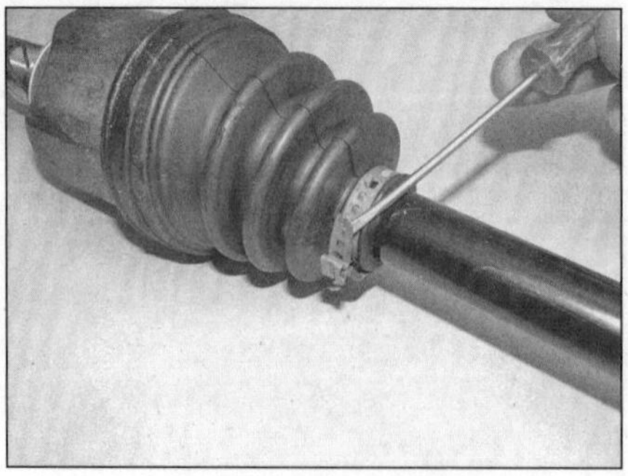

4.3b ...prise free the smaller clip...

4.3c ...and slide back the gaiter

4 Mark the driveshaft in relation to the joint housing, to ensure correct refitting.
5 Remove the inner joint housing from the tripod.
6 Extract the circlip retaining the tripod on the driveshaft **(see illustration)**. Some driveshafts may not have this circlip fitted; on these driveshafts, a simple peening of the splines retains the tripod. This can make removal difficult and a suitable puller may have to be employed to release the tripod.
7 Check that the inner end of the driveshaft is marked in relation to the splined tripod hub. If not, use dabs of paint on the driveshaft and one end of the tripod.
8 Using a soft-metal or wooden drift on the tripod centre hub (not on the outer rollers), tap off the tripod from the end of the driveshaft **(see illustrations)**.
9 Finally, slide off the inner gaiter.
10 If working on the right-hand driveshaft then this is an appropriate point to renew the support bearing. Remove the retaining clip and using a suitable press extract the bearing taking care not to damage the machined surface on the shaft. It should be born in mind that if this bearing is worn than it is more than likely that the entire driveshaft is due for renewal.
11 Clean the driveshaft, and obtain a new joint retaining circlip. The gaiter retaining clips must also be renewed.
12 Tape the end of the shaft to prevent damage to the gaiter and then slide the new gaiter onto the driveshaft, together with new clips **(see illustration)**.
13 Refit the tripod on the driveshaft splines, if necessary using a soft-faced mallet and a suitable socket to drive it fully onto the splines. It must be fitted with the previously-made marks aligned. Secure it in position using a new circlip. Ensure that the circlip is fully engaged in its groove. On driveshafts with no circlip, peen the ends of the shaft splines with a suitable punch.
14 Scoop out all of the old grease from the joint housing. Recover the spring and cup (if fitted) and then thoroughly clean all the components. Pack the joint and gaiter with new grease (see Specifications at the beginning of this Chapter). Guide the joint housing onto the tripod joint, making sure that the previously-made marks are aligned **(see illustrations)**.
15 Slide the gaiter along the driveshaft, and locate it on the tripod joint housing. The small diameter end of the gaiter must be located in the groove on the driveshaft, while the larger end of the gaiter should also locate in a groove on the housing.
16 Ensure that the gaiter is not twisted or distorted, and then insert a small screwdriver under the lip of the gaiter at the housing end. This will allow trapped air to escape.
17 Remove the screwdriver, then fit the retaining clips and tighten them **(see illustrations)**.

4.6 Remove the circlip

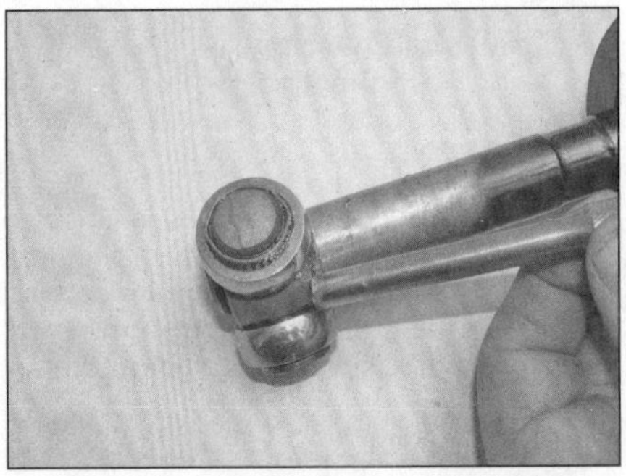
4.8a Use a drift to drive of the tripod...

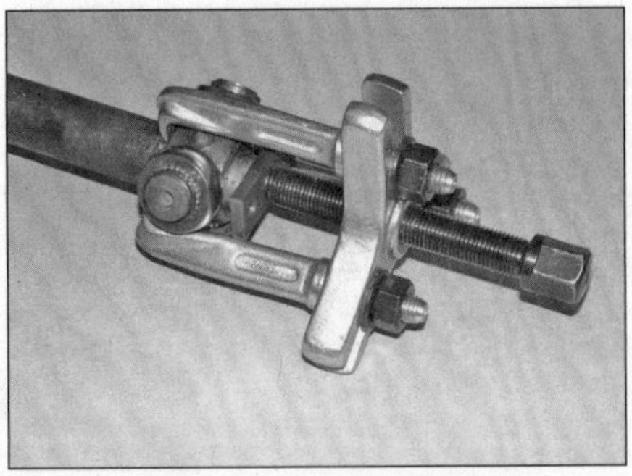
4.8b ...or a suitable puller

4.12 Cover the splines with tape to prevent damage to the new gaiter

4.14a Where applicable fit the spring and clip...

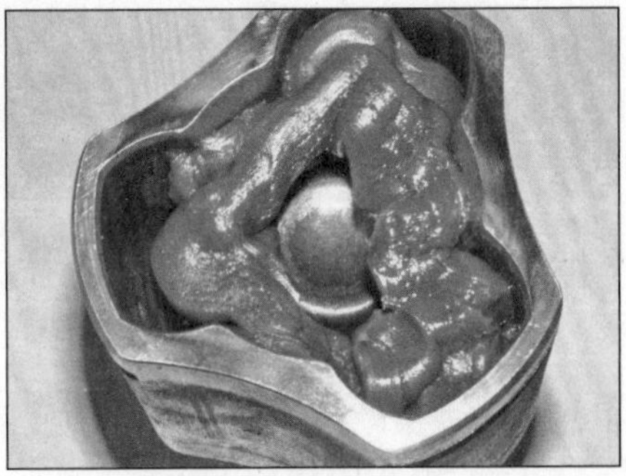
4.14b ...and then pack the joint with fresh grease

4.17a Slide on the new clip...

4.17b ...and tighten

5 Driveshaft overhaul – general information

1 If any of the checks described in Chapter 1A or 1B reveal wear in a driveshaft joint, first remove the roadwheel trim or centre cap (as appropriate) and check that the driveshaft retaining nut is still correctly tightened; if in doubt, use a torque wrench to check it. Refit the centre cap or trim, and repeat the check on the other driveshaft.

2 Road test the vehicle, and listen for a metallic clicking from the front as the vehicle is driven slowly in a circle on full lock. If a clicking or knocking noise can be heard, this may indicate wear in the outer constant velocity joint.

3 If vibration, consistent with roadspeed, is felt through the vehicle when accelerating, there is a possibility of wear in the inner constant velocity joints or support bearing.

4 Constant velocity joints can be dismantled and inspected for wear. Motor factors may be able to supply the outer CV joint as a reconditioned separate assembly. The inner joint can only be renewed with a complete driveshaft.

Chapter 9
Braking system

Contents

	Section number
Anti-lock braking system (ABS) – general information	18
Anti-lock braking system (ABS) components – removal and refitting	19
Brake pedal – removal and refitting	2
Brake pedal cross-shaft – removal and refitting	3
Front brake caliper – removal, overhaul and refitting	10
Front brake disc – inspection, removal and refitting	11
Front brake pad wear check	See Chapter 1A or 1B
Front brake pads – renewal	9
General information	1
Handbrake cables – removal and refitting	16
Handbrake check and adjustment	See Chapter 1A or 1B
Handbrake lever – removal and refitting	15
Hydraulic fluid level check	See *Weekly checks*
Hydraulic fluid renewal	See Chapter 1A or 1B
Hydraulic pipes and hoses – renewal	7
Hydraulic system – bleeding	6
Master cylinder – removal and refitting	8
Rear brake caliper – removal, overhaul and refitting	13
Rear brake disc – inspection, removal and refitting	14
Rear brake pad wear check	See Chapter 1A or 1B
Rear brake pads – inspection and renewal	12
Stop-light switch – removal, refitting and adjustment	17
Vacuum pump (diesel engines) – removal and refitting	20
Vacuum pump (diesel engines) – testing and overhaul	21
Vacuum servo unit – testing, removal and refitting	4
Vacuum servo unit check valve – removal, testing and refitting	5

Degrees of difficulty

Easy, suitable for novice with little experience	**Fairly easy,** suitable for beginner with some experience	**Fairly difficult,** suitable for competent DIY mechanic	**Difficult,** suitable for experienced DIY mechanic	**Very difficult,** suitable for expert DIY or professional

Specifications

General

System type	Servo-assisted hydraulic circuit, split diagonally with ABS anti-locking braking system
Front brakes	Disc, with single-piston sliding caliper
Rear brakes	Disc, with single-piston sliding caliper
Handbrake	Cable-operated, to rear wheels

Front brakes

Disc diameter	280 mm
Disc run-out	0.03 mm maximum
Disc thickness:	
New	24.0 mm
Minimum	21.8 mm
Brake pad thickness (friction material and backing plate):	
New	19.0 mm
Minimum	10.0 mm

Rear brakes

Disc diameter	260 mm
Disc run-out	0.06 mm maximum
Disc thickness:	
New	8.0 mm
Minimum	7.0 mm
Brake pad thickness (friction material and backing plate):	
New	19.0 mm
Minimum	10.0 mm

Vacuum servo

Pushrod setting dimension	133.2 mm

Torque wrench settings

	Nm	lbf ft
ABS system components:		
Hydraulic unit brake pipe union nuts	13	10
Hydraulic unit mounting bolts	8	6
ABS computer	3	2
Brake disc retaining screw	15	11
Brake hose and pipe unions	17	13
Brake pedal mounting nuts	21	15
Front brake caliper bleed screw	10	7
Front brake caliper mounting bracket bolts*	105	77
Front brake caliper guide pin bolts	27	20
Master cylinder brake pipe union nuts	14	10
Master cylinder mounting nuts	27	20
Rear brake caliper bleed screw	11	8
Rear brake caliper guide pin bolts*	35	26
Rear brake caliper mounting bracket bolts*	80	59
Rear hub nut**	220	162
Roadwheel bolts	110	81
Vacuum servo unit mounting bolts	21	15
Yaw speed and transversal acceleration sensor	8	6

** Use thread-locking fluid*
*** Use a new nut*

1 General information

The braking system is of the servo-assisted, dual circuit hydraulic type. All models are fitted with front and rear disc brakes. An anti-lock braking system (ABS) is fitted to all models as standard. Refer to Sections 18 and 19 for further information on ABS operation and components.

The front and rear disc brakes are actuated by single-piston sliding type calipers, which ensure that equal pressure is applied to each disc pad.

The rear disc brake calipers incorporate mechanical handbrake mechanisms, providing an independent mechanical means of rear brake application. Some models have an Electronic Parking Brake (EPB) fitted. On these models the parking brake is actuated by an electric motor.

The vacuum servo unit uses inlet manifold depression (generated only when a petrol engine is running) to boost the effort applied by the driver at the brake pedal and transmits this increased effort to the master cylinder pistons. Because there is no throttling of the inlet manifold on a diesel engine, it is not a suitable source of vacuum for brake servo operation. Vacuum is therefore derived from a separate vacuum pump, driven via a pushrod operated by an eccentric on the camshaft.

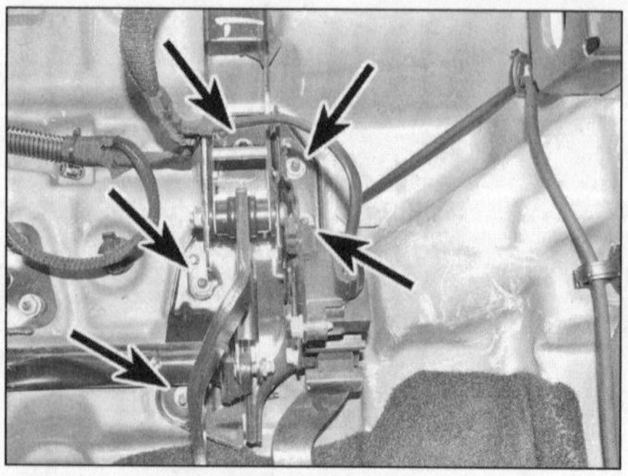

2.4 Brake pedal mounting bracket nuts (arrowed)

Precautions

The car's braking system is one of its most important safety features. When working on the brakes, there are a number of points to be aware of, to ensure that your health (or even your life) is not being put at risk.

Warning: Brake fluid is poisonous. Take care to keep it off bare skin, and in particular not to get splashes in your eyes. The fluid also attacks paintwork and plastics – wash off spillages immediately with cold water. Finally, brake fluid is highly inflammable, and should be handled with the same care as petrol.

- ***Make sure the ignition is off (take out the keycard) before disconnecting any braking system hydraulic union, and do not switch it on until after the hydraulic system has been bled. Failure to do this could lead to air entering the ABS hydraulic unit. If air enters the hydraulic unit pump, it will prove very difficult (in some cases impossible) to bleed the unit (see Section 6).***
- ***When servicing any part of the system, work carefully and methodically – do not take short-cuts; also observe scrupulous cleanliness when overhauling any part of the hydraulic system.***
- ***Always renew components in axle sets, where applicable – this means renewing brake pads on BOTH sides, even if only one set of pads is worn. In the instance of uneven brake wear, the cause should be investigated and fixed (sticking caliper pistons is a likely problem).***
- ***Use only genuine Renault parts, or at least those of known good quality.***
- ***Although genuine Renault brake pads are asbestos-free, the dust created by wear of non-genuine parts may contain asbestos, which is a health hazard. Never blow it out with compressed air, and don't inhale any of it.***
- ***DO NOT use petroleum-based solvents to clean brake parts; use brake cleaner or methylated spirit only.***
- ***DO NOT allow any brake fluid, oil or grease to contact the brake pads or disc.***

2 Brake pedal – removal and refitting

Removal

1 Remove the facia lower panel on the drivers side as described in Chapter 11.

2 Remove the accelerator pedal as described in Chapter 4A or 4B and then unclip the wiring loom from the top of the brake pedal.

3 Remove the brake pedal cross shaft as described below in Section 3.

4 Unscrew the five nuts securing the pedal mounting bracket to the bulkhead **(see illustration)**, then remove the pedal, twisting it sideways to release it.

Refitting

5 Refitting is a reversal of removal, noting the following points:

a) Tighten the pedal mounting bracket nuts to the specified torque.
b) A new pedal-to-cross-shaft clevis pin spring clip must befitted.
c) Check the operation of the brakes before taking the car out on the road.

3 Brake pedal cross-shaft – removal and refitting

Removal

1 Remove the glovebox **(see illustration)** as described in Chapter 11.
2 To further improve access, unclip and remove the plastic air duct fitted below the glovebox location.
3 Remove the facia lower panel on the drivers side as described in Chapter 11.
4 Working in the passenger footwell, disconnect the wiring plug from the brake light switch at the top of the servo operating lever. Turn the brake light switch 90° anti-clockwise and remove it.
5 Unclip the clutch hydraulic lines from the brackets on the shaft support plate **(see illustration)**.
6 Remove the spring clip and pin used to secure the servo operating lever to the cross shaft. **Note:** *A new pin and spring clip must be used when refitting – this is a small but vital component in the braking system.*
7 Remove the circlip and then unscrew the two nuts securing the cross-shaft to the servo operating lever **(see illustration)**. Dispose of the circlip – a new one must be used
8 Working in the drivers footwell disconnect the steering column at the pinch bolt (as described in Chapter 10, Section 15) and then remove the circlip from the cross shaft to brake pedal link **(see illustration)**. Dispose of the clip – a new one must be fitted.
9 Remove the brake pedal assembly as described in Section 2 of this Chapter.
10 Unbolt the servo mounting plate from the bulkhead, after removing the mounting nuts **(see illustration)**.
11 Taking care not to damage the clutch master cylinder pipes, withdraw the cross-shaft into the driver's footwell, and remove it from the car.
12 Examine the shaft, and all related components, very carefully. If there are signs of damage to any component, new parts should be fitted – never take risks where brakes are concerned.

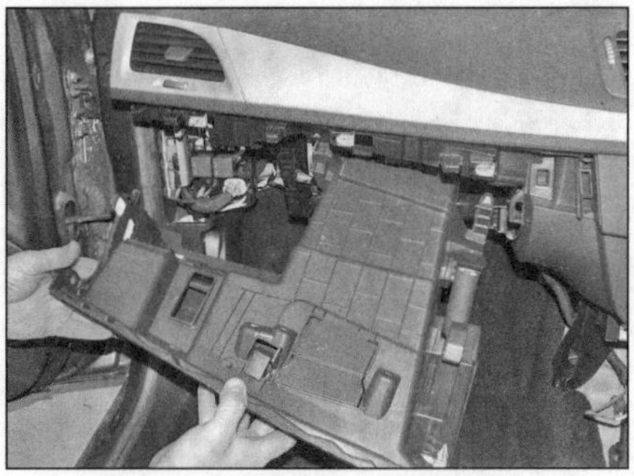

3.1 Removing the glovebox

Refitting

13 Refitting is a reversal of removal, noting the following points:

a) Use new circlips and clevis pin on the servo operating lever.
b) Fit a new circlip/spring clip to the brake pedal.
c) Tighten all fasteners securely, or to the specified torque.
d) Refit the glovebox as described in Chapter 11, and the brake pedal as described in Section 2.
e) Check the operation of the brakes before taking the car out on the road.

4 Vacuum servo unit – testing, removal and refitting

Testing

1 To test the operation of the servo unit, depress the footbrake several times to exhaust the vacuum, then start the engine whilst keeping the pedal firmly depressed.
2 As the engine starts, there should be a noticeable 'give' in the brake pedal as the vacuum builds-up. Allow the engine to run for at least two minutes, then switch it off. If the brake pedal is now depressed it should feel normal, but further applications should result in the pedal feeling firmer, with the pedal stroke decreasing with each application.
3 If the servo does not operate as described, inspect the servo unit check valve as described in Section 5.

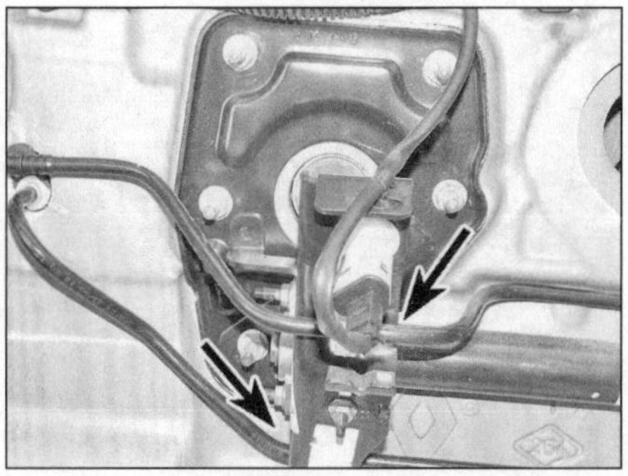

3.5 Unclip the hydraulic lines (arrowed)

4 If the servo unit still fails to operate satisfactorily, the fault lies within the unit itself. Apart from external components, no spares are available, so a defective servo must be renewed.

Removal

5 Remove the master cylinder as described in Section 8.
6 Disconnect and move to the side the gear selector cables as described in Chapter 7.
7 Remove the glovebox as described in Chapter 11.
8 To further improve access, unclip and remove the plastic air duct fitted below the glovebox location.
9 Remove the circlip and clevis pin securing the servo operating push rod the cross shaft. **Note:** *A new pin and circlip must be used when refitting – this is a small but vital component in the braking system.*
10 Prise out the servo check valve from the front of the servo unit, and move the hose to one side.
11 Unscrew and remove the servo mounting bolts **(see illustration 3.10)**.
12 Carefully withdraw the servo unit through the bulkhead into the engine compartment, and remove it.

Refitting

13 Prior to refitting, check that the servo unit pushrod is adjusted to the correct specified dimension.
14 Refitting is a reversal of removal, noting the following points:

a) Use a new circlip and clevis pin on the servo operating lever.

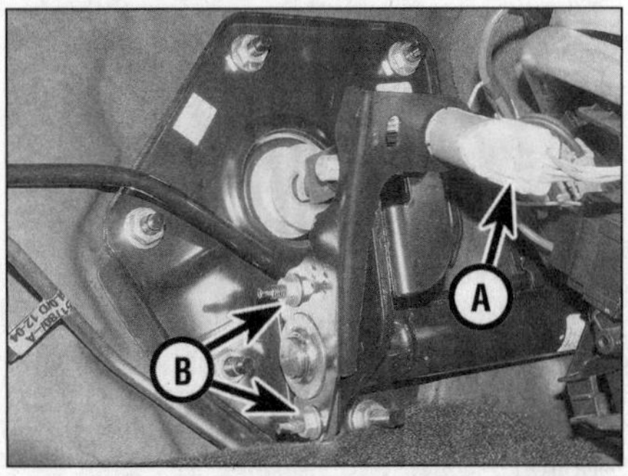

3.7 Disconnect the brake light switch (A) and remove the cross-shaft end nuts (B)

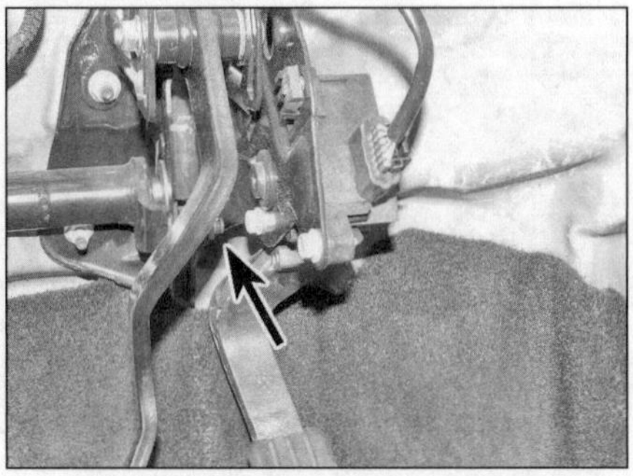

3.8 Remove the circlip (arrowed)

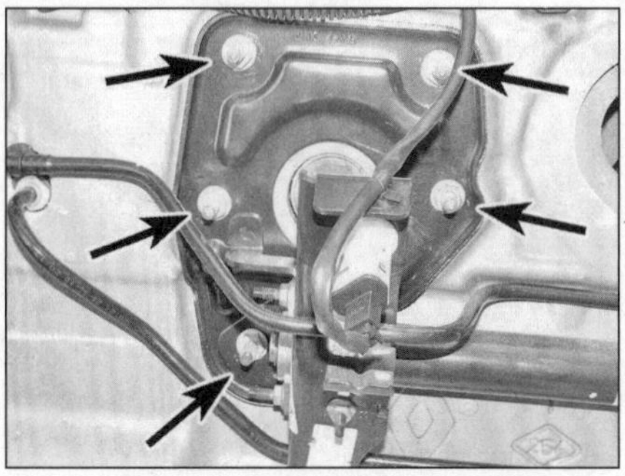

3.10 Remove the servo mounting nuts

5.1 Remove the air cleaner duct to access the check valve

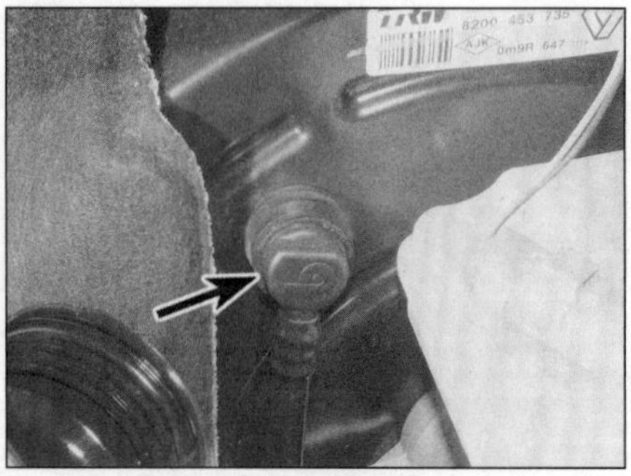

5.2 The check valve is located in the front of the servo

b) Tighten all fasteners securely, or to the specified torque.
c) Refit the glovebox as described in Chapter 11, and the brake pedal as described in Section 2.
d) Check the operation of the brakes before taking the car out on the road.

5 Vacuum servo unit check valve – removal, testing and refitting

Removal

1 Referring to Chapter 4A or 4B if necessary, remove the air cleaner duct for access to the servo unit vacuum hose **(see illustration)**.

2 Withdraw the valve from its rubber sealing grommet, using a pulling and twisting motion **(see illustration)** Remove the grommet from the servo.

3 To remove the hose completely, squeeze the tabs at the other end of the hose, and disconnect it from the inlet manifold or vacuum pump **(see illustrations)**.

Testing

4 Examine the check valve for signs of damage, and renew if necessary. The valve may be tested by blowing through it in both directions. Air should flow through the valve in one direction only – when blown through from the servo unit end of the valve. Renew the valve if this is not the case.

5 Examine the rubber sealing grommet and flexible vacuum hose for signs of damage or deterioration, and renew as necessary.

Refitting

6 Fit the sealing grommet into position in the servo unit.

7 Ease the check valve into position, taking care not to displace or damage the grommet. Reconnect the vacuum hose to the inlet manifold or vacuum pump.

8 On completion, start the engine and check that there are no air leaks. Check the operation of the brakes before taking the car onto the road.

6 Hydraulic system – bleeding

Note: *Refer to the precautions in Section 1 before proceeding.*

Caution: Make sure the ignition is off (take out the keycard) before bleeding the system.

General

1 The correct operation of any hydraulic system is only possible after removing all air from the components and circuit; this is achieved by bleeding the system.

2 During the bleeding procedure, add only clean, unused hydraulic fluid of the recommended type; never re-use fluid that has already been bled from the system. Ensure that sufficient fluid is available before starting work.

3 If there is any possibility of incorrect fluid being already in the system, the system must be flushed completely with uncontaminated, correct fluid, and new seals should be fitted to the various components.

4 If air has entered the hydraulic system because of a leak, ensure that the fault is cured before proceeding further.

5 Park the car on level ground, switch off the engine, remove the keycard and select first or reverse gear (or P on automatic transmission models). Chock the wheels and release the handbrake.

6 Check that all pipes and hoses are secure, unions tight and bleed screws closed. Clean any dirt from around the bleed screws – if they have not been opened for some time, apply a maintenance spray such as WD-40, and allow time for it to soak in.

7 Unscrew the master cylinder reservoir cap and top the master cylinder reservoir up to the MAX level line; refit the cap loosely. Remember to maintain the fluid level at least above the MIN level line throughout the procedure, or there is a risk of further air entering the system.

8 There are a number of one-man, do-it-yourself brake bleeding kits currently available from motor accessory shops. It is recommended that one of these kits is used whenever possible, as they greatly simplify the bleeding operation, and also reduce the risk of expelled air and fluid being drawn back into the system. If such a kit is not available, the basic (two-man) method must be used, which is described in detail below.

9 If a kit is to be used, prepare the car as described previously, and follow the kit manufacturer's instructions. The procedure may vary slightly according to the type of kit being used; general procedures are as outlined below in the relevant sub-section.

10 Whichever method is used, the same sequence must be followed (paragraphs 11 and 12) to ensure the removal of all air from the system.

Bleeding sequence

11 If the system has been only partially disconnected, and the correct precautions were taken to minimise fluid loss, it should be necessary only to bleed that part of the system (ie, the primary or secondary circuit).

12 If the complete system is to be bled, then it should be done working in the following sequence:

a) Right-hand rear brake.
b) Left-hand front brake.
c) Left-hand rear brake.
d) Right-hand front brake.

Bleeding

Basic (two-man) method

13 Collect a clean glass jar, a length of plastic or rubber tubing which is a tight fit over the bleed screw, and a ring spanner to fit the screw. The help of an assistant will also be required.

14 Remove the dust cap from the first screw in the sequence. Fit the spanner and tube to

5.3a Disconnect the servo hose from the vacuum pump (diesel)...

5.3b ...or inlet manifold (petrol)

the screw, place the other end of the tube in the jar, and pour in sufficient fluid to cover the end of the tube.

15 Ensure that the master cylinder reservoir fluid level is maintained at least above the MIN level line throughout the procedure.

16 Have the assistant fully depress the brake pedal several times to build-up pressure, then maintain it on the final stroke.

17 While pedal pressure is maintained, unscrew the bleed screw (approximately one turn) and allow the compressed fluid and air to flow into the jar. The assistant should maintain pedal pressure, following it down to the floor if necessary, and should not release it until instructed to do so. When the flow stops, tighten the bleed screw again. Have the assistant release the pedal slowly.

18 Repeat the steps given in paragraphs 16 and 17 until the fluid emerging from the bleed screw is free from air bubbles. Remember to recheck the fluid level in the master cylinder reservoir every five strokes or so. If the master cylinder has been drained and refilled, and air is being bled from the first screw in the sequence, allow approximately five seconds between strokes for the master cylinder passages to refill.

19 When no more air bubbles appear, tighten the bleed screw securely, remove the tube and spanner, and refit the dust cap. Do not overtighten the bleed screw.

20 Repeat the procedure on the remaining screws in sequence until all air is removed from the system and the brake pedal feels firm.

Using a one-way valve kit

21 As their name implies, these kits consist of a length of tubing with a one-way valve fitted to prevent expelled air and fluid being drawn back into the system; some kits include a translucent container, which can be positioned so that the air bubbles can be more easily seen flowing from the end of the tube **(see illustration)**.

22 The kit is connected to the bleed screw, which is then opened. The user returns to the driver's seat and depresses the brake pedal with a smooth, steady stroke and slowly releases it; this is repeated until the expelled fluid is clear of air bubbles.

23 Note that these kits simplify work so much that it is easy to forget the master cylinder reservoir fluid level; ensure that this is maintained at least above the MIN level line at all times.

Using a pressure-bleeding kit

24 These kits are usually operated by the reservoir of pressurised air contained in the spare tyre, although it may be necessary to reduce the pressure in the tyre to lower than normal; refer to the instructions supplied with the kit.

25 By connecting a pressurised, fluid-filled container to the master cylinder reservoir, bleeding can be carried out simply by opening each screw in turn (in the specified sequence) and allowing the fluid to flow out until no more air bubbles can be seen in the expelled fluid.

26 This method has the advantage that the large reservoir of fluid provides an additional safeguard against air being drawn into the system during bleeding.

27 Pressure-bleeding is particularly effective when bleeding 'difficult' systems, or when bleeding the complete system at the time of routine fluid renewal.

All methods

28 When bleeding is complete and firm pedal feel is restored, wash off any spilt fluid, tighten the bleed screws securely and refit their dust caps.

29 Check the hydraulic fluid level, and top-up if necessary (see *Weekly checks*).

30 Discard any hydraulic fluid that has been bled from the system; it will not be fit for re-use.

31 Check the feel of the brake pedal. If it feels at all spongy, air must still be present in the system, and further bleeding is required. Failure to bleed satisfactorily after several repetitions of the bleeding procedure may be due to worn master cylinder seals.

6.21 Using a one-man brake bleeding kit

7 Hydraulic pipes and hoses – renewal

Note: *Refer to the precautions in Section 1 before proceeding.*

1 If any pipe or hose is to be renewed, minimise fluid loss by removing the master cylinder reservoir cap and then tightening it down onto a piece of polythene (taking care not to damage the sender unit) to obtain an airtight seal. Alternatively, flexible hoses can be sealed, if required, using a proprietary brake hose clamp; metal brake pipe unions can be plugged (if care is taken not to allow dirt into the system) or capped immediately they are disconnected. Place a wad of rag under any union that is to be disconnected, to catch any spilt fluid.

2 If a flexible hose is to be disconnected, unscrew the brake pipe union nut before removing the spring clip which secures the hose to its mounting bracket **(see illustrations)**.

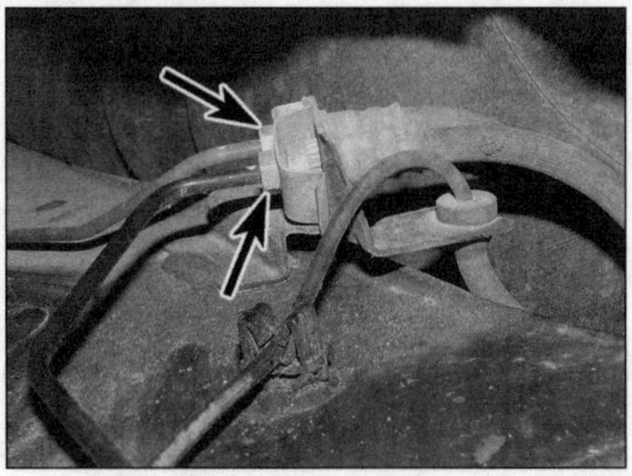

7.2a Unscrew the union nuts...

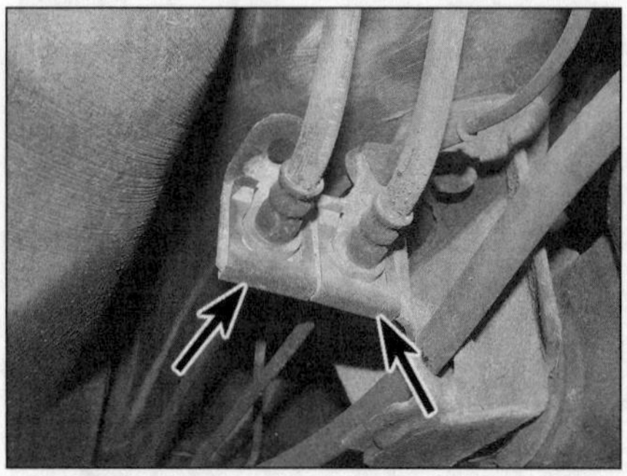

7.2b ...and pull out the spring clips securing the hoses

3 To unscrew the union nuts, it is preferable to obtain a brake pipe spanner of the correct size (split ring); these are available from motor accessory shops. Failing this, a close-fitting open-ended spanner will be required, though if the nuts are tight or corroded, their flats may be rounded off if the spanner slips. In such a case, a self-locking wrench is often the only way to unscrew a stubborn union, but it follows that the pipe and the damaged nuts must be renewed on reassembly. Always clean a union and surrounding area before disconnecting it. If disconnecting a component with more than one union, make a careful note of the connections before disturbing any of them.

4 If a brake pipe is to be renewed, it can be obtained, cut to length and with the union nuts and end flares in place, from Renault dealers. All that is then necessary is to bend it to shape, following the line of the original, before fitting it to the car. Alternatively, most motor accessory shops can make up brake pipes from kits, but this requires very careful measurement of the original to ensure that the new pipe is of the correct length. The safest answer is usually to take the original to the shop as a pattern.

5 On refitting, do not over tighten the union nuts. The specified torque wrench settings (where given) are not high, and it is not necessary to exercise brute force to obtain a sound joint.

6 Ensure that the pipes and hoses are correctly routed with no kinks, and that they are secured in the clips or brackets provided. In the case of flexible hoses, make sure that they cannot contact other components during

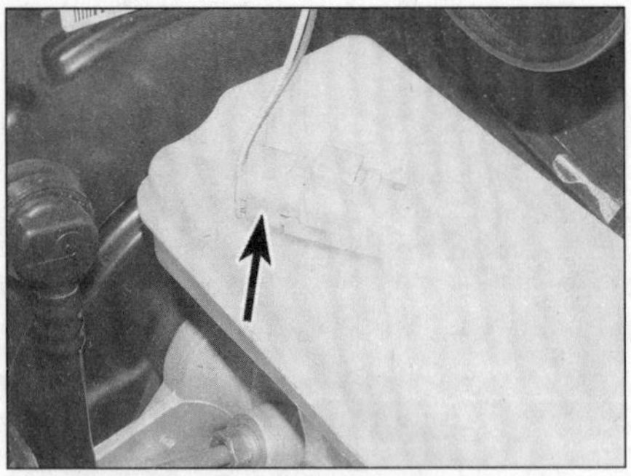
8.3 Disconnect the fluid level sender wiring connector

8.6 Master cylinder mounting nuts

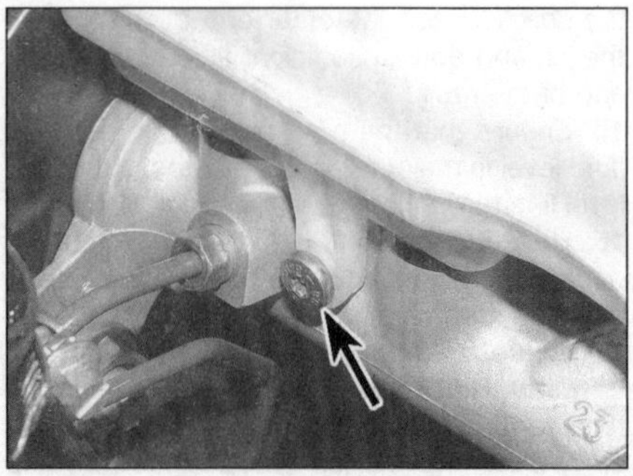
8.8 Reservoir-to-master cylinder mounting bolt

movement of the steering and/or suspension assemblies.

7 After fitting, remove the polythene from the reservoir (or remove the plugs or clamps, as applicable), and bleed the hydraulic system as described in Section 6. Wash off any spilt fluid, and check carefully for fluid leaks.

8 Master cylinder – removal and refitting

Note: *Refer to the precautions in Section 1 before proceeding.*

Removal

1 Remove the battery, battery tray and ECU as described in Chapter 5A.

2 Remove the air filter outlet and the air filter housing as described in Chapter 4A or 4B.

3 Remove the master cylinder reservoir cap, having disconnected the sender unit wiring connector, and syphon the hydraulic fluid from the reservoir **(see illustration). Note:** *Do not syphon the fluid by mouth, as it is poisonous; use a syringe or an old antifreeze hydrometer.* Alternatively, open any convenient pair of bleed screws in the system (one in each hydraulic circuit) and gently pump the brake pedal to expel the fluid through plastic tubes connected to the screws (see Section 6).

4 Release the clip and disconnect the clutch fluid supply hose. Seal the hose immediately.

5 Wipe clean the area around the brake pipe unions on the side of the master cylinder, and place absorbent rags beneath the pipe unions to catch any surplus fluid. Make a note of the correct fitted positions of the unions, then unscrew the union nuts and carefully withdraw the pipes. Plug or tape over the pipe ends and master cylinder orifices, to minimise the loss of brake fluid and to prevent the entry of dirt into the system. Wash off any spilt fluid immediately with cold water.

6 Unscrew and remove the two master cylinder to servo nuts **(see illustration)**.

7 Unclip the bulkhead soundproofing as necessary, then remove the master cylinder from the servo.

8 If necessary, the reservoir can be separated from the cylinder after removing the mounting bolt/clip **(see illustration)**.

9 No parts are available, so overhauling the master cylinder is not an option. If it is faulty, it must be replaced. The O-ring seal fitted between the master cylinder and the vacuum servo must be renewed as a matter of course, as should the seals between the reservoir and the master cylinder.

Refitting

10 Remove all traces of dirt from the master cylinder and servo unit mating surfaces. Fit a new O-ring seal to the groove on the master cylinder body.

11 Fit the master cylinder to the servo, ensuring that the servo pushrod enters the master cylinder bore centrally. Refit the master cylinder mounting nuts, and tighten them to the specified torque.

12 Wipe clean the brake pipe unions, then refit them to the master cylinder ports. Tighten the union nuts to the specified torque.

13 Further refitting is a reversal of removal, noting the following points:

a) On completion, fill the reservoir with fresh fluid and bleed the brakes as described in Section 6.

b) Bleed the clutch as described in Chapter 6.

c) Check the operation of the brakes before taking the car out on the road.

9 Front brake pads – renewal

Note: *Refer to the precautions in Section 1 before proceeding. Always renew the pads on both front brakes, never just on one side.*

1 Apply the handbrake, then jack up the front of the car and support it on axle stands (see *Jacking and vehicle support*). Remove the front roadwheels.

2 Using a suitable screwdriver, small pry bar or pliers remove the retaining spring **(see illustration)**.

3 Mark the position and then release the brake flexible hose from the base of the suspension strut.

4 At the rear of the caliper remove the dust caps from the guide bolts and then remove the bolts **(see illustrations)**.

5 Lift the caliper from the brake disc, remove the brake pad and then support the caliper from the coil spring with a suitable length of wire or stout cord **(see illustrations)**.

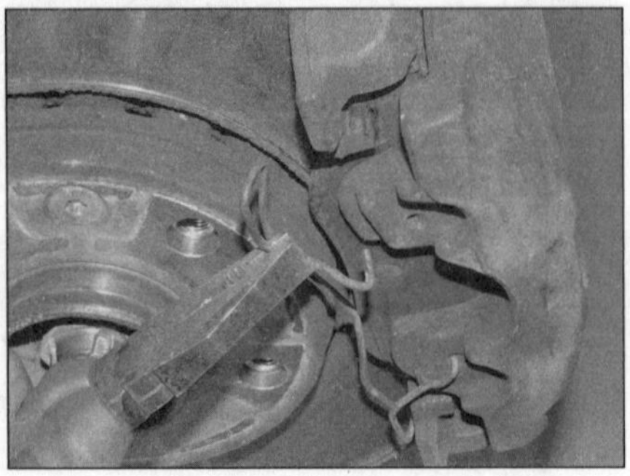
9.2 Remove the spring

9.4a Remove the caps and...

9.4b ...remove the bolts

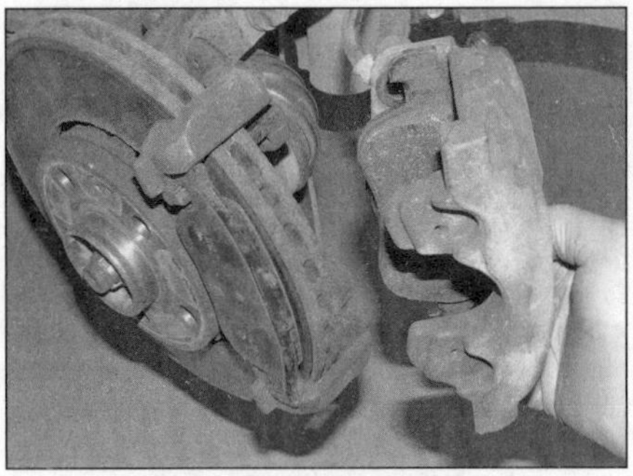

9.5a Remove the caliper...

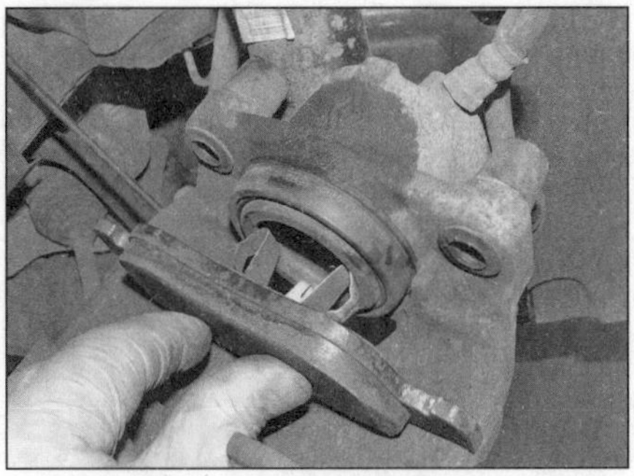

9.5b ...recover the pad...

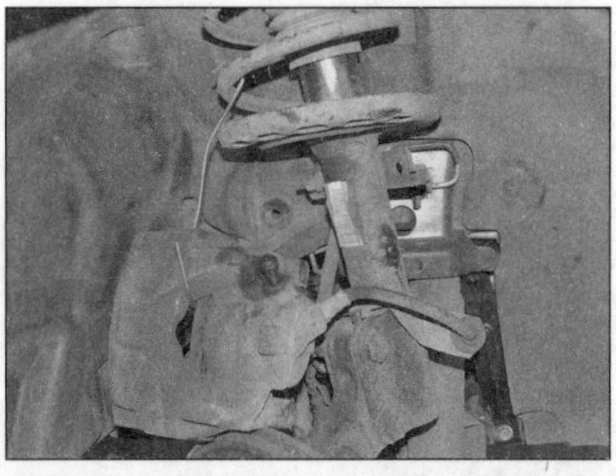

9.5c ...and hang the caliper from the strut

6 Remove the brake pad from the disc **(see illustration)**.

7 With the pads removed, measure the thickness of each brake pad (friction material and backing plate) **(see illustration)**. If any pad is worn at any point to the specified minimum thickness or less, all four pads must be renewed. If in doubt always replace the brake pads. Also, the pads should be renewed if any are fouled with oil or grease; there is no satisfactory way of degreasing friction material once contaminated.

8 If any of the brake pads are worn unevenly or fouled with oil or grease, trace and rectify the cause before reassembly. New brake pads and spring kits are available from Renault dealers and reputable motor factors.

9 If the brake pads are still serviceable, carefully clean them using a clean, fine wire brush or similar, paying particular attention to the sides and back of the metal backing. Carefully clean the pad locations in the caliper body/mounting bracket.

10 Prior to fitting the pads, check that the guide sleeves are free to slide easily in the caliper body, and check that the rubber guide sleeve gaiters are undamaged. Brush the dust and dirt from the caliper and piston, but *do not inhale it, as it may be a health hazard.* Inspect the dust seal around the piston for damage, and the piston for evidence of fluid leaks, corrosion or damage. If attention to any of these components is necessary, refer to Section 10. Also inspect the brake disc as described in Section 11.

9.6 Remove the outer brake pad from the disk

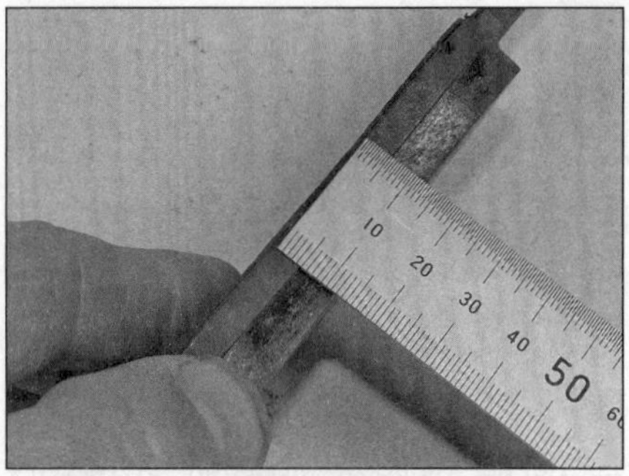

9.7 Check the thickness of the pad material

11 The caliper piston must be pushed back into the caliper to make room for the new pads – this may require considerable effort. Either use the correct tool, a G-clamp, sliding-jaw (water pump) pliers, or suitable pieces of wood as levers **(see illustrations)**.

Caution: Pushing back the piston causes a reverse-flow of brake fluid, which has been known to 'flip' the master cylinder rubber seals, resulting in a total loss of braking. To avoid this, clamp the caliper flexible hose and open the bleed screw – as the piston is pushed back, the fluid can be directed into a suitable container using a hose attached to the bleed screw. Close the screw just before the piston is pushed fully back, to ensure no air enters the system.

12 If the recommended method of opening a bleed screw before pushing back the piston is not used, the fluid level in the reservoir will rise, and possibly overflow. Make sure that there is sufficient space in the brake fluid reservoir to accept the displaced fluid, and if necessary, syphon some off first. Any brake fluid spilt on paintwork should be washed off with clean water without delay – brake fluid is also a highly-effective paint-stripper.

13 Most replacement brake pads will have an anti-squeal coating (often seen as an adhesive pad) applied to the pad backplates. If there is any doubt, apply a little copper based anti-seize grease to the backs of the pads (none should be applied to the friction material) before fitting **(see illustration)**.

14 Fit the piston side brake pad first by pushing the spring lugs into the piston **(see illustration)**. Apply a little lubricant (copper anti seize grease is ideal) if necessary to the spring lugs on the rear of the brake pad.

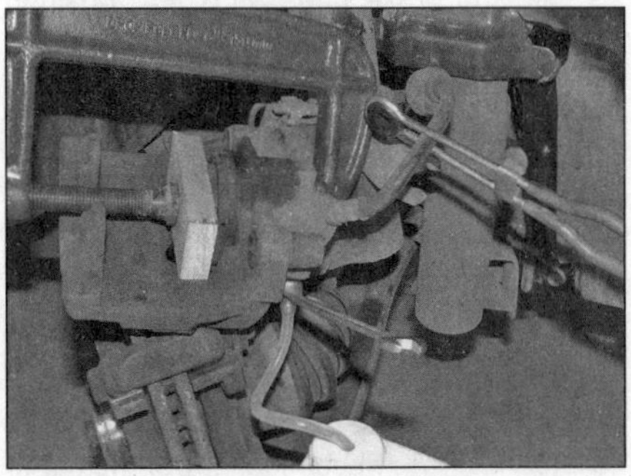

9.11a Use a clamp or...

9.11b ...the correct tool

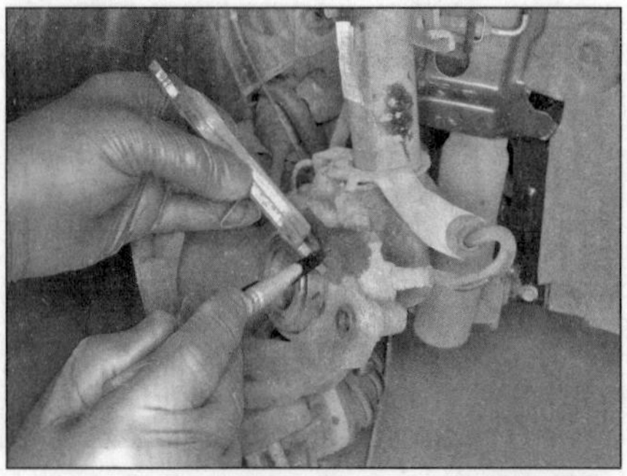

9.13 Apply a little anti-seize to the pad contact points

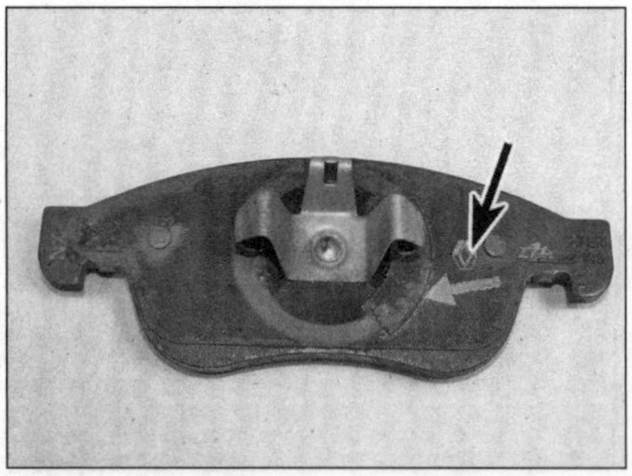

9.14 Observe the rotation arrows on the rear of the brake pads

15 Install the other pad into the caliper mounting bracket and then fit the caliper.

16 Fit the guide pin bolts and tighten them to the specified torque **(see illustration)**. Refit the dust covers to the guide pins.

17 Refit the retaining spring and then place the wheels in the straight ahead position.

18 Refit the brake flexible hose to the bracket on the base of the suspension tower.

19 Depress the brake pedal several times to bring the pads into firm contact with the brake disc.

20 Repeat the above procedure on the other front brake caliper.

21 Refit the roadwheels, then lower the car to the ground and tighten the bolts to the specified torque.

22 Check the hydraulic fluid level as described in *Weekly checks*.

23 If new pads have been fitted, full braking efficiency will not be obtained until the linings have bedded-in. Be prepared for longer stopping distances, and avoid harsh braking as far as possible for the first hundred miles or so after fitting new pads.

10 Front brake caliper – removal, overhaul and refitting

Note: *Refer to the precautions in Section 1 before proceeding.*

Removal

1 Apply the handbrake, then jack up the front of the car and support it on axle stands (see *Jacking and vehicle support*). Remove the appropriate roadwheel.

10.3 Loosen the brake hose union nut

9.16 Tighten the caliper guide bolts to the correct torque

2 Minimise fluid loss, either by removing the master cylinder reservoir cap and then tightening it down onto a piece of polythene to obtain an airtight seal (taking care not to damage the sender unit), or by using a brake hose clamp, a G-clamp or a similar tool with protected jaws to clamp the flexible hose.

3 Clean the area around the hose union, then loosen the brake hose union nut **(see illustration)**.

4 Remove the dust covers and then remove the caliper guide pin bolts.

5 With the guide pin bolts removed, lift the caliper away from the brake disc **(see illustration 9.5a)**. Remove the pad from the caliper. Unclip the brake hose from the clip on the suspension strut, then unscrew the caliper from the end of the brake hose.

Overhaul

Note: *Ensure that an appropriate caliper overhaul kit is obtained before starting work.*

6 With the caliper on the bench, wipe away all traces of dust and dirt, but avoid inhaling the dust, as it is injurious to health.

7 Using a small flat-bladed screwdriver, carefully prise the dust seal retaining clip out of the caliper bore.

8 Withdraw the partially-ejected piston from the caliper body and remove the dust seal. The piston can be withdrawn by hand, or if necessary forced out by applying compressed air to the union bolt hole.

Caution: The piston may be ejected with some force. Only low pressure should be required, such as is generated by a foot pump.

9 Extract the piston hydraulic seal using a blunt instrument such as a knitting needle or a crochet hook, taking care not to damage the caliper bore.

10 Remove the rubber gaiters from the guide pins housings.

11 Thoroughly clean all components using only methylated spirit, isopropyl alcohol or clean hydraulic fluid as a cleaning medium. Never use mineral-based solvents, such as petrol or paraffin, which will attack the hydraulic system rubber components. Dry the components immediately, using compressed air or a clean, lint-free cloth. Use compressed air to blow clear the fluid passages.

12 Check all components and renew any that are worn or damaged. Check particularly the cylinder bore and piston; if they are scratched, worn or corroded in any way, they must be renewed (note that this means the renewal of the complete body assembly). If there is any doubt about the condition of a component, renew it.

13 If the assembly is fit for further use, obtain the appropriate repair kit.

14 Renew all rubber seals, dust covers and caps disturbed on dismantling as a matter of course; these should never be re-used.

15 Before commencing reassembly, ensure that all components are absolutely clean and dry.

16 Dip the piston and the new piston (fluid) seal in clean hydraulic fluid. Smear clean fluid on the cylinder bore surface.

17 Fit the new piston (fluid) seal, using only the fingers to manipulate it into the cylinder bore groove. Fit the new dust seal to the piston. Refit the piston to the cylinder bore using a twisting motion, ensuring that the piston enters squarely into the bore. Press the piston fully into the bore, then press the dust seal into the caliper body.

18 Apply the grease supplied in the repair kit, or a good quality high-temperature brake grease or anti-seize compound to the guide pins.

Refitting

19 Screw the caliper body fully onto the flexible hose union nut. Check that the brake pads are still correctly fitted in the caliper mounting bracket.

20 Fit the outer pad to the caliper bracket and then fit the inner pad to the brake caliper.

21 Refit the caliper to the brake caliper mounting bracket and then refit the guide pins.

22 Refit the caliper guide pin dust covers and then refit the retaining spring.

23 Clip the brake hose back into position on the suspension strut, making sure it is not twisted.

24 Tighten the brake hose union nut to the specified torque.

25 Remove the brake hose clamp or polythene, where fitted, and bleed the hydraulic system as described in Section 6. Providing the precautions described were taken to minimise brake fluid loss, it should only be necessary to bleed the relevant front brake.

26 Refit the roadwheel, then lower the car to the ground and tighten the roadwheel bolts to the specified torque.

11.3 Checking the disc thickness with a micrometer

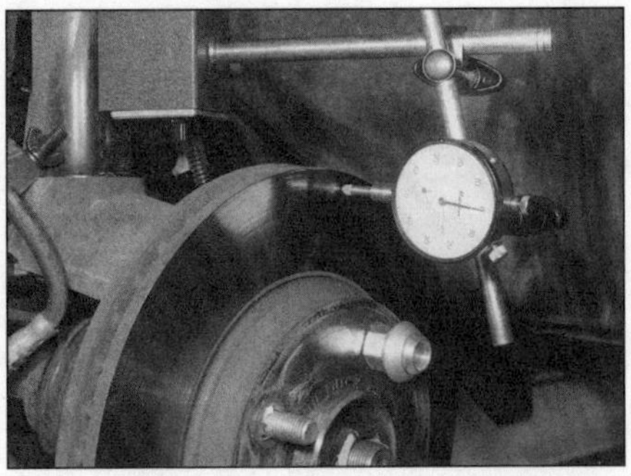

11.4 Checking for disc run-out with a dial gauge

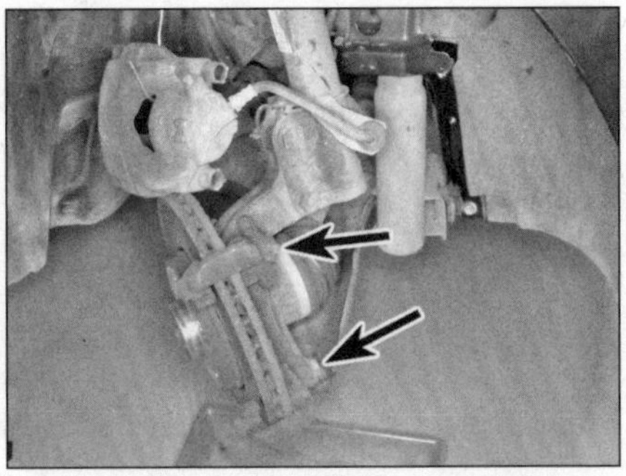

11.8 Remove the bolts (arrowed)

11 Front brake disc – inspection, removal and refitting

Note: *Refer to the precautions in Section 1 before proceeding.*

Inspection

1 Chock the rear wheels, firmly apply the handbrake, jack up the front of the car and support on axle stands (see *Jacking and vehicle support*). Remove the appropriate front roadwheel.

2 Slowly rotate the brake disc so that the full area of both sides can be checked; remove the brake pads, as described in Section 9, if better access is required to the inboard surface. Light scoring is normal in the area swept by the brake pads, but if heavy scoring is found, the disc must be renewed.

3 It is normal to find a lip of rust and brake dust around the disc's perimeter; this can be scraped off if required. If, however, a lip has formed due to wear of the brake pad swept area, the disc thickness must be measured using a micrometer **(see illustration)**. Take measurements at several places around the disc at the inside and outside of the pad swept area; if the disc has worn at any point to the specified minimum thickness or less, it must be renewed.

4 If the disc is thought to be warped, it can be checked for run-out, ideally by using a dial gauge mounted on any convenient fixed point, while the disc is slowly rotated **(see illustration)**. In the absence of a dial gauge, use feeler blades to measure (at several points all around the disc) the clearance between the disc and a fixed point such as the caliper mounting bracket.

5 If the measurements obtained are at the specified maximum or beyond, the disc is excessively warped, and must be renewed; however, it is worth checking first that the hub bearing is in good condition (Chapters 1A or 1B and 10). Also try the effect of removing the disc and turning it through 180° to reposition it on the hub; if run-out is still excessive, the disc must be renewed.

6 Check the disc for cracks (especially around the wheel bolt holes), and for any other wear or damage. Renew the disc if necessary.

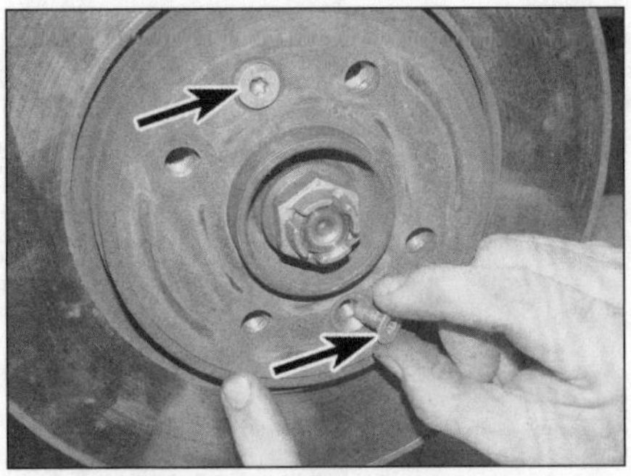

11.9a Remove the two Torx screws securing the brake disc...

11.9b ...then remove the disc from the hub

Removal

7 Remove the brake caliper and pads as described in Sections 9 and 10.

8 Unscrew the two bolts securing the brake caliper mounting bracket to the swivel hub, and slide the bracket off the disc **(see illustration)**.

9 If the same disc is to be refitted, use chalk or paint to mark the relationship of the disc to the hub. Remove the two screws securing the brake disc to the hub, and remove the disc **(see illustrations)**. If it is tight, lightly tap its rear face with a hide or plastic mallet.

Refitting

10 Refitting is the reverse of the removal procedure, noting the following points:

a) *Ensure that the mating surfaces of the disc and hub are clean and flat. To reduce the risk of corrosion, apply copper grease to the hub before fitting the disc (ensure that the grease does not get on the disc friction surfaces)* ***(see illustration)****.*

b) *If applicable, align the marks made on removal.*

c) *Securely tighten the disc retaining screws. Note that Renault recommend that the screws are replaced.*

d) *If a new disc has been fitted, use a suitable solvent to wipe any preservative coating from the disc before refitting the caliper.*

e) *Fit new brake caliper bracket mounting bolts, and tighten them to the specified torque* ***(see illustration)****.*

f) *Refit the roadwheel, then lower the car to the ground and tighten the roadwheel bolts to the specified torque. On completion, depress the brake pedal several times to bring the brake pads into contact with the disc.*

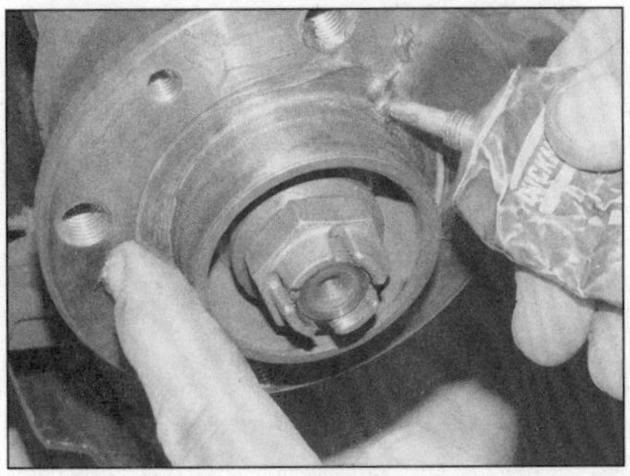

11.10a Apply copper grease to the hub before fitting the disc

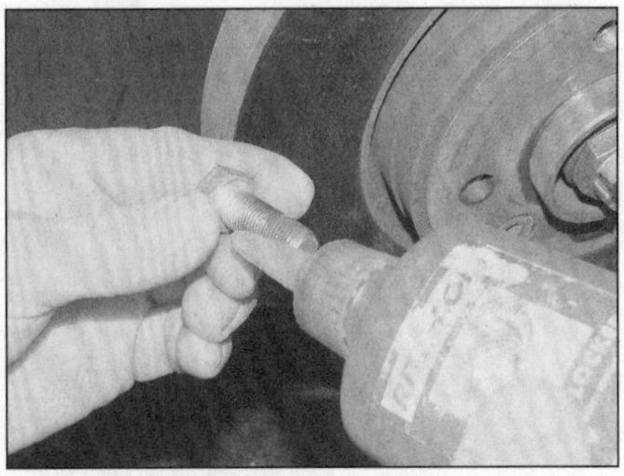

11.10b Apply locking fluid to the caliper mounting bracket bolts

12.2a The pads friction material (arrowed) can be viewed through the window...

12.2b ...and from the side (arrowed)

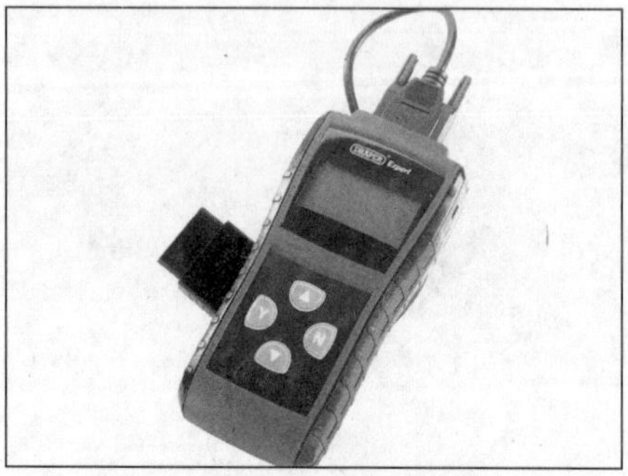

12.4 Parking brake tools are increasingly available to the home mechanic

12.5 Unscrew the caliper guide pin bolts, using two spanners

12 Rear brake pads – inspection and renewal

Note: *Refer to the precautions in Section 1 before proceeding. Always renew the pads on both rear brakes, never just on one side.*

Note: *On models fitted with an Electronic Parking Brake (EPB) a suitable diagnostic tool will be required to place the rear brake in 'maintenance mode'.*

Inspection

1 Chock the front wheels, engage reverse gear and release the handbrake. Jack up the rear of the car and support it on axle stands (see *Jacking and vehicle support*). Remove the rear wheels.

2 The pad thicknesses can be viewed without removing them from the caliper **(see illustrations)**. Wear rates for rear pads are generally far lower than for front pads, but if the friction material remaining is low, remember that this may also adversely affect the operation of the handbrake.

3 If either pad is worn at any point to the specified minimum thickness or less, all four pads must be renewed. Also, the pads should be renewed if any are fouled with oil or grease – there is no satisfactory way of degreasing friction material once contaminated. If any of the brake pads are worn unevenly, or fouled with oil or grease, trace and rectify the cause before reassembly. New brake pads and spring kits are available from Renault dealers.

Renewal

4 On models fitted with an electronic parking brake place the brake in 'maintenance mode' using a suitable diagnostic tool **(see illustration)**. Release the wiring loom from the retaining clips at the rear.

5 Unscrew the caliper guide pin bolts, using a second spanner on the pin outer hex fitting to prevent the pin turning **(see illustration). Note:** *To just access the pads, only the lower pin need be unscrewed – the caliper could then be swung upwards. However, fitting new pads involves 'screwing' the caliper piston back into the caliper, which is more easily achieved with the caliper removed from its mounting bracket, which means removing both guide pin bolts.*

6 Remove the caliper from the mounting bracket, and suspend it under the wheel arch so that the fluid hose is not strained **(see illustration)**. Alternatively rest the caliper on the rear suspension.

7 Unclip the inner and outer pads from the caliper mounting bracket, and remove them **(see illustration)**. Remove the anti-squeal shims from the caliper.

8 Carefully clean the pad locations in the caliper body/mounting bracket. Brush the dust and dirt from the caliper and piston, but *do not inhale it, as it may be a health hazard*.

9 Prior to fitting the pads, check that the guide sleeves are free to slide easily in the caliper body, and check that the rubber guide sleeve gaiters are undamaged **(see illustration)**. Inspect the dust seal around the piston for damage, and the piston for evidence of fluid leaks, corrosion or damage. If attention to any of these components is necessary, refer to Section 13. Also inspect the brake disc as described in Section 14.

10 If new brake pads are to be fitted, it will be necessary to retract the piston fully into the caliper bore by rotating it in a clockwise direction. This can be achieved using sturdy circlip pliers, noting that as well as being turned, the piston has to be pressed in very firmly. Special tools are available from companies such as Draper to achieve this with less effort **(see illustrations)**.

Caution: Pushing back the piston causes a reverse-flow of brake fluid, which has been known to 'flip' the master cylinder rubber seals, resulting in a total loss of braking. To avoid this, clamp the caliper flexible hose and open the bleed screw – as the piston is

12.6 Lift the caliper off the mounting bracket

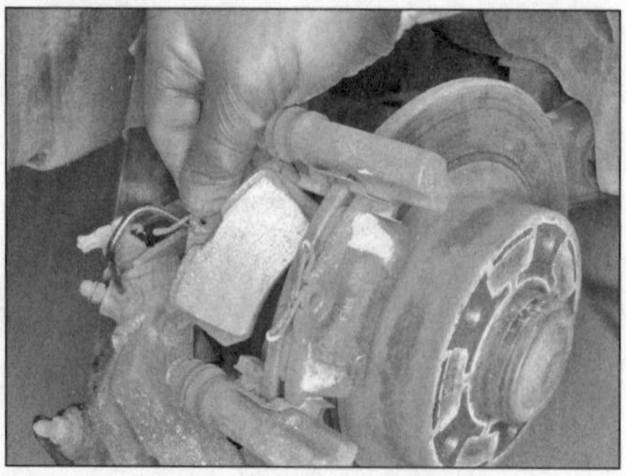

12.7 Unclip the brake pads from the mounting bracket

12.9 Check that the slides move freely

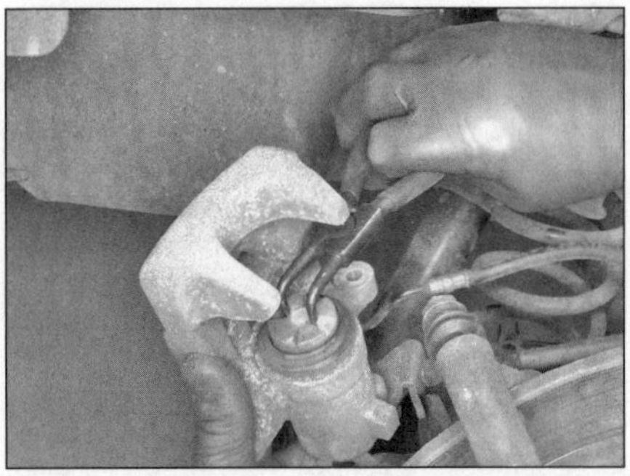

12.10a Circlip pliers can be used to retract the piston...

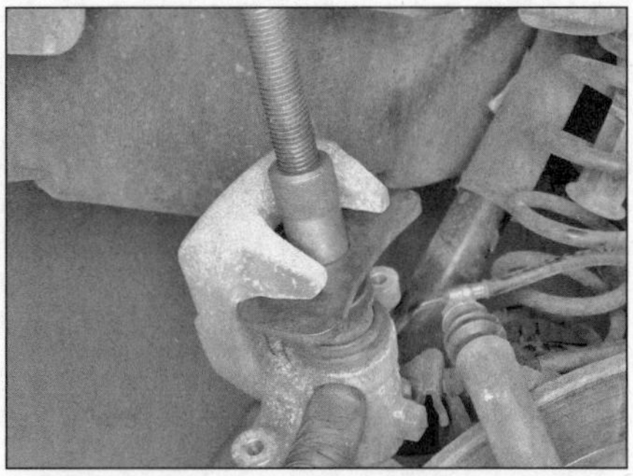

12.10b ...or more conveniently the correct tool

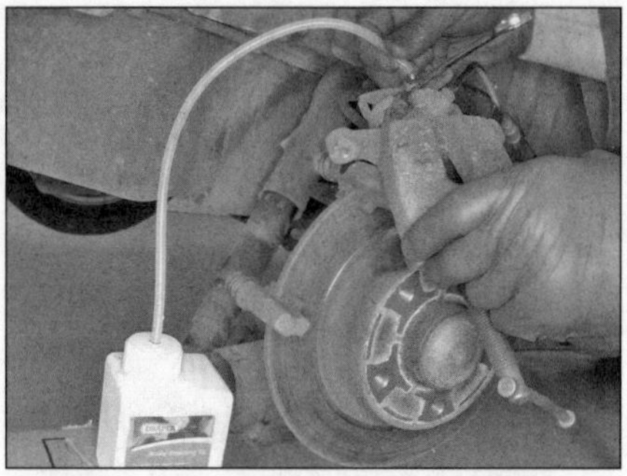

12.10c Clamp the flexible hose, open the bleed nipple, retract the piston and the brake fluid will fill the container

pushed back, the fluid can be directed into a suitable container using a hose attached to the bleed screw. Close the screw just before the piston is pushed fully back, to ensure no air enters the system.

11 If the recommended method of opening a bleed screw before pushing back the piston is not used, the fluid level in the reservoir will rise, and possibly overflow. Make sure that there is sufficient space in the brake fluid reservoir to accept the displaced fluid and, if necessary, syphon some off first. Any brake fluid spilt on paintwork should be washed off with clean water without delay – brake fluid is also a highly-effective paint-stripper.

12 Fit new anti-squeal shims to the caliper. These must be replaced and will normally be supplied with the replacement brake pads.

13 Genuine Renault pads appear to have an anti-squeal coating applied to the pad backplates. If other pads are being fitted, or if there is any doubt, apply a little copper brake grease to the backs of the pads (none should be applied to the friction material) before fitting.

14 Install the pads in the caliper mounting bracket, ensuring that the friction material of each pad is against the brake disc.

15 Lower the caliper over the pads.

16 Fit new clipper guide pin bolts and tighten to the specified torque.

17 Repeat the above procedure on the other front brake caliper.

18 On models fitted with EPB use the diagnostic tool to deactivate the maintenance mode.

19 Depress the brake pedal several times to bring the pads into firm contact with the brake disc.

20 Refit the roadwheels, then lower the car to the ground and tighten the bolts to the specified torque.

21 Check the hydraulic fluid level as described in *Weekly checks*.

22 Check the handbrake cable adjustment as described in Chapter 1A or 1B.

23 If new pads have been fitted, full braking efficiency will not be obtained until the linings have bedded-in. Be prepared for longer stopping distances, and avoid harsh braking as far as possible for the first hundred miles or so after fitting new pads.

13 Rear brake caliper – removal, overhaul and refitting

Note: *Refer to the precautions in Section 1 before proceeding.*

Note: *On models fitted with an Electronic Parking Brake (EPB) a suitable diagnostic tool will be required to place the rear brake in 'maintenance mode'.*

Removal

1 Chock the front wheels, engage reverse gear and release the handbrake. Jack up the rear of the car and support it on axle stands (see *Jacking and vehicle support*). Remove the relevant rear wheel.

2 On models fitted with an electronic parking brake place the brake in 'maintenance mode' using a suitable diagnostic tool. Disconnect the wiring plug and then release the wiring loom from the retaining clips at the rear.

3 On models fitted with a conventional parking brake, free the handbrake inner cable from the caliper handbrake operating lever, then unclip the outer cable from its bracket on the caliper body **(see illustrations)**.

4 Minimise fluid loss, either by removing the master cylinder reservoir cap and then tightening it down onto a piece of polythene to obtain an airtight seal (taking care not to damage the sender unit), or by using a brake hose clamp, a G-clamp or a similar tool with protected jaws to clamp the flexible hose at the nearest convenient point to the brake caliper.

5 Wipe away all traces of dirt around the brake pipe union on top of the caliper, and unscrew the union nut. Carefully ease the pipe out of position, and plug or tape over its end to prevent dirt entry. Wipe off any spilt fluid immediately.

6 Unscrew the caliper guide pin bolts, using a second spanner on the pin outer hex fitting to prevent the pin turning. Lift the caliper off the pads, and remove it.

Overhaul

Note: *Ensure the correct caliper overhaul kit is obtained before starting work.*

7 With the caliper on the bench, wipe away all traces of dust and dirt, but avoid inhaling the dust, as it is injurious to health.

8 Using a small screwdriver, carefully prise out the dust seal from the caliper bore, taking care not to damage the piston.

9 Remove the piston from the caliper bore by rotating it in an anti-clockwise direction. This can be achieved by using a square-section bar, such as the shaft of a screwdriver, which locates snugly in the caliper piston slots. Once the piston turns freely but does not come out any further, the piston can be withdrawn by hand, or if necessary pushed out by applying compressed air to the union bolt hole.

Caution: The piston may be ejected with some force – only low pressure should be required, such as is generated by a foot pump.

10 Using a blunt instrument such as a knitting needle or a crochet hook, extract the piston hydraulic seal, taking care not to damage the caliper bore.

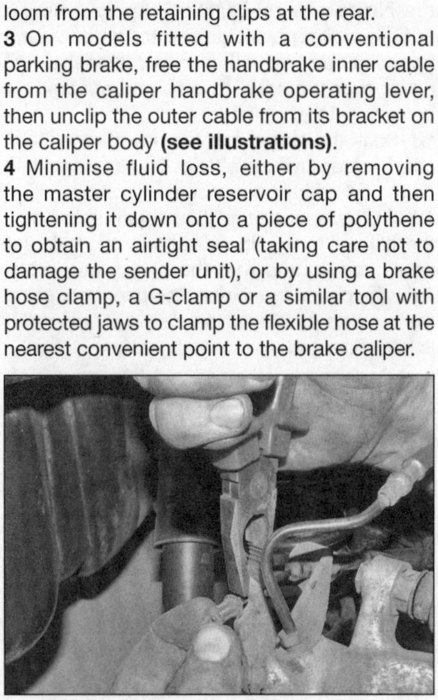

13.3a Release the handbrake cable end fitting from the lever...

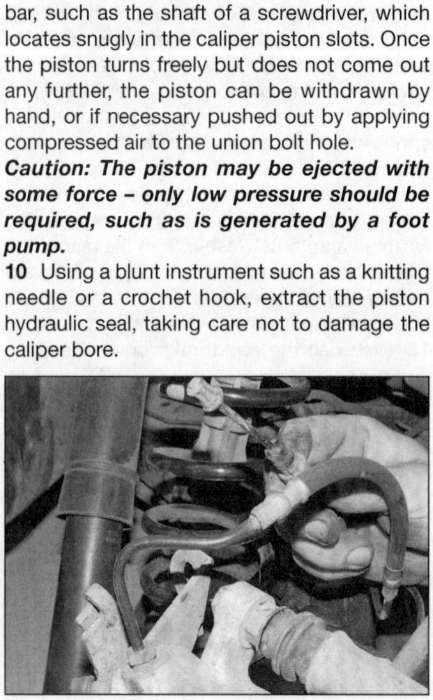

13.3b ...then unclip the cable outer from its bracket

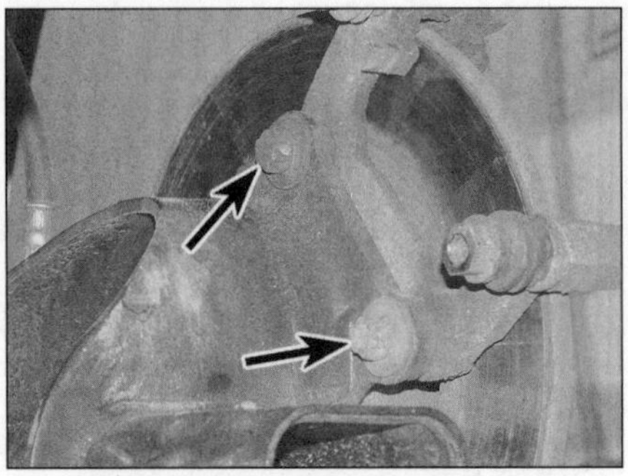

14.4a Unscrew the mounting bolts...

14.4b ...and lift off the caliper mounting bracket

11 Withdraw the guide sleeves from the caliper body, and remove the guide sleeve gaiters.

12 Inspect the caliper components as described in Section 10 for the front calipers. Renew as necessary, noting that the inside of the caliper piston must **not** be dismantled. If necessary, where a conventional parking brake is fitted the operating mechanism can be overhauled as described in the following paragraphs. If it is not wished to overhaul the handbrake mechanism, proceed to paragraph 18.

13 On models fitted with EPB do not attempt to overhaul the motor assembly. Removal of the motor is possible, but Renault recommend that if the motor assembly is removed then the complete caliper should be replaced. Note however that if the parking brake (on EPB models) is stuck on, it is possible to remove the motor and (using a hex key) the piston can be retracted to free off the parking brake.

14 Release the handbrake dust cover retaining clip, and peel the cover away from the rear of the caliper. Make a note of the correct fitted positions of the relative components to use as a guide on reassembly. Remove the circlip from the base of the operating lever shaft, then compress the adjusting screw spring washers, and withdraw the operating lever and dust cover from the caliper body. With the lever withdrawn, remove the return spring, plunger cam, adjusting screw, spring washers and thrustwasher from the rear of the caliper body. Using a pin punch, carefully tap the adjusting screw bush out of the caliper body and remove the O-ring.

15 Clean all the handbrake components in methylated spirit, and examine them for wear. If there is any sign of wear or damage, the complete handbrake mechanism assembly should be renewed.

16 Ensure that all components are clean and dry. Install the O-ring, then press the adjusting screw bush into position until its outer edge is flush with the rear of the caliper body; if necessary, tap the bush into position using a tubular drift. Fit the thrustwasher, then install the adjusting screw and spring washers, ensuring that the washers are correctly positioned. Locate the plunger cam in the end of the adjusting screw, and position the return spring in the caliper housing.

17 Fit the new dust cover to the operating lever, then compress the adjusting screw spring washers and insert the lever shaft through the caliper body, ensuring that it is correctly engaged with the return spring and plunger cam. Secure the operating lever in position with the circlip, then release the spring washers and check the operation of the handbrake mechanism. Apply a smear of high-melting point grease to the operating lever shaft and adjusting screw. Slide the dust cover over the caliper body, and secure it in position with a cable tie.

18 Soak the piston and the new piston (fluid) seal in clean hydraulic fluid. Smear clean fluid on the cylinder bore surface.

19 Fit the new piston (fluid) seal, using only the fingers to manipulate it into the cylinder bore groove, and refit the piston assembly. Turn the piston in a clockwise direction, using the method employed on dismantling, until it is fully retracted into the caliper bore.

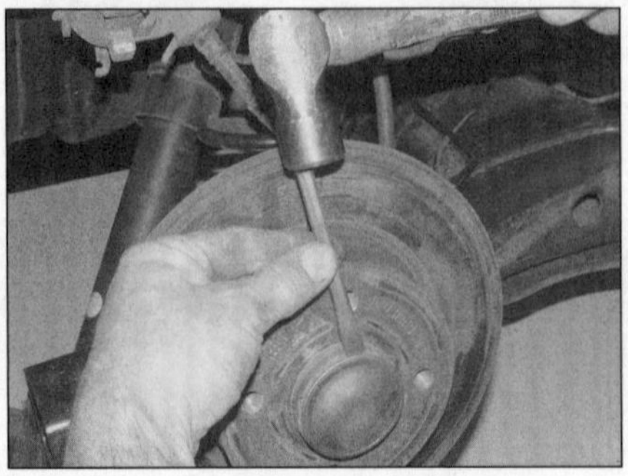

14.5a Using a hammer and punch...

14.5b ...tap off and remove the centre cap

20 Fit the dust seal to the caliper, ensuring that it is correctly located in the caliper and also the groove on the piston.

21 Apply the grease supplied in the repair kit, or a good-quality high-temperature brake grease or anti-seize compound to the guide sleeves. Fit the guide sleeves to the caliper body, and fit the new gaiters, ensuring that the gaiters are correctly located in the grooves on both the guide sleeve and caliper body.

Refitting

22 Position the caliper over the brake disc. Refit the two caliper guide pin bolts and tighten to the specified torque.

23 Wipe clean the brake pipe union. Refit the pipe to the caliper, and tighten its union nut securely.

24 Remove the clamp from the brake hose, or the polythene from the master cylinder reservoir (as applicable).

25 Clip the handbrake outer cable into position, then reconnect the inner cable to the caliper operating lever.

26 Bleed the hydraulic system as described in Section 6. Note that, providing the precautions described were taken to minimise brake fluid loss, it should only be necessary to bleed the relevant rear brake.

27 On models fitted with EPB, deactivate the 'maintenance mode' on the diagnostic tool.

28 Repeatedly apply the brake pedal to bring the pads into contact with the disc. Check and if necessary adjust the handbrake cable as described in Chapter 1A or 1B.

29 Refit the roadwheel, lower the car to the ground and tighten the wheel bolts to the specified torque. On completion, check the hydraulic fluid level as described in *Weekly checks*.

14 Rear brake disc – inspection, removal and refitting

Note: *Refer to the precautions in Section 1 before proceeding.*

Inspection

1 Chock the front wheels, engage reverse gear (or P) and release the handbrake. Jack up the rear of the car and support it on axle stands (see *Jacking and vehicle support*). Remove the appropriate rear roadwheel.

2 Inspect the disc as described in Section 11.

Removal

3 Remove the brake pads as described in Section 12.

4 Remove the two caliper mounting bracket bolts, and lift the bracket off **(see illustrations)**.

5 Using a hammer and a suitable punch (or a large flat-bladed screwdriver), carefully tap and prise the cap out of the centre of the brake disc **(see illustrations)**.

14.6 Unscrew and remove the rear hub nut

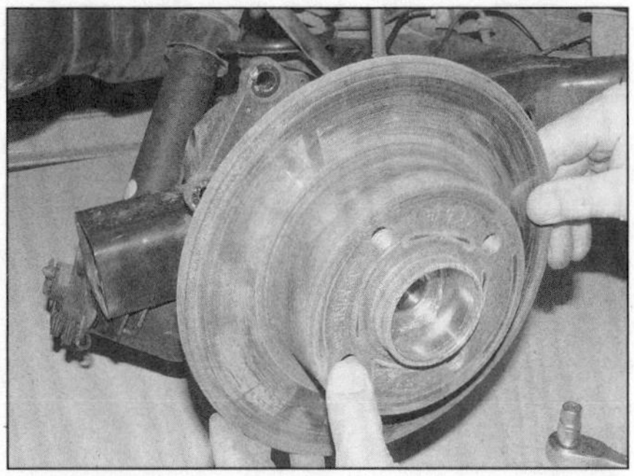

14.7 Withdraw the disc from the stub axle

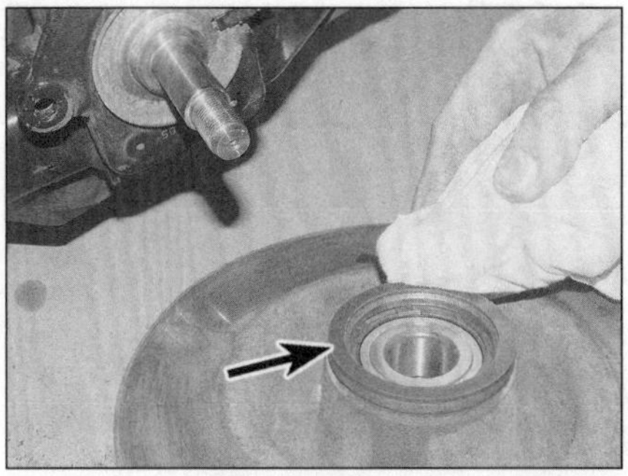

14.9 Clean the magnetic ring on the back of the disc/hub

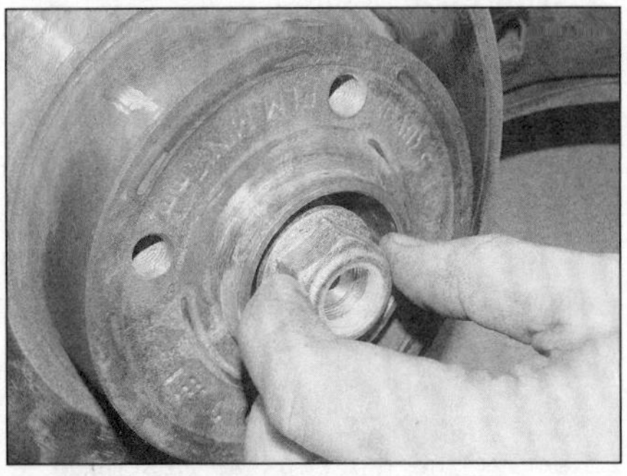

14.10a Fit the new rear hub nut...

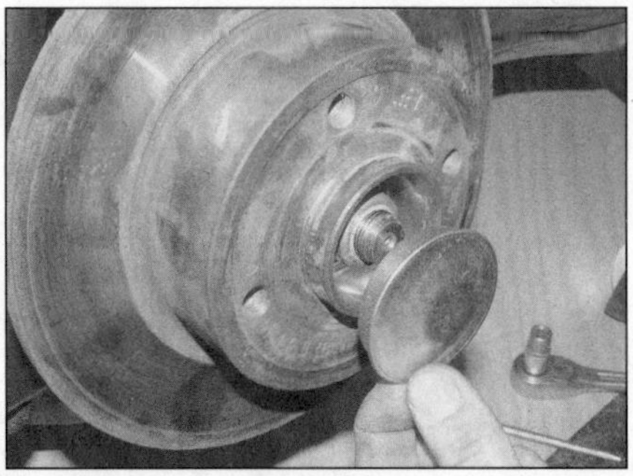

14.10b ...then tap the centre cap into position

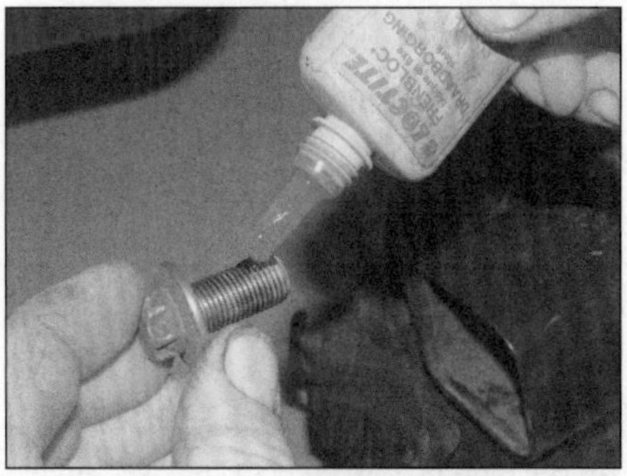

14.11 Apply thread-locking fluid to the caliper mounting bolts

6 Using a socket and long bar, slacken and remove the rear hub nut – this will be very tight, so ensure that the car is well-supported, and that only good-quality, close-fitting tools are used **(see illustration)**. Discard the hub nut; a new nut must be used on refitting.

7 It should now be possible to withdraw the brake disc and hub bearing assembly from the stub axle by hand **(see illustration)**. If the disc is tight, tap the periphery of the disc using a hide or plastic mallet.

Refitting

8 If new discs are being fitted, use a suitable solvent to wipe any preservative coating from its surface. Note that new discs (or at least genuine Renault ones) are supplied with new rear wheel bearings prefitted – the bearings can, however, be renewed separately as described in Chapter 10, Section 9.

9 Before refitting the disc, carefully clean the ABS magnetic ring on the back, surrounding the hub bearing **(see illustration)**.

10 Fit the new rear hub nut and tighten it to the specified torque. Tap the cap back into position in the centre of the disc (if the cap is in poor condition, a new one should be fitted) **(see illustrations)**.

11 Apply a few drops of locking fluid to the threads of the caliper mounting bracket bolts **(see illustration)**. Offer up the bracket and refit the bolts, tightening them to the specified torque.

12 Refit the brake pads as described in Section 12.

13 Check the handbrake cable adjustment as described in Chapter 1A or 1B.

14 Refit the roadwheels and lower the car to the ground. Tighten the roadwheel bolts to the specified torque.

15 Handbrake lever – removal and refitting

Removal

1 Chock the front wheels and engage reverse gear. Release the handbrake. Jack up the rear of the car and support it on axle stands (see *Jacking and vehicle support*).

2 On models fitted with a conventional handbrake, remove the centre console as described in Chapter 11, Section 23. Though not essential, access to the handbrake is greatly improved by removing one of the front seats (also Chapter 11).

3 On models with EPB connect the diagnostic tool and select the 'repair' or 'maintenance' mode. Prise free the upper section on the centre console as described in Chapter 11. Disconnect the wiring plug and unbolt the lever/switch.

4 To fully access the handbrake lever the carpet must be cut **(see illustration)**.

5 Pull up and remove the cover from the airbag control unit **(see illustration)**. Renault insist that this cover is replaced with a new one on refitting. Remove the sound proofing insulation from in front of the handbrake.

6 Before slackening the handbrake adjuster nut, measure the length of exposed thread on the adjuster rod and make a note of it – this way, the adjustment can be reset to its original setting when refitting.

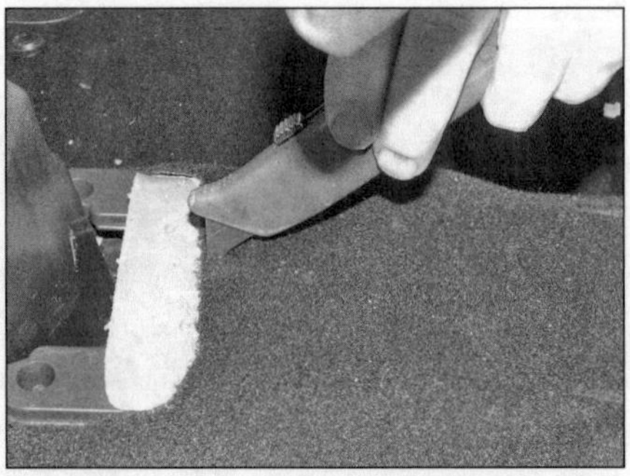

15.4 Make a cut in the carpet between the gear lever and the handbrake lever

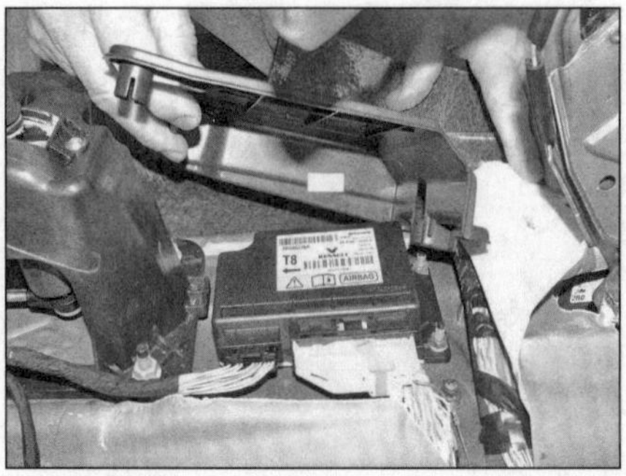

15.5 Remove the cover from the control unit

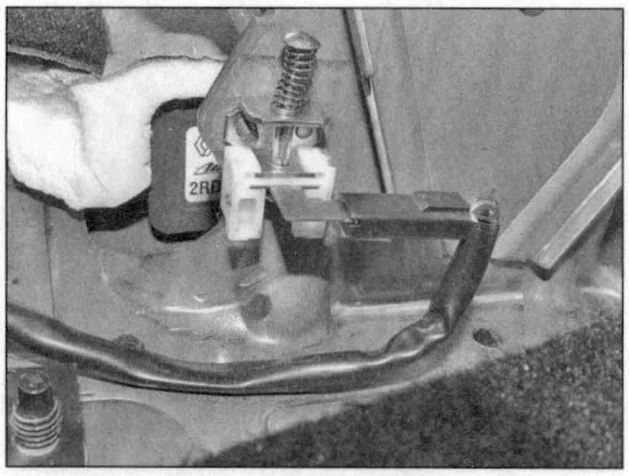

15.8 Disconnect the handbrake warning light switch wiring plug

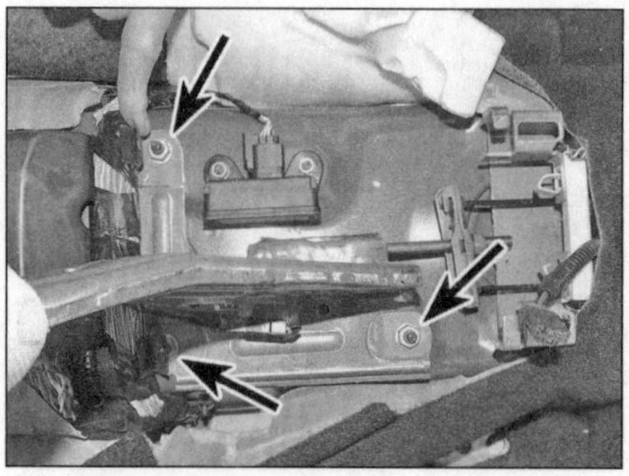

15.9 Remove the handbrake lever mounting nuts (arrowed)

7 Loosen the adjuster nut until both handbrake cables can be unhooked from the equaliser bar by moving them sideways.

8 Disconnect the wiring plug from the handbrake warning light switch **(see illustration)**.

9 Unclip the wiring loom at the front of the handbrake lever and then unscrew the handbrake lever mounting nuts **(see illustrations).** Remove the lever assembly out of the car.

Refitting

10 Refitting is a reversal of removal. Adjust the handbrake as described in Chapter 1A or 1B, setting the adjuster nut to the dimension noted on removal as a starting point. Fit a new cover to the airbag control unit. On models with EPB connect the diagnostic tool and follow the 'after repair' instructions displayed on the tool.

16 Handbrake cables – removal and refitting

Removal

1 The right- and left-hand cables are linked to the lever assembly by an equaliser plate. Each cable can be removed individually as follows.

2 Chock the front wheels, engage reverse gear and release the handbrake. Jack up the rear of the car and support it on axle stands (see *Jacking and vehicle support*).

3 To gain the best access to the cables, remove the centre console and one front seat as described in Chapter 11. Alternatively, prise off the rear storage compartment to access the cables **(see illustrations)**.

4 Loosen the handbrake adjuster nut, and disconnect the cables from the equaliser bar.

5 Disengage the inner cable from the caliper handbrake lever, then unclip the outer cable from its mounting bracket **(see illustrations)**.

6 Working along the length of the cable, remove any retaining bolts and screws, and free the cable from the retaining clips and ties **(see illustrations)**. Remove the cable from under the car.

Refitting

7 Refitting is a reversal of removal. Adjust the handbrake as described in Chapter 1A or 1B.

17 Stop-light switch – removal, refitting and adjustment

Note: *Renault recommend that the switch is replaced if removed.*

Removal

1 The stop-light switch is located on the passenger-side end of the brake pedal cross-shaft, and is accessed from the front passenger footwell.

2 Remove the glovebox as described in Chapter 11.

3 To further improve access, unclip and remove the plastic air duct fitted below the glovebox location **(see illustration)**.

4 Disconnect the wiring plug from the brake light switch **(see illustration)** then turn the switch approximately one eighth of a turn

16.3a Unclip the centre console rear panel...

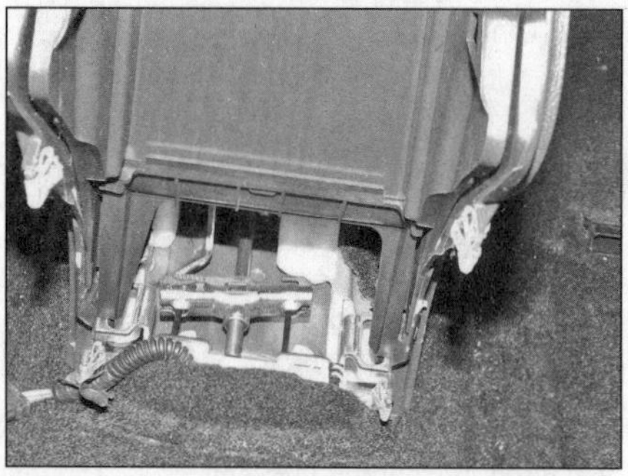

16.3b ...for access to the handbrake cables

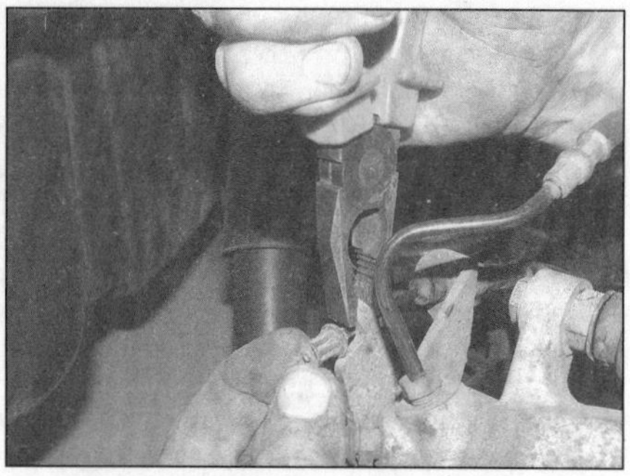

16.5a Release the handbrake cable end fitting from the lever...

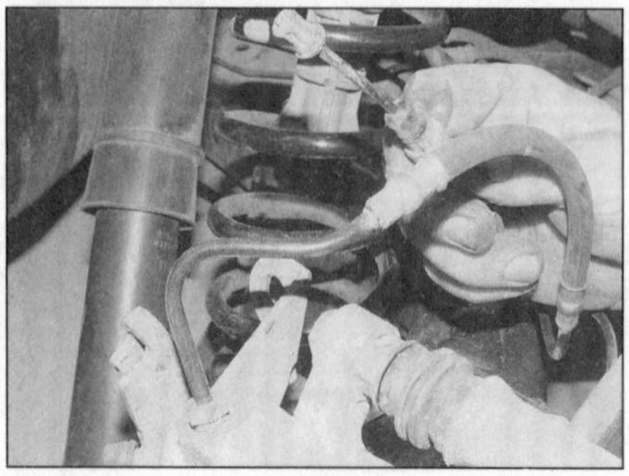

16.5b ...then unclip the cable outer from its bracket

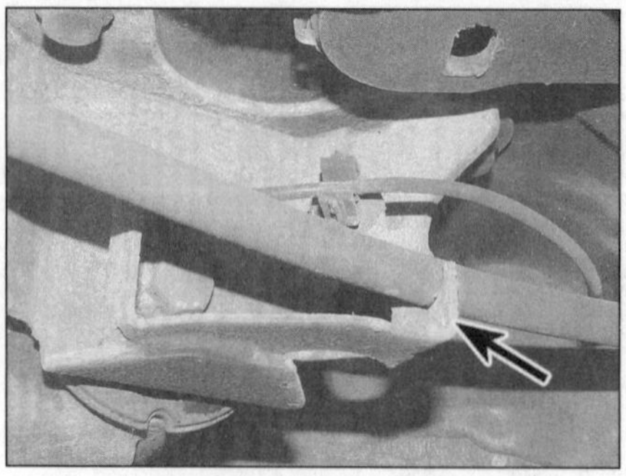

16.6a The handbrake cables may be supported in metal holders . . .

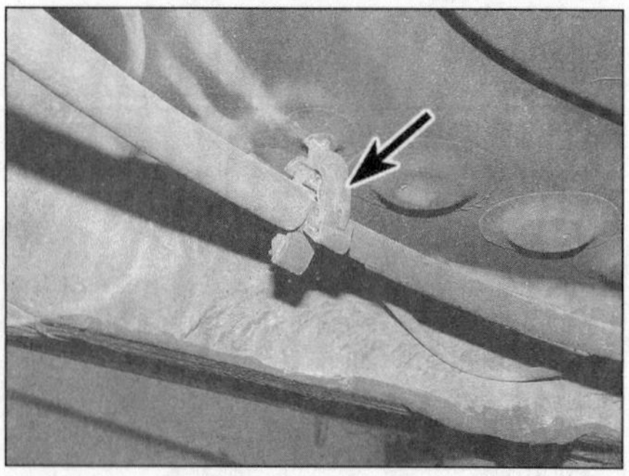

16.6b . . . or retained in plastic clips to the underside of the car

anti-clockwise and remove it. Recover the retaining ring from the mounting bracket.

Refitting and adjustment

5 Refitting is a reversal of removal, but note that:

a) A new switch and lock ring should be fitted.
b) Fully raise the brake pedal.
c) Insert the new switch and ensure the end of the switch is in contact with the yoke on the link bar.
d) Turn the switch clockwise to lock the switch in position and release the brake pedal
e) Check that a gap of between 1 and 2.5 mm exists between the switch plunger and the link bar yoke. Adjust the position of switch if necessary.
f) Reconnect the wiring plug.
g) Check the operation of the brake lights.

6 On completion, check the operation of the stop-lights.

18 Anti-lock braking system (ABS) – general information

The purpose of the system is to prevent the wheel(s) locking during heavy braking. This is achieved by automatic release of the brake on the relevant wheel before it can lock up, followed by rapid reapplication of the brake.

The main components of the system are four wheel sensors (one per wheel), and a modulator block which contains the ABS computer, the hydraulic solenoid valves and accumulators, and an electrically-driven return pump.

The solenoids are controlled by the computer, which receives signals from the wheel sensors. The sensors detect the speed of rotation of a reluctor ring, attached to the wheel hub. By comparing the speed signals from the four wheels, the computer can determine when a wheel is decelerating at an abnormal rate, and can therefore predict when a wheel is about to lock. During normal operation, the system functions in the same way as a non-ABS braking system does.

If the computer senses that a wheel is about to lock, the ABS system enters the 'pressure-maintain' phase. The computer operates the relevant solenoid valve in the modulator block; this isolates the brake on the wheel in question from the master cylinder, effectively sealing-in the hydraulic pressure.

If the speed of rotation of the wheel continues to decrease at an abnormal rate, the ABS system then enters the 'pressure-decrease' phase. The return pump operates and pumps the hydraulic fluid back into the master cylinder, releasing pressure on the brake. When the speed of rotation of the wheel returns to an acceptable rate, the pump stops and the solenoid valve opens, allowing hydraulic pressure to return and reapply the

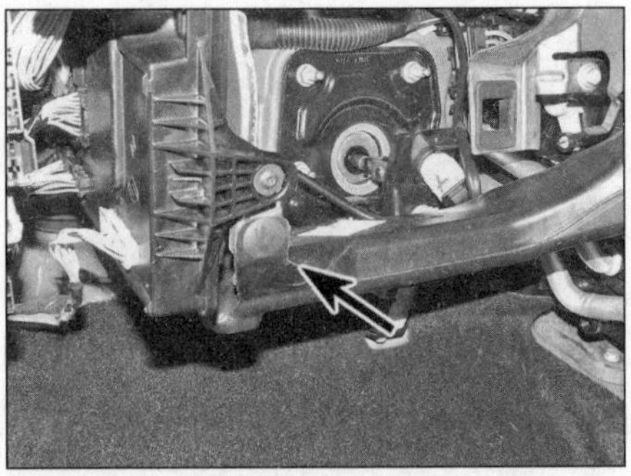

17.3 Prise out the retaining clip (arrowed) and remove the duct

brake. This cycle can be carried out at up to 10 times a second.

The action of the solenoid valves and return pump creates pulses in the hydraulic circuit. When the ABS system is functioning, these pulses can be felt through the brake pedal.

The Mégane is also equipped with an additional safety feature built into the ABS system, called EBD (Electronic Brake force Distribution), which automatically apportions braking effort between the front and rear wheels. The EBD function is built into the system's software, and the intention is to limit braking effort (fluid pressure) to the rear wheels, to prevent them locking up under heavy braking.

Another feature of the ABS is Brake Assist, which monitors how rapidly the brake pedal is pressed, and determines whether an emergency stop is required – in this case, maximum braking effort is applied more quickly than the driver would normally be able to, unaided.

The Electronic Stability Programme (ESP) is available as an option. This system uses the ABS to prevent wheel spin or skidding during acceleration or cornering, by selectively and partially applying the brakes individually or in pairs, to either 'steer' the car, or slow the front wheels (traction control). A yaw sensor mounted on the transmission tunnel **(see illustration)** informs the system ECU of the lateral (sideways) forces acting on the car, indicating the direction and speed of cornering. An integral steering angle sensor in the steering system is used to indicate

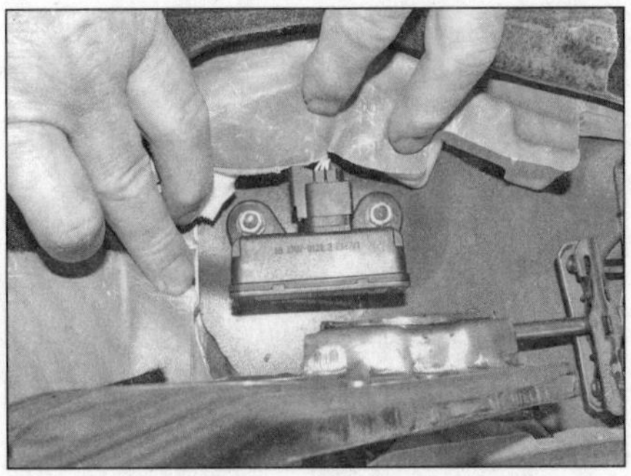

18.8 The yaw sensor

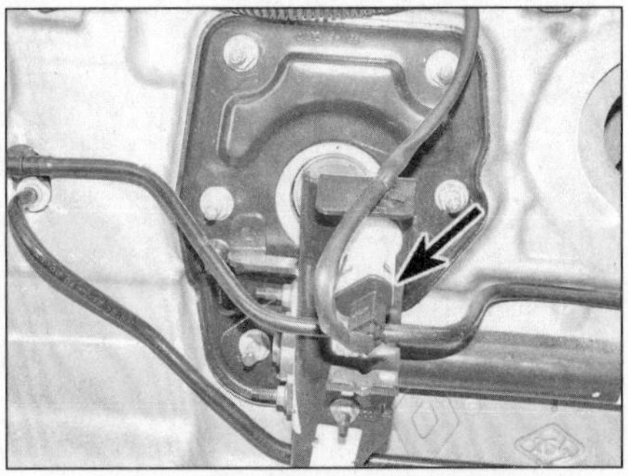

17.4 Disconnect the brake light switch plug, then twist and remove it

the amount of steering lock applied. A front-wheel drive car will typically understeer (run wide) if excess power is used when cornering on a slippery road – if the yaw sensor detects this condition, one or more brakes will be applied to help turn the car, and engine power will be momentarily reduced. Similarly, the traction control function uses the front wheel sensors to detect abnormally-fast wheel rotation, relative to the vehicle speed – when wheel spin is occurring, the engine power will be reduced, and the front brakes applied slightly

The operation of the ABS system is entirely dependent on electrical signals. To prevent the system responding to any inaccurate signals, a built-in safety circuit monitors all signals received by the computer. If an inaccurate signal or low battery voltage is detected, the ABS system is automatically shut down, and the warning light on the instrument panel is illuminated to inform the driver that the ABS system is not operational. Normal braking is unaffected, apart from the loss of the Electronic Brake force Distribution function (which may result in premature rear wheel lock-up under braking).

If a fault does develop in the ABS system, the car must be taken to a Renault dealer or suitably equipped garage for fault diagnosis and repair. Check first, however, that the problem is not due to loose or damaged wiring connections, or badly-routed wiring picking up spurious signals from the ignition system.

19 Anti-lock braking system (ABS) components – removal and refitting

Note: *Refer to the precautions in Section 1 before proceeding.*

Hydraulic unit

Removal

1 Have the AC system drained at a suitably equipped garage – or alternatively have a mobile air conditioning service drain the refrigerant.

2 The hydraulic unit is located in the far right-hand rear corner of the engine compartment, right up against the bulkhead. Access to the unit is far from easy.

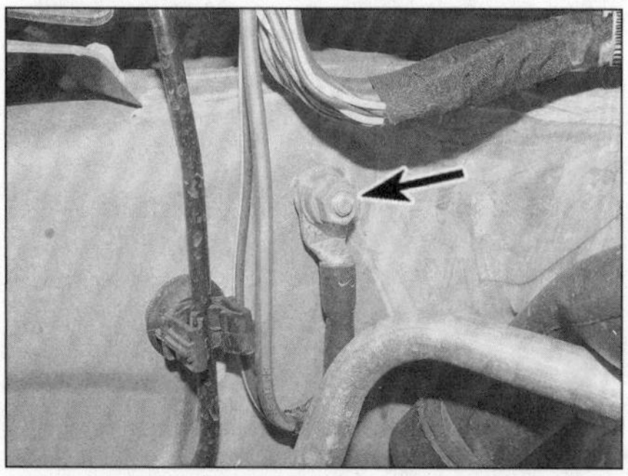

19.15 Unscrew the nut and disconnect the unit's earth lead

3 Disconnect the battery negative lead (refer to *Disconnecting the battery* Chapter 5A) and then remove the battery.
4 Where fitted, remove the engine top cover and then remove the air filter assembly as described in Chapter 4A or 4B.
5 Remove the windscreen cowl panels as described in Chapter 11.
6 Jack up and support the front of the vehicle (see *Jacking and vehicle support* in the reference section).
7 Remove both front wheels and then remove the engine undershield. Remove the front section of both front wing liners.
8 With reference to Chapter 10 remove the front subframe.
9 Disconnect the exhaust at the manifold and move it to one side. Support the pipe.
10 On diesel models remove the catalytic convertor and inter cooler pipe as described in Chapter 4B.
11 Release the heat shield from above the exhaust and move it to the rear of the vehicle.
12 Release the clips and remove the heat shield from the bulkhead.
13 Release the fuel lines from above the modulator.
14 At the bulkhead, disconnect the AC pipes from the expansion valve.
15 Unscrew the nut and disconnect the hydraulic unit's earth lead from the inner wing **(see illustration)**.
16 Turn the locking catch on the unit's wiring connector plug, then disconnect the plug and move the harness to one side **(see illustration)**.
17 Before removing the hydraulic unions from

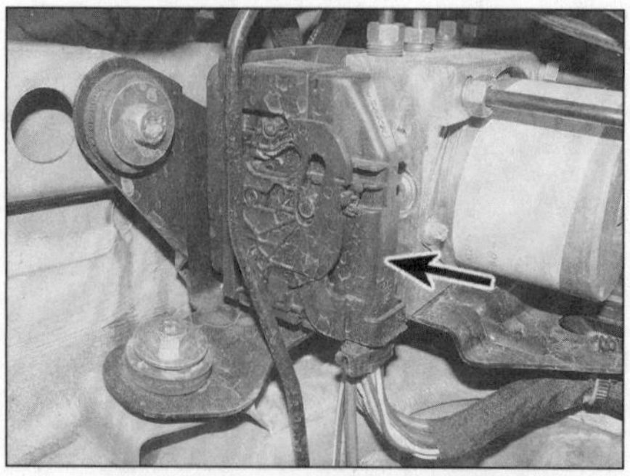

19.16 Turn the locking catch and disconnect the unit wiring plug

the unit, it may be advisable to mark them for position, perhaps by attaching labels, or marked pieces of tape, to each pipe.
18 Loosen the hydraulic unions, then disconnect and unclip the pipes from the unit – avoid bending the pipes at all costs.
19 Unscrew the three bolts securing the unit's mounting bracket, then remove the unit/bracket assembly from its location. If required, the unit and bracket can be separated after removal.

Caution: Do not attempt to dismantle the hydraulic unit assembly. Overhaul of the unit is a complex job, and should be entrusted to a Renault dealer.

Refitting

20 Refitting is the reverse of the removal procedure, noting the following points:

a) *Tighten the hydraulic unit mounting bolts to the specified torque.*
b) *Refit the brake pipes to the correct unions, and tighten the union nuts to the specified torque.*
c) *Reconnect the wiring plug securely.*
d) *Before reconnecting the battery, bleed the complete braking system as described in Section 6. Ensure the system is bled in the correct order, to prevent air entering the return pump.*

ABS computer

Note: *The computer can be removed from the modulator, but it is not available as a separate part*
21 Remove the hydraulic unit as described earlier in this Section.

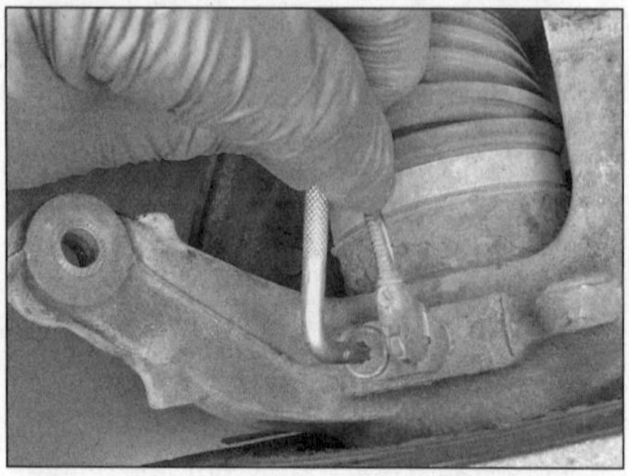

19.27 Remove the wheel speed sensor

20.4 Disconnect the hoses from the vacuum pump

22 Using a multi-spline socket, unscrew the four retaining bolts and remove the ABS computer. Discard the bolts as new ones must be used on refitting. **Note:** *When handling the computer, always hold it by its edge to prevent any stray electrical discharge.*
23 Refitting is a reversal of removal, but tighten the retaining bolts to the specified torque.

Wheel sensors

Front wheel sensor

24 Jack up the front of the car and support on axle stands (see *Jacking and vehicle support*). Remove the appropriate front wheel.
25 Unclip the front section of the wheel arch liner for access to the wiring connector.
26 Release the sensor wiring support clip then release the wiring connector.
27 Remove the bolt and then pull out the sensor **(see illustration)**.
28 Refitting is a reversal of removal.

Rear wheel sensor

29 Jack up the rear of the car and support on axle stands (see *Jacking and vehicle support*). Remove the rear wheel.
30 Using a flat-blade screwdriver, carefully press the retaining clip and remove the sensor from the backplate.
31 Release the sensor wiring support clips then release the wiring connector and remove the sensor and wiring.
32 Refitting is a reversal of removal.

Yaw speed and transversal acceleration sensor

33 Remove the centre console as described in Chapter 11, Section 23.
34 A small cut will need to be made in the soundproofing to access the sensor.
35 Note the forward facing arrow on the sensor **(see illustration 18.8)**, then disconnect the wiring, unscrew the mounting nuts and remove the sensor.
36 Refitting is a reversal of removal, but make sure the sensor is located with the arrow pointing forwards and tighten the mounting nuts to the specified torque.

20 Vacuum pump (diesel engines) – removal and refitting

Removal

1 Where fitted remove the engine cover.
2 Unbolt the support bracket from the right-hand end of the engine.
3 Unbolt the turbo boost control solenoid from the battery tray and move it to one side.
4 Squeeze together the tabs on the hose end fitting, and disconnect the vacuum hose from the pump **(see illustration)**. Pull off the vacuum supply hose.
5 Slacken and remove the two mounting bolts securing the pump to the end of the cylinder

head **(see illustration)**, then remove the pump. Recover the pump gasket and discard it; a new one should be used on refitting.

Refitting

6 Ensure that the pump and cylinder head mating surfaces are clean and dry, and fit the new gasket to the head **(see illustration)**.

7 Manoeuvre the pump into position, then refit the pump mounting bolts and tighten them securely.

21 Vacuum pump (diesel engines) – testing and overhaul

1 The operation of the braking system vacuum pump can be checked using a vacuum gauge.

2 Disconnect the vacuum pipe from the pump, and connect the gauge to the pump union using a length of hose.

3 Start the engine and allow it to idle, then measure the vacuum created by the pump. As a guide, after one minute, a minimum of approximately 500 mm Hg should be recorded. If the vacuum registered is significantly less than this, it is likely that the pump is faulty. However, seek the advice of a Renault dealer before condemning the pump.

4 Overhaul of the vacuum pump may not be possible; check for availability of spares.

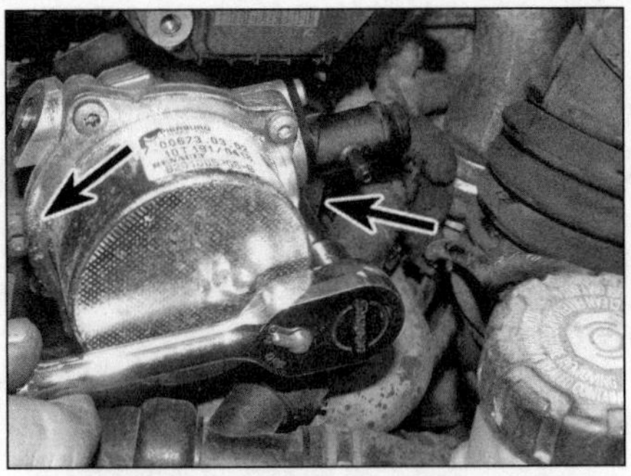

20.5 Remove the two pump mounting bolts (arrowed) – one out of view

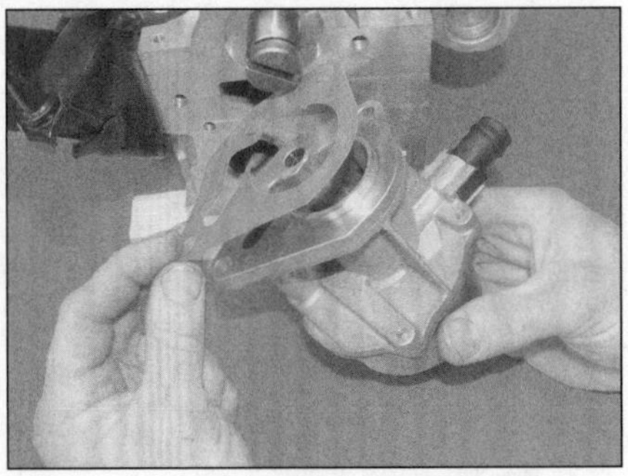

20.6 Use a new gasket when fitting the vacuum pump

Chapter 10
Suspension and steering

Contents

	Section number
Front anti-roll bar – removal and refitting	6
Front lower arm – removal, overhaul and refitting	7
Front strut – dismantling, inspection and reassembly	5
Front strut – removal and refitting	4
Front subframe – removal and refitting	8
Front suspension and steering check	See Chapter 1A or 1B
Front swivel hub assembly – removal and refitting	2
Front wheel bearings – checking, removal and refitting	3
General information	1
Rear axle – removal and refitting	12
Rear coil spring – removal and refitting	11
Rear shock absorber – removal, testing and refitting	10
Rear wheel bearings – checking, removal and refitting	9
Ride height – general information and checking	13
Steering column – removal, overhaul and refitting	15
Steering gear assembly – removal, inspection and refitting	17
Steering gear rubber gaiter – renewal	16
Steering wheel – removal and refitting	14
Track rod end balljoint – removal and refitting	18
Tyre pressure monitoring system – general information	20
Wheel alignment and steering angles – general information	19
Wheel and tyre maintenance and tyre pressure checks	See *Weekly checks*

Degrees of difficulty

Easy, suitable for novice with little experience	**Fairly easy,** suitable for beginner with some experience	**Fairly difficult,** suitable for competent DIY mechanic	**Difficult,** suitable for experienced DIY mechanic	**Very difficult,** suitable for expert DIY or professional

Specifications

Front suspension

Type	Independent, MacPherson struts, with coil springs and integral shock absorbers. Anti-roll bar fitted to all models
Hub bearing endfloat	0 to 0.05 mm

Rear suspension

Type	Semi-independent twist-beam axle, telescopic dampers and separate coil springs
Hub bearing endfloat	0 to 0.05 mm

Steering

Type	Power-assisted steering, rack-and-pinion, assistance provided by electric motor integrated into steering column

Wheel alignment and steering angles*

Front wheel toe setting:	+0° 10’ ± 10’ toe-out
Castor angle (not adjustable):	
Hatchback	5° 42’ ± 2°
Estate	5° 42’ ± 2°
Coupe	7° 18’ ± 2°
Front wheel camber angle at ride height (not adjustable):	
Hatchback	-31’ ± 30’
Estate	-31’ ± 30’
Coupe	-51’ ± 30’
Steering axis/kingpin inclination at ride height (not adjustable):	
Hatchback	13°0’ ± 30’
Estate	13°0’ ± 30’
Coupe	9°28’ ± 30’
Ride height**	
Front:	
Hatchback	164 mm
Estate	164 mm
Coupe	153 mm
Rear:	
Hatchback	246 mm
Estate	245 mm
Coupe	234 mm

* *All measurements are taken with the vehicle unladen, but with a full tank of fuel*

** *Refer to Section 13 for details of measuring ride height*

Tyres

Tyre sizes and pressures	See end of *Weekly checks* on page 0•16

Roadwheels

Type	Pressed-steel or aluminium alloy
Size	6.5J x 15, 6.5J x 16 or 6.5J x 17
Maximum run-out at rim	1.2 mm

Torque wrench settings

	Nm	lbf ft
Front suspension		
Anti-roll bar drop link rod balljoint nut	44	32
Anti-roll bar mounting clamp bolts	21	15
Driveshaft (hub) nut*	280	207
Lower arm balljoint clamp bolt	62	46
Lower arm mounting bolts/nuts	70	52
Radiator crossmember:		
Front mounting bolt	180	133
Side support plate bolts	21	15
Rear crossmember bolts	62	46
Strut lower pinch-bolts*	180	133
Strut piston rod nut*	62	46
Strut upper mounting bolt (to body)	21	15
Subframe front bolts*	105	77
Subframe rear bolts	180	133
Rear suspension		
Rear hub nut:*	220	162
Rear axle-to-chassis securing bolts	105	77
Rear stub axle bolts	185	137
Rear trailing arm pivot bolt nut	125	92
Shock absorber lower mounting bolt	105	77
Shock absorber upper mounting bolt	62	46
Steering		
Steering column mounting nuts	21	15
Steering column universal joint bolt*	62	46
Steering rack mounting bolts*	180	133
Steering wheel bolt*	44	32
Track rod end balljoint-to-swivel hub retaining nut*	37	27
Track rod end locknut	53	39
Roadwheels		
Wheel bolts	110	81

** Use a new nut/bolt*

1 General information

The independent front suspension is of the MacPherson strut type, incorporating coil springs and integral telescopic shock absorbers. The MacPherson struts are located by transverse lower suspension arms, which utilise rubber inner mounting bushes and incorporate a balljoint at the outer ends. The front swivel hubs, which carry the wheel bearings, brake calipers and the hub/disc assemblies, are bolted to the MacPherson struts and connected to the lower arms via the balljoints. A front anti-roll bar is fitted to all models. The anti-roll bar is rubber-mounted onto the subframe, and connects both the lower suspension arms.

The rear suspension is a twist-beam axle, with coil springs and separate telescopic dampers. At the pivot points (in front of the 'trailing arms') the axle is attached to the vehicle underbody by rubber bushes, and the rear ends are located by the inclined shock absorbers, which are bolted to the underbody at their upper ends. The coil springs are mounted separately from the shock absorbers, and act directly between the axle and the underbody.

The steering column is connected by a universal joint to an intermediate shaft, which has a second universal joint at its lower end. The lower universal joint is attached to the steering gear pinion by means of an eccentric clamp bolt.

The steering gear is mounted onto the front subframe. It is connected by two track rods and balljoints to steering arms projecting rearwards from the swivel hubs. The track rod ends are threaded to enable wheel alignment (toe) adjustment.

An electrically-powered motor is used to provide the steering's power assistance, rather than the conventional engine-driven hydraulic pump. The motor is attached to the steering column, and at the time of writing could only be purchased as a complete unit with the steering column shaft – check with your local dealer for availability of parts.

2 Front swivel hub assembly – removal and refitting

Removal

1 Remove the wheel trim or wheel centre cap, as applicable. Have an assistant firmly apply the footbrake, then slacken the driveshaft nut – the nut is extremely tight, so use good-quality, close-fitting tools **(see illustration)**. Remove the hub nut.

2 Loosen the front wheel bolts, then jack up the front of the car and support it on axle stands (see *Jacking and vehicle support*). Remove the front wheel.

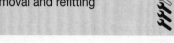

2.1 Loosen the driveshaft nut while the car is resting on its wheels, if possible

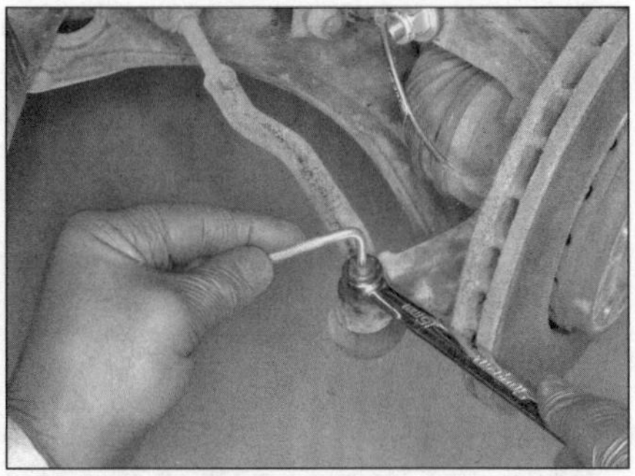

2.3a Unscrew the track rod end balljoint nut...

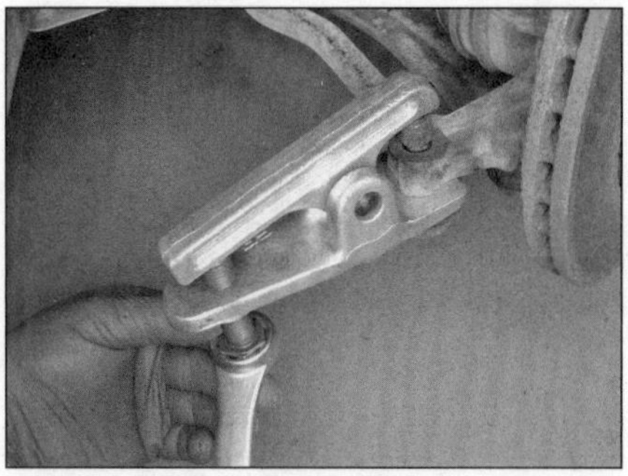

2.3b ...then use a balljoint separator tool to free the balljoint...

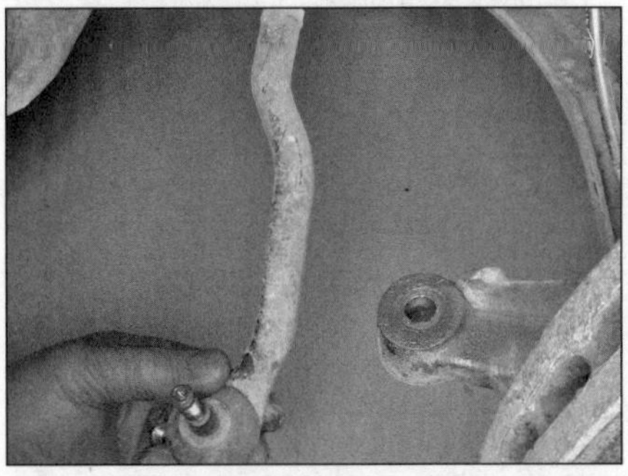

2.3c ...and disconnect the track rod end from the hub

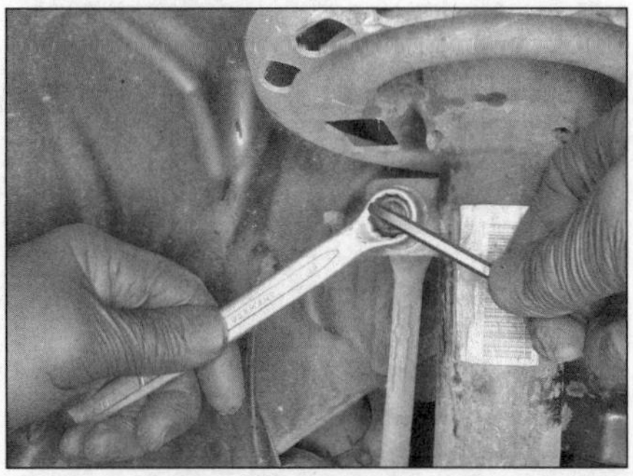

2.5a Unscrew the anti-roll bar drop link nut, using an Allen key to hold the stud...

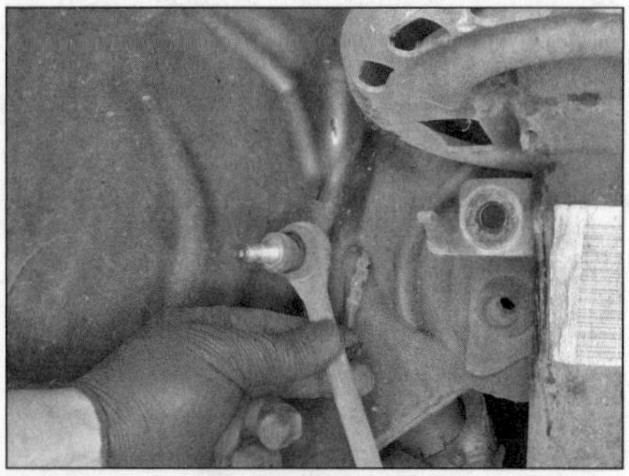

2.5b ...then separate the link rod from the strut

3 Loosen the track rod end balljoint nut, unscrewing it almost to the end of its threads (if the nut will not unscrew, hold the balljoint stud on top using a small spanner). Use a balljoint separator tool to free the balljoint, then unscrew the nut completely, and disconnect the track rod from the swivel hub **(see illustrations)**.

4 Remove the front brake caliper, caliper mounting bracket and brake disc as described in Chapter 9, Section 10. Secure the caliper to the strut assembly with stout cord or a cable tie.

5 Unscrew the upper nut from the anti-roll bar drop link, using an Allen key if necessary to prevent the balljoint stud turning as this is done **(see illustrations)**.

6 Unclip the ABS sensor wiring loom from the support bracket at the base of the strut **(see illustration)**. Remove the bolt from the sensor, pull out the sensor and secure the loom and sensor to one side.

7 Where fitted disconnect the link arm for the headlight adjustment sensor – zenon headlights only.

8 Apply penetrating fluid to the end of the driveshaft and push the driveshaft into the hub. If this proves difficult, refit the hub nut and use a copper or hide headed hammer to drive the driveshaft into the hub. It only needs to move to confirm that it is free from the hub.

9 Unscrew the nut from the lower balljoint. Leave the nut on the shank until the ball joint is freed from the hub.

10 The lower balljoint must now be separated, by pulling the lower arm downwards. Apply plenty of penetrating spray to begin with. We used a long pole, fitted into a wooden block under the car, with a chain wrapped around the end of the lower arm, to provide sufficient leverage **(see illustration)**. A conventional forked ball joint tool could also be used, but this carries the risk of damaging the ball joint sealing boot. Note that there is insufficient room to fit a scissor type ball joint tool. Free the taper on the ball joint, but do not release the hub completely at this point.

11 Remove both bolts from the base of the strut **(see illustration)**. Discard the nuts – they must be replaced.

12 Remove the hub nut and the ball joint nut and discard them – they must be replaced.

13 Pull the hub outwards, press down on the lower arm and free the hub from the base of the strut. It's helpful to have an assistant on hand here, to pull the hub outwards, while you hold back the driveshaft **(see illustration)**. **Note:** *Once the left-hand driveshaft has been removed from the hub, there is nothing to prevent it dropping out of the transmission.*

2.6 Unclip the sensor loom from the base of the strut

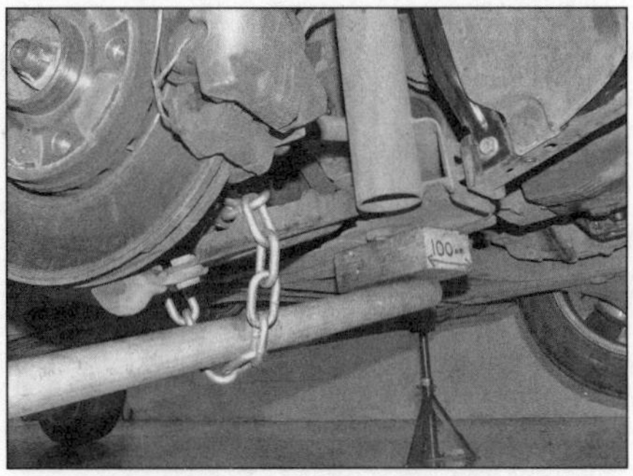

2.10 Using a long pole, wood block and chain to lever down the lower arm

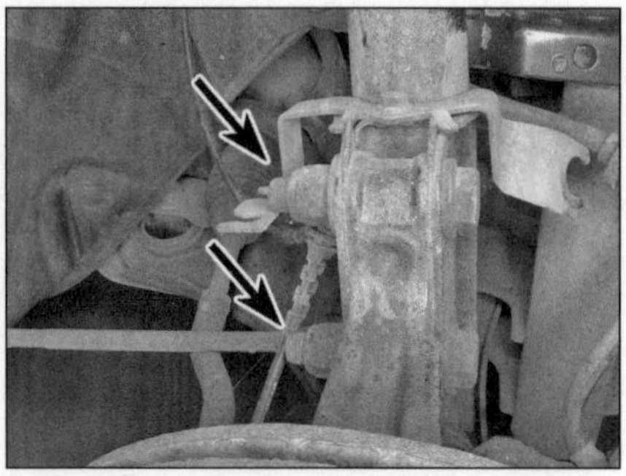

2.11 Remove the nut/bolts (arrowed) from the strut

2.13 Separate the hub from the base of the strut

14 Secure the driveshaft with stout cord, so that no strain is placed on the inner driveshaft joint.

Refitting

15 Refitting is a reversal of removal, noting the following points:

a) Lubricate the driveshaft splines with a little grease before inserting into the hub.

b) Tighten all nuts/bolts to the specified torque, but delay tightening the driveshaft nut fully until the car it back on the ground.

c) Remember to refit the ABS sensor wiring bracket to the strut.

d) Ensure that the brake hose and ABS wiring are routed correctly, and clipped into their respective brackets securely.

f) On completion, if new components have been fitted, it is advisable to have the wheel alignment checked.

3 Front wheel bearings – checking, removal and refitting

Note: *The bearing is a sealed, pre-adjusted and prelubricated, double-row roller type, and is intended to last the car's entire service life without maintenance or attention. Do not attempt to remove the bearing unless absolutely necessary, as it will be damaged during the removal operation. Never overtighten the driveshaft nut in an attempt to 'adjust' the bearing.*

Note: *A press will be required to dismantle and rebuild the assembly; if such a tool is not available, a large bench vice, big nuts/bolts and spacers (such as large sockets) will serve as an adequate substitute. A punch or chisel will also be needed to remove the bearing inner race from the hub flange.*

Checking

1 Wear in the front hub bearings can be checked for as described in Chapter 1A or 1B. However, the most common first symptom of bearing wear is a rumbling noise, noted at a particular roadspeed, or when the offending wheel is loaded-up during cornering. In this case, besides rocking the wheel, spin it and listen carefully, to distinguish between the sound of the brake pads rubbing the disc, and the rumble of bearing wear. Compare the sound with the other front wheel to confirm.

2 Wheel bearings do not have to be renewed in pairs. However, if the bearing on one side has worn, it may only be a short while before the other one needs renewal.

Removal

3 With the swivel hub removed as described in Section 2, proceed as follows.

4 The hub flange must first be removed from the bearing/swivel hub assembly. It is preferable to use a press to do this, but it is possible to drive out the hub using a metal tube of suitable diameter. Alternatively, a suitable puller can be used.

5 Securely support the hub carrier, on two metal bars for instance, with the inner face uppermost then, using a metal bar or tube of suitable diameter, press or drive out the hub flange – we used a bolt and large washer (the same diameter as the end of the hub's splined end) **(see illustrations)**. Alternatively, use the puller to separate the hub flange from the bearing. Note that the bearing inner race will remain on the hub.

6 The bearing inner race left on the hub flange must now be removed. To do this, grip the edge of the flange in a vice, and tap the race off with a chisel **(see illustrations)**. Tap the race at the top and both sides (even turn the flange over in the vice) to stop it jamming as it comes off.

7 To remove the bearing itself, the retaining circlip must first be removed, which requires the use of a sturdy pair of circlip pliers **(see illustrations)**. A new circlip should be used

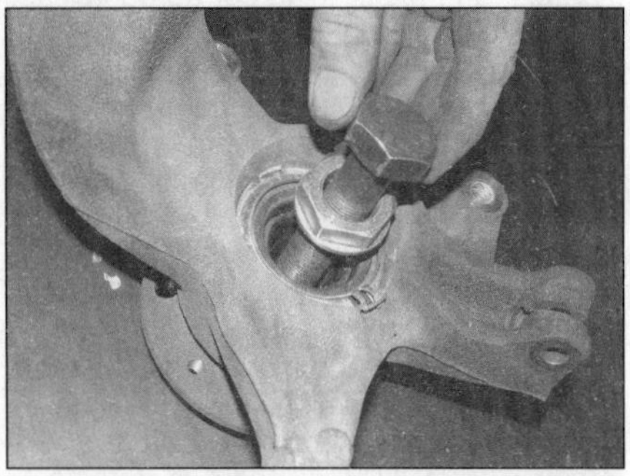

3.5a Insert a large bolt and flanged nut of the right diameter...

3.5b ...and using a large hammer...

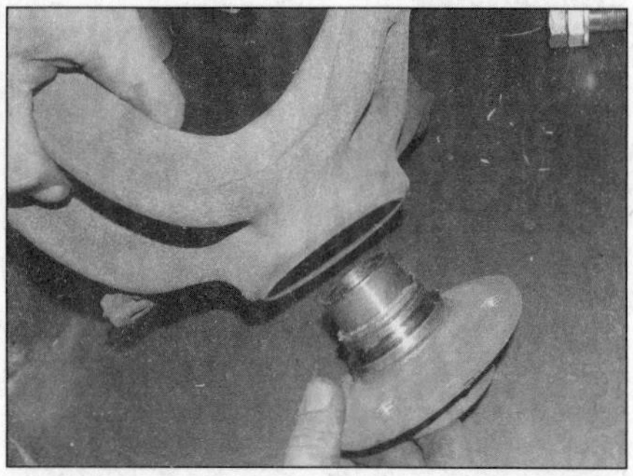

3.5c ...drive out the hub flange

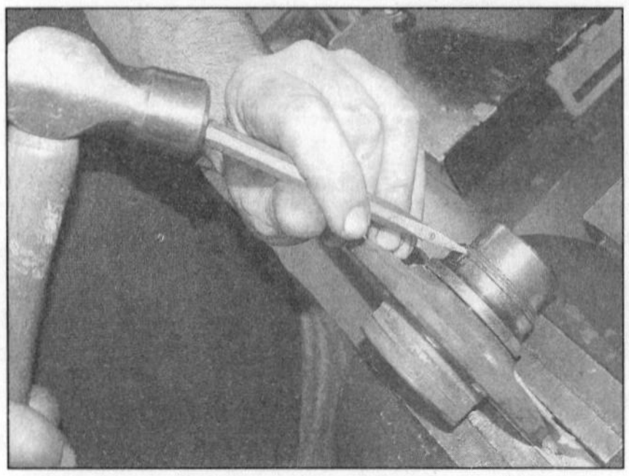

3.6a Using a hammer and suitable chisel...

3.6b ...tap the inner race off the hub flange

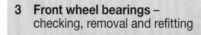

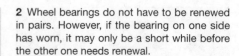

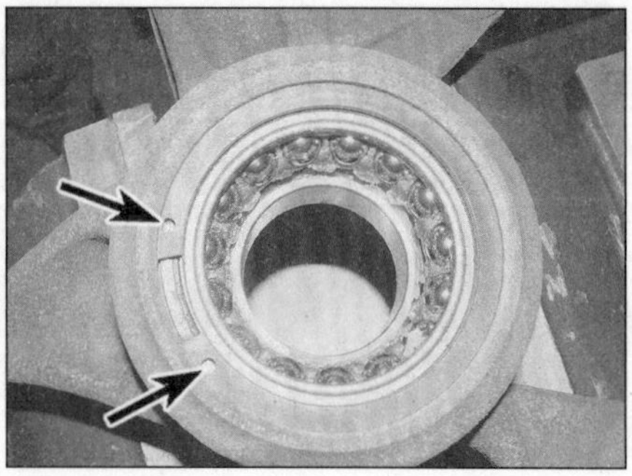

3.7a Using circlip pliers in the holes provided...

3.7b ...compress the circlip...

3.7c ...and remove it from the hub

3.8a Apply some spray lubricant...

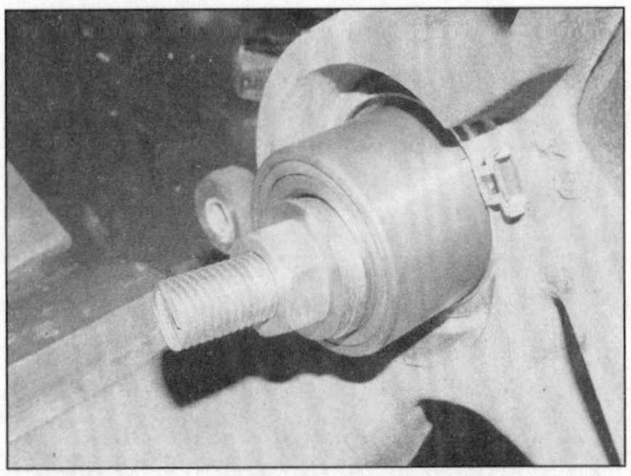
3.8b ...then use a nut, bolt, and some suitable spacers...

3.8c ...'wind' out the bearing from the hub

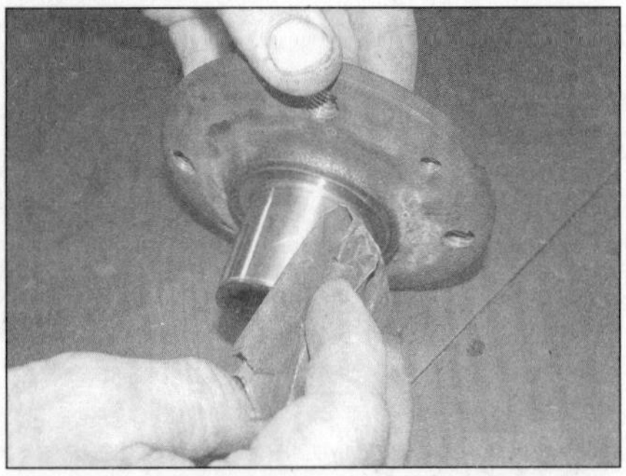
3.9 Clean any burrs from the hub flange

when refitting – one is supplied in the bearing kits supplied by Renault dealers.

8 Now the bearing itself must be removed. After applying a generous amount of spray lubricant, we were able to pull the bearing out, using another old bearing, together with a large nut and bolt, and several washers/ spacers **(see illustrations)**. Mount the swivel hub in a vice, then tighten the nut and bolt to apply pressure to the bearing – this, and a few hammer blows, should be enough to get the bearing moving, and extract it.

Refitting

9 Using emery paper, clean off any burrs or raised edges from the hub flange and hub, which might stop the components going back together **(see illustration)**. Clean and lightly lubricate the bearing location in the hub.

10 The new bearing has a magnetic reluctor ring fitted to its inner face (for the ABS sensor), which means that it should not be roughly handled during fitting. This means that, unlike a normal bearing, heavy hammer blows cannot be used to drive it into the swivel hub. It also means that the new bearing should be kept clean, and the protective cover fitted over the magnetic ring should only be removed just prior to fitting.

11 As for removal, mount the swivel hub in a sturdy bench vice. First, start the bearing into position by gently tapping it squarely into the hub, using a small hammer and protective wooden block.

12 Using the same nut/bolt and spacers as for removal, tighten the nut and bolt to press the bearing into place **(see illustration)**.

13 The bearing is fully seated when the circlip groove is visible. Fit the new circlip using suitable circlip pliers to retain the bearing **(see illustration)**.

14 The hub flange can be pressed into the new bearing using a very similar method to the one just used **(see illustrations)**.

15 On completion, refit the swivel hub as described in Section 2.

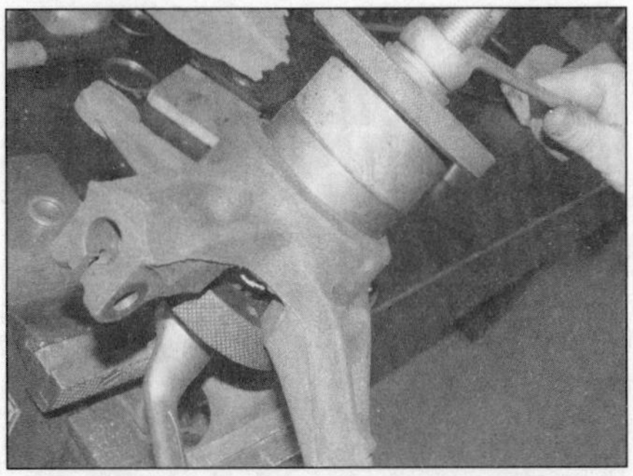
3.12 Using a nut/bolt and spacers to press the new bearing into place

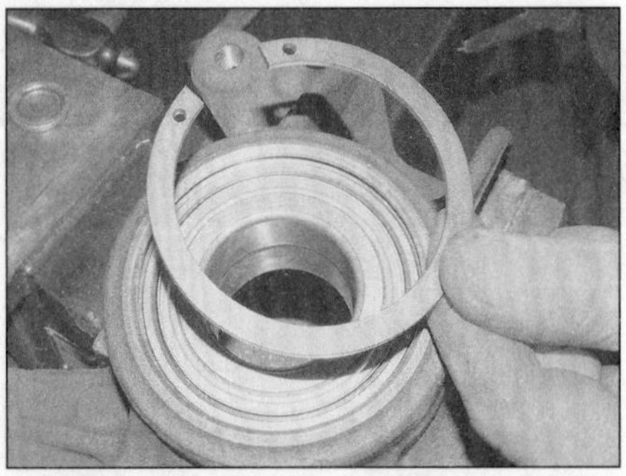
3.13 Fit the new circlip into the hub to retain the bearing

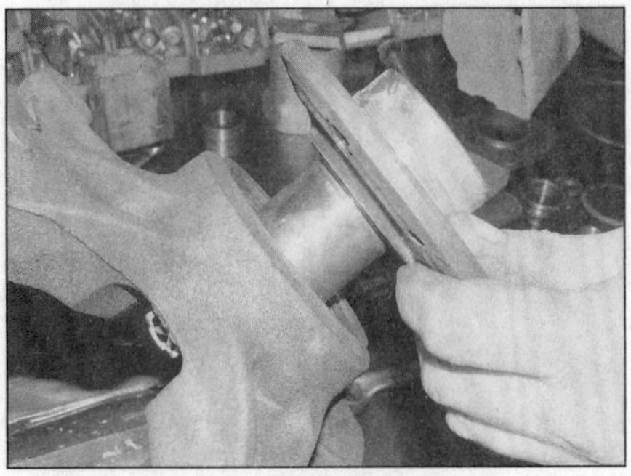
3.14a Fit the hub flange into the new bearing...

3.14b ...and press it into place using the nut/bolt and spacer method

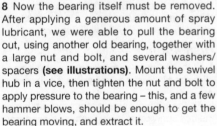

4.2a Unclip the brake hose and ABS wiring...

4.2b ...and them remove the bracket

4.3 Remove the anti-roll bar drop link nut, using an Allen key to hold the stud

4 Front strut – removal and refitting

Removal

1 Loosen the relevant front wheel bolts, then jack up the front of the car and support it on axle stands (see *Jacking and vehicle support*). Remove the appropriate roadwheel.

2 Remove the bracket and unclip the brake hose and ABS wiring from the strut assembly **(see illustrations)**.

3 Unscrew the upper nut from the anti-roll bar drop link, using an Allen key if necessary to prevent the balljoint stud turning as this is done **(see illustration)**.

4 Unscrew and remove the bolts from the base of the strut, noting which way round they are fitted. Discard the nuts – they must be replaced **(see illustration)**.

5 Using a lever if necessary separate the hub from the strut **(see illustration)**.

6 On the left-hand side especially, once the strut has been separated from the hub, there is a danger that the driveshaft may be pulled out of the transmission. To avoid this possibility, support the hub assembly underneath the lower arm, or tie it up.

7 Remove the windscreen cowl panels as described in Chapter 11. This is necessary to gain access to all of the strut upper mounting bolts in the engine compartment.

8 Unscrew and remove the three strut upper mounting bolts – do not loosen the centre nut at this stage. Lower the strut assembly out from under the wheel arch. The strut assembly is heavy, so have an assistant remove the strut whilst the last bolt is removed from the suspension tower **(see illustrations)**.

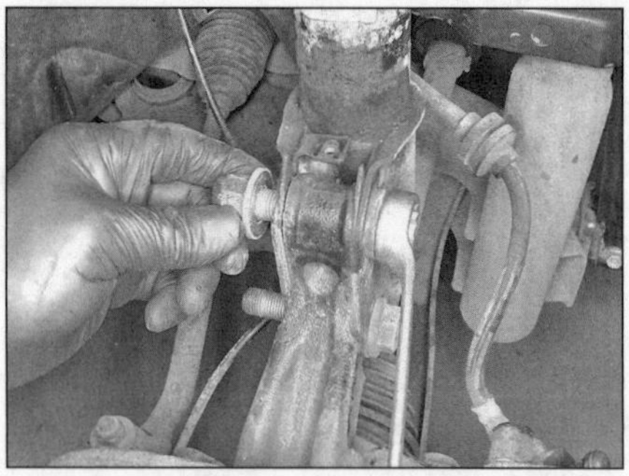

4.4 Unbolt the strut from the hub

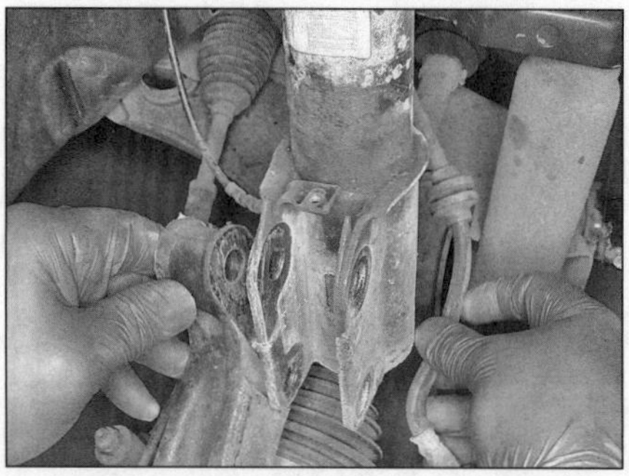

4.5 Separate the hub from the base of the strut

Refitting

9 Refitting is a reversal of removal, but note that new nuts must be fitted to the base of the strut. Tighten all the bolts to the specified torque.

5 Front strut – dismantling, inspection and reassembly

Warning: Before attempting to dismantle the front suspension strut, a special tool to hold the coil spring in compression must be obtained. Adjustable coil spring compressors are readily available, and are recommended for this operation. Any attempt to dismantle the strut without such a tool is likely to result in damage or personal injury.

Dismantling

1 With the strut removed from the car as described in Section 4, clean away all external dirt.

2 Fit the spring compressor, and compress the coil spring until all tension is relieved from the upper mounting plate. Ensure that the compressor tool is securely located on the spring according to the tool manufacturer's instructions. We found that the type of compressor which hooks onto the spring coils was insufficient, and had to use one with 'plates' or 'cups' for trapping the spring coils **(see illustration)**.

3 Slacken and remove the strut piston rod nut

4.8a Mark the position of the bolts and then...

4.8b ...remove them

4.8c Lower the strut from the wheel arch

5.2 Fit a spring compressor, and tighten until the strut upper plate is released

5.3a Hold the piston rod using an Allen key, while the nut is loosened...

5.3b ...and removed

5.4 Remove the upper plate/bearing and the spring seat...

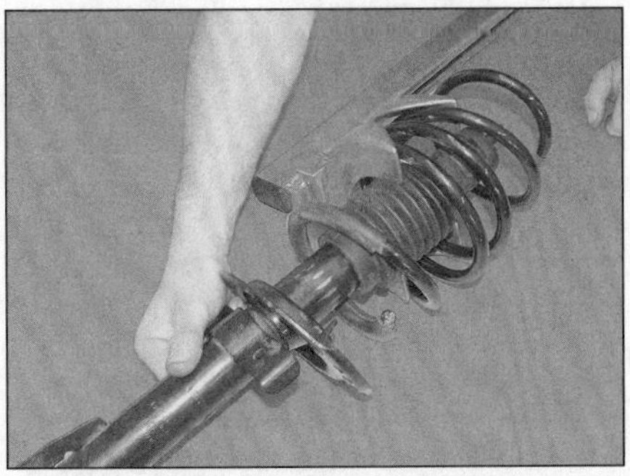

5.5 ...followed by the spring and compressor

5.6 Finally, remove the bump stop/dust cover from the strut piston

(18 mm on our car), using a 6 mm Allen key to prevent the rod from turning as this is done **(see illustrations)**.

4 Remove the upper mounting plate/bearing and the upper spring seat **(see illustration)**.

5 Carefully remove the coil spring, complete with the spring compressor, and store in a safe place for refitting **(see illustrations)**. If the spring will not be refitted for some time, it may be safer to release the spring compressor from the spring while it is stored.

6 Slide the rubber bump stop/dust cover off the strut piston **(see illustration)**.

Inspection

7 With the strut assembly now completely dismantled, examine all the components for wear, damage or deformation, and check the upper bearing for smoothness of operation. Renew any of the components as necessary.

8 Examine the strut for signs of fluid leakage. Check the strut piston for signs of pitting along its entire length, and check the strut body for signs of damage. Test the operation of the strut, while holding it in an upright position, by moving the piston through a full stroke and then through short strokes of 50 to 100 mm. In both cases, the resistance felt should be smooth and continuous. If the resistance is jerky or uneven, or if there is any visible sign of wear or damage, renewal is necessary.

9 If any doubt exists about the condition of the coil spring, gradually release the spring compressor (if not already done), and check the spring for distortion and signs of cracking. Since no minimum free length is specified by Renault, the only way to check the tension of the spring is to compare it to a new component. Renew the spring if it is damaged or distorted, or if there is any doubt as to its condition.

10 Inspect all other components for signs of damage or deterioration, and renew any that are suspect.

Reassembly

Note: *Apply grease between the ends of the spring and its stops.*

11 Ensure that all components are clean and dry. Slide the bump stop/dust cover into position over the strut piston.

12 Refit the compressed coil spring, followed by the upper spring seat. Ensure that both ends of the spring are correctly located in the spring seats **(see illustrations)**.

13 Refit the strut upper mounting plate/bearing. Fit a new piston rod nut, and tighten it while holding the rod using the Allen key as for removal. There is a specified torque for the piston rod nut, which should be observed where possible, but if the required special tools for tightening it are not available, ensure the nut is tightened very securely.

5.12a Ensure that the spring ends are located against the stops at the strut base...

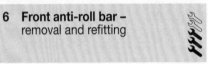

5.12b ...and against the spring seat at the top

14 Slowly and carefully release the spring compressor, watching to make sure that both ends of the spring remain correctly located in the spring seats.

15 Refit the strut to the car as described in Section 4.

6 Front anti-roll bar – removal and refitting

Removal

1 Loosen the front wheel bolts, then jack up the front of the car and support it on axle stands (see *Jacking and vehicle support*). Remove both front roadwheels.

6.2a Unscrew the anti-roll bar drop link nut, using an Allen key to hold the stud...

2 The anti-roll bar drop link rods can be renewed by unscrewing the nuts at either end, using an Allen key if necessary to prevent the balljoint stud turning as this is done **(see illustrations)**.

3 To remove the anti-roll bar itself, remove the front subframe as described in Section 8.

4 Unscrew the anti-roll bar clamp bolts, and remove the anti-roll bar **(see illustration)**.

5 Carefully examine the anti-roll bar components for signs of wear, damage or deterioration, paying particular attention to the mounting bushes. Renew worn components as necessary.

Refitting

6 Refitting is a reversal of removal, noting the following points:

a) *The anti-roll bar mountings have pegs which locate into holes in the subframe.*
b) *Tighten the clamp bolts to the specified torque.*
c) *Refit the subframe as described in Section 8.*
d) *Tighten the drop link nuts to the specified torque while holding the balljoint studs with an Allen key.*

7 Front lower arm – removal, overhaul and refitting

Removal

1 Loosen the relevant front wheel bolts, then jack up the front of the car and support it on axle stands (see *Jacking and vehicle support*). Remove the appropriate front roadwheel.

7.4 Slacken the ball joint nut

6.2b ...then separate the link rod from the strut

2 Where fitted disconnect the link arm from the headlight adjustment sensor. This is only fitted to models with Zenon headlights.

3 Use a ball joint separator and disconnect the track rod end from the swivel hub.

4 Unscrew the nut from the lower balljoint bolt, but do not fully remove it at this point **(see illustration)**.

5 The balljoint must now be separated, by pulling the lower arm downwards. Apply plenty of penetrating spray to begin with. We used a long pole, fitted into a wooden block under the car, with a chain wrapped around the end of the lower arm, to provide sufficient leverage **(see illustration 2.10)**.

6 Considerable force may be required to free the taper. If a forked type tool is used the rubber boot will be damaged. Renault do not supply this as a separate part, although they may be available in the after market. Where force is used to free the taper consideration should be given to replacing the ball joint as a matter of course.

7 Remove the rear mounting nut and bolt. Remove the nut from the ball joint and then manoeuvre the arm from the vehicle.

Overhaul

8 Renault supply a replacement ball joint kit, but no other parts **(see illustration)**.

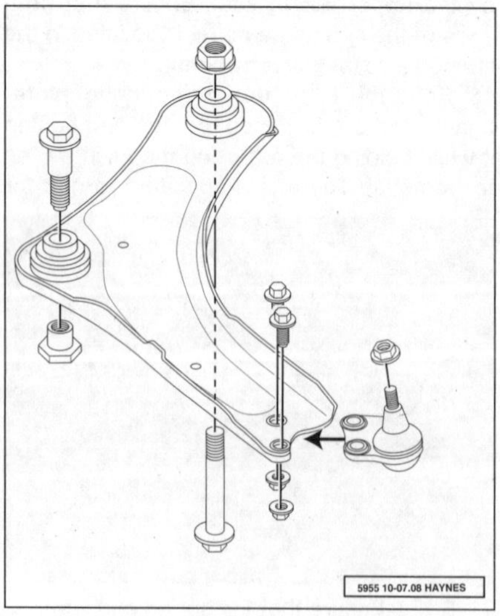

7.8 Typical lower arm and ball joint

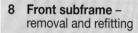

6.4 Unscrew the anti-roll bar clamp bolts, and remove the bar from the subframe

Reputable after market parts suppliers do list the ball joint and the arm bushes.

9 To replace the ball joint drill out (or grind the head off and punch out) the rivets. Pull the old ball joint out of the arm and fit the new one. Secure it in place with then new nuts and bolts supplied with the new ball joint.

10 If the rubber bushes require replacement they can be removed using a combination of threaded bar, nuts, washers and sockets to remove and replace the bushes. Note however that if both arm bushes are worn, it is more than likely that the ball joint itself will also be worn. If this is the case it will be more cost effective to replace the complete arm.

Refitting

11 Refitting is a reversal of removal, noting the following points:

a) *Tighten the suspension arm pivot and rear bolt nuts by hand only until the car is resting on its wheels.*
b) *Tighten all nuts and bolts to the specified torque.*
c) *Ensure that the ABS wiring is routed correctly, and clipped into its brackets securely.*
d) *On completion, with the car resting on its wheels, tighten the suspension arm pivot and rear bolt nuts to the specified torque.*
e) *If new components have been fitted, it is advisable to have the wheel alignment checked.*

8 Front subframe – removal and refitting

Removal

Note: *The front subframe is removed complete with the steering rack, both lower arms and the anti-roll bar.*

1 Set the front wheels in the straight-ahead position and then disconnect the battery - *see Disconnecting the battery in Chapter 5A*.

2 Inside the car, pull back the floor covering at the base of the steering column, then unscrew the universal joint bolt and separate the column from the steering gear pinion **(see illustration)**. Discard the bolt, a new one must be fitted.

3 Slacken the wheel nuts then jack up and

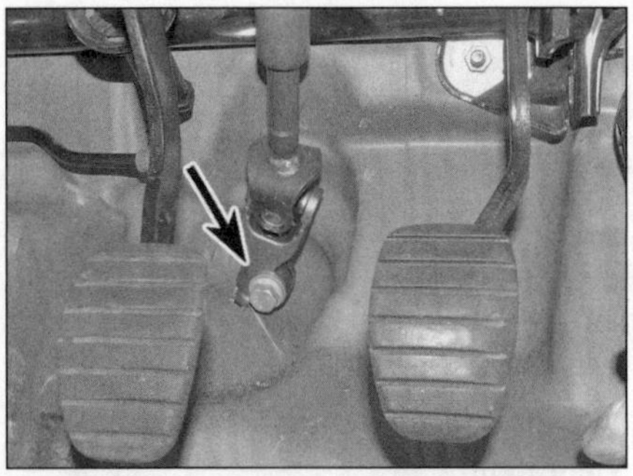

8.2 Pull back the carpet, then unscrew the bolt

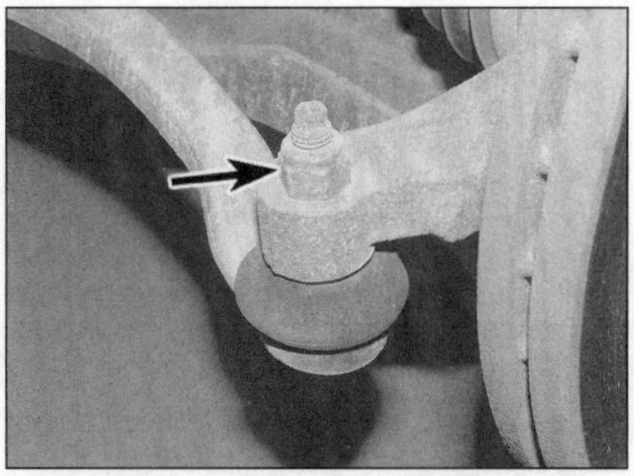

8.9a Unscrew the track rod end balljoint nut

8.9b ...then use a balljoint separator tool to free the balljoint...

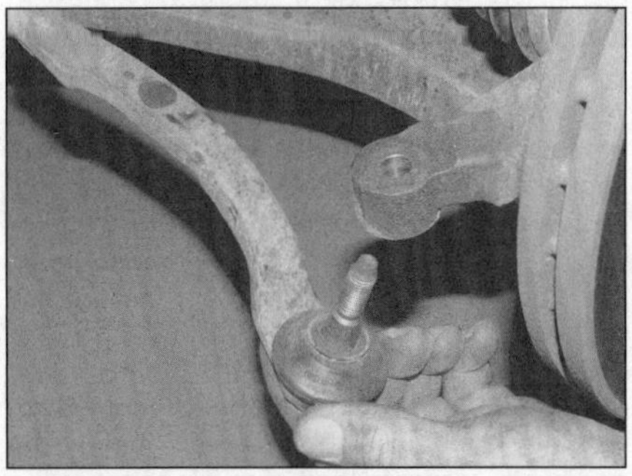

8.9c ...and disconnect the track rod end from the hub

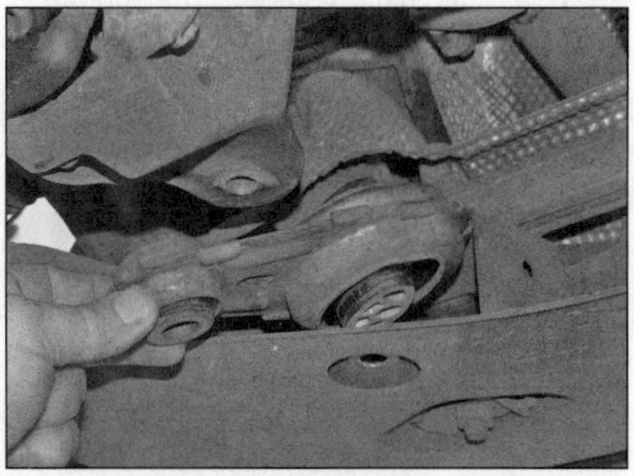

8.11 Remove the engine lower mounting/steady bar

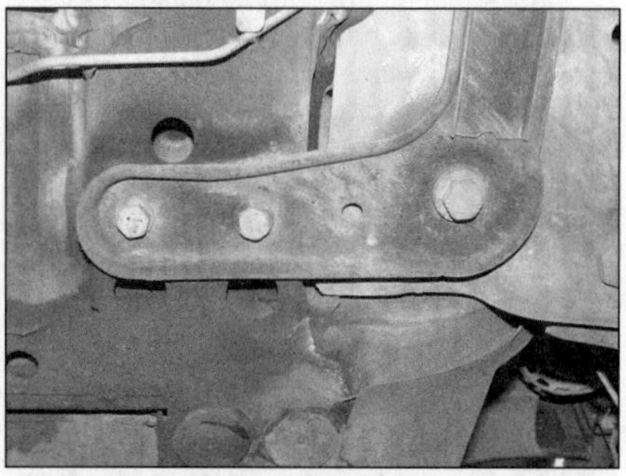

8.12 Remove the subframe rear mounting bolts (one side shown)

support the front of the vehicle (see *Jacking and vehicle support*).

4 Remove both front road wheels and then remove the engine undershield and wing liners.

5 Where fitted disconnect the link arm from the headlight adjustment sensor. The sensor is only fitted to models with Zenon headlights.

6 Unclip the brake hose and the wiring loom for the ABS sensors at the base of the suspension strut.

7 Disconnect the lower arm ball joints as described in Section 7.

8 Unbolt and remove the support bracket from the radiator support panel.

9 Loosen the track rod end balljoint nut each side, unscrewing it almost to the end of its threads (if the nut will not unscrew, hold the balljoint stud on top using a small spanner). Use a balljoint separator tool to free the balljoint, then unscrew the nut completely, and disconnect the track rods from the swivel hubs **(see illustrations)**.

10 Disconnect the anti-roll bar drop links at the strut.

11 Working at the rear of the subframe, disconnect the engine lower mounting tie-bar from the engine **(see illustration)**.

12 Remove the rear subframe mounting bolts (discard the bolts) and then remove the rear crossmember bolts **(see illustration)**. Remove the crossmember from the vehicle.

13 Support the weight of the subframe, using at least two sturdy jacks.

14 Remove the main subframe mounting bolts **(see illustration)**. These are located in the vertical cylinders. Discard the bolts – new ones must be used on refitting.

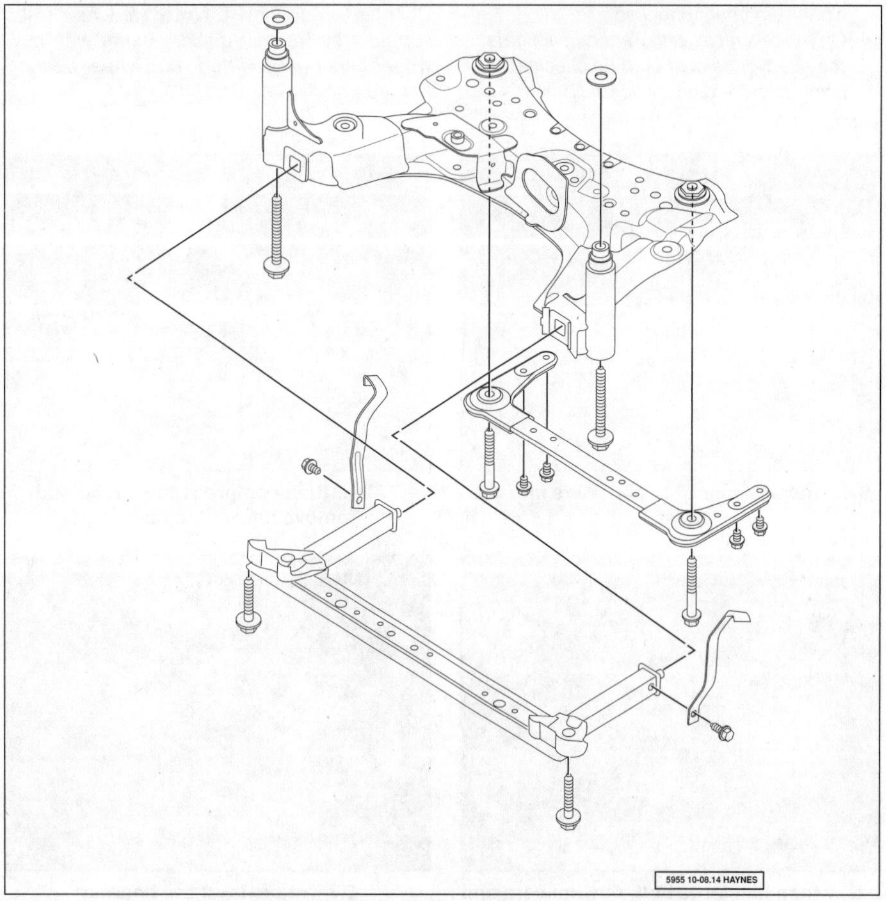

8.14 Details of the front subframe, crossmember and support panel

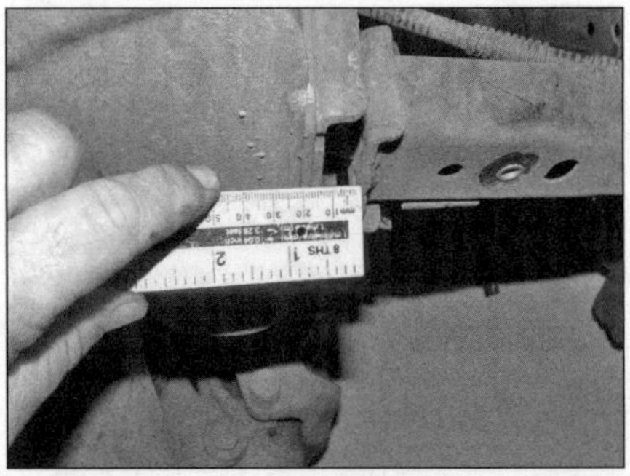

8.16 The gap between the subframe and the radiator support panel must 13mm

15 Check that all the components have been removed or detached from the subframe and then slowly lower the subframe to the ground.

Refitting

16 Refitting is a reversal of removal, noting the following points:

a) Use new subframe bolts.

b) Tighten all nuts/bolts to the specified torque.

c) Check the space between the subframe and the radiator mounting panel. This should be 13mm **(see illustration)**.

d) Fit a new nut and bolt when reconnecting the steering column universal joint.

e) On completion, it is advisable to have the wheel alignment checked.

f) On models fitted with Zenon headlights the headlight aim should be checked using suitable diagnostic equipment.

9 Rear wheel bearings – checking, removal and refitting

Note: *The bearing is a sealed, pre-adjusted and prelubricated, double-row tapered-roller type, and is intended to last the car's entire service life without maintenance or attention. Never overtighten the hub nut in an attempt to 'adjust' the bearings.*

Checking

1 Wear in the rear hub bearings can be checked for as described in Chapter 1A or 1B. However, the most common first symptom of bearing wear is a rumbling noise, noted at a particular roadspeed, or when the offending wheel is loaded-up during cornering. In this case, besides rocking the wheel, spin it and listen carefully, to distinguish between the sound of the brake pads rubbing the disc, and the rumble of bearing wear. Compare the sound with the other rear wheel to confirm.

2 Wheel bearings do not have to be renewed in pairs. However, if the bearing on one side has worn, it may only be a short while before the other one needs renewal.

Removal

3 Remove the rear brake disc as described in Chapter 9, Section 14. **Note:** *New rear discs supplied by Renault dealers come with new wheel bearings prefitted, but wheel bearing kits are also available.*

4 To remove the bearing, the retaining circlip must first be removed, which requires the use of a sturdy pair of circlip pliers **(see illustrations)**. A new circlip should be used when refitting – one is supplied in the bearing kits supplied by Renault dealers.

5 Care must be taken during bearing renewal, as there is a magnetic (reluctor) ring fitted to the rear of the disc/hub which must not be damaged. Mount the disc over the open jaws of a sturdy bench vice, with the magnetic ring facing upwards **(see illustration)**.

6 After applying a generous amount of spray lubricant, we were able to pull the bearing out, using two blocks of wood, together with a large nut and bolt, and several washers/spacers **(see illustration)**.

7 Tighten the nut and bolt to apply pressure to the bearing – this, and a few hammer blows, should be enough to get the bearing moving, and extract it **(see illustration)**.

Refitting

8 Using emery paper, clean off any burrs or raised edges from the hub, which might stop the components going back together – take care not to damage the magnetic ring. Clean and lightly lubricate the bearing location in the hub **(see illustrations)**.

9 Offer the bearing into position, and using a suitable spacer, tap it gently around its edge to start it squarely into the disc/hub **(see illustrations)**.

10 Using the same nut/bolt and spacers as

9.4a Insert a pair of circlip pliers into the holes...

9.4b ...then compress the circlip and remove it from the disc/hub

9.5 Mount the disc over the open jaws of a vice...

9.6 ...then fit a large bolt, nut, spacers and two blocks of wood...

9.7 ...to extract the bearing

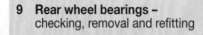

9.8a Clean off any burrs from the bearing location

9.8b Lightly oil the bearing location

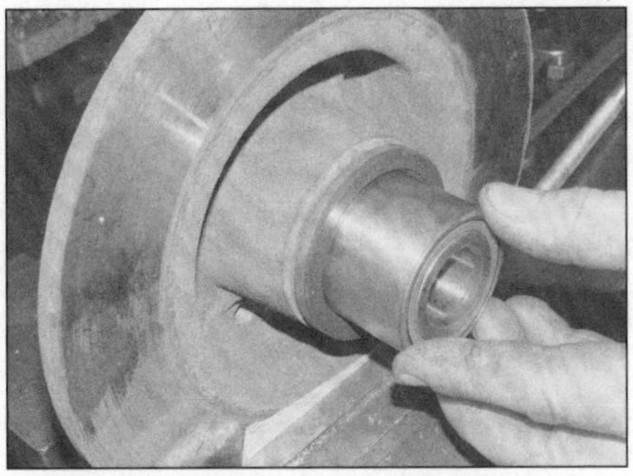
9.9a Offer the bearing into place...

9.9b ...then tap it gently to start it into the hub

9.10a Fit the same nut, bolt and spacers used for removal...

9.10b ...then tighten the nut/bolt to press the bearing into place

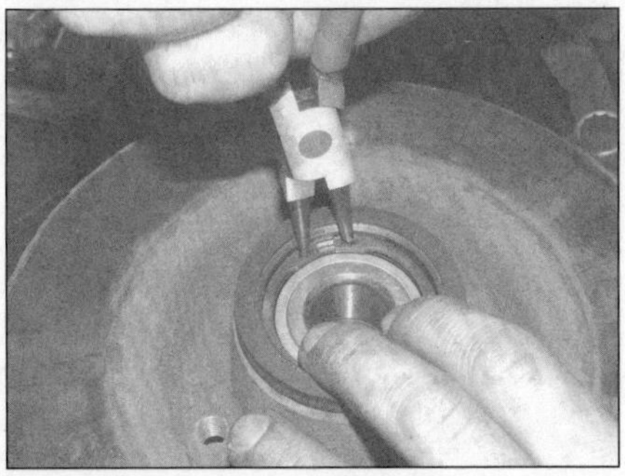
9.11 Fit the new bearing retaining circlip

for removal, tighten the nut and bolt to press the bearing into place **(see illustrations)**.

11 The bearing is fully seated when the circlip groove is visible. Fit the new circlip using suitable circlip pliers to retain the bearing **(see illustration)**.

12 Refit the brake disc as described in Chapter 9, Section 14.

10 Rear shock absorber – removal, testing and refitting

Removal

1 Chock the front wheels and engage reverse gear. (Loosen the relevant rear wheel bolts, then jack up the rear of the car and support it on axle stands (see *Jacking and vehicle support*). Remove the appropriate rear roadwheel.

10.2c ...then unscrew the small bolt...

2 Prise out the large plastic clip which secures the plastic cover fitted under the trailing arm and rear axle, then unscrew the small bolt underneath the trailing arm and lower the plastic cover for access to the shock absorber lower mounting **(see illustrations)**.

3 Using a jack and block of wood under the rear spring cup, lift the trailing arm slightly **(see illustration)**.

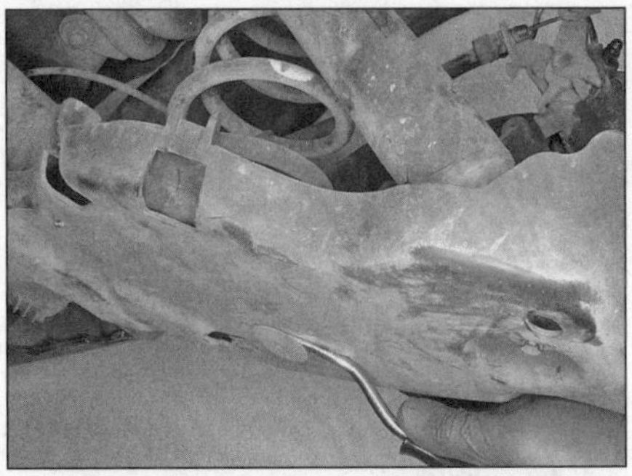
10.2a Prise out the large plastic clip...

10.2b ...and remove it...

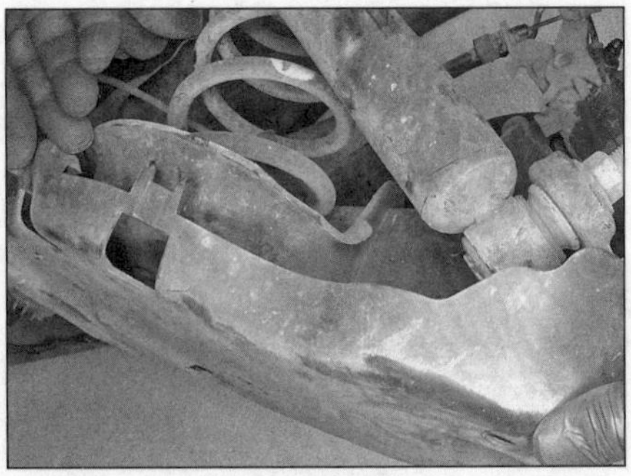
10.2d ...and lower the plastic cover from the trailing arm

10.3 Raise the trailing arm slightly using a jack

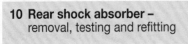

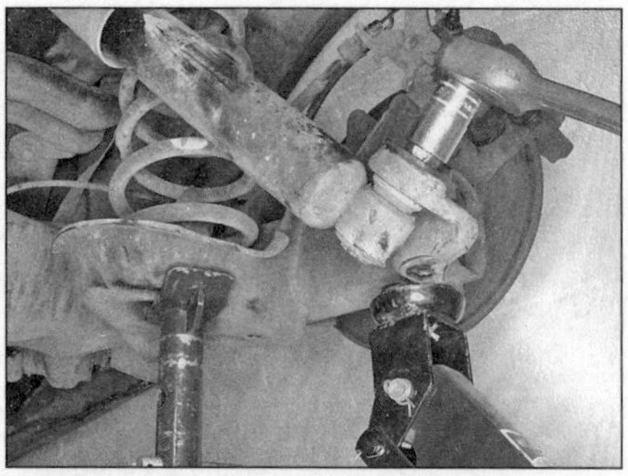

10.4a Unscrew the lower mounting nut...

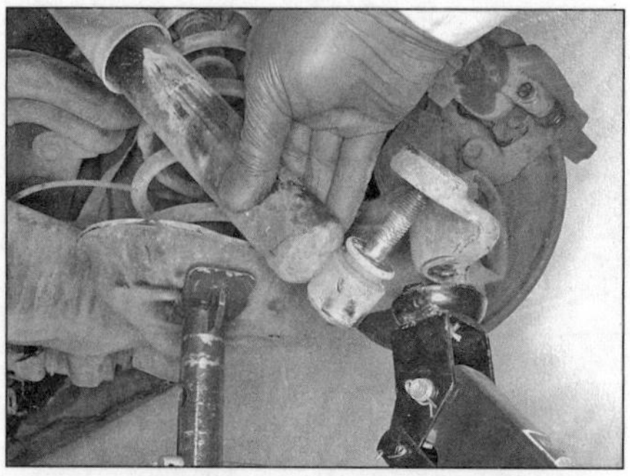

10.4b ...and detach the shock absorber from the trailing arm

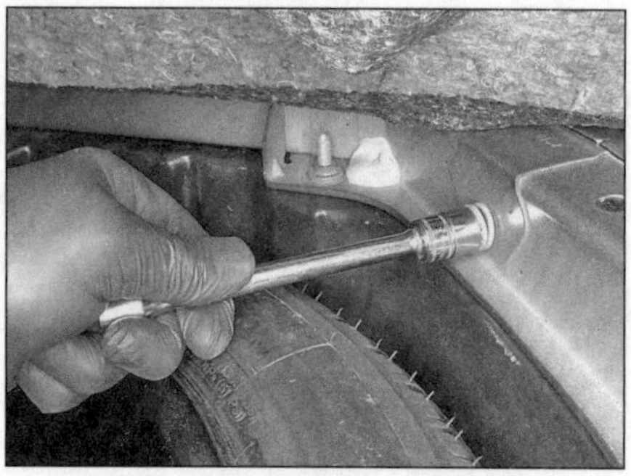

10.6a Remove the upper bolt

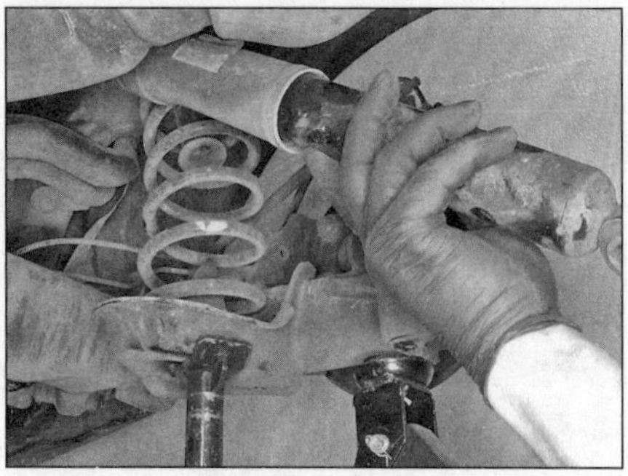

10.6b Lower the shock absorber out from under the wheel arch

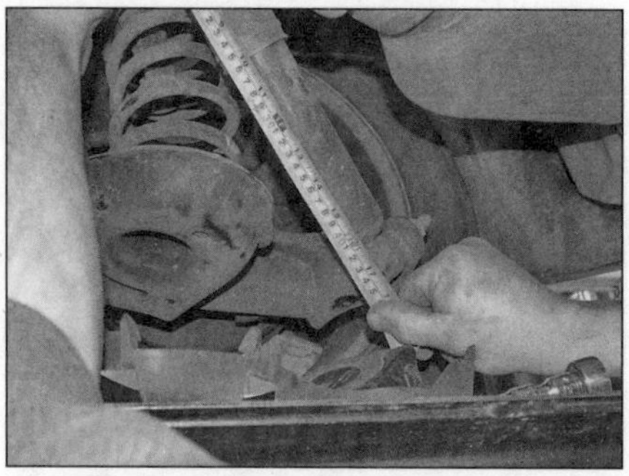

10.10a Set the eye to eye length to 432.5mm and then...

10.10b ...tighten the bolts to the specified torque

4 Unscrew the nut and disengage the shock absorber lower mounting bolt from the trailing arm **(see illustrations)**.

5 Inside the boot area, lift the floor carpet to gain access to the shock absorber upper mounting bolt.

6 Unscrew the upper mounting bolt, then remove the shock absorber from under the car **(see illustrations)**.

Testing

7 Mount the shock absorber in a vice, and test as described in Section 5 for the front suspension strut. Also check the rubber mounting bushes for damage and deterioration. Renew the shock absorber complete if any damage or wear is evident; the mounting bushes are not available separately. Inspect the mounting bolts for signs of wear or damage, and renew as necessary. Shock absorbers should always be renewed in pairs.

Refitting

8 Offer the shock absorber into position in its upper mounting, then insert the bolt and tighten by hand only at this stage.

9 Similarly, locate the lower mounting bolt, and tighten its nut by hand. If a new unit is being fitted, it may be restrained in its fully-compressed state by a special cord or strap – once the unit is in place, this restraining device should be cut.

10 Raise the jack, so that the shock absorber eye to eye length is 432.5 mm. Fully tighten the upper and lower bolts at this point **(see illustrations)**.

11 Remove the jack supporting the trailing arm. Refit the roadwheel, lower the car to the ground and tighten the roadwheel bolts to the specified torque.

12 Refit the plastic cover to the trailing arm, securing with the bolt and round clip.

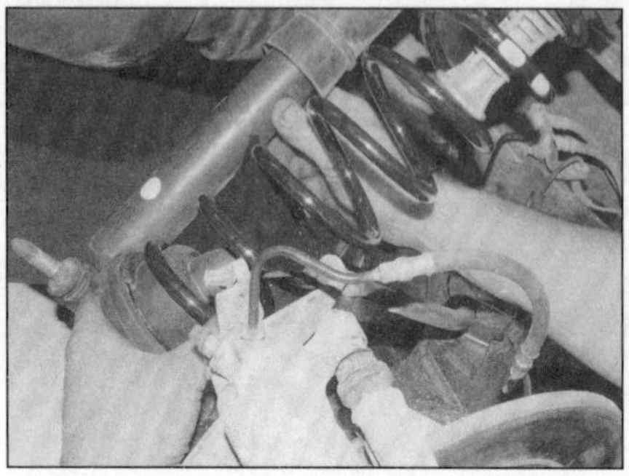

11.3 Lower the trailing arm, and remove the spring

11.4 Check the condition of the lower mounting rubber

11 Rear coil spring – removal and refitting

Removal

1 Disconnect the shock absorber lower mounting on the side concerned as described in Section 10, paragraphs 1 to 4.

2 Before removing the spring, mark it for position relative to the car – the spring should already have a paint code mark on it, which can be used to ensure it is orientated properly when refitting.

3 Carefully lower the jack supporting the trailing arm, and remove the coil spring and its lower mounting rubber from the trailing arm. Lever the trailing arm down slightly if necessary to remove the spring **(see illustration)**.

4 Check the condition of the lower mounting rubber, and renew if necessary **(see illustration)**. If new springs are being fitted, note that these should always be fitted in pairs.

5 If required, the spring upper mounting/ bump stop can be unclipped from the body, and a new one fitted **(see illustration)**.

Refitting

6 Refitting is a reversal of removal, remembering the following points:

a) Align the spring as noted before removal, so that it sits properly in the trailing arm.

b) Refit the shock absorber lower mounting as described in Section 10 and follow the procedure described in Section 10 to tighten the lower shock absorber bolt.

12 Rear axle – removal and refitting

Note: *Renewal of the rear axle bushes requires the use of a press. Check on parts availability before removing the rear axle for bush renewal.*

Removal

1 Chock the front wheels and engage reverse gear. Loosen the rear wheel bolts, then jack up the rear of the car and support it on axle stands. Remove both rear roadwheels.

2 On models fitted with an electronic parking brake (EPB), the brake must placed in the repair mode, using a suitable diagnostic tool - as described in Chapter 9.

3 If a new rear axle is to be fitted, remove the brake discs as described in Chapter 9. Otherwise, to make refitting the axle easier, remove the rear brake pads and tie up the calipers as described in Chapter 9.

4 Disconnect the wiring plugs from the ABS rear wheel sensors (behind the discs, facing forwards). Trace the wiring back, and unclip it from the axle.

5 Unhook the handbrake cable ends from the operating levers on the calipers, then unclip the cable outers from the calipers. Trace the cables back, and ensure they are disconnected from the clips relevant to the rear axle.

6 Use a brake hose clamp, a G-clamp or a similar tool with protected jaws to clamp the brake flexible hoses at the nearest convenient point. Disconnect the rear brake pipes at the caliper **(see illustration)**. Plug or tape over the union ends to prevent dirt entry. Wash off any spilt fluid immediately.

7 Remove the plastic cover **(see illustration)** and then disconnect the rear shock absorber lower mountings as described in Section 10.

8 Remove the rear springs as described in Section 11.

9 On models with xenon headlights, it may be necessary to disconnect the wiring from, and to unbolt, the ride height level sensor attached to the rear axle.

10 Clean the area under the car around the axle mounting plates, and mark their positions relative to the floor using paint. Loosen the three axle mounting plate bolts either side **(see illustration)**.

11 With the aid of an assistant, position two sturdy jacks under the ends of the axle, and just take its weight.

12 Remove the three mounting plate bolts each side progressively, then, with the assistant on hand to steady the axle on the jacks, lower the axle out from under the car.

13 If a new axle is being fitted, remove the brake pipes from the original and fit them to the new axle. Also transfer the brake assemblies using the information in Chapter 9 **(see illustration)**.

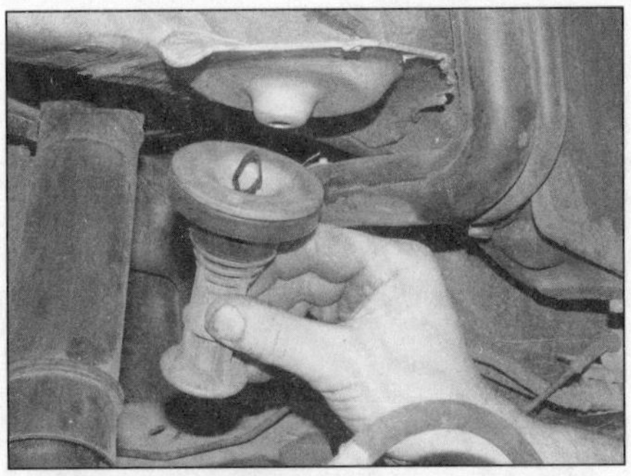

11.5 If necessary, unclip the upper mounting/bump stop

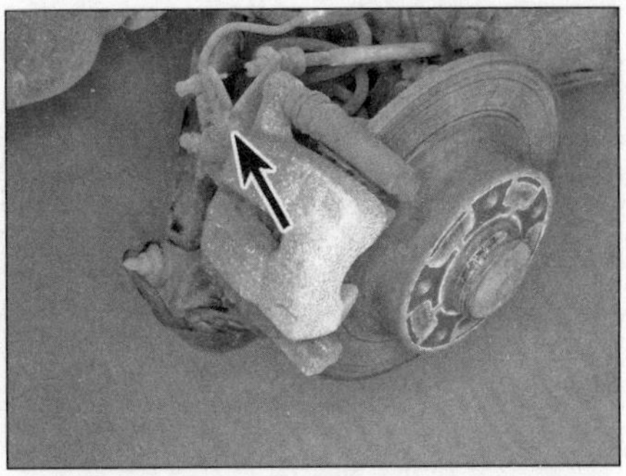

12.6 Disconnect the brake hose at the caliper (arrowed)

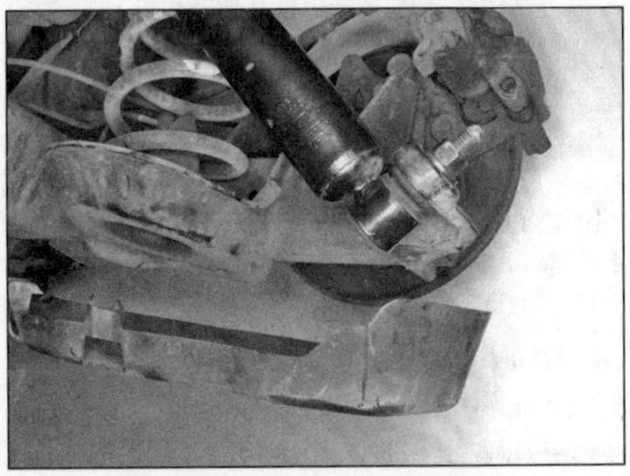

12.7 Remove the plastic cover

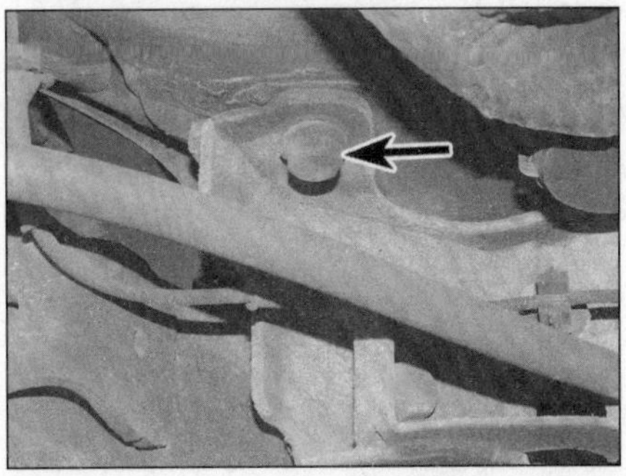

12.10 One of the rear axle mounting plate bolts

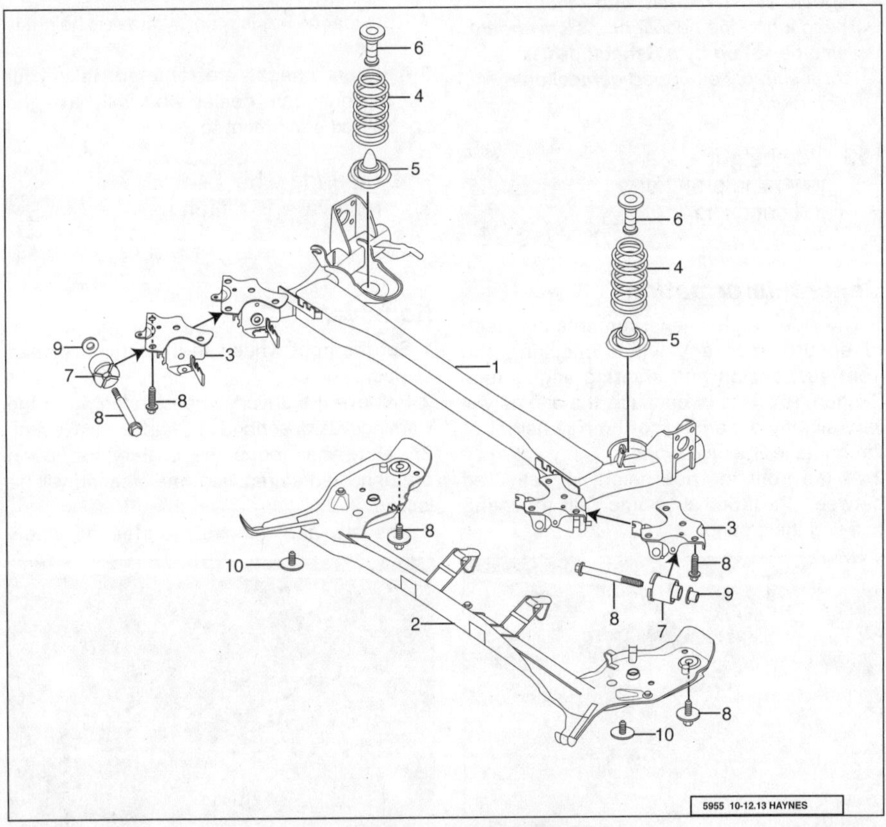

12.13 The rear axle assembly

1 Axle	*3 Body bracket*	*6 Bump stop*	*9 Nut*
2 Axle protector (cover)	*4 Coil spring*	*7 Bush*	*10 Clip*
	5 Spring seat	*8 Bolt*	

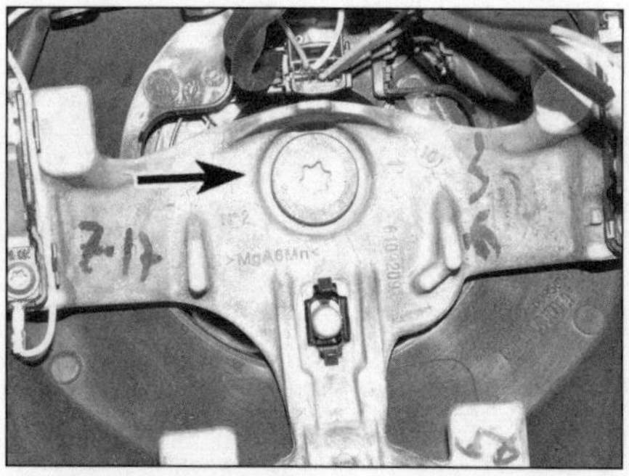

14.3 Unscrew and remove the steering wheel bolt (arrowed)

14.4 Note the factory paint mark (arrowed)

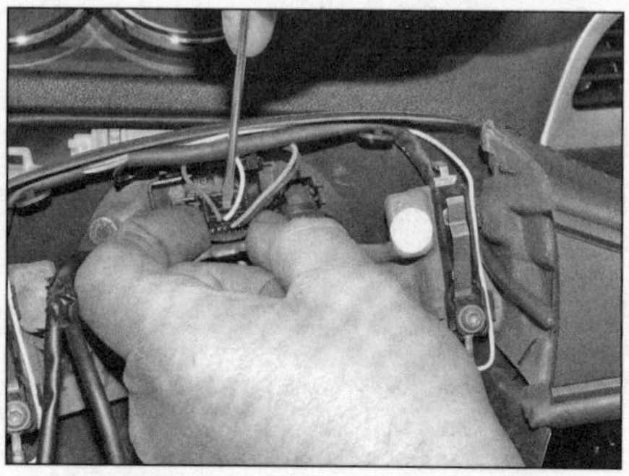

14.5 Disconnect the wiring plug

Refitting

14 Refitting is a reversal of removal, noting the following points:

a) Align the axle mounting plates with the marks made prior to removal, then tighten the bolts to the specified torque.

b) Refit the springs and reconnect the shock absorbers as described in Sections 11 and 10.

c) Refit the brake components, then on completion bleed the braking system as described in Chapter 9.

d) On completion, it may be advisable to have the rear wheel alignment checked by a Renault dealer or competent specialist. On models with xenon headlights, the headlight system should also be set up by a Renault dealer (or a suitably equipped garage) on completion.

13 Ride height – general information and checking

General information

1 The ride height measurements are used to ensure accuracy when checking the front suspension and steering angles (see Section 19). This is because the angles will vary slightly according to the ride height of the car (see Specifications).

2 At the front the ride height is measured between the front subframe rear mounting bolt and the ground.

3 At the rear the height is measured between the rear axle pivot bolt and the ground.

4 The values given in the specifications should be considered nominal values – a badly worn tyre for example will lower the ride height on one side. The important factor to consider is that the values are similar across each axle. Any deviation of more than 5 mm from side to side will require further investigation.

Checking

5 Position the unladen car on a level surface, with the tyres correctly inflated and the fuel tank full.

6 Measure and record the required dimensions as necessary.

7 Note that no adjustment of the ride height is possible.

8 If further checks are required, take your car to your local dealer who will have the specialised equipment to do this.

14 Steering wheel – removal and refitting

Removal

1 Set the front wheels in the straight-ahead position.

2 Remove the driver's airbag (referring to the warnings) as described in Chapter 12, Section 27. Note that, once the battery has been disconnected as required, the steering will be locked.

3 Unscrew and remove the steering wheel bolt, holding the wheel rim with one hand, and loosening the bolt with the other – do not rely on the steering lock to prevent the wheel turning, otherwise it may be damaged **(see illustration)**.

4 Before removing the wheel, note that there should be a master spline, a paint mark or punched alignment markings on the wheel and the end of the column, to ensure that the wheel is correctly refitted. If not, make your own marks with a pin punch or paint **(see illustration)**.

5 Where fitted disconnect the wiring plug for the steering wheel controls **(see illustration)**.

6 Pull the wheel from its splines, then feeding the wiring through the wheel, remove it completely. **Note:** *Do not turn the airbag contact ring assembly or the steering column shaft whilst the steering wheel is removed.*

Refitting

7 Refitting is a reversal of removal, bearing in mind the following points:

a) Make sure the steering wheel splines are aligned correctly, using the marks noted prior to removal.

b) Fit a new steering wheel bolt, and tighten to the specified torque **(see illustrations)**.

c) Check that all the wiring plugs are connected securely.

d) Refit the airbag as described in Chapter 12 (referring to the warnings).

15 Steering column – removal, overhaul and refitting

Removal

1 Disconnect the battery positive lead.

2 Remove the steering wheel as described in Section 14.

3 Remove the steering column switch assembly as described in Chapter 12, Section 5.

4 Remove the driver's side facia lower trim panel as described in Chapter 11, Section 24.

5 Pull back the floor covering at the base of the steering column, then unscrew the universal joint bolt **(see illustration)** and separate the column from the steering gear pinion. Discard the bolt – a new one must be used.

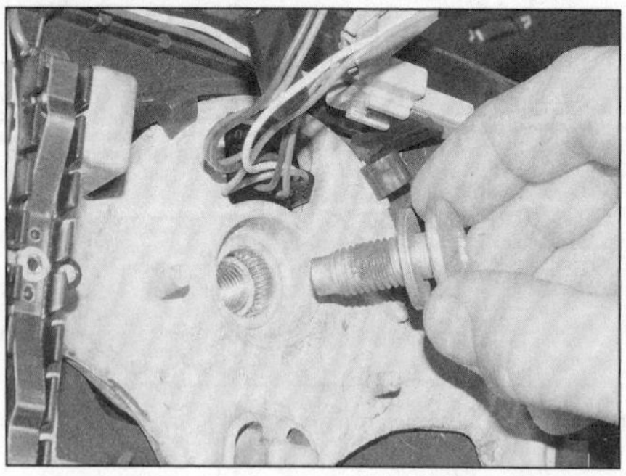

14.7a Fit a new steering wheel bolt...

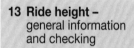

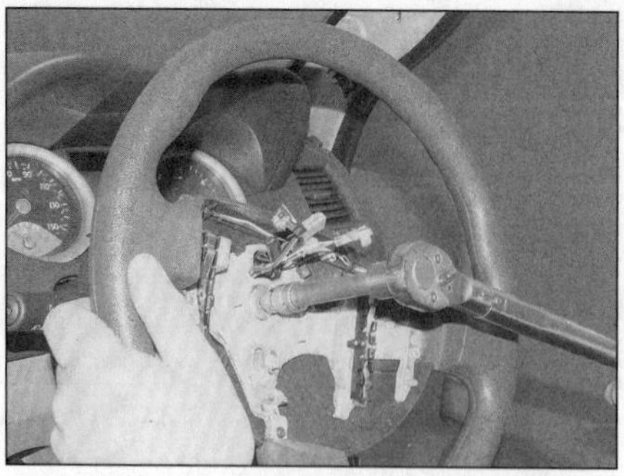

14.7b ...and tighten to the specified torque, holding the wheel rim

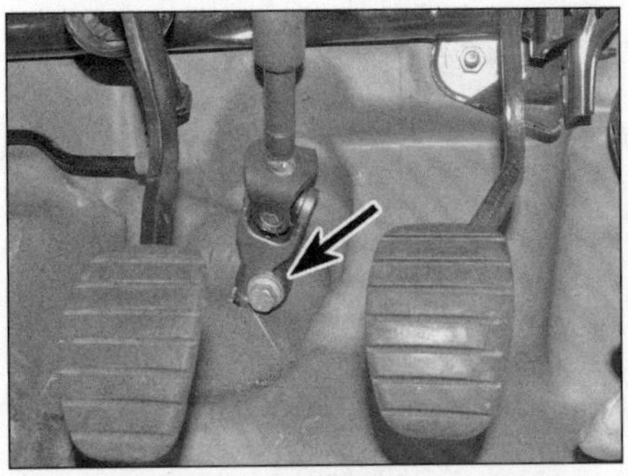

15.5 Remove the bolt (arrowed)

15.6a Disconnect the small motor wiring plug...

15.6b ...the main wiring plug...

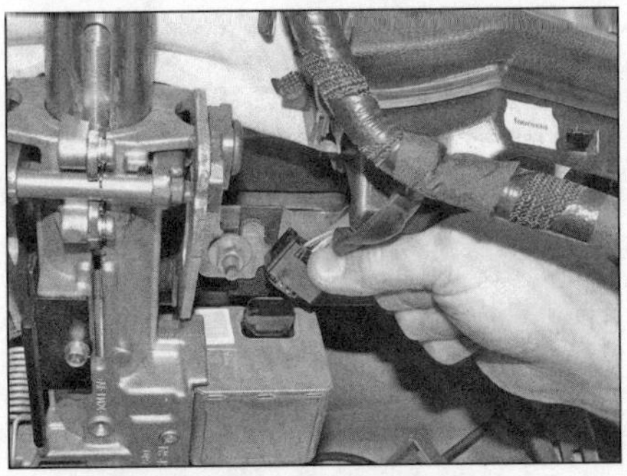

15.6c ...the steering lock plug...

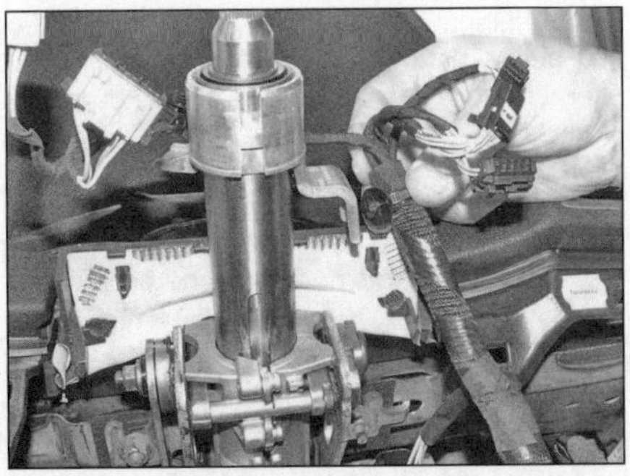

15.6d ...and then unclip the wiring loom

15.8 Remove the mounting nuts (arrowed)

6 Disconnect the wiring plugs from the steering column lock, and from the motor. Unclip the wiring harness so that the column is free to be removed **(see illustrations)**.

7 The steering column and motor are heavy items. The use of an assistant is strongly recommended when removing the column and motor assembly.

8 The column is held in place by four nuts **(see illustration)**. Working from below remove the nuts.

9 Lower the column/motor assembly into the footwell and remove it from the car **(see illustrations)**.

Overhaul

10 Check the steering shaft for signs of free play in the column bushes, and check the universal joints for signs of damage or roughness in the joint bearings. If damage or wear is found on the steering shaft universal joints or shaft bushes, the column must be renewed as an assembly.

Steering motor

11 The electric power steering motor is not available separately at the time of writing, and must be renewed with the column as an assembly.

Steering lock

12 The (electric) steering column lock is attached using a bolt with a **left-hand thread**. The lock can be removed with the column in place, as described in Chapter 12, Section 25.

13 Refer to Chapter 12, Section 4, for information on removing the keycard reader slot.

Refitting

14 Refitting is a reversal of removal, noting the following points:

a) *Check very carefully that the motor wiring plugs are securely connected – if the plugs were to work loose, this could result in a loss of power assistance.*

b) *Fit a new bolt when reconnecting the steering column universal joint.*

c) *When the battery has been reconnected, the steering must be initialised by turning it to full lock in either direction a few times, holding in the full-lock position for a few seconds each time.*

16 Steering gear rubber gaiter – renewal

1 Disconnect the track rod end balljoint from the swivel hub, using the information in Section 18. The track rod end does not have to be removed completely, though it is advisable to tape over the track rod balljoint threads, to avoid damaging the new gaiter during fitting.

2 Mark the correct fitted position of the gaiter on the track rod. Release or cut the retaining clips, and slide the gaiter off the steering gear housing and track rod end.

3 Thoroughly clean the track rod and the steering gear housing, using fine abrasive paper to polish off any corrosion, burrs or sharp edges which might damage the sealing lips of the new gaiter on installation.

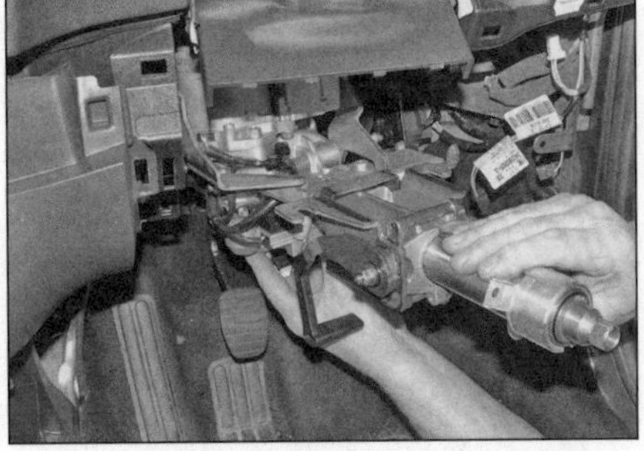

15.9a Lower the column...

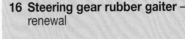

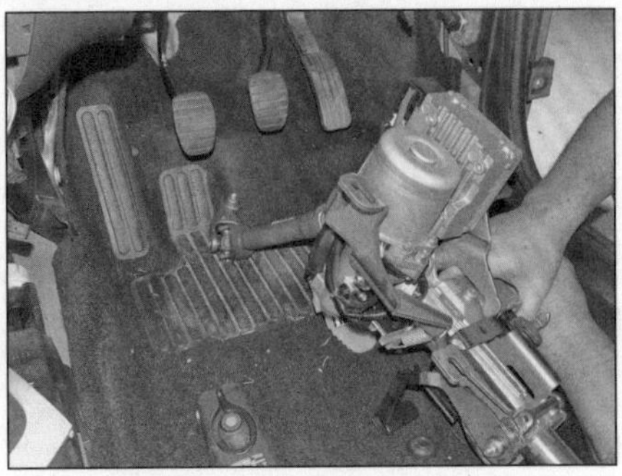

15.9b ...and then remove it

4 Recover the grease from inside the old gaiter. If it is uncontaminated with dirt or grit, apply it to the track rod inner balljoint. If the old grease is contaminated, or it is suspected that some has been lost, apply some new molybdenum disulphide grease.
5 Grease the inside of the new gaiter. Carefully slide the gaiter onto the track rod, and locate it on the steering gear housing. Align the outer edge of the gaiter with the mark made on the track rod prior to removal, then secure it in position with new retaining clips.
6 Reconnect the track rod balljoint as described in Section 18.

17 Steering gear assembly – removal, inspection and refitting

Removal

1 Remove the front subframe as described in Section 8.
2 Unscrew the two steering gear mounting bolts, and remove the steering gear assembly from the subframe **(see illustration)**. Discard the steering gear mounting bolts – new ones must be used when refitting.

Inspection

3 Renewal procedures for the gaiters and track rod end balljoints are given in Sections 16 and 18 respectively.
4 Examine the steering gear assembly for signs of wear or damage. Check that the rack moves freely over the full length of its travel, with no signs of roughness or excessive free play between the steering gear pinion and rack. Internal wear or damage can only be cured by renewing the steering gear assembly.

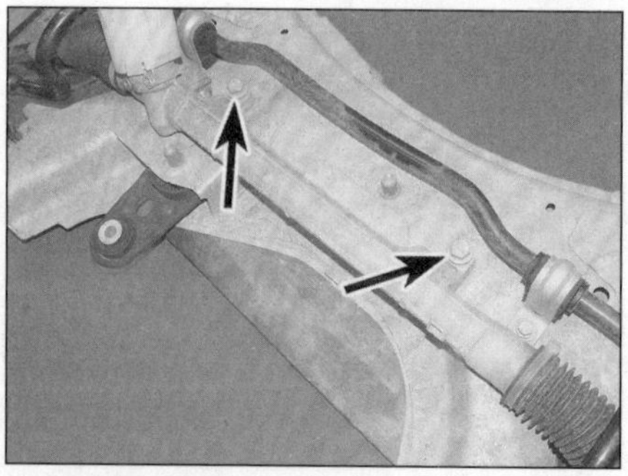

17.2 Unscrew and remove the steering gear mounting bolts

5 Overhaul of the steering rack and pinion assembly is not possible. The only components which can be renewed are the steering gear gaiters and track rod balljoints.

Refitting

6 Refitting is a reversal of removal, noting the following points:
a) Fit new steering gear mounting bolts, and tighten them to the specified torque.
b) Refit the subframe as described in Section 8.
c) When the battery has been reconnected, the steering must be initialised by turning it to full lock in either direction a few times, holding in the full-lock position for a few seconds each time.
d) On completion, it is advisable to have the wheel alignment checked.

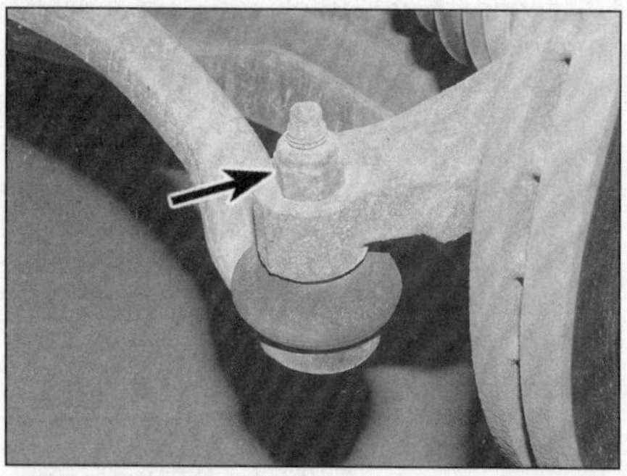

18.3a Unscrew the track rod end balljoint nut...

18.3b ...then use a balljoint separator tool to free the balljoint...

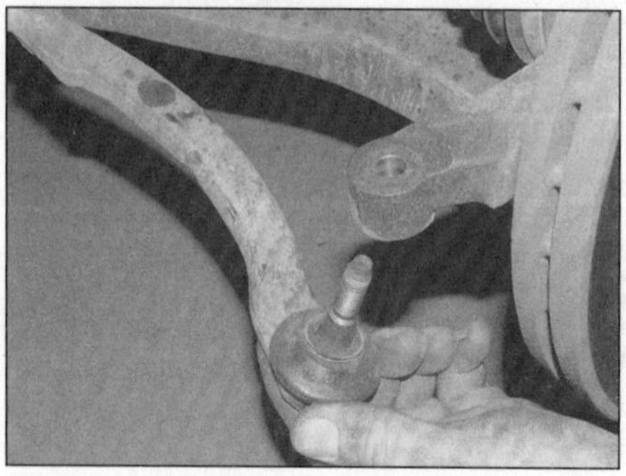

18.3c ...and disconnect the track rod end from the hub

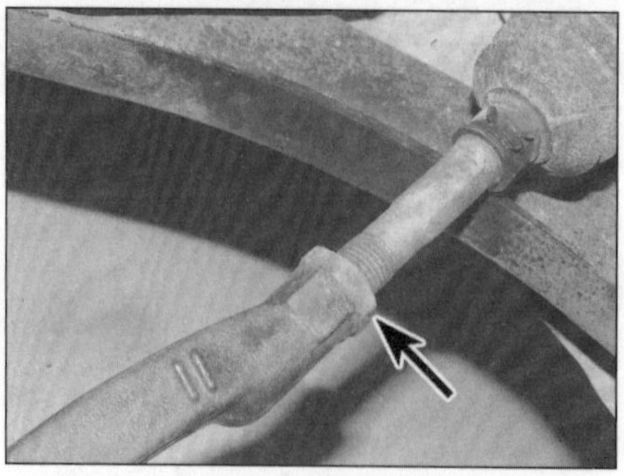

18.4 Hold the track rod end, and unscrew the locknut (arrowed)

18 Track rod end balljoint – removal and refitting

Removal

1 Apply the handbrake, then jack up the front of the car and support it on axle stands (see *Jacking and vehicle support*). Remove the appropriate front roadwheel.
2 If the balljoint is to be re-used, use a straight-edge and a scriber, or similar, to mark its relationship to the track rod.
3 Loosen the track rod end balljoint nut, unscrewing it almost to the end of its threads (if the nut will not unscrew, hold the balljoint stud on top using a small spanner). Use a balljoint separator tool to free the balljoint, then unscrew the nut completely, and disconnect the track rod from the swivel hub **(see illustrations)**.
4 Holding the balljoint on the hex fitting provided, unscrew its locknut by half a turn only – do not move the locknut from this position as it will serve as a reference mark on refitting **(see illustration)**.
5 Counting the **exact** number of turns necessary to do so, unscrew the balljoint from the track rod end.
6 Count the number of exposed threads between the end of the balljoint and the locknut, and record this figure. If a new balljoint is to be fitted, unscrew the locknut from the old balljoint.
7 Carefully clean the balljoint and the threads. Renew the balljoint if its movement is sloppy or if it is too stiff, if it is excessively worn, or if it is damaged in any way. Carefully check the shank taper and threads. If the balljoint gaiter is damaged, the complete balljoint must be renewed; it is not possible to obtain the gaiter separately.

Refitting

8 If applicable, screw the locknut onto the new balljoint, and position it so that the same number of exposed threads are visible as was noted prior to removal.
9 Screw the balljoint into the track rod by the number of turns noted on removal. This should bring the balljoint locknut to within a quarter of a turn of the end of the track rod, with the alignment marks that were made (if applicable) on removal lined up. Tighten the balljoint locknut to the specified torque.
10 Refit the balljoint shank to the swivel hub, and tighten the retaining nut to the specified torque. If difficulty is experienced due to the balljoint shank rotating, jam it by exerting pressure on the underside of the balljoint, using a tyre lever or a jack – alternatively, hold the balljoint stud on top using a small spanner.
11 Refit the roadwheel, lower the car to the

ground and tighten the roadwheel bolts to the specified torque.

12 Have the front wheel toe setting (tracking) checked on completion.

19 Wheel alignment and steering angles – general information

General information

1 A car's steering and suspension geometry is defined in four basic settings **(see illustration)**. For this purpose, all angles are expressed in degrees (toe settings are also expressed as a measurement of length). The steering axis is defined as an imaginary line drawn through the axis of the suspension strut, extended where necessary to contact the ground.

2 **Camber** is the angle between each roadwheel and a vertical line drawn through its centre and tyre contact patch, when viewed from the front or rear of the car. Positive camber is when the roadwheels are tilted outwards from the vertical at the top; negative camber is when they are tilted inwards.

3 Camber is not adjustable. Values are given for reference only. Checking is possible using a camber checking gauge, but if the figure obtained is significantly different from that specified, the car must be taken for careful checking by a professional. Wrong camber settings can only be caused by wear or damage to the body or suspension components.

4 **Castor** is the angle between the steering axis and a vertical line drawn through each roadwheel's centre and tyre contact patch, when viewed from the side of the car. Positive castor is when the steering axis is tilted so that it contacts the ground ahead of the vertical; negative castor is when it contacts the ground behind the vertical.

5 Castor is not adjustable. As with camber, values are given for reference only; deviation can only be due to wear or damage.

6 **Steering axis inclination/SAI** – also known as **kingpin inclination/KPI** – is the angle between the steering axis and a vertical line drawn through each roadwheel's centre and tyre contact patch, when viewed from the front or rear of the car.

7 SAI/KPI is not adjustable, and is given for reference only.

8 **Toe** is the amount by which the roadwheels point outwards or inwards, viewed from above. Toe-in is when the roadwheels point inwards, towards each other at the front, while toe-out is when they splay outwards from each other at the front. The value for toe can be expressed as an angle (taking the centre-line of the car as zero), or as a measurement of length (taking measurements between the inside rims of the wheels at hub height).

9 The front wheel toe setting is adjusted by screwing the balljoints in or out of their track rods to alter the effective length of the track rod assemblies.

10 Rear wheel toe setting is not adjustable, and is given for reference only. While it can be checked, if the figure obtained is significantly different from that specified, the car must be taken for careful checking by a professional, as the fault can only be caused by wear or damage to the body or suspension components.

Checking – general

11 Due to the special measuring equipment necessary to check the wheel alignment, and the skill required to use it properly, the checking and adjustment of these settings is best left to a Renault dealer or similar expert. Most tyre-fitting shops now possess sophisticated checking equipment.

12 For accurate checking, the car must be at the kerb weight specified in *Dimensions and weights* in the Reference Section.

13 Before starting work, check first that the tyre sizes and types are as specified, then check tyre pressures and tread wear. Also check roadwheel run-out, the condition of the hub bearings, the steering wheel free play and the condition of the front suspension components (Chapter 1A or 1B). Correct any faults.

14 Park the car on level ground, with the front roadwheels in the straight-ahead position. Rock both ends to settle the suspension. Release the handbrake and roll the car backwards 1 metre (3 feet), then forwards again, to relieve any stresses in the steering and suspension components.

Front wheel toe setting

Checking

15 Two methods are available to the home mechanic for checking the front wheel toe setting. One method is to use a gauge to measure the distance between the front and rear inside edges of the roadwheels. The other method is to use a scuff plate, in which each front wheel is rolled across a movable plate which records any deviation, or scuff, of the tyre from the straight-ahead position as it moves across the plate. Such gauges are available in relatively-inexpensive form from accessory outlets. It is up to the owner to decide whether the expense is justified, in view of the small amount of use such equipment would normally receive.

16 Prepare the car as described previously in paragraphs 12 to 14.

17 If the measurement procedure is being used, carefully measure the distance between the front edges of the roadwheel rims and the rear edges of the rims. Subtract the rear measurement from the front measurement, and check that the result is within the specified range. If not, adjust the toe setting as described in paragraph 19.

18 If scuff plates are to be used, roll the car backwards, check that the roadwheels are in the straight-ahead position, then roll it across the scuff plates so that each front roadwheel passes squarely over the centre of its respective plate. Note the angle recorded by the scuff plates. To ensure accuracy, repeat the check three times, and take the average of the three readings. If the roadwheels are running parallel, there will of course be no angle recorded; if a deviation value is shown on the scuff plates, compare the reading obtained for each wheel with that specified. If the value recorded is outside the specified tolerance, the toe setting is incorrect, and must be adjusted as follows.

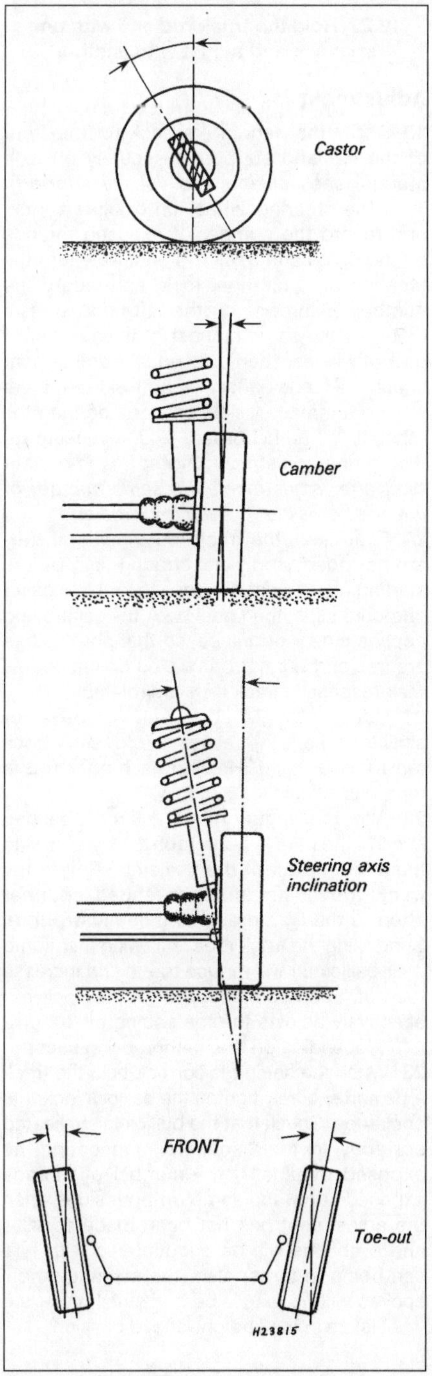

19.1 Wheel alignment and steering angles

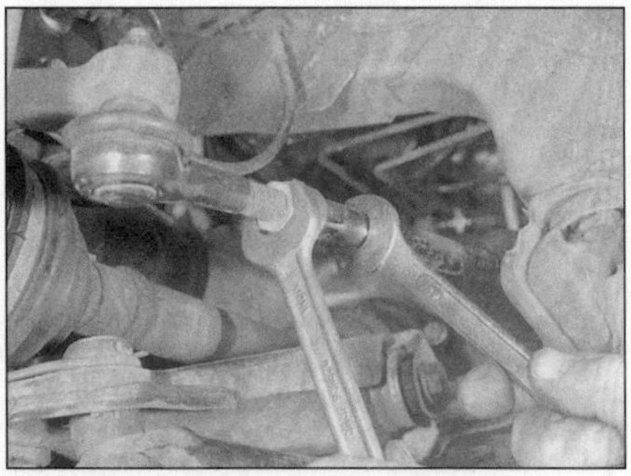

19.22 Hold the track rod end with one spanner, and adjust with another

Adjustment

19 Apply the handbrake, jack up the front of the car and support it securely on axle stands (see *Jacking and vehicle support*). Turn the steering wheel onto full-left lock, and record the number of exposed threads on the right-hand track rod end. Now turn the steering onto full-right lock, and record the number of threads on the left-hand side. If there are the same number of threads visible on both sides, then subsequent adjustment should be made equally on both sides. If there are more threads visible on one side than the other, it will be necessary to compensate for this during adjustment. **Note:** *It is important that, after adjustment, the same number of threads be visible on each track rod end.*

20 First clean the track rod threads; if they are corroded, apply penetrating fluid before starting adjustment. Release the rubber gaiter outboard clips, then peel back the gaiters and apply a smear of grease, so that both gaiters are free and will not be twisted or strained as their respective track rods are rotated.

21 Use a straight-edge and a scriber or similar to mark the relationship of each track rod to its balljoint. Holding each track rod in turn, unscrew its locknut fully.

22 Alter the length of the track rods, bearing in mind the note in paragraph 19, by screwing them into or out of the balljoints. Rotate the track rod using an open-ended spanner fitted to the flats provided **(see illustration)**. Shortening the track rods (screwing them onto their balljoints) will reduce toe-in and increase toe-out. Each complete turn of the track rod effectively adjusts the toe setting by 30' or 3 mm (depending on the method being used).

23 When the setting is correct, hold the track rods and securely tighten the balljoint locknuts or clamps. Check that the balljoints are seated correctly in their sockets, and count the exposed threads. If the number of threads exposed is not the same on both sides, then the adjustment has not been made equally, and problems will be encountered with tyre scrubbing in turns; also, the steering wheel spokes will no longer be horizontal when the wheels are in the straight-ahead position.

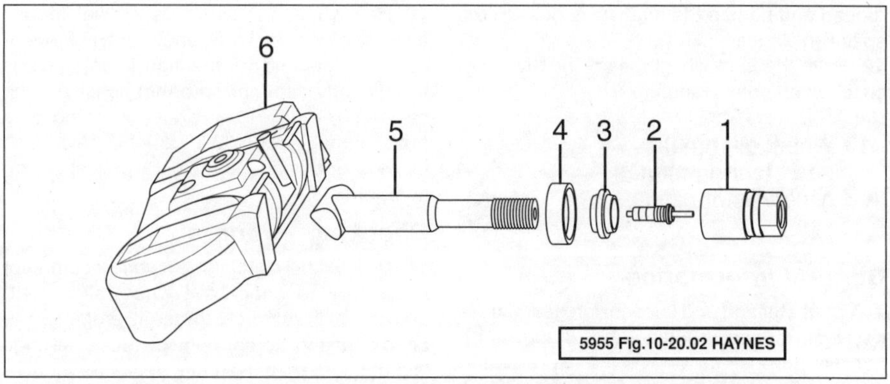

20.2 The component parts of the tyre pressure monitoring system

1 Dust cap
2 Valve core
3 Valve seal
4 Cup washer
5 Valve
6 Pressure sensor

24 When the track rod lengths are the same, lower the car to the ground and recheck the toe setting; readjust if necessary. Ensure that the rubber gaiters are seated correctly and are not twisted or strained; secure them in position with new retaining clips.

Rear wheel toe setting

25 The procedure for checking the rear toe setting is same as described for the front in paragraph 17. However, no adjustment is possible.

20 Tyre pressure monitoring system – general information

This system continuously monitors the tyre pressures of the four tyres in use on the car, and warns of any tyre pressure issues as they develop.

A sensor unit is fitted to each wheel, and forms an integral assembly with the tyre valve **(see illustration)**. Besides the conventional valve, the unit contains sensors for pressure, temperature and acceleration, a radio transmitter and a non-removable battery. Each sensor is programmed to monitor one 'corner' of the car, meaning that the wheels cannot be interchanged without a fault being signalled – a coloured band around the valve indicates each sensor's intended working position, as shown below. The units can be transferred between wheels once the tyres have been removed.

Green	*Front left*
Yellow	*Front right*
Red	*Rear left*
Black	*Rear right*

Information on the pressure, temperature and acceleration of each tyre is sent to the multiplex unit inside the car, via the radio senders. The multiplex unit then processes this information, determines whether a fault is present, and signals the driver using the information display in the centre of the instrument panel. The system warns the driver in the event of:

a) Overinflation.
b) Moderate or extreme underinflation.
c) A puncture.
d) A tyre pressure which is inappropriate for the vehicle speed.
e) Slow punctures between left- and right-hand tyres.
f) Pressure left-right imbalance when starting.
g) Sensor failure.

Precautions

The spare wheel is not equipped with a sensor, so while the spare is in use, a fault will be signalled continuously. A spare wheel sensor would not work with this system, since each sensor is coded for one position on the car – the spare wheel gets fitted wherever it is needed.

Similarly, even the four wheels with sensors cannot be interchanged (from front to rear, for instance, to compensate for uneven tyre wear) with this system, otherwise a fault will be signalled.

When new tyres are being fitted, make sure the fitter is made aware of the special sensor units, which have integrated valves, not the 'disposable' kind more commonly used. It is common practice for new valves to be fitted with new tyres, but this should not be attempted. Care is also required when removing old tyres (and when fitting new ones), as the sensors are located just inside the rim edge.

If new sensors have been fitted, they must be programmed to the car using suitable diagnostic equipment before they will work properly. Any problems with the system should also be referred to a Renault dealer or suitably equipped garage.

Chapter 11
Bodywork and fittings

Contents

	Section number
Body exterior fittings – removal and refitting	19
Bonnet – removal and refitting	9
Bonnet lock components – removal and refitting	10
Bumpers – removal and refitting	6
Centre console – removal and refitting	23
Door handle and lock components – removal and refitting	12
Door trim panel – removal and refitting	13
Door window glass and regulator – removal and refitting	14
Doors – removal and refitting	11
Facia panel and crossmember – removal and refitting	24
General information	1
Interior trim panels – removal and refitting	22
Maintenance – bodywork and underframe	2
Maintenance – upholstery and carpets	3
Major body damage – repair	5
Minor body damage – repair	4
Mirrors – removal, refitting and glass renewal	16
Radiator grille panel – removal and refitting	7
Seat belt components – removal and refitting	21
Seats – removal and refitting	20
Sunroof components – removal and refitting	18
Tailgate and related components – removal and refitting	15
Windscreen cowl panels – removal and refitting	8
Windscreen, tailgate and fixed window glass – general information	17

Degrees of difficulty

Easy, suitable for novice with little experience	**Fairly easy,** suitable for beginner with some experience	**Fairly difficult,** suitable for competent DIY mechanic	**Difficult,** suitable for experienced DIY mechanic	**Very difficult,** suitable for expert DIY or professional

Specifications

Torque wrench settings	Nm	lbf ft
Front seat mounting bolts*	35	26
Rear seat mountings	21	15
Seat belt mountings	21	15
Seat belt inertia reel*	21	15

** Use new bolts*

1 General information

The bodyshell and floorpan are manufactured from pressed-steel, and form an integral part of the car's structure , without the need for a separate chassis. The Mégane is available as a 5-door Hatchback , 5-door Estate (called the 'Sports Tourer' by Renault and a 3- door Coupe. A Cabriolet version is also available, but this model is not covered by this manual.

Various areas of the structure are strengthened to provide for suspension, steering and engine mounting points, and load distribution.

Corrosion protection is applied to all new cars. Various anti-corrosion preparations are used, including galvanising, zinc phosphatisation, and PVC underseal. An 'anti-gravel' undercoat is applied to the front section of the bonnet, to prevent corrosion and paint chipping caused by stones and other road debris hitting the front of the car. Protective wax is injected into the box sections and other hollow cavities.

Extensive use is made of plastic for peripheral components, such as the radiator grille, bumpers and wheel trims, and for much of the interior trim. Plastic wheel arch liners are fitted, to protect the metal body panels against corrosion due to a build-up of road dirt.

2 Maintenance – bodywork and underframe

The general condition of a car's bodywork is the one thing that significantly affects its value. Maintenance is easy, but needs to be regular. Neglect, particularly after minor damage, can lead quickly to further deterioration and costly repair bills. It is important also to keep watch on those parts of the car not immediately visible, for instance the underside, inside all the wheel arches, and the lower part of the engine compartment.

The basic maintenance routine for the bodywork is washing – preferably with a lot of water, from a hose. This will remove all the loose solids which may have stuck to the car. It is important to flush these off in such a way as to prevent grit from scratching the finish. The wheel arches and underframe need washing in the same way, to remove any accumulated mud which will retain moisture and tend to encourage rust. Strange as it sounds, the best time to clean the underframe and wheel arches is in wet weather, when the mud is thoroughly wet and soft. In very wet weather, the underframe is usually cleaned of large accumulations automatically, and this is a good time for inspection.

Periodically, except on cars with a wax-based underbody protective coating, it is a good idea to have the whole of the underframe of the car steam-cleaned, engine compartment included, so that a thorough inspection can be carried out to see what minor repairs and renovations are necessary. Steam-cleaning is available at many garages, and is necessary for the removal of the accumulation of oily grime, which sometimes is allowed to become thick in certain areas. If steam-cleaning facilities are not available, there are one or two excellent grease solvents available, which can be brush-applied; the dirt can then be simply hosed off. Note that these methods should not be used on cars with wax-based underbody protective coating, or the coating will be removed. Such cars should be inspected annually, preferably just prior to Winter, when the underbody should be washed down, and any damage to the wax coating repaired. Ideally, a completely fresh coat should be applied. It would also be worth considering the use of such wax-based protection for injection into door panels, sills, box sections, etc, as an additional safeguard against rust damage, where such protection is not provided by the car manufacturer.

After washing paintwork, wipe off with a chamois leather to give an unspotted clear finish. A coat of clear protective wax polish will give added protection against chemical pollutants in the air. If the paintwork sheen has dulled or oxidised, use a cleaner/polisher combination to restore the brilliance of the shine. This requires a little effort, but such dulling is usually caused because regular washing has been neglected. Care needs to be taken with metallic paintwork, as special non-abrasive cleaner/polisher is required to avoid damage to the finish. Always check that the door and ventilator opening drain holes and pipes are completely clear, so that water can be drained out. Brightwork should be treated in the same way as paintwork. Windscreens and windows can be kept clear of the smeary film which often appears, by the use of proprietary glass cleaner. Never use any form of wax or other body or chromium polish on glass.

3 Maintenance – upholstery and carpets

Mats and carpets should be brushed or vacuum-cleaned regularly, to keep them free of grit. If they are badly stained, remove them from the car for scrubbing or sponging, and make quite sure they are dry before refitting. Seats and interior trim panels can be kept clean by wiping with a damp cloth. If they do become stained (which can be more apparent on light-coloured upholstery), use a little liquid detergent and a soft nail brush to scour the grime out of the grain of the material. Do not forget to keep the headlining clean in the same way as the upholstery. When using liquid cleaners inside the car, do not over-wet the surfaces being cleaned. Excessive damp could get into the seams and padded interior, causing stains, offensive odours or even rot. If the inside of the car gets wet accidentally, it is worthwhile taking some trouble to dry it out properly, particularly where carpets are involved. *Do not leave oil or electric heaters inside the car for this purpose.*

4 Minor body damage – repair

Repair of minor scratches

If the scratch is very superficial, and does not penetrate to the metal of the bodywork, repair is very simple. Lightly rub the area of the scratch with a paintwork renovator, or a very fine cutting paste, to remove loose paint from the scratch, and to clear the surrounding bodywork of wax polish. Rinse the area with clean water.

In the case of metallic paint, the most commonly-found scratches are not in the paint, but in the lacquer top coat, and appear white. If care is taken, these can sometimes be rendered less obvious by very careful use of paintwork renovator (which would otherwise not be used on metallic paintwork); otherwise, repair of these scratches can be achieved by applying lacquer with a fine brush.

Apply touch-up paint to the scratch using a fine paint brush; continue to apply fine layers of paint until the surface of the paint in the scratch is level with the surrounding paintwork. Allow the new paint at least two weeks to harden, then blend it into the surrounding paintwork by rubbing the scratch area with a paintwork renovator or a very fine cutting paste. Finally, apply wax polish.

Where the scratch has penetrated right through to the metal of the bodywork, causing the metal to rust, a different repair technique is required. Remove any loose rust from the bottom of the scratch with a penknife, then apply rust-inhibiting paint, to prevent the formation of rust in the future. Using a rubber or nylon applicator, fill the scratch with bodystopper paste. If required, this paste can be mixed with cellulose thinners, to provide a very thin paste which is ideal for filling narrow scratches. Before the stopper-paste in the scratch hardens, wrap a piece of smooth cotton rag around the top of a finger. Dip the finger in cellulose thinners, and quickly sweep it across the surface of the stopper-paste in the scratch; this will ensure that the surface of the stopper-paste is slightly hollowed. The scratch can now be painted over as described earlier in this Section.

Repair of dents

When deep denting of the car's bodywork has taken place, the first task is to pull the dent out, until the affected bodywork almost attains its original shape. There is little point in trying to restore the original shape completely, as the metal in the damaged area will have stretched on impact, and cannot be reshaped fully to its original contour. It is better to bring the level of the dent up to a point which is about 3 mm below the level of the surrounding bodywork. In cases where the dent is very shallow anyway, it is not worth trying to pull it out at all. If the underside of the dent is accessible, it can be hammered out gently from behind, using a mallet with a wooden or plastic head. Whilst doing this, hold a block of wood firmly against the outside of the panel, to absorb the impact from the hammer blows and thus prevent a large area of the bodywork from being 'belled-out'.

Should the dent be in a section of the bodywork which has a double skin, or some other factor making it inaccessible from behind, a different technique is called for. Drill several small holes through the metal inside the area – particularly in the deeper section. Then screw long self-tapping screws into the holes, just sufficiently for them to gain a good purchase in the metal. Now the dent can be pulled out by pulling on the protruding heads of the screws with a pair of pliers.

The next stage of the repair is the removal of the paint from the damaged area, and from an inch or so of the surrounding 'sound' bodywork. This is accomplished most easily by using a wire brush or abrasive pad on a power drill, although it can be done just as effectively by hand, using sheets of abrasive paper. To complete the preparation for filling, score the surface of the bare metal with a screwdriver or the tang of a file, or alternatively, drill small holes in the affected area. This will provide a really good 'key' for the filler paste.

To complete the repair, see the Section on filling and respraying.

Repair of rust holes or gashes

Remove all paint from the affected area, and from an inch or so of the surrounding 'sound' bodywork, using an abrasive pad or a wire brush on a power drill. If these are not available, a few sheets of abrasive paper will do the job most effectively. With the paint removed, you will be able to judge the severity of the corrosion, and therefore decide whether to renew the whole panel (if this is possible) or to repair the affected area. New body panels are not as expensive as most people think, and it is often quicker and more satisfactory to fit a new panel than to attempt to repair large areas of corrosion.

Remove all fittings from the affected area, except those which will act as a guide to the original shape of the damaged bodywork (e.g. headlight shells etc). Then, using tin snips or a hacksaw blade, remove all loose metal and any other metal badly affected by corrosion. Hammer the edges of the hole inwards, in order to create a slight depression for the filler paste.

Wire-brush the affected area to remove the powdery rust from the surface of the remaining metal. Paint the affected area with rust-inhibiting paint; if the back of the rusted area is accessible, treat this also.

Before filling can take place, it will be necessary to block the hole in some way. This can be achieved by the use of aluminium or plastic mesh, or aluminium tape.

Aluminium or plastic mesh, or glass-fibre matting is probably the best material to use for a large hole. Cut a piece to the approximate size and shape of the hole to be filled, then position it in the hole so that its edges are below the level of the surrounding bodywork. It can be retained in position by several blobs of filler paste around its periphery.

Aluminium tape should be used for small or very narrow holes. Pull a piece off the roll, trim it to the approximate size and shape required, then pull off the backing paper (if used) and stick the tape over the hole; it can be overlapped if the thickness of one piece is insufficient. Burnish down the edges of the tape with the handle of a screwdriver or similar, to ensure that the tape is securely attached to the metal underneath.

Filling and respraying

Before using this Section, see the Sections on dent, deep scratch, rust holes and gash repairs.

Many types of bodyfiller are available, but generally speaking, those proprietary kits which contain a tin of filler paste and a tube of resin hardener are best for this type of repair. A wide, flexible plastic or nylon applicator will be found invaluable for imparting a smooth and well-contoured finish to the surface of the filler.

Mix up a little filler on a clean piece of card or board – measure the hardener carefully (follow the maker's instructions on the pack), otherwise the filler will set too rapidly or too slowly. Using the applicator, apply the filler paste to the prepared area; draw the applicator across the surface of the filler to achieve the correct contour and to level the surface. As soon as a contour that approximates to the correct one is achieved, stop working the paste – if you carry on too long, the paste will become sticky and begin to 'pick-up' on the applicator. Continue to add thin layers of filler paste at 20-minute intervals, until the level of the filler is just proud of the surrounding bodywork.

Once the filler has hardened, the excess can be removed using a metal plane or file. From then on, progressively-finer grades of abrasive paper should be used, starting with a 40-grade production paper, and finishing with a 400-grade wet-and-dry paper. Always wrap the abrasive paper around a flat rubber, cork, or wooden block – otherwise the surface of the filler will not be completely flat. During the smoothing of the filler surface, the wet-and-dry paper should be periodically rinsed in water. This will ensure that a very smooth finish is imparted to the filler at the final stage.

At this stage, the 'dent' should be surrounded by a ring of bare metal, which in turn should be encircled by the finely 'feathered' edge of the good paintwork. Rinse the repair area with clean water, until all of the dust produced by the rubbing-down operation has gone.

Spray the whole area with a light coat of – this will show up any imperfections in the surface of the filler. Repair these imperfections with fresh filler paste or bodystopper, and once more smooth the surface with abrasive paper. If bodystopper is used, it can be mixed with cellulose thinners, to form a really thin paste which is ideal for filling small holes. Repeat this spray-and-repair procedure until you are satisfied that the surface of the filler, and the feathered edge of the paintwork, are perfect. Clean the repair area with clean water, and allow to dry fully.

The repair area is now ready for final spraying. Paint spraying must be carried out in a warm, dry, windless and dust-free atmosphere. This condition can be created artificially if you have access to a large indoor working area, but if you are forced to work in the open, you will have to pick your day very carefully. If you are working indoors, dousing the floor in the work area with water will help to settle the dust which would otherwise be in the atmosphere. If the repair area is confined to one body panel, mask off the surrounding panels; this will help to minimise the effects of a slight mis-match in paint colours. Bodywork fittings (e.g. chrome strips, door handles etc) will also need to be masked off. Use genuine masking tape, and several thicknesses of newspaper, for the masking operations.

Before commencing to spray, agitate the aerosol can thoroughly, then spray a test area (an old tin, or similar) until the technique is mastered. Cover the repair area with a thick coat of primer; the thickness should be built up using several thin layers of paint, rather than one thick one. Using 400 grade wet-and-dry paper, rub down the surface of the primer until it is really smooth. While doing this, the work area should be thoroughly doused with water, and the wet-and-dry paper periodically rinsed in water. Allow to dry before spraying on more paint.

Spray on the top coat, again building up the thickness by using several thin layers of paint. Start spraying at the top of the repair area, and then, using a side-to-side motion, work downwards until the whole repair area and about 2 inches of the surrounding original paintwork is covered. Remove all masking material 10 to 15 minutes after spraying on the final coat of paint.

Allow the new paint at least two weeks to harden, then, using a paintwork renovator or a very fine cutting paste, blend the edges of the paint into the existing paintwork. Finally, apply wax polish.

Plastic components

With the use of more and more plastic body components by the car manufacturers (e.g.

6.3 Remove the bolts from both sides (one side shown only)

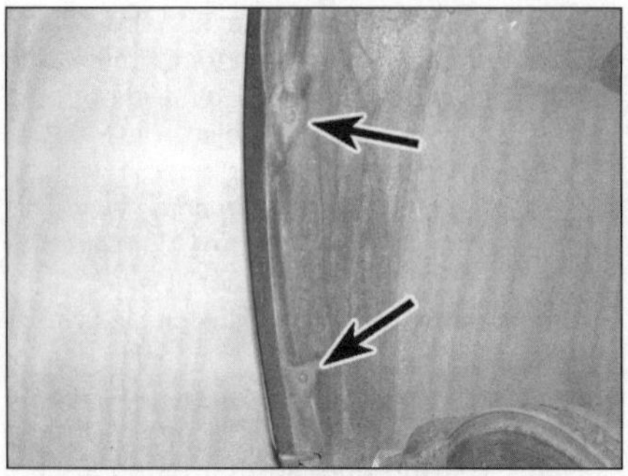

6.4 Remove the screws (arrowed)

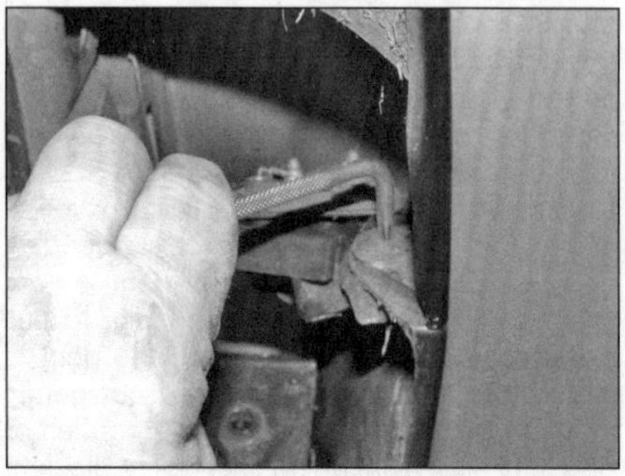

6.5 Remove the upper mounting screws

bumpers, spoilers, wings and in some cases major body panels), rectification of more serious damage to such items has become a matter of either entrusting repair work to a specialist in this field, or renewing complete components. Repair of such damage by the DIY owner is not really feasible, owing to the cost of the equipment and materials required for effecting such repairs. The basic technique involves making a groove along the line of the crack in the plastic, using a rotary burr in a power drill. The damaged part is then welded back together, using a hot air gun to heat up and fuse a plastic filler rod into the groove. Any excess plastic is then removed, and the area rubbed down to a smooth finish. It is important that a filler rod of the correct plastic is used, as body components can be made of a variety of different types (e.g. polycarbonate, ABS, polypropylene).

Damage of a less serious nature (abrasions, minor cracks etc) can be repaired by the DIY owner using a two-part epoxy filler repair. Once mixed in equal, this is used in similar fashion to the bodywork filler used on metal panels. The filler is usually cured in twenty to thirty minutes, ready for sanding and painting.

If the owner is renewing a complete component himself, or if he has repaired it with epoxy filler, he will be left with the problem of finding a suitable paint for finishing which is compatible with the type of plastic used. At one time, the use of a universal paint was not possible, owing to the complex range of plastics encountered in body component applications. Standard paints, generally speaking, will not bond to plastic or rubber satisfactorily, but suitable paints to match any plastic or rubber finish, can be obtained from dealers. However, it is now possible to obtain a plastic body parts finishing kit which consists of a pre-primer treatment, a primer and coloured top coat. Full instructions are normally supplied with a kit, but basically, the method of use is to first apply the pre-primer to the component concerned, and allow it to dry for up to 30 minutes. Then the primer is applied, and left to dry for about an hour before finally applying the special-coloured top coat. The result is a correctly-coloured component, where the paint will flex with the plastic or rubber, a property that standard paint does not normally posses.

5 Major body damage – repair

Where serious damage has occurred, or large areas need renewal due to neglect, it means that complete new panels will need welding-in, and this is best left to professionals. If the damage is due to impact, it will also be necessary to check completely the alignment of the bodyshell, and this can only be carried out accurately by a Renault dealer using special jigs. If the body is left misaligned, it is primarily dangerous, as the car will not handle properly, and secondly, uneven stresses will be imposed on the steering, suspension and possibly transmission, causing abnormal wear, or complete failure, particularly to such items as the tyres.

6 Bumpers – removal and refitting

Front bumper

1 On models fitted with front foglights, make sure the ignition is off (take out the keycard).

2 To improve access, jack up the front of the car and support it securely on axle stands (see *Jacking and vehicle support*).

3 Remove bolts from the underside of the bumper where it joins the engine undertray **(see illustration)**.

4 Inside the wheel arch on each side, remove the screws securing the outer edge of the bumper. Unclip and remove the front section of the wheel arch liner **(see illustration)**.

5 Remove both front headlights as described in Chapter 12, Section 8 and then remove the bumper upper mounting screws **(see illustration)**.

6 At the top of the bumper, remove the air intake duct. And remove all but 2 of the upper bumper bolts **(see illustrations)**.

7 Using a plastic trim tool if necessary release the bumper ends from the front wings on both sides **(see illustration)**.

8 The bumper should now only be supported by the 2 remaining upper bolts. On models with headlight washers, the washer tubing must be disconnected before the bumper can be fully removed – the washer jets themselves are each secured by a single nut.

9 With the aid of an assistant supporting the bumper, remove the remaining 2 bolts and

6.6a Remove the air intake duct

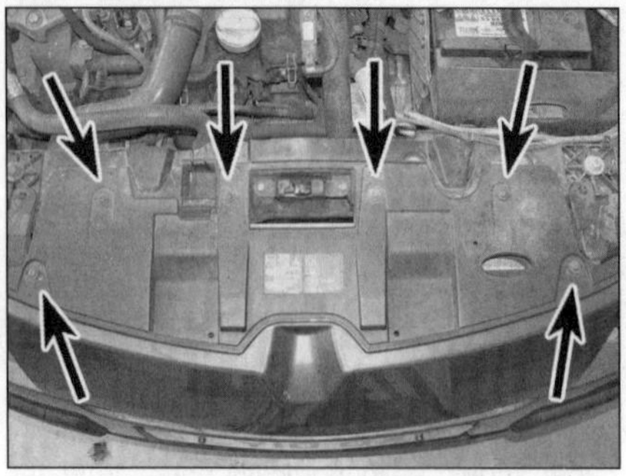

6.6b Remove the bolts (arrowed)

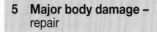

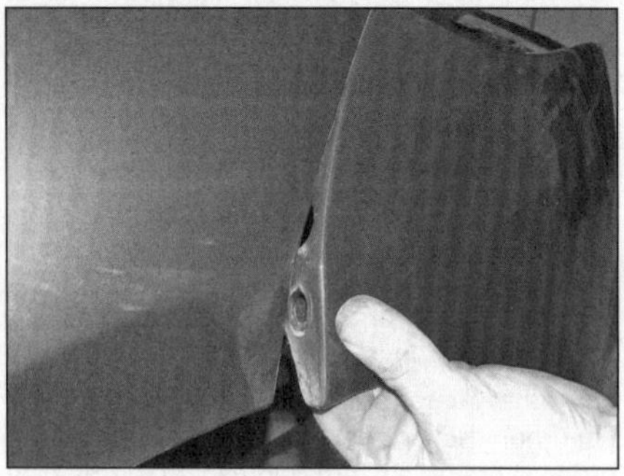

6.7 Free the bumper cover from the wing and mounting

6.9 Remove the bumper

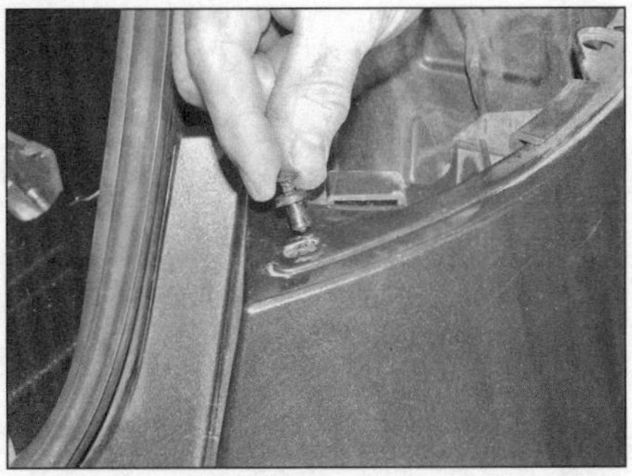

6.14a Remove the clip or screw (on some models)...

6.14b ...and the bump stops

6.15 Remove the wing liners

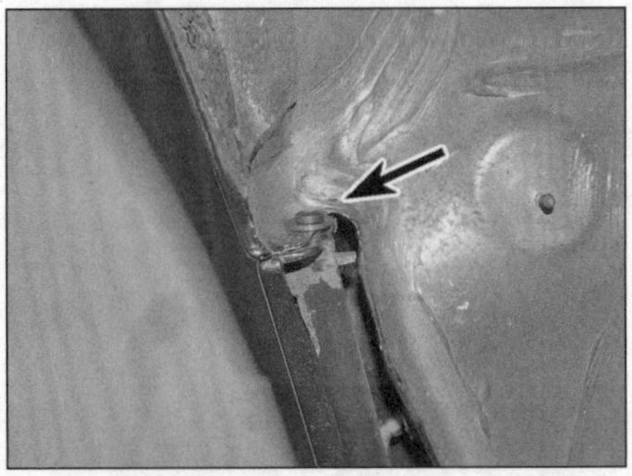

6.16 Remove the screw (arrowed)

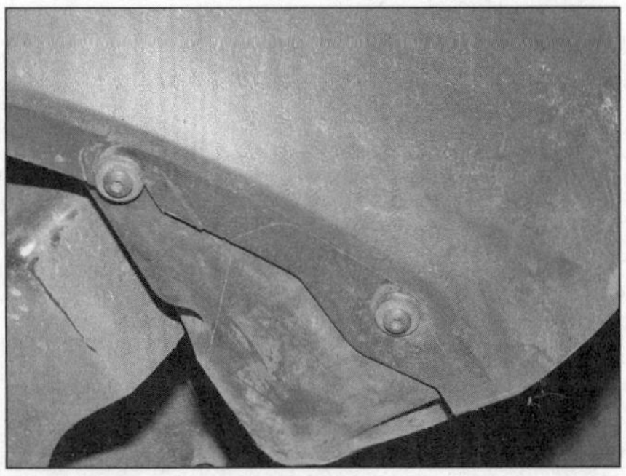

6.17 Remove the lower screws (side ones shown)

then remove the bumper from the vehicle **(see illustration)**.

10 Refitting is a reversal of removal.

Rear bumper

11 The removal procedure is similar for all models.

12 Chock the front wheels, then jack up the rear of the car and support it securely on axle stands (see *Jacking and vehicle support*).

13 Remove the rear light units as described in Chapter 12, Section 8.

14 Prise out the plastic clip (or remove the screw) on each side securing the top of the bumper and then remove the tailgate bump stops **(see illustrations)**.

15 Remove both rear wing liners **(see illustration)**. These are held in place by a combination of screws and plastic clips.

16 Remove the upper screw from the bumper from inside the wheel arch **(see illustration)**.

17 On the underside of the bumper, remove the screws on each side **(see illustration)** and in the centre.

18 Have an assistant support the bumper and then pull the bumper outwards at each side to release the clips. Unclip it along the top and bottom edges, and remove it **(see illustrations)**. At the same time on models fitted with a parking aid system, disconnect the wiring from the sensors, and if necessary remove the sensors as described in Chapter 12, Section 28.

19 Refitting is a reversal of removal.

7 Radiator grille panel – removal and refitting

The grille is part of the front bumper assembly, which is removed as described in Section 6. With the bumper removed, it appears that the grille panel and its inner cover can be unclipped and unscrewed as required **(see illustration)**. For availability of parts, you will need to check with your local Renault dealer.

8 Windscreen cowl panels – removal and refitting

Removal

1 Open the bonnet and remove the windscreen wiper arms as described in Chapter 12, Section 17.

2 Noting how it fits remove the weatherseal from the bulk head **(see illustration)**.

3 At each side remove the small trim pieces **(see illustration)**.

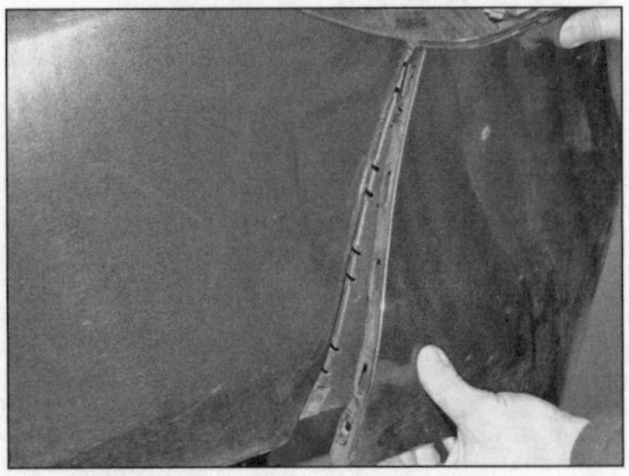

6.18a Release the bumper from the rear wing...

6.18b ...and remove it from the vehicle

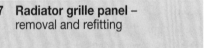

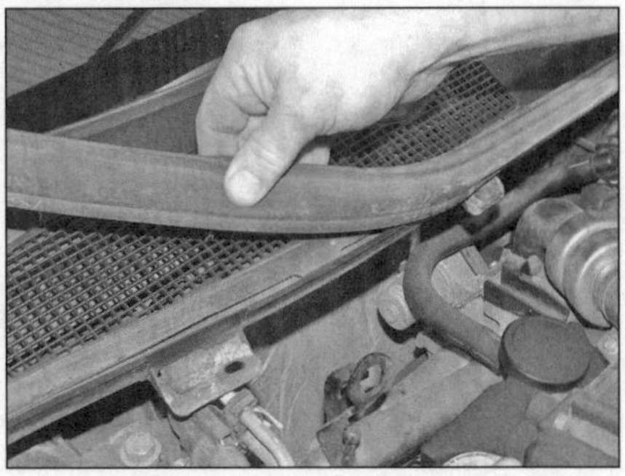

8.2 Remove the weatherseal

8.3 Remove the seals from both sides

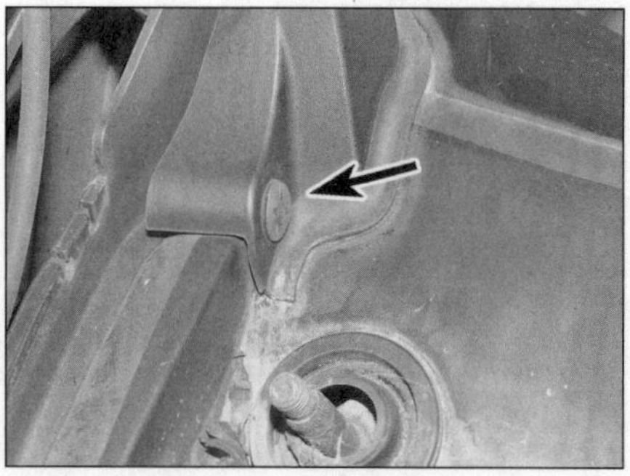
8.4a Prise out the clip (arrowed)...

8.4b ...and then remove the side deflectors

8.5a Remove the cowl panel

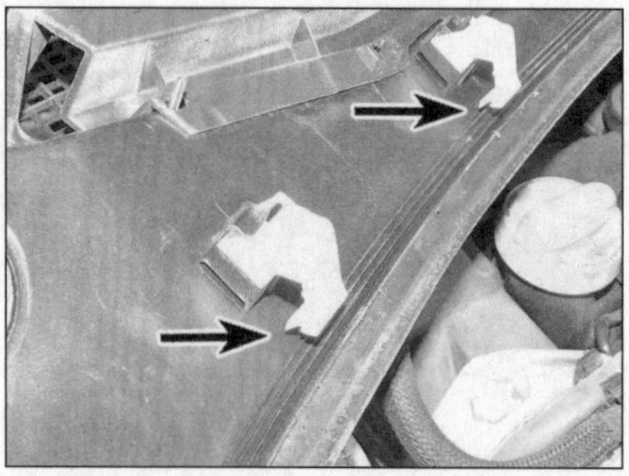
8.5b Note how the retaining clips lock into the base of the windscreen (arrowed)

4 Carefully unclip the side trim panels **(see illustrations)**.

5 Unclip and remove the main centre section of the panel **(see illustrations)**.

Refitting

6 Refitting is a reversal of removal, but note that Renault recommend replacing the small clips that secure the small side panels .

9 Bonnet – removal and refitting

Removal

1 Disconnect the windscreen washer hose at the T-piece or alternatively remove the screen washer jets complete with the washer hose. Trace the hose back to the right-hand hinge (right as seen from the driver's seat), unclipping it from the locations under the bonnet.

2 If the original bonnet is to be refitted, mark the position of the hinges on the bonnet to aid alignment on refitting **(see illustration)**.

3 Have an assistant support the bonnet in the open position.

4 Remove the locking clip from the support strut and remove the strut from the bonnet.

5 Remove the bolts securing the bonnet to the hinges (two bolts and a torx head screw at each side). With the aid of an assistant carefully remove the bonnet from the car. Store the bonnet safely.

Refitting

6 Refitting is a reversal of removal, bearing in mind the following points:

a) Where applicable, align the hinges with the marks made on the bonnet before removal.

b) Close the bonnet (carefully, in case it fouls the surrounding bodywork), and check the alignment with the surrounding body panels.

c) If necessary, the alignment of the bonnet can be adjusted by altering the position of the bonnet on the hinges, using the elongated holes provided.

10 Bonnet lock components – removal and refitting

Lock assembly

Removal

1 Open the bonnet.

2 Note and mark the position of the lock on the panel, to aid correct alignment when refitting.

3 Unscrew the two securing bolts, then remove the lock assembly from the panel. Remove the left-hand front headlight as described in Chapter 12 and release the cable from the mounting clips – this will provide enough play to pull the lock forward without the need to remove the bumper cover. Pull the lock assembly forward, unclip the release cable and disconnect the wiring plug **(see illustrations)**.

Refitting

4 Refitting is a reversal of removal, but align the assembly with the marks made on the panel before removal.

Lock release cable/lever

Removal

5 Remove the glovebox (see Section 22).

9.2 Mark the position of the hinges

10.3a Release the cable

10.3b Remove the bolts

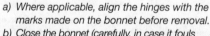

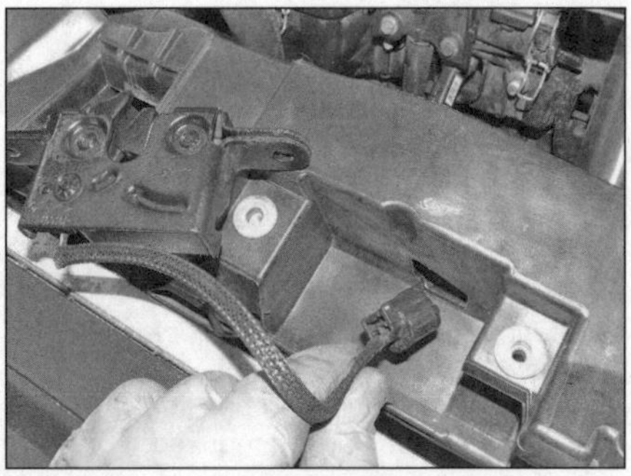
10.3c Disconnect the wiring plug

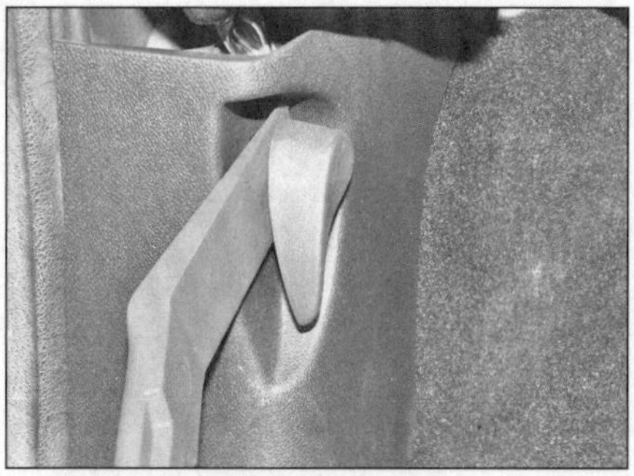
10.6 Remove the lever

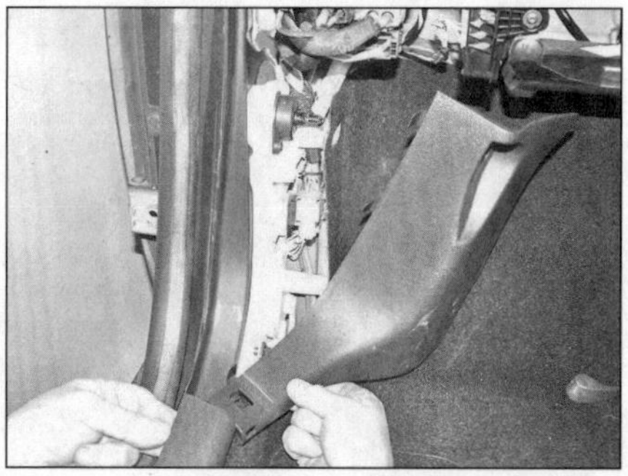
10.7a Remove the trim

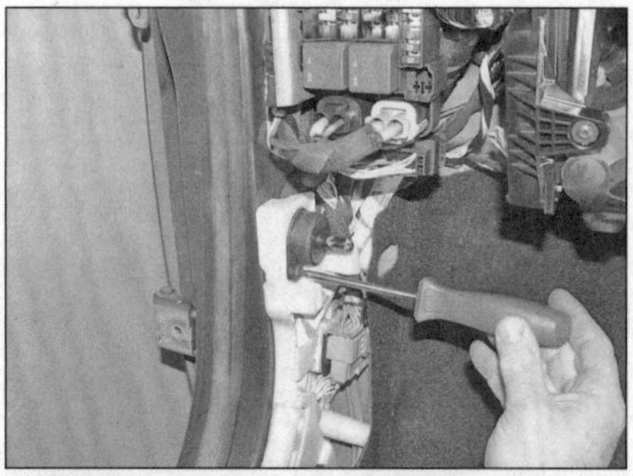
10.7b Remove the screws and then...

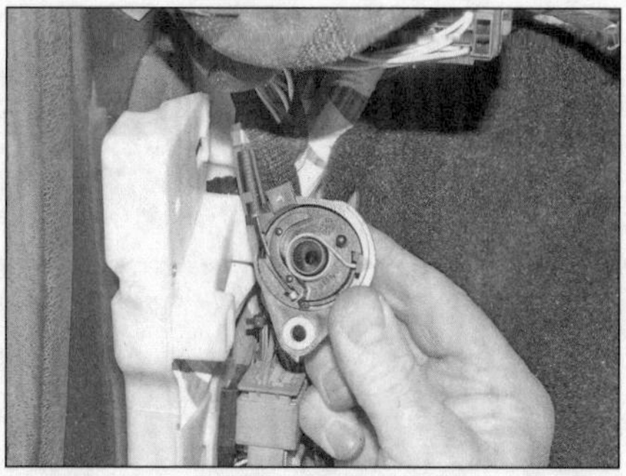
10.7c ...unhook the cable

6 Prise free the release handle with a suitable trim tool **(see illustration)**.

7 Remove the trim panel and then remove the main section of the release mechanism **(see illustrations)**.

8 Remove the bonnet lock, the battery, battery tray and the left-hand headlight. Locate the cable (it runs along the top of the left-hand chassis leg) and free it from the cable clips.

9 Tie a length of stout cord around the cable in the cabin and then pull the cable into the engine bay. Remove the cord from the cable.

Refitting

10 Refitting is a reversal of removal, but tie the replacement cable to the cord and use it to pull the new cable into the cabin.

Safety catch

Removal

11 The release catch is secured to the bonnet crossmember by two Torx screws. Open the bonnet and remove the screws. Remove the handle.

Refitting

12 Refitting is a reversal of removal.

11 Doors – removal and refitting

Removal

1 To remove a door, open it fully, and support it under its lower edge on a jack. Cover the head of the jack with pads of rag **(see illustration)**. Alternatively, have an assistant on hand to support the door.

2 Disconnect the battery negative lead.

3 Disconnect the door wiring connector by swinging the securing catch upwards, then pull the connector from its socket **(see illustration)**.

4 Unbolt the door check strap **(see illustration)**.

5 Mark the position on the hinges on the door frame and then (with the door supported) unscrew the upper and lower hinge nuts **(see illustrations)**. Remove the door from the car.

11.1 Support the door

11.3 Disconnect the wiring plug

11.4 Unbolt the door check strap (arrowed)

11.5a Remove the upper and...

11.5b ...lower hinge mounting nuts

12.1a Prise out the trim cover . . .

12.1b . . . and remove the screw behind it

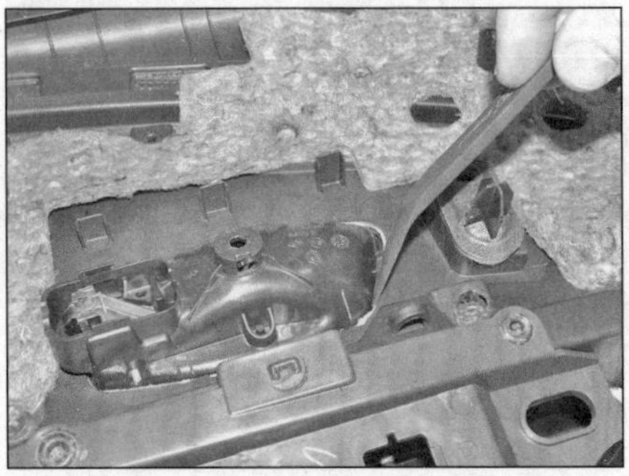

12.2 Remove the handle from the door trim panel

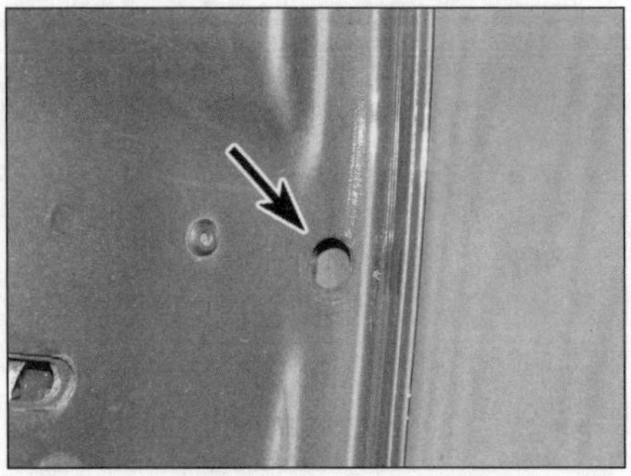

12.4 Prise out the trim cap (arrowed) at the rear of the door

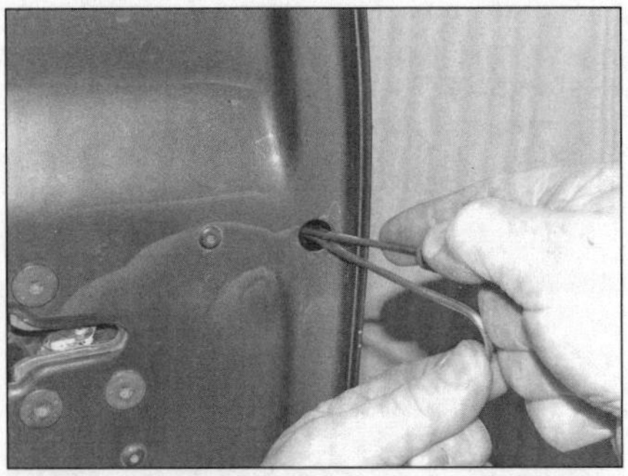

12.5a Insert a piece of hooked wire and small screwdriver into the hole and pull outwards to disengage the lock barrel

12.5b Note how the hook and screwdriver release the lock cylinder – removed from the door for clarity. The arrow shows where the metal rotating section hits the plastic stop

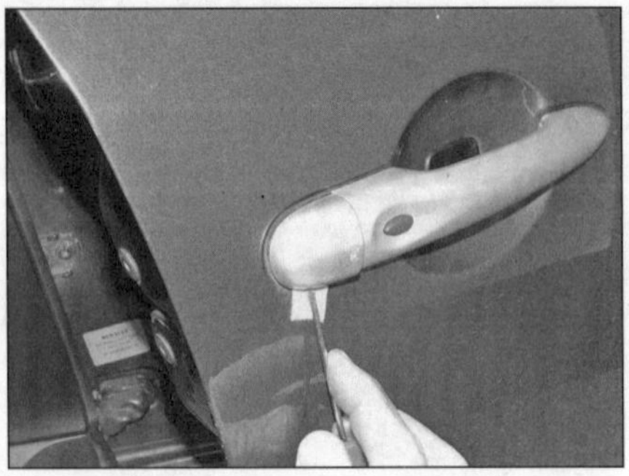

12.6a Release the cover (keyless model shown)...

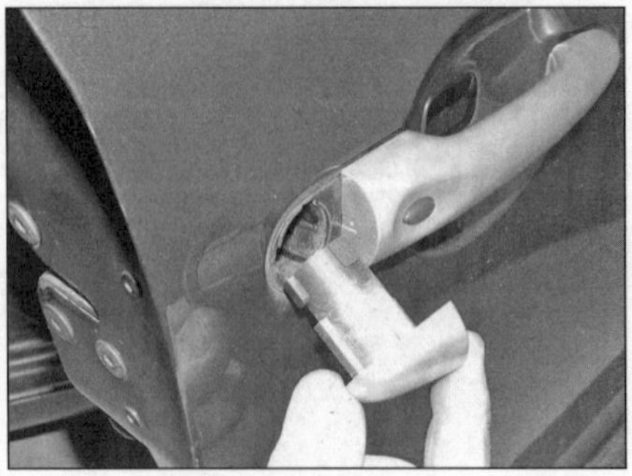

12.6b ...and remove it

Refitting

6 Refitting is a reversal of removal. Tighten the hinge nuts securely, and check the operation of the door. If the same doors are refitted, no adjustment should be required.

Adjustment

7 Door closure may be most easily adjusted by altering the position of the lock striker on the body pillar, using a Torx bit.
8 The hinges are bolted in position, and their position can be adjusted if required.

12 Door handle and lock components – removal and refitting

Door interior handle

1 Prise out the trim cover, and remove the single screw securing the door interior handle to the door **(see illustrations)**.
2 Prise out the handle and unclip the operating cable from the rear of it. Remove the handle from the door. Note that if you are removing the door trim panel to access internal components it is simpler to leave the handle in position (after removing the screw) and unhook the cable from the rear of the panel. Removing the handle with the door panel removed is also an option **(see illustration)**.
3 Refitting is a reversal of removal.

Front door lock cylinder/trim

4 Open the door, and prise out the trim cap from the back edge **(see illustration)**.
5 Release the door lock cylinder retaining catch by inserting a hooked piece of wire into the hole, and pulling the catch outwards. A small screwdriver will also be required to lift the retaining stop **(see illustrations)**.
6 Protect the paint on the outside of the door, then prise out the door lock cylinder and remove it **(see illustrations)**.
7 Refitting is a reversal of removal. Re-engage the door lock cylinder catch on completion by pushing it forwards.

Door exterior handle

8 On models with 'hands-free' locking (identifiable by the pushbutton on the handle), remove the door trim panel as described in Section 13 until access is gained to the inside of the handle. Disconnect the wiring plug from the handle module.
9 Remove the lock barrel or handle rear trim piece as described in paragraphs 4 to 6.
10 Pull the rear end of the handle outwards, and unhook it at the front. On models with 'hands-free' locking, take care not to damage the wiring plug as the handle is withdrawn. Recover the rubber gasket from the door, and check its condition – fit a new one if necessary, to prevent water getting into the door **(see illustrations)**.
11 Refitting is a reversal of removal. Refit

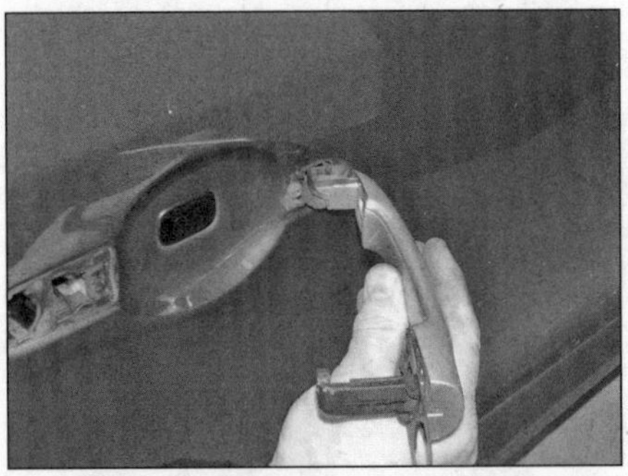
12.10a Release the handle...

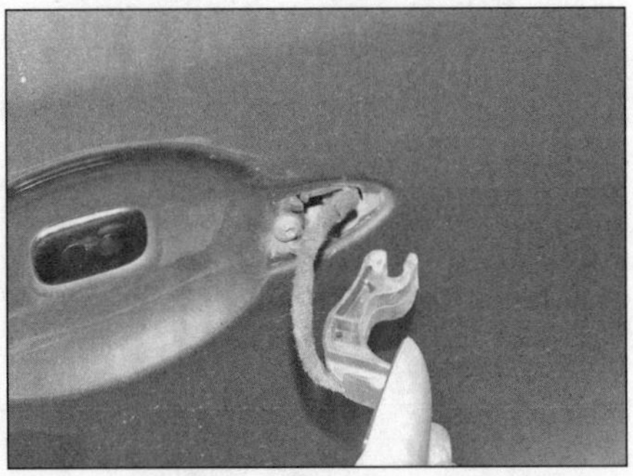
12.10b ...and unhook it

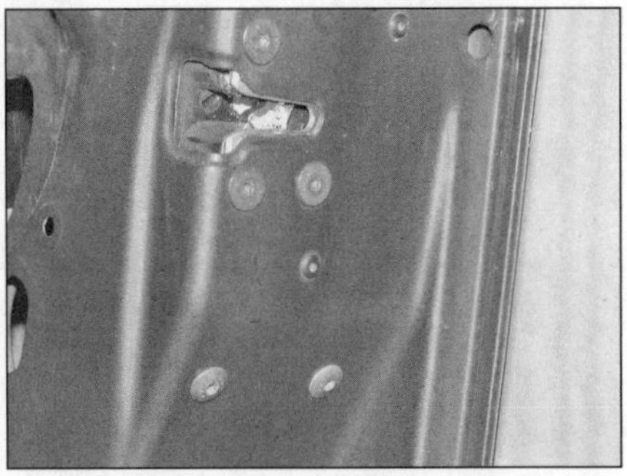
12.15 Remove the lock securing screws

12.16a Remove the gasket...

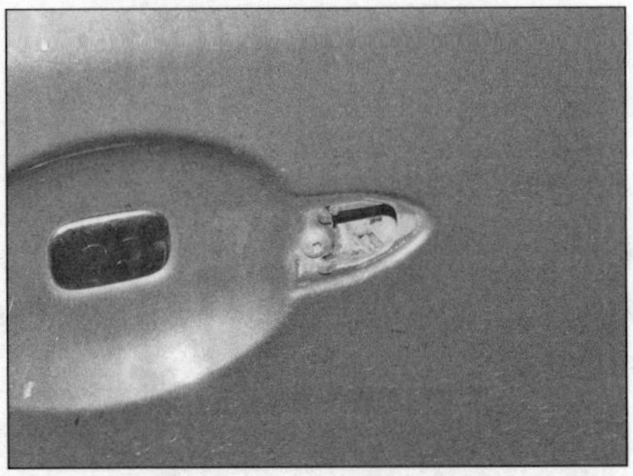
12.16b ...and the screw

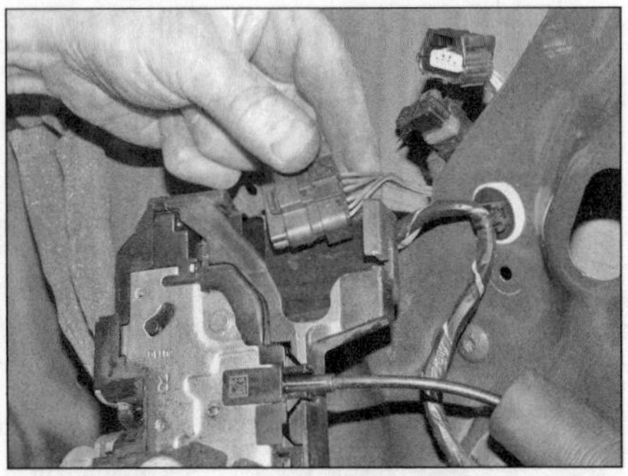
12.16c Manoeuvre the lock from the door and disconnect the wiring plug

the lock barrel/trim piece as described in paragraph 7. Where applicable, refit the door trim panel as described in Section 13.

Door lock

12 The lock assembly is best removed with the inner section of the outer handle, the interconnecting cable and the inner handle release cable as a complete assembly.

13 Remove the exterior handle as described previously in this Section.

14 Remove the door inner trim panel as described in Section 13. Disconnect the door lock wiring plug with the help of a small screwdriver.

15 Unscrew the lock securing screws from the rear edge of the door **(see illustration)**.

16 From outside, remove the small gasket and screw. Unclip the inner part of the door handle. The lock and the inner section of the handle assembly can now be manoeuvred out of the door frame – note that the lock assembly rests on a hidden hook in the end of the door frame **(see illustrations)**.

17 Refitting is a reversal of removal. Refit the exterior handle as described previously. Where applicable, refit the door trim panel as described in Section 13.

Central locking components

18 All the central locking components are integrated into the locks and handles.

13 Door trim panel – removal and refitting

1 Disconnect the battery negative lead, and move the lead away from the battery (see *Disconnecting the battery*).

Front door

2 Unclip the triangular trim panel at the front of the door. On models with manual door mirrors, pull off the mirror adjuster handle cover first, then work the trim panel off over the handle. Remove the screw from the panel **(see illustrations)**

3 Remove the door interior handle retaining screw as described in Section 12.

4 Prise off the cover from the door pull handle **(see illustration)**.

5 Remove the two screws inside the door pull handle **(see illustration)**.

6 Where applicable, prise out and disconnect the footwell illumination light at the base of the door **(see illustration)**.

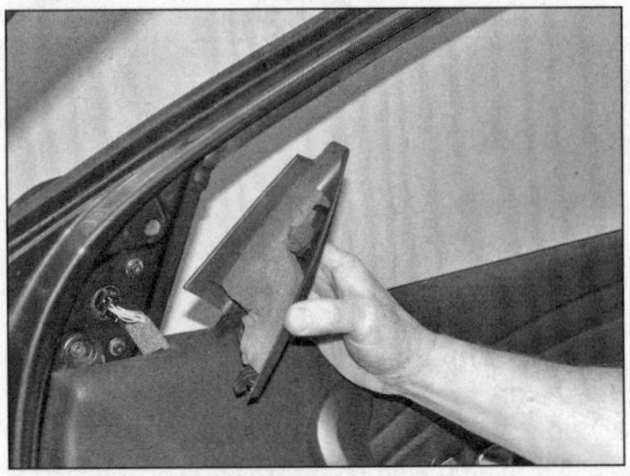
13.2a Unclip the mirror trim panel...

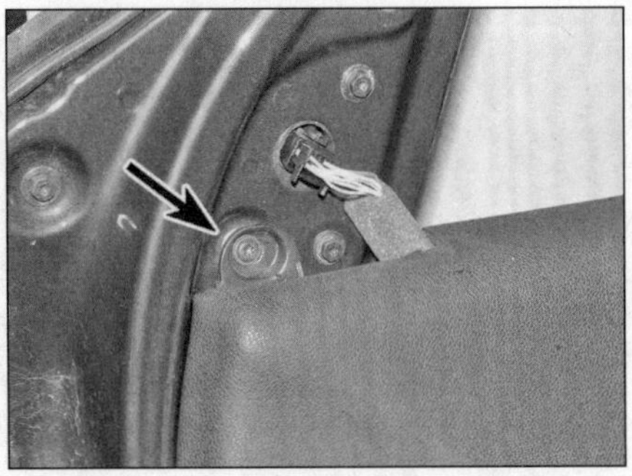
13.2b ...and then remove the screw (arrowed)

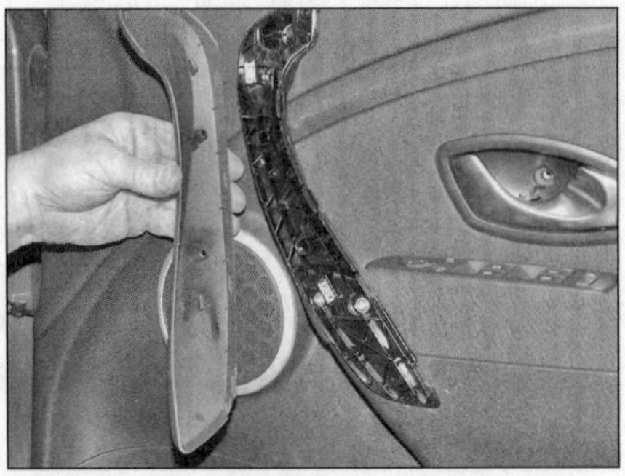
13.4 Prise off the door pull handle cover

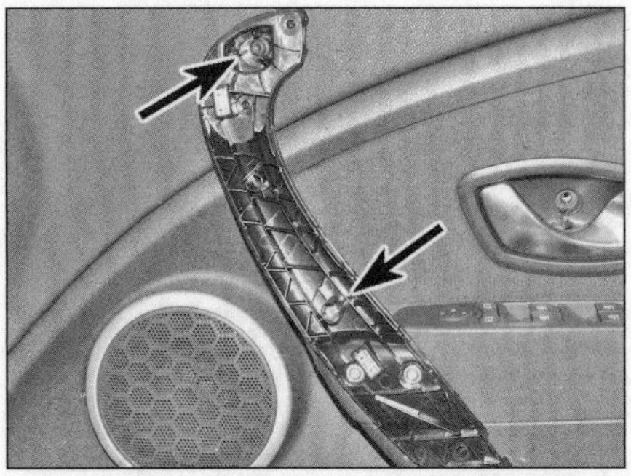

13.5 Remove the screws (arrowed)

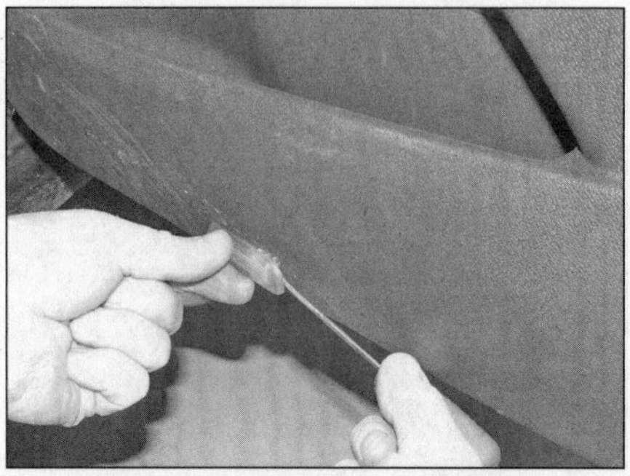

13.6 At the base of the door, prise out and disconnect the footwell light

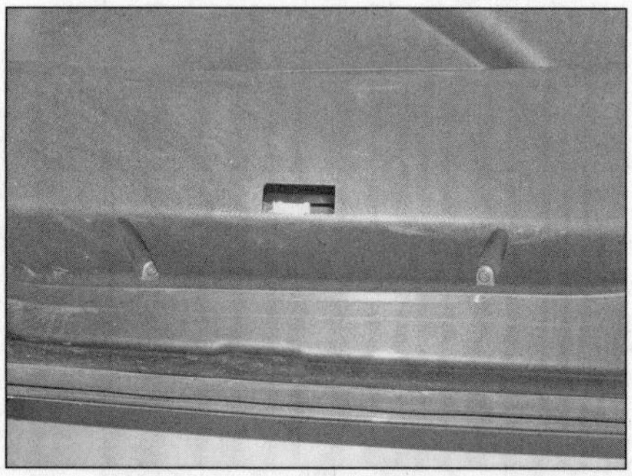

13.7a Remove the two screws from the base of the trim panel...

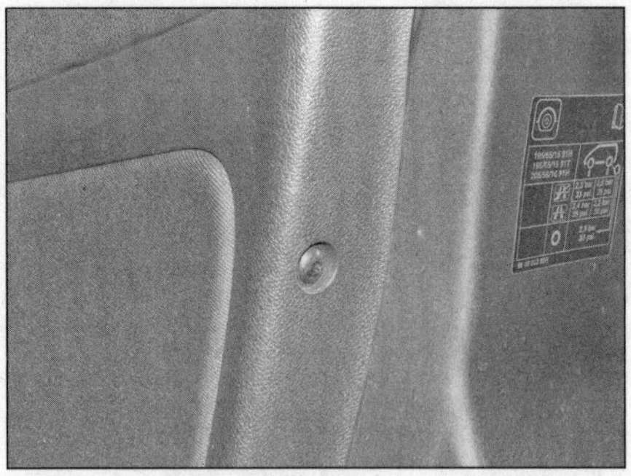

13.7b ...and at the upper rear

13.9 Disconnect the cable

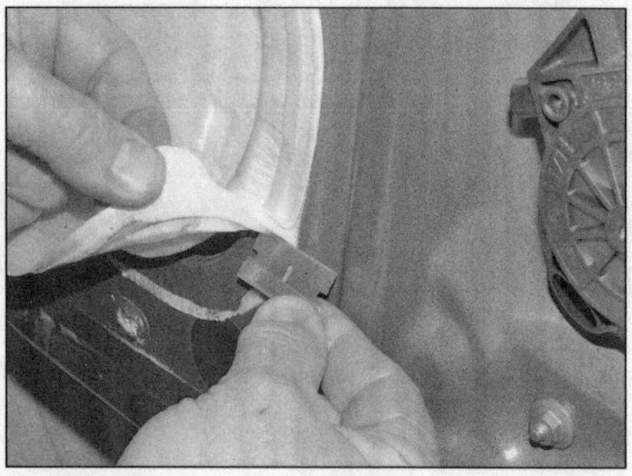

13.11 Remove the membrane carefully

7 Remove the two screws from the bottom of the trim panel and then remove the upper rear screw **(see illustrations)**.

8 Using a plastic trim tool release the door panel retaining clips. Anticipate some damaged clips as the panel is released.

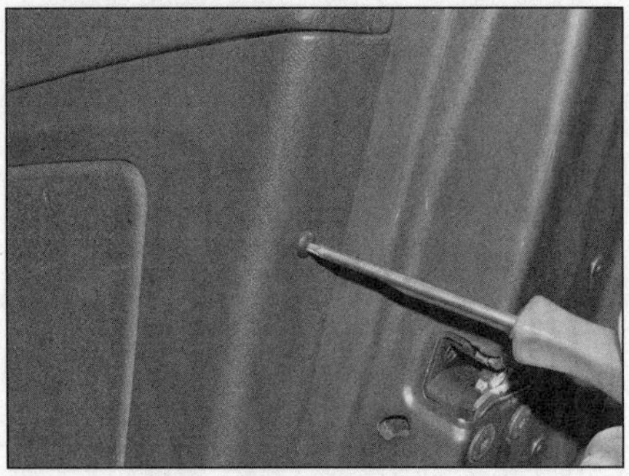

13.14 Remove the screw

13.15 Work around the panel releasing the retaining clips

9 Fully release the panel by pushing it up and away from the door. Disconnect the lock release cable **(see illustration)** and the window/mirror switch wiring plug before finally removing the panel.

10 Refitting is a reversal of removal.

11 If access to the interior of the door is required remove the membrane with a sharp knife or blade **(see illustration)**. Renault recommend that the membrane is replaced whenever it is removed, however in practise it is possible to remove it, and successfully refit it.

Rear door

12 Remove the door interior handle as described in Section 12.

13 On models fitted with manual rear window remove the window wider handle by releasing the spring retaining clip. Suitable tools are widely available. Alternatively a polishing cloth dragged around the handle will release the spring clip.

14.2 Remove the blanking plug

14 Where applicable, prise out and disconnect the footwell illumination light at the base of the door. Also remove the single trim panel screw at the rear of the panel **(see illustration)**.

15 Using a plastic trim tool release the door panel retaining clips **(see illustration)**. Anticipate some damaged clips as the panel is released.

16 Lift off the panel and disconnect the lock release cable and (where electric windows are fitted) wiring plug as the panel is removed.

17 Refitting is a reversal of removal, but note that replacement panel retaining clips may be required. On models fitted with manual rear windows, Renault recommend replacement of the winder handle retaining spring clip.

14 Door window glass and regulator – removal and refitting

Front door

Door glass

1 Remove the door trim panel and membranes, as described in the previous Section.

2 Remove the blanking plug from the inner door skin **(see illustration)** refit the power window switch and lower the glass so that the glass retaining clamp screws can be accessed.

3 Disconnect the battery as described in Chapter 5A.

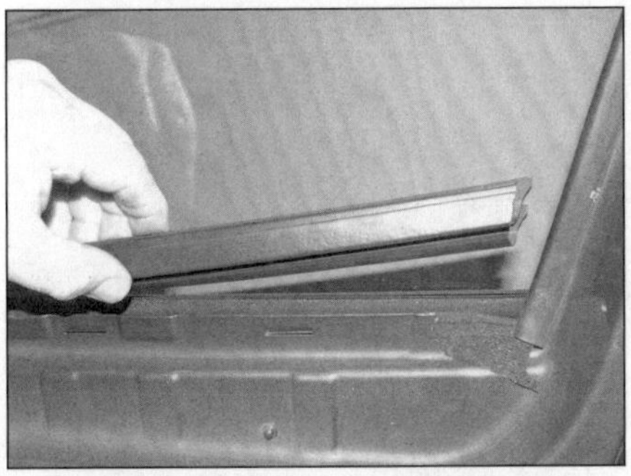

14.5 Remove the inner weatherseal

14.6a Remove the front...

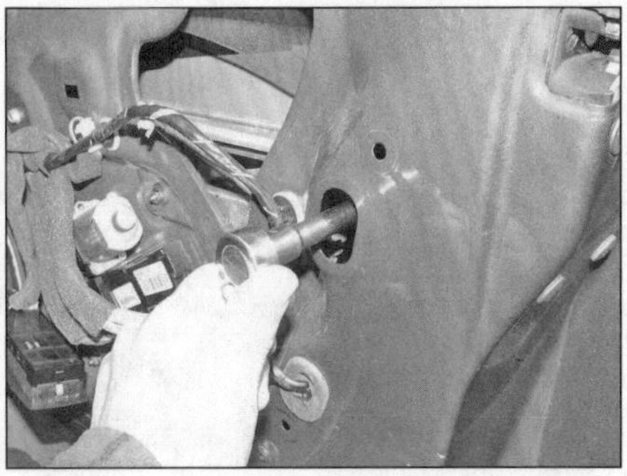

14.6b ...and rear glass clamp bolts

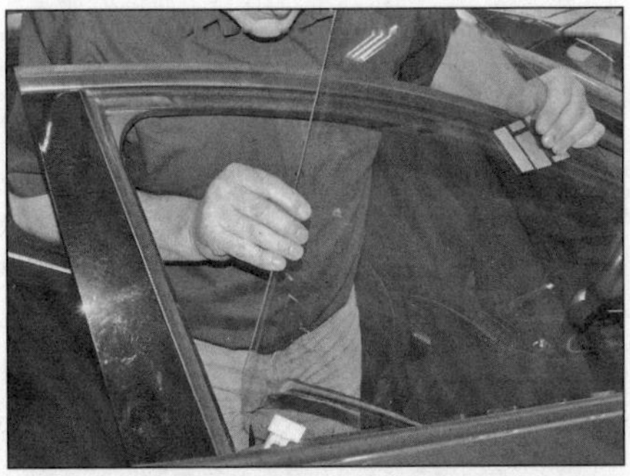

14.7 Remove the glass from the door frame

14.11a Disconnect the wiring plug...

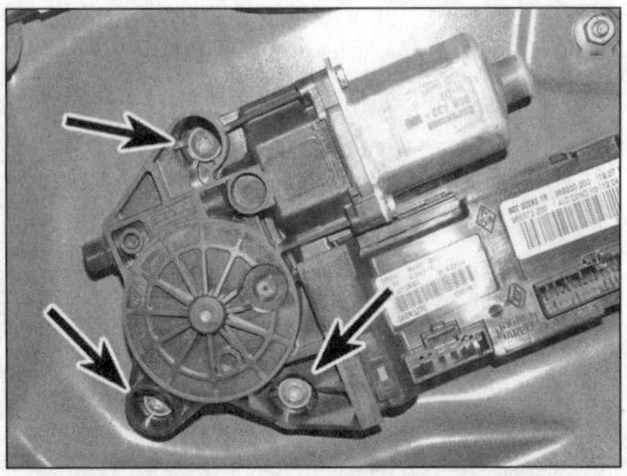

14.11b ...remove the bolts (arrowed)...

4 Where fitted, remove or protect the side impact sensor.

5 Using a suitable tool work free and then remove the inner weatherseal **(see illustration)**.

6 Remove the bolts on the glass retaining brackets **(see illustrations)**.

7 Pull the glass free and remove it outwards from the door frame **(see illustration)**.

8 Refitting is a reversal of removal, but note that Renault recommend that the glass clamp bolts are replaced. Where a new piece of glass is to be fitted, then a replacement foam strip must be fitted to the lower edge of the glass.

Regulator

9 Remove the door trim panel and membrane (as described in the previous Section).

10 Position the door glass so that the glass retaining clamp screws are accessible. Disconnect the battery - as described in Chapter 5A.

14.13a Remove the front glass guide channel...

11 Disconnect the wiring plugs from the regulator motor and then remove the 3 mounting bolts. Remove the motor **(see illustrations)**.

12 Slacken the mounting screws and then pull the glass free from the retaining clamps. Pull the glass up to the fully closed position and locate it in place with strong adhesive tape **(see illustration)**.

13 Remove the regulator mounting bolts and then carefully manoeuvre the regulator from the door frame **(see illustrations)**.

14.11c ...and remove the motor

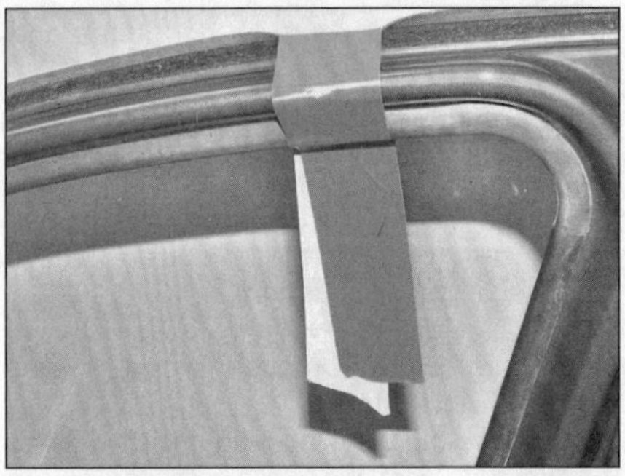

14.12 Secure the glass with adhesive tape

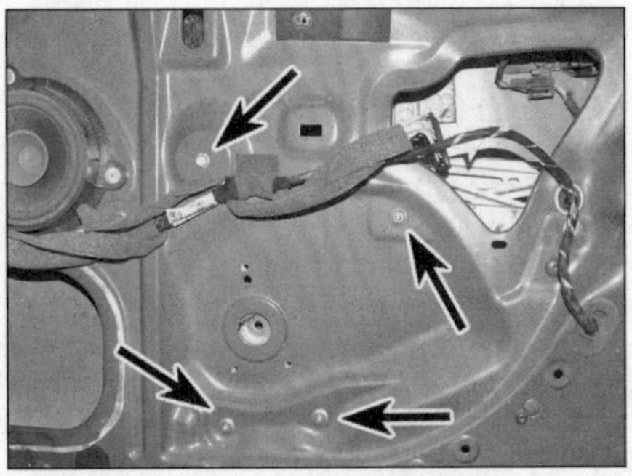

14.13b ...remove the bolts (arrowed)...

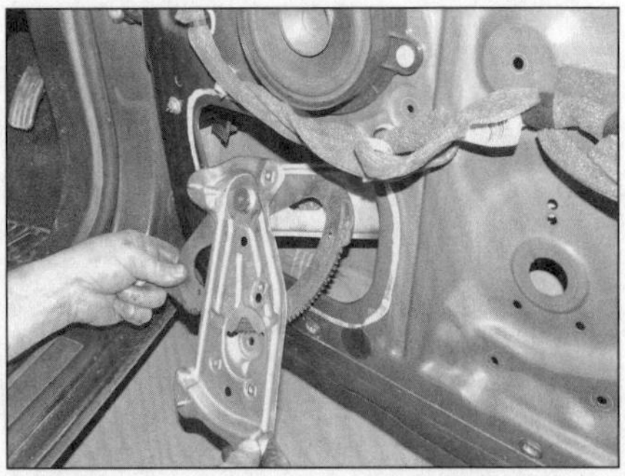

14.13c ...and then remove the regulator assembly

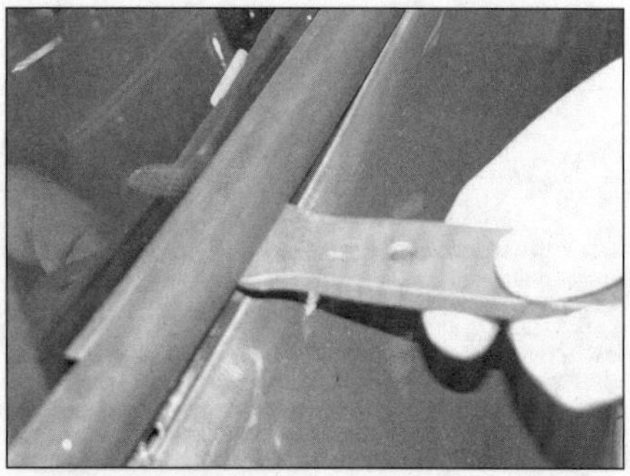

14.16a Prise up and remove the outer weatherseal...

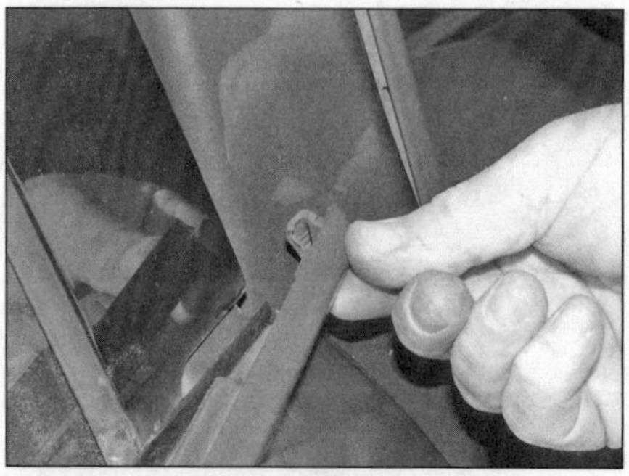

14.16b ...noting how it fits into the door frame

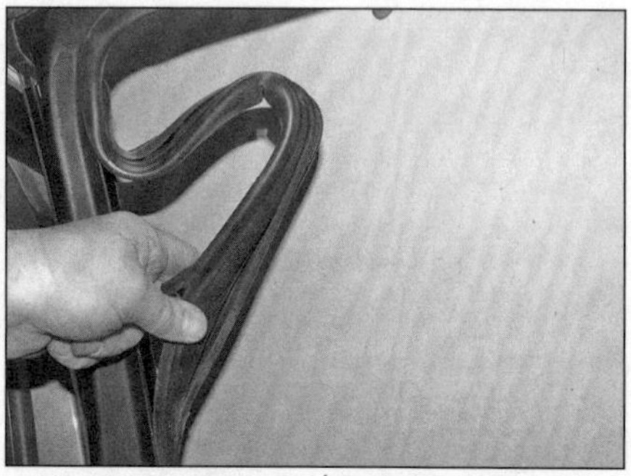

14.17 Pull out the seal from the glass guide channel

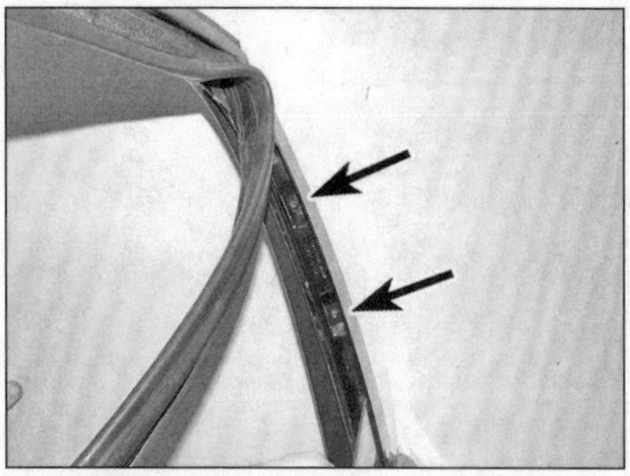

14.18a Remove the screws (arrowed)

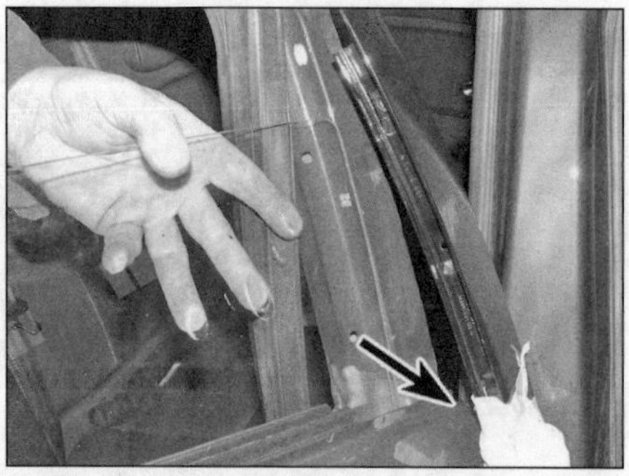

14.18b Note the protective cloth wrapped around the panel

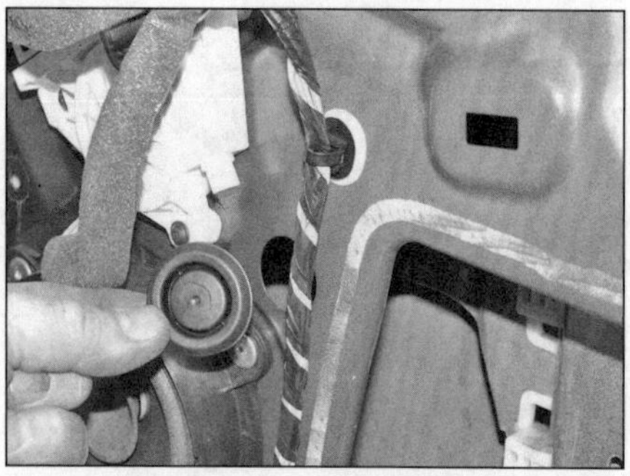

14.19a Remove the blanking plug

14 Refitting is a reversal of removal, but note that Renault recommend replacement of the motor mounting bolts.

Rear door

Sliding glass

15 Follow the procedure for door trim panel and membrane removal in the previous Section.

16 If necessary protect the outer door skin and then remove the outer weather strip **(see illustrations)**.

17 Fully lower the glass and then pull up and partially remove the front glass guide channel rubber seal **(see illustration)**.

18 Remove the screws from the metal trim, protect the door and move the panel to one side **(see illustrations)**.

19 Remove the blanking plug and then lower the glass so that the glass retaining clamp bolts are accessible **(see illustrations)**.

20 Remove the bolts from the regulator lower mounting and slacken the regulator/motor mounting bolts – this will allow the glass to pivot slightly as it is removed.

21 Lift up and remove the glass to the outside of the door **(see illustration)**.

22 Refitting is a reversal of removal.

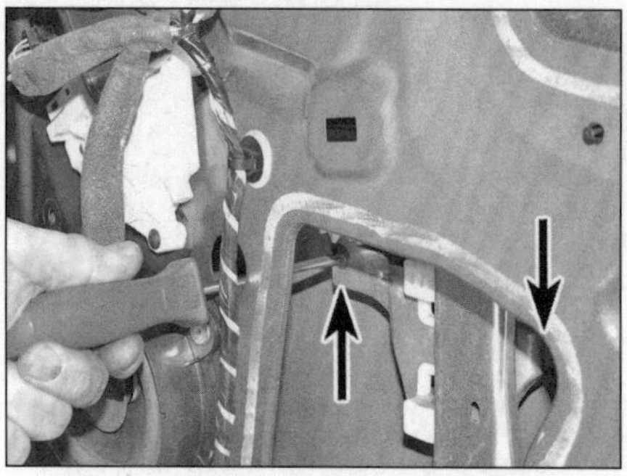

14.19b ...and remove the glass clamp bolts (arrowed)

Fixed glass

23 Remove the sliding glass as described previously in this Section.

24 Partially remove the sliding glass guide channel rubber strip out of the window frame.

14.21 Remove the glass

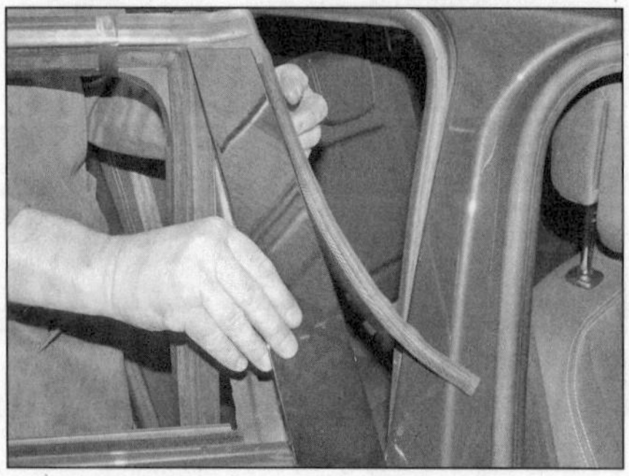

14.25a Remove the exterior trim panel

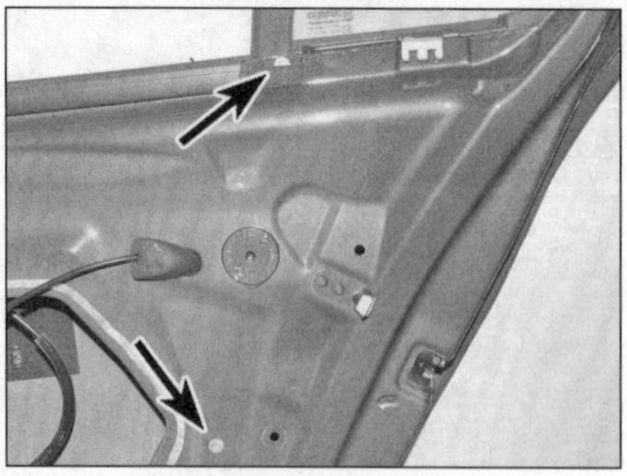

14.25b Unbolt the rear glass guide channel bolts (arrowed)

14.25c Remove the guide channel

25 Fully release the exterior metal trim panel and then remove the upper and lower mounting bolts from the rear sliding window guide. Note that the upper bolt is hidden behind the guide channel rubber. Remove the guide channel **(see illustrations)**.

26 Work the seal from the door frame, complete with the fixed glass.

27 With the seal and glass removed to a suitable working area, the glass can be withdrawn from the seal and removed **(see illustration)**.

28 Refitting is a reversal of removal.

Regulator

29 Remove the door trim panel as described previously in this Section.

30 Position the glass so that the glass clamp screws are accessible. Slacken the screws, pull up the glass and tape it securely in the fully closed position.

31 Where an electric window is fitted disconnect the wiring plug and remove the three motor retaining screws **(see illustration)**.

32 Remove the upper and lower regulator mounting bolts and manoeuvre the assembly form the door frame **(see illustrations)**.

33 Refitting is a reversal of removal.

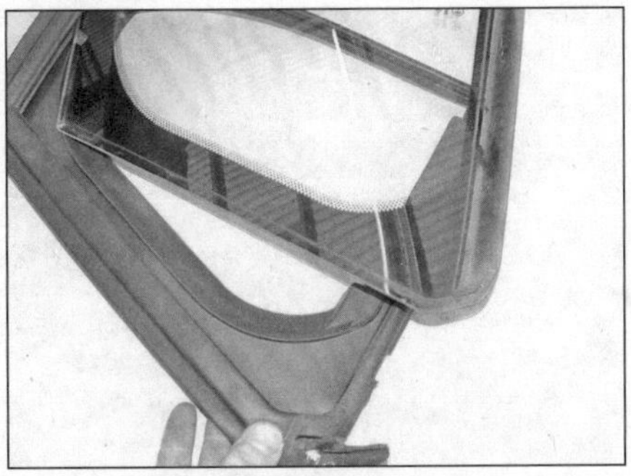

14.27 Remove the glass from the seal

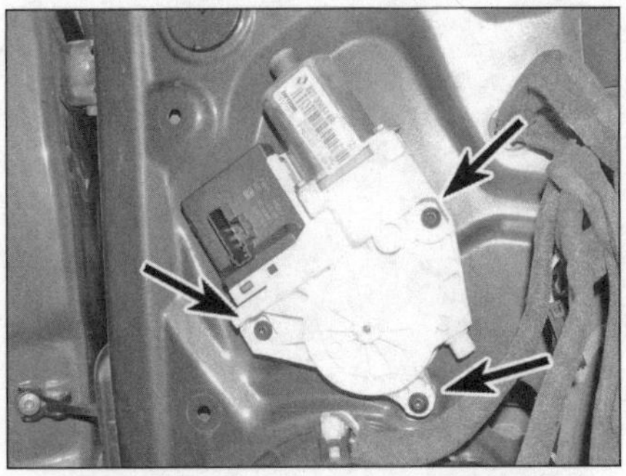

14.31 Remove the bolts (arrowed)

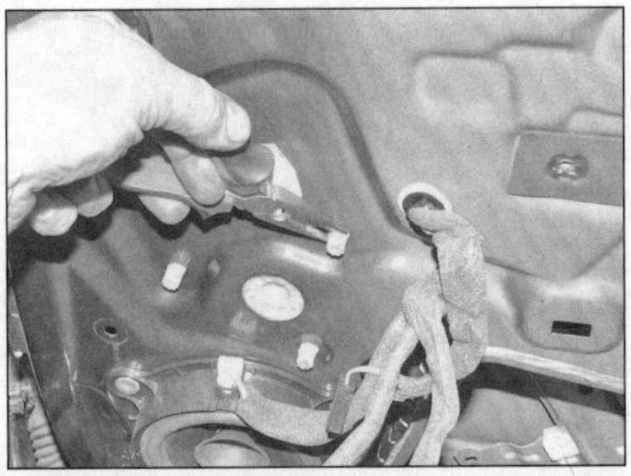

14.32a Where electric windows are fitted the motor mounting bolts and the regulator share a common mounting. Depress the clips to release the regulator

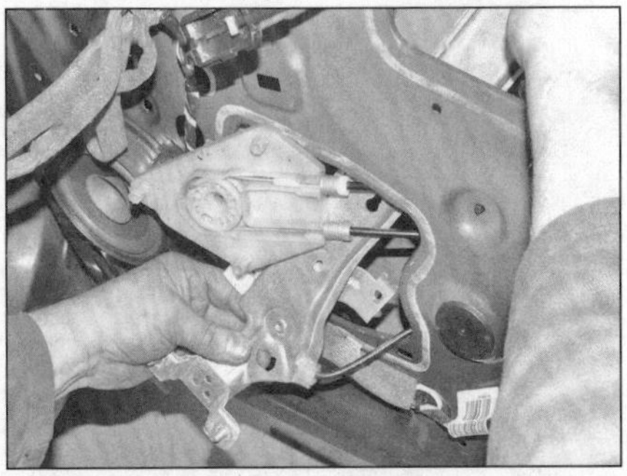

14.32b Remove the regulator from the door frame

15 Tailgate and related components – removal and refitting

Tailgate trim panel

1 Open the tailgate and remove the upper centre panel by prising it free **(see illustration)**.

2 Use a suitable trim tool and prise both side panels free from the tailgate **(see illustration)**.

3 Several screws hold the main panel in position, there exact location varies according to the model. Locate and remove the screws and then prise free the panel **(see illustrations)**.

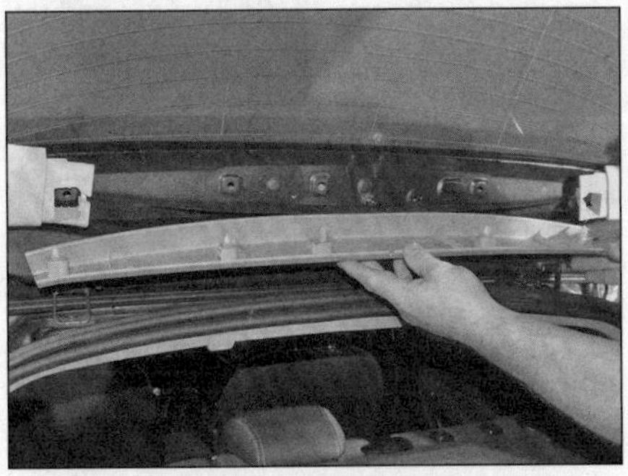

15.1 Remove the upper panel (hatchback shown)

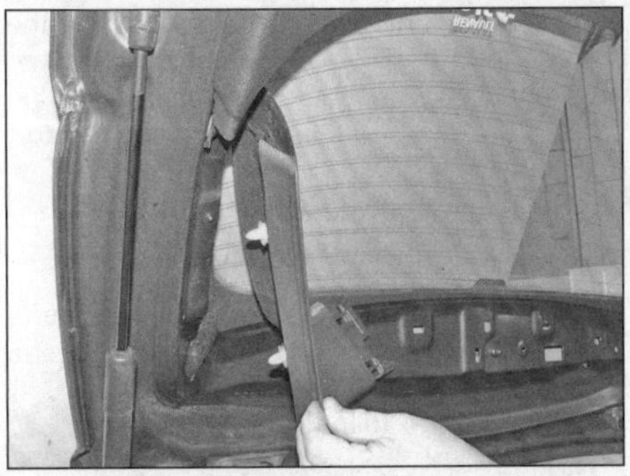

15.2 Remove the side panels (estate shown)

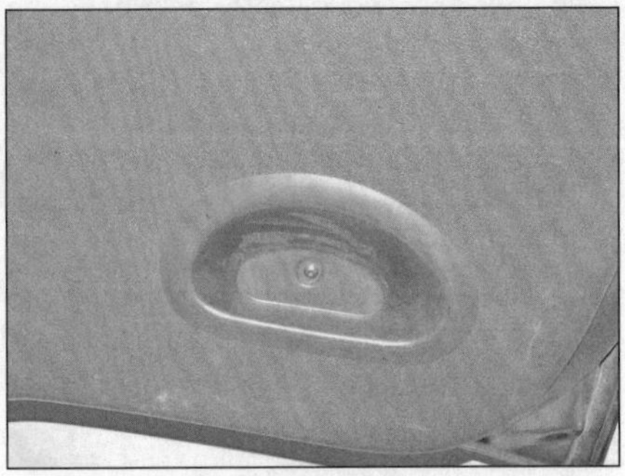

15.3a Remove the screws in the grab handles...

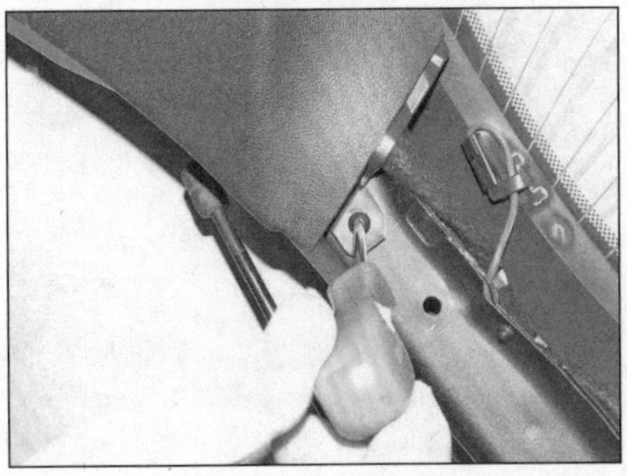

15.3b ...at the side...

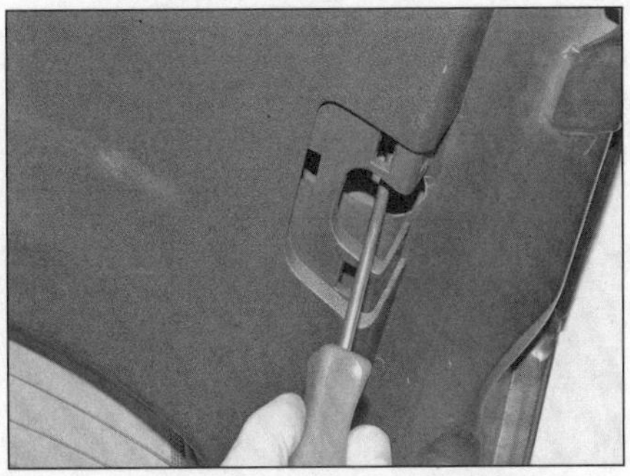

15.3c ...and behind the trim piece on estate models

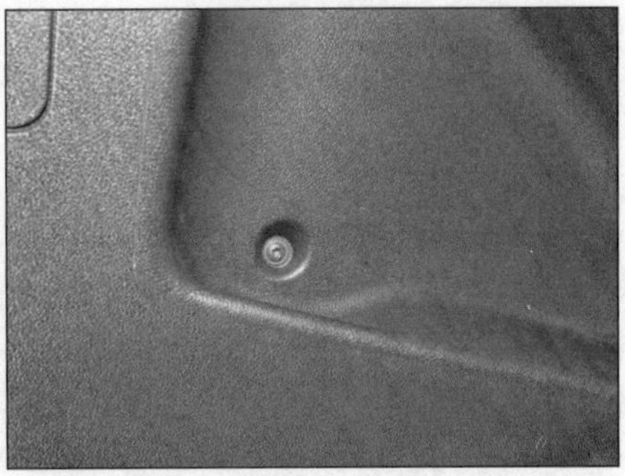

15.3d On hatchback models the screws are visible

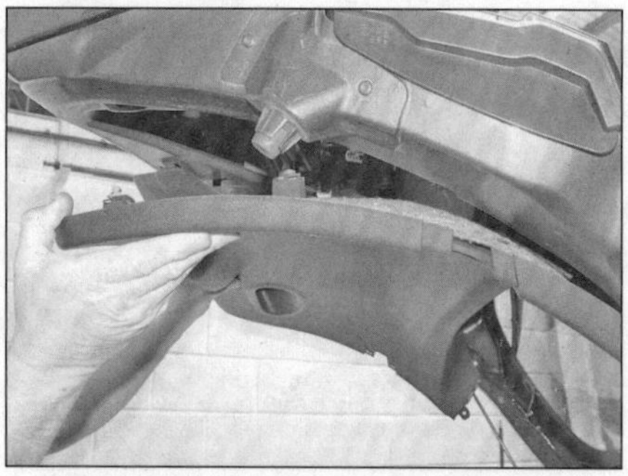

15.3e Remove the panel

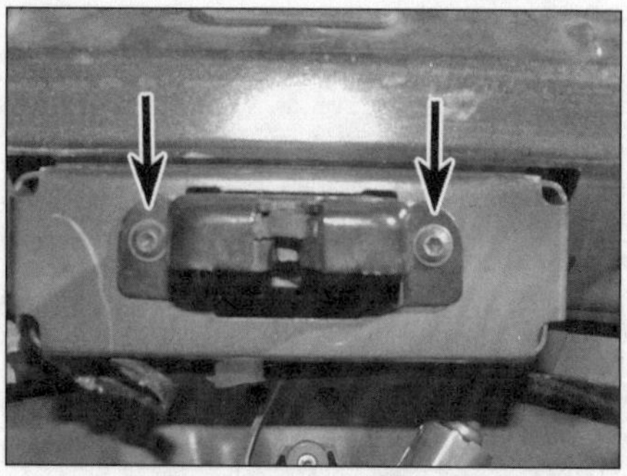

15.6 Remove the screws (arrowed)

15.7 Lower the lock and disconnect the wiring plug

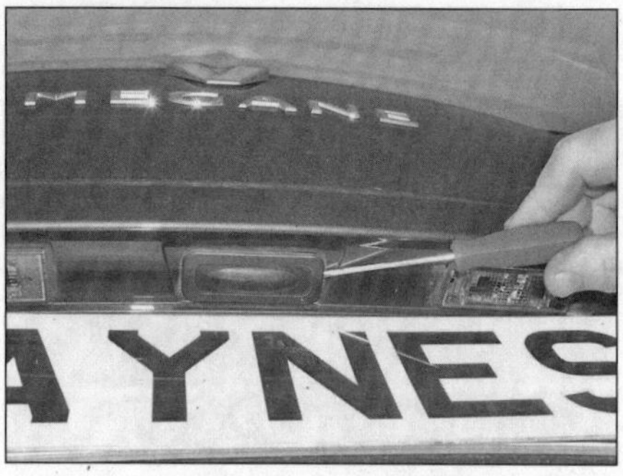

15.10 Release the switch

15.11 Disconnect the wiring plug

15.14 Prise open the spring clip

4 Refitting is a reversal of removal.

Tailgate lock

5 Remove the main trim panel as described in paragraph 3.

6 Remove the two tailgate lock mounting screws **(see illustration)**.

7 Release the lock retaining catch, and ease the lock out of the tailgate **(see illustration)**.

8 Disconnect the wiring plug from the lock, and remove it completely.

9 Refitting is a reversal of removal.

Tailgate release switch

10 Using a screwdriver, release the switch securing clips, and withdraw it from its location **(see illustration)**.

11 Disconnect the wiring plug, and remove the switch **(see illustration)**.

12 Refitting is a reversal of removal.

Support struts

13 Open the tailgate, and have an assistant support it in the fully-open position.

14 Disconnect the support strut from the tailgate by prising out the securing clip using a small screwdriver, then pull the end of the strut off the ball fitting **(see illustration)**.

15 Repeat the procedure for the clip securing the strut to the body, and withdraw the strut from the car.

16 Refitting is a reversal of removal

Tailgate

17 Disconnect the battery negative lead, and move the lead away from the battery (see *Disconnecting the battery*).

18 Remove the tailgate main trim panel as previously described.

19 Disconnect the wiring from the heated rear window, tailgate wiper motor, and central locking motor, referring where necessary to the relevant removal procedures. Release the wiring loom from any securing clips **(see illustrations)**.

20 Remove the high-level brake light as described in Chapter 12, Section 8. Feed the wiring plug and tailgate washer hose back into the tailgate.

21 Disconnect the wiring plug from the harness which supplies the number plate lights.

22 Unclip the rest of the wiring from its support clips and ties, then feed it up to the top of the tailgate, noting its routing.

23 Release the wiring and washer tube grommets **(see illustration)** at the top of the tailgate, and pull the wiring clear.

24 Have an assistant support the tailgate, then pull out the spring clips and pull the ends of the support struts from the ball fittings.

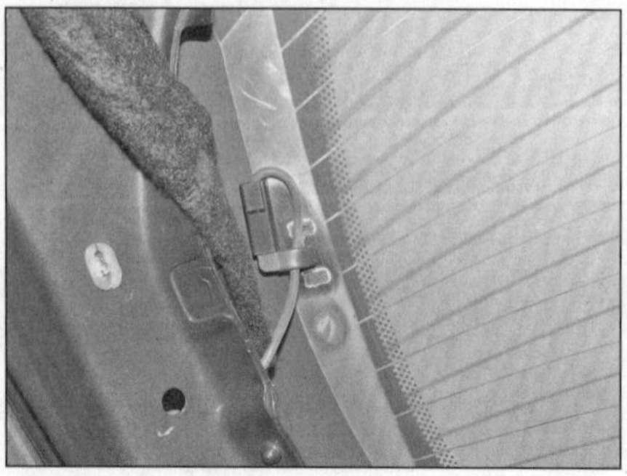

5.19a Disconnect the rear screen heater wiring plugs

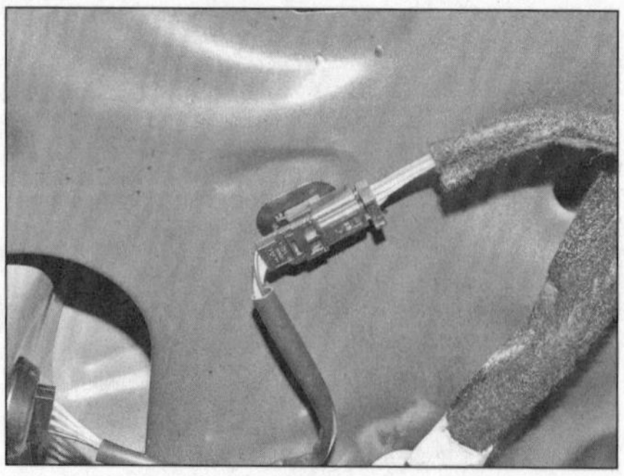

5.19b Disconnect the wiring plugs...

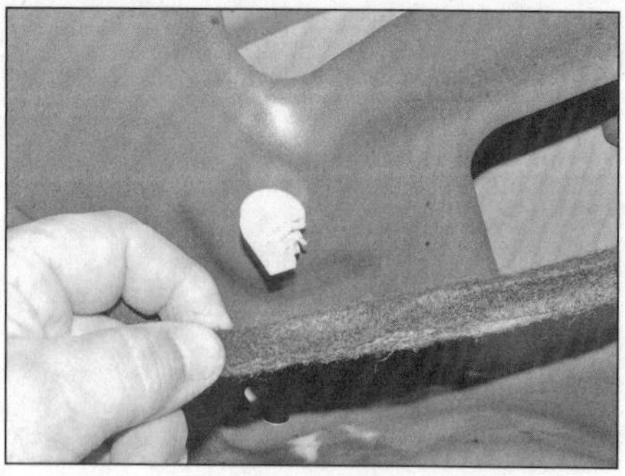

5.19c ...and release the wiring loom

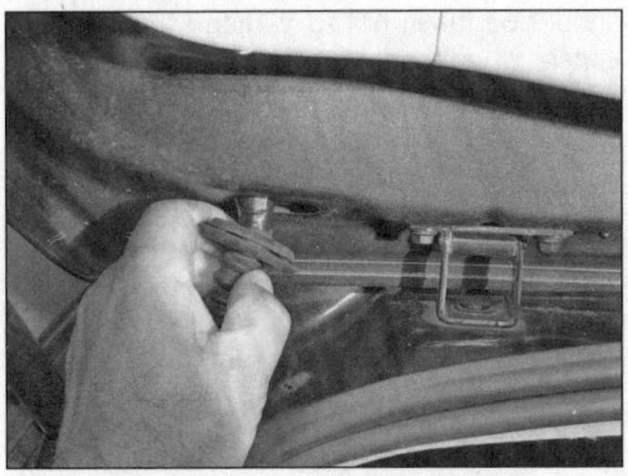

15.23 Prise free the grommet

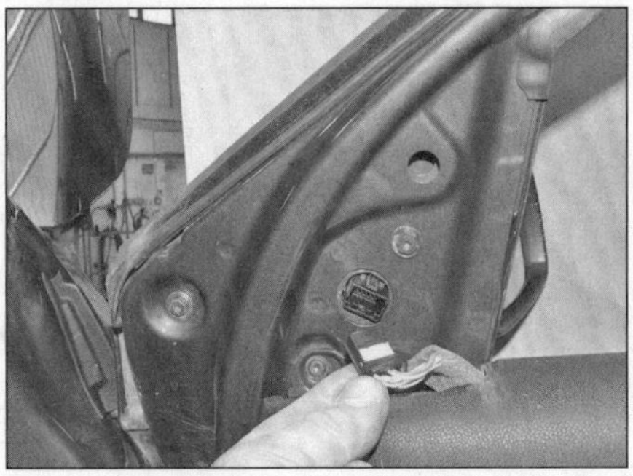

16.3a Disconnect the wiring

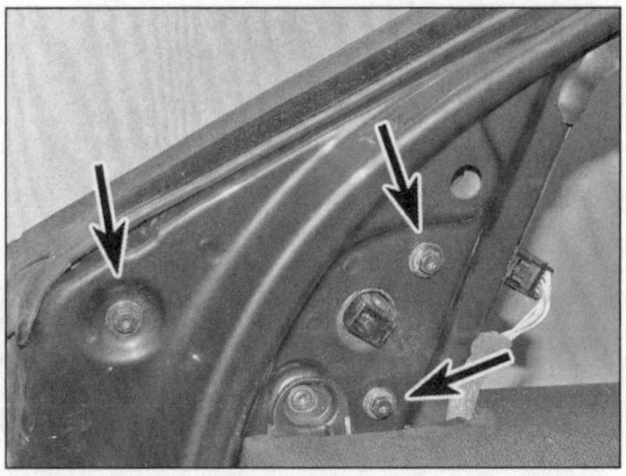

16.3b Remove the screws (arrowed)

25 Again with the help of an assistant, unscrew the hinge bolts and lift the tailgate clear of the car.

26 Refitting is a reversal of removal.

16 Mirrors – removal, refitting and glass renewal

Door mirror

1 Disconnect the battery negative lead, and move the lead away from the battery (see *Disconnecting the battery*).

2 Carefully prise the mirror trim panel from the front edge of the door **(see illustration 13.2a)**.

3 Disconnect the wiring plug and then remove the mirror retaining screws. Remove the mirror **(see illustrations)**.

4 Refitting is a reversal of removal.

Glass renewal

5 Using a flat-bladed tool, carefully prise behind the top edge of the mirror glass **(see illustration)**. Support the glass, lever the tool forwards and the mirror glass will unclip from the mirror assembly. Take care not to drop the mirror glass as the clip is released.

6 Where applicable, disconnect the wiring connectors from the rear of the mirror glass **(see illustration)**.

7 To refit the glass, press the glass into position until it engages securely, taking care not to damage the glass.

Shell renewal

8 Remove the mirror glass as described previously in this Section.

9 Using a small screwdriver, release the four retaining tabs, then carefully prise the shell from the mirror **(see illustrations)**.

10 Refitting is a reversal of removal.

Temperature sensor

11 The left-hand mirror contains an outside air temperature sensor.

12 Remove the glass and mirror shell as previously described.

13 Unscrew and remove the mirror motor **(see illustration)**.

14 Remove the side repeater lamp (as described in Chapter 12, Section 8) and work free the front section of the mirror **(see illustration)**.

15 Prise free the temperature sensor **(see illustration)**. Replacement will require the cutting of the wires and the connection of the replacement, ideally with a soldered connection.

Interior mirror

16 Slide the upper section of trim towards the roof, and remove it. Extreme caution is

16.5 Prise the glass free

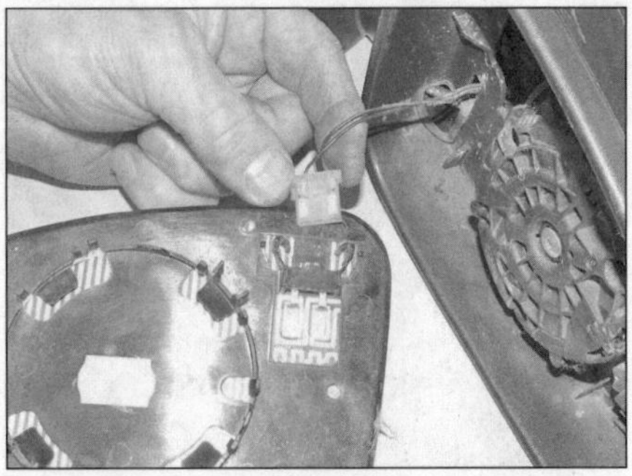

16.6 Disconnect the wiring plugs

16.9a Release the tabs (arrowed)...

16.9b ...and remove the cover

16.13 Remove the motor screws (arrowed)

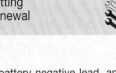

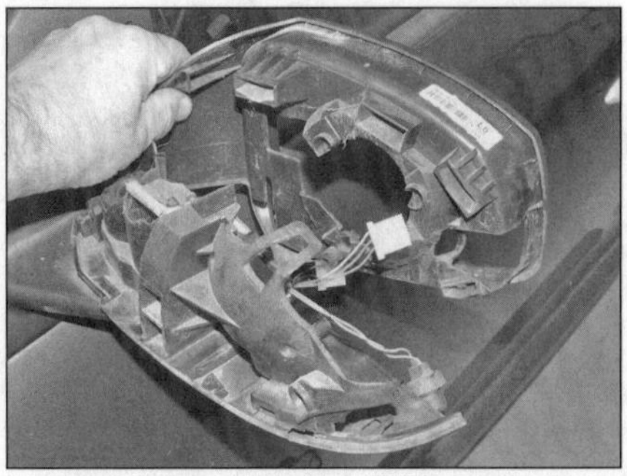

16.14 Remove the front section of the mirror

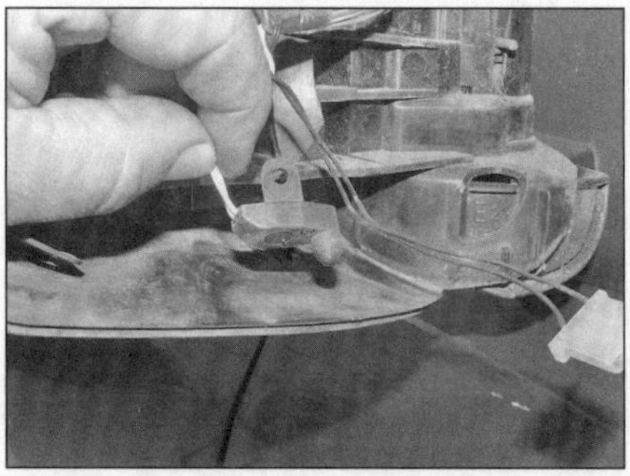

16.15 Remove the sensor

16.16 Remove the upper cover

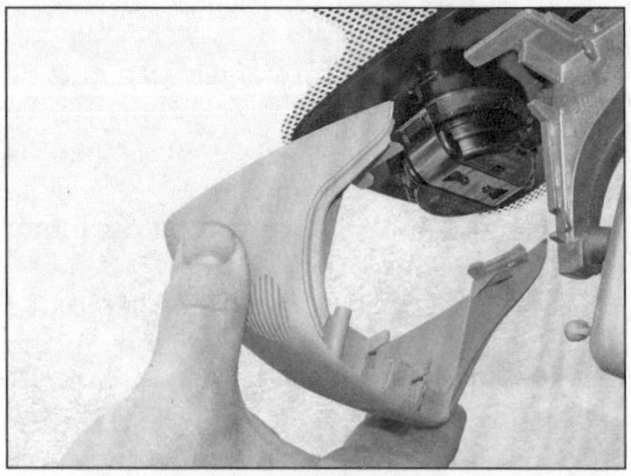

16.17 Remove the lower cover

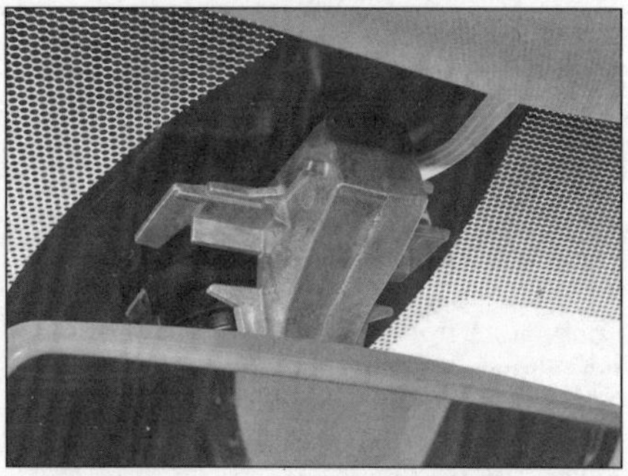

16.19 Slide the mirror up to remove it

advised, as the retaining tabs are very fragile **(see illustration)**.

17 Using a small screwdriver, unclip the front section of trim surrounding the mirror base **(see illustrations)**.

18 Disconnect the wiring plugs behind the mirror – the number of these will depend on equipment level.

19 The interior mirror is very firmly attached, but can be removed by sliding it towards the roof **(see illustration)**. Note, however, that considerable effort may be required, and care should be taken not to damage the light/rain sensor when the mirror is released.

20 Refitting is a reversal of removal.

17 Windscreen, tailgate and fixed window glass – general information

These areas of glass are secured by the tight fit of the weatherseal in the body aperture, and are bonded in position with a special adhesive. Renewal of such fixed glass is a difficult, messy and time-consuming task, which is considered beyond the scope of the home mechanic. It is difficult, unless one has plenty of practice, to obtain a secure, waterproof fit. Furthermore, the task carries a high risk of breakage; this applies especially to the laminated glass windscreen. In view of this, owners are strongly advised to have this sort of work carried out by one of the many specialist windscreen fitters.

18 Sunroof components – removal and refitting

A sunroof is available as an option on most models in the Megane range. This type of sunroof is a complex piece of equipment, consisting of a large number of components. It is strongly recommended that the sunroof mechanism is not disturbed unless absolutely necessary. If the sunroof mechanism is faulty, or requires overhaul, consult a Renault dealer for advice. Even removing the sunroof motor requires that the headlining be taken down, which is not a job to be taken on lightly.

19 Body exterior fittings – removal and refitting

Wheel arch liners

1 Plastic shields are fitted to the wheel arches and various engine components to protect against road dirt and moisture.

2 The shields are secured by a combination of plastic clips or screws **(see illustrations)**. Removal and refitting should be self-evident. Take particular care not to break plastic clips when removing them – renew where necessary.

Rubbing strips

Note: *Take care not to damage the paintwork when removing the rubbing strips.*

3 On all door the rubbing strips are secured by a screw fitting at the rear, and a bayonet type fitting at the front. Some models also have the strip held in place with adhesive tape.

4 Remove the blanking plug at the rear of the door **(see illustration)** to access the screw. Remove the screw and move the strip away from the door. Pull it rearward to release it from the fitting at the front edge.

5 Refitting is a reversal of removal.

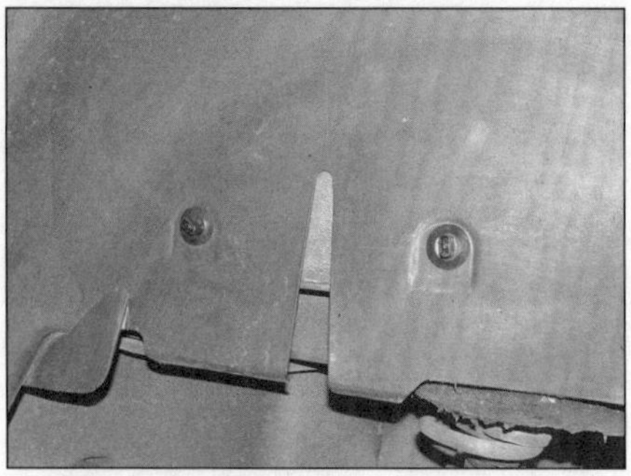

19.2a Remove the plastic clips...

19.2b ...and screws

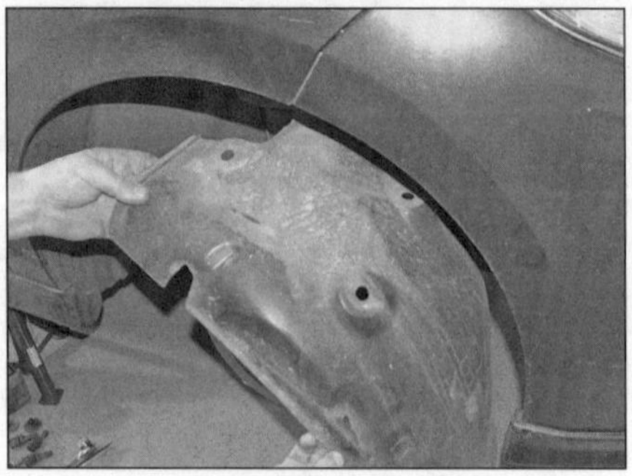

19.2c Remove the liner

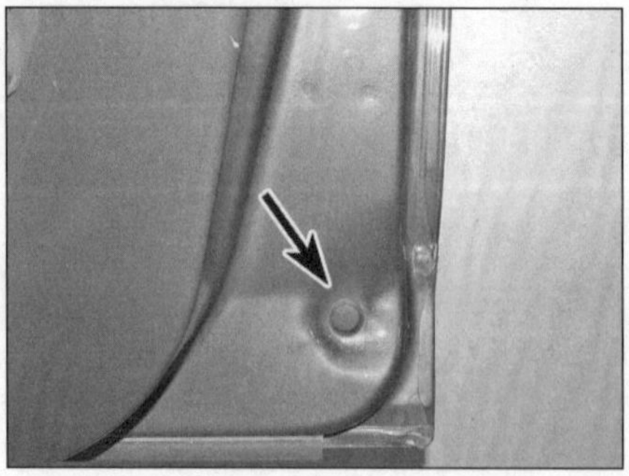

19.4 Remove the blanking plug (arrowed)

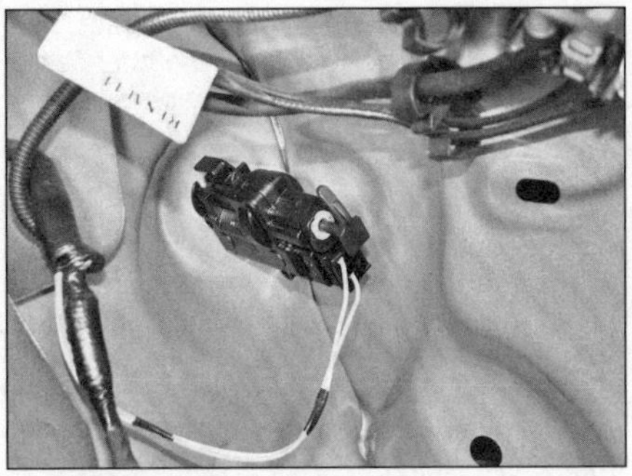

19.10 Remove the locking solenoid

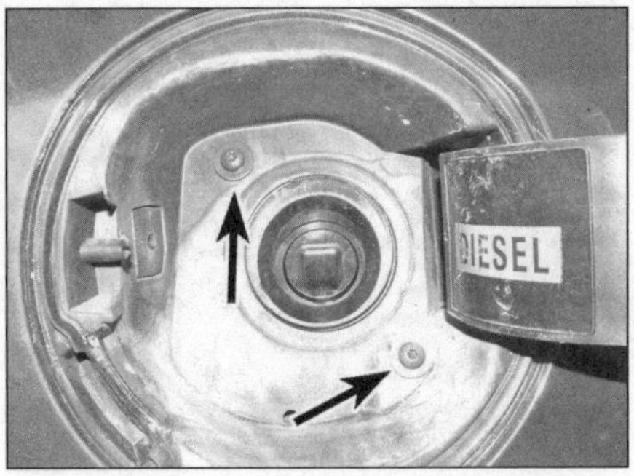

19.14 Remove the screws (arrowed)

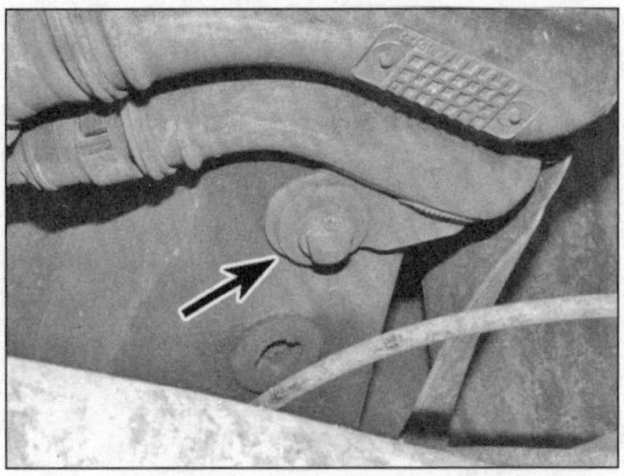

19.18 Remove the bolt (arrowed)

Badges

6 The various badges may be secured with adhesives. To remove them, either soften the adhesive using a hot-air gun or hairdryer (taking care to avoid damage to the paintwork), or separate the badge from the body by 'sawing' through the adhesive using a length of nylon cord. **Note:** *Some badges are located by pegs in plastic grommets – these will need to be carefully prised from the bodywork.*

7 Clean off all traces of adhesive using white spirit, then wash the area with warm soapy water to remove all traces of spirit, and allow to dry. Ensure that the surface to which the new badge is to be fastened is completely clean, and free from grease and dirt.

8 Use the hot-air gun to soften the adhesive on the new badge, then press it firmly into position.

Fuel filler flap solenoid

9 Remove the boot side trim panels as described in Section 22.

10 Depress the solenoid mounting clip, and release the solenoid **(see illustration)**.

11 Disconnect the wiring plug from the solenoid, and remove it completely.

12 Refitting is a reversal of removal.

Fuel filler flap

13 The filler flap is part of the fuel filler neck. Ensure the fuel tank is virtually empty before starting work.

14 Open the filler flap, then remove the two screws inside **(see illustration)**.

15 Remove the locking solenoid as described above.

16 Jack up and support the rear of the vehicle (see *Jacking and vehicle support* in the reference section).

17 Remove the right-hand rear wing liner and then release the hose clips from the filler neck – dispose of the clips, they must be replaced.

18 Remove the bolt **(see illustration)** and then work the filler assembly free from the inner wing.

19 Refitting is a reversal of removal, but new hose clips must be fitted.

20 Seats – removal and refitting

Front seat

Warning: Disconnect the battery negative lead (see 'Disconnecting the battery'), then wait for five minutes before proceeding. If this waiting period is not observed, there is danger of activating the side airbags and seat belt tensioners.

1 Using a small screwdriver in the hole provided, depress the catch to release the belt from the buckle on the outside of the seat **(see illustrations)**.

2 Slide the seat forwards, and unscrew the seat mounting bolt at the rear of each runner **(see illustration)**.

3 Slide the seat fully to the rear, and unscrew the seat mounting bolts at the front ends of the runners **(see illustration)**.

4 Fold back the carpet at the front of the seat, then swing the locking lever to the side and disconnect the seat wiring plug **(see illustration)**.

5 The seat is a very heavy assembly – take care when lifting it from the car. Also, be careful that the seat runners do not scratch any trim or paintwork as the seat is removed.

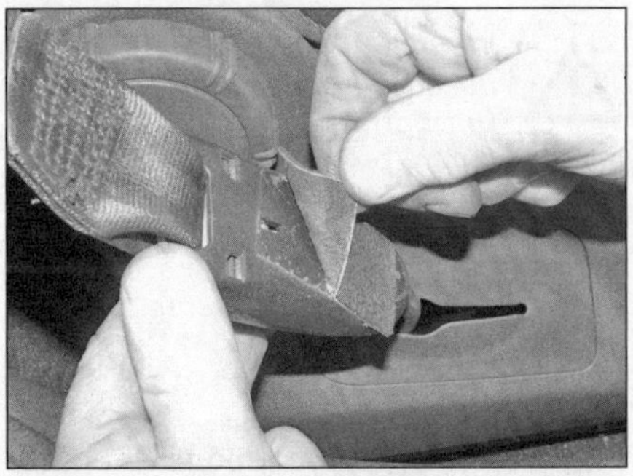

20.1a Peel back the fabric cover

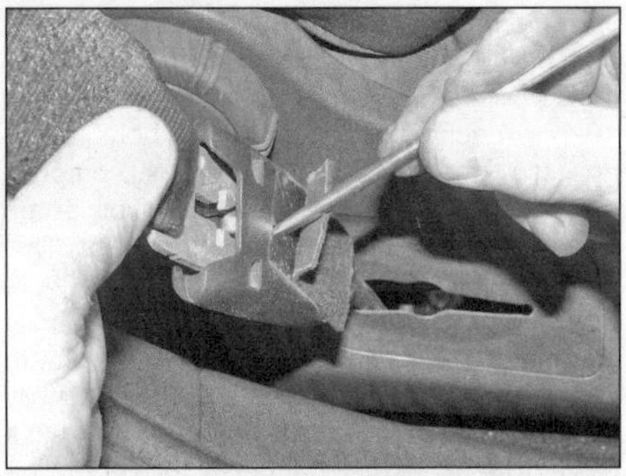

20.1b Release the seat belt

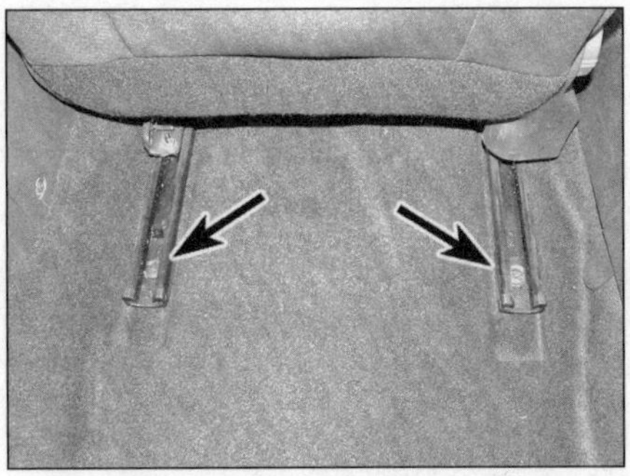

20.2 Remove the rear mounting bolts (arrowed)

20.3 Remove the front bolts

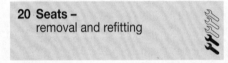

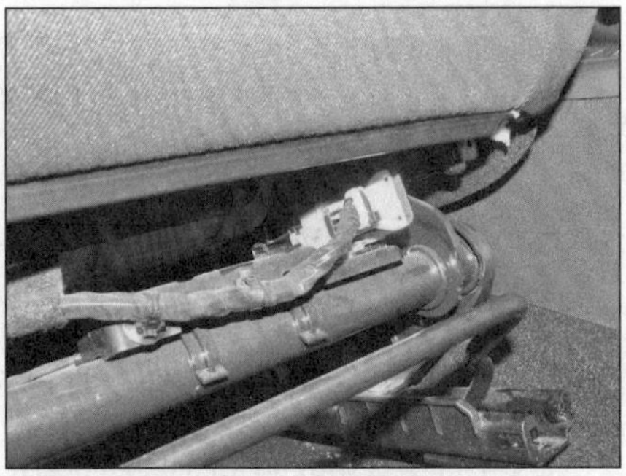

20.4 Disconnect the wiring plug

20.7 The seat cushion hinge

20.10 Remove the bolts and the buckle

Remember that the seat contains at least one airbag – handle it gently.

6 Refitting is a reversal of removal, noting the following points:

a) Reconnect the seat wiring plug securely before reconnecting the battery.

b) Tighten the mounting bolts to the specified torque, starting with the inner bolts.

Rear seat cushion

7 Tip the seat cushion forwards, then insert a small screwdriver in the hole on top of each 'hinge' and release the securing clip. Lift the hinges out of their locations in the floor, and remove the cushion from the car **(see illustration)**.

8 Refitting is a reversal of removal. Ensure that the seat cushion is securely retained by its clips.

Rear seat backrest

9 Either fold forwards the seat cushion, or remove it completely as described previously in this Section.

10 The backrest 'front' mounting bolts (those accessed from in front of the backrest) comprise both the seat mounting bolts and on some models those for the seat belt buckles. This means the buckles must also be removed – note the fitted order of all components when the bolts are removed **(see illustration)**. On models with a 'split' backrest, the sections can theoretically be removed independently, however we found it easier to remove the seat backs as a complete assembly and separate them on the bench.

11 With the front bolts removed, move to the boot area and release the boot carpet from the base of the backrest – depending on model, this will either mean prising up some plastic clips, or releasing some Velcro.

12 The backrest mounting brackets have key hole slots. Release the seats from the upper catches and then push the base back to release the rear brackets from the fitting .

13 Refitting is a reversal of removal, noting the following points:

a) Hook the seat over the rear mounting points first.

b) When refitting the seat belt buckles, pay attention to the fitted order of components noted before removal.

c) Tighten the mounting bolts to the specified torque.

21 Seat belt components – removal and refitting

Warning: Disconnect the battery negative lead (see 'Disconnecting the battery'), then wait for five minutes before proceeding. If this waiting period is not observed, there is danger of activating the seat belt tensioners.

Note: *If the car has been in an accident, all affected seat belt components must be renewed.*

Seat belt tensioners

Information and precautions

1 Seat belt pretensioners are fitted to remove any slack from the front and outer rear seat belts in the event of a frontal impact. The system is designed to reduce the chances of injury to the driver and front seat passenger in the event of an accident, by pulling your body back into the seat.

2 The system consists of two special seat belt tensioner/stalk assemblies mounted directly on the front seats, or on the outer rear belt inertia reels, connected to the airbag control unit. **Note:** *Coupe models have just one tensioner per front seat, but are additionally fitted with an 'anti-submarining' airbag in the front seat cushion.*

3 Each tensioner/stalk assembly consists of a special buckle attached to a cable. The end of the cable is attached to a piston inside the tensioner cylinder.

4 In the event of a sufficiently-severe frontal impact, the seat belt tensioners will be triggered by the airbag control unit (for more information on the airbag system, refer to Chapter 12).

5 When a tensioner ignition module is triggered, a small capsule is energised, which rapidly releases gas into the tensioner cylinder. As the gas is released, the piston is forced along the cylinder, pulling the cable (approximately 70 mm) and hence the seat belt stalk, which in turn removes any slack from the seat belt, pulling the belt tight against the wearer. The rear belt reels contain similar systems, to spin the reel and retract the belt.

6 Once a seat belt tensioner has been triggered, it must be renewed.

7 Take care, when working on the car, not to expose the pretensioner system components to excess heat, impact, or even magnetic field, as this may cause inadvertent triggering or a malfunction in an accident.

Front belt

8 Using a small screwdriver in the hole provided, depress the catch to release the belt from the buckle on the outside of the seat **(see illustration 20.1b)**. On three door (Coupe) models remove the door step panel and unbolt the sliding rail. Unhook the rail from the inner sill.

9 Remove the cover from the upper mounting – on the B-pilllar **(see illustrations)**.

10 Remove the upper bolt and the guide **(see illustrations)**.

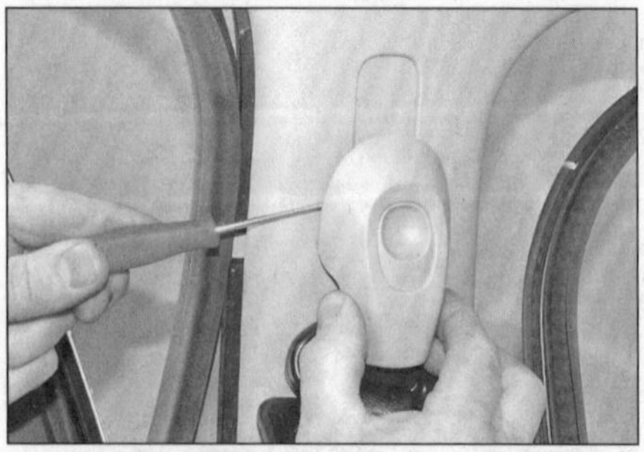

21.9a On models with an adjustable upper mounting use a small screwdriver to release the cover

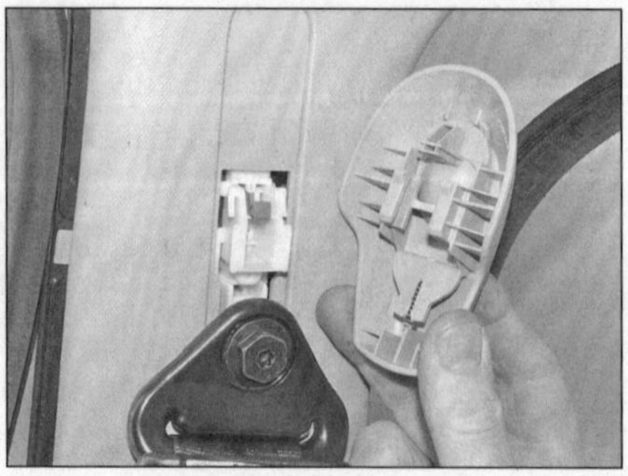

21.9b Note how the cover locks into the sliding bracket

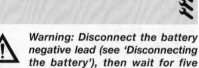

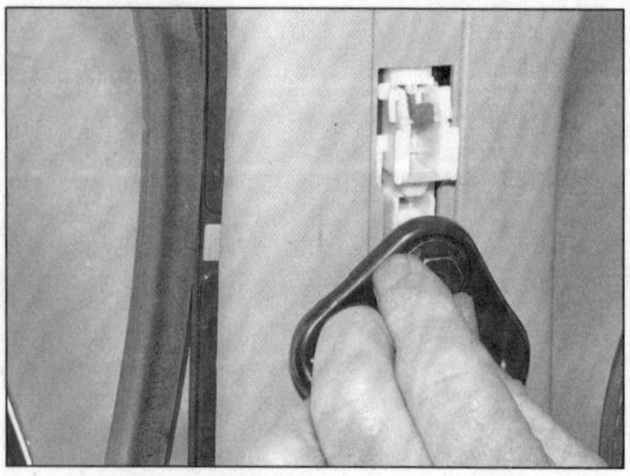

21.10a Remove the upper bolt...

21.10b ...and the guide bracket bolt

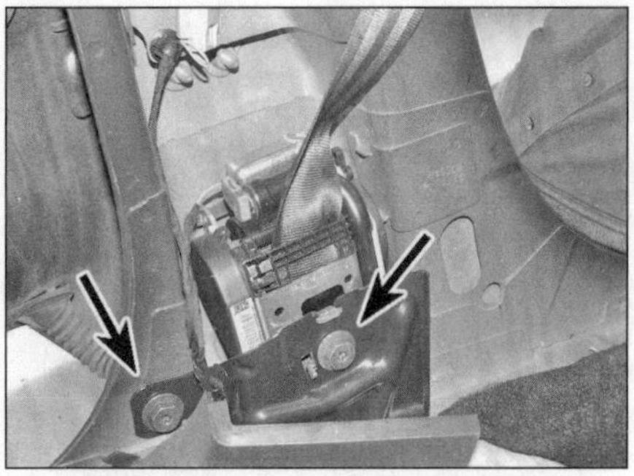

21.12 Remove the bolts (arrowed)

21.16 Remove the bolt (arrowed)

11 Remove the B-pillar trim and door step panels as described in Section 22.

12 Remove the bolt - or bolts depending on the model **(see illustration).** Remove the reel from the base of the pillar and then disconnect the wiring plug.

13 Refitting is a reversal of removal, but use a new bolt for the inertia reel and tighten the belt mountings to the specified torque.

Front belt height adjuster

14 Remove the B-pillar trim panel, as described in Section 24.

15 To remove the adjuster completely, unscrew the seat belt upper mounting bolt.

16 Unscrew the adjuster bolt **(see illustration)** then lift the adjuster to unhook the lower mounting, and withdraw the adjuster from the pillar.

17 Refitting is a reversal of removal. Tighten the mountings to the specified torque.

Front belt tensioners

18 Remove the front seat (see Section 20).

19 Fully raise the seat and then remove the single screw securing the relevant seat side trim panel, then unclip and remove it.

20 Disconnect the wiring plug from the belt tensioner **(see illustration)**.

21 Unscrew the tensioner mounting bolt, and remove the tensioner from the seat, unclipping the operating cable as required **(see illustration)**.

22 Refitting is a reversal of removal. Ensure the wiring plugs are securely reconnected before refitting the battery lead, and tighten the mounting bolts to the specified torque.

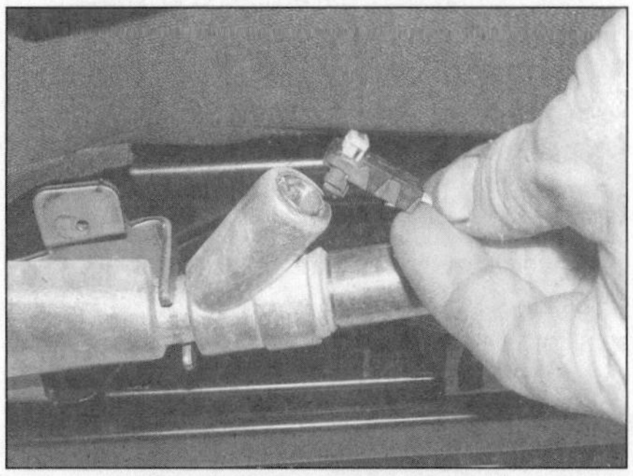

21.20 Disconnect the wiring plug

Rear side belt

23 Remove the rear sill and wheel arch trim panels (or the rear side trim panel on three door models) as described in Section 22.

24 Unscrew the seat belt lower anchor bolt **(see illustration)**.

25 Where the seat belt passes through the C-pillar trim panel, remove the trim panel as described in Section 22.

26 Where applicable, unscrew the seat belt upper mounting bolt (on Estate models, prise off the trim cap first) **(see illustration)**.

27 Remove further side trim panels as necessary, as described in Section 22, to access the inertia reel. Disconnect the belt tensioner wiring plug. Unscrew the inertia reel mounting bolt, then unhook and lift out the reel **(see illustration)**. Remove the seat belt from the car.

28 Refitting is a reversal of removal. Tighten the mountings to the specified torque.

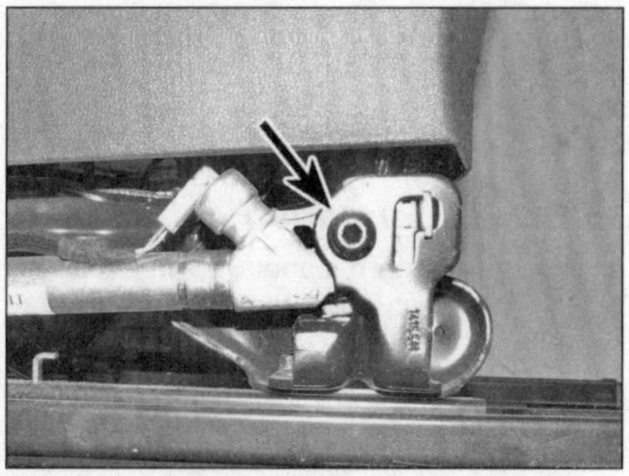

21.21 Remove the bolt (arrowed)

Rear centre belt

29 Remove the rear seat cushion as described in Section 20.

30 Remove the bolt from the centre belt buckle, which also secures the belt lower mounting – note the fitted order of the components.

31 The belt's inertia reel is contained inside the seat backrest, which can be removed as described in Section 21. First inspection reveals a zip fastener around the edge of the backrest, to 'open' the seat for access to the internal components. However, this zip has no 'handle', so whilst it can be opened, it cannot be closed without the use of a Renault tool Car.1558. For this reason, take the backrest to your dealer for work on the centre belt.

32 Refitting is a reversal of removal. Tighten the lower mounting to the specified torque.

21.24 Remove the lower anchor point

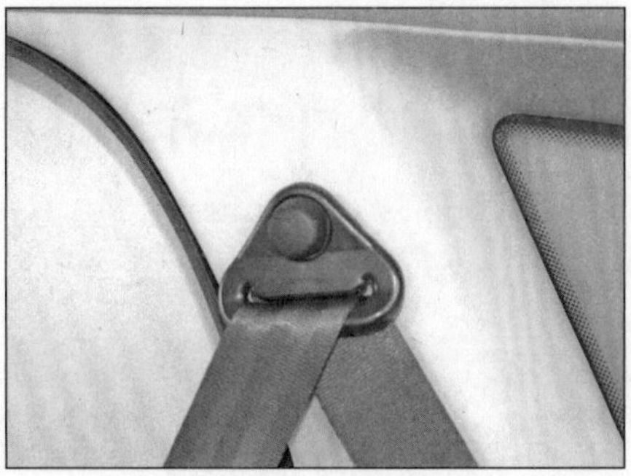

21.26 Remove the cap and then the bolt

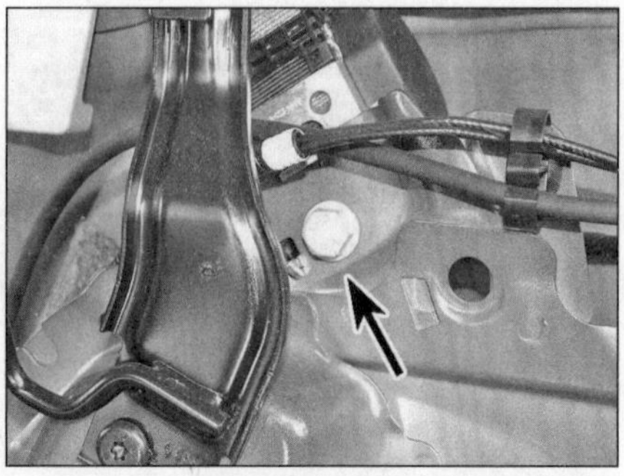

21.27 Remove the bolt (arrowed) and disconnect the wiring plug

22.8a Prise the panel free and...

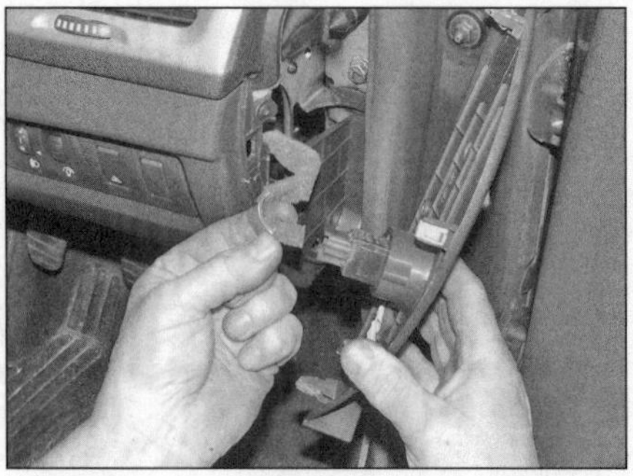
22.8b ...disconnect the wiring plug

22.10 Remove the screws (arrowed)

22 Interior trim panels – removal and refitting

General information

1 The interior trim panels are all secured using either plastic clips built into the panel, or screws.

2 Before removing a panel, study it carefully, noting how it is secured. Often, other panels or ancillary components (such as seat belt mountings, grab handles, etc) must be removed before a particular panel can be withdrawn.

3 Once any such components have been removed, check that there are no other panels overlapping the one to be removed. Usually, the sequence to be followed will become obvious on close inspection.

4 Remove all obvious fasteners, such as screws, which may have plastic covers fitted. If the panel cannot be freed, it is probably secured by hidden clips or fasteners on the rear of the panel. Such fasteners are usually situated around the edge of the panel, and can be prised up to release them. Note that plastic clips can break quite easily, so it is advisable to have a few new clips of the correct type available for refitting. Generally, the best way of releasing such clips is to use a wide flat-bladed tool, designed for the purpose – these are available from tool suppliers such as Draper. If this is not available, an old, broad-bladed screwdriver with the edges rounded-off and wrapped in insulating tape will serve as a good substitute.

5 The following paragraphs and the accompanying illustrations describe removal and refitting of all the major trim panels. Note that the type and number of fasteners used often varies during the production run of a particular model, so differences may be found to the procedures provided.

6 When removing a panel, **never** use excessive force, or the panel may be damaged. Always check carefully that all fasteners have been removed or released before attempting to withdraw a panel.

7 When refitting, secure the fasteners by pressing them firmly into place. Ensure that all disturbed components are correctly secured, to prevent rattles.

Driver's lower facia panel

Warning: Disconnect the battery negative lead (see 'Disconnecting the battery'), then wait for five minutes before proceeding. If this waiting period is not observed, there is danger of activating the passenger airbag.

8 Partially remove the door weatheseal and then (using a suitable trim tool) prise off the facia end panel. Disconnect the wiring plug from the Passenger Airbag Deactivation switch (PAD switch) as the panel is removed **(see illustrations)**.

9 The switch panel can now be pushed out (in theory), but we removed the panel and then disconnected the wiring to the switch as the panel was removed.

10 Remove the screws from the end of the facia and then release the panel from the facia **(see illustration)**.

11 Refitting is a reversal of removal.

Glovebox

12 Working slowly and carefully along the facia, remove the trim piece from above the glovebox **(see illustrations)**.

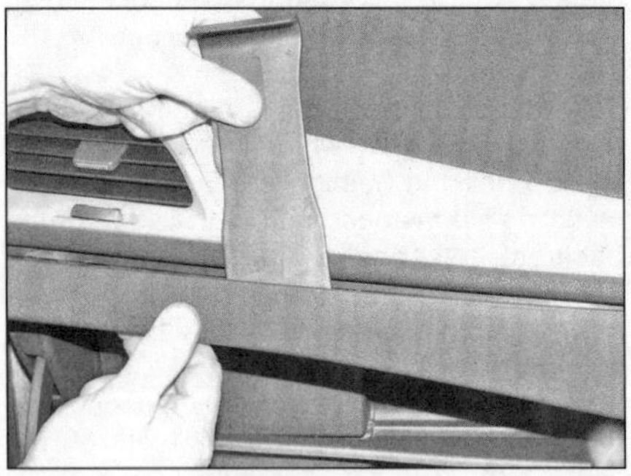
22.12a Prise free...

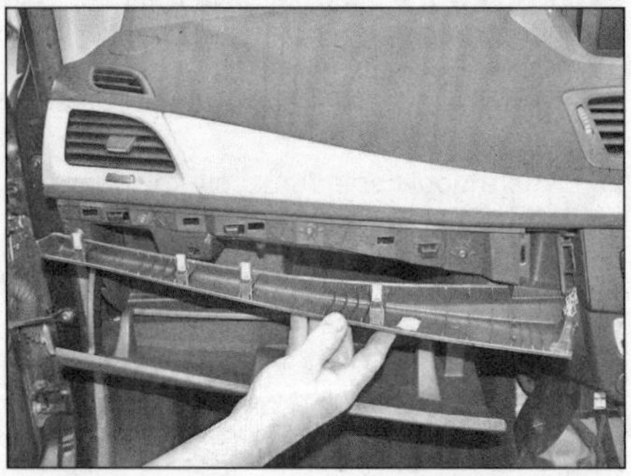
22.12b ...and then remove the trim panel

22.13 Remove the end panel

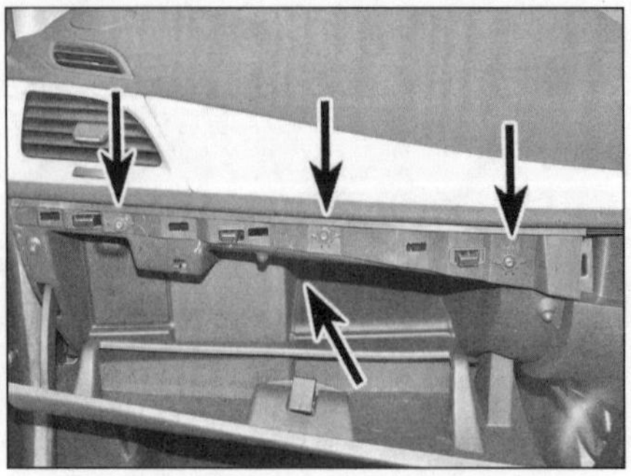
22.14a Remove the screws (arrowed)...

22.14b ...and then the glovebox

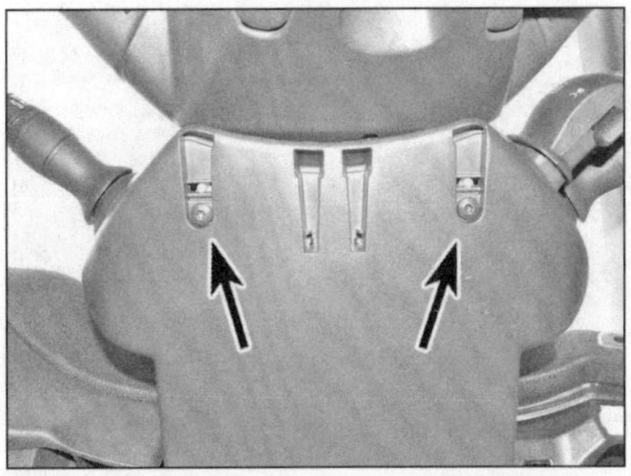
12.16 Remove the screw (arrowed)

12.17a Remove the upper shroud...

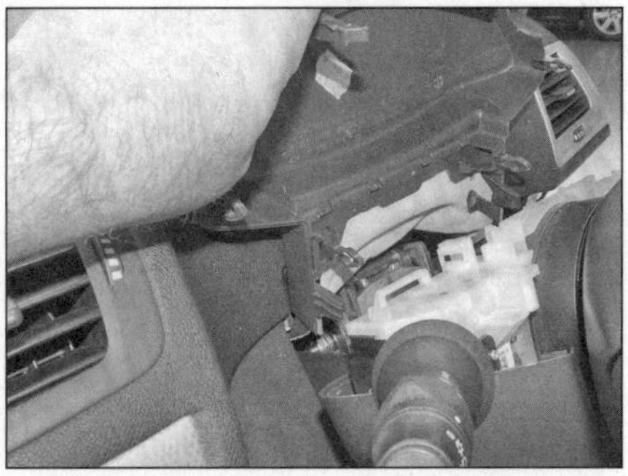
22.17b ...and unclip the gaiter

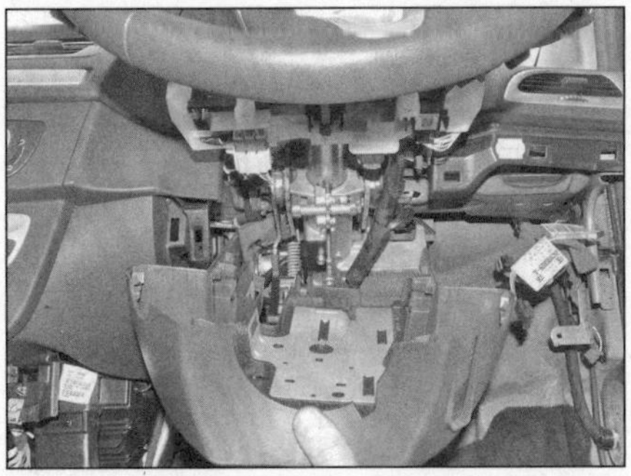
22.18 Remove the lower shroud

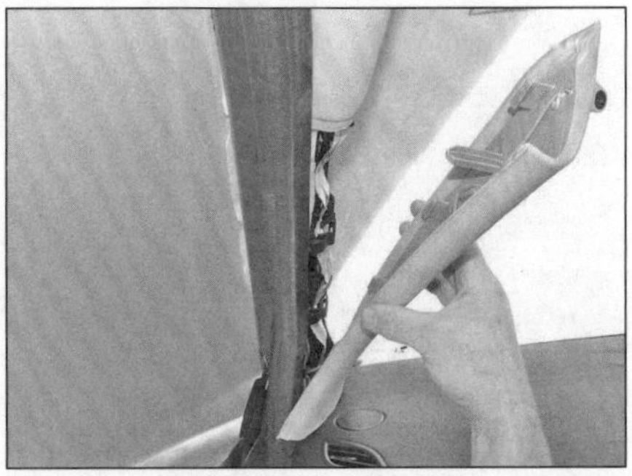
22.21 Remove the A-pillar trim panel

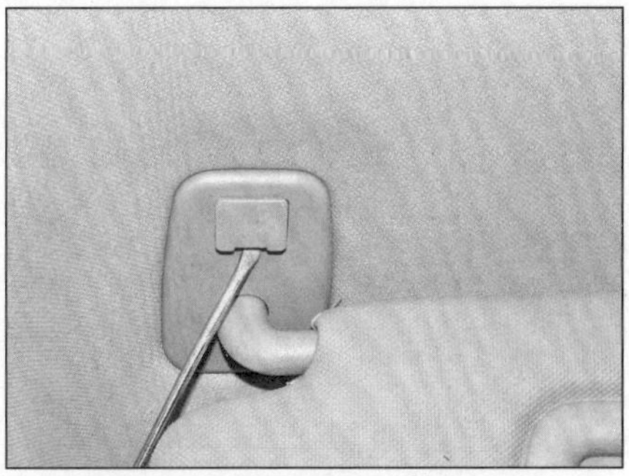
22.23 Prise out the locking peg

13 Partially remove the door weatheseal and then (using a suitable trim tool) prise off the facia end panel **(see illustration)**.

14 Remove the screws from the end of the facia and from above the glovebox (note the single screw inside the glovebox) and then withdraw the glovebox **(see illustrations)**.

15 Refitting is a reversal of removal.

Steering column shrouds

16 Raise and pull out the steering column to access the lower mounting screws. Remove the screws **(see illustration)**.

17 Lower the steering column and separate the upper shroud from the lower. Unclip the shroud from the flexible section and then remove the upper shroud **(see illustrations)**.

18 Raise the column and work free the lower cover **(see illustration)**.

19 Refitting is a reversal of removal.

A-pillar trim panel

20 Partially remove the door weatherseal from the door aperture.

21 Use a trim tool and release the panel from the A-pillar **(see illustration)**. Remove it by pulling it up and inwards at the same time.

22 Refitting is a reversal of removal.

Sunvisors

23 Prise down the cover panel using a small screwdriver **(see illustration)**.

24 Release the retaining tab inside, and withdraw the sunvisor mounting from the headlining **(see illustrations)**.

25 A similar method is used to remove the sunvisor centre mounting **(see illustrations)**.

26 Refitting is a reversal of removal.

Footwell trim panel

27 If working on the left-hand side prise free the bonnet release handle **(see illustration)**.

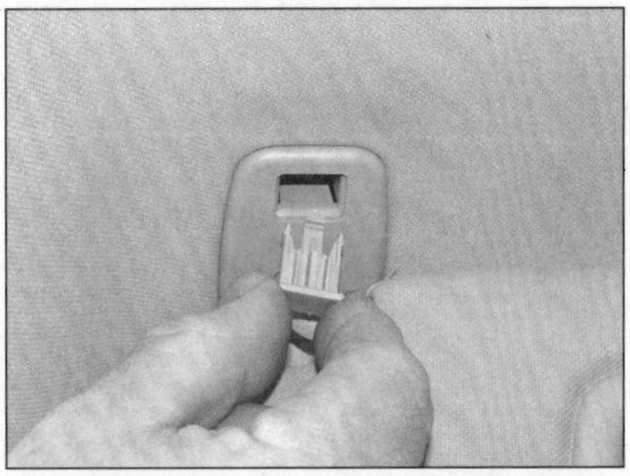
22.24a Remove the peg and then...

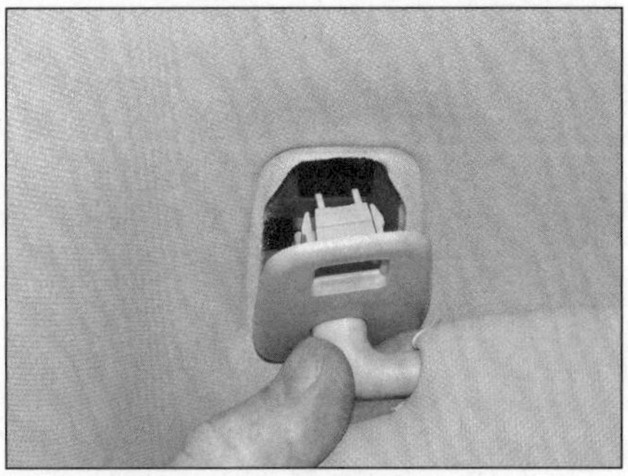
22.24b ...remove the visor

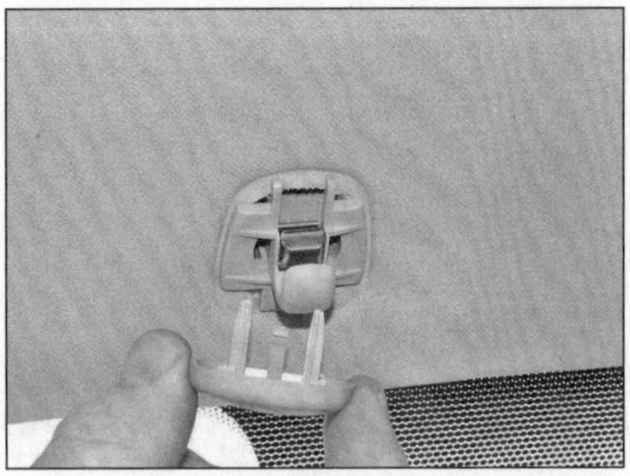
22.25a Remove the locking peg...

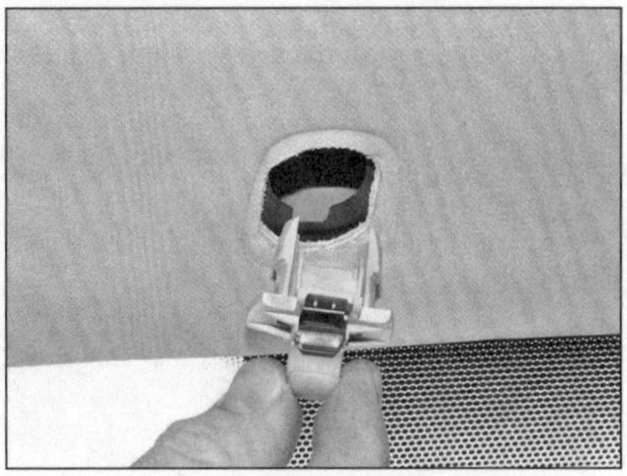
22.25b ...and then remove the catch

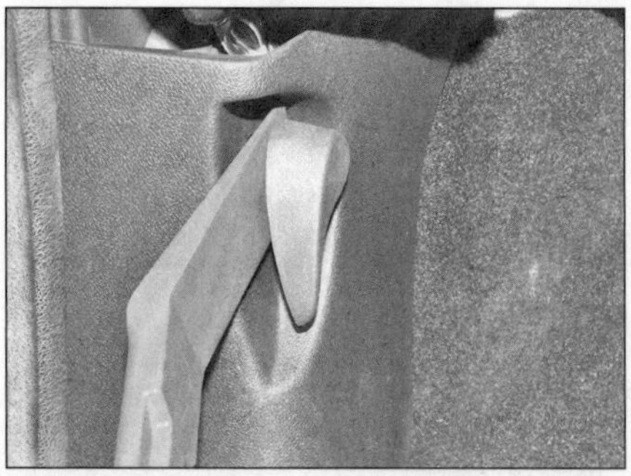

22.27 Prise off the bonnet release handle

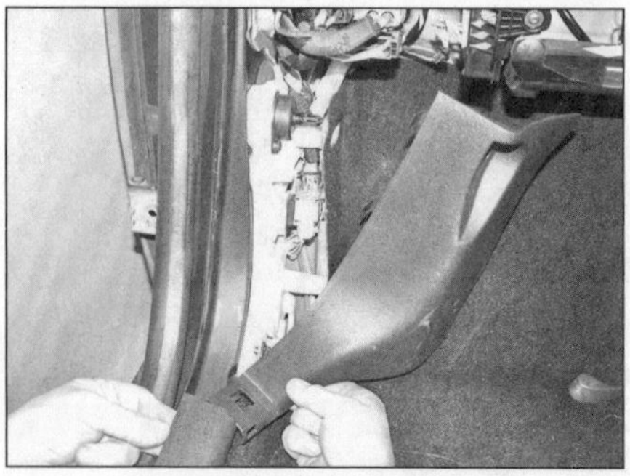

22.29 Remove the panel

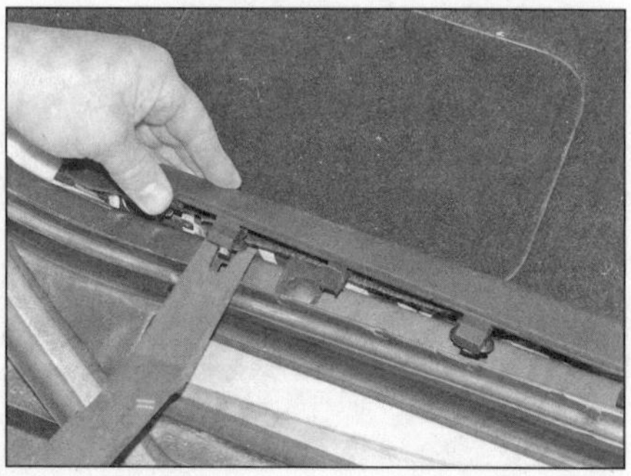

22.33a Prise up and...

22.33b ...then remove the panel

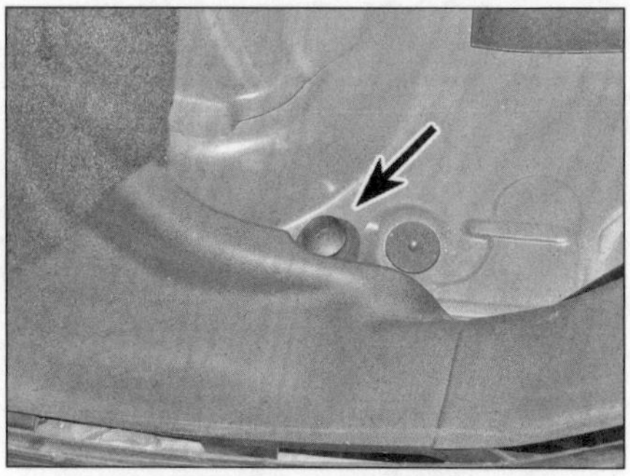

22.37 Remove the clip (arrowed)

28 Release the door weatherseal and then prise up and unclip the front edge of the sill trim panel.

29 Pull the footwell trim panel outwards at the bottom, then unclip it at the top and remove it from the car **(see illustration)**.

30 Refitting is a reversal of removal.

22.40a Release the weatherseal

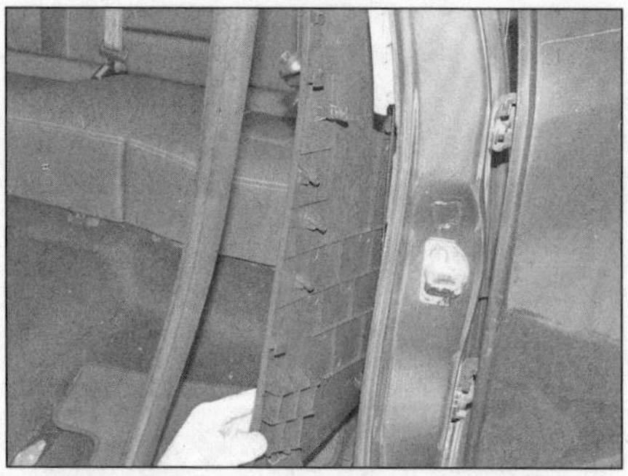

22.40b Remove the lower section of the panel

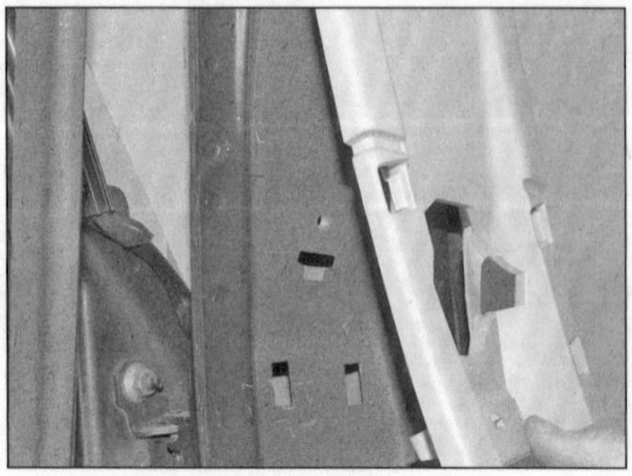

22.44a Pull down and...

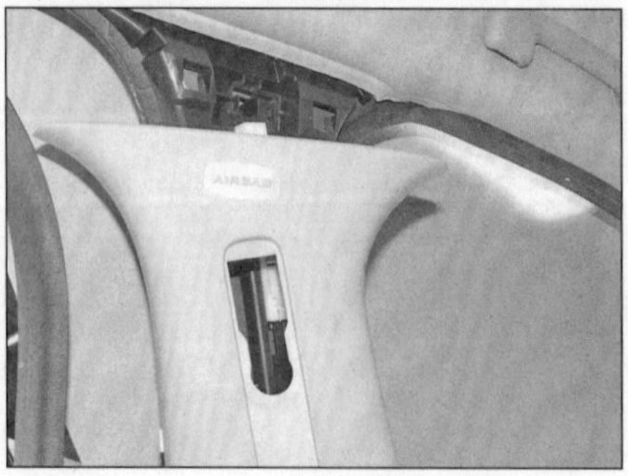

22.44b ...then out to release the panel

Sill trim panels

Front

31 Pull up the sill panel at the front edge to release the clips **(see illustration 24.25)**.

32 On 3-door models, pull up on the sill panel at the rear, and remove it.

33 Work along the panel with a suitable plastic trim tool and release it from the various clips **(see illustrations)**.

34 Refitting is a reversal of removal.

Rear (not coupe)

35 Pull up the sill panel at the front edge to release the clips.

36 Fold the rear seat cushion forwards.

37 At the rear, the panel is held by a separate plastic clip at floor level, which must be prised out. When this is done, the panel can be unclipped at the rear and removed **(see illustration)**.

38 Refitting is a reversal of removal.

B-pillar trim panels

Lower panel

39 Remove the sill trim panel as described previously in this Section.

40 Pull back the rubber weatherstrip in front and behind the panel as necessary, then carefully unclip and remove it **(see illustrations)**.

41 Refitting is a reversal of removal.

Upper panel

42 Remove the lower B-pillar trim panel as described previously in this Section.

43 Unbolt and remove the seatbelt upper mounting **(see illustration 21.10)**

44 Pull back the rubber weatherstrip in front of and behind the panel as necessary, then squeeze together the retaining tabs at the base of the panel, and lower it to free the two lugs at the top **(see illustrations)**.

45 Withdraw the panel from the pillar.

46 Refitting is a reversal of removal.

Upper panel (Coupe)

47 Remove the rear side trim panel as described later in this Section. It may be possible, with care, to just locally detach the rear side trim panel, rather than remove it completely.

48 Prise free the upper seat belt anchor cover and then remove the mounting bolt.
49 At the base of the panel remove the screws.
50 Pull back the rubber weatherstrip in front of the panel, then use a wide-bladed tool to release the panel securing clips, and remove it.
51 Refitting is a reversal of removal.

Rear side upper trim panel (5 door models)

52 On estate models remove the upper seat belt mounting bolt as described in Section 21.
53 Remove the parcel shelf support panel as described below.
54 Prise free the D-pillar trim – on estate models this is part of the window surround trim panel.
55 Refitting is a reversal of removal.

Rear side trim panel (Coupe)

56 Fold down the rear seat back and then prise free the smaller upper from above the window glass.
57 Remove the sill trim panel as described previously in this Section.
58 Remove the front seat belt sliding rail as described in Section 21.
59 Remove the rear seat back as described in Section 20.
60 Remove the parcel shelf support panel as described below and then remove the small panel from beneath the window .
61 Remove the screw from the front of the trim panel and then free the panel by pulling the panel free at the top.
62 Work around the panel releasing the clips. Disconnect the wiring plug from the rear speaker when the panel is free. Remove the panel from the vehicle.
63 Refitting is a reversal of removal.

Parcel shelf support panel

64 Remove the parcel shelf itself.
65 Where applicable, prise out and disconnect the boot light from the panel.
66 Remove the securing screws, and withdraw the trim panel from the car **(see illustrations)**. Where a 12 volt power outlet is fitted disconnect the wiring plug as the panel is withdrawn.
67 Refitting is a reversal of removal.

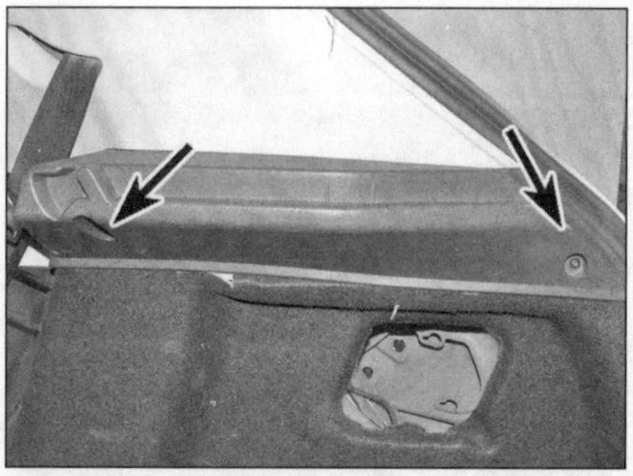

22.66a Remove the screws - hatchback model shown (arrowed)...

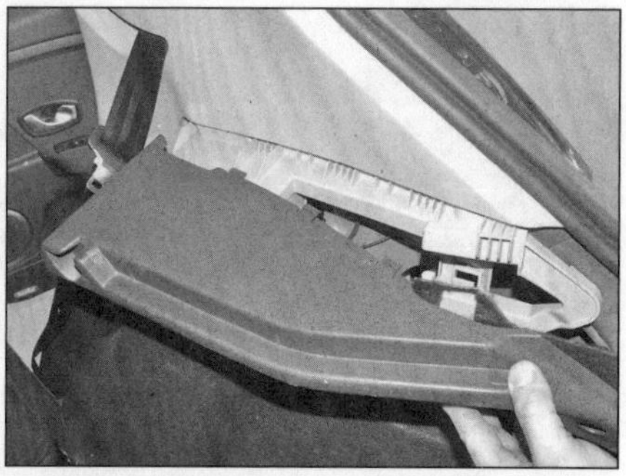

22.66b ...and then remove the panel

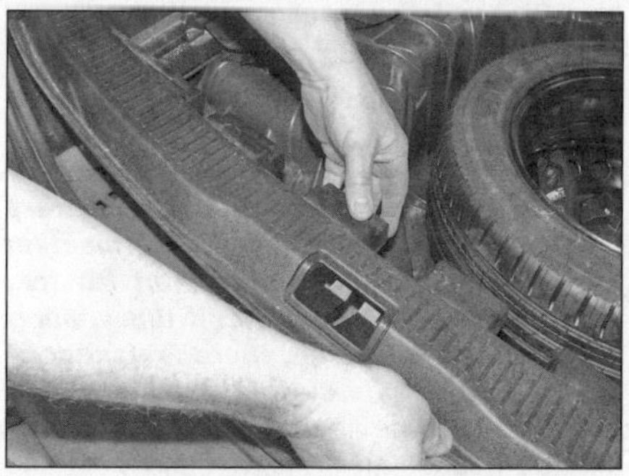

22.68 Prise up the panel

22.69 Remove the trim clip with a suitable tool

Load area side trim panel

68 Remove the rear door slam panel trim by prising it up **(see illustration)**.
69 Remove the plastic screw fastener at the rear of the panel **(see illustration)**.
70 Partially remove (by slackening the screws) the parcel shelf support panel and then work the panel free from behind the panel. If necessary remove the parcel shelf panel completely.
71 Remove the load area floor cover and then where fitted, remove the floor support panel **(see illustrations)**.
72 Free the panel and remove it to the rear **(see illustration)**.
73 Refitting is a reversal of removal.

C-pillar trim panel

Hatchback

74 Open the appropriate door and tailgate. Remove the parcel shelf support panel
75 Pull away the rubber weatherstrips from the C-pillar D-pillar.
76 Lift up the rear seat cushion.
77 Prise free the upper and lower sections of the panel
78 Refitting is a reversal of removal.

Estate

79 The upper section is removed as part of the upper trim panel. Removal is described in paragraphs 52 to 54.
80 Prise off the lower panel to release the clips, and remove it.
81 Refitting is a reversal of removal.

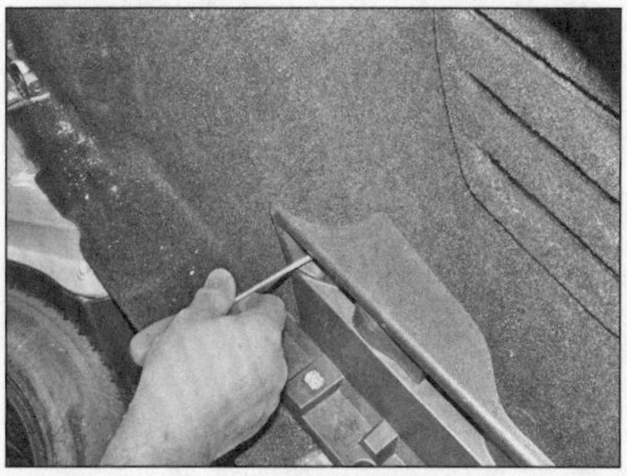

22.71a Unscrew and...

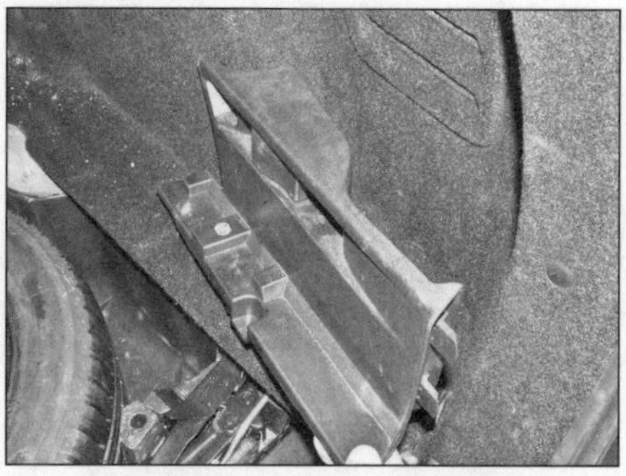

22.71b ...remove the panel

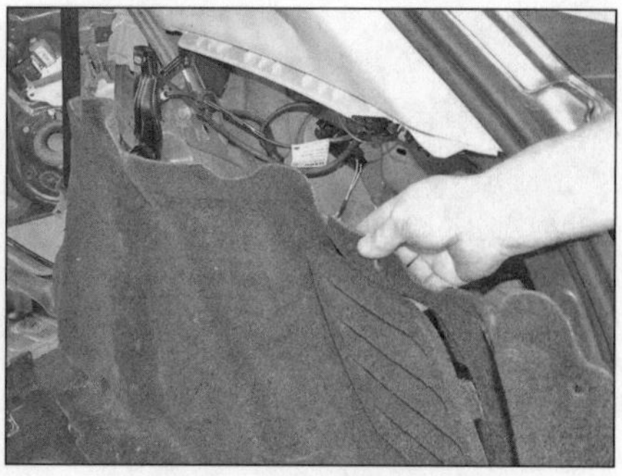

22.72 Remove the side panel

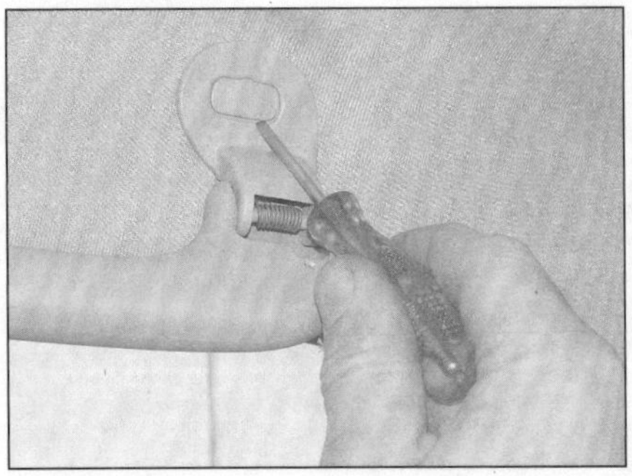

22.85a Using a small screwdriver . . .

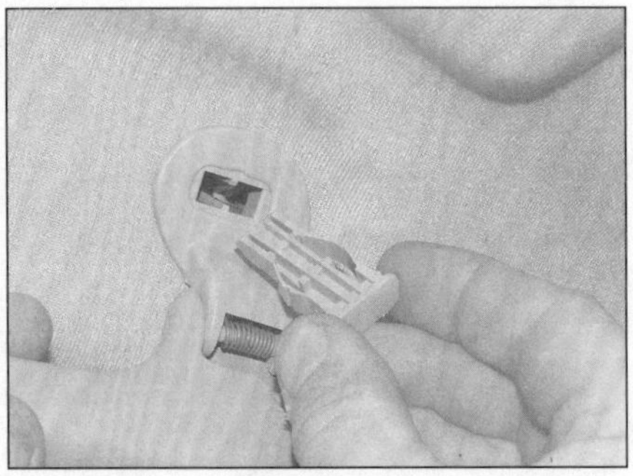

22.85b . . . prise out the grab handle retaining pegs

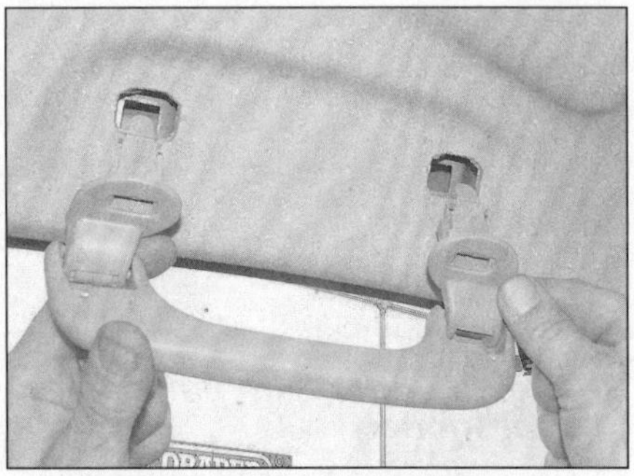

22.86 Lower the handle from the headlining, and remove it

Coupe

82 The panel is part of the rear side trim panel. Remove the panel as described previously in this Section.

Carpets

83 The carpet is held in position by the sill trim panels, and other surrounding panels and components.

84 Carpet removal and refitting is reasonably straightforward, but very time-consuming, due to the fact that many of the adjoining trim panels must be removed first. It will also be necessary to remove components such as the seats and their mountings, the centre console, etc.

Grab handles

85 Using a small screwdriver, prise out the retaining peg at each end of the grab handle **(see illustrations)**.

86 Lower the grab handle from the headlining and remove it **(see illustration)**.

87 Refitting is a reversal of removal.

Headlining

Warning: Disconnect the battery negative lead (see 'Disconnecting the battery'), then wait for five minutes before proceeding. If this waiting period is not observed, there is danger of activating the side curtain airbags, which are located in the headlining.

88 The headlining is held in place by the grab handles, sunvisors, sunroof trim, door pillar trim panels, rear quarter trim panels, weatherseals, etc. When all the fittings have been removed or prised clear, it can then be withdrawn out through the tailgate aperture. Disconnect the wiring plugs for the side curtain airbags as they become accessible.

89 Note that headlining removal requires considerable skill and patience if it is to be carried out without damage, and is therefore best entrusted to an expert.

23.1 Remove the console extension panels

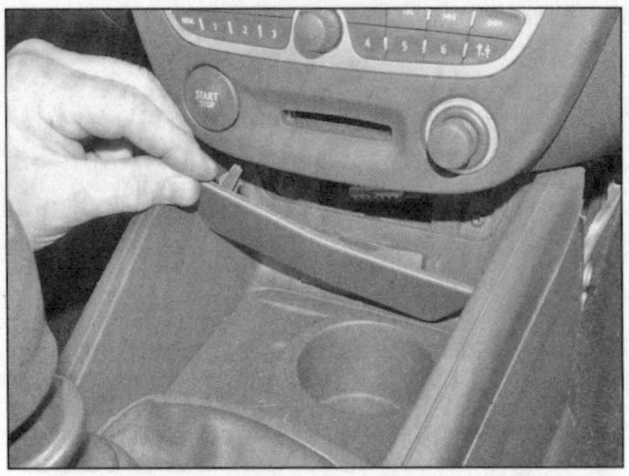

23.2 Remove the cover

23 Centre console – removal and refitting

Removal

1 Unclip the front extension panels from both sides **(see illustration)**.

2 Remove the diagnostic socket cover from the front of the gear lever **(see illustration)**.

3 Unclip the trim surrounding the base of the gear lever gaiter, then pull upwards to remove the gaiter and gear knob. If required, the gear knob can be unclipped and removed separately **(see illustration)**.

4 Where a conventional handbrake is fitted, prise free the handbrake lever gaiter **(see illustration)**.

5 Unclip and remove the cup holder **(see illustration)**.

6 Using a suitable trim tool, prise free the main upper trim panel. Disconnect the audio auxiliary socket, navigation control and hand brake switch (where fitted) as the panel is removed **(see illustrations)**.

7 Prise free the rear cover from the console, disconnecting the wiring plug from the 12 volt power outlet as the panel is removed **(see illustrations)**.

8 At the front of the console, remove both of the screws next to the diagnostic socket **(see illustration)**.

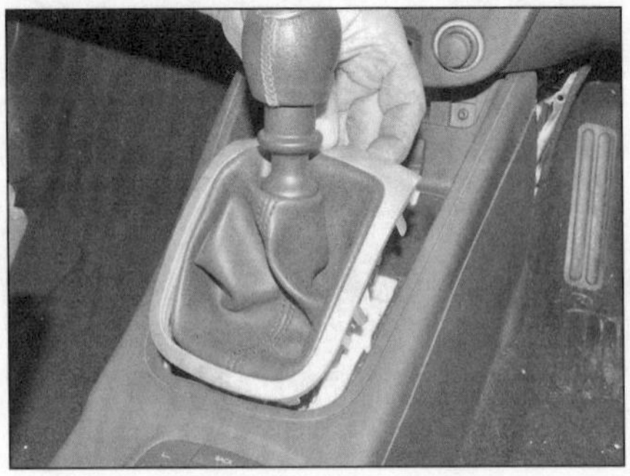

23.3 Prise up the gaiter

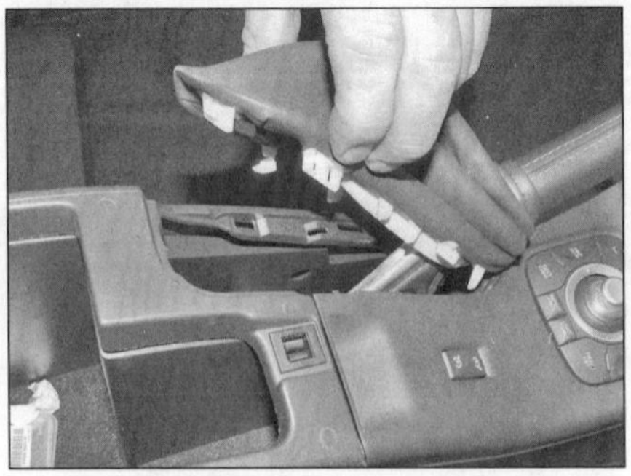

23.4 Prise free the handbrake gaiter

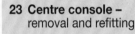

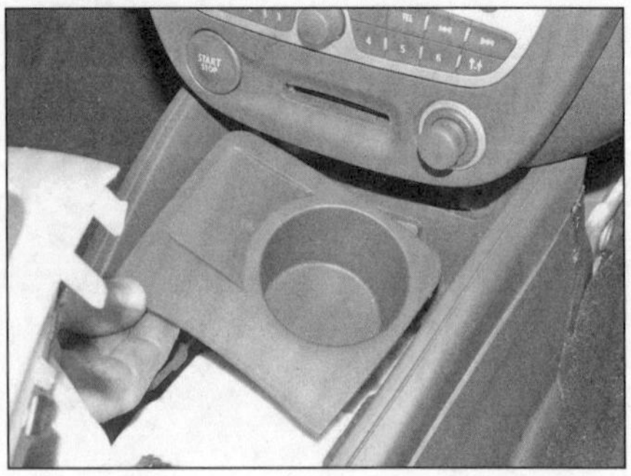

23.5 Remove the cup holder

23.6a Prise up the main panel...

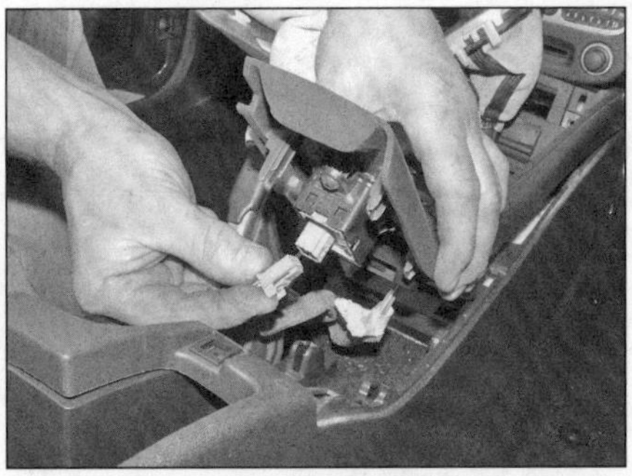
23.6b ...and disconnect the wiring plug as the panel is removed

23.7a Prise free...

23.7b ...and remove the end panel

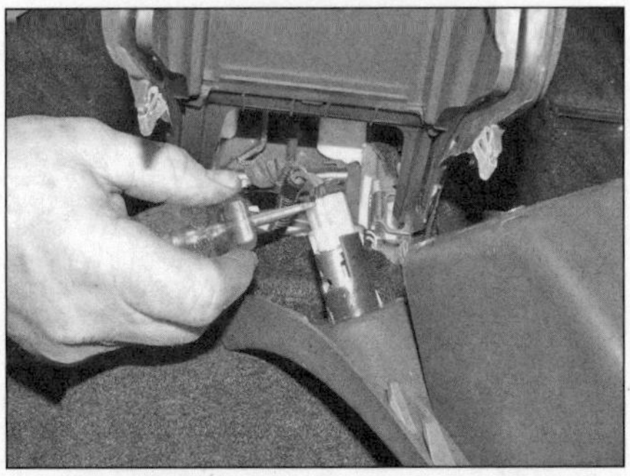
23.7c Disconnect the wiring plug

23.8 Remove the screws

9 Remove the rear fixing screws from the console. Slide the console back and then up. Manoeuvre the console over the handbrake lever and gear lever **(see illustrations)**. Remove the console from the vehicle.

Refitting

10 Refitting is a reversal of removal.

24 Facia panel and crossmember – removal and refitting

Removal

Facia panel

1 Disconnect the battery negative lead (see *Disconnecting the battery*), then wait for five minutes before proceeding. If this waiting period is not observed, there is danger of activating the airbags.

2 Remove the centre console as described in Section 23.

3 Remove the A-pillar and footwell trim panels as described in Section 22.

4 Taking care not to scratch the top of the facia, prise up the tweeter speaker grilles **(see illustration)**. On models fitted with speakers, prise out the speakers themselves, then disconnect each one's wiring plug and remove them. On models not fitted with speakers release the connectors from the holder and pull the wiring loom down towards the crossmember.

5 Remove the driver's side lower facia panel and glovebox as described in Section 22.

6 Remove the steering wheel (as described in Chapter 10, Section 14) and then remove the steering column switch assembly and the instrument panel as described in Chapter 12, Section 11.

7 If only the facia is being removed, there is no need to remove the column itself, but access can be improved by unbolting the column from the crossmember and allowing it to rest on the floor. If you are removing the facia panel to access the crossmember, now is a good time to remove the column completely from the vehicle.

8 Remove the heater control panel, audio unit and centre vent panel as described in Chapter 3 and Chapter 12.

9 Remove both facia end panels.

10 Release the key card reader and disconnect the wiring plug **(see illustrations)**.

11 With reference to Chapter 12, prise up the trim and remove the information display unit

23.9a Remove the screw (arrowed)

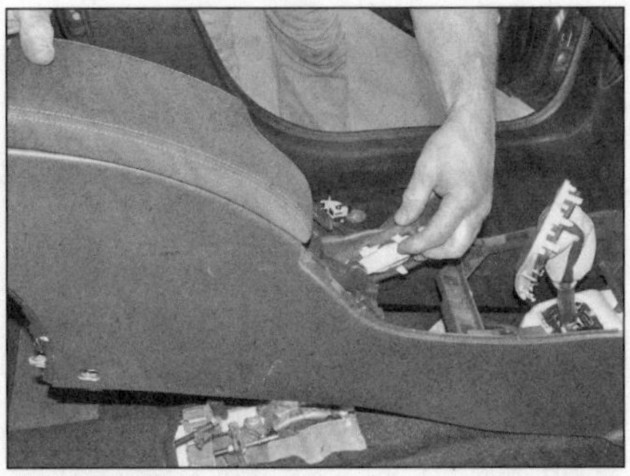
23.9b Lift the console over the gear lever and hand brake

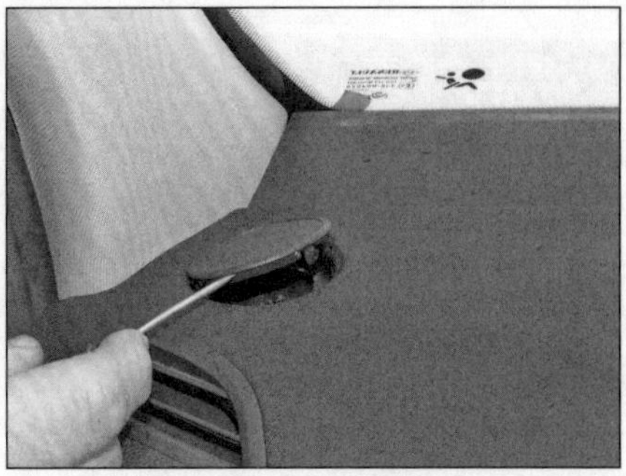
24.4 Remove the speaker grilles

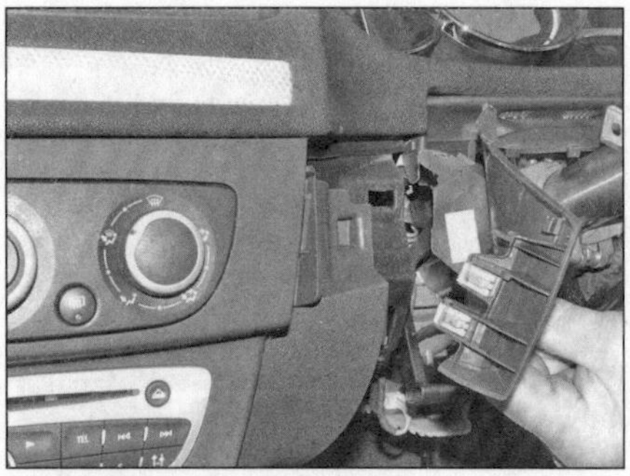

24.10a Prise free the right-hand trim panel

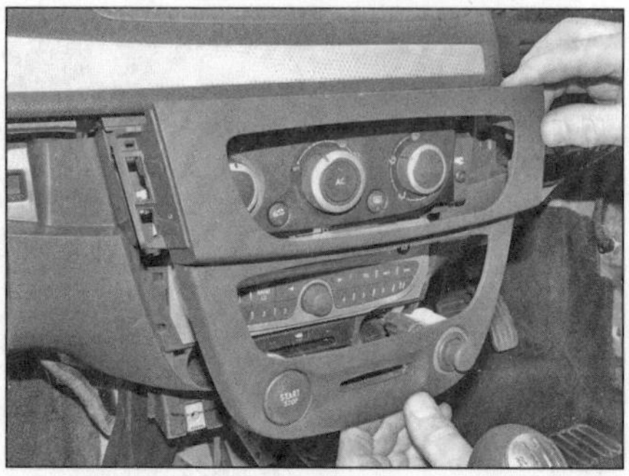

24.10b Release the main panel...

24.10c ...disconnecting the wiring plugs as the panel is removed

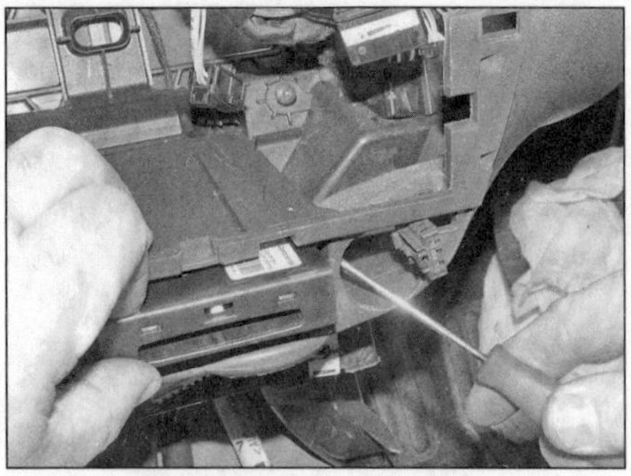

24.10d Use a small screwdriver to release the key card reader...

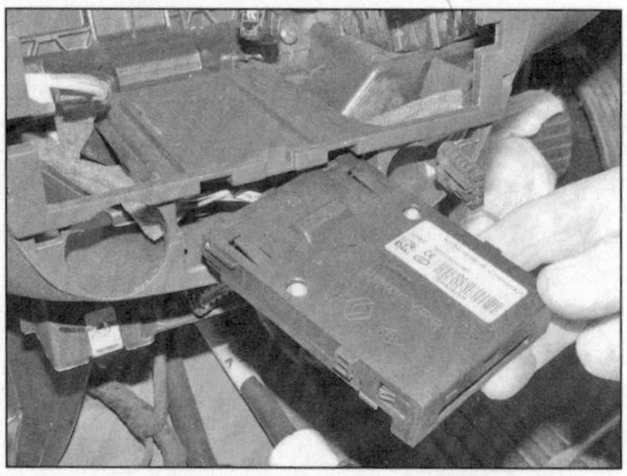

24.10e ...and then remove it

24.11 Remove the trim

(or satellite navigation display) where fitted **(see illustration)**.

12 Prise out and disconnect the wiring plug from the glovebox light unit.

24.13 Disconnect the wiring plugs

13 Unbolt and then lower the body control module (UCH). Disconnect the wiring plugs and remove it from the vehicle **(see illustration)**.

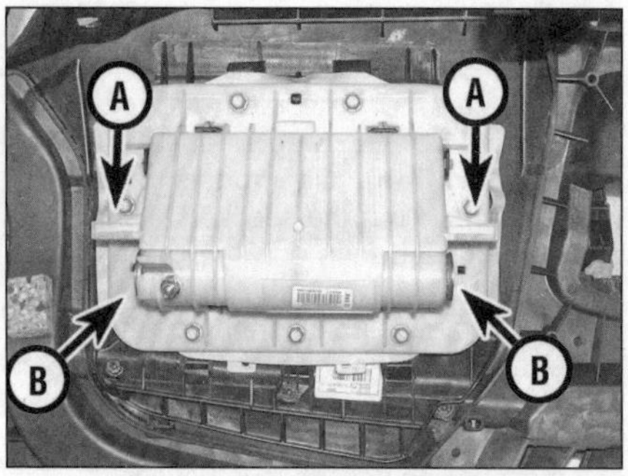

24.15 With the facia removed, note the location of the retaining bolts (A) and the wiring connectors (B)

14 Reach up under the facia and disconnect the two wiring connectors (one at each end) from the passenger airbag unit. Access is extremely difficult.

15 Remove the bolts that secure the airbag to the crossmember. The air duct will require compressing to fully access the bolts, even then access to these bolts is both difficult and awkward **(see illustration)**.

16 The facia panel is now held in place by a number of screws, as follows **(see illustrations)**:

a) Two at each end of the facia panel.
b) One underneath the passenger airbag.
c) One behind the instrument panel location.
d) One recessed in behind the facia top panel location.
e) Two in the centre, securing the facia to the heater unit.

17 With all the above-mentioned screws

24.16a Remove the lower screws at the centre (arrowed)...

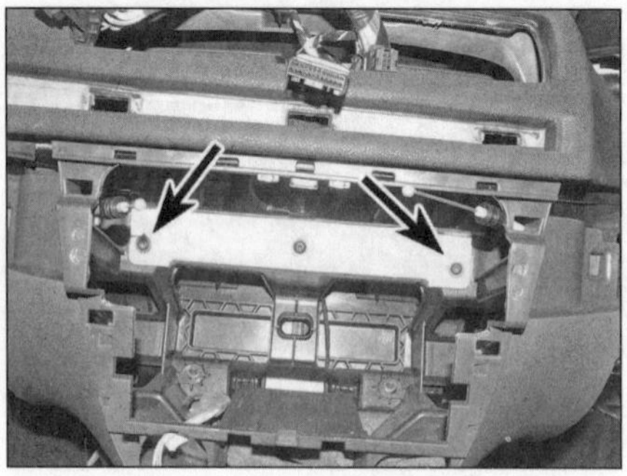

24.16b ...the upper centre...

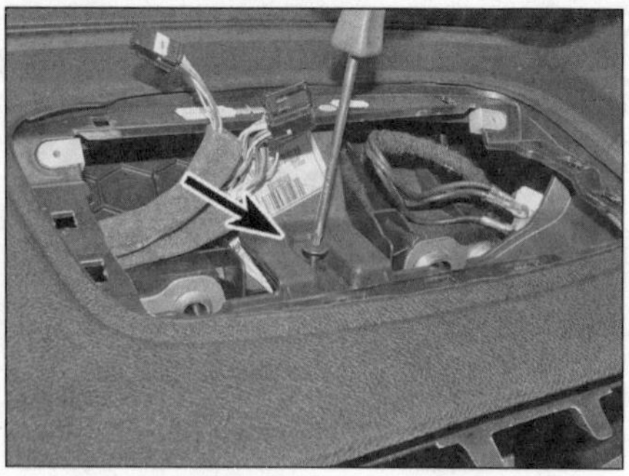

24.16c ...at the top centre (arrowed)...

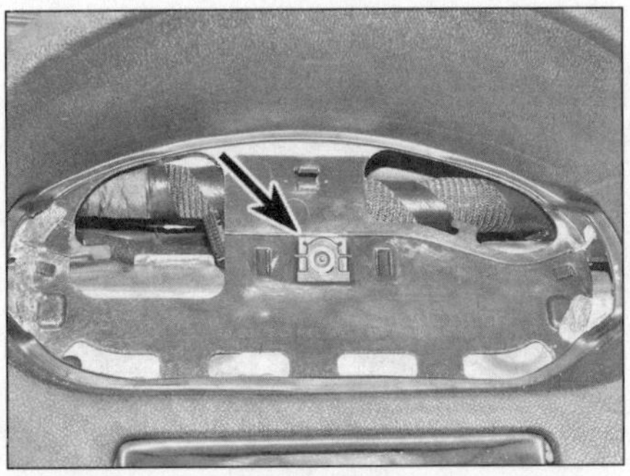

24.16d ...behind the instrument panel (arrowed)...

24.16e ...and at both ends of the facia (arrowed)

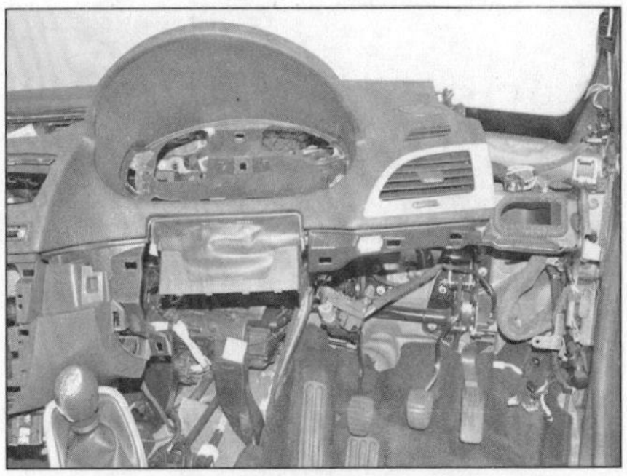

24.17 Remove the facia

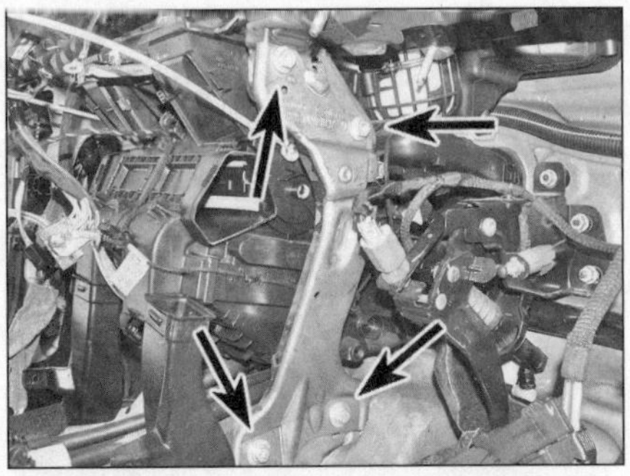

24.20a Remove the main bolts (arrowed)...

24.20b ...the hidden bolt (arrowed)...

24.20c ...and then remove the support strut

removed, and with the help of an assistant, withdraw the facia panel into the car **(see illustration)**.

Crossmember

18 If not already done so, remove the steering column as described in Chapter 10, Section 15 – as the facia panel is removed, there will be no problem accessing the mounting nuts.

19 With reference to Section 11 of this Chapter, remove both front doors.

20 Release the wiring clip and then unbolt and remove the vertical support strut from the right-hand side of the transmission tunnel **(see illustrations)**.

21 On the left-hand side remove the bolt that secures the heater assembly to the crossmember **(see illustration)** and then remove the two upper bolts from the heater assembly.

22 Work around the crossmember, disconnecting the cable-tied and clipped-on wiring harness as necessary, noting how it is routed **(see illustrations)**. Most of the cable ties are reusable, however we found several on the left-hand side that required cutting to remove them – these will require replacement on reassembly.

23 Remove the ventilation ducts from the metal crossmember, noting how they are fitted **(see illustrations)**.

24.21 Remove the bolt (arrowed)

24.22a Unclip the wiring loom...

24.22b ...and remove it

24.23a Remove the left-hand air distribution duct

24.23b Remove the screw and then remove the central air distribution ducting

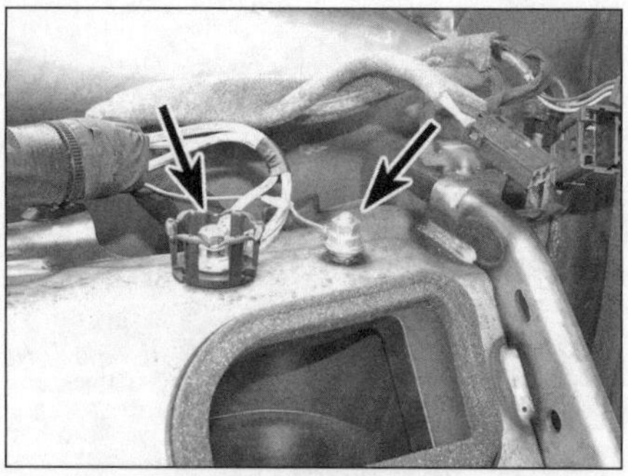

24.24a Unbolt the earth connections (arrowed) on both sides...

24.24b ...and then remove the loom

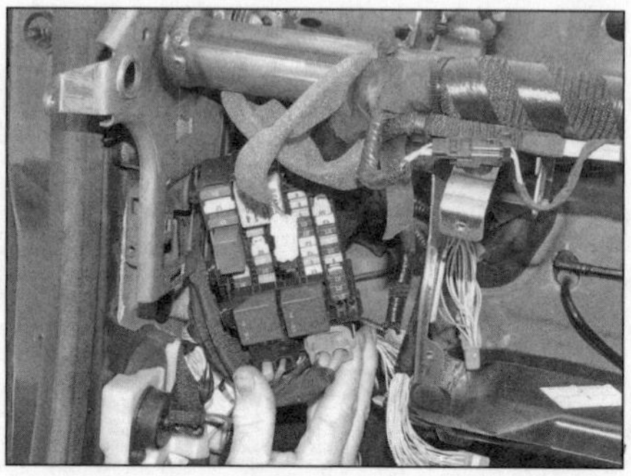

24.25a Unclip the fuse box...

24.25b ...and disconnect the wiring plugs

24.27 Make alignment marks around the bolts and locating peg

24.28a Remove the blanking plugs and...

24 Unbolt the earth straps at either end of the crossmember **(see illustrations)** – note that one is also fitted to the left-hand side of the transmission tunnel.

25 Unclip the fusebox from the left-hand end of the crossmember **(see illustrations)**.

26 Remove the bolt from the upper support at the base of the windscreen.

27 Make suitable alignment marks on the crossmember in relation to the A-pillars **(see illustration)**.

28 Remove the blanking plugs from the outside of the A-pillars and then remove the bolts **(see illustrations)**.

29 Remove the remaining bolts on the inside of the A-pillars and then (after checking that all the wiring has been released) remove with the aid of an assistant the crossmember from the vehicle **(see illustration)**.

Refitting

30 Refitting is a reversal of removal, bearing in mind the following points:

a) *If the facia is to be refitted at a later date, ensure that the battery is disconnected before starting. It is dangerous, for example, to reconnect the airbag wiring with the battery connected.*

b) *Before refitting the cross member fully wind home the adjustment bolts of the end of the crossmember* **(see illustration)**. *Note that these are a left-hand thread.*

c) *Fit the crossmember and then fit (but do not fully tighten)the crossmember bolts.*

d) *Fit the main long end bolts through the A-pillars and tighten them until the adjustable nut starts to bite into the A-pillars. Adjust each bolt in turn until the crossmember aligns with the previously made marks.*

e) *Fully tighten the main crossmember bolts and then tighten the long end bolts. Note that Renault do not supply a torque figure for the crossmember bolts.*

f) *Ensure that the wiring harnesses, cable clips, etc, are routed as noted before removal.*

24.28b ...then remove the bolts

24.29 Remove the crossmember

24.30 Fully wind in the adjustable spacer nut (arrowed)

Chapter 12
Body electrical system

Contents

Section number

Airbag system – general information and precautions 26
Airbag system components – removal and refitting 27
Anti-theft alarm and immobiliser systems – general information 24
Audio unit – removal and refitting 21
Auxiliary display – removal and refitting 12
Bulbs (exterior lights) – renewal 6
Bulbs (interior lights) – renewal 7
Cigar lighter – removal and refitting 15
Electrical connectors - general information 4
Electrical fault finding – general information 2
Exterior light units – removal and refitting 8
Fuses, relays and electronic control units – general information 3
General information and precautions 1
Headlight beam alignment – general information 10
Horn – removal and refitting 16
Instrument panel – removal and refitting 11

Section number

Interior light units – removal and refitting 9
Outside air temperature sensor – removal and refitting 13
Parking aid components – general information, removal and refitting 28
Radio aerial – removal and refitting 23
Rain sensor and automatic headlight sensor – removal and refitting . . 14
Speakers – removal and refitting 22
Steering column lock – removal and refitting 25
Switches – removal and refitting 5
Tailgate wiper motor – removal and refitting 19
Windscreen wiper motor and linkage – removal and refitting 18
Windscreen/tailgate washer system components – removal and refitting 20
Windscreen/tailgate wiper blade check and renewal . . . . See *Weekly checks*
Wiper arms – removal and refitting 17

Degrees of difficulty

Easy, suitable for novice with little experience	**Fairly easy,** suitable for beginner with some experience	**Fairly difficult,** suitable for competent DIY mechanic	**Difficult,** suitable for experienced DIY mechanic	**Very difficult,** suitable for expert DIY or professional

Specifications

General

System type	12 volt, negative earth	

Bulbs

Exterior lights	**Wattage**	**Type**
Direction indicator	21	PY21W
Direction indicator side repeater	5	W5W
Front foglight	55	H11
Front sidelight	5	W5W
Headlight with halogen bulbs:		
Main beam	55	H7
Dip beam	55	H7
Headlight with xenon bulbs:		
Main beam	55	H7*
Dip beam	37	D1S*
High-level brake light	LEDs (no bulbs fitted)	
Number plate light (festoon)	5	C5W
Rear foglight/sidelight (Hatchback)	21/4	P21/4W
Rear foglight (Coupe)	21	H21W
Rear foglight (Estate)	21/4	P21W
Reversing light (Hatchback)	16	W16W
Reversing light (Coupe and Estate)	21	P21
Stop/tail	21/5	P21/5W
Interior lights		
Boot/glovebox light (festoon)	5	C5W
Interior/footwell lights (wedge-base)	5	W5W

* **Note:** *As the headlights have plastic lenses,* **anti-UV type bulbs** *are used (the headlight may be damaged if any other type of bulb is used).*

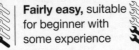

1 General information and precautions

Warning: Before carrying out any work on the electrical system, read through the precautions given in 'Safety first!' at the beginning of this manual, and in Chapter 5A.

The electrical system is of 12 volt negative earth type. Power for the lights and all electrical accessories is supplied by a lead-acid type battery, which is charged by the alternator.

This Chapter covers repair and service procedures for the various electrical components not associated with engine. Information on the battery, alternator and starter motor can be found in Chapter 5A.

It should be noted that, prior to working on any component in the electrical system, the battery negative terminal should first be disconnected, to prevent the possibility of electrical short-circuits and/or fires.

Caution: Before disconnecting the battery, refer to the information given in 'Disconnecting the battery' in the Reference Section of this manual.

2 Electrical fault finding – general information

Note: *Refer to the precautions given in 'Safety first!' and at the beginning of Chapter 5A before starting work.*

Warning: Since this is a multiplex wiring system, every circuit in the car passes through at least one 'ECU'. For this reason, it is inadvisable to use any kind of self-powered test equipment, as this may cause damage to the electronic modules fitted.

General

1 A typical electrical circuit consists of an electrical component, any switches, relays, motors, fuses, fusible links or circuit breakers related to that component, and the wiring and connectors which link the component to both the battery and the chassis. To help to pinpoint a problem in an electrical circuit, wiring diagrams are included at the end of this Chapter.

2 Before attempting to diagnose an electrical fault, first study the appropriate wiring diagram, to obtain a more complete understanding of the components included in the particular circuit concerned. The possible sources of a fault can be narrowed down by noting whether other components related to the circuit are operating properly. If several components or circuits fail at one time, the problem is likely to be related to a shared fuse or earth connection.

3 Multiplex wiring makes traditional electrical fault finding more difficult, as inter-related circuits are connected together as required by the multiplex modules. This factor makes tracing faults from one end of the car to the other almost impossible, with the added factor that the multiplex modules may also be at fault, in not switching/connecting the circuits correctly. Once testing has passed beyond the basic stage, it may be more time-efficient to have the fault diagnosed by a Renault dealer or suitably equipped garage.

4 Electrical problems usually stem from simple causes, such as loose or corroded connections, a faulty earth connection, a blown fuse, a melted fusible link, or a faulty relay (refer to Section 3 for details of testing relays). Visually inspect the condition of all fuses, wires and connections in a problem circuit before testing the components. Use the wiring diagrams to determine which terminal connections will need to be checked, in order to pinpoint the trouble-spot.

5 The basic tools required for electrical fault-finding include a voltmeter (a 12 volt bulb with a set of test leads can also be used for certain tests), an ohmmeter (to measure resistance), and a jumper wire, preferably with a circuit breaker or fuse incorporated, which can be used to bypass suspect wires or electrical components. Before attempting to locate a problem with test instruments, use the wiring diagram to determine where to make the connections.

6 To find the source of an intermittent wiring fault (usually due to a poor or dirty connection, or damaged wiring insulation), a 'wiggle' test can be performed on the wiring. This involves wiggling the wiring by hand, to see if the fault occurs as the wiring is moved. It should be possible to narrow down the source of the fault to a particular section of wiring. This method of testing can be used in conjunction with any of the tests described in the following sub-Sections.

7 Apart from problems due to poor connections, two basic types of fault can occur in an electrical circuit – open-circuit, or short-circuit.

8 Open-circuit faults are caused by a break somewhere in the circuit, which prevents current from flowing. An open-circuit fault will prevent a component from working, but will not cause the relevant circuit fuse to blow.

9 Short-circuit faults are caused by a 'short' somewhere in the circuit, which allows the current flowing in the circuit to 'escape' along an alternative route, usually to earth. Short-circuit faults are normally caused by a breakdown in wiring insulation, which allows a feed wire to touch either another wire, or an earthed component such as the bodyshell. A short-circuit fault will normally cause the relevant circuit fuse to blow.

Finding an open-circuit

10 To check for an open-circuit, connect one lead of a test light or voltmeter to either the negative battery terminal or a known good earth.

11 Connect the other lead to a connector in the circuit being tested, preferably nearest to the battery or fuse.

12 Switch on the circuit, bearing in mind that some circuits are live only when the ignition is on (with the keycard in position, and neither brake nor clutch depressed, press the starter button to switch on the ignition).

13 If voltage is present (indicated either by the tester bulb lighting or a voltmeter reading, as applicable), this means that the section of the circuit between the relevant connector and the battery is problem-free.

14 Continue to check the remainder of the circuit in the same fashion.

15 When a point is reached at which no voltage is present, the problem must lie between that point and the previous test point with voltage. Most problems can be traced to a broken, corroded or loose connection.

Finding a short-circuit

16 To check for a short-circuit, first disconnect the load(s) from the circuit (loads are the components which draw current from a circuit, such as bulbs, motors, heating elements, etc).

17 Remove the relevant fuse from the circuit, and connect a test light or voltmeter to the fuse connections.

18 Switch on the circuit, bearing in mind that some circuits are live only when the ignition is on (with the keycard in position, and neither brake nor clutch depressed, press the starter button to switch on the ignition).

19 If voltage is present (indicated either by the test bulb lighting or a voltmeter reading, as applicable), this means that there is a short-circuit.

20 If no voltage is present, but the fuse still blows with the load(s) connected, this indicates an internal fault in the load(s).

Finding an earth fault

21 The battery negative terminal is connected to 'earth' – the metal of the engine/transmission unit and the car body – and most systems are wired so that they only receive a negative feed, the current returning via the metal of the car body. This means that the component mounting and the body form part of that circuit. Loose or corroded mountings can therefore cause a range of electrical faults, ranging from total failure of a circuit, to a puzzling partial fault.

22 In particular, lights may shine dimly (especially when another circuit sharing the same earth point is in operation), motors (eg, wiper motors or the radiator cooling fan motor) may run slowly, and the operation of one circuit may have an apparently-unrelated effect on another.

23 Note that on many vehicles, earth straps are used between certain components, such as the engine/transmission and the body, usually where there is no metal-to-metal contact between components, due to flexible rubber mountings, etc.

24 To check whether a component is properly earthed, disconnect the battery, and connect one lead of an ohmmeter to a known good earth point. Connect the other lead to the wire or earth connection being tested. The resistance reading should be zero; if not, check the connection as follows.

25 If an earth connection is thought to be faulty, dismantle the connection, and clean back to bare metal both the bodyshell and the wire terminal or the component earth connection mating surface. Be careful to remove all traces of dirt and corrosion, then use a knife to trim away any paint, so that a clean metal-to-metal joint is made.

26 On reassembly, tighten the joint fasteners securely; if a wire terminal is being refitted, use serrated washers between the terminal and the bodyshell, to ensure a clean and secure connection.

27 When the connection is remade, prevent the onset of corrosion in the future by applying a coat of petroleum jelly or silicone-based grease, or by spraying on (at regular intervals) a proprietary ignition sealer.

3 Fuses, relays and electronic control units – general information

Fuses

1 Fuses are designed to break a circuit when a predetermined current is reached, in order to protect the components and wiring which could be damaged by excessive current flow. Any excessive current flow will be due to a fault in the circuit, usually a short-circuit (see Section 2).

2 The main fuses are located in the fusebox, inside the glovebox.

3 Open the glovebox, then prise down the fusebox cover panel to the left – the cover holds the fuse puller tool and spare fuses **(see illustration)**.

4 A blown fuse can be recognised from its melted or broken wire **(see illustration)**.

5 To remove a fuse, first ensure that the relevant circuit is switched off – for maximum safety, disconnect the battery (see *Disconnecting the battery*).

6 Pull the fuse from its location, using the plastic tweezer tool provided **(see illustrations)**. Spare fuses are provided in the cover panel, and below the fusebox.

7 Before renewing a blown fuse, trace and rectify the cause, and always use a fuse of the correct rating. Never substitute a fuse of a higher rating, or make temporary repairs using wire or metal foil; more serious damage, or even fire, could result.

8 Additional fuses are located the engine compartment fusebox. These are located at the left-hand rear of the battery, to the left of the main engine management ECU (behind the headlight) and beneath the protection and switching control unit (under the cover to the left of the battery).

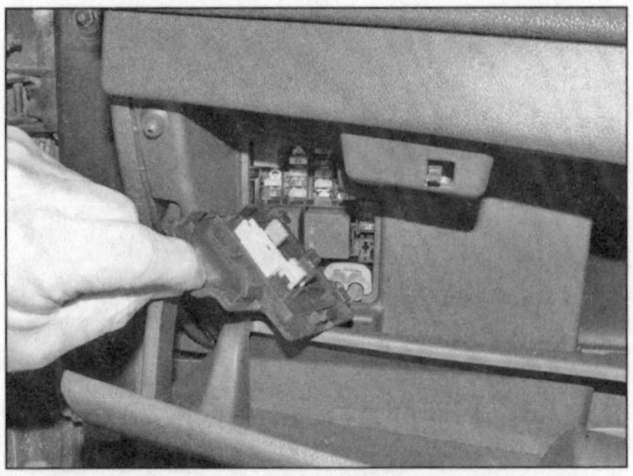

3.3 Open the fusebox cover panel to the left of the glovebox opening

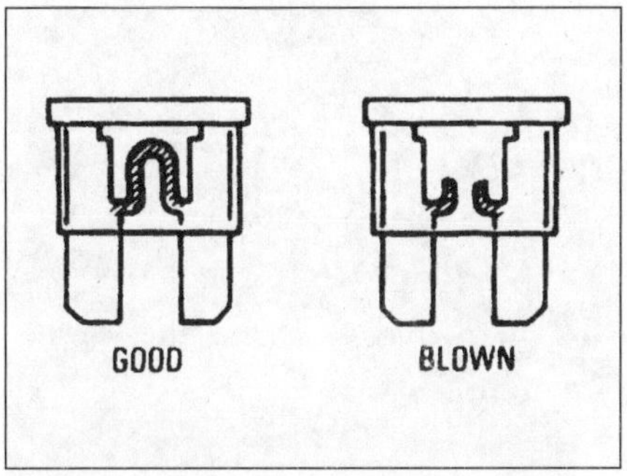

3.4 The fuses can be checked visually to see if they have blown

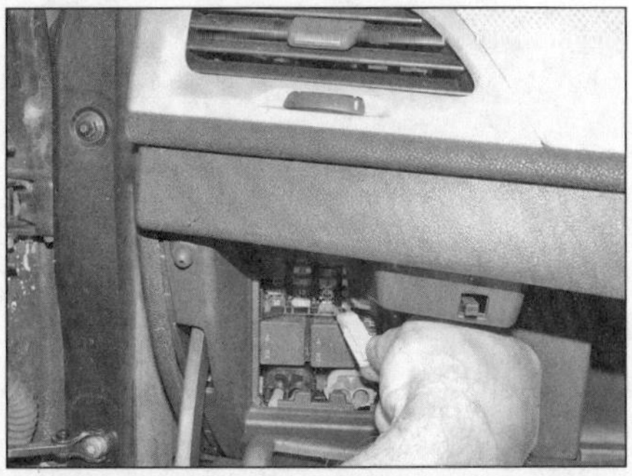

3.6a Use the tool provided in the fusebox cover to remove a fuse

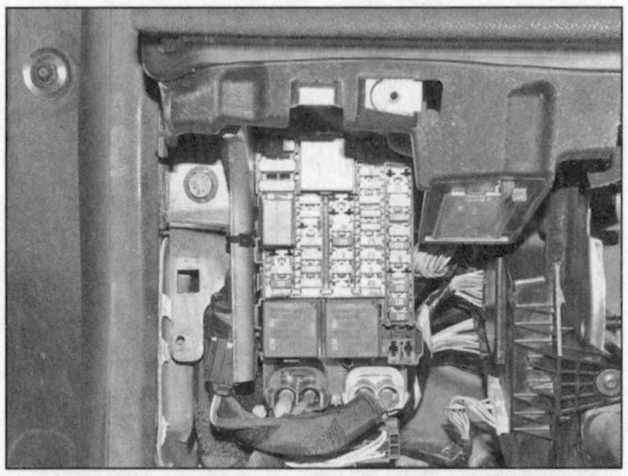

3.6b Full access to the fusebox can only be gained by removing the glovebox

9 Access is gained by removing the appropriate cover. The fusebox behind the headlight **(see illustration)** is best accessed by removing the headlight as described in Section 8.

10 The fusebox to the rear of the battery must be unbolted before the cover can be removed. Disconnect the battery first - as described in Chapter 5A, Section 4 – remove the nuts and then release the locking clip at the rear. Pull up the fusebox and open the cover to access the fuses.

Relays

11 A relay is an electrically-operated switch, which is used for the following reasons:

a) A relay can switch a heavy current remotely from the circuit in which the current is flowing, allowing the use of lighter-gauge wiring and switch contacts.

b) A relay can receive more than one control input, unlike a mechanical switch.

c) A relay can have a timer function – for example, the intermittent wiper relay.

3.9 Remove the headlight to access the fusebox (arrowed)

12 As a result of the switching functions contained within the multiplex modules, fewer relays are fitted than normal. Those that are fitted are located in the main fuseboxes in the passenger and engine compartments. Refer to the wiring diagrams at the end of this Chapter for more information.

13 If a circuit or system controlled by a relay develops a fault, and the relay is suspect, operate the system. If the relay is functioning, it should be possible to hear it 'click' as it is energised. If this is the case, the fault lies with the components or wiring of the system. If the relay is not being energised, then either the relay is not receiving a main supply or a switching voltage, or the relay itself is faulty. Testing is by the substitution of a known good unit, but be careful – while some relays are identical in appearance and in operation, others look similar but perform different functions.

Electronic control units

Note: *If the control unit is to be replaced, the vehicle software (in the control unit) must be first downloaded to a suitable diagnostic tool and then uploaded to the replacement control unit.*

14 The main engine control unit (ECU) is located in front of the battery. Disconnect the battery before proceeding -see *Disconnecting the battery in Chapter 5A.*

3.15a Remove the ECU cover and air intake duct

3.15b Disconnect the wiring plugs

3.15c Note the location of the lower mounting bolt (arrowed and shown with the front panel removed for clarity). Unbolt the ECU from the bracket...

3.15d ...and then remove the ECU

15 Remove the air intake duct . This can be removed complete with the ECU cover. To improve access remove the left-hand headlight and battery cover. Disconnect the wiring plugs and then remove the ECU form the mounting bracket **(see illustrations)**. Alternatively, remove the mounting bracket complete with the ECU and then separate the ECU from the bracket on the bench.

16 The interior ECU (also known as the UCH, or Unité de Commande d'Habitacle) is located under the facia panel, on the passenger side. To gain access to the module, remove the glovebox as described in Chapter 11, Section 22.

17 Unscrew the single bolt securing the ECU to the underside of the facia crossmember, then unclip and lower it into the footwell. Release the locking catches from the module wiring plugs, and remove the module **(see illustrations)**.

18 Any suspected problems with either module are best referred to a Renault dealer or suitably equipped garage, who will have the dedicated diagnostic equipment available to determine the problem. Simply swapping another ECU from a similar donor vehicle will not work as the donor ECU will not be programmed with the correct software and security information.

4 Electrical connectors - general information

1 Most electrical connections on these vehicles are made with multiwire plastic connectors. The mating halves of many connectors are secured with locking clips molded into the plastic connector shells. The mating halves of some large connectors, such as some of those under the instrument panel, are held together by a bolt through the center of the connector.

2 To separate a connector with locking clips, use a small screwdriver to pry the clips apart carefully, then separate the connector halves. Pull only on the shell, never pull on the wiring harness, as you may damage the individual wires and terminals inside the connectors. Look at the connector closely before trying to separate the halves. Often the locking clips are engaged in a way that is not immediately clear. Additionally, many connectors have more than one set of clips.

3 Each pair of connector terminals has a male half and a female half. When you look at the end view of a connector in a diagram, be sure to understand whether the view shows the harness side or the component side of the connector. Connector halves are mirror images of each other, and a terminal shown on the right side end-view of one half will be on the left side end-view of the other half.

4 It is often necessary to take circuit voltage measurements with a connector connected. Whenever possible, carefully insert a small straight pin (not your meter probe) into the rear of the connector shell to contact the terminal inside, then clip your meter lead to the pin. This kind of connection is called "backprobing." When inserting a test probe into a terminal, be careful not to distort the terminal opening. Doing so can lead to a poor connection and corrosion at that terminal later. Using the small straight pin instead of a meter probe results in less chance of deforming the terminal connector. "T" pins are a good choice as temporary meter connections. They allow for a larger surface area to attach the meter leads too.

3.17a Remove the mounting screw

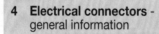

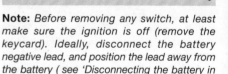

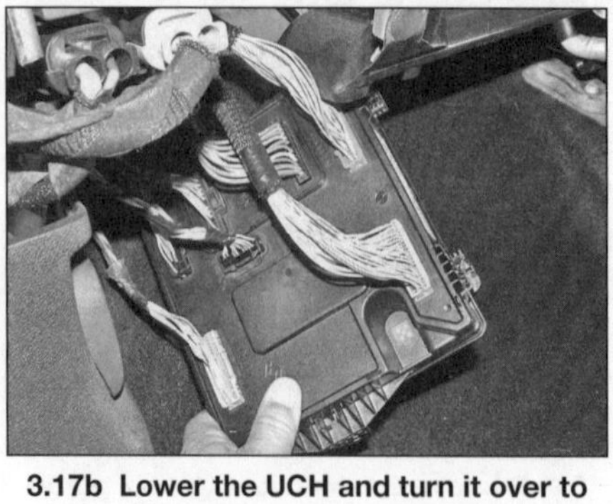

3.17b Lower the UCH and turn it over to access the wiring plugs

5 Switches - removal and refitting

Note: *Before removing any switch, at least make sure the ignition is off (remove the keycard). Ideally, disconnect the battery negative lead, and position the lead away from the battery (see 'Disconnecting the battery in Chapter 5A).*

Ignition keycard reader

1 Carefully remove the side trim panels from above the glovebox and next to the steering column. Remove the central trim panel **(see illustrations)**.

2 Use a small screwdriver and release the key card reader **(see illustration)**. Disconnect the wiring plug as the reader is removed.

3 Refitting is a reversal of removal.

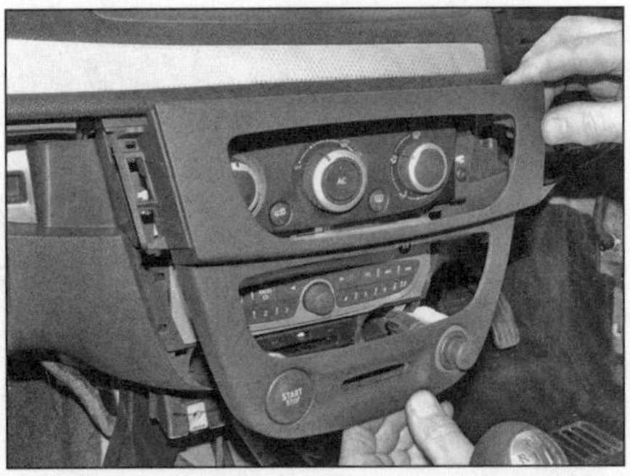

5.1a Remove the centre trim panel

5.1b Disconnect the wiring plugs as the panel is removed

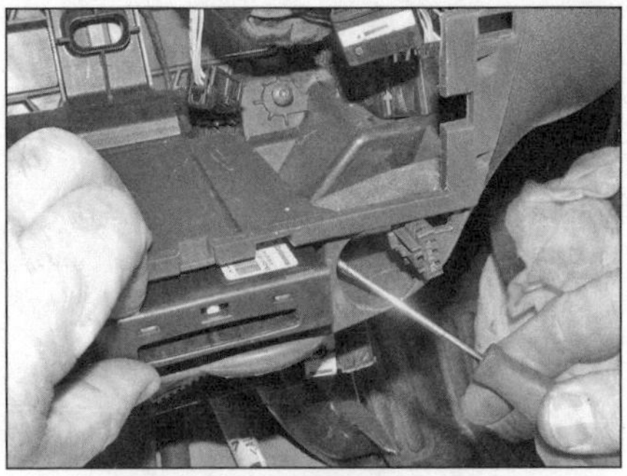

5.2 Release the keycard reader using a small screwdriver

5.8 Remove the central air distribution panel

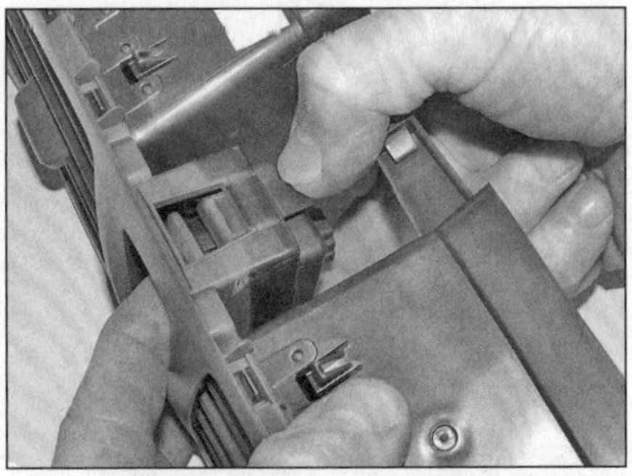

5.10a Depress the locking tabs and...

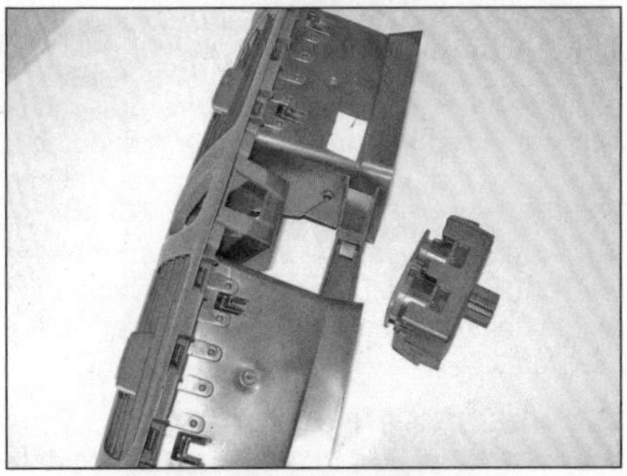

5.10b ...remove the switch

Starter button

4 Remove the facia centre panel as described in paragraphs **(see illustrations 5.1a and 5.1b)**.

5 Disconnect the wiring plugs from the back of the starter button and the12v power outlet.

6 Using two small screwdrivers, release the switch securing tabs, and remove it from the facia centre panel.

7 Refitting is a reversal of removal.

Hazard warning light switch

8 Using a plastic trim tool prise free the centre air distribution vent **(see illustration)**.

9 Disconnect the wiring plug from the back of the combined hazard warning light/central locking switch unit.

10 Release the locking tabs from the rear of the panel and then release the switch securing tabs. Remove the switch **(see illustrations)**. The hazard warning light switch and central door locking switch are a combined unit and can not be separated.

11 Refitting is a reversal of removal.

Central locking switch

12 The switch is integrated into the hazard warning switch and is removed with hazard warning switch as described above.

Steering column switches

Note: *The steering column switch assembly includes the rotary connector ('clockspring') for the drivers airbag and the steering wheel position sensor. It is a complete single assembly and if any one component is faulty the entire assembly must be replaced.*

13 Remove the upper and lower steering column cowls **(see illustrations)**.

14 Disconnect the battery and then remove the steering wheel as described in Chapter 10, Section 14.

15 The steering column switch assembly is retained by a single screw. Slacken the screw and use a flat blade screwdriver to gently prise apart the locking clamp. Partially free the switch assembly from the steering column and disconnect the wiring plugs **(see illustrations)**.

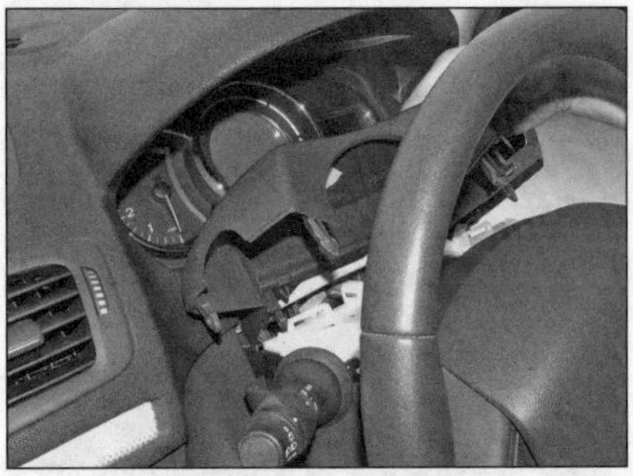

5.13a Remove the upper and then...

5.13b ...the lower cowl

5.15a Use a screwdriver to release the switch assembly. Note the tape holding the 'clockspring' in position

5.15b Disconnect the wiring plugs

5.18a Slide the switch down to remove it

16 Refitting is a reversal of removal.

Radio remote controls

17 Raise the steering column and remove the screws from the shroud. Lower the column and remove the upper section of the column shroud.

18 Remove the single retaining screw and unclip the control. Disconnect the wiring plug as the control is removed **(see illustrations)**.

19 Refitting is a reversal of removal.

Blower and air conditioning switches

20 These switches are built into the heater control panel – remove the panel as described in Chapter 3, Section 11.

Headlight adjuster switch

21 Remove the driver's side lower facia panel as described in Chapter 11.

5.27 Disconnect the wiring plug

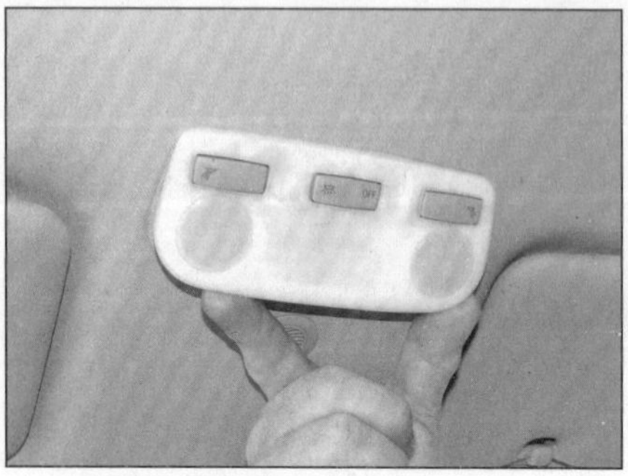

5.35a Prise the lamp free and...

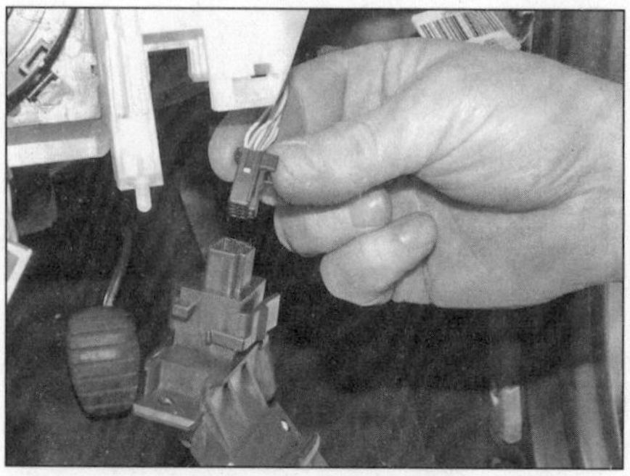

5.18b Disconnect the wiring plug

22 Disconnect the wiring plugs from the rear of the panel.

23 Release the switch retaining tabs from the back, then remove the switch assembly from the front.

24 Refitting is a reversal of removal.

Instrument dimmer switch

25 The instrument dimmer switch is integrated into the headlight adjuster switch and is removed with the switch.

Passenger airbag selector switch

Warning: Disconnect the battery negative lead (see 'Disconnecting the battery' in Chapter 5A), then wait for five minutes before proceeding. If this waiting period is not observed, there is danger of activating the passenger airbag.

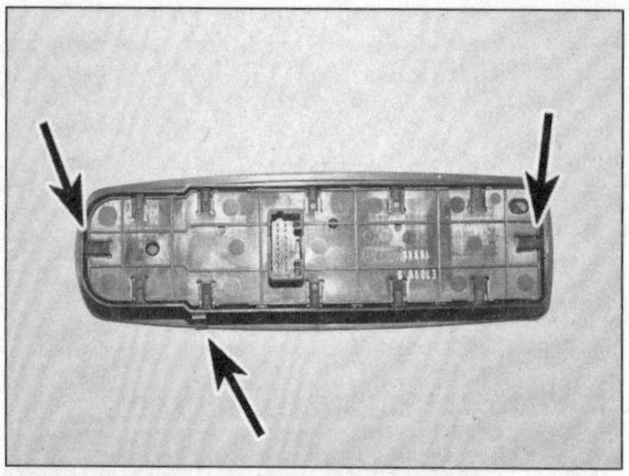

5.30 With the switch removed, note the location of the locking tabs (arrowed). Front door switch shown, but the rear is similar

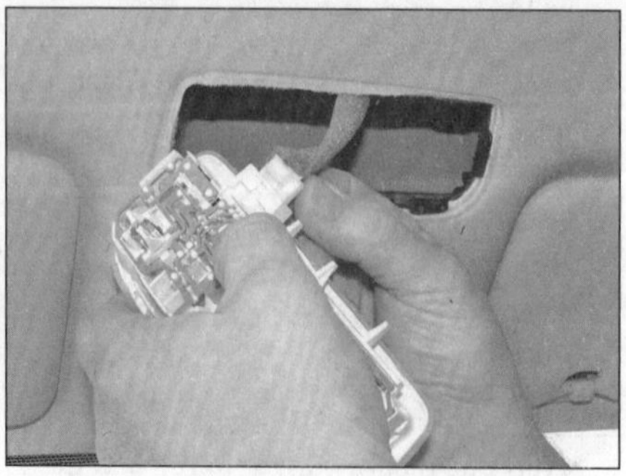

5.35b ...disconnect the wiring plug

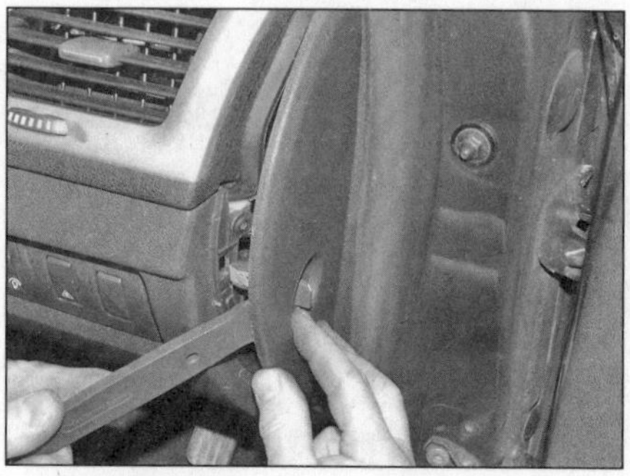

5.26 Prise the end panel free

26 Unclip the facia end cover panel at the driver's side **(see illustration)**.

27 Disconnect the wiring plug from the switch**(see illustration)** then unclip and push out the switch.

28 Refitting is a reversal of removal. Reconnect the switch before reconnecting the battery.

Electric window switches

29 It should be possible to prise up the power window switches from the door trim panel, however we found this impossible.

30 Remove the door trim panel as described in Chapter 11, Section 13 and then push the switch free from the rear **(see illustration)**.

31 Refitting is a reversal of removal.

Electric mirror switch

32 The switch is integrated into the electric window switch and is removed with window switch panel as described above. It is not available as a separate item.

Interior light switches

33 The interior/courtesy lights are operated by the interior multiplex unit (UCH), using information from the central locking system. Conventional switches are therefore not used.

34 The switches to turn on or off the courtesy lights and for the reading lights are part of the interior lamp assembly.

35 Prise free the lamp and disconnect the wiring plug **(see illustrations)**. If any of the switches are faulty the complete lamp assembly must be replaced.

Heated rear window switch

36 The switch is built into the heater control panel. It is not available as a separate part – remove the panel as described in Chapter 3.

Heated seat switches

37 Remove the single screw from the seat side trim panel and then using a plastic trim tool prise free the side panel.

38 Disconnect the heated seat wiring plugs, then use a small screwdriver to prise the switch out.

39 Refitting is a reversal of removal.

5.46a Remove the screw (arrowed)

Sunroof switch

40 Prise the switch panel out of the headlining, and disconnect the wiring plug from it.
41 Use a small screwdriver, release the tabs around the switch body, and remove it from the panel.
42 Refitting is a reversal of removal.

Brake light switch

43 The brake light switch is removed as described in Chapter 9.

Handbrake warning light switch

44 Remove the centre console as described in Chapter 11, Section 23.
45 Disconnect the wiring plug from the warning light switch.
46 Pull back the carpet as necessary. Remove the securing screw and then remove the switch **(see illustrations)**.
47 Refitting is a reversal of removal. Check the switch operation before refitting the centre console.

Parking aid switch

48 Prise free the gear lever gaiter and the release the surrounding trim panel.
49 Disconnect the wiring connector, release the retaining clips and remove the switch.
50 Refitting is a reversal of removal.

6 Bulbs (exterior lights) – renewal

General

1 Whenever a bulb is renewed, note the following points.

a) *Disconnect the battery negative lead, or at least make sure that the lighting circuit is switched off, before starting work.*
b) *Remember that if the light has recently been in use, the bulb may be extremely hot.*
c) *Always check the bulb contacts and/or holder (as applicable). Ensure that there is clean metal-to-metal contact between the bulb contacts and the contacts in the holder, and/or the holder and the wiring plug. Clean off any corrosion or dirt before fitting a new bulb.*
d) *Ensure that the new bulb is of the correct rating and that it is completely clean before fitting; this applies particularly to headlight bulbs.*

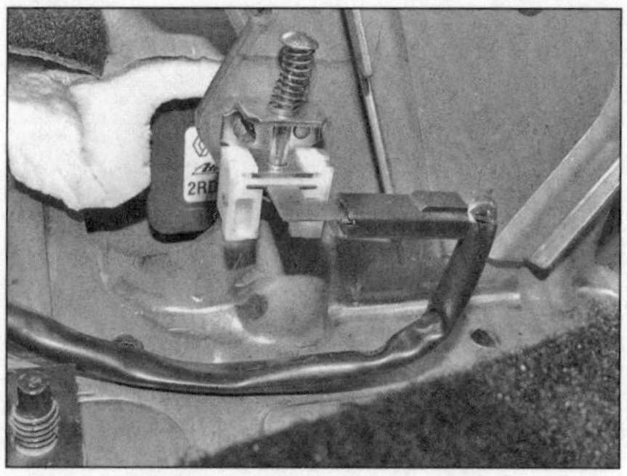

5.46b Remove the switch

Headlight (halogen)

Note: *The headlight lenses are plastic, and may melt if the correct bulbs are not fitted.*
2 On all models pull up the locking peg and remove the 2 mounting bolts **(see illustrations)**. Slide the headlight forwards to access the bulbs.
3 Remove the relevant round cover from the back of the light unit . The inner, rubber, cover is for the main beam bulb, with the outer plastic one for the dipped beam **(see illustrations)**.
4 Bulb removal itself is the same for either bulb. Disconnect the wiring plug from the bulb, then unhook the wire retaining clip, fold it down, and withdraw the bulb **(see illustrations)**.
5 When handling the new bulb, use a tissue or clean cloth to avoid touching the glass with the fingers; moisture and grease from the skin

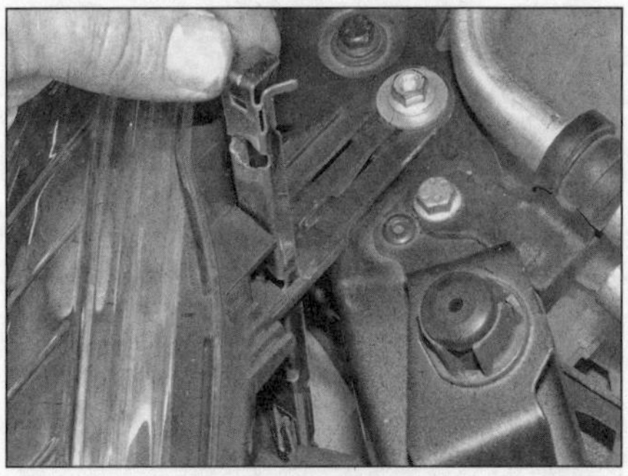

6.2a Pull up the locking peg to release the headlight

6.2b The locking peg doubles up as a spanner to remove the bolts

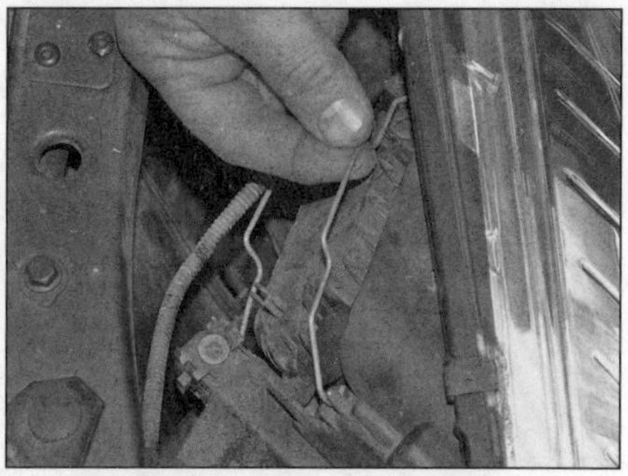

6.3a Release the spring clips and...

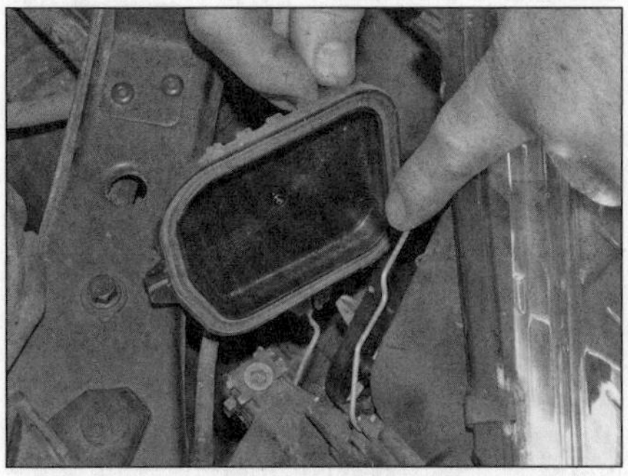

6.3b ...remove the cover from the dipped beam bulb

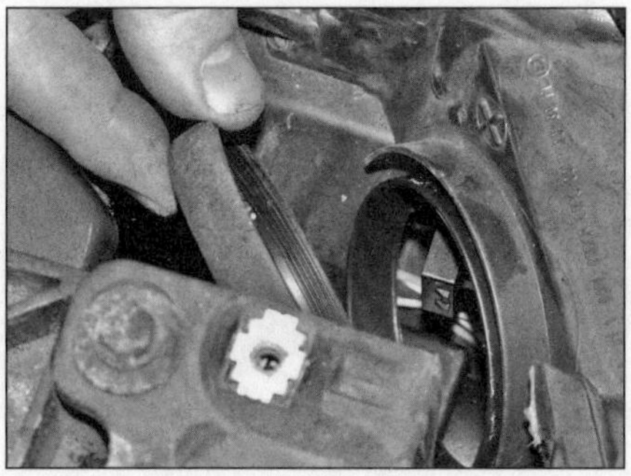

6.3c Pull off the rubber cover from the main beam bulb

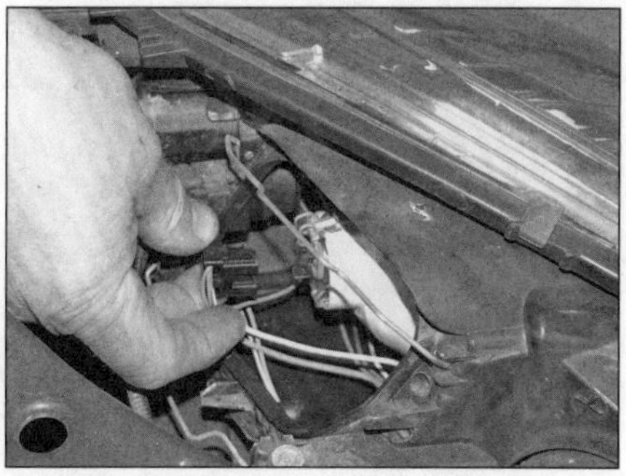

6.4a Disconnect the wiring plug...

6.4b ....release the spring clips...

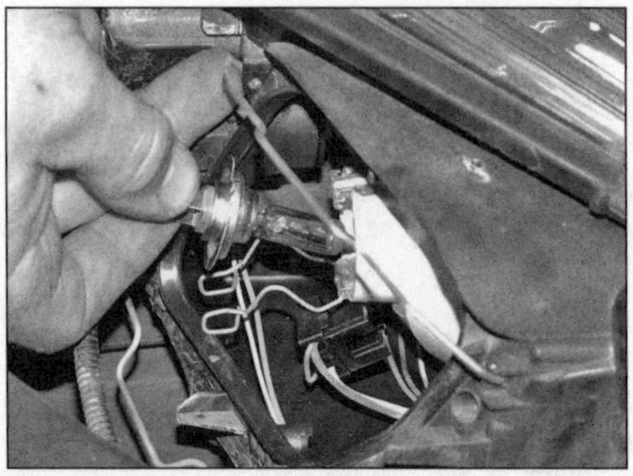

6.4c ...and withdraw the bulb

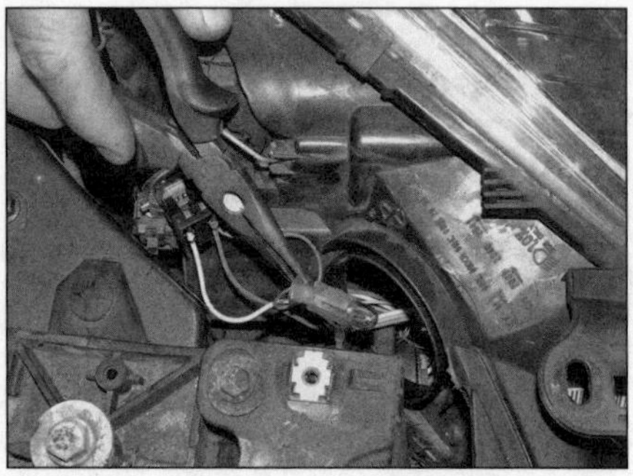

6.14 Pliers can be used to release the bulb

can cause blackening and rapid failure of this type of bulb.

6 Refitting is a reversal of removal.

Headlight (xenon)

Note: *Renewal of the main beam bulb is as described for the halogen light previously in this Section – for renewal of the xenon dipped beam bulb, proceed as follows.*

Warning: Before carrying out any operations on xenon headlight units, it is recommended that protective gloves and safety glasses are worn. It is essential that the wiring connectors are disconnected from the rear of the headlight unit, then wait until the bulbs have cooled down before removal. DO NOT switch the headlights on with the bulb removed as it is harmful to the eyes.

7 Follow the procedure outlined above and pull the headlight unit forwards.

8 Swing the wire clip to the side, and remove the cover from the rear of the headlight unit.

9 Pull the bulb rearwards slightly and disconnect the wiring plug.

10 Rotate the bulb anti-clockwise about a quarter of a turn and withdraw it from the light unit. The external conductor of the bulb is fragile, take care not to damage or knock it.

11 When handling the new bulb, use a tissue or clean cloth to avoid touching the glass with the fingers; moisture and grease from the skin can cause blackening and rapid failure of this type of bulb.

12 Refitting is a reversal of removal. When a Xenon bulb has been replaced headlight alignment should be checked and adjusted with a suitable diagnostic tool. Entrust this task to a Renault dealer or suitably equipped garage.

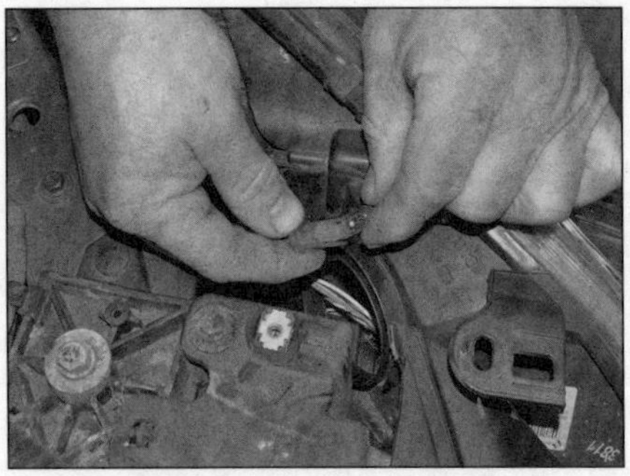

6.15 Pull the bulb from the bulb holder

6.19 Remove the direction indicator bulb

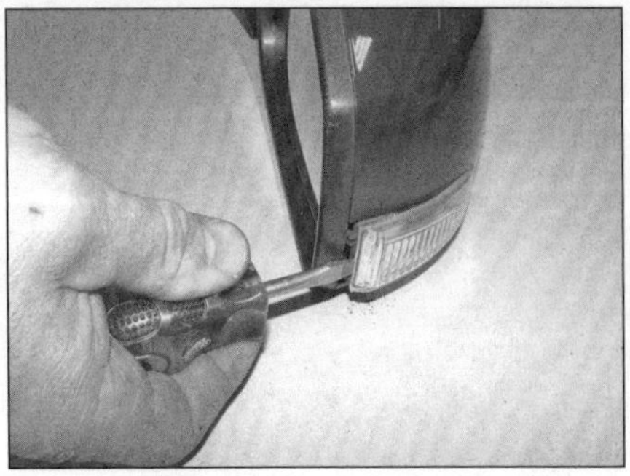

6.27 Prise the lamp free from the door mirror

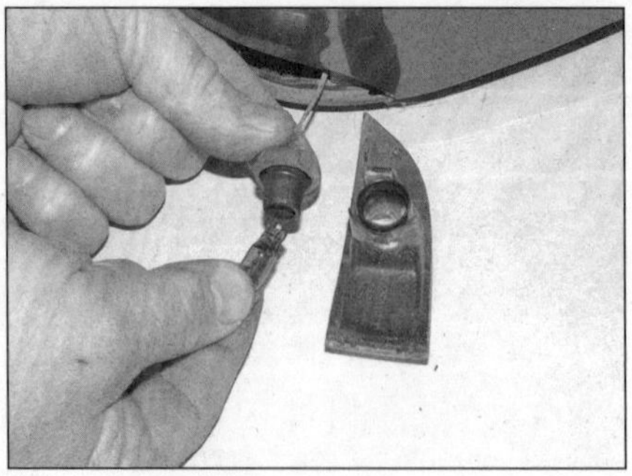

6.28 Remove the bulb from the bulb holder

Front sidelight

13 Remove the main beam cover from the rear of the headlight unit, as described previously in this Section.

14 Withdraw the bulbholder from the rear of the headlight assembly **(see illustration)**.

15 The bulb is a push-fit (capless) in the bulbholder **(see illustration)**.

16 Refitting is a reversal of removal.

Front indicator

17 The indicator bulb is the outermost one in the headlight unit.

18 Gain access to the back of the headlight as described in paragraph 2.

19 The bulbholder has a flat 'handle' on the back, which makes it easier to twist anti-clockwise for removal **(see illustration)**.

20 With the bulbholder removed, twist and remove the indicator bulb.

21 Refitting is a reversal of removal.

Daytime running lights

22 The daytime running lights are mounted inboard of the direction indicators.

23 Remove the sealing cover.

24 Release the bulb by turning it a quarter turn anti-clockwise. Disconnect the wiring plug.

25 Refitting is a reversal of removal.

Front indicator side repeater

26 The light unit is mounted in the door mirror.

27 Use a suitable plastic trim tool or small screwdriver and prise the lamp free by unhooking the narrow (forward) end of the lamp first **(see illustration)**.

28 Twist the bulb holder free from the lamp and then pull out the wedge-base bulb **(see illustration)** from the bulb holder.

29 Refitting is a reversal of removal.

Front foglight

30 Remove the front bumper as described in Chapter 11, Section 6 and then disconnect the wiring plug from the base of the foglight **(see illustration)**.

31 Twist the wiring socket anti-clockwise, and withdraw the bulb from the light unit – note that the wiring socket is integral with the bulb **(see illustration)**.

6.30 Disconnect the wiring plug

6.31 Remove the bulb

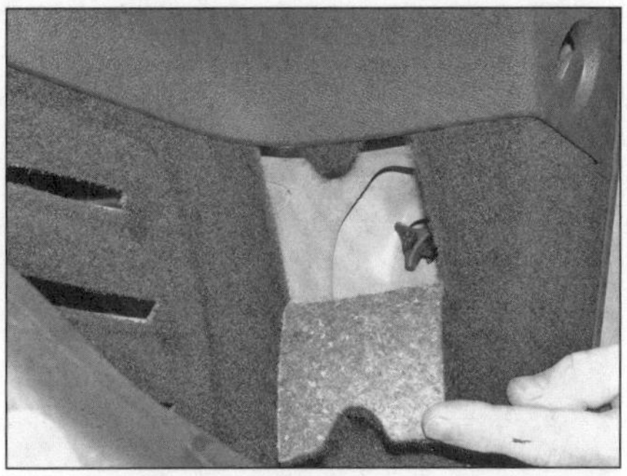

6.35a Remove the access panels (Estate shown)

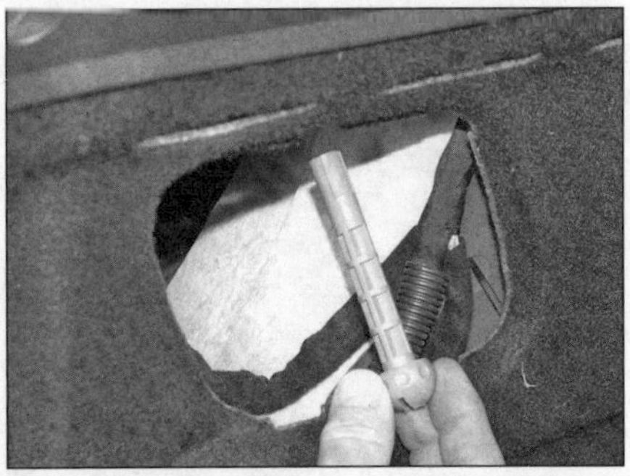

6.35b Unscrew to plastic 'nuts' (Hatchback shown)

6.36a Removing the rear wing mounted lamp on Hatchback models...

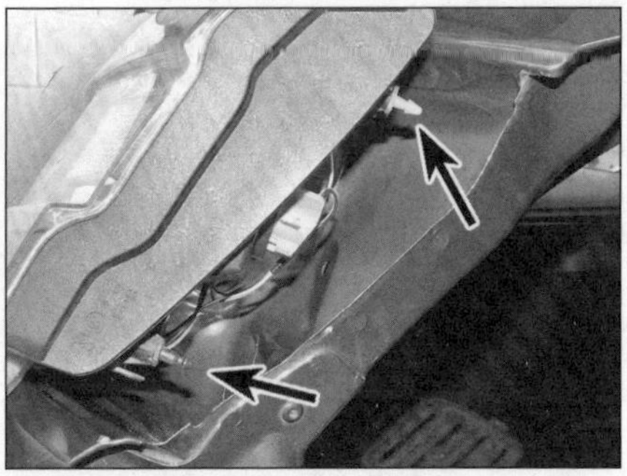

6.36b ...and on Estate models. Note the locating pegs (arrowed)

32 When handling the new bulb, use a tissue or clean cloth to avoid touching the glass with the fingers; moisture and grease from the skin can cause blackening and rapid failure of this type of bulb. If the glass is accidentally touched, wipe it clean using methylated spirit.

33 Refitting is a reversal of removal.

Rear light cluster

34 The direction indicators, brake and side lights are wing mounted. The fog, reversing and additional side light are mounted on the tailgate. On Coupe models all rear lights are wing mounted. The method of removal and replacement is similar for all models.

35 Open the tailgate, remove or lower the access flaps and then unscrew the plastic fixing nuts **(see illustrations)**.

36 Unhook the lamp and pull it from the rear wing. Disconnect the wiring plug and then release the bulb holder from the lamp by opening the retaining clips **(see illustrations)**.

37 Remove the bulb by depressing it slightly and then rotating it anti-clockwise **(see illustration)**.

38 To remove the tailgate mounted bulbs open the tailgate and remove the access cover **(see illustrations)**.

39 Remove the now exposed mounting bolts and release the lamp from the tailgate **(see illustrations)**.

6.36c Disconnect the wiring plug...

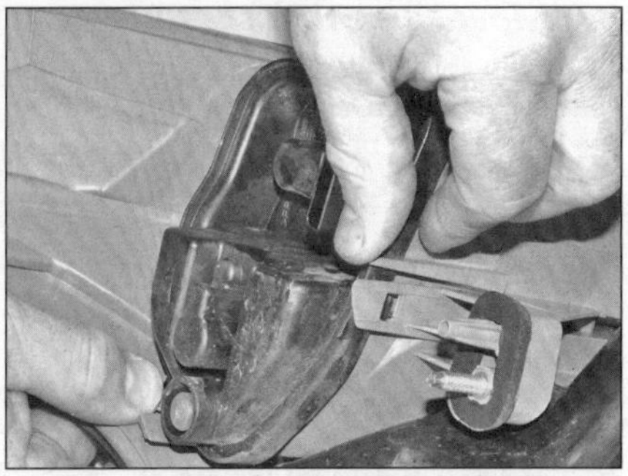

6.36d ...release the locking tabs and...

6.36e ...remove the bulb holder (Hatchback model shown)

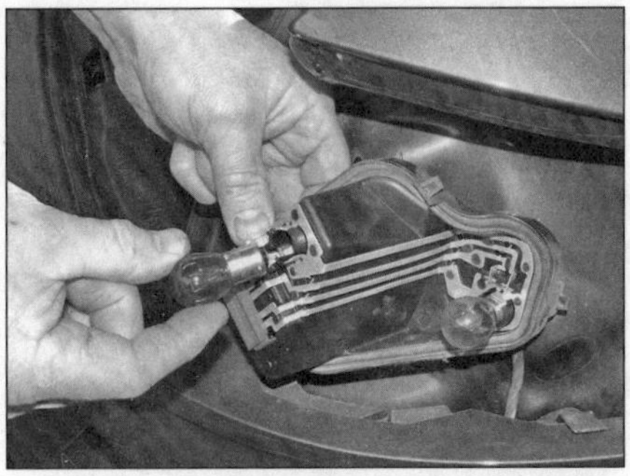

6.37 Remove the appropriate bulb from the bulb holder (Estate model shown)

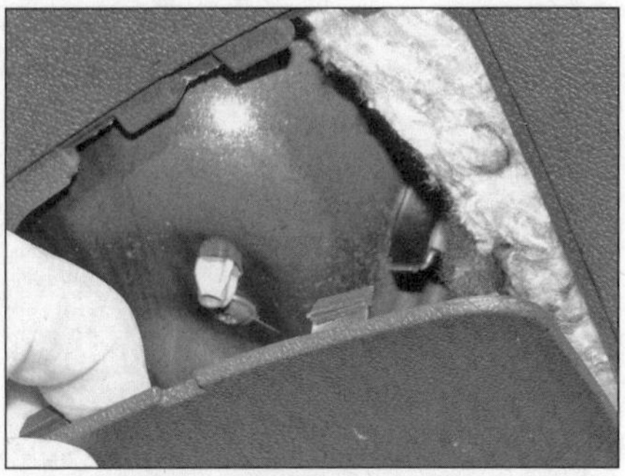

6.38a Removing the cover on Hatchback models...

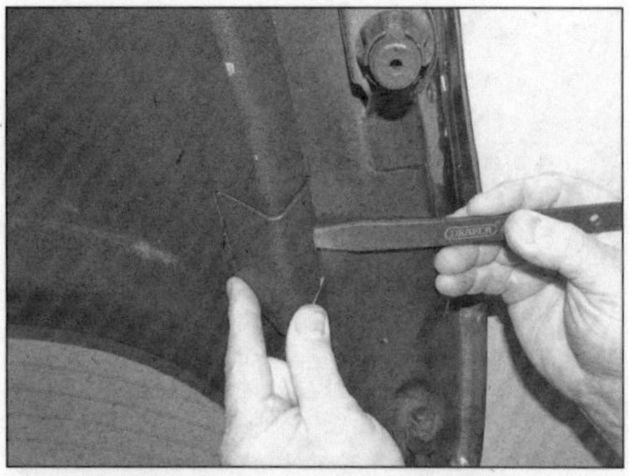

6.38b ...and on Estate models

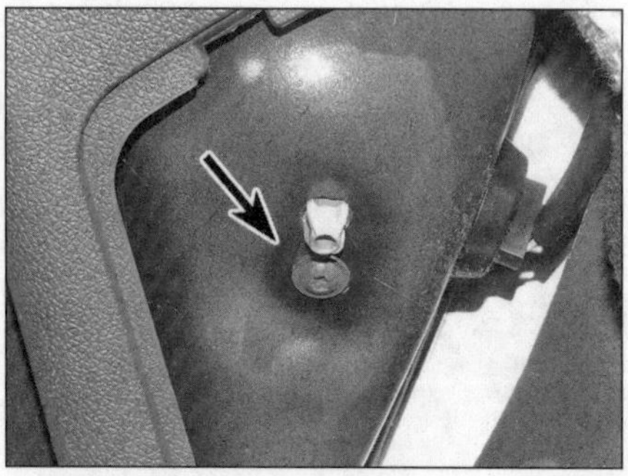

6.39a Remove the inner fixing screw (arrowed)...

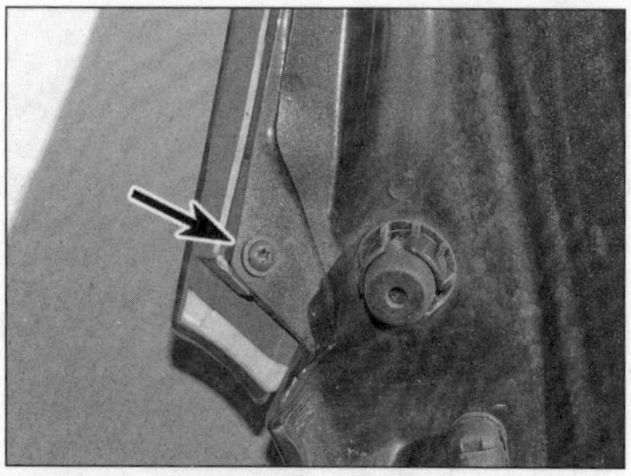

6.39b ...and on Hatchback models the outer screw (arrowed)

6.43 Remove the lamp from the tailgate

6.44a Remove the lens and...

6.44b ...pull out the bulb

40 Rotate the bulb holders anti-clockwise to access the bulbs. Remove the appropriate bulb by depressing it slightly and then rotating it anti-clockwise.

41 Refitting is a reversal of removal.

High-level stop-light

42 The 'bulbs' in the high-level stop-light are non-renewable LEDs (Light Emitting Diodes). The light unit can be removed as described in Section 8.

Rear number plate light

43 Prise out the light unit with a small screwdriver **(see illustration)**.

44 Prise off the lens from the light, for access to the bulb. Pull the wedge type bulb from the lamp and remove it **(see illustrations)**.

45 Refitting is a reversal of removal.

7 Bulbs (interior lights) – renewal

General

1 Refer to Section 6, paragraph 1.

Interior light

2 Unclip the light unit lens for access to the bulbs. Pull the bulb to remove it **(see illustrations 5.35a and 5.35b)**.

3 Refitting is a reversal of removal.

Footwell light

4 Prise out the light unit from the base of the door trim panel, and disconnect the wiring plug **(see illustration)**.

5 Pull out the wedge-base bulb, and remove it.

6 Refitting is a reversal of removal.

Instrument panel and warning lights

7 The instrument panel is a 'solid-state' type, which means the 'bulbs' are non-renewable LEDs. The instrument panel is removed as described in Section 11.

Auxiliary display illumination

8 Refer to Section 12.

Glovebox light

9 Remove the glovebox as described in Chapter 11, Section 22.

10 Prise down the light unit, then disconnect its wiring plug and remove it **(see illustration)**. Unclip the festoon-type bulb from its contacts.

11 Refitting is a reversal of removal.

Heater control illumination

12 A single bulb fitted to the control panel provides the panel illumination. Remove the control panel as described in Chapter 3.

13 Turn the panel over and using long nose pliers rotate the bulb holder and remove it from the control panel **(see illustration)**. The bulb is renewed with the bulb holder.

14 Refitting is a reversal of removal.

Luggage compartment light

15 Unclip the light from its location in the luggage compartment, then disconnect the wiring plug and remove it.

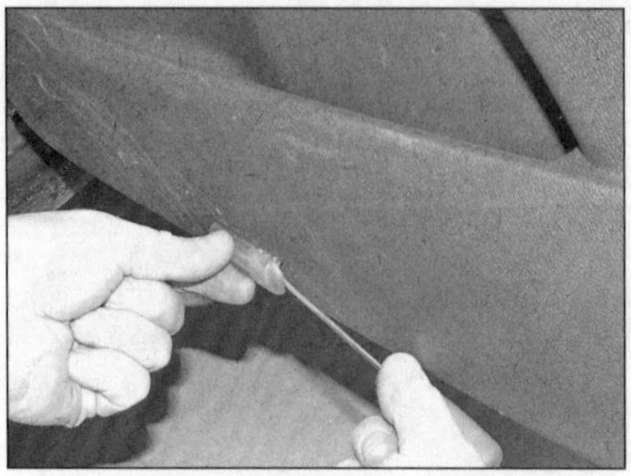

7.4 Prise the lamp from the door panel

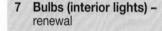

7.10 Prise free the glovebox lamp

16 Unclip the lens, then unclip and remove the festoon bulb.

17 Refitting is a reversal of removal.

8 Exterior light units – removal and refitting

Note: *Before removing any light, at least make sure the light concerned is switched off, and that the ignition is also off (remove the keycard). Ideally, disconnect the battery negative lead, and position the lead away from the battery (also see 'Disconnecting the battery').*

Headlight

Warning: Before carrying out any operations on xenon headlight units, it is recommended that protective gloves and safety glasses are worn. It is essential that the wiring connectors are disconnected from the rear of the headlight unit, then wait until the bulbs have cooled down before removal. DO NOT switch the headlights on with the bulb removed, as it is harmful to the eyes.

1 Remove the front bumper as described in Chapter 11, Section 6.

2 Remove the locking clip and the two headlight mounting screws **(see illustration 6.2a and 6.2b)**. Slide the headlight unit forward until it hits the stops built into the support panel. Rock slightly and then lift the headlight from the panel. Turn the headlight to access the wiring plug and then disconnect

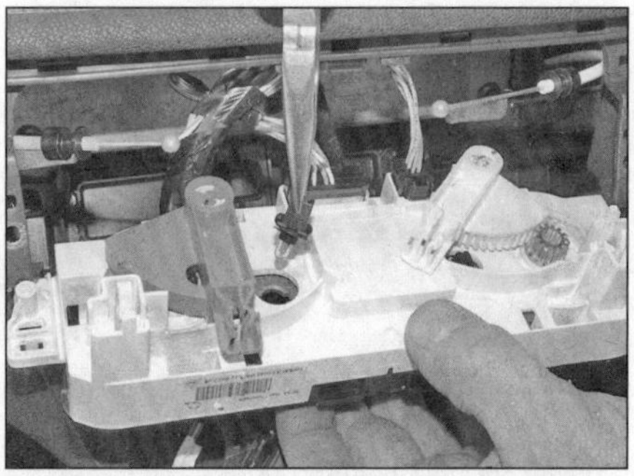

7.13 Remove the bulb holder using pliers

the wiring plugs from the back of the light **(see illustration)**. Remove the headlight

3 Refitting is a reversal of removal.

4 On completion, the headlight beam alignment should be checked, ideally using optical setting equipment. This check should be carried out by a Renault dealer or a suitably-equipped garage (see Section 10). Models fitted with Xenon headlights will require the alignment adjusted with suitable diagnostic equipment.

Front foglight

5 Remove the front bumper as described in Chapter 11, Section 6. Disconnect the wiring plug.

6 Unscrew the two foglight mounting bolts, and remove the light from the bumper **(see illustration)**.

7 Refitting is a reversal of removal. It is advisable to have the foglight beam alignment checked on completion.

8.2 Disconnect the headlight wiring plugs (one shown, but two fitted)

Front indicator side repeater

8 The procedure is described in the bulb renewal sequence in Section 6.

Rear light cluster

9 The procedure is described in the bulb renewal sequence in Section 6.

10 Refitting is a reversal of removal.

High-level stop-light

Hatchback and Estate

11 Open the tailgate and unclip the top section of the tailgate window trim panel **(see illustration)**.

12 Using a small screwdriver, press the retaining lugs at either end of the light unit to release it from the tailgate **(see illustrations)**.

13 Disconnect the washer jet tubing and the wiring plug, and remove the light completely **(see illustrations)**.

8.6 Remove the screws (arrowed)

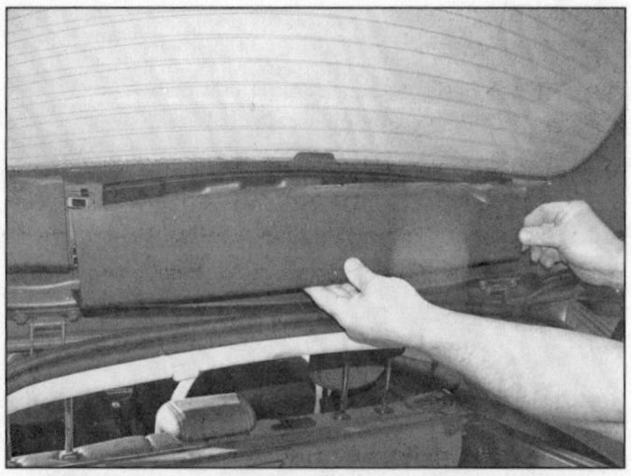

8.11 Remove the upper centre panel

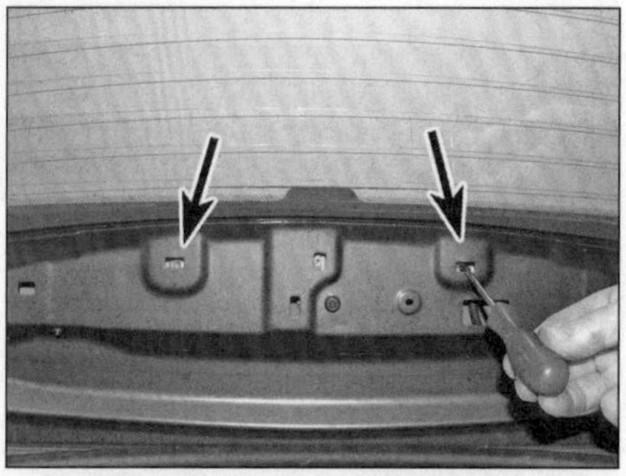

8.12a Release the retaining lugs (arrowed) using a small screwdriver...

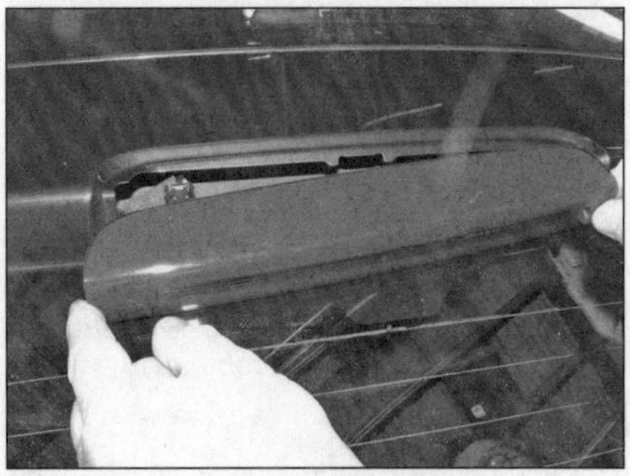

8.12b ...and release the lamp

8.13a Disconnect the wiring plug...

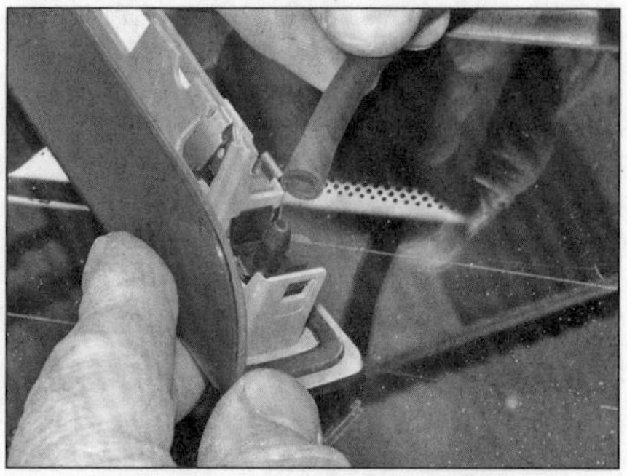

8.13b ...and the washer jet hose

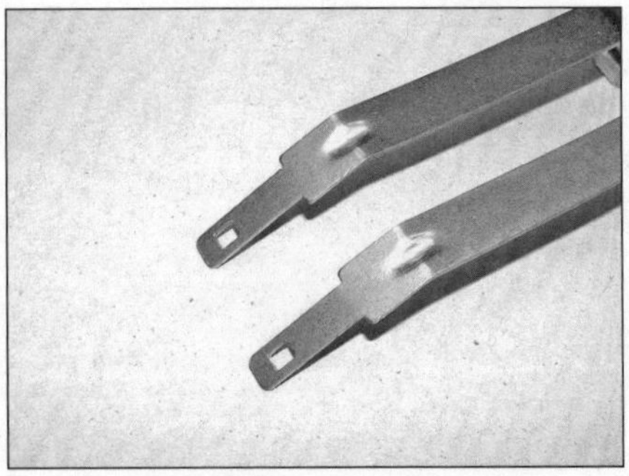

11.2 The Renault special tools

14 Other than the washer jet, which can be removed as described in Section 20, the light unit cannot be dismantled further.
15 Refitting is a reversal of removal.

Coupe

16 Open the tailgate and carefully unclip the tailgate top centre trim panel and then remove both side sections.
17 Remove the foam blanking pads from the tailgate to access the spoiler retaining bolts.
18 Lift the spoiler from the tailgate. Disconnect the wiring plug and screen washer jet supply pipe from the spoiler as it is removed
19 Remove the two mounting screws, then squeeze together the two centre retaining tabs and lift out the light unit
20 Other than the washer jet, which can be removed as described in Section 20, the light unit cannot be dismantled further.
21 A new sealing kit will be required when refitting.

Rear number plate light

22 The procedure is described in the bulb renewal sequence, in Section 6.

9 Interior light units – removal and refitting

Interior lights

1 The procedure is described in the switch renewal sequence, in Section 5.

Glovebox light

2 The procedure is described in the bulb renewal sequence, in Section 7.

Footwell lights

3 The procedure is described in the bulb renewal sequence, in Section 7.

Luggage compartment light

4 The procedure is described in the bulb renewal sequence, in Section 7.

10 Headlight beam alignment – general information

Accurate adjustment of the headlight beam is only possible using optical beam-setting equipment, and this work should therefore be carried out by a Renault dealer or suitably-equipped workshop.

To make a temporary adjustment of the headlights, position the car on a level surface 10 metres from a wall. The tyres must all be at the correct pressure, and the manual adjustment switch inside the car set at 0. Use the adjuster screws at the rear of the headlight to reset the beams accordingly.

All models have a headlight beam manual adjustment control, which allows the aim of the headlights to be adjusted to compensate for variation in the car's payload. The aim is altered by means of facia-mounted switch, which controls electric adjuster motors located in the rear of the headlight assemblies.

Models with xenon headlights have an automatic levelling system. If a fault occurs in the system, a warning light will show up on the instrument panel, and the headlights will be angled down to avoid dazzling oncoming traffic. If this happens, the driving speed must be adjusted accordingly to allow for decreased visibility.

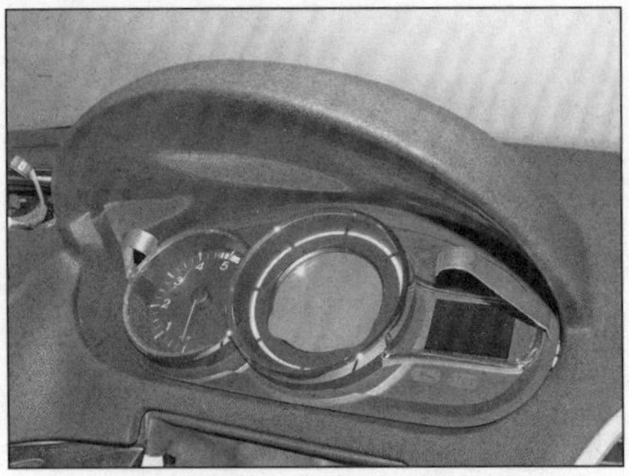

11.4a Insert the tools...

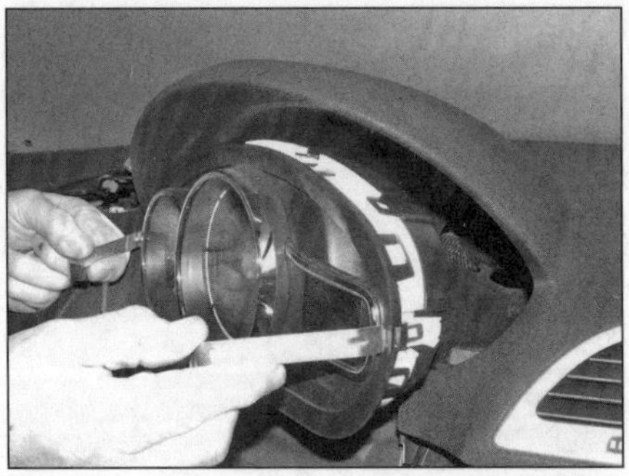

11.4b ...and release the instrument panel

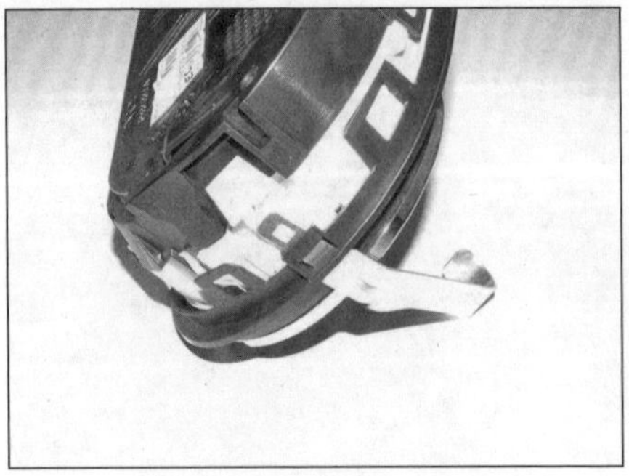

11.4c Note how the tools engage into the instrument panel

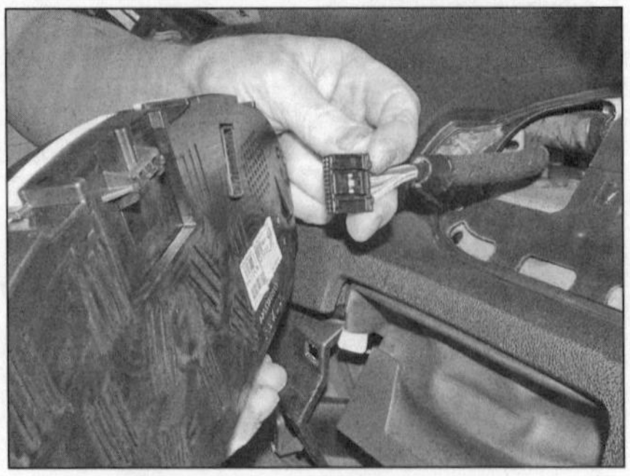

11.5 Disconnect the wiring plug

11 Instrument panel – removal and refitting

Note: *If the instrument panel is being replaced a suitable diagnostic tool will be required to download the programmed information from the old panel. This must then be uploaded to the replacement instrument panel.*

Removal

1 Disconnect the battery negative lead, and move the lead away from the battery (see *Disconnecting the battery*).
2 Fully lower the steering column and where available insert Renault special tool Ms 1872 **(see illustration)** into the slots provided.
3 Where the special tool is not available it may be possible to fabricate a suitable tool, note however that the factory tool is not expensive.
4 Insert the tools into the panel and gently lever them to release the locking clips **(see illustrations)**.
5 Lift out the panel and disconnect the wiring plug **(see illustration)**.

Refitting

6 Refitting is a reversal of removal.

12 Auxiliary display – removal and refitting

Note: *The auxiliary display is fitted in the top of the facia panel at the centre. This display is for the radio, temperature, clock and, where fitted, satellite navigation system.*
Note: *Replacement displays must be initialised with a suitable diagnostic tool.*

Removal

1 Disconnect the battery negative lead, and move the lead away from the battery (see *Disconnecting the battery*).

2 Using a plastic trim tool, prise free the mounting panel. On models fitted with a satellite navigation system prise free the trim panel **(see illustrations)**.
3 Pull the display forward and disconnect the wiring plug.
4 On models with satellite navigation remove the 2 mounting screws, pull the display forward and disconnect the wiring plug **(see illustrations)**.
5 On models with a standard display unit unclip and remove the facia top panel.

Refitting

6 Refitting is a reversal of removal.

13 Outside air temperature sensor – removal and refitting

Removal

1 The exterior temperature sensor is located in the left-hand exterior mirror.
2 Remove the mirror glass, the motor and the mirror front shell as described in Chapter 11, Section 16.
3 Unclip the sensor from its mounting on the mirror body **(see illustration)**.
4 No wiring plug is provided, so the two sensor wires have to be cut to remove the sensor. When doing this, leave as much wire as possible on the car, to make fitting the new sensor easier.

Refitting

5 Refitting is a reversal of removal. Solder the new sensor wires to the old ones, observing the wire colour-coding, and insulate the two joints with tape or heat-shrink tubing.

14 Rain sensor and automatic headlight sensor – removal and refitting

Note: *This sensor is not really intended for DIY removal and refitting. It works through a clear gel coating on the inside of the windscreen, which if damaged or contaminated in any way will result in faulty operation of the sensor.*

General information

1 The sensor used to automatically switch on the headlights and wipers, on models so equipped, consists of several photo-electric cells fitted at the top of the windscreen, detecting the amount of light coming through. If the light is refracted by raindrops on the glass, the sensor signals the interior multiplex module to operate the wipers, independently of the driver. Similarly, if the light level is reduced (as in the evening, or when entering a tunnel, for example), the headlights are automatically switched on (and then off again, if the light level increases).
2 Since the sensor is highly sensitive, it is vital for its correct operation that the windscreen

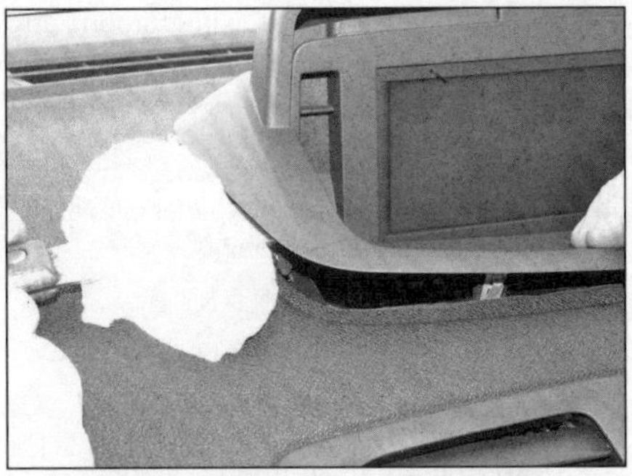

12.2a Protect the fascia, prise free...

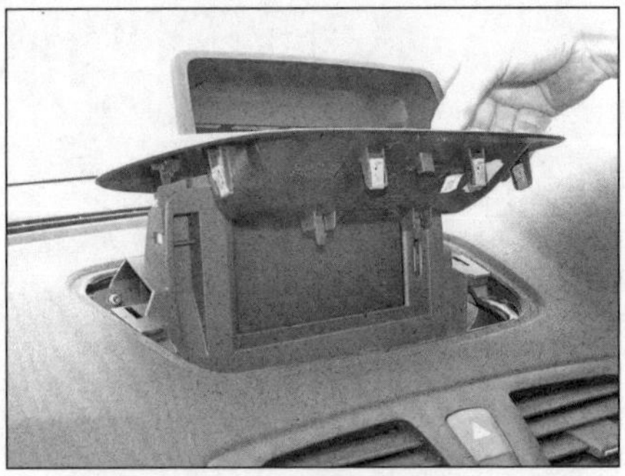

12.2b ...and remove the surround

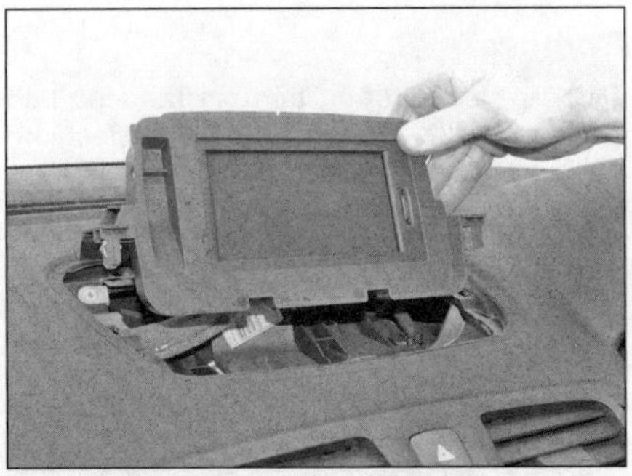

12.4a Lift out the display...

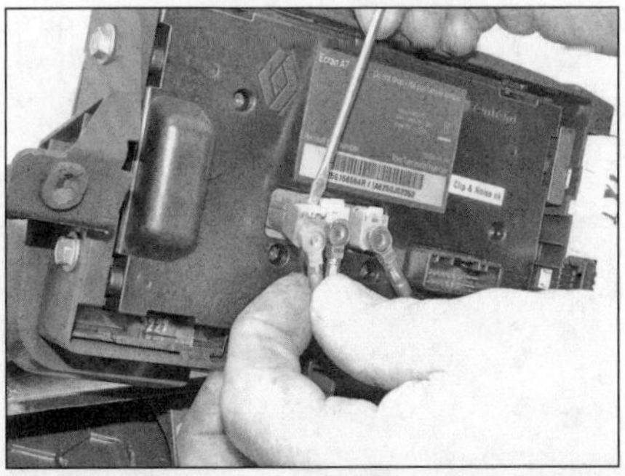

12.4b ...and disconnect the wiring plugs (satnav model shown)

be as clean as possible. Also, any damage to the glass, such as a stone chip in the vicinity of the sensor, will seriously affect it.

Removal

3 Unclip the front section of the interior mirror surround, then slide off the rear section **(see illustrations)**.
4 Use a small screwdriver to release the metal clip from either side of the sensor body, then carefully lower the sensor from the screen – this operation can result in damage to the clear

13.3 Remove the temperature sensor

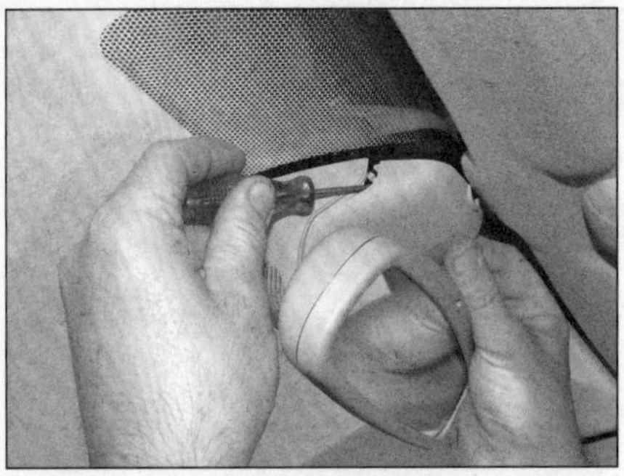

14.3a Unclip the front section of the interior mirror surround...

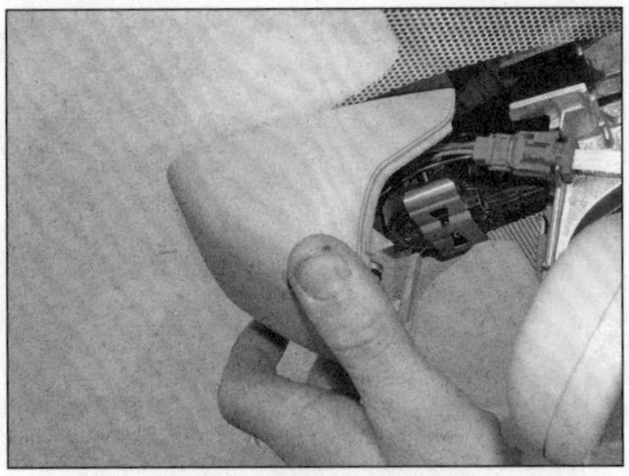

14.3b ...then slide the rear section towards the screen

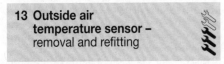

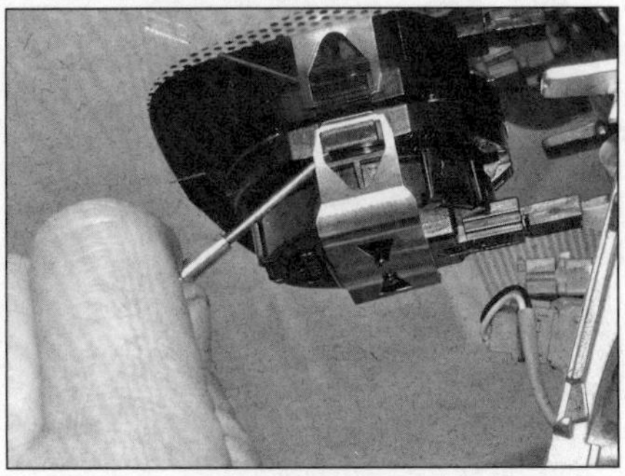

14.4a Release the metal clips either side...

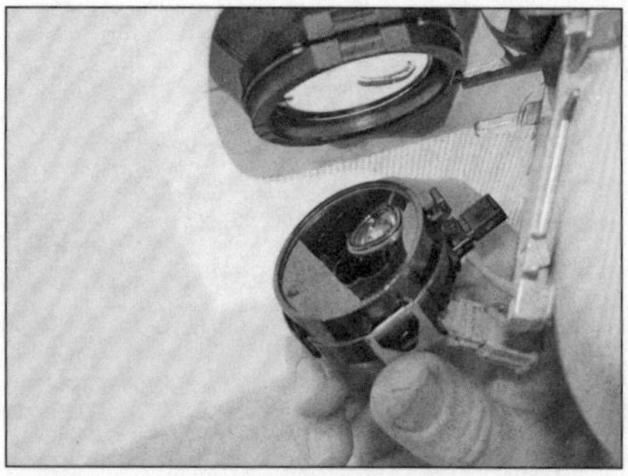

14.4b ...and separate the sensor from the base

gel in the sensor base, which might require a new base to be fitted **(see illustrations)**. Disconnect the wiring plug from the sensor and remove it.

5 The sensor base (which contains the clear gel) is stuck firmly to the windscreen, and there is a great risk of damage to the screen in removing it. This operation may be better entrusted to a Renault dealer, or possibly to a windscreen specialist. A new base must be fitted in conditions of absolute cleanliness, to avoid the sensor malfunctioning.

Refitting

6 Refitting is a reversal of removal.

15 Cigar lighter – removal and refitting

Removal

1 Unclip the centre front trim panel as described in Chapter 11, Section 22. Disconnect the wiring plug as the panel is removed.

16.3 Disconnect the wiring plug

16.4 Unbolt and remove the horns

17.1 Mark the resting position of the wiper blades with adhesive tape

17.3a Remove the cover

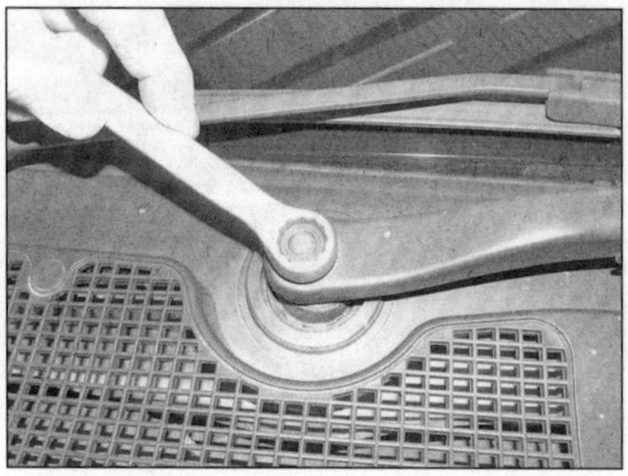

17.3b Unbolt the wiper arm

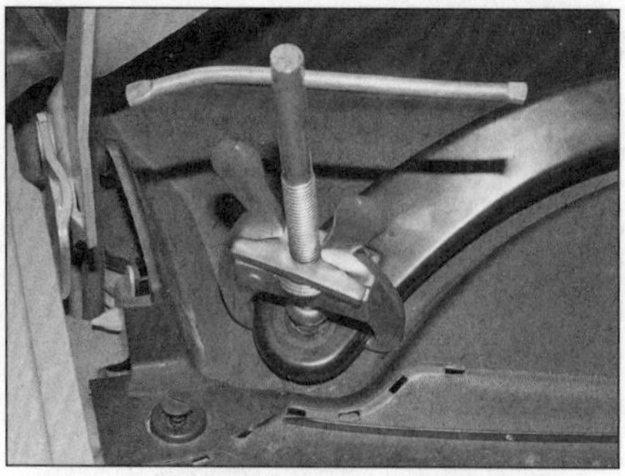

17.4 Use a suitable puller if necessary

2 Use a flat blade screwdriver and release the clips securing the cigar lighter to the panel.

Refitting

3 Refitting is a reversal of removal.

16 Horn – removal and refitting

Removal

1 Jack up and support the front of the vehicle (see *Jacking and vehicle support* in the reference section) and then remove the front bumper as described in Chapter 11, Section 6.

2 Unclip and remove the air deflector from the bonnet slam panel.

3 Disconnect the wiring plug from the horn **(see illustration)**.

4 Unscrew the mounting bolt, and withdraw the horn (or horns) from the front crossmember **(see illustration)**.

Refitting

5 Refitting is a reversal of removal.

17 Wiper arms – removal and refitting

Removal

1 The wiper motor should be in the parked position before removing the wiper arm. Mark the position of the blade on the glass with adhesive tape, as a guide to refitting **(see illustration)**.

2 If both windscreen wiper arms are to be removed, identify them so that they can be refitted in their original positions.

3 Lift the hinged cover (if working on the rear arm) or unclip the plastic cap, and remove the nut underneath securing the arm to the spindle **(see illustrations)**.

4 Pull or prise the arm from the spindle. If the arm is stubborn use a suitable puller to remove it **(see illustration)**. Take care not to damage the trim or paintwork.

Refitting

5 Refitting is a reversal of removal. Position the arms so that the blades align with the tape applied to the glass before removal.

18 Windscreen wiper motor and linkage – removal and refitting

Removal

1 Make sure that the wipers are in the parked position (switch the wipers on, then off).

2 Remove the windscreen wiper arms as described in Section 17.

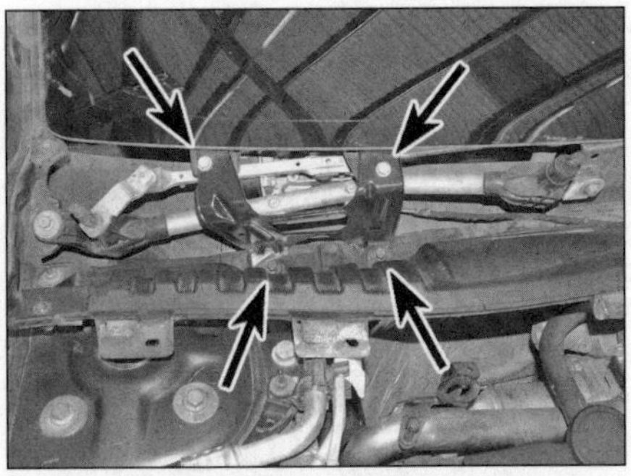

18.4a Remove the bolts (arrowed) and...

3 Remove the windscreen cowl panels, as described in Chapter 11, Section 8.
4 Unbolt and remove the centre support panel **(see illustrations)**.
5 Remove the two wiper linkage mounting bolts, then lift the linkage/motor assembly out. Disconnect the wiring plug from the wiper motor as the assembly is lifted out **(see illustrations)**.
6 To remove the motor, mark the relative positions of the motor shaft and crank, then unscrew the retaining nut and washer and free the wiper linkage from the motor spindle. Unscrew the three motor retaining bolts and separate the motor from the linkage.

Refitting

7 Refitting is a reversal of removal.

19 Tailgate wiper motor – removal and refitting

Removal

1 Remove the tailgate wiper arm with reference to Section 17.
2 With reference to Chapter 11, Section 15 remove the tailgate trim panel and then disconnect the wiring plug.
3 The motor is secured by three rivets, which must be drilled out. Take care not to damage the tailgate in the process **(see illustration)**. When fitting the new motor, it's likely that suitable self-tapping screws/bolts could be found to secure it – or use new rivets.

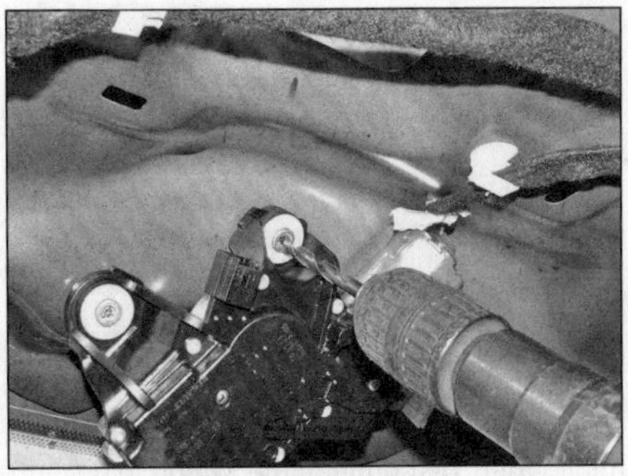

19.3 Drill out the rivets

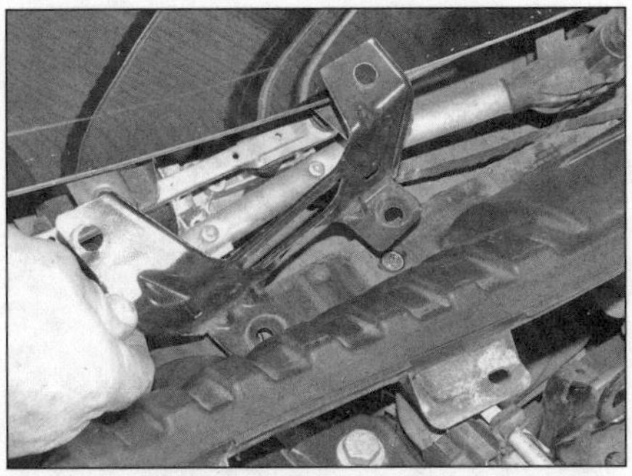

18.4b ...then remove the support bracket

18.5b ...disconnect the wiring plug...

Refitting

4 Refitting is a reversal of removal.

20 Windscreen/tailgate washer system components – removal and refitting

Washer jets

Windscreen

1 Open the bonnet. The windscreen washer jets are located under the rear edge of the bonnet, clipped into rectangular holes – use a small screwdriver to prise them out, taking care not to damage the paint **(see illustration)**.
2 Disconnect the washer tube from the jet, and remove it.
3 The washer supply tubing can be disconnected from the underbonnet T-pieces

20.1 Remove the washer jet

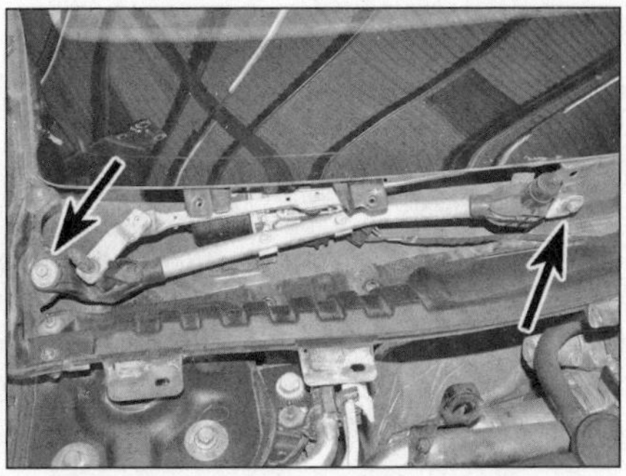

18.5a Remove the bolts (arrowed)...

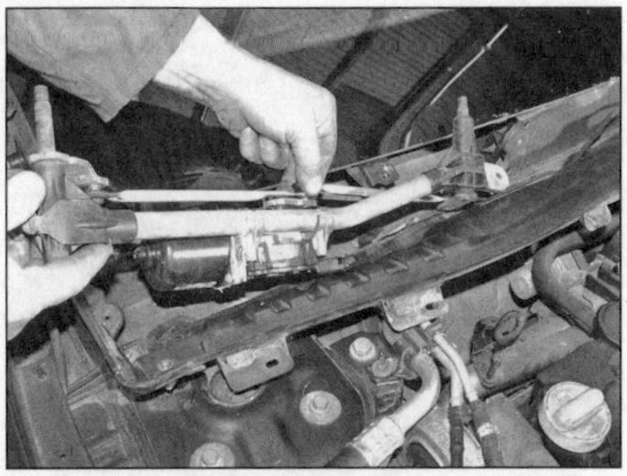

18.5c ...and then remove the linkage and motor assembly

and released from the mounting clips as required.
4 Refitting is a reversal of removal. Ensure that the jets are clipped in and the hoses reconnected securely.

Tailgate

Note: *The jet is part of the high level brake light and is not available as a separate part from Renault*

5 Remove the high-level stop-light as described in Section 8.
6 Use a small screwdriver to release the jet securing tabs, then withdraw it from the light unit **(see illustration)**
7 Refitting is a reversal of removal. Ensure that the jet is clipped in and the hose reconnected securely.

Washer reservoir

8 Remove the front bumper and front section of the wing liner as described in Chapter 11 Section 6.

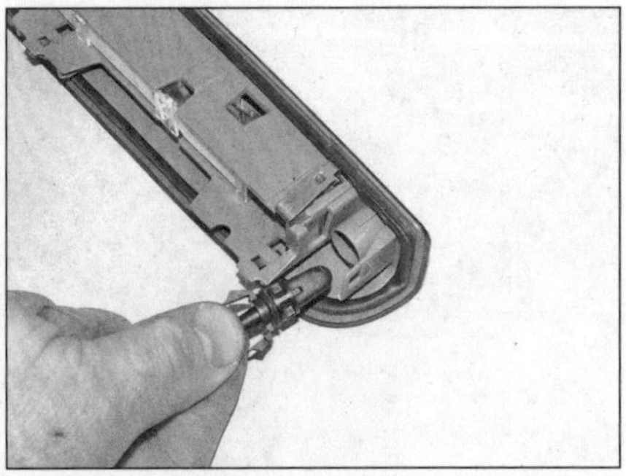

20.6 Remove the washer jet from the high level brake light

20.11 Remove the reservoir retaining bolt

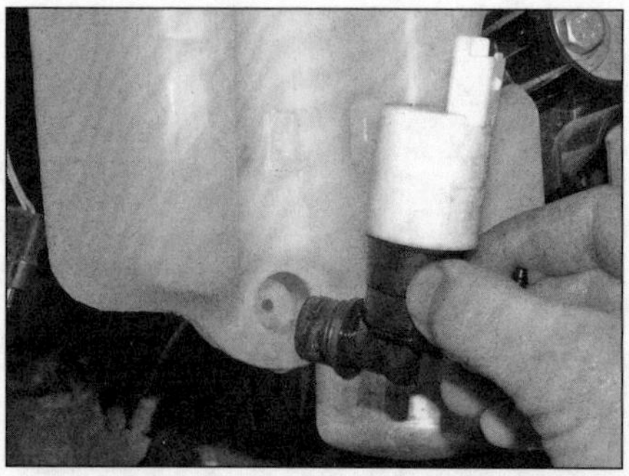

20.15a Pull the washer pump out of the reservoir

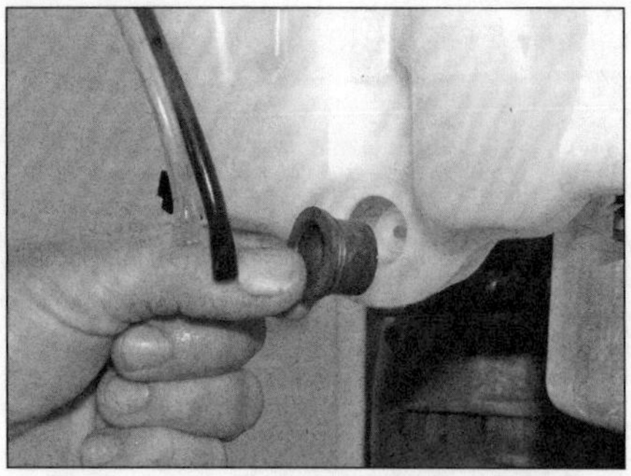

20.15b If the rubber grommet gets pulled out...

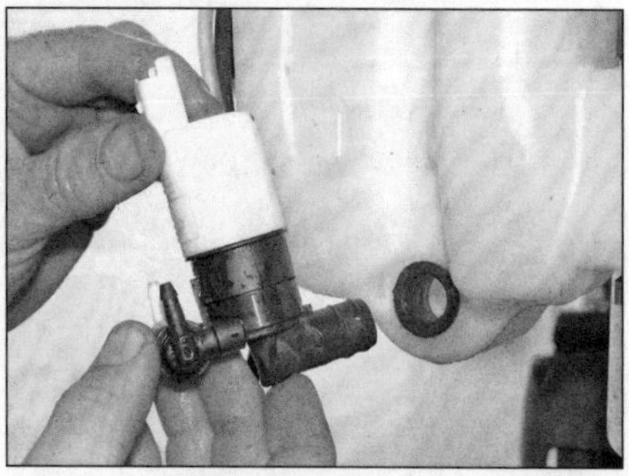

20.15c ...refit it before fitting the pump

9 Disconnect the wiring plug and washer tubes from the washer pump – anticipate losing the entire contents of the reservoir when the tubes are disconnected.

10 At the top of the reservoir, compress the concertina section of the filler neck, and pull it out.

11 Remove the mounting bolt and release the reservoir from under the front wing **(see illustration)**.

21.4 A small screwdriver can be used instead of the correct tools to release the audio unit

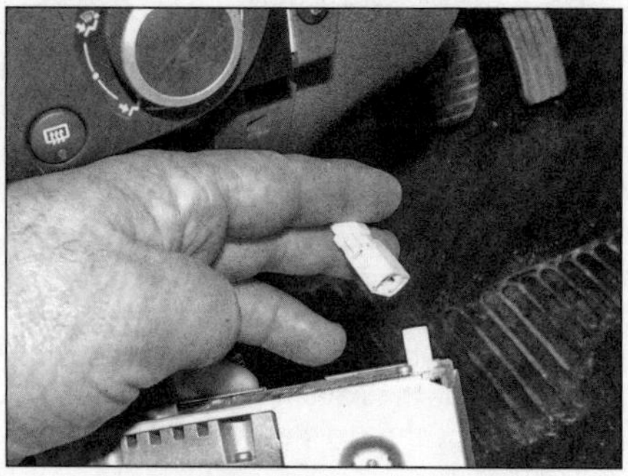

21.5a Disconnect the aerial lead...

21.5b ...and then the main wiring plug

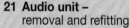

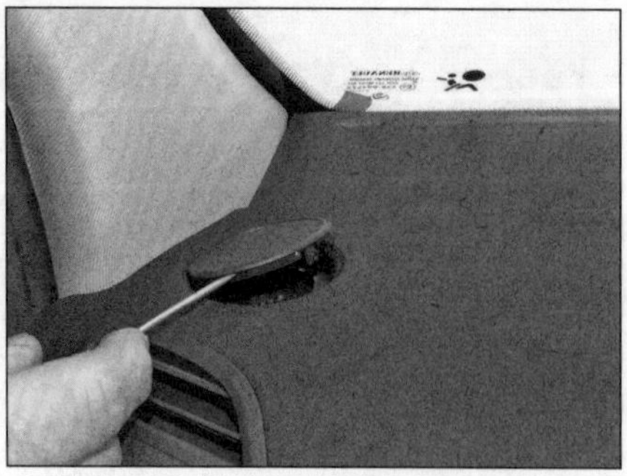

22.1 Release the speaker cover

12 Refitting is a reversal of removal. Partially fill the reservoir and check for leaks before refitting the bumper.

Washer pump

13 Remove the front bumper as described in Chapter 11, Section 6.

14 Disconnect the wiring plug and washer tubes from the washer pump – anticipate losing the entire contents of the reservoir when the tubes are disconnected.

15 Pull the washer pump sideways out of the reservoir – it's likely that the rubber grommet will come with it, in which case this should be refitted to the reservoir before the pump goes back in **(see illustrations)**.

16 Refitting is a reversal of removal. Partially fill the reservoir and check for leaks before refitting the bumper.

21 Audio unit – removal and refitting

Removal

1 All the audio units fitted to the Mégane range have DIN standard fixings. However the front cover is unique, so a simple swap for an alternative make is not possible. A pair of removal tools, obtainable from in-car entertainment specialists, will be required for removal.

2 Disconnect the battery negative lead. **Note:** *If the car has a security-coded radio check that you have a copy of the code number before disconnecting the battery.*

3 Remove the trim panel from around the audio unit as described in Chapter 11, Section 22.

4 Insert the tools into the holes at the sides of the unit, and push home until they click. Pull the tools outwards and rearwards to release the unit and pull it from the facia **(see illustration)**.

5 Disconnect the aerial lead and the wiring plugs from the rear of the unit **(see illustrations)**.

Refitting

6 Refitting is a reversal of removal. Where necessary re-enter the radio code.

22 Speakers – removal and refitting

Facia speakers (tweeters)

Note: *Not all models have the speakers fitted.*

1 Taking care not to mark the facia, use a small screwdriver to prise out the speaker grille **(see illustration)**.

2 Use the screwdriver to lift out the speaker itself, then disconnect the wiring plug and remove it.

3 Refitting is a reversal of removal.

Front door speakers

4 Remove the door panel as described in Chapter 11, Section 13.
5 A suitable drill will be required to remove the three mounting rivets. Disconnect the wiring plug, drill out the rivets and then withdraw the speaker **(see illustrations)**.
6 Refitting is a reversal of removal.

Rear door speakers

7 Remove the rear door trim panel as described in Chapter 11, Section 13.
8 Disconnect the speaker wiring plug and then drill out the rivets. Withdraw the speaker from the door.
9 Refitting is a reversal of removal.

Rear speakers (Coupe)

10 Remove the rear side trim panel as described in Chapter 11, Section 22.
11 Disconnect the wiring plug.
12 Drill out the rivets and remove the speaker.
13 Refitting is a reversal of removal.

Subwoofer

14 The subwoofer is located beneath the front right-hand seat (where fitted).
15 Disconnect the battery (see *Disconnecting the battery* in Chapter 5A) wait at least 5 minutes and then remove the front right-hand seat as described in Chapter 11, Section 20.
16 Remove the A-pillar lower scuff panel, the door step trim panel and then the lower section of the B-pillar panel – as described in Chapter 11.
17 Unclip the wiring loom and feed it through the carpet.
18 Unclip, and then lift up the carpet. Fold the carpet over the centre console and then remove the false floor section from the floor.
19 Disconnect the wiring plug and then remove the subwoofer mounting bolts. Remove the subwoofer from the floor.
20 Refitting is a reversal of removal.

23 Radio aerial – removal and refitting

Aerial

Note: *Some models do not have a conventional aerial fitted. The aerial on these models may be integrated into the rear tailgate glass or concealed in the headlining.*
1 Where a conventional aerial is fitted the aerial mast can be unscrewed from the base of the aerial if required.
2 Open the tailgate, then peel back the rubber seal from the edge of the headlining.
3 To gain extra movement of the headlining, to expose the base of the aerial, it may be necessary to remove the right- and left-hand C-pillar trim panels as described in Chapter 11, Section 22.

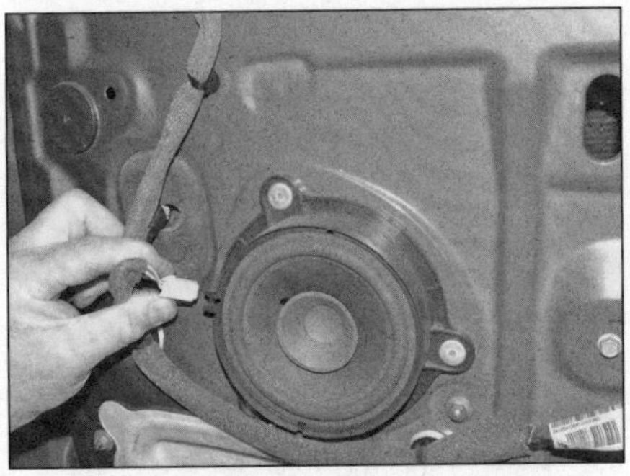

22.5a Disconnect the wiring plug and then...

4 Carefully lower the rear of the headlining for access to the aerial.
5 Unscrew the securing nut, and disconnect the aerial lead from the base of the aerial. Lift the aerial from the roof panel.
6 Refitting is a reversal of removal.

Aerial lead

7 With the lead disconnected from the aerial as described previously in this Section, observe the routing of the lead – it appears to run down the right-hand side of the car.
8 Remove the radio unit as described in Section 21, then disconnect the aerial lead from the rear of the unit.
9 The routing of the lead behind the facia can be judged by studying the facia removal procedure in Chapter 11 – to do the job properly would require the facia to be removed.
10 By removing the relevant trim panels as described in Chapter 11, Section 22, it should be possible, with patience, to fit a new lead without necessarily bothering to remove the old one. In routing a new cable, ensure that it will not be kinked or crushed in any way, and that it cannot drop down to interfere with the foot pedals.

24 Anti-theft alarm and immobiliser systems – general information

Certain models are fitted with an anti-theft alarm system, which uses various sensing

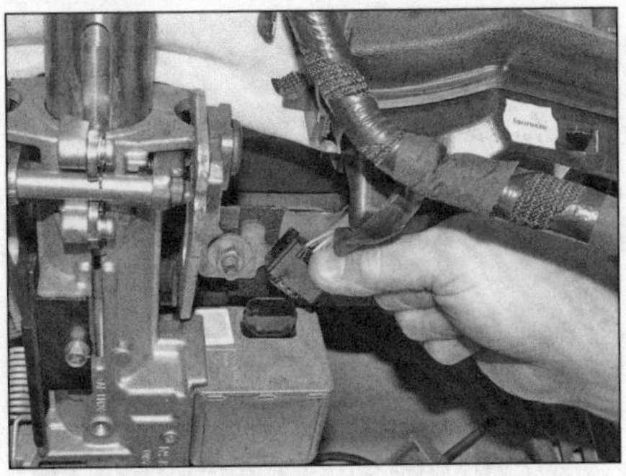

25.5 Disconnect the wiring plug

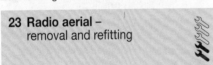

22.5b ...drill out the rivets

systems and warning sirens, depending on model. No information was available for the alarm systems at the time of writing. Any faults should be referred to a Renault dealer for diagnosis.

All models are fitted with an engine immobiliser device which is activated by the coded ignition keycard. When the immobiliser is armed, the indicator light on the instrument panel will flash continuously. When the keycard is inserted, the code from the card is read by the card reader unit and transmits it to the interior multiplex module (see Section 3). If the multiplex module recognises the code, the engine can be started.

In the event of a non-starting car, remember that the system also relies on the brake or clutch being pressed, and on the transmission being in neutral. Therefore, a fault with the clutch pedal switch, brake stop-light switch or transmission neutral switch will result in the wrong signal being sent to the multiplex modules. Refer to the relevant Chapters for more details.

25 Steering column lock – removal and refitting

Caution: The column lock can only be removed when it is unlocked. A suitable diagnostic tool will be required to safely disable the airbag and to initialise the replacement column lock. Do not proceed unless a suitable tool is available.
1 The steering column lock is an electrically-operated mechanical lock. It is controlled by the body systems electronic control unit (UCH) and is activated when the keycard is inserted or removed.

Removal

2 Remove the driver's lower facia panel as described in Chapter 11.
3 Remove the driver's side air distribution duct.
4 Lift up and pull out the steering column.
5 Disconnect the wiring plug from the front of the steering column lock **(see illustration)**.
6 Remove the single bolt securing the lock, and withdraw it from the column **(see**

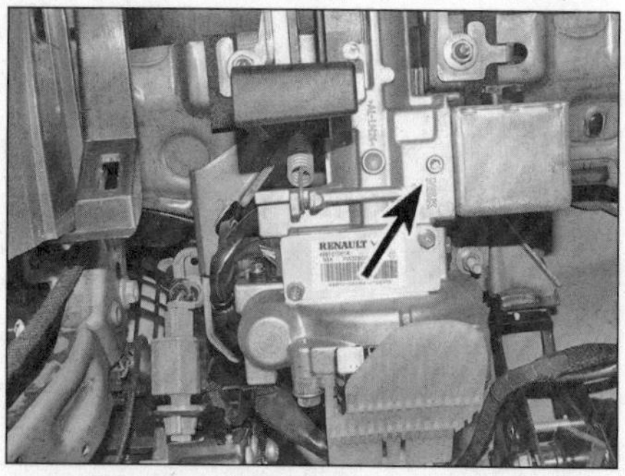

25.6 Steering column lock mounting bolt (arrowed)

illustration). This bolt has a **left-hand thread** – ie, it unscrews **clockwise**. Where a 'shear' type bolt has been fitted this must be drilled out.

Refitting

7 Refitting is a reversal of removal. A new bolt must be fitted to the steering column lock. If a new steering column lock is fitted it must be programmed to the vehicle using suitable diagnostic equipment. If a new lock is required both the removal and fitting of the new lock should be entrusted to a suitable equipped garage or Renault dealer.

26 Airbag system – general information and precautions

General information

All Megane models are equipped with a comprehensive airbag system. In addition to adaptive front airbags for the driver and front passenger, there are side airbags fitted to the front seats, and side curtain airbags which are deployed from modules in the headlining. Rear side airbags are available as an option.

The airbag system is triggered in the event of a heavy frontal or side impact above a predetermined force; depending on the point of impact, not all the airbags will necessarily be fired. The airbags inflate within milliseconds to form a safety cushion which prevents contact with the internal surfaces of the car, greatly reducing the risk of injury. The airbags then deflate almost immediately.

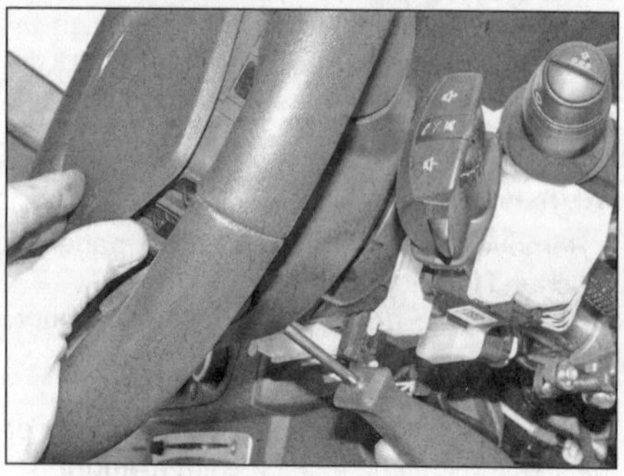

27.4a Release the airbag

The system is armed only when the ignition is on. However, a reserve power source maintains power to the system in the event of a break in the main electrical supply for a short period – for this reason, it is essential to wait before disconnecting any of the system wiring.

The system is activated by a 'g' sensor (deceleration sensor), incorporated in the electronic control unit, fitted under the rear of the centre console. Note that the airbag control unit also controls the seat belt tensioners. Impact sensors in the B-pillars detect side impacts, which if severe enough, will cause the side and curtain airbags to be fired on the side concerned.

The airbags are inflated by gas generators, which force the bags out from their locations. Although these are safety items, their deployment is violently rapid, and this may cause injury if they are triggered unintentionally.

Linked to the airbag system are the seat belt tensioners fitted to each seat belt (except the centre belt on the rear seat). All except coupe models have two tensioners fitted to the front seats. Coupe models have additional 'anti-submarining' airbags in the front seats, intended to prevent the occupants sliding under their seat belts). The seat belt tensioners are fired with the airbags in the event of an accident, to take up the slack in the belts, and hold the occupants in their seats.

Precautions

Warning: The following precautions must be observed when working on vehicles equipped with an airbag system, to prevent the possibility of personal injury.

General precautions

The following precautions must be observed when carrying out work on a vehicle equipped with an airbag:

a) Do not disconnect the battery with the engine running.
b) Before carrying out any work in the vicinity of the airbag, removal of any of the airbag components, or any welding work on the car, de-activate the system as described in the following sub-Section.
c) Do not attempt to test any of the airbag system circuits using test meters or any other test equipment.
d) If the airbag warning light comes on, or any fault in the system is suspected, consult a Renault dealer without delay. Do not attempt to carry out fault diagnosis, or any dismantling of the components.

When handling an airbag

a) Transport the airbag by itself, bag upward.
b) Do not put your arms around the airbag.
c) Carry the airbag close to the body, bag outward.
d) Do not drop the airbag or expose it to impacts.
e) Do not attempt to dismantle the airbag unit.
f) Do not connect any form of electrical equipment to any part of the airbag circuit.

When storing an airbag unit

a) Store the unit in a cupboard with the airbag upward.
b) Do not expose the airbag to temperatures above 80°C.
c) Do not expose the airbag to flames.
d) Do not attempt to dispose of the airbag – consult a Renault dealer.
e) Never refit an airbag which is known to be faulty or damaged.

De-activation of airbag system

The system must be de-activated as follows, before carrying out any work on the airbag components or surrounding area.

a) Switch off the engine.
b) Remove the ignition keycard – on models with the 'hands-free' system, the keycard should be kept well away from the car.
c) Switch off all electrical equipment.
d) Disconnect the battery negative lead (see 'Disconnecting the battery').
e) Insulate the battery negative terminal and the end of the battery negative lead to prevent any possibility of contact.
f) Wait for at least five minutes before carrying out any further work.

27 Airbag system components – removal and refitting

Note: *Refer to the precautions in Section 26 before carrying out the following operations.*

1 Disconnect the battery negative lead and wait for at least five minutes. This will allow the reserve power capacitors in the control unit to discharge and disable the airbag system (see Section 26).

Driver's airbag

Removal

2 Unclip and lift off the column upper shroud **(see illustration 5.13a).**

3 Remove the screws underneath the steering column lower shroud, then unclip it and lower it out **(see illustration 5.13b).**

4 Use a small T30 screwdriver in the hole provided at the back of the steering wheel, prise the end of the spring clip used to retain

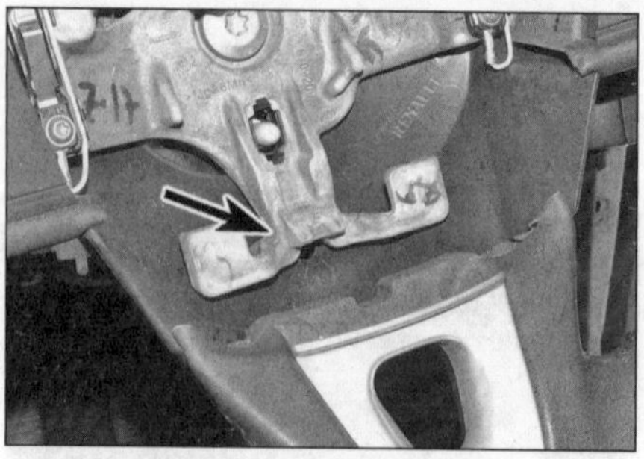

27.4b With the airbag removed note the retaining peg (arrowed) on the steering wheel...

the airbag – as this is done, pull up and backwards on the airbag to release it **(see illustrations)**.

5 Pull the airbag out from the wheel to access the two airbag wiring plugs. Release the plugs by prising out the yellow locking clip with a small screwdriver, and disconnect them **(see illustration)**.

6 Remove the airbag from the car, taking care not to knock or drop it, and keeping the front uppermost. Store it somewhere safe while it is removed.

Refitting

7 Ensure that the wiring connectors are securely reconnected and seat the airbag unit centrally in the steering wheel, making sure the wires do not become trapped. Slide the airbag downwards, and press it squarely into place until the retaining clip at the base engages.

8 Ensuring no one is inside the car, reconnect the battery. From the passenger seat, insert the keycard and check the operation of the airbag warning light.

Airbag rotary connector (clockspring)

Removal

9 Remove the driver's airbag as described previously in this Section, and the steering wheel as described in Chapter 10, Section 14.

10 First, check that the window on the front of the clockspring is aligned correctly with its index mark **(see illustrations)**. It should be, by default, if the front wheels were set straight-ahead when the steering wheel was removed. The steering cannot turn since it will automatically be locked.

11 The airbag rotary connector is an integral part of the steering column switch module, meaning that the whole assembly must be removed. Follow the procedure for switch replacement in Section 5 of this Chapter.

12 Slide the module back off the column for access to the wiring plugs at the bottom. Slide the locking lever to the side to release the central wiring plug. Once all plugs have been disconnected, the module, including the rotary connector, can be removed.

13 While the module is removed, take care that the rotary connector is not turned from its aligned position. If the clockspring becomes dislodged it is possible to reset it. To do this fully turn the movable section fully clockwise and then (counting the number of turns) turn the clockspring fully anti-clockwise. Divide the number of turns by two and rotate the clockspring by the result to find the central (neutral) position – the window should be aligned with the index mark. Tape the two sections together.

Refitting

14 Check that the window is still aligned with

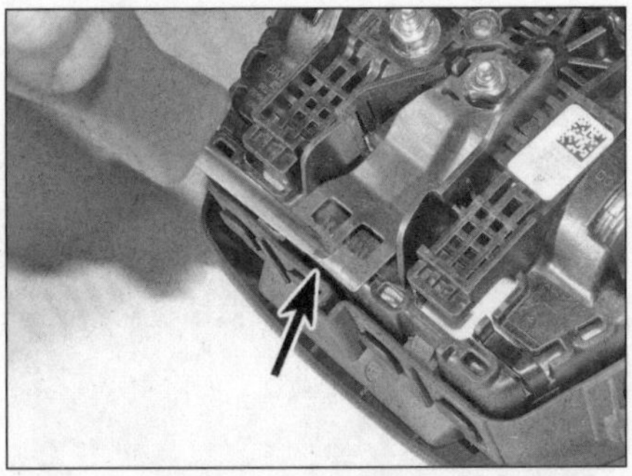

27.4c ...and the position of the screwdriver on the spring clip (arrowed) of the airbag

27.10a The window (arrowed) must be aligned with the index mark

the index mark, then refit the module using a reversal of the removal procedure.

15 Refit the steering wheel as described in Chapter 10, and the airbag as described previously in this Section.

Passenger's airbag

Removal

16 Remove the facia panel as described in Chapter 11, Section 24 – the crossmember does not have to be removed.

17 Turn the facia panel over and remove the airbag unit mounting bolts **(see illustration)**. Remove the airbag and store it safely.

Refitting

18 Refitting is a reversal of removal, but note that the airbag to facia and airbag to crossmember bolts must be replaced with new ones.

27.17 The passenger airbag mounting bolts

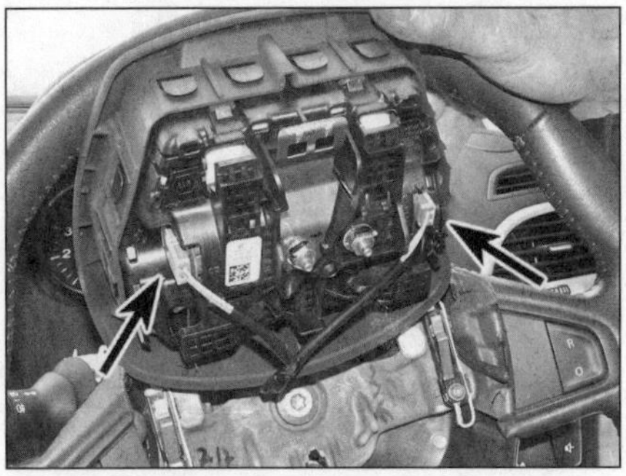

27.5 Disconnect the wiring plugs (arrowed)

27.10b To ensure the clockspring can not move tape the sections together

Front side airbags

19 The side airbags are located internally within the front seat backrest, and no attempt should be made to remove them. Any suspected problems with the side airbag system should be referred to a Renault dealer.

Anti-submarining airbags

20 The anti-submarining airbags are located internally within the front seat cushion, and no attempt should be made to remove them. Any suspected problems with the side airbag system should be referred to a Renault dealer.

Side curtain airbags

21 The modules for the side curtain airbags are located at the sides of the headlining. It is strongly recommended that any work which requires even just the removal of the headlining, never mind any work on the side curtain airbags, be referred to a Renault dealer.

Airbag control unit

Removal

22 Remove the centre console as described in Chapter 11, Section 23.

23 The airbag control unit is located behind the gear/selector lever, appearing as a bulge in the carpet. To access the unit, a cut must be made in the carpet and sound-deadening **(see illustration)**.

24 Fold back the carpeting, then unclip the cover fitted over the unit. Disconnect the wiring plug after releasing the locking catch,

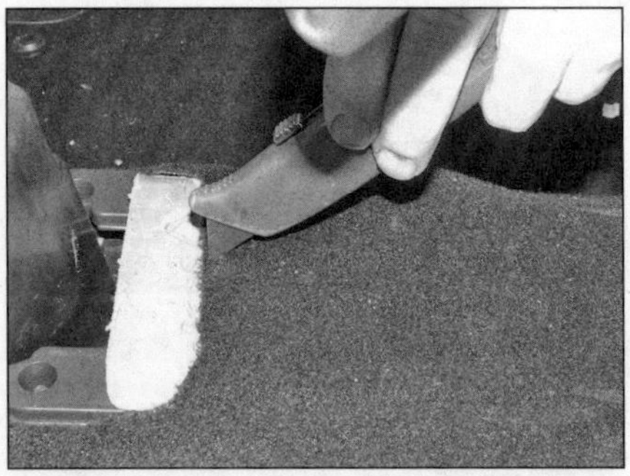

27.23 Make a 200mm cut in the carpet

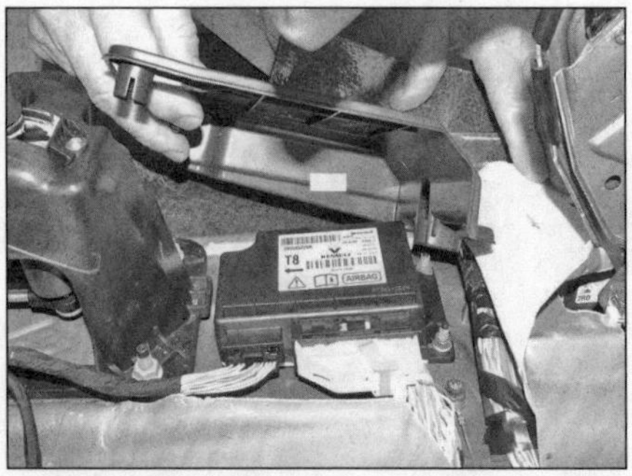

27.24a Remove the cover

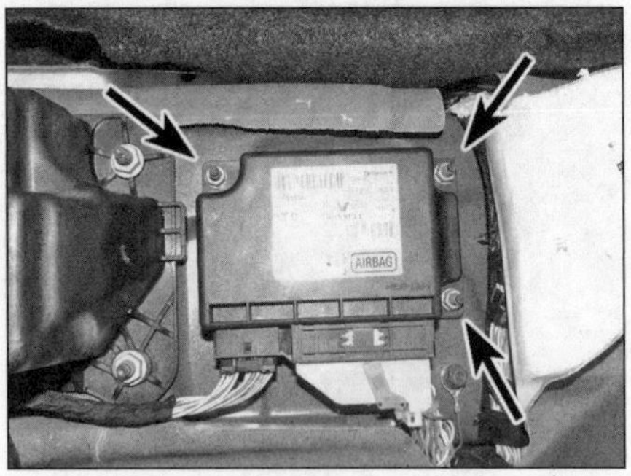

27.24b Remove the mounting nuts (arrowed)

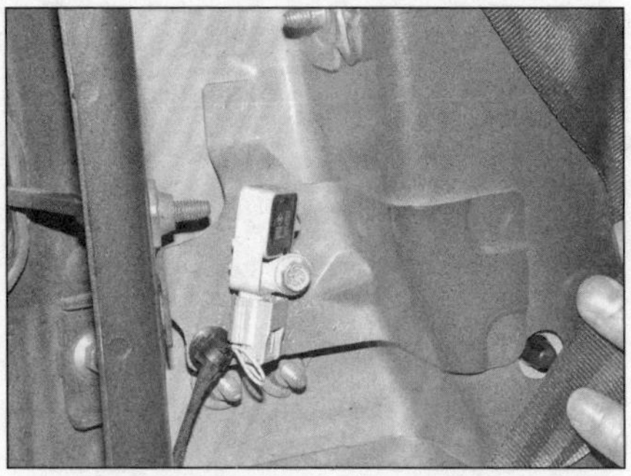

27.32 The side impact sensor

then unscrew the three mounting nuts and remove the unit **(see illustrations)**.

Refitting

25 Refit the control unit, tightening the mounting nuts securely.

26 Reconnect the wiring connector, and secure with the locking catch. Renault insist that the protective cover is replaced every time it is removed. Obtain a new cover and fit it.

27 Refit the centre console as described in Chapter 11.

28 Ensuring no one is inside the car, reconnect the battery. From the passenger seat, insert the keycard and check the operation of the airbag warning light.

Passenger airbag selector switch

29 Refer to Section 5.

Side impact sensors

Removal

30 Except on Coupe models, remove the B-pillar lower trim panel as described in Chapter 11, Section 22.

31 On Coupe models, remove the rear side trim panel as described in Chapter 11, Section 22.

32 Disconnect the wiring plug, then unscrew the mounting bolt and remove the sensor **(see illustration)**.

Refitting

33 Refitting is a reversal of removal. Tighten the sensor mounting bolt securely.

Seat belt tensioners

34 Refer to the seat belt procedures in Chapter 11, Section 21.

28 Parking aid components – general information, removal and refitting

General information

1 The parking aid system is available as an option on certain models. Four ultrasound sensors located in the rear bumper measure the distance to the closest object behind the car, and inform the driver using acoustic signals from a buzzer located under the rear trim. The nearer the object, the more frequent the acoustic signals. A switch located on the centre console allows the driver to switch the system on or off (see Section 5).

2 The system includes a control unit and self-diagnosis program, and therefore, in the event of a fault, the vehicle should be taken to a Renault dealer for investigation.

Control unit

3 Remove the left-hand rear load area side panel and the left-hand wheel arch trim panel as described in Chapter 11.

4 Unbolt the control unit from the body inner panel, then disconnect the wiring and remove the unit.

5 Refitting is a reversal of removal. If a new unit is being fitted, it will be necessary to have a Renault dealer (or suitably equipped garage) program the unit using a specialist diagnostic tool.

Range/distance sensor

6 Remove the rear bumper as described in Chapter 11, Section 6.

7 If only one sensor is being removed, disconnect the wiring at the sensor then release the clips and remove the sensor from the rear bumper. Take care not to scratch or damage the sensor as it is fragile.

8 Refitting is a reversal of removal.

Warning buzzer

9 The warning buzzer is located next to the control unit. Follow the procedure for the removal of the control unit.

10 Disconnect the wiring plug and unbolt the buzzer from the panel.

11 Refitting is a reversal of removal.

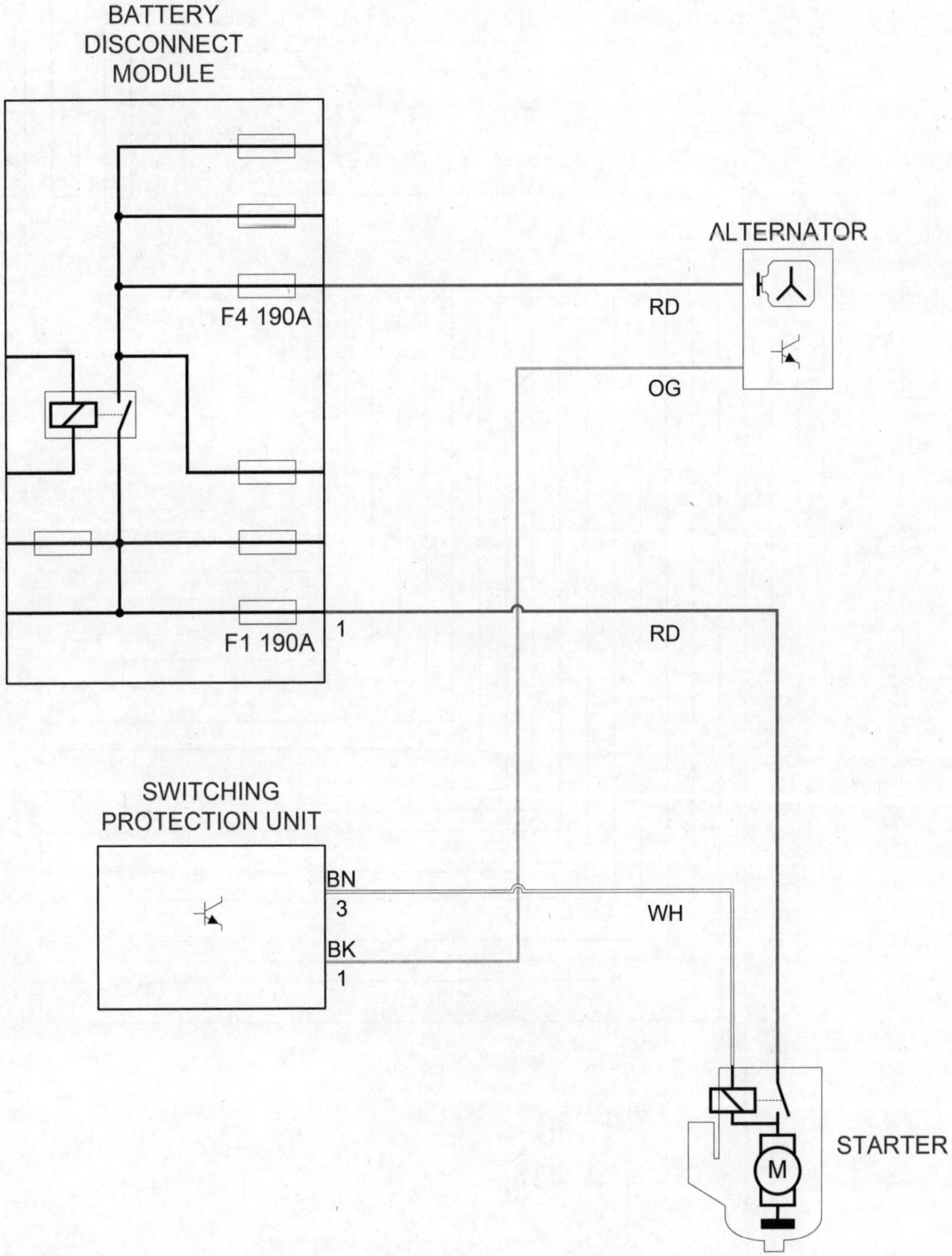

Diagram 1 – Starting and Charging

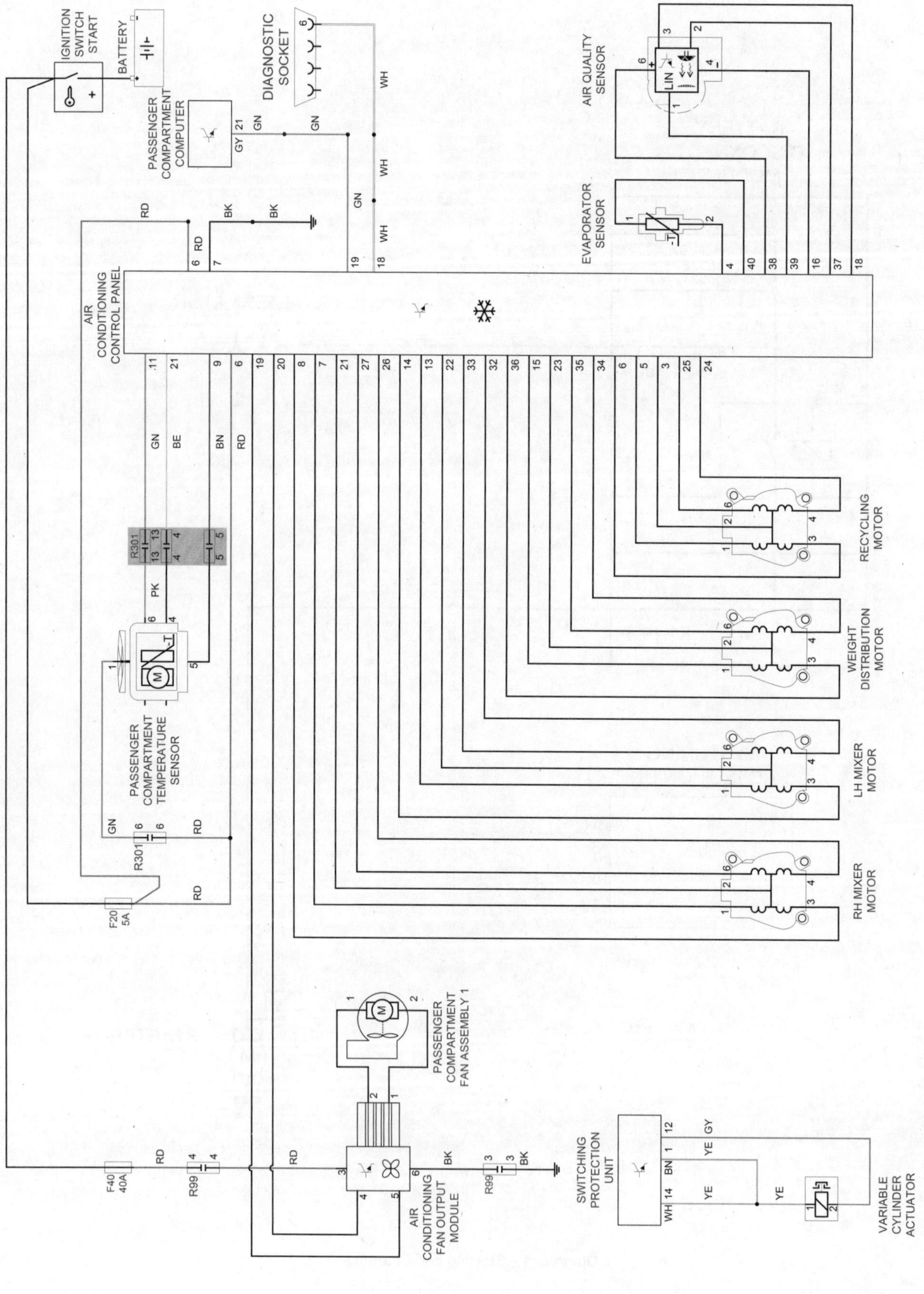

Diagram 2 – Climatronic air conditioning

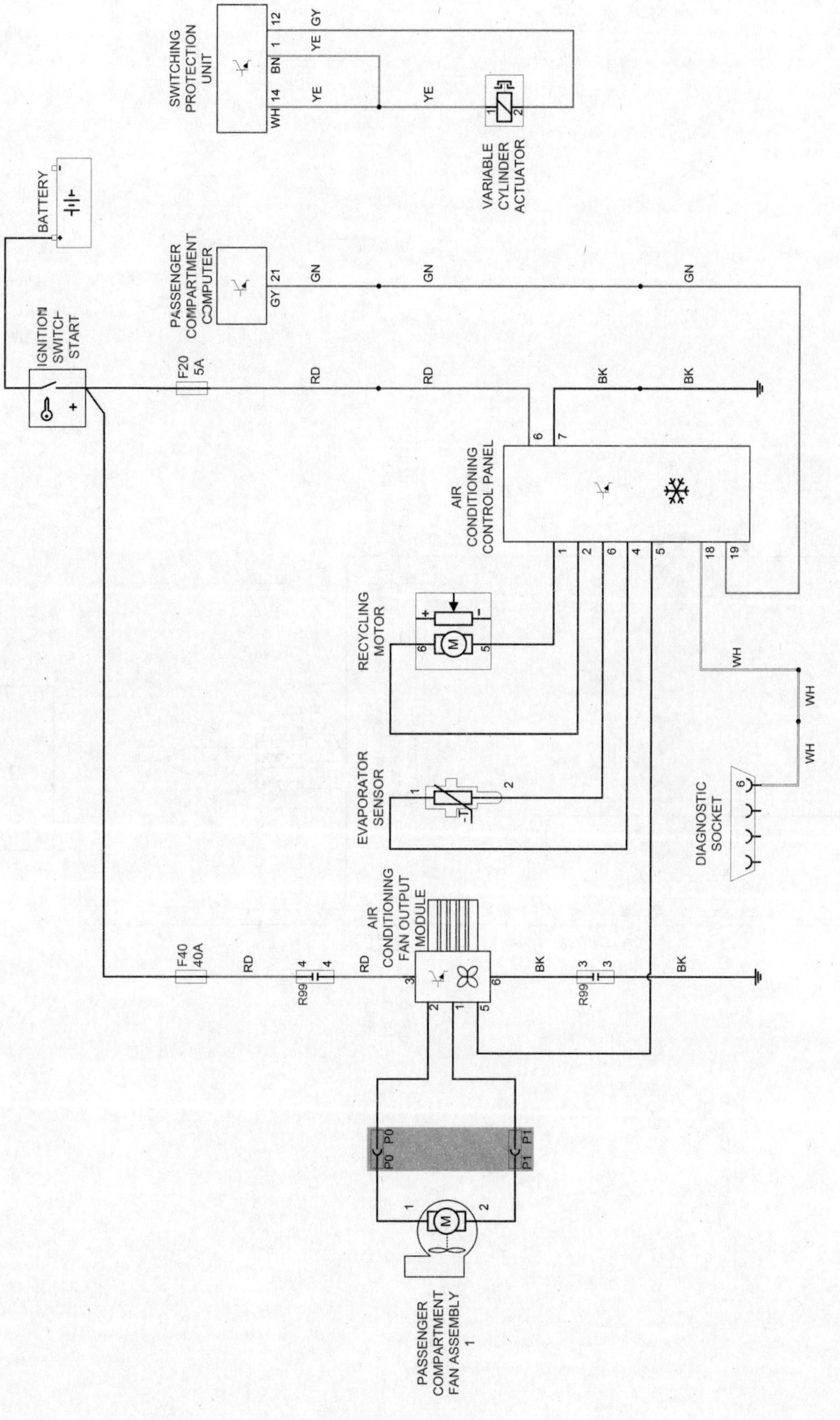

Diagram 3 – Manual air conditioning

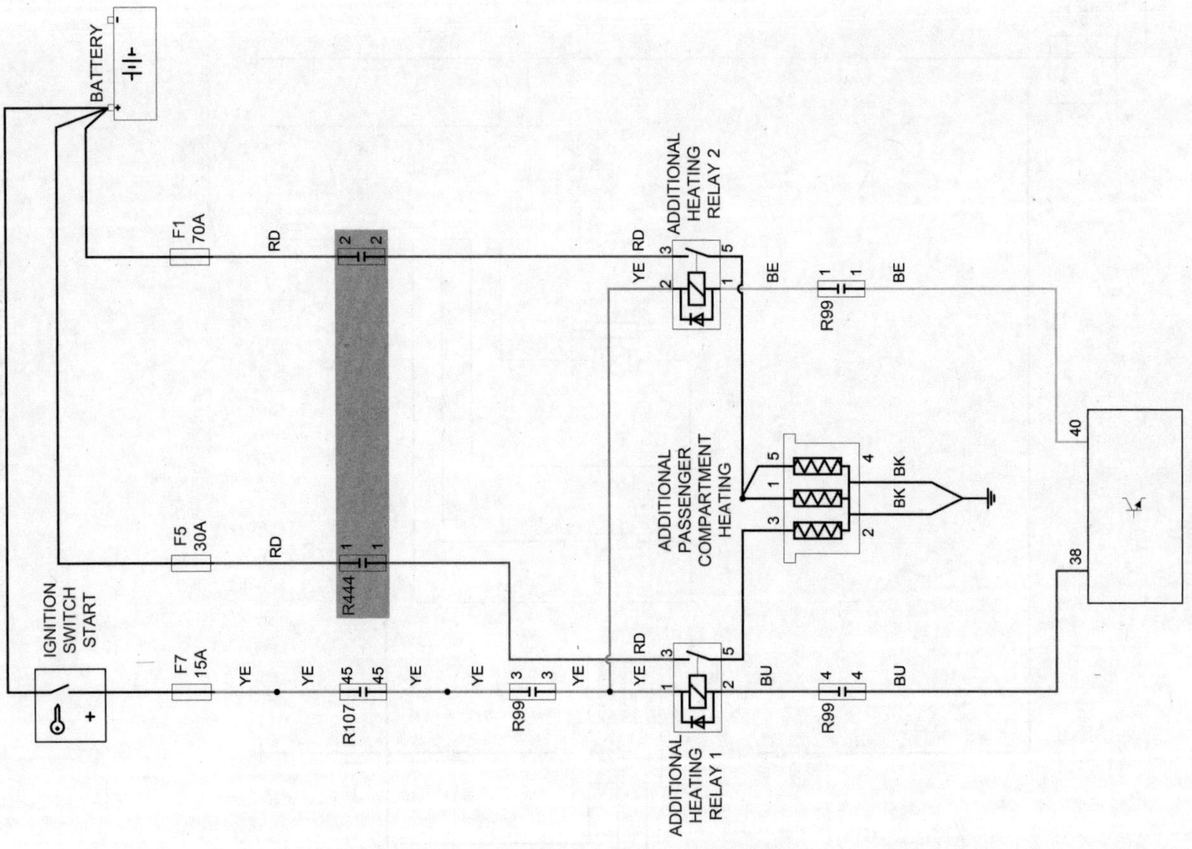

Diagram 4 – Additional heating

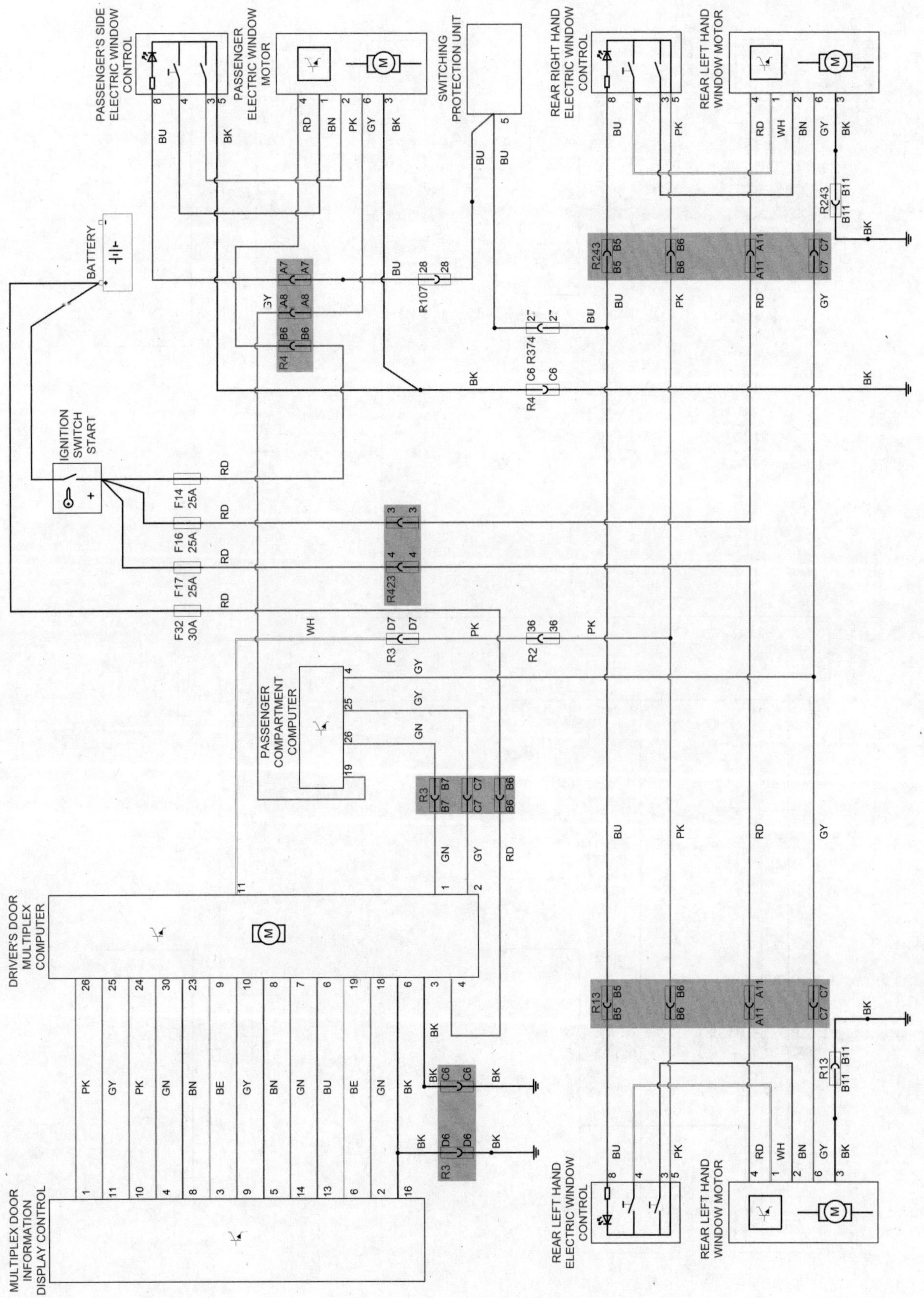

Diagram 5 – Electric windows

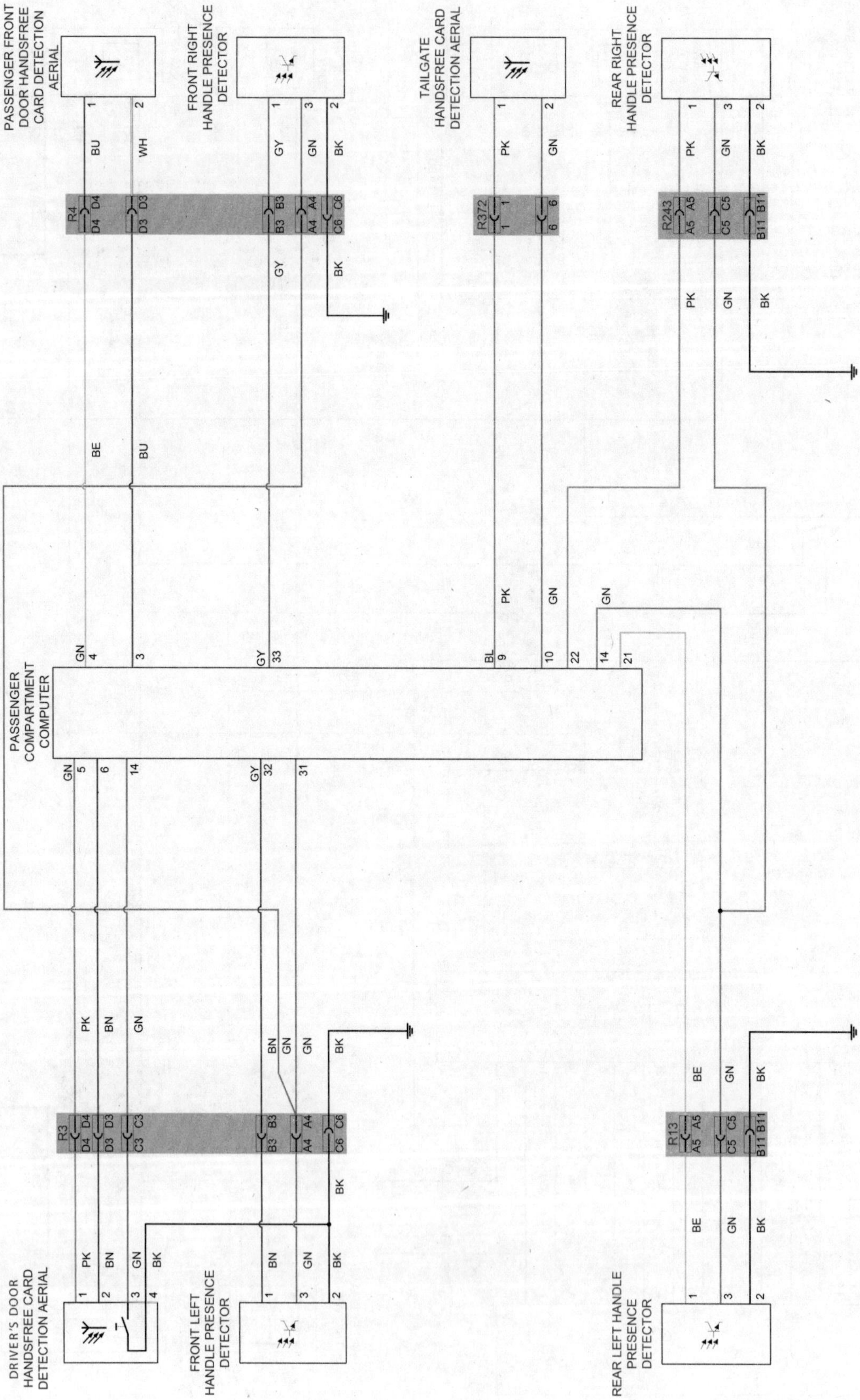

Diagram 6 – Central locking with Keyless

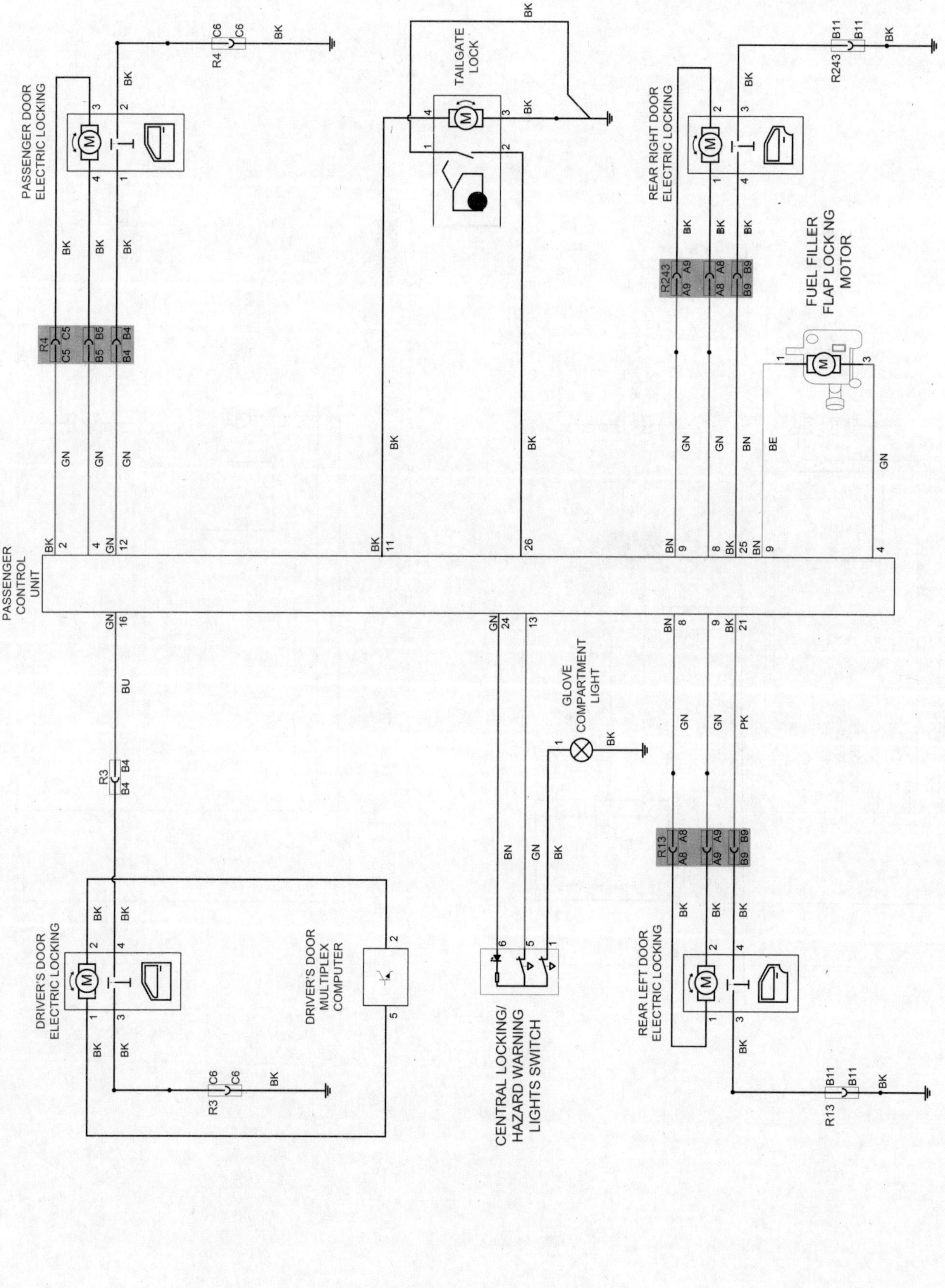

Diagram 7 – Central locking without Keyless

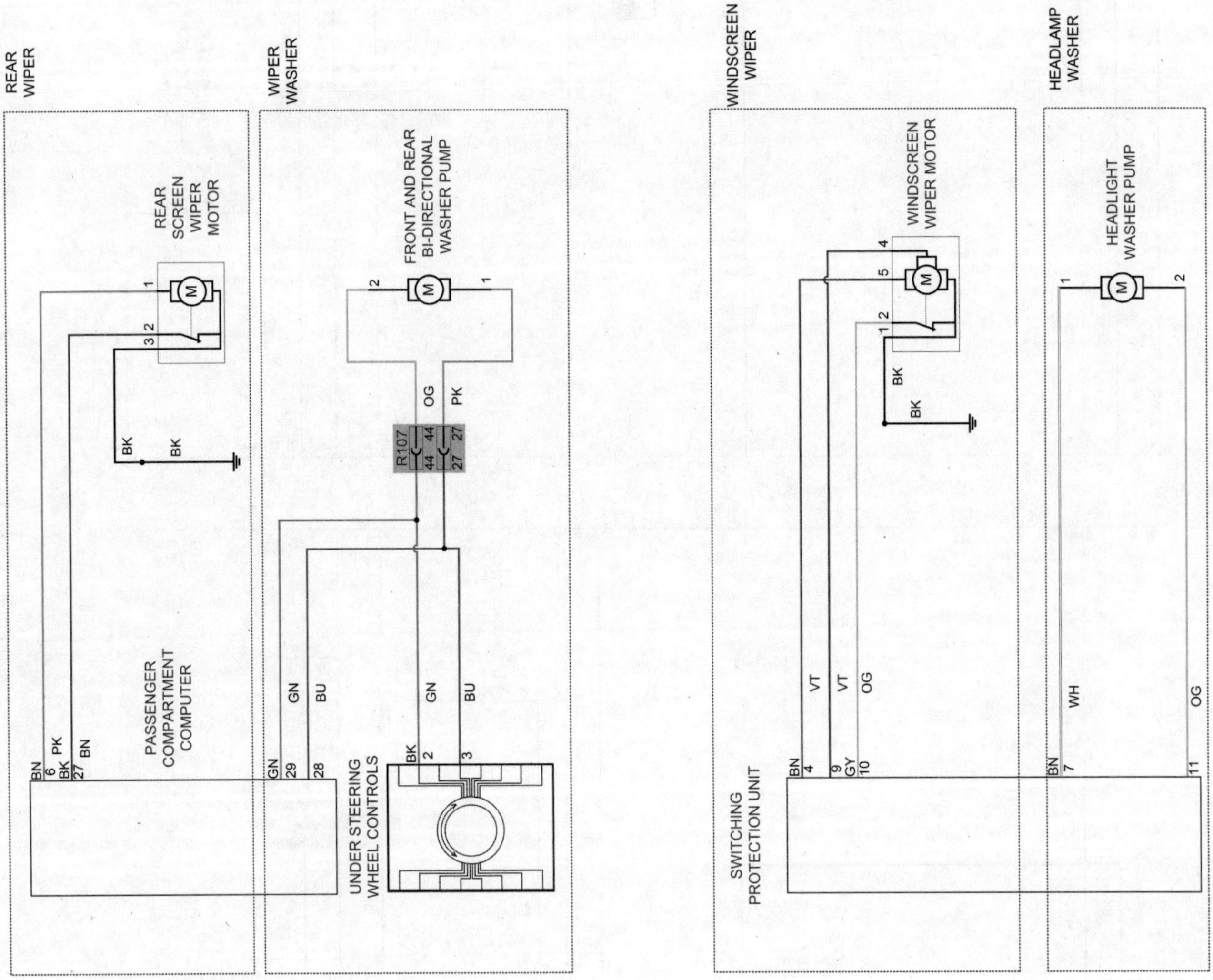
REAR WIPER
REAR SCREEN WIPER MOTOR
PASSENGER COMPARTMENT COMPUTER
WIPER WASHER
FRONT AND REAR BI-DIRECTIONAL WASHER PUMP
R107
UNDER STEERING WHEEL CONTROLS
WINDSCREEN WIPER
WINDSCREEN WIPER MOTOR
SWITCHING PROTECTION UNIT
HEADLAMP WASHER
HEADLIGHT WASHER PUMP
BN
PK
BK
GN
BU
OG
VT
GY
WH

Diagram 8 – Wipers and washers

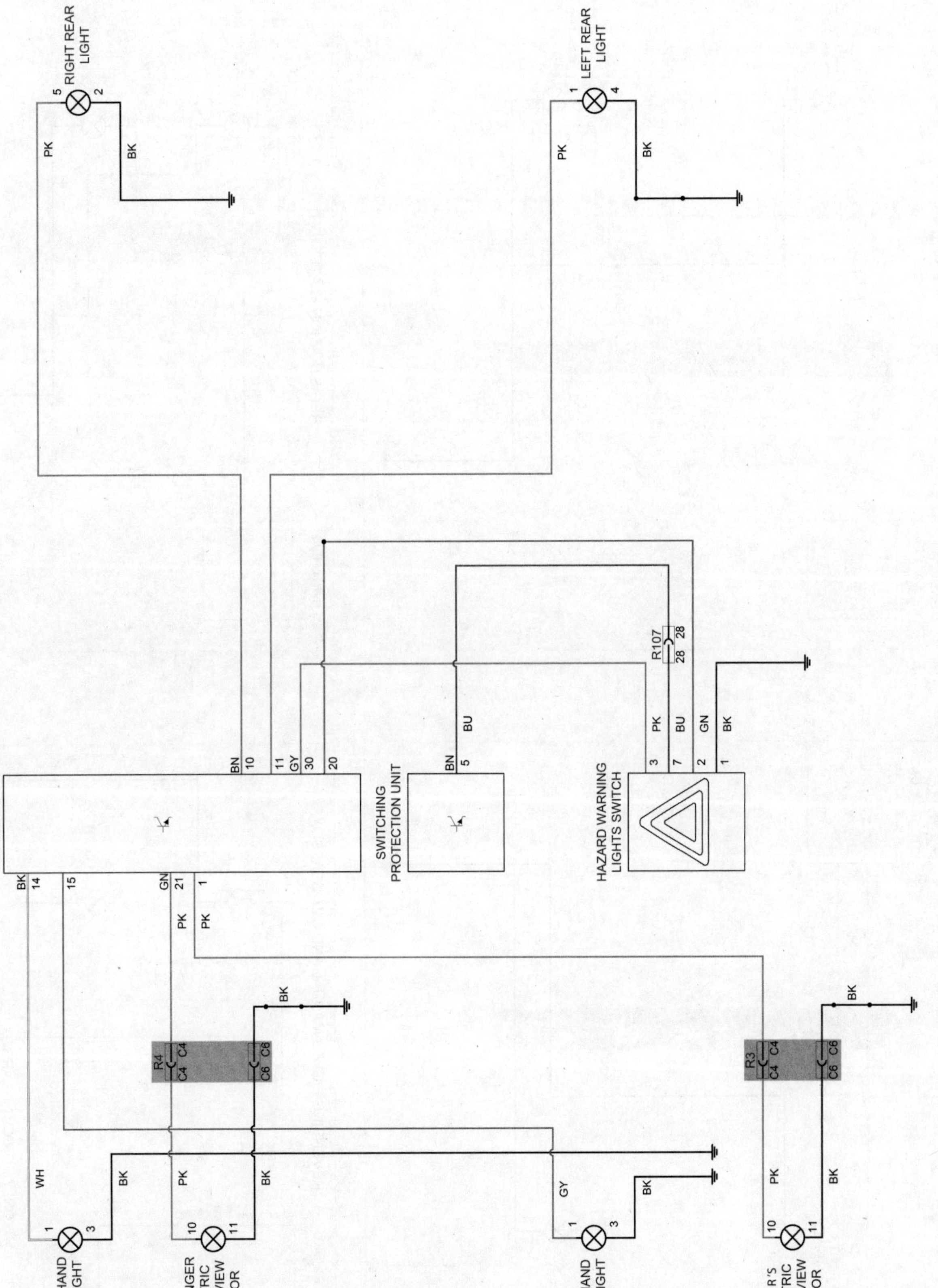

Diagram 9 – Indicators and hazard warning lights

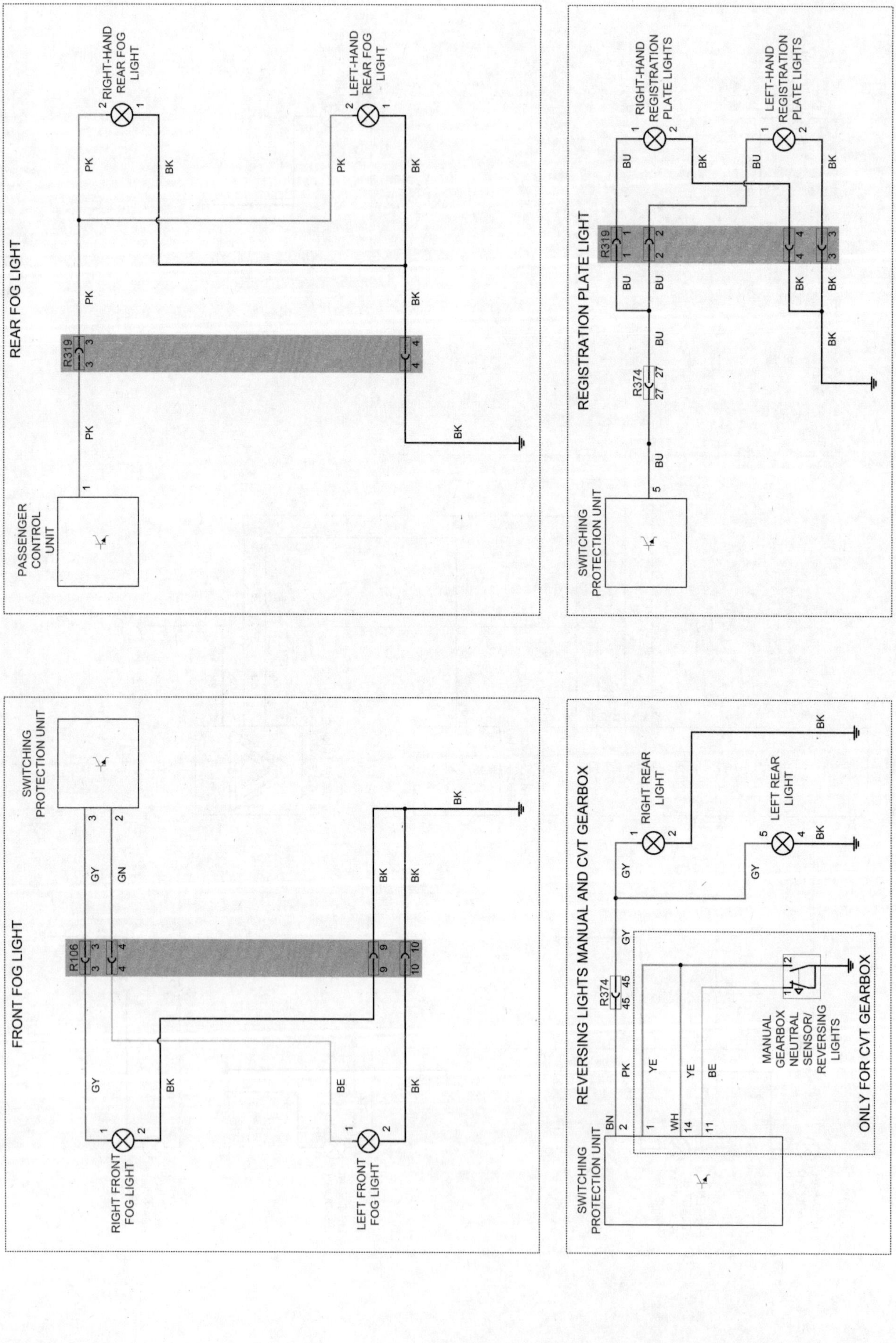

Diagram 10 – Fog, reversing and number Lights

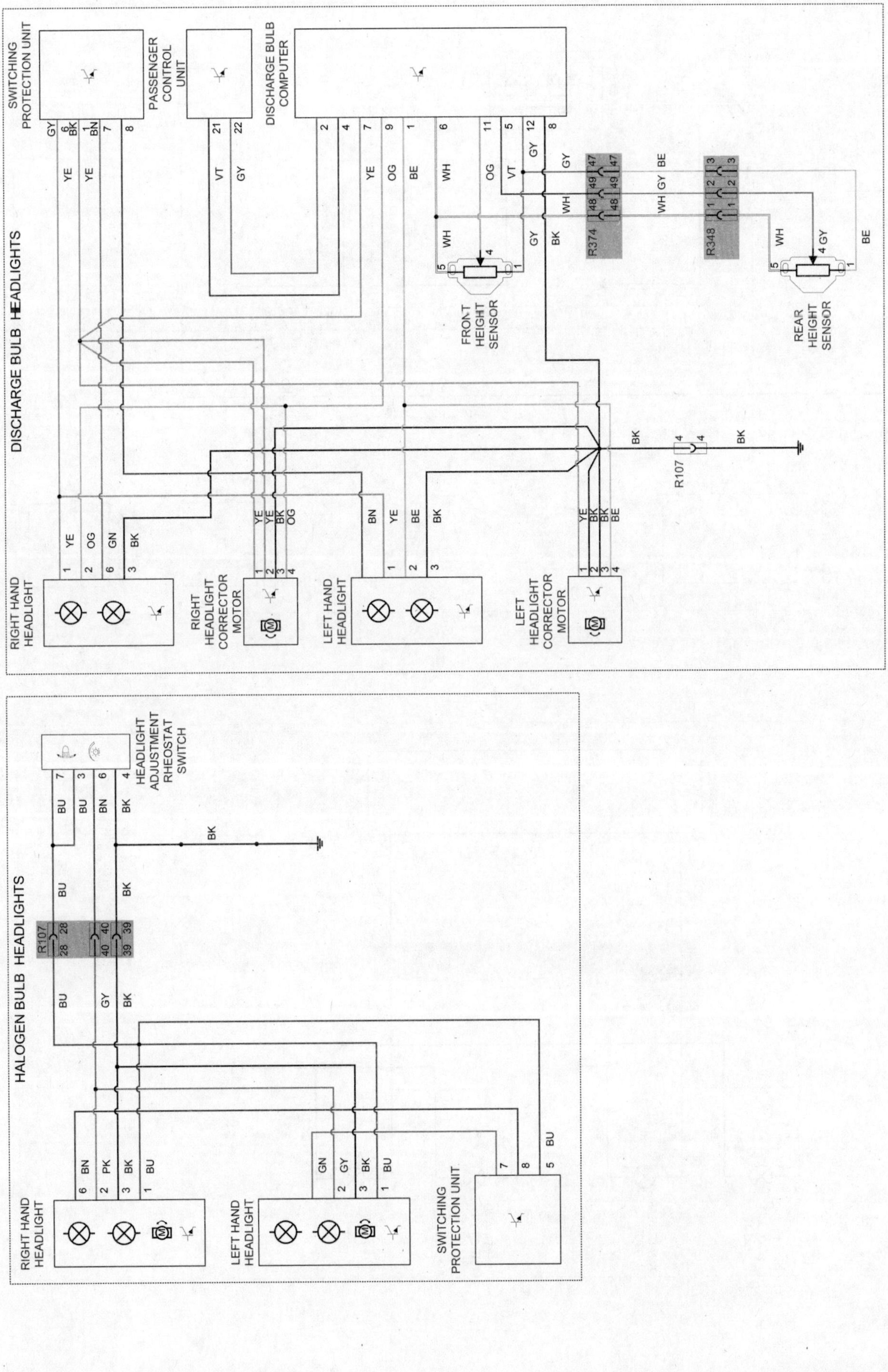

Diagram 11 – Headlights

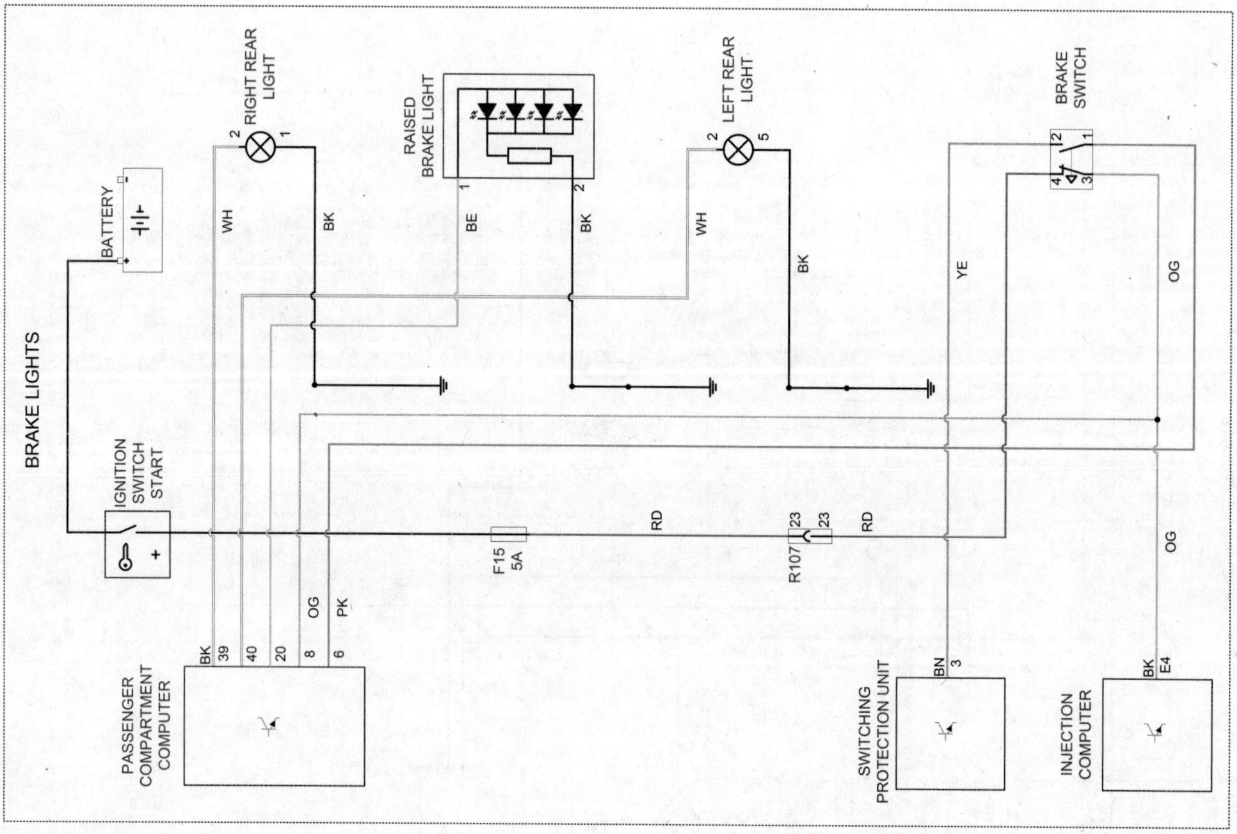

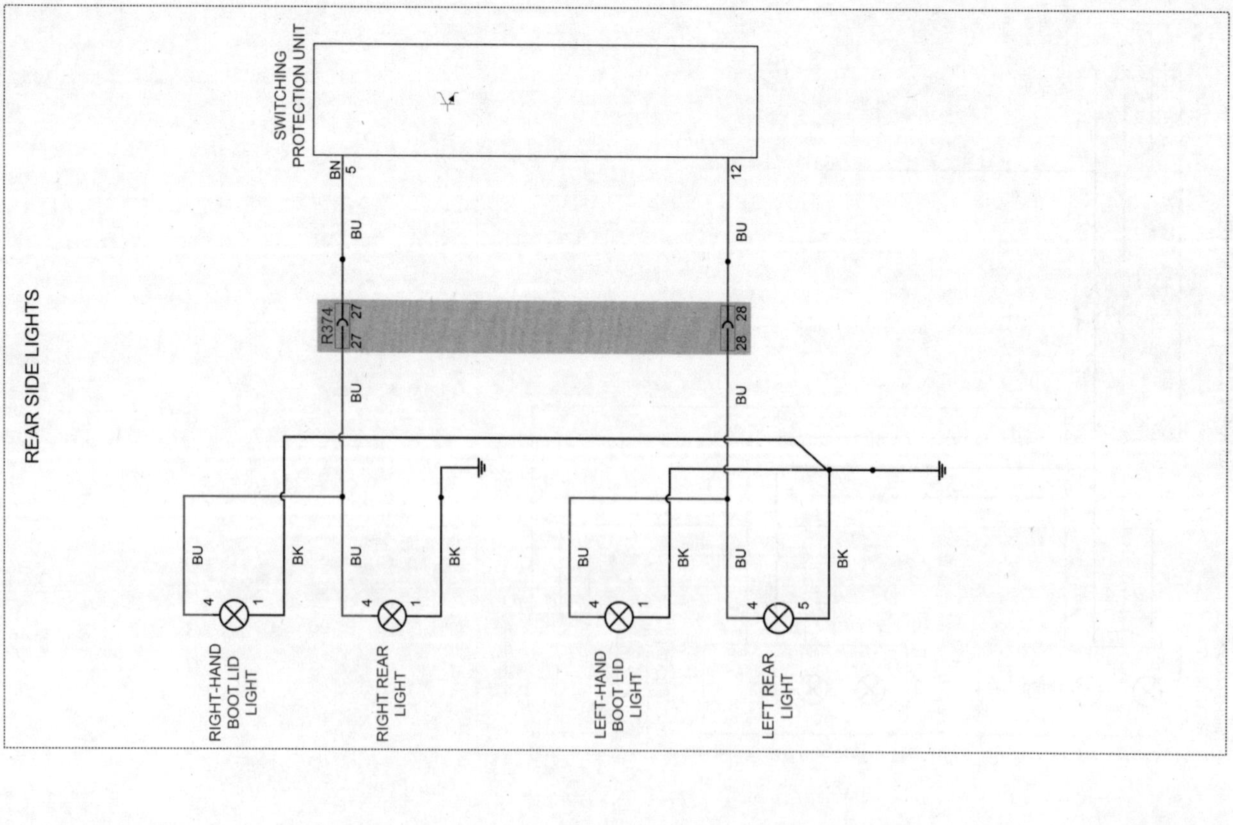

Diagram 12 – Tail lights and brake lights

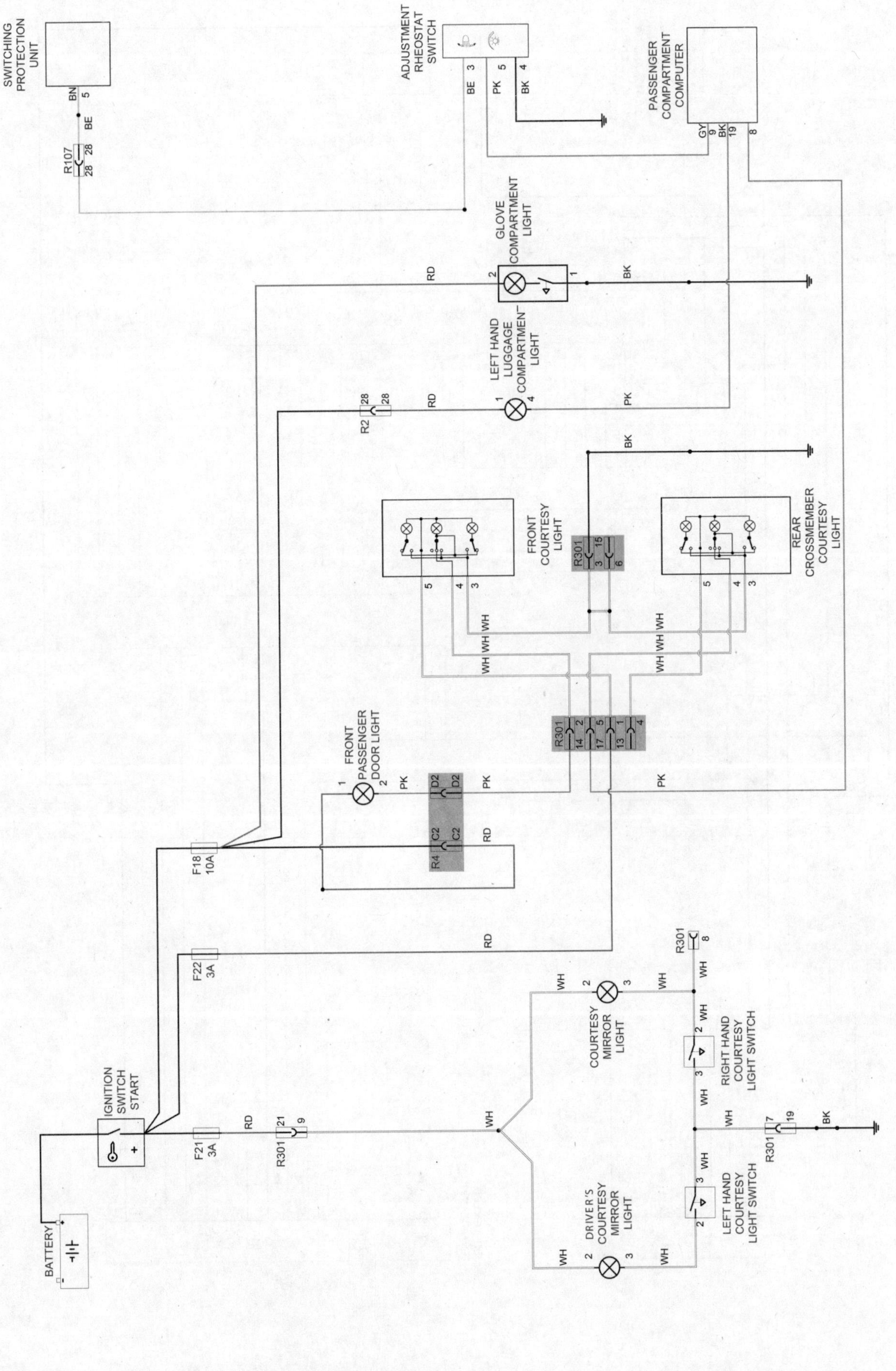

Diagram 13 – Interior lights

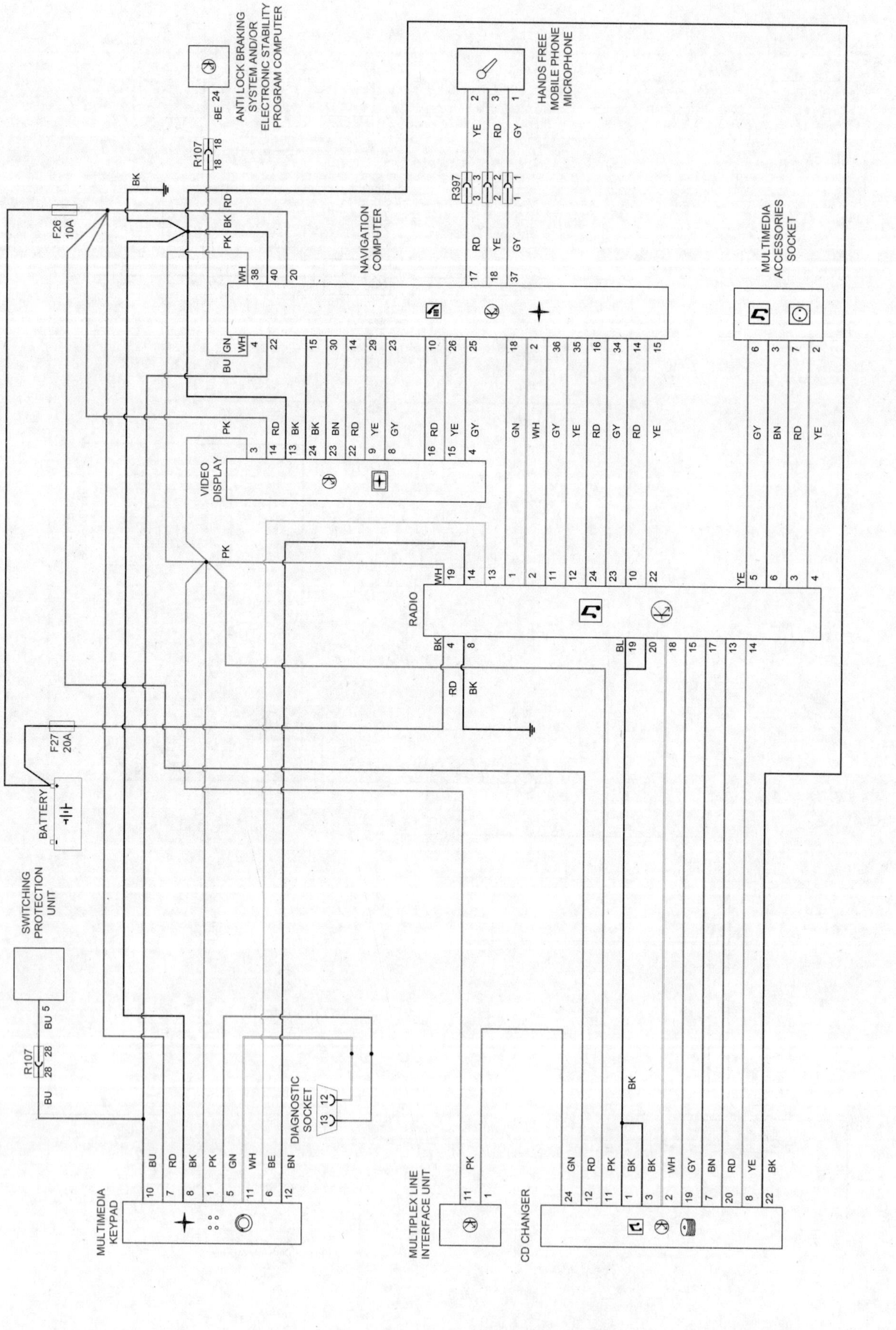

Diagram 14 – Audio and navigation

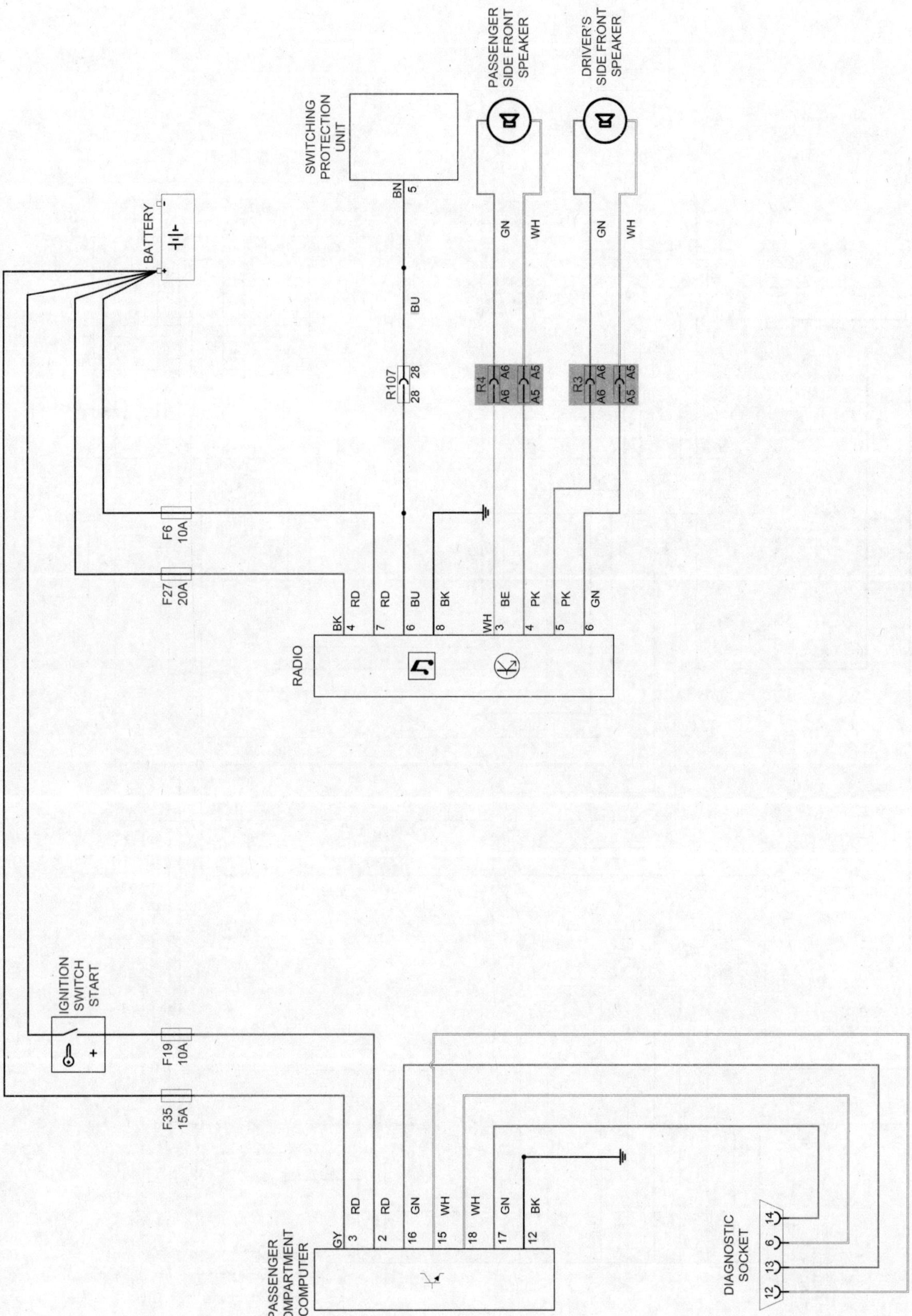

Diagram 15 – Audio pre-equipped

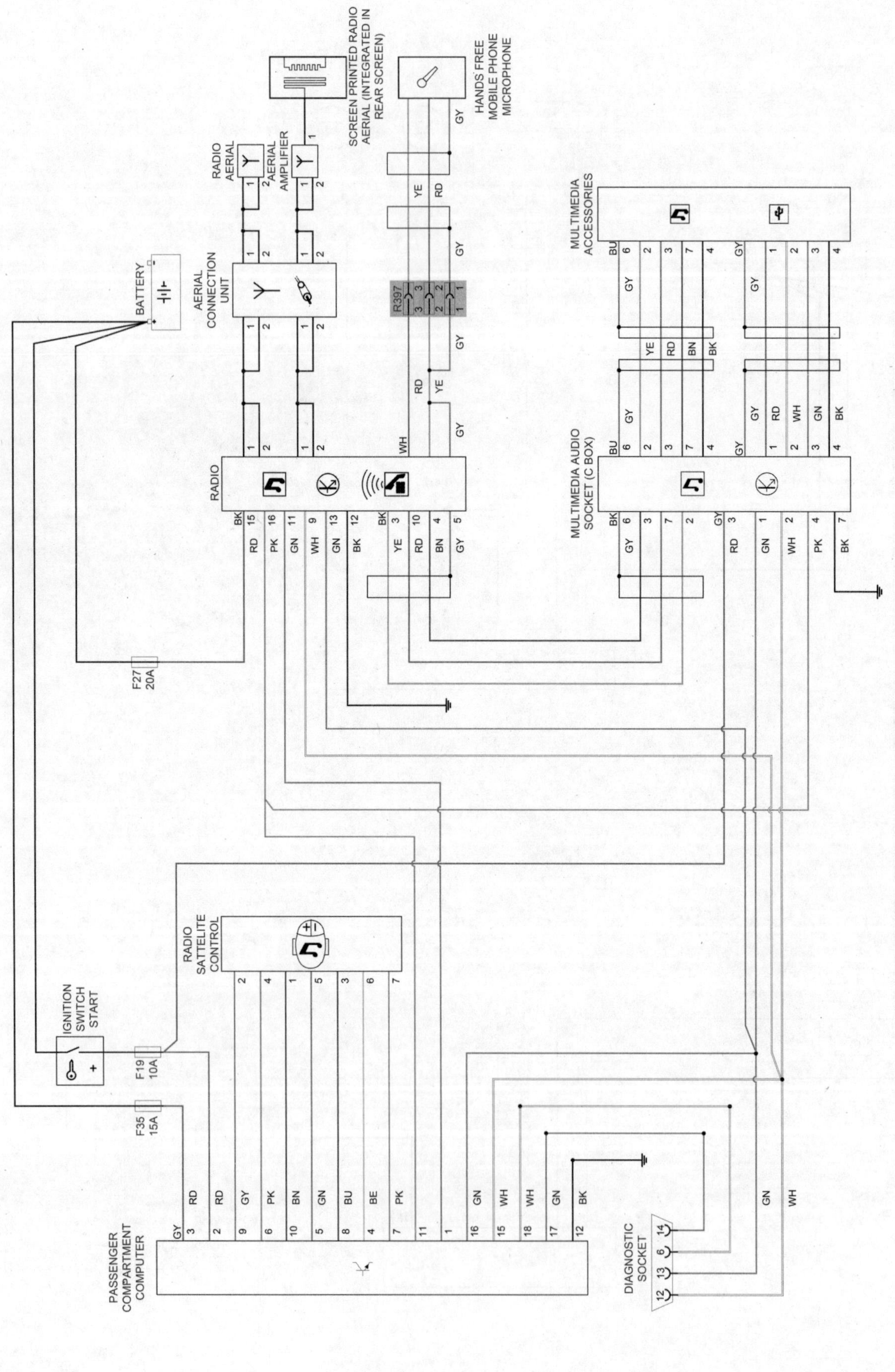

Diagram 16 – Standard audio

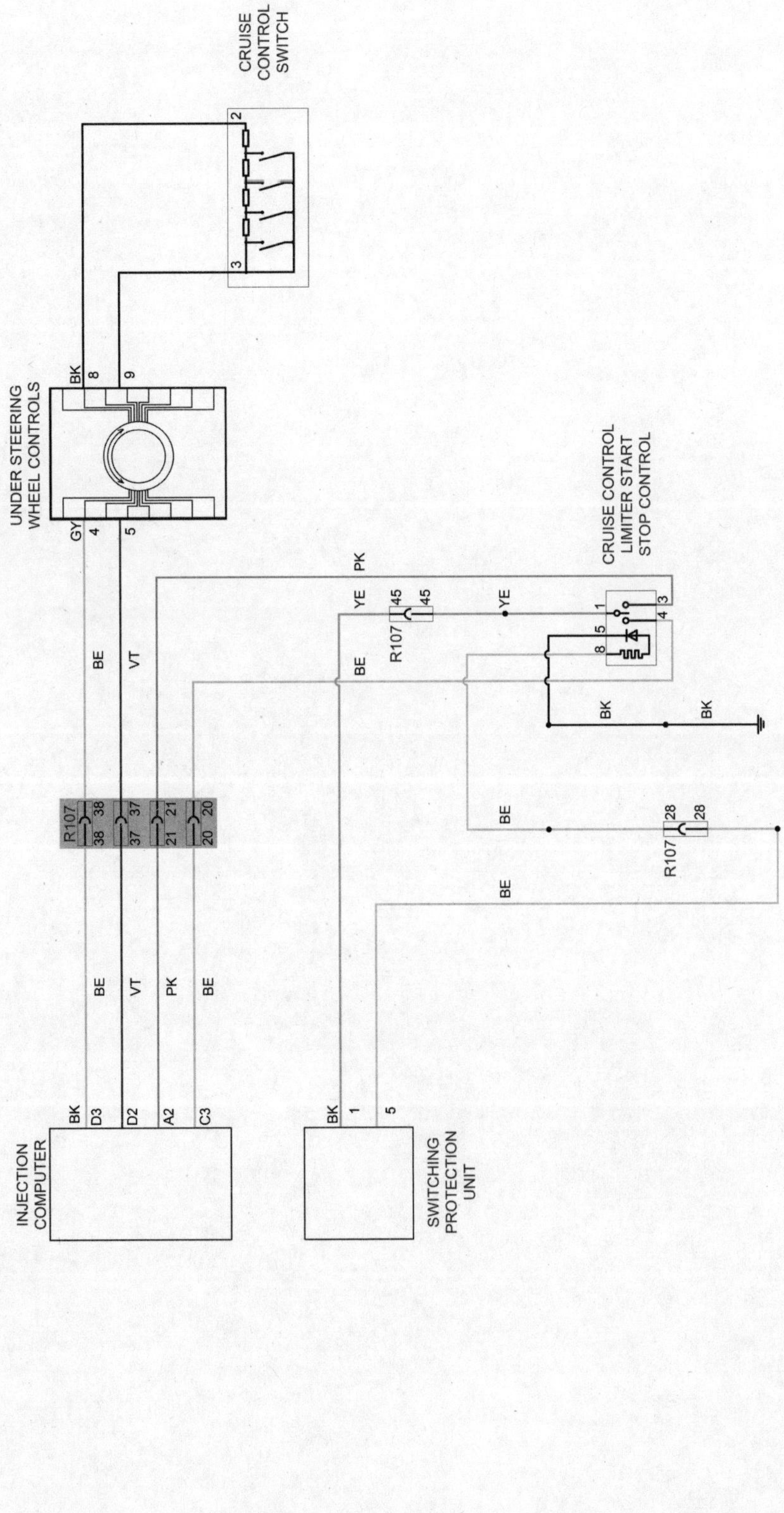

Diagram 17 – Cruise control

Dimensions and weights . . . . REF•1
Fuel economy . . . . REF•2
Conversion factors . . . . REF•6
Buying spare parts . . . . REF•7
Jacking and vehicle support . . . . REF•7
General repair procedures . . . . REF•8
Vehicle identification . . . . REF•9
Tools and working facilities . . . . REF•10
MOT test checks . . . . REF•12
Fault finding . . . . REF•16
Glossary of technical terms . . . . REF•23
Index . . . . REF•27

Dimensions and weights

Note: *All figures are approximate, and may vary according to model. Refer to manufacturer's data for exact figures.*

Dimensions

Overall length:	
Hatchback	4292 mm
Estate	4558 mm
Coupe	4299 mm
Overall width – excluding mirrors:	
Hatchback	1808 mm
Estate	1766 mm
Coupe	1785 mm
Overall height (unladen, according to model):	
Hatchback	1471 mm
Estate (including roof bars)	1461 mm
Coupe	1423 mm
Wheelbase	
Hatchback	2641 mm
Estate	2703 mm
Coupe	2640 mm
Front track	1546 mm
Rear track	1547 mm

Weights

Kerb weight*:	
Petrol models (typical)	1145 to 1230 kg
Diesel models (typical)	1175 to 1327 kg
Maximum gross vehicle weight	1520 to 1580 kg
Maximum roof rack load	80 kg
Maximum towing weight	Refer to your Renault dealer

** Exact kerb weight varies depending on model – refer to VIN plate.*

Fuel economy

Although depreciation is still the biggest part of the cost of motoring for most car owners, the cost of fuel is more immediately noticeable. These pages give some tips on how to get the best fuel economy.

Working it out

Manufacturer's figures

Car manufacturers are required by law to provide fuel consumption information on all new vehicles sold. These 'official' figures are obtained by simulating various driving conditions on a rolling road or a test track. Real life conditions are different, so the fuel consumption actually achieved may not bear much resemblance to the quoted figures.

How to calculate it

Many cars now have trip computers which will display fuel consumption, both instantaneous and average. Refer to the owner's handbook for details of how to use these.

To calculate consumption yourself (and maybe to check that the trip computer is accurate), proceed as follows.

1. Fill up with fuel and note the mileage, or zero the trip recorder.
2. Drive as usual until you need to fill up again.
3. Note the amount of fuel required to refill the tank, and the mileage covered since the previous fill-up.
4. Divide the mileage by the amount of fuel used to obtain the consumption figure.

For example:

Mileage at first fill-up (a) = 27,903
Mileage at second fill-up (b) = 28,346
Mileage covered (b - a) = 443
Fuel required at second fill-up = 48.6 litres

The half-completed changeover to metric units in the UK means that we buy our fuel in litres, measure distances in miles and talk about fuel consumption in miles per gallon. There are two ways round this: the first is to convert the litres to gallons before doing the calculation (by dividing by 4.546, or see Table 1). So in the example:

48.6 litres ÷ 4.546 = 10.69 gallons
443 miles ÷ 10.69 gallons = 41.4 mpg

The second way is to calculate the consumption in miles per litre, then multiply that figure by 4.546 (or see Table 2).

So in the example, fuel consumption is:

443 miles ÷ 48.6 litres = 9.1 mpl
9.1 mpl x 4.546 = 41.4 mpg

The rest of Europe expresses fuel consumption in litres of fuel required to travel 100 km (l/100 km). For interest, the conversions are given in Table 3. In practice it doesn't matter what units you use, provided you know what your normal consumption is and can spot if it's getting better or worse.

Table 1: conversion of litres to Imperial gallons

litres	1	2	3	4	5	10	20	30	40	50	60	70
gallons	0.22	0.44	0.66	0.88	1.10	2.24	4.49	6.73	8.98	11.22	13.47	15.71

Table 2: conversion of miles per litre to miles per gallon

miles per litre	5	6	7	8	9	10	11	12	13	14
miles per gallon	23	27	32	36	41	46	50	55	59	64

Table 3: conversion of litres per 100 km to miles per gallon

litres per 100 km	4	4.5	5	5.5	6	6.5	7	8	9	10
miles per gallon	71	63	56	51	47	43	40	35	31	28

Maintenance

A well-maintained car uses less fuel and creates less pollution. In particular:

Filters

Change air and fuel filters at the specified intervals.

Oil

Use a good quality oil of the lowest viscosity specified by the vehicle manufacturer (see *Lubricants and fluids*). Check the level often and be careful not to overfill.

Spark plugs

When applicable, renew at the specified intervals.

Tyres

Check tyre pressures regularly. Under-inflated tyres have an increased rolling resistance. It is generally safe to use the higher pressures specified for full load conditions even when not fully laden, but keep an eye on the centre band of tread for signs of wear due to over-inflation.

When buying new tyres, consider the 'fuel saving' models which most manufacturers include in their ranges.

Driving style

Acceleration

Acceleration uses more fuel than driving at a steady speed. The best technique with modern cars is to accelerate reasonably briskly to the desired speed, changing up through the gears as soon as possible without making the engine labour.

Air conditioning

Air conditioning absorbs quite a bit of energy from the engine – typically 3 kW (4 hp) or so. The effect on fuel consumption is at its worst in slow traffic. Switch it off when not required.

Anticipation

Drive smoothly and try to read the traffic flow so as to avoid unnecessary acceleration and braking.

Automatic transmission

When accelerating in an automatic, avoid depressing the throttle so far as to make the transmission hold onto lower gears at higher speeds. Don't use the 'Sport' setting, if applicable.

When stationary with the engine running, select 'N' or 'P'. When moving, keep your left foot away from the brake.

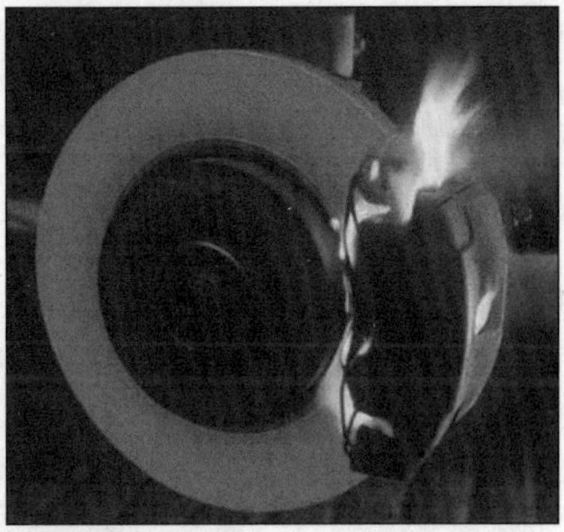

Braking

Braking converts the car's energy of motion into heat – essentially, it is wasted. Obviously some braking is always going to be necessary, but with good anticipation it is surprising how much can be avoided, especially on routes that you know well.

Carshare

Consider sharing lifts to work or to the shops. Even once a week will make a difference.

Electrical loads

Electricity is 'fuel' too; the alternator which charges the battery does so by converting some of the engine's energy of motion into electrical energy. The more electrical accessories are in use, the greater the load on the alternator. Switch off big consumers like the heated rear window when not required.

Freewheeling

Freewheeling (coasting) in neutral with the engine switched off is dangerous. The effort required to operate power-assisted brakes and steering increases when the engine is not running, with a potential lack of control in emergency situations.

In any case, modern fuel injection systems automatically cut off the engine's fuel supply on the overrun (moving and in gear, but with the accelerator pedal released).

Gadgets

Bolt-on devices claiming to save fuel have been around for nearly as long as the motor car itself. Those which worked were rapidly adopted as standard equipment by the vehicle manufacturers. Others worked only in certain situations, or saved fuel only at the expense of unacceptable effects on performance, driveability or the life of engine components.

The most effective fuel saving gadget is the driver's right foot.

Journey planning

Combine (eg) a trip to the supermarket with a visit to the recycling centre and the DIY store, rather than making separate journeys.

When possible choose a travelling time outside rush hours.

Load

The more heavily a car is laden, the greater the energy required to accelerate it to a given speed. Remove heavy items which you don't need to carry.

One load which is often overlooked is the contents of the fuel tank. A tankful of fuel (55 litres / 12 gallons) weighs 45 kg (100 lb) or so. Just half filling it may be worthwhile.

Lost?

At the risk of stating the obvious, if you're going somewhere new, have details of the route to hand. There's not much point in achieving record mpg if you also go miles out of your way.

Parking

If possible, carry out any reversing or turning manoeuvres when you arrive at a parking space so that you can drive straight out when you leave. Manoeuvering when the engine is cold uses a lot more fuel.

Driving around looking for free on-street parking may cost more in fuel than buying a car park ticket.

Premium fuel

Most major oil companies (and some supermarkets) have premium grades of fuel which are several pence a litre dearer than the standard grades. Reports vary, but the consensus seems to be that if these fuels improve economy at all, they do not do so by enough to justify their extra cost.

Roof rack

When loading a roof rack, try to produce a wedge shape with the narrow end at the front. Any cover should be securely fastened – if it flaps it's creating turbulence and absorbing energy.

Remove roof racks and boxes when not in use – they increase air resistance and can create a surprising amount of noise.

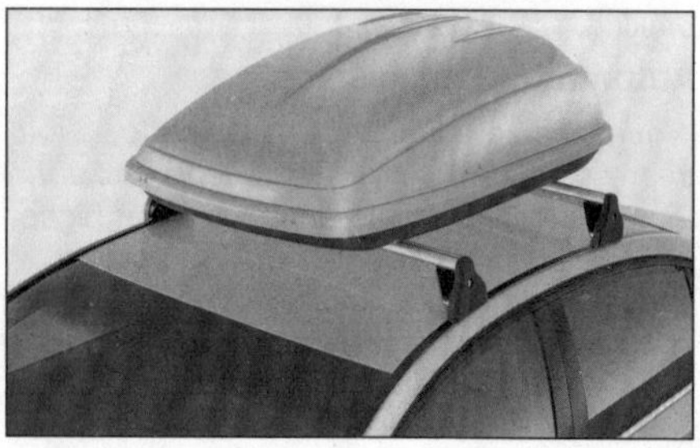

Short journeys

The engine is at its least efficient, and wear is highest, during the first few miles after a cold start. Consider walking, cycling or using public transport.

Speed

The engine is at its most efficient when running at a steady speed and load at the rpm where it develops maximum torque. (You can find this figure in the car's handbook.) For most cars this corresponds to between 55 and 65 mph in top gear.

Above the optimum cruising speed, fuel consumption starts to rise quite sharply. A car travelling at 80 mph will typically be using 30% more fuel than at 60 mph.

Supermarket fuel

It may be cheap but is it any good? In the UK all supermarket fuel must meet the relevant British Standard. The major oil companies will say that their branded fuels have better additive packages which may stop carbon and other deposits building up. A reasonable compromise might be to use one tank of branded fuel to three or four from the supermarket.

Switch off when stationary

Switch off the engine if you look like being stationary for more than 30 seconds or so. This is good for the environment as well as for your pocket. Be aware though that frequent restarts are hard on the battery and the starter motor.

Windows

Driving with the windows open increases air turbulence around the vehicle. Closing the windows promotes smooth airflow and reduced resistance. The faster you go, the more significant this is.

And finally . . .

Driving techniques associated with good fuel economy tend to involve moderate acceleration and low top speeds. Be considerate to the needs of other road users who may need to make brisker progress; even if you do not agree with them this is not an excuse to be obstructive.

Safety must always take precedence over economy, whether it is a question of accelerating hard to complete an overtaking manoeuvre, killing your speed when confronted with a potential hazard or switching the lights on when it starts to get dark.

Conversion factors

Length (distance)

Inches (in)	x 25.4	=	Millimetres (mm)	x 0.0394	=	Inches (in)
Feet (ft)	x 0.305	=	Metres (m)	x 3.281	=	Feet (ft)
Miles	x 1.609	=	Kilometres (km)	x 0.621	=	Miles

Volume (capacity)

Cubic inches (cu in; in^3)	x 16.387	=	Cubic centimetres (cc; cm^3)	x 0.061	=	Cubic inches (cu in; in^3)
Imperial pints (Imp pt)	x 0.568	=	Litres (l)	x 1.76	=	Imperial pints (Imp pt)
Imperial quarts (Imp qt)	x 1.137	=	Litres (l)	x 0.88	=	Imperial quarts (Imp qt)
Imperial quarts (Imp qt)	x 1.201	=	US quarts (US qt)	x 0.833	=	Imperial quarts (Imp qt)
US quarts (US qt)	x 0.946	=	Litres (l)	x 1.057	=	US quarts (US qt)
Imperial gallons (Imp gal)	x 4.546	=	Litres (l)	x 0.22	=	Imperial gallons (Imp gal)
Imperial gallons (Imp gal)	x 1.201	=	US gallons (US gal)	x 0.833	=	Imperial gallons (Imp gal)
US gallons (US gal)	x 3.785	=	Litres (l)	x 0.264	=	US gallons (US gal)

Mass (weight)

Ounces (oz)	x 28.35	=	Grams (g)	x 0.035	=	Ounces (oz)
Pounds (lb)	x 0.454	=	Kilograms (kg)	x 2.205	=	Pounds (lb)

Force

Ounces-force (ozf; oz)	x 0.278	=	Newtons (N)	x 3.6	=	Ounces-force (ozf; oz)
Pounds-force (lbf; lb)	x 4.448	=	Newtons (N)	x 0.225	=	Pounds-force (lbf; lb)
Newtons (N)	x 0.1	=	Kilograms-force (kgf; kg)	x 9.81	=	Newtons (N)

Pressure

Pounds-force per square inch (psi; lbf/in^2; lb/in^2)	x 0.070	=	Kilograms-force per square centimetre (kgf/cm^2; kg/cm^2)	x 14.223	=	Pounds-force per square inch (psi; lbf/in^2; lb/in^2)
Pounds-force per square inch (psi; lbf/in^2; lb/in^2)	x 0.068	=	Atmospheres (atm)	x 14.696	=	Pounds-force per square inch (psi; lbf/in^2; lb/in^2)
Pounds-force per square inch (psi; lbf/in^2; lb/in^2)	x 0.069	=	Bars	x 14.5	=	Pounds-force per square inch (psi; lbf/in^2; lb/in^2)
Pounds-force per square inch (psi; lbf/in^2; lb/in^2)	x 6.895	=	Kilopascals (kPa)	x 0.145	=	Pounds-force per square inch (psi; lbf/in^2; lb/in^2)
Kilopascals (kPa)	x 0.01	=	Kilograms-force per square centimetre (kgf/cm^2; kg/cm^2)	x 98.1	=	Kilopascals (kPa)
Millibar (mbar)	x 100	=	Pascals (Pa)	x 0.01	=	Millibar (mbar)
Millibar (mbar)	x 0.0145	=	Pounds-force per square inch (psi; lbf/in^2; lb/in^2)	x 68.947	=	Millibar (mbar)
Millibar (mbar)	x 0.75	=	Millimetres of mercury (mmHg)	x 1.333	=	Millibar (mbar)
Millibar (mbar)	x 0.401	=	Inches of water (inH$_2$O)	x 2.491	=	Millibar (mbar)
Millimetres of mercury (mmHg)	x 0.535	=	Inches of water (inH$_2$O)	x 1.868	=	Millimetres of mercury (mmHg)
Inches of water (inH$_2$O)	x 0.036	=	Pounds-force per square inch (psi; lbf/in^2; lb/in^2)	x 27.68	=	Inches of water (inH$_2$O)

Torque (moment of force)

Pounds-force inches (lbf in; lb in)	x 1.152	=	Kilograms-force centimetre (kgf cm; kg cm)	x 0.868	=	Pounds-force inches (lbf in; lb in)
Pounds-force inches (lbf in; lb in)	x 0.113	=	Newton metres (Nm)	x 8.85	=	Pounds-force inches (lbf in; lb in)
Pounds-force inches (lbf in; lb in)	x 0.083	=	Pounds-force feet (lbf ft; lb ft)	x 12	=	Pounds-force inches (lbf in; lb in)
Pounds-force feet (lbf ft; lb ft)	x 0.138	=	Kilograms-force metres (kgf m; kg m)	x 7.233	=	Pounds-force feet (lbf ft; lb ft)
Pounds-force feet (lbf ft; lb ft)	x 1.356	=	Newton metres (Nm)	x 0.738	=	Pounds-force feet (lbf ft; lb ft)
Newton metres (Nm)	x 0.102	=	Kilograms-force metres (kgf m; kg m)	x 9.804	=	Newton metres (Nm)

Power

Horsepower (hp)	x 745.7	=	Watts (W)	x 0.0013	=	Horsepower (hp)

Velocity (speed)

Miles per hour (miles/hr; mph)	x 1.609	=	Kilometres per hour (km/hr; kph)	x 0.621	=	Miles per hour (miles/hr; mph)

Fuel consumption*

Miles per gallon, Imperial (mpg)	x 0.354	=	Kilometres per litre (km/l)	x 2.825	=	Miles per gallon, Imperial (mpg)
Miles per gallon, US (mpg)	x 0.425	=	Kilometres per litre (km/l)	x 2.352	=	Miles per gallon, US (mpg)

Temperature

Degrees Fahrenheit = (°C x 1.8) + 32

Degrees Celsius (Degrees Centigrade; °C) = (°F - 32) x 0.56

** It is common practice to convert from miles per gallon (mpg) to litres/100 kilometres (l/100km), where mpg x l/100 km = 282*

Buying spare parts

Spare parts are available from many sources, including maker's appointed garages, accessory shops, and motor factors. To be sure of obtaining the correct parts, it will sometimes be necessary to quote the vehicle identification number (see *Vehicle identification*). If possible, it can also be useful to take the old parts along for positive identification. Items such as starter motors and alternators may be available under a service exchange scheme – any parts returned should always be clean.

Our advice regarding spare part sources is as follows.

Officially-appointed garages

This is the best source of parts which are peculiar to your car, and which are not otherwise generally available (eg badges, interior trim, certain body panels, etc). It is also the only place at which you should buy parts if the car is still under warranty.

Accessory shops

These are very good places to buy materials and components needed for the maintenance of your car (oil, air and fuel filters, spark plugs, light bulbs, drivebelts, oils and greases, brake pads, touch-up paint, etc). Components of this nature sold by a reputable shop are of the same standard as those used by the car manufacturer.

Besides components, these shops also sell tools and general accessories, usually have convenient opening hours, charge lower prices, and can often be found not far from home. Some accessory shops have parts counters where the components needed for almost any repair job can be purchased or ordered.

Motor factors

Good factors will stock all the more important components which wear out comparatively quickly, and can sometimes supply individual components needed for the overhaul of a larger assembly (eg brake seals and hydraulic parts, bearing shells, pistons, valves, alternator brushes). They may also handle work such as cylinder block reboring, crankshaft regrinding and balancing, etc.

Tyre and exhaust specialists

These outlets may be independent, or members of a local or national chain. They frequently offer competitive prices when compared with a main dealer or local garage, but it will pay to obtain several quotes before making a decision. When researching prices, also ask what 'extras' may be added – for instance, fitting a new valve and balancing the wheel are both commonly charged on top of the price of a new tyre. **Note:** *Many models in the Mégane range have a tyre pressure monitoring system, which means that new valves should not be fitted when tyres are changed – see Chapter 10.*

Other sources

Beware of parts or materials obtained from market stalls, car boot sales or similar outlets. Such items are not invariably sub-standard, but there is little chance of compensation if they do prove unsatisfactory. In the case of safety-critical components such as brake pads, there is the risk not only of financial loss but also of an accident causing injury or death.

Second-hand components or assemblies obtained from a car breaker can be a good buy in some circumstances, but this sort of purchase is best made by the experienced DIY mechanic.

Jacking and vehicle support

The jack supplied with the car's tool kit should only be used for changing the roadwheels – see *Wheel changing* at the front of this book. When carrying out any other kind of work, raise the car using a hydraulic (or 'trolley') jack, and always supplement the jack with axle stands positioned under the jacking/support points. If the roadwheels do not have to be removed, consider using wheel ramps – if wished, these can be placed under the wheels once the car has been raised using a hydraulic jack, and then lowered onto the ramps so that it is resting on its wheels.

Only ever jack the car up on a solid, level surface. If there is even a slight slope, take great care that the car cannot move as the wheels are lifted off the ground. Jacking up on an uneven or gravelled surface is not recommended, as the weight of the car will not be evenly distributed, and the jack may slip as the car is raised.

As far as possible, do not leave the car unattended once it has been raised, particularly if children are playing nearby.

Before jacking up the front of the car, ensure that the handbrake is firmly applied. When jacking up the rear of the car, place wooden chocks in front of the front wheels, and engage first gear.

To raise the front of the car, position the jack head forward of the sill jacking point. Use a flat piece of wood to spread the load or use a jack fitted with a rubber pad **(see illustration)**. Always supplement the jack with axle stands under the sill jacking points.

To raise the rear position the jack – with a suitable block of wood – to the rear of the sill jacking point **(see illustration)**. It is also possible at the rear (provided that work is not being carried out on the rear suspension) to lift the vehicle with a jack placed under the rear spring seat – note, however, that this must only be attempted with a substantial jack and with the car on solid, level ground.

Do not jack the car under any other part of the sill, sump, floor pan, or (except as described) directly under any of the steering or suspension components.

Never work under, around, or near a raised vehicle, unless it is adequately supported on stands. Do not rely on a jack alone, as even a hydraulic jack could fail under load.

Place the jack just forward of the sill jacking point

Place the jack just to the rear of the sill jacking point

Whenever servicing, repair or overhaul work is carried out on the car or its components, observe the following procedures and instructions. This will assist in carrying out the operation efficiently and to a professional standard of workmanship.

Joint mating faces and gaskets

When separating components at their mating faces, never insert screwdrivers or similar implements into the joint between the faces in order to prise them apart. This can cause severe damage which results in oil leaks, coolant leaks, etc upon reassembly. Separation is usually achieved by tapping along the joint with a soft-faced hammer in order to break the seal. However, note that this method may not be suitable where dowels are used for component location.

Where a gasket is used between the mating faces of two components, a new one must be fitted on reassembly; fit it dry unless otherwise stated in the repair procedure. Make sure that the mating faces are clean and dry, with all traces of old gasket removed. When cleaning a joint face, use a tool which is unlikely to score or damage the face, and remove any burrs or nicks with an oilstone or fine file.

Make sure that tapped holes are cleaned with a pipe cleaner, and keep them free of jointing compound, if this is being used, unless specifically instructed otherwise.

Ensure that all orifices, channels or pipes are clear, and blow through them, preferably using compressed air.

Oil seals

Oil seals can be removed by levering them out with a wide flat-bladed screwdriver or similar implement. Alternatively, a number of self-tapping screws may be screwed into the seal, and these used as a purchase for pliers or some similar device in order to pull the seal free.

Whenever an oil seal is removed from its working location, either individually or as part of an assembly, it should be renewed.

The very fine sealing lip of the seal is easily damaged, and will not seal if the surface it contacts is not completely clean and free from scratches, nicks or grooves. If the original sealing surface of the component cannot be restored, and the manufacturer has not made provision for slight relocation of the seal relative to the sealing surface, the component should be renewed.

Protect the lips of the seal from any surface which may damage them in the course of fitting. Use tape or a conical sleeve where possible. Where indicated, lubricate the seal lips with oil before fitting and, on dual-lipped seals, fill the space between the lips with grease.

Unless otherwise stated, oil seals must be fitted with their sealing lips toward the lubricant to be sealed.

Use a tubular drift or block of wood of the appropriate size to install the seal and, if the seal housing is shouldered, drive the seal down to the shoulder. If the seal housing is unshouldered, the seal should be fitted with its face flush with the housing top face (unless otherwise instructed).

Screw threads and fastenings

Seized nuts, bolts and screws are quite a common occurrence where corrosion has set in, and the use of penetrating oil or releasing fluid will often overcome this problem if the offending item is soaked for a while before attempting to release it. The use of an impact driver may also provide a means of releasing such stubborn fastening devices, when used in conjunction with the appropriate screwdriver bit or socket. If none of these methods works, it may be necessary to resort to the careful application of heat, or the use of a hacksaw or nut splitter device. Before resorting to extreme methods, check that you are not dealing with a left-hand thread!

Studs are usually removed by locking two nuts together on the threaded part, and then using a spanner on the lower nut to unscrew the stud. Studs or bolts which have broken off below the surface of the component in which they are mounted can sometimes be removed using a stud extractor.

Always ensure that a blind tapped hole is completely free from oil, grease, water or other fluid before installing the bolt or stud. Failure to do this could cause the housing to crack due to the hydraulic action of the bolt or stud as it is screwed in.

For some screw fastenings, notably cylinder head bolts or nuts, torque wrench settings are no longer specified for the latter stages of tightening, "angle-tightening" being called up instead. Typically, a fairly low torque wrench setting will be applied to the bolts/nuts in the correct sequence, followed by one or more stages of tightening through specified angles.

When checking or retightening a nut or bolt to a specified torque setting, slacken the nut or bolt by a quarter of a turn, and then retighten to the specified setting. However, this should not be attempted where angular tightening has been used.

Locknuts, locktabs and washers

Any fastening which will rotate against a component or housing during tightening should always have a washer between it and the relevant component or housing.

Spring or split washers should always be renewed when they are used to lock a critical component such as a big-end bearing retaining bolt or nut. Locktabs which are folded over to retain a nut or bolt should always be renewed.

Self-locking nuts can be re-used in non-critical areas, providing resistance can be felt when the locking portion passes over the bolt or stud thread. However, it should be noted that self-locking stiffnuts tend to lose their effectiveness after long periods of use, and should then be renewed as a matter of course.

Split pins must always be replaced with new ones of the correct size for the hole.

When thread-locking compound is found on the threads of a fastener which is to be re-used, it should be cleaned off with a wire brush and solvent, and fresh compound applied on reassembly.

Special tools

Some repair procedures in this manual entail the use of special tools such as a press, two or three-legged pullers, spring compressors, etc. Wherever possible, suitable readily-available alternatives to the manufacturer's special tools are described, and are shown in use. In some instances, where no alternative is possible, it has been necessary to resort to the use of a manufacturer's tool, and this has been done for reasons of safety as well as the efficient completion of the repair operation. Unless you are highly-skilled and have a thorough understanding of the procedures described, never attempt to bypass the use of any special tool when the procedure described specifies its use. Not only is there a very great risk of personal injury, but expensive damage could be caused to the components involved.

Environmental considerations

When disposing of used engine oil, brake fluid, antifreeze, etc, give due consideration to any detrimental environmental effects. Do not, for instance, pour any of the above liquids down drains into the general sewage system, or onto the ground to soak away, as this is likely to pollute your local environment. Many local council refuse tips provide a facility for waste oil disposal, as do some garages. You can find your nearest disposal point by calling the Environment Agency on 03708 506 506 or by visiting www.oilbankline.org.uk.

Note: It is illegal and anti-social to dump oil down the drain. To find the location of your local oil recycling bank, call 03708 506 506 or visit www.oilbankline.org.uk.

Modifications are a continuing and unpublicised process in car manufacture, quite apart from major model changes. Spare parts manuals and lists are compiled upon a numerical basis, the individual vehicle identification numbers being essential to correct identification of the component concerned.

When ordering spare parts, always give as much information as possible. Quote the car model, year of manufacture, body and engine numbers as appropriate. Most factors and dealers have access to a vehicle look up system based on the vehicles registration number and this is often the only information required.

The *vehicle identification plate* is located on the right-hand C-pillar on hatchback and estate models. On coupe models the plate is located of the right-hand door B-pillar, and can be viewed with the door open. In addition to many other details, it carries the Vehicle Identification Number (VIN), maximum vehicle weight information, and codes for interior trim and body colours. A further VIN may be found on the B-pillar of some models **(see illustrations)**.

All models also have the VIN on the left-hand end of the facia – visible through the windscreen glass **(see illustration)**.

The *engine number* is stamped on the front of the engine. Even with the engine top cover removed (where applicable), the number can be hard to see – this is especially true of the diesel engines **(see illustration)**.

The vehicle identification plate on the base of the B-pillar

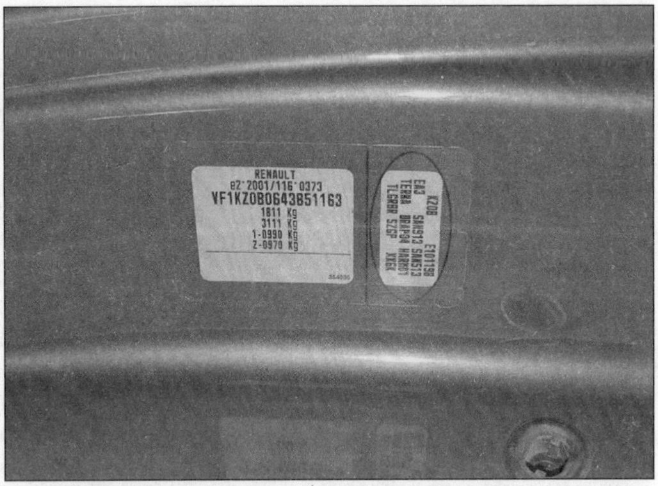

A comprehensive VIN plate is also mounted on the door shut

The VIN is also visible through the windscreen

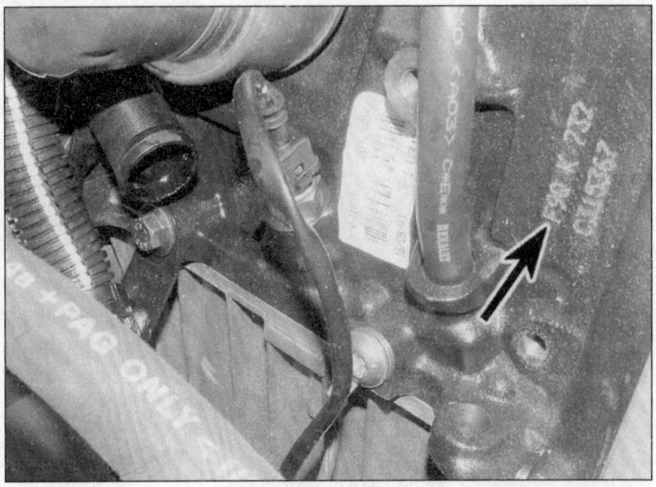

The engine number is stamped on the front of the block and may be hard to see

Introduction

A selection of good tools is a fundamental requirement for anyone contemplating the maintenance and repair of a motor vehicle. For the owner who does not possess any, their purchase will prove a considerable expense, offsetting some of the savings made by doing-it-yourself. However, provided that the tools purchased meet the relevant national safety standards and are of good quality, they will last for many years and prove an extremely worthwhile investment.

To help the average owner to decide which tools are needed to carry out the various tasks detailed in this manual, we have compiled three lists of tools under the following headings: *Maintenance and minor repair*, *Repair and overhaul*, and *Special*. Newcomers to practical mechanics should start off with the *Maintenance and minor repair* tool kit, and confine themselves to the simpler jobs around the vehicle. Then, as confidence and experience grow, more difficult tasks can be undertaken, with extra tools being purchased as, and when, they are needed. In this way, a *Maintenance and minor repair* tool kit can be built up into a *Repair and overhaul* tool kit over a considerable period of time, without any major cash outlays. The experienced do-it-yourselfer will have a tool kit good enough for most repair and overhaul procedures, and will add tools from the *Special* category when it is felt that the expense is justified by the amount of use to which these tools will be put.

Maintenance and minor repair tool kit

The tools given in this list should be considered as a minimum requirement if routine maintenance, servicing and minor repair operations are to be undertaken. We recommend the purchase of combination spanners (ring one end, open-ended the other); although more expensive than open-ended ones, they do give the advantages of both types of spanner.

- ☐ *Combination spanners:*
  Metric - 8 to 19 mm inclusive
- ☐ *Adjustable spanner - 35 mm jaw (approx.)*
- ☐ *Spark plug spanner (with rubber insert) - petrol models*
- ☐ *Spark plug gap adjustment tool - petrol models*
- ☐ *Set of feeler gauges*
- ☐ *Brake bleed nipple spanner*
- ☐ *Screwdrivers:*
  Flat blade - 100 mm long x 6 mm dia
  Cross blade - 100 mm long x 6 mm dia
  Torx - various sizes (not all vehicles)
- ☐ *Combination pliers*
- ☐ *Hacksaw (junior)*
- ☐ *Tyre pump*
- ☐ *Tyre pressure gauge*
- ☐ *Oil can*
- ☐ *Oil filter removal tool (if applicable)*
- ☐ *Fine emery cloth*
- ☐ *Wire brush (small)*
- ☐ *Funnel (medium size)*
- ☐ *Sump drain plug key (not all vehicles)*

Repair and overhaul tool kit

These tools are virtually essential for anyone undertaking any major repairs to a motor vehicle, and are additional to those given in the *Maintenance and minor repair* list. Included in this list is a comprehensive set of sockets. Although these are expensive, they will be found invaluable as they are so versatile - particularly if various drives are included in the set. We recommend the half-inch square-drive type, as this can be used with most proprietary torque wrenches.

The tools in this list will sometimes need to be supplemented by tools from the *Special* list:

- ☐ *Sockets to cover range in previous list (including Torx sockets)*
- ☐ *Reversible ratchet drive (for use with sockets)*
- ☐ *Extension piece, 250 mm (for use with sockets)*
- ☐ *Universal joint (for use with sockets)*
- ☐ *Flexible handle or sliding T "breaker bar" (for use with sockets)*
- ☐ *Torque wrench (for use with sockets)*
- ☐ *Self-locking grips*
- ☐ *Ball pein hammer*
- ☐ *Soft-faced mallet (plastic or rubber)*
- ☐ *Screwdrivers:*
  Flat blade - long & sturdy, short (chubby), and narrow (electrician's) types
  Cross blade – long & sturdy, and short (chubby) types
- ☐ *Pliers:*
  Long-nosed
  Side cutters (electrician's)
  Circlip (internal and external)
- ☐ *Cold chisel - 25 mm*
- ☐ *Scriber*
- ☐ *Scraper*
- ☐ *Centre-punch*
- ☐ *Pin punch*
- ☐ *Hacksaw*
- ☐ *Brake hose clamp*
- ☐ *Brake/clutch bleeding kit*
- ☐ *Selection of twist drills*
- ☐ *Steel rule/straight-edge*
- ☐ *Allen keys (inc. splined/Torx type)*
- ☐ *Selection of files*
- ☐ *Wire brush*
- ☐ *Axle stands*
- ☐ *Jack (strong trolley or hydraulic type)*
- ☐ *Light with extension lead*
- ☐ *Universal electrical multi-meter*

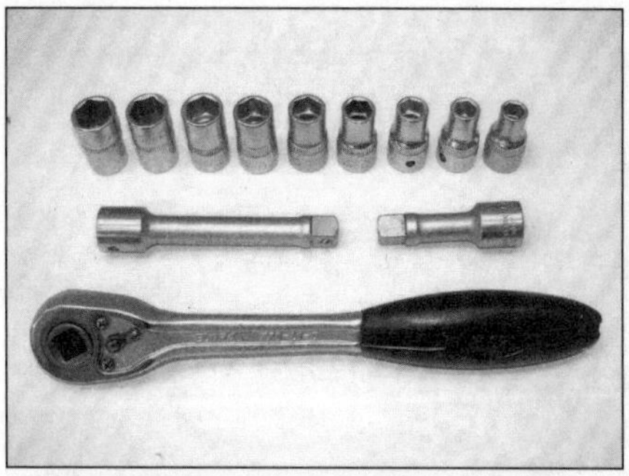

Sockets and reversible ratchet drive

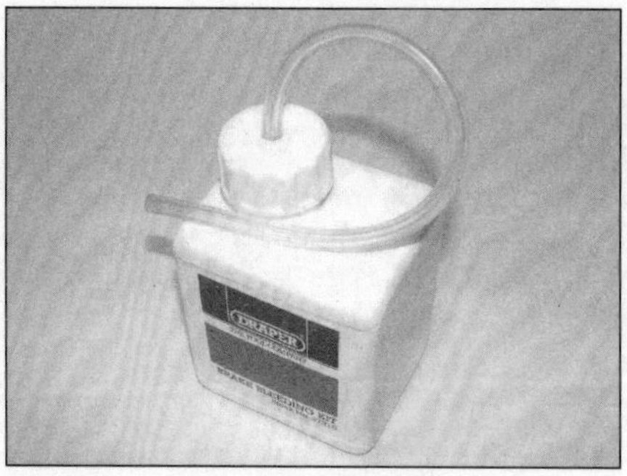

Brake bleeding kit

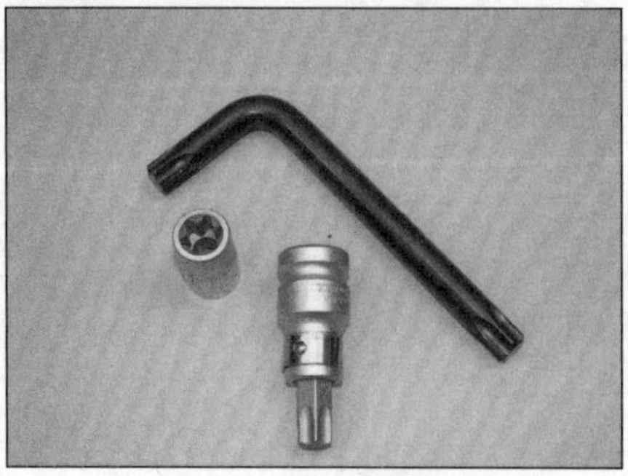

Torx key, socket and bit

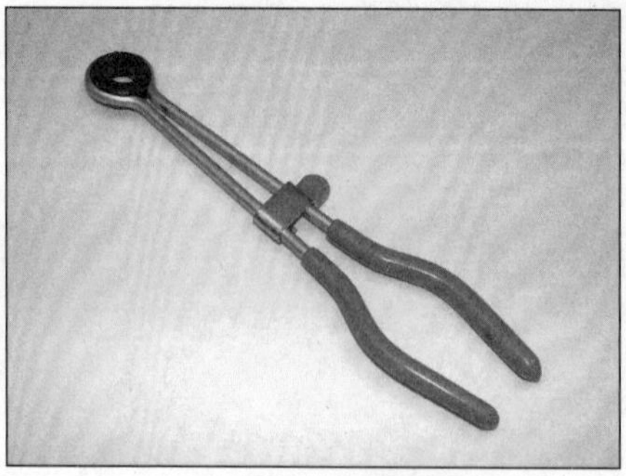

Hose clamp

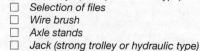

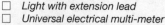

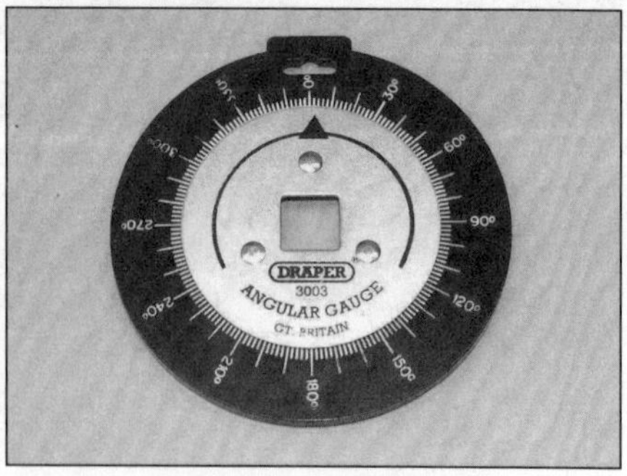

Angular-tightening gauge

Special tools

The tools in this list are those which are not used regularly, are expensive to buy, or which need to be used in accordance with their manufacturers' instructions. Unless relatively difficult mechanical jobs are undertaken frequently, it will not be economic to buy many of these tools. Where this is the case, you could consider clubbing together with friends (or joining a motorists' club) to make a joint purchase, or borrowing the tools against a deposit from a local garage or tool hire specialist.

The following list contains only those tools and instruments freely available to the public, and not those special tools produced by the vehicle manufacturer specifically for its dealer network. You will find occasional references to these manufacturers' special tools in the text of this manual. Generally, an alternative method of doing the job without the vehicle manufacturers' special tool is given. However, sometimes there is no alternative to using them. Where this is the case and the relevant tool cannot be bought or borrowed, you will have to entrust the work to a dealer.

- ☐ *Angular-tightening gauge*
- ☐ *Valve spring compressor*
- ☐ *Valve grinding tool*
- ☐ *Piston ring compressor*
- ☐ *Piston ring removal/installation tool*
- ☐ *Cylinder bore hone*
- ☐ *Balljoint separator*
- ☐ *Coil spring compressors (where applicable)*
- ☐ *Two/three-legged hub and bearing puller*
- ☐ *Impact screwdriver*
- ☐ *Micrometer and/or vernier calipers*
- ☐ *Dial gauge*
- ☐ *Tachometer*
- ☐ *Fault code reader*
- ☐ *Cylinder compression gauge*
- ☐ *Hand-operated vacuum pump and gauge*
- ☐ *Clutch plate alignment set*
- ☐ *Brake shoe steady spring cup removal tool*
- ☐ *Bush and bearing removal/installation set*
- ☐ *Stud extractors*
- ☐ *Tap and die set*
- ☐ *Lifting tackle*

Buying tools

Reputable motor accessory shops and superstores often offer excellent quality tools at discount prices, so it pays to shop around.

Remember, you don't have to buy the most expensive items on the shelf, but it is always advisable to steer clear of the very cheap tools. Beware of 'bargains' offered on market stalls, on-line or at car boot sales. There are plenty of good tools around at reasonable prices, but always aim to purchase items which meet the relevant national safety standards. If in doubt, ask the proprietor or manager of the shop for advice before making a purchase.

Care and maintenance of tools

Having purchased a reasonable tool kit, it is necessary to keep the tools in a clean and serviceable condition. After use, always wipe off any dirt, grease and metal particles using a clean, dry cloth, before putting the tools away. Never leave them lying around after they have been used. A simple tool rack on the garage or workshop wall for items such as screwdrivers and pliers is a good idea. Store all normal spanners and sockets in a metal box. Any measuring instruments, gauges, meters, etc, must be carefully stored where they cannot be damaged or become rusty.

Take a little care when tools are used. Hammer heads inevitably become marked, and screwdrivers lose the keen edge on their blades from time to time. A little timely attention with emery cloth or a file will soon restore items like this to a good finish.

Working facilities

Not to be forgotten when discussing tools is the workshop itself. If anything more than routine maintenance is to be carried out, a suitable working area becomes essential.

It is appreciated that many an owner-mechanic is forced by circumstances to remove an engine or similar item without the benefit of a garage or workshop. Having done this, any repairs should always be done under the cover of a roof.

Wherever possible, any dismantling should be done on a clean, flat workbench or table at a suitable working height.

Any workbench needs a vice; one with a jaw opening of 100 mm is suitable for most jobs. As mentioned previously, some clean dry storage space is also required for tools, as well as for any lubricants, cleaning fluids, touch-up paints etc, which become necessary.

Another item which may be required, and which has a much more general usage, is an electric drill with a chuck capacity of at least 8 mm. This, together with a good range of twist drills, is virtually essential for fitting accessories.

Last, but not least, always keep a supply of old newspapers and clean, lint-free rags available, and try to keep any working area as clean as possible.

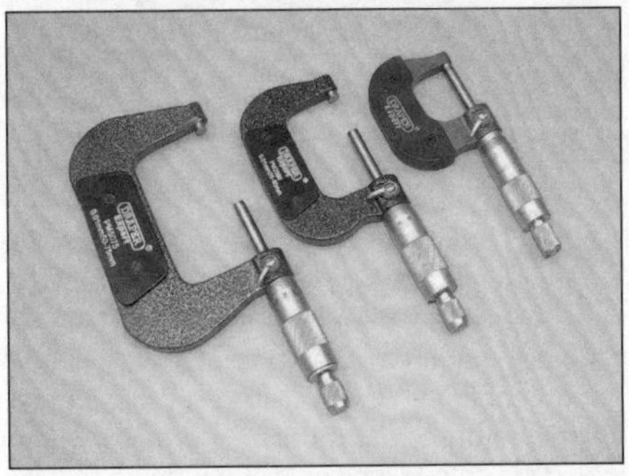

Micrometers

Dial test indicator ("dial gauge")

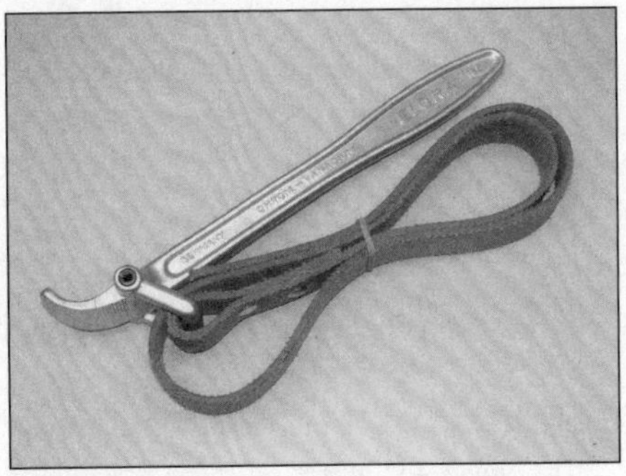

Oil filter removal tool (strap wrench type)

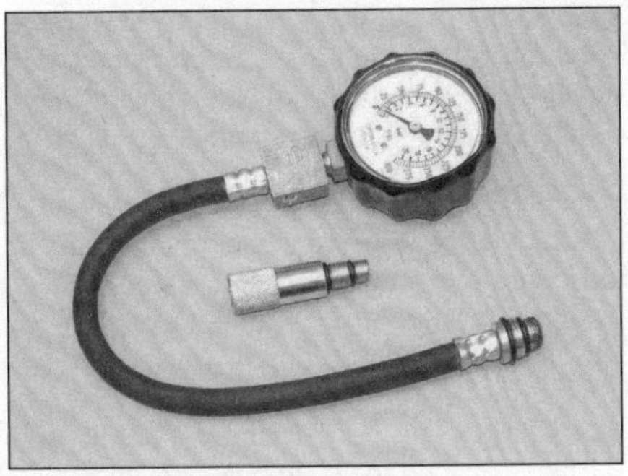

Compression tester

Bearing puller

This is a guide to getting your vehicle through the MOT test. Obviously it will not be possible to examine the vehicle to the same standard as the professional MOT tester. However, working through the following checks will enable you to identify any problem areas before submitting the vehicle for the test.

It has only been possible to summarise the test requirements here, based on the regulations in force at the time of printing. Test standards are becoming increasingly stringent, although there are some exemptions for older vehicles.

An assistant will be needed to help carry out some of these checks.

The checks have been sub-divided into four categories, as follows:

1 Checks carried out **FROM THE DRIVER'S SEAT**

2 Checks carried out **WITH THE VEHICLE ON THE GROUND**

3 Checks carried out **WITH THE VEHICLE RAISED AND THE WHEELS FREE TO TURN**

4 Checks carried out on **YOUR VEHICLE'S EXHAUST EMISSION SYSTEM**

1 Checks carried out FROM THE DRIVER'S SEAT

Handbrake (parking brake)

☐ Test the operation of the handbrake. Excessive travel (too many clicks) indicates incorrect brake or cable adjustment.

☐ Check that the handbrake cannot be released by tapping the lever sideways. Check the security of the lever mountings.

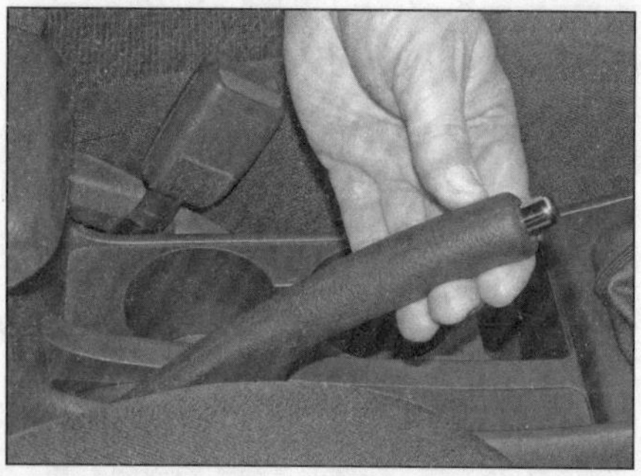

☐ If the parking brake is foot-operated, check that the pedal is secure and without excessive travel, and that the release mechanism operates correctly.

☐ Where applicable, test the operation of the electronic handbrake. The brake should engage and disengage without excessive delay. If the warning light does not extinguish when the brake is disengaged, this could indicate a fault which will need further investigation.

Footbrake

☐ Depress the brake pedal and check that it does not creep down to the floor, indicating a master cylinder fault. Release the pedal, wait a few seconds, then depress it again. If the pedal travels nearly to the floor before firm resistance is felt, brake adjustment or repair is necessary. If the pedal feels spongy, there is air in the hydraulic system which must be removed by bleeding.

☐ Check that the brake pedal is secure and in good condition. Check also for signs of fluid leaks on the pedal, floor or carpets, which would indicate failed seals in the brake master cylinder.

☐ Check the servo unit (when applicable) by operating the brake pedal several times, then keeping the pedal depressed and starting the engine. As the engine starts, the pedal will move down slightly. If not, the vacuum hose or the servo itself may be faulty.

Steering wheel and column

☐ Examine the steering wheel for fractures or looseness of the hub, spokes or rim.

☐ Move the steering wheel from side to side and then up and down. Check that the steering wheel is not loose on the column, indicating wear or a loose retaining nut. Continue moving the steering wheel as before, but also turn it slightly from left to right.

☐ Check that the steering wheel is not loose on the column, and that there is no abnormal movement of the steering wheel, indicating wear in the column support bearings or couplings.

☐ Check that the ignition lock (where fitted) engages and disengages correctly.

☐ Steering column adjustment mechanisms (where fitted) must be able to lock the column securely in place with no play evident.

Windscreen, mirrors and sunvisor

☐ The windscreen must be free of cracks or other significant damage within the driver's field of view. (Small stone chips are acceptable.) Rear view mirrors must be secure, intact, and capable of being adjusted.

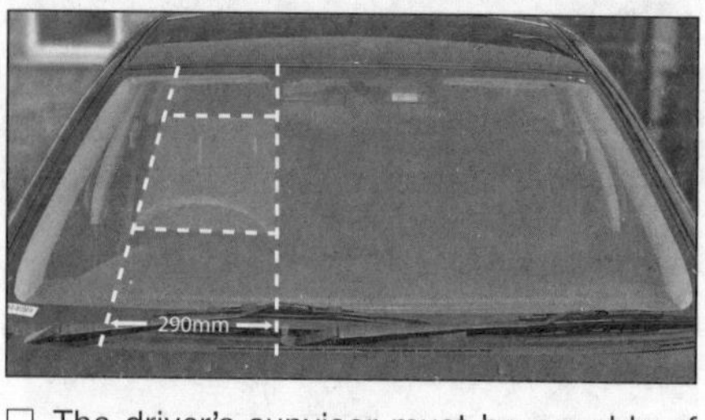

☐ The driver's sunvisor must be capable of being stored in the "up" position.

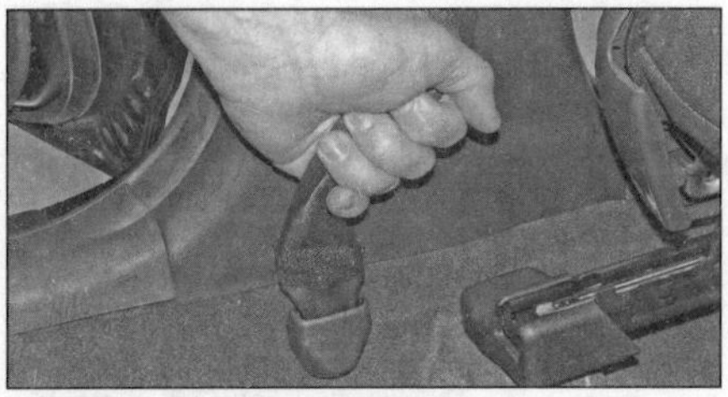

Seat belts and seats

Note: *The following checks are applicable to all seat belts, front and rear.*

☐Examine the webbing of all the belts (including rear belts if fitted) for cuts, serious fraying or deterioration. Fasten and unfasten each belt to check the buckles. If applicable, check the retracting mechanism. Check the security of all seat belt mountings accessible from inside the vehicle, ensuring any height adjustable mountings lock securely in place.

☐Seat belts with pre-tensioners, once activated, have a "flag" or similar showing on the seat belt stalk. This, in itself, is not a reason for test failure.

☐The front seats themselves must be securely attached and the backrests must lock in the upright position.

Doors

☐Both front doors must be able to be opened and closed from outside and inside, and must latch securely when closed.

Bonnet and boot/tailgate

☐The bonnet and boot/tailgate must latch securely when closed.

2 Checks carried out WITH THE VEHICLE ON THE GROUND

Vehicle identification

☐Number plates must be in good condition, secure and legible, with letters and numbers correctly spaced – spacing at (A) should be 33 mm and at (B) 11 mm. At the front, digits must be black on a white background and at the rear black on a yellow background. Other background designs (such as honeycomb) are not permitted.

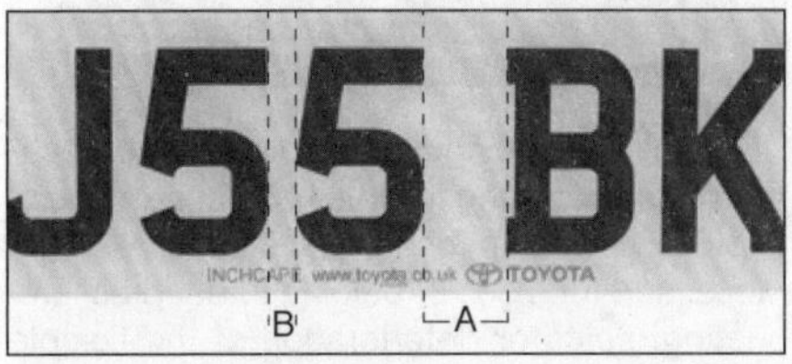

☐The VIN plate and/or homologation plate must be permanently displayed and legible.

Electrical equipment

☐Switch on the ignition and check the operation of the horn.

☐Check the windscreen washers and wipers, examining the wiper blades; renew damaged or perished blades. Also check the operation of the stop-lights.

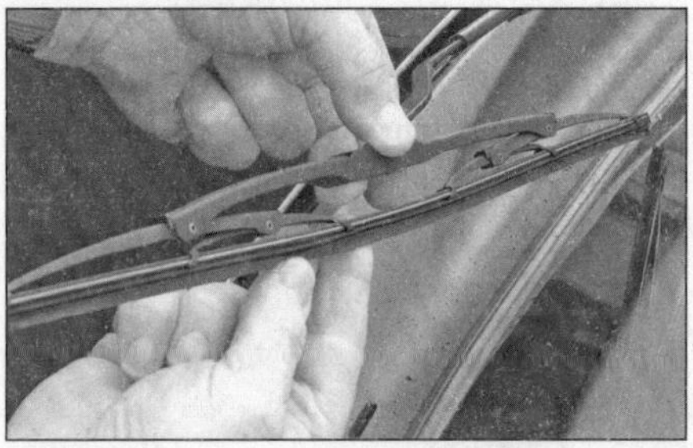

☐Check the operation of the sidelights and number plate lights. The lenses and reflectors must be secure, clean and undamaged.

☐Check the operation and alignment of the headlights. The headlight reflectors must not be tarnished and the lenses must be undamaged.

☐Switch on the ignition and check the operation of the direction indicators (including the instrument panel tell-tale) and the hazard warning lights. Operation of the sidelights and stop-lights must not affect the indicators - if it does, the cause is usually a bad earth at the rear light cluster. Indicators should flash at a rate of between 60 and 120 times per minute – faster or slower than this could indicate a fault with the flasher unit or a bad earth at one of the light units.

☐Check the operation of the rear foglight(s), including the warning light on the instrument panel or in the switch.

☐The warning lights must illuminate in accordance with the manufacturer's design. For most vehicles, the ABS and other warning lights should illuminate when the ignition is switched on, and (if the system is operating properly) extinguish after a few seconds. Refer to the owner's handbook.

Footbrake

☐Examine the master cylinder, brake pipes and servo unit for leaks, loose mountings, corrosion or other damage. If ABS is fitted, this unit should also be examined for signs of leaks or corrosion.

☐The fluid reservoir must be secure and the fluid level must be between the upper (**A**) and lower (**B**) markings.

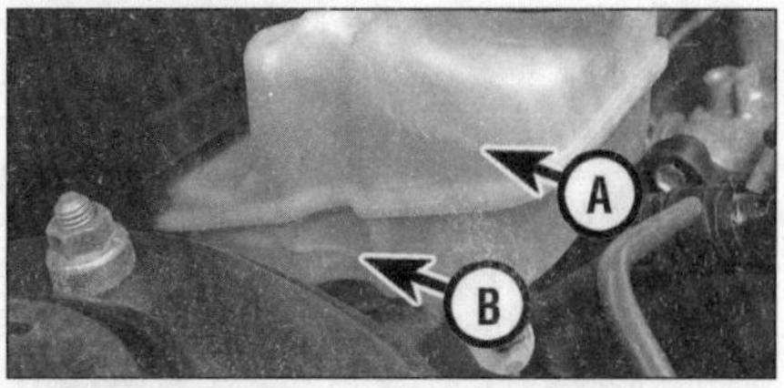

☐Inspect both front brake flexible hoses for cracks or deterioration of the rubber. Turn the steering from lock to lock, and ensure that the hoses do not contact the wheel, tyre, or any part of the steering or suspension mechanism. With the brake pedal firmly depressed, check the hoses for bulges or leaks under pressure.

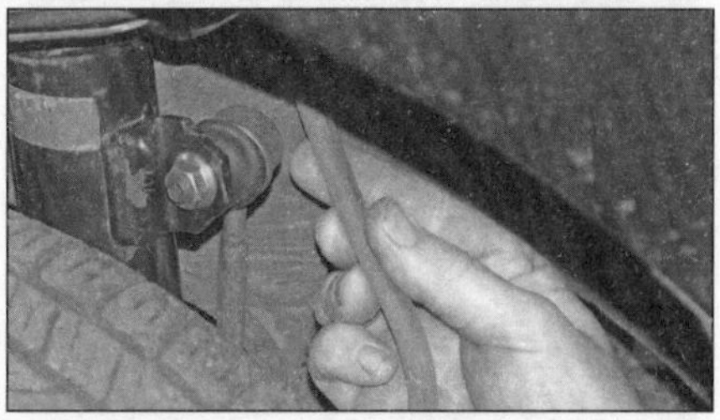

Steering and suspension

☐Have your assistant turn the steering wheel from side to side slightly, up to the point where the steering gear just begins to transmit this movement to the roadwheels. Check for excessive free play between the steering wheel and the steering gear, indicating wear or insecurity of the steering column joints, the column-to-steering gear coupling, or the steering gear itself.

☐Have your assistant turn the steering wheel more vigorously in each direction, so that the roadwheels just begin to turn. As this is done, examine all the steering joints, linkages, fittings and attachments. Renew any component that shows signs of wear or damage. On vehicles with power steering, check the security and condition of the steering pump, drivebelt and hoses.

☐Check that the vehicle is standing level, and at approximately the correct ride height.

Shock absorbers

☐Depress each corner of the vehicle in turn, then release it. The vehicle should rise and then settle in its normal position. If the vehicle continues to rise and fall, the shock absorber is defective. A shock absorber which has seized will also cause the vehicle to fail.

Exhaust system

□Start the engine. With your assistant holding a rag over the tailpipe, check the entire system for leaks. Repair or renew leaking sections.

3 Checks carried out **WITH THE VEHICLE RAISED AND THE WHEELS FREE TO TURN**

Jack up the front and rear of the vehicle, and securely support it on axle stands. Position the stands clear of the suspension assemblies. Ensure that the wheels are clear of the ground and that the steering can be turned from lock to lock.

Steering mechanism

□Have your assistant turn the steering from lock to lock. Check that the steering turns smoothly, and that no part of the steering mechanism, including a wheel or tyre, fouls any brake hose or pipe or any part of the body structure.

□ Examine the steering rack rubber gaiters for damage or insecurity of the retaining clips. If power steering is fitted, check for signs of damage or leakage of the fluid hoses, pipes or connections. Also check for excessive stiffness or binding of the steering, a missing split pin or locking device, or severe corrosion of the body structure within 30 cm of any steering component attachment point.

Front and rear suspension and wheel bearings

□Starting at the front right-hand side, grasp the roadwheel at the 3 o'clock and 9 o'clock positions and rock gently but firmly. Check for free play or insecurity at the wheel bearings, suspension balljoints, or suspension mount-ings, pivots and attachments.

□Now grasp the wheel at the 12 o'clock and 6 o'clock positions and repeat the previous inspection. Spin the wheel, and check for roughness or tightness of the front wheel bearing.

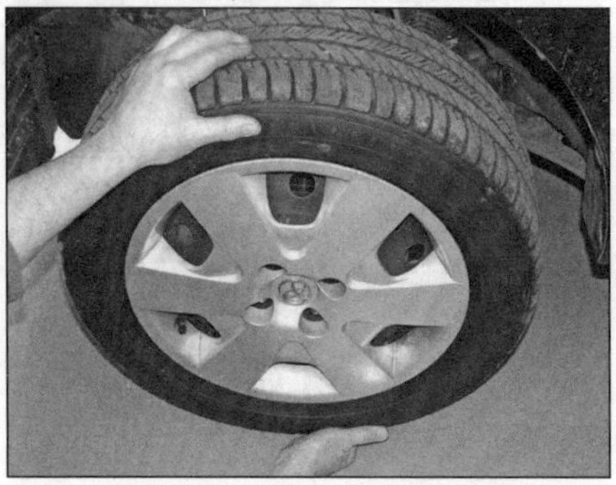

□If excess free play is suspected at a component pivot point, this can be confirmed by using a large screwdriver or similar tool and levering between the mounting and the component attachment. This will confirm whether the wear is in the pivot bush, its retaining bolt, or in the mounting itself (the bolt holes can often become elongated).

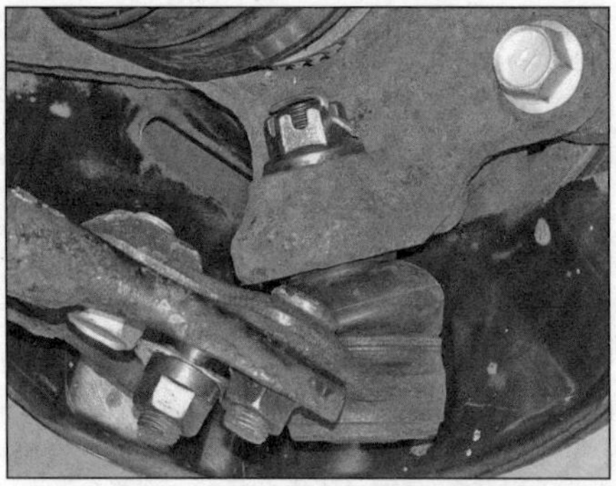

□Carry out all the above checks at the other front wheel, and then at both rear wheels.

Springs and shock absorbers

□Examine the suspension struts (when applicable) for serious fluid leakage, corrosion, or damage to the casing. Also check the security of the mounting points.

□If coil springs are fitted, check that the spring ends locate in their seats, and that the spring is not corroded, cracked or broken.

□If leaf springs are fitted, check that all leaves are intact, that the axle is securely attached to each spring, and that there is no deterioration of the spring eye mountings, bushes, and shackles.

□The same general checks apply to vehicles fitted with other suspension types, such as torsion bars, hydraulic displacer units, etc. Ensure that all mountings and attachments are secure, that there are no signs of excessive wear, corrosion or damage, and (on hydraulic types) that there are no fluid leaks or damaged pipes.

□Inspect the shock absorbers for signs of serious fluid leakage. Check for wear of the mounting bushes or attachments, or damage to the body of the unit.

Driveshafts (fwd vehicles only)

□Rotate each front wheel in turn and inspect the constant velocity joint gaiters for splits or damage. Also check that each driveshaft is straight and undamaged.

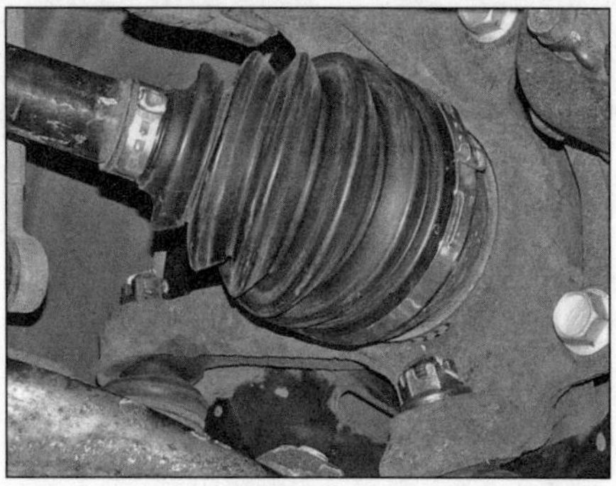

Braking system

□If possible without dismantling, check brake pad wear and disc condition. Ensure that the friction lining material has not worn excessively, (A) and that the discs are not fractured, pitted, scored or badly worn (B).

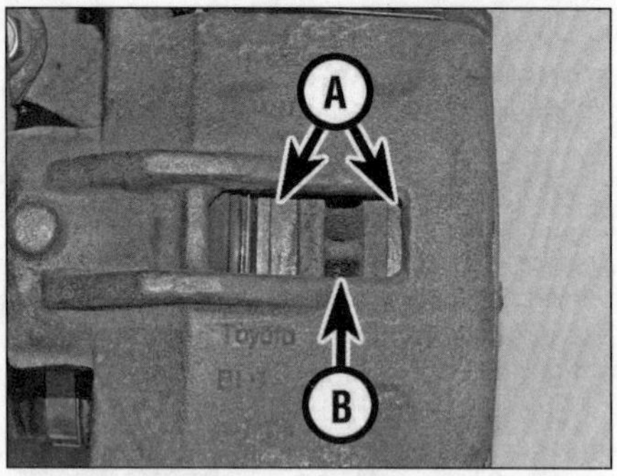

□Examine all the rigid brake pipes underneath the vehicle, and the flexible hose(s) at the rear. Look for corrosion, chafing or insecurity of the pipes, and for signs of bulging under pressure, chafing, splits or deterioration of the flexible hoses.

□Look for signs of fluid leaks at the brake calipers or on the brake backplates. Repair or renew leaking components.

□Slowly spin each wheel, while your assistant depresses and releases the footbrake. Ensure that each brake is operating and does not bind when the pedal is released.

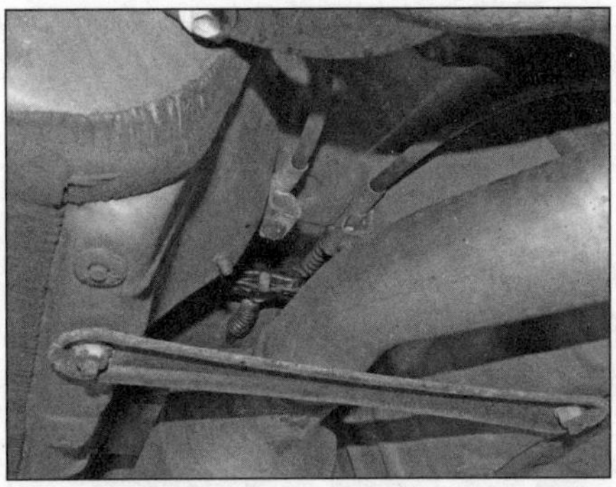

☐Examine the handbrake mechanism, checking for frayed or broken cables, excessive corrosion, or wear or insecurity of the linkage. Check that the mechanism works on each relevant wheel, and releases fully, without binding.

☐It is not possible to test brake efficiency without special equipment, but a road test can be carried out later to check that the vehicle pulls up in a straight line.

Fuel and exhaust systems

☐Inspect the fuel tank (including the filler cap), fuel pipes, hoses and unions. All components must be secure and free from leaks. Locking fuel caps must lock securely and the key must be provided for the MOT test.

☐Examine the exhaust system over its entire length, checking for any damaged, broken or missing mountings, security of the retaining clamps and rust or corrosion.

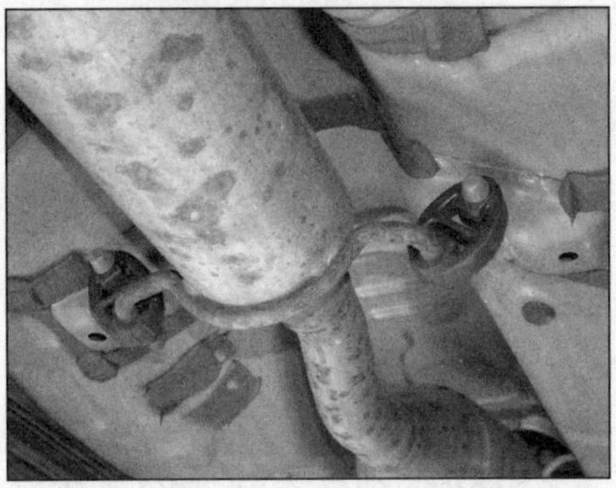

Wheels and tyres

☐Examine the sidewalls and tread area of each tyre in turn. Check for cuts, tears, lumps, bulges, separation of the tread, and exposure of the ply or cord due to wear or damage. Check that the tyre bead is correctly seated on the wheel rim, that the valve is sound and properly seated, and that the wheel is not distorted or damaged.

☐Check that the tyres are of the correct size for the vehicle, that they are of the same size and type on each axle, and that the pressures are correct.

☐Check the tyre tread depth. The legal minimum at the time of writing is 1.6 mm over the central three-quarters of the tread width. Abnormal tread wear may indicate incorrect front wheel alignment or wear in steering or suspension components.

☐If the spare wheel is fitted externally or in a separate carrier beneath the vehicle, check that mountings are secure and free of excessive corrosion.

Body corrosion

☐Check the condition of the entire vehicle structure for signs of corrosion in load-bearing areas. (These include chassis box sections, side sills, cross-members, pillars, and all suspension, steering, braking system and seat belt mountings and anchorages.) Any corrosion which has seriously reduced the thickness of a load-bearing area (or is within 30 cm of safety-related components such as steering or suspension) is likely to cause the vehicle to fail. In this case professional repairs are likely to be needed.

☐Damage or corrosion which causes sharp or otherwise dangerous edges to be exposed will also cause the vehicle to fail.

Towbars

☐Check the condition of mounting points (both beneath the vehicle and within boot/ hatchback areas) for signs of corrosion, ensuring that all fixings are secure and not worn or damaged. There must be no excessive play in detachable tow ball arms or quick-release mechanisms.

4 Checks carried out on YOUR VEHICLE'S EXHAUST EMISSION SYSTEM

Petrol models

☐The engine should be warmed up, and running well (ignition system in good order, air filter element clean, etc).

☐Before testing, run the engine at around 2500 rpm for 20 seconds. Let the engine drop to idle, and watch for smoke from the exhaust. If the idle speed is too high, or if dense blue or black smoke emerges for more than 5 seconds, the vehicle will fail. Typically, blue smoke signifies oil burning (engine wear); black smoke means unburnt fuel (dirty air cleaner element, or other fuel system fault).

☐An exhaust gas analyser for measuring carbon monoxide (CO) and hydrocarbons (HC) is now needed. If one cannot be hired or borrowed, have a local garage perform the check.

CO emissions (mixture)

☐The MOT tester has access to the CO limits for all vehicles. The CO level is measured at idle speed, and at 'fast idle' (2500 to 3000 rpm). The following limits are given as a general guide:

At idle speed – Less than 0.5% CO
At 'fast idle' – Less than 0.3% CO
Lambda reading – 0.97 to 1.03

☐If the CO level is too high, this may point to poor maintenance, a fuel injection system problem, faulty lambda (oxygen) sensor or catalytic converter. Try an injector cleaning treatment, and check the vehicle's ECU for fault codes.

HC emissions

☐The MOT tester has access to HC limits for all vehicles. The HC level is measured at 'fast idle' (2500 to 3000 rpm). The following limits are given as a general guide:

At 'fast idle' – Less then 200 ppm

☐Excessive HC emissions are typically caused by oil being burnt (worn engine), or by a blocked crankcase ventilation system ('breather'). If the engine oil is old and thin, an oil change may help. If the engine is running badly, check the vehicle's ECU for fault codes.

Diesel models

☐The only emission test for diesel engines is measuring exhaust smoke density, using a calibrated smoke meter. The test involves accelerating the engine at least 3 times to its maximum unloaded speed.

Note: *On engines with a timing belt, it is VITAL that the belt is in good condition before the test is carried out.*

☐With the engine warmed up, it is first purged by running at around 2500 rpm for 20 seconds. A governor check is then carried out, by slowly accelerating the engine to its maximum speed. After this, the smoke meter is connected, and the engine is accelerated quickly to maximum speed three times. If the smoke density is less than the limits given below, the vehicle will pass:

Non-turbo vehicles: 2.5m-1
Turbocharged vehicles: 3.0m-1

☐If excess smoke is produced, try fitting a new air cleaner element, or using an injector cleaning treatment. If the engine is running badly, where applicable, check the vehicle's ECU for fault codes. Also check the vehicle's EGR system, where applicable. At high mileages, the injectors may require professional attention.

Engine
- ☐ Engine fails to rotate when attempting to start
- ☐ Engine rotates, but will not start
- ☐ Engine difficult to start when cold
- ☐ Engine difficult to start when hot
- ☐ Starter motor noisy or excessively-rough in engagement
- ☐ Engine starts, but stops immediately
- ☐ Engine misfires, or idles unevenly
- ☐ Engine stalls, or lacks power
- ☐ Engine backfires
- ☐ Engine noises
- ☐ Oil consumption excessive
- ☐ Oil pressure warning light illuminated with engine running

Cooling system
- ☐ Overheating
- ☐ Overcooling
- ☐ External coolant leakage
- ☐ Internal coolant leakage
- ☐ Corrosion

Fuel and exhaust systems
- ☐ Fuel consumption excessive
- ☐ Fuel leakage and/or fuel odour
- ☐ Black smoke in exhaust
- ☐ Blue or white smoke in exhaust
- ☐ Excessive noise or fumes from exhaust system

Clutch
- ☐ Pedal travels to floor – no pressure or very little resistance
- ☐ Clutch fails to disengage (unable to select gears)
- ☐ Clutch slips (engine speed increases, with no increase in vehicle speed)
- ☐ Judder as clutch is engaged
- ☐ Noise when depressing or releasing clutch pedal

Manual transmission
- ☐ Noisy in neutral with engine running
- ☐ Noisy in one particular gear
- ☐ Difficulty engaging gears
- ☐ Jumps out of gear
- ☐ Vibration
- ☐ Lubricant leaks

Driveshafts
- ☐ Vibration when accelerating or decelerating
- ☐ Clicking or knocking noise on turns (at slow speed on full-lock)

Braking system
- ☐ Car pulls to one side under braking
- ☐ Noise (grinding or high-pitched squeal) when brakes applied
- ☐ Excessive brake pedal travel
- ☐ Brake pedal feels spongy when depressed
- ☐ Excessive brake pedal effort required to stop vehicle
- ☐ Judder felt through brake pedal or steering wheel when braking
- ☐ Brakes binding
- ☐ Rear wheels locking under normal braking

Suspension and steering
- ☐ Car pulls to one side
- ☐ Wheel wobble and vibration
- ☐ Excessive pitching and/or rolling around corners, or during braking
- ☐ Wandering or general instability
- ☐ Excessively-stiff steering
- ☐ Excessive play in steering
- ☐ Lack of power assistance
- ☐ Tyre wear excessive

Electrical system
- ☐ Battery will only hold a charge for a few days
- ☐ Ignition (no-charge) warning light remains illuminated with engine running
- ☐ Ignition (no-charge) warning light fails to come on
- ☐ Lights inoperative
- ☐ Instrument readings inaccurate or erratic
- ☐ Horn faults
- ☐ Windscreen/tailgate wiper faults
- ☐ Windscreen/tailgate washer faults
- ☐ Electric window faults
- ☐ Central locking system faults

Introduction

The car owner who does his or her own maintenance according to the recommended service schedules should not have to use this section of the manual very often. Modern component reliability is such that, provided those items subject to wear or deterioration are inspected or renewed at the specified intervals, sudden failure is comparatively rare. Faults do not usually just happen as a result of sudden failure, but develop over a period of time. Major mechanical failures in particular are usually preceded by characteristic symptoms over hundreds or even thousands of miles. Those components which do occasionally fail without warning are often small and easily carried in the car.

With any fault-finding, the first step is to decide where to begin investigations. Sometimes this is obvious, but on other occasions, a little detective work will be necessary. The owner who makes half a dozen haphazard adjustments or replacements may be successful in curing a fault (or its symptoms), but will be none the wiser if the fault recurs, and ultimately may have spent more time and money than was necessary. A calm and logical approach will be found to be more satisfactory in the long run. Always take into account any warning signs or abnormalities that may have been noticed in the period preceding the fault – power loss, high or low gauge readings, unusual smells, etc – and remember that failure of components such as fuses may only be pointers to some underlying fault.

The pages which follow provide an easy reference guide to the more common problems which may occur during the operation of the car. These problems and their possible causes are grouped under headings denoting various components or systems, such as Engine, Cooling system, etc. The Chapter and/or Section which deals with the problem is also shown in brackets. Whatever the fault, certain basic principles apply. These are as follows:

Verify the fault. This is simply a matter of being sure that you know what the symptoms are before starting work. This is particularly important if you are investigating a fault for someone else, who may not have described it very accurately.

Don't overlook the obvious. For example, if the car won't start, is there fuel in the tank? (Don't take anyone else's word on this particular point, and don't trust the fuel gauge either!) If an electrical fault is indicated, look for loose or broken wires before using the test gear.

Cure the disease, not the symptom. Substituting a flat battery with a fully-charged one will get you off the hard shoulder, but if the underlying cause is not attended to, the new battery will go the same way.

Don't take anything for granted. Particularly, don't forget that a 'new' component may itself be defective (especially if it's been rattling around in the boot for months), and don't leave components out of a fault diagnosis sequence just because they are new or recently fitted. When you do finally diagnose a difficult fault, you'll probably realise that all the evidence was there from the start.

Consider what work, if any, has recently been carried out. Many faults arise through careless or hurried work. For instance, if any work has been performed under the bonnet, could some of the wiring have been dislodged or incorrectly routed, or a hose trapped? Have all the fasteners been properly tightened? Were new, genuine parts and new gaskets used? There is often a certain amount of detective work to be done in this case, as an apparently-unrelated task can have far-reaching consequences.

Diesel fault diagnosis

The majority of starting problems on small diesel engines are electrical in origin. The mechanic who is familiar with petrol engines but less so with diesel may be inclined to view the diesel's injectors and pump in the same light as the spark plugs and distributor, but this is generally a mistake.

When investigating complaints of difficult starting for someone else, make sure that the correct starting procedure is understood and is being followed. Some drivers are unaware of the significance of the preheating warning light – many modern engines are sufficiently forgiving for this not to matter in mild weather, but with the onset of winter problems begin.

As a rule of thumb, if the engine is difficult to start but runs well when it has finally got going, the problem is electrical (battery, starter motor or preheating system). If poor performance is combined with difficult starting, the problem is likely to be in the fuel system. The low pressure (supply) side of the fuel system should be checked before suspecting the injectors and injection pump. The most common fuel supply problem is air getting into the system, and any pipe from the fuel tank forwards must be scrutinised if air leakage is suspected. Normally the pump is the last item to suspect, since unless it has been tampered with there is no reason for it to be at fault.

Engine

Engine fails to rotate when attempting to start

- ☐ Battery terminal connections loose or corroded (*Weekly checks*).
- ☐ Battery discharged or faulty (Chapter 5A).
- ☐ Broken, loose or disconnected wiring in the starting circuit (Chapter 5A).
- ☐ Defective starter solenoid, ignition keycard reader, or starter button (Chapter 5A or 12).
- ☐ Defective starter motor (Chapter 5A).
- ☐ Flywheel ring gear or starter pinion teeth loose or broken (Chapter 2A, 2B, or 5A).
- ☐ Engine earth strap broken or disconnected.
- ☐ Engine suffering 'hydraulic lock' (eg from water ingested after traversing flooded roads, or from a serious internal coolant leak) – consult a Renault dealer for advice.
- ☐ Clutch or brake pedal not depressed, or transmission not in neutral.
- ☐ Clutch pedal switch, transmission neutral switch, or stop-light switch faulty (Chapter 6, 7 or 9).

Engine rotates, but will not start

- ☐ Fuel tank empty.
- ☐ Battery discharged or inadequate capacity (engine rotates slowly) (Chapter 5A).
- ☐ Battery terminal connections loose or corroded (*Weekly checks*).
- ☐ Ignition components damp or damaged – petrol engines (Chapter 1A or 5B)
- ☐ Worn, faulty or incorrectly-gapped spark plugs – petrol engines (Chapter 1A)
- ☐ Incorrect use of diesel preheating system, or preheating system fault (Chapter 5B).
- ☐ Diesel fuel waxing (in very cold weather).
- ☐ Immobiliser or anti-theft alarm faulty or incorrectly used, or 'uncoded' ignition keycard being used (Chapter 12).
- ☐ Crankshaft sensor, or other engine management system sensor, fault (Chapter 4A or 4B)
- ☐ Air filter element dirty or clogged (Chapter 1A or 1B).
- ☐ Blockage in exhaust system (Chapter 4A or 4B).
- ☐ Poor compressions (Chapter 2A or 2B).
- ☐ Air in diesel fuel system (Chapter 4B).
- ☐ Valve timing incorrect, possibly through a poorly-fitted timing belt (Chapter 2A or 2B).
- ☐ Major mechanical failure (eg camshaft drive) (Chapter 2A or 2B).

Engine difficult to start when cold

- ☐ Battery discharged (Chapter 5A).
- ☐ Battery terminal connections loose or corroded (see *Weekly checks*).
- ☐ Worn, faulty or incorrectly-gapped spark plugs – petrol models (Chapter 1A).
- ☐ Other ignition system fault – petrol models (Chapter 5B).
- ☐ Fuel system fault (Chapter 4A or 4B).
- ☐ Diesel glow plug(s) defective (Chapter 5C).
- ☐ Wrong grade of engine oil used (*Weekly checks* or Chapter 1A or 1B).
- ☐ Low cylinder compressions (Chapter 2A or 2B)

Engine difficult to start when hot

- ☐ Air filter element dirty or clogged (Chapter 1A or 1B).
- ☐ Fuel system fault (Chapter 4A or 4B).
- ☐ Low cylinder compressions (Chapter 2A or 2B).

Starter motor noisy or excessively-rough

- ☐ Starter pinion or flywheel ring gear teeth loose or broken (Chapter 2A, 2B or 5A).
- ☐ Starter motor mounting bolts loose or missing (Chapter 5A).
- ☐ Starter motor internal components worn or damaged (Chapter 5A).

Engine starts, but stops immediately

- ☐ Loose or faulty electrical connections in the ignition circuit – petrol models (Chapter 1A or 5B).
- ☐ Vacuum leak at the throttle body, inlet manifold or associated hoses – petrol models (Chapter 4A).
- ☐ Blocked injectors/fuel system fault (Chapter 4A or 4B).
- ☐ Fuel very low in tank.
- ☐ Restriction in fuel feed or return.
- ☐ Air in diesel fuel system (Chapter 4B).
- ☐ Air cleaner dirty or blockage in air intake system (Chapter 1A, 1B, 4A or 4B).
- ☐ Blockage in exhaust system (Chapter 4A or 4B).

Engine (continued)

Engine misfires, or idles unevenly

- ☐ Air cleaner dirty or blockage in air intake system (Chapter 1A, 1B, 4A or 4B).
- ☐ Vacuum leak at the throttle body, inlet manifold or associated hoses – petrol models (Chapter 4A).
- ☐ Worn, faulty or incorrectly-gapped spark plugs – petrol models (Chapter 1A).
- ☐ Valve clearances incorrect (Chapter 2A or 2B).
- ☐ Uneven or low cylinder compressions (Chapter 2A or 2B)
- ☐ Camshaft lobes worn (Chapter 2A or 2B).
- ☐ Timing belt/chain incorrectly fitted (Chapter 2A or 2B).
- ☐ Blocked injectors/fuel injection system fault (Chapter 4A or 4B).
- ☐ Valve(s) sticking, valve spring(s) weak or broken, or poor compressions (Chapter 2A or 2B).
- ☐ Overheating (Chapter 3).
- ☐ Cylinder head gasket blown (Chapter 2A or 2B).

Engine stalls, or lacks power

- ☐ Fuel filter choked (Chapter 1B or 4A).
- ☐ Petrol in-tank fuel pump faulty, or delivery pressure low (Chapter 4A).
- ☐ Diesel lift pump (in injection pump) faulty, or delivery pressure low (Chapter 4B).
- ☐ Air in diesel fuel system (Chapter 4B).
- ☐ Valve clearances incorrect (Chapter 2A or 2B).
- ☐ Vacuum leak at the throttle body, inlet manifold or associated hoses – petrol models (Chapter 4A).
- ☐ Worn, faulty or incorrectly-gapped spark plugs – petrol models (Chapter 1).
- ☐ Faulty ignition coils – petrol models (Chapter 5B).
- ☐ Uneven or low cylinder compressions (Chapter 2A or 2B).
- ☐ Blocked injector/fuel system fault (Chapter 4A or 4B).
- ☐ Blocked catalytic converter (Chapter 4A or 4B).
- ☐ Engine overheating (Chapter 3).
- ☐ Air filter element blocked (Chapter 1).
- ☐ Throttle position sensor fault (Chapter 4A or 4B).
- ☐ Engine warning light on (fault code in system) (Chapter 4A or 4B).
- ☐ Timing belt worn, or incorrectly fitted (Chapter 2A or 2B).
- ☐ Turbo boost pressure inadequate – diesel models (Chapter 4B).
- ☐ Brakes binding (Chapter 1 or 9).
- ☐ Clutch slipping (Chapter 6).

Engine backfires

- ☐ Timing belt incorrectly fitted (Chapter 2A or 2B).
- ☐ Vacuum leak at the throttle body, inlet manifold or associated hoses – petrol models (Chapter 4A).
- ☐ Blocked catalytic converter (Chapter 4A or 4B).
- ☐ Ignition coil faulty – petrol models (Chapter 5B).

Engine noises

Pre-ignition (pinking) or knocking during acceleration or under load

- ☐ Ignition system fault – petrol models (Chapter 1A or 5B).
- ☐ Incorrect grade of spark plug – petrol models (Chapter 1A).
- ☐ Incorrect grade (or type) of fuel used (Chapter 4A or 4B).
- ☐ Vacuum leak at the throttle body, inlet manifold or associated hoses – petrol models (Chapter 4A).
- ☐ Excessive carbon build-up in cylinder head/pistons (Chapter 2A or 2B).
- ☐ Blocked injector/fuel injection system fault (Chapter 4A or 4B).

Whistling or wheezing noises

- ☐ Leaking inlet manifold or throttle body gasket – petrol models (Chapter 4A or 4B).
- ☐ Leaking exhaust manifold gasket, or pipe-to-manifold joint (Chapter 4A or 4B).
- ☐ Leaking vacuum hose (Chapter 4 or 9).
- ☐ Blowing cylinder head gasket (Chapter 2A or 2B).
- ☐ Partially blocked or leaking crankcase ventilation system (Chapter 4C).

Tapping or rattling noises

- ☐ Valve clearances incorrect (Chapter 2A or 2B).
- ☐ Worn camshaft (Chapter 2A or 2B)
- ☐ Ancillary component fault (coolant pump, alternator, etc) (Chapter 3, 5A, etc).
- ☐ Air in diesel fuel system (Chapter 4B).

Knocking or thumping noises

- ☐ Worn big-end bearings (regular heavy knocking, perhaps less under load) (Chapter 2C).
- ☐ Worn main bearings (rumbling and knocking, perhaps worsening under load) (Chapter 2C).
- ☐ Piston slap – most noticeable when cold, caused by piston/bore wear (Chapter 2C).
- ☐ Ancillary component fault (coolant pump, alternator, etc) (Chapter 3, 5A, etc).
- ☐ Engine mountings worn or defective (Chapter 2A or 2B).
- ☐ Front suspension or steering components worn (Chapter 10).

Oil consumption excessive

- ☐ External leakage (standing or running) – eg sump gasket, crankshaft oil seals (Chapter 2A or 2B).
- ☐ New engine not yet run-in.
- ☐ Engine oil incorrect grade/poor quality, or oil level too high (*Weekly checks*).
- ☐ Crankcase ventilation system obstructed (Chapter 1 or 4C).
- ☐ Burning oil due to general engine wear – pistons and/or bores, valve stem oil seals, etc (Chapter 2C).

Oil pressure warning light illuminated with engine running

- ☐ Low oil level or incorrect oil grade (*Weekly checks*).
- ☐ Faulty oil pressure warning light switch (Chapter 2A or 2B).
- ☐ Worn engine bearings and/or oil pump (Chapter 2).
- ☐ High engine operating temperature (Chapter 3).
- ☐ Oil pick-up strainer clogged – remove sump to check (Chapter 2A, 2B or 2C).

Cooling system

Overheating

- ☐ Insufficient coolant in system (*Weekly checks*).
- ☐ Thermostat faulty (Chapter 3).
- ☐ Radiator core blocked or grille restricted (Chapter 3).
- ☐ Radiator electric cooling fan(s) or coolant temperature sensor faulty (Chapter 3).
- ☐ Pressure cap faulty (Chapter 3).
- ☐ Inaccurate coolant temperature gauge sender (Chapter 3).
- ☐ Airlock in cooling system (Chapter 1A or 1B).
- ☐ Engine management system fault (Chapter 4A or 4B).
- ☐ Blockage in exhaust system (Chapter 4A or 4B).
- ☐ Cylinder head gasket blown (Chapter 2A or 2B).

Overcooling

- ☐ Thermostat faulty (Chapter 3).
- ☐ Inaccurate coolant temperature gauge sender (Chapter 3).

External coolant leakage

- ☐ Deteriorated or damaged hoses or hose clips (Chapter 1A or 1B).
- ☐ Radiator core or heater matrix leaking (Chapter 3).
- ☐ Pressure cap faulty (Chapter 1A or 1B).
- ☐ Water pump or thermostat housing leaking (Chapter 3).
- ☐ Boiling due to overheating (Chapter 3).
- ☐ Core plug leaking (Chapter 2C).

Internal coolant leakage

- ☐ Leaking cylinder head gasket (Chapter 2A or 2B).
- ☐ Cracked cylinder head or cylinder bore (Chapter 2C).

Corrosion

- ☐ Infrequent draining and flushing (Chapter 1A or 1B).
- ☐ Incorrect antifreeze mixture, or inappropriate antifreeze type (*Weekly checks* and Chapter 1A or 1B).

Fuel and exhaust systems

Fuel consumption excessive

- ☐ New engine not yet run-in.
- ☐ Air cleaner element dirty, or blockage in air intake system (Chapter 1A, 1B, 4A or 4B).
- ☐ Fuel system fault (Chapter 4A or 4B).
- ☐ Crankcase ventilation system blocked (Chapter 4C).
- ☐ Unsympathetic driving style, or adverse conditions.
- ☐ Tyres under-inflated (see *Weekly checks*).
- ☐ Brakes binding (Chapter 1 or 9).
- ☐ Fuel leak, causing apparent high consumption (Chapter 1A, 1B, 4A or 4B).
- ☐ Valve timing incorrect, possibly through a poorly-fitted timing belt (Chapter 2A or 2B).

Fuel leakage and/or fuel odour

- ☐ Damaged or corroded fuel tank, pipes or connections (Chapter 1A or 1B).
- ☐ Evaporative emissions system fault – petrol models (Chapter 4C).

Black smoke in exhaust

- ☐ Air cleaner element dirty, or blockage in air intake system (Chapter 1A, 1B, 4A or 4B).
- ☐ Turbo boost pressure inadequate – diesel models (Chapter 4B).
- ☐ Exhaust gas recirculation system fault – diesel models (Chapter 4C).
- ☐ Fuel system fault (Chapter 4A or 4B).

Blue or white smoke in exhaust

- ☐ Engine oil incorrect grade or poor quality, or fuel passing into sump (worn piston rings/bores).
- ☐ Diesel glow plug(s) defective (white smoke at start-up only) (Chapter 5C).
- ☐ Air cleaner element dirty, or blockage in air intake system (Chapter 1A, 1B, 4A or 4B).
- ☐ Injector(s) faulty (Chapter 4A or 4B).
- ☐ Blocked or damaged emissions system hoses or components (Chapter 4C).
- ☐ General engine wear – pistons and/or bores, valve stem oil seals, etc (Chapter 2C).

Excessive noise or fumes from exhaust system

- ☐ Leaking exhaust system or manifold joints (Chapter 1A, 1B, 4A or 4B).
- ☐ Leaking, corroded or damaged silencers or pipe (Chapter 1A, 1B, 4A or 4B).
- ☐ Exhaust gas recirculation system fault – diesel models (Chapter 4C).
- ☐ Oxygen sensors loose or damaged – petrol models (Chapter 4C).
- ☐ Broken mountings, causing body or suspension contact (Chapter 1A, 1B, 4A or 4B).

Clutch

Pedal travels to floor – no pressure or very little resistance

- ☐ Air in hydraulic system/faulty master or slave cylinder (Chapter 6).
- ☐ Faulty hydraulic release system (Chapter 6).
- ☐ Clutch pedal return spring detached or broken (Chapter 6).
- ☐ Broken clutch release bearing or fork (Chapter 6).
- ☐ Broken diaphragm spring in clutch pressure plate (Chapter 6).

Clutch fails to disengage (unable to select gears)

- ☐ Air in hydraulic system/faulty master or slave cylinder (Chapter 6).
- ☐ Faulty hydraulic release system (Chapter 6).
- ☐ Clutch disc sticking on transmission input shaft splines (Chapter 6).
- ☐ Clutch disc sticking to flywheel or pressure plate (Chapter 6).
- ☐ Faulty pressure plate assembly (Chapter 6).
- ☐ Clutch release mechanism worn or incorrectly assembled (Chapter 6).

Clutch slips (engine speed increases, with no increase in vehicle speed)

- ☐ Faulty hydraulic release system (Chapter 6).
- ☐ Clutch disc linings excessively worn (Chapter 6).
- ☐ Clutch disc linings contaminated with oil or grease (Chapter 6).
- ☐ Faulty pressure plate or weak diaphragm spring (Chapter 6).

Judder as clutch is engaged

- ☐ Clutch disc linings contaminated with oil or grease (Chapter 6).
- ☐ Clutch disc linings excessively worn (Chapter 6).
- ☐ Faulty or distorted pressure plate or diaphragm spring (Chapter 6).
- ☐ Worn or loose engine/transmission mountings (Chapter 2A or 2B)
- ☐ Clutch disc hub or transmission input shaft splines worn (Chapter 6 or 7).

Noise when depressing or releasing clutch pedal

- ☐ Worn clutch release bearing (Chapter 6).
- ☐ Worn or dry clutch pedal bushes (Chapter 6).
- ☐ Worn or dry clutch master cylinder piston (Chapter 6).
- ☐ Faulty pressure plate assembly (Chapter 6).
- ☐ Pressure plate diaphragm spring broken (Chapter 6).
- ☐ Broken clutch disc cushioning springs (Chapter 6).

Manual transmission

Noisy in neutral with engine running

- ☐ Lack of oil (Chapter 1A or 1B).
- ☐ Input shaft bearings worn (noise apparent with clutch pedal released, but not when depressed) (Chapter 7).*
- ☐ Clutch release bearing worn (noise apparent with clutch pedal depressed, possibly less when released) (Chapter 6).

Noisy in one particular gear

- ☐ Worn, damaged or chipped gear teeth (Chapter 7).*

Difficulty engaging gears

- ☐ Clutch fault (Chapter 6).
- ☐ Worn or damaged gear cables (Chapter 7).
- ☐ Incorrectly-adjusted gear cables (Chapter 7).
- ☐ Worn synchroniser assemblies (Chapter 7).*

Jumps out of gear

- ☐ Worn or damaged gear cables (Chapter 7).
- ☐ Incorrectly-adjusted gear cables (Chapter 7).
- ☐ Worn synchroniser assemblies (Chapter 7).*
- ☐ Worn selector forks (Chapter 7).*

Vibration

- ☐ Lack of oil (Chapter 1).
- ☐ Worn bearings (Chapter 7).*

Lubricant leaks

- ☐ Leaking differential side gear oil seal (Chapter 7).
- ☐ Leaking housing joint (Chapter 7).*
- ☐ Leaking input shaft oil seal (Chapter 7).*
- ☐ Leaking selector shaft oil seal (Chapter 7).

** Although the corrective action necessary to remedy the symptoms described is beyond the scope of the home mechanic, the above information should be helpful in isolating the cause of the condition, so that the owner can communicate clearly with a professional mechanic.*

Driveshafts

Vibration when accelerating or decelerating

- ☐ Worn inner constant velocity joint (Chapter 1A, 1B or 8).
- ☐ Bent or distorted driveshaft (Chapter 8).
- ☐ Worn intermediate bearing (Chapter 8).
- ☐ Loose or damaged driveshaft nut (Chapter 1A, 1B or 8).

Clicking or knocking noise on turns (at slow speed on full-lock)

- ☐ Lack of constant velocity joint lubricant (Chapter 8).
- ☐ Worn outer constant velocity joint (Chapter 1A, 1B or 8).
- ☐ Worn intermediate bearing (Chapter 8).
- ☐ Loose or damaged driveshaft nut (Chapter 1A, 1B or 8).

Braking system

Note: *Before assuming that a brake problem exists, make sure that the tyres are in good condition and correctly inflated, that the front wheel alignment is correct, and that the car is not loaded with weight in an unequal manner. Apart from checking the condition of all pipe and hose connections, any faults occurring on the Anti-lock Braking System (ABS) should be referred to a Renault dealer for diagnosis.*

Car pulls to one side under braking

- ☐ Worn, defective, damaged or contaminated front or rear brake pads on one side (Chapter 1A or 1B).
- ☐ Seized or partially-seized caliper piston (Chapter 9).
- ☐ A mixture of brake pad lining materials fitted between sides (Chapter 1A or 1B).
- ☐ Brake caliper mounting bolts loose (Chapter 9).
- ☐ Worn or damaged steering or suspension components (Chapter 10).

Noise (grinding or high-pitched squeal) when brakes applied

- ☐ Brake pad friction lining material worn down to metal backing Chapter 1A or 1B).
- ☐ Excessive corrosion of brake disc (may be apparent after the car has been standing for some time) (Chapter 1A or 1B).

Excessive brake pedal travel

- ☐ Faulty master cylinder (Chapter 9).
- ☐ Air in hydraulic system (Chapter 9).

Brake pedal feels spongy when depressed

- ☐ Air in hydraulic system (Chapter 9).
- ☐ Deteriorated flexible rubber brake hoses (Chapter 9).
- ☐ Master cylinder mounting nuts loose (Chapter 9).
- ☐ Faulty master cylinder (Chapter 9).

Excessive brake pedal effort required to stop car

- ☐ Faulty vacuum servo unit (Chapter 9).
- ☐ Disconnected, damaged or insecure brake servo vacuum hoses (Chapter 9).
- ☐ Brake vacuum pump leaking or faulty – diesel models (Chapter 9).
- ☐ Primary or secondary hydraulic circuit failure (Chapter 9).
- ☐ Seized brake caliper piston (Chapter 9).
- ☐ Brake pads incorrectly fitted (Chapter 9).
- ☐ Incorrect grade of brake pads fitted (Chapter 1A or 1B).
- ☐ Brake pads contaminated (Chapter 1A or 1B).

Judder felt through brake pedal or steering wheel when braking

- ☐ Excessive run-out or distortion of front or rear discs (Chapter 9).
- ☐ Brake pads worn (Chapter 1A or 1B).
- ☐ Brake caliper mounting bolts loose (Chapter 9).
- ☐ Wear in suspension or steering components or mountings (Chapter 10).

Brakes binding

- ☐ Seized brake caliper piston (Chapter 9).
- ☐ Faulty handbrake mechanism (Chapter 9).
- ☐ Faulty master cylinder (Chapter 9).

Rear wheels locking under normal braking

- ☐ Rear brake pads contaminated (Chapter 1A or 1B).
- ☐ Faulty ABS unit (Chapter 9).

Suspension and steering

Note: *Before diagnosing suspension or steering faults, be sure that the trouble is not due to incorrect tyre pressures, mixtures of tyre types, or binding brakes.*

Car pulls to one side

- ☐ Defective tyre (Chapter 1A or 1B).
- ☐ Excessive wear in suspension or steering components (Chapter 10).
- ☐ Incorrect front wheel alignment (Chapter 10).
- ☐ Accident damage to steering or suspension components (Chapter 10).

Wheel wobble and vibration

- ☐ Front roadwheels out of balance (vibration felt mainly through the steering wheel) (Chapter 1A or 1B).
- ☐ Rear roadwheels out of balance (vibration felt throughout the car) (Chapter 1A or 1B).
- ☐ Roadwheels damaged or distorted (Chapter 1A or 1B).
- ☐ Faulty or damaged tyre (*Weekly checks*).
- ☐ Worn steering or suspension joints, bushes or components (Chapter 10).
- ☐ Roadwheel bolts loose (Chapter 1A or 1B).
- ☐ Wear in driveshaft joint, or loose driveshaft nut (vibration worst when under load) (Chapter 1A, 1B or 8).

Excessive pitching and/or rolling around corners, or during braking

- ☐ Defective shock absorbers (Chapter 10).
- ☐ Broken or weak coil spring and/or suspension components (Chapter 10).
- ☐ Worn or damaged anti-roll bar or mountings (Chapter 10).

Wandering or general instability

- ☐ Incorrect front wheel alignment (Chapter 10).
- ☐ Worn steering or suspension joints, bushes or components (Chapter 10).
- ☐ Tyres out of balance (*Weekly checks*).
- ☐ Faulty or damaged tyre (*Weekly checks*).
- ☐ Roadwheel bolts loose (Chapter 1A or 1B).
- ☐ Defective shock absorbers (Chapter 10).

Excessively-stiff steering

- ☐ Lack of steering gear lubricant (Chapter 10).
- ☐ Seized track rod end balljoint or suspension balljoint (Chapter 10).
- ☐ Steering motor failure (Chapter 10).
- ☐ Incorrect front wheel alignment (Chapter 10).
- ☐ Steering rack or column bent or damaged (Chapter 10).

Excessive play in steering

- ☐ Worn steering column universal joint (Chapter 10).
- ☐ Worn steering track rod end balljoints (Chapter 10).
- ☐ Worn rack-and-pinion steering gear (Chapter 10).
- ☐ Worn steering or suspension joints, bushes or components (Chapter 10).

Lack of power assistance

- ☐ Steering motor failure (Chapter 10).

Tyre wear excessive

Tyres worn on inside or outside edges

- ☐ Tyres under-inflated (wear on both edges) (*Weekly checks*).
- ☐ Incorrect camber or castor angles (wear on one edge only) (Chapter 10).
- ☐ Worn steering or suspension joints, bushes or components (Chapter 10).
- ☐ Excessively-hard cornering.
- ☐ Accident damage.

Tyre treads exhibit feathered edges

- ☐ Incorrect toe setting (Chapter 10).

Tyres worn in centre of tread

- ☐ Tyres over-inflated (*Weekly checks*).

Tyres worn on inside and outside edges

- ☐ Tyres under-inflated (*Weekly checks*).

Tyres worn unevenly

- ☐ Tyres out of balance (*Weekly checks*).
- ☐ Excessive wheel or tyre run-out (Chapter 1A or 1B).
- ☐ Worn shock absorbers (Chapter 10).
- ☐ Faulty tyre (*Weekly checks*).

Electrical system

- ☐ For problems associated with the starting system, refer to the faults listed under Engine earlier in this Section.

Battery will only hold a charge for a few days

- ☐ Battery defective internally (Chapter 5A).
- ☐ Battery electrolyte level low (Chapter 5A).
- ☐ Battery terminal connections loose or corroded (*Weekly checks*).
- ☐ Auxiliary drivebelt worn or slipping (Chapter 1A or 1B).
- ☐ Alternator not charging at correct output (Chapter 5A).
- ☐ Alternator or voltage regulator faulty (Chapter 5A).
- ☐ Short-circuit causing continual battery drain (Chapters 5A and 12).

Ignition (no-charge) warning light remains illuminated with engine running

- ☐ Auxiliary drivebelt broken, worn, or slipping (Chapter 1A or 1B).
- ☐ Alternator brushes worn, sticking, or dirty (Chapter 5A).
- ☐ Alternator brush springs weak or broken (Chapter 5A).
- ☐ Internal fault in alternator or voltage regulator (Chapter 5A).
- ☐ Disconnected or loose wiring in charging circuit (Chapter 5A).

Ignition (no-charge) warning light fails to come on

- ☐ Warning light bulb blown (Chapter 12).
- ☐ Broken, disconnected, or loose wiring in warning light circuit (Chapters 5A and 12).
- ☐ Alternator faulty (Chapter 5A).

Lights inoperative

- ☐ Bulb blown (Chapter 12).
- ☐ Corrosion of bulb or bulbholder contacts (Chapter 12).
- ☐ Blown fuse (Chapter 12).
- ☐ Faulty relay (Chapter 12).
- ☐ Broken, loose, or disconnected wiring (Chapter 12).
- ☐ Multiplex module fault (Chapter 12).
- ☐ Faulty switch (Chapter 12).

Electrical system (continued)

Instrument readings inaccurate or erratic

Gauges give no reading

- ☐ Faulty gauge sender unit (Chapter 3 or 4A).
- ☐ Wiring open-circuit (Chapter 12).
- ☐ Faulty gauge (Chapter 12).

Gauges give continuous maximum reading

- ☐ Faulty gauge sender unit (Chapter 3 or 4A).
- ☐ Wiring short-circuit (Chapter 12).
- ☐ Faulty gauge (Chapter 12).

Horn faults

Horn fails to operate

- ☐ Blown fuse (Chapter 12).
- ☐ Cable or cable connections loose or disconnected (Chapter 12).
- ☐ Faulty horn (Chapter 12).

Horn emits intermittent or unsatisfactory sound

- ☐ Cable connections loose (Chapter 12).
- ☐ Horn mountings loose (Chapter 12).
- ☐ Faulty horn (Chapter 12).

Horn operates all the time

- ☐ Horn push either earthed or stuck down (Chapter 12).
- ☐ Horn cable to horn push earthed (Chapter 12).

Windscreen/tailgate wiper faults

Wipers fail to operate, or operate very slowly

- ☐ Wiper blades stuck to screen, or linkage seized (Chapter 12).
- ☐ Blown fuse (Chapter 12).
- ☐ Cable or cable connections loose or disconnected (Chapter 12).
- ☐ Faulty relay (Chapter 12).
- ☐ Faulty wiper motor (Chapter 12).
- ☐ Multiplex module fault (Chapter 12).

Wiper blades sweep over the wrong area of glass

- ☐ Wiper arms incorrectly-positioned on spindles (Chapter 12).
- ☐ Excessive wear of wiper linkage (Chapter 12).
- ☐ Wiper motor or linkage mountings loose or insecure (Chapter 12).

Wiper blades fail to clean the glass effectively

- ☐ Wiper blade rubbers worn or perished (*Weekly checks*).
- ☐ Wiper arm tension springs broken, or arm pivots seized (Chapter 12).
- ☐ Insufficient windscreen washer additive to adequately remove road film (*Weekly checks*).

Windscreen/tailgate washer faults

One or more washer jets inoperative

- ☐ Blocked washer jet (*Weekly checks* or Chapter 12).
- ☐ Disconnected, kinked or restricted fluid hose (Chapter 12).
- ☐ Insufficient fluid in washer reservoir (*Weekly checks*).

Washer pump fails to operate

- ☐ Broken or disconnected wiring or connections (Chapter 12).
- ☐ Blown fuse (Chapter 12).
- ☐ Faulty washer switch (Chapter 12).
- ☐ Faulty washer pump (Chapter 12).

Washer pump runs for some time before fluid is emitted from jets

- ☐ Faulty one-way valve in fluid supply hose (Chapter 12).

Electric window faults

Window glass will only move in one direction

- ☐ Faulty switch (Chapter 12).

Window glass slow to move

- ☐ Regulator seized or damaged, or lack of lubrication (Chapter 11).
- ☐ Door internal components or trim fouling regulator (Chapter 11).
- ☐ Faulty motor (Chapter 12).

Window glass fails to move

- ☐ Blown fuse (Chapter 12).
- ☐ Faulty relay (Chapter 12).
- ☐ Broken or disconnected wiring or connections (Chapter 12).
- ☐ Faulty motor (Chapter 12).

Central locking system faults

Complete system failure

- ☐ Blown fuse (Chapter 12).
- ☐ Faulty relay (Chapter 12).
- ☐ Broken or disconnected wiring or connections (Chapter 12).
- ☐ Multiplex module fault (Chapter 12).

Latch locks but will not unlock, or unlocks but will not lock

- ☐ Faulty lock (Chapter 11).

One lock motor fails to operate

- ☐ Broken or disconnected wiring or connections (Chapter 12).
- ☐ Faulty lock motor (Chapter 11).
- ☐ Fault in door latch (Chapter 11).

A

ABS (Anti-lock brake system) A system, usually electronically controlled, that senses incipient wheel lockup during braking and relieves hydraulic pressure at wheels that are about to skid.

Air bag An inflatable bag hidden in the steering wheel (driver's side) or the dash or glovebox (passenger side). In a head-on collision, the bags inflate, preventing the driver and front passenger from being thrown forward into the steering wheel or windscreen.

Air cleaner A metal or plastic housing, containing a filter element, which removes dust and dirt from the air being drawn into the engine.

Air filter element The actual filter in an air cleaner system, usually manufactured from pleated paper and requiring renewal at regular intervals.

Air filter

Allen key A hexagonal wrench which fits into a recessed hexagonal hole.

Alligator clip A long-nosed spring-loaded metal clip with meshing teeth. Used to make temporary electrical connections.

Alternator A component in the electrical system which converts mechanical energy from a drivebelt into electrical energy to charge the battery and to operate the starting system, ignition system and electrical accessories.

Ampere (amp) A unit of measurement for the flow of electric current. One amp is the amount of current produced by one volt acting through a resistance of one ohm.

Anaerobic sealer A substance used to prevent bolts and screws from loosening. Anaerobic means that it does not require oxygen for activation. The Loctite brand is widely used.

Antifreeze A substance (usually ethylene glycol) mixed with water, and added to a vehicle's cooling system, to prevent freezing of the coolant in winter. Antifreeze also contains chemicals to inhibit corrosion and the formation of rust and other deposits that would tend to clog the radiator and coolant passages and reduce cooling efficiency.

Anti-seize compound A coating that reduces the risk of seizing on fasteners that are subjected to high temperatures, such as exhaust manifold bolts and nuts.

Asbestos A natural fibrous mineral with great heat resistance, commonly used in the composition of brake friction materials. Asbestos is a health hazard and the dust created by brake systems should never be inhaled or ingested.

Axle A shaft on which a wheel revolves, or which revolves with a wheel. Also, a solid beam that connects the two wheels at one end of the vehicle. An axle which also transmits power to the wheels is known as a live axle.

Axleshaft A single rotating shaft, on either side of the differential, which delivers power from the final drive assembly to the drive wheels. Also called a driveshaft or a halfshaft.

B

Ball bearing An anti-friction bearing consisting of a hardened inner and outer race with hardened steel balls between two races.

Bearing The curved surface on a shaft or in a bore, or the part assembled into either, that permits relative motion between them with minimum wear and friction.

Bearing

Big-end bearing The bearing in the end of the connecting rod that's attached to the crankshaft.

Bleed nipple A valve on a brake wheel cylinder, caliper or other hydraulic component that is opened to purge the hydraulic system of air. Also called a bleed screw.

Brake bleeding Procedure for removing air from lines of a hydraulic brake system.

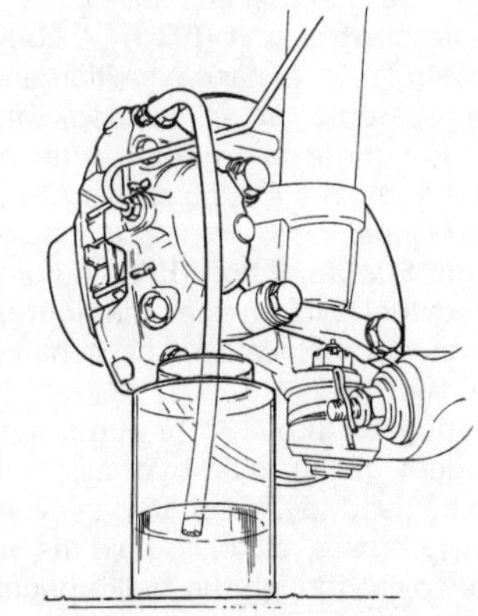

Brake bleeding

Brake disc The component of a disc brake that rotates with the wheels.

Brake drum The component of a drum brake that rotates with the wheels.

Brake linings The friction material which contacts the brake disc or drum to retard the vehicle's speed. The linings are bonded or riveted to the brake pads or shoes.

Brake pads The replaceable friction pads that pinch the brake disc when the brakes are applied. Brake pads consist of a friction material bonded or riveted to a rigid backing plate.

Brake shoe The crescent-shaped carrier to which the brake linings are mounted and which forces the lining against the rotating drum during braking.

Braking systems For more information on braking systems, consult the *Haynes Automotive Brake Manual*.

Breaker bar A long socket wrench handle providing greater leverage.

Bulkhead The insulated partition between the engine and the passenger compartment.

C

Caliper The non-rotating part of a disc-brake assembly that straddles the disc and carries the brake pads. The caliper also contains the hydraulic components that cause the pads to pinch the disc when the brakes are applied. A caliper is also a measuring tool that can be set to measure inside or outside dimensions of an object.

Camshaft A rotating shaft on which a series of cam lobes operate the valve mechanisms. The camshaft may be driven by gears, by sprockets and chain or by sprockets and a belt.

Canister A container in an evaporative emission control system; contains activated charcoal granules to trap vapours from the fuel system.

Canister

Carburettor A device which mixes fuel with air in the proper proportions to provide a desired power output from a spark ignition internal combustion engine.

Castellated Resembling the parapets along the top of a castle wall. For example, a castellated balljoint stud nut.

Castor In wheel alignment, the backward or forward tilt of the steering axis. Castor is positive when the steering axis is inclined rearward at the top.

Glossary of technical terms

Catalytic converter A silencer-like device in the exhaust system which converts certain pollutants in the exhaust gases into less harmful substances.

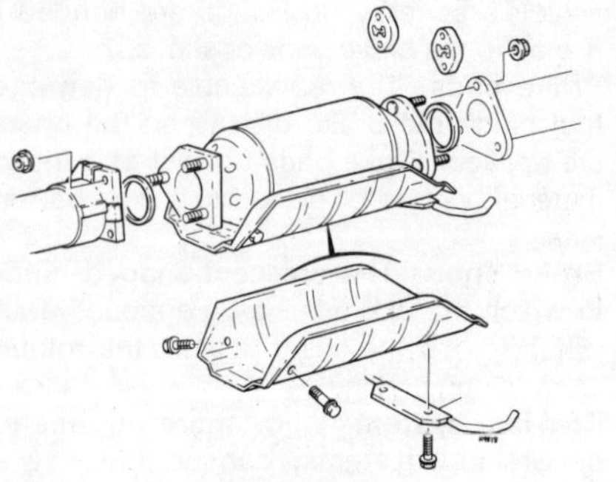

Catalytic converter

Circlip A ring-shaped clip used to prevent endwise movement of cylindrical parts and shafts. An internal circlip is installed in a groove in a housing; an external circlip fits into a groove on the outside of a cylindrical piece such as a shaft.

Clearance The amount of space between two parts. For example, between a piston and a cylinder, between a bearing and a journal, etc.

Coil spring A spiral of elastic steel found in various sizes throughout a vehicle, for example as a springing medium in the suspension and in the valve train.

Compression Reduction in volume, and increase in pressure and temperature, of a gas, caused by squeezing it into a smaller space.

Compression ratio The relationship between cylinder volume when the piston is at top dead centre and cylinder volume when the piston is at bottom dead centre.

Constant velocity (CV) joint A type of universal joint that cancels out vibrations caused by driving power being transmitted through an angle.

Core plug A disc or cup-shaped metal device inserted in a hole in a casting through which core was removed when the casting was formed. Also known as a freeze plug or expansion plug.

Crankcase The lower part of the engine block in which the crankshaft rotates.

Crankshaft The main rotating member, or shaft, running the length of the crankcase, with offset "throws" to which the connecting rods are attached.

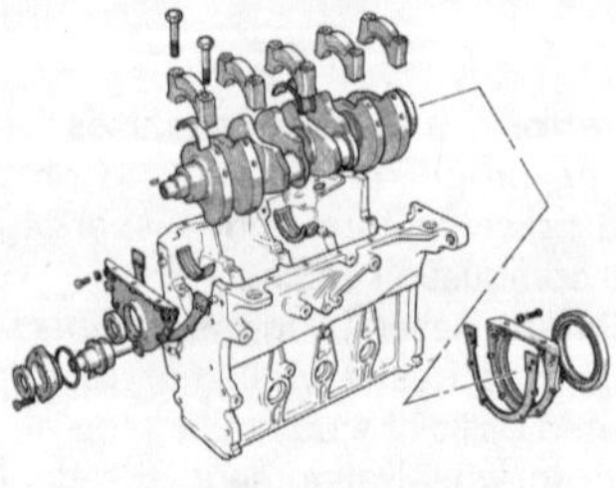

Crankshaft assembly

Crocodile clip See Alligator clip

D

Diagnostic code Code numbers obtained by accessing the diagnostic mode of an engine management computer. This code can be used to determine the area in the system where a malfunction may be located.

Disc brake A brake design incorporating a rotating disc onto which brake pads are squeezed. The resulting friction converts the energy of a moving vehicle into heat.

Double-overhead cam (DOHC) An engine that uses two overhead camshafts, usually one for the intake valves and one for the exhaust valves.

Drivebelt(s) The belt(s) used to drive accessories such as the alternator, water pump, power steering pump, air conditioning compressor, etc. off the crankshaft pulley.

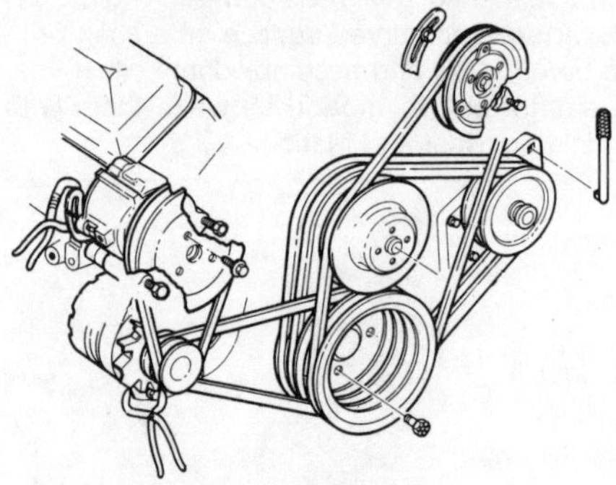

Accessory drivebelts

Driveshaft Any shaft used to transmit motion. Commonly used when referring to the axleshafts on a front wheel drive vehicle.

Drum brake A type of brake using a drum-shaped metal cylinder attached to the inner surface of the wheel. When the brake pedal is pressed, curved brake shoes with friction linings press against the inside of the drum to slow or stop the vehicle.

E

EGR valve A valve used to introduce exhaust gases into the intake air stream.

Electronic control unit (ECU) A computer which controls (for instance) ignition and fuel injection systems, or an anti-lock braking system. For more information refer to the *Haynes Automotive Electrical and Electronic Systems Manual*.

Electronic Fuel Injection (EFI) A computer controlled fuel system that distributes fuel through an injector located in each intake port of the engine.

Emergency brake A braking system, independent of the main hydraulic system, that can be used to slow or stop the vehicle if the primary brakes fail, or to hold the vehicle stationary even though the brake pedal isn't depressed. It usually consists of a hand lever that actuates either front or rear brakes mechanically through a series of cables and linkages. Also known as a handbrake or parking brake.

Endfloat The amount of lengthwise movement between two parts. As applied to a crankshaft, the distance that the crankshaft can move forward and back in the cylinder block.

Engine management system (EMS) A computer controlled system which manages the fuel injection and the ignition systems in an integrated fashion.

Exhaust manifold A part with several passages through which exhaust gases leave the engine combustion chambers and enter the exhaust pipe.

F

Fan clutch A viscous (fluid) drive coupling device which permits variable engine fan speeds in relation to engine speeds.

Feeler blade A thin strip or blade of hardened steel, ground to an exact thickness, used to check or measure clearances between parts.

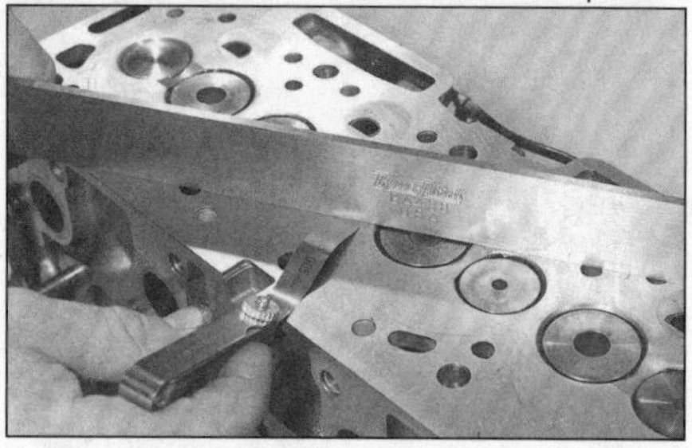

Feeler blade

Firing order The order in which the engine cylinders fire, or deliver their power strokes, beginning with the number one cylinder.

Flywheel A heavy spinning wheel in which energy is absorbed and stored by means of momentum. On cars, the flywheel is attached to the crankshaft to smooth out firing impulses.

Free play The amount of travel before any action takes place. The "looseness" in a linkage, or an assembly of parts, between the initial application of force and actual movement. For example, the distance the brake pedal moves before the pistons in the master cylinder are actuated.

Fuse An electrical device which protects a circuit against accidental overload. The typical fuse contains a soft piece of metal which is calibrated to melt at a predetermined current flow (expressed as amps) and break the circuit.

Fusible link A circuit protection device consisting of a conductor surrounded by heat-resistant insulation. The conductor is smaller than the wire it protects, so it acts as the weakest link in the circuit. Unlike a blown fuse, a failed fusible link must frequently be cut from the wire for replacement.

G

Gap The distance the spark must travel in jumping from the centre electrode to the side electrode in a spark plug. Also refers to the spacing between the points in a contact breaker assembly in a conventional points-type ignition, or to the distance between the reluctor or rotor and the pickup coil in an electronic ignition.

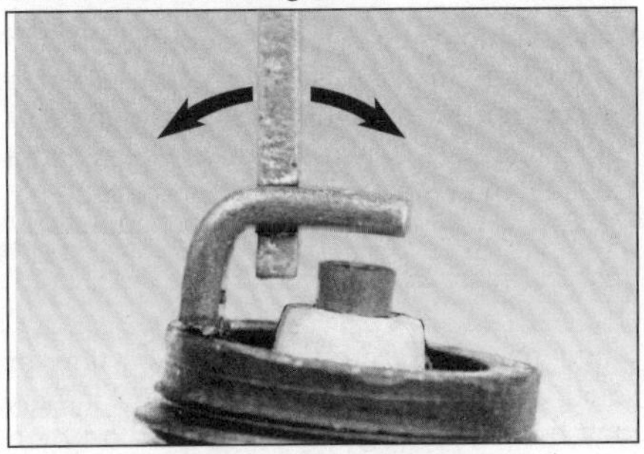

Adjusting spark plug gap

Gasket Any thin, soft material - usually cork, cardboard, asbestos or soft metal - installed between two metal surfaces to ensure a good seal. For instance, the cylinder head gasket seals the joint between the block and the cylinder head.

Gasket

Gauge An instrument panel display used to monitor engine conditions. A gauge with a movable pointer on a dial or a fixed scale is an analogue gauge. A gauge with a numerical readout is called a digital gauge.

H

Halfshaft A rotating shaft that transmits power from the final drive unit to a drive wheel, usually when referring to a live rear axle.

Harmonic balancer A device designed to reduce torsion or twisting vibration in the crankshaft. May be incorporated in the crankshaft pulley. Also known as a vibration damper.

Hone An abrasive tool for correcting small irregularities or differences in diameter in an engine cylinder, brake cylinder, etc.

Hydraulic tappet A tappet that utilises hydraulic pressure from the engine's lubrication system to maintain zero clearance (constant contact with both camshaft and valve stem). Automatically adjusts to variation in valve stem length. Hydraulic tappets also reduce valve noise.

I

Ignition timing The moment at which the spark plug fires, usually expressed in the number of crankshaft degrees before the piston reaches the top of its stroke.

Inlet manifold A tube or housing with passages through which flows the air-fuel mixture (carburettor vehicles and vehicles with throttle body injection) or air only (port fuel-injected vehicles) to the port openings in the cylinder head.

J

Jump start Starting the engine of a vehicle with a discharged or weak battery by attaching jump leads from the weak battery to a charged or helper battery.

L

Load Sensing Proportioning Valve (LSPV) A brake hydraulic system control valve that works like a proportioning valve, but also takes into consideration the amount of weight carried by the rear axle.

Locknut A nut used to lock an adjustment nut, or other threaded component, in place. For example, a locknut is employed to keep the adjusting nut on the rocker arm in position.

Lockwasher A form of washer designed to prevent an attaching nut from working loose.

M

MacPherson strut A type of front suspension system devised by Earle MacPherson at Ford of England. In its original form, a simple lateral link with the anti-roll bar creates the lower control arm. A long strut - an integral coil spring and shock absorber - is mounted between the body and the steering knuckle. Many modern so-called MacPherson strut systems use a conventional lower A-arm and don't rely on the anti-roll bar for location.

Multimeter An electrical test instrument with the capability to measure voltage, current and resistance.

N

NOx Oxides of Nitrogen. A common toxic pollutant emitted by petrol and diesel engines at higher temperatures.

O

Ohm The unit of electrical resistance. One volt applied to a resistance of one ohm will produce a current of one amp.

Ohmmeter An instrument for measuring electrical resistance.

O-ring A type of sealing ring made of a special rubber-like material; in use, the O-ring is compressed into a groove to provide the sealing action.

Overhead cam (ohc) engine An engine with the camshaft(s) located on top of the cylinder head(s).

Overhead valve (ohv) engine An engine with the valves located in the cylinder head, but with the camshaft located in the engine block.

Oxygen sensor A device installed in the engine exhaust manifold, which senses the oxygen content in the exhaust and converts this information into an electric current. Also called a Lambda sensor.

P

Phillips screw A type of screw head having a cross instead of a slot for a corresponding type of screwdriver.

Plastigage A thin strip of plastic thread, available in different sizes, used for measuring clearances. For example, a strip of Plastigage is laid across a bearing journal. The parts are assembled and dismantled; the width of the crushed strip indicates the clearance between journal and bearing.

Plastigage

Propeller shaft The long hollow tube with universal joints at both ends that carries power from the transmission to the differential on front-engined rear wheel drive vehicles.

Proportioning valve A hydraulic control valve which limits the amount of pressure to the rear brakes during panic stops to prevent wheel lock-up.

R

Rack-and-pinion steering A steering system with a pinion gear on the end of the steering shaft that mates with a rack (think of a geared wheel opened up and laid flat). When the steering wheel is turned, the pinion turns, moving the rack to the left or right. This movement is transmitted through the track rods to the steering arms at the wheels.

Radiator A liquid-to-air heat transfer device designed to reduce the temperature of the coolant in an internal combustion engine cooling system.

Refrigerant Any substance used as a heat transfer agent in an air-conditioning system. R-12 has been the principle refrigerant for many years; recently, however, manufacturers have begun using R-134a, a non-CFC substance that is considered less harmful to the ozone in the upper atmosphere.

Rocker arm A lever arm that rocks on a shaft or pivots on a stud. In an overhead valve engine, the rocker arm converts the upward movement of the pushrod into a downward movement to open a valve.

Rotor In a distributor, the rotating device inside the cap that connects the centre electrode and the outer terminals as it turns, distributing the high voltage from the coil secondary winding to the proper spark plug. Also, that part of an alternator which rotates inside the stator. Also, the rotating assembly of a turbocharger, including the compressor wheel, shaft and turbine wheel.

Runout The amount of wobble (in-and-out movement) of a gear or wheel as it's rotated. The amount a shaft rotates "out-of-true." The out-of-round condition of a rotating part.

S

Sealant A liquid or paste used to prevent leakage at a joint. Sometimes used in conjunction with a gasket.

Sealed beam lamp An older headlight design which integrates the reflector, lens and filaments into a hermetically-sealed one-piece unit. When a filament burns out or the lens cracks, the entire unit is simply replaced.

Serpentine drivebelt A single, long, wide accessory drivebelt that's used on some newer vehicles to drive all the accessories, instead of a series of smaller, shorter belts. Serpentine drivebelts are usually tensioned by an automatic tensioner.

Serpentine drivebelt

Shim Thin spacer, commonly used to adjust the clearance or relative positions between two parts. For example, shims inserted into or under bucket tappets control valve clearances. Clearance is adjusted by changing the thickness of the shim.

Slide hammer A special puller that screws into or hooks onto a component such as a shaft or bearing; a heavy sliding handle on the shaft bottoms against the end of the shaft to knock the component free.

Sprocket A tooth or projection on the periphery of a wheel, shaped to engage with a chain or drivebelt. Commonly used to refer to the sprocket wheel itself.

Starter inhibitor switch On vehicles with an automatic transmission, a switch that prevents starting if the vehicle is not in Neutral or Park.

Strut See MacPherson strut.

T

Tappet A cylindrical component which transmits motion from the cam to the valve stem, either directly or via a pushrod and rocker arm. Also called a cam follower.

Thermostat A heat-controlled valve that regulates the flow of coolant between the cylinder block and the radiator, so maintaining optimum engine operating temperature. A thermostat is also used in some air cleaners in which the temperature is regulated.

Thrust bearing The bearing in the clutch assembly that is moved in to the release levers by clutch pedal action to disengage the clutch. Also referred to as a release bearing.

Timing belt A toothed belt which drives the camshaft. Serious engine damage may result if it breaks in service.

Timing chain A chain which drives the camshaft.

Toe-in The amount the front wheels are closer together at the front than at the rear. On rear wheel drive vehicles, a slight amount of toe-in is usually specified to keep the front wheels running parallel on the road by offsetting other forces that tend to spread the wheels apart.

Toe-out The amount the front wheels are closer together at the rear than at the front. On front wheel drive vehicles, a slight amount of toe-out is usually specified.

Tools For full information on choosing and using tools, refer to the *Haynes Automotive Tools Manual*.

Tracer A stripe of a second colour applied to a wire insulator to distinguish that wire from another one with the same colour insulator.

Tune-up A process of accurate and careful adjustments and parts replacement to obtain the best possible engine performance.

Turbocharger A centrifugal device, driven by exhaust gases, that pressurises the intake air. Normally used to increase the power output from a given engine displacement, but can also be used primarily to reduce exhaust emissions (as on VW's "Umwelt" Diesel engine).

U

Universal joint or U-joint A double-pivoted connection for transmitting power from a driving to a driven shaft through an angle. A U-joint consists of two Y-shaped yokes and a cross-shaped member called the spider.

V

Valve A device through which the flow of liquid, gas, vacuum, or loose material in bulk may be started, stopped, or regulated by a movable part that opens, shuts, or partially obstructs one or more ports or passageways. A valve is also the movable part of such a device.

Valve clearance The clearance between the valve tip (the end of the valve stem) and the rocker arm or tappet. The valve clearance is measured when the valve is closed.

Vernier caliper A precision measuring instrument that measures inside and outside dimensions. Not quite as accurate as a micrometer, but more convenient.

Viscosity The thickness of a liquid or its resistance to flow.

Volt A unit for expressing electrical "pressure" in a circuit. One volt that will produce a current of one ampere through a resistance of one ohm.

W

Welding Various processes used to join metal items by heating the areas to be joined to a molten state and fusing them together. For more information refer to the *Haynes Automotive Welding Manual*.

Wiring diagram A drawing portraying the components and wires in a vehicle's electrical system, using standardised symbols. For more information refer to the *Haynes Automotive Electrical and Electronic Systems Manual*.

Note: *References throughout this index are in the form* **"Chapter number" • "Page number"**. *So, for example, 2C•15 refers to page 15 of Chapter 2C.*

A

Accelerator pedal – 4A•3, 4B•6
Aerial – 12•17
Air cleaner/inlet ducts – 4A•2, 4B•3
Air conditioning system – 1A•14, 3•13
Air filter – 1A•13, 1B•12
Airbag – 12•18
Alternator – 5A•4
Anti-lock braking system (ABS) – 9•15
Anti-roll bar – 10•7
Anti-theft alarm and immobiliser – 12•17
Audio unit – 12•16
Auxiliary display – 12•12
Auxiliary drivebelt – 1A•8, 1A•10, 1B•8, 1B•13
Auxiliary heater – 3•12

B

Battery – 0•14, 5A•2
Blower motor – 3•10
  resistor – 3•11
  switch – 3•11
Body electrical system – 12•1 *et seq*
Body exterior fittings – 11•16
Bodywork and fittings – 11•1 *et seq*
Bonnet – 11•6
  lock components – 11•6
Braking system – 9•1 *et seq*
  bleeding – 9•4
  caliper – 9•8, 9•11
  check – 1A•8, 1B•8
  disc – 9•9, 9•12
  fault finding – REF•20
  fluid – 0•12, 1A•14, 1B•15
  master cylinder – 9•6
  pads – 9•6, 9•10
  pedal – 9•2
  pedal cross-shaft – 9•3
  pipes and hoses – 9•5
Bulbs – 12•7, 12•10
Bumpers – 11•4

C

Camshafts – 2A•8
  and tappets – 2B•11
  oil seal – 2A•7, 2B•10
Catalytic converter and particulate filter – 4C•6
Centre console – 11•24
Charging system – 5A•4
Cigar lighter – 12•14
Clutch – 6•1 *et seq*
  bleeding – 6•4
  check – 1A•8, 1B•8
  fault finding – REF•19
  fluid – 0•12
  hydraulic hoses – 6•3
  master cylinder – 6•2
  pedal – 6•4
  pedal switches – 6•4
  slave cylinder – 6•3
Compression and leakdown test – 2A•3, 2B•3
Conversion factors – REF•6
Coolant – 0•11, 1A•14, 1B•15
Coolant temperature sensor – 3•7, 5C•4
Cooling system fault finding – REF•19
Cooling system hoses – 3•2
Cooling, heating and air conditioning systems – 3•1 *et seq*
Crankshaft – 2C•10, 2C•13, 2C•14
  oil seals – 2A•14, 2B•17
Cylinder block/crankcase – 2C•11
Cylinder head – 2A•10, 2B•12, 2C•7, 2C•9
  and valves – 2C•8

D

Diesel engine fuel and exhaust systems – 4B•1 *et seq*
Diesel engine in-car repair procedures – 2B•1 *et seq*
Dimensions and weights – REF•1
Doors – 11•7
  handle – 11•8
  trim panel – 11•9
  window glass and regulator – 11•10
Driveshafts – 8•1 *et seq*
  fault finding – REF•20
  gaiter – 1A•10, 1B•11, 8•4
  seals – 7•4

E

Electrical system fault finding – 12•2, REF•21
Electrical systems check and testing – 0•15, 1A•9, 1B•9
Emission control systems – 4C•1 *et seq*
Engine fault finding – REF•17
Engine management ECU – 4B•6
Engine mountings – 2B•17
Engine oil and filter – 0•11, 1A•6, 1B•6
Engine removal and overhaul procedures – 2C•1 *et seq*
Engine/transmission mountings – 2A•14
Exhaust system – 4A•10, 4B•13, 1A•9, 1B•9
Expansion bottle – 3•4

Note: *References throughout this index are in the form* **"Chapter number" • "Page number"**. *So, for example, 2C•15 refers to page 15 of Chapter 2C.*

F

Facia panel and crossmember – 11•25
Fault finding – REF•16
braking system – REF•20
clutch – REF•19
cooling system – REF•19
driveshafts – REF•20
electrical system – 12•2, REF•21
engine – REF•17
fuel and exhaust systems – REF•19
manual transmission – REF•20
steering and suspension – REF•21
Flywheel – 2A•16, 2B•17
Front lower arm – 10•8
Front strut – 10•6
Front swivel hub assembly – 10•2
Fuel and exhaust systems fault finding – REF•19
Fuel economy – REF•2
Fuel filler flap – 11•17
solenoid – 11•17
Fuel filter – 1B•12
water draining – 1B•9
Fuel gauge sender unit – 4B•3
and pressure regulator – 4A•5
Fuel injection depressurization – 4A•4
Fuel injection systems – 4A•3, 4A•7
Fuel injectors – 4B•7
Fuel pipes and fittings – 4A•4, 4B•5
Fuel pump – 4A•4
Fuel system priming and bleeding – 4B•5
Fuel tank – 4A•6, 4B•3
Fuses, relays and electronic control units – 12•3

G

Gearchange mechanism – 7•3
Glossary of technical terms – REF•23
Glow plugs – 5C•2

H

Handbrake cables – 9•14
Handbrake check and adjustment – 1A•8
Handbrake lever – 9•13
Headlight beam alignment – 12•12
Heater assembly/air distribution housing – 3•12
Heater control panel – 3•9
Heater matrix – 3•11
Heating system – 3•9
High-pressure pump – 4B•6
Horn – 12•14

I

Idle speed – 4B•5
Ignition HT coils – 5B•2
Ignition system – petrol engines – 5B•1 *et seq*
Ignition timing – 5B•2
Injector rail – 4B•10
Input shaft seal – 7•4
Instrument panel – 12•12
Intercooler – 4B•13
Interior trim panels – 11•20

J

Jacking and vehicle support – REF•7
Jump starting – 0•7

K

Knock sensor – 5B•2

L

Leaks – 0•9, 1A•11, 1B•11
Light units – 12•11, 12•12
Lubricants and fluids – 0•16

M

Main and big-end bearings – 2C•13
Manifolds – 4A•9, 4B•10
Manual transmission – 7•1 *et seq*
Manual transmission fault finding – REF•20
oil level – 1A•13, 1B•14
Mirrors – 11•15
MOT test checks – REF•12
Multipoint injection system – 4A•8

O

Oil pressure switch – 2B•19
Oil pump and sprockets – 2A•12, 2B•16
Outer constant velocity joint gaither – 8•4
Outside air temperature sensor – 12•13

Note: *References throughout this index are in the form* **"Chapter number" • "Page number"**. *So, for example, 2C•15 refers to page 15 of Chapter 2C.*

P

Parking aid components – 12•20
Petrol engine fuel and exhaust systems – 4A•1 *et seq*
Petrol engine in-car repair procedures – 2A•1 *et seq*
Piston/connecting rod assemblies – 2C•10, 2C•11, 2C•15
Pollen filter – 1A•7, 1B•7
Pre/post-heating system – diesel engines – 5C•1 *et seq*

R

Radiator – 3•3
cooling fan – 3•5
cooling fan switch – 3•7
grille panel – 11•5
Rain sensor and automatic headlight sensor – 12•13
Rear axle – 10•13
Rear coil spring – 10•12
Reversing light switch – 7•4
Ride height – 10•14
Road test – 1A•12, 1B•12
Roadside repairs – 0•6
Routine maintenance and servicing – diesel models – 1B•1 *et seq*
Routine maintenance and servicing – petrol models – 1A•1 *et seq*

S

Safety first – 0•5
Screen washer fluid – 0•12
Seats – 11•17
belts – 1A•9, 1B•9, 11•18
Shock absorber – 10•11
Spark plugs – 1A•12
Speakers – 12•16
Starting and charging systems – 5A•1 *et seq*
motor – 5A•6
system – 5A•6
Steering column – 10•14
lock – 12•17
Steering gear assembly – 10•16
Steering gear rubber gaiters – 10•15
Steering wheel – 10•14
Stop-light switch – 9•14
Subframe – 10•8
Sump – 2A•12, 2B•15
Sunroof – 11•16
Suspension and steering – 10•1 *et seq*
check – 1A•9, 1B•10
fault finding – REF•21
Switches – 12•4

T

Tailgate – 11•13
Tailgate wiper motor – 12•15
TDC for No 1 piston – 2A•3
Thermostat – 3•5
Throttle body/housing – 4A•7
Timing belt – 2A•4, 2B•7
sprockets, idler pulley and tensioner – 2A•7, 2B•10
Towing – 0•9
Track rod end balljoint – 10•16
Transmission oil – 7•2
Turbocharger – 4B•11
Tyres – 0•13, 0•16
pressure monitoring system – 10•18

U

Unleaded petrol – 4A•3

V

Vacuum pump – 9•16, 9•17
Vacuum servo unit – 9•3
check valve – 9•4
Valve clearances – 2B•6
Valve cover – 2B•5
Valve timing holes – 2B•3
Vehicle identification – REF•9

W

Washer jets and reservoir – 12•15
Water pump – 3•8
Wheel alignment and steering angles – 10•17
Wheel bearings – 10•4, 10•10
Wheel changing – 0•8
Windscreen cowl panels – 11•5
Windscreen wiper motor and linkage – 12•14
Windscreen, tailgate and fixed window glass – 11•16
Wipers – 0•14, 12•14
Wiring diagrams – 12•21 *et seq*